Short forms

adj	adjective
adv	adverb
C	countable noun
etc	etcetera
I	intransitive verb
n	noun
sb	someone
sth	something
T	transitive verb
U	uncountable noun
US	United States of America
v	verb

Labels

AMERICAN	used in American English, but not in British En ...
BRITISH	used in British English, but not in American En ...
ESPECIALLY AMERICAN	used more in American English than British En ...
ESPECIALLY BRITISH	used more in British English than in American ...
FORMAL	suitable for formal writing or speech, but not n ... in ordinary conversation
INFORMAL	used in normal conversation, but not suitable f ... situations, such as writing an essay or business ...
SPOKEN	used mainly in speech, but not often in writing ...
WRITTEN	used mainly in writing, but not often in speech ...

Symbols

⚠ help box warning about common mistakes and how to avoid them

◯ word or phrase used mainly in speech

Pearson Education Limited
Edinburgh Gate
Harlow
Essex CM20 2JE
England
and associated companies throughout the world

Visit our website: http://www.longman.com/dictionaries

Longman Essential Activator
©Addison Wesley Longman Limited 1997
©Pearson Education Limited 2006

First edition 1997
Second edition 2006

ISBN-10: 1-4058-1559-0 (paper)
ISBN-10: 1-4058-1568-X (paper + CD)
ISBN-10: 1-4058-1569-8 (cased + CD)
ISBN-13: 978-1-4058-1559-8 (paper)
ISBN-13: 978-1-4058-1568-0 (paper + CD)
ISBN-13: 978-1-4058-1569-7 (cased + CD)

A British Library Cataloguing-in-Publication Data
A catalogue record for this book is available from the British Library.

Typeset by Kerrypress, UK
Printed in India

LONGMAN

Essential
Activator

Longman

**NEW
EDITION**

Acknowledgements

The publishers and editorial team would like to thank the many people who have contributed to the making of this dictionary, in particular the Linglex Dictionary and Corpus Advisory Committee who have reviewed and commented on the book at several stages from concept planning to final text:

Lord Quirk (chair), Professor Douglas Biber, Rod Bolitho, Professor Gillian Brown, Professor David Crystal, Professor Geoffrey Leech, Dr Paul Meara, Philip Scholfield, Professor Peter Trudgill, Professor Katie Wales, Professor John Wells

and also Professor Yoshihiko Ikegami and Professor Thomas Herbst.

Thanks also go to Yuri Komuro, and all the teachers and students throughout the world who have given us feedback and advice, as well as all those who have contributed to the Longman Learner's Corpus.

Director
Della Summers

Senior Publisher
Laurence Delacroix

Projects Director
Michael Mayor

Managing Editor
Stephen Bullon

Senior Associate Lexicographer
Chris Fox

Associate Lexicographers
Elizabeth Manning
Michael Murphy
Stella O'Shea
Sue Engineer

Editors
Evadne Adrian-Vallance
Karen Cleveland Marwick
Martin Stark
Emma Campbell
Ted Jackson

Lexicographers
Rebecca Campbell
Dileri Borunda Johnston
Carol Pomeroy Zhong
Paula Biswas
Pat Bulhosen
Lucy Hollingworth
Jill Leatherbarrow
Joanna Leigh
Glennis Pye
Patrick Gillard
Fiona McIntosh
Elaine Pollard

Pronunciation Editor
Dinah Jackson

Proofreaders
Sandra Anderson
Philippa Logan

Grammar section
David Crystal

Project Manager
Alan Savill

Production Manager
Clive McKeough

Senior Production Editor
Paola Rocchetti

Corpus development
Steve Crowdy
Allan Orsnes

Technical support
Trevor Satchell
Kim Lee-Amies

Administrative Assistant
Janine Trainor

Database Administrator
Denise McKeough

Design
Mick Harris

Keyboarder
Pauline Savill

Illustrator
Chris Pavely

Picture research
Kevin Brown
Valerie Mulcahy

CONTENTS

How to use the Longman Essential Activator

The **Longman Essential Activator** will help you make your language more accurate, more varied, and more like that of a native speaker. For example, imagine you want to find a better word to use instead of 'very happy' in this sentence:

I was <u>very happy</u> to hear about your new job.

(Longman Learner's Corpus extract, intermediate level student.)

This is what you do:

1. Think of a word which expresses the basic meaning of what you want to say.

HAPPY

2. Find that word in the *Essential Activator*, and choose the most suitable section.

2 happy because something good has happened

3. Read the definitions of the words in that section, and decide which is the best one for you to use.

delighted /dɪˈlaɪtɪd/ [*adj* not before noun] extremely happy because something very good has happened: *She's been offered a job in Japan, and she's delighted of course.*

4. Now use this word to improve your sentence.

I was <u>delighted</u> to hear about your new job.

You can also find help when you need to write about a particular subject or topic, by using the **Word Banks**. For example, if you want to write an article about the environment, look up the Word Banks section on pages A26–A29, where you will find vocabulary, information, and ideas related to this subject.

When you are dealing with real situations in English, such as apologizing, complaining, or having a conversation, use the **ESSENTIAL COMMUNICATION** section, like this:

1. Choose the type of situation you need to deal with in English.

2. Decide which box best describes the situation you are in.

3. Read the options you are given and select the one which is most suitable ...

4. ... and use this to communicate in English.

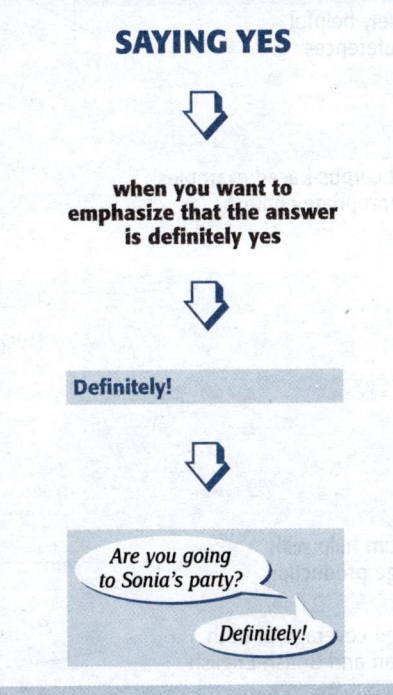

If you need help with grammar, turn to the **ESSENTIAL GRAMMAR** section, where you will find help with all the major grammar problems.

Every word and phrase in the **Longman Essential Activator** also appears in the index at the back, so if you know which word you want, but need more information about it, you can see exactly where to find it:

The **Longman Essential Activator** is the essential one-stop resource for language production.

Guide to the Dictionary

Vocabulary is divided into meaning areas

Genuinely helpful cross-references

Natural corpus-based examples give appropriate context

Maximum help with language production

Balanced coverage of both American and British English

Spoken as well as written examples

Irregular comparatives, superlatives and inflections are spelled out in full

---

ANGRY

➡ if you mean 'not angry or upset', go to **CALM**

1 feeling angry

angry /ˈæŋgri/ [adj] if you are **angry**, you feel a strong emotion, for example about someone who has treated you badly or about something that you think is wrong or unfair: *I was so angry that I could hardly speak.* | *A crowd of angry demonstrators gathered outside the embassy.* | *After the programme, the TV station received hundreds of angry phone calls.*
+with *She was angry with him because he had lied to her.*
+about *Don't you feel angry about the way you've been treated?*
+at *At first I was angry at him.*
+that *Local people are angry that they weren't consulted about plans to expand the airport.*
angry – angrier – angriest

> ⚠ Use **angry with** about people: *I was really angry with him.* Use **angry about** about things: *I was really angry about it.* Use **angry at** about people and things.

angrily [adv] *Rachel slammed the door angrily on her way out.*

mad /mæd/ [adj not before noun] INFORMAL, ESPECIALLY AMERICAN angry: *Tom will be real mad when he sees what you've done to his car.*
+at *She used to get mad at Harry because he was always changing his mind.*
+about *Come on, Maria – what are you so mad about?*
mad – madder – maddest

annoyed /əˈnɔɪd/ [adj not before noun] a little angry, but not very angry: *I'll be annoyed if he's forgotten to post my letter.*
+with *Joe was annoyed with her for being late.* | *I was annoyed with myself for playing so badly.*
+at/by *Kay was clearly annoyed at John's remark.*
+that *I was really annoyed that she didn't tell me herself.*

irritated /ˈɪrɪteɪtɪd/ [adj not before noun] a little angry and not patient about something, especially an annoying situation: *She got irritated because they hadn't cleaned up after themselves.*
+by/at *Coleman was irritated by all the questions.*

+**with** *She was irritated with herself for feeling nervous.*

furious /ˈfjʊəriəs/ [*adj*] very angry: *I've never been so furious in all my life.* | *a furious argument (=when people shout at each other in an angry way)*
+**with** *She'd be furious with me if she knew I was reading her diary.*
+**at/about** *He came home furious at something his boss had said.*

> Don't say 'very furious'. Say **absolutely furious**.

furiously [*adv*] *"Stop it,"* shouted *Ralph furiously.*

livid /ˈlɪvɪd/ [*adj*] so angry that it is difficult for you to speak properly or think clearly: *"Was he angry when you got in so late?" "Angry? He was livid!"* | *I know I shouldn't have spoken to her like that, but I was absolutely livid.*

> Don't say 'very livid'. Say **absolutely livid** or just **livid**.

offended /əˈfendɪd/ [*adj* not before noun] angry and upset because someone has said or done something rude or has insulted you: *A lot of Muslims were offended when the book came out.* | *I hope you won't be offended if I leave early.*
+**by** *Many readers were offended by the newspaper's anti-Irish comments.*

🔍 **cross** /krɒs‖krɔːs/ [*adj*] BRITISH, ESPECIALLY SPOKEN angry – used especially by children or when you are talking to children: *Do you think Dad will be cross when he finds out what happened?*
+**with** *Are you cross with me?*

fed up with sth/sick of sth /ˌfed ˈʌp wɪð (stʰ), ˈsɪk ɒv (stʰ)/ INFORMAL annoyed because something bad has been happening for a long time and you want it to stop: *I'm really fed up with this awful weather.* | *Joe was getting sick of Carol's stupid comments.* | *I left the job because I got fed up with being treated like a servant.*

2 to become angry

get angry/get mad /get ˈæŋɡri, get ˈmæd/ to become angry: *He tends to get angry if he loses.*
+**at** *Just calm down. There's no need to get mad at me.*

Formal or informal?

Don't say 'become angry' except in fairly formal written English. **Get angry** and **get mad** are the usual expressions.

Collocating prepositions and grammar patterns are highlighted and illustrated

Potential errors are highlighted and avoidance strategies given – all information based on Longman Learner's Corpus

Extensive coverage of spoken English

Formality is clearly indicated

Photo Acknowledgements

The publishers are grateful to the following for their permission to reproduce copyright photographs:

20th Century Fox / DreamWorks / Kobal Collection: p. 31(r); **Actionplus**: p. 67; **Agripictures**: p. 36(r); **Alamy**: p. 2 (Pacific Press Service), p. 27(l) (Mark Boulton), p. 36(l) (Leslie Garland Picture Library), p. 51 (Stockbyte Platinum), p. 78 (Acestock); **Arenapal**: p. 56(l), p. 74; **Corbis**: p. 11(r), p. 31(m), p. 31(l) (Bureau L.A. Collection), p. 43(l), p. 71, p. 75(r), p. 85(l), p. 90(r), p. 91; **DK Images**: p. 39(r); **Getty Images**: p. 47(l), p. 63, p. 75(l), p. 89(all), p. 93(l), p. 94(r); **Sally & Richard Greenhill**: p. 47(r); **Robert Harding Picture Library**: p. 46(l); **Hemera Technologies Inc "Photo Objects"** "Copyright ©2005 (Pearson Education) and its licensors. All rights reserved.": p. 28 (all), p. 42, p. 55(all), p. 56(r),p. 79(r), p. 86(l); **Pearson Education**: p. 35(r), p. 46(r); **Photodisc "Office, Gadgets & People"**: p. 6(all); **Photolibrary.com**: p. 27(r), p. 35(l); **Punchstock**: p. 7 (Bananastock), p. 11(l) (Rubberball), p. 19(r) (Brand X Pictures), p. 19(l), p. 34, p. 59, p. 84 (Digital Vision), p. 29(r) (Photodisc), p. 43(m) (Image Source), p. 56(r) (Stockbyte), p. 86(r) (Comstock); **Rex Features**: p. 9(l), p. 36(l), p. 58(l), p. 85(l); **Science Photo Library**: p. 90(l); **Superstock**: p. 38; **Topfoto**: p. 43(r), p. 79(l), p. 93(r), p. 94(l).

Cover image by Hemera Technologies Inc

Picture research by Kevin Brown

Every effort has been made to trace the copyright holders and we apologise in advance for any unintentional omissions. We would be pleased to insert the appropriate acknowledgement in any subsequent edition of this publication.

A, a

ABOUT

➡ look here for . . .
• about a person or subject
• not exact
➡ if you mean 'be about to', go to the
ESSENTIAL GRAMMAR (Section 5)

1 about a person or subject

about /əˈbaʊt/ [*preposition*] concerned with or relating to a particular subject or person: *She talks about him all the time.* | *I'm reading a story about some children who get lost on a mountain.* | *I've been thinking about what you said, and I've decided that you're right.* | *Does anyone have any questions about tonight's homework?*
be about *"It's a really good film."* *"What's it about?" "It's about some students in New York."*
all about sth (all the details about something) *Mom wanted to know all about my new job.*

on /ɒnǁɑːn, ɔːn/ [*preposition*] about a particular subject: *a book on 18th century European literature* | *Professor Dodd is giving a lecture on medieval history.*
opinions/ideas/views on *a survey of young people's opinions on marriage*
+how/why/what etc *We would like to hear your views on how services could be improved.*

⚠ Don't use **on** when talking about books, films etc that tell stories. Use it about opinions, or about writing or talks about factual things.

concerning/regarding /kənˈsɜːʳnɪŋ, rɪˈgɑːʳdɪŋ/ [*preposition*] FORMAL about – use this to talk about information, ideas, questions, or discussions, not to talk about books, films, or stories: *The police have new information concerning the identity of the murder victim.* | *Thank you for your letter regarding my student loan.*

Formal or informal?
Concerning and **regarding** are used in writing and in formal spoken English.

deal with sth /ˈdiːl wɪð (sth)/ [*phrasal verb* T] if a book, film, play, speech etc **deals with** a subject, it is about that subject: *The book deals with the problems of poverty and unemployment.* | *These issues are dealt with again in Chapter 4.*
dealing – dealt – have dealt

⚠ Only use **deal with** about serious subjects that are related to real life.

2 not an exact number or amount

about (also **around** ESPECIALLY AMERICAN) /əˈbaʊt, əˈraʊnd/ [*adv*] a little more or a little less than a particular number, amount, distance, or time: *The church is about a mile away.* | *It's about 2 years since I last saw him.* | *"What time would you like me to come?" "Oh, about 9 o'clock."* | *The murder was committed at around noon on Friday.* | *It cost around $1500.*

approximately /əˈprɒksɪ̩mɪ̩tlɪǁəˈprɑːk-/ [*adv*] close to a particular number but possibly a little more or a little less than it – used when you do not know the exact number: *We will be landing at Heathrow in approximately 30 minutes.* | *Approximately 30% of the community is Polish.*

Formal or informal?
Approximately is more formal than **about** or **around**, and is mostly used in writing.

roughly /ˈrʌfli/ [*adv*] a little more or a little less than a number – use this when you are making a guess which you know is not at all exact: *A new computer like this one would cost roughly $2000.* | *There were roughly 50 people there.*

🔍 **odd** /ɒdǁɑːd/ [*adv*] SPOKEN INFORMAL **a hundred/forty/twenty etc odd** a little more or less than a hundred, forty etc – use this after numbers in tens, hundreds, or thousands: *It's been thirty odd years since I've seen him.* | *There's fifty odd channels, and still nothing to watch.*

or so /ɔːʳ ˈsəʊ/ use this after a number or amount to show that it may be a little more or a little less: *"How many people are coming?" "Oh, about a dozen or so."* | *A month or so later, they heard that Blake was dead.*

> **Formal or informal?**
> Don't use **or so** in formal writing.

give or take /ˌgɪv ɔːʳ ˈteɪk/ **give or take a few days/miles/dollars etc** ESPECIALLY SPOKEN use this after a number, to show that it is not exact but it is nearly correct: *She's been working there for two years, give or take a few weeks.*

ACCEPT

➡ look here for . . .
• accept an offer or gift
• accept an idea or suggestion
• accept a situation that you cannot change

1 to accept an offer, invitation, or request

➡ opposite **REFUSE**
➡ see also ❚❚ **SAYING YES,**
    ❚❚ **INVITATIONS,** ❚❚ **OFFERS**

accept /əkˈsept/ [v T] to say yes to an offer, an invitation, or a chance to do something: *I decided to accept the job.* | *The President has accepted an invitation to visit Beijing.* | *If they offered you a place on the course, would you accept it?*

> Don't say 'I accepted to do it'. Say **I agreed to do it.**

take /teɪk/ [v T] if you **take** an opportunity or a job that someone offers you, you accept it: *He says he'll take the job if they offer it to him.* | *This is a wonderful opportunity – I think you should take it.*
taking – took – have taken

> **Formal or informal?**
> **Take** is more informal than **accept.**

say yes /ˌseɪ ˈjes/ ESPECIALLY SPOKEN to say you will do what someone has invited you to do or asked you to do: *We'd love you to come with us to France this summer. Please say yes!* | *He doesn't usually lend his CDs, so I was surprised when he said yes.*

agree /əˈgriː/ [v I] to say you will do what someone has asked you to do, especially something that may be difficult, inconvenient etc: *They've asked me to do a talk at the conference, and I've agreed.*
agree to do sth *I wish I had never agreed to teach him to drive.*
agreeing – agreed – have agreed

take sb up on sth/take up sb's offer /-ˌteɪk (sb) ˈʌp ɒn (sth), ˌteɪk ʌp (sb's) ˈɒfəʳ‖-ˈɔːf-/ to accept someone's offer to do something for you, at some time after the offer was originally made: *"If you need a babysitter, give me a call." "Thanks – I may take you up on that some time!"* | *In the end he took up his parents' offer of a loan.*

> **Formal or informal?**
> **Take sb up on sth** is more informal than **take up sb's offer.**

2 to take money or a gift that someone offers you

➡ opposite **REFUSE**

take /teɪk/ [v T] to accept something that is offered or given to you: *Take my advice and go to see a doctor.*
take sth from sb *My mother always warned us never to take candy from strangers.*
take it or leave it SPOKEN (used to tell someone that you will not change your offer) *$100 is my final offer – take it or leave it.*
taking – took – have taken

accept /əkˈsept/ [v T] to take money or a gift from someone: *We hope you'll accept this small gift.* | *Jerry wouldn't accept any payment for helping Mr Smythe.*
accept sth from sb *The minister was accused of accepting bribes from oil companies.*

Formal or informal?
Accept is more formal than take.

---

3 to agree that a suggestion or idea is right

➡ opposite **DISAGREE, AGAINST**
➡ see also ℂ **SAYING YES,**
   ℂ **AGREEING,** ℂ **SUGGESTIONS**

accept /ək'sept/ [v T] to agree that an idea or fact is true or right, especially when you did not previously think so: *He was beginning to accept the idea that there may be some truth in what she was saying.*
+that *The judge accepted that Carter had not intended to harm anyone.*

agree /ə'griː/ [v I/T] to accept that a plan or suggestion is good, especially when you have the power to decide whether it will be allowed to happen: *I spoke to my boss yesterday about postponing the meeting, and she agreed.*
+to *We want to have a big party, but I don't think my parents will agree to it.*
+that *Everyone agreed that Dave should be in the team.*

welcome /'welkəm/ [v T] to think that a plan, suggestion, or decision is very good, and eagerly accept it: *Most companies have welcomed the idea of job-sharing.*
be warmly welcomed *These new proposals were warmly welcomed by the German Chancellor.*

---

4 to accept a situation which you do not like

accept /ək'sept/ [v T] to realize that you cannot change a situation which you do not like: *There's nothing we can do – we have to accept the voters' decision.*
+that *We have to accept that the airport will carry on getting bigger.*

◯ **put up with sth** /,pʊt 'ʌp wɪð (sth)/ [phrasal verb T] ESPECIALLY SPOKEN to accept an annoying situation or someone's annoying behaviour, without trying to stop it or change it:

I don't know how you put up with all this noise day after day. | You see what I have to put up with – the kids never stop quarrelling.

tolerate /'tɒləreɪt‖'tɑː-/ [v T] to accept an unpleasant situation, without trying to change it even though you would like to: *For years the workers have had to tolerate low wages and terrible working conditions. | I don't know why his mother tolerates his behaviour.*

Formal or informal?
Tolerate is used in writing. It can also be used in spoken English by a parent, teacher etc who is angry and is showing their authority: *I will not tolerate this kind of behaviour.*

◯ **live with sth** /'lɪv wɪð (sth)/ [phrasal verb T] ESPECIALLY SPOKEN to accept an unpleasant situation as a permanent part of your life which you cannot change: *You have to learn to live with stress. | We don't really like the new system, but I suppose we'll just have to live with it.*

be resigned to sth/resign yourself to sth /biː rɪ'zaɪnd tuː (sth), rɪ'zaɪn jɔːʳself tuː (sth)/ ESPECIALLY WRITTEN to realize that you must accept an unpleasant situation, because you cannot prevent it or avoid it: *Joe is resigned to the fact that he will miss tomorrow's big race. | Pat knew her husband wasn't coming back and she was resigned to being alone. | She had resigned herself to a life of cooking and cleaning.*

◯ **make the best of it/make the most of it** /,meɪk ðə 'best əv ɪt, ,meɪk ðə 'məʊst əv ɪt/ ESPECIALLY SPOKEN to accept a situation that you do not like, and try to enjoy it or use it in the best or most complete way possible: *It's not the college I really wanted to go to, but I suppose I'll just have to make the best of it. | It rained every day we were in Paris, but we made the most of it.*

---

5 to officially accept a new law or proposal

pass /pɑːs‖pæs/ [v T] if a parliament or similar group **passes** a law or proposal, the members vote to accept it: *The State Assembly passed a law* which banned smoking in public places. | The bill was passed by 197 votes to 50.

approve /ə'pruːv/ [v T] to officially accept a plan or proposal to do something: *The Medical Research Council said it could not approve the use of the new drug.* | *The deal has already been approved by shareholders.*

approval /ə'pruːvəl/ [n U] when a suggestion or plan is officially accepted: *The parking proposals have been given the mayor's approval.* (=he has approved them)

ACCIDENT

➡ if you mean 'by accident', go to **ACCIDENTALLY**

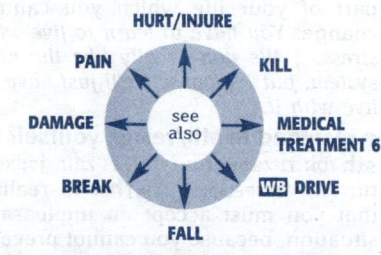

HURT/INJURE

PAIN   KILL

DAMAGE   see also   MEDICAL TREATMENT 6

BREAK   WB DRIVE

FALL

1   at home, at work, when doing a sport etc

accident /'æksɪ̞dənt/ [n C] when someone gets hurt or something gets damaged, without anyone intending them to be: *Jim was rushed to the hospital after an accident at work.*

have an accident *She had an accident while she was playing basketball and broke her arm.*

serious accident *The park is now closed following a serious accident last week.*

riding/climbing/skiing etc accident *Greg has been unable to walk since he was injured in a riding accident.*

2   in a car, train, plane etc

accident /'æksɪ̞dənt/ [n C] when a car, train etc hits an object, a person, or another vehicle: *We saw an accident on the motorway this morning.*

have an accident *Older drivers have fewer accidents on the roads than people under 25.*

bad/serious accident *There are delays on the main road into town following a serious accident.*

fatal accident (=when someone dies as a result) *There were two fatal accidents in the factory last year.*

road/car accident *Road accidents are the biggest cause of death among young people.*

crash /kræʃ/ [n C] an accident in which a car, plane, train etc hits something and is badly damaged or destroyed: *Wearing a seat belt can save your life in a crash.*

plane/train/car crash *Her husband died in a plane crash when he was only 30.*

have a crash/be in a crash (=in a car) *Have you ever had a crash?*

crash /kræʃ/ [v I/T] to have an accident in a car, train etc by hitting something: *The plane crashed just after take-off.* | *Prost lost control on the first bend and crashed.* | *Someone stole my car and crashed it.*

+into *The truck skidded across the road before crashing into a wall.*

> ⚠ Don't say 'crash with something'. Say **crash into something**.

wreck /rek/ [n C] AMERICAN a serious accident in which a car hits another vehicle: *The wreck caused a 5-mile traffic jam.*

collision /kə'lɪʒən/ [n C] an accident in which two or more cars, planes etc hit each other while they are moving: *Several cars were involved in a collision on the expressway this morning.*

+with *The 25-year-old man was thrown from his motorcycle in a collision with a truck.*

+between *a mid-air collision between two planes*

head-on collision (=between two cars etc moving directly towards each other)

pile-up /'paɪl ʌp/ [n C] a serious road accident in which a lot of vehicles hit each other: *The pile-up happened in thick fog.*

get run over/get run down /ˌget rʌn 'əʊvər, ˌget rʌn 'daʊn/ if someone **gets run over** or **gets run down**, a car or other vehicle hits them, and they get hurt or killed: *I could cross the street tomorrow and get run over by a truck, and no one would care. | I nearly got run down by some crazy taxi driver.*

3 an extremely bad accident when people are killed

disaster /dɪ'zɑːstər‖-'zæs-/ [n C] an extremely bad accident in which a lot of people are killed: *Thousands of people were killed or injured in the Chernobyl nuclear disaster. | Could your hospitals cope with a major disaster like a train crash?*
natural disaster (=caused by wind, rain, or other natural forces) *Natural disasters such as earthquakes are common in this part of the world.*
catastrophe /kə'tæstrəfi/ [n C] a terrible event that causes death, damage, and destruction over a very large area: *The destruction of the ozone layer could lead to an environmental catastrophe. | fears of a possible nuclear catastrophe*

ACCIDENTALLY

when you do something that you did not intend to do

➡ opposite **DELIBERATELY**

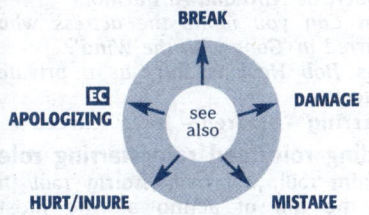

accidentally/by accident /ˌæks¦-'deˌntli◂, baɪ 'æks¦dənt/ [adv] if you do something **accidentally** or **by accident**, you do it even though you did not intend to: *I accidentally burnt a hole in her sofa with my cigarette. | Doctors discovered the new drug quite by accident, while they were researching something else.*

> ⚠ **Accidentally** can come between the subject and the verb (*I accidentally broke it*), but **by accident** usually comes at the end of a sentence or clause (*I broke it by accident*).

by mistake /baɪ mɪ'steɪk/ [adv] if you do something **by mistake**, you intend to do one thing but you make a mistake and do something else instead: *Gary wandered into the wrong hotel room by mistake. | Police believe Burton may have shot the woman by mistake.*

> ⚠ **By mistake** usually comes at the end of a sentence or clause.

unintentionally /ˌʌnɪn'tenʃənəli/ [adv] ESPECIALLY WRITTEN if you do something **unintentionally**, especially something bad, you do it even though you did not intend to: *Some male science teachers unintentionally discourage the girls in their classes.*

◌ didn't mean to /ˌdɪdnt 'miːn tuː/ ESPECIALLY SPOKEN if you **didn't mean to** do something bad or wrong, you did not intend to do it
didn't mean to do sth *Sorry, I didn't mean to upset you. | I'm sure Rachel didn't mean to leave the door unlocked.*

> ⚠ You often say **I didn't mean to** when you are saying sorry to someone: *I'm sorry I shouted at you. I didn't mean to.*

accidental /ˌæks¦'dentl◂/ [adj] use this about bad or dangerous things that happen, which no one intended to happen: *The court recorded a verdict of accidental death on a man who drowned in the river. | Villagers were in shock after the accidental shooting of a 10-year-old last week.*

> **Formal or informal?**
> **Accidental** is mainly used in formal writing or news reports, although it is sometimes used in ordinary conversation after 'be': *Was his death accidental?*

unintentional /ˌʌnɪn'tenʃənəl◂/ [adj] ESPECIALLY WRITTEN said or done accidentally, especially when you were trying to say or do something completely different: *Any offence these remarks might have caused was wholly unintentional.*

🔍**it was an accident** /ɪt wəz ən ˈæksɪ̆dənt/ SPOKEN say this to tell someone that you did not intend to do something, for example when you have broken something or made a mistake, and someone is angry with you: *It was an accident – the handle just came off when I picked it up.*

ACTOR/ACTRESS

➡ see also WB **FILMS/MOVIES,**
WB **THEATRE/PLAYS,** WB **TELEVISION AND RADIO**

1 someone who performs in plays or films

actor /ˈæktəʳ/ [n C] someone whose job is to perform in plays or films: *Keanu Reeves is my favourite actor.* | *The actor who played Macbeth was really good.*
lead/leading actor *She's starred with many leading actors.*
actress /ˈæktrɪ̆s/ [n C] a woman whose job is to perform in plays or films: *I've always wanted to be an actress.*

> ⚠ You can use **actor** about a man or a woman. Some women prefer to be called **actors** and do not like the word **actress**.

star /stɑːʳ/ [n C] a very famous and successful actor, especially in films: *Hundreds of fans gathered to watch the stars arriving at the Oscar ceremony.*
film/movie star a glamorous Hollywood movie star

2 to be in a play or film

act /ækt/ [v I] to be an actor in plays or films, especially as a job: *I first started acting when I was twelve years old.* | *She always enjoyed acting.*
acting /ˈæktɪŋ/ [n U] the job or skill of being an actor: *Before he became famous, James Dean studied acting in New York.* | *a career in acting*
play /pleɪ/ [v T] to act as a particular character in a play or film

play Hamlet/Cleopatra/James Bond etc *Timothy Dalton was the fourth actor to play James Bond.* | *The taxi driver is played by Jamie Foxx.*
play the part (of sb) *We still need someone to play the part of the messenger.*

🔍**be in sth** /biː ˈɪn (sth)/ [phrasal verb T] ESPECIALLY SPOKEN to act in a particular play or film: *He was very young when he was in "Home Alone".*

perform /pəʳˈfɔːʳm/ [v T] if a group of actors **perform** a play, they act in it for people to watch: *The children perform a Christmas play every year.* | *The group will be performing 'Cats' in the Open Air Theatre.*
performance /pəʳˈfɔːʳməns/ [n C] the way someone acts in a play or film – use this to talk about how good or bad someone's acting is: *She won an Oscar for her performance in 'Monster'.*
give a good/bad etc performance *Meryl Streep gave a marvellous performance as the mother.*

3 to be the most important actor in a play or film

star /stɑːʳ/ [v I/T] if an actor **stars** in a film or a play, he or she is one of the most important actors in it; if a film or play **stars** an actor, he or she plays one of the most important characters in it: *'Heat' is a police drama starring Robert de Niro and Al Pacino.*
+in *Can you name the actress who starred in 'Gone with the Wind'?*
+as *Bob Hoskins stars as a private detective.*
starring – starred – have starred

leading role/lead role/starring role /ˌliːdɪŋ ˈrəʊl, ˌliːd ˈrəʊl, ˌstɑːrɪŋ ˈrəʊl/ [n C] the job of acting as the most important character in a film: *Judy Garland became famous after her starring role in 'The Wizard of Oz'.*
play the leading/lead/starring role (=act as the most important character) *Michael Keaton played the leading role in the first two 'Batman' movies.*

lead /liːd/ [n C] the most important actor or character in a play or film
play the lead (=be the main actor) *She was given the chance to play the lead when Pamela Anderson became ill.*

4   the person that an actor pretends to be in a play or film

character /ˈkærɪ̧ktəʳ/ [n C] one of the people in the story of a play or film: *Moore's character is a New York policeman who drinks too much.*

part /pɑːʳt/ [n C] the job of acting as a particular character in a play or film: *She knew she wanted the part as soon as she read the script.*

play the part of sb (=act as a particular character) *She played the part of the Wicked Stepmother in 'Snow White'.*

ADD

➡ see also **MORE, INCREASE, INCLUDE/ NOT INCLUDE**

1   to add a new part to something

add /æd/ [v T] to put a new part or piece onto or into something, especially in order to improve it: *The book would look a lot more attractive if they added a few colour pictures.*

add sth to sth *Adding fertilizer to the soil will help the plants to grow more quickly.* | *The fresh chillies add a spicy flavour to the sauce.*

add on /ˌæd ˈɒn‖-ˈɑːn/ [phrasal verb T] to add another part to something so that it becomes bigger

add on sth *We're having a bedroom added on at the back of the house.*

2   to put two or more numbers together

➡ see also **COUNT/CALCULATE**

add /æd/ [v T] if you add numbers or amounts together, you calculate their total

add sth and sth/add sth to sth *"What do you get when you add 68 and 32?" "100."*

3   to increase an amount or cost

add /æd/ [v I/T] to add more to an amount or to the cost of something:

The builder added an extra £150 to the bill for no reason.

add (sth) to sth *Watson's recent victory added $30,000 to his total prize money in 1996.* | *Using better quality paper will add to the cost.*

increase /ɪnˈkriːs/ [v T] to make an amount or cost become larger: *The company will increase your salary after six months, provided your work is satisfactory.*

increase sth by sth *We need to increase our prices by 8%.*

put sth on sth /ˌpʊt (sth) ˈɒn (sth) ‖-ˈɑːn-/ [phrasal verb T] to add an amount of money or tax to the cost of something: *The new tax will put another ten cents on the price of gas.*

4   something that is added

addition /əˈdɪʃən/ [n C/U] something that is added to something else

+to *The latest addition to the museum's collection is a picture by Salvador Dali.*

make an addition *The chair makes a good addition to the room.*

additive /ˈædɪ̧tɪv/ [n C] a chemical substance that is added to food in order to make it taste better or stay fresh longer: *This product contains no artificial additives.*

ADMIRE

to respect and like someone

1   to admire someone

admire /ədˈmaɪəʳ/ [v T] to have a very good opinion of someone, either because they have achieved something good or because they have skills or qualities that you think are good: *I admire the way she's brought up those children on her own.* | *Which world leader do you most admire?*

admire sb for sth *She had to admire him for the way he handled the situation.*

respect /rɪˈspekt/ [v T] to have a good opinion of someone even if you do not like them, because they have high standards or good personal qualities: *All the staff respected him.*

respect sb for doing sth *I don't agree with him, but I respect him for sticking to his principles.*

⚠ Don't say 'I respect to him'. Just say **I respect him**.

look up to sb /ˌlʊk ˈʌp tuː (sb)/ [*phrasal verb* T] to admire and respect someone who is older than you or who has authority over you: *I always looked up to my older brothers.*

idolize (also **idolise** BRITISH) /ˈaɪdəl-aɪz/ [v T] to admire someone very much, especially a famous person, so that you think everything about them is perfect: *Marilyn Monroe was idolized by movie fans all over the world.*

2 the feeling of admiring someone

admiration /ˌædməˈreɪʃən/ [n U] the feeling you have about someone when you think that they have achieved something good or that they have skills or qualities that are good
in/with admiration *We listened with admiration as she played the violin.*
+for *The other players were full of admiration for him.*

respect /rɪˈspekt/ [n U] the feeling you have when you admire someone because they have high standards or good personal qualities
+for *My respect for my teacher grew as the months passed.*
great respect (=a lot of respect) *I have great respect for Tony's judgment.*
earn/win sb's respect (=make someone respect you) *She always managed to win the kids' respect.*

3 someone you admire

hero/heroine /ˈhɪərəʊ, ˈherəʊɪn/ [n C] your **hero** or **heroine** is a man or woman who you admire very much because of their achievements, skills, or personal qualities: *When I was young, David Bowie was my hero.*
plural **heroes**

idol /ˈaɪdl/ [n C] a famous actor, actress, musician, or sports player that a lot of

people admire: *Thousands of fans were at the airport to greet their idol.* | *pop idol, Robbie Williams*

ADMIT

➡ see also **CRIME, MISTAKE, GUILTY/ NOT GUILTY**

1 to agree that you have done something wrong

admit /ədˈmɪt/ [v I/T] to say that you have done something wrong or illegal, especially when someone asks or persuades you to do this
+(that) *Blake finally admitted he had stolen the money.* | *She admitted that she had made a mistake.*
admit (to) doing sth *Many workers admit to taking time off work when they are not sick.* | *He admitted taking the car without the owner's permission.*
admit responsibility *The hospital has refused to admit responsibility for his death.*
admitting – admitted – have admitted

confess /kənˈfes/ [v I/T] to tell the police or someone in a position of authority that you have done something illegal or bad, especially after they have persuaded you to do this: *After two days of questioning, he finally confessed.*
+(that) *She later confessed that she had killed her husband.*
confess to a robbery/murder/crime etc *People were forced to confess to crimes they had not committed.*
confess to doing sth *Edwards eventually confessed to being a spy.*

own up /ˌəʊn ˈʌp/ [*phrasal verb* I] to admit that you did something, especially something that is not very serious: *Unless the guilty person owns up, the whole class will be punished.*
own up to (doing) sth *No-one owned up to breaking the window.*

Formal or informal?
Own up is more informal than **admit** or **confess**.

2 a statement admitting something

confession /kən'feʃən/ [n C] an official statement that someone makes to the police, admitting that they have done something illegal and explaining what happened: *He says that he was beaten and forced to sign a confession.*
make a confession *At 3 a.m., Higgins broke down and made a full confession.*

admission /əd'mɪʃən/ [n C usually singular] when you admit that you were wrong or that you have done something bad or illegal: *I'm surprised to hear you make such an admission.*
+(that) *The Senator's admission that he had lied to Congress shocked many Americans.*
admission of guilt/failure/defeat (=when you admit that you are guilty, you have failed etc) *The court may assume that your silence is an admission of guilt.*

Formal or informal?
Admission is formal when used in spoken English.

3 to agree that something is true, although you do not want to

admit /əd'mɪt/ [v I/T] to accept that something is true or that someone is right, although you do not want to accept it, or you feel embarrassed about accepting it: *"Yes, I was frightened," he admitted.*
+(that) *I know you don't like her, but you have to admit that she's good at her job.*
admit (to) doing sth *He admitted to lying to his wife and her family.*
🗩 **I must admit (that)/I have to admit (that)** SPOKEN *I must admit I really enjoy watching soap operas.*
🗩 **admit it** SPOKEN *You were wrong, weren't you? Come on, admit it!*
admitting – admitted – have admitted

admittedly /əd'mɪtᵻdli/ [adv] use this when you are admitting that something is true: *Admittedly, the questions were fairly easy, but you all did very well. | The treatment is painful, admittedly, but it is usually very successful.*

Formal or informal?
Don't use **admittedly** in very informal conversation.

ADULT

➡ opposite **CHILD**
➡ see also **AGE, OLD, YOUNG**

1 not a child

adult /'ædʌlt, ə'dʌlt/ [n C] someone who is not a child – use this to talk about someone who is at least 18: *The cost of the trip is $59 for adults and $30 for children. | Some children find it difficult to talk to adults.*

⚠ You can also use **adult** before a noun, like an adjective: *The book is intended for adult readers. | adult education*

⚠ Don't say 'adult people'. Just say **adults**.

grown-up /ˌgrəʊn 'ʌp◂/ [n C] an adult – used especially by children or when you are talking to children: *Grown-ups are so boring! All they ever do is talk!*
grown-up [adj] *Margaret has two grown-up sons. | Ryan felt very grown-up being allowed to stay up so late.*

full grown/fully grown /ˌfʊl 'grəʊn◂, ˌfʊli 'grəʊn◂/ [adj] a person, animal, or plant that is **full grown** or **fully grown** has reached its full adult size: *A fully grown blue whale may be up to 30m long.*

2 to become an adult

grow up /ˌgrəʊ 'ʌp/ [phrasal verb I] to develop from being a child to being an adult: *What do you want to do when you grow up? | We plan to go and live in Florida when the children have grown up.*

3 the time when someone is an adult

adult life /ˌædʌlt ˈlaɪf, əˌdʌlt-/ [n U] the part of someone's life when they are an adult: *He has spent most of his adult life in the US.*

adulthood /ˈædʌlthʊd, əˈdʌlthʊd/ [n U] FORMAL the time when you are an adult – use this especially to talk about people reaching this time: *Children with the disease have little chance of surviving to adulthood.*

reach adulthood (=become an adult) *By the time we reach adulthood our heart-rate has dropped to around 70 beats per minute.*

ADVANTAGE/ DISADVANTAGE

➡ look here for . . .
- the good and bad points about something
- something that makes some people more successful than others

➡ see also **GOOD, BAD**

1 a good feature of something

advantage /ədˈvɑːntɪdʒ‖ədˈvæn-/ [n C] a good feature of something, for example a way in which it is useful or better than other things of the same kind: *There are several methods of saving money, but this one has obvious advantages.*

+of *The advantage of cycling to work is that I get some exercise.*

big advantage *One of the biggest advantages of a digital camera is that you can see the photos as soon as you've taken them.*

🔾 **the good thing about sth** /ðə ˈɡʊd θɪŋ əbaʊt (sth)/ ESPECIALLY SPOKEN use this when you are talking about one of the main advantages of something: *The good thing about this job is that I can work from home whenever I want.*

benefit /ˈbenɪfɪt/ [n C/U] a feature of something that has a good effect on people's lives: *Tourism has brought many benefits to the area.*

+of *the benefits of a healthy lifestyle* |

What are the benefits, for Britain, of belonging to the European Union?

2 a bad feature of something

disadvantage /ˌdɪsədˈvɑːntɪdʒ‖-ˈvæn-/ [n C] a bad feature of something, for example a way in which it causes problems or is worse than other things of the same kind: *Nuclear power has a lot of disadvantages – for example what do you do with all the nuclear waste?*

+of *The main disadvantage of being a nurse is working irregular hours.*

drawback /ˈdrɔːbæk/ [n C] a disadvantage of something, which makes it seem less attractive – use this especially when something seems good in other ways: *It's a good-looking car – the only drawback is the price.*

+of *One of the drawbacks of working for a large company is that you never know who is really in charge.*

+to *The only drawback to her new job was having to get up really early in the morning.*

3 when you compare what is good and bad about something

advantages and disadvantages /ədˌvɑːntɪdʒɪz ən ˌdɪsədvɑːntɪdʒɪz‖-ˌvæn-/ the good and bad features of something – use this especially when you are comparing what is good and what is bad about something

+of *We had to write about the advantages and disadvantages of living in a big city.*

pros and cons /ˌprəʊz ən ˈkɒnz‖-ˈkɑːnz/ the advantages and disadvantages of something, which you need to think about in order to make a decision

+of *Your doctor should explain the pros and cons of the different treatments available.*

weigh up the pros and cons (=think carefully about all the advantages and disadvantages) *Students should weigh up the pros and cons of each university.*

pluses and minuses /ˌplʌsɪz ən ˈmaɪnəsɪz/ INFORMAL the advantages and disadvantages of something such as a plan or method, that you consider before you do something or that you notice after it has been done **+of** *She talked about some of the pluses and minuses of being self-employed.*

4 something that helps someone to be more successful than others

advantage /əd'vɑːntɪdʒ‖əd'væn-/ [n C] something that makes you more likely to succeed than other people
have an advantage *The American team seemed to have all the advantages – better training, better facilities, and much better financial support.*
give sb an advantage (=make them more likely to succeed)
+over *I had already lived in France for a year, and this gave me a big advantage over the other students.*

privilege /'prɪvɪlɪdʒ/ [n C] a special advantage or right that only a few people have, for example because their family is rich or because they have an important job: *MPs have a number of special privileges, such as free travel on the railways.*
the privilege of sth *Not everyone has the privilege of a private education.*
privileged [adj] having a lot of privileges: *At that time, the universities were only open to a privileged minority.*

5 something that makes it more difficult for someone to succeed

disadvantage /ˌdɪsəd'vɑːntɪdʒ‖-'væn-/ [n C] something that makes it more difficult for you to succeed or do what you want, especially as compared with other people
have a disadvantage *She has one big disadvantage – she lacks experience.*
be at a disadvantage (=have a disadvantage compared with other people) *In basketball, smaller players are at a disadvantage.*

ADVERTISING

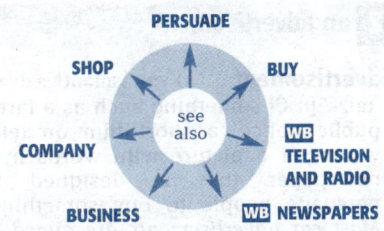

PERSUADE
SHOP   BUY
see also
COMPANY   **WB** TELEVISION AND RADIO
BUSINESS   **WB** NEWSPAPERS

1 advertising

advertising /'ædvətaɪzɪŋ/ [n U] the business of persuading people to buy things, using pictures, words, songs etc on TV and radio, large public notices, and newspapers and magazines: *How much does Coca-Cola spend on advertising?* | *Cigarette advertising isn't allowed on TV any more.* | *Beth wants a job in advertising.* (=in a company that makes advertisements) | *How much do you think you are influenced by advertising?*
advertising campaign (=a planned series of advertisements for a new product) *a nationwide advertising campaign for a new range of soap*

publicity /pʌ'blɪsɪti/ [n U] the business of making sure that people know about a new product, a new film, a famous person etc, for example by talking about them on TV or writing about them in magazines: *The show's organizers spent over $500,000 on publicity alone.*
good/bad publicity *The band appeared on the Larry King show, which was good publicity for their US tour.*

marketing /'mɑːkɪtɪŋ/ [n U] the business of trying to sell a product by deciding which type of people are likely to buy it and making it attractive and interesting to them: *I'm looking for a job in marketing.* | *Good marketing has always been a major factor in the company's success.*

hype /haɪp/ [n U] INFORMAL attempts to make people interested in a product, entertainer, film etc, using television, radio, and newspapers – use this especially to show that you do not trust this kind of information: *Despite all the hype, I thought the film was pretty boring.*

2 an advertisement

advertisement /əd'vɜːtᵻsmənt‖ˌædvər-'taɪz-/ [n C] something such as a large public notice, a short film on television, or a picture with words in a newspaper that is designed to persuade people to buy something: *Most car advertisements are aimed at men.*
+for *In the autumn, the newspapers are full of advertisements for winter breaks.*

ad (also **advert** BRITISH) /æd, 'ædvɜːˈt/ [n C] INFORMAL an advertisement: *He began his acting career by doing shampoo adverts on TV.*
+for *The local papers are full of ads for cheap furniture and washing machines and things.*

commercial /kə'mɜːˈʃəl/ [n C] an advertisement on television or radio: *Have you seen the new Levi's commercial?*
commercial break (=when there are commercials in the middle of a programme) *We'll be right back with you after a short commercial break.*

pop-up /'pɒp ʌp‖'pɑːp-/ [n C] an advertisement that appears in a small box on your computer screen when you are using the Internet, and which is sent there from the website you are looking at: *A lot of people find pop-ups really annoying.*

flyer /'flaɪəˈ/ [n C] a sheet of paper advertising a shop, club, concert, or other event, that is handed out to people in the street: *People were handing out flyers all along Oxford Street.*

slogan /'sləʊgən/ [n C] a short clever phrase used in an advertisement: *a dry-cleaning company that used the slogan 'We know the meaning of cleaning'*

hoarding BRITISH **billboard** AMERICAN /'hɔːˈdɪŋ, 'bɪlbɔːˈd/ [n C] a large flat board in a public place, where large printed advertisements are shown: *Beside the freeway was a huge billboard covered in ads for washing powder.*

3 to advertise something

advertise /'ædvəˈtaɪz/ [v I/T] to use advertisements on television or radio, in newspapers etc, in order to try to persuade people to buy something: *There was a big poster advertising a well-known brand of cola. | a small company that can't afford to advertise on TV*
be advertised on TV/the radio *"How did you find out about the new software?" "It was advertised on TV."*
be advertised in a newspaper/ magazine etc *The concert was advertised in all the national newspapers.*

> Don't write 'advertize'. **Advertise** is never spelled with a 'z'.

promote /prə'məʊt/ [v T] to try to make people buy a new product, see a new film etc, for example by selling it at a lower price or talking about it on television: *Meg Ryan is in Europe to promote her new movie.*
promote sth as sth *They're trying to promote Dubai as a tourist destination.*

ADVISE

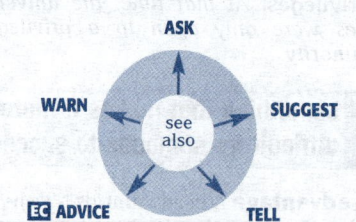

ASK
WARN
see also
SUGGEST
EC ADVICE
TELL

1 to advise someone

advise /əd'vaɪz/ [v T] to tell someone what you think they should do, especially when you have more knowledge or experience than they have
advise sb to do sth *I advise you to think very carefully before making a decision. | All US citizens in the area have been advised to return home.*
advise sb against doing sth (=advise them not to do it) *Her lawyers have*

advised her against saying anything to the newspapers.

advise sb on/about sth *Your teacher will be able to advise you about what qualifications you will need.*

strongly advise *I'd strongly advise you to get medical insurance if you're going skiing.*

> **Formal or informal?**
> **Advise** is more formal than **say sb should do sth**. It can be used in spoken English when giving someone professional advice or advice about something serious.

 Don't confuse 'advise' and 'advice'. **Advise** is a verb and **advice** is a noun.

say sb should do sth/say sb ought to do sth /ˌseɪ (sb) ʃʊd 'duː (sth), ˌseɪ (sb) ɔːt tə 'duː (sth)/ to give your personal opinion about what someone should do: *My friends keep saying I ought to learn to drive.* | *Her mother said she should call the police immediately.*

> This is the most common way of saying 'to **advise** someone'.

tell /tel/ [v T] to tell someone that you think they should do something, especially in order to avoid problems
tell sb to do sth *I told him to go and see a doctor if he was worried.*
tell sb (that) they should do sth *I told him he should take more exercise.*
telling – told – have told

> **Formal or informal?**
> Use **tell** especially in spoken English or informal writing.

suggest /sə'dʒest‖səg-/ [v T] to tell someone your ideas about what they should do, where they should go etc: *"Why not ask Dad?" he suggested.*
+(that) *Sarah suggested that I should apply for this job.*

give advice /ˌgɪv əd'vaɪs/ to advise someone about a problem or subject, especially something that they have asked you about: *The centre gives advice to young people who have drug problems.*

give sb advice *Can you give me some advice? I'm thinking of buying a new computer.*

> Don't say 'give someone advices' or 'give someone an advice'. **Advice** is an uncountable noun.

2　to ask someone to advise you

ask sb's advice /ˌɑːsk (sb's) əd'vaɪs‖ˌæsk-/ to ask someone to advise you about something: *Can I ask your advice? I need to find somewhere to stay in London.*
+on/about *I always ask my brother's advice about computers.*

consult /kən'sʌlt/ [v T] FORMAL to get advice from someone who is paid to advise people, for example a lawyer or a doctor: *If the symptoms persist, consult your doctor.* | *I want to consult my lawyer before I say anything.*
consult sb about sth *Tonight the President will consult his military advisers about the likelihood of an attack.*

3　to do what someone advises you to do

take sb's advice/follow sb's advice /ˌteɪk (sb's) əd'vaɪs, ˌfɒləʊ (sb's) əd'vaɪs‖ˌfaː-/ *I've decided to take your advice and go to art school.* | *If she had followed my advice, this would never have happened.*

listen to sb /'lɪsən tuː (sb)/ to do what someone advises you to do, especially because you respect them and trust their judgement: *You tell him, Dad – I'm sure he'll listen to you.* | *Bob warned us about this. I wish we'd listened to him.*

on sb's advice/on the advice of sb /ɒn (sb's) əd'vaɪs, ɒn ði əd'vaɪs ɒv (sb)/ FORMAL if you do something **on someone's advice** or **on the advice of someone**, you do it because they have advised you to do it: *On her doctor's advice, she took a few days off work.* | *The decision was made by the president on the advice of a Supreme Court judge.*

A

4 someone's opinion about what you should do

advice /əd'vaɪs/ [n U] what someone advises you to do: *Get some advice from the people in the tourist office.*
+on/about *For advice on AIDS, phone this free number.*
give sb advice *My doctor gave me some good advice about how to eat sensibly.*
piece of advice (=some advice) *Years ago, my father gave me a piece of advice that I've never forgotten.*
medical/legal/professional advice *You should get legal advice before you sign the contract.*

> ⚠ **Advice** is an uncountable noun, so don't say 'an advice' or 'some advices'. Say **a piece of advice** or **some advice**.

tip /tɪp/ [n C] a simple but useful piece of advice about how to do something more easily or more effectively: *Here's a good tip: if you spill red wine on a carpet, pour salt on it to get rid of the stain.*
+on *useful tips on how to take better photos*

guidance /'gaɪdəns/ [n U] advice about what to do in your job, your education, or your private life – use this especially about advice you get from your parents or from someone whose job is to advise and help people
give guidance on sth *Your teacher can give you guidance on choosing a career.* | *Parents should give moral guidance to their children.*

counselling BRITISH **counseling** AMERICAN /'kaʊnsəlɪŋ/ [n U] support given by an expert, to help someone who has personal problems or who has had a very unpleasant experience: *The college provides counselling for students who have emotional problems.* | *Victims of violent crimes often need counseling.*

5 someone who advises people

adviser (also **advisor** AMERICAN) /əd'vaɪzər/ [n C] someone whose job is to give advice, especially in business, law, or politics

financial/legal/careers adviser *Talk to an independent financial adviser before you invest your money.*
+on *the government's senior adviser on the environment*
+to *She's been appointed as scientific advisor to the President.*

AFTER

➡ opposite **BEFORE**
➡ see also **LATER/AT A LATER TIME**

1 after something happens or after someone does something

after /'ɑːftər‖'æf-/ [preposition/conjunction/adv] *After the party Jo stayed behind to help clean up the mess.* | *What are you going to do after you finish college?* | *Let's eat after the movie.* | *Less than a month after he left England, he wanted to go home.*
after that *In the summer Joni left him, and after that he always looked sad.*
just after (=a short time after) *My mother died just after Mark was born.*
straight after/right after (=immediately after) *We'll be starting the class straight after lunch.*

> ⚠ **After** can be used as an adverb, but only in expressions like **soon after** and **not long after**: *I left college when I was 21, and got married soon after.* Don't use **after** on its own as an adverb. Instead, use **then**, **after that**, or **afterwards** in sentences like this: *We had a game of tennis, and then/after that/afterwards we went for a cup of coffee.*

> ⚠ Don't use 'will' with **after**. Don't say 'after I will leave school, I am going to university'. Say **after I leave school ...**

afterwards (also **afterward** AMERICAN) /'ɑːftərwərd(z)‖'æf-/ [adv] after an event or a time that you have just mentioned: *Afterwards, Nick said he'd never been so nervous in his life.* | *What's the point of going to the gym if you always eat a chocolate bar afterwards?*
two years/three months etc afterwards *A couple of years*

afterwards I met him by chance in the street.

soon/shortly afterwards (=a short time later) *Her husband became ill and died soon afterwards.*

next /nekst/ [*adv*] after something happens or after someone does something – use this when you are describing a series of events in the order they happened: *Can you remember what happened next? | First we asked Jim what to do. Next we tried asking Dad.*

then /ðen/ [*adv*] after you have done something – use this when you are describing a series of things you did, or when you are giving instructions: *First we played tennis, and then we went swimming. | Add a cup of sugar. Then beat in three eggs.*

2 after a particular time or date

after /ˈɑːftəʳ‖ˈæf-/ [*preposition*] *Could you call again after 6 o'clock? | After 1800, more and more people worked in factories.*

just after (=a short time after) *If they left just after twelve, they should be here soon.*

past /pɑːst‖pæst/ [*preposition*] ESPECIALLY BRITISH after a particular time, usually a short time later: *Wake up! It's past 9 o'clock!*

past midnight *We didn't get home till past midnight.*

way/well past INFORMAL (=a long time after) *Sorry, it's way past closing time.*

> **Past** is often used to emphasize that it is after a particular time.

from/as from /frəm, ˈæz frəm/ [*preposition*] use this to say that a new rule or arrangement will start at a particular time and will continue from then: *We will be at our new address from next week. | As from tomorrow, all accidents must be reported to me.*

from then on /frəm ˌðen ˈɒn/ use this to talk about something that started to happen at a time in the past, and continued from that time: *He went to his first football game when he was four, and from then on he was crazy about it.*

3 after a period of time has passed

after /ˈɑːftəʳ‖ˈæf-/ [*preposition*] **after a week/several hours/a long time etc** a week, several hours etc after a period of time has passed: *After half an hour we got tired of waiting and went home. | Jane was very shy, but after a while* (=after a short time) *she became more confident.*

after a week/a year etc of (doing) sth *The war ended after another six months of fighting.*

in /ɪn/ [*preposition*]

in a minute/a few hours/a month etc a minute, a few hours etc after the present time: *I'll be with you in a minute. | Rosie should be home in a week or two. | He gets his exam results in a couple of days.*

in an hour's time/a few minutes' time etc *In a few weeks' time I'll be off to university.*

> You can use **after** when talking about the past or the future. But use **in** only when talking about the future.

within /wɪðˈɪn‖wɪðˈɪn, wɪθˈɪn/ [*preposition*]

within a month/two weeks/a year etc less than a month, two weeks etc after something happens, especially when this is an unusually short time: *One of the soldiers was bitten by a snake and was dead within three hours. | Within minutes the building was full of smoke.*

within a month/a few days etc of doing sth *The plane got into difficulties within a few minutes of taking off.*

later /ˈleɪtəʳ/ [*adv*] some time after the present time or after the time you are talking about: *See you later. | He later became Governor of California.*

three months/two years/ten days etc later *A couple of days later I saw her in a downtown bar.*

later on (=at a later time during the same day, event etc) *The first half of the movie is really boring, but it gets better later on.*

much later (=a long time afterwards) *Eventually he got married, but that was much later.*

later that day/month/year etc (=use

this when telling stories or describing past events) *Later that month we got another letter, asking for more money.*
later in the morning/evening/day etc *Let's meet for dinner later in the week.*

> ⚠ Don't use **after** and **later** in the same sentence.

4 the next day/month/year etc

next /nekst/ [*adj* only before noun]
the next day/week etc the day, week etc that comes just after the one you were talking about: *I finished my classes on the 5th, and the next day I went home to Cleveland.*
next Monday/week/August etc (=the one after this Monday, this week, this August etc) *Next Thursday is my birthday.*

> ⚠ Don't confuse **next week** and **the next week**. Use **next week**, **next Friday** etc (without **the**) to talk about the future: *See you next Saturday!* Use **the next week**, **the next day** etc to talk about the past: *She got married and spent the next five years in Boston.*

> ⚠ Don't say 'on next Sunday'. Just say **next Sunday**.

> ⚠ Don't say 'next Tuesday/Friday' etc when you are talking about a day in the present week. Say **this Tuesday/Friday** etc: *The concert's this Saturday, not next Saturday.*

after /ˈɑːftəʳ‖ˈæf-/ [*adv/preposition/ conjunction*] **the day/Monday/ month/year after** the day, Monday, month etc that comes after the time or event that you are talking about: *The party's not this Saturday but the Saturday after.* | *The weather changed the morning after we arrived.* | *I felt rather tired the day after the party.*

following /ˈfɒləʊɪŋ‖ˈfɑː-/ [*adj* only before noun] **the following day/ month/year etc** the next day, month, year etc – use this especially in stories and descriptions, to talk about

what happened in the past: *The following day she woke up with a splitting headache.* | *They agreed to meet the following week.*

5 to happen or exist after something else

come after /ˌkʌm ˈɑːftəʳ‖-ˈæf-/ [*phrasal verb* T] to happen after something else and often as a result of something else: *The agreement came after six months of negotiations.*
come three weeks/five days etc after sth *My first chance to talk to her again came three days after the argument.*

follow /ˈfɒləʊ‖ˈfɑː-/ [*v* I/T] if an event or period **follows** another event or period, it happens after it: *We saw each other a lot in the months that followed.* | *the long period of stability that followed the war*
be followed by sth *The wedding was followed by a big party at the Chelsea Hotel.*
be closely followed by sth (=come very soon after) *His release from prison was closely followed by the sudden death of his father.*

6 the person, thing, or time that comes after the present one

next /nekst/ [*adj/adv*] the **next** person or thing is the one that comes just after the present one in a series, list etc: *Could you ask the next patient to come in, please?* | *Look at the diagram on the next page.* | *I'm afraid you'll have to wait for the next train.*
come next (=come immediately after something that has just been mentioned) *Kennedy, Johnson, Nixon ... who comes next?*
◯ **be next** (=be the next person or thing in a list, line etc) SPOKEN *Hey, I'm next! I was here before you!*

be after sth/come after sth /biː ˈɑːftəʳ (sth), ˌkʌm ˈɑːftəʳ (sth)‖-ˈæf-/ [*phrasal verb* T] if someone or something **is after** or **comes after** another person or thing in a list, line etc, they are the one just after, with no others in between: *My name is after hers on the list.* | *In American addresses, the name of the city always comes after the name of the street.*

later /ˈleɪtəʳ/ [adj only before noun] happening some time later, not immediately afterwards
a later date/time/chapter/meeting etc *We can decide on the final details at a later stage.* | *This will be discussed more fully in a later chapter.*
in later years/months/centuries etc ESPECIALLY WRITTEN *In later years, he became a Buddhist.*

subsequent /ˈsʌbsɪ̩kwənt/ [adj only before noun] FORMAL happening after something you have just mentioned: *Many of Marx's theories were disproved by subsequent events.* | *The first meeting will be in the City Hall, but all subsequent meetings will be held in the school.*

> ⚠ **Subsequent** is often followed by a plural noun.

follow /ˈfɒləʊ‖ˈfɑː-/ [v I/T] to come after something in a book, series, or list: *Taylor explains his theory in the pages that follow.*
be followed by sth *In English words, the letter Q is normally followed by a U.* | *Each chapter is followed by a set of exercises.*

7 when several things happen one after another

in a row /ɪn ə ˈrəʊ/ **four days in a row/three times in a row etc** when someone does something on four days, on three occasions etc, one after the other, with no other days etc in between: *He won the competition five years in a row.* | *I was late for school four days in a row.*

one after another /ˌwʌn ɑːftər əˈnʌðəʳ‖ -æf-/ if several things happen **one after another**, each thing happens immediately after the previous one: *There were three loud explosions, one after another.*

consecutive /kənˈsekjʊ̩tɪv/ [adj only before noun] FORMAL **consecutive** days, years, or occasions come one after the other, with no other days, years etc in between: *If you miss work*

for more than three consecutive days, you need a letter from your doctor.*
fourth/seventh etc consecutive *It was their fourth consecutive win this season.*

series /ˈsɪəriːz/ [n C] a **series** of events or actions is several of them that happen one after another
+of *She gave a series of talks at the university.* | *Harris finally resigned after a series of public scandals.*
plural **series**

AGAIN

➡ if you mean 'say something again', go to **SAY**

1 again

again /əˈgen, əˈgeɪn‖əˈgen/ [adv] *Would you say that again? I didn't hear you.* | *Julie! It's your sister on the phone again.* | *Nice to see you again.* | *Oh no! Here comes that boy again.* | *I rang the bell again, but no-one answered.*

> ⚠ **Again** usually comes at the end of a sentence or clause.

once again/once more /ˌwʌns əˈgen, ˌwʌns ˈmɔːʳ/ FORMAL again – use this to emphasize that something very worrying, serious, or annoying has happened before: *Once again I must remind you of the seriousness of the problems we face.* | *The crops had failed, and once more famine threatened the region.*

yet again /ˌjet əˈgen/ again – use this to emphasize that something has happened too many times before in a way that is very annoying: *Yet again, Flora had changed her mind.* | *It seems that yet again the police have allowed a very dangerous man to escape.*

again and again /əˌgen ənd əˈgen/ many times: *I've told you again and again – don't play ball in the house!*

over and over (again) /ˌəʊvər ənd ˌəʊvər əˈgen/ many times – use this especially when something is annoying or boring: *I've told him over and*

over again not to call me at work. |
She practised the lines over and over
until she had them memorized.

one more time/once more /ˌwʌn mɔːʳ
'taɪm, wʌn 'mɔːʳ/ again, and usually
for the last time: *He kissed her one
more time before he left.*
just one more time/just once more
Can we practise that just once more?

back /bæk/ [*adv*] again – use this about
telephoning or writing to someone
again, or asking someone to come to
your house again
call (sb) back *I'll call back as soon as
I have some news.* | *Can I call you
back later?*
write back (to sb) (=write a letter to
someone who has written a letter to
you) *I wrote back to them, thanking
them for their invitation.*
invite/ask sb back *Her kids wrecked
the house last time they were here –
that's why I've never asked them back.*

2 to do something again

do sth again /ˌduː (sth) ə'gen/ *I'd like
you to do this exercise again.* | *She
spilled coffee on the application form
and had to do it all again.*

repeat /rɪ'piːt/ [*v* T] to do something
again, especially many times, in
order to achieve something useful
**repeat a test/experiment/exercise/
process/performance** *Repeat the
process again and again until you can
do it in 30 seconds.* | *If you repeat the
exercise 20 times a day, you'll soon
have firmer, more muscular arms.*

> **Repeat** is used especially in instructions
> and technical writing.

over /'əʊvəʳ/ [*adv*] AMERICAN if you do
something **over**, you do it again from
the beginning: *I'm afraid you'll have
to do it over.* | *I'm sorry I messed it up
– let's start over.*

all over again /ˌɔːl ˌəʊvər ə'gen/
ESPECIALLY SPOKEN if you do something
long or difficult **all over again**, you
do it again from the beginning: *At the
police station they asked me the same
questions all over again.*
start (sth) all over again *The
computer crashed and I had to start the
essay all over again.*

redo /riː'duː/ [*v* T] to do a piece of work
again: *I can't read a word of this –
you'll have to redo it.*
redoing – redid – have redone

retake /riː'teɪk/ [*v* T] to do a test again
because you failed it: *She retook her
driving test five times before she
passed.*
retaking – retook – have retaken

3 to start again

start again /ˌstaːʳt ə'gen/ [*phrasal verb*
I/T] to start doing something again,
or to start happening again: *The drill-
ing noise started again in the next
room.*
start work/school etc again *After
her vacation Trish really didn't feel like
starting her classes again.*
start doing sth again *Have Jill and
Larry started talking to each other
again?*
start to do sth again *It's starting to
snow again.*

bring back sth /ˌbrɪŋ 'bæk (sth)/ [*phrasal
verb* T] to start to use a law, method,
or system again: *Do you think they
should bring back the death penalty?*

revival /rɪ'vaɪvəl/ [*n* C] when something
becomes popular or fashionable
again – use this especially about
ideas, customs, or styles in art or
music: *a seventies revival* (=when
things from the 1970s become
fashionable again)
+of *the recent revival of interest in
alternative medicine*

go back to sth /gəʊ 'bæk tuː (sth)/
[*phrasal verb* T] to start doing a job or
activity again after a period when you
stopped it: *I wouldn't like to go back to
full-time work again.*
go back to doing sth *Tim was
determined he would never go back to
using drugs.*

When you see **EC**, go to the
ESSENTIAL COMMUNICATION section.

AGAINST

when you think that something is wrong and should not be allowed

➡ opposite **SUPPORT**

➡ see also **DISAGREE, EC DISAGREEING, EC OPINIONS**

1 to think something is wrong and try to prevent it

be against sth/be opposed to sth /biː əˈgenst (sth), biː əˈpəʊzd tuː (sth)/ to think that something is wrong and that it should not be allowed, especially because you think it is morally wrong: *I'm not against people eating meat, but I don't think people should kill animals for sport.* | *60% of the population is opposed to the war.*
be strongly opposed to sth *They are strongly opposed to any form of violence.*

object to sth /əbˈdʒekt tuː (sth)/ to believe that something is wrong, unfair, or unreasonable, especially when this makes you angry: *What I object to most is the way the book portrays women.*
strongly object to sth *Most of the students strongly object to the new rules.*

> **Formal or informal?**
> **Object to sth** is formal when used in spoken English.

not agree with sth /nɒt əˈgriː wɪð (sth)/ ESPECIALLY SPOKEN to be against something, for example because it is new or different and you do not like things to change: *I don't agree with all these new anti-smoking laws, do you?* | *My grandmother doesn't agree with divorce.*

not approve of sth /nɒt əˈpruːv əv (sth)/ to think that something is not good or right, especially because it is different from the way things were done before: *These guys didn't approve of women cops.* | *He doesn't really approve of drinking, let alone drinking and driving.*

not believe in sth /nɒt bᵻˈliːv ɪn (sth)/ to be against something, especially because you think it is wrong or immoral: *She doesn't believe in sex before marriage.* | *I don't believe in hitting children for any reason.*

anti- /ˈæntɪ‖ˈæntɪ, -taɪ/ [*prefix*] **anti-war/anti-smoking/anti-American etc** against war, smoking, America etc: *Anti-war demonstrators gathered on Capitol Hill.* | *anti-Communist propaganda*

2 someone who is against something

opponent /əˈpəʊnənt/ [*n* C] someone who thinks that a plan, type of behaviour etc is wrong, and tries to prevent it or change it: *a debate between an anti-abortion group and its opponents*
+of *All opponents of the government are likely to be imprisoned.*
life-long opponent (=someone who has opposed something since they were young) *a life-long opponent of nuclear weapons*

3 things you say or do to show that you are against something

opposition /ˌɒpəˈzɪʃən‖ˌɑːp-/ [*n* U] things that people say or do in order to show that they are against something: *Plans to build the airport faced a lot of opposition from local people.*
+to *Opposition to the war was growing rapidly.*
strong opposition *The new law was passed, despite strong opposition.*
widespread opposition (=when a lot of people are against something) *Widespread opposition to the military government led to violence on the streets.*

> **Opposition** is used especially in newspapers and news reports.

objection /əbˈdʒekʃən/ [*n* C] a reason that you give to explain why you are against something
have an objection *If anyone has any objections, please let us know as soon as possible.*

+to *What were her father's objections to their marriage?*

raise an objection (=state that you have an objection) *Club members raised a number of objections to the proposals.*

have no objection (=not be against something) FORMAL *I'll give them your name as a witness, if you have no objection.*

AGE

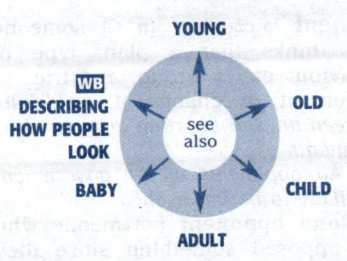

YOUNG

WB
DESCRIBING HOW PEOPLE LOOK

see also

OLD

BABY

CHILD

ADULT

1 how long someone has lived, or how long something has existed

age /eɪdʒ/ [n C/U] the number of years that someone has lived or something has existed

the age of sb/sth *The average age of the students is 18. | Can anyone tell me the approximate age of the Earth?*

sb's age *I tried to guess her age. | The children's ages range from three to 17.*

be sb's age (=be the same age as someone) *When I was your age I was already working.*

the same age as sb/sth *Their house is about the same age as ours.*

of my age/her age etc (=about the same age as me, her etc) *I'm surprised a girl of your age didn't know that!*

at the age of 10/20 etc WRITTEN (use this to say how old someone was when something happened) *He died in 1995 at the age of 73.*

over/under the age of 16/30 etc (=older or younger than that age) *Anyone over the age of 14 had to pay the full fare.*

be small/tall etc for your age (=be small, tall etc compared with other people of the same age) *Jimmy's very tall for his age. | She's 86, but very fit for her age.*

> Don't say 'His age is 49' or 'I'm at the age of 27'. Say **He is 49** or **I'm 27**.

> Don't use **in** before **age**. Don't say 'children in my age'. Say **children of my age**. Don't say 'he died in the age of 25'. Say **he died at the age of 25**.

how old /haʊ ˈəʊld/ use this to ask or talk about the age of a person or thing: *"How old are you?" "I'm 24." | I'm not sure how old my grandfather is. | How old were you when you got married? | Archaeologists are trying to discover how old these buildings are.*

be /biː/ [v]

be 5/10/27 etc (only use this about people) *Julie will be 30 on her next birthday.*

be 5/10/27 years old (use this about people or things) *Simon's almost 15 years old. | The school is 100 years old next year.*

be 5/10/27 years of age FORMAL (only use this about people) *He appeared to be about 35 years of age.*

5-year-old/60-year-old etc [adj only before noun] use this to say how old someone or something is: *27-year-old Susan Walker is the new world champion. | an eight-year-old car | a six-week-old baby*

> Don't say 'a 14 years old boy'. Say **a 14-year-old boy** or **a boy of 14**.

a man of 50/a child of 5 etc a man aged 50, a child aged 5 etc: *If a man of 55 loses his job in this city he'll never get another. | This calculator is so simple a child of five could use it.*

in your 20s/40s/80s etc use this to say that someone is between the age of 20 and 29, 40 and 49, 80 and 89 etc: *I'm not sure how old she is – I think she's in her 50s.*

in your late 20s/30s/40s etc (=between 27 and 29, 37 and 39 etc) *Police say that the man is tall, has dark hair, and is in his late thirties.*

in your early 20s/30s/40s etc (=between 20 and 23, 30 and 33 etc)

He first visited Europe when he was in his early twenties.

in your mid 20s/30s/40s etc (=between 24 and 26, 34 and 36 etc) *My grandparents are both in their mid eighties.*

aged /eɪdʒd/ [adj] ESPECIALLY WRITTEN
aged 5/10/27 etc use this to say how old someone is, usually when you are writing about them: *McIntosh died on April 25th, aged 67.* | *He wrote a song for his daughter Soraya, now aged six.* | *A man aged 20 has been arrested on suspicion of murder.*

2 people who are the same age

generation /ˌdʒenəˈreɪʃən/ [n C usually singular] all the people in a country or in a society who are about the same age: *preserving the environment for future generations* | *There was now a whole generation of people who had never experienced peace.*
of sb's generation *People of my father's generation aren't used to computers.* | *She was one of the best writers of her generation.*
the younger/older generation (=use this to talk about young or old people in general) *There is not much interest in politics among the younger generation.* | *Saga specializes in holidays for the older generation.*

age group /ˈeɪdʒ gruːp/ [n C] all the people who are between two particular ages - use this to talk about the problems, behaviour, interests etc of people of a particular age: *Boys in this age group watch TV for an average of five hours a day.* | *a competition for the 11–15 age group*

the over-60s/under-5s etc /ðiː əʊvəʳ (60s), ʌndəʳ (5s, etc)/ ESPECIALLY BRITISH people who are older than 60, younger than 5 etc: *an aerobics class for the over-50s* | *She teaches young children, mostly the under-5s.*

AGREE

➡ look here for . . .
   • have the same opinion as someone else
   • say you will do what someone else asks you

1 to have the same opinion as someone else

➡ opposite **DISAGREE 1**
➡ see also **EC AGREEING**, **EC OPINIONS, SUPPORT 1**

agree /əˈɡriː/ [v I/T] *I think it's too expensive. Do you agree?* | *"That's right," Richard agreed.*
+with *Everyone agreed with Karen.*
+on/about *I agree with you about the colour – it looks awful.* | *The one thing all the parties agreed on was the need for fair elections.*
+that *Many experts agree that the best way to lose weight is to do more exercise.*
agreeing – agreed – have agreed

 Don't say 'I am agreeing', 'he is agreeing' etc. Say **I agree**, **he agrees** etc.

 If you want to say that two people agree with each other, you can just say they **agree**: *Jack and I agree about most things.*

 Don't say 'I agree you' or 'I am agree you'. Say **I agree with you**.

be in agreement /biː ɪn əˈɡriːmənt/ FORMAL if people **are in agreement**, they agree about something, especially after discussing it a lot and trying to agree: *No decision can be made until everybody is in agreement.*

share sb's view /ˌʃeəʳ (sb's) ˈvjuː/ FORMAL to agree with someone else's opinion, especially about something important, in politics, business, science etc: *Many people shared Davidson's view, and thought the plan should be stopped.*
share this/that view *This view is shared by many doctors.*

unanimous /juːˈnænɪ̩məs/ [adj] a **unanimous** decision, agreement etc is one about which all the people involved agree
unanimous decision/vote/verdict *Harvey was elected by a unanimous vote.* (=everyone voted for him) | *The committee reached a unanimous decision.* | *The decision to end his contract was almost unanimous.*

unanimously [*adv*] *The members voted unanimously to appoint her as chairperson.*

2 to agree with someone else's plan or suggestion

➡ see also **LET 1, EG SAYING YES, EG SUGGESTIONS, EG PERMISSION**

agree /ə'griː/ [*v* I] to say yes to someone else's plan or suggestion: *Charles suggested going for a picnic, and we all agreed.*
agree to sth (=agree to allow something to happen) *The Council of Ministers would never agree to such a plan.*
agreeing – agreed – have agreed

go along with sb/sth /ˌɡəʊ ə'lɒŋ wɪð (sth) ‖-ə'lɔːŋ-/ [*phrasal verb* T] to agree with someone else's plan or suggestion, even though you are not sure if it is the right thing to do: *We went along with Eva's idea, as no-one could think of a better one. | Often it was easier just to go along with him, rather than risk an argument.*

> **Formal or informal?**
> **Go along with sb/sth** is more informal than **agree**.

3 when people make a decision or plan after talking about it

➡ opposite **DISAGREE 2**

agree /ə'griː/ [*v* I/T] if two or more people **agree**, they reach a decision about what to do, and they are all satisfied with it
+on *We've finally agreed on a date for the party.*
agree to do sth *They agreed to meet again later in the week.*
+that *In the end, everyone agreed that the best thing to do was to wait.*
it is agreed (=a group of people have agreed about something) *It was agreed that the price should be fixed at $200.*
◯ **we're (all) agreed** SPOKEN (say this when everyone in a group has agreed about something) *Right then, are we all agreed?*
agreeing – agreed – have agreed

reach an agreement/come to an agreement /ˌriːtʃ ən ə'griːmənt, ˌkʌm tʊ ən ə'griːmənt/ to agree on something, after discussing it until everyone involved is satisfied with the decision: *After two years of talks, the Russians and Americans finally reached an agreement. | British Airways and the unions hope to come to an agreement before Monday.*

compromise /'kɒmprəmaɪz‖'kɑːm-/ [*v* I] to reach an agreement with someone, in which both of you accept less than you really want: *The employers will have to be ready to compromise if they want to avoid a strike.*
+on *We are not prepared to compromise on safety standards.*

◯ **make a deal/do a deal** /ˌmeɪk ə 'diːl, ˌduː ə 'diːl/ ESPECIALLY SPOKEN to make an agreement with someone so that you get what you want, and they get what they want
+with *The government denied making a deal with the kidnappers.*

4 to tell someone you will do what they asked you to do

➡ opposite **REFUSE 1**

agree to do sth /əˌgriː tə 'duː (sth)/ to say that you will do what someone has asked you to do, especially something that may be difficult, inconvenient etc: *I've agreed to look after Pat's children next weekend. | Why did I ever agree to teach him to drive?*

> ⚠ Don't use 'accept' in this meaning. Don't say 'he accepted to wait'. Say **he agreed to wait**.

5 something that has been agreed

agreement /ə'griːmənt/ [*n* C] an arrangement that is made when two or more people, countries, or organizations agree to do something
make an agreement *They made a secret agreement not to tell anyone about their plans.*
sign an agreement *The US has signed a trade agreement with China.*
under an agreement (=according to

an agreement) *Under the agreement, UN troops will remain in Bosnia for another year.*

compromise /ˈkɒmprəmaɪz‖ˈkɑːm-/ [n C] an agreement in which both people or groups accept less than they really want
reach/find a compromise *After several hours of discussions, they managed to reach a compromise.*
+between *The treaty represented a compromise between the Communists and the Nationalists.*

treaty /ˈtriːti/ [n C] a written agreement between two or more countries, especially to end a war: *The Treaty of Versailles ended the First World War.*
sign a treaty *A peace treaty was signed in 1975.*
plural **treaties**

contract /ˈkɒntrækt‖ˈkɑːn-/ [n C] a written legal agreement with all the details of a job or business arrangement, for example what someone must do and how much they will be paid: *My contract says I have to work 35 hours per week.*
sign a contract (with sb) *REM signed an $80 million dollar contract with Warner Brothers.*

ALIVE

➡ opposite **DEAD**
➡ see also **EXIST, DIE, LIFE**

1 not dead

alive /əˈlaɪv/ [adj not before noun] not dead: *Are all your grandparents still alive? | He was badly injured, but at least he was alive.*
alive and well (=alive and not injured or ill) *The children were found alive and well after two days.*

living /ˈlɪvɪŋ/ [adj only before noun] still living now: *Mary's brother is her only living relative, and he lives in Australia. | Seamus Heaney is Ireland's greatest living poet.*

the living /ðə ˈlɪvɪŋ/ [n plural] all the people who are alive, as opposed to dead people: *Funerals help the living accept the death of a loved one.*

2 to continue to be alive

live /lɪv/ [v I] to continue to be alive: *She's seriously ill, but the doctor thinks she'll live. | Without light plants cannot live. | People are living longer these days.*
live for 2 years/3 months/a long time etc *He lived for five years after his heart operation. | Cats normally live for about 12 years.*

stay alive /ˌsteɪ əˈlaɪv/ to not die, even though you are in a dangerous situation: *They managed to stay alive by eating insects and berries.*

keep sb alive /ˌkiːp (sb) əˈlaɪv/ [phrasal verb T] to prevent someone from dying by giving them food, medicine etc: *He is being kept alive on a life-support machine.*

survive /səˈvaɪv/ [v I/T] to not die in an accident or war, or from an illness or operation: *Only two of the passengers survived. | She survived the war, but died of old age six months later. | My grandmother is too old to survive another operation.*

survivor /səˈvaɪvər/ [n C] someone who has not died in an accident or war
+of *survivors of the First World War*
sole survivor (=only survivor) *The sole survivor of the crash was the pilot.*

ALL

➡ if you mean 'all the time' (=through all of a period of time), go to **TIME 8**
➡ if you mean 'all the time' (=without stopping), go to **ALWAYS 4**
➡ see also **EVERYWHERE**

1 all things or all people

> ⚠ **All, all of**, and **every** mean the same thing: *All the computers in the school were stolen = All of the computers in the school were stolen = Every computer in the school was stolen.*

all /ɔːl/ [predeterminer/quantifier] all the things or people in a group: *They're all having lunch. | The new government banned all political parties.*

we all/you all/them all etc *We all passed our English test.* | *He thanked us all for coming.* | *Have you all finished your dinner?*

all the/these/their/my etc *All the teachers at my school are women.* | *Did you take all these photos yourself?* | *I invited all my friends to the party.*

all of *I invited all of my friends to the party.* | *Do we have to read all of the books on this list?* | *It's going to be a difficult day for all of us.*

almost/nearly all *Almost all my friends have got cars.* | *The plates rolled off the shelf and nearly all of them broke.*

all dogs/all cars/all children etc (use this to make a general statement about things or people of the same kind) *All mammals are warm-blooded.* | *The new law will affect all cars over 5 years old.*

> Word order with auxiliary or modal verbs (like **have, will, can, should** etc): **all** goes after the auxiliary or modal verb, and before the main verb: *The new students will all arrive tomorrow.* | *You should all go and visit her in the hospital.*

> Don't use 'all the ...' to make general statements about people or things. Don't say 'all the dogs have four legs'. Say **all dogs have four legs**.

every /ˈevri/ [*determiner*] all – use this only with singular nouns: *Every room in the house was painted white.* | *The bank has branches in every city in France.* | *She bought presents for every member of her family.* | *Every teacher knows the problems that difficult children can cause.*

every single (used to emphasize that you really mean everyone or everything, especially when this is surprising) *It rained every single day of our vacation.* | *The police questioned every single passenger on the plane.*

> Use **every** with a singular noun and a singular verb.

each /iːtʃ/ [*determiner/pronoun*] all – use this to emphasize that you mean every separate person or thing in a group: *The calendar has a different picture for each month of the year.* |

She had a ring on each finger of her right hand. | *The president shook hands with each member of the team.*

each of *She gave each of them a hug.* | *Each of the bedrooms has its own shower.*

we each/they each/us each etc *My brother and I each have our own room.* | *She gave us each a pen and a piece of paper.*

in each/for each/to each etc *She dug several tiny holes in the soil, planting a seed in each.*

> You can use **each** before a singular noun or after a plural pronoun: *Each child has a desk and a chair.* | *They each have a desk and a chair.* Use **each of** with a plural noun and a singular verb: *Each of the children has a desk and a chair.*

everything /ˈevriθɪŋ/ [*pronoun*] all the things in a group, or all the things that someone says or does: *Everything in the store costs less than $10.* | *I agree with everything she said.*

> Use **everything** with a singular verb. Don't say 'everything were very expensive'. Say **everything was very expensive**.

> Don't write this word as 'every thing'. The correct spelling is **everything**.

everyone/everybody /ˈevriwʌn, ˈevribɒdiǁ-baːdi/ [*pronoun*] all the people in a group: *I think everyone enjoyed the party.* | *If everybody is ready, I'll begin.* | *Has everyone gone home?*

> Use **everyone** and **everybody** with a singular verb. Don't say 'everyone were late'. Say **everyone was late**.

> You can also use **everyone** and **everybody** to talk about people in general: *Everyone knows that smoking is bad for your health.*

unanimous /juːˈnænɪ̥məs/ [*adj*] if a group of people or a decision they make is **unanimous**, all the members of the group agree about something: *Many party members agreed with their*

leader, but they certainly weren't unanimous.
unanimous decision/agreement/ verdict *The committee made a unanimous decision to expel the three students.*

2 the whole of something

all /ɔːl/ [*predeterminer/quantifier*] all of something – use this especially with uncountable nouns
all the/this/that/my etc *He spends all his money on beer and cigarettes.* | *I've finished all my homework.* | *Did you eat all that bread?*
all of the/this/my/it etc *I enjoyed the book although I didn't understand all of it.*
it all *Is there any left, or did you spend it all?*
all day/week/year etc (=the whole of a period of time) *I spent all day cleaning the house.*

> ⚠ **All** and **all of** mean the same: *The children ate all the food = The children ate all of the food.*

whole /həʊl/ [*adj/quantifier*] all of something that is large or has a lot of parts, for example a large area of land, a long period of time, or a large group of people: *Police searched the whole area for the murder weapon.* | *She was so frightened, her whole body was shaking.* | *I didn't see her again for a whole year.*
the whole of *She spent the whole of the journey complaining about her boyfriend.* | *The Romans conquered almost the whole of western Europe.*

> ⚠ Don't use **the whole** directly before 'it' or before the name of a place or an organization. Use **the whole of**. Don't say 'the whole Mexico', say **the whole of Mexico**.

complete /kəmˈpliːt/ [*adj*] use this to say that something includes all the parts that it should have, with nothing missing: *They discovered the complete skeleton of a dinosaur.* | *He has a complete collection of Elvis records.*

full /fʊl/ [*adj*] all of something, with everything included – use **full** with these words: **name, address, details, set, report, statement, price, cost, amount, refund**: *Please write your full name and address.* | *I used my student card, so I didn't have to pay the full price.*
a full refund (=when a shop or company gives you back all the money you paid for something)

entire /ɪnˈtaɪəʳ/ [*adj* only before noun] all of something – use this especially to emphasize that you are annoyed or surprised by something: *It was the worst day of my entire life.* | *A single CD-ROM can hold the entire text of a 20-volume encyclopedia.* | *We wasted an entire day waiting at the airport.*

3 any person or thing

any /ˈeni/ [*determiner/pronoun*] use this to talk about each one of the people or things in a group, when it is not important to say exactly which one: *Any student who wishes to go on the trip should sign this list.* | *You can buy the magazine at any good bookstore.*
any of the/these/my/them etc *You are welcome to borrow any of these books.* | *Will any of your friends be going to the same university?*

> ⚠ **Any of** can be used with a plural verb or a singular verb, but is more commonly used with a plural verb: *If any of these items are offered to you, please contact the police.*

anything /ˈeniθɪŋ/ [*pronoun*] any object, action, idea etc: *I went shopping with Kathy, but we didn't buy anything.* | *You can write about anything you enjoy doing.* | *Do you know anything about computer networks?* | *If anything goes wrong with the car, call the garage straight away.*

anyone/anybody /ˈeniwʌn, ˈenibədi‖ -bɑːdi/ [*pronoun*] any person: *This would be an ideal job for anyone who speaks French and Italian.* | *Peter's more intelligent than anybody I know.* | *If anyone needs more information, come and see me after the class.*

⚠️ **Anyone** and **anybody** are singular and take a singular verb: *Has anyone seen my keys?* But we usually use **they**, **them**, and **their** with these words: *If anyone phones me, tell them I'll be back later.* In more formal situations, you can use **he or she** etc instead of 'they' etc: *If anyone wishes to speak to the Principal, he or she should make an appointment.*

whatever /wɒt'evəʳ‖wɑːt-/ [*pronoun*] anything at all – use this to emphasize that it does not matter which object, action, idea etc
whatever sb does/says/wants etc *They told me I could eat whatever I wanted from the fridge.* | *We'll do whatever we can to help.* | *It's best just to agree with whatever he says.*

whoever /huː'evəʳ/ [*pronoun*] any person at all – use this to emphasize that it does not matter which one: *You can invite whoever you want to your party.* | *It seems that whoever is in charge of the team, we always lose.*

4 affecting everything or every part of a situation

total/complete /'təʊtl, kəm'pliːt/ [*adj* only before noun] affecting everything or every part of a situation: *They want a total ban on cigarette advertising.* | *My parents had complete control over my life.* | *the complete destruction of the rainforest*

ALMOST

1 almost

almost/nearly /'ɔːlməʊst, 'nɪəʳli/ [*adv*] use this to say that something is a little less than a number or amount, or to say that something almost happens or is almost true

⚠️ You can use **almost** or **nearly a)** with numbers: *There were almost 200 people at the meeting.* **b)** with verbs: *I was laughing so much I almost fell off my chair.* | *She nearly died of her injuries.* **c)** with **all**, **every**, **everyone**, **everything**, **always**: *She lost almost all her money.* | *We see each other nearly every day.* **d)** with **as** + adjective + **as**: *She's almost as tall as her big sister.*

⚠️ Don't say 'almost my friends came' or 'almost of my friends came'. Say **almost all my friends came** or **almost all of my friends came**.

⚠️ In American English, **almost** is much more common than **nearly**, but in British English both words are common.

⚠️ You can use 'very' with **nearly**, but you can't use it with **almost**. Don't say 'Brazil very almost lost the game', say **Brazil very nearly lost the game**.

practically/virtually /'præktɪkli, 'vɜːʳtʃuəli/ [*adv*] almost completely: *The old part of town remains virtually unchanged.*
+full/empty/impossible/the same etc *The theatre was practically empty.* | *It's virtually impossible for a woman to become president in this country.*
+all/every/everyone (=very nearly all) *Tom knew practically everyone at the party.* | *Virtually all the children come to school by car.*

⚠️ Don't use **practically** or **virtually** with numbers. But you can use them with 'nothing': *She had eaten virtually nothing at supper.*

🔍 **just about/more or less** /ˌdʒʌst ə'baʊt, ˌmɔːr ɔːʳ 'lesˏ/ ESPECIALLY SPOKEN very nearly – use this when the statement is so close to being absolutely true that there is no real difference in meaning: *I had more or less convinced her that I was telling the truth.*
+ready/finished/straight/the same etc *Dinner's just about ready.* | *All the rooms are more or less the same size.*
+every/everyone/everything *She's invited just about everyone she knows.*

not quite /nɒt 'kwaɪt/ not completely, but almost – use this to say that

something is not true or has not happened yet, but that it is almost true or has almost happened: *She hasn't quite finished her homework yet.* | *This skirt isn't quite long enough.* | *Give me five minutes – I'm not quite ready.*
not quite as good/big/strong etc as *The female bird isn't quite as big as the male.*

> ⚠ Don't use **not quite** with numbers, unless you are talking about someone's age: *He was not quite sixteen.*

2 when something happens, but almost does not

just /dʒʌst/ [*adv*] use this to talk about something that happens, but which almost does not happen: *I just managed to get there before the train left.* | *We could just see the coast in the distance.*
only just *These pants only just fit me.* (=they are almost too small)
just big enough/old enough etc *The tunnel is just wide enough for two trucks to pass each other.*
hardly /'hɑːʳdli/ [*adv*] almost not: *I hadn't seen him for 12 years, but he'd hardly changed at all.*
can/could hardly do sth (=can only do it with difficulty) *I was so tired I could hardly keep my eyes open.*
hardly any/anyone/anything (=almost none, almost no one, almost nothing) *There's hardly any fuel left in the tank.*
hardly ever (=almost never) *She hardly ever goes to church.*

> ⚠ Be careful with the word order. **Hardly** goes before the verb: *She hardly spoke to me all day.* If there is an auxiliary or modal verb (like **have**, **will**, **should** etc), **hardly** goes after this and before the main verb: *She had hardly spoken to me all day.* | *The writing was so small, I could hardly read it.*

ALONE

➡ see also **INDEPENDENT**

1 when there are no other people with you

alone/on your own/by yourself /ə'ləʊn, ɒn jɔːr 'əʊn, baɪ jɔːʳˈself/ [*adj/ adv*] when you are in a place and no one else is there with you: *She was sitting alone on a park bench.* | *I wanted to be on my own.* | *Do you share the apartment, or do you live by yourself?*
all alone/on your own/by yourself (=completely alone) *Wendy was frightened, all alone in that big old house.*
leave sb alone/on their own/by themselves *The first time his parents left him alone in the house, he set fire to the kitchen.* | *Mark's not well. I can't go out and leave him on his own.*

> **Formal or informal?**
> **On your own** and **by yourself** are more informal than **alone**. **Alone** is often used in written stories and descriptions.

> ⚠ Don't confuse **alone** (=when no-one else is there) and **lonely** (=when you feel unhappy because you are alone).

2 when you do something without anyone else

on your own/by yourself /ɒn jɔːr 'əʊn, baɪ jɔːʳˈself/ if you do something **on your own** or **by yourself**, you do it without anyone with you or helping you: *I don't like going to restaurants on my own.* | *Surely he's old enough to get dressed by himself, isn't he?*
all on your own/all by yourself (=when it is surprising that someone has done something without anyone's help) *How did you manage to prepare so much food all on your own?*
single-handed/single-handedly /ˌsɪŋgəl 'hændɪd, ˌsɪŋgəl 'hændɪdli/ [*adv*] if you do something **single-handed**

or **single-handedly**, especially something very difficult or impressive, you do it without any help from anyone else: *She brought up three children single-handedly.* | *In 1992, he rowed across the Atlantic single-handed.*

solo /'səʊləʊ/ [adv] if you do something **solo**, you do something alone that people often do in groups, for example playing music, climbing mountains, or sailing a boat: *I flew solo for the first time this weekend.*

go solo (=start to do something on your own instead of in a group) *He played in a band for five years before going solo.*

solo [adj only before noun] *Her first solo album will be released next week.*

solitary /'sɒlɪtəriǁ'sɑːlɪˌteri/ [adj] FORMAL done or experienced when there is no one else with you: *He took a long, solitary walk.*

solitary confinement (=when a prisoner is kept alone and not allowed to see anyone)

3 alone and unhappy

lonely (also **lonesome** AMERICAN) /'ləʊnli, 'ləʊnsəm/ [adj] unhappy because you are alone or you have no friends: *Martha felt very lonely when she first arrived in New York.* | *a lonely old woman* | *I get so lonesome here with no-one to talk to.*

loneliness [n U] the feeling you have when you are lonely: *Many old people complain of loneliness.*

isolated /'aɪsəleɪtɪd/ [adj] if you feel **isolated**, you feel that there is no one you can talk to or have as a friend, because your situation makes it difficult for you to meet people: *Young single parents often feel isolated and forgotten.*

miss /mɪs/ [v T] to feel lonely because someone that you like very much is not with you: *When are you coming home? I miss you.* | *It was great living in Prague, but I really missed all my friends.*

4 someone who spends a lot of time alone

loner /'ləʊnəʳ/ [n C] someone who likes to do things alone and does not have many friends: *Jo has always been a bit of a loner.*

recluse /rɪ'kluːsǁ'rekluːs/ [n C] someone who lives alone and avoids meeting other people: *After her husband died, she became a complete recluse.*

ALWAYS

➡ opposite **NEVER**
➡ if you mean 'continuing for a long time', go to **CONTINUE 5**
➡ see also **OFTEN, USUALLY, SOMETIMES**

> ⚠ Word order with **always**. **Always** usually goes between the subject and the verb: *I always play tennis on Saturdays.* However, when the verb is **be**, **always** comes after it: *He's always late for class.* If there is an auxiliary or modal verb (like **have**, **will**, **should** etc), **always** goes after this and before the main verb: *Karen had always wanted to visit Thailand.*

1 when someone always does something or something always happens

always /'ɔːlwɪz, -weɪz/ [adv] *She was always ready to listen to my problems.* | *Why do you always blame me for everything?* | *He always has sandwiches for his lunch.* | *We always meet for lunch on Thursdays.*

all (of) the time /ˌɔːl əv ðə 'taɪm/ always or very often: *They quarrelled all the time.*

every time /ˌevri 'taɪm/ [adv/conjunction] on every occasion – use this to say that when one thing happens, something else always happens: *My neck hurts every time I move.* | *He jumped every time he heard his father's voice.* | *The coach says we should go out on the field expecting to win every time.*

whenever /wen'evə^r/ [*conjunction*] every time that something happens: *He goes to visit Amy whenever he's in town.* | *You can use my computer whenever you like.*
whenever possible (=whenever you can) *Try to use public transport whenever possible.*

every /'evri/ [*determiner*] **every day/week/Monday etc** use this to say that something happens regularly on each day, each week etc: *We use the car almost every day.* | *Thousands of tourists visit Bali every year.*

○ **nine times out of ten** /,naɪn taɪmz aʊt əv 'ten/ ESPECIALLY SPOKEN almost always – use this to emphasize that something almost always happens in a particular way: *I often leave work early, and nine times out of ten no-one notices.*

2   always in the future

always /'ɔːlwз̩z, -weɪz/ [*adv*] *I'll always remember the first time I went to Paris.* | *She said she would always love him.* | *Don't worry! Things won't always seem this hard!*

forever/for ever /fər'evə^r/ [*adv*] for all time in the future – use this to emphasize that something will continue for a very long time: *I'd like to stay here forever.* | *If you wait for Victor to make up his mind, you'll be waiting for ever.*

> Use **forever** or **for ever** at the end of a sentence or clause.

permanent /'pɜː^rmənənt/ [*adj*] something that is **permanent** will exist for all time in the future and cannot be changed or removed: *a disease which can cause permanent brain damage*
permanently [*adv*] *The accident left him permanently disabled.*

for life /fə^r 'laɪf/ for the rest of your life: *There's no such thing as a job for life any more.* | *If you help me, I'll be your friend for life!*
be jailed for life *She was jailed for life in 1965 for the murder of her husband and children.*

for good /fə^r 'gʊd/ if someone does something **for good**, they do something that causes a permanent

change in their situation: *He said he was tired of boxing and was giving it up for good.* | *I'm leaving her, and this time it's for good.*

> **Formal or informal?**
> **For good** is informal. It is used at the end of a sentence or clause.

3   always in the past

always /'ɔːlwз̩z, -weɪz/ [*adv*] *Have you always lived here?* | *He's always wanted to work in TV.* | *I always thought there was something strange about him.*

○ **all along** /ɔːl ə'lɒŋǁ-ə'lɔːŋ/ ESPECIALLY SPOKEN if something has been true **all along**, it has been true all the time but you did not know it: *He realized that she'd been right all along.* | *I spent all morning looking for my keys, and they were in my purse all along!*

from the start /frəm ðə 'stɑː^rt/ always, from the time when something first began: *Their marriage was a disaster from the start.*
right from the start (=use this to emphasize that something has always been true or has always been happening since it first began) *They liked each other right from the start.*

4   all the time, without stopping

all (of) the time /,ɔːl əv ðə 'taɪm/ without stopping: *I seem to be tired all the time these days.* | *Do you wear your glasses all the time, or just for reading?*

always /'ɔːlwз̩z, -weɪz/ [*adv*] all the time – use this especially about something bad or annoying: *There's always loud music coming from the room upstairs.* | *As Jim is always telling us, things were different when he was a boy.*

○ **the whole time** /ðə ˌhəʊl 'taɪm/ SPOKEN all the time while something is happening – use this about something annoying or surprising: *He talked about himself the whole time.* | *We realized that Duncan had been standing there the whole time.*

constant /'kɒnstəntǁ'kɑːn-/ [*adj* usually before noun] continuing all the time without ever changing or stopping:

His constant complaining is really beginning to annoy me. | *a constant supply of fresh water*

constantly [adv] *We were constantly in debt.* | *The English language is constantly changing.*

permanent /'pɜːˈmənənt/ [adj] remaining the same for a very long time or for ever: *a country in a permanent state of crisis* | *He seems to have a permanent smile on his face.*

permanent feature/fixture (=someone or something that is always there) *He's become a permanent fixture in this Arsenal side.*

permanently [adv] *This door is kept permanently locked.*

AMOUNT/NUMBER

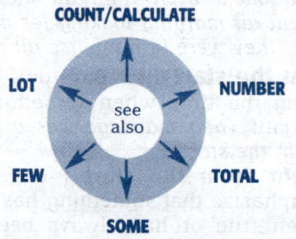

COUNT/CALCULATE

LOT   NUMBER

see also

FEW   TOTAL

SOME

1 an amount of something such as money, food, time, or crime

amount /əˈmaʊnt/ [n C]

the amount of sth *The amount of tax you pay depends on how much you earn.* | *Try to reduce the amount of fat in your diet.*

a small/tiny amount *The water here contains small amounts of calcium and other minerals.*

a large / enormous / considerable amount *Finding the right house takes a considerable amount of time and effort.*

 Don't say 'a big amount'.

how much /ˌhaʊ ˈmʌtʃ/ use this to ask or talk about the size of an amount of money, time, food etc: *I'll get you some paint if you'll tell me how much you need.* | *How much did your jeans cost?*

how much time/money/food etc *How much money do I owe you?* | *Do you realize how much trouble you caused?* | *How much gas is left in the tank?*

 Only use **how much** with uncountable nouns like 'money' and 'time'.

 Only say 'how much is ...' when you are asking about the cost of something: *How much is this dress?* Don't say 'how much is the temperature?' Say **what is the temperature**?

quantity /'kwɒntɪtɪ‖ˈkwɑːn-/ [n C] ESPECIALLY WRITTEN use this, especially in written descriptions or instructions, to talk about amounts of food, liquid, or other substances that can be measured

+of *Make sure that you add the correct quantity of water.* | *Use equal quantities of flour and butter.*

a large/small/enormous etc quantity *An enormous quantity of chemical waste had been dumped in the river.*

 Don't use **quantity** to talk about amounts of money or time.

level /'levəl/ [n C] use this to talk about the exact amount of something at one time, even though this amount may go up or go down at other times

the level of sth *a device that measures the level of carbon monoxide in the air* | *the rising level of crime in the inner-cities*

a high/low level *At that time Spain had a very high level of unemployment.*

100 pounds' worth/ten dollars' worth etc /(£100 etc) wɜːˈθ/ an amount of something that is worth £100, $10 etc

+of *Over £10 million worth of heroin was seized in the raid.* | *The company owns millions of dollars' worth of real estate in downtown Tokyo.*

extent /ɪkˈstent/ [n C] use this to talk about how large and how serious a problem is

the extent of sth *Government inspectors will assess the extent of the damage.* | *Considering the extent of his injuries, he's lucky to be alive.*

sum /sʌm/ [n C] an amount of money
a large/enormous sum *It cost over $25,000, which was an enormous sum in those days.*
a sum of money *She left a small sum of money to her two granddaughters.*

> **Formal or informal?**
> **Sum** is more formal than **amount** and is usually used in written English.

volume /ˈvɒljuːm‖ˈvɑːljəm/ [n singular] use this to talk about amounts of business activity or amounts of traffic that are continually increasing or decreasing
the volume of trade/sales/traffic/business *The volume of traffic on our roads increases every year.* | *After 1929, there was a rapid fall in the volume of trade.*

 2   a number of people or things

number /ˈnʌmbəʳ/ [n C]
the number of *We need to know the number of students in each class.*
a number of (=several) *Sally had spent a number of years in Italy.*
a large/small number *A large number of reporters had gathered outside the house.* | *Thousands of men apply to join the Marines but only a small number are accepted.*

> ⚠ Don't say 'a big number'. Say **a large number**.

> ⚠ **Number** is used with a plural verb: *Only a small number of people were injured.*

> ⚠ **Number** can be used in the plural with the same meaning: 'large numbers of people' means the same as 'a large number of people'.

how many /ˌhaʊ ˈmeni/ use this to talk about or ask about the number of people or things that there are
how many people/things/years etc *How many cups of coffee do you have a day?* | *He wouldn't tell us how many girlfriends he'd had.*
+of *How many of you can swim?*

> ⚠ Only use **how many** with countable nouns.

quantity /ˈkwɒntɪti‖ˈkwɑːn-/ ESPECIALLY WRITTEN [n C] a number of things – use this especially to talk about things that are being sold, stored, or carried
a quantity of *Thieves escaped with £850 in cash and a quantity of cigarettes.*
a large/small/huge etc quantity *We had no sugar, just a large quantity of coffee.*

> ⚠ **Quantity** can be used in the plural with the same meaning: 'large quantities of weapons' means the same as 'a large quantity of weapons'.

100 pounds' worth/ten dollars' worth etc /(£100 etc) wɜːʳθ/ a number of things that together are worth £100, $10 etc
+of *Police recovered over a million pounds' worth of stolen diamonds.* | *$100,000 worth of rugs were destroyed in the fire.*

 3   a number that is compared with another number

percentage /pəʳˈsentɪdʒ/ [n C usually singular] a number or amount that is calculated as part of a total of 100, and is shown using a % sign
+of *The percentage of women students at the university has increased steadily.* | *a slight fall in the percentage of nitrogen in the air*
a high/large percentage *A high percentage of the population lives in poverty here.*
a low/small percentage *The disease is serious, and in a small percentage of cases it can be fatal.*

proportion /prəˈpɔːʳʃən/ [n singular] the number or amount of a particular type of person or thing, compared with the whole number or amount that exists of all types of people or things
+of *a program to increase the proportion of women and black people in the police service*
a high/low/large/small proportion *Part-time workers now make up a high proportion of employees.*

ratio /'reɪʃiəʊ‖'reɪʃəʊ/ [n singular] a set of numbers, such as '20:1' or '5:1', that shows how much larger one quantity is than another

the ratio of sth to sth *The ratio of students to teachers is about 5:1.*

> ⚠ Don't confuse **ratio** and **rate**.

rate /reɪt/ [n C] a measurement showing the number of times that something happens during a particular period, which is used especially for talking about social changes or problems

the crime/divorce/suicide/murder etc rate *The city has a murder rate of more than one a day.*

fraction /'frækʃən/ [n singular] a very small part of an amount or number: *Computers can now do the same job at a fraction of the cost.* | *The disease affects only a tiny fraction of the population.*

ANGRY

➡ if you mean 'not angry or upset', go to **CALM**

1 feeling angry

angry /'æŋgri/ [adj] if you are **angry**, you feel a strong emotion, for example about someone who has treated you badly or about something that you think is wrong or unfair: *I was so angry that I could hardly speak.* | *A crowd of angry demonstrators gathered outside the embassy.* | *After the programme, the TV station received hundreds of angry phone calls.*

+with *She was angry with him because he had lied to her.*

+about *Don't you feel angry about the way you've been treated?*

+at *At first I was angry at him.*

+that *Local people are angry that they weren't consulted about plans to expand the airport.*

angry – angrier – angriest

> ⚠ Use **angry with** about people: *I was really angry with him.* Use **angry about** about things: *I was really angry about it.* Use **angry at** about people and things.

angrily [adv] *Rachel slammed the door angrily on her way out.*

mad /mæd/ [adj not before noun] INFORMAL, ESPECIALLY AMERICAN angry: *Tom will be real mad when he sees what you've done to his car.*

+at *She used to get mad at Harry because he was always changing his mind.*

+about *Come on, Maria – what are you so mad about?*

mad – madder – maddest

annoyed /ə'nɔɪd/ [adj not before noun] a little angry, but not very angry: *I'll be annoyed if he's forgotten to post my letter.*

+with *Joe was annoyed with her for being late.* | *I was annoyed with myself for playing so badly.*

+at/by *Kay was clearly annoyed at John's remark.*

+that *I was really annoyed that she didn't tell me herself.*

irritated /'ɪrɪteɪtɪd/ [adj not before noun] a little angry and not patient about something, especially an annoying situation: *She got irritated because they hadn't cleaned up after themselves.*

+by/at *Coleman was irritated by all the questions.*

+with *She was irritated with herself for feeling nervous.*

furious /'fjʊəriəs/ [adj] very angry: *I've never been so furious in all my life.* | *a furious argument* (=when people shout at each other in an angry way)

+with *She'd be furious with me if she knew I was reading her diary.*

+at/about *He came home furious at something his boss had said.*

> Don't say 'very furious'. Say **absolutely furious**.

furiously [adv] *"Stop it," shouted Ralph furiously.*

livid /'lɪvɪd/ [adj] so angry that it is difficult for you to speak properly or think clearly: *"Was he angry when you* got in so late?" "Angry? He was livid!" | I know I shouldn't have spoken to her like that, but I was absolutely livid.

> ⚠ Don't say 'very livid'. Say **absolutely livid** or just **livid**.

offended /əˈfendɪd/ [adj not before noun] angry and upset because someone has said or done something rude or has insulted you: A lot of Muslims were offended when the book came out. | I hope you won't be offended if I leave early.
+by Many readers were offended by the newspaper's anti-Irish comments.

🔍 **cross** /krɒs‖krɔːs/ [adj] BRITISH, ESPECIALLY SPOKEN angry – used especially by children or when you are talking to children: Do you think Dad will be cross when he finds out what happened?
+with Are you cross with me?

fed up with sth/sick of sth /ˌfed ˈʌp wɪð (sth), ˈsɪk ɒv (sth)/ INFORMAL annoyed because something bad has been happening for a long time and you want it to stop: I'm really fed up with this awful weather. | Joe was getting sick of Carol's stupid comments. | I left the job because I got fed up with being treated like a servant.

2 to become angry

get angry/get mad /get ˈæŋgri, get ˈmæd/ to become angry: He tends to get angry if he loses.
+at Just calm down. There's no need to get mad at me.

> **Formal or informal?**
>
> **Get angry** and **get mad** are the usual phrases to use. The phrase **become angry** is only used in more formal written English, for example in descriptions in novels.

lose your temper /ˌluːz jɔːʳ ˈtempəʳ/ to suddenly become very angry, especially after you have been trying not to: I've never seen Denise lose her temper before. | "I've told you already," said Kathryn, trying hard not to lose her temper.
+with Whatever you do, don't lose your temper with the students – you'll only make things worse.

throw a tantrum/have a tantrum /ˌθrəʊ ə ˈtæntrəm, ˌhæv ə ˈtæntrəm/ to shout and cry angrily, especially because you cannot have what you want – use this especially about children: Josie threw a tantrum in the supermarket again today.

3 behaving in an angry unfriendly way

bad-tempered /ˌbæd ˈtempəʳd◂/ [adj] someone who is **bad-tempered** behaves in an angry and unfriendly way: Our teacher was a bad-tempered old woman. | Pressure at work was making her more and more bad-tempered.

be in a bad mood /biː ɪn ə ˌbæd ˈmuːd/ if someone **is in a bad mood**, they are annoyed and upset about something, and this makes them behave in an unfriendly way: Why's Jenny in such a bad mood this morning?
put sb in a bad mood (=make someone annoyed) I missed the bus, which put me in a bad mood for the rest of the day.

grumpy/grouchy /ˈgrʌmpi, ˈgraʊtʃi/ [adj] INFORMAL someone who is **grumpy** or **grouchy** is angry and unfriendly, and complains a lot: a grumpy old man | Her illness made her grumpy and impatient. | Dan is always tired and grouchy in the mornings.
grumpy – grumpier – grumpiest
grouchy – grouchier – grouchiest

moody /ˈmuːdi/ [adj] someone who is **moody** often becomes annoyed or unhappy, even though there does not seem to be a good reason for feeling that way: moody teenagers | Tara had been moody and difficult all day.
moody – moodier – moodiest

irritable /ˈɪrɪtəbəl/ [adj] ESPECIALLY WRITTEN someone who is **irritable** easily gets annoyed by things that are not important: The heat was making me irritable. | Zoe hadn't had much sleep and was feeling tired and irritable.

touchy /ˈtʌtʃi/ [adj] if someone is **touchy**, they easily get offended, so you have to be careful what you say to them: She always gets a little touchy when you ask her about her parents.
+about Don't say anything about his

bald patch – he's a little touchy about it.

touchy – touchier – touchiest

sulky /'sʌlki/ [adj] ESPECIALLY WRITTEN someone who is **sulky** has an angry, unhappy look on their face and does not talk much, especially because they think they have been treated unfairly: *a sulky child* | *After a while, he stopped looking sulky.*

sulky – sulkier – sulkiest

sulkily [adv] *She just sat in the corner and stared sulkily at the floor.*

4 someone or something that makes you angry

annoying /ə'nɔɪ-ɪŋ/ [adj] an **annoying** person, fact, or situation makes you feel annoyed or impatient: *Henry's the most annoying person I have ever met.* | *Just as I got into the shower the phone rang. It was so annoying.*

irritating /'ɪrɪ̩teɪtɪŋ/ [adj] something that is **irritating** is very annoying and it keeps happening: *Steve has an irritating habit of leaving the fridge door open.* | *I do find it irritating when people keep interrupting me.*

frustrating /frʌ'streɪtɪŋ‖'frʌstreɪtɪŋ/ [adj] a **frustrating** situation makes you feel annoyed because it stops you from doing what you want to do: *It's so frustrating when you're in a hurry and the traffic isn't moving.* | *Learning a new language can be a frustrating experience.*

be a nuisance /biː ə 'njuːsəns‖-'nuː-/ ESPECIALLY SPOKEN someone or something that **is a nuisance** is annoying because they cause problems or inconvenience for you: *My car's broken down again. It's a nuisance, isn't it?*

what a nuisance! SPOKEN *Oh, what a nuisance! I've left my sandwiches at home.*

infuriating /ɪn'fjʊərieɪtɪŋ/ [adj] something that is **infuriating** makes you very angry, especially because there is nothing you can do to stop it: *He always pretends he doesn't understand what I'm saying. It's absolutely infuriating.* | *infuriating delays*

5 to make someone angry

make sb angry (also **make sb mad** ESPECIALLY AMERICAN) /ˌmeɪk (sb) 'æŋgri, ˌmeɪk (sb) 'mæd/ *Sophie tried not to do anything that would make Henry angry.*

it makes sb angry/mad when *It always makes me mad when people drive up behind me and start flashing their lights.*

annoy /ə'nɔɪ/ [v T] to make someone feel annoyed: *The only reason she went out with him was to annoy her parents.* | *Are you doing that just to annoy me?*

it annoys sb that/when *It annoys me that Kim never returns the books she borrows.*

irritate /'ɪrɪ̩teɪt/ [v T] to annoy someone – use this about things that keep happening or things that people keep doing: *That silly smile of hers always irritated him.* | *After a while, the loud ticking of the clock began to irritate me.*

offend /ə'fend/ [v T] to make someone feel angry and upset by doing or saying something rude or insulting: *I'm sorry if I offended you.* | *Some people were offended by Leary's racist jokes.*

get on sb's nerves /ˌget ɒn (sb's) 'nɜːˈvz/ INFORMAL if someone or something **gets on your nerves**, they make you feel more and more annoyed, especially because they keep saying or doing something that you do not like: *The noise from the apartment upstairs was beginning to get on my nerves.* | *I hope Diane isn't going to be there – she really gets on my nerves.*

drive sb crazy (also **drive sb mad** BRITISH) /ˌdraɪv (sb) 'kreɪzi, ˌdraɪv (sb) 'mæd/ INFORMAL, ESPECIALLY SPOKEN if someone or something **drives you crazy** or **drives you mad**, they annoy you so much that you cannot feel calm or think clearly: *Turn that music down – it's driving me mad!* | *Being alone all day with three small kids is enough to drive anyone crazy.*

provoke /prə'vəʊk/ [v T] to deliberately try to make someone angry: *She would never have hit you if you hadn't provoked her.*
provoke sb into doing sth *Charlie was trying to provoke him into losing his temper.*

6 angry feelings

anger /'æŋgəʳ/ [n U] an angry feeling: *He was finding it difficult to control his growing anger.* | *Her heart was filled with sadness more than anger.*
with anger (=because of anger) *His face went bright red with anger.*

rage /reɪdʒ/ [n U] ESPECIALLY WRITTEN a very strong feeling of anger that often makes you feel violent as well
with rage (=because of rage) *By now Samuel was white in the face and absolutely shaking with rage.*
a fit of rage (=when someone suddenly feels very angry) *Verlaine shot Rimbaud in a fit of jealous rage.*

frustration /frʌ'streɪʃən/ [n U] a feeling of being annoyed and impatient because you cannot do what you want to do or you cannot change a bad situation
in/with frustration (=because of frustration) *Jess stared out of the window, almost crying with frustration.* | *Kay stamped her foot in frustration and marched out of the room.*

7 to talk angrily to someone because they have done something wrong

tell sb off /ˌtel (sb) 'ɒf‖-'ɔːf/ [phrasal verb T] to talk to someone, especially a child, in an angry way because they have done something wrong: *She's always telling her kids off or shouting at them.*
+for *He's upset because the teacher told him off for talking in class.*
Q **get told off** SPOKEN *I got told off by my dad when I got home.*
yell at sb /'jel æt (sb)/ [phrasal verb T] ESPECIALLY AMERICAN to shout or talk angrily to someone because they have done something wrong or annoying: *It was so embarrassing – he just started yelling at his wife.*

Q **get yelled at** SPOKEN *I got yelled at at school because I was wearing the wrong shirt.*

ANOTHER

➡ see also **MORE**

one more of the same kind

another /ə'nʌðəʳ/ [determiner/pronoun] use this to talk about one more person or thing that is similar to the one you already have: *"I've lost my pencil." "Don't worry, here's another."*
another person/thing/glass etc *Would you like another drink?* | *You'll get another chance to see him after the show.*
another one *"That was a good cup of coffee." "Would you like another one?"*
+of *This is just another of his crazy ideas. Ignore it.*

⚠ Only use **another** with a singular countable noun. With uncountable nouns, use **more**. Compare: *Would you like another glass of wine?* | *Would you like some more wine?*

⚠ Don't say 'also another'. Just say **another**: *There's another way of doing this.* (not 'there's also another'.)

Q **one more** /ˌwʌn 'mɔːʳ/ ESPECIALLY SPOKEN another – use this when you mean that this will be the last one: *One more drink and then I really have to go.* | *I'll give you one more chance to tell the truth.*

Formal or informal?
One more is not used in formal written English.

extra /'ekstrə/ [adj only before noun] in addition to the usual amount or number – use this about something useful that you may need: *Bring an extra set of clothes in case you decide to stay overnight.* | *We need an extra pint of milk for tomorrow.*

spare /speəʳ/ [adj only before noun]
spare room/key/tyre etc another room, key etc that you do not usually use but you can use if you need to:

You can sleep in the spare bedroom if you like. | *I always leave a set of spare keys with my neighbour.*

ANSWER

➡ see also **ASK**

1 to say something after someone has asked you a question or spoken to you

answer /'ɑːnsəʳ‖'æn-/ [v I/T] *Jamie thought carefully before answering.* | *I said hello to her, but she didn't answer.* | *"Why don't you just leave?" "I'd like to," she answered, "but I have nowhere else to go."*
answer a question *You still haven't answered my question.*
+that *Hugh answered that he knew nothing about the robbery.*
answer sb *Why don't you answer me?*

> ⚠ Don't say 'she didn't answer to me' or 'she didn't answer to my question'. Say **she didn't answer me** or **she didn't answer my question**.

answer /'ɑːnsəʳ‖'æn-/ [n C] something you say when someone asks you a question or speaks to you: *I called out her name, but there was no answer.* | *Each time I ask him when the work will be done, I get a different answer.*
give sb an answer *I should be able to give you a definite answer tomorrow.*
the answer is (that) *Why don't people complain?The answer is that they are frightened of losing their jobs.*
+to *These are important questions, and we want answers to them.*

reply /rɪ'plaɪ/ [v I/T] ESPECIALLY WRITTEN to answer someone when they have asked you a question or spoken to you – use this especially in written English to report what someone said: *"I'm so sorry," he replied.* | *Before she could reply, Grant put the phone down.*
+that *Lisa replied that she didn't like playing tennis.*
reply to a question *The Senator refused to reply to any more questions.*
replying – replied – have replied

> ⚠ Don't say 'he replied me'. Say **he replied**.

reply /rɪ'plaɪ/ [n C] ESPECIALLY WRITTEN something you say after someone has asked you a question or spoken to you: *Kathy murmured a reply, but I couldn't hear it.*
reply to a question/request *He turned and left the room, without waiting for a reply to his question.*
plural **replies**

2 to answer a letter, invitation, or advertisement

write back /ˌraɪt 'bæk/ [phrasal verb I] to write a letter to someone who has written a letter to you: *I wrote back and said that of course they could stay with us.*
+to *You must write back to Amy and tell her all the news.*

reply /rɪ'plaɪ/ [v I] to write a letter to someone who has written to you, or to someone who has put an advertisement in a newspaper: *I wrote to Franca three weeks ago but she hasn't replied yet.*
reply to a letter/invitation/advertisement etc *Becky hasn't replied to our invitation so I assume she isn't coming.*
replying – replied – have replied

> ⚠ Don't say 'reply a letter', 'reply an advertisement' etc. Say **reply to a letter/advertisement** etc: *If you want to reply to this ad, write to the above address.*

reply /rɪ'plaɪ/ [n C] a written answer to a letter, invitation, or advertisement: *Any customer who complains to the bank will receive a reply within 48 hours.*
+to *We got over a hundred replies to our advertisement.*
plural **replies**

answer /'ɑːnsəʳ‖'æn-/ [v T] if you **answer** a letter or advertisement, you write a letter to the person who has written it: *He spent the morning answering letters in his study.* | *Paola got the job by answering an ad in the paper.*

> ⚠ Don't say 'answer to a letter,' 'answer to an advertisement' etc. Say **answer a letter/advertisement** etc.

3 telephone/door

answer /ˈɑːnsəʳ‖ˈæn-/ [v I/T] to pick up the telephone and speak when it rings, or go to the door and open it when someone knocks: *I knocked and knocked but no one answered.*
answer the phone/the door/a call *A strange man answered the phone.* | *He still isn't answering my calls.*

> ⚠ Don't say 'answer to the phone/door'. Say **answer the phone/door**.

◯ **get** /get/ [v T] SPOKEN to answer the telephone, or go to the door when someone knocks: *"I think that's the phone." "It's OK – I'll get it."* | *Can someone get the door – I'm in the shower!*
getting – got – have got

there was no answer/there was no reply /ðeəʳ wəz nəʊ ˈɑːnsəʳ, ðeəʳ wəz nəʊ rɪˈplaɪ‖-ˈæn-/ BRITISH use this to say that no one answered the telephone or the door: *She knocked on Mike's door but there was no answer.* | *I've been trying to call Cathy all day and there's no reply.*

4 in a test or competition

answer /ˈɑːnsəʳ‖ˈæn-/ [n C] an answer to a question in a test or competition: *Write your answers on a postcard and send it to this address.*
the answer (=the correct answer) *And the answer is ... Washington DC!*
+to *What's the answer to question 4?*
the right/wrong answer *The first person to call us with the right answer will win 10 CDs of their choice.*
answer /ˈɑːnsəʳ‖ˈæn-/ [v I/T] to give an answer to a question in a test or competition
answer a question *You have 20 minutes to answer all the questions.*
answer correctly/wrongly *If you answer correctly, you could win a video camera.*

solution /səˈluːʃən/ [n C] the correct answer to a complicated problem in a test or competition: *Have you worked out the solution yet?*
+to *The solution to last week's crossword puzzle is on page 25.*

5 the answer to a problem

answer /ˈɑːnsəʳ‖ˈæn-/ [n C] a way of dealing with a problem
+to *There are no easy answers to our environmental problems.*
the answer (=the best way of dealing with a problem) *Some people think cars should be banned from the city, but I don't think that's the answer.*
solution /səˈluːʃən/ [n C] a way of dealing with a problem, especially a complicated or difficult problem
+to *Nuclear power can never be the only solution to our energy problems.*
find a solution/come up with a solution *So far, all attempts to find a solution have failed.*
solve /sɒlv‖sɑːlv, sɔːlv/ [v T] to successfully deal with a problem
solve a problem *The only way to solve the city's housing problems is to build new homes.*
◯ **know what to do** /nəʊ ˌwɒt tə ˈduː/ ESPECIALLY SPOKEN to know what you should do in order to deal with a problem: *Go and ask Larry – he'll know what to do.*
+about *Carrie thought her boyfriend was seeing another girl, but she didn't know what to do about it.*

> When you see **WB**, go to the **WORD BANKS** section.

AREA

a part of the world, a country, or a surface

➡ see also **SPACE, PLACE, LAND AND SEA**

1 an area of the world or of a country

area /'eəriə/ [n C] *There will be sunshine in most areas tomorrow.*
+of *A substantial area of Brazil is still covered by rainforest.*
industrial/agricultural/rural area *The news hadn't reached the rural areas yet.*

region /'riːdʒən/ [n C] a large area that is part of a country or of the world: *There have been reports of fighting throughout the region.* | *They finally settled in the north-west region.*
+of *Wild dogs are rare, even in the more remote regions of Africa.*

> **Formal or informal?**
> **Region** is not used in ordinary informal conversation.

zone /zəʊn/ [n C] an area that is in some way special or different from the areas around it, for example because it has a particular type of problem: *San Francisco and Tokyo are both located in earthquake zones.* | *They want the Pacific Ocean to become a nuclear-free zone.*
war/battle zone *UN troops are unwilling to enter the war zone.*

2 an area in or around a town or city

area /'eəriə/ [n C]
+of *They used to live in Marylebone, an area of London.*
poor/rich area *Diego was brought up in a very poor area of Buenos Aires.*
the surrounding area (=the area around a town or city) *Police are searching Blickling and the surrounding area for the missing child.*

district /'dɪstrɪkt/ [n C] part of a town or city that is either one of its officially fixed divisions or is a place where a particular group of people live or a particular activity takes place: *The financial district is in the centre of Manila.*
+of *Their apartment is in the Chongwen district of Peking.*

neighbourhood BRITISH **neighborhood** AMERICAN /'neɪbəˈhʊd/ [n C] one of the parts of a town or city where people live: *Freddie and his family lived in a big house in a wealthy neighbourhood.* | *Everyone in the neighborhood seemed to have heard the news.*

suburb /'sʌbɜːrb/ [n C] an area away from the centre of a city, where people live, especially an area where there are houses with gardens
+of *Amy teaches at a school in a suburb of Boston.*
the suburbs *It took about an hour to drive through the suburbs.*

block /blɒk‖blɑːk/ [n C] ESPECIALLY AMERICAN a group of buildings in a city, with four streets around it – often used as a way of talking about distances in the city: *She lived three blocks away, on 32nd Street.* | *Most of the families on our block are Italian Americans.*

precinct /'priːsɪŋkt/ [n C] AMERICAN an area in an American town or city that has its own local government and police: *the fourteenth precinct*

3 an area that is a part of a surface

area /'eəriə/ [n C] a part of a surface that has a particular size or shape: *There were several damp areas on the living room walls.*
+of *The garden has a small area of grass, with a few fruit trees around it.*

patch /pætʃ/ [n C] a small area that is different from the parts around it: *a white kitten with black patches*
damp/dirty/icy etc patch *Icy patches on the road are making driving dangerous.*
patch of dirt/damp/grease etc *a patch of dirt in the middle of the rug*
plural **patches**

ARGUE

➡ see also **DISAGREE, SHOUT,**
EC DISAGREEING

1 to argue

> ⚠ You can use **argue** about anyone, but people who **quarrel**, **squabble**, or **have a fight/have a row** usually know each other well or belong to the same family.

argue /ˈɑːʳgjuː/ [v I] if people **argue**, they speak angrily to each other because they disagree about something: *Jim and Beth seem to spend all their time arguing.*
+with *Don't argue with me, John. Just do what I tell you.*
+about/over *Out in the street, a cab driver and his passenger were arguing about the fare. | A lot of time was spent arguing over the details of the contract.*

quarrel /ˈkwɒrəl‖ˈkwɔː-, ˈkwɑː-/ [v I] if two people **quarrel**, they argue angrily and may stop being friends with each other: *They haven't spoken to each other since they quarrelled.*
+with *She left home after quarrelling with her parents.*
+about/over *The two brothers had quarreled over ownership of the farm.*
quarrelling – quarrelled – have quarrelled BRITISH
quarreling – quarreled – have quarreled AMERICAN

have a fight (also **have a row** BRITISH) /hæv ə ˈfaɪt, hæv ə ˈraʊ/ INFORMAL if two people **have a fight** or **have a row**, they argue very angrily and noisily
+with *I had another fight with Mom last night.*
+about *Kelvin and his wife have endless rows about money.*

squabble /ˈskwɒbəl‖ˈskwɑː-/ [v I] to argue noisily about something that is not really important – use this especially about children or when you think people are behaving like children: *Oh, for goodness sake, stop squabbling, you two!*
+about/over *The kids always squabble about who should do the dishes.*

fall out with sb /ˌfɔːl ˈaʊt wɪð (sb)/ [phrasal verb T] to stop having a friendly relationship with someone, because you have quarrelled with them: *I think she's fallen out with her boyfriend.*
+about/over *I don't want to fall out with you over something so unimportant.*

2 an argument

➡ if you mean 'the reason that someone gives why something is right, wrong etc', go to **REASON**

argument /ˈɑːʳgjɵmənt/ [n C] when people speak angrily to each other because they disagree about something
have an argument *My sister and I had a terrible argument and haven't spoken since.*
+about/over *the usual family arguments about what time we should be home at night*
+with *I could hear her on the phone, having an argument with someone from the bank.*
get into an argument INFORMAL (=start arguing, without intending to) *Phil got into an argument with a guy at the bar.*
start an argument (=say something that makes someone argue with you) *I didn't want to start an argument, so I kept quiet.*

quarrel /ˈkwɒrəl‖ˈkwɔː-, ˈkwɑː-/ [n C] an angry argument between people who know each other well: *a family quarrel*
+with *I was tired of these stupid quarrels with my parents.*
have a quarrel *They had some sort of quarrel years ago, and they haven't spoken to each other since.*

disagreement /ˌdɪsəˈgriːmənt/ [n C] a situation in which people disagree with each other, but without shouting or getting angry
+about/over *There were the occasional disagreements about money, but mostly we got on well.*
+with *Ginny had left the company after a disagreement with her boss.*
+between *a disagreement between the USA and China*

row /raʊ/ [n C] BRITISH an argument, when two people shout angrily at each other: *There were always rows when my dad got home.*

a blazing row (=a very angry, noisy argument) *The couple in the house next door were having a blazing row.*

squabble /'skwɒbəl‖'skwɑː-/ [n C] a noisy argument about something that is not important, especially between children: *Uncle Matt bought them a computer game to share, which led to endless squabbles.*

+about/over *a noisy squabble over who should sit in the front of the car*

dispute /dɪ'spjuːt, 'dɪspjuːt/ [n C] FORMAL when two people, organizations, or countries publicly disagree and argue with each other about something important

+over/about *an international dispute over fishing rights*

+with *Morris has been involved in a long legal dispute with his publisher.*

+between *a bitter dispute between the two countries*

settle a dispute (=end it by agreement) *All efforts to settle the dispute have so far failed.*

3 someone who likes arguing

argumentative/quarrelsome /,ɑːrɡjʊ'mentətɪv,   'kwɒrəlsəm‖'kwɔːr-, 'kwɑː-/ [adj] someone who is **argumentative** or **quarrelsome** seems to like arguing or starting arguments: *When he drinks too much, he becomes very argumentative.* | *She had had enough of all her quarrelsome relatives.*

4 to stop arguing

⌕ make up/make it up /,meɪk 'ʌp, ,meɪk ɪt 'ʌp/ [phrasal verb I] ESPECIALLY SPOKEN if two people who know each other well **make up** or **make it up**, they stop arguing and start being friendly to each other again: *I'm glad to see that you two have made up at last.*

+with *Have you made it up with your sister yet?*

settle your differences /,setl jɔːr 'dɪfərənsɨz/ if two people or organizations **settle their differences**, they stop arguing and discuss things in a sensible way until they come to an

agreement: *By the early 1970s, France and Britain had settled their differences over European trade.* | *Is it at all possible that you and your husband could settle your differences?*

> **Formal or informal?**
> **Settle your differences** is used in writing and in formal spoken English.

ARMY

WAR

POSITION/RANK   PEACE

EXPLODE   see   ATTACK
                 also

SHOOT   DEFEND

WEAPON

1 the army, navy etc

army /'ɑːrmi/ [n C] a large organized group of people trained to fight on land in a war: *the armies of Britain and France*

be in the army *Both my brothers are in the army.*

join the army/go into the army *He joined the army when he was seventeen.*

plural **armies**

> ⚠ You can also use **army** before a noun, like an adjective: *army officers* | *army uniform*

> ⚠ In British English, you can use **army** with a singular or plural verb: *The army has/have been heavily criticized.* In American English, always use a singular verb: *The army has been heavily criticized.*

the armed forces /ðɪ ,ɑːrmd 'fɔːrsɨz/ [n plural] FORMAL the army, navy, and air force of a country: *people who served in the armed forces during the war*

the military /ðə 'mɪlɨtəri‖-teri/ [n singular] ESPECIALLY AMERICAN the army, navy, and air force of a country: *The* company supplies electronic equipment to the US military. | In 1976 there was a coup and the military seized power.

military /'mɪlɪ̯təri‖-teri/ [adj only before noun] use this about things or people that belong to or are connected with the armed forces
military power/aircraft/training/ uniform etc the supreme US military commander in Europe | The airport is used by civilian and military planes.

2 someone who is in the army, navy etc

soldier /'səʊldʒəʳ/ [n C] a member of an army, especially someone who is not an officer

troops /truːps/ [n plural] soldiers – use this especially to talk about soldiers taking part in a military attack: Thousands of French troops died in the attack. | Troops were sent in to stop the riots.

men /men/ [n plural] a group of soldiers who are under the authority of a particular officer: The captain ordered his men to fire.

officer /'ɒfɪsəʳ‖'ɔː-, 'ɑː-/ [n C] a member of the army, navy etc who is in charge of a group of soldiers, sailors etc: More than 30 officers and men are still missing.
commanding officer the commanding officer of the 1st Battalion

3 to join the army, navy etc

join /dʒɔɪn/ [v T] **join the army/navy/ air force/marines** to become a member of the army, navy etc: He wants to join the air force when he finishes school.

join up /ˌdʒɔɪn 'ʌp/ [phrasal verb I] to join the armed forces during a war: My dad joined up at the beginning of the war.

enlist /ɪn'lɪst/ [v I] to join the armed forces, either in peacetime or during a war: By the end of 1915, over 700,000 men had enlisted.
+in Frank enlisted in the Marines at the age of 19.

4 when people must join the army, navy etc

conscription (also **the draft** AMERICAN) /kən'skrɪpʃən, ðə 'drɑːft‖-'dræft/ [n U] when people are officially ordered to join the armed forces, especially during a war: When was conscription introduced in Britain? | Many young men went abroad to avoid the draft.

military service /ˌmɪlɪtəri 'sɜːʳvɪ̯s‖-teri-/ [n U] the system in which everyone has to be a member of the armed forces for a period of time: All males between the ages of 18 and 30 were liable for military service.
do military service (=be a member of the armed forces as part of this system) Did you have to do military service?

 Don't say 'the military service'. Just say **military service**.

be called up BRITISH **be drafted** AMERICAN /biː ˌkɔːld 'ʌp, biː 'drɑːftɪ̯d‖ -'dræf-/ to be officially ordered to join the armed forces during a war: I was called up three months after the war started. | Thousands of young Americans were drafted to fight in Vietnam.

AROUND

➡ if you mean 'turn around', go to **TURN**

1 around someone or something

around (also **round** BRITISH) /(ə)'raʊnd/ [adv/preposition] surrounding or enclosing someone or something: A group of students sat around the table chatting. | She was wearing a silver chain round her neck. | a package with tape wrapped around it
all around/all round Enemy soldiers were now all around us. | a long garden with high walls all round

be surrounded by /bɪ: sə'raʊndɪ̩d baɪ/ if someone or something **is surrounded by** people or things, those people or things are around them on every side: *The lake was surrounded by trees.* | *Jill sat on the floor surrounded by boxes.*

on/from all sides /ɒn, frəm ˌɔːl 'saɪdz/ ESPECIALLY WRITTEN surrounding you in all directions, or coming from all directions, often in a way that may make you feel that you are unable to move or escape: *Mountains rose steeply on all sides.* | *There was the sound of gunfire from all sides.*

2 to move into a position around someone or something

surround /sə'raʊnd/ [v T] if people surround someone or something, they form a circle around them, especially to prevent someone escaping: *Police surrounded the house.* | *Football fans ran onto the field and surrounded the referee.*

gather around (also **gather round** BRITISH) /ˌgæðəʳ (ə)'raʊnd/ [phrasal verb I/T] if a group of people **gathers around** someone or something, they move nearer to them in order to see or hear them: *A crowd of young boys had gathered round.*
gather around sth/sb *People were gathering around the TV to watch the game.*

crowd around (also **crowd round** BRITISH) /ˌkraʊd (ə)'raʊnd/ [phrasal verb I/T] ESPECIALLY WRITTEN if a group of people **crowds around** someone or something, they stand near them closely together, often pushing forward to see what is happening: *The children crowded round, eager and excited.*
crowd around sb/sth *Dozens of journalists crowded around the Princess and started asking her questions.*

3 moving in a circle or moving around something

around (also **round** BRITISH) /(ə)'raʊnd/ [adv/preposition] use this after verbs of movement, to show that someone or something is moving in a circle or moving around something
go/fly/travel/run etc around sth *The Earth goes around the Sun.*
round and round *The helicopter flew round and round above us.*

in circles /ɪn 'sɜːʳkəlz/ if someone or something moves **in circles**, they move around in a circle several times: *Birds flew in circles above the lake.* | *As the dog got more and more excited, it started running around us in circles.*

circle /'sɜːʳkəl/ [v I/T] ESPECIALLY WRITTEN to move around someone or something in a circle: *The plane circled the airport several times before landing.*
+around/above *Seagulls were circling above the cliffs.*

> **Formal or informal?**
> Use **circle** especially when you are writing stories or descriptions.

orbit /'ɔːʳbɪ̩t/ [v T] to go around the Earth, the Moon, the Sun etc in a continuous circular movement: *a TV satellite that orbits the Earth every 48 hours*

ARRIVE

➡ opposite **LEAVE**
➡ see also **LATE/NOT LATE, EARLY**

1 to arrive somewhere

arrive /ə'raɪv/ [v I] *What time do you think we'll arrive?*
arrive at the house/hotel/airport etc *It was already dark by the time they arrived at their hotel.*
arrive in France/Tokyo etc *The British Prime Minister arrived in Tokyo today.*
arrive here/there/back/home *When I first arrived here none of the other students would talk to me.*

+from *Some friends were arriving from Australia for Christmas.*

 Don't say 'arrive to' a place. Say **arrive at** (a building or public place) or **arrive in** (a city or country).

 Don't say 'arrive at home' or 'arrive to home'. Say **arrive home**.

Formal or informal?
Arrive is more formal than **get to**.

get to /'get tu:/ [phrasal verb T] to arrive at a place: *It'll take us about half an hour to get to the airport.*
get back to sth *I'll call her when I get back to Chicago.*
get there/here/home *What time do you usually get home in the evening? | I want to get there before the stores close.*

come /kʌm/ [v I] if someone or something **comes**, they arrive at the place where you are waiting for them: *When the visitors come, bring them up to my office. | Has the mail come yet?*
come home *What time is Dad coming home?*
coming – came – have come

reach /ri:tʃ/ [v T] ESPECIALLY WRITTEN to arrive at a place, especially after a long or difficult journey: *It took them over three days to reach the top of the mountain. | On March 3rd the US 1st Army finally reached Cologne.*

 Don't say 'reach to' or 'reach at'.

be here /bi: 'hɪəʳ/ SPOKEN you say someone **is here** when they have arrived at the place where you are waiting for them: *Susan, your friends are here. | Is Nick here yet?*
turn up/show up /,tɜːʳn 'ʌp, ,ʃəʊ 'ʌp/ [phrasal verb I] INFORMAL to arrive – use this about someone you are expecting to arrive, especially when they arrive late: *Steve turned up half an hour late as usual. | Some of the people I invited never showed up.*

2 when a plane, ship, or train arrives

arrive /ə'raɪv/ [v I] *The plane arrived two hours late.*
+in/at/from *I'm catching a train that arrives in Osaka at 5.30. | Planes carrying military supplies have been arriving at the airbase.*

Formal or informal?
Arrive is more formal than **get in**.

get in /,get 'ɪn/ [phrasal verb I] to arrive – use this when you are talking about the time when a train, ship, or plane arrives: *What time does your train get in?*
+to *The ferry gets in to Milwaukee around noon.*
land /lænd/ [v I] if a plane or its passengers **land**, they arrive at an airport
+at *When the plane landed at JFK, it was three hours late.*
+in *What time did you land in Miami?*
come in to land (=go down slowly towards the ground at an airport) *There's a plane coming in to land now.*

 Planes **land at** an airport, or **land in** a city or country.

come in /,kʌm 'ɪn/ [phrasal verb I] if a plane, ship, or train **comes in**, it arrives in the place that it is travelling to: *Crowds had gathered at the harbour to watch the ship come in. | Has the Air India flight come in yet?*

3 when someone or something arrives

arrival /ə'raɪvəl/ [n singular/U]
sb's arrival *Joe's sudden arrival spoiled all our plans.*
the arrival of sb/sth *We apologize for the late arrival of flight 605.*
+at/in *The TV crew went to film his arrival at Heathrow. | the day after our arrival in Paris*
on sb's arrival FORMAL (=when someone arrives) *On his arrival, he was greeted by the President.*
dead on arrival *She was rushed to hospital but she was dead on arrival.*

4 to arrive somewhere without intending to

end up /ˌend ˈʌp/ [phrasal verb I] to arrive in a place that you did not intend to go to
+in/at *I fell asleep on the bus and ended up in Denver.* | *We had planned to go straight home, but we all ended up at Tom's place.*

come to sth /ˈkʌm tuː (sth)/ [phrasal verb T] ESPECIALLY WRITTEN to arrive at a place that you did not know was there: *We were walking through the forest when we came to a waterfall.*

 Use come to especially when you are writing stories.

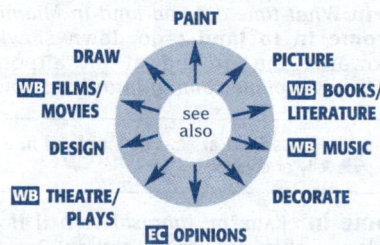

ART

PAINT

DRAW   PICTURE

WB FILMS/   **WB** BOOKS/
MOVIES   LITERATURE

see
also

DESIGN   **WB** MUSIC

WB THEATRE/   DECORATE
PLAYS
EC OPINIONS

1 something that an artist has produced

art /ɑːʳt/ [n U] a way of representing things or expressing ideas, using pictures, sculpture, and other objects that people can look at: *a book about German art in the 19th century* | *What kind of art do you like?* | *the History of Art* (=a subject, often taught at school and university)

work of art /ˌwɜːʳk əv ˈɑːʳt/ [n C] something produced by an artist, especially something that is of very high quality: *Several priceless works of art were badly damaged when the palace was bombed.*
plural **works of art**

work /wɜːʳk/ [n C] a picture, statue, sculpture etc – use this especially when you are also saying who the

artist was: *Tracy Emin's latest work has just gone on display.* | *Her later works reflected her growing depression.*

masterpiece /ˈmɑːstəʳpiːs‖ˈmæs-/ [n C] a picture, statue etc that is of extremely high quality, especially one that is believed to be the best work of a particular artist: *one of the great Italian masterpieces* | *Many people regard this painting as Raphael's masterpiece.*

 You can use **work of art**, **work**, and **masterpiece** about art in any form.

2 types of picture

picture /ˈpɪktʃəʳ/ [n C] a general word for something painted or drawn on a surface to represent something or someone, or a photograph: *The walls of the room were covered with pictures.*
+of *I like that picture of the cathedral.*
draw/paint a picture *Did you draw that picture?* | *He asked her permission to paint her picture.*
take sb's picture/take a picture of sb (=use a camera to take a photograph of someone) *Stand over there and I'll take your picture.*
wedding/holiday etc pictures (=photographs of someone's wedding/holiday etc)

painting /ˈpeɪntɪŋ/ [n C] a picture made using paint: *a 17th century Dutch painting*
+of *a painting of a woman lying on a bed*
+by *a painting by Turner*
oil painting (=done using a special type of paint made with oil)

drawing /ˈdrɔːɪŋ/ [n C] a picture drawn with pencils or pens
+of *a 16th century drawing of the canals in Venice*

photograph /ˈfəʊtəɡrɑːf‖-ɡræf/ [n C] a picture made using a camera

illustration /ˌɪləˈstreɪʃən/ [n C] a picture in a book or article that shows an event, person etc from the story or helps explain something: *the wonderful illustrations in Van Allsburg's children's books*

print /prɪnt/ [n C] a picture made by cutting lines into a piece of metal or wood and then putting ink onto it and printing it on paper; or a copy of a painting that is made by taking a photograph of it and then printing it onto paper

sketch /sketʃ/ [n C] a simple drawing that you make quickly and that does not show much detail

mosaic

mosaic /məʊˈzeɪ-ɪk/ [n C] a picture made using very small pieces of glass or stone

collage /ˈkɒlɑːʒ‖kəˈlɑːʒ/ [n C] a picture made by sticking pieces of paper, cloth, or other pictures onto a surface

watercolour BRITISH **watercolor** AMERICAN /ˈwɔːtərˌkʌlərˈ‖ˈwɔː-,ˈwɑː-/ [n C] a picture painted using a special type of paint that is mixed with water, so the colours are pale

portrait /ˈpɔːrtrət/ [n C] a painting, drawing, or photograph of a person

still life /ˌstɪl ˈlaɪf◂/ [n C] a picture of an object or several objects, especially fruit or flowers

landscape /ˈlændskeɪp/ [n C] a picture of the countryside

seascape /ˈsiːskeɪp/ [n C] a picture of the sea

3 other types of art

sculpture /ˈskʌlptʃərˈ/ [n C/U] a work of art that someone shapes from materials such as stone, metal, or wood

statue /ˈstætʃuː/ [n C] an image of a person or animal made from a hard material such as stone or metal, especially one that represents a famous person or an important idea

ceramics /sɪˈræmɪks/ [n plural] pots, bowls etc made of clay

⚠️ **Ceramics** is always used in the plural: *an exhibition of Japanese ceramics*. Don't use **ceramics** when you are talking about one clay object. Say **a bowl**, **a plate** etc.

4 the subject of a picture, painting etc

show /ʃəʊ/ [v T] if a picture, painting etc **shows** something, you can see it in the picture, painting etc: *The painting shows a young couple sitting at a pavement café. | I want a photograph that shows his face clearly.*

depict /dɪˈpɪkt/ [v T] FORMAL if a painting or other piece of art **depicts** something, it shows or represents it: *Her drawings depict life in an African village.*

portray /pɔːˈtreɪ/ [v T] FORMAL if a painting or other piece of art **portrays** something, it shows or represents it: *The first painting portrays the Battle of Trafalgar.*

5 someone who draws, paints etc

artist /ˈɑːrtɪst/ [n C] someone who produces paintings, sculptures, or any kind of art: *an exhibition of work by young artists*

painter /ˈpeɪntərˈ/ [n C] someone who produces paintings: *Pissarro was a famous French painter.*

sculptor /ˈskʌlptərˈ/ [n C] someone who makes sculptures

photographer /fəˈtɒɡrəfərˈ‖-ˈtɑː-/ [n C] someone who takes photographs as an art or a profession

6 to make drawings, pictures etc

paint /peɪnt/ [v I/T] to make a picture using paint: *Botticelli painted 'The Birth of Venus'.*

draw /drɔː/ [v I/T] to make a picture using a pencil or pen: *The students were drawing a Chinese vase that stood on the table. | Small children love to draw with coloured pens.*

photograph /ˈfəʊtəɡrɑːf‖-ɡræf/ [v T] to take a photograph of someone or something: *Eve Arnold photographed Marilyn Monroe many times.*

⚠ Don't say 'I photographed my friends on the beach'. Say **I took a photo of my friends** or **I took a picture of my friends**. Only use the verb **photograph** when saying what a professional photographer does.

7 a place where art is shown

gallery (also **art gallery**) /ˈgæləri, ˈɑːˈt ˌgæləri/ [n C] a building or room where you can go to look at paintings, sculptures etc: *There's a small art gallery in the centre of the town.* | *the National Gallery*

⚠ In American English, **gallery** is only used to refer to a room or a small building, not a large building.

museum /mjuːˈziːəm‖mjʊ-/ [n C] AMERICAN a large building where you can go to look at paintings, sculptures etc: *The museum has a few of Van Gogh's early works.* | *the Museum of Modern Art*

exhibition /ˌeksɨˈbɪʃən/ [n C] a collection of paintings, sculptures etc, often the work of one artist or from a particular period, which you can go to see – use this especially when they are only being shown for a limited period of time: *Have you been to the Picasso exhibition yet?*
+of *an exhibition of black and white photographs*

8 styles of art

classical

classical /ˈklæsɪkəl/ [adj] the main style of art in 18th century Europe, based on the styles of ancient Greece and Rome

romantic

romantic /rəʊˈmæntɪk, rə-/ [adj] a style of art popular in 19th century Europe, often showing the sea or the countryside, and usually expressing strong emotions

impressionist

impressionist /ɪmˈpreʃənɨst/ [adj] a style of art that was developed in France in the late 19th century, which uses colours to show the effects of light on people, objects, and places, and does not show small details

modern

modern /ˈmɒdən‖ˈmɑːdərn/ [adj] the style of art in the 20th century that is deliberately different from art of the 18th and 19th centuries, and does not show people, objects, or places as they appear in real life

abstract /ˈæbstrækt/ [adj] a type of modern art that uses shapes, colours,

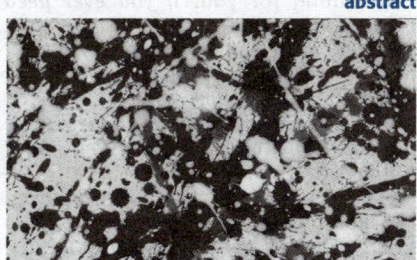

abstract

and patterns to express ideas and feelings, rather than making pictures that look like people, objects, or places

ASHAMED

➡ see also **EMBARRASSED, GUILTY/NOT GUILTY, SORRY**

> Don't confuse **ashamed** and **embarrassed**. If you are **ashamed**, you feel guilty and bad about yourself, because you have done something that you know is wrong. If you are **embarrassed**, you worry about what other people think of you, especially because you have said or done something silly. **Ashamed** is a much stronger word.

ashamed /əˈʃeɪmd/ [*adj* not before noun] someone who is **ashamed** feels very sorry because they know they have done something bad, and they think people may no longer respect them
be/feel ashamed *When she thought about what she'd said, she felt ashamed.*
ashamed of doing sth *Frank was ashamed of having lied to his mother.*
ashamed of yourself *You ought to be ashamed of yourself – coming home drunk like that!*
ashamed of sb (=when you wish you were not connected with someone because they have behaved badly) *No one wants their own children to feel ashamed of them.*
+(that) *Later, he felt ashamed that he had not offered to help.*
shame /ʃeɪm/ [*n* U] the feeling that you have when you know that you have behaved badly or that you have lost

other people's respect: *"Please don't tell my dad about this," he said, blushing with shame.*
+of *I suppose he wants to avoid the shame of a public confession.*
in shame (=because you are ashamed) *As Philip entered the courtroom, he hung his head in shame.*

> Don't say 'I feel shame'. Say **I feel ashamed**.

disgrace /dɪsˈɡreɪs/ [*n* U] when you have completely lost other people's respect because of something bad you have done
in disgrace *Browne was caught selling drugs, and was sent home from college in disgrace.*
+of *Garton killed himself because he could not bear the disgrace of a public scandal.*
humiliating /hjuːˈmɪlieɪtɪŋ/ [*adj*] a **humiliating** experience makes you seem weak or stupid in a way that many other people can see: *I had to apologize in front of all the other students – it was so humiliating!*

ASK

➡ if you want to know how to form questions, go to the **ESSENTIAL GRAMMAR** (Section 1)

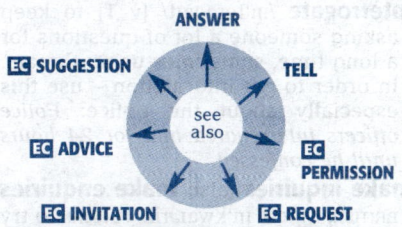

1 **to ask questions**

ask /ɑːsk‖æsk/ [*v* I/T] to ask someone a question because you want to get information from them: *I knew there was something wrong, but I didn't like to ask.*
ask (sb) what/how/why etc *Ask Kim what she'd like for her birthday.* | *I asked why, but they wouldn't give a reason.*

ask (sb) if/whether *I asked her if she was English.* | *He asked whether I was looking for accommodation.*

ask (sb) about sth *At the interview, they're sure to ask you about your work experience.*

ask (sb) a question *Would anyone like to ask me any questions?*

ask sb *If you need any more information, ask your doctor.*

> ⚠ Don't say 'ask to someone'. Say **ask someone**: *If you don't understand, ask your teacher.*

consult /kən'sʌlt/ [v T] FORMAL to ask for information or advice from someone whose job is to give people information or advice

consult a doctor/lawyer/expert etc *Before starting any exercise programme, you should consult your doctor.*

consult sb about sth *He should have consulted his advisors about this before taking any action.*

question /'kwestʃən/ [v T] to ask someone a lot of questions, in order to find out what they think, or to get information about something that has happened: *Half of the people we questioned thought the President should resign.*

question sb about sth *The police have already questioned him about the missing $50,000.*

interrogate /ɪn'terəgeɪt/ [v T] to keep asking someone a lot of questions for a long time, sometimes using threats, in order to get information – use this especially about the police: *Police officers interrogated him for 24 hours until he confessed.*

make inquiries (also **make enquiries** BRITISH) /ˌmeɪk ɪn'kwaɪəriz/ FORMAL to try to get information about something or someone by politely asking people questions about them: *We went to the French Embassy to make inquiries.*

+about *A detective was here earlier, making inquiries about your friend Gary.*

2 to ask for something

ask /ɑːsk‖æsk/ [v I/T] to ask for something, or to ask someone to do

something for you: *If you ever need any help, just ask.* | *I need some more money, but I don't dare ask my dad.*

ask (sb) for sth *A lot of people don't like asking for help.*

ask sb to do sth/if *Ask him to wait outside for a moment.* | *I asked him if he would teach me German.*

ask to do sth/if (=ask to be allowed to do something) *She walked right in here and asked to speak to the manager.* | *He asked if he could join in.*

> ⚠ Don't say 'ask to someone'. Say **ask someone**.

order /'ɔːʳdəʳ/ [v T] to ask for the food or drink that you want in restaurants, or to ask companies to send you some goods that they sell: *Have you ordered the wine yet?* | *Nina orders a lot of her clothes from mail-order catalogues.*

demand /dɪ'mɑːnd‖dɪ'mænd/ [v T] to ask for something, or ask someone to do something, in a firm or angry way that shows you expect them to do it: *Parents are demanding greater control over their children's education.*

demand to know/see etc sth *They stopped me and demanded to see my passport.*

> **Formal or informal?**
> **Demand** is not used in informal conversation. You can use **I demand** when you want to formally ask for something in a firm way: *I demand to see my husband.*

beg /beg/ [v I/T] to ask for something, or ask someone to do something, in a way that shows you want it very much: *She begged and begged until finally they agreed to let her come.*

beg sb to do sth *I begged Greg not to tell Cindy about it.*

+for *The prisoners were begging for mercy.*

begging – begged – have begged

nag /næg/ [v I/T] to keep asking someone to do something, in a very annoying way: *Oh, stop nagging – I'll do it later!*

nag sb to do sth *My parents keep nagging me to get my hair cut.*

nagging – nagged – have nagged

3 to ask for something officially

apply /əˈplaɪ/ [v I] to write officially to someone asking for something such as a job, an opportunity to study at a university, or permission to do something: *There was a job vacancy at the radio station, and 150 people applied.*
+for *Why don't you apply for a loan?*
apply to do sth *In the 1960s, thousands of people applied to emigrate to South Africa.*
applying – applied – have applied

claim /kleɪm/ [v T] to ask for something that you have a legal right to have, from a government, company etc: *Thousands of people who should get welfare payments never even bother to claim them.*
claim sth from sb *If you were unfairly dismissed, you will be able to claim compensation from your employer.*

appeal /əˈpiːl/ [v I] to make a public request, for example on television or in the newspapers, for money, food, information etc, especially in order to help someone who is in a very bad situation
+for *Aid agencies are appealing for food and clothes for the refugees.*
appeal to sb for sth *Police appealed to the public for any information about the missing girl.*

request /rɪˈkwest/ [v T] FORMAL to officially ask someone for something or ask someone to do something: *The pilot requested permission to land.*
+that *His lawyer requested that the case should be heard immediately.*
request sb to do sth *All members are requested to attend the annual meeting.*

> Don't say 'request for something'. Say **request something**.

4 to ask for money or food because you do not have any

beg (also **panhandle** AMERICAN) /beg, ˈpænhændl/ [v I] to ask people in the street for money or food because you do not have any: *In London there are* more and more homeless kids begging in the streets. | *An old man was panhandling outside the bus terminal.*
begging – begged – have begged

5 something that you ask

question /ˈkwestʃən/ [n C] what you say or write when you are asking for information: *There were several questions she wanted to ask.*
+about *Does anyone have any questions about the homework?*
answer a question *The teacher never answered my question.*
a difficult/awkward question (=one that it is hard to answer) *I hope the interviewers don't ask too many difficult questions.*

request /rɪˈkwest/ [n C] a statement, letter etc in which you ask for something politely or formally
+for *The bank refused his request for a loan.*
make a request *We've already made a request for some new equipment.*
on request FORMAL (=when you can get something by formally asking for it) *Information about the test is available on request.*

demand /dɪˈmɑːnd‖dɪˈmænd/ [n C] a strong request saying very clearly what you want, especially when it is something that someone does not want to give you: *The kidnappers sent a list of demands to a national newspaper.*
+for *a demand for a 10% pay increase*

6 a set of questions that you ask in order to find out what people think

survey /ˈsɜːrveɪ/ [n C] a set of questions that you ask a large number of people in order to find out about their opinions or behaviour: *A recent survey showed that 50% of 18–22-year-olds had tried drugs.*
+of/into *a survey of people's eating habits*
carry out/conduct a survey *We are carrying out a survey into the effects of TV violence on children.*

opinion poll /əˈpɪnjən ˌpəʊl/ [n C] the process of finding out about people's opinions, especially their political opinions, by asking them how they intend to vote etc: *Opinion polls show that the Democrats are way ahead.*

questionnaire /ˌkwestʃə'neəʳ, ˌkes-/ [n C] a piece of paper with a set of questions on it, which is given to a large number of people to find out what they think
complete a questionnaire (=answer all the questions on it) *Complete our questionnaire and you might win a car!*

ATTACK

➡ opposite **DEFEND**

THREATEN   CRITICIZE
SUFFER   VIOLENT
            see
            also
PROTECT   WAR
CRIME   ARMY
        SHOOT

1 to attack a person

attack /ə'tæk/ [v T] to use violence against someone and try to hurt them: *She was attacked on her way to the station. | A big dog jumped out and attacked me.*
attack sb with sth *He'd been attacked with some kind of heavy object.*
attacker [n C] someone who attacks another person: *Could you give me a description of your attacker?*

mug /mʌg/ [v T usually in passive] to attack someone and take money from them in a public place such as a street: *He's been mugged twice since he moved to London.*
mugging – mugged – have mugged

ambush /'æmbʊʃ/ [v T] if a group of people **ambush** someone, they hide and wait for them and then suddenly attack them: *An armed gang ambushed a security vehicle and killed the driver.*

assault /ə'sɔːlt/ [v T] FORMAL to attack someone violently and hurt them – use this especially to emphasize that this was a crime: *Several police officers were assaulted by demonstrators.*

2 to attack a place or country

attack /ə'tæk/ [v I/T] to attack a place or country using weapons, aircraft, soldiers etc: *Enemy planes attacked the city throughout the night. | General McArthur gave the order to attack.*

invade /ɪn'veɪd/ [v I/T] if a country's army **invades** another country, it enters it and tries to take control of it: *In the summer of 1968, Soviet troops invaded Czechoslovakia.*

raid /reɪd/ [v T] if a group of soldiers **raids** a place belonging to an enemy, they attack it suddenly and cause a lot of damage in a short time: *Shortly after dawn a small group of commandos raided the enemy camp.*

3 to attack someone because they attacked you

retaliate /rɪ'tælieɪt/ [v I] to attack a person, country, or group because they have attacked you first
retaliate by doing sth *Protestors retaliated by throwing stones at the police.*
retaliation /rɪˌtæli'eɪʃən/ [n U] when you attack someone because they attacked you
in retaliation for sth (=as retaliation when someone attacks you) *The rockets were fired in retaliation for Tuesday's bomb attack.*
counter-attack /'kaʊntərəˌtæk/ [n C] an attack that an army makes after it has been attacked by an enemy: *The British counter-attack forced the French back into their own territory.*
counter-attack [v I] to attack an enemy after they have attacked you: *The General ordered two divisions to counter-attack.*

4 an attack against a person

attack /ə'tæk/ [n C] when someone uses violence against another person and tries to hurt them: *The attack took place as Mr Owen was leaving his home. | Police are investigating a series of racial attacks in the city.*
+on *a serious attack on a young Turkish worker in Germany yesterday*

mugging /'mʌgɪŋ/ [n C] an attack on someone in a public place such as a street, in order to steal something from them: *Every year there are thousands of muggings on the subway.*

assault /ə'sɔːlt/ [n C/U] a violent attack on someone – use this especially to talk about the crime of attacking someone: *Reed was serving a 5-year jail sentence for burglary and assault.*
+on *Statistics show an increase in the number of assaults on women.*

5 a military attack

attack /ə'tæk/ [n C] when a military force attacks a place or country, using weapons, aircraft, soldiers etc: *The attack began at dawn.* | *a terrorist attack*
+on *a carefully planned attack on American air bases*
launch/mount an attack (=start an attack) *Troops launched an attack on the city in the early hours of the morning.*

invasion /ɪn'veɪʒən/ [n C] when an army from one country enters another country and tries to take control of it: *Troops spent three months preparing to launch the invasion.*
+of *the invasion of Normandy in 1944*
American/French/British etc invasion *the Soviet invasion of Afghanistan*

raid /reɪd/ [n C] a short, quick attack by a group of soldiers, planes, or ships on a place that belongs to an enemy
+on *Several raids were made on nearby villages.*
air raid (=when aircraft drop bombs on a place) *A series of air raids almost totally destroyed the ancient city centre.*

ambush /'æmbʊʃ/ [n C] a sudden attack on someone by people who have been hiding and waiting for them, especially in a place where there is a war or fighting: *Four soldiers were killed in an ambush outside the camp.*
plural **ambushes**

6 a person or place that is attacked

victim /'vɪktɪ̱m/ [n C] someone who has been attacked: *The victim received serious head injuries.*
be the victim of a crime/assault/attack etc *Saleem, aged 16, was the victim of a vicious racial attack yesterday evening.*

target /'tɑː^rgɪ̱t/ [n C] a person or place that someone decides to attack
+for *Government buildings have recently been a target for terrorist attacks.*
prime target (=a very likely target) *Airports are a prime target.*

AVAILABLE/NOT AVAILABLE

➡ see also **GET**

1 available for someone to have or use

available /ə'veɪləbəl/ [adj] if something is **available**, you can get it, buy it, or use it: *Coffee, tea, and snacks will be available throughout the day.* | *This treatment is not available in all hospitals.* | *Every available space on the walls was covered with posters.*
+to *Only a few documents were available to him.*
+from *His latest book is available from all good bookstores.*
readily/freely available (=very easy to get) *Drugs like heroin are readily available on the streets.*
make sth available *These statistics are never sold or made available to the public.*

> **Formal or informal?**
> **Available** is rather a formal word. For example, in conversation you would say **When can we have the money?** not 'When will the money become available?'

spare /speə^r/ [adj] something that is **spare** is not being used now, but it can be used if someone needs it: *There are some spare chairs in the next room if you need them.* | *Bring plenty of spare clothes if you want to stay for the weekend.*

spare change/cash (=money available to use for a particular purpose because you do not need it for anything else at the time) *I need 50 pence for the coffee machine – do you have any spare change?*

free /friː/ [adj] a room or seat that is **free** is available for anyone to use because no one is using it yet: *Is this seat free?* | *The conference room is free this morning.*

have sth free *The hotel never has any rooms free over the Christmas period.*

2 not available

unavailable/unobtainable /ˌʌnəˈveɪl-əbəl, ˌʌnəbˈteɪnəbəl/ [adj not before noun] if something is **unavailable** or **unobtainable**, it is impossible to get it or buy it: *Fresh fruits were unavailable in winter.* | *Good apartments to rent had become almost unobtainable.*

AVOID

1 to make sure that something bad does not happen

avoid /əˈvɔɪd/ [v T] to prevent a difficult situation, an accident, a mistake etc from happening: *If we learn from our mistakes, we can avoid future problems.* | *It's important to take measures to avoid the risk of fire.* | *helping students to avoid common errors*

avoid doing sth (=not do something, in order to prevent problems) *Students should try to avoid getting into debt.* | *It's best to avoid going out alone after dark.*

> ⚠ Don't say 'avoid to do something'. Say **avoid doing something**.

get out of sth /ˌget ˈaʊt ɒv (sth)/ [phrasal verb T] INFORMAL to find a way of not doing something that you should do or that you have promised to do: *I'm supposed to stay at home with my sister this evening, but I'll try to get out of it.*

get out of doing sth *He always manages to get out of paying for the drinks.*

get around sth (also **get round sth** BRITISH) /ˌget (ə)ˈraʊnd (sth)/ [phrasal verb T] INFORMAL to find a way of avoiding a difficult situation or problem, so that you do not have to deal with it or be limited by it: *There's no getting around it – you're going to have to tell her the truth.* | *Isn't there any way of getting round these regulations?*

2 to keep away from a person or place

avoid /əˈvɔɪd/ [v T] to keep away from a person because you do not want to talk to them, or to keep away from a place because there are problems there: *I'm sure Sarah's been avoiding me recently.* | *It's best to avoid the city centre during the rush hour.*

avoid sb/sth like the plague INFORMAL (=try very hard to avoid them) *Since their divorce, they've avoided each other like the plague.*

stay away/keep away /ˌsteɪ əˈweɪ, ˌkiːp əˈweɪ/ [phrasal verb I] to not go near a person or place, because they may be dangerous or may cause problems

+from *That evening he received a note warning him to stay away from the camp.* | *Keep away from my children, or I'll call the police.*

stay/keep well away (=completely avoid) *She walked along the path, keeping well away from the cliff's edge.*

steer clear of sb/sth /ˌstɪə^r ˈklɪər ɒv (sb/sth)/ INFORMAL to make an effort to avoid a person or place, because there could be serious problems if you do not: *We were told to steer clear of the main roads, where we might be recognized.* | *She advised me to steer clear of Matthew – she said he couldn't be trusted.*

3 to avoid a difficult question or subject

avoid /ə'vɔɪd/ [v T] to not talk about a subject or to not answer a question directly, because you do not want to cause embarrassment or problems for yourself: *Try to avoid subjects like sex or religion that might offend people.* | *Like a lot of politicians, he just kept avoiding the question.*

steer clear of sth /ˌstɪər 'klɪər ɒv (sth)/ INFORMAL to make an effort to avoid talking about a subject which may cause embarrassment or arguments: *Steer clear of controversial topics.*

evasive /ɪ'veɪsɪv/ [adj] deliberately trying to avoid answering questions directly or explaining something clearly, in order to hide information: *All of the journalists' questions were met with vague, evasive answers.* | *When we asked him where his wife was, O'Hare suddenly became evasive.*

4 to avoid being hit

avoid /ə'vɔɪd/ [v T] to move so that you do not hit something or get hit by it: *I had to swerve to avoid the truck.*
avoid doing sth *Penny jumped out of the way to avoid being hit by the falling branch.*

get out of the way /ˌget ˌaʊt əv ðə 'weɪ/ to move quickly in order to avoid something dangerous that is moving towards you: *"Get out of the way!" he yelled, as the wall began to crumble.*
+of *He ran off the track to get out of the way of the horses.*

duck /dʌk/ [v I] to move your head and the top part of your body down in order to avoid something: *If she hadn't ducked, the ball would have hit her.* | *I forgot to duck and hit my head on the doorway.*

duck

dodge /dɒdʒ‖dɑːdʒ/ [v I/T] ESPECIALLY WRITTEN to avoid something or someone by quickly moving sideways: *He managed to dodge the traffic as he ran across the road.* | *If I hadn't dodged at the last second, they would have caught me.*

dodge

+behind/into/through
He saw the policeman and dodged into an alley.

B

B, b

BABY

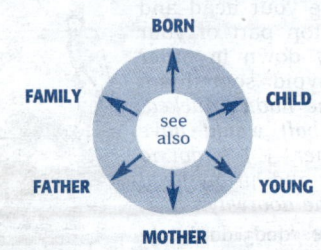

BORN

FAMILY   CHILD

see
also

FATHER   YOUNG

MOTHER

1 a baby

baby /'beɪbi/ [n C] a very young child
who has not yet learned to speak or
walk: *Who will look after the baby
when you go back to work?*
new baby (=a baby that was born
only recently) *Have you seen Rachel's
new baby?*
newborn baby (=a baby that has just
been born) *The average weight of a
newborn baby is about seven pounds.*
baby boy/girl *a four-day-old baby
boy*
baby son/daughter *Steve and Martha
are proud to announce the birth of their
baby daughter, Kate Louise.*
unborn baby (=a baby that is still
growing inside its mother) *There are a
lot of sounds that an unborn baby can
hear.*
plural **babies**

child /tʃaɪld/ [n C] a baby: *They had
their first child after ten years of
marriage.*
unborn child (=a baby that is still
growing inside its mother) *The rubella
virus can seriously harm the unborn
child.*
plural **children**

> **Formal or informal?**
> **Child** is used with this meaning in writing and
> in formal speech.

2 to be born

be born /biː 'bɔːʳn/ when a baby **is
born**, it comes out of its mother's
body and begins its life: *The baby was
born two months early.* | *Where were
you born?*

> Don't say 'I borned'. Say **I was born**.

birth /bɜːʳθ/ [n C/U] the process of
being born, or the time when
someone is born
+of *It's quite common for fathers to be
present at the birth of their babies.*
at birth (=at the time when a baby is
born) *He only weighed 1.5 kg at birth.*
premature /'premətʃəʳ, -tʃʊəʳ, ˌpremə-
'tʃʊəʳ‖ˌpriːmə'tʃʊər/ [adj] a **premature**
baby is born too early and is often
small or weak: *Many premature babies
have breathing problems.*
**three months/seven weeks etc
premature** (=born three months etc
before the normal time) *The baby was
six weeks premature.*

3 have a baby

have a baby /ˌhæv ə 'beɪbi/ if a woman
has a baby, it comes out of her body:
Helen had her second baby at home.
have a boy/girl *Val's just had another
baby boy!*
have twins (=have two babies at the
same time)

give birth /ˌgɪv 'bɜːʳθ/ if a woman **gives
birth**, a baby comes out of her body:
*An Italian woman has given birth at
the age of 61.*
**give birth to a boy/girl/son/
daughter** *The King hoped she would
give birth to a son.*

> **Formal or informal?**
> **Give birth** is more formal than **have a baby**,
> and is not often used in conversation.

childbirth /'tʃaɪldbɜːʳθ/ [n U] the process during which a baby is coming
out of its mother's body: *drugs that
ease the pain of childbirth*
natural childbirth (=without drugs,
medical operations etc)

in labour BRITISH **in labor** AMERICAN /ɪn
'leɪbəʳ/ a woman is **in labour** during

the hours when her baby is being born: *She was in labour for over 16 hours with her first child.*
go into labour (=to start the process of giving birth to a baby) *Anna was at work when she went into labour.*

4 going to have a baby

pregnant /'pregnənt/ [adj] a **pregnant** woman has a baby growing inside her body: *Have you heard that Liz is pregnant?*
get pregnant (=become pregnant) *She got pregnant while she was only 15.*
twelve weeks/eight months etc pregnant *Helen's three months pregnant.*
○ **be going to have a baby** /biː ˌgəʊɪŋ tə hæv ə 'beɪbi/ ESPECIALLY SPOKEN to have a baby growing inside your body: *I've got something to tell you all: I'm going to have a baby!*

⚠ Use **be going to have a baby** especially when you are telling someone for the first time that you or someone else is pregnant.

pregnancy /'pregnənsi/ [n C/U] the time when a woman has a baby growing inside her body: *This drug should not be taken during pregnancy.*
teenage pregnancy (=when teenagers become pregnant) *an increase in the number of teenage pregnancies* plural **pregnancies**

maternity /mə'tɜːʳnₑti/ [adj only before noun] intended or designed for women who are going to have a baby
maternity hospital/ward/unit (=a hospital or part of a hospital where women go to have their babies)
maternity clothes (=clothes specially designed for women who are going to have a baby)
maternity leave (=the period of time that a mother is allowed to spend away from work when she has a baby)

5 when a baby is not born alive

have a miscarriage /ˌhæv ə 'mɪskærɪdʒ/ if a woman **has a miscarriage**, the

baby is born dead when it is still only partly developed: *She had a miscarriage when she was three months pregnant.*
lose the baby /ˌluːz ðə 'beɪbi/ if a woman **loses a baby**, it dies before it is born, or at the time it is born: *Patricia lost the baby six months into her pregnancy.*

Formal or informal?
Lose a baby is a less technical and more emotional expression than **have a miscarriage** and is used more in informal conversation.

abortion /ə'bɔːʳʃən/ [n C/U] when a woman has a medical operation to remove a baby that is developing inside her, before the baby is ready to be born: *In Europe there are over 2 million abortions a year.* | *The Catholic Church remains strongly opposed to abortion.*
have an abortion *She had an abortion when she was only 15.*

6 a baby animal

kitten /'kɪtn/ [n C] a young cat
puppy /'pʌpi/ [n C] a young dog plural **puppies**
lamb /læm/ [n C] a young sheep
piglet /'pɪglₑt/ [n C] a young pig
calf /kɑːfǁkæf/ [n C] a young cow plural **calves**
foal /fəʊl/ [n C] a young horse
chick /tʃɪk/ [n C] a young bird
young /jʌŋ/ [n plural] an animal's babies: *The mother bird will stay with her young until they are four weeks old.*

Formal or informal?
Young is used especially in written English and in descriptions of the way animals live and behave.

baby /'beɪbi/ [adj only before noun]
baby rabbit/elephant/monkey etc a very young animal: *The baby monkey was following its mother.*

B

7 how animals and humans produce babies

breed /briːd/ [v I] if animals **breed**, they produce babies: *Rabbits breed very quickly.*
breeding – bred – have bred

reproduce /ˌriːprə'djuːs‖-'duːs/ [v I] FORMAL to produce babies: *Fish reproduce by laying eggs.*
reproduction /ˌriːprə'dʌkʃən/ [n U] the process of producing babies, young animals, or young plants: *Reproduction is the main aim of almost all life forms.*

> **Formal or informal?**
> **Reproduce** is used in formal scientific writing, programmes etc.

BAD

➡ opposite **GOOD**

WORSE

EC OPINIONS

HORRIBLE/
UNPLEASANT

VIOLENT

WRONG

see also

CARELESS

CRUEL

FRIGHTENING/
FRIGHTENED

SERIOUS

DISAPPOINTING/
DISAPPOINTED

1 bad films/books/methods/ plans/food

bad /bæd/ [adj] something that is **bad** is of a low standard, because it has been done badly, designed badly, performed badly etc: *The movie was so bad that we left halfway through.* | *This is the worst book she's ever written.* | *Opponents of the plan say it is a bad way of managing city traffic.* | *The food we get at school is really bad.*
bad – worse – worst

◯ **no good** /nəʊ 'gʊd/ SPOKEN used for saying that something is not good at all: *I wouldn't go there – the food's no good.* | *I've tried that diet, and it's no good.*

no good at all *The buses only run twice a day, which is no good at all.*

awful/terrible/appalling /'ɔːfəl, 'terᵻbəl, ə'pɔːlɪŋ/ [adj] very bad: *Some of the meat you get in supermarkets is awful.* | *I think that's a terrible idea!* | *Your handwriting is appalling!*

◯ **garbage** ESPECIALLY AMERICAN **rubbish** BRITISH /'gɑːbɪdʒ, 'rʌbɪʃ/ [n U] SPOKEN INFORMAL something that is very bad or very stupid, especially things people say or write: *I don't know why you're watching that programme. It's complete garbage.* | *I've never read such rubbish in my life!*

2 products that are badly made or of bad quality

poor quality/low quality /pʊə' 'kwɒlᵻti, ləʊ 'kwɒlᵻti‖-'kwɑː-/ **poor quality** products have been made badly: *Poor quality housing often leads to health problems.* | *It's never worth buying low quality goods.*
be of poor/low quality *The steel was of poor quality.*

badly made /ˌbædli 'meɪdᵻ/ made without care or skill: *Her clothes looked cheap and badly made.* | *Badly made furniture like that doesn't last long.*

cheap /tʃiːp/ [adj] **cheap** furniture, jewellery, clothes etc look unattractive and badly made, and seem to have been produced using low quality materials: *The room was depressing, with a dim light and cheap furniture.* | *young men wearing cheap suits and fake gold watches*

3 not very bad, but not very good

◯ **not very good** /nɒt veri 'gʊd/ ESPECIALLY SPOKEN not good – use this when you were expecting something to be better: *"What was the movie like?" "Not very good, really."* | *He's been learning English for five years, but his pronunciation isn't very good.*

◯ **all right/OK** /ɔːl 'raɪt, əʊ'keɪ/ SPOKEN if something is **all right** or **OK**, it is good in some ways but there are some bad parts too: *The movie was all* right, but it wasn't as good as his last one. | "How was the meal?" "It was OK. | I've had better."

🔍 **nothing special** /ˌnʌθɪŋ ˈspeʃəl/ SPOKEN not especially good, but not very bad either: *The town's nice, but the beach is nothing special.* | *"Was the food good?" "It was okay, but nothing special."*

second-rate /ˌsekənd ˈreɪt◂/ [adj] not very good, especially not as good as other things of the same kind: *a second-rate horror movie* | *It was a pretty awful speech, full of second-rate jokes.*

mediocre /ˌmiːdiˈəʊkəʳ◂/ [adj] something that is **mediocre** is of a lower standard than it should be, and does not show much quality or skill: *The team gave another mediocre performance last night.* | *A lot of the teaching was pretty mediocre.*

4 **unpleasant events/ experiences/weather**

bad /bæd/ [adj] not at all pleasant, enjoyable, or successful: *If the weather's bad, we could go to the museum instead.* | *I'm afraid I have some bad news.* (=news of a bad event) | *bad housing conditions* | *Terry started shouting at me, which just made things worse.*
a bad day/year/time etc (=when a lot of unpleasant things happen) *It had been a bad day, and I just wanted to go home.* | *The company has had a very bad year, and profits have fallen dramatically.*
bad – worse – worst

awful/terrible/horrible /ˈɔːfəl, ˈterᵻbəl, ˈhɒrᵻbəl‖-ˈhɔː-, -ˈhɑː-/ [adj] very bad: *I just burst into tears in front of everyone. It was awful!* | *That's terrible! Surely they can't just fire you for no reason.* | *She had a horrible nightmare that night.*

unpleasant /ʌnˈplezənt/ [adj] an **unpleasant** experience is one that you do not like or enjoy at all: *a drug with unpleasant side effects* | *The news came as an unpleasant shock.* | *It has an unpleasant taste and smell.*
unpleasantly [adv] *The room was unpleasantly damp.*

appalling /əˈpɔːlɪŋ/ [adj] so bad that you are shocked: *the appalling suffering caused by the civil war* | *No ship could leave port in such appalling weather.*

5 **a bad problem/accident/illness**

bad /bæd/ [adj] use this about something that affects people or things in a very severe and unpleasant way: *a bad car crash* | *"How are things at home?" "Bad!"* | *It was the worst mistake I ever made.*
a bad cold/headache etc *Jane's not at school today – she has a bad cold.* | *a bad attack of asthma*
bad – worse – worst
badly [adv] *Several people were killed or badly injured.* | *The furniture was badly damaged in the fire.*

⚠ Don't say 'her hands were burned badly'. Say **her hands were badly burned**. **Badly** comes before a past participle.

serious /ˈsɪəriəs/ [adj] use this about problems, accidents, or illnesses that affect people very severely and are difficult to deal with: *There was a serious accident on the freeway.* | *serious head injuries* | *Youth unemployment is a serious problem in Britain.*
seriously [adv] *Her father is seriously ill with pneumonia.* | *a legal case that seriously damaged her political career*

horrific /hɒˈrɪfɪk‖hɔː-/ [adj] use this about accidents or injuries that are extremely serious, and make you feel shocked or upset: *Her husband was killed in a horrific riding accident.* | *a horrific attack on an innocent child*

🔍 **nasty** /ˈnɑːstɪ‖ˈnæsti/ [adj] ESPECIALLY SPOKEN use this about accidents, injuries, or illnesses that are not very serious, but are quite unpleasant: *That cough sounds nasty – you ought to see a doctor.* | *He had a nasty cut on his head.*
nasty – nastier – nastiest

B

6 when a situation is so bad that you cannot bear it

can't stand sth/can't bear sth /ˌkɑːnt ˈstænd (sth), ˌkɑːnt ˈbeəʳ (sth)‖ˌkænt-/ to be unable to accept or deal with something unpleasant or difficult: *Marcia couldn't stand the pain any longer.*
can't stand/bear the thought of sth *They can't bear the thought of selling their home.*
can't bear to do sth *I couldn't bear to see her with another man.*
⚬ **can't take sth** /ˌkɑːnt ˈteɪk (sth)‖ˌkænt-/ ESPECIALLY SPOKEN to be unable to accept something unpleasant without becoming angry or upset, especially when someone's behaviour is not fair or reasonable: *Careful what you say – he can't take criticism.*
can't take any more of sth *I can't take any more of this – she's always complaining about something.*
unbearable /ʌnˈbeərəbəl/ [adj] something that is **unbearable**, such as a pain or a bad situation, is too bad for you to deal with or live with: *Without him, life would be unbearable. | Richard was in unbearable pain.*

7 a situation that is very bad

➡ see also **ACCIDENT**

emergency /ɪˈmɜːʳdʒənsi/ [n C] a very serious and dangerous situation that happens suddenly and needs to be dealt with immediately: *Lifeguards are trained to deal with any emergency.*
in an emergency *In an emergency dial 911 for the police, the fire department, or an ambulance.*
the emergency services BRITISH (=the organizations and people that come immediately to help you if there is an emergency) *The emergency services in this area couldn't cope if there was a major terrorist attack.*
plural **emergencies**

⚠ You can also use **emergency** before a noun, like an adjective: *emergency surgery | The plane made an emergency landing.*

crisis /ˈkraɪsɪs/ [n C] a very bad situation in which there is a risk that serious problems will become suddenly worse: *The Cuban missile crisis of 1960 was probably the closest we have been to nuclear war. | Their marriage was going through a crisis which almost ended in divorce. | an economic crisis*
plural **crises**

disaster /dɪˈzɑːstəʳ‖dɪˈzæ-/ [n C] a terrible event that causes a lot of damage or a lot of deaths: *a mining disaster in which 108 people lost their lives | the 1986 Chernobyl nuclear disaster*
natural disaster (=caused by storms, floods etc) *a fund set up to deal with natural disasters such as earthquakes or floods*

8 bad people or bad behaviour

bad /bæd/ [adj] use this about behaviour that is morally wrong, or about people who do things that are morally wrong: *In spite of all the bad things he had done, I still loved him. | In most movies, the bad guy gets caught in the end. | Is there any crime worse than murdering a child? | He had a bad influence on his younger brothers.*
bad – worse – worst

wrong /rɒŋ‖rɔːŋ/ [adj not before noun] use this about behaviour, actions, or situations that are not morally right: *He knew it was wrong, but he couldn't resist taking the money.*
it is wrong to do sth *It is wrong to tell lies.*
it is wrong that *It's wrong that so many people are starving, when there is plenty of food in the world.*
immoral /ɪˈmɒrəl‖ɪˈmɔː-/ [adj] use this about actions which you believe are morally wrong and unacceptable, even if they are not illegal: *Many people think that testing drugs on animals is immoral. | Letting children go hungry is immoral.*

Formal or informal?
Immoral is more formal than **wrong**

> ⚠ Don't say 'very immoral'. Say **totally immoral** or **highly immoral**.

evil/wicked /'iːvəl, 'wɪkɪ̷d/ [adj] deliberately very bad and very cruel to other people: *an evil dictator* | *They spread terrible rumours about him. It was wicked!*

9 a bad child

naughty /'nɔːtɪllˈnɔːti, 'nɑːti/ [adj] a child who is **naughty** behaves badly, for example by being rude or by doing things that are not allowed: *Should parents smack children if they're naughty?* | *We've been looking for you everywhere, you naughty boy!*

naughty – naughtier – naughtiest

spoiled (also **spoilt** BRITISH) /spɔːld, spɔɪlt/ [adj] children who are **spoiled** or **spoilt** behave badly because their parents always let them do what they want and have what they want: *He's a very spoilt little boy.* | *Those kids are definitely spoiled – they need to learn some manners.*

mischievous /'mɪstʃɪ̷vəs/ [adj] ESPECIALLY WRITTEN a child who is **mischievous** behaves badly, but in a way that makes people laugh rather than making them angry: *She was a mischievous little girl, who was always playing tricks on people.*

mischievously [adv] *Ben smiled mischievously.*

badly-behaved /ˌbædli bɪˈheɪvd◂/ [adj] a **badly-behaved** child behaves badly and causes a lot of trouble: *Two or three badly-behaved children are causing all the problems in the class.*

brat /bræt/ [n C] INFORMAL a child that you do not like, who behaves badly and is rude: *The school is full of rich brats.*

spoiled/spoilt brat (=a child who behaves badly because they have always been allowed to do whatever they want)

10 bad at doing something

bad /bæd/ [adj] not able to do something well, for example a job, sport, or activity

bad teacher/driver/player etc *He's the worst driver I've ever seen.* | *The problem was caused by bad management.*

+at *I was always bad at French!*

bad at doing sth *I'm very bad at remembering people's names.*

bad – worse – worst

> ⚠ Only use **bad** about other people if you want to criticize them strongly. If you want to be more polite, use **not very good** instead.

badly /'bædli/ [adv] if you do something **badly**, you do it without skill, or in an unsatisfactory way: *Kate plays the violin very badly.* | *The company had been badly managed from the start.*

> ⚠ Don't say 'I speak English very bad'. Say **I speak English very badly**. Remember that **bad** is an adjective and **badly** is an adverb.

🔍 not very good /nɒt veri 'gʊd/ ESPECIALLY SPOKEN not able to do something well: *He's a nice guy, but he's not a very good actor.*

+at *I'm afraid I'm not very good at algebra!*

not very good at doing sth *She's not very good at communicating with other people.*

not very well *"Do you play the piano?" "Not very well."*

🔍 no good at sth /ˌnəʊ 'gʊd æt (sth)/ SPOKEN very bad at a skill or activity: *I'm no good at tennis.*

no good at doing sth *He can drive quite well, but he's still no good at parking.*

🔍 terrible/useless/hopeless /'terɪ̷bəl, 'juːsləs, 'həʊpləs/ [adj] ESPECIALLY SPOKEN very bad at doing something, or very badly made or done: *I can speak a bit of French, but my accent's terrible.* | *She's very intelligent but she's a hopeless cook.*

+at *I'm useless at spelling.*

incompetent /ɪnˈkɒmpɪ̷təntll-ˈkɑːm-/ [adj] someone who is **incompetent** lacks the skills they need to do their job – use this to criticize someone who is very bad at something and makes a lot of mistakes: *This government is totally incompetent.* | *incompetent management*

B

> ⚠ Don't say 'very incompetent'. Say **totally/completely incompetent**.

11 in bad condition

in bad condition /ɪn ˌbæd kənˈdɪʃən/ if something is **in bad condition**, it needs repairing, cleaning etc: *When we bought the house, it was in pretty bad condition.* | *The city's drains are ancient and in very bad condition.*

> ⚠ Don't say 'in a bad condition'. Say **in bad condition**.

⊂ be falling apart /biː ˌfɔːlɪŋ əˈpɑːʳt/ ESPECIALLY SPOKEN if something **is falling apart**, it is gradually breaking into pieces, because it is old or it was not well made: *My trainers were falling apart so I threw them out.*

battered /ˈbætəʳd/ [adj usually before noun] something that is **battered** is old and in bad condition because it has been used a lot: *a battered old suitcase* | *Professor Dewey got out a battered copy of Shakespeare's plays.* | *a couple of battered wooden chairs*

rotten /ˈrɒtn‖ˈrɑːtn/ [adj] wood that is **rotten** has decayed and become very soft, so that it breaks easily: *The window frames were rotten, so we had to replace them.*

rusty /ˈrʌsti/ [adj] metal that is **rusty** is red-brown in colour, because it has been damaged by the effects of water: *A few rusty nails held the door in place.* | *The railings were old and rusty.*

rusty – rustier – rustiest

rust [n U] *You can't see it, but underneath the car is covered in rust.*

shabby /ˈʃæbi/ [adj] ESPECIALLY WRITTEN clothes, furniture, or places that are **shabby** are no longer in good condition because they have been worn or used a lot: *Paul was wearing a shabby old suit.* | *Their hotel room was dark and shabby.*

shabby – shabbier – shabbiest

dilapidated /dɪˈlæpɪdeɪtɪd/ [adj] a building that is **dilapidated** is in very bad condition, because it has not been looked after or repaired: *Most of the factories are now empty and dilapidated.* | *The dilapidated building was barely fit for storage.*

bad /bæd/ [adj] food that is **bad** is not good to eat, because it has started to decay: *Do you think this meat smells bad?* | *Bad eggs can make you sick.*

⊂ go off/go bad /gəʊ ˈɒf, gəʊ ˈbæd/ ESPECIALLY SPOKEN if food **goes off** or **goes bad**, it starts to decay because it has been kept for too long: *In this heat, fish goes off very quickly.* | *The fruit went bad before we could eat it all.*

12 to think something or someone is bad or morally wrong

disapprove /ˌdɪsəˈpruːv/ [v I] to think that a person or action is bad, morally wrong, or very stupid: *I wanted to be an actor but my parents disapproved.*

+of *Debbie's father disapproves of her boyfriend.*

disapprove of sb doing sth *My friends disapprove of me smoking.*

strongly disapprove (=disapprove very much) *I strongly disapprove of any form of gambling.*

think sth is wrong /ˌθɪŋk (sth) ɪz ˈrɒŋ‖-ˈrɔːŋ/ to think that something is morally bad and should not happen: *Do you think abortion is always wrong?*

think it is wrong to do sth *I think it's wrong to hit a child, whatever the circumstances.*

disapproval /ˌdɪsəˈpruːvəl/ [n U] ESPECIALLY WRITTEN how you feel when you think someone's ideas, behaviour, or actions are bad or morally wrong

with/in disapproval *She looked at my clothes with obvious disapproval.*

sb's disapproval/the disapproval of sb *Pete was determined to go to art school, despite his parents' disapproval.*

+of *They tried not to show any disapproval of Sandy's lifestyle.*

disapproving /ˌdɪsəˈpruːvɪŋ◂/ [adj] WRITTEN if someone speaks to you or looks at you in a **disapproving** way, they show by the way they talk or look that they disapprove of you: *John gave me* *a disapproving look when I suggested another drink.* | *"Do you think you should be doing that?" he said, in a disapproving voice.*

13 so bad that it makes you very angry

Q **outrageous/disgraceful** /aʊt'reɪdʒəs, dɪs'ɡreɪsfəl/ [adj] ESPECIALLY SPOKEN use this about actions or situations that are very bad or very unfair and should not be allowed to happen: *an outrageous waste of public money* | *I thought their behaviour was disgraceful.*

Q **be a disgrace** /biː ə dɪs'ɡreɪs/ ESPECIALLY SPOKEN if you say that something **is a disgrace**, you are angry about it and think that it should not be allowed to happen: *The state of some of these classrooms is a disgrace.* **it's a disgrace that** *It's an absolute disgrace that my wife had to wait five hours to see a doctor.*

BANKS

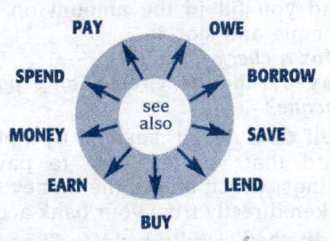

PAY   OWE
SPEND   BORROW
MONEY   see also   SAVE
EARN   LEND
BUY

1 places where you keep your money

bank /bæŋk/ [n C] a business that keeps and lends money and provides other financial services, or an office of this business: *Which bank do you use?* | *She works for a bank in Manhattan.* | *I need to go to the bank on the way home.*

building society BRITISH **savings and loan association** AMERICAN /'bɪldɪŋ sə,saɪəti, ,seɪvɪŋz ən 'ləʊn əsəʊsi,eɪʃən/ [n C] a type of bank in which you can save money, and that will lend you money to buy a house or apartment: *I've been to see my building society about getting a mortgage.*

bank account (also **account**) /'bæŋk ə,kaʊnt, ə'kaʊnt/ [n C] if you have a bank account with a particular bank, you keep your money there, and take some out when you need it **open a bank account** (=start a new bank account)

current account BRITISH **checking account** AMERICAN /'kʌrənt ə,kaʊnt, 'tʃekɪŋ ə,kaʊnt/ [n C] a bank account that you use regularly for making payments for things and for getting cash

deposit account BRITISH **savings account** AMERICAN /dɪ'pɒzɪt ə,kaʊnt, 'seɪvɪŋz ə,kaʊnt‖dɪ'pɑː-/ [n C] a bank account where you leave money for longer periods of time and which makes more money for you if you leave it there

2 things you do at the bank

pay in/into /,peɪ 'ɪn, 'ɪntuː/ if you **pay in** money, or if you **pay** it **into** your account, you put money into your account: *I have a cheque for £100 that I want to pay in.*

withdraw /wɪð'drɔː‖wɪð-, wɪθ-/ [v T] FORMAL if you **withdraw** money, you take it out of your bank account by using a cash machine or by going into a bank **withdraw £100/$200 etc** *You may withdraw up to $500 a day.*

take out (also **get out**) /,teɪk 'aʊt, ,get 'aʊt/ if you **take** money **out**, you get it out of your bank account by using a cash machine or by going into a bank **take out £50/$70 etc** *How much are you going to take out?*

check your balance /,tʃek jɔːʳ 'bæləns/ if you **check your balance**, you find out exactly how much money you have in your account: *I'd like to check the balance in my deposit account, please.*

B

transfer (also **make a transfer**) /træns'fɜː^r, ˌmeɪk ə 'trænsfɜː^r/ if you **transfer** money from one account to another, you move it from one account to the other: *Can I transfer £500 from my deposit account to my current account?* | *I need to make a transfer to my son's account.*

3 services provided by a bank

bank statement /'bæŋk ˌsteɪtmənt/ [n C] a printed list that your bank sends you regularly, which shows what money you have paid into and taken out of your bank account

bank loan (also **loan**) /'bæŋk ləʊn, ləʊn/ money that the bank agrees to lend you in order to buy something, such as a new car: *I went to see my bank manager to ask about a loan.*

mortgage /'mɔː^rgɪdʒ/ [n C] an arrangement to borrow money from a bank or building society in order to buy a house or apartment, and to pay back the money over a period of years: *Your building society will be able to arrange a mortgage for you.*

overdraft /'əʊvə^rdrɑːft‖-dræft/ [n C] BRITISH an amount that you arrange to owe your bank, because you need to spend more money than you have in your account
have a £50/$300 overdraft (=when you owe the bank this amount of money) *I've got a £200 overdraft.*
give sb an overdraft (=when a bank agrees to let someone have an overdraft) *The bank manager gave me an overdraft.*

overdraft limit /'əʊvə^rdrɑːft ˌlɪmɪt‖ -dræft-/ [n C] the largest amount of money that the bank has agreed that you can owe them
go over your overdraft limit (=spend more money than the bank has agreed that you can)

online banking (also **Internet banking**) /ˌɒnlaɪn 'bæŋkɪŋ, ˌɪntə^rnet 'bæŋkɪŋ‖ˌɔːn-/ [n U]) a service provided by banks so that people can find out information about their bank account, and pay bills etc using the Internet: *Online banking allows customers instant access to their accounts.*

4 ways of getting your money out of a bank and paying for things

cash machine (also **ATM**) (also **hole-in-the-wall** /'kæʃ məˌʃiːn, ˌeɪ tiː 'em, ˌhəʊl ðə 'wɔːl/ BRITISH INFORMAL) [n C] a machine in the wall of a bank, shop etc that lets you take money out of your bank account using a special card

bank card /'bæŋk kɑː^rd/ [n C] a small plastic card given to you by your bank, which you show when you write a cheque, and which also lets you get money out of a cash machine. A bank card can often also be used as a debit card.

cash card BRITISH **ATM card** AMERICAN /'kæʃ kɑː^rd, ˌeɪ tiː 'em kɑː^rd/ [n C] a plastic card given to you by your bank, that you use to get money out of a cash machine

cheque BRITISH **check** AMERICAN /tʃek/ [n C] a printed piece of paper that you get from your bank which you can use instead of money to pay for things. Your bank gives you several cheques in the form of a small book, called a **cheque book** or **check book** and you fill in the amount on each cheque and sign it.
+for *a check for $300*
pay by cheque/check *Can I pay by cheque?*

debit card /'debɪt ˌkɑː^rd/ [n U] a plastic card that you can use to pay for things, which allows the money to be taken directly from your bank account

credit card /'kredɪt ˌkɑː^rd/ [n C] a plastic card that you can use to pay for things with money you borrow from a financial organization such as VISA or MasterCard. A **credit card** lets you pay for things, and then pay what you owe to the organization later: *We accept all major credit cards.* | *credit card fraud* (=dishonest use of credit cards)

direct debit /dɪˌrekt 'debɪt/ [n C,U] BRITISH an arrangement that you make with your bank for them to pay money directly out of your account regularly to a particular person or organization: *You can arrange to pay your bills by direct debit.*

BEAUTIFUL

➡ opposite **UGLY**
➡ see also **WB DESCRIBING HOW PEOPLE LOOK**

1 women

beautiful /'bju:tɪ̩fəl/ [adj] use this about a woman who is extremely attractive in a way that is fairly unusual and special, so that people notice and admire her: *a beautiful woman with long black hair and green eyes | Karen was even more beautiful than I had remembered. | She has a beautiful smile.*

good-looking /ˌgʊd 'lʊkɪŋ◂/ [adj] use this about a woman who is nice to look at and has an attractive face and body: *Ginny was tall and good-looking. | A good-looking woman dressed in black came into the room. | If anything, she seems to get better-looking with age.*
good-looking – better-looking – best-looking

pretty /'prɪti/ [adj] use this about a young woman or girl who has an attractive face and is good-looking, but not in an unusual way: *Maureen's really pretty, isn't she? | a pretty girl in white jeans | She has a pretty face.*
pretty – prettier – prettiest

attractive /ə'træktɪv/ [adj] use this about a woman who is good-looking in a way that makes people sexually interested in her: *Frances was a charming and attractive girl. | Your wife's a very attractive woman.*
find sb attractive *A lot of men find plump women attractive.*

◌ nice-looking /ˌnaɪs 'lʊkɪŋ◂/ [adj] ESPECIALLY SPOKEN use this about a woman who looks pleasant and friendly but is not extremely pretty: *A nice-looking girl came up and offered to help.*

cute /kju:t/ [adj] INFORMAL, ESPECIALLY AMERICAN use this about a girl or young woman who is pretty and sexually attractive: *Look at that girl – isn't she cute?*

◌ gorgeous /'gɔːʳdʒəs/ [adj] ESPECIALLY SPOKEN use this to emphasize that a woman is extremely attractive, in a sexual way: *What was the name of that gorgeous girl you met in France?*
look gorgeous *You look absolutely gorgeous in that dress!*

glamorous /'glæmərəs/ [adj] use this about a woman who looks like a beautiful actress or film star, and has an attractive body and wears expensive clothes: *The picture showed a glamorous young woman sitting in a sports car. | With her blonde hair, blue eyes, and long legs, she was really glamorous.*

stunning /'stʌnɪŋ/ [adj] use this about a woman who is extremely beautiful and sexually attractive, in a way that everyone notices and admires: *stunning French actress Juliette Binoche*
look stunning *Beth looked stunning in a beautiful green silk dress.*

elegant /'elɪ̩gənt/ [adj] ESPECIALLY WRITTEN use this about a woman who is tall and attractive, and wears clothes that look good: *An elegant young woman sat at the next table, sipping a cocktail.*
look elegant *a woman in a well-cut navy coat who, despite the rain, still looked elegant*

2 men

good-looking /ˌgʊd 'lʊkɪŋ◂/ [adj] use this about a man who is nice to look at: *A tall good-looking man asked me if I wanted to dance. | She showed me a photo of a good-looking young soldier.*
good-looking – better-looking – best looking

attractive /ə'træktɪv/ [adj] use this about a man who is good-looking in a way that makes people sexually interested in him: *He was a tall, attractive man in his mid-forties.*
find sb attractive *Do you find Sam attractive?*

cute /kju:t/ [adj] INFORMAL, ESPECIALLY AMERICAN use this about a young man who looks nice and is sexually attractive: *I don't know why she won't go out with him. I think he's kind of cute.*

◌ gorgeous /'gɔːʳdʒəs/ [adj] ESPECIALLY SPOKEN use this to emphasize that a man is extremely attractive in a sexual way: *Look at that guy over there. Isn't he gorgeous?*

handsome /'hænsəm/ [adj] ESPECIALLY WRITTEN use this about a man who is good-looking, especially one who is tall and strong-looking: *Richard was a handsome man with a lot of charm.* | *My brother was two years older than me, taller, and more handsome.*
look handsome *He looks really handsome in his uniform, doesn't he?*

 Use **handsome** especially when you are writing stories and descriptions.

🔍 **nice-looking** /ˌnaɪs ˈlʊkɪŋ◂/ [adj] ESPECIALLY SPOKEN use this about a man who looks pleasant and friendly but is not extremely attractive: *I suppose he's quite nice-looking, but he's not really my type.*

3 children

beautiful /'bjuːtɪfəl/ [adj] use this about a child who is so good-looking that everyone notices and admires him or her: *Parents always think their baby is the most beautiful baby in the world.* | *On her desk there was a photograph of two beautiful children.*

lovely /'lʌvli/ [adj] use this about a child who looks nice and has a pleasant, friendly character: *They've got three lovely kids.* | *Rosie's a lovely baby.*
look lovely *Your daughter looks lovely.*
lovely – lovelier – loveliest

⚠ Don't say 'very lovely'. Just say **lovely**.

cute /kjuːt/ [adj] INFORMAL use this about a child who looks attractive and has a happy or amusing character: *He's really naughty, but he's so cute.* | *You were such a cute baby!*
look cute *Doesn't he look cute in that baseball cap!*

4 animals

beautiful /'bjuːtɪfəl/ [adj] use this about animals that look extremely attractive and impressive

beautiful bird/horse/animal/feathers/fur etc *a beautiful bird with bright blue feathers* | *A beautiful grey horse trotted up to the gate.*

cute/sweet /kjuːt, swiːt/ [adj] use this about pets and baby animals that look nice in a way that makes people want to look after them
+kitten/puppy/dog/baby bird etc *Look at those cute kittens!* | *She has a funny little dog – he's really sweet!*

magnificent /mæg'nɪfɪsənt/ [adj] use this about animals and large birds that are very beautiful and impressive because they are large and strong or beautifully coloured: *She owned a magnificent pair of racehorses.* | *a magnificent golden eagle* | *The Siberian Tiger is a magnificent animal.*

5 things/buildings

beautiful (also **lovely** ESPECIALLY BRITISH) /'bjuːtɪfəl, 'lʌvli/ [adj] use this about things or buildings that look extremely good, and give you a feeling of pleasure: *a beautiful painting* | *"Do you like the house?" "Like it? It's beautiful!"* | *Thanks for the flowers – they're lovely!* | *one of Europe's loveliest churches*
lovely – lovelier – loveliest

beautifully [adv] *a beautifully decorated house* | *The presents were all beautifully wrapped in pink paper.*

pretty /'prɪti/ [adj] use this about objects that are small and delicate, or things in your home such as curtains and carpets: *pretty wallpaper with yellow flowers on it* | *What a pretty vase!*
pretty – prettier – prettiest

magnificent /mæg'nɪfɪsənt/ [adj] very beautiful and impressive – use this about large and impressive buildings or pieces of furniture, especially old ones: *In the middle of the room was a magnificent oak dining table.* | *a magnificent 15th century castle*

🔍 **gorgeous** /'gɔːrdʒəs/ [adj] ESPECIALLY SPOKEN use this about beautiful things that you admire very much
gorgeous dress/coat/colour etc *I love your dress! It's such a gorgeous colour!* | *The apartment had been furnished in rich, deep colours and gorgeous fabrics.*

exquisite /ɪkˈskwɪzɪ̩t, ˈekskwɪ-/ [adj] very beautiful – use this about jewellery or small things that have been designed with great care and made with a lot of skill: *an exquisite gold and diamond ring* | *Look at this handbag – it's exquisite.*

elegant /ˈelɪ̩gənt/ [adj] use this about buildings, furniture, and clothes that are beautifully designed in a simple but usually expensive way: *They were staying in an elegant 18th century hotel in Oxfordshire.* | *an elegant rosewood dining table* | *She was wearing an elegant black suit.*

<h2>6   places/countryside/views</h2>

beautiful /ˈbjuːtɪ̩fəl/ [adj] use this about places that everyone admires and likes to visit: *Florence is such a beautiful city.* | *Cornwall has some of the most beautiful stretches of coastline in Britain.* | *a restaurant with beautiful views over Sorrento and the Gulf of Naples*

lovely /ˈlʌvli/ [adj] use this about places that are beautiful in a way that makes you feel relaxed and gives you a lot of pleasure: *The woods are lovely at this time of year.* | *You are so lucky to live here with all this lovely countryside around you.* | *The garden was looking lovely.*

lovely – lovelier – loveliest

> Don't say 'very lovely'. Just say **lovely**.

stunning/breathtaking /ˈstʌnɪŋ, ˈbreθˌteɪkɪŋ/ [adj] use this about views that are extremely beautiful and extremely impressive: *The view from the top of the mountain was stunning.* | *breathtaking views of the Himalayas*

magnificent /mægˈnɪfɪsənt/ [adj] use this about areas where there are beautiful, large, and impressive mountains, valleys, rivers etc: *magnificent views across the valley* | *the magnificent mountains around Lake Titicaca*

picturesque /ˌpɪktʃəˈresk‹/ [adj] use this about villages and towns that are pretty and old-fashioned: *We visited the picturesque fishing village of Lochinver.* | *The old part of the town is very picturesque.*

scenic /ˈsiːnɪk/ [adj] use this about roads that go through beautiful countryside

scenic route/journey/drive/road *a scenic road through the Welsh mountains* | *We had plenty of time so we took the scenic route.*

<h2>7   the beautiful appearance of someone or something</h2>

beauty /ˈbjuːti/ [n U] the beautiful appearance of a place or person: *the beauty of the countryside in spring* | *He had written a poem about Sylvia, praising her charm and beauty.*

of great beauty FORMAL (=very beautiful) *ancient carvings of great beauty*

good looks /ˌgʊd ˈlʊks/ [n plural] someone's attractive appearance: *Although over 50, she had not lost her good looks.*

<h1>BECOME</h1>

<h2>1   with adjectives</h2>

> **Formal or informal?**
> Word choice - **become** and **get**: 1. **Become** is more formal than **get** and is used mainly in written English. **Get** is the usual word to use in conversation: say **it's getting cold**, **I'm getting hungry** etc (not 'it's becoming cold'). 2. You can use **become** with most adjectives, but **get** can only be used with some adjectives; see the note at **get** for details.

become /bɪˈkʌm/ [v] if you **become** rich, famous, worried etc, you start to be rich, famous, worried etc: *Julian's book was a big success and he quickly became rich and famous.* | *The weather was becoming warmer.* | *After a while, my eyes became accustomed to the dark.*

it becomes clear/difficult/quiet etc *It soon became clear that the fire was out of control.*

becoming – became – have become

get /get/ [v] to become: *The man got annoyed and started shouting at me.* | *The situation doesn't seem to be getting any better.* | *I'm getting too old for this kind of thing.*
it gets dark/cold etc *It normally gets dark at about 8.30 p.m.*
getting – got – have got BRITISH **have gotten** AMERICAN

 Don't use **get** with these words: **available**, **calm**, **clear**, **famous**, **happy**, **important**, **necessary**, **obvious**, **poor**, **powerful**, **proud**, **sad**, **silent**, **successful**, **useful**. But you can use **get** with comparatives such as: **clearer**, **happier**, **more famous**, **more important**. You can also use **get** with past participles, such as: **damaged**, **lost**, **broken**.

grow /grəʊ/ [v]
grow old/tired/worse/larger etc to gradually become old, tired etc: *As we grow old, we worry more about our health.* | *The sound of footsteps grew louder.* | *They had grown tired of waiting.* | *The children were late, and she was growing anxious.*
growing – grew – have grown

 Use **grow** especially when you are writing stories or descriptions.

go /gəʊ/ [v] to become – only use **go** with these words
go grey/white/red/dark *Her face went bright red with embarrassment.*
go mad/wild/crazy *Your dad'll go crazy when he finds out.*
go quiet/silent *As soon as the band started playing, the crowd went quiet.*
go bad/sour/cold *My coffee's gone cold.*
going – went – have gone

turn /tɜːʳn/ [v]
turn red/blue/white etc to become a different colour because of a natural change: *My father's hair turned grey when he was only 40.* | *In autumn the leaves turn red and yellow.*

2 with nouns

 Don't use **get** with nouns.

become /bɪˈkʌm/ [v] *In the 19th century, the city became a major trading centre.* | *Since she won all that money, she's become a very unpleasant person.*
become a doctor/writer/teacher etc *Theroux decided to give up teaching and become a writer.*
becoming – became – have become

 You can also use **be** when saying what someone wants to become: *I want to be a doctor when I leave college.*

change into sth/turn into sth /ˈtʃeɪndʒ ɪntuː (sth), ˈtɜːʳn ɪntuː (sth)/ [*phrasal verb* T] to completely change and become something else, often in a surprising way: *A caterpillar eventually changes into a beautiful butterfly.* | *During the brewing process, all the sugar turns into alcohol.*

develop into sth /dɪˈveləp ɪntuː (sth)/ [*phrasal verb* T] to gradually become something that is much better, bigger, more important, or more serious: *In 20 years, the company has developed into a huge multinational organization.* | *a minor illness which developed into a serious chest infection*

BEFORE

➡ opposite **AFTER**
➡ see also **EARLY**

1 before something happens, or before someone does something

before /bɪˈfɔːʳ/ [*preposition/conjunction/adv*] **before** you do something or **before** an event happens: *Think carefully before you give your final answer.* | *The family left France just before the war.* | *Before I could say anything, Dave walked away.*

before doing sth *Before taking the medicine, read the instructions carefully.* | *You should check the oil before starting a long drive.*

before this/that *We spent two years in America, and before that we lived in Japan.*

the night before/the day before/the week before etc *The night before the wedding she was really nervous.*

a week/2 days/5 years etc before *I was born just 11 months before my brother.*

⚠️ **Before** can be used as an adverb, but only in expressions like **a week before** and **the day before**: *When we got there, we found out he had left the day before.* Don't use **before** on its own as an adverb – use **before this** or **before that**: *I had a job as a waiter, and before that I worked in a supermarket.*

⚠️ Don't use 'will' with **before**. Don't say 'before I will leave England, I want to visit Cambridge'. Say **before I leave England ...**

beforehand (also **ahead of time** AMERICAN) /bɪˈfɔːʰhænd, əˌhed əv ˈtaɪm/ [*adv*] if you do something **beforehand** or **ahead of time**, you do it before you do something else, especially in order to make a situation easier: *We had agreed beforehand exactly where to meet.* | *Everything had been laid out for the party ahead of time.*

in advance /ɪn ədˈvɑːns‖-ˈvæns/ if you do something **in advance**, you do it before another event happens, especially so that you will be well prepared: *This is a meal you can easily prepare in advance.*

tell/warn sb in advance (=warn them that something may happen) *I wish you'd told me in advance that you might be late.*

six months in advance/a year in advance etc *Preparations for the visit had been made months in advance.*

pre- /priː/ [*prefix*] **pre-war/pre-school/pre-Christmas etc** before the war, before starting school etc: *life in pre-war Britain* | *The government seems to have forgotten all its pre-election promises.*

2 before a particular time or date

before /bɪˈfɔːʰ/ [*preposition*] before a particular time or date: *Call me back before 4.30.*

just before *She was born just before Christmas.*

the day before yesterday (=two days ago) *I saw Jean the day before yesterday.*

by /baɪ/ [*preposition*] **by 6 o'clock/Friday/next winter etc** at some time before 6 o'clock, Friday etc, and certainly not later than this: *I'll be home by 6, I promise.* | *Make sure you get the work done by Friday.* | *By 9 o'clock, all the guests had arrived.*

3 before now

before /bɪˈfɔːʰ/ [*adv*] before now or before the time you are talking about: *I've never seen such a big spider before.* | *Have you ever been to the States before?*

the day/week/month etc before *He was in Norway last week, and Denmark the week before.*

ago /əˈgəʊ/ [*adv*]

five minutes/two weeks/20 years etc ago five minutes, two weeks etc before now: *He went out half an hour ago, but he'll be back soon.* | *She died two months ago.*

a long time ago *"When did you live in Germany?" "Oh, it was a long time ago – in 1967."*

🔍 **ages ago** SPOKEN (=a very long time ago) *He wrote to me once, but that was ages ago.*

⚠️ Use **ago**, not **before**, when you are saying how much time has passed since something happened. For example, don't say 'he died 10 years before'. Say **he died 10 years ago**.

⚠️ Don't use **ago** with verbs in the present perfect. Don't say 'she has left 10 minutes ago'. Say **she left 10 minutes ago**.

earlier /ˈ3ːʰliəʰ/ [*adv*] at some time, date, year etc before now or before the time you are talking about: *This is an example of what I was talking about earlier.*

B

earlier in the day/year etc *I saw Barbara earlier in the day – she looked very upset.*
20 years earlier/10 minutes earlier/moments earlier etc *Three years earlier, he had been happily married with a good job.*

previously /ˈpriːviəsli/ [adv] before now or before a time or event in the past: *This is the simplest method, as I mentioned previously.* | *The attack was carried out by a previously unknown group of terrorists.*
two days/three weeks/six months etc previously *A few weeks previously I had met him at a conference.*

Formal or informal?
Previously is more formal than **earlier**.

formerly /ˈfɔːʳməʳli/ [adv] FORMAL during a period in the past but not now: *He was formerly editor of a national newspaper.* | *Zimbabwe was formerly known as Rhodesia.*

Formal or informal?
In conversation and informal writing, use **used to**: *Zimbabwe used to be known as Rhodesia.*

4 someone or something that existed before, or that you had before

previous /ˈpriːviəs/ [adj only before noun] the **previous** person, thing, or time is the one that existed just before now or before the time you are talking about: *She has two children from her previous marriage.* | *In her previous job, she had an office in the centre of town.* | *The previous owner kept the car in a garage.*
the previous day/week/year etc (=the day, week etc before the time in the past that you are talking about) *The previous day my father had looked perfectly healthy.*
in previous years *The weather that summer was much better than in previous years.*

last /lɑːst‖læst/ [adj only before noun] the **last** person or thing is the one that you had just before now, or the one that existed just before now: *The*

last apartment we lived in was much smaller than this one.* | *Clare broke up with her last boyfriend because he drank too much.*
last night/week/year etc (=the one before this one) *I couldn't sleep last night because of the heat.*

| ⚠ Don't say 'the last week/night/Tuesday'. Say **last week/night/Tuesday**: *What did you do last Saturday?* |

ex- /eks/ [prefix] **ex-wife/ex-boyfriend/ex-policeman/ex-soldier etc** someone who used to be someone's wife, used to be a policeman etc, but is not any more: *I don't have much contact with my ex-husband.* | *Joe's father's an ex-policeman.*

old /əʊld/ [adj only before noun] **sb's old job/car/girlfriend/boss etc** the job, car etc that someone had before the one they have now: *How much did you sell your old car for?* | *I tried to call Jim, but I only have his old phone number.* | *We had a big family room in our old house.*

Formal or informal?
Old is less formal than **previous**, and you usually use it in conversation. You use it about things that you used to have, or people that you used to work with or have a relationship with.

the one before /ðə ˌwʌn bɪˈfɔːʳ/ the person or thing that existed before the one that you have just mentioned: *The new hospital is a big improvement on the one before.*
the day before/the week before/the year before etc (=the day, week etc before the time in the past that you are talking about) *The day before had been rainy.*

former /ˈfɔːʳməʳ/ [adj only before noun] FORMAL existing or being something at some time in the past, but not now – use this especially to talk about someone who used to have a particular job or position: *In his will, he left everything to his former wife.*
the former president/chairman/director etc *the former president of Chile*
the former East Germany/Yugoslavia etc (used about a country

that has changed its name) *the former
Soviet Union*

predecessor /ˈpriːd₃ˌsesəʳ‖ˈpre-/ [n C]
FORMAL someone's **predecessor** is the
person who had the same job before
them: *Sally's predecessor had warned
her that the class could be very dif-
ficult.* | *Kennedy's predecessor,
President Eisenhower*

5 when you do something before anyone else does it

first /fɜːʳst/ [adv] if you do something
first, go somewhere **first** etc, you do
it, go there etc before anyone else:
*Did the Americans really get to the
moon first?* | *Let Michael choose first.
He's the youngest.*
be the first to do sth *My sister always
said I would be the first to get married,
but she was wrong.*

6 before something else in a list or series

before /bɪˈfɔːʳ/ [preposition] before
something or someone else in a list,
series, or set: *I think you were before
me in line, weren't you?* | *What hap-
pened in the programme before this
one?* | *Harajuku station is one stop
before Shibuya station on the
Yamanote Line.*

in front of/ahead of /ɪn ˈfrʌnt ɒv, əˈhed
ɒv/ [preposition] before another
person in a group of people who are
waiting to do something: *The man in
front of me let me go first.* | *There were
about fifty people ahead of us in the
queue.*

previous /ˈpriːviəs/ [adj only before
noun] coming before the one that you
are dealing with now: *In a previous
chapter we considered how children
learn language.* | *He played the part of
Tommy in a previous series of the
show.*

earlier /ˈɜːʳliəʳ/ [adj only before
noun] coming at some time before the one
you have just mentioned – use this
especially about something that is
very different from what is happening
now: *His later plays lack the wit and
energy of his earlier work.* | *The

minister had denied the accusations in
his earlier statement.*

the one before /ðə ˌwʌn bɪˈfɔːʳ/ the
thing that comes before another in a
series: *I don't like this song – the one
before was much better.* | *In the series
2, 4, 8, 16, each number is twice as big
as the one before.*

above /əˈbʌv/ [adj only before noun]
FORMAL WRITTEN use this to talk about
information that is given higher up a
page in a letter, book etc: *Write to the
above address for more information.* |
*The above diagram shows a normal car
engine.*
the above (=the people or things
mentioned earlier) *Contact any of the
above for more details.*
above [adv] *the organizations
mentioned above*

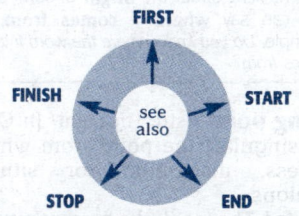

BEGINNING

1 the beginning of something

the beginning /ðə bɪˈɡɪnɪŋ/ [n singular]
the first part of an event, period of
time, story etc
+of *It will be ready by the beginning of
next week.* | *The beginning of the
movie is very violent.*
at the beginning (of sth) *There's
always a spelling test at the beginning
of each class.*
from the beginning (=all the time,
from the beginning of a long period)
*It was obvious from the beginning that
the plan would fail.*
in the beginning *In the beginning, I
didn't trust her at all.*

start /staːʳt/ [n singular] the time or
moment when something begins, or
the way that something begins
the start of sth *The runners are now
lining up for the start of the race.*

B

at the start *At the start, their relationship was very good.*

right from the start (=use this to emphasize that something has been true all the time from when it started) *We've had problems with this car right from the start.*

from start to finish (=from the beginning to the end) *a book that holds your attention from start to finish*

a good/bad start to sth *First the car broke down – which wasn't a very good start to the vacation.*

get off to a good/bad start (=start well/badly) *The year got off to a good start.*

origin /ˈɒrɪdʒɪn‖ˈɔː-, ˈɑː-/ [n C] the **origin** of something is where it came from or how it first started to exist: *AIDS became widespread in the 1980s, but no-one is certain of its origin.*
+of *a dictionary that explains the origins of words*

> **Formal or informal?**
> When talking about the **origin** of something, you can say **where** it **comes from**, for example. *Do you know where the word Internet comes from?*

starting point /ˈstɑːtɪŋ pɔɪnt/ [n C usually singular] the point from which a process, discussion, or situation develops
+for/of *They took the present situation in South Africa as the starting point for their discussion.* | *The assassination of Archduke Ferdinand is seen as the starting point of the war.*

a good starting point (=a point from which something is likely to be able to develop well) *If you want to learn about financial management, this book is a good starting point.*

2 at the beginning

at the beginning/at the start /ət ðə bɪˈɡɪnɪŋ, ət ðə ˈstɑːt/ *We agreed at the start that we would discuss any problems openly.*
+of *Your rent is due at the beginning of every month.* | *The team was doing well at the start of the season.*

at first /ət ˈfɜːst/ at the beginning of an event or period, especially when the situation later gets worse or better:

Barney was shy at first, but gradually he became more confident.

initially /ɪˈnɪʃəli/ [adv] at first – use this to say what happened at the beginning of a process or situation, especially when something different happened later: *They offered her the job, initially on a temporary basis.* | *Initially, the President didn't support this proposal.*

initial [adj only before noun] happening at first: *My initial impression was that she was shy and a little unhappy.*

> **Formal or informal?**
> **Initially** is more formal than **at first**.

originally /əˈrɪdʒɪnəli, -dʒənəli/ [adv] at the beginning – use this to talk about the situation at the time when something first existed: *Our family originally came from Scotland.* | *Originally, the book was published as a series of magazine articles.*

original /əˈrɪdʒɪnəl, -dʒənəl/ [adj only before noun] existing at the beginning: *Our original aim was to raise around $5,000.*

early /ˈɜːli/ [adv] near the beginning of an event, story, or period: *I'll be seeing him early next week.*

early in the game/story/century etc *United scored early in the game.*

early – earlier – earliest

early [adj only before noun] *We're spending two weeks in Malaysia in early May.* | *a man in his early thirties* (=between 30 and 33 years old) | *the story of her early life in India.*

3 a speech or piece of writing that comes at the beginning

introduction /ˌɪntrəˈdʌkʃən/ [n C] a short part at the beginning of a book or speech, explaining what it is about: *You'll understand the poems better if you read the introduction first.*
+to *The lecture began with a brief introduction to the topic.*

preface /ˈprefɪs/ [n C] a part of a book that comes before the main part and explains what it is about
+to *Mead writes in the preface to his book that he enjoyed researching it.*

foreword /ˈfɔːwɜːd/ [n C] a short piece of writing at the beginning of a book that introduces the book or its writer and is often written by someone other than the writer of the book: *Gore wrote the foreword to this book on the environment.*

introductory /ˌɪntrəˈdʌktəriˌ/ [adj]
FORMAL **introductory remark/ paragraph/sentence** something that someone says or writes at the beginning of a book, speech etc to explain what it is about: *Write an introductory paragraph giving the background to your research.*

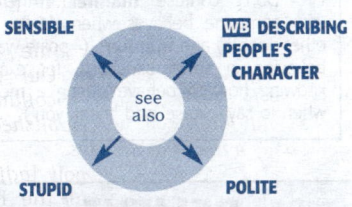

BEHAVE

SENSIBLE   **WB** DESCRIBING
                    PEOPLE'S
                    CHARACTER

          see
          also

STUPID   POLITE

1 to behave in a particular way

behave /bɪˈheɪv/ [v I] the way someone **behaves** is the things that they do and say, especially in relation to other people: *How does Sam behave at school?*
behave well/badly/unreasonably etc *I'm not going to talk to him until he starts behaving reasonably.*
behave as if *The next time I saw him, Frank behaved as if nothing had happened.*
behave like sb/sth *Oh, be quiet! You're behaving like a two-year-old.*
behave towards sb *William was behaving very strangely towards me.*
behave in a sensible/silly/strange etc way *Sally behaved in a very responsible way.*
be /biː/ [v] **be rude/helpful/silly etc** to behave in a rude, helpful, silly etc way: *Don't be so rude!* | *The waiter was really friendly and helpful.* | *Stop being silly!* | *Why is she being so nice to us?*
act /ækt/ [v I] to behave in a particular way, especially in a way that seems unusual, surprising, or annoying to other people

act strangely/stupidly/oddly etc *Tina's been acting very strangely lately.*
act like sb/sth *He has been accused of acting like a dictator.*
act as if *She acts as if she owns the place and we're her servants.*

react /riˈækt/ [v I] to say or do something because of what another person has said or done, or because of something that has happened: *How did she react when you told her the news?*
react angrily/violently/calmly *Parents reacted angrily when the school asked them to keep their children at home.*
react to sth *People are likely to react badly to the announcement.*
react by doing sth *The crowd reacted by shouting and booing.*

treat /triːt/ [v T] to behave towards someone or deal with someone in a particular way
treat sb well/badly *Amy's treated him really badly – no wonder he's upset.*
treat sb like sb/sth *I'm sick of my parents treating me like a child.*
treat sb with respect/contempt/ kindness *Employers should always try to treat their staff with respect.*

treatment /ˈtriːtmənt/ [n U] the way that a person, organization etc treats someone: *I decided to complain about the unfair treatment I'd received.*
+of *The council promised to improve its treatment of homeless people.*
special/preferential treatment (=when one person is treated better than everyone else) *Although I was the boss's daughter, I didn't get preferential treatment.*

2 to behave well

behave /bɪˈheɪv/ [v I] ESPECIALLY SPOKEN to do what people tell you and not cause any trouble – use this especially about children: *If you two don't behave, I'm taking you straight home.*
behave well/beautifully *All of the children behaved very well.*
behave yourself (=behave well) *Make sure you behave yourselves when we visit Grandma.*

good /ɡʊd/ a child who is **good** does not cause trouble and does what he

B

or she is told to do: *I was always very good at school.* | *He's a good little boy.*

well-behaved /ˌwel bɪˈheɪvd◂/ [adj] someone who is **well-behaved** does not cause any trouble and does what other people tell them to do – use this especially about children, pets, or large groups of people: *Can I bring my dog? She's very well-behaved.* | *The crowd was noisy but well-behaved.*

be on your best behaviour BRITISH **behavior** AMERICAN /biː ɒn jɔːʳ ˌbest bɪˈheɪvjəʳ/ to make a special effort to behave well by doing and saying the right things and being very polite, because you know other people are watching you: *Dinner was very formal, with everyone on their best behaviour.*

3 to behave badly

behave badly /bɪˌheɪv ˈbædli/ to be rude, unhelpful, or unpleasant and not do what you are told to do: *I knew I'd behaved very badly and I was sorry.* | *The kids behaved so badly that I was embarrassed.*

misbehave /ˌmɪsbɪˈheɪv/ [v I] if children **misbehave**, they behave badly by being noisy, fighting etc: *Kids often misbehave when they are bored or tired.* | *We never dared to misbehave in Miss Dill's classes.*

> **Formal or informal?**
> **Misbehave** is more formal than **behave badly**.

mess around/fool around /ˌmes əˈraʊnd, ˌfuːl əˈraʊnd/ [phrasal verb I] INFORMAL to behave in a silly way when you should be working or paying attention: *Some of the kids were just messing around in the back of the classroom.*
+with *Instead of doing his homework, he's fooling around with the computer.*

act up /ˌækt ˈʌp/ [phrasal verb I] INFORMAL to behave badly by being very active and noisy: *During his parents' divorce, Robert began acting up in class.*

4 the way someone behaves

behaviour BRITISH **behavior** AMERICAN /bɪˈheɪvjəʳ/ [n U] *His behaviour in*

school is beginning to improve. | *That kind of behavior is not acceptable.*
+towards *Eric's behaviour towards his family surprised me.*
good/bad behaviour *Reward your children for good behaviour.*

> ⚠️ Don't say 'behaviours' or 'a behaviour'. **Behaviour** is an uncountable noun.

manner /ˈmænəʳ/ [n singular] the way someone behaves when they are talking to or dealing with other people: *The driver's manner was very unfriendly.* | *She impressed everyone with her businesslike manner.*

> ⚠️ Don't confuse **manner** (=the way someone behaves when dealing with other people) and **manners** (=polite ways of behaving in social situations, for example knowing how to behave during a meal or when to say 'please' and 'thank you').

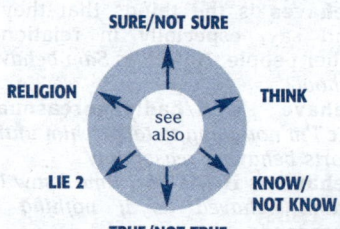

BELIEVE/
NOT BELIEVE

SURE/NOT SURE

RELIGION — see also — THINK

LIE 2 — KNOW/NOT KNOW

TRUE/NOT TRUE

1 to believe something

believe /bɪˈliːv/ [v T] to think that something is true or that someone is telling the truth: *Did the police believe her story?* | *No-one believed me when I explained that the gun wasn't mine.*
+(that) *People used to believe the Earth was flat.* | *The government believes that its campaign against drugs is working.*
believe in sth/sb (=believe that something or someone exists) *Do you believe in ghosts?* | *If you don't believe in God, why are you getting married in church?*

firmly/strongly believe *Kit firmly believed that he was doing the right thing.*

 Don't say 'I am believing', 'he is believing' etc. Say **I believe**, **he believes**.

accept /ək'sept/ [v T] to believe something because someone has told you it is true: *Most people accepted the official explanation.* | *I'm not sure whether your story would be accepted by a jury.*
+that *I don't accept that he knew nothing about these payments until now.*

 Don't say 'I am accepting', 'he is accepting' etc. Say **I accept**, **he accepts**.

be taken in /biː ˌteɪkən 'ɪn/ to believe that someone is telling the truth, when in fact they are lying in order to trick you: *He told me that it was a genuine diamond, and I was completely taken in.*
+by *Don't be taken in by products claiming to make you lose weight quickly.*

gullible /'gʌlɪbəl/ [adj] too willing to believe what other people tell you, so that it is easy for people to cheat you: *I was so gullible – I thought he loved me!* | *cheap goods sold at high prices to gullible tourists*

2 something that someone believes

belief /bɪ'liːf/ [n C/U] something you believe to be true
religious/political beliefs *They were put in prison because of their religious beliefs.*
+that *He never lost his belief that democracy would finally come to Russia.*
a strong/firm belief *our strong belief in the importance of education*
contrary to popular belief (=despite what most people believe) FORMAL *Contrary to popular belief, eating carrots does not improve your eyesight.*
faith /feɪθ/ [n U] a strong belief that something is true or can be trusted, especially a religious belief
+in *Marion's strong faith in God*

have faith (in sb/sth) *Many people no longer have faith in the government.*
superstition /ˌsuːpəˈstɪʃən, ˌsjuː-ǁˌsuː-/ [n C/U] a belief that some things are lucky and some are unlucky, even though there are no scientific reasons for believing this: *There is an old superstition that walking under a ladder is unlucky.* | *These people lived in an age of superstition and ignorance.*

3 when something seems to be true

convincing /kən'vɪnsɪŋ/ [adj] a **convincing** explanation, argument, reason, etc seems likely to be true: *There was a lot of convincing evidence that he was guilty.* | *I didn't find any of their arguments very convincing.*
plausible /'plɔːzəbəl/ [adj] something that is **plausible** seems reasonable and likely to be true, even though it may actually be untrue – use this especially with these words: **explanation**, **excuse**, **answer**, **theory**: *His explanation sounds fairly plausible to me.* | *I need to think of a plausible excuse for not going to the meeting.*

Formal or informal?
Plausible is more formal than **convincing**.

4 to not believe something

not believe /nɒt bɪ'liːv/ [v T] *Don't believe everything you read in the newspapers.* | *I told her I was sorry, but she didn't believe me.*
+(that) *I can't believe he's only 25!*
not believe a word of it (=not believe it at all) SPOKEN *They say they're going to send me the money, but I don't believe a word of it.*
find sth hard to believe (=think that something is unlikely to be true) *I found his explanation hard to believe.*

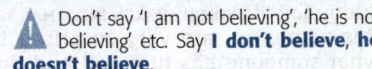 Don't say 'I am not believing', 'he is not believing' etc. Say **I don't believe**, **he doesn't believe**.

doubt /daʊt/ [v T] to think that something is probably not true: *Kim never doubted his story.*

+if/whether *You can complain, but I doubt if it will make any difference.*
I doubt it *He might come, but I doubt it.*
doubt very much (=think something is almost certainly not true) *She says she'll leave him, but I doubt very much if she will.*

> Don't say 'I am doubting', 'he is doubting' etc. Say **I doubt, he doubts**.

sceptical BRITISH **skeptical** AMERICAN /ˈskeptɪkəl/ [adj] someone who is **sceptical** about something is not sure whether it is true, or does not really believe it: *"You can trust me," he said. Roxie looked sceptical. | Russell's sceptical attitude towards the Christian religion*
+about *I wish him luck, but I'm sceptical about his chances of success.*
highly sceptical *You should be highly sceptical about what you read in the press.*

cynical /ˈsɪnɪkəl/ [adj] someone who is **cynical** is not willing to believe that people have good or honest reasons for doing something: *You can't believe what politicians say – but maybe I'm too cynical. | an author with a cynical view of human nature*
+about *Since her divorce, she's become very cynical about men.*

disbelief /ˌdɪsbɪˈliːf/ [n U] ESPECIALLY WRITTEN the feeling that you have when you are very surprised by something and do not believe that it is true: *Disbelief is a common reaction to bad news.*
stare/watch in disbelief *I stared at him in disbelief. "You're not serious, surely?"*

5 what you say when you do not believe what someone is telling you

⚲ you're kidding/you're joking /jɔːʳ ˈkɪdɪŋ, jɔːʳ ˈdʒəʊkɪŋ/ SPOKEN INFORMAL say this when you are very surprised by what someone has just said and find it difficult to believe it: *They got married! You're kidding!*

> ⚠ Only say this to friends and people who you know well.

⚲ come off it /kʌm ˈɒf ɪt/ SPOKEN INFORMAL say this when you cannot believe what someone has said, and you think they do not really believe it themselves: *"I'm going to fail!" "Oh come off it, you couldn't possibly fail after all the work you've done."*

> ⚠ Only say this to friends and people who you know well. If you use **come off it** to people who you do not know well, it will seem rude.

BEND

➡ opposite **STRAIGHT**

1 to bend your body, or part of your body

bend /bend/ [v I/T] if you **bend**, you move the top part of your body forwards or down; if you **bend** your arm, leg, or knee, you move it so that it folds at the joint: *Bend your arms and then stretch them upwards.*
+forward/towards/across *Martha bent towards me and whispered in my ear.*
bending – bent – have bent

bend over/bend down /ˌbend ˈəʊvəʳ, ˌbend ˈdaʊn/ [phrasal verb I] to bend the top part of your body down, for example to pick something up: *She bent over to pick up the coin. | I can't bend down because I've hurt my back.*

bow /baʊ/ [v I] to bend your head and the upper part of your body forward slightly, in order to show respect or as a formal greeting: *Remember to bow when you meet the Princess.*

bow

crouch /kraʊtʃ/ [v I]
WRITTEN to bend your
legs under you and
bring your body
close to the ground:
*He crouched behind
some bushes until the
police had passed.*
crouch down *Emma
was crouching down,
watching the spider.*

crouch

curl up

curl up /ˌkɜːˈl ˈʌp/ [phrasal verb I] to lie
or sit with your arms and legs bent
close to your body, especially when
you are relaxing or sleeping: *I just
want to curl up with a good book.*

2 to bend something

bend /bend/ [v T] to
push or press
something into a
curved shape, or fold
it to form an angle: *I
hit the nail too hard
and bent it a little.*
bend sth into sth
*Bend the wire into an
'S' shape.*
**bend sth back/
down** *He grabbed the man and bent
his arm back.*
bending – bent – have bent

bend

twist /twɪst/ [v T] to
bend and turn
something such as a
piece of wire, cloth,
or rope several times:
*Laura twisted the
handkerchief in her
hands nervously.*
**twist sth into/
around/through sth**
*Her hair was twisted
into a knot at the back
of her head.*

twist

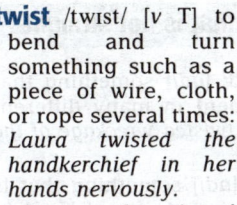

3 easy to bend

flexible /ˈfleksɪ̩bəl/ [adj] something that
is **flexible** is easy to bend: *shoes with
flexible rubber soles | A long flexible
hose is attached to the tap.*

pliable /ˈplaɪəbəl/ [adj] FORMAL able to
bend without breaking or cracking:
High quality leather is firm yet pliable.

bendy /ˈbendi/ [adj] BRITISH INFORMAL
easy to bend: *a bendy rubber doll*

4 not easy to bend

stiff /stɪf/ [adj] hard, and difficult to
bend: *a sheet of stiff cardboard | The
plant's leaves are stiff and prickly.*

rigid /ˈrɪdʒɪ̩d/ [adj] an object that is
rigid cannot be bent at all: *The
framework of the aircraft is rigid but
light. | a rigid metal structure*

> **Formal or informal?**
> **Rigid** is a more technical word than **stiff**.

firm /fɜːˈrm/ [adj] not completely hard,
but not soft, and not easy to bend into
a different shape: *The sofa cushions
are fairly firm.*

5 someone who finds it easy to bend their arms, back etc

supple /ˈsʌpəl/ [adj] someone who is
supple can bend and stretch very
easily and comfortably: *a supple
young gymnast*

B

6 something that is not straight

twisted /'twɪstɪd/ [adj] something that is **twisted** is bent in many different directions: *the twisted wreckage of the plane*

curved /kɜːʳvd/ [adj] something that is **curved** has a smooth round bend in it: *a sword with a curved blade*

wavy /'weɪvi/ [adj] **wavy** lines or hair have a lot of smooth curves in a regular pattern: *A series of wavy lines appeared on the screen.* | *She had long wavy brown hair.*

curly /'kɜːʳli/ [adj] **curly** hair has a lot of curls and is not at all straight: *Anna's long curly hair*

7 a road/river/path etc

bend /bend/ [n C] a place on a road, river, or path where it turns to go in a different direction: *We came to a bend in the river.* | *The car came round the bend too fast.*
a sharp bend (=one that turns suddenly) *After you've passed the church, you go around a sharp bend.*

curve /kɜːʳv/ [v I] WRITTEN a road, river, or path that **curves** has a long smooth bend in it, like part of a circle: *From here the railway curves away towards the town.* | *a sandy beach curving gently around the bay*
curving /'kɜːʳvɪŋ/ [adj only before noun] *a wide curving staircase*

wind

a winding river

wind /waɪnd/ [v I] WRITTEN a road, river, or path that **winds** has a lot of curved bends over a long distance
+through/along/around *The trail winds through the forest, then descends towards the lake.*

 Use **wind** when you are writing descriptions.

winding /'waɪndɪŋ/ [adj only before noun] *a peaceful little town on the banks of a winding river*
winding – wound – have wound

zigzag /'zɪgzæg/ [v I] a road or path that **zigzags** keeps turning to the left and then the right with a lot of sharp bends
+down/across/through *Ski routes zigzag down the mountainside.*
zigzagging – zigzagged – have zigzagged

BEST

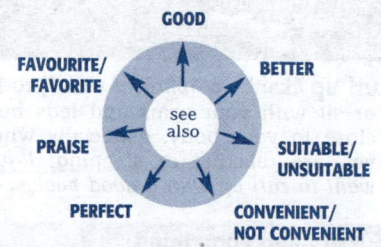

GOOD

FAVOURITE/
FAVORITE

BETTER

see
also

PRAISE

SUITABLE/
UNSUITABLE

PERFECT

CONVENIENT/
NOT CONVENIENT

1 better than all the others

best /best/ [adj usually before noun] better than anything or anyone else: *The best ice-cream in the world is made in Italy.* | *Two of their best players were injured.* | *She got the award for 'Best Actress' for her part in the movie.* | *What's the best way to cook sweet potatoes?*
the best (=someone or something that is better than all the others) *I chose a Japanese camera because I wanted to buy the best.*
the best in the country/the world/the class etc *Woods is the best player in the team.* | *Their heart surgery unit is the best in the country.*
by far the best/easily the best (=much better than any others) *It was by far the best vacation I've ever had.*
the best thing to do *I think the best thing to do would be to call a doctor.*

sb's best friend (=a friend you like and know better than anyone else) *Maria's my best friend at school.*

best [adv] *I've tried a lot of shampoos but this is the one I like best.* | *Nadia was the best-dressed woman at the conference.*

greatest /'greɪt‿ɪst/ [adj] the best and most important that there has ever been – use this about artists, political leaders, sports players etc, or about paintings, books, music, achievements etc: *Picasso was one of the greatest artists of the 20th century.* | *The First World War produced some of the greatest poetry ever written.* | *What do you consider your greatest achievement?*

finest /'faɪn‿ɪst/ [adj] the best and most skilful, or the best and highest quality – use this about artists, writers, performances, or achievements, or about wines, foods, products, or materials: *Marlon Brando was perhaps the finest film actor of them all.* | *Many people regard Beethoven's Fifth Symphony as his finest work.* | *We use only the finest ingredients.*

> **Formal or informal?**
> **Finest** is more formal than **best**.

top /tɒp‖tɑːp/ [adj only before noun] the most skilful, most successful, and most famous – use this about people such as sports players, lawyers, entertainers, photographers, or designers: *one of the world's top tennis players* | *Several top rock acts will be performing at the charity concert.* | *By the age of 18, she was already a top fashion model.*

> **Formal or informal?**
> **Top** is used especially in informal news reports and on television.

star /stɑːʳ/ [adj only before noun] **star player/performer/student/pupil etc** the best player in a team, the best student in a class etc: *Their star player earns millions of dollars.* | *the Washington Post's star reporter*

> **Formal or informal?**
> **Star** is used in conversation and informal writing, and in news reports.

star [n C] *They're a pretty good class, but Laura's undoubtedly the star.*

2 when you do something better than ever before

at your best /ət jɔːʳ 'best/ if you are **at your best**, you are performing at your highest level of skill: *At his best, Maradona was one of the most exciting players in the world.* | *This recording shows Grappelli at his very best.*

be at your peak /biː ət jɔːʳ 'piːk/ to be at the time in your life when you are playing a sport, doing your job etc better than at any other time: *Long distance runners are usually at their peak in their mid-30s.* | *At his peak, he was making $500,000 a year.*

3 the thing that you do best

best /best/ [adj only before noun] your **best** subject, sport etc is the one that you do better than anything else: *My best subject at school was history.* | *He's good at lots of sports but his best event is the high-jump.*

speciality BRITISH **specialty** AMERICAN /ˌspeʃi'æl‿ti, 'speʃəlti/ [n C] the thing that you do best and that you do more than anything else: *She loved baking, and cakes were her speciality.* | *He also runs the 200 metres, but the 100 is his speciality.*
plural **specialities** BRITISH
specialties AMERICAN

BETTER

➡ opposite **WORSE**

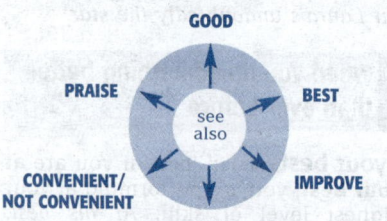

1 better than someone or something else

better /'betə^r/ [adj] A better job with a better salary – that's what I want.
+than Your stereo's better than mine.
better at sth (=able to do something better) Paul's better at tennis than I am. | Here, let me do it – I'm better at drawing.
it is better to do sth I think it would be better to go tomorrow instead.
much/far/a lot better The sales figures are much better than we expected.
better [adv] You can probably explain this better than I can.

superior /suː'pɪərɪə^r, sjuː-‖suː-/ [adj] better – use this about people's skills, or about products or services that you can buy: His superior technique helped him win the game.
+to Are French wines really superior to British ones?
vastly superior (=very much better) a vastly superior army

> **Formal or informal?**
>
> **Superior** is more formal than **better**, and is mostly used in writing.

preferably /'prefərəbli/ [adv] use this to say that something would be better than other possibilities, or more suitable: Come early next week – on Monday preferably. | We need well-qualified people, preferably with good computer skills.

2 better than before

better /'betə^r/ [adj] I hope the weather's better next week.
+than The food here's a lot better than it used to be.
get better His work got better after he changed schools.
much/far/a lot better I'm still not very good at Japanese, but I'm much better than I used to be.

be an improvement /biː ən ɪm'pruːvmənt/ to be better than something similar that you had or did before or that existed before
+on The new heating system needs to be a clear improvement on the old one.
a big/dramatic improvement There has been a big improvement in our profits.

improved /ɪm'pruːvd/ [adj only before noun] better than before, because changes have been made: a new and improved version of the two litre engine | improved relations between the two countries | The improved quality of health care in recent years has resulted in people living longer.

that's more like it /,ðæts mɔː^r 'laɪk ɪt/ SPOKEN say this when a situation is better than before, or when someone starts to do something better: Can't you walk faster – that's more like it. | He's reduced his price to $800. Now that's more like it!

3 to do something better

do better /duː 'betə^r/ to do something better than you did before, or do something better than someone else: You'd do better if you practised more often.
+than John did better than most of the other students in the class. | Come on – you can do better than that!

improve on sth /ɪm'pruːv ɒn (sth)/ [phrasal verb T] to do something better than before, especially by trying very hard: We have improved on last year's results. | Smithson has 165 points, and I don't think anyone will improve on that.

outdo /aʊt'duː/ [v T] to be more successful at something than someone else: *Clare is always trying to outdo her sister.*
outdoing – outdid – have outdone

4 better after an illness

◯ **better** /'betəʳ/ [adj not before noun] ESPECIALLY SPOKEN better after you have been ill: *Is Helen better yet?*
get better *I hope you get better soon.*
feel better *Are you feeling better today?*

well /wel/ [adj not before noun] when you are no longer ill: *Do you think you'll be well enough to go to the party?*
◯ **get well soon** SPOKEN (say this when someone is ill)

recover /rɪ'kʌvəʳ/ [v I] to get well again after you have had an illness or injury: *She had chickenpox, and it took her ten days to recover.*
+from *Rooney is recovering from a knee injury.*
be fully recovered (=be completely well again) *Mitchell is fully recovered and will be taking part in the race.*

> **Formal or informal?**
> **Recover** is more formal than **get better**, and is usually used when talking about serious illnesses or injuries.

When you see **EC**, go to the **ESSENTIAL COMMUNICATION** section.

BIG

➡ if you want to know about word order with adjectives, go to the **ESSENTIAL GRAMMAR** (Section 13)
➡ opposite **SMALL**

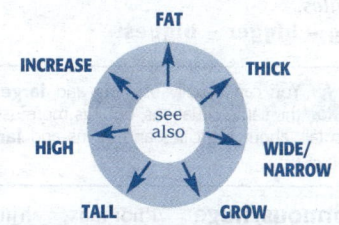

1 things/groups/organizations

big/large /bɪg, lɑːʳdʒ/ [adj] *a big red car | a large class of between thirty and forty students | My old computer was a lot bigger than this one. | Do you have this T-shirt in a larger size? | Boeing is the world's largest commercial airplane manufacturer.*
big – bigger – biggest

> **Formal or informal?**
> **Big** and **large** mean the same thing. **Large** is a little more formal than **big**, so **large** is more common in written English, and **big** is more common in spoken English.

enormous/huge /ɪ'nɔːʳməs, hjuːdʒ/ [adj] very big and impressive: *a huge leather chair | The company is enormous, employing around 10,000 people worldwide. | Huge crowds had gathered outside the embassy.*

> Don't say 'very enormous' or 'very huge'. Just say **enormous** or **huge**.

gigantic /dʒaɪ'gæntɪk/ [adj] something that is **gigantic** is much bigger than other things of the same type, often in a slightly strange or frightening way: *Gigantic waves more than 40 feet high crashed against the boat. | These gigantic creatures became extinct in the Jurassic period.*

B

2 places/areas/cities/buildings/rooms

big/large /bɪg, lɑːʳdʒ/ [adj] London is the biggest city in Europe. | Their new house isn't as big as the old one. | Flooding spread over a large area of Wales.

big – bigger – biggest

> ⚠ You can usually use **big** and **large** in the same situations, but it is more usual to talk about **big** cities and towns and **large** areas.

enormous/huge /ɪˈnɔːʳməs, hjuːdʒ/ [adj] very big and impressive: They have a huge garden. | The kitchen was enormous. | The family once owned huge areas of land.

spacious /ˈspeɪʃəs/ [adj] use this about the inside of a room or building that has a lot of space: a spacious apartment in Manhattan | All the bedrooms are spacious, light, and airy. | the company's spacious offices in Oxford

vast /vɑːst‖væst/ [adj] use this about very large areas of land, sea, or space: China is a vast country. | Whales can communicate across vast distances.

> **Formal or informal?**
> **Vast** is more formal than **enormous** and **huge**, and is not used much by young people.

3 people

➡ see also **TALL, FAT**

big/large /bɪg, lɑːʳdʒ/ [adj] use this about someone who is tall and has a large body: My grandfather was a very big man. | A large woman in her early 50s answered the door.

big – bigger – biggest

> **Formal or informal?**
> **Large** is more formal than **big** and is used especially in written descriptions. It is not polite to tell a woman that she is **big** or **large**.

well-built /ˌwel ˈbɪlt◂/ [adj] use this about someone who is big and strong and has a lot of muscles: He was well-built, with broad shoulders and long muscular legs.

huge/enormous /hjuːdʒ, ɪˈnɔːʳməs/ very big and tall, in a way that is impressive or frightening: A huge policeman stood outside the gate. | To a small child, Miss Trunchball seemed enormous.

4 numbers/amounts

> ⚠ Don't use **big** to talk about numbers and amounts.

large /lɑːʳdʒ/ [adj]
large amount/quantity/number The thieves escaped with a large amount of money. | Large quantities of nuclear waste have been dumped into the sea.
large sum (=a large amount of money) He had invested a large sum of money in stocks and shares.
in large numbers People turned out in large numbers to vote in Thursday's election.

huge / massive / enormous /hjuːdʒ, ˈmæsɪv, ɪˈnɔːʳməs/ [adj] very large, in a way that is impressive or shocking **+ amount / number / increase / reduction etc** The government spends huge amounts of money on health care. | There has been a massive increase in the number of people living below the poverty line. | An enormous number of studies have been done on this subject.

high /haɪ/ [adj] use this about prices and levels, especially when you think that something is too expensive or there is too much of it: Many old people cannot afford the high cost of heating their homes. | Levels of pollution are unacceptably high. | very high interest rates on bank loans

> ⚠ Don't say 'high amount'. Say **large amount**.

5 problems/changes/differences/effects

> ⚠ Don't use **large** about problems, changes, differences, or effects.

big /bɪg/ [*adj* only before noun] *Our biggest problem is lack of money.* | *There will have to be some big changes around here.* | *Your clothes can make a big difference to the way you feel about yourself.*
big – bigger – biggest

huge/enormous /hjuːdʒ, ɪˈnɔːʳməs/ [*adj*] very big, and very important, or serious: *Advances in technology have had a huge impact on the way people work.* | *The show was apparently an enormous success.*

major /ˈmeɪdʒəʳ/ [*adj* only before noun] use this about something that has serious and important effects on many people, many places etc
major difference/change/difficulty/problem *We have been told to expect major changes in the Earth's climate.* | *There is one major difference between these two systems of government.*

6 how big something is

size /saɪz/ [*n* C/U] *Teachers and parents are protesting about class sizes in schools.* | *It takes a cat two years to reach full adult size.*
+of *plans to reduce the size of the army*
of this/that size (=as big as this) *You'd need six litres of paint for a room of that size.*
the size of sth (=the same size as something) *A whole library of information can be stored on a microchip the size of a fingernail.*
a good/fair/nice size (=fairly big) *The kitchen is a good size.*

how big /ˌhaʊ ˈbɪg/ use this to talk about or ask about the size of something: *I'm not sure how big the apartment is.* | *How big do these fish grow?*

scale /skeɪl/ [*n* singular] the size of something such as a problem or a change, not of an object, vehicle etc

the scale of sth *Rescue workers are trying to assess the scale of the disaster.* | *Scientists are only just beginning to realize the scale of the problem.*
on a large/massive/huge scale (=when something very big or serious happens) *The rainforest is being destroyed on a massive scale.*

7 to become bigger

➡ see also **GROW, INCREASE**

get bigger /ˌget ˈbɪgəʳ/ to become bigger: *The hole in the ozone layer is getting bigger every year* | *a problem that's getting bigger all the time*
get bigger and bigger (=continue to become bigger) *The waves were getting bigger and bigger as the wind grew stronger.*

grow /grəʊ/ [*v* I] to become bigger – use this especially about amounts, organizations, and places: *Mark's business grew rapidly in the first year.* | *Our annual profits grew by 24% last year.* | *Tokyo has grown a lot over the last ten years.*
growing – grew – have grown

expand /ɪkˈspænd/ [*v* I] to become bigger and more successful – use this about businesses and other organizations: *The sports and leisure market is expanding more quickly than ever before.* | *The computer industry has expanded rapidly over the last decade.*

swell up /ˌswel ˈʌp/ [*phrasal verb* I] use this about parts of your body that have become bigger because you are ill or injured: *One side of his face had swollen up.*
swelling up – swelled up – have swollen up

swollen /ˈswəʊlən/ [*adj*] *The boy's right knee was badly swollen.* (=it had become much bigger because he was injured)

stretch /stretʃ/ [*v* I] if something such as a piece of clothing **stretches**, it gets bigger and changes its shape because it is being pulled or pressed: *The jeans will stretch a little when you start wearing them.*

B

8 to make something bigger

stretch /stretʃ/ [v T] to pull cloth, plastic, leather, etc so that it gets bigger and changes its shape: *Stretch the canvas so that it covers the whole frame.*

enlarge /ɪnˈlɑːʳdʒ/ [v T] to make a photograph, picture, or document bigger: *a photocopier that can enlarge documents by up to 100%*
have/get sth enlarged *That's a lovely photo of Amy. Why don't you get it enlarged?*

magnify /ˈmæɡnɪ̩faɪ/ [v T] to make something look bigger than it is, for example by using a microscope: *a microscope that can magnify an object up to forty times*
magnifying – magnified – have magnified

extend /ɪkˈstend/ [v T] BRITISH to make a building bigger by adding more rooms or more space: *The hotel has been recently renovated and extended.* | *We're thinking of extending the kitchen.*

BITE

➡ see also **EAT**, WB **FOOD**

bite /baɪt/ [v I/T] to cut or crush something with your teeth: *She sat there nervously biting her fingernails.* | *Don't worry about the dog – he won't bite.*
+into/through *Hannah bit into the juicy apple.* | *A shark had bitten right through our nets.*
bite sb on the hand/leg etc *I was bitten on the leg by a snake.* •
bite sth off (=remove something by biting it) *He took a cigar and bit the end off.*
biting – bit – have bitten

have a bite/take a bite /ˌhæv ə ˈbaɪt, ˌteɪk ə ˈbaɪt/ to take a piece from some food by biting it: *"This looks delicious," he said, taking a bite.* | *Sandy picked up a doughnut and took an enormous bite.*
+of *Can I have a bite of your candy bar?*

chew /tʃuː/ [v I/T] to keep biting something that is in your mouth: *It's healthier if you chew your food slowly.* | *Helen chewed her pencil, trying to think what to write next.*

peck /pek/ [v I/T] if a bird **pecks** something, it makes quick movements with its beak to try to bite it: *Stand very still, and the pigeons will peck the breadcrumbs straight from your hand.*
+at *Hens pecked at the corn on the ground.*

peck

gnaw

gnaw /nɔː/ [v I/T] if an animal **gnaws** something, it bites it repeatedly in order to eat it or destroy it: *Rats had gnawed holes in the boxes.*
+at/on *The dog was gnawing on a bone.*

BLAME

to say or think that someone is responsible for something bad that has happened

➡ see also **GUILTY/NOT GUILTY**, **CRITICIZE**

1 to blame someone

blame /bleɪm/ [v T] to say or think that someone is responsible for something bad that has happened: *He always*

blames someone else when things go wrong. | *It was your idea so don't blame me if it hasn't worked.*
blame sb for sth *At first, everyone blamed the pilot for the crash.*
blame sth on sb/sth *You can't blame everything on the government.*
blame yourself *For many years I blamed myself for her death.*

⊙ say sth is sb's fault /ˌseɪ (sth) ɪz (sb's) 'fɔːlt/ ESPECIALLY SPOKEN to say that someone is responsible for something bad that has happened
+(that) *How can you say it's my fault you lost your job?*

put the blame on sb /ˌpʊt ðə 'bleɪm ɒn (sb)/ to say or think that someone is responsible for something bad that has happened, especially when this is unfair: *Don't try to put the blame on me!*
put the blame for sth on sb *Richard still puts the blame for the divorce on his wife.*

accuse /əˈkjuːz/ [v T] to say that someone is guilty of a crime or of doing something bad
accuse sb of doing sth *Are you accusing me of telling lies?*
be accused of murder/armed robbery etc *West has been accused of murder.*

<hr>

2 | **to be blamed for something**

get the blame /ˌget ðə 'bleɪm/ to be blamed for something, especially something that you did not do: *The other kids all ran off, and I was the one who got the blame.*
+for *I always seem to get the blame for other people's mistakes.*

scapegoat /ˈskeɪpɡəʊt/ [n C] someone who is unfairly blamed for something, because people want to see that someone is blamed or punished for it: *Clark's wife accused the government of using her husband as a scapegoat.*

<hr>

3 | **to be responsible for something bad that has happened**

⊙ be sb's fault /biː (sb's) 'fɔːlt/ ESPECIALLY SPOKEN if something **is someone's fault**, they are responsible for it, especially because

they made a mistake: *Parents usually feel that it's their fault when things go wrong.*
be sb's own fault (=when someone is responsible for something bad that happens to them) *If you miss the train, it'll be your own fault.*
+(that) *I'm sorry. It's my fault that we're late.*
be sb's fault for doing sth *It's my fault for not checking the tickets.*

be to blame /biː tə 'bleɪm/ if someone or something **is to blame** for a bad situation, they caused it, especially by doing something wrong: *Anna's family say the authorities are to blame.*
+for *Some people think television is to blame for a lot of the problems in modern society.*

be responsible /biː rɪˈspɒnsᵻbəl‖-ˈspɑːn-/ if someone **is responsible** for an accident, a crime etc, they caused it and they should be punished for it
+for *The police are trying to find out who was responsible for the attack.*
feel responsible (=think that something is your fault) *Dan spent the rest of his life feeling responsible for the accident.*

> ⚠ Don't say 'be responsible of something'. Say **be responsible for something**: *The truck driver was responsible for the crash.*

<hr>

4 | **to not be responsible for something bad that has happened**

⊙ not be sb's fault /nɒt biː (sb's) 'fɔːlt/ ESPECIALLY SPOKEN if something **is not someone's fault**, they did not make it happen and they should not be blamed for it: *Don't worry – it's not your fault.* | *She felt guilty, even though the accident wasn't her fault.*
+(that) *It wasn't Carl's fault that you didn't get the message.*

⊙ sb can't help it /(sb) ˌkɑːnt 'help ɪt‖ˌkænt-/ ESPECIALLY SPOKEN if you say someone **can't help it**, you mean they should not be blamed because they cannot prevent something from happening: *"Stop worrying all the time!" "Sorry, I can't help it."*
+if *I can't help it if the computer keeps crashing.*

B

be not to blame /biː ˌnɒt tə ˈbleɪm/ to not be responsible for something bad that happens – use this especially when other people think you might have done something to make it happen
+for *The report said that no-one was to blame for the accident.* | *Hospital workers were not to blame for the nine-year-old's death, a court decided yesterday.*

5 to say that you are responsible for something bad that has happened

take the blame /ˌteɪk ðə ˈbleɪm/ to accept punishment or criticism for something bad that has happened, even if it was not your fault: *It's not my fault and I don't see why I should take the blame.*
+for *The coach took the blame for the team's defeat.*

take full responsibility/accept full responsibility /teɪk ˌfʊl rɪˌspɒnsɪ̩ˈbɪlɪ̩ti, əksept ˌfʊl rɪˌspɒnsɪ̩ˈbɪlɪ̩tɪ‖-spɑːn-/ FORMAL if you **take** or **accept full responsibility** for something bad that has happened, you admit that you are completely responsible for it – use this especially about managers and leaders admitting that they are responsible
+for *The Chairman of the airline said he accepted full responsibility for the accident and immediately resigned.*

When you see **WB**, go to the **WORD BANKS** section.

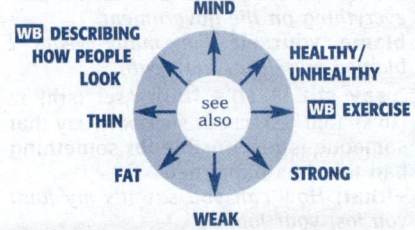

BODY

➡ If you mean 'dead body', go to **DEAD**

WB DESCRIBING HOW PEOPLE LOOK

THIN

MIND

HEALTHY/ UNHEALTHY

WB EXERCISE

see also

FAT

STRONG

WEAK

1 the body of a person or animal

body /ˈbɒdiǁˈbɑːdi/ [n C] your **body** is your head, arms, chest, waist, legs, feet, and all the other physical parts of you: *Exercise is good for your body and mind.* | *My body ached all over, and I knew I was getting the flu.* | *The cancer may have spread to other parts of her body.*
the human body (=the body of any person) *There are over 1000 muscles in the human body.*
plural **bodies**

⚠ You can also use **body** to talk about the main part of someone's body, not including the head, arms, or legs: *a spider with orange markings all over its body* | *The victim had bruises all over his face, neck, and body.*

2 the shape of someone's body

figure /ˈfɪɡəʳǁˈfɪɡjər/ [n C usually singular] the shape of a woman's body – use this especially to talk about a woman whose body has an attractive shape: *Tina has a very good figure.*
keep your figure (=keep your body slim and an attractive shape) *She'd managed to keep her figure and youthful appearance.*
body /ˈbɒdiǁˈbɑːdi/ [n C] the shape, size, and appearance of someone's body: *Teenagers are often embarrassed about their bodies.*
have a good/wonderful/great body (=a very attractive body) *At the age of fifty, she still has a great body.*
plural **bodies**

physique /fɪ̩'ziːk/ [n C usually singular] the shape and size of someone's body – use this especially to talk about the body of a man who is very strong and has a lot of muscles: *Brad was strong, with the physique of a rugby player.*

⚠ **Physique** is a used mostly in writing.

3 concerning your body

physical /'fɪzɪkəl/ [adj] concerning your body, not your mind: *You seem to be in good physical health.* | *During the war, people suffered terrible physical and emotional hardships.*
physically [adv] *At the end of the week I was physically and mentally exhausted.*

BOOKS/LITERATURE

➡ see Word Banks section

BORING/BORED

➡ opposite **INTERESTING/INTERESTED**

⚠ Don't confuse **boring** and **bored**. If something is **boring**, it is not interesting. If you feel **bored**, you are not interested in something, or you have nothing interesting to do.

1 boring jobs, books, films, activities etc

boring /'bɔːrɪŋ/ [adj] something that is **boring** is not interesting in any way and makes you feel tired: *a boring job in an office* | *a long boring lecture on economic planning* | *I thought the movie was really boring.* | *What a boring way to spend an evening!*

⚠ Be careful not to say 'I am boring' when you mean 'I am bored'.

🔍 **not very interesting** /nɒt veri 'ɪntrɪ̩stɪŋ/ ESPECIALLY SPOKEN very ordinary, and not really interesting or enjoyable: *I watched a documentary on medical research, but it wasn't very interesting.* | *There was nothing very interesting in the local newspaper this week.*

dull /dʌl/ ESPECIALLY WRITTEN boring because nothing different, interesting, or exciting happens: *The weekly sales meeting tends to be very dull.* | *It was a really dull movie.*

monotonous /məˈnɒtənəs‖məˈnɑː-/ [adj] something that is **monotonous** is boring because it is always continues in the same way and it never changes
monotonous work/job/routine *a monotonous factory job*
monotonous sound/voice/rhythm *The teacher's low monotonous voice almost sent me to sleep.*

tedious /'tiːdiəs/ [adj] something that is **tedious** is boring and tiring because it continues for too long: *a tedious journey* | *Card games can be extremely tedious.*

bore /bɔːʳ/ [v T] to make someone feel bored, for example by talking too much about the same thing: *I hope I'm not boring you.*
bore sb with sth *He's one of those people who bore you with their holiday photographs.*
bore sb to death/to tears INFORMAL (=make someone very bored) *Being alone with a baby all day bored her to tears.*

2 boring people

boring/dull /'bɔːrɪŋ, dʌl/ [adj] someone who is **boring** or **dull** never says or does anything interesting: *He's so boring – all he ever talks about is football.* | *Diana's husband is the most boring person I've ever met.* | *Our neighbours are OK, but they're a bit dull.*

Formal or informal?
Dull is more formal than **boring**, and is used especially in written English.

bore /bɔːʳ/ [n C usually singular] a boring person who talks too much about themselves or about the same

B

things all the time: *Alison, don't be such a bore! | He was being a bore, so I made an excuse and left.*

3 boring places

boring /'bɔːrɪŋ/ [adj] not at all interesting or exciting to live in: *My family lived in a boring little town miles from anywhere. | It's so boring here. I wish we lived in New York!*

dead /ded/ [adj not before noun] a town that is **dead** is boring because there is nothing interesting to do and not many people there: *In summer we get a few visitors, but most of the time this place is dead. | It's absolutely dead here when all the students go away for the summer vacation.*

nothing ever happens /,nʌθɪŋ evəʳ 'hæpənz/ SPOKEN if you say that **nothing ever happens** in a place, you mean that nothing interesting or exciting happens there: *Nothing ever happens around here. Why can't we move to the city?*

dreary /'drɪəri/ [adj] a **dreary** place is one which is not attractive or cheerful: *I was sent to yet another dreary government office. | Laurie gazed out over a dreary landscape of factories and waste ground.*

dreary – drearier – dreariest

dull /dʌl/ ESPECIALLY WRITTEN a **dull** place is not interesting or exciting, and very little happens there: *a dull Midwestern town*

4 when you feel bored

bored /bɔːʳd/ [adj] tired and wanting something to change or happen, either because something is not interesting, or because you have nothing to do: *Dad, can we go home now? I'm bored! | gangs of bored teenagers wandering around the streets*
get bored *She seems to get bored very easily.*
bored with doing sth *Julia soon got bored with lying on the beach.*
+with *I'm bored with pasta. Let's have something else for a change.*
bored to tears/bored stiff INFORMAL (=extremely bored) *There's nothing to do here – I'm bored stiff!*

 Be careful not to say 'I am boring' when you mean 'I am bored'.

fed up /,fed 'ʌp/ ESPECIALLY SPOKEN bored and annoyed with something that has continued for too long: *Her husband's out working all the time, and she's really fed up.*
+with *We were getting the same computer problems every day, and we were all fed up with it.*
fed up with doing sth *I'm fed up with listening to her complaints the whole time.*
get fed up *When you have to stay in and study every night you just get fed up with it.*

be tired of sth/be sick of sth /bi: 'taɪəʳd ɒv(sth), bi: 'sɪk ɒv (sth)/ to feel very annoyed and impatient with a situation that has continued for too long, or with a person who has done something for too long: *We're always arguing, and I'm just tired of it. | I'm really sick of him – he's always criticizing.*
be tired/sick of doing sth *People are tired of hearing politicians make promises that they never keep. | I'm sick of cleaning up after you!*
get tired/sick of sth *He couldn't make a decision, and I got tired of waiting.*

 Don't say 'very tired of something' or 'very sick of something'. Say **really tired of something** or **really sick of something**.

have had enough /həv ,hæd ɪ'nʌf/ to be so bored with something that has continued for a long time that you decide to leave, do something different, or change the situation: *After 10 years of teaching, Allan had had enough.*
have had enough of (doing) sth *I'd had enough of living abroad, and I wanted to go home.*

5 the feeling of being bored

boredom /'bɔːʳdəm/ [n U] the feeling you have when you are bored: *the boredom of office life*

out of boredom (=because of boredom) *Some kids cause trouble at school out of boredom.*

relieve the boredom (=make a situation less boring) *On long journeys we would play games, just to relieve the boredom.*

BORN

➡ see also **BABY**

1 to be born

be born /biː ˈbɔːʳn/ a baby **is born** when it comes out of its mother's body and begins its life: *Until recently most babies were born at home.*

born in July/in 1961 etc (=in a particular month or year) *Shakespeare was born in 1564.*

born on February 8th/29th August etc (=on a particular day) *Katie was born on 23rd of May, 1992.*

born in Russia/Texas/Oxford etc *Jodie was born in a small town in Nebraska.*

> ⚠ Don't say 'I borned' or 'I have been born'. Say **I was born**.

come from/be from /ˈkʌm frɒm, biː ˈfrɒm/ [*phrasal verb* T] if you **come from** or **are from** a particular country, area, or town, you were born there or spent the early part of your life there: *We live in California now, but we're from Boston originally.* | *"Where do you come from?" "Bari, in southern Italy."*

2 the place where you were born

home town /ˌhəʊm ˈtaʊn/ [*n* C] the town where you were born or where you spent the early part of your life: *She left her home town of Glasgow at the age of 18, and never returned.*

place of birth /ˌpleɪs əv ˈbɜːʳθ/ WRITTEN the town where you were born – used especially in official documents: *Please write your name, address, and place of birth on the form.*

birthplace /ˈbɜːʳθpleɪs/ [*n* C] the place where a famous person was born
+of *The city of Assisi is known as the birthplace of St Francis.*

BORROW

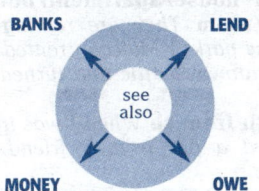

1 to borrow something

borrow /ˈbɒrəʊǁˈbaː-, ˈbɔː-/ [*v* I/T] if you **borrow** something from someone, they let you have it, and you agree to give it back to them later: *Can I borrow your calculator? I left mine at home.* | *She asked if she could borrow 50 cents to get a coffee.*

borrow sth from sb/sth *You're allowed to borrow six books from the library at a time.* | *Rwanda applied to borrow $12 million from the World Bank.*

borrow heavily (=borrow a lot of money from a bank or financial organization) *Companies that borrowed heavily are now having trouble paying their debts.*

> ⚠ Be careful not to use **borrow** when you mean **lend**. You **lend** money, your car etc to someone (=you let them have it), but you **borrow** it from someone (=they let you have it). Don't say 'she borrowed me her car'. Say **she lent me her car**.

take out a loan /ˌteɪk aʊt ə ˈləʊn/ to borrow a large amount of money from a bank or company, which you pay back over a long period of time: *We had to take out a three-year loan to buy the car.*

B

2 to pay money to use someone else's car, house, equipment etc

rent /rent/ [v T] to pay money to use a house, office, shop etc that belongs to someone else
rent a house/apartment/building/office/room *They are renting a flat near the park.* | *Malcolm rented a shop in downtown Seattle and turned it into a bar.*
rent sth from sb *When I was in Paris, I rented a flat from a friend of my father's.*
rented [adj] *Rented accommodation is very expensive in this part of town.*
rent (also **hire** BRITISH) /rent, haɪəʳ/ [v T] to pay money to use a car, piece of equipment etc for a short period of time: *I don't feel like going out – why don't we rent a DVD instead?* | *We hired a car at the airport and drove to our hotel.*
rent/hire sth from sb/sth *You can hire skis and boots from the ski school.*

3 money that you borrow

loan /ləʊn/ [n C] an amount of money that you borrow, especially from a bank, which you agree to pay back by the end of a period of time: *If you need more money, we can arrange a loan.*
a £5000/$20,000 loan *The organization asked for a $2 million loan to plant new trees in the rainforest.*
take out a loan (=get a loan) *We took out a loan to buy a new car.*
pay off/repay a loan (=finish paying back what you borrowed) *It will take over three years to repay the loan.*
bank loan (=money you borrow from a bank)
mortgage /ˈmɔːʳgɪdʒ/ [n C] a large amount of money that you borrow from a bank or a company in order to buy a house or apartment; **mortgages** are usually paid back by regular payments over a long period: *First, find a property you would like, then apply for a mortgage.*
take out a mortgage (=get a mortgage) *I didn't want to take out a mortgage until I had a steady job.*
pay the mortgage (=make regular

payments to pay it back) *Some months we only just have enough to pay the mortgage.*
pay off a mortgage (=to make the last payment on a mortgage) *We paid off the mortgage early, after Jeff inherited some money.*
a mortgage on a house/apartment (=the money you have borrowed to buy it) *They have a large mortgage on their home in Central Park West.*
a £60,000/$85,000 mortgage (=the amount of money you have borrowed)

BRAVE/NOT BRAVE

➡ see also **WB** **DESCRIBING PEOPLE'S CHARACTER**

1 not afraid when you are in a dangerous or frightening situation

brave /breɪv/ [adj] someone who is **brave** does not show that they are afraid in a frightening situation or when they have to do something dangerous, painful, or unpleasant: *You have to be very brave to be a firefighter.* | *Your husband is a very brave man.* | *a brave rescue attempt* (=done by someone who is brave)
◯ **be brave** (=behave bravely) SPOKEN *This may hurt a little, so be brave!*
it is brave of sb to do sth *It was very brave of you to tell her the truth.*
bravely [adv] *soldiers who fought bravely for their country*
courageous /kəˈreɪdʒəs/ [adj] ESPECIALLY WRITTEN someone who is **courageous** behaves very bravely, often for a long period, especially when they are fighting for something they believe in or suffering great pain: *Throughout his life, he was a courageous fighter for justice.* | *She died yesterday, after a long and courageous battle with cancer.*
courageously [adv] *He courageously opposed apartheid for over 20 years.*
daring /ˈdeərɪŋ/ [adj] someone who is **daring** is not afraid of taking risks, and seems to like doing dangerous things: *His sister was very daring, and*

swam the English Channel when she was only 16. | a daring attack on an enemy village

hero /'hɪərəʊ/ [n C] a man who is remembered and admired for doing something very brave: *a famous war hero*

plural **heroes**

heroine /'herəʊɪn/ [n C] a woman who is remembered and admired for doing something very brave: *The women who died for the cause became heroines.*

2　not afraid to do something new and different

daring /'deərɪŋ/ [adj] someone who is **daring** is not afraid of doing something new, unusual, or shocking, often in areas such as art, fashion, and design: *Many architects copied Nash's new and daring style.* | *In those days, girls who smoked were considered very daring.*

bold /bəʊld/ [adj] not afraid of making big changes or taking difficult decisions – use this especially when describing a leader or what they do: *The company needs a leader who is bold enough to make some tough decisions.* | *bold new policies for reviving the inner-city areas*
a bold move/step (=something you do that shows you are bold) *In a bold move, the company sacked its chairman and chief executive.*

3　to be brave enough to do something

dare /deə^r/ [v I] to be brave enough to do something that most people would be too frightened to do: *You can also go hang-gliding or bungee-jumping, if you dare.*
dare to do sth *She was the only one who dared to stand up and ask questions.*

!　**Dare** is not usually used in positive sentences. Don't say 'he dared to tell them the truth'. It is more usual to say something like **he wasn't afraid to tell them the truth** or **he was brave enough to tell them the truth**.

have the guts /ˌhæv ðə 'gʌts/ INFORMAL to be brave enough to do something very difficult or unpleasant: *He wouldn't have the guts!*
have the guts to do sth *OK, she made a mistake, but at least she had the guts to admit it.*

have the nerve /ˌhæv ðə 'nɜːʳv/ to be brave enough to do something very difficult or unpleasant: *I knew that I should leave him, but I didn't have the nerve.*
have the nerve to do sth *She didn't have the nerve to ask him.*

4　the ability to behave bravely

courage /'kʌrɪdʒ‖'kɜː-/ [n U] the ability to behave bravely and calmly in a situation where most people would be afraid or would lose confidence: *Martha showed great courage during her long illness.*
have the courage to do sth *Governments must have the courage to deal firmly with terrorism.*
it takes courage to do sth (=you need courage to do something) *It takes courage to get back on a horse after falling off.*

bravery /'breɪvəri/ [n U] ESPECIALLY WRITTEN when you behave bravely in a war or in a situation where your life is in danger: *Both sides fought with great bravery.* | *Two police officers received medals for bravery.*

guts /gʌts/ [n plural] INFORMAL someone who has **guts** is brave enough to do something difficult or dangerous, and you admire them for it: *You need guts and determination to succeed in motor racing.*
it takes guts to do sth (=you need to be brave to do something) *It took a lot of guts to tell the boss he was wrong.*

5　not brave

coward /'kaʊəʳd/ [n C] someone who is not brave enough to do something

B

dangerous or unpleasant that they ought to do: *If you refused to fight, you were accused of being a coward.* | *I hated myself for acting like a coward.*

cowardly /'kaʊəʳdli/ [*adj*] not brave – use this especially when someone is not brave enough to accept the unpleasant results of a situation they have caused: *The bombing was described as 'a cowardly attack on innocent citizens'.* | *He was a weak, cowardly man.* | *She was too cowardly to tell him what had happened.*

> **Formal or informal?**
> In ordinary informal conversation, it is more usual to say that someone is **not very brave** or **not brave enough to do something**.

> ⚠ Remember that **coward** is a noun and **cowardly** is an adjective.

🔍 **wimp** /wɪmp/ [*n C*] SPOKEN INFORMAL someone that you do not respect because they are afraid to do something that is a little difficult or unpleasant: *Don't be such a wimp! Just jump.*

6 to not be brave enough to do something

not dare /nɒt 'deəʳ/ to not be brave enough to do something: *I wanted to go with the other boys, but I didn't dare.*

not dare to do sth/not dare do sth *I wouldn't dare do a parachute jump, would you?* | *We stood outside the old house, not daring to go in.*

hardly dare (=almost not dare) *Velda hid behind the door, hardly daring to breathe.*

lose your nerve /ˌluːz jɔːʳ 'nɜːʳv/ to suddenly lose the confidence that you need in order to do something difficult or dangerous: *At the top of the ski slope I lost my nerve.* | *Jane went to the police right away, before she lost her nerve.*

🔍 **wimp out** /ˌwɪmp 'aʊt/ [*phrasal verb I*] SPOKEN INFORMAL to not be brave enough to do something you intended to do or said you would do: *We've come all this way to talk to her, so you'd better not wimp out now.*

wimp out of (doing) sth *I bet he wimps out of giving that speech tomorrow.*

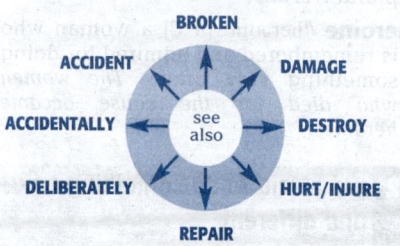

BREAK

1 object/window/plate/cup etc

break /breɪk/ [*v I/T*] if something **breaks**, or if you **break** it, it separates into two or more pieces because it has been hit, dropped, or bent: *He dropped the vase and it broke.* | *I'm sorry, but I've broken one of your plates.*

get broken (=be broken accidentally) *A few of the cups got broken when we moved to the new house.*

break (sth) in two/break (sth) in half (=into two fairly equal pieces) *A tile came off the roof and broke in two as it hit the ground.* | *I broke the chocolate in half and gave a piece to my brother.*

breaking – broke – have broken

crack /kræk/ [*v I/T*] if a window, plate, cup etc **cracks**, or if you **crack** it, it becomes damaged and lines appear in its surface: *One of the wine glasses cracked while I was washing it.* | *A stone hit the car window and cracked it.*

smash /smæʃ/ [*v I/T*] if something **smashes**, or if you **smash** it, it breaks into pieces because it has been dropped, thrown, or hit, and it makes a loud noise: *I heard something smash on the floor in the kitchen.* | *Angry crowds smashed windows in the city centre.*

be smashed to pieces/bits *Their little boat hit the rocks and was smashed to bits.*

smash (sth) to pieces/bits *The ball*

went straight through the window, smashing it to pieces.

snap /snæp/ [v I/T] if something long and thin **snaps**, or if you **snap** it, it breaks into two pieces and makes a sudden short noise as it breaks: *A twig snapped under his feet.* | *High winds snapped power lines in the city.*

snap

snap (sth) in two/half *The hurricane snapped telephone poles in two.*
snap off (sth) *The handle on the pan snapped off.*

shatter /'ʃætəʳ/ [v I/T] if a window, plate, mirror etc **shatters**, or if something **shatters** it, it breaks into many small pieces, making a loud noise: *A big water jug slid off the table and shattered into a thousand pieces as it hit the floor.* | *The huge blast shattered office windows 500 metres away.*

shatter

---

2   **machine/camera/television etc**

break /breɪk/ [v T] if you **break** a machine, camera etc, you damage it so that it does not work any more: *"Can I use your camera, Dad?" "OK, but be careful you don't break it."* | *I'm afraid I might have broken the video machine.*
breaking – broke – have broken

---

3   **paper/clothes/things made of cloth**

 Don't use **break** about paper, clothes, and things made of cloth.

tear /teəʳ/ [v T] to pull paper or cloth apart, or to accidentally make a hole in it: *She unwrapped the present carefully, trying not to tear the paper.* | *Mark had torn his jacket climbing over a fence.*

tear up sth/tear sth up (=tear it into many pieces) *Crying bitterly, she tore up his letter.*

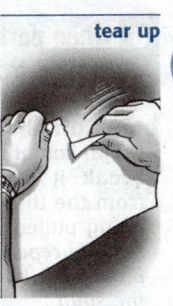
tear up

tear sth in half (=tear it into two pieces) *He took my ticket and tore it in half.*
tearing – tore – have torn

---

4   **a bone in your body**

break /breɪk/ [v T] to break or crack a bone in your body
break your arm/leg/ankle *Nicola broke her leg when she went skiing.*
breaking – broke – have broken

fracture /'fræktʃəʳ/ [v T] to damage a bone in your body so that a line appears along it
fracture your skull/leg/ribs *The X-ray showed that he had fractured his skull.*

> **Formal or informal?**
> **Fracture** is the usual formal medical word that is used when someone breaks a bone in their body.

---

5   **ball/tyre/water pipe etc**

 Don't use **break** about a ball, tyre, or water pipe.

burst /bɜːʳst/ [v I] if a tyre, ball, pipe etc **bursts**, it breaks open, and air, gas, or liquid comes out: *One of the front tyres burst, causing the car to swerve and crash.* | *Thousands of gallons of oil flowed into the river when an oil pipeline burst.*
bursting – burst – have burst

burst

blow /bləʊ/ [v I] AMERICAN if a tyre **blows**, it breaks open suddenly and all the air comes out of it: *The front tire blew and we skidded off the freeway.*

B

6 when part of something is broken from the main part

break off /ˌbreɪk ˈɒf‖-ˈɔːf/ [phrasal verb I/T] if something **breaks off**, or if you **break** it **off**, it becomes separated from the thing that it was fixed to, by being pulled very hard: *The handle on the saucepan just broke off.* | *She broke off a bit of bread and dipped it in the soup.*

come off /ˌkʌm ˈɒf‖-ˈɔːf/ [phrasal verb I/T] if something **comes off**, it accidentally becomes separated from the thing that it is fixed to, because it is not fastened firmly enough: *Can you fix the door? The handle has come off.*

come off sth *A wheel had come off a car and rolled to the side of the road.*

7 easily broken

fragile /ˈfrædʒaɪl‖-dʒəl/ [adj] a **fragile** object is not strong, and can be easily broken or damaged: *Be careful with those glasses – they're fragile.* | *The package was marked FRAGILE – HANDLE WITH CARE.*

BREATHE

1 to breathe

breathe /briːð/ [v I] to take air into your lungs and send it out again through your nose or mouth: *The air was so smoky it was difficult to breathe.* | *The boy was unconscious, but he was still breathing.*

breathe deeply (=slowly take a lot of air into your lungs) *I want you to breathe deeply and relax.*

breathe heavily (=with long slow breaths because you are tired, frightened etc) *Grandad climbed the stairs, breathing heavily.*

> ⚠ Don't confuse **breathe** (verb) and **breath** (noun).

breathe in /ˌbriːð ˈɪn/ [phrasal verb I/T] to take air into your lungs, through your nose or mouth: *My chest hurts every time I breathe in.*

breathe in air/fumes etc *They stood on the cliff breathing in the fresh sea air.*

breathe out /ˌbriːð ˈaʊt/ [phrasal verb I] to send air out of your lungs, through your nose or mouth: *The doctor told him to breathe in, then breathe out slowly.*

blow /bləʊ/ [v I] to make air come out of your mouth quickly, with your lips close together: *I blew as hard as I could, but couldn't get a sound out of the trumpet.*

+on/into *She blew on her coffee to cool it.*

blowing – blew – have blown

2 the action of breathing

breathing /ˈbriːðɪŋ/ [n U] when you breathe in and out – use this especially to talk about whether someone is breathing easily or with difficulty: *Breathing became more difficult as we got higher up the mountain.* | *She bent over the crib and listened to her baby's breathing.*

breath /breθ/ [n U] the air that you breathe out: *His breath smelt of alcohol and cigarettes.*

hold your breath (=stop yourself from breathing for a short time) *I can swim underwater, but I can't hold my breath for very long.*

bad breath (=breath that smells unpleasant) *His teeth were rotten and he had bad breath.*

3 to breathe noisily

sniff /snɪf/ [v I] to breathe in noisily through your nose, especially because you have a cold or because you are crying: *She was sniffing all the way through the movie.*

snore /snɔːʳ/ [v I] to breathe very noisily when you are asleep: *Hank was fast asleep with his mouth open, snoring loudly.*

snoring [n U] when someone snores: *Does your partner's snoring keep you awake?*

sigh /saɪ/ [v I] to breathe in and out noisily, either because you are disappointed, tired, or sad, or because you can begin to relax after worrying about something

sigh deeply *My father put his head in his hands and sighed deeply.*

sigh with relief (=because you no longer have to worry) *"Thank God that's over," she said, sighing with relief.*

sigh /saɪ/ [n C] ESPECIALLY WRITTEN the action of sighing, or the sound you make when you sigh: *"What's Jake done this time?" Dad said with a sigh.*

breathe/give a sigh of relief *Irene closed the door behind her and breathed a big sigh of relief.*

gasp /gɑːsp‖gæsp/ [v I/T] WRITTEN to suddenly breathe in noisily, with your mouth open, because you are surprised, shocked, or in pain: *The crowd gasped as the plane burst into flames.*

gasp with amazement/shock/pain etc *One of the boys hit him in the face, and he gasped with pain.*

 Use **gasp** when you are writing stories.

gasp /gɑːsp‖gæsp/ [n C] WRITTEN the sound you make when you gasp

gasp of astonishment/pain/admiration etc *There were gasps of astonishment from the audience.*

4   to breathe with difficulty

breathless/out of breath /ˈbreθləs, ˌaʊt əv ˈbreθ/ if you are **breathless** or **out of breath**, it is difficult to breathe, because you have just been running, climbing etc: *Do you get breathless going up and down stairs? | By the time we reached the top of the hill, we were all out of breath.*

pant /pænt/ [v I] ESPECIALLY WRITTEN to breathe quickly and loudly with your mouth open, for example because you have been running: *Matt was still panting after his run. | The dog was panting in the heat.*

gasping for breath /ˌgɑːspɪŋ fər ˈbreθ‖ˌgæsp-/ breathing very quickly and with great difficulty: *His mother was coughing and gasping for breath.*

5   to start to breathe normally again after running, playing sport etc

get your breath back /ˌget jɔːr ˈbreθ bæk/ to start to breathe normally again after you have been running, playing sport etc: *Hang on a minute while I get my breath back.*

6   when you cannot breathe

can't breathe /ˌkɑːnt ˈbriːð‖ˌkænt-/ if you **can't breathe**, you feel as though you cannot breathe: *I couldn't breathe in there – there were too many people. | The worst thing about asthma is the feeling that you can't breathe.*

choke /tʃəʊk/ [v I] if you **choke**, you try to breathe but you cannot get enough air or there is something in your throat that stops the air going into your lungs: *Scott was on the floor, red in the face and choking.*

+on *People can die by choking on a chicken bone.*

suffocate /ˈsʌfəkeɪt/ [v I] to die because there is not enough air to breathe: *Many of the birds had suffocated in their boxes. | It was very hot inside the car, and I felt as though I was suffocating.*

suffocation /ˌsʌfəˈkeɪʃən/ [n U] when someone dies by suffocating: *Glue-sniffing carries the risk of suffocation.*

BRIGHT/NOT BRIGHT

➡ for bright colours, go to **COLOUR/ COLOR**

➡ see also **SHINE, LIGHT, DARK**

1   bright light

bright /braɪt/ [adj] a **bright** light shines strongly: *From the top of the hill they could see the bright lights of the city below them. | We set off in bright sunshine.*

B

brightly [*adv*] *The fire was burning brightly now.* | *a brightly lit hall*
brightness [*n* U] *She closed her eyes against the brightness of the sun.*

strong /strɒŋ‖strɔːŋ/ [*adj*] a **strong** light is very bright and it helps you to see things clearly: *The light from the flashlight wasn't strong enough to read by.* | *The plant prefers strong light, and if possible direct sunlight.*

blazing /ˈbleɪzɪŋ/ [*adj* only before noun] ESPECIALLY WRITTEN very bright – use this about the sun, or about lights that you can see from a long way away: *Very few people went outside in the blazing midday sun.* | *The blazing lights of the casino shone out across the bay.*

dazzling /ˈdæzəlɪŋ/ [*adj*] a **dazzling** light is so bright that it hurts your eyes: *We emerged from the cinema into dazzling sunshine.*

blinding /ˈblaɪndɪŋ/ [*adj*] ESPECIALLY WRITTEN a **blinding** light is so bright that you cannot see for a short time after you have looked at it: *There was a blinding flash and then a loud bang.*

2 a bright place

bright /braɪt/ [*adj*] a **bright** place is full of light, especially in a way that seems pleasant and attractive: *The kitchen was always bright and cheerful.* | *Claire had a nice bright bedroom, decorated in yellow and white.*

well-lit /ˌwel ˈlɪt◂/ [*adj*] a **well-lit** place is bright because there are electric lights, so it is easy for you to see what you are doing: *She always tried to park in a well-lit area at night.* | *To avoid eye problems, make sure that your desk is well-lit.*

light /laɪt/ [*adj*] a **light** building or room has plenty of light in it, especially because it has big windows: *The kitchen is light and airy, with a fantastic view.*

3 not bright

dim /dɪm/ [*adj*] **dim** light is not very bright and makes it difficult for you to see: *I struggled to read by the dim light of the fire.*
dim – dimmer – dimmest

soft /sɒft‖sɔːft/ [*adj* only before noun] **soft** light is not too bright, in a way that is pleasant and relaxing: *The restaurant has a romantic atmosphere, with soft lights and background music.*

BROKEN

➡ opposite **WORKING**

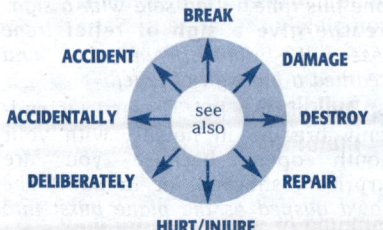

1 objects/cups/furniture/clothes etc

broken /ˈbrəʊkən/ [*adj*]
something that is **broken** has become separated into pieces, for example by being hit or dropped: *The floor was covered in broken glass.* | *The handle on her suitcase was broken.* | *In the hut there was an old table and a couple of broken chairs.*

broken

cracked /krækt/ [*adj*]
something that is **cracked** has a line on its surface where it is slightly damaged – use this especially about cups, plates, and things made of glass or clay: *Cracked glasses should always be thrown away.* | *The tiles were old and cracked.*

cracked

torn /tɔːʳn/ [*adj*] **torn** paper, clothes, curtains etc have been damaged and have holes in them: *His jeans were torn at the knees.* | *a thick book with a torn green cover* | *The cover on the bed was torn in several places.*

2 broken bones

broken /'brəʊkən/ [adj] a **broken** bone or a **broken** arm, leg etc has been damaged so that the bone is cracked or has separated into two or more pieces: *One little boy had a broken arm.* | *The doctor thought it was unlikely that the bone was broken.*

fractured /'fræktʃəʳd/ [adj] a **fractured** bone has been cracked, but it has not completely separated: *She suffered several fractures in the fall.*

3 buildings that are in bad condition

be falling down /bi: ˌfɔːlɪŋ 'daʊn/ if a building or wall **is falling down**, it is in very bad condition and many parts of it are broken: *Several of the farm buildings were falling down.*

crumbling

a crumbling wall

crumbling /'krʌmblɪŋ/ [adj] ESPECIALLY WRITTEN a **crumbling** building or wall has small pieces of stone, brick etc falling from it and it is in very bad condition, especially because it is very old: *the crumbling walls of a medieval castle*

derelict /'derɪlɪkt/ [adj] a **derelict** building or piece of land is in very bad condition because it has not been used for a long time: *some derelict houses near the docks*

4 machines, cars, phones etc that do not work

not working/doesn't work /nɒt 'wɜːʳkɪŋ, ˌdʌzənt 'wɜːʳk/ ESPECIALLY SPOKEN if a machine or piece of equipment **isn't working** or **doesn't work**, it does not do the job it is supposed to do: *The dishwasher's not working.* | *Do you know your brake lights aren't working?* | *Take the camera back to the store if it doesn't work.*

there's something wrong with /ðeəʳz ˌsʌmθɪŋ 'rɒŋ wɪð‖-'rɔːŋ-/ ESPECIALLY SPOKEN if **there's something wrong with** a machine, car etc, it does not work properly, but you do not know exactly why: *If there's something wrong with your computer, call the IT helpdesk.*

broken /'brəʊkən/ [adj] not working – use this especially about small machines or equipment: *"What's the time?" "I don't know, my watch is broken."* | *a broken old fax machine*

out of order /ˌaʊt əv 'ɔːʳdəʳ/ [not before noun] not working – use this about machines in public places: *Every phone I tried was out of order.* | *The toilets were out of order.*

faulty /'fɔːlti/ [adj] something that is **faulty**, especially a piece of electrical equipment, is not working properly and may be dangerous: *Fires in the home are often caused by faulty electrical equipment.*

be down /bi: 'daʊn/ if a computer system **is down**, it is not working, usually for a short time: *The system's down so you won't be able to use email or the Internet until it's working again.*
go down (=stop working) *When the system went down, many passengers were stranded at the airport.*

5 to stop working

break down /ˌbreɪk 'daʊn/ [phrasal verb I] if a car, bus, train, or large machine **breaks down**, it stops working completely: *I took the bus because my car broke down.* | *The elevators in this block are always breaking down.*

go wrong /ˌgəʊ 'rɒŋ‖-'rɔːŋ/ to stop working normally – use this especially

about complicated equipment, when you do not know what the problem is: *Our TV went wrong last night.*
+**with** *Something keeps going wrong with the heating system.*

crash /kræʃ/ [v I] if a computer or a computer system **crashes**, it suddenly stops working, and information is often lost because of this: *The network crashed and we lost half a day's work.*

BUILD

➡ see also **DESIGN,** ⬛ **HOUSES/WHERE PEOPLE LIVE**

1 to build something

build /bɪld/ [v T]
build a house/church/school/road/bridge etc to make a house, church etc using bricks, stone, wood, or other materials: *Our house was built in the early 1930s.* | *The Romans built roads all over Europe.* | *The cost of building the new football stadium was over £3 million.*
be built of concrete/stone/wood etc *In those days most of the houses were built of wood, and were easily destroyed by fire.*
building – built – have built

building /'bɪldɪŋ/ [n C] something that has walls and a roof, for example a house, an office, or a church: *The church is one of the oldest buildings in the city.*
a farm/office/government building *a brand new office building in the centre of Tokyo*

builder /'bɪldə^r/ [n C] someone whose job is to build houses, offices etc: *The roof is being fixed by a local builder.*

construct /kən'strʌkt/ [v T] to build a large public building, a road, bridge etc: *There are plans to construct a new bridge across the river.* | *The building was constructed using local stone.*
construction [n U] the process of building houses, roads, bridges etc: *the construction of the new library.*

Formal or informal?
Construct is more formal than **build**.

2 the design of buildings

architecture /'ɑː^rkɪtektʃə^r/ [n U] the way in which buildings are designed, or the work of designing buildings: *We spent the afternoon walking around Rome, admiring the architecture.* | *a fine example of Gothic architecture* | *She studied architecture at university.*

architect /'ɑː^rkɪtekt/ [n C] someone whose job is to design buildings: *St Paul's Cathedral was designed by the famous architect, Sir Christopher Wren.*

BURN

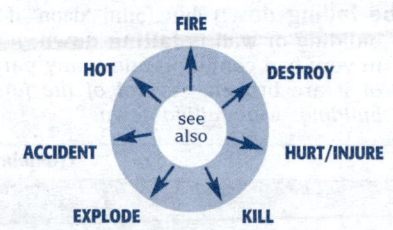

1 to burn something

burn /bɜː^rn/ [v T] to damage or destroy something with fire or heat: *She lit a fire and burned his letters one by one.*
badly burned *The paintings were badly burned in the fire.*
burn a hole in sth (=make a hole by burning it) *Someone had dropped a cigarette and burned a hole in the carpet.*
burning – burned (also **burnt** BRITISH) **– have burned** (also **have burnt** BRITISH)

burned/burnt [adj] *The cake is slightly burnt, I'm afraid.* | *The kitchen smelled of burned toast.*

> ⚠ Don't use **burn** when you want to say that someone destroys a building. Use **burn down**.

burn down /ˌbɜː^rn 'daʊn/ [phrasal verb T] to completely destroy a building by burning it
burn down sth *Police believe students are responsible for burning down the school.*

burn sth down *Her ex-husband threatened to burn the house down with her and the kids inside.*

scorch /skɔːʳtʃ/ [v T] to burn the surface of something and make a dark mark on it: *The walls of the house were still scorched and blackened from the fire.* | *I scorched my shirt when I was ironing.*

2 to burn yourself

burn /bɜːʳn/ [v T] if you **burn** yourself, you hurt yourself by accidentally touching something hot
burn yourself *Don't touch the iron. You'll burn yourself.*
burn your hand/leg/mouth etc *The soup was so hot it burnt my mouth.*
badly burned *Jerry was badly burned in the explosion.*
burning – burned (also **burnt** BRITISH) **– have burned** (also **have burnt** BRITISH)

scald /skɔːld/ [v T] to burn yourself with very hot liquid: *The coffee scalded his tongue.*
scald yourself *It's easy to knock a pan off the stove and scald yourself.*

burn /bɜːʳn/ [n C usually plural] a mark on your skin where you have been burned
severe/serious burns *Billy was taken to the hospital with severe burns.*
minor burns (=not very serious)

3 to make something start burning

set fire to sth/set sth on fire /ˌset ˈfaɪəʳ tuː (sth), ˌset (sth) ɒn ˈfaɪəʳ/ to make something start to burn, so that it gets damaged: *Vandals set fire to an empty warehouse near the docks last night.* | *In the dry season, the slightest spark can set fire to the grass.* | *Rioters set cars on fire and attacked the police.*

light /laɪt/ [v T]
light a cigarette/fire/candle to make a cigarette, fire etc start to burn: *Ricky sat down and lit a cigarette.* | *We searched around for twigs, so we could light a fire.*
lighting – lit – have lit

4 to make something stop burning

put out /ˌpʊt ˈaʊt/ [phrasal verb T] to make a fire stop burning, or make a cigarette, pipe etc stop burning
put out the fire/the blaze *It took firefighters four hours to put out the blaze.*
put out a cigarette/pipe *I put out my cigarette and went back into the house.*
put sth out *She threw sand on the fire to put it out.*

extinguish /ɪkˈstɪŋgwɪʃ/ [v T] FORMAL to make a fire stop burning, or make a cigarette stop burning – used especially in official notices and requests: *Would all passengers please extinguish their cigarettes? Thank you.* | *It took six days to extinguish the fires on the slopes of Table Mountain.*

blow out /ˌbləʊ ˈaʊt/ [phrasal verb T] to make a flame or fire stop burning by blowing on it
blow out a candle/a match/a fire *See if you can blow out all the candles on your cake!*
blow sth out *We tried to light a fire but the wind kept blowing it out.*

stub out /ˌstʌb ˈaʊt/ [phrasal verb T] to make a cigarette or a cigar stop burning by pressing the end of it against something
stub out a cigarette/cigar *Butler stubbed out his cigarette in the ashtray and reached for the phone.*
stub a cigarette/cigar out *He worked without a break, pausing only to stub his cigarette out and light another.*

5 when something is burning

burn /bɜːʳn/ [v I] to produce flames and heat: *They could smell wood burning in the yard.*
burn brightly WRITTEN *At one end of the room a coal fire burned brightly.*
burning – burned (also **burnt** BRITISH) **– have burned** (also **have burnt** BRITISH)

burning [adj only before noun] *He escaped by jumping from the fourth floor of a burning apartment block.*

be on fire /biː ɒn ˈfaɪəʳ/ if a building, vehicle, or piece of clothing **is on fire**, it is burning and the fire needs to be stopped: *The whole house was on fire by the time the firefighters arrived.*

burn down /ˌbɜːˈn ˈdaʊn/ [phrasal verb I] if a building **burns down**, it is completely destroyed by fire: *The hotel burned down in 1990.*

be in flames /biː ɪn ˈfleɪmz/ if a building or vehicle **is in flames**, it is burning strongly with a lot of flames, causing a lot of damage: *A large part of the building was in flames, and some people were trapped on the roof.*

blazing /ˈbleɪzɪŋ/ [adj only before noun] a **blazing** fire, building etc is producing a lot of flames and heat while it burns: *We sat in front of a blazing log fire.* | *An old woman was rescued from the blazing house by a neighbour.*

 Blazing is used especially in stories and descriptions, and in news reports.

smoulder BRITISH **smolder** AMERICAN /ˈsməʊldəʳ/ [v I] ESPECIALLY WRITTEN to burn slowly, producing smoke but no flames: *A cigarette was smoldering in the ashtray.* | *The remains of the fire still smouldered in the grate.*

6   when something starts burning

catch fire /ˌkætʃ ˈfaɪəʳ/ to start burning accidentally: *Two farm workers died when a barn caught fire yesterday.* | *The car turned over, but luckily it didn't catch fire.*

burst into flames /ˌbɜːʳst ɪntə ˈfleɪmz/ to suddenly start burning and produce a lot of flames that cause serious damage: *The plane burst into flames on the runway.*

 Burst into flames is used especially in news reports and stories.

go up in flames /ˌgəʊ ʌp ɪn ˈfleɪmz/ if a building or vehicle **goes up in flames**, it starts burning and is destroyed by fire: *If the firefighters hadn't arrived when they did, the whole place might have gone up in flames.*

break out /ˌbreɪk ˈaʊt/ [phrasal verb I] if a fire **breaks out**, it starts burning accidentally and spreads very quickly:

£200,000 worth of damage was caused when fire broke out in the hospital.

7   something that burns easily

flammable /ˈflæməbəl/ [adj] **flammable** chemicals, gases, and other materials burn easily and quickly and are therefore dangerous: *Caution! Flammable substances.*

highly flammable (=extremely flammable) *Petrol is highly flammable.*

Formal or informal?

Flammable is a technical word, used especially when warning about a substance.

BUSINESS

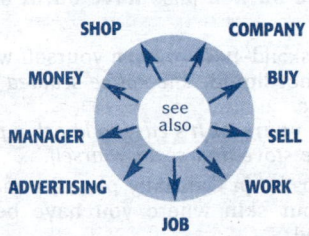

1   the work that companies do

business /ˈbɪznɪ̥s/ [n U] the work that companies do when they buy and sell goods and services: *Business in Europe has been badly affected by economic conditions.*

do business (with sb) *We do business with a number of Italian companies.*

on business (=when someone goes somewhere for business reasons) *She'll be back next week – she's in Korea on business.*

in business (=active in this area of work) *The company has been in business for over 30 years.*

the music/entertainment/advertising etc business (=the work of companies that are involved in music etc)

go into business (=start working in business, or start your own business company) *A lot of graduates decide to go into business.*

⚠️ You can also use **business** before a noun, like an adjective: *a business meeting* | *studying at business school*

⚠️ Don't confuse **business** [U] (=when you buy and sell goods or services) with **a business** [C] (=a company).

trade /treɪd/ [*n* U] the activity of buying and selling large quantities of goods, especially between one country and another: *international trade*
+with/between *Trade between the two countries has increased.* | *Britain's trade with the United States*
the fur/arms/diamond trade (=the buying and selling of fur, weapons etc)
trade in rice/textiles/gold etc (=the buying and selling of rice, cloth etc)

⚠️ You can also use **trade** before a noun, like an adjective: *a trade agreement between China and the US*

industry /ˈɪndəstri/ [*n* C/U] the production of goods to be sold, especially in factories: *The region has tried to attract new industry in order to reduce unemployment.*
steel / textile / automobile / manufacturing industry *the recent decline in the manufacturing industry*
in industry *Salaries are much higher for people in industry.* (=people whose jobs are in industry)
heavy industry (=the production of oil, metals, and coal, and of large goods such as cars and aircraft)
light industry (=the production of goods such as kitchen equipment, TVs, and computers)
plural **industries**

industrial /ɪnˈdʌstriəl/ [*adj* usually before noun] connected with industry: *industrial waste* | *industrial pollution*

⚠️ Don't confuse **industry** (=the production of goods) with **factory** (=a place where goods are made) or **company** (=an organization that makes or sells goods or services).

⚠️ Don't say 'the industry' when you mean all industries. Just say **industry**: *Industry is one of the main causes of pollution.*

commercial /kəˈmɜːrʃəl/ [*adj* only before noun] concerned with business: *Commercial pressures are forcing many companies to cut jobs.* | *We need to protect our commercial interests.*
commercially [*adv*] concerned with whether something is successful and makes a profit: *Commercially, the movie was a disaster.*

e-commerce (also **e-business** ESPECIALLY AMERICAN /ˈiː ˌkɒmɜːrs, ˈiː ˌbɪznəs‖-ˌkɑː-/) [*n* U] electronic commerce; when companies buy and sell goods and services and do other business activities on a computer, using the Internet: *The company is a leading supplier of e-commerce services.*

2 a business agreement

deal /diːl/ [*n* C] a business agreement, especially when one company agrees to provide goods or services, and another company agrees to buy them: *I had a business deal to complete in Turin.* | *Wicks lost a lot of money on property deals.*
+with *a $55 million deal with a Japanese automobile company*
sign a deal *He recently signed a deal with a major record company worth over three million dollars.*

3 to take part in business activities

do business /ˌduː ˈbɪznəs/ if a company **does business** with another company, it buys things from them or sells things to them: *STC is one of our regular customers – we've done business for years.*
+with *They do a lot of business with Italian companies.*
be in business /biː ɪn ˈbɪznəs/ if someone **is in business**, they own a company or shop, and they are involved in business activities: *Her father was in business in Korea.* | *They've been in business for about 10 years, and are doing quite well.*
set up in business BRITISH (=start a

B

company, shop etc) *I decided to set up in business as a financial consultant.*

trade /treɪd/ [v I] if one country or company **trades** with another country or company, it buys things from them, or sells things to them: *Slater's company continued to trade, even though it was in trouble.*
+in *a French firm that trades in farm machinery*
+with *The two nations have not traded with each other for over thirty years.*
trading partner (=a country that regularly does business with another country) *Japan is one of our major trading partners.*

deal with sb /ˈdiːl wɪð (sb)/ [phrasal verb T] to buy goods from another company or person, or to sell goods to them: *The firm deals directly with the manufacturers.* | *I've dealt with Bill Harrison for years and always found him very reliable.*

4 someone who works in business

businessman / businesswoman / business person /ˈbɪznɪˌsmən, ˈbɪznɪˌswʊmən, ˈbɪznɪs ˌpɜːˌsən/ [n C] someone who works in business, especially as the manager or owner of a company: *Tim Knight is a highly successful businessman who runs his own electronics company.*
plural **businessmen – businesswomen**

entrepreneur /ˌɒntrəprəˈnɜːʳ‖ˌɑːn-/ [n C] someone who starts a new business or arranges new business deals, especially someone who is willing to risk their own money in order to make a profit: *Local entrepreneur Tony Ridley started his computer company five years ago and is now a millionaire.*

BUSY/NOT BUSY

➡ see also [WB] **FREE TIME, WORK**

1 a busy person

busy /ˈbɪzi/ [adj] if you are **busy**, you have a lot of things to do: *Sorry I haven't called you, but I've been really busy.* | *Can I speak with you for a moment, or are you too busy?*
busy doing sth *Alex is busy studying for his exams.*
+with *Marion was busy with preparations for the wedding.*
keep sb busy (=give someone plenty to do) *There were plenty of activities to keep the kids busy.*
busy – busier – busiest

> ⚠ Don't say 'she's busy with studying'. Say **she's busy studying** or **she's busy with her studies**.

have a lot to do /hæv ə ˌlɒt tə ˈduːǁ -ˌlɑːt-/ if you **have a lot to do**, you have to do a lot of things, and you need to hurry or work hard: *She had a lot to do before she could go home.*

◯ **be snowed under** /biː ˌsnəʊd ˈʌndəʳ/ INFORMAL, ESPECIALLY SPOKEN if you **are snowed under**, you have so much work that it is difficult for you to do it all: *I can't stop for lunch today. I'm completely snowed under.*
+with *We've been snowed under with emergency calls this morning.*

◯ **be rushed off your feet** /biː ˌrʌʃt ɒf jɔːʳ ˈfiːt/ INFORMAL, ESPECIALLY SPOKEN to be very busy and in a hurry, because you have a lot of things to do: *I've been rushed off my feet getting ready for the party.*

2 a busy place or time

➡ see also **CROWD**

busy /ˈbɪzi/ [adj] use this about places where a lot of people are travelling, shopping, or doing things, or about times when you have a lot to do: *By 10 o'clock the supermarket was really busy.* | *a busy main road* | *a doctor in a busy hospital* | *July and August are our busiest times.*
a busy day *I've had a terribly busy day at the office.*
busy – busier – busiest

hectic /ˈhektɪk/ [adj] a **hectic** time or situation is very busy, so you are always in a hurry and you often feel worried or excited: *It was really hectic at work today.* | *The band had a hectic recording schedule.* | *When she lived in London she had a hectic social life.*

the rush hour /ðə ˈrʌʃ aʊəʳ/ [n singular] the time in the morning and evening when a lot of people are travelling to or from work: *In the rush hour the trains are always crowded.*
rush hour traffic *She got held up in rush hour traffic.*

the rush /ðə ˈrʌʃ/ [n singular] a time when a lot of people are shopping or travelling: *Sam got to the theatre early to avoid the rush.*
the Christmas/summer/weekend rush *Shop by mail and beat the Christmas rush!*

---

3   a person who is not busy

not busy /nɒt ˈbɪzi/ *Let's find a time when you're not so busy, and talk about this calmly.* | *Hopefully by March we won't be so busy.*

○ **not have much to do** /nɒt hæv ˌmʌtʃ tə ˈduː/ ESPECIALLY SPOKEN to not be busy – use this especially to say that you have enough time to do other things: *I could help if you want – I don't have much to do this weekend.*

free /friː/ [adj] not busy, because you have not arranged to do anything, or you do not have to go to work or school: *I'm busy all day today, but I'm free tomorrow morning.* | *Which days is she free next week?*
free time (=time when you do not have to work and can do what you want) *What do you do in your free time?*

---

4   a place or time that is not busy

quiet /ˈkwaɪət/ [adj] a **quiet** place or time is one in which there is not much happening or not many people are travelling, shopping etc: *a quiet suburb of Seattle* | *I spent a quiet weekend at home.*

out of season BRITISH **in the off season** AMERICAN /aʊt əv ˈsiːzən‹ , ɪn ði ˈɒf ˌsiːzən‖-ˈɔːf-/ if you visit a tourist area **out of season**, you go there at a time of the year when there are not a lot of people: *It's much cheaper if you go there out of season.* | *Rooms, in the off season, are as cheap as $52 a night.*

BUY

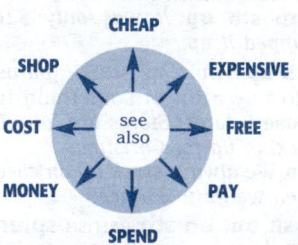

B

---

1   to buy something

buy /baɪ/ [v T] to pay money so that you can have something: *He's just gone to buy some cigarettes.* | *The painting was bought by a museum in New York.*
buy sb sth *Let me buy you a drink.*
buy sth for sb/sth *The money was used to buy new equipment for the hospital.*
buy sth from sb/sth *Ella buys a lot of her clothes from second-hand stores.*
buy sth for $10/£50 etc *They bought their house for $200,000.*
buying – bought – have bought

○ **get** /get/ [v T not in passive] ESPECIALLY SPOKEN to buy something, especially ordinary things such as food, clothes, or things for your house: *Did you get some bread?*
get sb sth *I'm getting Dad a bottle of whiskey for his birthday.*
get sth for sb *Why don't you get a video game for Greg?*
get sth for $10/£50 etc *She got that skirt for £10 in the market.*
getting – got – have got BRITISH **have gotten** AMERICAN

purchase /ˈpɜːʳtʃɪ̩s/ [v T] FORMAL to buy something, especially something large and expensive: *The cost of purchasing new equipment for the science laboratories was over £100,000.*
+from *Tickets may be purchased in advance from the box office.*

> **Formal or informal?**
> **Purchase** is used especially in formal business situations.

snap up /ˌsnæp ˈʌp/ [phrasal verb T] INFORMAL to buy something as soon as you see it, because it is very cheap or because you want it very much

snap up sth *You can snap up some real bargains in the sales.*

snap sth up *It was only $10, so I snapped it up.*

stock up /ˌstɒk 'ʌp‖ˌstɑːk-/ [phrasal verb I] to buy a lot of something in order to use it later: *Stores are full of people stocking up for Christmas.*

+on *We always stock up on cheap wine when we go to France.*

splash out on sth BRITISH **splurge (on sth)** AMERICAN /ˌsplæʃ 'aʊt ɒn (sth) 'splɜːʳdʒ ɒn (sth)/ [phrasal verb T] INFORMAL to buy something expensive that you would not usually buy: *Why don't you splash out on a new dress for the party?* | *We splurged on an expensive hotel for the last night of the holiday.*

2 to go to shops to buy things

go shopping /ˌgəʊ 'ʃɒpɪŋ‖-'ʃɑː-/ to go to shops in order to look at things and buy things: *That afternoon, Jo and Emma went shopping in Oxford Street.*

> ⚠ Don't say 'go to shopping'. Say **go shopping**.

do the shopping /ˌduː ðə 'ʃɒpɪŋ‖-'ʃɑː-/ to go to shops in order to buy the things that you need regularly, especially food: *I spent all day Saturday doing the shopping and cleaning the apartment.*

do your/my/his etc shopping *We do all our shopping at the supermarket.*

🔍 **go to the shops** BRITISH **go to the store** AMERICAN /ˌgəʊ tə ðə 'ʃɒps, ˌgəʊ tə ðə 'stɔːʳ‖-'ʃɑːps/ ESPECIALLY SPOKEN to go to the shops near your house in order to buy food or to buy one or two other small things that you need: *I'm just going to the shops for a newspaper – do you want anything?* | *If you go to the store could you get me some milk?*

shop /ʃɒp‖ʃɑːp/ [v I not in progressive] if you **shop** at a particular shop, you go there regularly to buy things

+at *I usually shop at Tesco.*

shopping – shopped – have shopped

shop around /ˌʃɒp ə'raʊnd‖ˌʃɑːp-/ [phrasal verb I] to compare the price of something in several shops, before deciding where to buy it: *You could probably get the same camera cheaper if you shop around.*

window shopping /'wɪndəʊ ˌʃɒpɪŋ‖-ˌʃɑːp-/ [n U] when you look at things in shop windows without intending to buy anything: *We went to the city centre, just to do some window shopping.*

3 someone who buys something

customer /'kʌstəməʳ/ [n C] someone who buys things from a shop or company, or who uses a restaurant, bar etc: *Several customers complained about how rude the waiters were.* | *We offer a 10% discount to regular customers.*

best/biggest customer (=a person or company who uses a shop or company the most)

shoppers /'ʃɒpəʳz‖'ʃɑːp-/ [n plural] the people in a shop or town who are buying things: *streets crowded with Christmas shoppers*

buyer /'baɪəʳ/ [n C] someone who buys something expensive such as a house or car: *Have you found a buyer for your house yet?* | *Potential buyers can view the paintings the day before the sale.*

> ⚠ Don't use **buyer** about people buying things in shops.

consumers / the consumer /kən'sjuːməʳz, ðə kən'sjuːməʳ‖-'suː-/ [n] all the people who buy and use goods and services: *Consumers are demanding cheaper food.* | *The consumer is interested in high quality goods, not just low prices.*

Formal or informal?

Consumers/the consumer is used especially in formal writing or news reports about business. **Consumers** is plural and **the consumer** is singular, but they are both used to refer to people who buy things.

C, c

CALM

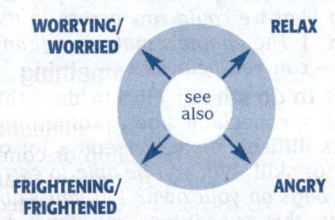

not angry or upset, even in a difficult situation

WORRYING/WORRIED   RELAX

see also

FRIGHTENING/FRIGHTENED   ANGRY

1 calm

calm /kɑːm‖kɑːm, kɑːlm/ [adj] not getting angry or upset, even in a difficult situation: *Everyone praised Douglas for the calm way in which he handled the situation.* | *We'll talk about this when you're feeling calmer.*
keep/stay calm *Keep calm and try not to panic.*

calmly [adv] *The other kids were screaming, but Ellie calmly picked up the snake and threw it out of the window.*

relaxed /rɪˈlækst/ [adj] someone who is **relaxed** is very calm and does not seem to be worried about anything, and it is pleasant for other people to be with them: *George greeted us in his friendly relaxed way.* | *You seem much more relaxed since you changed jobs.*

stay cool/keep cool /ˌsteɪ ˈkuːl, ˌkiːp ˈkuːl/ to stay calm and not show your emotions, especially when other people are getting excited or angry: *He's the kind of player who always manages to stay cool, even under pressure.*
keep your cool (=not become angry) *Mark managed to keep his cool and ignore her last comments.*

coolly [adv] *She walked coolly to the front of the hall and picked up the microphone.*

keep your head /ˌkiːp jɔːʳ ˈhed/ to manage to stay calm and to behave in a sensible way when something is likely to make you feel frightened or worried: *In this job, you need to be good at keeping your head in a crisis.*

laid-back /ˌleɪd ˈbæk◂/ [adj] INFORMAL someone who is **laid-back** is always relaxed and never seems to worry about things that other people worry about: *Nigel's fun and very laid-back.*
laid-back attitude/manner/approach *I really liked his laid-back attitude to life.*

2 to become calm, or to make someone calm

calm down /ˌkɑːm ˈdaʊn‖ˌkɑːm-, ˌkɑːlm-/ [phrasal verb I/T] to become calm again after you have been angry or upset, or to make someone do this: *It took Mum a little while to calm down.*
calm sb down *He put his arms around Christine and tried to calm her down.*

3 what you say to someone when you want them to be calm

○ **calm down** /ˌkɑːm ˈdaʊn‖ˌkɑːm-, ˌkɑːlm-/ SPOKEN say this when someone is angry, upset, or excited and you want them to think calmly or speak calmly again: *Calm down! There's nothing to worry about.*

○ **relax** /rɪˈlæks/ SPOKEN say this to someone who is worried or frightened about something, in order to stop them worrying: *Relax! Everything will be fine.*

○ **take it easy** /ˌteɪk ɪt ˈiːzi/ SPOKEN INFORMAL say this when someone is angry or upset, and you want to stop them reacting in such an emotional way: *Hey, take it easy! Nobody's saying you're not good at your job.*

○ **it's okay/it's all right** /ɪts əʊˈkeɪ, ɪts ˌɔːl ˈraɪt/ SPOKEN say this to someone to try to make them stop being worried: *It's okay, I'll be home by midnight.* | *It's all right, don't cry. Mummy's here.*

CAN/CAN'T

➡ look here for ...
  • be able to do something
  • be allowed to do something
➡ if you want to know about modal verbs, go to the **ESSENTIAL GRAMMAR** (Section 7)
➡ see also **EG** **REQUESTS**

> ⚠ Don't say 'I can to come'. Say **I can come**.

> ⚠ The past
> If you just want to say that someone had the ability, money etc to do something at some time in the past, use **could**: *He could read by the time he was four.* | *He was a rich man who could afford to buy anything he wanted.* If you want to say that someone succeeded in doing something because they had the opportunity, ability, money etc, use **was able to do sth**: *When the rain stopped we were able to finish the game.*

> ⚠ The future
> Use **will be able to do sth** (often shortened to 'I'll be able', 'we'll be able', 'he'll be able' etc): *When everyone comes back from their vacations, we'll be able to get a lot more work done.* | *I'll be able to see my friends and family again very soon.* In spoken English you can use **can** to talk about tomorrow, next week etc: *I can come with you on Sunday.*

> ⚠ The time up to the present
> Use **have been able to do sth** to say that someone has succeeded in doing something: *Up to now no-one has been able to break the record set by Lewis.* Use **could have done sth** to say that someone was able to do something but did not do it: *He could have become president, but he wasn't ambitious.*

> ⚠ If you need to use an infinitive, use **to be able to do sth**: *He wants to be able to speak French.*

1 to have the ability, opportunity, time, or equipment that you need in order to do something

can /kən, *strong* kæn/ [*modal verb*] *"Can you speak Japanese?" "Yes, I can."* | *Can you come for lunch on Saturday?* | *Adrian could read when he was four.* | *Even a small computer can store huge amounts of information.* | *If we had a boat we could row across to the island.* | *The engine's making a funny noise – can you hear it?*

be able to do sth /bi: ,eɪbəl tə 'du: (sth)/ use this especially about something that is difficult or that needs a lot of effort or skill: *Will you be able to carry those bags on your own?* | *If you want to join this expedition, you must be able to speak some Spanish.* | *Three weeks after the accident, she was able to walk and even exercise in the gym.*

> ⚠ Use **can**, not **be able to**, with verbs like 'see', 'hear', or 'feel' when describing your present situation. Don't say 'I am able to see him' or 'I am not able to hear her'. Say **I can see him** and **I can't hear her**.

be capable of sth /bi: 'keɪpəbəl ɒv (sth)/ to have the power or ability to do something, especially something very difficult or unusual: *The car is capable of a top speed of 200 mph.* | *No one thought he was capable of murder.*
be capable of doing sth *He's a very good player, and capable of beating anyone in the world when he's at his best.*
be perfectly capable of doing sth (=used to emphasize that someone has the ability to do something, especially without help) *Don't worry, she's perfectly capable of dealing with the situation.*

have the ability to do sth /hæv ði ə,bɪlịti tə 'du: (sth)/ to be able to do something, especially something that is unusual or that most people cannot do: *She seemed to have the ability to make people do anything she wanted.*

it is possible for sb to do sth /ɪt ɪz ,pɒsịbəl fəʳ (sb) tə 'du: (sth)‖-,pɑː-/ FORMAL use this especially when you are making an arrangement with someone, to ask or say what someone will be able to do: *Would it be possible* *for you to come to a meeting on Tuesday? | It might be possible for him to stay with friends of mine in Florida.*

> ⚠️ Don't use this when you are simply saying what you can do. Don't say 'it is possible for me to go'. Say **I can go**.

2 to be allowed to do something or have the power to do it

➡ see also **EC PERMISSION, LET/ALLOW**

can /kən, *strong* kæn/ [modal verb] *If you want to come with us, you can.*
can do sth *It's my house and I can do what I want here. | Can I borrow your car? | Only the Supreme Court can change these laws.*

be able to do sth /biː ˌeɪbəl tə ˈduː (sth)/ use this especially when a law or rule makes it possible for someone to do something: *You might be able to get a temporary passport. | As senior students, we were able to attend some university classes.*

have the power to do sth /hæv ðə ˌpaʊəʳ tə ˈduː (sth)/ to be able to do something because your official position gives you the power to do it: *The judge has the power to order a witness to give evidence. | Each state had the power to make its own laws.*

be in a position to do sth /biː ɪn ə pəˌzɪʃən tə ˈduː (sth)/ FORMAL to be able to do something because you have the power or authority to do it: *You should talk to the police – at least they are in a position to do something about it.*

be authorized to do sth (also **be authorised to do sth** BRITISH) /biː ˌɔːθəraɪzd tə ˈduː (sth)/ to be able to do something because you have been given official authority or permission to do it: *If the police have a search warrant, they are authorized to enter the building, by force if necessary. | The ship is legally authorized to carry 203 passengers.*

3 the ability to do something

ability /əˈbɪlɪti/ [n C/U] something that you are able to do because you have the physical skill, intelligence, or

knowledge to do it
ability to do sth *Our ability to speak makes us different from other animals. | You'll need the ability to communicate with a wide range of people.*
have the ability *Are you confident he has the ability to do this job?*
plural **abilities**

> ⚠️ Don't say 'ability of speaking'. Say **ability to speak**.

skill /skɪl/ [n C] a special ability that you need to learn in order to do a particular job or activity: *These exercises develop the student's reading and writing skills. | You need computing skills for most office jobs.*

capability /ˌkeɪpəˈbɪlɪti/ [n C/U] the ability, skill, or power that makes a machine, person, or organization able to do something, especially something difficult that needs special skills, knowledge, or equipment
capability to do sth *There's a huge question mark over the organization's capability to adapt and change.*
+of *The task is well within the capabilities of the machine.*
capability of doing sth *He has this unique capability of bringing the best out in people.*
plural **capabilities**

4 to make someone able to do something

enable sb to do sth /ɪˌneɪbəl (sb) tə ˈduː (sth)/ to make it possible for someone to do something: *The money from my grandmother enabled us to buy the house. | This training and advice will enable them to get new jobs.*

> **Formal or informal?**
> **Enable sb to do sth** is not used in informal conversation. For example, don't say 'This enables us to go to the party'. Say **This means we can go to the party.**

make it possible /ˌmeɪk ɪt ˈpɒsɪbəl‖-ˈpɑː-/ if a situation, event, or change **makes it possible** for someone to do something, they are able to do something as a result of this situation, event etc
make it possible to do sth *The direct*

flight makes it possible to get from London to Tokyo in 12 hours.
make it possible for sb to do sth *Loans are available to make it possible for people to continue their education.*

mean sb can do sth /ˌmiːn (sb) kən 'duː (sth)/ if an event, situation, system etc **means someone can do something**, it makes it possible for them to do it: *This facility means you can easily change the layout of the text.* | *I live just a mile away, which means I can walk to work in the morning.*

allow sb to do sth/let sb do sth /əˌlaʊ (sb) tə 'duː (sth), ˌlet (sb) 'duː (sth)/ if a piece of equipment or a service **allows you to do something** or **lets you do something**, it provides what you need to be able to do it: *The Internet allows us to access information almost instantly.* | *Your card lets you get cash from machines all over the world.*

5 to be unable to do something

can't/cannot /kɑːnt, 'kænət, -nɒt‖kænt, 'kænɑːt/ [*modal verb*] to be unable to do something, because you do not have the ability, time, equipment etc: *"Can you drive?" "No, I can't."*
can't/cannot do sth *Tom can't see anything without his glasses.* | *I packed so much into my suitcase that I couldn't lift it!* | *I'm afraid Mr Martin can't see you now – he's with a client.*

> **Formal or informal?**
> **Cannot** is more formal than **can't**, and is used especially in written English: *Human beings cannot survive for long without water.* **Cannot** is always written as one word.

not be able to do sth /ˌnɒt biː ˌeɪbəl tə 'duː (sth)/ *Unfortunately, I wasn't able to help them.* | *I don't think I'll be able to come to the meeting after all.* | *The doctor told Tina she wouldn't be able to have children.*

> ⚠ **Not be able to** is used mostly in past or future tenses. In the present tense, use **can't** or **cannot** instead. For example, don't say 'I am not able to drive'. Say **I can't drive**.

be unable to do sth /biː ʌnˌeɪbəl tə 'duː (sth)/ ESPECIALLY WRITTEN to not be able to do something, especially something important that you want to do or need to do: *He lay awake all night, unable to sleep.* | *Many passengers were unable to reach the lifeboats in time.*

not know how to do sth /ˌnɒt nəʊ haʊ tə 'duː (sth)/ to not have the necessary knowledge or skill to be able to do something: *I still don't know how to drive.* | *I don't know how to get there. Do you?*

be incapable/not be capable /biː ɪnˈkeɪpəbəl, nɒt biː ˈkeɪpəbəl/ to not have the physical strength or mental ability to do something
+of *She's no longer capable of looking after herself.* | *Matthew seemed to be incapable of keeping a job.* | *Some people believe that his party is incapable of government.*

not be in a position to do sth /ˌnɒt biː ɪn ə pəˌzɪʃən tə 'duː (sth)/ FORMAL to not be able to do something, because you do not have enough knowledge, authority, or money: *I'm afraid I'm not in a position to answer your questions.* | *We are not in a position to publish the results of the survey yet.*

it is not possible for sb to do sth /ɪt ɪz nɒt ˌpɒsəbəl fəʳ (sb) tə 'duː (sth)‖-ˌpɑː-/ FORMAL use this to explain to someone that the situation prevents you or another person from doing something: *It won't be possible for the Director to see you this morning.* | *Unfortunately, it wasn't possible for my daughter to come with me.*

inability to do sth /ˌɪnəˌbɪləti tə 'duː (sth)/ when someone is not able to do something, especially something that you think they should be able to do: *Her actions show an inability to distinguish between fantasy and reality.*
sb's inability to do sth *I felt frustrated by his inability to accept new ideas.*

6 to not be allowed to do something or not have the power to do it

can't/cannot /kɑːnt, 'kænət, -nɒt‖kænt, 'kænɑːt/ [*modal verb*] *"I really want to see that film." "I'm sorry, you can't. You're too young."* | *The President* cannot change a law that has been approved by Congress.

can't do sth You can't get married until you're 16. | I found out that you can't work in the States without getting a work permit.

Formal or informal?

Cannot is more formal than **can't**, and is used especially in written English: *Members of the public cannot enter the building without official permission.* **Cannot** is always written as one word.

not be able to do sth /ˌnɒt biː ˈeɪbəl tə ˈduː (sth)/ use this when a law or rule does not allow someone to do something: *If you don't have a library card, you won't be able to borrow any books.*

powerless /ˈpaʊəˈləs/ [adj] not before noun] FORMAL not able to control or stop something, because you do not have the power or legal right to do it **powerless to do sth** Although we all thought the decision was unfair, we were powerless to change it.

CAREFUL

➡ opposite **CARELESS**

1 when you try to avoid danger or accidents

careful /ˈkeəˈfəl/ [adj] someone who is **careful** tries to avoid danger, risks, or accidents: *You'll be OK with Jane – she's a very careful driver.* | *Everyone learns to be careful when dealing with electricity.*

Q **careful!/be careful!** SPOKEN (=say this when you are warning someone that they must be careful) *That vase is very delicate. Be careful!*
+with *Hey! Careful with that cigarette!*
careful (not) to do sth *You have to be careful not to slip on the ice.*
+(that) *We were always very careful that the teachers didn't catch us.*
careful how/what/who etc *Be very careful how you handle those glasses!*
carefully [adv] *Goodbye, Sarah – drive carefully!*

cautious /ˈkɔːʃəs/ [adj] someone who is **cautious** does not like taking risks

and is always very careful to avoid them: *If we're too cautious, we might lose a good business opportunity.* | *My dad always goes really slowly – he's a very cautious driver.*
+about *I've always been cautious about giving people my phone number.*
cautiously [adv] *Slowly and cautiously, we made our way along the edge of the cliff.*

Q **watch out!/look out!** /ˌwɒtʃ ˈaʊt, ˌlʊk ˈaʊt‖ˌwɑːtʃ-, ˌwɔːtʃ-/ SPOKEN say this to warn someone that they are going to have an accident and they must do something quickly to avoid it: *Watch out – you're going to spill the paint.* | *Look out, Phil – there's a car coming!*

with care/with caution /wɪð ˈkeəˈ, wɪð ˈkɔːʃən/ if you do something **with care** or **with caution**, you are very careful to avoid accidents when you do it: *Some roads may be icy and motorists are advised to drive with caution.*
be handled with care *The paintings are fragile and must be handled with care.*

Formal or informal?

With care and **with caution** are often used when giving advice, and in written instructions on bottles, packages etc that contain things that are dangerous or easy to break: *Toxic materials – handle with caution.*

be on your guard /biː ɒn jɔːˈ ˈgɑːˈd/ to be paying attention to what is happening around you, in order to avoid danger or being tricked: *Police are warning women in the area to be on their guard.*
+against *People were advised to be on their guard against doorstep salesmen.*

not take any chances/take no chances /ˌnɒt teɪk eni ˈtʃɑːnsz, ˌteɪk nəʊ ˈtʃɑːnsz‖-ˈtʃæn-/ to organize something in a very careful way, because you want to avoid any possible risks: *I've lost a lot of money in the past, so I'm not taking any chances this time.*

2 when you try not to make mistakes or do things badly

careful /ˈkeəˈfəl/ [adj] someone who is **careful** tries not to make mistakes, and tries to do everything correctly: *a careful, hard-working student*

+with *Try to be more careful with your punctuation.*
careful to do sth *They were careful not to touch anything until the police arrived.*
carefully [adv] *Check your essay carefully for spelling mistakes.*

take care /,teɪk 'keəʳ/ to do a piece of work carefully because you want it to be right, and you do not want to make mistakes
+with *You need to take a little more care with your work.*
+over *Martin always took great care over every detail.*
take care to do sth *Take care to label all the disks with the correct file names.*

thorough /'θʌrə‖'θʌrəʊ, 'θʌrə/ [adj] not usually before noun] someone who is **thorough** is careful that all the work they do is complete and correct: *Our mechanics will check everything – they're very thorough.*
thoroughly [adv] *All the equipment has been thoroughly tested.*

conscientious /,kɒnʃi'enʃəs‹ ‖,kɑːn-/ [adj] someone who is **conscientious** has a careful and responsible attitude to their work or duties, and works hard to do everything that needs to be done: *Ryan has always been a conscientious worker.* | *a conscientious mother*
conscientiously [adv] *The chairman carried out his duties conscientiously.*

meticulous /mɪ'tɪkjʊləs/ [adj] someone who is **meticulous** is very careful about every small detail, and always makes sure that everything is done correctly: *The jewellery was beautifully made, and obviously the work of a meticulous craftsman.*
+about *John's very meticulous about keeping accounts.*
meticulously [adv] *Investigators worked meticulously through the evidence for several months.*

pay attention to sth /,peɪ ə'tenʃən tuː (sth)/ to be careful that a particular thing is done in the right way: *In financial matters, it helps to pay careful attention to the details.*

methodical /mɪ'θɒdɪkəl‖-'θɑː-/ someone who is **methodical** always does their work in a careful planned way and checks that everything is done correctly: *They have a reputation for carrying out methodical research and they always publish their findings.* | *I learned to take my time and be more methodical.*

3 careful work/actions

careful /'keəʳfəl/ [adj only before noun] a **careful** test, study, piece of work etc is done carefully and correctly, with a lot of attention to details: *A careful inspection showed cracks in the foundation of the building.* | *Her book is the result of years of careful research.*

thorough /'θʌrə‖'θʌrəʊ, 'θʌrə/ [adj] a **thorough** search, check, examination etc is done carefully so that no detail is missed: *The police have made a thorough search of the area.* | *The doctor gave me a thorough check-up.*

systematic /,sɪstə'mætɪk‹/ [adj] a **systematic** way of doing something is organized carefully and done thoroughly, especially using a fixed plan: *It's essential to have a systematic way of organizing your work.* | *a systematic approach to record-keeping*
systematically [adv] *The whole area was systematically explored, mapped, and investigated.*

painstaking /'peɪnz,teɪkɪŋ/ [adj] very careful and thorough, and taking a lot of time and effort: *They began the long and painstaking task of compiling a bibliography.*
painstakingly [adv] *The poet's house has been painstakingly restored.*

Formal or informal?

Painstaking is not used in informal conversation.

CARELESS

➡ opposite **CAREFUL**

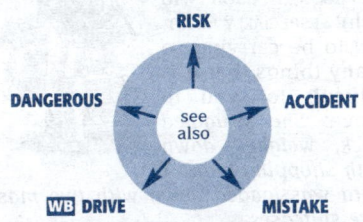

RISK

DANGEROUS → see also ← ACCIDENT

WB DRIVE — MISTAKE

1 careless, so that accidents happen

careless /ˈkeəʳləs/ [adj] someone who is **careless** does not take care to avoid accidents and is likely to damage something or hurt someone: *a careless driver* | *the careless handling of explosives*
+about *The airline was accused of being careless about security.*
carelessly [adv] *Someone had carelessly dropped a cigarette end into the wastebasket.*
carelessness [n U] *Her injuries were caused by someone else's carelessness.*

clumsy /ˈklʌmzi/ [adj] someone who is **clumsy** moves or handles things in a careless or awkward way, so that they often drop things or break things: *As a child, I was tall and clumsy.* | *Paula always felt clumsy when she had to serve food to people.* | *a large man with big, clumsy hands*
clumsy – clumsier – clumsiest
clumsily [adv] *I got up, clumsily knocking against the table.*

irresponsible /ˌɪrɪˈspɒnsɨbəl‖-ˈspɑːn-/ [adj] someone who is **irresponsible** does not do the things they should do, or does things they should not do, usually with harmful results: *I think teenage boys are far more irresponsible than girls.* | *The government has joined the police in condemning the irresponsible behaviour of a small minority of fans.*

reckless /ˈrekləs/ [adj] ESPECIALLY WRITTEN someone who is **reckless** does dangerous or stupid things without thinking that they or someone else might get hurt: *He was angry and that always made him reckless.*
reckless driving *The driver of the car was arrested for reckless driving.* | *a reckless disregard for human life*
recklessly [adv] *people who recklessly risk their lives in a dangerous sport*

negligence /ˈneglɪdʒəns/ [n U] FORMAL when someone does not do an important job carefully enough, especially with the result that there is an accident and they are punished for causing it: *Dr Forbes was found guilty of medical negligence.* | *You can claim compensation if your injury is a result of your employer's negligence.*
negligent [adj] *The court said that the teacher had been negligent in not reporting the accident.*

2 careless, so that you make mistakes

careless /ˈkeəʳləs/ [adj] someone who is **careless** makes mistakes because they do not think carefully enough about what they are doing: *I made a few careless mistakes.*
+with *Don't be so careless with your money.*
it is careless of sb (to do sth) *It was very careless of you to leave your purse lying on the desk.*
carelessly [adv] *He had carelessly switched off his computer without saving the data.*
carelessness [n U] *Lyra's weaknesses are carelessness and a lack of organizational skills.*

sloppy /ˈslɒpi‖ˈslɑːpi/ [adj] INFORMAL done in a careless and lazy way – use this about someone's work or the way someone writes or speaks: *At school, his work was always sloppy.* | *The company's failure was blamed on sloppy management.*
sloppy – sloppier – sloppiest

3 when you decide too quickly

rash /ræʃ/ [adj] if you do something **rash**, you do not think carefully about the effect it will have, and you wish later you had not done it: *I advised him to think carefully and not do anything rash.*

a rash promise/statement etc *Don't make any rash promises that you may regret later.*

rashly [*adv*] *I rashly offered to lend her the money.*

hasty /ˈheɪsti/ [*adj*] too quick to do or say something, without taking time to think about it first: *I think I was a little hasty. I shouldn't have accused him of lying.*

a hasty decision *Don't make any hasty decisions.*

hastily [*adv*] *He later admitted that he had acted too hastily.*

CARRY

➡ see also **TAKE/BRING, LIFT, HOLD**

1 to carry something or someone

carry /ˈkæri/ [*v* T] to take something from one place to another, by holding it in your hands, supporting it on your back etc: *A porter helped me carry my bags.*

carry

carry sth to/out of/around etc *The women have to carry water from the well to the village. | I've been carrying this tape-recorder around with me all day.*

carrying – carried – have carried

> ⚠ Don't confuse **carry** (=take something somewhere, usually by holding it in your hands) with **hold** (=have something in your hands) and **lift** (=move something to a higher position, usually with your hands).

> ⚠ Don't confuse **carry** and **take**. Don't say 'I carried him home in my car'. Say **I took him home in my car**.

be weighed down with sth/be loaded down with sth /biː ˌweɪd ˈdaʊn wɪð (sth), biː ˌləʊdɪd ˈdaʊn wɪð (sth)/ ESPECIALLY WRITTEN to be carrying so many things that it is difficult for you to move: *She struggled back, weighed down with shopping bags. |*

be weighed down

Cora was loaded down with two massive suitcases.

be loaded with sth /biː ˈləʊdɪd wɪð (sth)/ if a vehicle **is loaded with** something, it is carrying a lot of it: *A truck loaded with cement had crashed into the wall.*

be heavily loaded *a bus heavily loaded with passengers*

2 easy to carry

portable /ˈpɔːrtəbəl/ [*adj* usually before noun]

portable TV/computer/typewriter/heater etc a television, computer etc that is fairly small and easy to carry around with you: *She has a small portable TV in the kitchen. | He still writes his novels on an old portable typewriter.*

CATCH

➡ look here for ...
- catch a ball
- catch someone after chasing them
- see someone doing something wrong
- catch an animal

1 to catch a ball or other moving object

➡ see also **THROW, WB SPORT**

catch /kætʃ/ [*v* T] to get hold of a ball or other object that is moving through the air: *I caught the ball with my left hand and threw it back to Ted.*

🔍 **catch!** (say this when you throw something to someone) SPOKEN *Here's your lighter – catch!*

catching – caught – have caught

2 to catch someone who is trying to escape

➡ see also **RUN, FOLLOW, ESCAPE, PRISON**

catch /kætʃ/ [v T] to stop someone who is trying to escape, especially by running after them and holding them: *"I bet you can't catch me!" Katie said, running off.* | *The police caught two of the three bank robbers after a car chase through the city.*
catching – caught – have caught

capture /'kæptʃəʳ/ [v T] to catch an enemy, especially after defeating them in a war or battle: *The rebel leader was captured and publicly executed.* | *They captured twenty enemy soldiers.*

take sb prisoner /ˌteɪk (sb) 'prɪzənəʳ/ to catch someone, especially in a war, and keep them as a prisoner: *350 enemy soldiers were killed, and 300 more were taken prisoner.*

3 when the police catch a criminal

see also **WB POLICE, TELL 5**

catch /kætʃ/ [v T] if the police **catch** someone who has done something illegal, they find that person and stop them from escaping: *Police have so far failed to catch the murderer.* | *The thieves were never caught.*
catching – caught – have caught

arrest /ə'rest/ [v T] if the police **arrest** someone, they take them to a police station because they believe that person has done something illegal: *Police arrested nine men in a drugs raid.*
arrest sb for sth *Wayne was arrested for dangerous driving.*

arrest [n C/U] when someone is arrested by the police: *His confessions led to the arrest of several well-known gangsters.*
make an arrest (=arrest someone) *Police made a number of arrests after a fight in a city bar.*
be under arrest (=to have been arrested) *A man is now under arrest for the assault.*
place/put sb under arrest (=to arrest

someone) *He was brought in for questioning and placed under arrest.*

◯ **get** /get/ [v T] SPOKEN INFORMAL to find the person who has done something illegal, and punish them: *They never actually got the man who did it.* | *Did the police get the people who stole your car?*
getting – got – have got

4 to catch someone while they are doing something wrong

catch /kætʃ/ [v T] to find or see someone while they are doing something wrong
catch sb doing sth *Monica caught her son stealing money from her purse.*
get caught *Be careful you don't get caught!*
be/get caught doing sth *Paul was caught cheating in a test.*
catch sb red-handed/catch sb in the act (=while they are in the process of doing something wrong, especially stealing) *"Are you sure Gavin took it?" "I caught him red-handed!"*
catching – caught – have caught

5 to catch an animal

catch /kætʃ/ [v T] to get an animal, for example by using a net or trap, and stop it from escaping: *Did you catch any fish?* | *a trap to catch mice*
catching – caught – have caught

trap /træp/ [v T] to catch an animal or bird using special equipment that will hold them so that they cannot escape: *Some of the birds had been shot, others trapped.*
trapping – trapped – have trapped

trap /træp/ [n C] a piece of equipment used to trap animals and birds: *The wolf had been caught in a trap.*

When you see **EC**, go to the
ESSENTIAL COMMUNICATION section.

CAUSE

➡ see also **REASON**

1 to make something happen

cause /kɔːz/ [v T] to make something happen, especially something bad: *Smoking causes cancer.* | *The fire caused $30,000 worth of damage.* | *A lot of traffic accidents are caused by carelessness.*
cause sb embarrassment/anxiety/pain (=make someone feel embarrassed, anxious etc) *Robert's behaviour is causing his family a lot of anxiety.*
cause sth to do sth FORMAL *Inflation has caused fuel prices to rise sharply in recent months.*

> **Formal or informal?**
> The usual verb for saying that one thing makes another thing happen is **make**, not **cause**: *The smoke made me cough.* **Cause**, followed by an infinitive, is used mostly in formal or technical writing: *This reaction causes the body temperature to rise.*

> ⚠ Don't say 'cause that something happens'. Say **cause something to happen**.

make /meɪk/ [v T] to make someone do something or make something happen
make sb/sth do sth *Sarah's really funny – she always makes me laugh.* | *A new hairstyle can make you look years younger.*
make sb angry/happy/nervous etc *Stop staring at me – you're making me nervous!*
make sth better/worse/easier etc *The senator's recent remarks seem to have made the situation worse.*
make it easy/difficult/impossible etc for sb to do sth *The new rail service should make it easier for commuters to get to work.*
making – made – have made

> ⚠ Don't say 'she made him to cry'. Say **she made him cry**.

be responsible for sth /biː rɪˈspɒnsɪbəl fɔːʳ (sth)‖-ˈspɑːn-/ if a person, or something that they do, **is responsible for** an accident, problem, mistake etc, it is their fault that it happens: *I felt partly responsible for the fact that her boyfriend left her.* | *Who is responsible for all this mess?*

> Don't use 'of' after **responsible**.

bring about sth /ˌbrɪŋ əˈbaʊt (sth)/ [*phrasal verb* T] to make something happen, especially a change or an improved situation: *The war brought about huge social and political changes.* | *Many improvements in public health have been brought about by advances in medical science.*

result in sth /rɪˈzʌlt ɪn (sth)/ [*phrasal verb* T] if an action or event **results in** something, it makes something happen: *The train crash resulted in the deaths of all 52 passengers.* | *All these changes in the rules have resulted in great confusion.*

lead to sth /ˈliːd tuː (sth)/ [*phrasal verb* T] if an action or event **leads to** something, it starts a process which finally makes something happen: *His research eventually led to the development of a vaccine.* | *The bank has offered a reward for any information leading to the arrest of the robbers.*

trigger off sth /ˌtrɪgər ˈɒf (sth)‖-ˈɔːf-/ [*phrasal verb* T] if a small action or event **triggers off** something more serious, it makes it happen very quickly: *the events that triggered off World War I*

2 the thing that makes something else happen

cause /kɔːz/ [n C] the thing that makes something else happen, especially something bad: *The increase in violent crime has several causes.*
+of *They still haven't found out the cause of the fire.*
root cause (=the most basic and important cause) *The root cause of Britain's economic problems is lack of investment.*

Don't say 'the cause for something'. Say **the cause of something**.

factor /ˈfæktəʳ/ [n C] one of several reasons that explain why something happens or why a situation exists: *The rise in crime is mainly due to factors such as unemployment.*
+in *Wright's skill and experience has been an important factor in the team's success.*

CHANCE

➡ look here for ...
• the chance to do something interesting, exciting etc
• when something happens without being planned

1 when you have the chance to do something

chance /tʃɑːnsǁtʃæns/ [n C] a situation in which it is possible for you to do something enjoyable or exciting, or something that you want to do
get/have the chance *It's a beautiful building – you should go and see it if you have the chance.*
+to do sth *I never got the chance to thank him for all his help.*
give sb the chance to do sth *I wish he'd just give me the chance to explain.*
a second chance (=another chance after you have failed the first time) *Viewers will have a second chance to see Saturday's concert on Channel 4 tonight.*
take the chance to do sth (=use a chance when you have it) *Take the chance to travel while you're still young.*
sb's last chance (=when you will not have another chance) *It was her last chance to see him before she left town.*
miss a chance (=not use a chance when you have it) *Diane never misses the chance of a free meal.*
jump at the chance (of doing sth) (=eagerly do something exciting when you get the chance) *You're so lucky. I'd jump at the chance of going to Hollywood.*

opportunity /ˌɒpəˈtjuːnᵻtiǁˌɑːpərˈtuː-/ [n C] a chance to do something, especially something that is important or useful to you, or something that you want to do very much
have the opportunity (to do sth) *He didn't have the opportunity to go to university when he was younger.*
opportunity for sb (to do sth) *Companies should provide more opportunities for workers to broaden their skills.*
take/seize an opportunity (=use an opportunity) *I'd like to take this opportunity to thank you all for your support.*
miss an opportunity (to do sth) (=not use an opportunity when you have one)
career/job opportunities (=chances to find a job) *There are a wide range of career opportunities for young people.*
plural **opportunities**

golden opportunity /ˌgəʊldən ɒpəˈtjuːnᵻtiǁ-ˌɑːpərˈtuː-/ [n C] an extremely good opportunity that is very unlikely to happen again: *I saw it as a golden opportunity – the chance I'd been waiting for.*
a golden opportunity (for sb) to do sth *This is a golden opportunity for you to go back to college. Don't waste it.*

the chance of a lifetime /ðə ˌtʃɑːns əv ə ˈlaɪftaɪmǁ-ˌtʃæns-/ the chance to do something very exciting or important, that you might never have the opportunity to do again: *It was the chance of a lifetime – I had to go.*

2 when something happens for no reason or without being planned

➡ see also **LUCKY/UNLUCKY**

by chance /baɪ ˈtʃɑːnsǁ-ˈtʃæns/ if something happens **by chance**, it is not deliberate or planned and you did not expect it to happen: *I met an old friend by chance on the train.*
quite/purely/entirely by chance (=completely by chance) *Quite by chance, we both ended up working for the same company.*

by accident /baɪ ˈæksᵻdənt/ if something happens **by accident**, it happens in a way that is not planned or intended: *I* got involved in this field of research almost by accident.

quite/entirely/purely by accident (=completely by accident) We met quite by accident.

coincidence /kəʊˈɪnsɪ̩dəns/ [n C/U] a surprising situation, when two similar things happen at the same time, or two or more people do the same thing, but no one planned or intended this to happen:

🔍 **what a coincidence!** SPOKEN What a coincidence! I didn't know you were going to be in Geneva too.

by coincidence By coincidence, Jill was wearing the same dress as me.

by a strange / curious / amazing coincidence By a strange coincidence, all three girls had boyfriends called Simon.

happen to do sth /̩hæpən tə ˈduː (sth)/ if you **happen to** meet someone, go somewhere, or see something, you do it by chance and not because you planned to do it: A police car just happened to be driving past when the robbery took place.

🔍 **as it happens** /əz ɪt ˈhæpənz/ SPOKEN say **as it happens** when you are mentioning a fact that is connected, by chance, with what you have just been talking about: "I'm thinking of selling my guitar." "Well, as it happens, I know someone who's thinking of buying one."

luck /lʌk/ [n U] the way in which good or bad things happen to people by chance, not because they were planned or intended

it's a matter of luck/it's just luck (=it depends on luck) There's no skill in roulette; it's all a matter of luck.

fate /feɪt/ [n U] the power which some people believe controls what happens in everyone's lives: It was fate that we should meet.

by a twist of fate (=because fate made things happen in an unexpected way) By a strange twist of fate, the twin brothers married twin sisters.

CHANGE

➡ see also **DIFFERENT, SAME, BECOME**

1 to become different

change /tʃeɪndʒ/ [v I] The city has changed a lot in recent years. | She's really changed since she went to college. | the changing role of women in society

+into The caterpillar eventually changes into a beautiful butterfly.

change from sth to/into sth In the 18th century, Britain changed from a mainly agricultural society to an industrial one.

change colour BRITISH **change color** AMERICAN It was October, and the leaves on the trees were starting to change colour.

alter /ˈɔːltəʳ/ [v I] ESPECIALLY WRITTEN to change – use this especially about someone's feelings or behaviour, or about a situation: His mood suddenly altered and he seemed a little annoyed. | The political situation altered dramatically in 1979.

Formal or informal?

Alter is more formal than **change**, and is used mostly in writing.

---

vary /ˈveəri/ [v I] if something **varies**, it changes according to what the situation is: Ticket prices to New York vary depending on the time of year.

vary considerably/widely (=change a lot) Her income varies considerably from one month to the next.

+according to These dates may vary according to the requirements of the course.

🔍 **it varies** SPOKEN (used to say that something changes according to the situation) "What kind of food do you like best?" "Well, it varies."

varying – varied – have varied

turn into sth /ˈtɜːʳn ɪntuː (sth)/ [phrasal verb T] to become something completely different: a story about a frog that turns into a prince | A trip to the beach turned into a nightmare for a local family yesterday.

🔍 **go from ... to ...** /ˈgəʊ frɒm ... tuː .../ ESPECIALLY SPOKEN to stop being on thing and start being something else, especially something very different: *In less than five years, he went from being a communist to being a member of the military government.* | *His face went from pink to bright red.*

2 to make someone or something different

change /tʃeɪndʒ/ [v T] to make someone or something different and usually better: *Unfortunately, there's nothing we can do to change the situation.* | *Being at college has changed her – she seems much more confident now.*

alter /ˈɔːltəʳ/ [v T] to change something so that it is better or more suitable: *The border was closed, and they were forced to alter their plans.* | *You can alter the colour and size of the image using a remote control.*

> **Formal or informal?**
> **Alter** is more formal than **change**.

make changes /ˌmeɪk ˈtʃeɪndʒɪz/ to change some parts of a system or the way something is done, but not all of it: *Williams intends to make a few changes.*
+to/in *When you get married, you'll have to make some changes to your lifestyle.*

reform /rɪˈfɔːʳm/ [v T] to change a law, system, or organization, so that it is fairer or more effective: *plans to reform the voting system* | *Health care needs to be completely reformed.*

adapt/modify /əˈdæpt, ˈmɒdɪ̥faɪ‖ˈmɑː-/ [v T] to change something slightly in order to improve it or make it suitable for a different purpose: *How much would it cost to adapt the existing equipment?* | *a modified version of the original computer program* | *You can adapt the recipe to suit your own requirements.*
adapt/modify sth for sth *All our facilities have been modified for use by people in wheelchairs.*
modifying – modified – have modified

> **Formal or informal?**
> **Adapt** and **modify** are used especially in formal or technical writing and speech.

revise /rɪˈvaɪz/ [v T] to change an existing plan, idea, or law etc because of new information or ideas: *Canada has promised to revise its rules that prevent foreign ownership in the broadcast industry.* | *a revised business plan*

3 to make something completely different

transform /trænsˈfɔːʳm/ [v T often in passive] to completely change something, especially so that it is much better: *When she smiled, her face was completely transformed.*
transform sth into sth *In the last 20 years, Korea has been transformed into a major industrial nation.*

turn sth into sth /ˈtɜːʳn (sth) ɪntuː (sth)/ [phrasal verb T] to make something become a completely different thing, for example because you want to use it for a different purpose: *We're planning to turn the study into an extra bedroom.* | *The book was later turned into a movie.*

revolutionize (also **revolutionise** BRITISH) /ˌrevəˈluːʃənaɪz/ [v T] to completely and permanently change the way people do something or think about something, especially because of a new idea or invention: *Computers have revolutionized the way we work.*

4 easy to change

flexible /ˈfleksɪ̥bəl/ [adj] methods, systems, or rules that are **flexible** can easily be changed if necessary: *flexible working hours* | *Your schedule should be flexible enough to cope with interruptions or unexpected tasks.*

5 a change

change /tʃeɪndʒ/ [n C/U] when people or things become different: *In the future, we are sure to see a lot of changes.* | *Many people are frightened of change.*
+in *House plants are often sensitive to changes in the temperature.*

social / economic / political / techno-logical change *1989 was a year of great political change in Eastern Europe.*

big/major change *There have been big changes in the way languages are taught in schools.*

a change for the better/worse (=one that makes a situation better or worse) *For most ordinary workers, the new tax laws represent a change for the worse.*

alteration /ˌɔːltəˈreɪʃən/ [n C/U] a change, especially a small change in someone's behaviour, or in a plan, design, or document

+in *Recently, there had been a definite alteration in his manner.*

make alterations (to sth) *We've made one or two small alterations to the house.*

minor alteration (=small alteration) *After a few minor alterations, the proposal was accepted.*

Formal or informal?

Alteration is more formal than **change**

---

reform /rɪˈfɔːrm/ [n C/U] a change that is made to a political, legal, or social system, in order to make it fairer or more effective

+of *the reform of local government*

radical reform (=when things are changed very thoroughly) *The Socialists have promised a programme of radical social reform.*

economic/educational/welfare etc reform *the slow process of economic reform*

revolution /ˌrevəˈluːʃən/ [n C] a complete and permanent change in the way people do things or think about things

+in *Piaget's ideas caused a revolution in education.*

scientific/technological/social etc revolution *The 1970s saw the beginnings of a new technological revolution, based on microelectronics.*

upheaval /ʌpˈhiːvəl/ [n C/U] a big change in your life or in the way things are organized, especially when this causes problems and anxiety

+for *Moving to a different school can be a major upheaval for young children.*

social / political / emotional etc

upheaval *The recent civil war caused enormous social and economic upheaval.*

---
6 to change where you live, what you do etc
---

change /tʃeɪndʒ/ [v I/T] to change what you do or use, where you go etc, and start doing or using something else instead: *I'm thinking of changing my car.* (=selling it and getting another one)

change jobs/schools/doctors etc (=change your job, the school you go to, the doctor you go to etc) *Alex will be changing schools in September.*

change places/seats (=when two people sit in each other's seats) *Would you mind changing places so I can sit next to my girlfriend?*

change from sth to sth *Nowadays, people change from one cellphone to another all the time.*

switch /swɪtʃ/ [v I/T] to change from doing or using one thing to doing or using something completely different, especially suddenly

switch (from sth) to sth *She worked as a librarian before switching to journalism. | We hope more and more travellers will switch from road to rail.*

switch jobs/sides etc (=change your job, the group you support etc) *School-leavers often switch jobs several times before finding one that suits them.*

Formal or informal?

Switch is more informal than **change**

---

move /muːv/ [v I/T] to go to live in a different house or city, or move the place where you work to a different office or city: *Karen doesn't live here anymore – she's moved.*

+to *We moved to Memphis when I was eight.*

+into *The new offices should be ready for the company to move into very soon.*

move house/office BRITISH (=move from one house or office to a different one)

convert to sth /kənˈvɜːrt tuː (sth)/ [phrasal verb T]

convert to Christianity/Islam/Juda-ism etc to change to a different religion from the one that you believed in before: *She converted to Catholicism at the time of her marriage.*

used to a new situation: *Children are often more adaptable than adults.* | *All my life I've moved around and I've learnt to be adaptable.*

7 to change your plans, opinions, or decisions

change your mind /ˌtʃeɪndʒ jɔːʳ 'maɪnd/ to change your plans, opinions, or decisions: *Are you still coming out tonight, or have you changed your mind?*
+about *I've changed my mind about Terry – he's actually a pretty nice guy.*

have second thoughts /hæv ˌsekənd 'θɔːts/ to feel less sure about something that you intended to do, and begin to think it may not be a good idea: *At first she agreed, but then she seemed to have second thoughts.*
+about *Martin was having second thoughts about accepting the job.*

get cold feet /get ˌkəʊld 'fiːt/ INFORMAL to suddenly feel that you are not sure or confident enough about something that you had intended to do: *The whole project failed after the biggest sponsor got cold feet.*

come around (also **come round** BRITISH) /ˌkʌm (ə)'raʊnd/ [*phrasal verb* I] to gradually change your mind and begin to agree with someone, although you did not agree with them before: *We had to work hard to persuade her, but she finally came around.*
come around to sb's point of view/ come around to an idea *Give him time, and I'm sure he'll come round to your point of view.*

8 willing to change your ideas, opinions, or the way you do something

flexible /'fleksɪbəl/ [*adj*] willing to change your ideas, plans, or methods according to the situation: *Which day do you want to meet? I'm fairly flexible.*
+about *It's easier to find a job if you can be flexible about where you work.*

adaptable /ə'dæptəbəl/ [*adj*] someone who is **adaptable** does not get upset or annoyed if they have to change the way they do things, and easily gets

9 not changing and always the same

permanent /'pɜːʳmənənt/ [*adj*] something that is **permanent** continues forever or for a very long time: *We're hoping to find a permanent solution to the problem.* | *a permanent job* | *The accident left her with permanent brain damage.*

fixed /fɪkst/ [*adj*] use this about amounts, prices, or times that cannot be changed: *The classes begin and end at fixed times.*
fixed income/price/rate etc *Workers are paid a fixed rate per hour.*

constant /'kɒnstənt‖'kɑːn-/ [*adj*] use this about an amount or level that remains the same over a long period: *An animal's fur helps it to maintain a constant body temperature.*
remain/stay constant *The noise level remained constant throughout the day.*

> **Formal or informal?**
> **Constant** is often used in formal scientific writing.

steady /'stedi/ [*adj*] use this about an amount that remains the same or a process that continues in the same way over a long period, especially when this is a good thing: *a steady improvement* | *They drove along at a steady 80 kilometres per hour.*
a steady stream/flow *There's been a steady stream of visitors at the centre.*
steady – steadier – steadiest
steadily [*adv*] *The standard of living has been rising steadily for 20 years.*

stable /'steɪbəl/ [*adj*] use this about prices, amounts, or levels that are no longer changing, after a period when they were changing a lot: *Fuel prices have become more stable after several increases last year.*
remain stable *His temperature remained stable throughout the night.*

10 unwilling to change your ideas or opinions

➡ see also EC **DETERMINED**

stubborn /'stʌbəʳn/ [adj] someone who is **stubborn** refuses to change their ideas or opinions, even when other people think they are being unreasonable: *Myra had strong views and could be very stubborn at times.*

be set in your ways /bi: ˌset ɪn jɔːʳ 'weɪz/ INFORMAL someone who **is set in their ways** does not want to change the way they do things, because they have done them in the same way for a long time: *I'm too old and set in my ways to get married again now.*

rigid /'rɪdʒɪd/ [adj] someone who is **rigid** will never change their mind about what is right or wrong or about how things should be done: *The opposition has accused the government of being too rigid in opposing the Kyoto treaty on global warming.* | *the rigid sexual morals of Victorian Britain*

11 changing a lot

changeable /'tʃeɪndʒəbəl/ [adj] something that is **changeable** changes often, so that you do not know what to expect next: *In the mountains the weather is very changeable.* | *the changeable international situation*

variable /'veəriəbəl/ [adj] changing according to the situation – use this about amounts, prices, speeds, temperatures etc: *The price of petrol is variable, depending on where you buy it.*

When you see **WB**, go to the **WORD BANKS** section.

CHEAP

➡ opposite **EXPENSIVE**

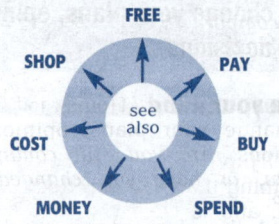

1 not costing much money

cheap /tʃiːp/ [adj] something that is **cheap** costs very little money, or costs less than you expected: *My shoes were really cheap – they only cost $15.* | *The cheapest way to get to Chicago is to take the bus.*

it is cheap to do sth *It's cheaper to phone after six o'clock.*

relatively cheap (=cheap compared with other things) *Wooden houses are relatively cheap to build.*

get sth cheap (=buy something for a lower price than you expected) *If you want to get something cheap, go to the market.*

cheaply [adv] *You can buy electronic diaries fairly cheaply nowadays.*

inexpensive /ˌɪnɪk'spensɪv◂/ [adj] not expensive – use this especially about things that are of good quality, even though they do not cost a lot: *The furniture is inexpensive but well-made.* | *a simple, inexpensive meal* | *Beans and lentils are an inexpensive source of protein.*

> **Formal or informal?**
> **Inexpensive** is more formal than **cheap**.

🔾 **not cost much** /nɒt 'kɒst ˌmʌtʃ‖ -'kɔːst-/ ESPECIALLY SPOKEN to not be expensive: *We had a very good meal and it didn't cost much.*

it doesn't cost much to do sth *It doesn't cost much to rent a TV.*

economical /ˌekə'nɒmɪkəl◂, ˌiː-‖-'nɑː-/ [adj] cheap to use or cheap to do – use this about cars, machines, or ways of doing things that do not waste any money, fuel etc: *Gas is* usually the most economical fuel for heating a house.

be economical to use/run/operate This is a well-designed car that is also very economical to run.

it is more economical to do sth If you compare the prices, it's more economical to buy the big packet.

2 cheap but bad quality

cheap /tʃiːp/ [adj usually before noun] something that is **cheap** does not cost much, and is clearly of bad quality: The tourist shops were full of cheap souvenirs. | a woman smelling of cheap perfume

cheap and nasty BRITISH (=cheap and unattractive because it is of very bad quality) The jewellery in this catalogue looks really cheap and nasty.

3 when you get something good for a low price

be good value /biː gʊd 'væljuː/ to be worth the price that you pay for it: The meals at Charlie's Pizza are really good value.

good value for money There's a special ticket that means you can see six concerts, which is definitely good value for money.

bargain /'bɑːrgɪn/ [n C] something that costs a lot less than you expect or a lot less than it usually costs: Did you get any bargains at the market? | I got this shirt when I was in Thailand. It was a real bargain.

be a good buy /biː ə ˌgʊd 'baɪ/ something that **is a good buy** is worth the price you pay for it, because it is not expensive but is still good: The Brazilian white wine is a good buy at only £2.99 a bottle.

> ⚠ Use **a good buy** about goods or products, but not about services such as travel, entertainment, or meals.

good deal /ˌgʊd 'diːl/ [n C] if something is a **good deal**, it is worth the price you pay, especially because it includes a lot of extra things or services: They're selling three litres for the price of two, so it's a really good deal.

give sb a good deal They gave me a pretty good deal on my camera.
get a good deal We got a good deal on the tickets, which meant we could afford to stay in a better hotel.

reasonable /'riːzənəbəl/ [adj] **reasonable** prices seem fair because they are not too high: They sell good-quality computer equipment at reasonable prices. | Only £15 a night? That's very reasonable!

4 when the price has been reduced

sale /seɪl/ [n C] a time when a shop sells things more cheaply than usual: The bookstore is having a closing-down sale.

the sales BRITISH (=when a lot of shops sell things at reduced prices) The sales start in January. | I bought this coat half price in the sales.

on sale /ɒn 'seɪl/ AMERICAN something that is **on sale** is being sold at a specially low price in a shop: "How much was your jacket?" "I got it on sale for $45."

reduced /rɪ'djuːst‖-'duːst/ [adj not before noun] goods that are **reduced** are being sold at a lower price than usual: Everything is reduced because the store's closing down next month.
+from ... to ... The CDs were reduced from $10 to $5.

£5/$20/10% etc off /(£5 etc) 'ɒf‖-'ɔːf/ if there is **£5, $20, 10% etc off** something, its usual price has been reduced by that amount: There's 20% off all computers in Dixon's summer sale.

discount /'dɪskaʊnt/ [n C] a reduction in the price you pay for something, which is given for a special reason
get a discount (=pay less) Do you get a discount if you pay in cash?
+on Workers at the store get a discount on books and records.
30%/£50 etc discount a 30% discount on all electrical goods.
at a discount (=at a reduced price) Air UK are currently offering tickets to students at a special discount.

special offer /ˌspeʃəl 'ɒfəʳ‖-'ɔːf-/ [n C] a very low price that a shop, restaurant etc sells something for, in order to persuade more people to buy things

there: *There's a special offer of two meals for the price of one.*
+on *Look out for this week's special offer on Australian wines.*

cut-price /ˌkʌt ˈpraɪs‹/ [*adj* only before noun] **cut-price** goods or services are cheaper than normal: *cut-price cigarettes | a travel operator offering cut-price deals on winter holidays*

CHEAT

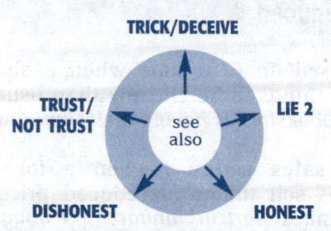

TRICK/DECEIVE

TRUST/ NOT TRUST — see also — **LIE 2**

DISHONEST — **HONEST**

---

1 to get money or possessions from someone dishonestly

cheat /tʃiːt/ [*v* T] *Be careful of salesmen who come to the door. They may be trying to cheat you.*
cheat sb out of sth *The woman claims that the company cheated her out of £36,000.*

swindle /ˈswɪndl/ [*v* T] to get money from a person or organization by cheating them, especially using clever and complicated methods: *He was jailed in 1992 for attempting to swindle the insurance company he worked for.*
swindle sb out of sth *Investors have been swindled out of millions of pounds.*

con /kɒnǁkɑːn/ [*v* T] INFORMAL to persuade someone to buy something or to give you money by telling them lies
con sb out of sth *Baker conned his followers out of £100 million.*
con sb into doing sth *The gang conned an elderly woman into giving her cash card away.*
conning – conned – have conned

fiddle /ˈfɪdl/ [*v* T] BRITISH INFORMAL to give false information or make dishonest changes in financial records, in order to get money or

avoid paying money: *My boss thinks I've been fiddling my travel expenses.*
fiddle the books/fiddle the accounts (=change a company's financial records) *The company secretary had been fiddling the books for years.*

embezzle /ɪmˈbezəl/ [*v* T] to steal a lot of money from the place where you work: *He has been charged with embezzling money from public funds, and could face up to 10 years in jail.*

fleece /fliːs/ [*v* T] INFORMAL to cheat someone by tricking or persuading them into giving you a lot of money: *As she made her wedding vows, she was already planning how she could fleece him of every penny he had. | The authorities are trying to recover the money he fleeced from investors.*

---

2 to make someone pay too much money for something

overcharge /ˌəʊvəˈtʃaːˈdʒ/ [*v* I/T] to make someone pay too much for something in a shop, a restaurant, a taxi etc: *The cab driver overcharged us by $20.*
overcharge sb for sth *The meal was good, but we were overcharged for the wine.*

rip off /ˌrɪp ˈɒfǁ-ˈɔːf/ [*phrasal verb* T] SPOKEN INFORMAL to make someone pay much more than the usual price for something
rip sb off *They really ripped us off at that hotel.*
rip off sb *Bars by the sea make huge profits by ripping off tourists.*

a rip-off /ə ˈrɪp ɒfǁ-ɔːf/ [*n* singular] SPOKEN INFORMAL if something is **a rip-off**, it is much too expensive and you think that someone is trying to cheat you: *"It cost £200 to get it fixed." "What a rip-off!"*
a complete/total rip-off *The meal cost me $80 – it was a total rip-off.*

3 to cheat in an examination or game

cheat /tʃiːt/ [v I] to use dishonest methods in order to pass an examination or win a game: *Anyone caught cheating will automatically fail the exam.*
+at *Jenny always cheats at cards.*
cheating [n U] when someone cheats in an examination or game: *Some of the boys were suspected of cheating.*

copy /ˈkɒpi‖ˈkɑːpi/ [v I/T] to cheat in an examination, schoolwork etc by looking at someone else's work and writing the same thing as they have
+from *Jenny was accused of copying from the girl next to her.*

4 when people are dishonest in order to get money

fraud /frɔːd/ [n C/U] the crime of getting money dishonestly from a big organization, for example by giving false information or changing documents, especially over a long period: *Big losses due to theft and fraud forced the company to close.* | *Credit card fraud is very common.*

scam /skæm/ [n C] INFORMAL a clever plan for dishonestly getting money or advantages for yourself: *There was a scam in which thousands of people sent £20 to register with a non-existent agency.*
a tax scam (=a way to dishonestly avoid paying tax)

swindle /ˈswɪndl/ [n C] a complicated or clever plan for getting money from people by cheating or deceiving them: *a $2 million insurance swindle* | *The newspaper exposed the swindle in July.*

5 someone who cheats

cheat /tʃiːt/ [n C] someone who behaves dishonestly, especially in an examination or game: *Bergstrom accused his opponent of being a cheat.*

conman/con artist /ˈkɒnmæn, ˈkɒn ˌɑːˈtɪst‖ˈkɑːn-/ [n C] INFORMAL someone who gets money by cheating people

or lying to them: *He was a handsome conman who charmed women into giving him money.*
plural **conmen**

swindler /ˈswɪndləʳ/ [n C] someone who regularly cheats people or organizations to get money: *a convicted swindler*

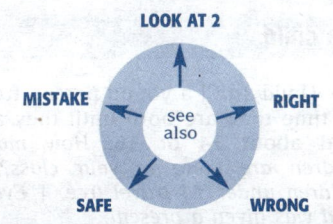

CHECK

LOOK AT 2

MISTAKE — see also — RIGHT

SAFE — WRONG

to make sure that something is true or correct

check /tʃek/ [v I/T] to do something in order to find out whether something is really true or correct: *"Are you sure this is the right phone number?" "Yes, I've just checked."* | *Remember to check your spellings in a dictionary.*
+(that) *I'll just check I locked the door.* | *Check that the meat is cooked thoroughly before serving it.*
+if/whether *Before your trip, check if your insurance covers you abroad.*

make sure /ˌmeɪk ˈʃʊəʳ/ to check that a situation really is the way you want or expect it to be: *I don't think Sarah's back yet, but knock on her door just to make sure.*
+(that) *I phoned the hotel to make sure that they had reserved a room for us.* | *Make sure there are no cars behind you before you drive off.*

double-check /ˌdʌbəl ˈtʃek/ [v I/T] to check a second time, so that you are completely sure: *"Did you switch the heating off?" "Yes, I double-checked."* | *I can't have got it wrong. I checked and double-checked all my calculations.*

CHILD

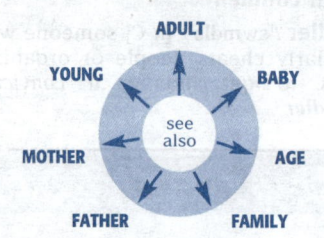

ADULT

YOUNG   BABY

see
also

MOTHER   AGE

FATHER   FAMILY

1 a child

child /tʃaɪld/ [n C] a young person from
the time they are born until they are
aged about 14 or 15: *How many
children are there in your class?* |
Children under 14 travel free. | *Every
child was given a present.*
plural children

> ⚠ You usually call a very young child that
> cannot walk or talk a **baby**.

kid /kɪd/ [n C] INFORMAL a child: *A gang
of kids were playing in the yard.* | *I
really enjoy working with kids.* |
Jamie's a bright kid.

boy /bɔɪ/ [n C] a male child: *I used to
live in Spain when I was a boy.* | *Harry
teaches in a boys' school in Glasgow.*
little boy (=a very young boy) *Her
best friend was a little boy called Sam.*

girl /gɜːʳl/ [n C] a female child: *What's
that girl's name?* | *More girls than ever
before are choosing to study science.*
little girl (=a very young girl) *A little
girl was sitting on the front doorstep.*

toddler /'tɒdləʳ‖'tɑːd-/ [n C] a very young
child who has just learned to walk: *a
playgroup for mothers and toddlers*

2 someone's son or daughter

child /tʃaɪld/ [n C] someone's son or
daughter, of any age: *She called her
first child Katrin.* | *The house seems
very quiet now all the children have left
home.* | *One of her children lives in
Australia now.*
only child (=a child who has no
brothers or sisters)
plural children

kid /kɪd/ [n C] INFORMAL someone's son
or daughter – use this about children
aged up to 14 or 15: *All I ever wanted
was to get married and have kids.*
the kids (use this especially to talk
about your own children) *Could you
look after the kids this evening?*

son /sʌn/ [n C] someone's male child:
We have two teenage sons. | *Her son
used to work in Scotland.*

daughter /'dɔːtəʳ/ [n C] someone's
female child: *Our eldest daughter has
just left university.* | *My aunt had five
daughters and three sons.*

⟢ little boy/little girl /ˌlɪtl 'bɔɪ, ˌlɪtl
'gɜːʳl/ [n C] SPOKEN someone's young
son or daughter: *Paula's had to go
home – her little girl's sick.* | *"How
old's your little boy?" "He's three."*

> ⚠ Use **little boy** or **little girl** when you
> are talking about very young children.

3 a child whose parents have died

orphan /'ɔːʳfən/ [n C] a child whose
parents have died: *Leila was an
orphan whose parents had been killed
in the war.*

4 the time when someone is a child

childhood /'tʃaɪldhʊd/ [n U] the time
when someone is a child: *They've
known each other since childhood.*
early childhood (=the time when you
are very young) *I spent my early childhood in California.*

> ⚠ You can also use **childhood** before a
> noun, like an adjective: *childhood ill-
> nesses* | *He was deeply affected by his early
> childhood experiences.*

in infancy/during infancy /ɪn 'ɪnfənsi,
ˌdjʊərɪŋ 'ɪnfənsi‖ˌdʊr-/ FORMAL while
someone is a baby or a very young
child – use this especially to talk
about children dying or getting
diseases: *Three of her children died in
infancy.*

CHOOSE

➡ see also **DECIDE, VOTE, MUST**

1 to choose something

choose /tʃuːz/ [v I/T] to decide which one of several things or possibilities you want: *I can't decide what I want. You choose.* | *Will you help me choose a present for Warren?*
choose to do sth *I chose to learn Spanish rather than German or French.*
+whether/which/when etc *It took her three hours to choose which dress to wear.*
+between (=choose one of two things) *We had to choose between two houses that were in our price range.*
+from (=choose from among several things) *When hiring a car, you can choose from a wide range of vehicles.*
choosing – chose – have chosen

pick /pɪk/ [v T] to choose something, especially from a particular range that is available: *Pick a number from one to five.* | *Students have to pick two modules during their first year.*

> **Formal or informal?**
> **Pick** is more informal than **choose**.

select /sɪˈlekt/ [v T] FORMAL to choose something by carefully thinking about which is best or most suitable: *We asked Steve to help us select the music for the wedding.* | *Our wines have been carefully selected from vineyards throughout Europe.*

decide on sth /dɪˈsaɪd ɒn (sth)‖-ɑːn-/ [phrasal verb T] to finally choose something, especially when making the decision has been difficult or has taken a long time: *Have you decided on a name for the baby yet?*

○ **go for sth** /ˈgəʊ fɔːʳ (sth)/ [phrasal verb T] SPOKEN INFORMAL to choose something because you think it is the most attractive, interesting, or enjoyable: *She always goes for the most expensive thing on the menu.*

make a choice /ˌmeɪk ə ˈtʃɔɪs/ to make a decision, especially a difficult decision, about which thing to choose: *You don't have to make a choice yet. Think about it a bit longer.*

make the right/wrong choice *He's decided to study law. I hope he's made the right choice.*

opt /ɒpt‖ɑːpt/ [v I] to choose something after thinking carefully about all the possibilities
+for *The government is likely to opt for an election early next spring.*
opt to do sth *When her parents divorced, Mary Ann opted to live with her father.*

> **Formal or informal?**
> **Opt** is more formal than **choose**, and is used especially when talking about choosing a course of action or a product from a range that is available.

2 to choose someone for a job or a team

choose /tʃuːz/ [v T] to decide who is the best person for a job, team, prize etc: *Companies are now using computers to help them choose new workers.*
choose sb as sth *He was chosen as team captain because of his age and experience.*
choose sb to do sth *Eventually, they chose Jane to be their representative.*
choosing – chose – have chosen

select /sɪˈlekt/ [v T] FORMAL to choose someone for a particular job, team, place at school etc, after considering a lot of different people who might be suitable: *The college selects only 12 students from the thousands who apply.*
select sb for sth *We selected four applicants for interview.*
select sb to do sth *Ernst had been selected to play in the game against Belgium.*

appoint /əˈpɔɪnt/ [v T] to officially choose someone to do an important job: *The company has appointed a new Sales Director.*
appoint sb as sth *They have appointed Jane Staller as their new East Coast manager.*
appoint sb to do sth *A committee was appointed to consider changes to the Prison Service.*

pick /pɪk/ [v T] to choose someone for a sports team or an important job: *Joe*

C

picked Steve and Terry to be on his team. | a change in the way the Conservative Party picks its leader

Formal or informal?
Pick is more informal than **choose**.

3 the decision you make when you choose

choice /tʃɔɪs/ [n C] *It was a difficult choice, but we finally decided that Hannah should have the prize. | Of course, financial considerations will influence your choice.*

4 something or someone that has been chosen

choice /tʃɔɪs/ [n singular] something or someone that has been chosen
first/second etc choice (=the thing you wanted most, the thing you wanted most after that etc) *Greece was our first choice for a vacation, but all the flights were full.*
sb's choice of sth (=the thing someone chooses) *I don't like his choice of friends.*

selection /sɪˈlekʃən/ [n C] a small group of the best things that have been chosen from a larger group
+of *She showed me a selection of her drawings. | a selection of songs from 'West Side Story'*

5 the things or people that you can choose from

choice /tʃɔɪs/ [n singular/U]
+of *The school seems OK, but there isn't a great choice of courses.*
have a choice of (=be able to choose from several things) *You will have a choice of twelve questions in the exam.*
wide/good choice (=a lot of things to choose from) *There is a wide choice of hotels and hostels in the town.*

option /ˈɒpʃən‖ˈɑːp-/ [n C] one of the possible things that you can choose to do in a situation
have an option *You have only two options.*
+for *We've considered a range of options for dealing with the situation.*

keep your options open (=delay choosing so that you continue to have several things to choose from) *Anne hasn't decided which college to go to yet. She's keeping her options open.*

alternative /ɔːlˈtɜːʳnətɪv/ [n C] a different way of doing something that you could choose
+to *Is there an alternative to the present system? | The company has already explored possible alternatives to job cuts.*
have no alternative (=to not have a choice about what to do or how to do it) *I didn't want to go to the police, but I had no alternative.*

selection /sɪˈlekʃən/ [n singular] a **selection** of cakes, wines, clothes, books etc is a lot of different cakes, wines etc for you to choose from, especially in a shop
+of *A wonderful selection of cakes and pastries was displayed in the window.*
wide/large selection (=a lot of things to choose from) *The restaurant offers you a wide selection of local dishes.*

6 someone who is very careful about choosing things

choosy /ˈtʃuːzi/ [adj not before noun] INFORMAL someone who is **choosy** chooses things carefully and only wants the things that they think are the best: *I get offered a lot of work now, so I can be more choosy.*
+about *She's very choosy about what airline she travels on.*

fussy/picky /ˈfʌsi, ˈpɪki/ [adj] INFORMAL someone who is **picky** or **fussy** is difficult to please because they only like a few things and will only accept exactly what they want: *Don't be so picky! Eat what you are given.*
+about *She was always very fussy about her clothes.*
fussy/picky eater (=someone who will only eat the few things they like)

selective /sɪˈlektɪv/ [adj not before noun] careful about what you choose, so that you only choose the best or most suitable things
+about *People are becoming more and more selective about what foods they buy.*

Formal or informal?
Selective is more formal than **choosy**.

CLASS IN SOCIETY

social class based on your job, your family, how much you earn etc

➡ if you mean 'a class in a school', go to [WB] **EDUCATION**
➡ see also **POSITION/RANK**

1 someone's social class

class /klɑːsǁklæs/ [n C/U] the social group that you belong to because of your job, the type of family you come from, or the amount of money you have: *At one time, success was based on class rather than on ability.* | *the professional and managerial classes*
the class system (=the system by which society is divided into classes) *The old class system is slowly disappearing.*
social class (=the class in society you come from) *There is a clear link between social class and educational achievement.*
plural **classes**

background /ˈbækɡraʊnd/ [n C] the type of home and family that you come from, and its social class: *The school takes kids from all sorts of backgrounds.* | *We come from the same town and have a similar background.*
working-class/middle-class etc background *The changes are designed to encourage children from working-class backgrounds to go to university.*

2 the highest class

upper-class /ˌʌpəʳ ˈklɑːs◂ǁ-ˈklæs◂/ [adj] belonging to the class of people who originally had most of the money and power, especially families that own a lot of land: *Like many upper-class Englishmen, he was proud of his athletic abilities.* | *He spoke with an upper-class accent.*

the upper class/the upper classes (=people who are upper-class) *the privileges of the upper classes*

 The **upper classes** means the same as **the upper class**.

posh /pɒʃǁpɑːʃ/ [adj] BRITISH SPOKEN someone who is **posh** behaves and speaks in a way in which upper-class people usually behave or speak: *Her parents are terribly posh.*
posh school/hotel/restaurant etc (=one that is very expensive, that rich people go to) *She went to a posh girls' school in Switzerland.*

⚠ People often use the word **posh** when they are making fun of other people who belong to a higher social class.

the aristocracy /ði ˌærɪˈstɒkrəsiǁ-ˈstɑː-/ [n singular] the people who belong to families that own a lot of land and used to have a lot of power, and have special titles before their names, like 'Lord' or 'Lady' – used especially when you are talking about the past: *members of the British aristocracy* | *the French aristocracy*

3 the middle class

middle-class /ˌmɪdl ˈklɑːs◂ǁ-ˈklæs◂/ [adj] belonging to the class of people who are usually well educated, fairly rich, and who work in jobs which they have trained for a long time to do; for example, doctors, lawyers, and managers are middle-class: *a newspaper whose readers are mostly middle-class* | *They live in a middle-class neighbourhood on the edge of town.*
the middle class/the middle classes (=people who are middle-class) *The government needs the support of the middle classes to win the next election.*

 The **middle classes** means the same as **the middle class**.

white-collar /ˌwaɪt ˈkɒləʳ◄ ‖-ˈkɑː-/ [adj only before noun] **white-collar worker/job/employee** someone who works in an office, not a factory, mine etc: *The economic recession has put many white-collar workers in danger of losing their jobs.*

4 the lowest class

working-class /ˌwɜːʳkɪŋ ˈklɑːs◄ ‖-ˈklæs◄/ [adj] belonging to the class of people who do not have much money or power, and who have jobs where they do physical work; for example, factory workers, builders, and drivers are working-class: *Most of the people who live round here are working-class. | He's from a working-class background.*
the working class/the working classes (=people who are working-class) *Cuts in welfare spending affect the working class most.*

> ⚠ **The working classes** means the same as **the working class**.

lower-class /ˌləʊəʳ ˈklɑːs◄ ‖-ˈklæs◄/ [adj] an impolite word meaning belonging to the class of people that has less money, power, or education than people from other social classes: *He was born into a lower-class family in the East End of London.*
the lower class/the lower classes (=lower-class people) *Rich people look down on the lower classes.*

blue-collar /ˌbluː ˈkɒləʳ◄ ‖-ˈkɑː-/ [adj only before noun] **blue-collar worker/job/employee** someone who does physical work, for example in a factory or a mine, and does not work in an office: *His political support comes mainly from blue-collar workers.*

underclass /ˈʌndəʳklɑːs‖-klæs/ [n singular] a very low social class, who are very poor and may not have jobs, homes etc: *Increasing unemployment led to the creation of an underclass.*

5 someone who cares too much about social class

snob /snɒb‖snɑːb/ [n C] someone who thinks that they are better than people from a lower social class, and does not want to talk to them or be friends with them: *My mother was such a snob she wouldn't let me play with the local children.*

snobbish /ˈsnɒbɪʃ‖ˈsnɑːb-/ [adj] someone who is **snobbish** thinks that they are better than people from a lower social class: *Some of the other parents seemed very rich and very snobbish.*

CLEAN

not dirty

➡ opposite **DIRTY**
➡ see also **TIDY, SHINE, WASH**

> ⚠ Don't confuse **clean** (=not dirty) and **tidy** (=when everything is neatly arranged and is in the right place).

1 clean

clean /kliːn/ [adj] not dirty: *He changed into a clean shirt. | I'll put some clean sheets on the bed. | New houses are much easier to keep clean.*
🔍 **nice and clean/lovely and clean** BRITISH, ESPECIALLY SPOKEN (=very clean) *Our hotel room was lovely and clean.*
clean water/air (=with no harmful substances in it) *What the villagers need most is a supply of clean drinking water.*

spotlessly clean/spotless /ˌspɒtləsli ˈkliːn, ˈspɒtləs‖ˌspɑːt-/ [adj] completely clean – use this about clothes, rooms, or houses: *Nina keeps the kitchen absolutely spotless. | He was wearing a spotlessly clean white shirt.*

hygienic /haɪˈdʒiːnɪk‖-ˈdʒe-, -ˈdʒiː-/ [adj] clean so that diseases cannot spread: *You shouldn't let the cat walk on the table. It's not hygienic. | Meat products must always be kept in hygienic conditions.*

2 to make something clean

clean /kliːn/ [v I/T] to make something clean by removing the dirt, dust etc: *I clean the windows every Saturday.* | *Tony was cleaning his car.* | *How often do you clean the kitchen?*

clean sth up/clean up sth (=remove dirt by cleaning, especially in a room, from a floor etc) *There was mud all over the carpet, and it took me a long time to clean it up.*

clean your teeth BRITISH *Dentists recommend that you should clean your teeth at least twice a day.*

+behind/under etc *Make sure you clean behind the stove.*

cleaning [n U] when you clean things, especially in a room, or a house: *I hate cleaning!*

do the cleaning *Her husband does most of the cleaning.*

⚠ You can also say **give something a clean** in British English. It means the same as **clean something**: *I decided to give my bedroom a clean.*

---

spring-clean /ˌsprɪŋ ˈkliːn/ [v I/T] to clean your whole house very thoroughly, including things that you do not clean very often: *Barry spent the weekend spring-cleaning.* | *I want to spring-clean the whole apartment before Easter.*

3 to clean something with a cloth

wipe /waɪp/ [v T] to remove dirt or liquid from something using a slightly wet cloth: *The waiter was wiping the tables.*

wipe

wipe sth up/wipe up sth (=remove something from a surface by wiping) *If you spill any paint, wipe it up immediately.*

dust /dʌst/ [v I/T] to remove dust from furniture, shelves etc using a soft cloth: *I had to stand on a chair to dust the top shelf.*

dust

+behind/under etc *How often do you dust behind the pictures on your walls?*

polish /ˈpɒlɪʃǁˈpɑː-/ [v T] to make something clean and shiny, for example your shoes or a piece of furniture, by rubbing it with a cloth or brush: *She polished the piano until the wood shone.* | *a polished wooden floor*

shine /ʃaɪn/ [v T] to make shoes clean and shiny by rubbing them with a brush or cloth and shoe polish: *My mom used to iron my dad's shirts, shine his shoes and press his trousers.*

4 to clean something with a brush

brush /brʌʃ/ [v T] *You should brush your jacket – it's covered in dust.*

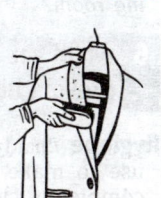
brush

brush sth off sth *I brushed the crumbs off the sofa.*

brush your teeth *Have you brushed your teeth yet?*

scrub /skrʌb/ [v T] to clean something by rubbing it hard with a brush and some water or soap: *I had a job in a restaurant, washing the dishes and scrubbing the floors.* | *Scrub the potatoes and boil them for 5–10 minutes.*

scrub

scrubbing – scrubbed – have scrubbed

sweep /swiːp/ [v T] to clean the floor or the ground using a brush with a long handle: *When everyone had left, Ed swept the floor.*

sweep

sweep up sth/sweep sth up (=remove something from a floor by sweeping) *Can you help me sweep up all the pieces of glass?*

sweeping – swept – have swept

---

5 to clean something with a special cleaning machine

vacuum (also **hoover** BRITISH) /'vækjuəm, -kjʊm, 'huːvəʳ/ [v I/T] to clean something using a special machine that sucks dirt into a bag inside the machine: *Have you vacuumed the living room?*

vacuum

---

6 when you keep things clean to prevent disease

hygiene /'haɪdʒiːn/ [n U] methods you use to make sure that everything is completely clean, especially in order to prevent disease: *Lack of hygiene in the restaurant had attracted rats.*

personal hygiene (=keeping your body clean) *Young people need to learn about the importance of personal hygiene.*

disinfect /ˌdɪsɪ̩n'fekt/ [v T] to use chemicals to clean a place, a piece of equipment, or a wound, in order to prevent disease: *She cleaned and disinfected the cuts on his hands.* | *Disinfect the toilet regularly using bleach.*

sterilize (also **sterilise** BRITISH) /'sterɪ̩laɪz/ [v T] to make something safe to use by heating it or using chemicals, in order to prevent disease – use this about medical or scientific equipment or babies' bottles: *Has the needle been sterilized?* | *Babies' bottles can be sterilized simply by boiling them in water.*

---

7 someone whose job is to clean things

cleaner /'kliːnəʳ/ [n C] someone who is paid to clean a house or office: *We finish work at six, and then the cleaners come in.* | *a window cleaner*

cleaner's/dry cleaner's /'kliːnəʳz, ˌdraɪ 'kliːnəʳz/ [n C] a shop where you can take your clothes to be cleaned, especially with chemicals, not water: *My best suit is at the dry cleaner's.* | *Can you collect my dress from the cleaner's?*

---

8 what you use to clean things with

detergent /dɪ'tɜːʳdʒənt/ [n C/U] a liquid or powder that you use to wash dishes or clothes: *What brand of detergent do you use?*

cleaner /'kliːnəʳ/ [n C/U]

toilet/carpet/oven etc cleaner a substance that you use to clean toilets, carpets, ovens etc

disinfectant /ˌdɪsɪ̩n'fektənt/ [n C/U] a chemical that you use for cleaning toilets, sinks etc, and also cuts on the skin, which helps prevent disease

bleach /bliːtʃ/ [n U] a strong chemical that you use to clean a place or surface completely, in order to prevent disease

---

CLEAR/NOT CLEAR

➡ look here for ...
　• easy or difficult to see
　• easy or difficult to understand

➡ if you mean 'something that you can see through', go to **SEE 7**

---

1 instructions/rules/explanations etc

➡ see also **UNDERSTAND/NOT UNDERSTAND, EXPLAIN, INSTRUCTIONS**

clear /klɪəʳ/ [adj] something that is **clear** is easy to understand because it is said or written in a simple way –

use this especially about explanations, instructions, or rules: *The instructions in the manual aren't very clear.*

clear about/on sth *Your contract should be absolutely clear about your conditions of employment.*

clear to sb *The rules seem clear enough to me.*

make it clear (that) *Barlow made it very clear that he did not agree with us.*

clearly [adv] *The teacher explained everything to us very clearly.*

plain /pleɪn/ [adj] only before noun] **plain** language, instructions etc are easy to understand because they are written clearly and use simple words: *She spoke clearly and carefully, using plain simple language.* | *We now write documents in plain English, and words like 'vendor' and 'purchaser' have been replaced by 'buyer' and 'seller'.*

plainly [adv] *He told her plainly what he thought of her work.* | *The conditions of sale are stated plainly on the bill.*

2 objects/views etc

clear /klɪəʳ/ [adj] something that is **clear** is easy to see: *There was a clear view across the valley.*

clearly [adv] *We could see the harbour lights shining clearly in the distance.*

the naked eye /ðə ˌneɪkɪd̬ ˈaɪ/ if you can see something with **the naked eye**, you can see it without using any special equipment such as a telescope: *These tiny creatures are invisible to the naked eye.*

with the naked eye *On a clear night, it's just possible to see the planet with the naked eye.*

3 facts/reasons/situations etc

obvious /ˈɒbviəs‖ˈɑːb-/ [adj] something that is **obvious** is very easy to notice or understand: *There is an obvious connection between the two murders.* | *"Why is she leaving?" "Well, it's obvious, isn't it?"*

it is obvious that *It was obvious that there was something wrong.*

obvious to sb *The answer might be obvious to you, but it isn't to me.*

for obvious reasons (=when the reasons are so obvious that you do not need to say what they are) *For obvious reasons we have had to cancel tonight's performance.*

clear /klɪəʳ/ [adj] if it is **clear** that something is true, it is easy to notice that it is true and you feel sure about it and have no doubts

it is clear (that) *It was clear that she was very upset by what had happened.*

it is clear to sb *It was clear to me that my father was dying.*

it becomes clear *It soon became clear that more police officers were needed to deal with the situation.*

clear evidence/example/sign *There is clear evidence that unemployment and crime are related.*

> **Formal or informal?**
> **Clear** is more formal than **obvious** and is used more in writing than in speech.

obviously/clearly /ˈɒbviəsli, ˈklɪəʳli‖ˈɑːb-/ [adv] use this to emphasize that it is easy to see that something is true: *We're obviously going to need more help.* | *Clearly, the situation is more complicated than we first thought.* | *"Is she pleased with the decision?" "Obviously not!"* | *The children were clearly upset.*

> Don't say 'it is obviously that' or 'it is clearly that'. Say **it is obvious that** or **it is clear that**.

> **Formal or informal?**
> **Clearly** is more formal than **obviously**.

can tell /kən ˈtel/ to know that something must be true because you can see signs that show this

+(that) *I can tell that he isn't happy.* | *Den could tell that they wanted to be left alone.*

+by *I could tell by her face that she didn't like him.*

it is easy to see /ɪt ɪz ˌiːzi tə ˈsiː/ if **it is easy to see** that something is true, it is very easy for anyone to notice or understand that fact

+(that) *It's easy to see that he isn't well.*

+**how/why/what** *It's easy to see why this car is so popular.* | *It's easy to see how the mistake was made.*

noticeable /'nəʊtɪ̩səbəl/ [adj] a **noticeable** change, difference, or fact is easy to notice: *a noticeable difference in temperature*
it is noticeable that (=it is easy for people to notice something) *It was noticeable that she had invited everyone except Gail.*
noticeably [adv] *When he was shown the letter, Simmons became noticeably nervous.*

blatant /'bleɪtənt/ [adj usually before noun] use this about something that someone does which is clearly bad, but which they do not seem to be ashamed of: *This is a lie, a blatant lie!* | *The company's refusal to hire him was a blatant act of discrimination.*
blatantly [adv] *blatantly racist comments*

4 not easy to understand

unclear/not clear /ʌnˈklɪəʳ, nɒt ˈklɪəʳ/ [adj] use this about something that is difficult to understand because there is not enough information or it has not been explained well: *The reasons for his resignation are still unclear.*
+**whether/what/why etc** *It's not clear why the local police did not start the search immediately.* | *It is still unclear whether the drug will reduce heart disease.*
+**about** *His ideas are good, but he's very unclear about how he's going to achieve them.*

ambiguous /æmˈbɪgjuəs/ [adj] use this about something that someone says or writes that has more than one meaning so that it is possible to understand it in more than one way: *The last part of her letter was deliberately ambiguous.*
ambiguously [adv] *The contract was worded ambiguously.*

vague /veɪg/ [adj] use this about something that someone says or writes that is not clear because they do not give enough details: *Politicians are always making vague promises.*
+**about** *He was rather vague about the reasons why he never finished school.*
vaguely [adv] *The man was vaguely*

described as 'medium build with brown hair'.

confusing /kənˈfjuːzɪŋ/ [adj] a **confusing** situation, explanation, story etc is difficult to understand because it is complicated or badly explained: *All these rules and regulations are very confusing.* | *I found the movie confusing because several of the characters looked almost exactly the same.*

5 not easy to see or notice

faint /feɪnt/ [adj] ESPECIALLY WRITTEN a **faint** sound, smell, image etc is difficult to hear, smell, or see: *His voice on the phone was so faint I could hardly hear it.* (=because it sounded a long way away) | *the faint light of dawn* | *There was a faint smell of lavender in the bathroom.*

subtle /'sʌtl/ [adj] a **subtle** change or difference is difficult to notice unless you look closely or think about it carefully: *The patterns look the same at first, but there are subtle differences between them.*

blurred /blɜːʳd/ [adj] if a picture or image is **blurred**, you can see its general shape, but the edges are not clear: *The photographs were very blurred.* | *Everything looks blurred when I take my glasses off.*

CLIMB

➡ see also **UP, DOWN, LAND AND SEA**

1 to climb up something

climb /klaɪm/ [v I/T] to move up towards the top of a wall, mountain, tree etc, using your hands and feet: *Most kids love climbing trees.* | *Trying not to look down, Alan began to climb.*
+**up/over/onto etc** *Several fans climbed onto the roof of the arena to get a better view.*
climb down (=go down a wall etc using your hands and feet) *The prisoner had escaped by climbing down a drainpipe.*

scale /skeɪl/ [v T] ESPECIALLY WRITTEN to climb to the top of something very high and very difficult or dangerous to climb: *The rescue team had to scale a 300 metre cliff to reach the injured climbers.*

Formal or informal?

Scale is used especially in formal writing or news reports.

2 climbing hills or mountains as a sport

climbing /ˈklaɪmɪŋ/ [n U] the sport of climbing hills or mountains: *Eva's hobbies are horse-riding, climbing, and aerobics.* | *climbing boots*
rock climbing (=the sport of climbing up steep rocks and cliffs)
mountaineering /ˌmaʊntɨˈnɪərɪŋ/ [n U] the sport of climbing high mountains using special equipment: *Mountaineering can be a very dangerous sport.*
climber /ˈklaɪməʳ/ [n C] someone who climbs hills, mountains, or rocks as a sport, especially using special equipment: *a mountain climber* | *The search is continuing for a group of climbers reported missing in the region.*

CLOTHES

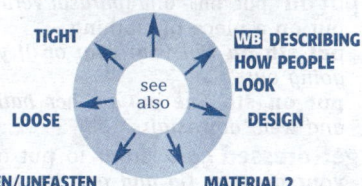

FASHIONABLE/UNFASHIONABLE

TIGHT

WB DESCRIBING HOW PEOPLE LOOK

see also

LOOSE

DESIGN

FASTEN/UNFASTEN

MATERIAL 2

1 clothes

clothes /kləʊðz, kləʊz/ [n plural] things that you wear, for example, coats, shirts, and dresses: *I need to buy some new clothes.* | *She always wears very nice clothes.*
baby/school/work etc clothes (=for babies, for school etc) *He quickly changed out of his work clothes.*
casual clothes (=ordinary clothes that you wear every day)

best clothes (=clothes that you wear for special occasions)

> Don't confuse **clothes** (=things you wear) and **cloth** (=the material that clothes are made from).

> Don't say 'a nice clothes'. Just say **nice clothes**.

> You can also use **clothes** before a noun, like an adjective: *a clothes shop* | *a clothes line* (=for hanging wet clothes on)

clothing /ˈkləʊðɪŋ/ [n U] clothes in general – use this either to talk about a particular type of clothes, or to talk about a large quantity of clothes: *basic necessities such as food and clothing*
warm/light/protective/outdoor clothing *Make sure that you take plenty of warm clothing – it can be very cold up there.*
piece/item/article of clothing (=one thing that you wear, for example a shirt or a dress) FORMAL *There was nothing in the chest apart from a few items of clothing.*

Formal or informal?

Don't use **clothing** to talk about your own clothes or a particular person's clothes, except when speaking or writing formally: *I spilled coffee all over my clothes.* (not 'my clothing') | *The police said that some blood was found on the dead woman's clothing.*

> You can also use **clothing** before a noun, like an adjective: *the clothing industry*

something to wear /ˌsʌmθɪŋ tə ˈweəʳ/ SPOKEN clothes, especially clothes that you can wear for a particular event or occasion: *I must buy something to wear for Julia's wedding.*

> In questions and negatives, use **anything to wear** or **nothing to wear**: *I haven't got anything to wear to Jim's party.* | *I had nothing to wear.*

2 clothes that you wear together as a set

suit /suːt, sjuːtǁsuːt/ [n C] a pair of trousers or a skirt, which you wear with a short coat made of the same material: *She wore a black suit for the interview.* | *Bob was wearing a business suit.*

outfit /'aʊtˌfɪt/ [n C] a set of clothes that look attractive together, which you wear for a special occasion: *I've bought a new outfit for Kate's birthday party.* | *Natalie was wearing a blue and purple outfit.*

> ⚠ Use **outfit** to describe clothes worn by women and children. Don't use it about men's clothes.

uniform /'juːnɪˌfɔːˈm/ [n C/U] a set of clothes that are worn by all the people who belong to a particular organization, for example by soldiers, police officers, or schoolchildren: *Do you have to wear a uniform if you work at McDonald's?*
school uniform *I used to hate wearing school uniform.*
in uniform (=wearing uniform) *Most of the old soldiers came to the ceremony in uniform.*

○ **things** /θɪŋz/ [n plural] **swimming/ football/tennis etc things** SPOKEN the clothes that you wear for swimming, playing football etc: *Don't forget to bring your swimming things when we go to Brighton.*

costume /'kɒstjʊmǁ'kɑːstuːm/ [n C/U] a set of clothes that you wear for acting in a play or performance: *The play was great and the costumes were brilliant.*
national costume (=the traditional clothes of a country) *The dancers were dressed in Ukrainian national costume.*

3 to wear clothes

wear /weəˈ/ [v T] to have clothes, shoes, glasses, jewellery etc on your body: *She was wearing shorts and sandals.* | *What do you think I should wear for the party?*
wear black/red/green etc (=wear black clothes, red clothes etc) *A lot of people wear black for work.*
wearing – wore – have worn

> ⚠ Be careful with the verb form. Say **he/she is wearing** when you are talking about what clothes someone is wearing now: *Catriona is wearing a green jacket and jeans.* Say **he/she wears** when talking about the clothes that someone usually wears: *Gina always wears a suit for work.*

in /ɪn/ [preposition]
in a suit/in a red dress etc wearing a suit, a red dress etc: *There was a man in a linen suit standing at the bar.* | *a couple of girls in jeans and T-shirts*

have on /ˌhæv 'ɒnǁ-'ɑːn/ [phrasal verb T] to be wearing clothes, shoes, glasses, or jewellery: *She had on a red hat and a pair of matching shoes.*
have a coat/jacket/suit etc on *All the men had suits on.*

be dressed /biː 'drest/ to be wearing clothes: *It's 11 o'clock and you still aren't dressed!*
+in *Each child was dressed in a clean shirt.* | *a woman dressed in green*
be dressed as sb (=wearing clothes that are meant make you look like someone else) *Some of the children were dressed as soldiers.*

4 to put on clothes

put on /ˌpʊt 'ɒnǁ-'ɑːn/ [phrasal verb T] to put on a piece of clothing
put sth on *Put your coat on if you're going out.*
put on sth *She put on her bathrobe and went downstairs.*

get dressed /ˌget 'drest/ to put on all your clothes: *Go and get dressed. It's nearly time for school.* | *Sandra's in the bedroom getting dressed.*

try on /ˌtraɪ 'ɒnǁ-'ɑːn/ [phrasal verb T] to put on a piece of clothing so that you can see if it fits you and if it looks nice on you, especially in a shop
try sth on *If you like the shoes, why don't you try them on?*
try on sth *I tried on a beautiful coat, but it was too big.*

dress up/get dressed up /ˌdres 'ʌp, get ˌdrest 'ʌp/ to put on clothes that are suitable for a special or formal occasion: *Most teenagers hate getting dressed up.* | *It's an informal party, so you don't need to dress up.*

5 to take off clothes

take off /,teɪk 'ɒf‖-'ɔːf/ [phrasal verb T] to remove a piece of clothing that you were wearing
take sth off *Why don't you take your coat off?* | *If I take my glasses off, I can hardly see anything.*
take off sth *He took off his jacket and put it around my shoulders.*

> ⚠ Don't say 'he put off his clothes'. Say **he took off his clothes**.

get undressed /,get ʌn'drest/ to take off all your clothes, especially before going to bed: *She got undressed and went to bed.*

undress /ʌn'dres/ [v I] WRITTEN to take off all your clothes, especially before going to bed: *Paul went into the bathroom to undress.*

get changed /,get 'tʃeɪndʒd/ to take off your clothes and put on different clothes: *The boys ran upstairs to get changed.* | *Are you going to get changed before the party?*

change /tʃeɪndʒ/ [v I/T] to take off all or some of your clothes and put some different clothes on: *I'll just change my shirt and I'll be with you in a minute.*
+into *She changed into a sweater and some jeans.*
+out of *Can you wait while I change out of these dirty clothes?*

strip off /,strɪp 'ɒf‖-'ɔːf/ [phrasal verb I/T] to quickly take off all your clothes or a piece of clothing: *The guys stripped off and dived into the pool.*
strip sth off *She ran upstairs, stripped off her jeans and put on a nice dress.*

6 describing people's clothes

tight /taɪt/ [adj] **tight** clothes fit your body very closely: *These jeans are too tight – I can't get them on.* | *a tight miniskirt*

loose /luːs/ [adj] **loose** clothes do not fit your body tightly, so you feel comfortable when you wear them: *Loose clothes are best in summer.* | *She wore a loose sweater and leggings.*

tight   baggy

baggy /'bægi/ [adj] **baggy** trousers, shirts etc are designed to be big and loose and they hide the shape of your body: *a comfortable baggy sweater* | *He was wearing baggy jeans and a T-shirt.*

well-dressed /,wel 'drest◂/ [adj] ESPECIALLY WRITTEN someone who is **well-dressed** is wearing good quality clothes and looks as if they have taken a lot of care about how they look: *The photograph showed a well-dressed man in his early 50s.*

fashionable /'fæʃənəbəl/ [adj] **fashionable** clothes are in a style that is popular at the moment: *Shorter skirts are fashionable these days.* | *a pair of fashionable and expensive-looking trainers*

smart /smɑːʳt/ [adj] BRITISH if you look **smart** or your clothes are **smart**, you are dressed in an attractive way and you look very tidy: *a smart suit* | *You're looking very smart today, Paul.*

casual /'kæʒuəl/ [adj] **casual** clothes are comfortable clothes that you wear when you are relaxing or when you do not need to wear formal clothes: *a casual jacket*

scruffy /'skrʌfi/ [adj] people or clothes that are **scruffy** look dirty and untidy: *Change out of those scruffy jeans.* | *You look too scruffy to go to a restaurant.*

match /mætʃ/ [v I/T] if clothes **match** each other, or if they **match**, they look good together, especially because they are a similar colour: *That shirt doesn't really match your jacket.*

hat/scarf/tie to match (=the same colour as something else) *I've got some blue shoes – now I need a bag to match.*

suit /suːt, sjuːt‖suːt/ [v T] if a piece of clothing or a type of clothing **suits** you, it looks good on you: *Short skirts don't really suit me.*

fit /fɪt/ [v I/T] if clothes **fit**, they are the right size: *Do those shoes still fit you? | I've put on so much weight that this skirt doesn't fit any more.*

fitting – fitted (also **fit** AMERICAN) – **have fitted**

---

7 the way that clothes look

style /staɪl/ [n C] the way that clothes look and how they have been designed: *I like the colour, but I don't really like the style. | 70s styles are coming back into fashion.*

fashion /'fæʃən/ [n C] the style of clothes that are popular at a particular time: *shops selling all the latest fashions | the fashions of the 1960s*

---

8 wearing no clothes

◯ **have nothing on/not have anything on** /hæv ˌnʌθɪŋ 'ɒn, ˌnɒt hæv ˌeniθɪŋ 'ɒn/ ESPECIALLY SPOKEN to not be wearing any clothes: *Don't come in yet – I haven't got anything on! | She seemed to have nothing on underneath her dress.*

naked /'neɪkɪd/ [adj] wearing no clothes – use this especially when it is surprising that someone is not wearing clothes: *He was lying on the bed completely naked. | The magazine was full of pictures of naked men.*

stark naked (also **buck naked** AMERICAN) (=completely naked) *Lizzie was standing there stark naked.*

undressed /ʌn'drest/ [adj] wearing no clothes, because you have just taken them off, for example to have a bath or go to bed: *Upstairs, George was already undressed and in bed.*

bare /beəʳ/ [adj] a part of your body that is **bare** is not covered by any clothes: *Her dress left her shoulders completely bare. | In summer, the kids go around in bare feet.*

nude /njuːd‖nuːd/ [adj] wearing no clothes – use this especially about images of people in paintings, films etc: *an oil painting of a nude model reclining on a bed | She has refused in the past to do nude scenes.*

COLD

➡ opposite **HOT**
➡ see also **WET, DRY, WEATHER**

---

1 weather

cold /kəʊld/ [adj] *a cold January morning | This is the coldest winter we've had for years.*

it's cold (=the weather is cold) *Put your gloves on – it's cold outside today!*

freezing cold (=extremely cold) *It gets freezing cold at night in the mountains.*

bitterly cold (=extremely cold and unpleasant) *a bitterly cold north wind*

cold weather *We've been warned to expect very cold weather next week.*

the cold /ðə 'kəʊld/ [n singular] cold weather – use this to emphasize how unpleasant and uncomfortable it is outside: *Come in. Don't stand out there in the cold!*

cool /kuːl/ [adj] cold in a pleasant way, especially after the weather has been hot: *a cool sea breeze*

it's cool (=the weather is cool) *Although the days are very hot, it's much cooler at night.*

chilly /'tʃɪli/ [adj] cold, but not extremely cold: *a chilly morning in April*

it's chilly (=the weather is chilly) *It's getting chilly – I think we'll go inside.*

frosty /'frɒsti‖'frɔːsti/ [adj] very cold, when everything is covered in a thin white layer of ice, and the sky is often very bright and clear: *a bright frosty morning*

freezing /'friːzɪŋ/ [adj] extremely cold, so that rivers, streams etc turn to ice: *The freezing weather continued all through February.*

it's freezing/it's freezing cold (=the weather is extremely cold) *It was freezing cold outside. | Take your gloves – it's freezing.*

wintry /ˈwɪntri/ [*adj*] cold with rain or snow, and typical of the weather in winter: *Tonight, we can expect some wintry showers on the hills.* | *wintry weather* | *a wintry day*

icy /ˈaɪsi/ [*adj*] if there is an **icy** wind, or if the weather is **icy** cold, it is extremely cold: *The next day was icy cold, and frost covered the ground.* | *An icy wind blew through the house.*

2 person

cold /kəʊld/ [*adj* not before noun] feeling cold
be cold *Dad, I'm cold. Can I put the heater on?*
feel cold *He woke up in the middle of the night feeling cold.*
look cold *Come and sit by the fire. You look cold.*
○ **freezing** /ˈfriːzɪŋ/ (also **frozen** /ˈfrəʊzən/) [*adj* not before noun] SPOKEN feeling very cold and uncomfortable: *"Are you warm enough?" "No, I'm absolutely freezing!"* | *You must be frozen! Come and sit by the fire.*
shiver /ˈʃɪvəʳ/ [*v* I] to shake because you are cold: *I was shivering in my thin sleeping bag.*
shiver with cold *We stood in the doorway shivering with cold.*
have goosepimples BRITISH **have goosebumps** AMERICAN /hæv ˈguːs-ˌpɪmpəlz, hæv ˈguːsbʌmps/ to have small raised areas on your skin, because you are cold

3 place/room

cold /kəʊld/ [*adj*] *He waited an hour for the train on a cold platform.*
it's cold *Why is it always so cold in this office?*
cool /kuːl/ [*adj*] cold in a pleasant way, especially when the weather is hot: *Our hotel room was cool, even during the day*
it's cool *It's much cooler downstairs.*
chilly /ˈtʃɪli/ [*adj*] a little too cold for you to feel comfortable: *I slept in a chilly little room at the top of the house.*
it's chilly *It's chilly in here – why don't you turn the heater on?*
draughty BRITISH **drafty** AMERICAN /ˈdrɑːfti‖ˈdræfti/ [*adj*] a room that is **draughty** has cold air blowing into it from outside, especially because the doors and windows do not fit very well: *a draughty old farmhouse*

freezing /ˈfriːzɪŋ/ [*adj*] extremely cold, so that you feel very uncomfortable: *The heating broke down and the classrooms were freezing.*
it's freezing *It's freezing in here!*

4 liquid/object/surface

cold /kəʊld/ [*adj*] *I wanted a bath but the water was cold.* | *a cold stone floor*
freezing /ˈfriːzɪŋ/ [*adj*] extremely cold: *His friends pulled him from the freezing water.*
freezing cold *The river was freezing cold.*
cool /kuːl/ [*adj*] cold in a pleasant way, but not very cold: *Ruth put her cool hand on my burning forehead.*

5 food/drink

cold /kəʊld/ [*adj*] **cold** food has been cooked, but is no longer hot: *a selection of cold meats* | *Serve the quiche hot or cold, with a salad.*
get cold/go cold (=become cold, especially when it should be hot) *Come and eat your dinner before it gets cold.*
stone cold (=completely cold when it should be hot) *By the time I'd finished on the phone my coffee was stone cold.*
cool /kuːl/ [*adj*] **cool** drinks are pleasantly cold, especially when the weather is warm: *I really need a cool drink.*
chilled /tʃɪld/ [*adj*] **chilled** food or drink has been made very cold, especially by putting it on ice: *a bottle of chilled champagne* | *This soup is delicious served chilled.*
frozen /ˈfrəʊzən/ [*adj*] **frozen** food is stored at a very low temperature so that you can keep it for a long time: *All I had in the freezer was a couple of frozen pizzas.*
ice-cold /ˌaɪs ˈkəʊld◄/ [*adj*] very cold – use this about drinks that have been made very cold so that they are pleasant to drink in hot weather: *an ice-cold beer*

C

6 to become colder

get cold/get colder /get 'kəʊld, get 'kəʊldə^r/ to become cold or colder: *It's got a lot colder recently.* (=the weather has become colder) | *Tell John his coffee's getting cold.*

cool down /ˌkuːl 'daʊn/ [phrasal verb I] to become colder after being hot: *Leave the bread on a wire tray to cool down.* | *It begins to cool down around 6 o'clock.* (=the weather becomes cooler)

cool /kuːl/ [v I] if hot food or other hot substances **cool**, they become colder: *As the metal cools, it will decrease in size.*

COLLECT

to keep things because you think they are attractive or interesting

collect /kə'lekt/ [v T] to get and keep things that are all of a similar kind, because you think they are attractive or interesting: *Do you collect stamps? | I've started collecting old bottles.*

collector /kə'lektə^r/ [n C] someone who collects things: *a coin collector | The auction room was full of art collectors and dealers.*

collection /kə'lekʃən/ [n C] a group of things that someone has collected because they are attractive or interesting
+of *The museum has one of the world's finest collections of impressionist paintings.*
a stamp/coin etc collection (=a collection of stamps, coins, etc)

set /set/ [n C] a complete group of one type of object that someone has collected: *I'm collecting American league baseball cards – I only need one more to have the set.*
+of *a complete set of magazines from 1984 to 1992*

COLOUR/COLOR

➡ if you mean 'colour of hair', go to **HAIR**

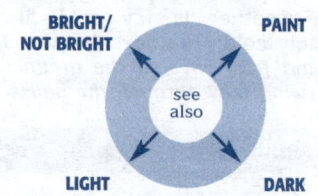

BRIGHT/
NOT BRIGHT   PAINT

see
also

LIGHT   DARK

1 a colour

colour BRITISH **color** AMERICAN /'kʌlə^r/ [n C/U] *Blue is my favorite color. | Yellow is a nice bright colour. | Her hair was the same colour as mine.*
what colour is...? *"What color is your new car?" "Silver."*
change colour *In September the leaves start to change colour.*

shade /ʃeɪd/ [n C] a particular type of red, green, blue etc, which is darker or lighter than usual: *Softer shades are in fashion this season.*
shade of blue/green etc *Valerie's eyes are a beautiful shade of blue.*

colouring BRITISH **coloring** AMERICAN /'kʌlərɪŋ/ [n U] the colour of a person's or animal's hair, skin, or eyes: *This lipstick is perfect for your colouring. | He had his mother's looks and colouring.*

2 to be a particular colour

be /bi, *strong* biː/ [v] **be red/green/ blue etc** *Frogs are green, toads are brown – that's how you can tell the difference. | The Japanese flag is white with a red sun on it.*

> ⚠ Use **is**, **are** etc when mentioning the colour of something: *My dad's car is red. | Her eyes were blue.* Don't use **have**, and don't use the word **colour** itself: *Her new bike is green.* (not *'Her bike has green.'* or *'Her bike is green colour.'*) Only use **colour** when you are asking a question: *"What colour is your new bike?" "It's green."*

coloured BRITISH **colored** AMERICAN /ˈkʌləʳd/ [adj usually before noun] a **coloured** or **colored** object has one or more colours, but not black or white: *The town hall was decorated with hundreds of coloured ribbons.* | *panels of colored glass*

3 bright colours

bright /braɪt/ [adj] a **bright** colour is strong and very easy to notice: *an artist who loved bright colours* | *If you are cycling at night, always wear something bright.*
bright blue/red/yellow etc *The front door was painted bright red.* | *a bright yellow van*
brightly [adv] *a brightly painted boat* | *brightly coloured balloons*
colourful BRITISH **colorful** AMERICAN /ˈkʌləʳfəl/ [adj] something that is **colourful** or **colorful** has a lot of different colours, especially bright colours: *women in colourful summer dresses* | *Children's books need to have large clear letters and colorful pictures.*
brilliant /ˈbrɪljənt/ [adj usually before noun] ESPECIALLY WRITTEN
brilliant white/blue/green etc so bright that it almost hurts your eyes to look at it: *a brilliant blue sky* | *The room was painted a brilliant white.*

4 light colours

light /laɪt/ [adj] **light** colours are closer to white than to black: *They both have brown hair, but Tina's is slightly lighter than Jan's.*
light blue/green/brown etc *The leaves are light green with small purple markings.*
pale /peɪl/ [adj] very light in colour: *The wine has a pale colour but a lively flavour.*
pale blue/pink/yellow etc *a pale pink blouse* | *pale yellow wallpaper with a white daisy pattern*
pastel /ˈpæstl‖pæˈstel/ [adj only before noun] **pastel** colours, especially pink, yellow, green, or blue, are soft and light and not at all bright – use this about clothes and about paint, wallpaper etc for rooms: *The bedrooms have all been painted in cool pastel shades.*

5 dark colours

dark /dɑːʳk/ [adj] **dark** colours are not at all light and are close to black: *Everyone at the funeral was dressed in dark colours, except for Rita, who wore a pink dress.*
dark blue/brown/green etc *She has beautiful dark brown hair.* | *a dark grey suit*
deep /diːp/ [adj only before noun] **deep** colours are strong, dark, and attractive: *a deep, rich shade of crimson*
deep blue/purple/red *A few stars began to appear in the deep blue sky.*

6 photograph/film/television

colour BRITISH **color** AMERICAN /ˈkʌləʳ/ [adj usually before noun] showing pictures in all colours, not just in black, white, and grey: *a delightful book containing 200 colour photographs of wild flowers* | *My parents didn't buy a color TV until the late 1970s.*
in colour (=showing all the colours) *All the pictures are in colour.*
black and white /ˌblæk ən ˈwaɪt◂/ showing pictures only in black, white, and grey: *an old black and white movie starring Charlie Chaplin*
in black and white (=showing only black, white, and grey) *Karsh's famous photographs of Churchill were all in black and white.*

7 to change colour or lose colour

dye /daɪ/ [v T] to change the colour of material or hair by using a special coloured liquid: *I bet she dyes her hair.*
dye sth blue/yellow etc *I'm going to dye this skirt dark blue.*
dyeing – dyed – have dyed
fade /feɪd/ [v I] if a colour or coloured material **fades**, its colour becomes lighter, for example because it has been washed a lot of times or been in sunlight for a long time: *Over the years the green curtains had faded.* | *Her red T-shirt had faded to pink.*
faded [adj] *faded blue jeans*

COMFORTABLE/ UNCOMFORTABLE

➡ see also **RELAX**

1 feeling comfortable

comfortable /'kʌmftəbəl, 'kʌmfət- ‖'kʌmfərt-, 'kʌmft-/ [adj] not before noun] feeling physically relaxed, for example because you are sitting on a soft chair or lying on a soft bed: *I was so warm and comfortable in bed I didn't want to get up.* | *Are you comfortable lying on the floor like that?*
make yourself comfortable *Sit down and make yourself comfortable.*
get comfortable (=get into a comfortable position) *My shoulder was hurting and I couldn't get comfortable.*
comfortably [adv] *Brian was sitting comfortably in front of the television.*

Q **comfy** /'kʌmfi/ [adj not before noun] SPOKEN INFORMAL feeling comfortable: *"Comfy?" "Yes, thanks."*

snug /snʌg/ [adj not before noun] feeling comfortable, warm, and happy because you are in bed, wearing warm clothes etc: *She looks really snug under all those blankets.*

in comfort /ɪn 'kʌmfəˈt/ if you do something **in comfort**, you feel comfortable and relaxed while you are doing it: *Jardine sat down by the fire to enjoy his whiskey in comfort.* | *The car is big enough for the whole family to travel in comfort.*

2 comfortable furniture, clothes, places etc

comfortable /'kʌmftəbəl, 'kʌmfət- ‖'kʌmfərt-, 'kʌmft-/ [adj] use this about clothes, furniture, or rooms that make you feel comfortable: *Our hotel room was very comfortable.* | *a comfortable leather armchair* | *Can you just wait a moment while I change into something more comfortable?*
comfortable to sit on/lie on/wear *Harder mattresses are often more comfortable to lie on.*
comfortably [adv] *a comfortably furnished apartment*

Q **comfy** /'kʌmfi/ [adj] SPOKEN INFORMAL use **comfy** about clothes, furniture, or rooms that make you feel comfortable: *a comfy little cabin in the woods* | *a comfy chair*

cosy BRITISH **cozy** AMERICAN /'kəʊzi/ [adj] a **cosy** room or place is small, warm, and comfortable, and you feel relaxed and happy there: *a small cozy apartment* | *The bar looked lovely and cosy, with a log fire burning brightly.*

luxurious /lʌg'zjʊəriəs, ləg'ʒʊəriəs‖ ləg'ʒʊəriəs/ [adj] a **luxurious** house, hotel, ship etc makes you feel very comfortable because it has large rooms and expensive furniture, carpets etc: *a luxurious yacht, once owned by Aristotle Onassis* | *The hotel we stayed in was really luxurious.*

3 not comfortable

uncomfortable / not comfortable /ʌn'kʌmftəbəl, nɒt 'kʌmftəbəl, -'kʌmfət- ‖-'kʌmfərt-, -'kʌmft-/ [adj] not comfortable: *You can't be very comfortable on that stool.* | *The heat was making us all feel very uncomfortable.* | *She was wearing very uncomfortable-looking shoes.*

4 something that makes you feel uncomfortable

cramped /kræmpt/ [adj] a **cramped** room, apartment, car etc is uncomfortable because there is not enough space: *cramped living conditions* | *They worked from cramped offices near the main station.*

bumpy /'bʌmpi/ [adj] a **bumpy** journey in a car or plane is uncomfortable because the car or plane shakes a lot, as the result of bad roads or bad weather: *a bumpy ride up the mountainside in an old bus*

rough /rʌf/ [adj] a **rough** journey by sea is uncomfortable because the weather is bad and the boat goes up and down a lot: *We had a rough crossing and most of the passengers were seasick.* | *It'll be rough out there today with all this wind.*

COMPANY

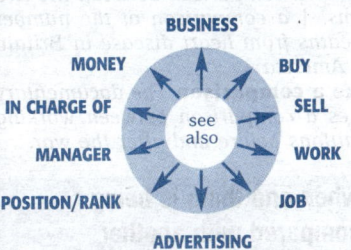

BUSINESS
MONEY
IN CHARGE OF
MANAGER
POSITION/RANK
ADVERTISING
see also
BUY
SELL
WORK
JOB

1 different types of company

company /ˈkʌmpəni/ [n C] any organization, either large or small, that produces goods or provides services in order to make a profit: *The company employs over 10,000 people worldwide.*
oil/insurance/phone etc company *the second largest insurance company in Japan*
work for a company (=have a job there) *My father used to work for one of the big oil companies.*
join a company (=start to work there) *This year, we have had several new executives joining the company.*
set up/start a company *The company was set up in 1975.*
plural **companies**

⚠ You can also use **company** before a noun, like an adjective: *a company car* (=one that is provided for you by your company)| *Company profits have doubled in the last four years.*

firm /fɜːʳm/ [n C] a company, especially one that provides services rather than producing goods, often financial or legal services: *The firm employs about 15 full-time staff.*
law/electronics/building etc firm *She works for a law firm in Amsterdam.*
firm of lawyers/accountants etc BRITISH *Ed's just got a job with a firm of accountants in Boston.*
join a firm (=start working for a firm) *Sara joined the firm when she was only 16.*
business /ˈbɪznɨs/ [n C] a company, shop, or factory that sells goods or provides services, especially one that

employs only a small number of people or only one person: *Norm's a gardener – he has his own business.*
manage/run a business *She's running her own printing business now.*
set up/start a business *Profits have slowly increased since we started the business three years ago.*
small business (=one that employs only one person or very few people)
family business (=one that was started by and employs members of the same family)

corporation /ˌkɔːʳpəˈreɪʃən/ [n C] a large company that employs a lot of people, especially one that includes several different departments or several smaller companies: *IBM is one of the biggest corporations in the US. | the British Broadcasting Corporation*

multinational /ˌmʌltɪˈnæʃənəl◂/ [adj only before noun] **multinational company/corporation/business** a very large company that has offices or factories in many different countries: *Mitsubishi is a multinational company, whose head office is in Japan.*
multinational [n C] a very large company with offices or factories in many different countries: *the power of the big multinationals*

subsidiary /səbˈsɪdiəriǁ-dieri/ [n C] a company that is owned and controlled by a larger company
+of *The Isle of Man Bank is now a subsidiary of NatWest Bank plc.*
plural **subsidiaries**

employer /ɪmˈplɔɪəʳ/ [n C] a company – use this when you are talking about a company as something that provides jobs, not as something that produces and sells things: *Parker Plastics is the city's biggest employer, with about 3000 workers. | Your employer* (=the company you work for) *is responsible for ensuring safety in the workplace.*

2 abbreviations for different types of company

Ltd BRITISH **Inc.** AMERICAN the written abbreviations of 'Limited' and 'Incorporated' – used after the name of a large or small company to show that it is legally established and that its owners are legally responsible for only a limited amount of money if the company gets into debt: *Stevenson Securities Ltd | Syquest Technology Inc.*

Corp. the written abbreviation of 'Corporation' – used after the name of a large company, especially in the US: *Federal Express Corp.*

Co. /kəʊ/ the abbreviation of 'Company' – used after the name of a company: *American Express Co.*

and Co./& Co. (often used after the name of a company when the name is the owner's name) *He joined Young and Co. of Bristol.*

plc /ˌpiː el ˈsiː/ the abbreviation of 'public limited company' – used in Britain after the name of a large company that ordinary people can buy shares in: *Marks & Spencer plc*

Pty the written abbreviation of 'Proprietary' – used in Australia, New Zealand, and South Africa after the name of a company: *Australian Wine Growers Pty*

COMPARE

to think about two or more things or people, in order to see how similar or different they are

➡ see also **SAME, DIFFERENT**

1 to compare things

compare /kəmˈpeəʳ/ [v T] to think about two or more things or people, in order to see how similar or different they are: *Compare prices before you buy a new DVD player.*
compare sth/sb with sth/sb *If you compare rents in London with rents in Paris, you'll find they are about the same. | I hate the way you always compare me with your ex-boyfriend.*

> ⚠ **Compare sth/sb to sth/sb** usually means to say that someone or something is like another person or thing. For example: *a new young singer that some people have compared to Pavarotti* (=they say he is as good as Pavarotti)

comparison /kəmˈpærɪsən/ [n C] something that you say or write that shows how similar or different two things or people are
+of/between *The students were asked to write a comparison between the two poems. | a comparison of the number of deaths from heart disease in Britain and America*
make a comparison *The documentary makes a comparison between working conditions before and after the war.*

2 when one thing is being compared with another

compared to/compared with /kəmˈpeəʳd tuː, kəmˈpeəʳd wɪð/ use this when you are comparing two or more things or people: *Their house seems like a palace compared to our apartment. | Compared with some other EU countries, Britain has a low standard of living.*

in comparison/by comparison /ɪn kəmˈpærɪsən, baɪ kəmˈpærɪsən/ ESPECIALLY WRITTEN use this when you are comparing two or more things or people: *After months of living in a tropical climate, Spain seemed cool by comparison.*
+with *In comparison with London, life in our small town was very quiet.*

> **Formal or informal?**
> **In comparison** and **by comparison** are more formal than **compared to** and **compared with**, and are more common in written English.

in contrast/by contrast /ɪn ˈkɒntrɑːst, baɪ ˈkɒntrɑːst‖-ˈkɑːntræst/ ESPECIALLY WRITTEN use this when you are emphasizing the difference between two or more things or people: *These stocks have gone up by 5%. By contrast, technology stocks have gone down 2%.*
in contrast to/by contrast with *In contrast to his previous visit, there was little publicity.*

relative /ˈrelətɪv/ [adj] **relative importance/advantage/amount/size** the importance, advantage etc that one thing has when it is compared to other things: *the relative importance of money and job satisfaction | the relative advantages of different methods of transporting goods*

relatively [adv] *We have a relatively small budget.* | *This technique is relatively simple.*

COMPETITION

➡ look here for ...
  • a game or sports event
  • when people or companies are trying to be more successful than others
➡ see also WB **SPORT, TAKE PART**

1 a game or event in which people try to do better than each other

competition /ˌkɒmpɪˈtɪʃən‖ˌkɑːm-/ [n C] an organized event in which people try to do an activity or sport better than other people, especially in order to win a prize: *He was awarded first prize in the National Poetry Competition.*
win a competition *A student from St. Paul won the speechwriting competition.*
enter a competition (=be in a competition) *Enter our free competition and win a weekend in Paris.*
a competition to do sth *a competition to think of a name for the new building*

championship /ˈtʃæmpiənʃɪp/ [n C] a competition in a sport or game in which players or teams play against each other to decide who is the best in an area, the country, or the world: *the World Chess Championship*
win a championship *At 17, Becker was the youngest player to win the Men's Tennis Championship.*

tournament /ˈtʊənəmənt, ˈtɔː-‖ˈtɜːr-, ˈtʊər-/ [n C] a competition in a sport or game in which each player or team plays a series of games until one person or team wins: *an international golf tournament*
win a tournament *Telford won the local five-a-side football tournament.*

> ⚠ A **tournament** is usually not as important as a **championship**, and does not involve as many players or teams.

contest /ˈkɒntest‖ˈkɑːn-/ [n C] a competition in which a person or team does an activity, and a group of judges decide which of them is the best
win a contest *The singing contest was won by Sven from Sweden.*
beauty contest (=a contest in which judges decide who is the most beautiful woman)

> ⚠ **Contest** is not usually used about sports events.

2 someone who takes part in a competition

competitor /kəmˈpetɪtər/ [n C] someone who takes part in a competition: *Two of the competitors failed to turn up for the first race.*
contestant /kənˈtestənt/ [n C] someone who takes part in a contest, a TV game, test of knowledge etc: *The next contestant is Alice Jones from Vancouver.* | *Each contestant has to answer questions on a variety of subjects.*

3 to take part in a competition, sports event etc

compete /kəmˈpiːt/ [v I] to take part in a competition, sporting event etc
+in *Athletes from 197 countries competed in the last Olympic Games.*
+against *Ten teams will compete against each other for the National Trophy.*

4 to try to do better than another person or organization

compete /kəmˈpiːt/ [v I] to try to do better than another person or organization, for example in business or politics
+with *Today we compete more and more with foreign companies.*
+for (=in order to get something) *two little children competing for their mother's attention*
can't compete with (=not have enough skill, money etc to compete successfully with another person,

company etc) *Small British car companies just can't compete with giants like BMW and Volkswagen.*

compete to do sth *Fujitsu, Hitachi, and NEC are competing with US firms to build the world's fastest supercomputer.*

fight /faɪt/ [v I/T] to try extremely hard to get an important job or political position which other people are also trying to get

+for *Both aircraft companies are fighting for the contract.*

fight sb for sth *Williams fought several rivals for the leadership of the party.*

fighting – fought – have fought

 Fight is used especially in news reports.

5 a situation in which people try to do better than each other

competition /ˌkɒmpə'tɪʃən‖ˌkɑːm-/ [n U] when people or organizations try hard to get something that they all want but only one of them can get

+for *Competition for these jobs is very tough – we've had over 200 applications.*

+between *There's a lot of competition between the big supermarket chains.*

fierce / strong / tough competition (=when a lot of people are all trying very hard to get something) *There is fierce competition for places in the Olympic team.*

competitive /kəm'petɪtɪv/ [adj] a **competitive** situation is one in which people try hard to do better than each other, for example in business or at school: *Advertising is a very competitive industry.*

highly competitive (=very competitive) *The atmosphere at our school was highly competitive.*

rivalry /'raɪvəlri/ [n U] when two people, teams, or companies try to do better than each other, especially over a long period

+between *Rivalry between brothers and sisters is quite normal.* | *the longstanding rivalry between Coca-Cola and Pepsi.*

intense/fierce rivalry (=very strong

rivalry) *There was intense rivalry between the Brazilian and Italian teams.*

battle /'bætl/ [n C] a situation in which people or organizations fight against each other to get power or control of something, and they are all very determined to win

+for *The President's advisors were engaged in a battle for power.*

 Battle is used especially in news reports and writing.

6 people who are trying to do better than each other

competitor /kəm'petɪtər/ [n C] a person or company that tries to do better than another which offers similar goods or services: *Their major competitors are IBM and Sun Microsystems.*

rival /'raɪvəl/ [n C] a person, team, or company that tries to do better than another similar one, especially over a long period: *The two teams had always been rivals.*

 You can also use **rival** before a noun, like an adjective: *A fight broke out between rival gangs in the city centre.* | *rival companies*

the competition /ðə ˌkɒmpə'tɪʃən‖ -ˌkɑːm-/ [n singular/U] all the people or groups that are trying to do better than you, especially in business or in a sport: *Our sales figures are 10% ahead of the competition.*

strong competition (=when the people you are competing against are very good) *The team overcame strong competition to gain their place in the finals.*

7 someone who likes competing

competitive /kəm'petɪtɪv/ [adj] someone who is **competitive** seems to enjoy competing and is always trying to do better than other people: *I hate playing tennis with her – she's so competitive.*

COMPLAIN

➡ see also **EC** **COMPLAINING, SATISFIED/DISSATISFIED**

1 to complain

complain /kəm'pleɪn/ [v I/T] to say that you are annoyed about something or not satisfied with it, for example because it is unfair or not as good as it should be: *We had to remove the advertisement because so many people complained.*
+about *Local residents have complained about the noise from the club.*
+that *Jenny's always complaining that her boss gives her too much work.*
+to *If the hotel isn't satisfactory, you should complain to the Tourist Office.*

> ⚠ Don't say 'complain against something' or 'complain for something'. Say **complain about something**.

make a complaint /ˌmeɪk ə kəm'pleɪnt/ to tell someone in an official position that you are not satisfied with something that they are responsible for: *Write to this address if you wish to make a complaint.*
+to *Parents made a complaint to the principal about bullying in the school.*

protest /prə'test/ [v I/T] to complain about something that you think is wrong and should not be allowed to happen – use this especially about groups of people who meet in a public place to show that they do not approve of something
+about/against/at *Workers protested angrily about job losses.*
protest sth AMERICAN *a large crowd protesting the war*

object /əb'dʒekt/ [v I] to say that you do not agree with something or you do not approve of it, because it annoys you or offends you: *The neighbours might object if you park your car in front of their house.*
+to *Does anyone object to these proposals?*

2 to complain a lot in an annoying way

moan /məʊn/ [v I] INFORMAL, ESPECIALLY BRITISH to keep complaining in an annoying way – use this about someone who complains all the time, even about things that are not important: *I'm fed up with hearing you moaning the whole time!*
+about *Why do people always moan about the weather?*

grumble /'grʌmbəl/ [v I] to keep complaining in a bad-tempered way, especially when you think you have been treated unfairly: *The old man turned away, grumbling as he went.*
+about *She was grumbling about having to work so late.*

make a fuss /ˌmeɪk ə 'fʌs/ ESPECIALLY BRITISH to complain angrily and noisily about something, so that everyone hears you or notices you
+about *The couple sitting next to us made a big fuss about their bill.*

3 something that you do or say when you complain

complaint /kəm'pleɪnt/ [n C/U] something that you say or write when you are complaining, especially to someone in an official position: *If you have any complaints, please contact our customer relations department.*
+about *Channel 4 received hundreds of complaints about the show.*

protest /'prəʊtest/ [n C/U] a public complaint about something that people think is wrong or unfair and should not be allowed to happen: *Students' fees were increased, despite protests on all the college campuses.*
in protest (=as a way of making a protest) *When two members of the team were fired, the rest of them walked out in protest.*

outcry /'aʊtkraɪ/ [n C usually singular] an angry protest by a lot of people about something that they think is very wrong or unfair
+about/over *the international outcry over French nuclear tests in the Pacific*
public outcry *The shooting of a teenager by police caused a public outcry.*

C

COMPLETELY

not partly, but in every way

➡ see also **ALL**
➡ for words meaning the opposite, go to **PARTLY**

completely /kəm'pli:tli/ [*adv*] not partly, but in every way: *The drug is completely safe.* | *Make sure that the tank is completely full.* | *I was fed up with school, and I felt like trying something completely different.*

complete /kəm'pli:t/ [*adj* only before noun]
complete success/failure/disaster (=when something is completely successful or unsuccessful) *Our first date was a complete disaster.*
make a complete recovery (=completely recover from an illness) *Doctors say he will make a complete recovery.*
a complete waste of time/money (=when something wastes time or money and is not useful at all) *To me, fishing seems like a complete waste of time.*

absolutely /'æbsəlu:tli/ [*adv*] use this to show that you strongly agree with something or approve of something, or to emphasize strong adjectives
absolutely right/correct *They said it would be a waste of money, and they were absolutely right.*
absolutely marvellous/amazing/brilliant *That's an absolutely brilliant idea.*
absolutely certain/sure *Are you absolutely sure you don't mind?*
absolutely exhausted/soaked/ruined etc *By the end of the day, I was absolutely exhausted.*

> ⚠ Use **absolutely** especially with words that express a strong feeling or opinion, for example: *We had an absolutely fantastic time.* | *He was absolutely furious.* | *They don't let us wear T-shirts at school – it's absolutely crazy.*

fully /'fʊli/ [*adv*] use this especially to say that you completely understand something, or that you have all the things or information you need
fully understand/realize/appreciate *I fully appreciate your concern.*
fully aware/informed *Please keep me fully informed of any developments.*
fully furnished/equipped *The house is fully furnished, and has a dishwasher and a microwave.*

totally /'təʊtl-i/ [*adv*] use this especially to show that you strongly disagree with something or that you are very annoyed about it
totally refuse/ignore/reject/fail *He totally ignored my advice.*
totally impossible/unacceptable/ridiculous *The whole thing is totally ridiculous.*

entirely /ɪn'taɪəʳli/ [*adv*] in every possible way – use this especially in negative sentences, or with 'almost'
not entirely *I'm not entirely sure what he meant.* | *The reasons for his departure weren't entirely clear.*
almost entirely *The class consisted almost entirely of girls.*

utterly /'ʌtəʳli/ [*adv*] use this especially to say how bad or wrong something is
utterly ridiculous/impossible/useless etc *At first the idea sounded utterly ridiculous.* | *The map was utterly useless.* | *The town was utterly destroyed by bombing.*

in every way /ɪn ˌevri 'weɪ/ use this to say that something is true in every detail or part: *The two drawings are the same in every way.* | *It was an excellent course in every way.*

COMPUTERS/ INTERNET

➡ see Word Banks section

CONFIDENT/NOT CONFIDENT

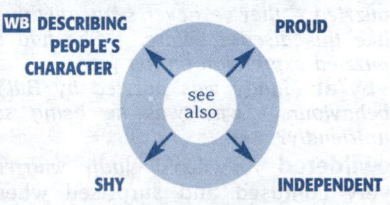

WB DESCRIBING PEOPLE'S CHARACTER

PROUD

see also

SHY

INDEPENDENT

1 a confident person

confident /'kɒnfᵻdənt‖'kɑːn-/ [adj] sure that you have the ability to do something well, and not worried about failing: *It's a difficult test, but she seems fairly confident.* | *He read his speech in a strong, confident voice.*
confident about (doing) sth *I'm much more confident about the race than I was.*
feel confident *I don't feel very confident about going back to work.*
confidently [adv] *She answered each question confidently and competently.* | *He was smiling confidently.*

> ⚠ Don't say 'confident of yourself' or 'confident about yourself'. Say **self-confident**.

self-confident /self 'kɒnfᵻdənt‖-'kɑːn-/ [adj] someone who is **self-confident** is very confident about their own abilities, and is not shy or nervous in social situations: *Jess was only 12, but she was very self-confident.* | *When you have had more experience, you become more self-confident about speaking in front of groups of people.*
sure of yourself /'ʃʊər əv jɔːˌʳself/ very sure that what you do and think is right, even when other people do not

agree with you: *He sounded so sure of himself that I didn't bother to argue.* | *Barnes looked older, and seemed less sure of himself.*

brash /bræʃ/ [adj] ESPECIALLY WRITTEN someone who is **brash** is very confident in an annoying way, for example because they talk too loudly and never listen to other people: *The hotel bar was full of brash, noisy journalists.* | *a brash young salesman from New York*

extrovert /'ekstrəvɜːˌʳt/ [n C] someone who enjoys being with other people, and getting a lot of attention from other people: *Most actors are natural extroverts.*

2 a confident feeling

confidence /'kɒnfᵻdəns‖'kɑːn-/ [n U] the feeling that you have the ability to do things well, and to not make mistakes or be nervous in new situations
give sb confidence *If you understand the grammar, it will give you a lot more confidence.*
have the confidence to do sth (=be confident enough to do something) *In this job you have to have the confidence to make tough decisions.*
give sb the confidence to do sth *Going to college was good for me – it gave me the confidence to work on my own.*
full of confidence (=very confident) *I went into the test full of confidence, but it was more difficult than I had expected.*

self-confidence /self 'kɒnfᵻdəns‖-'kɑːn-/ [n U] a strong belief that you can do things well and that other people will like you, which means you behave confidently in most situations: *He's only 19 but he has plenty of self-confidence.*

morale /məˈrɑːl‖məˈræl/ [n U] the amount of confidence, satisfaction, and hope that people feel, especially a group of people who work together
low/high morale (=a low/high level of confidence) *We've had a lot of problems recently and the morale among the teachers is pretty low.*
keep up morale (=prevent people losing confidence) *They sang songs to keep up their morale until the rescuers arrived.*

3 not confident

shy /ʃaɪ/ [adj] someone who is **shy** feels nervous and embarrassed about talking to people, especially people they do not know: *She was very shy, and didn't like using the phone.* | *Five years ago, I was a shy, clumsy, overweight teenager.*

too shy to do sth *I wanted to ask a question, but I was too shy to say anything.*

lack confidence /ˌlæk 'kɒnfɪdəns‖-'kɑːn-/ to not feel confident about your own abilities or about the way you look: *Francine lacks confidence and needs a lot of encouragement and support.*

lose confidence /ˌluːz 'kɒnfɪdəns‖-'kɑːn-/ to stop feeling confident, especially after something bad has happened: *Men who are out of work for a long time tend to lose confidence.*

be unsure of yourself /biː ʌnˈʃʊər əv jɔːʳˌself/ to not be confident, especially because you are young or you do not have much experience of something: *He was only 21 and still very unsure of himself with women.*

insecure /ˌɪnsɪˈkjʊəʳ/ [adj] not confident about making decisions, trying new experiences, or forming new relationships, especially because you are worried that you are not good enough: *Ben's parents' divorce left him lonely and insecure.*

+about *Even though she's a model, she's very insecure about how she looks.*

CONFUSED

when you cannot understand something or you do not know what to do

➡ see also **UNDERSTAND/ NOT UNDERSTAND**

1 confused

confused /kənˈfjuːzd/ [adj] unable to understand what is happening, what someone is saying etc, especially when this makes you feel worried: *I'm a little confused – could you explain it again?* | *She felt hurt and confused when her husband left her.*

+about *Andrea is still confused about what happened on the night of the accident.*

get confused (=become confused) *It's easy for bank customers to get confused and take out a loan they don't really understand.*

puzzled /ˈpʌzld/ [adj] completely unable to understand why or how something happened: *The doctors are puzzled – they've never seen anything like this disease before.* | *She had a puzzled expression on her face.*

+by/at *Mandy was puzzled by Bill's behaviour – why was he being so unfriendly?*

bewildered /bɪˈwɪldəʳd/ [adj] WRITTEN very confused and surprised when something unusual and unexpected happens to you: *He was bewildered to find three policemen at the front door.*

+by *At first she was bewildered by all the noise and activity of the city.*

 Use **bewildered** when you are writing stories or descriptions.

confusion /kənˈfjuːʒən/ [n U] the feeling you have when you feel confused, or a situation in which people are confused: *The new rules have caused a lot of confusion.*

+about/over *There is some confusion about how the new law actually works.*

2 something that makes you feel confused

confusing /kənˈfjuːzɪŋ/ [adj] **confusing** instructions, explanations, situations etc make you feel confused, because it is not clear what they mean or what you should do: *The road signs were very confusing and we ended up getting lost.* | *I found some of the questions really confusing.*

puzzling /ˈpʌzlɪŋ/ [adj] a **puzzling** action or situation makes you feel confused because you do not understand why or how it happened:

Jan's decision not to take part in the race was very puzzling. | I find it puzzling that no-one noticed them leave.

bewildering /bɪ'wɪldərɪŋ/ [adj] a **bewildering** situation is very confusing, especially because it is strange or new, or because a lot of different things are happening at once: *Elderly people often find hospitals bewildering and frightening places.*
bewildering choice/variety/range (=so many things that it is difficult for you to choose) *There was a bewildering variety of styles to choose from.*

3 to make someone feel confused

confuse /kən'fjuːz/ [v T] *You will confuse the students if you give them too much new information at once.*

4 to think one person or thing is another person or thing

confuse /kən'fjuːz/ [v T] to wrongly think that one person or thing is someone or something else: *Try not to confuse 'your' and 'you're'.*
confuse sb with sb *I always confuse Anthea with her sister – they look so alike.*

mix up /ˌmɪks 'ʌp/ [phrasal verb T] ESPECIALLY SPOKEN to wrongly think one person or thing is someone or something else, especially because they are very similar
mix sth up/mix up sth *Children often mix up 'b' and 'd' when they're learning to write.*
get sb/sth mixed up *Which one's Jane and which one's Jen? I always get their names mixed up.*

> **Formal or informal?**
> **Mix up** is more informal than **confuse** and is used especially in spoken English.

CONNECTED/ NOT CONNECTED

when there is a relationship/no relationship between two things

➡ see also **JOIN, STICK**

1 to be connected with something

be connected/be related /biː kə'nektɪd, biː rɪ'leɪtɪd/ if two things **are connected** with each other or **related** to each other, there is a relationship between them
be connected with sth *The police want to talk to people who saw anything that might be connected with the crime.*
be related to sth *Most of my problems were related to work.*
be closely connected/related *The two languages are closely related. | Achievement at school is closely connected with a child's home life.*

be linked /biː 'lɪŋkt/ to be directly connected in some way – use this especially when there is one fact or cause that connects two things
be closely/strongly linked *Diet and health are strongly linked.*
+to/with *Drug dealing has always been closely linked with organized crime.*

have/be something to do with /hæv, biː ˌsʌmθɪŋ tə 'duː wɪð/ ESPECIALLY SPOKEN to be connected in a way that you do not understand clearly: *I don't know much about his job, but it has something to do with finance. | "What's wrong with your car?" "I'm not sure. I think it's something to do with the starter motor."*

2 something that connects two facts, events, or people

link/connection /lɪŋk, kə'nekʃən/ [n C] something that connects two facts, events, or people with each other: *How can the weather affect the way people vote? I don't see any connection.*
+between *The link between smoking*

and lung cancer has been definitely proved. | the connection between sports and gambling

+with The firm has formed a trading link with Japan. | Do they think her murder has any connection with her political activities?

relationship /rɪˈleɪʃənʃɪp/ [n C] the way in which two facts, events, or situations affect each other

+between the relationship between poverty and crime

3 connected with the subject you are talking about

relevant /ˈrelɪvənt/ [adj] directly connected with the subject you are talking about or considering: Make sure that everything you write in your answer is relevant. | We can't make a decision until we have all the relevant information.

+to I don't think your arguments are relevant to this discussion.

> **Formal or informal?**
> **Relevant** is used in writing and in formal spoken English.

4 not connected with someone or something

not connected/not related /nɒt kəˈnektɪd, nɒt rɪˈleɪtɪd/ The two diseases seem similar, but they are not related in any way.

+with The group is not connected with any political party.

○ **have/be nothing to do with** /hæv, biː ˈnʌθɪŋ tə ˈduː wɪð/ ESPECIALLY SPOKEN to not be connected with something or someone in any way: Your age has nothing to do with your ability to do the job. | Those boxes are nothing to do with me. Sally left them there.

have no connection with sth /hæv ˌnəʊ kəˈnekʃən wɪð (sth)/ ESPECIALLY WRITTEN to not be connected with something in any way: The first chapter of the book seems to have no connection with the main story.

unrelated/unconnected /ˌʌnrɪˈleɪtɪd◂, ˌʌnkəˈnektɪd◂/ [adj] FORMAL not connected in any way: The two robberies are said to be unconnected.

unrelated to/unconnected with Most of his books seem completely unrelated to real life.

5 not connected with the subject you are talking about

irrelevant /ɪˈrelɪvənt/ [adj] She kept asking irrelevant questions. | His age is irrelevant, as long as he can do the job.

completely/totally irrelevant What you are saying is true, but it's totally irrelevant.

> **Formal or informal?**
> **Irrelevant** is used in writing and in formal spoken English.

○ **that's beside the point** /ðæts bɪˌsaɪd ðə ˈpɔɪnt/ SPOKEN say this when you think that what someone has said does not have any real connection with what you are talking about: "He wasn't drunk." "That's beside the point. He shouldn't have been driving at all."

○ **what has that got to do with ...?** BRITISH SPOKEN **what does that have to do with ...?** AMERICAN SPOKEN /wɒt həz ˌðæt gɒt tə ˈduː wɪð, wɒt dəz ˌðæt hæv tə ˈduː wɪðǁ-gɑːt-/ say this when someone has mentioned something and you cannot understand how it is connected with the subject you are talking about: You already told me you had to work Saturday. What's that got to do with me?

CONTAIN

1 to have something inside

contain /kənˈteɪn/ [v T] to have something inside, or to have something as a part: The bag contained a razor, some soap and a towel. | Some paints contain lead, which can be poisonous. | Try to avoid foods that contain a lot of fat.

Don't say 'the box is containing apples'. Say **the box contains apples**.

have sth in it /'hæv (sth) ɪn ɪt/ if a container, room, or food or drink **has something in it**, something has been put into it: *Does this coffee have sugar in it?* | *She can't eat anything that has nuts in it.* | *The bedroom had a huge double bed in it.*

Formal or informal?
Have sth in it is more informal than **contain**.

2 to be able to contain a particular amount

hold /həʊld/ [v T] if something **holds** 50 people, 10 litres etc, that is the largest amount that can go in it: *This jug holds about two litres.* | *The lecture theatre can hold up to 200 students.*

take /teɪk/ [v T not in passive] to have only enough space to contain a particular number or amount, but no more: *The car only takes five people, so the rest of you will have to take a taxi.* | *Our bookshelves won't take any more books.*

can carry /kən 'kæri/ if a vehicle or ship **can carry** a particular amount of things or a particular number of people, it has enough space inside for them to go in it: *The new plane can carry up to 450 people.*

CONTINUE

➡ opposite **STOP**
➡ look here for ...
  • when something does not stop
  • when something starts again after stopping

1 when you continue to do something

continue /kən'tɪnjuː/ [v I/T] to not stop doing something that you are already doing: *We will continue our struggle for independence.*
continue to do sth *She continued to*

live in the same room after Benny left. | *Despite all the warnings, many people continue to smoke.*
continue doing sth *Senator Gramm continued speaking for another ten minutes.*
+with *My teacher advised me to continue with my studies.*

go on/carry on /ˌgəʊ 'ɒn, ˌkæri 'ɒn‖-'ɑːn/ [phrasal verb I] to continue to do something and not let anything stop you
go on/carry on doing sth *She ignored my question and carried on talking.* | *Why do they go on living together if they argue so much?*
+with *Don't stop. Carry on with your work.* | *They decided to go on with their meeting instead of going to lunch.*

Formal or informal?
Continue is more formal than **go on** and **carry on**.

keep doing sth/keep on doing sth /ˌkiːp 'duːɪŋ (sth), ˌkiːp ɒn 'duːɪŋ (sth)/ to continue to do something for a long time, especially in order to get somewhere or achieve something: *Keep driving till you come to a crossroads.* | *We were all tired but we knew we had to keep moving.* | *If you keep on trying, I'm sure you'll get what you want.*

still /stɪl/ [adv] if someone is **still** doing something, they continue to do it – use this especially to show surprise: *He's 35 and he's still living with his parents.* | *You're not still working, are you?* | *Why are you still wearing your sweater? It's hot in here.*

maintain /meɪn'teɪn, mən-/ [v T] ESPECIALLY WRITTEN to make sure that something good continues to happen or continues to exist: *He always tried to maintain the old family traditions.* | *It is important that the US maintains its relationship with China.*

2 when something continues to happen

continue /kən'tɪnjuː/ [v I] to continue happening: *The good weather seems likely to continue.* | *We don't know how long the strike will continue.*

continue for three months/several weeks/a long time etc *The war continued for another two months.*

continue happening/continue to happen *Several people have lost work, and this will continue to happen until we get the computer system fixed.*

last /lɑːst‖læst/ [v I] to continue – use this to say how long something continues

last two hours/six months/a long time etc *The concert lasted all day. | It's not certain how long the ceasefire will last.*

+from/until *The meeting lasted until lunchtime.*

go on /ˌɡəʊ ˈɒn‖-ˈɑːn/ [phrasal verb I] to continue, especially for a long time: *How long does this TV show go on for?*

+until/till *The party went on till three in the morning.*

go on and on (=continue for a very long time) *The noise went on and on – it was driving us crazy.*

> **Formal or informal?**
> **Continue** is more formal than **go on**.

drag on /ˌdræɡ ˈɒn‖-ˈɑːn/ [phrasal verb I] if something that is happening **drags on**, it is boring and seems to continue for much longer than is necessary: *The lesson dragged on for another hour.*

3 to continue to be the same as before

stay /steɪ/ [v]

stay open/warm/calm etc to continue to be open, warm etc: *The library stays open until 8pm on Fridays. | It will stay cold for the next few days.*

remain /rɪˈmeɪn/ [v] FORMAL

remain silent/calm/loyal etc to continue to be silent, calm etc: *She remained calm and waited till he had finished shouting at her. | Can you please remain seated.*

remain a secret/mystery/problem etc *The details of his death remain a closely guarded secret.*

remain the same (=when someone or something does not change) *His doctors say that his condition remains the same.*

remain friends *They remained friends after their divorce.*

still /stɪl/ [adv] use this to emphasize that something or someone has not changed and continues to be the same: *At the age of 50, Marlene was still a beautiful woman. | I'm still confused. Would you explain it again?*

4 to continue after stopping

continue /kənˈtɪnjuː/ [v I/T] to start again after stopping: *After a short time the rain stopped and the game continued. | Can we continue this discussion later?*

continue doing sth *When the audience had stopped cheering, he continued speaking.*

go on/carry on /ˌɡəʊ ˈɒn, ˌkæri ˈɒn‖-ˈɑːn/ [phrasal verb I] to continue doing something or continue speaking, after a short pause: *It's one o'clock now – shall we carry on after lunch? | Go on, I'm listening.*

go on/carry on doing sth *The doctor looked up from her desk for a moment and then went on writing.*

+with *As soon as Mr Saunders gets back we'll carry on with the meeting. | Do you want me to go on with my story?*

> **Formal or informal?**
> **Continue** is more formal than **go on** and **carry on**.

go back to sth /ˌɡəʊ ˈbæk tuː (sth)/ [phrasal verb T] to start doing something again after a short period when you were doing something else: *Melanie made herself a cup of coffee and went back to her reading.*

5 continuing for a long time

continuous /kənˈtɪnjuəs/ [adj] continuing for a long time without stopping: *The north coast has had several days of continuous rain. | Education does not stop when you finish school – it's a continuous process.*

continuously [adv] *Radio Moscow played solemn music continuously throughout the day.*

constant /'kɒnstənt‖'kɑːn-/ [adj only before noun] use this about an unpleasant or worrying situation that seems as if it will never end: He suffered constant pain in the months before his death. | The refugees live in constant fear of being attacked.

constantly [adv] We need to be constantly aware of the risk of accidents.

non-stop /ˌnɒn 'stɒp◂‖ˌnɑːn 'stɑːp◂/ [adv] use this to emphasize that something happens continuously, and never stops even when you expect it to stop or want it to stop: She talked non-stop for over an hour.

Formal or informal?

Non-stop is more informal than **continuously**.

---

non-stop [adj only before noun] 48 hours of non-stop rain

steady /'stedi/ [adj only before noun] a **steady** change or improvement happens gradually, and continues without stopping or being interrupted: There has been a steady increase in the number of students going to college. | a steady drop in road accidents.

steady – steadier – steadiest

steadily [adv] The divorce rate has risen steadily since the 1950s.

day after day/week after week etc /ˌdeɪ ɑːftəʳ 'deɪ, ˌwiːk ɑːftəʳ 'wiːk(etc)‖ -æf-/ ESPECIALLY WRITTEN every day, every week etc for a long time: The fighting went on week after week and there seemed no end to it. | She sits at home day after day, waiting for a message from her husband.

day and night/around the clock /ˌdeɪ ən 'naɪt, əˌraʊnd ðə 'klɒk‖-'klɑːk/ continuously, all day and all night without ever stopping: Security guards watch the fence around the clock. | She nursed him day and night until he recovered.

24/7 /ˌtwenti fɔːʳ 'sevən/ all day and all night, and every day of the week: Our local convenience store is open 24/7.

CONTROL

to make things happen in the way that you want, or make someone do what you want

➡ see also **POWER, LIMIT, IN CHARGE OF**

⚠ Don't confuse **control** (=make someone or something do what you want) with **check** or **inspect** (=look at something to see if it is correct or safe): A guard got on the train and inspected our passports. (See **LOOK AT**.)

---

1 to control what happens

control /kən'trəʊl/ [v T] to make things happen in the way that you want by using your power, skill, money etc: The company used to control half of the world's oil trade. | Republican politicians now control the main congressional committees. | the parts of the brain that control the breathing process **controlling – controlled – have controlled**

be in control /ˌbiː ɪn kən'trəʊl/ to control a situation, organization, country etc – use this especially about someone who got their power by using force or by clever planning, but not by being elected: The President has been arrested, and rebel forces are now in control.
+of He is in control of over half the TV channels in the country.

keep/get sth under control /ˌkiːp, ˌget (sth) ʌndəʳ kən'trəʊl/ to control a difficult or dangerous situation by doing everything that you can to stop it from getting any worse: Firefighters struggled to keep the blaze under control. | We aim to be able to get the virus under control by 2005.

2 to control a person

control /kən'trəʊl/ [v T] to make someone behave in the way that you want: It was obvious that the teacher couldn't control the class. | Religion was just another way in which the

country's rulers tried to control the people.
controlling – **controlled** – **have controlled**

keep sb under control /ˌkiːp (sb) ʌndər kənˈtrəʊl/ to prevent someone from causing trouble or problems: *Police were struggling to keep the demonstrators under control.* | *Can't you keep that dog under control?*

dominate /ˈdɒmɪneɪt‖ˈdɑː-/ [v T] ESPECIALLY WRITTEN if someone who has a strong character **dominates** another person, they have a very powerful effect on that person's mind and the way that they behave: *It was obvious that her husband completely dominated her.* | *his dominating manner*

manipulate /məˈnɪpjʊleɪt/ [v T] to make someone do what you want them to do by cleverly influencing them, especially when they do not realize what you are doing: *The group's manager skilfully manipulated the media, and they quickly became as famous as the Beatles.*
manipulative [adj] clever at manipulating people – use this when you disapprove of this behaviour: *Sweet as she was, there was a manipulative side to her character.*

3 to control the temperature, speed, or amount of something

control /kənˈtrəʊl/ [v T] to make the temperature, speed, or amount of something change in the way that you want or stay at the level you want: *This button controls the temperature in the building.* | *How do you control the speed of the drill?*
controlling – **controlled** – **have controlled**

keep sth under control /ˌkiːp (sth) ʌndər kənˈtrəʊl/ to prevent the amount of something from becoming too great: *He's been trying for years to keep his drinking under control.* | *The administration has certainly succeeded in keeping inflation under control.*

regulate /ˈregjʊleɪt/ [v T] to keep the temperature, speed, or amount of something at exactly the right level: *Sweating helps you regulate your body temperature.*

Formal or informal?
Regulate is used especially in technical and formal scientific writing.

4 to control your feelings

control /kənˈtrəʊl/ if you **control** yourself or **control** your feelings, you continue to behave calmly and sensibly and do not become too angry, excited, or upset
control yourself *She was really annoying me, but I managed to control myself and not say anything.*
control your temper/anger *I wish he'd learn to control his temper.*
controlling – **controlled** – **have controlled**

self-control /ˌself kənˈtrəʊl/ [n U] the ability to behave calmly and sensibly and not become too angry, excited, or upset: *The German team showed amazing self-control throughout the game.*

5 unable to control your feelings

lose control /ˌluːz kənˈtrəʊl/ to become unable to control your feelings and become very angry or upset: *He made her so angry that she lost control and hit him.*

get carried away /get ˌkærid əˈweɪ/ ESPECIALLY SPOKEN to feel so excited, interested etc that you cannot control what you are saying or doing: *It's easy to get carried away and buy a lot of things that you don't need.* | *Tony got a bit carried away on the dance floor.*

6 to no longer be able to control a situation, vehicle, group of people etc

lose control /ˌluːz kənˈtrəʊl/ to no longer be able to control a situation, vehicle, group of people etc: *The car skidded on the ice, and I lost control.*
+of *parents who lose control of their children* | *O'Connor recently lost control of the company he had run for seven years.*

7 **to get control of a situation, organization, country etc**

take control /ˌteɪk kənˈtrəʊl/ to get control of a situation, organization, or place, often by using violent or illegal methods: *In 1949 the Chinese Communist Party took control.*
+of *Troops were called in to take control of the prison.*

take over /ˌteɪk ˈəʊvəʳ/ [phrasal verb I/T] to get control of a company or organization, or become the leader, president etc after someone else: *People are wondering who's going to take over when the old dictator dies.*
take over sth/take sth over *CBS records was taken over by Sony.*
+from *She took over from Barton as Managing Director in 1994.*

8 **difficult or impossible to control**

uncontrollable /ˌʌnkənˈtrəʊləbəl◂/ [adj] WRITTEN **uncontrollable** emotions or actions are difficult or impossible to control: *Barbara was shaking with uncontrollable laughter.* | *an uncontrollable rage*

out of control /ˌaʊt əv kənˈtrəʊl/ a situation that is **out of control** has got much worse and can no longer be controlled: *The fire was out of control.* | *Teenage crime was now out of control.*
get out of control (=become impossible to control) *It's easy to let spending on credit cards get out of control.*

CONVENIENT/ NOT CONVENIENT

➡ see also **SUITABLE/UNSUITABLE**

1 **a suitable time to do something**

convenient /kənˈviːniənt/ [adj] a **convenient** time to do something is a time that does not cause you any problems, for example because you were not planning to do anything else: *I'd like to talk to the manager – can you suggest a convenient time?*

+for *We need to arrange a meeting. Would 11 o'clock on Tuesday be convenient for you?*

> **Formal or informal?**
> **Convenient** is used in writing and in formal spoken English.

🗨 **a good time** /ə ɡʊd ˈtaɪm/ ESPECIALLY SPOKEN a convenient time to do something: *"I'm too busy to talk to you now." "When would be a good time?"*
a good time to do sth *Now might be a good time to think about what you really want to do.*
+for *I'm afraid Friday isn't a good time for me – I have to go to the dentist.*

suit /suːt, sjuːt‖suːt/ [v T] if a time or date **suits** you, it is convenient for you: *Let's go to see a film next week. Which day would suit you best?* | *Finding a time that suits everyone is going to be difficult.*

🗨 **be OK/be okay** /biː ˌəʊˈkeɪ/ SPOKEN INFORMAL if a time or date **is OK** or **is okay**, it is convenient for you: *I'll drive over and get you. Is 10 o'clock OK?*
+for *Friday's probably okay for me, but I'll check with Jean.*

fit in with sth /ˌfɪt ˈɪn wɪð (sth)/ [phrasal verb T] if something **fits in with** your plans, you do not need to change your plans in order to do it: *We'd like to take you out for a meal on Thursday – does that fit in with what you're doing?*

2 **a useful object, place, or method**

➡ see also **NEAR**

convenient /kənˈviːniənt/ [adj] a **convenient** place or way of doing something is useful because it is quick and easy, and does not cause you any problems: *Credit cards are probably the most convenient way of paying for concert tickets.*
it is convenient to do sth *I could take the train, but it's more convenient to go in the car.*
convenient for the school/shops/ station etc BRITISH (=near to the school etc, so it is easy to get there) *The hotel is very convenient for the station – it's only a two minute walk.*

handy /'hændi/ [*adj*] INFORMAL a **handy** object, method, place etc is easy to use, easy to do, or easy to get to: *Many fruit juices are now available in handy little cartons.* | *It's a handy way of keeping a record of your spending.*

handy for the school/shops/station etc BRITISH (=near to the school etc, so it is easy to get there) *Our house is very handy for the shops.*

3 not convenient

inconvenient/not convenient /ˌɪnkən-'viːniənt◂, nɒt kən'viːniənt/ [*adj*] not convenient: *I'm afraid he's come at an inconvenient time.*

+for *I can call you back later if it's not convenient for you to talk now.* | *The trouble with living in the country is that it's not very convenient for work.*

it is inconvenient to do sth *If you find it inconvenient to come to the office, we can mail the papers to you.*

> **Formal or informal?**
>
> **Inconvenient** and **not convenient** are used in writing and in formal spoken English when talking about a time.

a bad time /ə ˌbæd 'taɪm/ ESPECIALLY SPOKEN a time that is not convenient because you are busy or you have made other plans: *Sorry – have I come at a bad time?*

a bad time to do sth *It was definitely a bad time to ask Mr Field for more money.*

> When you see **EC**, go to the **ESSENTIAL COMMUNICATION** section.

COOK

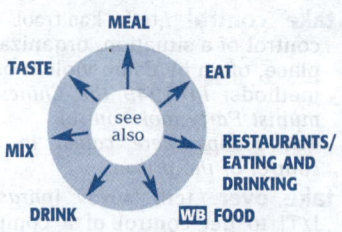

1 to hook a meal or make something such as bread, soup etc

cook /kʊk/ [*v* I/T] to prepare food or a meal by heating it, boiling it, frying it etc: *I'm usually too tired to cook when I get home from work.* | *Prick the sausages with a fork before cooking them.*

cook lunch/supper/a meal etc *I usually cook lunch on Sunday.*

cook (sth) for sb (=cook a meal for someone) *I helped Mom cook Christmas dinner for the whole family.*

cooked [*adj*] *Mix the vegetables and the mayonnaise with the cooked rice.* | *Is that pasta cooked yet?*

make /meɪk/ [*v* T] to make a meal or type of food, either by cooking it or by preparing it in some other way: *My mother used to make delicious strawberry jam.* | *I think I'll make fish pie for supper.* | *I'll make the salad.*

make lunch/dinner/supper etc *Martin was in the kitchen making lunch.*

make sb sth *I'll make you some sandwiches to take with you.*

making – made – have made

get /get/ [*v* T not in passive] SPOKEN to cook or prepare a meal

get breakfast/lunch/dinner *Sit down and let me get dinner.*

get sb their lunch/dinner etc *Joey was downstairs getting the kids their breakfast.*

getting – got – have got BRITISH
getting – got – have gotten AMERICAN

fix /fɪks/ [*v* T] INFORMAL, ESPECIALLY AMERICAN to make a meal or dish – use this about meals you make quickly, not about big, formal meals

fix breakfast/lunch/dinner etc *I have to fix lunch now.*

fix sb sth *You're too late for supper but I can fix you some scrambled eggs.*

prepare /prɪˈpeər/ [v T] to make a meal or dish, especially something that needs time, effort, or skill: *Prepare a sauce with cream, lemon juice, and mustard.* | *Mrs Fujimoto had prepared a delicious meal for them when they got home.*

> **Formal or informal?**
>
> **Prepare** is more formal than **make**. It is used in writing and in cookery programmes on TV.

2 ways of heating or cooking food

boil /bɔɪl/ [v I/T] to cook food in very hot water: *Boil the potatoes until they are soft.* | *The beans should be boiled for at least 20 minutes.*

boiled [*adj* only before noun] *boiled eggs*

simmer /ˈsɪmər/ [v I/T] to cook food over a low heat so that it is boiling very gently: *Let the soup simmer for five minutes.*

simmer gently/slowly *Simmer the sauce gently until it thickens.*

fry /fraɪ/ [v I/T] to cook food in hot oil, butter, or fat: *Fry the onions gently for five minutes.* | *Mushrooms are best when fried in olive oil.*

fried [*adj* only before noun] *fried bacon*

frying – fried – have fried

bake /beɪk/ [v I/T] to cook food in an oven, without any liquid or fat: *Put the cake into a hot oven and bake for 35 minutes.* | *Do you bake your own bread?*

baked [*adj* only before noun] *baked potatoes*

roast /rəʊst/ [v I/T] to cook meat or vegetables, in an oven or over a fire using a small amount of fat: *Roast the chicken for three hours in a hot oven.*

roast [*adj* only before noun] *roast potatoes* | *There's some cold roast beef in the fridge.*

grill BRITISH **broil** AMERICAN /grɪl, brɔɪl/ [v I/T] to cook food, especially meat or fish, by putting it directly underneath a flame or a heated electric object: *Grill the steak for about five minutes on each side.* | *Brush the ribs lightly with oil and broil them.*

grilled/broiled [*adj* only before noun] *grilled fish*

steam /stiːm/ [v I/T] to cook food in steam: *Steam the courgettes for 3–4 minutes.*

steamed [*adj* only before noun] *a steamed pudding*

barbecue /ˈbɑːrbɪkjuː/ [v T] to cook meat, fish, or vegetables on a metal frame over a fire outdoors: *Why don't we barbecue some chicken and pork ribs tonight?*

barbecued [*adj* only before noun] *barbecued kebabs*

grill sth over flames/charcoal /ˌgrɪl əʊvər ˈfleɪmz, ˈtʃɑːrkəʊl/ AMERICAN to cook meat, fish, or vegetables on a metal frame over a fire, either outdoors or indoors, for example in a restaurant: *Grill the burgers over flames for 3 or 4 minutes each side.* | *swordfish grilled over charcoal*

3 ways of preparing food before you cook it

mix /mɪks/ [v I/T] to put two or more types of food together so that they become a single substance: *Add eggs to the flour and butter, and mix well.*

mix sth with sth *I usually make salad dressing by mixing olive oil with vinegar and adding a little mustard.*

mix sth together *Mix all the ingredients together in a large bowl.*

stir /stɜːr/ [v I/T] to mix things together by moving them slowly around with a spoon or fork: *She kept stirring the mixture until it was completely smooth.* | *Heat the soup in a pan, stirring constantly.*

stir

stir in sth (=add an ingredient to a sauce or mixture and stir it) *When the sauce has cooled, stir in the grated cheese.*

stirring – stirred – have stirred

beat /biːt/ [v T] to mix eggs, cream etc together thoroughly with a fork or a special tool, using quick, strong movements: *Carry on beating the*

margarine and sugar until they are light and fluffy.
beating – beat – have beaten

whisk /wɪsk/ [v T] to mix eggs, cream etc very quickly with a special tool or machine, so that they get air in them and become thicker: *My mother whisked the eggs and sugar in a large bowl.*

whisk

4 not cooked

raw /rɔː/ [adj] **raw** food has not been cooked: *a salad made with raw carrots, nuts, and raisins | Sushi consists of raw fish and rice.*

uncooked /ˌʌnˈkʊkt◂/ [adj only before noun] **uncooked** food has not yet been cooked, but must be cooked before it is eaten: *uncooked pastry | Uncooked meat should be stored separately.*

underdone/undercooked /ˌʌndəˈdʌn◂, ˌʌndəˈkʊkt◂/ [adj] not cooked enough: *It can be dangerous to eat undercooked pork. | The potatoes were underdone.*

5 cooked too much

overcooked/overdone /ˌəʊvəˈkʊkt◂, ˌəʊvəˈdʌn◂/ [adj] food that is **overcooked** or **overdone** has been cooked too much and does not taste nice: *This steak's a little overdone. | I hate overcooked vegetables.*

burn /bɜːrn/ [v T] to cook food for too long, or too close to the heat, so that it becomes black on the outside: *Oh no! I've burnt the turkey!*
burned/burnt [adj] *the smell of burnt toast*
burning – burned (also **burnt** BRITISH) **– have burned** (also **have burnt** BRITISH)

6 the activity of cooking

cooking /ˈkʊkɪŋ/ [n U] the activity of cooking: *His hobbies include cooking and cycling.*
do the cooking *Who does the cooking in your house?*

sb's cooking (=the way that someone cooks) *Stop criticizing my cooking!*

> ⚠ You can also use **cooking** before a noun, like an adjective: *Follow the cooking instructions carefully. | cooking utensils*

cookery /ˈkʊkəri/ [n U] ESPECIALLY BRITISH the activity or study of cooking: *My favourite subject at school was cookery.*

> ⚠ You can also use **cookery** before a noun, like an adjective: *cookery classes | a cookery book*

cuisine /kwɪˈziːn/ [n U] FORMAL the style of cooking of a particular country or place, especially when the food is very good: *The restaurant is famous for its excellent cuisine.*
French/Italian/Chinese cuisine (=the French etc style of cooking)

7 instructions for cooking

recipe /ˈresɪpi/ [n C] a set of instructions for cooking a particular dish or meal: *rabbit pie made to a traditional country recipe*
+for *Could you give me the recipe for that chocolate cake?*

cookbook (also **recipe book** BRITISH) /ˈkʊkbʊk, ˈresɪpi bʊk/ [n C] a book that has instructions for preparing various dishes

8 someone who cooks

cook /kʊk/ [n C] someone who cooks food, either as their job or for pleasure: *Jane works as a cook in an Italian restaurant.*
a good/excellent/terrible cook (=someone who is very good or very bad at cooking)

chef /ʃef/ [n C] someone who has been trained to prepare and cook food, especially the most important cook in a hotel or restaurant: *Marco's a chef in a big hotel in Oxford.*

COPY

➡ Look here for
• copy a document or photograph
• copy the way someone behaves

1 to copy a picture or piece of writing

copy /'kɒpi‖'kɑːpi/ [v T] to produce something that is the same as something else: *They were arrested for illegally copying video recordings.* | *Copy the graph on page 25, then answer the questions.*
copy sth from/into/onto sth *The drawings had been copied from photographs.* | *I copied her address onto a piece of paper.* | *We had to copy all our files onto floppy disks.*
copying – copied – have copied

make a copy /ˌmeɪk ə 'kɒpi‖-'kɑːpi/ to copy something using a machine
+of *I'll make a copy of my report for you.* | *Are you allowed to make copies of this software?*

photocopy (also **Xerox** TRADEMARK, ESPECIALLY AMERICAN) /'fəʊtəkɒpi, 'zɪərɒks‖-kɑːpi, -rɑːks/ [v T] to copy a piece of paper with writing or pictures on it, using a special machine that makes a photograph of the original: *I photocopied the letter before sending it off.* | *Where can I get these papers Xeroxed?*
photocopying – photocopied – have photocopied

2 something that has been copied from something else

copy /'kɒpi‖'kɑːpi/ [n C] something that has been made to look exactly like something else
+of *This statue is a copy of the one in the Louvre.*
exact copy *The movie's set was an exact copy of the one used in the original TV series.*
plural copies

photocopy (also **Xerox** TRADEMARK, ESPECIALLY AMERICAN) /'fəʊtəkɒpi, 'zɪərɒks‖-kɑːpi, -rɑːks/ [n C] a copy of a document, letter, or picture etc, made by a machine that photographs the original
+of *Please send a photocopy of your birth certificate.* | *Xeroxes of the company's accounts*
plural photocopies

duplicate /'djuːplɪk⅟ɪt‖'duː-/ [adj only before noun] a **duplicate** key, bill etc is an exact copy of a key, bill etc and can be used in the same way, especially if the original one is lost: *a duplicate set of keys* | *It's a good idea to keep duplicate files on floppy disk.*

model /'mɒdl‖'mɑːdl/ [n C] a small copy of a building, vehicle, or machine, made to look exactly like the original building, vehicle etc
+of *We bought a little plastic model of the Eiffel Tower as a souvenir.*
model ship/airplane etc *There was a shelf in his bedroom full of model planes.*

replica /'replɪkə/ [n C] a copy of a well-known vehicle, building, or weapon, especially one that is the same size as the original: *a replica gun*
+of *You can now drive a perfect replica of this classic racing car.* | *The building is an exact replica of the original Globe theatre.*

reproduction /ˌriːprə'dʌkʃən/ [n C] a copy of an old or valuable work of art or piece of furniture: *Of course this picture isn't the original – it's only a reproduction.*
+of *a reproduction of a beautiful Ming vase*
reproduction furniture/chair/table etc *beautiful pieces of reproduction furniture*

3 to copy something without permission

copy /'kɒpi‖'kɑːpi/ [v I/T] to copy something and dishonestly pretend it is your own work: *Any student caught copying from someone else will be sent out.* | *She was furious when she discovered that another scientist had copied her ideas.*
copy sth from/out of sth *She had copied the article from the encyclopedia.*
copying – copied – have copied

forge /fɔːʳdʒ/ [v T] to illegally copy something written or printed, such as a bank note or official document, for dishonest purposes: *The thief had forged my signature on a cheque.* | *He must have entered the country using a forged passport.*

4 an illegal copy

forgery /'fɔːʳdʒəri/ [n C] an illegal copy of something such as a bank note or official document: *The passports were forgeries.* | *Further investigation showed that the so-called 'Hitler Diaries' were a forgery.*
plural **forgeries**

counterfeit /'kaʊntəʳfɪt/ [adj] **counterfeit** money looks exactly like real money but has been produced illegally: *Police have warned stores to look out for counterfeit $50 bills.*

pirate /'paɪərət/ [adj only before noun] **pirate copies/videos/CDs** copies of books, records, films etc that have been made illegally and are sold without the permission of the people who originally produced them: *They were selling pirate copies of Harry Potter.*

5 to do the same as someone else

copy /'kɒpi‖'kɑːpi/ [v T] to do the same things that someone else does: *Girls all over the country copied her hairstyle.* | *Whatever Billy does, his little brother copies him.*
copying – copied – have copied

imitate /'ɪmɪ̩teɪt/ [v T] to copy the way someone behaves, speaks, writes, or moves, especially because you admire them or want to be like them: *When children play, they frequently imitate adults.* | *A lot of writers have tried to imitate Lawrence's style.*

> **Formal or informal?**
> **Imitate** is more formal than **copy**.

○ **do what sb does** /,duː wɒt (sb) 'dʌz/ ESPECIALLY SPOKEN to do the same things as someone else, especially in order to learn from them: *Just watch the other kids and do what they do.*

follow sb's example /,fɒləʊ (sb's) ɪg'zɑːmpəl‖,fɑːləʊ (sb's) ɪg'zæm-/ ESPECIALLY WRITTEN to do the same as someone else, especially because you admire them or because they have got good results by doing it: *Perhaps Britain should follow America's example and keep religion and education separate.*

6 to copy someone's behaviour or voice in order to make people laugh

imitate /'ɪmɪ̩teɪt/ [v T] to copy what someone says or does, in order to make people laugh: *She's really good at imitating our teacher's Scottish accent.*

do an impression of sb/do an impersonation of sb /,duː ən ɪm'preʃən ɒv (sb), ,duː ən ɪmpɜːʳsə'neɪʃən ɒv (sb)/ to copy the way a famous person speaks, walks, or behaves in order to make people laugh: *He did a pretty stupid impression of Charlie Chaplin.*

COST

1 what you have to pay for something

cost /kɒst‖kɔːst/ [n C] the amount of money you must pay for services, activities, or things you need all the time like food and electricity
+of *The cost of bread went up by 200%.* | *Many old people cannot afford the cost of heating their homes.*
high/low cost *the high cost of building land in Tokyo*

heating/transportation/legal etc costs *Delaney still owes his lawyer over £20,000 in legal costs.*
the cost of living (=the amount of money you need for things such as food, clothes, and rent) *The cost of living is much higher in London than in the north of England.*

 Don't use 'cost' about things you buy in shops. Use **price**.

 Don't say 'the cost is expensive'. Say **it is expensive**.

price /praɪs/ [n C] the amount of money you must pay to buy something that is for sale, for example in a shop: *There's a great new clothes store on Main Street, and the prices seem very reasonable.*
+of *What's the price of a pack of cigarettes nowadays?*
half price (=half the usual price) *I bought these jeans half price in the sale.*
reduce/cut prices *Comet has reduced the prices of most electrical goods by 25%.*
rising prices (=prices that keep increasing) *Football fans have been complaining about rising ticket prices.*
oil/food/house etc prices *House prices have increased a lot in recent years.*
asking price (=the price that someone wants for something they are selling) *I didn't think the house was worth the asking price, so I made a lower offer.*

 Don't say 'the price is expensive' or 'the price is cheap'. Say **it is expensive** or **it is cheap**.

 You can also use **price** before a noun, like an adjective: *price increases | price controls*

fare /feəʳ/ [n C] the cost of a journey on a bus, train, plane etc: *My folks want me to go home for Christmas, and said they'd pay my fare.*
taxi/bus/plane etc fare *How much is the taxi fare home?*

rent /rent/ [n C/U] the amount of money that you must pay to live in or use a place that you do not own
pay rent *She pays £350 a month rent for a one-bedroomed apartment.*
high/low rent *Office rents are highest in the centre of town.*
put up the rent/raise the rent (=increase it) *Our landlord has just raised the rent again.*

charge /tʃɑːʳdʒ/ [n C/U] the amount of money that you must pay for a service or for being allowed to use something
bank/delivery/electricity etc charges *How much do you pay in bank charges a month?*
+for *Is there an extra charge for using the swimming pool? | There's no charge for disabled parking.*

fee /fiː/ [n C] the amount of money that you must pay to someone such as a doctor, lawyer, or teacher for a professional service: *My lawyer has increased his fee to $200 an hour.*
school/legal/medical etc fees *My insurance paid all the medical fees.*

2   ways of saying or asking how much something costs

cost /kɒst‖kɔːst/ [v] if something **costs** £10, $100 etc, that is what you have to pay in order to buy it: *How much did that coat cost?*
cost £10/$20/a lot etc *The holiday costs £600 per person. | It only costs 50 cents.*
cost sb £10/$20 etc *That sofa cost me nearly $1000.*
🔍 **cost (sb) a fortune** INFORMAL, ESPECIALLY SPOKEN (=use this to emphasize that something costs a lot of money, or costs a lot more than you expected) *This is costing us a fortune in phone bills.*
it costs £10/$20/a lot etc to do sth *It costs about £500 to fly to America.*
costing – cost – have cost

 Don't say 'it costs expensive'. Say **it is expensive** or **it costs a lot**.

🔍 **how much** /haʊ ˈmʌtʃ/ SPOKEN say **how much** to ask what the price or cost of something is: *How much is that table?* | *That's a beautiful ring – how much did you pay for it?* | *By the way, how much does it cost to use the swimming pool?*

> ⚠ Don't say 'how much costs this?' or 'how much cost was it?' Say **how much does this cost?** or **how much did it cost?**

○ **be** /biː/ [v] ESPECIALLY SPOKEN if something **is** £100, $1000 etc, that is how much it costs – use this especially when you are asking or replying to a question about the cost of something
be £5/$20/a lot of money etc *"That's a nice shirt – how much was it?" "It was only five pounds."* | *I can't remember how much it cost. I think it was around $400.*

3 how much something would cost if it was sold

value /'væljuː/ [n C/U] the amount of money that something expensive, rare, or old would cost if it was sold – use this to talk about things like houses, cars, jewellery, paintings, or furniture
+of *The value of the painting was estimated at $500,000.*
increase/fall in value *Some fine wines increase in value as they get older.*

> **Formal or informal?**
> **Value** is not used in informal conversation.

be worth /biː 'wɜːʳθ/ if something **is worth** £10, $100 etc, that is how much money it would cost if it was sold: *How much is your ring worth?*
be worth $500/£10 etc *I guess their house must be worth about £500,000.* | *That old piano can't be worth more than $200.*

4 to ask for a particular amount of money for something

charge /tʃɑːʳdʒ/ [v I/T] if someone **charges** an amount of money, that is how much you must pay them for providing a service or doing work for you

charge £10/$50 etc (for sth) *He charges $200 an hour.* | *The engineer charged £70 for labour and £45 for parts.*
charge sb £10/$50 *How much are they charging you for the repairs?* | *The bank will charge its customers 6% interest from next week.*

ask /ɑːsk‖æsk/ [v T] to state a price for something that you are selling, especially when it is not a fixed price and can be changed – use this when you are talking about a person, not a shop or a company
ask £100/$3000 etc for sth *He was asking £2000 for it, and was happy to take £1800.*

○ **want** /wɒnt‖wɑːnt/ [v T] ESPECIALLY SPOKEN to want an amount of money for something you are selling or for doing work for someone
want £20/$50 etc for sth *How much do you want for the video recorder?*

5 a statement that says how much something will probably cost

estimate /'estɪmət/ [n C] a statement that says how much money it will probably cost to build or repair something: *The final cost was £2000 higher than the original estimate.*
+for *I've asked the builders to give us an estimate for fixing the roof.*

quotation (also **quote** INFORMAL) /kwəʊ'teɪʃən, kwəʊt/ [n C] a written statement of exactly how much money something will cost: *Get a few quotations from different firms so you can compare prices.*

> When you see WB, go to the **WORD BANKS** section.

COUNT/CALCULATE

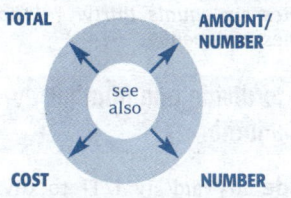

TOTAL

AMOUNT/ NUMBER

see also

COST

NUMBER

1 to count numbers, objects etc in order to find the total

count/count up /kaʊnt, ˌkaʊnt 'ʌp/ [v T] to find the total number of things or people in a group by counting them all: *Katherine counted her money. There was almost $50 left.* | *Count up the number of calories you have each day.* | *The teacher was counting the children as they got onto the bus.*

add up /ˌæd 'ʌp/ [phrasal verb T] to put several numbers or amounts together and calculate the total
add up sth *When we added up the receipts we realized we had spent too much.*
add sth up *The books cost quite a lot of money, when you added them all up.*

tot up /ˌtɒt 'ʌp ‖ ˌtɑːt-/ [phrasal verb T] INFORMAL to put several numbers or amounts together and calculate the total, especially quickly
tot up sth *Dan took his calculator and totted up some figures.*
tot sth up *I reckon there are around 230, if you tot them all up.*
tot – totting – totted

keep count /ˌkiːp 'kaʊnt/ to keep a record, either on paper or in your memory, of numbers or amounts that increase over a period of time, so that you always know what the total is: *I don't know what the score was. I wasn't keeping count.*
+of *She was trying to keep count of how many stations they'd passed.*

2 to calculate an amount or price

calculate /'kælkjˌ̩leɪt/ [v T] to find out how much something will cost, how long something will take etc, by using

numbers: *Their accountant calculated the total cost of the project.*
calculate how much/how many/ how far etc *I'll try to calculate how long it will take us to get home from here.*
+that *Sally calculated that she needed $300 to pay all her bills.*

calculation /ˌkælkjˌ̩'leɪʃən/ [n C often plural] a process by which you calculate a total, price, time etc: *NASA calculations put the cost of the space program at $118 billion.*

work out /ˌwɜːˈk 'aʊt/ [phrasal verb T] ESPECIALLY SPOKEN to calculate an answer, amount, price, or value
work out sth *I always use a calculator to work out percentages.*
work sth out *"How much do I owe you?" "I haven't worked it out yet."*
work out how much/ how many/ how far etc *We need to work out how much food we'll need to take with us.*

estimate /'estˌ̩meɪt/ [v T] to guess an amount, price, or number, as exactly as you can
+that *It's been estimated that the number of car-owners will increase by about 15%.*
estimate what/how many/how much etc *It is impossible to estimate how many illegal guns there are on the streets.*

estimate /'estˌ̩mˌ̩t/ [n C] an amount that is guessed, not calculated exactly: *As a rough estimate, we currently recycle about 5% of the paper we use.*

3 to add one number to another

add /æd/ [v T] to put two or more numbers together and calculate the answer
add sth and sth *If you add 24 and 36 you get 60.*
add sth to sth *Add 10% to the total.*
addition [n U] when you add a number

plus /plʌs/ [preposition] SPOKEN use **plus** between numbers or amounts to show that you are adding one to another: *Eight plus six is fourteen.* | *The cost is £45 plus £5 for delivery.*

 The written sign for **plus** is '+': 8 + 6 = 14

4 to take one number from another

Q **take/take away** /teɪk, ˌteɪk ə'weɪ/ [v T] ESPECIALLY SPOKEN to take one number from another and calculate the answer

take sth (away) from sth If you take 17 from 100 you get 83. | Take 19 away from 48 and then add 15.

subtract /səb'trækt/ [v T] to take one number from another and calculate the answer: To convert the temperature into Celsius, subtract 32, then multiply by 5 and divide by 9.

subtract sth from sth Subtract 12 from 32.

subtraction [n U] when you subtract a number

Formal or informal?

Subtract is more formal than **take** or **take away**.

Q **minus** /'maɪnəs/ [preposition] SPOKEN use **minus** between numbers or amounts to show that you are taking one from another: 30 minus 5 leaves 25.

⚠ The written sign for **minus** is '–': 10 − 6 = 4

5 to multiply one number by another

multiply /'mʌltɪplaɪ/ [v I/T] to add a number to itself a particular number of times

multiply sth by sth If you multiply ten by seven you get seventy.

+by To find the price in yen, you must multiply by 86.

multiplied by 11 multiplied by 10 is 110.

multiplying – multiplied – have multiplied

multiplication /ˌmʌltɪplɪ'keɪʃən/ [n U] when you multiply a number: Use your calculator for multiplication.

⚠ The written sign for **multiplied by** is '×': 6 × 3 =18

Q **times** /taɪmz/ [preposition] SPOKEN use **times** between numbers or amounts to show that you are multiplying one by another: Five times six equals thirty. | What's nine times eighteen?

6 to divide one number by another

divide /dɪ'vaɪd/ [v I/T] to divide one number by another, usually smaller, number

+by It is easier to divide by 10 than by 12.

divide sth by sth If you divide thirty by five you get six.

divided by 36 divided by 2 is 18.

division /dɪ'vɪʒən/ [n U] when you divide a number: We didn't learn division until we were older.

⚠ The written sign for **divided by** is '÷': 10 ÷ 2 = 5

COUNTRY

 if you mean 'land where there are trees and fields and not many buildings', go to **COUNTRYSIDE**

➡ see also **LAND AND SEA**, **WB** **ENVIRONMENT**

1 country

country /'kʌntri/ [n C] an area of land with its own government, army etc, for example, France, Japan, or the USA: Brazil is one of the biggest countries in the world. | How many countries are there in Europe? | The northeast of the country was badly hit by the hurricane. | I've travelled all over the country. (=to a lot of places within a country)

the country (=all the people in a country) The explosion in Paris shocked the whole country.

plural **countries**

⚠ Don't say 'what is your country?'. Say **where are you from?** or **where do you come from?**

nation /ˈneɪʃən/ [n C] a country – use this especially to talk about a country's history, way of life, and social and economic conditions: *Indonesia is the world's largest Muslim nation.* | *Representatives from the world's eight leading industrial nations will meet in Geneva this week.* | *The flag symbolizes a new united, democratic South African nation.*
the nation (=all the people in a nation) *The President will broadcast to the nation this evening.* | *a celebration that united the whole nation*

state /steɪt/ [n C] a country – use this to talk about a country as a political organization with its own political system: *In 1830 Greece became an independent state.* | *the member states of the European Union* (=the countries that belong to the EU)
one-party/capitalist/democratic etc state (=with that particular form of government) *For more that 70 years the Soviet Union was a one-party state.*

land /lænd/ [n C] ESPECIALLY WRITTEN a country – used mainly in poetry and stories: *Long ago, in a far away land, there lived a wicked queen.* | *His journey took him to many foreign lands.*
your native land (=the country where you were born) *They were honest men who loved their native land.*
a land of opportunity (=a country where there are new and exciting opportunities) *Australia represented a land of opportunity for thousands of people.*

republic /rɪˈpʌblɪk/ [n C] a country that has an elected government, and is led by a president, not a king or queen: *the Czech Republic* | *the Republic of Ireland*

empire /ˈempaɪəʳ/ [n C] a group of countries that are all controlled by one ruler or government: *the Roman Empire* | *the government of an empire*

colony /ˈkɒləni‖ˈkɑː-/ [n C] a country that has no independent government of its own, but is controlled by a more powerful country, especially one that is a long way away: *Algeria was formerly a French colony.*
plural **colonies**

monarchy /ˈmɒnəʳkiː‖ˈmɑːn-/ [n C] a country whose head of state is a king or queen: *In Britain, we live in a monarchy.*
plural **monarchies**

2　the country that you come from

be from/come from /biː ˈfrɒm, ˈkʌm frɒm/ [phrasal verb T] if you **are from** or **come from** a country, that is where you were born or is the place that you consider to be your home: *Maya's father is from Sri Lanka and her mother is from Brazil.* | *"Where do you come from?" "Australia."*

> ⚠ Don't say 'he is coming from Hong Kong'. Say **he comes from Hong Kong**.

home /həʊm/ [n U] the country that you consider to be your home, especially when you are living in a different country: *I've lived abroad most of my life but I still think of England as my home.*
🔍 **back home** SPOKEN (=in the country you come from) *Back home we never had to lock our doors at night.*
go/travel/fly home *Air fares go up in December because everyone flies home for Christmas.*

> ⚠ Don't say 'I'm going back to my country'. Say **I'm going home**.

3　the line where one country ends and another begins

border /ˈbɔːʳdəʳ/ [n C] the official line that separates two countries
+with *The river runs along Mexico's border with the US.*
the Brazilian/Nigerian etc border (=the border where Brazil, Nigeria etc begins)
on the border *Jeumont is a small town on the French-Belgian border.*
cross the border *The refugees crossed the border at night.*

4 someone who has the right to live in a country

citizen /'sɪtˌɪzən/ [n C] a person from a particular country who has the legal right to vote, work, and live there: *He became a Dutch citizen after working there for eight years.* | *The US government is advising all American citizens in the war zone to come home.*

nationality /ˌnæʃəˈnælˌti/ [n C/U] your **nationality** is the fact that you are American, Japanese, French etc: *We had to write our name and nationality on the form.* | *people of different nationalities*
plural **nationalities**

> ⚠ **Nationality** is not used to tell someone where you come from. Don't say 'my nationality is French'. Say **I am French** or **I come from France**.

citizenship /'sɪtˌɪzənʃɪp/ [n U]
US/Japanese etc citizenship the legal right of being an American, Japanese etc citizen, especially when you were born in another country: *She married him so that she could get Swiss citizenship.*

5 existing in or happening in a country

national /'næʃənəl/ [adj usually before noun] use **national** about things that happen in or affect a whole country and not just a part of it: *Ice hockey is the national sport of Canada.* | *The Day of the Dead is a national holiday in Latin American countries.* | *national and local news*
nationally [adv] *Nationally there was a 12% drop in crime last year.*

domestic /dəˈmestɪk/ [adj usually before noun] FORMAL use **domestic** about things that happen or exist within a country and do not affect any other country: *All domestic flights have been cancelled, but a few international flights are still running.* | *The factory produces cars mainly for the domestic market.*

> ⚠ **Domestic** is used mainly in business and political contexts.

6 existing in or happening in many countries

international /ˌɪntərˈnæʃənəl/ [adj usually before noun] use **international** about things that involve or affect people from several different countries: *an international conference on human rights* | *international trade agreements* | *Hal Hartley's latest movie has been an international success.*

multinational /ˌmʌltiˈnæʃənəl/ [adj only before noun]
multinational company/bank/corporation a large company that has offices or factories in many different countries: *a huge multinational oil corporation*

7 someone who loves their country

patriotic /ˌpætriˈɒtɪk, ˌpeɪ-‖ˌpeɪtriˈɑtɪk/ [adj] someone who is **patriotic** loves their country and is very loyal to it: *We're just good, patriotic Americans ready to defend our freedom.* | *At school we had to raise the flag and sing patriotic songs every morning.*
patriotism /'pætriətɪzəm, 'peɪ-‖'peɪ-/ [n U] love for your country

nationalistic /ˌnæʃənəˈlɪstɪk/ [adj] someone who is **nationalistic** believes that their country is better than any other, and often has no respect for other countries: *As nationalistic feelings grew, life became increasingly difficult for immigrants.*
nationalism /'næʃənəlɪzəm/ [n U] nationalistic feelings: *the rise of nationalism and military power that led to war in 1914*

8 people who want to form a separate country

nationalist /'næʃənəlˌɪst/ [n C] someone who wants a separate independent country for people of their own race, religion, or origin

Scottish/Welsh/Quebec etc nationalists *The Scottish nationalists won a record number of votes in the local elections.*
nationalist [*adj*] *the nationalist campaign in French-speaking Canada*
nationalism [*n* U] *nationalist ideas and activities: Basque nationalism*

COUNTRYSIDE

the parts of a country that are far from towns or cities

➡ see also **WB** ENVIRONMENT

countryside /ˈkʌntrisaɪd/ [*n* U] the parts of a country that are not near any big towns or cities, where there are farms, fields, villages etc: *a villa with wonderful views over the surrounding countryside*
the French/Sussex etc countryside *Cezanne's paintings of the French countryside*
the country /ðə ˈkʌntri/ [*n* singular] an area that is not in or near a big town or city – use this when you are comparing this kind of area with towns and cities
in the country *I'd hate to live in the country – I'd get really bored. | They have an apartment in town and a cottage in the country.*

> ⚠ You can also use **country** before a noun, like an adjective: *a country house* (=a big house in the country) | *country people*

rural /ˈrʊərəl/ [*adj* only before noun] use **rural** about places and situations that exist far away from big towns and cities, especially when you are talking about employment, education, and social conditions: *People living in rural areas depend on having a car. | a shortage of rural housing*
rural France/India etc *In many parts of rural India there is no electricity.*

nature /ˈneɪtʃər/ [*n* U] everything in the physical world that is not made or controlled by humans, such as wild plants and animals, rocks, and the weather: *We grew up in the countryside surrounded by nature. | the beauty of nature*

nature reserve (=an area where animals and plants are protected)

> ⚠ Don't use **nature** when you mean **countryside**. Don't say 'The nature around here is very beautiful'. Say **The countryside around here is very beautiful.**

COURT/TRIAL

➡ see Word Banks section

COVER

1 to put something over, on, or around something else

cover /ˈkʌvər/ [*v* T] to put something over, on, or around something else, in order to hide it, protect it, or improve its appearance: *Prepare the salad, and cover it until it's time to serve.*
cover sth with sth *She covered her face with her hands and ran upstairs.*
cover up sth/cover sth up (=cover something completely) *They used special paint to cover up the cracks in the wall.*
put over /ˌpʊt ˈəʊvər/ [*phrasal verb* T] to put a cloth or piece of material loosely over the top of something in order to cover it: *The stewardess gave him a blanket to put over his legs.*
put sth over sth *Before you paint the walls, put some old sheets over the furniture.*
wrap up/wrap /ˌræp ˈʌp, ræp/ [*v* T] to put paper, plastic, cloth etc tightly around something in order to protect it or decorate it: *Have you wrapped all your Christmas presents yet?*
wrap sth up/wrap up sth *Open it if you want to, I can always wrap it up again.*
wrap sth (up) in sth *Her gift was wrapped in beautiful gold paper.*
coat /kəʊt/ [*v* T] ESPECIALLY WRITTEN to thinly cover the whole surface of something, especially food, with something soft or liquid

coat sth with/in sth *Coat the chicken with garlic butter and cook it at 200° C.*

2 something that is used to cover something else

cover /ˈkʌvəʳ/ [n C] a piece of paper, plastic, cloth etc that is used to cover something: *I've bought some cushion covers to brighten up my room.* | *It's a good idea to buy a dust cover for your computer keyboard.* | *There were old record covers scattered all over the floor.* | *a duvet cover*

covering /ˈkʌvərɪŋ/ [n C] something that is used to cover a large flat area, especially in order to protect it from damage, dirt etc
floor/wall covering *The prison cells have no electricity and no floor coverings.*

lid /lɪd/ [n C] a flat part that fits on top of a container, a pan, a box etc in order to close it: *a saucepan lid* | *She wiped the lid and screwed it back on.*
+of *Sam lifted the lid of his desk and took out a calculator.*

top /tɒpǁtɑːp/ [n C] a thing that you put on or over an object to cover it, protect it, or prevent liquid coming out of it: *Why don't you ever put the top back on the toothbottle?* | *I can't get the top off this bottle.*

wrapper /ˈræpəʳ/ [n C] a piece of paper, or very thin plastic or metal, that covers food, chocolate etc when you buy it: *The empty stadium was littered with burger wrappers and empty cans.* | *chewing-gum wrappers*

3 a thin flat layer that covers a surface

layer /ˈleɪəʳ/ [n C] a thin flat quantity of something that covers the whole of a surface
+of *A layer of dust covered everything in the room.* | *The original wallpaper was hidden under several layers of paint.*

film /fɪlm/ [n C] ESPECIALLY WRITTEN a very thin clear layer, especially of something liquid, that has formed on a surface

a film of oil/grease/sweat/dust *There was a film of oil floating on the surface of the water.*

coating /ˈkəʊtɪŋ/ [n C] a layer of a liquid or soft substance that has been put on the surface of something, for example in order to protect it or make it taste better: *The tent is made from nylon with a waterproof coating.*
+of *ice-cream with a thick coating of chocolate*

4 when an object or area has been covered with something

be covered in/with sth /biː ˈkʌvəʳd ɪn, wɪð (sth)/ if something is **covered in** or **covered with** something, it has that substance lying all over the top of it or spread all over it: *The ground was covered with snow.* | *Look at your clothes! They're covered in mud.* | *a wall covered with ivy*

be coated in/with sth /biː ˈkəʊtʲd ɪn, wɪð (sth)/ if an object **is coated in** or **coated with** a liquid or soft substance, it has a layer of that substance all over its surface: *Serve the chicken with new potatoes coated in butter.*

CRAZY

very strange and not at all sensible

➡ if you mean that someone has a mental illness, go to **MENTALLY ILL**

1 people

🔍 **crazy** (also **mad** BRITISH) /ˈkreɪzi, mæd/ [adj] ESPECIALLY SPOKEN someone who is **crazy** or **mad** behaves in a way that is strange or not sensible: *My parents think I'm crazy, but I've always enjoyed dangerous sports.* | *You agreed to marry him? Are you mad?* | *Both his brothers are such crazy drivers.*
go crazy/mad (=start to feel crazy) *I'll go crazy if I stay in this house much longer.*
drive sb crazy/mad (=make them start to feel crazy) *Stop that noise! You're driving me crazy.*

be **crazy/mad to do sth** *You must be crazy to lend him all that money!*
crazy – crazier – craziest
mad – madder – maddest

> ⚠ Don't say 'become crazy' or 'become mad'. Say **go crazy** or **go mad**.

> ⚠ Don't say 'very crazy' or 'very mad'. Say **completely crazy/mad** or **totally crazy/mad**: *If I don't take a holiday soon, I'm going to go totally crazy.*

◌ **insane/out of your mind** /ɪnˈseɪn, ˌaʊt əv jɔːr ˈmaɪnd/ [adj] ESPECIALLY SPOKEN you say someone is **insane** or **out of their mind** if they do something or intend to do something that is completely crazy: *Anyone who takes a boat out in this weather must be insane.* | *Tell the police? Are you out of your mind?*

◌ **maniac/lunatic** /ˈmeɪniæk, ˈluːnətɪk/ [n C] ESPECIALLY SPOKEN someone who behaves in a stupidly dangerous way: *He drives like a maniac.* | *Some lunatic threw paraffin on the fire.*

◌ **barmy** /ˈbɑːrmi/ [adj] BRITISH SPOKEN INFORMAL you say someone is **barmy** if they do or say things that seem slightly strange or crazy: *You must be barmy, hanging around outside on a night like this.*
barmy – barmier- barmiest

zany /ˈzeɪni/ [adj] INFORMAL crazy or unusual in a way that is funny: *zany comedian Vic Reeves* | *Some of my colleagues are pretty zany.*
zany – zanier – zaniest

◌ **be nuts** (also **be crackers** BRITISH) /biː ˈnʌts, biː ˈkrækəʳz/ SPOKEN INFORMAL to be crazy: *People will think you're crackers if you go around talking to yourself.* | *That guy is nuts!*

◌ **nutcase** /ˈnʌtkeɪs/ [n C] SPOKEN INFORMAL someone who behaves strangely and has very unusual ideas: *He's a complete nutcase.*

2 things/ideas/situations

◌ **crazy** (also **mad** BRITISH) /ˈkreɪzi, mæd/ [adj] ESPECIALLY SPOKEN ideas, actions, or situations that are **crazy** or **mad** are not at all sensible and are

likely to cause problems or danger: *You see drivers do some crazy things.* | *Jade wants to build a swimming pool in the garden. I think it's a mad idea.*
it's crazy *The farmers get more money from the government if they don't plant crops – it's crazy.*
crazy – crazier – craziest
mad – madder – maddest

> ⚠ Don't say 'very crazy' or 'very mad'. Say **absolutely crazy/mad** or **completely crazy/mad**: *How can we do all this work in one day? It's absolutely crazy.*

insane /ɪnˈseɪn/ [adj] an **insane** idea or plan is stupid or dangerous, and is very unlikely to succeed: *For some insane reason, he decided to do the whole drive in one day.*
it is insane to do sth *It would be insane to try to climb the mountain in weather like this.*

◌ **be lunacy** (also **be madness** BRITISH) /biː ˈluːnəsi, biː ˈmædnɪs/ ESPECIALLY SPOKEN you say that a situation or action **is lunacy** or **is madness** if you think it is completely crazy: *They can't close the hospital – it's madness!*
it is sheer lunacy/madness to do sth (=it is completely crazy to do it) *It would be sheer lunacy to turn down such a good job offer.*

CRIME

WB COURT/TRIAL   THREATEN
STEAL   **TELL 5**
                 see
                 also
DRUGS   **WB** POLICE
KILL   **LAW**
                 ATTACK

1 something that is not legal

crime /kraɪm/ [n C] an action that is against the law, such as stealing something, taking drugs, or deliberately hurting someone: *The number of crimes reported to the police has increased.*

commit a crime (=do something that is a crime) *We believe that the crime was committed around 7:30 p.m.*
+against *Violent crimes against the elderly are on the increase.*
serious crime *The police say that 50% of serious crimes are drug-related.*
solve a crime (=find out who did it) *a terrible crime which was never solved*

> ⚠ Don't say 'make a crime' or 'do a crime'. Say **commit a crime**.

offence BRITISH **offense** AMERICAN /ə'fens/ [n C] any action that can be punished by law: *He has been charged with several offenses, including homicide.*
commit an offence (=do something that is an offence) *Bates is being tried for offences committed in the 1980s.*
criminal offence *Driving when drunk is a criminal offence.*
serious offence *The number of women convicted of serious offences is still relatively small.*
minor offence (=not very serious) *a minor traffic offence*
speeding/parking offence *Speeding offenses are usually punishable by a fine.*

> **Formal or informal?**
> **Offence** is used especially in formal situations by the police, judges, and lawyers.
> **Offence** can be used both for serious crimes like murder and robbery, and for less serious actions like parking your car in the wrong place or not paying your taxes.

> ⚠ Don't say 'do an offence'. Say **commit an offence**.

illegal /ɪ'liːgəl/ [adj] not legal: *He was caught selling illegal drugs.* | *fraud and other illegal activities*
it is illegal to do sth *In Britain, it is illegal to sell cigarettes to anyone under 16.*

be against the law /beː ə,genst ðə 'lɔː/ if something **is against the law**, it is illegal to do it: *Drinking alcohol in a public place is against the law.*
it is against the law to do sth *In Sweden, it is against the law to hit a child.*

break the law /,breɪk ðə 'lɔː/ to do something that is illegal: *People who break the law must expect to be punished.* | *I didn't realize I was breaking the law.*

criminal /'krɪmɪnəl/ [adj only before noun] FORMAL connected with crimes: *James made around £100,000 from his criminal activities.*
criminal record (=a list of someone's crimes that is kept by the police) *It's very difficult to get a job if you have a criminal record.*
criminal charge (=an official statement by the police that someone has done something illegal) *West's wife faced serious criminal charges in connection with the murders.*

2 crimes in general

crime /kraɪm/ [n U] crimes in general – use this to talk generally about the reasons for crimes, the problems they cause, and the number of crimes: *a support group for victims of crime* | *Voters are increasingly concerned about the level of crime.*
violent crime *Violent crime increased by 36% last year.*
serious crime *Victims of serious crime are often too scared to talk about their experiences.*
petty crime (=crime that is not very serious) *Leo became involved in petty crime at a very young age.*

> ⚠ You can also use **crime** before a noun, like an adjective: *an increase in the crime rate* (=the number of crimes that happen) | *crime prevention*

> ⚠ Don't say 'the crime' when you are talking about crimes in general: *People are worried about the increase in crime* (not 'in the crime').

3 someone who commits a crime

criminal /'krɪmɪnəl/ [n C] someone who is guilty of a serious crime or of several crimes: *The police described him as a violent and dangerous criminal.*
convicted criminal (=someone that a court has found guilty of a crime)

offender /ə'fendə^r/ [n C] someone who has broken the law and is being punished for doing this: *The courts should impose tougher punishments on offenders.*
young offender BRITISH **juvenile offender** AMERICAN (=under 18 years old) *The system for dealing with young offenders doesn't really work.*

gang /gæŋ/ [n C] a group of criminals who work together: *Gangs of thieves used to hang around the station.*
armed gang (=carrying weapons) *An armed gang robbed a warehouse in the south of the city.*

murderer /'mɜː^{r}dərə^r/ [n C] someone who kills another person deliberately: *A massive police hunt for the murderer has begun.*
convicted murderer (=someone that a court has found guilty of murder)

burglar /'bɜː^{r}glə^r/ [n C] someone who goes into buildings, especially houses, to steal things: *Burglars broke into their house took two computers and some cash.*

robber /'rɒbə^r‖'rɑː-/ [n C] someone who steals money or other things from a bank, shop etc
bank robber (=someone who steals from a bank)
armed robber (=carrying weapons) *Armed robbers shot a security guard and escaped with $6000 in cash.*

mugger /'mʌgə^r/ [n C] someone who attacks another person in a public place and steals things from them: *Three muggers beat him up and stole his money and mobile phone.*

organized crime /,ɔː^{r}gənaɪzd 'kraɪm/ [n U] large criminal organizations that plan and control serious crimes such as robbing banks and selling drugs: *Police need more resources to fight organized crime.*

CRITICIZE

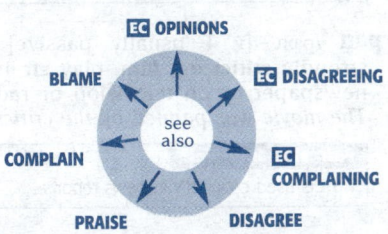

EC OPINIONS
BLAME
EC DISAGREEING
see also
COMPLAIN
EC COMPLAINING
PRAISE
DISAGREE

1 to say what is bad about a person, plan, performance etc

criticize (also **criticise** BRITISH) /'krɪtɪsaɪz/ [v I/T] *Stop criticizing my driving!* | *People are always criticizing the royal family, but I think they do a good job.* | *It's easy to criticize, but managing a football team can be an extremely difficult job.*
criticize sb for doing sth *The United Nations was criticized for failing to react sooner to the crisis.*
criticize sb/sth as sth *The TV show was criticized as racist and inaccurate.*

attack /ə'tæk/ [v T] to strongly and publicly criticize a person, plan, or belief that you completely disagree with: *Several actors have attacked proposals to cut the theatre's budget.*
attack sb for (doing) sth *Newspapers attacked the government for raising taxes.*

 Attack is used especially in news reports.

be critical /biː 'krɪtɪkəl/ to strongly criticize a plan, system etc, especially when you give detailed reasons why you think it is bad: *Why do you always have to be so critical?*
+of *Miller was critical of the way the company was managed.*
be highly critical (=very critical) *The judge was highly critical of the Los Angeles Police Department.*

When you see **EC**, go to the **ESSENTIAL COMMUNICATION** section.

Formal or informal?

Be critical is not often used in informal conversation.

pan /pæn/ [v T usually passive] to strongly criticize a film, play etc in a newspaper or on television or radio: *The movie was panned by the critics.*

Formal or informal?

Pan is used especially in news reports.

2 to criticize someone or something in an annoying, unfair, or unkind way

find fault with sth /ˌfaɪnd ˈfɔːlt wɪð (sth)/ to criticize things that are wrong with someone or something, especially small and unimportant things: *No-one enjoys working for a boss who always finds fault with their work.*

pick holes in sth /ˌpɪk ˈhəʊlz ɪn (sth)/ INFORMAL, ESPECIALLY BRITISH to criticize small details in someone's ideas or plan – use this about someone who seems to be looking for problems and mistakes: *As soon as she stopped talking, Janet's colleagues began to pick holes in the idea.*

talk about sb behind their back /ˌtɔːk əbaʊt (sb) bɪˌhaɪnd ðeəᵊ ˈbæk/ to criticize someone when they are not there: *I was very upset when I found out that they'd all been talking about me behind my back.*

make fun of sb/poke fun at sb /ˌmeɪk ˈfʌn ɒv (sb), ˌpəʊk ˈfʌn æt (sb)/ to say unkind things about someone or about the things they do, in order to make them look silly: *The kids at school make fun of Jack because he's fat.* | *a comedian who pokes fun at TV celebrities and politicians*

3 to tell someone that they should not have done something

tell sb off /ˌtel (sb) ˈɒf‖-ˈɔːf/ [phrasal verb T] to tell someone that they should not have done something, and warn them that they must not do it again – use this especially about

teachers and parents talking to children
+for *When I got home my dad told me off for staying out so late.*
get told off (=be told off) *She was always getting told off by her teachers.*

chew sb out /ˌtʃuː (sb) ˈaʊt/ [phrasal verb T] AMERICAN INFORMAL if someone in authority chews you out, they talk to you angrily for a long time because they disapprove of what you have done: *She called him into her office to chew him out for not doing his job.*
get chewed out *I was always getting chewed out for coming home late.*

4 something that you write or say in order to criticize

criticism /ˈkrɪtɪsɪzəm/ [n C/U] what you say or write when you criticize someone or something: *Bill's very sensitive to any kind of criticism.*
+of *The report makes many criticisms of the nation's prison system.*
severe/strong criticism *There has been strong criticism of these proposals.*
come in for criticism (=be criticized) *Taylor has come in for a lot of criticism for his part in the affair.*

attack /əˈtæk/ [n C/U] a statement that criticizes someone publicly, especially in politics
+on *The communist newspapers often contained attacks on the Church.*
come under attack from sb (=be criticized by someone) *Once again the oil companies have come under attack from environmentalists.*

⚠ **Attack** is used especially in news reports.

critical /ˈkrɪtɪkəl/ [adj] a **critical** statement, report, or description criticizes someone or something: *She was offended whenever anyone made critical remarks about her acting ability.*
highly critical (=very critical) *The article is highly critical of US policy towards Central America.*

scathing /ˈskeɪðɪŋ/ [adj] criticizing someone or something very strongly, because you think they are completely wrong or of low quality

scathing attack/comment/remark
etc *Her new book is a scathing attack
on the President.*
+about *'The New York Times' was
particularly scathing about his
performance.*

5 someone who criticizes

critic /'krɪtɪk/ [n C] someone who
criticizes a person, such as a politician or business leader, or their plans
or methods, especially in public: *The
Prime Minister answered his critics in a
televised speech.*
+of *Critics of nuclear power say that it
is dangerous and that no one knows
what to do with nuclear waste.*

CROWD

➡ if you mean 'when there are a lot of
people travelling, shopping etc', go
to **BUSY/NOT BUSY**

1 a large number of people together in a public place

crowd /kraʊd/ [n C] a large number of
people together in one place: *I don't
often go to football games because I
don't like big crowds.*
+of *a crowd of angry protesters*
crowds of people/shoppers/tourists
etc *The exhibition is expected to attract
huge crowds of visitors.*
horde /hɔː'd/ [n C] a large crowd of
people who are behaving in a noisy
uncontrolled way that you disapprove
of
+of *A horde of screaming kids ran out
of the building.* | *She was chased by
hordes of reporters and camera crews.*
mob /mɒb‖mɑːb/ [n C] a crowd of noisy
and violent people who are difficult
to control: *The mob set fire to cars and
buildings.*
+of *A mob of 200 rioters caused millions of pounds worth of damage.*

Formal or informal?

Mob is used especially in news reports or in
formal writing about historical events.

2 when a place is full of people

crowded /'kraʊdᶾd/ [adj] so full of
people that it is difficult to move or to
find a place to sit or stand: *The train
was really crowded.* | *James walked
into the crowded bar.*
+with *It was two weeks before
Christmas and the mall was crowded
with shoppers.*
packed /pækt/ [adj] so full of people
that there is almost no space left: *The
club is so popular that it's packed by 9
o'clock.* | *A bomb exploded this morn-
ing in a packed department store in the
city centre.*
+with *St Peter's Square was packed
with tourists.*
jam-packed (=completely full) *The
stadium was absolutely jam-packed.*
overcrowded /ˌəʊvə'ˈkraʊdᶾd◂/ [adj] a
place that is **overcrowded** has too
many people in it and is unpleasant
and uncomfortable: *The buses were all
filthy and overcrowded.* | *overcrowded
prisons*
be swarming with /biː 'swɔː'mɪŋ wɪð/ if
a place **is swarming with** people, it
is crowded with so many people that
it is difficult to go where you want to
go – use this when you are annoyed
that a place is crowded with people,
especially people you disapprove of:
*The place was swarming with noisy
kids.*
packed out /ˌpækt 'aʊt/ [adj not before
noun] BRITISH INFORMAL a cinema,
restaurant etc that is **packed out** is
completely full of people: *The
theatre's been packed out every night
this week.*
+with *There's good live music most
nights and it's always packed out with
students.*

3 when a crowd fills a place

crowd /kraʊd/ [v I/T] WRITTEN if people
crowd a place, they fill it and move
around in it: *Shoppers and tourists
crowded the market square every day.*

+**around** (also **round** BRITISH) *Fans crowded around the entrance, hoping to see the band as they arrived.*

fill /fɪl/ [v T] ESPECIALLY WRITTEN if a lot of people **fill** a place, there are so many of them that there is no room for any more: *An audience of over 50,000 had filled the arena.*

4 when people come together to make a crowd

gather /ˈgæðəʳ/ [v I] if people **gather**, they meet or come together and become a crowd: *By the time the President arrived, a large crowd had gathered to watch.*
+**around/at/in etc** *Angry workers were gathering around the steps of the City Hall.*

form /fɔːʳm/ [v I] ESPECIALLY WRITTEN if a crowd **forms**, more and more people join a group of people who are already watching or listening to something: *A crowd was beginning to form at the scene of the accident.*

congregate /ˈkɒŋgrɪgeɪt‖ˈkɑːŋ-/ [v I] if people **congregate** in a place, a large number of them meet there, especially regularly in the same place, and at the same time
+**at/in/around etc** *On Friday evening, teenagers would congregate outside the bars on the main street.*

5 when a crowd separates

disperse /dɪˈspɜːʳs/ [v I] if a crowd **disperses**, the people in it begin to move away in different directions: *Once the ambulance left, the crowd began to disperse.*

> **Formal or informal?**
> **Disperse** is more formal than **break up**.

break up /ˌbreɪk ˈʌp/ [phrasal verb I] if a crowd **breaks up**, people start to leave and move away in small groups: *When the police arrived, the crowd broke up very quickly.*

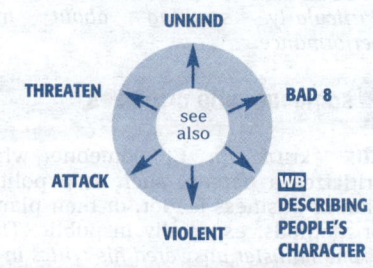

CRUEL

UNKIND

THREATEN

see also

BAD 8

ATTACK

WB
DESCRIBING
PEOPLE'S
CHARACTER

VIOLENT

1 cruel people

cruel /ˈkruːəl/ [adj] someone who is **cruel** deliberately causes pain and does not care if other people suffer: *Children can sometimes be very cruel.*
+**to** *She loved him even though he was often cruel to her.*
it is cruel to do sth *I think it's cruel to keep dogs locked up inside all day.*
cruelly [adv] *Women prisoners were treated especially cruelly.*
cruel – crueller – cruellest BRITISH
cruel – crueler – cruelest AMERICAN

mean /miːn/ [adj] someone who is **mean** is very unkind in the way they treat people, especially by saying unkind things to them: *Why are you being so mean?*
+**to** *Sharon was really mean to me at school today.*
it is mean of sb to do sth *It was mean of you not to invite her.*
real mean AMERICAN SPOKEN (=very unkind or rude) *He said something real mean to Jake.*

ruthless /ˈruːθləs/ [adj] so determined to get what you want that you do not care how much other people suffer: *These men are ruthless terrorists. | the ruthless dictator, Joseph Stalin*
ruthlessly [adv] *His political opponents were ruthlessly executed.*

sadist /ˈseɪdɪst/ [n C] someone who enjoys making people suffer: *Andrea's father was a real sadist. I'm not surprised that she hates him.*

sadistic /səˈdɪstɪk/ [adj] someone who is **sadistic** enjoys hurting people or being cruel to them: *He took a sadistic* pleasure in embarrassing her in front of her friends. | The head teacher was a violent and sadistic man.

2 cruel punishments/behaviour

cruel /'kruːəl/ [adj] intended to upset someone or make them suffer: *Lyle was always playing cruel jokes on his little sister.* | *The electric chair is possibly the cruelest method of execution.*
cruel – crueller – cruellest BRITISH
cruel – crueler – cruelest AMERICAN

barbaric /baːˈbærɪk/ [adj] extremely cruel, in a way that shocks people: *the barbaric treatment of prisoners* | *The custom of stoning criminals to death seems simply barbaric.*

cold-blooded /ˌkəʊld ˈblʌd̮ɪd◂/ [adj only before noun]
cold-blooded murder/killing/attack a murder etc done without showing any feeling or pity for the person who is attacked: *The country has been shocked by the cold-blooded murder of the two girls.*

cruelty /'kruːəlti/ [n U] cruel treatment or behaviour: *Walter's wife left him because of his cruelty.*
+to *She has been campaigning against cruelty to animals for years.*

abuse /əˈbjuːs/ [n U] deliberately cruel treatment of someone, especially someone in your family that you are supposed to care for: *a woman who had suffered abuse from her husband for many years*
child abuse (=when a child is harmed physically or sexually) *There has been an increase in the number of cases of child abuse.*
sexual abuse (=when someone forces another person to take part in sexual activities) *a victim of sexual abuse*

3 to treat someone cruelly

be cruel to sb /biː ˈkruːəl tuː (sb)/ *Teachers at the school were often accused of being cruel to the children in their care.*

be mean to sb /biː ˈmiːn tuː (sb)/ to treat someone in a very unkind way, especially by saying unkind things to them: *She was mean to her sister.*

abuse /əˈbjuːz/ [v T] to treat someone in your family or someone that you

are responsible for in a cruel way, especially violently or sexually: *The children's father abused them for years.* | *Erica runs a hostel for women who have been abused by their husbands.*
sexually abuse (=force someone to take part in sexual activities) *He was accused of sexually abusing five children.*

persecute /'pɜːˈsɪkjuːt/ [v T] to be cruel to a person or group of people over a long period because of their race or their religious or political beliefs: *Countries all over Europe have persecuted gypsies for centuries.*
be persecuted *Jewish families were relentlessly persecuted.*
persecution /ˌpɜːsɪˈkjuːʃən/ [n U] *They left the country to escape persecution.*

bully /'bʊli/ [v T] to be cruel to someone who is smaller, younger, or weaker than you – use this especially about children being cruel to other children: *A group of girls would bully the younger kids, and force them to give them money.*
be bullied *He killed himself after being bullied at school.*
bullying – bullied – have bullied

bullying [n U] when people are being bullied: *a campaign to put an end to bullying in schools*

CRY

➡ opposite **LAUGH**
➡ see also **SAD, WORRYING/WORRIED, SHOUT**

1 to cry

cry /kraɪ/ [v I] if you **cry**, tears come from your eyes, for example because you are sad or upset, or because you have hurt yourself: *I could hear the baby crying in the next room.* | *A little boy was crying because he'd fallen off his bike.* | *Don't cry. I'll be back soon.*
make sb cry *The film was so sad, it made me cry.*
○ **cry and cry** ESPECIALLY SPOKEN (=cry for a long time) *I couldn't believe it – I just cried and cried.*
○ **cry your eyes out** ESPECIALLY SPOKEN (=cry a lot because you are very

upset) *The poor kid's so miserable, he's upstairs crying his eyes out.*
cry with happiness/joy/relief *She cried with joy when she heard that the children were safe.*
crying – cried – have cried

crying [n U] *We could hear the sound of crying coming from his room.*

weep /wiːp/ [v I] WRITTEN to cry a lot because you feel sad: *Caroline wept when she heard the news.* | *Weeping mourners followed the coffin into the churchyard.*
weep with emotion/grief/joy *Ivan wept with emotion as he waved goodbye to his family.*
weeping – wept – have wept

> ⚠ Use **weep** when you are writing stories and descriptions.

sob /sɒbǁsɑːb/ [v I] if you **sob**, you cry noisily and your body shakes, because you are very sad or because someone has upset you: *She collapsed, sobbing, in his arms.* | *"Please don't leave me," she sobbed.*
sobbing – sobbed – have sobbed

> ⚠ Use **sob** especially when you are writing stories and descriptions.

in tears /ɪn ˈtɪəʳz/ crying because someone has upset you, or because a film, story etc is very sad: *Frank ran out of the room in tears.* | *Most of us were in tears by the time he'd finished his story.*

tear /tɪəʳ/ [n C usually plural] a drop of water that comes from your eyes when you are crying: *Grandpa wiped the tears from his eyes.*
have tears in your eyes (=when you are nearly crying) *Ahmed had tears in his eyes, and I knew he was thinking of home.*
tears run down sb's face/cheeks (=someone is crying a lot) *Tears of joy ran down her face.*
be close to tears (=be almost crying) *Howell was close to tears as he told the court what had happened.*

sb's eyes water /(sb's) ˈaɪz ˌwɔːtəʳ/ if your **eyes water**, they feel painful and you start to cry, for example when you are cutting onions or when there is a lot of smoke

make sb's eyes water *The cigarette smoke was making my eyes water.*

2 to start to cry

start to cry/start crying /ˌstɑːʳt tə ˈkraɪ, ˌstɑːʳt ˈkraɪ-ɪŋ/ *What should I do if the baby starts crying?* | *He started crying when I told her I wanted to end our relationship.*

burst into tears /ˌbɜːʳst ɪntə ˈtɪəʳz/ to suddenly start to cry because you are very upset about something: *Janet burst into tears and ran out of the room.*

break down /ˌbreɪk ˈdaʊn/ [phrasal verb I] ESPECIALLY WRITTEN to suddenly start to cry a lot, after trying not to cry
break down and cry *As the funeral service began, Paolo broke down and cried.*
break down in tears *All the worry and anxiety had been too much for her, and she suddenly broke down in tears.*

CUT

➡ see also **SHARP/NOT SHARP, PIECE, HURT/INJURE**

1 with scissors or a knife

cut /kʌt/ [v I/T] to divide something into two or more pieces, using a knife or scissors: *He poured some coffee and cut a slice of bread.* | *Using scissors, cut carefully along the dotted line.*
cut sth in two/cut sth in half *Mandy cut the paper in half and gave a piece to each child.*
cut sth up/cut up sth (=into several pieces) *Can you cut the pizza up, please?* | *Tommy sat on the floor, cutting up old magazines.*
cut sth open *Rescue workers had to use special equipment to cut the steel door open.*
cutting – cut – have cut

slit /slɪt/ [v T] to make a long narrow cut through something, especially skin or cloth: *He killed the sheep by slitting its throat.*
slit sth open *Diane slit the envelope open with a knife.*
slitting – slit – have slit

slash /slæʃ/ [v T] to cut something quickly and violently with a knife, because you want to damage it or cause injury: *Vandals got in and slashed the painting.* | *Maria was slashed across the face with a razor.*

2   to cut food

cut /kʌt/ [v T] *Look! The bride and groom are going to cut the cake.*
cut sth into pieces/chunks *I'm going to cut the meat into four pieces.*
cutting – cut – have cut

chop/chop up /tʃɒp, ˌtʃɒp ˈʌp‖tʃɑːp-/ [v T] to cut something such as vegetables or meat into small pieces when you are preparing a meal: *Chop two onions for the stew.* | *Do you want me to chop up the vegetables?*

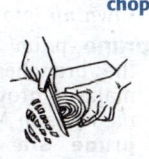
chop

chop sth into pieces/chunks/cubes *Chop the eggplant into cubes.*
chopped [adj only before noun] *Add some chopped nuts to the salad.*
finely chopped (=in very small pieces) *finely chopped onions*
chopping – chopped – have chopped

slice /slaɪs/ [v T] to cut food such as bread, meat, or vegetables into thin flat pieces: *My grandmother sliced the carrots and put them in a saucepan of water.*

slice

sliced [adj only before noun] *sliced white bread*

carve /kɑːʳv/ [v I/T] to cut a large piece of cooked meat into pieces: *Who's going to carve the turkey?* | *Will you carve or shall I?*

carve

mince BRITISH **grind** AMERICAN /mɪns, graɪnd/ [v T] to cut raw meat into very small pieces, using a machine: *Will you ask the butcher to mince the lamb very finely?*
minced/ground [adj only before noun] *minced meat* | *ground beef*
grinding – ground – have ground

grate /greɪt/ [v T] to cut cheese or vegetables into very small thin pieces by rubbing them against a metal surface with holes in it: *Grate some cheese over the potatoes before serving.*

grate

grated [adj] *grated orange peel*

3   to cut part of your body

➡ see also **HURT/INJURE**

cut /kʌt/ [v T] to accidentally injure part of your body, so that it bleeds: *Don't cut your finger on that glass.*
cut yourself *I cut myself shaving this morning.*
cut [n C] a wound on your skin where it has been cut: *Several passengers were treated for cuts and bruises.*
cutting – cut – have cut

scratch /skrætʃ/ [v T] to cut part of your body very slightly, and not at all deeply: *The cat scratched me while I was playing with her.* | *I got scratched by the bushes trying to find that ball.*
scratch [n C] a slight cut that is not at all deep: *Don't cry, it's only a scratch.*

graze /greɪz/ [v T] to accidentally injure yourself by rubbing your skin against something hard and rough: *Tommy fell and grazed his knee in the yard.*
graze [n C] a slight wound on your skin where it has been rubbed against something hard and rough: *Kids are always getting cuts and grazes.*

4   to cut someone's hair, beard, or fingernails

➡ see also **HAIR**

cut /kʌt/ [v T] *My sister usually cuts my hair.* | *I wish you wouldn't cut your toenails in the living-room.*
have/get your hair cut (=pay someone to cut it for you) *Beth's at the hairdresser's having her hair cut.*
cut [n singular] *Your hair needs a cut.*
cutting – cut – have cut

trim /trɪm/ [v T] to cut a small amount off someone's hair, beard, or nails, so that they look tidier: *Could you just trim my hair at the back?* | *Mark was trimming his nails in the bath.*

trim [n singular] *I usually have a trim every month or so.*
trimming – trimmed – have trimmed

shave /ʃeɪv/ [v I/T] to cut the hair on your face or body, using a special blade, so that your skin feels smooth: *Have you shaved today? | I didn't have time to shave my legs.*
shave off sth/shave sth off *I wish you'd shave off that awful beard!*
shave [n singular] *He went upstairs and had a quick shave.*

manicure /ˈmænɪkjʊəʳ/ [v T usually passive] to carefully cut, shape, polish etc your fingernails so that they look very well cared for: *Her long nails were pink and beautifully manicured.*
manicure [n C] *I sometimes have a manicure when I go to the hairdresser's.*

5   to cut wood, plants, or grass

cut down/chop down /ˌkʌt ˈdaʊn, ˌtʃɒp ˈdaʊn‖ˌtʃɑːp-/ [phrasal verb T] to make trees or bushes fall down by cutting them with a sharp tool
cut/chop down sth *Cutting down the rainforests has created serious ecological problems.*
cut/chop sth down *The tree was dangerous so we had to chop it down.*

> ⚠ Don't use 'cut' on its own about trees. Don't say 'he cut the tree'. Say **he cut the tree down**.

chop /tʃɒp‖tʃɑːp/ [v T] to cut wood into pieces using an axe (=a tool with a long handle and a sharp blade): *We soon got warm, chopping wood.*
chop sth up/chop up sth (=into several pieces) *I chopped the old fence up for firewood.*
chopping – chopped – have chopped

chop

cut /kʌt/ [v T] to cut grass and make it shorter or to cut off parts of a plant: *It's time I cut the hedge.*
cutting – cut – have cut

mow /məʊ/ [v T] to cut grass shorter, using a special machine
mow the lawn/the grass *It only takes me half an hour to mow the lawn.*

saw /sɔː/ [v T] to cut wood using a sharp tool that you push backwards and forwards across the surface of the wood: *Jane was in the basement, sawing wood.*

saw

saw sth up/saw up sth (=into several pieces) *The logs are sawn up into six foot lengths.*

prune /pruːn/ [v T] to cut off some of the branches of a tree or bush to make it grow better: *I usually prune the roses in March.*
prune sth back/prune back sth *Some shrubs need to be pruned back every year.*

6   to cut something from something else

cut off /ˌkʌt ˈɒf‖-ˈɔːf/ [phrasal verb T] to cut part of something away from the rest of it
cut off sth *Van Gogh cut off his ear.*
cut sth off *Remove the cake from the oven and cut any burnt edges off.*

chop off /ˌtʃɒp ˈɒf‖ˌtʃɑːp ˈɔːf/ [phrasal verb T] to cut something off by hitting or cutting it with a sharp tool
chop off sth *Chop off the tops of the carrots, and then peel them.*
chop sth off *Be careful you don't chop your fingers off!*

amputate /ˈæmpjʊteɪt/ [v T] to cut off someone's arm, leg, or foot as a medical operation: *His leg had to be amputated after the accident.*

cut out /ˌkʌt ˈaʊt/ [phrasal verb T] to remove something from something else by cutting all around it
cut out sth *Did you cut out that photo of Tony in the newspaper?*
cut sth out *Wash the apples, and cut any bad parts out.*

D, d

DAMAGE

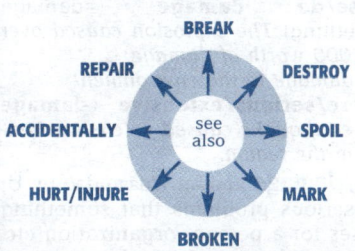

1 to damage objects, machines, buildings etc

damage /'dæmɪdʒ/ [v T] to cause physical harm to something, so that it no longer looks good or works properly: *The building was severely damaged by fire.* | *Don't put any hot pans on the table – you'll damage the surface.*
badly damaged *Luckily, the ship wasn't badly damaged.*

> ⚠ Don't use **damage** about people. Use **injure**: *The car was badly damaged and the driver was injured.*

break /breɪk/ [v T] to damage a machine or piece of equipment so that it does not work or cannot be used: *Leave that clock alone – you'll break it!* | *We used to have a remote-control for the TV, but Tommy broke it.*
breaking – broke – have broken

scratch /skrætʃ/ [v T] to damage a painted or polished surface by making long thin marks on it with something sharp or rough: *Be careful not to scratch the table with those scissors.* | *I'm afraid I've scratched your car.*

vandalize (also **vandalise** BRITISH) /'vændəlaɪz/ [v T] to deliberately damage buildings, vehicles, or public property, just for fun: *All the public telephones in the area had been vandalized.*

vandal [n C] someone who vandalizes

things: *Vandals broke into the school and wrecked two classrooms.*

vandalism [n U] the criminal activity of vandalizing things: *efforts to cut down on under-age drinking and vandalism in the shopping centre*

smash up/smash /ˌsmæʃ 'ʌp, smæʃ/ [v T] to deliberately damage a room or building by breaking windows, furniture etc
smash sth up *Some of the soldiers got drunk and smashed the place up.*
smash up sth *Angry protesters broke shop windows and smashed up everything inside.* | *In the past 12 months, hooligans have smashed her windows and stolen her car.*

trash /træʃ/ [v T] INFORMAL, ESPECIALLY AMERICAN to cause a lot of damage to a thing or place, either deliberately or by using it carelessly: *That kid of yours just trashed my VCR.*
🔍 **trash the place** SPOKEN (=cause a lot of damage to a room or building) *Dad says it's OK to have the party here, so long as we don't trash the place.*

sabotage /'sæbətɑːʒ/ [v T] to secretly damage machines or equipment so that they cannot be used, especially in order to harm an enemy: *The railway line had been sabotaged by enemy commandos.*

sabotage [n U] when people secretly damage machines or equipment: *The terrorists were planning acts of sabotage to destabilize the country.*

2 when things get gradually damaged over a long period

wear away /ˌweər ə'weɪ/ [phrasal verb T] if the wind, rain, sea etc **wears** something **away**, it makes it get gradually thinner until there is nothing left
wear away sth/wear sth away *places where the waves had worn away the cliff face* | *The cathedral steps were getting worn away by thousands of visitors.*

wear out /ˌweər 'aʊt/ [phrasal verb T] to damage clothes, material, or equipment by wearing them or using them a lot
wear sth out/wear out sth *After only a month Terry had worn out the soles*

of his shoes. | *The carpet on the stairs is getting very worn out.*

erosion /ɪˈrəʊʒən/ [n U] the gradual process by which the weather, water, or air damages or destroys rocks, buildings, land etc: *soil erosion*
+of *the erosion of the coastline*

3 to have a bad effect on something

harm/damage /hɑːʳm, ˈdæmɪdʒ/ [v T] to have a bad effect on something, in a way that makes it weaker, less effective, or less successful: *The scandal will damage the company's reputation.* | *Will this harm the President's chances of being re-elected?*

be bad for sth/have a bad effect on sth /biː ˈbæd fɔːʳ (sth), hæv ə ˌbæd ɪˈfekt ɒn (sth)/ to change or affect something in a harmful way: *Losing her job had a bad effect on Patty's confidence.* | *An increase in interest rates at the present time would definitely be bad for business.*

hurt /hɜːʳt/ [v T] ESPECIALLY AMERICAN to have a bad effect on an organization or activity, by making it less successful or effective: *new regulations that could hurt the farming industry*
hurting – hurt – have hurt

harmful /ˈhɑːʳmfəl/ [adj] causing physical damage or serious problems – use this especially about things that harm the environment or are dangerous for people's health: *harmful ultra-violet rays*
+to *These chemicals are harmful to the ozone layer.*
harmful effects *the harmful effects of smoking*

damaging /ˈdæmɪdʒɪŋ/ [adj] causing serious problems – use this especially about information, events, or situations that cause serious problems for a person or organization: *damaging rumors about the President's private life*
+to *If people found out about his divorce, it could be very damaging to his career.*

4 the physical damage caused by something

damage /ˈdæmɪdʒ/ [n U] physical damage that spoils the way something looks or the way it works: *It will take many years to repair the damage.*
cause/do damage (=damage something) *The explosion caused over $50,000 worth of damage.*
+to *damage to the environment*
severe/serious/extensive damage *The earthquake caused extensive damage in the region.*

harm/damage /hɑːʳm, ˈdæmɪdʒ/ [n U] the serious problems that something causes for a person, organization etc
do harm/damage *If you keep criticizing children, it can do a lot of harm.*
+to *The news caused serious damage to the minister's reputation.* | *The civil war did a lot of harm to the tourist industry.*

DANCE

1 to dance

dance /dɑːns‖dæns/ [v I] to move your body in time to music: *Everyone got up and danced.*
+with *Will you dance with me?*
+to *My parents were dancing to a sentimental old love song.*

dancing /ˈdɑːnsɪŋ‖ˈdæn-/ [n U] the activity of moving your feet and body to music: *My boyfriend doesn't like dancing.* | *There was music, Scottish dancing, and lots of food.*
go dancing (=go somewhere in order to dance) *We went dancing nearly every Saturday night.*

do /duː/ [v T] to do a particular kind of dance: *Can you do the twist?* | *She got up and did a little dance.*
doing – did – have done

2 different types of dance

dance /dɑːns‖dæns/ [n C] a set of movements that you do to a particular kind of music: *I prefer old-fashioned dances like the waltz and the tango.*

folk dance (=a traditional dance from a particular country or area) *Hungarian folk dances*

ballet /ˈbæleɪ‖bæˈleɪ, ˈbæleɪ/ [n U] a serious artistic performance in which movement and dancing are used to tell a story

ballroom dancing /ˌbɔːlrʊm ˈdɑːnsɪŋ‖-ˈdæn-/ [n U] a type of formal dancing in which people dance in pairs, and do different, fixed movements to different types of music

country dancing BRITISH **square dancing** AMERICAN /ˌkʌntri ˈdɑːnsɪŋ, ˈskweəʳ ˌdɑːnsɪŋ‖-ˈdæns-/ [n U] traditional dancing in which pairs of dancers move in rows and circles

3 someone who dances

dancer /ˈdɑːnsəʳ‖ˈdæn-/ [n C] someone who dances, either because it is their job or for enjoyment: *As a child, Alice dreamed of becoming a ballet dancer. | I'm not a very good dancer.*

partner /ˈpɑːʳtnəʳ/ [n C] someone that you dance with: *When I saw her again, she was dancing with a different partner. | I kept stepping on my partner's toes.*

4 a social event where people dance

dance /dɑːns‖dæns/ [n C] an organized social event where people go to dance: *Later on, there was a dance in the school hall. | the firm's annual dinner and dance* (=event at which there is a formal meal and dancing)

club /klʌb/ [n C] a place where people pay to go at night to dance to loud popular music: *I met some friends at a party and then we went on to a club.*
go clubbing (=go to one or more clubs) *We always go clubbing on Saturday night.*

disco /ˈdɪskəʊ/ [n C] a place or fairly informal social event at which people dance to popular music: *Every Friday night, the kids went to a disco in town.*

ball /bɔːl/ [n C] a formal social event at which people dance and wear formal clothes: *The Summer Ball will be held at the end of June.*

prom /prɒm‖prɑːm/ [n C] a social event for high school students in the US where there is music and dancing, and which people usually go to with a partner: *Joey walked me home after the prom.*
high school prom/senior prom (=a prom for students in the last year at school)

DANGEROUS

➡ opposite **SAFE**

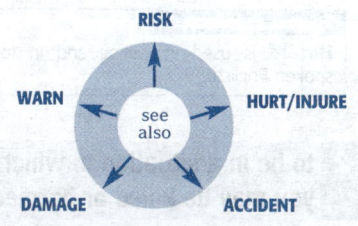

1 likely to cause death or serious harm

dangerous /ˈdeɪndʒərəs/ [adj] *Snow and ice are making driving conditions very dangerous. | dangerous drugs such as heroin | Motor-racing is a dangerous sport.*
highly/extremely dangerous (=very dangerous) *The police described the situation as highly dangerous.*
it is dangerous to do sth *It's dangerous to walk out on your own at night in this area.*
dangerously [adv] *The plane was flying dangerously close to the mountain.*

risky /ˈrɪski/ [adj] involving a risk that something bad might happen – use this about things that you decide to do although you know they may be dangerous: *Doctors cannot operate because it's too risky. | It's risky, but there's no alternative.*
risky – riskier – riskiest

poisonous /ˈpɔɪzənəs/ [adj] something that is **poisonous** will make you ill or kill you if you swallow it or breathe it: *The boy died after eating poisonous berries. | The river is full of poisonous chemicals.*

be a danger to sb/sth /biː ə ˈdeɪndʒəʳ tuː (sb/sth)/ to be likely to harm other people or things: *People who drink and drive are a danger to themselves and to others.* | *That man is a danger to the community.* | *sharp rocks that are a danger to the fishing boats*

hazard /ˈhæzəʳd/ [n C] something that may cause accidents or be dangerous to your health: *Signs warn drivers of hazards on the road ahead.* | *the potential hazards of using this machinery*
+to *Polluted water sources are a hazard to wildlife.*
health hazard (=something that may damage your health)

Formal or informal?
Hazard is used in writing and in formal spoken English.

2 to be in a situation in which you may be killed or harmed

be in danger /biː ɪn ˈdeɪndʒəʳ/ *Mr and Mrs Watkins are worried that their daughter may be in danger.*
be in danger of sth (=be in a situation when it is possible you may be killed or injured by something dangerous) *Some of the children were in danger of starvation.*
sb's life is in danger *The refugees believe their lives are in danger if they return home.*

> ⚠ Don't say 'be in a danger'. Say **be in danger**.

be at risk /biː ət ˈrɪsk/ if someone **is at risk**, they are in a dangerous situation, especially because they are weak and so they are likely to be harmed by disease or violence
+from *Those most at risk from the flu epidemic are old people and very young children.* | *women who are at risk from violent husbands*

3 to do something that may hurt or kill you

risk your life /ˌrɪsk jɔːʳ ˈlaɪf/ to do something very dangerous, especially in order to help someone: *Firemen risked their lives to save people from the flames.*

at your own risk /ət jɔːr ˌəʊn ˈrɪsk/ if you do something **at your own risk**, you must accept that it is dangerous and that it is your own fault if you are injured or killed: *Anyone who swims in this part of the river does so at their own risk.*

Formal or informal?
At your own risk is used especially in formal written warnings.

4 danger of death or serious harm

danger /ˈdeɪndʒəʳ/ [n C/U] the possibility that someone or something will be harmed or killed: *Danger! Keep out.* | *I waved my arms to warn other drivers of the danger.*
+of *Many people are still not aware of the dangers of drugs such as Ecstasy.*
risk /rɪsk/ [n C/U] the possibility of serious harm if you do something dangerous – use this especially when you want to say how great the possibility is: *Doctor, how much risk is there with this kind of operation?* | *A lot of children start smoking without realizing what the risks are.*
+of *Wearing a seat belt can reduce the risk of serious injury.*
+to *The disease affects cats but there is no risk to humans.*

DARK

➡ look here for ...
• when there is not much light
• dark colour, skin, hair
➡ see also **COLOUR/COLOR, LIGHT, BRIGHT/NOT BRIGHT**

1 place/room

dark /dɑːʳk/ [adj] if a place is **dark**, there is little or no light: *The church was dark and quiet.* | *I hid in the darkest corner of the yard and prayed that the soldiers would not find me.* | *No, you can't play outside now – it's too dark.*
it gets dark (=night comes) *It doesn't start to get dark until about ten o'clock in the summer.*

be pitch dark (=be completely dark) *It was pitch dark in the attic.*

> ⚠ Don't say 'it becomes dark' to talk about the time when night comes. Say **it gets dark**.

dimly-lit /ˌdɪmli ˈlɪt◂/ [adj] ESPECIALLY WRITTEN a **dimly-lit** street, room, building etc is almost dark because the lights there are not bright: *a long dimly-lit corridor*

gloomy /ˈgluːmi/ [adj] a **gloomy** place or room is not at all bright or cheerful: *Mr Casaubon would sit all day in his gloomy study.* | *It's a bit gloomy in here.*

dingy /ˈdɪndʒi/ [adj] a building, room, office etc that is **dingy** is fairly dark and usually dirty and in bad condition: *He ate lunch in a dingy little café near the station.*
dingy – dingier – dingiest

the dark /ðə ˈdɑːʳk/ [n singular] when there is no light, especially in a room: *Most children are afraid of the dark.*
in the dark *Why are you sitting there in the dark?*

darkness /ˈdɑːʳknᵻs/ [n U] when there is no light: *the long hours of darkness during winter* | *There was a sudden flash of light, then darkness again.*
in complete/total darkness (=with no light at all) *The lights suddenly went out and we found ourselves in total darkness.*
darkness falls WRITTEN (=it becomes night) *As darkness fell, we were still miles from the village.*

2 colour/hair/skin/clothes

➡ see also **HAIR**

dark /dɑːʳk/ [adj] **dark** colours are close to black and are not at all bright or pale: *There was a dark stain on the carpet that looked like blood.* | *a boy with dark curly hair*
dark blue/green/brown etc *She had beautiful dark brown eyes.* | *a dark blue dress*

DEAD

➡ opposite **ALIVE**
➡ see also **DIE, EXIST**

1 no longer alive

D

dead /ded/ [adj] *My mother has been dead for over ten years.* | *The dead man's wife is being questioned by the police.* | *She was found dead in her apartment, with a bottle of sleeping pills beside her.*

> ⚠ We do not usually say 'my dead mother', 'my dead husband' etc. It is more usual to use **late**.

late /leɪt/ [adj only before noun] FORMAL use this as a polite way of talking about someone who has died, especially someone who died recently
sb's late husband/wife/mother/father *She set up the fund in memory of her late husband.*
the late President Marcos/John Lennon etc *He is the last surviving son of the late Indira Gandhi.*

the dead /ðə ˈded/ [n plural] people who have died – use this especially to talk about people who died in wars or accidents: *a religious service to commemorate the dead of two World Wars* | *Four of the dead had been travelling in the same car.*

> ⚠ When you are talking about a group of people who have died, don't say 'the dead people'. Say **the dead**.

2 the body of a dead person

body /ˈbɒdiǁˈbɑːdi/ [n C] *Police found the body of a young boy in Epping Forest last night.* | *The woman sat down beside her son's body and wept.*
plural bodies

> ⚠ We usually just say **body**, not 'dead body'. Only say 'dead body' if it is not clear from the rest of the sentence that the person is dead: *Have you ever seen a dead body?*

D

corpse /kɔːˈps/ [n C] the body of a dead person – use this when you are talking about the body as an object, not as a person: *A corpse was found floating in the river.*

remains /rɪˈmeɪnz/ [n plural] all or parts of the body of a dead person, especially someone who has been dead for a long time
the remains of *They discovered the remains of a young woman hidden under the floorboards.*
sb's remains *His remains will be flown back to Ireland.*

ashes /ˈæʃəz/ [n plural] the powder that is left after a body has been burned as part of a funeral ceremony
sb's ashes *His ashes were scattered over the Jumna river.*

DEAL WITH

to deal with a difficult problem or with things that need to be done

➡ see also **PROBLEM, ANSWER 5**

1 to do things that need doing

deal with sth /ˈdiːl wɪð (sth)/ [phrasal verb T] to decide what needs to be done and make sure that it is done, especially when it is your job to do this: *Who is dealing with the accommodation arrangements for the conference? | I spend most of my working day dealing with customer inquiries.*

see to sth/attend to sth /ˈsiː tuː (sth), əˈtend tuː (sth)/ [phrasal verb T] to deal with all the practical details of something that needs to be done or organized: *I'll join you later – there are a few things I have to see to at the office first. | Their mother was too upset to attend to the funeral arrangements. | You'd better get someone to see to that leaking pipe.*

Formal or informal?
Attend to sth is more formal than **see to sth**.

take care of sth /ˌteɪk ˈkeər ɒv (sth)/ to deal with all the necessary work, arrangements etc, usually so that someone else will not have to: *My secretary will take care of the details. | Don't worry about your passport and visa – it's all taken care of.*

🗣 **leave it to me** /ˌliːv ɪt tə ˈmiː/ SPOKEN say this to tell someone that you will be responsible for doing something that needs doing: *Leave it to me. I'll make sure it gets posted tonight.*

2 to deal with a problem or difficult situation

tackle /ˈtækəl/ [v T] to begin to deal with a problem in a determined way, especially a big or complicated problem: *Many schools are now trying to tackle the problem of drug use. | policies aimed at tackling unemployment*

Formal or informal?
Tackle is not used in formal writing. Use **deal with** instead.

handle /ˈhændl/ [v T] to deal with a problem or a difficult situation, especially in an effective or confident way: *There were a few problems, but nothing I couldn't handle. | A lot of people find it difficult to handle criticism.*
handle sth well/badly *It's her first year as a doctor, but she is handling the pressures of the job very well.*

cope /kəʊp/ [v I] to succeed in dealing with difficult problems in your life, your job, or your relationships: *It's a tough job but I'm sure he'll cope.*
+with *She has to cope with five children all on her own.*

sort out /ˌsɔːt ˈaʊt/ [phrasal verb T] ESPECIALLY BRITISH to deal with all the small but difficult problems that are causing trouble or preventing you from doing something
sort out sth *I spent the weekend sorting out my tax affairs.*
sort sth out *We'll have to sort your immigration status out before we can offer you the job.*

Formal or informal?
Sort out is not used in formal writing.

get through sth /ˌget ˈθruː (sth)/ [phrasal verb T] to live through an unhappy or unpleasant time in your life, and deal with the problems that it brings: *Her friends helped her to get through the first awful weeks after Bill died.*

3 to have to deal with a problem you cannot ignore

face /feɪs/ [v T] if you **face** a difficult problem, or if a difficult problem **faces** you, you must deal with it and you cannot ignore it: *The new administration faces the difficult task of rebuilding the country's economy. | One of the problems facing the management is the shortage of skilled workers.*
be faced with/by sth *I was faced with the awful job of breaking the bad news to the girl's family.*

4 to find a successful way of dealing with a difficult problem

solve /sɒlv‖sɑːlv, sɔːlv/ [v T] *They thought money would solve all their problems. | The two countries are meeting for talks in an attempt to solve the crisis.*

find a solution /ˌfaɪnd ə səˈluːʃən/ to think of a way to solve a problem, especially a complicated political or social problem: *Both sides are trying to find a peaceful solution.*
+to *European governments are working together to find a solution to the problem of nuclear waste.*

DECIDE

➡ see also **DEPEND/IT DEPENDS, THINK**

1 to decide to do something

decide /dɪˈsaɪd/ [v I/T] to make a choice that you are going to do something: *I don't mind where we go. You decide.*
decide to do sth *She decided to tell her mother all about it that evening.*
decide not to do sth *If you decide not to accept our offer, let me know.*
+(that) *I've decided that I really must stop smoking.*
decide what/how/when etc *Have*

you decided whether to apply for that job? | Martha took hours deciding which dress to wear?*
decide against sth (=decide not to do something) *Marlowe thought about using his gun, but decided against it.*

make up your mind /ˌmeɪk ʌp jɔːʳ ˈmaɪnd/ to finally decide that you will definitely do something, after thinking about it for a long time
make up your mind what/which/how etc *I couldn't make up my mind which college I wanted to go to.*
make your mind up *Haven't they made their minds up yet?*
make up your mind to do sth *John had made up his mind to forget the past and make a fresh start.*
+(that) *He's made up his mind that he wants to study abroad.*

choose /tʃuːz/ [v T] to decide to do something because you want to, without worrying about what other people think
choose to do sth *More and more young couples are choosing not to get married. | I told him to drive more slowly, but he chose to ignore my advice.*
choosing – chose – have chosen

resolve /rɪˈzɒlv‖rɪˈzɑːlv, rɪˈzɔːlv/ [v T] FORMAL to decide that you will definitely do something and will not change your mind about it, especially because you have learned from your past experiences
resolve to do sth *After the divorce she resolved never to get married again. | I returned to Edinburgh, resolving to stay there until my book was finished.*

opt /ɒpt‖ɑːpt/ [v I/T] to decide to do one thing instead of another – use this especially when there are two or more particular things that you can choose between
opt to do sth *Students can now opt to spend their third year in Europe, if they wish.*
+for *Do you think I should opt for Economics or Maths?*

2 something that someone decides to do

decision /dɪˈsɪʒən/ [n C] *They're going to close the school, but I think that's the wrong decision.*

make/take a decision (=decide about something important) *As chief executive, I often have to take difficult decisions.* | *We don't have to make a decision right now. Let's talk about it tomorrow.*

decision to do sth *Brett's sudden decision to join the army surprised everyone.*

come to/reach a decision (=make a decision after thinking carefully or discussing it for a long time) *The jury took three days to reach a decision.*

big decision (=a difficult and important decision) *It's a big decision, don't rush it.*

3 to decide that something is true

decide /dɪ'saɪd/ [v T] to think that something is true, after thinking about it, checking it, or looking at it
+(that) *I decided that he was probably telling the truth.*
decide whether/which/what etc *She couldn't decide whether the hat suited her or not.*

come to the conclusion that /ˌkʌm tə ðə kən'kluːʒən ðət/ to decide that something is true after thinking carefully about all the facts: *I came to the conclusion that there was only one way of tackling the problem.* | *De Klerk eventually came to the conclusion that the apartheid system could not continue.*

jump to conclusions /ˌdʒʌmp tə kən'kluːʒənz/ to decide too quickly that something is true, without considering all the facts: *We mustn't jump to conclusions. There may be a perfectly good explanation for him being so late.*

judge /dʒʌdʒ/ [v T] FORMAL to decide that something is the case after examining a situation carefully and using your knowledge and experience
+that *Kaldor judged that the moment was exactly right to call an election.*
judge whether/which/what etc *It's difficult to judge whether this is the right time to tell him.*

4 when someone has the right to decide

it is up to sb /ɪt ɪz 'ʌp tuː (sb)/ ESPECIALLY SPOKEN if you say **it is up to him/her/you etc**, you mean that that person should make the decision about something, and no one else: *"Should we finish the job now, or leave it till later?" "I don't know – it's up to you."* | *It's up to them what they do with the money.*

it/that is for sb to decide /ɪt, ðæt ɪz fɔːʳ (sb) tə dɪ'saɪd/ FORMAL use this when only one person or group has the official power to make a decision about something important: *We cannot say if he is guilty or not. That is for the court to decide.*

5 able to make decisions quickly and firmly

decisive /dɪ'saɪsɪv/ [adj] someone who is **decisive** can make decisions firmly and confidently, without needing too much time to talk about them or think about them: *I wish he'd be more decisive.* | *The country needs strong decisive leadership.*
decisively [adv] *The police responded to the crisis quickly and decisively.*

6 when someone cannot decide

can't decide /ˌkɑːnt dɪ'saɪdǁˌkænt-/ to not be able to make a decision: *"Are you going to take the job or not?" "I don't know – I can't decide."*
can't decide what/whether/how etc *I can't decide what to wear.* | *Lucinda couldn't decide whether she wanted to marry Jerry or not.*

indecisive /ˌɪndɪ'saɪsɪv◂/ [adj] not good at making decisions quickly and firmly: *She's far too indecisive to ever make a good manager.*

dither /'dɪðəʳ/ [v I] INFORMAL to keep changing your mind – use this when you think someone is weak or stupid because they cannot decide about something: *Stop dithering and make up your mind.*

DECORATE

to improve the way something looks, by painting it or adding something attractive to it

➡ see also **PAINT, DESIGN, PATTERN**

1 to decorate something

decorate /'dekəreɪt/ [v T] to improve the way something looks by painting it or adding something attractive to it: *The children always enjoy decorating the Christmas tree.*
be decorated with sth *The room was decorated with balloons and coloured ribbons.* | *The king wore a robe decorated with fur and precious stones.*
decorated [adj] *a richly decorated room*

garnish /'gɑːnɪʃ/ [v T] to make food look nice by adding a small amount of another type of food, usually of a different colour – used especially in cooking instructions
garnish sth with sth *Garnish the pasta with olives and basil.*

2 things that are used to decorate something

decorations /ˌdekə'reɪʃənz/ [n plural] things that you use to decorate a place, object, piece of furniture etc, often for a special occasion: *Have you put up your Christmas decorations yet?* | *The bride's mother had made all the table decorations.*

decoration /ˌdekə'reɪʃən/ [n U] designs, patterns, and objects used to decorate buildings, clothes, furniture, food etc: *The altar is a fine example of Baroque decoration.* | *Keep some of the strawberries for decoration.*

decorative /'dekərətɪv‖'dekərə-, 'dekəreɪ-/ [adj] something that is **decorative** is intended to make a place, object, piece of furniture etc look attractive – use this especially about designs and patterns: *There are decorative tiles around the fireplace, with pictures of birds and flowers on them.* | *Inside the church there are many interesting decorative features.*

ornamental /ˌɔːnə'mentl‹/ [adj] designed to make an object, building or place look attractive rather than to be used for a particular purpose: *Ornamental pots will brighten up your garden.* | *an ornamental pond* | *The handles are purely ornamental.*

3 something that has a lot of decoration

fancy /'fænsi/ [adj] **fancy** clothes, patterns etc have a lot of decoration or bright colours – use this especially when you think something has too much decoration: *a velvet jacket with fancy buttons* | *I don't like his designs – they're too fancy for me.*
fancy – fancier – fanciest

ornate /ɔː'neɪt/ [adj]
ESPECIALLY WRITTEN an **ornate** object, picture, or part of a building has a lot of expensive or complicated decoration on it: *a pair of ornate gold candlesticks* | *An ornate mirror hung above the fireplace.*

ornate

an ornate mirror

elaborate /ɪ'læbərɪt/ [adj] carefully and skilfully decorated with a lot of small details and decorations: *We found elaborate carvings on the tomb.*

DEEP/NOT DEEP

➡ if you want to talk about solid objects made of wood, metal, stone etc, go to **THICK**
➡ if you mean 'a deep colour', go to **COLOUR/COLOR**
➡ if you mean 'a deep sound or voice', go to **LOW**

1 water/hole/snow/sand

deep /diːp/ [adj] use this about water, holes, snow etc where the bottom is a long distance from the top: *Be careful! The water's quite deep here.* | *Someone had dug a deep hole in the middle of the field.*
ankle-deep/waist-deep (=deep enough to reach the top of a person's foot or

their waist) *The snow was waist-deep in places.*

get deeper (=become deeper) *The pond gets much deeper in the middle.*

⚠ Don't use **deep** to talk about materials such as wood, metal, or stone. Use **thick**.

the depths /ðə 'depθs/ [n plural] **the depths** of the sea, the ocean, a lake etc are the very deepest parts of the sea, the ocean, or a large lake: *These strange creatures live in the depths of the ocean.*

Formal or informal?
Use **the depths** especially when you are writing stories and descriptions.

2 a long distance below the surface

deep /di:p/ [adv] **+below/under/in** *Earthquakes are caused by movements deep below the Earth's surface.*

3 how deep something is

how deep /haʊ 'di:p/ *How deep is the hole?* | *I wasn't sure how deep the water was and I didn't want to swim out too far.*

40 metres/100 feet etc deep /(40 metres etc) 'di:p/ use this to say how deep something is: *The snow was over two metres deep.*

depth /depθ/ [n C/U] the distance from the surface to the bottom of a hole, river, sea etc: *"What's the depth of the pool?" "It's 12 feet at this end."*
+of *The yard was flooded to a depth of 3 feet.*

4 not deep

not very deep /nɒt veri 'di:p/ when the bottom of a hole, river etc is not a long distance from the surface: *Come on in, the water isn't very deep.*

Formal or informal?
In informal spoken English, **not very deep** is much more common than **shallow**.

shallow /'ʃæləʊ/ [adj] not very deep – use this especially about the water in a river, lake, swimming pool etc: *The river is too shallow for our boat.* | *The babies splashed around at the shallow end of the pool.*

DEFEND

to protect yourself when someone is attacking you or criticizing you

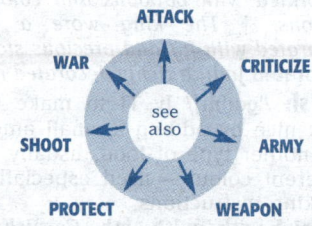

1 to defend your country or yourself

defend /dɪ'fend/ [v T] to use physical or military force to protect a person or place that is being attacked: *Hundreds of soldiers died while defending the town.* | *US troops in Panama will only be used to defend the Canal.*
defend sth against/from *The castle was built in 1549 to defend the island against invaders.*
defend yourself *Mandel died trying to defend himself and his children.*

defence BRITISH **defense** AMERICAN /dɪ'fens/ [n U] all the weapons, soldiers, systems, or activities that a country uses to protect itself from attack by an enemy: *The amount spent on defence has risen by 10%.* | *Defense is expected to be a big issue during the next election.*

⚠ You can also use **defence** before a noun, like an adjective, especially to talk about the money a government spends on defence: *defence spending* | *massive cuts in the defense budget*

defensive /dɪ'fensɪv/ [adj] used only for protecting your country or group, not for attacking someone else: *Police officers claimed that their actions during the riots were purely defensive.*
defensive weapons/position/measures *According to the report, only defensive weapons had been supplied to Iran.*

self-defence BRITISH **self-defense** AMERICAN /ˌself dɪ'fens/ [n U] the things a country or person does to stop themselves from being attacked or harmed: *All nations have the right to self-defence.* | *self-defence classes*
in self-defence (=in order to protect yourself) *She claims she shot him in self-defense.*

defences BRITISH **defenses** AMERICAN /dɪ'fensɪz/ [n plural] all the people, structures, and equipment that are available for defending a country or a place: *The invading army easily overcame the town's defences.* | *They responded to the threat by strengthening their defences.*

2 | to defend your ideas or your rights

defend /dɪ'fend/ [v T] to say something to support an idea or person when other people are criticizing them or trying to take something away from them: *It's difficult to defend a sport that involves hurting animals.* | *a speech defending the workers' right to strike* | *The Fire Chief defended his staff, and said that they had done everything possible to save the girl's life.*
defend sb/sth against *She has repeatedly tried to defend her husband against hostile criticism in the press.*
defend yourself *She tried to defend herself by saying that she was only obeying orders.*

stand up for sb/sth /ˌstænd 'ʌp fɔːr (sb/sth)/ [phrasal verb T] to strongly defend someone or something that is being criticized, or strongly defend your opinions or your rights: *You have to be ready to stand up for what you believe in.* | *Didn't anyone stand up for James and say it wasn't his fault?*
stand up for yourself *Politics can be*

a very tough business, and you have to learn to stand up for yourself.

stick up for sb /ˌstɪk 'ʌp fɔːr (sb)/ [phrasal verb T] INFORMAL to strongly defend someone who is being criticized, or to strongly defend your opinions or your rights, especially when no one else will defend them: *The only person who stuck up for me was Sarah.*
stick up for yourself *We've encouraged John to stick up for himself at school.*

DELIBERATELY

when you do something because you intended to do it

➡ opposite **ACCIDENTALLY**

deliberately /dɪ'lɪbərətli/ [adv] if you do something **deliberately**, you do it because you want to do it, and you hope it will have a particular result or effect: *She left the letter there deliberately so that you'd see it.* | *Police believe the fire was started deliberately.* | *I think he was deliberately ignoring me.*

deliberate /dɪ'lɪbərɪt/ [adj] use this about things that you do or say deliberately: *a deliberate attempt to prevent the truth from being known* | *His rudeness was quite deliberate.*

on purpose /ɒn 'pɜːrpəs/ [adv] ESPECIALLY SPOKEN if you do something **on purpose**, you do it deliberately, in order to annoy people or to get an advantage for yourself: *He always pronounces my name wrong. Do you think he does it on purpose?* | *He was being annoying on purpose.*

 Don't use **on purpose** about crimes.

intentionally /ɪn'tenʃənəli/ [adv] ESPECIALLY WRITTEN if you do something **intentionally**, you plan to do it and you hope it will have a particular result or effect: *The jury has to decide whether he killed John Bishop intentionally or whether it was an accident.* | *They arrived late intentionally, in order to avoid seeing him.*

Formal or informal?

Intentionally is more formal than **deliberately** or **on purpose** and is not common in spoken English.

intentional /ɪnˈtenʃənəl/ [adj] ESPECIALLY WRITTEN use this about things that you do or say deliberately in order to get a particular result or have a particular effect: *I made a mistake. I was wrong, but it was not intentional.* | *If their advertisements are shocking, this is entirely intentional.*

Formal or informal?

Intentional is more formal than **deliberate** and is not common in spoken English.

intend to do sth /ɪnˌtend tə ˈduː (sth)/ if you **intend** to do something, you decide that you want to do it, and you plan to do it: *I intend to win this game.* | *She clearly intended to kill him, and nearly succeeded.*

DEPEND/IT DEPENDS

when the way something happens is influenced by other facts or events

➡ if you mean 'depend on someone', go to **TRUST/NOT TRUST**

➡ see also **DECIDE, THINK**

depend /dɪˈpend/ [v I] if something **depends** on a fact, result, decision etc, it is directly affected or decided by it and will change if the fact, result, decision etc changes
+on *The amount of tax you pay depends on how much you earn.*
it depends how/where/what etc *I might not be able to go to France – it depends how much it costs.*
depending on *I kept getting different answers, depending on who I asked.*
🔍 **it depends/that depends** SPOKEN (say this when you cannot give a definite answer, because your decision may change according to what happens) *"Are you going to apply for that job?" "Well, it depends."*
🔍 **it all depends** SPOKEN (say this to emphasize that you cannot be certain about something at all) *We still don't*

know whether we'll have to move to a new house or not – it all depends.

 Don't say 'it is depending'. Say **it depends**.

according to sth /əˈkɔːˈdɪŋ tuː (sth)/ if something is done **according to** particular facts or principles, these facts or principles are what affect the way it is done: *Telephone charges vary according to the time of day.* | *The students were grouped according to age and ability.*

DESCRIBE

➡ see also **DETAIL, DESCRIBING PEOPLE, WB HOUSES/WHERE PEOPLE LIVE**

1 to describe someone or something

describe /dɪˈskraɪb/ [v T] to talk or write about a person, place, event etc, saying what they are like and giving details about them: *Could you try and describe the man you saw?* | *In her book, she describes her journey across the Sahara.*
describe sb/sth as *Police described the attack as particularly violent.*
describe sb/sth to sb *I tried to describe the feeling to my doctor, but she didn't understand.*
describe how/what *It's difficult to describe how I felt.*

 Don't say 'I described him the scenery'. Say **I described the scenery to him**.

write about sb/sth /ˈraɪt əbaʊt (sb/sth)/ [phrasal verb T] to describe a person, place, or situation by writing about it: *Thomas Hardy wrote about life in the countryside in nineteenth-century England.*

give an account of sth /ˌɡɪv ən əˈkaʊnt ɒv (sth)/ WRITTEN to describe something that happened, only giving the facts and not adding your own feelings or opinions: *Please give a brief account of your previous work experience.*

portray sb/sth as sth /pɔːˈtreɪ (sb/sth) æz (sth)/ [phrasal verb T] FORMAL to describe someone or something in a way that shows your opinion of them, especially when this is untrue or unfair: *In the book, Diana is portrayed as the victim of a loveless marriage.* | *The right-wing press portrayed the election result as a major defeat for the Socialists.*

what is sb/sth like /wɒt ɪz (sb/sth) ˈlaɪk/ SPOKEN use this when you are asking someone to describe or give an opinion about someone or something: *"I've just met Anna's new boyfriend." "What's he like?"* | *What's their new apartment like?*

2 a written or spoken description

description /dɪˈskrɪpʃən/ [n C] what you say or write when you are describing a person, place, thing etc
+of *Write a description of someone you know well.*
give sb a description *Tom gave the police a description of his car.*
a full/detailed description (=containing all the important details) *The guidebook contains a full description of the church.*

report /rɪˈpɔːt/ [n C] a description of a situation or event, that provides people with facts or other information about it: *the bank's annual report to shareholders*
+on *a government report on the effects of tobacco advertising*
newspaper/news/television report *News reports suggest that over 300 people may have died.*

account /əˈkaʊnt/ [n C] a written or spoken description of something that happened
+of *The newspaper printed a detailed account of the trial.*
give an account *His book gives a fascinating account of this dangerous journey.*

commentary /ˈkɒməntəriˌ ˈkɑːməntɛri/ [n C/U] a spoken description of a race or sports event on the radio or television, which is given while it is happening: *Don't miss tonight's game between the Bears and the Red Sox – commentary by Nick O'Ryan.*
+on *Now let's go over to our London studio for commentary on the game.*

plural **commentaries**

DESCRIBING HOW PEOPLE LOOK

➡ see Word Banks section

DESCRIBING PEOPLE'S CHARACTER

➡ see Word Banks section

DESERVE

1 to deserve something good

deserve /dɪˈzɜːv/ [v T] if you **deserve** something, it is right that you should have it, because you have worked hard, done something well etc: *After all that hard work, you deserve a rest.*
deserve to do sth *Barcelona played better than Real Madrid, and they deserved to win.*
thoroughly deserve sth (=deserve something very much) *Jill was awarded first prize, and she thoroughly deserved it.*

well-deserved/well-earned /ˌwel dɪˈzɜːvdˌ , ˌwel ˈɜːndˌ / [adj usually before noun] a **well-deserved** or **well-earned** rest, win, drink etc is one that you deserve to have, because you have worked hard: *The game ended in a well-deserved victory for the German team.* | *At 9 o'clock, she settled down for a well-earned rest.*

2 to deserve something bad

deserve /dɪˈzɜːv/ [v T] if you think that someone **deserves** something bad that happens to them, you think it is fair that it happens because they have done something wrong or stupid
deserve to do sth *Anyone who drives like that deserves to lose their licence.*
deserve it (=deserve the bad things

that happen) *"You really weren't very nice to her." "Well, she deserved it!"*
get what you deserve (=when something bad happens to you, and you deserve it) *In the end, the bully got what he deserved.*
thoroughly deserve sth *I can't help feeling sorry for him even though he thoroughly deserved to be fired.*

serve sb right /ˌsɜːʳv (sb) ˈraɪt/ SPOKEN use this to say you think someone deserves something bad that happens to them, because they have been unkind or done something stupid
+for *"I feel terrible." "Serves you right for drinking so much last night."*
it serves sb right *"It'd serve them right if something did happen to me,"* she thought.

DESIGN

the way that something has been planned to look or work

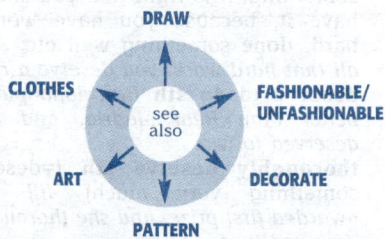

DRAW

CLOTHES   FASHIONABLE/
               UNFASHIONABLE
see also

ART   DECORATE

PATTERN

---

1   the design of something

design /dɪˈzaɪn/ [n C/U] the way that something has been planned and made, including its appearance and the way it works – use this about things like furniture, clothes, buildings, or machines: *Conran's furniture was based on simple, modern designs.* | *The success of the product was largely due to good design.* | *The problem was caused by a design fault.*
the design of sth *The basic design of the vehicle hasn't changed in ten years.*

---

2   to plan how something new will look or work

design /dɪˈzaɪn/ [v T] to make drawings or plans of something new that will be made or built: *Sally designs all her own clothes.* | *The car was designed and built in Korea.*
be well designed/badly designed *Everyone agreed that the new office building was well designed.*

plan /plæn/ [v T] to design a large space, such as a town or a park, and to decide how all the different parts should be arranged: *The campus was originally planned in the 1950s, when there weren't as many cars.*
planning – planned – have planned

---

3   someone whose job is designing things

designer /dɪˈzaɪnəʳ/ [n C] someone whose job is to design new machines, furniture, clothes etc: *He works as a designer for the Ford Motor Company.*
fashion/furniture/software etc designer *The show features clothes by famous fashion designers like Jean-Paul Gaultier.*
interior designer (=someone who plans and chooses the colours, materials, furniture etc for the inside of buildings, especially people's homes)

architect /ˈɑːʳkɪtekt/ [n C] someone whose job is to design buildings: *The Imperial Hotel in Tokyo was designed by the famous architect Frank Lloyd Wright.*

DESTROY

to damage something so badly that it cannot be repaired

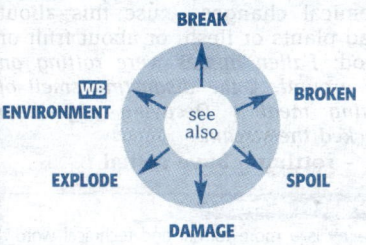

1 to destroy buildings, cities, trees etc

destroy /dɪˈstrɔɪ/ [v T] *The earthquake destroyed much of the city. | The rainforests are gradually being destroyed. | A force of 500 aircraft set out to destroy the US navy. | The factory was almost completely destroyed by fire.*

devastate /ˈdevəsteɪt/ [v T] to cause so much damage over a large area that most of the buildings, trees, and crops there are destroyed: *A huge explosion devastated the downtown area last night. | The country has been devastated by floods.*

be in ruins /biː ɪn ˈruːᵻnz/ if a town or building **is in ruins**, it has been completely destroyed: *Four days and nights of continuous bombing had left the city in ruins.*

wreck /rek/ [v T] to deliberately damage a building or room so badly that it cannot be used again: *The bar was wrecked by a gang of drunks. | A huge bomb wrecked the Opera House.*

destruction /dɪˈstrʌkʃən/ [n U] when something is destroyed: *The war caused widespread death and destruction.*
+of *a campaign to halt the destruction of the Amazonian forest*

demolish /dɪˈmɒlɪʃǁdɪˈmɑː-/ [v T] to completely destroy a building that is old or not safe, usually in order to build something new: *Eventually, in 1992, the apartment block was demolished. | When they demolished the church, a cave was discovered beneath it.*

demolition /ˌdeməˈlɪʃən/ [n U] when a building is demolished: *The plans involve the demolition of some 18th century houses.*

knock down /ˌnɒk ˈdaʊnǁˌnɑːk-/ [phrasal verb T] to destroy a building or part of a building in order to build something new
knock sth down *They'll have to knock these houses down when they build the new road.*
knock down sth *We knocked down the internal wall to make the room bigger.*

> **Formal or informal?**
> **Knock down** is more informal than **demolish**.

2 to completely destroy a car

wreck /rek/ [v T] to damage a car very badly in an accident: *They had stolen a car and wrecked it on the freeway.*
wrecked [adj] *Wrecked vehicles lay abandoned at the roadside.*

write off /ˌraɪt ˈɒfǁˈɔːf/ [phrasal verb T] BRITISH to damage a car so badly in an accident that it cannot be repaired
write off sth/write sth off *She wrote off her mother's car the first time she drove it.*

total /ˈtəʊtl/ [v T] AMERICAN SPOKEN to damage a car so badly in an accident that it cannot be repaired: *It was a terrible accident. Both cars were totaled.*
totaling – totaled – have totaled

3 causing a lot of damage

destructive /dɪˈstrʌktɪv/ [adj] something or someone that is **destructive** causes a lot of damage: *a wasteful and destructive war | Small children can be very destructive. | the destructive effects of mass tourism*

devastating /ˈdevəsteɪtɪŋ/ [adj] causing very serious damage to all the buildings, trees, crops etc in an area: *The palace was rebuilt in 1832 after a devastating fire.*
have a devastating effect on *The oil spill had a devastating effect on sea birds and other wildlife.*

D

4 a place or thing that has been destroyed

wreckage

wreckage /'rekɪdʒ/ [n U] the broken parts of a car, plane etc that has crashed: *Wreckage from the plane was scattered over a large area.* | *Passengers were trapped in the burning wreckage.*

ruins

ruins /'ruːɪnz/ [n plural] the parts of a building or town that remain after it has been destroyed
+of *We visited the ruins of an ancient temple.* | *the ruins of a bombed-out office block*

wreck /rek/ [n C] a ship that has been sunk, or a car that has been badly damaged in a crash: *Divers went down to search the wreck.* | *The car was a complete wreck, but the driver escaped with minor injuries.*

write-off /'raɪt ɒfǁ-ɔːf/ [n C] BRITISH a car that has been so badly damaged in a crash that it cannot be used again: *The car was a complete write-off.*

5 be gradually destroyed by a natural process

rot/decay /rɒt, dɪ'keɪǁraɪt/ [v I] to be gradually destroyed by natural chemical changes – use this about dead plants or flesh, or about fruit or wood: *Fallen apples were rotting on the ground.* | *the disgusting smell of rotting meat* | *Decaying vegetation blocked the stream.*
rot – rotting – have rotted

rust /rʌst/ [v I] if metal **rusts**, it becomes red-brown in colour because it has been damaged by the effects of water: *Your bike will rust if you leave it out in the rain.*

DETAIL

➡ see also **INFORMATION, DESCRIBE**

1 a specific piece of information

detail /'diːteɪlǁdɪ'teɪl/ [n C usually plural] a single fact or piece of information about something: *The story's very complicated – I can't remember all the exact details.*
+of *The details of the deal were kept secret.* | *Baker advises the President on the details of foreign policy.*
personal details (=information about someone, such as their age, their address, whether they are married etc) *To apply for a loan, first fill in the section marked 'Personal Details'.*

point /pɔɪnt/ [n C] a detail that you need to talk about when you are discussing a plan, statement, or written agreement: *There's one point in your letter that is not quite clear.*
small/minor point (=one that is not very important) *We only have a few small points left to discuss.*

⌕ **thing** /θɪŋ/ [n C] SPOKEN a detail in something such as a plan, statement, or written agreement: *There's one thing I'm not clear about, and that's* *how we are going to get to the airport. | I need to change a few things before I give the speech.*

the small print BRITISH **the fine print** AMERICAN /ðə ˌsmɔːl ˈprɪnt, ðə ˌfaɪn ˈprɪnt/ [*n singular*] the specific details in an agreement or document, which may be very important but which people do not always notice: *Be sure to read the small print before you sign anything.*

2 features of something you see

detail /ˈdiːteɪlǁdɪˈteɪl/ [*n U*] all of the features that you can see in something such as a picture, a building, or something that someone has made: *The cathedral has a carved ceiling which is full of interesting detail.*

3 with a lot of details

detailed /ˈdiːteɪldǁdɪˈteɪld/ [*adj*] a **detailed** description, explanation, picture etc contains a lot of details or detail: *The police have issued a detailed description of the man they are looking for. | Do you have a more detailed map of the area?*

in detail /ɪn ˈdiːteɪlǁ-dɪˈteɪl/ if you talk about or consider something **in detail**, you pay attention to all the details: *I haven't had time to look at the plans in detail yet. | This problem is discussed in more detail in Chapter 7.*

in great detail (=including a lot of detail) *Fortunately, she was able to describe her attacker in great detail.*

4 not containing many details

general /ˈdʒenərəl/ [*adj only before noun*] a general description or explanation of something contains the most basic information but does not include all the details: *The course is called 'A General Introduction to Computing'.*

a general idea (=basic knowledge) *This guidebook will give you a good general idea of the city.*

rough /rʌf/ [*adj only before noun*] **rough description/plan/outline etc** a description, plan etc that is not exact or complete, but has enough

information to help you understand it: *We've drawn up a rough plan but we haven't worked out all the costs.*

a rough idea (=a basic understanding) *Give us a rough idea of what you're trying to do.*

vague /veɪg/ [*adj*] something that is **vague** is not clear because it does not provide enough details: *Dave's instructions were rather vague. | I had heard vague rumours that they were getting married.*

not go into detail /nɒt gəʊ ɪntə ˈdiːteɪlǁ-dɪˈteɪl/ if you do **not go into detail** when you are telling someone about something, you only give them the basic facts without any details: *Wilson wouldn't go into detail about the arrangements because he said the press did not need to know.*

DETERMINED

when you have definitely decided to do something, and you will not let anything stop you

➡ see also WB **DESCRIBING PEOPLE'S CHARACTER**

1 determined to do something

determined /dɪˈtɜːˈmɪnd/ [*adj*] if you are **determined** to do something, you have decided that you are definitely going to do it, and you will not let anything stop you: *There's no point trying to stop her – it'll only make her more determined.*

determined to do sth *I was determined to be a professional dancer, and practised every day.*

+(that) *She was determined that her children should have the best possible education.*

be set on sth /biː ˈset ɒn (sth)/ to be determined to do something, especially something important that will affect your whole life, even if other people think you should not do it

be set on (doing) sth *Nina seems to be set on marrying him.*

be dead set on sth (=extremely determined to do something) *Bob's always been dead set on a career in advertising.*

D

2 someone who has a determined character

determined /dɪˈtɜːˈmɪnd/ [adj] someone who is **determined** works very hard to achieve what they want to achieve, and will not let problems stop them: *Dorothy was obviously a very determined woman.*

single-minded /ˌsɪŋɡəl ˈmaɪndɪd◂/ [adj] someone who is **single-minded** works very hard in order to achieve one thing, and thinks that everything else is much less important: *You have to be tough and single-minded if you want a career in the movies.*
single-minded determination/commitment/purpose etc *her single-minded devotion to her students*

3 determined to be successful in life or in your job

ambitious /æmˈbɪʃəs/ [adj] determined to become successful, rich, powerful, or famous: *John was very ambitious, and even at the age of 17 he began planning his career as a politician.* | *an ambitious young lawyer*

pushy /ˈpʊʃi/ [adj] INFORMAL someone who is **pushy** is so determined to do well and to get what they want that they behave in a way that is rude and annoying: *You have to be pushy to succeed in journalism.* | *Pushy parents can put their children under a lot of stress.*
pushy – pushier – pushiest

4 determined in a way that is annoying or silly

stubborn /ˈstʌbəˈn/ [adj] someone who is **stubborn** refuses to change their mind about something, even when other people think they are wrong or are being unreasonable: *I told him it was a bad idea, but Dave's so stubborn that he just never listens.* | *The oil companies face stubborn opposition from environmentalists.*
stubbornly [adv] *My grandmother stubbornly refused to eat any 'foreign' foods.*

obstinate /ˈɒbstɪnət‖ˈɑːb-/ [adj] someone who is **obstinate** always does what they want and refuses to change their mind, even when this is annoying and unreasonable: *How do you deal with an obstinate teenager who always says she isn't hungry?*
obstinately [adv] *She obstinately refused to admit she was wrong.*

pig-headed /ˌpɪɡ ˈhedɪd◂/ [adj] INFORMAL use this about someone who refuses to change their mind even if there are good reasons to do so: *He tried to warn me, but I was too pig-headed to listen.*

5 so determined that you do not care who you harm

ruthless /ˈruːθləs/ [adj] someone who is **ruthless** is so determined to get what they want, especially in business or politics, that they do not care if they harm other people: *Allan can be pretty ruthless if anyone gets in his way.* | *With ruthless efficiency, the new management fired half the workforce to increase company profits.*
ruthlessly [adv] *Pro-independence demonstrations were ruthlessly suppressed.*

go to any lengths/stop at nothing /ˌɡəʊ tʊ ˌeni ˈleŋθs, ˌstɒp ət ˈnʌθɪŋ‖ˌstɑːp-/ to be willing to do anything, even if it is cruel, dishonest, or illegal, in order to get what you want: *He was prepared to go to any lengths to find the men who killed his daughter.* | *Lawrence would stop at nothing to achieve power and wealth.*

6 when someone is determined

determination /dɪˌtɜːˈmɪˈneɪʃən/ [n U] when you continue trying to achieve what you want, even when this is difficult: *After the accident, Bill learned to walk again through sheer hard work and determination.*
determination to do sth *A spokesman stressed the police's determination to find the girl's killer.*

ambition /æmˈbɪʃən/ [n U] determination to become successful, rich, powerful, or famous: *Eric wasn't particularly intelligent but he had plenty of ambition.*

willpower /'wɪlˌpaʊəʳ/ [n U] the ability to control your mind and body in order to achieve whatever you decide to to do: *It takes a lot of willpower to give up smoking.*

perseverance /ˌpɜːʳsɪ̯'vɪərəns/ [n U] the ability to keep on trying to achieve something over a long period, even when there are problems and difficulties: *You need patience and perseverance to learn a foreign language.*

DIE

→ opposite **LIVE**
→ see also **DEAD, ALIVE, EXIST**

1 to die because you are old or ill

die /daɪ/ [v I] to stop being alive, as a result of old age or illness: *I want to see Ireland again before I die.* | *Many people are worried about growing old and dying alone.*
+of *Her youngest brother died of cancer when he was only thirteen.*
die young (=die when you are young) *His first wife had died young.*
dying – died – have died

> ⚠ The usual preposition after **die** is **of**: *He died of a heart attack.* You can also use **from**, especially when someone dies as a result of being injured: *She was shot twice, and died later from her wounds.* But don't use **with** after **die**

dying /'daɪ-ɪŋ/ [adj] if someone is **dying**, they will die very soon because they are very ill or very badly injured: *He gave the dying man a drop of water from his flask.* | *Her aunt lay dying upstairs.*

death /deθ/ [n C/U] when someone dies
the death of sb FORMAL (=when someone dies) *Over 100 years have passed since the death of Karl Marx.*
+from *The number of deaths from AIDS is still increasing.*
on sb's death FORMAL (=when they die) *Catherine will inherit a large sum of money on her father's death.*

pass away /ˌpɑːs ə'weɪ‖ˌpæs-/ [phrasal verb I] to die – use this when you want to avoid using the word 'die', because you think it might upset

someone: *"Your mother passed away during the night," the doctor told him.*

⟲ **drop dead** /ˌdrɒp 'ded‖ˌdrɑːp-/ INFORMAL, ESPECIALLY SPOKEN if someone **drops dead** they die very suddenly and unexpectedly, especially when they are in the middle of doing something: *Her husband dropped dead of a heart attack.*

2 to die in an accident, war, fight etc

die/be killed /daɪ, biː 'kɪld/ [v I] *Bob's parents died when their car was hit by a truck.*
die/be killed in an accident/explosion/the war etc *Two people were killed and four injured in a gas explosion this morning.*
die/be killed in action (=be killed while fighting in a war) *His brother was killed in action in Vietnam.*

death /deθ/ [n C/U] when someone dies in an accident or a war: *The number of deaths on Britain's roads continues to fall.*
the death of sb FORMAL (=when someone dies) *Police are investigating the mysterious deaths of two teenagers.*

to death /tə 'deθ/ **starve/freeze/bleed to death** to die because of having no food, being too cold, or losing blood: *The baby starved to death.* | *A young man was hit with a broken bottle and bled to death.*

lose your life /ˌluːz jɔːʳ 'laɪf/ to be killed in a terrible event – used in news reports and descriptions of past events: *Hundreds of people lost their lives when the ship overturned in a storm.* | *The Brazilian driver lost his life in an accident during a Formula One race in Germany.*

die for sth /'daɪ fɔːʳ (sth)/ [phrasal verb T] to die for your country or because of something you believe in: *brave men who were ready to die for their country*

D

3 an illness or accident that you die from

fatal /'feɪtl/ [adj] a **fatal** accident or medical condition kills someone, usually immediately: *a fatal heart attack* | *Meyer's car was involved in a fatal accident on the A1.*

> **Formal or informal?**
>
> **Fatal** is not usually used in informal conversation.

fatally [adv] **fatally injured/wounded** *His father had been fatally injured in an explosion.*

terminal /'tɜːrmɪnəl/. [adj] a **terminal** illness cannot be cured, and the person who has it will soon die: *She was recently told she had terminal cancer.*

terminally [adv] **terminally ill** *a ward for terminally ill patients*

4 when one of your relatives or friends dies

lose /luːz/ [v T] if you **lose** a friend or a close relative, they die: *Maya lost her mother when she was very young.* | *It's a terrible thing to lose someone very close to you.*

losing – lost – have lost

be widowed /biː 'wɪdəʊd/ if you **are widowed**, your husband or wife dies: *Becky was widowed only ten months after her marriage.*

widowed [adj only before noun] *He's gone to stay with his widowed mother in Florida.*

be orphaned /biː 'ɔːrfənd/ if you **are orphaned**, both your parents die when you are still young: *Thousands of Rwandan children were orphaned by the war.*

orphaned [adj only before noun] *a home for orphaned children*

5 when a type of animal or plant stops existing

die out /ˌdaɪ 'aʊt/ [phrasal verb I] if a type of animal or plant **dies out**, fewer and fewer of them exist, until in the end there are no more left: *The dinosaurs died out long ago.* | *Many species of wildflower are dying out as a result of pollution.*

extinct /ɪk'stɪŋkt/ [adj] a type of animal or plant that is **extinct** does not exist any more: *Animals such as the white rhino and the giant panda may soon be extinct.*

become extinct *Bears became extinct in this country over 100 years ago.*

6 places, ceremonies, etc connected with people who have died

funeral /'fjuːnərəl/ [n C] a religious ceremony when someone who has died is buried or burned

coffin (also **casket** AMERICAN) /'kɒfɪn, 'kɑːskət‖'kɔː-, 'kæs-/ [n C] the box in which a dead person's body is placed for their funeral

hearse /hɜːrs/ [n C] a large car used to carry a body in a coffin at a funeral

bury /'beri/ [v T] to put a dead person's body in a grave: *She was buried in the little churchyard, not far from the place where she was born.*

burying – buried – have buried

be cremated /biː krɪ'meɪtɪd‖ -'kriːmeɪtɪd/ to be burned, usually after a funeral – use this about a dead person's body

grave /greɪv/ [n C] a deep hole in the ground where a dead person's body is buried

graveyard /'greɪvjɑːrd/ [n C] an area of land where dead people are buried; **graveyards** are usually smaller than **cemeteries**, and in Britain they are usually next to a church

cemetery /'semətri‖-teri/ [n C] a large area of land where dead people are buried

war cemetery (=where soldiers killed in a war are buried)

plural cemeteries

DIFFERENT

➡ look here for
• different from someone or something else
• a different one, not the same one

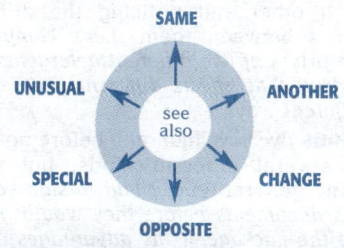

SAME

UNUSUAL   ANOTHER

see
also

SPECIAL   CHANGE

OPPOSITE

1 not like something or someone else

different /'dɪfərənt/ [adj] if something or someone is **different**, they are not like something or someone else, or they are not like they were before: *We've painted the door a different colour.* | *You look different. Have you had your hair cut?* | *Our two children are very different.*
different from sth/sb (also **different than sth/sb** AMERICAN) *This novel is quite different from her last book.*
completely/totally different *The living-room looks totally different with those new curtains.*
differently [adv] *The two words sound the same, but they're spelled differently.*

⚠ If you want to say that two people or things are different from each other, you can just say **they are different**: *Rap music and reggae are different in lots of ways.*

not like /nɒt 'laɪk/ [preposition] different from – use this especially when two things or people are not at all similar: *You should remember that walking in the hills isn't like walking down the street – it can be very dangerous.*
not at all like/nothing like (=completely different from) *She's very shy – not at all like her sister.*
not look/sound like *The voice on the answering machine did not sound like Anna at all.*

not the same /nɒt ðə 'seɪm/ different – use this especially when two things are similar but not exactly like each other: *The two patterns are similar but not the same.*
+as *I've tried Mexican food here in London, but it just isn't the same as in Mexico.*

vary /'veəri/ [v I] if things of the same type **vary**, they are all different from each other: *Methods of treatment vary according to the age and general health of the patient.*
vary considerably/greatly *Prices of video cameras vary considerably.*
vary in price/quality/size/flavour etc *The cheeses vary in flavour from mild to strong.*
varying – varied – have varied

differ /'dɪfər/ [v I] FORMAL if two things **differ**, they have different qualities or features
+from *Scottish law has always differed from English law.*
differ in cost/size/appearance etc *The two drugs have the same effect, but they differ in certain important respects.*
differ greatly/widely *Opinions on the subject differ widely.*

2 completely different from anyone or anything else

unique /juːˈniːk/ [adj] something **unique** is so different, special, or unusual that it is the only one of its kind: *a musician with a unique style* | *a mental ability which makes the human race unique among animals*

special /'speʃəl/ [adj] designed for one particular purpose, and therefore different from other things of its type: *Bob's been on a special diet since his heart attack.* | *You need a special tool for this job.*

distinctive /dɪˈstɪŋktɪv/ [adj] ESPECIALLY WRITTEN something that is **distinctive** has a special quality or appearance that makes it different from other things, and makes it easy to recognize: *Sarah dressed in a very distinctive style.* | *the distinctive taste of genuine malt whisky*

one-off /ˌwʌn 'ɒf/ [n C] BRITISH INFORMAL someone who is completely different

D

from anyone else: *I really liked Rohan. He was a complete one-off.*
plural **one-offs**

3 another one, not the same one as before

another /ə'nʌðəʳ/ [*determiner/pronoun*] one more of the same kind of thing or person: *creatures from another planet | Louise has one house in New York, and another in Florida.*
another one *I didn't like the dress I'd bought, so I changed it for another one.*

> ⚠ Don't say 'another countries'. Say **another country** or **other countries**. **Another** is not used before a plural or uncountable noun.

different /'dɪfərənt/ [*adj* only before noun] a **different** thing or person is not the same one that you have already mentioned: *The other portrait is by a different artist. | She used to be a teacher, but I think she's doing a different job now.*

new /njuː‖nuː/ [*adj* only before noun] use this about something or someone that replaces the one that was there before: *Have you met Keith's new girlfriend? | She's really enjoying her new job.*

else /els/ [*adv*] **something/some-where/someone else** another thing, place, or person instead of this one: *Go and play somewhere else. I'm trying to work. | He wants the best, and won't accept anything else.*

alternative /ɔːlˈtɜːʳnətɪv‖ɔːl-, æl-/ [*adj* only before noun] an **alternative** plan, arrangement, or system can be used instead of the usual one: *The company is trying to develop cars that run on alternative fuels. | For vegetarian guests there is an alternative menu.*

> **Formal or informal?**
> **Alternative** is used in writing and in formal spoken English.

4 several different things or people

different /'dɪfərənt/ [*adj* only before noun] use this about several people or things of the same general type, when you are comparing them with each other and noticing the differences between them: *Let's compare the prices of five different detergents. | a drug that affects different people in different ways*

various /'veəriəs/ [*adj* only before noun] of several different kinds, but the same general type: *I had to sign various documents before they would give me the package. | the advantages and disadvantages of the various teaching methods*

all sorts of/all kinds of /ɔːl 'sɔːʳts ɒv, ɔːl 'kaɪndz ɒv/ ESPECIALLY SPOKEN a lot of people or things that are different from each other, but of the same general type: *I meet all sorts of people in my job. | The bureau provides advice on all kinds of housing problems.*

a variety of /ə vəˈraɪəti ɒv/ ESPECIALLY WRITTEN a lot of things that are different from each other, but of the same general type: *Children do badly at school for a variety of reasons.*
a wide variety of (=very many different things) *The college offers a wide variety of language courses.*

varied /'veərid/ [*adj*] including many different things or people, especially in a way that seems interesting: *I really enjoy the work here – it's very varied. | It is important that a child gets a varied diet.*

separate /'sepərɪt/ [*adj* only before noun] use this about two or more things of the same general type that are not connected with each other: *a word that has three separate meanings | She has been warned on a number of separate occasions.*

5 the way in which two things are different

difference /'dɪfərəns/ [*n C*] what makes one thing or person different from another: *He's speaking Spanish, not Italian. Don't you know the difference?*

+between *Try and spot the differences between these two pictures.*

contrast /ˈkɒntrɑːst‖ˈkɑːntræst/ [n singular] a very clear difference that you can easily see when you compare two things or people
+between *The thing that surprised us was the contrast between the ancient temples and the ultra-modern office buildings.*

gap /gæp/ [n C] a big difference between two amounts, two ages, or two groups of people
+ between *There's a ten-year gap between Kay's two children. | The gap between rich and poor is getting wider.*

6 to notice that two things or people are different

can tell the difference /kən ˌtel ðə ˈdɪfərəns/ to be able to see how one thing or person is different from another very similar one – use this especially in questions and negative statements: *It looked just like a real diamond – I couldn't tell the difference.*
+between *Can you tell the difference between butter and margarine?*

can tell sb/sth apart /kən ˌtel (sb/sth) əˈpɑːˈt/ to be able to tell the difference between two very similar things or people – use this especially in questions and negative statements: *The twins are identical – even their parents can't always tell them apart.*

distinguish /dɪˈstɪŋgwɪʃ/ [v I/T] to be able to see the difference between two or more similar things or people
+between *Even an expert would find it hard to distinguish between the original painting and the copy.*
distinguish sb/sth from sb/sth *A tiny baby soon learns to distinguish its mother's face from other adults' faces.*

> **Formal or informal?**
> **Distinguish** is more formal than **can tell the difference**.

7 when one statement makes a different one seem untrue

contradict /ˌkɒntrəˈdɪkt‖ˌkɑːn-/ [v T] if one statement or fact **contradicts**

another one, it is so different that it makes the other one seem untrue or impossible: *The two newspaper reports totally contradict each other. | Their theories have been contradicted by the results of recent experiments.*

DIFFICULT

➡ opposite **EASY**

1 difficult to do or understand

difficult/hard /ˈdɪfɪkəlt, hɑːˈd/ [adj] not easy to do or understand: *The police have a difficult job to do. | Windsurfing is harder than it looks.*
difficult/hard to see/hear/read etc *His handwriting is very difficult to read.*
it is difficult/hard to do sth *It's difficult to explain these problems to a child. | It is hard to imagine what life was like in the 13th century.*
find it difficult/hard to do sth *People find it difficult to learn new skills as they get older.*
make it difficult/hard for sb to do sth *My mother's illness makes it very difficult for her to do a full-time job.*

> **Formal or informal?**
> **Difficult** is more formal than **hard**.

tough /tʌf/ [adj] very difficult to do or deal with – use this about jobs, decisions, questions, or problems: *People in government are always having to make tough decisions. | He'll have some pretty tough questions to answer.*

complicated /ˈkɒmplɪkeɪtɪd‖ˈkɑːm-/ [adj] a **complicated** problem, situation, or system is difficult to understand because it consists of many different parts or details: *the complicated problem of bringing peace to the Middle East | a complicated set of instructions*

complex /ˈkɒmpleks‖ˌkɑːmˈpleks/ [adj] a **complex** process or system is difficult to understand because it has a lot of parts that are all connected in different ways: *The way humans think is a complex process that scientists cannot fully explain. | complex laws relating to sex discrimination*

◯ **it's easier said than done** /ɪts ˌiːziəʳ ˌsed ðən ˈdʌn/ SPOKEN say this to tell someone that something is much more difficult than they think it is: *"You'll just have to find yourself a rich husband!" "Well, that's easier said than done."*

2 something that needs a lot of skill, hard work, and determination

challenging /ˈtʃælɪndʒɪŋ/ [adj] a **challenging** job or activity needs a lot of hard work and skill, but is interesting or enjoyable: *She finds working with handicapped children challenging but rewarding. | The job wasn't challenging enough for me – I wanted something more creative.*

be a challenge /biː ə ˈtʃælɪndʒ/ if a new job or activity **is a challenge**, it is difficult, but you are determined to do it because it is interesting and exciting: *You may find your first couple of months in the job quite a challenge. | We have to walk 60 kilometres in two days – it will be a real challenge.*

demanding /dɪˈmɑːndɪŋ‖dɪˈmæn-/ [adj] a **demanding** job or activity is very difficult and tiring, because it needs all your effort and skill and a lot of your time: *Being a nurse in a busy hospital is a demanding job.*

daunting /ˈdɔːntɪŋ/ [adj] if something is **daunting**, it seems almost impossible, and the idea of doing it makes you feel nervous: *Climbing Everest was a daunting challenge for any mountaineer.*
daunting task *I was faced with the daunting task of learning the entire script in 24 hours.*

3 a situation that is difficult to deal with or talk about

difficult /ˈdɪfɪkəlt/ [adj] a **difficult** situation or subject is not easy to deal with or talk about, and it makes you feel nervous or unhappy: *Things at*

home have been very difficult since my father died. | Their relationship had been difficult from the start.*
in a difficult position (=when someone has problems that are difficult to deal with) *His ex-wife's accusations have put the President in a very difficult position.*

awkward /ˈɔːkwəʳd/ [adj] an **awkward** situation or subject is difficult to deal with or talk about, especially because it might be embarrassing: *He's at the age when kids start asking awkward questions like 'Where do babies come from?'*

tricky /ˈtrɪki/ [adj] a **tricky** situation is one that you have to deal with very carefully, because there are a lot of things that could easily go wrong: *Teachers often have to deal with tricky situations, such as interviews with angry parents. | Although I was his boss I was much younger than him, so things were rather tricky at first.*
tricky – trickier – trickiest

sensitive /ˈsensɪtɪv/ [adj] a **sensitive** subject is one that you need to deal with very carefully, because it is likely to cause disagreement or upset someone: *the sensitive subject of homosexuality | The whole issue of abortion is very sensitive.*

4 someone who is unhelpful and causes problems

difficult /ˈdɪfɪkəlt/ [adj] someone who is **difficult** is not easy to live with or work with because they do not behave in a helpful, friendly way, or they do not do what you want: *When Darren was a little boy, he was very difficult at times. | Campbell has the reputation of being difficult to work with.*

awkward /ˈɔːkwəʳd/ [adj] BRITISH someone who is **awkward** is deliberately unhelpful and unfriendly, and seems to like causing problems for people: *I don't think she's really too sick to come with us. She's just being awkward.*

D

🔍 **impossible** /ɪmˈpɒsɪ̩bəl‖ɪmˈpɑː-/ [adj not before noun] SPOKEN someone who is **impossible** makes you annoyed and impatient, for example because they are never satisfied or they keep changing their mind: *Even when I offer to help her she always finds some reason to complain. She's impossible!*

🔍 **be a pain (in the neck)** /biː ə ˌpeɪn ɪn ðə ˈnek/ SPOKEN INFORMAL to be very annoying and difficult to deal with: *Lately he's been a real pain in the neck. | My brother is such a pain!*

5 a time when you have a lot of problems

difficult/hard/tough /ˈdɪfɪkəlt, hɑːʳd, tʌf/ [adj] use this about a period of time when you have a lot of problems or a lot of bad things happen to you: *The last few months have been especially difficult for her. | This was perhaps the hardest year we've faced so far.*
have a hard/difficult/tough time *Try to be nice to her. She's had a really tough time recently.*

6 to have problems when you are trying to do something

have difficulty /hæv ˈdɪfɪkəlti/ if you **have difficulty** when you are trying to do something, you cannot do it easily
have difficulty doing sth *I noticed that she was having difficulty breathing. | Kelly was having difficulty controlling his temper.*
+with *Do you have any difficulty with spelling?*

 Don't say 'I had difficulty to walk'. Say **I had difficulty walking**.

find sth difficult /ˌfaɪnd (sth) ˈdɪfɪkəlt/ to not be able to do something easily, especially because you do not have enough ability or skill: *I found the course difficult at first, but it gradually got easier.*
find it difficult to do sth *He's very shy, and finds it difficult to talk to people.*

with difficulty /wɪð ˈdɪfɪkəlti/ WRITTEN if you do something **with difficulty**, you do it, but only by using all your strength, all your determination etc: *With difficulty, the old man struggled up the stairs. | She spoke with difficulty, choking back her tears.*

have a hard time /hæv ə ˌhɑːʳd ˈtaɪm/ to find it difficult to do something, especially because there are particular problems involved or because it is difficult to persuade other people: *Anyone running their own business sometimes has a hard time.*
have a hard time doing sth *You're going to have a hard time proving he's not guilty.*

can hardly /kən ˈhɑːʳdli/ if you **can hardly** do something, you can only just do it, and it is very difficult: *He talks so fast, I can hardly understand what he's saying. | By the end of the day she could hardly walk.*

 Don't say 'we can't hardly move'. Say **we can hardly move**.

🔍 **have a job doing sth** /hæv ə ˈdʒɒb duːɪŋ (sth)‖-ˈdʒɑːb-/ BRITISH SPOKEN if you **have a job doing something**, it takes a lot of time or a lot of effort, and you may not be able to do it: *You'll have a job persuading him to give you any more money. | There was some kind of festival going on, and we had a job finding somewhere to park the car.*

DIRECTION

➡ see also **WAY**

the direction in which something or someone moves

direction /dɪ̩ˈrekʃən, daɪ-/ [n C usually singular] the direction that something or someone is moving towards or pointing towards
in sb's direction (=towards someone) *We crept past, hoping that the guard would not look in our direction.*
in the direction of sth (=towards something) *We carried on walking in the direction of the ocean.*

D

in the right/wrong direction *Are you sure we're going in the right direction?*

in the opposite direction *Bill marched off angrily in the opposite direction.*

from the direction of sth *Suddenly Anna heard a shout coming from the direction of the kitchen.*

way /weɪ/ [n C usually singular] the general direction that something or someone is moving towards or pointing towards: *"Which way does the garden face?" "South. It gets a lot of sun."*

this way/that way *The truck went that way – you can see its tracks in the snow.*

the right way/the wrong way *I think we're going the wrong way.*

the other way (=the opposite way) *Another train passed, going the other way.*

Formal or informal?

Way and **direction** mean the same, but **way** is more common in informal spoken English and **direction** is more common in formal written English.

⚠ Don't use 'in' before **way**. Don't say 'I'm going in this way'. Say **I'm going this way**.

DIRTY

➡ opposite **CLEAN**
➡ see also **WASH, MARK**

1 dirty

dirty /'dɜːʳti/ [adj] not clean: *Look how dirty your hands are! | dirty clothes | The children had made dirty fingermarks on the wall.*

get dirty (=become dirty) *This carpet's getting very dirty.*

get sth dirty (=make it dirty) *I don't want to get my new shoes dirty.*

dirty – dirtier – dirtiest

filthy /'fɪlθi/ [adj] extremely dirty: *We didn't go swimming because the water looked filthy. | She put the cake into the filthiest, greasiest oven he had ever seen.*

absolutely filthy *Your jeans are absolutely filthy.*

filthy – filthier – filthiest

muddy /'mʌdi/ [adj] covered in mud: *Take off your muddy boots. | She left a trail of muddy footprints behind her. | a muddy field*

muddy – muddier – muddiest

dusty /'dʌsti/ [adj] a **dusty** room, piece of furniture etc is covered in dust, especially because no one has cleaned it for a long time: *The room was dark and dusty. | dusty shelves*

dusty – dustier – dustiest

greasy /'griːsi, -zi/ [adj] something that is **greasy** looks dirty because it has an oily substance on it: *She had long greasy black hair. | He wiped his hands on a greasy cloth.*

greasy – greasier – greasiest

dingy /'dɪndʒi/ [adj] a **dingy** room, street, or building is dirty, dark, and in bad condition: *Marlowe's dingy little office was in a run-down block near the station.*

dingy – dingier – dingiest

2 dirty and bad for your health

➡ see also **WB ENVIRONMENT**

unhygienic /ˌʌnhaɪˈdʒiːnɪk‖-ˈdʒen-, -ˈdʒiːn-/ [adj] likely to cause disease – use this about dirty conditions in kitchens, restaurants, and hospitals: *It is unhygienic to store raw and cooked meats together. | Operations are carried out under the most unhygienic conditions.*

polluted /pəˈluːtɪd/ [adj] water or air that is **polluted** has a lot of harmful waste or poisonous chemicals in it: *an effort to clean up Britain's polluted rivers*

+with/by *Parts of the Mediterranean are polluted with toxic waste.*

heavily polluted (=very badly polluted) *The air is heavily polluted with exhaust fumes.*

contaminated /kənˈtæmɪneɪtɪd/ [adj] FORMAL food, water, or land that is **contaminated** is not safe to use or be in because dangerous chemicals or bacteria have come into it: *contaminated drinking water*

+with/by *Milk contaminated with lead has been on sale in the supermarkets.*

heavily contaminated (=very badly contaminated) *Crops cannot be grown in the heavily contaminated soil around Chernobyl.*

3 something that makes things dirty

dirt /dɜːʳt/ [n U] dust, mud, or anything else that makes things dirty: *She rubbed some dirt off the glass with her finger.* | *I've washed that shirt twice, but I can't get the dirt out.*

dust /dʌst/ [n U] dry powder that forms a layer on furniture, floors, clothes etc, especially when they have not been cleaned for a long time: *There was a thick layer of dust on the shelves.* | *Max brushed the dust off his coat.*

 Don't say 'a lot of dusts'. Say **a lot of dust. Dust** has no plural form.

mud /mʌd/ [n U] very wet earth that sticks to your shoes, clothes, car tyres etc: *The dog left mud all over the carpet.* | *Hayley scraped the dried mud off her boots.*
be covered in mud *Their expensive riding jackets were covered in mud.*

pollution /pəˈluːʃən/ [n U] the harmful effects on water, air, or land of chemicals and waste from factories, cars, modern farming methods etc: *Industrial pollution has killed all the fish in the river.* | *We moved to the country to get away from all the crime and pollution in Los Angeles.*

DISABLED

when someone cannot use part of their body

1 disabled

disabled /dɪsˈeɪbəld/ [adj] someone who is **disabled** has serious difficulty using part of their body or mind, and this makes it difficult for them to have a normal life: *David goes to a special school for disabled children.* | *Her son is disabled and she has to take care of him all the time.*
mentally/physically/learning

disabled *Several physically disabled children attend the local school.*
the disabled (=disabled people) *new laws to protect the rights of the disabled*
disabled toilets/parking etc (=special toilets, parking etc for disabled people)

special needs /ˌspeʃəl ˈniːdz/ [n plural] people with **special needs** need different teaching methods, special equipment etc because they have physical or mental problems – used especially by people who work with children like this: *a school for children with special needs*

disability /ˌdɪsəˈbɪlɪti/ [n C/U] a problem with part of your body which makes it difficult for you to walk, talk, see etc: *There are special courses for people with disabilities.* | *His disability didn't stop him from becoming a world-class scientist.*
learning/mental/physical disability *He was tutoring children with learning disabilities.*
plural **disabilities**

2 not disabled

able-bodied /ˌeɪbəl ˈbɒdid◄ ‖-ˈbɑː-/ [adj] not disabled – use this when you are comparing disabled people with people who are not disabled: *Disabled students face different problems from their able-bodied friends.*

DISAGREE

➡ opposite **AGREE**

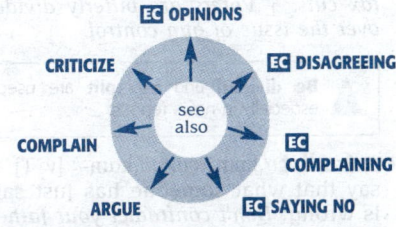

1 to have a different opinion from someone else

disagree/not agree /ˌdɪsəˈgriː, ˌnɒt əˈgriː/ [v I] to have a different opinion

from someone else: *This is what I'm suggesting. If you don't agree, just say so.* | *Anthea thought they should move to a bigger apartment, but Jim disagreed.*
+with *I understand what he's suggesting, but I just don't agree with it.* | *Other scientists disagree with her ideas.*
+about *Experts disagree about the effects of global warming.*

> ⚠ Don't say 'I am disagreeing', 'I am not agreeing etc'. Say **I disagree**, **I don't agree** etc.

> ⚠ If you want to say that two people disagree with each other, you can just say **they disagree** or **they don't agree**: *Bill and Larry disagreed about almost everything.*

> ⚠ Don't say 'I disagree to this view' or 'I disagree this view'. Say **I disagree with this view**.

🔍 **not see eye to eye** /nɒt siː ˌaɪ tʊ 'aɪ/ ESPECIALLY SPOKEN if two people do **not see eye to eye**, they have very different opinions and ideas, so that it is difficult for them to be friends or to work together
+on/about *Unfortunately, Sally and I don't see eye to eye on money matters.*
+with *She never saw eye to eye with her daughter-in-law.*

be divided/be split /biː dɪˈvaɪdɪd, biː 'splɪt/ if a group of people **is divided** or **is split** over something, some of them support one opinion and others support the opposite opinion
+over/on *The country's leaders appear to be split on the question of tax cuts.* | *Voters are bitterly divided over the issue of gun control.*

> ⚠ **Be divided** and **be split** are used especially in news reports.

contradict /ˌkɒntrəˈdɪkt‖ˌkɑːn-/ [v T] to say that what someone has just said is wrong: *Don't contradict your father.* | *One of his students contradicted something he said, and he got really angry.*

---

2 a situation in which people disagree

disagreement /ˌdɪsəˈɡriːmənt/ [n C/U] when people disagree with each other
+about/over *Disagreement over who should produce the next album caused the band to split.*
+between/among *There is some disagreement among medical experts about the best treatment for back pain.*
have a disagreement with sb (=disagree and argue with them) *She had a disagreement with her boss – that's why she's upset.*

argument /'ɑːrɡjʊmənt/ [n C] when people speak angrily to each other because they disagree about something
have an argument *Ron and I had an argument last night.*
+about/over *There had been a brief argument about what to do if the plan didn't work.*
+with *Dad had a huge argument with Vicky about politics.*

difference of opinion /ˌdɪfərəns əv əˈpɪnjən/ [n C] when people disagree, especially about something important – use this as a way of avoiding more direct words like 'argument' and 'disagreement'
+between/among *There were reports of a slight difference of opinion between the President and his advisers.*
+about/over *There are differences of opinion about what the document actually means.*
plural **differences of opinion**

controversy /'kɒntrəvɜːsi, kənˈtrɒvəsi‖'kɑːntrə,vɜːrsi/ [n C/U] serious disagreement about a decision, plan, or action, which causes arguments for a long time in the newspapers, on television etc: *Controversy surrounds the TV show, which many consider to be racist, sexist, and homophobic.*
+over *The controversy over the nuclear energy program is likely to continue.*
plural **controversies**

deadlock/stalemate /'dedlɒk, 'steɪl-meɪt‖-lɑːk/ [n singular/U] a situation in which two groups disagree with each other, and no agreement is possible because each group refuses to change its mind: *After two weeks, the discussions reached complete deadlock.* | *The long-running dispute ended in a stalemate.*

> ⚠ **Deadlock** and **stalemate** are used especially in news reports.

3 causing disagreement

controversial /,kɒntrə'vɜːʳʃəl‖,kɑːn-/ [adj] something that is **controversial** causes a lot of disagreement and angry argument, especially in the newspapers, on television etc: *He wrote a highly controversial article about the education system.*
controversial issue (=a subject that many people disagree about) *Abortion is always a controversial issue in the US.*

DISAPPEAR

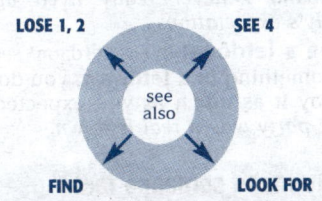

LOSE 1, 2   SEE 4

see also

FIND   LOOK FOR

1 when you can't find someone or something

disappear /,dɪsə'pɪəʳ/ [v I] if someone or something **disappears**, you cannot find them: *Where are my keys? They seem to have disappeared.*
+from *The money had disappeared from the table.*
disappear without (a) trace (=disappear and never be found again) *The plane disappeared without trace, and no survivors were ever found.*
disappearance [n U] when someone or something disappears: *Her sudden disappearance was very worrying.*

> ⚠ Don't say 'he was disappeared', 'they are disappeared' etc. Say **he disappeared, they have disappeared** etc.

> ⚠ If you say that a person **has disappeared**, this can mean either that you do not know where they are at the moment, or that they have been taken away by someone and they may be in danger: *"Where's Tom?" "I don't know – he's disappeared."* | *A 12-year-old boy disappeared from his home in Kansas City last night.*

vanish /'vænɪʃ/ [v I] if someone or something **vanishes**, you suddenly cannot find them and you cannot understand what has happened to them: *When she returned, her car had vanished.*
vanish into thin air (=vanish in a way that seems impossible) *He was here ten minutes ago; now he's vanished into thin air.*

go missing /,gəʊ 'mɪsɪŋ/ BRITISH if someone **goes missing**, they cannot be found anywhere, and they may be in danger: *Angela Priest went missing one year ago.*
+from *The police were called after a six-year-old girl went missing from a playground near her home.*

be/have gone /biː, həv 'gɒn‖-'gɔːn/ to have disappeared: *I didn't even notice it was gone.* | *When he returned minutes later, his equipment had gone.*

2 to become impossible to see

disappear /,dɪsə'pɪəʳ/ [v I] if someone or something **disappears**, you cannot see them any more
+behind/under/into/over etc *The sun disappeared behind a cloud.* | *She watched the boat sail out to sea until it disappeared over the horizon.*

vanish /'vænɪʃ/ [v I] to disappear suddenly and in a way that cannot be explained: *Jake thought he saw a woman at the window, but when he looked again she had vanished.*
+into/behind/under etc *A strange light appeared and then vanished again into the darkness.*

go /gəʊ/ [v I] to disappear by becoming hidden
+behind/under etc *He saw the plane just before it went behind a cloud.* | *The spider had gone under the fridge.*

DISAPPOINTING/ DISAPPOINTED

unhappy because things did not happen in the way that you hoped

➡ see also **SATISFIED/DISSATISFIED**

1 disappointed

disappointed /ˌdɪsə'pɔɪntɪd◂/ [adj] unhappy because things did not happen in the way you hoped they would, or were not as good as you expected them to be: *I felt a little disappointed when she didn't come to the party.* | *The hall was already full, and hundreds of disappointed fans were turned away at the door.*
+with/by *Were you disappointed with the way you played today?*
+in *I was disappointed in my performance.*
+that *The children were very disappointed that we couldn't go to the zoo.*
disappointed to find/learn/hear/ see *We were disappointed to find that the museum was closed.*
bitterly disappointed (=very disappointed) *Backley was bitterly disappointed when an injury prevented him from competing in the Olympic Games.*
disappointment [n U] the feeling of being disappointed: *She couldn't hide her disappointment when David told her he wasn't coming.*
feel let down /fiːl ˌlet 'daʊn/ to feel disappointed because someone did not do what they promised to do, or did not help you when you needed them: *No wonder the nurses feel let down – they were promised a big pay increase, but nothing has happened.*
disillusioned /ˌdɪsɪ'luːʒənd◂/ [adj] you feel **disillusioned** when you realize that a person, belief, way of life etc is not as good as you thought they were: *Disillusioned voters are turning against the government.*

+with *After three years of war, the army was becoming disillusioned with its leaders.*

2 something that makes you feel disappointed

disappointing /ˌdɪsə'pɔɪntɪŋ◂/ [adj] something that is **disappointing** makes you feel slightly unhappy or dissatisfied, because it is not as good as you hoped it would be: *The team had a disappointing season.* | *Company profits this year have been very disappointing.*
be a disappointment /biː ə ˌdɪsə'pɔɪntmənt/ something that **is a disappointment** does not happen in the way you hoped, or is not as good as you expected: *The holiday was a bit of a disappointment – it rained the whole time.*
+to *Failing the test was a real disappointment to me.*
be a great disappointment *It was a great disappointment to my parents that I didn't go to university.*
not live up to expectations /nɒt lɪv ˌʌp tʊ ekspek'teɪʃənz/ if an event or person **does not live up to expectations**, you expected them to be very good but in fact they are not: *I'm afraid as a husband I never really lived up to Kelly's expectations.*
◯ **be a letdown** /biː ə 'letdaʊn/ SPOKEN if something **is a letdown**, you do not enjoy it as much as you expected to: *The party was a real letdown.*

3 to make someone feel disappointed

disappoint /ˌdɪsə'pɔɪnt/ [v T] to make someone feel disappointed: *I'm sorry to disappoint you, but there aren't any tickets left.*
let sb down /ˌlet (sb) 'daʊn/ [phrasal verb T] if someone **lets you down**, they do not do what they promised to do, or they do not behave as well as you expected them to: *I said I would help them – I can't let them down.*
let sb down badly *Many disabled soldiers feel the government has let them down very badly.*

DISHONEST

→ opposite **HONEST**
→ see also **CHEAT, LIE 2, TRICK/DECEIVE, TRUST/NOT TRUST**

1 dishonest

dishonest /dɪs'ɒnɪst‖-'ɑː-/ [adj] someone who is **dishonest** tells lies or tries to trick people or steal things: *a dishonest car salesman* | *dishonest practices among financial dealers* | *I'm sure you can trust Bob – he wouldn't do anything dishonest.*
dishonestly [adv] *He was accused of dishonestly obtaining an American passport.*

○ **you can't trust sb** /juː kɑːnt 'trʌst (sb)‖-kænt-/ SPOKEN say this about someone when you think that they may tell lies or try to trick you: *You can't trust the tobacco companies – they'll say anything to protect their business.*

unscrupulous /ʌn'skruːpjʊləs/ [adj] FORMAL someone who is **unscrupulous** uses dishonest and unfair methods to get what they want, and does not care if they cause problems for other people: *Some unscrupulous employers hire illegal immigrants to work for very low wages.* | *unscrupulous landlords*

corrupt /kə'rʌpt/ [adj] a **corrupt** politician, official, or police officer uses their power in a dishonest way for their own advantage, for example by accepting money from people in return for helping them: *Corrupt customs officials allowed the drug trade to continue.*

devious /'diːviəs/ [adj] someone who is **devious** tries to get what they want by secretly using clever plans to trick people, so you can never be sure what their real intentions are: *a devious politician* | *one of Stalin's devious schemes*

suspicious /sə'spɪʃəs/ [adj] use this about behaviour or situations that make you think that someone is doing something dishonest: *It seems very suspicious to me. Where did he get all that money from?*

suspicious-looking *There was a suspicious-looking character standing in a doorway across the street.*
suspiciously [adv] *If you notice anyone behaving suspiciously, call the police.*

sneaky /'sniːki/ [adj] INFORMAL someone who is **sneaky** does things secretly and tricks people in order to get what they want: *the sneaky type of guy who pretends to be nice and friendly just so he can steal all your ideas*
sneaky – sneakier – sneakiest

crooked /'krʊkɪd/ [adj] INFORMAL someone who is **crooked** is dishonest or involved in illegal activities – use this especially about someone in a position of authority: *a crooked cop* (=policeman)

2 dishonest behaviour

dishonesty /dɪs'ɒnɪsti‖-'ɑː-/ [n U] dishonest behaviour: *Are you accusing me of dishonesty?* | *If a lawyer is suspected of dishonesty, he risks losing his job.*

corruption /kə'rʌpʃən/ [n U] when someone who works for the government, the police etc uses their power dishonestly to get money or gain an advantage: *The chief of police was forced to resign after allegations of corruption.*

bribery /'braɪbəri/ [n U] when someone offers money to a politician or government official in order to persuade them to do something: *US firms used bribery to win contracts.* | *a massive bribery scandal involving dozens of politicians*
bribery and corruption *The General promised to end bribery and corruption in the government.*

graft /grɑːft‖græft/ [n U] AMERICAN dishonest behaviour by someone in a position of authority, who uses their influence or power to gain an advantage or get money from someone: *The new police chief was committed to cleaning up graft, bribery, and corruption in the police force.*

DO

➡ see also **REFUSE, AGREE 4, LET**

1 to do something

do /duː/ [v T] *"What are you doing?"* *"I'm trying to fix the television."*
do work/housework/homework *95% of housework is done by women.* | *I did a lot of work in the garden today.*
do the washing/cooking/shopping etc *His mother still does all his washing.*
do a test/exam/course etc *He's doing an art course at Wrexham College.*
do sth well/badly *She enjoys her job and she does it very well.*
doing – did – have done

achieve /əˈtʃiːv/ [v T] to succeed in doing something good or getting the result that you wanted, after trying hard for a long time: *At the age of 40, he felt he had achieved nothing in his life.* | *She was determined to become a pilot, and finally achieved her goal.*

carry out /ˌkæri ˈaʊt/ [phrasal verb T] to do something that has been planned or that someone has told you to do: *They employed a builder to carry out the work.*
carry out tests/research/a survey/a search *Scientists are carrying out research into the effects of this drug.* | *Police carried out a thorough search of the building.*
carry out sb's orders/instructions/wishes (=do what someone told you to do) *The porter refused to let anyone into the building, but he was only carrying out orders.*
carry out a threat/promise (=do what you said you would do) *The terrorists carried out their threat and shot two of the hostages.*

commit /kəˈmɪt/ [v T]
commit a crime/murder/robbery etc to do something that is a crime, especially a serious crime: *Women commit far fewer crimes than men.* | *The murder must have been committed between 7 and 10pm.*
committing – committed – have committed

perform /pəˈfɔːrm/ [v T] FORMAL to do something, especially something difficult or useful
perform a duty/operation/task *The operation was performed by a team of surgeons at Addenbrookes Hospital.* | *Computers perform several tasks at the same time.*

◯ **get on with sth** /ˌget ˈɒn wɪð (sth)‖-ˈɑːn-/ [phrasal verb T] ESPECIALLY SPOKEN to start doing something that you should have started already, or that you have stopped doing for a short time: *Stop talking and get on with your work.*
get on with doing sth *As soon as the rain stops, I'll get on with painting the fence.*

◯ **be up to something** /bi ˈʌp tə ˌsʌmθɪŋ/ ESPECIALLY SPOKEN if someone **is up to something**, they are doing something but you do not know exactly what it is, and you think it is probably something bad: *There's a lot of whispering in the kitchen. I think the kids must be up to something.* | *I wish I knew what he was up to!*

2 to do something in order to deal with a bad situation

do something /ˈduː ˌsʌmθɪŋ/ to do something to deal with a problem, especially one that is urgent: *Quick, do something – there's water all over the floor!*
+about *Street crime is a real problem. It's time the police did something about it.*

intervene /ˌɪntərˈviːn/ [v I] to do something to try to stop people from fighting or quarrelling with each other: *After a few hours the police intervened to stop the rioting.*
+in *The government may have to intervene in the strike.*

> **Formal or informal?**
> **Intervene** is used in writing and in formal spoken English.

take action /ˌteɪk ˈækʃən/ to do something to stop a bad situation from happening or continuing – use this to talk about people in powerful positions, when they have a clear plan for dealing with a problem

Unless governments take action soon, the Earth's atmosphere will be damaged forever.
take action to do sth *Governments must take action to end the trade in rare and endangered animals.*
+against *The school will take strong action against any students using illegal drugs.*

act /ækt/ [I] FORMAL to do something to deal with an urgent problem, especially by using your power or authority: *If the UN does not act soon, more people will die.*
act to do sth *The government acted quickly to introduce tight controls.*

step in /ˌstep 'ɪn/ [phrasal verb I] to get involved in a situation in order to deal with a problem or to stop trouble: *Local parents have stepped in to provide extra help at the school. | The military may step in if the crisis continues.*

> ⚠ **Step in** is used especially in news reports.

3 something that someone does

thing /θɪŋ/ [n C] something that someone does – always use this with the verb **do**: *The first thing you should do is connect the computer to the printer.*
a stupid/clever/difficult etc thing to do *You left your bag on the train? What a stupid thing to do! | It's a very dangerous thing to do.*

action /'ækʃən/ [n C] FORMAL something that someone does: *Lavender's actions had been stupid, but he had not intended any harm.*
course of action (=something that you could do in order to deal with a situation) *There was only one possible course of action – he had to kill Siltz.*

> ⚠ Don't use **action** with 'do'. Use 'thing' or 'something' instead: *I think you did the right thing. | He might do something stupid.*

activities /æk'tɪvɪtiz/ [n plural] things that people do, especially things that people do as a group, for work or for pleasure: *Rebecca has always loved*

horse riding and other outdoor activities. | Police are investigating the company's activities.
leisure / social / cultural   activities *The school arranges social activities for students to take part in at the weekends.*

> **Formal or informal?**
> **Activities** is used in writing and in formal spoken English.

achievement /ə'tʃiːvmənt/ [n C] something you succeed in doing after trying hard, especially something that is difficult to do and that other people admire: *We opened a bottle of champagne to celebrate our achievement.*
great / remarkable / tremendous achievement (=one that you admire a lot) *They sold over 20 million copies of their album in the US, which is a tremendous achievement.*

4 to not do something that you should do

not do sth /nɒt 'duː (sth)/ *The translation? I'm sorry, I haven't done it yet. | She was terrified that he would hurt her if she didn't do what he said.*

fail to do sth /ˌfeɪl tə 'duː (sth)/ FORMAL to not do something that you should do, especially when this has serious results: *The driver of the car failed to stop in time, and the boy was killed.*

 not bother /nɒt 'bɒðəʳ‖-'bɑː-/ ESPECIALLY SPOKEN to not do something because it does not seem important or necessary
don't bother *"Would you like me to wait for you?" "No, don't bother."*
not bother to do sth *He didn't even bother to tell me he was going to be late.*

do nothing/not do anything /ˌduː 'nʌθɪŋ, nɒt duː 'eniθɪŋ/ to not try to help someone or prevent a bad situation, even though you know it is happening: *He admitted he had seen the attack and done nothing.*
+about *We told the police months ago, but they still haven't done anything about it.*
+to help/stop/prevent sth *No-one in*

the company did anything to stop this disaster from happening.

○ **just sit there/just stand there**
/dʒʌst ˈsɪt ðeəʳ, dʒʌst ˈstænd ðeəʳ/ SPOKEN to do nothing helpful or useful, especially when you should do something: *Don't just stand there – do something! | When the fire alarm went off she just sat there as if she hadn't heard a thing.*

leave /liːv/ [v T] to not do something now because you can do it later: *If you can't answer a question, leave it and go on to the next one.*
leave sth for now *Leave the details for now, we'll deal with them later.*
leave sth till later/tomorrow/next week etc *Can we leave the washing till tomorrow?*
leaving – left – have left

give sth a miss /ˌgɪv (sth) ə ˈmɪs/ BRITISH INFORMAL to decide not to do something that you had planned to do, for example because you are too tired: *I think I'll give my exercise class a miss tonight – I'm worn out.*

5 to not do anything

have nothing to do /hæv ˌnʌθɪŋ tə ˈduː/ if you **have nothing to do**, there is nothing interesting for you to do and you feel bored: *I get depressed if I have nothing to do.*
with nothing to do *She was sick of sitting around at home with nothing to do.*

sit around/stand around /ˌsɪt əˈraʊnd, ˌstænd əˈraʊnd/ [phrasal verb I] to sit or stand somewhere for a long time, feeling bored, when you are waiting for something to happen or when you are just being lazy: *I spent the whole morning sitting around waiting for news. | A group of teenagers were standing around outside the station.*

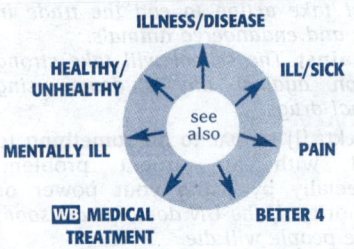

DOCTOR

ILLNESS/DISEASE
HEALTHY/UNHEALTHY
ILL/SICK
see also
MENTALLY ILL
PAIN
WB MEDICAL TREATMENT
BETTER 4

1 doctor

doctor /ˈdɒktəʳ‖ˈdɑːk-/ [n C] someone who is trained to treat people who are ill: *Sylvia's met a really nice man – he's a doctor.*
go to/see/visit a doctor *Rod though he had the flu, and went to the doctor.*
see a doctor about sth *I think you should see a doctor about your cough.*

⚠ Don't say 'I want to be doctor' or 'he is doctor'. Say **I want to be a doctor** or **he is a doctor**.

⚠ The written abbreviation **Dr** is used before the name of a doctor: *Dr Anderson is an expert in tropical diseases.*

physician /fɪˈzɪʃən/ [n C] AMERICAN FORMAL a doctor: *My physician told me to stop smoking. | His parents are both physicians in a busy hospital.*

GP /ˌdʒiː ˈpiː/ [n C] BRITISH a doctor who is trained to treat all kinds of illnesses, and treats people who live in one local area: *I went to my GP and she prescribed antibiotics.*

⚠ GP is short for **General Practitioner**.

the medical profession /ðə ˈmedɪkə prəˌfeʃən/ [n singular] FORMAL doctors, nurses, and other people who treat people who are ill

⚠ In British English, you can use **the medical profession** with a singular or plural verb: *The medical profession is unhappy/ are unhappy about the changes.*

2 the place where you go to see a doctor

🔍 **the doctor's** BRITISH **the doctor's office** AMERICAN /ðə 'dɒktəʳz, ðə ˌdɒktəz 'ɒfꜱ‖-ˌdɑːktərz 'ɔːfꜱ/ [*n* singular] SPOKEN the place where a doctor works, where people who are ill can go at certain times to be examined: *You'd better go to the doctor's if your sore throat doesn't get any better.*

clinic /'klɪnɪk/ [*n* C] in the US, a place where several doctors have offices or a place where poor people can get health care without paying a lot of money; in Britain, a place where people can go for advice about a specific medical condition: *a family-planning clinic* | *a clinic for people with alcohol problems* | *a health clinic in an inner-city area*

health centre BRITISH **health center** AMERICAN /'helθ ˌsentəʳ/ [*n* C] in Britain, a building where several doctors have offices and people can go to see them for treatment; in the US, a similar place in a college or university, where the students can go to see a doctor

surgery /'sɜːʳdʒəri/ [*n* C] BRITISH the office where a doctor works, where people can go to be examined and treated: *The waiting room at the surgery was full of people with colds and flu.*
plural **surgeries**

3 a doctor with special knowledge of particular illnesses

specialist /'speʃəlꜱst/ [*n* C] a doctor who has a lot of special knowledge about one type of illness or one part of the body: *His doctor sent him to see a specialist.*
heart/eye/skin etc specialist *a heart specialist*

surgeon /'sɜːʳdʒən/ [*n* C] a doctor who does operations in a hospital: *Her operation was performed by a well-known surgeon.*

consultant /kən'sʌltənt/ [*n* C] BRITISH an important hospital doctor who has a lot of knowledge about one type of medical treatment: *The consultant told Jean that an operation was necessary to save her life.*

4 a doctor who treats people who have mental or emotional problems

psychiatrist /saɪ'kaɪətrꜱst‖sə-/ [*n* C] a doctor who treats people who are mentally ill

psychologist /saɪ'kɒlədʒꜱst‖-'kɑː-/ [*n* C] a doctor who treats people who have mental problems that affect behaviour

analyst /'ænəlꜱst/ [*n* C] ESPECIALLY AMERICAN a doctor who treats people with mental or emotional problems, by talking with them about their experiences and feelings

5 a doctor who treats people's teeth

dentist /'dentꜱst/ [*n* C] someone who is trained to treat people's teeth
go to/see/visit a dentist *I'm going to the dentist tomorrow, just for a check-up.*

6 a doctor who treats animals

vet (also **veterinarian** AMERICAN) /vet, ˌvetərꜱ'neəriən/ [*n* C] someone who is trained to give medical treatment to animals: *The cat's not well – I'll have to take her to the vet.*

DON'T CARE

**when you do not care what happens
or what someone does**

1 to not care because something is not important to you

don't care /ˌdəʊnt ˈkeəʳ/ if you **don't care** about something, it is not important to you: *"What do you think I should do?" "I don't care. Do what you want."*

don't care what/whether/if etc *I don't really care how you do it, as long as it gets done. | I like George, and I don't care what anyone else thinks about him.*

+about *She doesn't care about anything except money.*

Q **who cares?/so what?** /ˌhuː ˈkeəʳz, ˌsəʊ ˈwɒt/ SPOKEN INFORMAL say this when you do not care about something, because you do not think it is important at all: *"Phil was really mad when he heard what you'd done." "So what? It's none of his business." | I ought to be working really, but who cares?*

> These phrases sound impolite if used to say that you do not care what someone thinks.

Q **couldn't care less** /ˌkʊdnt keəʳ ˈles/ SPOKEN INFORMAL to not care at all about something. Say **I couldn't care less** when you feel annoyed. Say another person **couldn't care less** when you think they are behaving in a rude or unkind way: *"Do you know what Rita told me?" "I really couldn't care less."*

couldn't care less what/whether etc *She does whatever she likes and couldn't care less what other people think.*

+about *To be honest, I couldn't care less about her stupid problems.*

Q **it's not my problem** /ɪts nɒt ˈmaɪ ˌprɒbləm‖-ˌprɑːb-/ SPOKEN INFORMAL say this when you do not care about a problem or difficult situation, because you will not have to deal with it:

"How am I going to explain this to my parents?" "Sorry, it's not my problem."

2 to not care because you will be happy with whatever happens

don't mind (also **don't care** AMERICAN) /ˌdəʊnt ˈmaɪnd, ˌdəʊnt ˈkeəʳ/ to not care because you will be happy with whatever happens or with whatever someone decides: *"What would you like to do tonight?" "I don't mind. You decide."*

don't mind where/what/how etc *Honestly, I don't mind whether Linda comes with us or not. | Bill was just happy to be with her, and he didn't care where they went.*

> Don't say 'I don't mind it'. Just say **I don't mind**.

Q **it makes no difference to me** /ɪt ˌmeɪks nəʊ ˌdɪfərəns tə ˈmiː/ SPOKEN say this when you do not mind what happens because it does not affect you or cause you any problems: *You can come on Thursday or Friday – it makes no difference to me.*

Q **I'm easy** /aɪm ˈiːzi/ SPOKEN INFORMAL say this when someone asks you which of two things you would prefer and you want to say that you do not mind: *"Do you want to stay in, or go out for a meal?" "I'm easy."*

3 someone who does not seem to care

unconcerned /ˌʌnkənˈsɜːʳnd/ [adj not before noun] ESPECIALLY WRITTEN not worried or not caring about something, especially when this is surprising: *They're threatening to fire him, but he seems unconcerned.*

+about *Many large companies remain completely unconcerned about the environment.*

indifferent /ɪnˈdɪfərənt/ [adj] ESPECIALLY WRITTEN not seeming to care about what is happening, especially about other people's problems or feelings *Their mother was cold and indifferent.*

+to *Both parties seem indifferent to the needs of the poor.*

apathetic /ˌæpə'θetɪk◂/ [adj] not interested in anything, or not caring about anything and not making any effort to change or improve things: *The students here aren't really apathetic. They just don't believe anyone will listen to what they say.*
+about *Many young people have now become totally apathetic about politics.*

DOWN

➡ if you mean 'a price or number goes down', go to **LESS**
➡ opposite **UP**

1 towards a lower position

down /daʊn/ [adv/preposition] to a lower position or place: *Tears ran down his face.*
+into/to/from/off *Get down off the table! | He's gone down to the basement to get some more beer.*
look/glance/gaze down *The doctor glanced down at his notepad.*

downwards ESPECIALLY BRITISH (also **downward** ESPECIALLY AMERICAN) /'daʊnwə'd(z)/ [adv] towards a lower level or towards the ground: *a path winding downwards through the trees to the valley below | He was gazing downward into the pit.*
downward [adj only before noun] *a gentle downward slope*

downhill /ˌdaʊn'hɪl◂/ [adv] if you move, walk, or drive **downhill**, you go down a slope: *We set off downhill towards the lake. | From this point, the path goes downhill all the way to the beach.*

downstairs /ˌdaʊn'steə'z◂/ [adv] down towards a lower floor of a building: *She said goodnight to the children and went downstairs. | Uncle Eric had fallen downstairs.*

2 to go down

go down /ˌgəʊ 'daʊn/ [phrasal verb I/T] to go down some stairs, a ladder, a slope etc: *You go down a steep slope, then turn left at the bottom of the hill. | Dan slipped as he was going down the stairs. | I'll go down to the kitchen and get you a glass of water.*

fall /fɔːl/ [v I] to come down through the air from a higher place: *Come back from the edge – I don't want you to fall.*
+from/down/on etc *Leaves were falling from the tree. | Ian tripped and fell down. | Two bombs fell on the parliament building.*
falling – fell – have fallen

land /lænd/ [v I] if a plane or bird **lands**, it comes down to the ground in a controlled way
+in/on/at *We will be landing at Singapore airport at 3am local time. | A flock of geese landed on the river in front of us.*

> ⚠ Say that a plane **lands** when it reaches the ground in the normal way. If you say that a plane **came down** somewhere, you mean it crashed: *One of the aircraft came down in the ocean off the Florida Keys.*

descend /dɪ'send/ [v I/T] WRITTEN to go down a slope, a mountain etc slowly and carefully: *We descended into the cave by a rope ladder. | Slowly the two climbers descended the cliff face.*

> ⚠ Use **descend** when you are writing stories or describing past events.

3 to go down under the water

sink /sɪŋk/ [v I] to go down below the surface of water, mud, sand etc without being able to control or prevent it: *Hundreds of passengers tried to escape as the ferry started to sink.*
+into *The heavy trucks were sinking deeper and deeper into the mud.*
sinking – sank – have sunk

> ⚠ Don't use **sink** about people who go down below the surface of the sea or a river. Use **drown** if they do this accidentally, or **dive** if they deliberately go down under the water.

dive /daɪv/ [v I] to jump head-first down into water: *She stood at the edge of the pool waiting to dive.*

+**into/in** *Ralph dived into the icy water.* | *A woman dived in to rescue the boy.*

diving – **dived** (also **dove** AMERICAN) – **have dived**

dive [*n* C] an act of diving: *She did a perfect dive from the top board.*

4 when the sun goes down

go down/set /ˌgəʊ ˈdaʊn, set/ [*v* I] when the sun **goes down** or **sets** at the end of the day, it moves downwards in the sky until it cannot be seen: *We sat on the balcony and watched the sun go down.* | *The sun was setting and the sky was red.*

setting – **set** – **have set**

sunset /ˈsʌnset/ [*n* C/U] the time when the sun goes down: *Everyone stopped work at sunset.* | *You get beautiful sunsets in Hawaii.*

5 to let something go down

drop /drɒp‖drɑːp/ [*v* T] if you **drop** something that you are holding, it suddenly falls from your hands: *You've dropped your handkerchief.* | *The second baseman dropped the ball.*

dropping – **dropped** – **have dropped**

put down /ˌpʊt ˈdaʊn/ [*phrasal verb* T] to put something that you are holding down onto the ground or onto a surface

put down sth *Putting down her book, Sally stood up to greet us.*

put sth down *Put that gun down now!*

lower /ˈləʊəʳ/ [*v* T] to let something you are holding, or a part of your body, move slowly downwards: *The coffin was lowered slowly into the ground.*

lower your head/arms/body *Lowering its head, the bull charged at him.*

lower yourself into/onto sth (=move slowly and carefully downwards, using your hands for support) *The old man lowered himself wearily into his chair.*

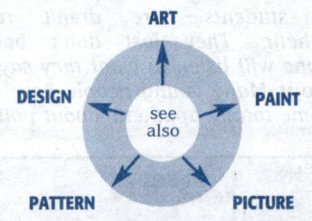

DRAW

ART

DESIGN   see also   PAINT

PATTERN   PICTURE

1 to draw a picture, pattern, line etc

draw /drɔː/ [*v* I/T] to make a picture, pattern, line etc using a pen or pencil: *What are you drawing?* | *She can draw really well.*

draw a picture of sb/sth *The teacher asked us to draw a picture of someone we know.*

draw a line/circle/square etc *Someone had drawn a line under my name.*

drawing – **drew** – **have drawn**

sketch /sketʃ/ [*v* I/T] to make a quick, simple drawing of a person, place etc, without many details: *Valerie sketched the view from her hotel window.* | *He sat by the river, sketching.*

doodle /ˈduːdl/ [*v* I] to draw shapes, lines, or patterns without thinking about what you are doing, while you are doing something else or when you feel bored: *Mark was doodling in his notebook during math class.*

2 something that you draw

drawing /'drɔːɪŋ/ [n C] a picture that you draw with a pen or pencil: *an original drawing by Pablo Picasso*
do a drawing of sb/sth *I did a drawing of the church.*

sketch /sketʃ/ [n C] a quick, simple drawing that does not show any details
do/draw a sketch *Phil drew a sketch to show us what the new school would look like.*
rough sketch (=a quick sketch that is not done very carefully)
plural **sketches**

DREAM

➡ see also **SLEEP, WAKE UP/GET UP, IMAGINE**

1 a dream

dream /driːm/ [n C] a series of thoughts, images, and experiences that come into your mind while you are asleep: *I can never remember my dreams when I wake up.*
have a dream *I had a strange dream last night.*
bad dream (=an unpleasant or frightening dream)

nightmare /'naɪtmeəʳ/ [n C] a very unpleasant and frightening dream: *I woke from the nightmare screaming.*
have a nightmare *Jim's been having nightmares about falling off a cliff.*

daydream /'deɪdriːm/ [n C] a series of pleasant thoughts and scenes that come into your mind while you are awake, so that you do not notice what is happening around you: *Neil seemed lost in a daydream.*

2 to have a dream

dream /driːm/ [v I/T] to have a dream or have dreams: *The dog must be dreaming – he keeps making funny noises!*
+(that) *She often dreamt that she was back in India.*
+about *I dreamt about you last night.*

dreaming – dreamt – have dreamt BRITISH
dreaming – dreamed – have dreamed ESPECIALLY AMERICAN

have a dream /ˌhæv ə 'driːm/ to imagine something while you are asleep: *Why do I have dreams about drowning?*

daydream /'deɪdriːm/ [v I] to think pleasant thoughts when you are awake, especially when you should be thinking about something else: *Stop daydreaming and pay attention!*
+about *Brian began to daydream about what he would do if he won the money.*

DRINK

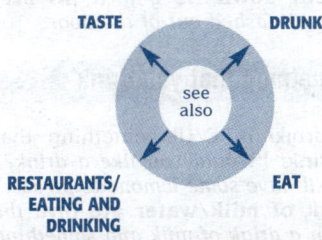

TASTE   DRUNK

see also

RESTAURANTS/   EAT
EATING AND
DRINKING

1 to drink something

drink /drɪŋk/ [v I/T] to take liquid into your mouth and swallow it: *Drink your milk, please, Ellie.* | *"What would you like to drink?" "Orange juice, please."*
drink from a cup/bottle *He didn't ask for a glass, he just drank straight from the bottle.*
drink up (=finish your drink) *Drink up your tea so that I can wash the cups.* | *Come on, drink up and we'll go home.*
drinking – drank – have drunk

> ⚠ We do not usually use the verb **drink** with objects like 'a cup of tea' or 'a glass of milk'. We usually say **have**: *After class, we had a cup of coffee.* (not 'we drank a cup of coffee').

have /hæv/ [v T] to drink an amount of something
have a cup of tea/a glass of milk/a beer etc *I'm going to have a cup of coffee. Do you want one?* | *I had a coke with my pizza.*

have a drink of sth *I had a drink of water as my throat was hurting.*
having – had – have had

take /teɪk/ [v T] to drink a small amount or a single mouthful of something
take a sip/mouthful/gulp etc *He took a long swig (=drink) from the brandy bottle.*
taking – took – have taken

sip /sɪp/ [v T] to drink something slowly, in very small amounts: *Sue sat at the bar sipping a Martini.*
sipping – sipped – have sipped

gulp down /ˌgʌlp ˈdaʊn/ [phrasal verb T] to swallow a large amount of drink quickly
gulp down sth *'I'm coming,' said Mary, gulping down her tea.*
gulp sth down *He gulped his beer down and dashed out of the door.*

2 something that you drink

drink /drɪŋk/ [n C/U] something that you drink: *"Would you like a drink?" "Yes, I'll have some lemonade please."*
a drink of milk/water etc *Give the children a drink of milk and something to eat.*
food and drink(s) (=things to eat and drink) *You can bring your own food and drink to the picnic.*
something to drink /ˌsʌmθɪŋ tə ˈdrɪŋk/ ESPECIALLY SPOKEN a drink: *I'm really thirsty. Let's stop for something to drink.*

3 when you need a drink

thirsty /ˈθɜːʳsti/ [adj not usually before noun] if you are **thirsty**, you feel that you want to drink something: *I'm really thirsty.*
feel thirsty *The nuts were salty and they made me feel thirsty.*
thirsty – thirstier – thirstiest

thirst /θɜːʳst/ [n singular/U] the feeling you have when you want a drink very much: *The soldiers suffered constantly from hunger and thirst.*

4 to drink alcohol

have a drink /ˌhæv ə ˈdrɪŋk/ to drink something alcoholic: *We had a few drinks to celebrate. | I won't have another drink because I have to drive home.*

drink /drɪŋk/ [v I] to drink alcohol, especially regularly: *The doctor told him he had to stop drinking. | It was obvious that Jim had been drinking.*
drink and drive (=drink alcohol before driving your car) *People who drink and drive make me very angry.*
drink heavily (=regularly drink too much) *His uncle drank heavily and had problems with his liver.*
I don't drink (=used to say that you never drink alcohol) *"Would you like a glass of wine?" "No thanks, I don't drink. I'll have an orange juice."*
drinking – drank – have drunk

> ⚠ Don't say 'I don't drink alcohol'. Just say **I don't drink.**

5 drinks that contain alcohol

alcohol /ˈælkəhɒl‖-hɔːl/ [n U] drinks that contain alcohol – used especially in rules and warnings about alcoholic drinks: *We're not allowed to serve alcohol to people under 18.*
alcoholic /ˌælkəˈhɒlɪk◂ ‖-ˈhɔːl-/ [adj] containing alcohol: *You can't sell alcoholic drinks unless you have a licence.*

drink /drɪŋk/ [n C] a drink that contains alcohol: *"Can I offer you a drink?" "I'll have a gin and tonic please." | After a few drinks, I began to feel better.*
go (out) for a drink (=go somewhere such as a bar to drink alcohol) *Do you feel like going out for a drink tonight?*

> ⚠ In British English, **drink** can also be an uncountable noun, meaning alcoholic drinks in general: *An enormous amount of drink is consumed over the Christmas period.*

booze /buːz/ [n U] INFORMAL drinks that contain alcohol: *The doctor told Jimmy to stay off the booze for a while.*

liquor /ˈlɪkəʳ/ [n U] ESPECIALLY AMERICAN drinks that contain alcohol, especially

strong alcoholic drinks: *Lambert spends all his money on liquor and gambling.* | *a liquor store*
hard liquor (=strong alcoholic drinks)

cocktail /'kɒkteɪl‖'kɑːk-/ [*n* C] an alcoholic drink which is a mixture of different drinks: *Pippa was already in the bar, sipping a colourful cocktail.*

spirits /'spɪrᵻts/ [*n* plural] ESPECIALLY BRITISH strong alcoholic drinks such as whisky or vodka: *I don't drink spirits. I prefer wine.*

6 drinks that do not contain alcohol

soft drink /ˌsɒft 'drɪŋk‖ˌsɔːft-/ [*n* C] in Britain, a cold drink, such as orange juice, which does not contain alcohol; in the US, a drink such as Coca-Cola which contains gas but no alcohol: *Do you want a beer, or would you prefer a soft drink?*

non-alcoholic /ˌnɒn ælkə'hɒlɪk◂ ‖-'hɔː-/ [*adj*] a **non-alcoholic** drink does not contain alcohol: *I've bought some non-alcoholic drinks for the drivers.* | *non-alcoholic wine*

low-alcohol /ˌləʊ 'ælkəhɒl◂ ‖-hɔːl◂/ [*adj* only before noun] **low-alcohol** beer or wine contains very little alcohol: *There is a growing market for low-alcohol beers.*

7 drinks that contain gas or do not contain gas

fizzy BRITISH **carbonated** ESPECIALLY AMERICAN /'fɪzi, 'kɑːʳbəneɪtᵻd/ [*adj*] **fizzy** drinks have gas in them: *fizzy lemonade* | *carbonated mineral water*

sparkling /'spɑːʳklɪŋ/ [*adj* only before noun] **sparkling** wine has gas in it: *a bottle of sparkling wine*

still BRITISH **uncarbonated** AMERICAN /stɪl, ʌn'kɑːʳbəneɪtᵻd/ [*adj*] **still** drinks do not have gas in them: *Do you prefer still mineral water?*

flat /flæt/ [*adj*] if a drink that should contain gas is **flat**, there is no gas left in it
go flat (=become flat) *The cola's gone flat.*

8 what people say when they drink alcohol together

⌕ **cheers** /tʃɪəʳz/ SPOKEN say this as you raise your glass when you are drinking with someone: *Cheers, everyone!*

⌕ **here's to ....** /'hɪəʳz tuː/ SPOKEN say this when you want other people to drink with you in order to wish someone happiness or success: *Here's to Clare and Malcolm! May they have a long and happy married life!*

DRIVE

➡ see Word Banks section

DRUNK

when you have drunk too much alcohol

➡ see also **DRINK, RESTAURANTS/ EATING AND DRINKING, ILL/SICK**

1 drunk

drunk /drʌŋk/ [*adj* not before noun] someone who is **drunk** has drunk too much alcohol and cannot think clearly: *She was so drunk, she could hardly stand up.* | *Gary was too drunk to remember what had happened that night.*
get drunk (=become drunk) *Everyone at the party got very drunk.*
blind drunk (=extremely drunk) *Getting blind drunk every night isn't going to solve anything!*

 Use **drunk**, not 'drunken', after a verb.

have had too much to drink /həv hæd ˌtuː mʌtʃ tə 'drɪŋk/ to have drunk too much alcohol, so that you feel drunk or sick: *I'd better take Phil home – he's had too much to drink.*

tipsy /'tɪpsi/ [*adj* not before noun] INFORMAL a little drunk: *After the second glass of wine I was feeling a little tipsy.*

drunken /'drʌŋkən/ [*adj* only before noun] WRITTEN a **drunken** person often gets drunk, or behaves in a way that shows that they are drunk: *A drunken man was singing loudly in the street below.* | *She was tired of living with her drunken husband.*

> ⚠ Use **drunken**, not 'drunk', before a noun.

wrecked /rekt/ [*adj* not before noun] BRITISH INFORMAL very drunk: *A lot of people go out on a Saturday night just to get wrecked.*

2 someone who is often drunk

alcoholic /ˌælkə'hɒlɪk‖-'hɔː-/ [*n* C] someone who drinks too much alcohol every day and cannot stop: *Many alcoholics do not realise they have a problem until it is too late.*

drunk /drʌŋk/ [*n* C] someone who is drunk or who often gets drunk – use this especially to talk about a person you see in a public place such as a street or a bar: *A drunk came staggering down the street towards me.*

3 to drive while you are drunk

drink and drive /ˌdrɪŋk ən 'draɪv/ to drive after you have been drinking alcohol: *He was arrested for drinking and driving.*

drunk/drunken driver /ˌdrʌŋk, ˌdrʌŋkən 'draɪvəʳ/ [*n* C] someone who drives when they have drunk too much alcohol

drunk/drunken driving (also **drink-driving** BRITISH) /ˌdrʌŋk, ˌdrʌŋkən 'draɪvɪŋ, ˌdrɪŋk 'draɪvɪŋ/ [*n* U] driving a vehicle when you have more alcohol in your body than the law allows a driver to have: *Following the accident, she faced charges of drunk driving.*

DUI /ˌdiː juː 'aɪ/ [*n* C/U] AMERICAN the crime of driving after drinking too much alcohol

4 feeling ill the day after you have been drinking

hangover /'hæŋəʊvəʳ/ [*n* C] the feeling you have the morning after you have drunk too much alcohol, when your head hurts and you feel sick: *Kevin woke up the next day with a terrible hangover.*

5 not drunk

sober /'səʊbəʳ/ [*adj* not before noun] not drunk: *I don't think I've ever seen Bill sober.*

sober up /ˌsəʊbər 'ʌp/ [*phrasal verb* I] if someone who has been drunk **sobers up**, they gradually become less drunk until they are not at all drunk: *He didn't sober up till he'd had a cup of strong coffee.*

DRY

➡ opposite **WET**
➡ see also **WEATHER**

1 not wet

dry /draɪ/ [*adj*] *The wood was dry and it burned easily.* | *You should change into some dry clothes.* | *The apples must be stored in a cool dry place.*
bone dry/dry as a bone (=completely dry and containing no water at all) *It hadn't rained for months, and the soil was bone dry.*
dry – drier – driest

2 when there is not much rain

dry /draɪ/ [*adj*] if the weather is **dry**, there is not much rain: *It was a very dry summer.* | *Tunisia's hot, dry climate*
dry – drier – driest

dusty /'dʌsti/ [*adj*] a **dusty** road, town, track etc is dry and covered with dust, because the weather is hot and there is not much rain: *The road to Agra was long, hot, and dusty.* | *a small, dusty village on the edge of the desert*
dusty – dustier – dustiest

drought /draʊt/ [n C/U] a long period when there is little or no rain, so that people and animals do not have enough water and plants die: *Southern Africa is suffering its worst drought of the century.*

3 to become dry

dry /draɪ/ [v I] *Wet clothes soon dry on a hot day.* | *Leave the dishes on the draining board to dry.*

hang sth out to dry (=hang clothes outside, so that they are dried by the sun or wind)

drying – dried – have dried

dry out /ˌdraɪ ˈaʊt/ [phrasal verb I] to become completely dry, on the inside and the outside: *Put your coat near the fire – it'll soon dry out.* | *Cover the pastry with a damp cloth to prevent it from drying out.*

dry up /ˌdraɪ ˈʌp/ [phrasal verb I] if a river or lake **dries up**, it becomes completely dry because there has not been any rain: *Last summer the river dried up and you could walk right across it.* | *The drought has made the reservoir dry up, and many homes are without water.*

shrivel up /ˌʃrɪvəl ˈʌp/ [phrasal verb I] if a plant or a fruit **shrivels up**, it becomes smaller and deep lines form on its surface, because it is so dry: *Without rain the crops will shrivel up and die.*

shrivelling – shrivelled – have shrivelled BRITISH
shriveling – shriveled – have shriveled AMERICAN

4 to make something dry or make yourself dry

dry /draɪ/ [v T] to make something dry: *Could you wait ten minutes while I dry my hair?* | *We built a fire to get ourselves warm and dry our clothes.*

drying – dried – have dried

dry yourself off /ˌdraɪ jɔːʳself ˈɒfǁ-ˈɔːf/ [phrasal verb T] to use a towel to make yourself dry, for example after a bath or a swim: *He got out of the pool and dried himself off.*

E, e

EARLY

➡ opposite **LATE/NOT LATE**
➡ see also **SOON, BEGINNING, FIRST, TIME**

1 before the usual or expected time

early /'ɜːʳli/ [adj/adv] if something happens **early**, it happens before the usual time or the most suitable time; if someone is **early**, they arrive before the time they are expected: *I finished work early today.* | *After an early lunch, we started the meeting at one o'clock.* | *If you plant the seeds outside too early, they won't grow.*
be early (=arrive early) *You're early – I wasn't expecting you till seven.*
seven months/three days etc early (=seven months/three days etc earlier than expected) *Our first child was born eight weeks early.*
far too early (=much too early) *We arrived far too early and had to wait outside for an hour.*
early – earlier – earliest

in good time/in plenty of time /ɪn ˌɡʊd 'taɪm, ɪn ˌplenti əv 'taɪm/ early, so that you do not have to rush, or so that you have time to get ready: *Don't worry, we'll get there in plenty of time.*
+for *It is important to arrive in good time for your interview.*

with time to spare /wɪð ˌtaɪm tə 'speəʳ/ if you arrive somewhere or finish something **with time to spare**, you arrive or finish earlier than you need to: *We reached London with plenty of time to spare.*
with ten minutes/half an hour etc to spare *I finished the test with just two minutes to spare.* (=two minutes before the end)

premature /'premətʃəʳ, -tʃʊəʳ, ˌpreməˈtʃʊəʳ‖ˌpriːməˈtʃʊəʳ/ [adj] happening before the normal or natural time – use this especially about medical conditions
premature death/birth/ageing *Alcoholism is one of the major causes of premature death.*
premature baby (=a baby that is born too early) *a hospital unit for premature babies*
prematurely [adv] *Hannah's hair went prematurely grey when she was only 24.*

2 early in the morning

early /'ɜːʳli/ [adj/adv] early in the morning: *I always wake up early when the weather's warm.* | *Early the next day, Jamie received a call from his mother.*
bright and early (=when you get up or go somewhere early, because you are excited or eager to do something) *Daphne woke bright and early and went for a walk along the beach.*
make an early start (=start an activity or journey early in the morning)
in the early hours (=very early in the morning) *The robbery took place in the early hours of Sunday morning.*
early – earlier – earliest

first thing /ˌfɜːʳst 'θɪŋ/ ESPECIALLY SPOKEN if you do something **first thing**, you do it immediately after you get up or as soon as you start work: *Don't worry – I'll phone her first thing.*
first thing tomorrow/Wednesday/in the morning *They promised to come and fix it first thing tomorrow.*

at the crack of dawn /ət ðə ˌkræk əv 'dɔːn/ INFORMAL use this to emphasize that something happens very early in the morning, when most people are still in bed: *My Dad used to get up at the crack of dawn every Sunday to go fishing.*

EARN

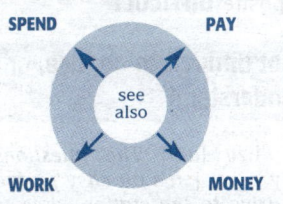

SPEND   PAY

see also

WORK   MONEY

1 to get money for your work

Formal or informal?

All these words mean 'to be paid money for working'. **Earn** is a little more formal than the others, so it is used less often in informal conversation. You use **make** or **get** when you are talking about the actual amount that someone earns, but **get** is more informal than **make**.

earn /ɜːʳn/ [v T] to be paid money for the work that you do: *People were willing to do any job to earn money.*
earn £15,000 a year/£12 an hour etc *people earning more than $50,000 a year*
earn more than/less than/a few dollars etc *It's quite common for women to earn more than their husbands.* | *I earned a few dollars playing in a bar.*
earn a living/earn your living (=earn enough money to pay for the things you need) *It's difficult to earn a living as a writer.*

make /meɪk/ [v T] to earn money – use this when you are saying or asking how much someone earns: *In the first three months I made over $45,000.* | *How much do you think she makes?*
make $500 a week/£25,000 a year/a lot etc *A supermodel can make millions of dollars a year.*
making – made – have made

get /get/ [v T] INFORMAL to earn money – use this when you are saying or asking how much someone earns
get £10 per hour/$350 a week etc *She gets £200 a day to run these training courses.*
get $25/£15 etc for doing sth *I got £5 for washing Nick's car.*
getting – got – have got

be paid/get paid /biː ˈpeɪd, get ˈpeɪd/ to earn money, when you work for an employer, and not for yourself
be paid £50/$200 etc *The cleaners are paid less than 1000 francs a week.*

2 earning a lot of money

highly paid/well-paid /ˌhaɪli ˈpeɪd◂, ˌwel ˈpeɪd◂/ [adj] earning a lot of money: *He's a lawyer, so he must be very well-paid.* | *highly paid and well-motivated workers*
well-paid job *She's got a really well-paid job.*

make a fortune /ˌmeɪk ə ˈfɔːʳtʃən/ to earn a lot of money from a particular job or activity: *Some of these company directors make an absolute fortune!*
make a fortune doing sth *Roger makes a fortune buying and selling yachts.*

3 not earning much money

low-paid/badly paid /ˌləʊ ˈpeɪd◂, ˌbædli ˈpeɪd◂/ [adj] earning less money than most people earn: *People who work in stores are usually very badly paid.*
low-paid job *I could only get a low-paid temporary job.*

4 the money that you earn

pay /peɪ/ [n U] the money that you earn by working: *I'm looking for a job with better pay.* | *There have been complaints about the level of nurses' pay.*
sick pay/holiday pay/maternity pay (=money your employer pays you when you are ill, on holiday, or when you have a new baby) *Joe's been receiving sick pay since the accident.*

⚠ You can also use **pay** before a noun, like an adjective: *a big pay increase* | *pay negotiations*

salary /ˈsæləri/ [n C] the money that someone is paid every month by their employer, especially someone who works in an office, bank etc: *Please give details of your present salary.*

a salary of £100,000/$10,000 etc
The university provided us with a salary of $2000 a month.
on a salary of £30,000/$40,000 etc
(=earning a particular salary) *I joined the company in 1985, on a salary of $15,000 a year.*
a good/high salary *She earns a good salary as an investment banker.*
plural **salaries**

wages /'weɪdʒɪz/ [n plural] the money that someone is paid every week by their employer, especially someone who works in a factory, or in a shop etc: *workers on low wages*
sb's wages *We collect our wages on Friday mornings. | I was paying for bills, food, and everything from my wages.*

wage /weɪdʒ/ [n singular] the amount of money that people receive when they are paid every day or week for their work, rather than every month: *What's the average weekly wage? | The hourly wage is $20.*

income /'ɪŋkʌm, 'ɪn-/ [n C/U] all the money that you receive regularly, for work or for any other reason: *Her annual income is just over $40,000. | We get some additional income from an investment in an oil company.*
be on a low income (=receive very little money) *Families on low incomes get extra welfare payments.*
+from *He has a comfortable income from his salary and his investments.*

fee /fiː/ [n C] the money paid to a lawyer, doctor etc for work that they have done: *Our legal fees came to more than $200,000. | consultant's fees for the design work*

5 the person in a family who earns money

the breadwinner /ðə 'bredwɪnəʳ/ [n singular] the person in a family who earns most or all of the money that the family needs: *In the past it was always the husband who was expected to be the breadwinner.*

EASY

➡ opposite **DIFFICULT**

1 not difficult to do, use, or understand

easy /'iːzi/ [adj] *The questions were really easy. | It's an easy journey – we just drive to the station, then take the direct train to Paris.*
be easy to read/use/learn etc (=when it is easy to read something, use something etc) *The machine is well-designed, and very easy to use.*
it is easy to do sth *It is easy to see why she didn't marry him.*
it is easy for sb to do sth *It wasn't easy for me to get a job.*
find sth easy (=when you have no difficulty doing something) *I can't operate the computer, but my children find it easy.*
easy – **easier** – **easiest**

easily /'iːzɪli/ [adv] if you can do something **easily**, you can do it without trying hard: *A burglar could easily climb through that window. | When I went to college I made friends very easily.*
be easily recognized/damaged/ done etc (=when something can be recognized, damaged etc easily) *These plates are easily damaged, so be careful.*

not difficult /nɒt 'dɪfɪkəlt/ fairly easy: *"Did you make this pizza yourself?" "Yes, it's not difficult."*
it is not difficult to do sth *It's not difficult to see why she's unhappy all the time.*

simple /'sɪmpəl/ [adj] easy to use or understand, because it is not complicated – use this about things like explanations or instructions, or about machines or systems: *She drew us a simple map so that we wouldn't get lost. | Try this simple recipe for pasta sauce.*
be simple to use/make/prepare etc *The new photocopier is much simpler to use than the one we had before.*

straightforward /ˌstreɪt'fɔːʳwəʳd/ [adj] easy to understand and easy to do – use this especially about a method or process: *It's very straightforward – you* *just type the file name, then press 'Enter'. | There's a straightforward calculation for working out how much tax you have to pay.*

user-friendly /ˌjuːzəˈ ˈfrendliˈ/ [adj] easy to use or understand – use this especially about computers or written instructions: *We are trying to develop software that is more user-friendly.*

2 ways of saying that something is very easy to do

○ **it's easy** /ɪts ˈiːzi/ SPOKEN *"How do you print out files?" "It's easy. You just click on the 'Print' icon."*

> **Formal or informal?**
>
> In informal spoken English, you can just say **easy** on its own: *"How can we make sure she comes?" "Easy. Just tell her that Mark will be there."*

○ **there's nothing to it** /ˌðeəʳz ˌnʌθɪŋ ˈtuː ɪt/ SPOKEN say this when you think something is easy to do, even though other people think it is difficult: *Anyone can use a computer – there's nothing to it.*

○ **be a piece of cake** /biː ə ˌpiːs əv ˈkeɪk/ SPOKEN INFORMAL say this about something that is very easy for someone to do, especially when compared with something more difficult: *If you can learn Japanese, learning French should be a piece of cake.*

3 to make something easier

make sth easier /ˌmeɪk (sth) ˈiːziəʳ/ to make it possible to do something more quickly and easily: *Large supermarkets have made shopping much easier.*
make it easier for sb to do sth *The Internet has made it easier for children to get access to pornography.*
make things/life easier *If the buses were on time, it would make life a lot easier.*

simplify /ˈsɪmpləfaɪ/ [v T] to make something easier to understand: *The whole procedure has been simplified.*
simplifying – simplified – have simplified

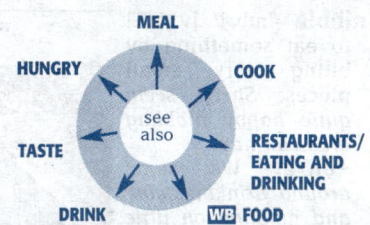

EAT

MEAL

HUNGRY   COOK

see also

TASTE   RESTAURANTS/ EATING AND DRINKING

DRINK   WB FOOD

E

1 to eat

eat /iːt/ [v I/T] *Don't eat so fast – you'll get indigestion. | She was sitting on the wall, eating an apple. | Hey! – someone's eaten all my chocolates.*
eating – ate – have eaten

have /hæv/ [v T] INFORMAL to eat a particular thing: *I wasn't very hungry, so I just had a sandwich. | I think I'll just have one more piece of cake.*
have sth for lunch/dinner/ breakfast *What shall we have for dinner? | I usually just have fruit for breakfast.*
having – had – have had

chew /tʃuː/ [v I/T] to bite food several times and turn it around in your mouth: *You have to chew toffee slowly. | There was a cow in the field, slowly chewing a mouthful of grass.*
+on *a dog chewing on a bone*

swallow /ˈswɒləʊ‖ˈswɑː-/ [v T] to make something go down your throat towards your stomach: *He swallowed the whole thing in one go. | If you drink some water it will make the pills easier to swallow.*

lick /lɪk/ [v T] to eat something soft by moving your tongue across its surface: *The children sat licking their ice-creams.*
lick sth off sth *Nina licked the melted chocolate off her fingers.*

lick

munch /mʌntʃ/ [v I/T] to eat something with continuous movements of your mouth, especially food that is noisy to

eat: *Jamie came out of the store munching a bag of potato chips.*
+on/at *We sipped black coffee and munched on homemade biscuits.*

nibble /ˈnɪbəl/ [*v* I/T] to eat something by biting very small pieces: *Sheep seem quite happy nibbling grass all day.*
+on/at *We stood around drinking wine and nibbling on little snacks.*

nibble

2 to have a meal

> ⚠ Don't say 'take dinner', 'take breakfast' etc. Say **have dinner**, **have breakfast** etc.

have /hæv/ [*v* T]
have breakfast/lunch/dinner *Make sure you have a good breakfast because lunch isn't until two o'clock.*
have a meal *We had an excellent meal in a Thai restaurant.*
have something to eat ESPECIALLY SPOKEN (=eat a meal) *Let's stop here and have something to eat.*
having – had – have had

eat /iːt/ [*v* I/T] *We usually eat at 7 o'clock.* | *I'm not hungry, thanks – I've already eaten.*
eat out (=eat a meal in a restaurant) *We eat out about once a month.*
eat lunch/dinner etc AMERICAN *We ate dinner at around six, then went out.*
eating – ate – have eaten

> ⚠ In British English, don't say 'eat breakfast', 'eat lunch' etc. Say **have breakfast**, **have lunch** etc.

3 to finish eating

finish /ˈfɪnɪʃ/ [*v* T] to finish eating something, or to eat all of something: *Alice finished her lunch and took the dishes into the kitchen.* | *If you finish your pasta you can have some ice-cream.*

4 to eat very little food or no food

diet /ˈdaɪət/ [*n* C] when you eat less food because you want to get thinner: *I've tried lots of diets but none of them work.*
be on a diet (=be eating less food) *Do you want some dessert, or are you still on a diet?*
go on a diet (=start a diet) *As soon as Christmas is over, I'm going on a diet.*
diet [*v* I] to eat less food in order to get thinner: *She first started dieting when she was only 12.*

fast /fɑːst‖fæst/ [*v* I] to stop eating food for a fixed period of time, especially for religious reasons: *Muslims fast during Ramadan.*
fast [*n* C] *At the end of our fast, we have a big party to celebrate.*

pick at sth /ˈpɪk æt (sth)/ [*phrasal verb* T] to eat only a small part of a meal, especially because you feel ill or unhappy: *I sat picking at my dinner, wishing I was somewhere else.*

hardly touch sth /ˌhɑːʳdli ˈtʌtʃ (sth)/ ESPECIALLY SPOKEN to not eat very much of your meal: *Rachel hardly touched her dinner – is she okay?* | *Don't you like the pudding? You've hardly touched it.*

5 when you have eaten enough food

have had enough /həv ˌhæd ɪˈnʌf/ SPOKEN to have eaten enough food, so that you do not want any more: *"Would you like some dessert?" "No thanks, I've had enough."* | *Leave the rest if you've had enough.*

be full (up) /biː ˌfʊl ˈʌp/ SPOKEN if you **are full** or **full up**, you have eaten a lot of food and you do not want to eat any more: *"Would you like some more pie?" "No thanks, I'm full."*

6 someone who eats too much

greedy /ˈgriːdi/ [*adj*] ESPECIALLY BRITISH someone who is **greedy** eats too much: *Don't be greedy – leave some cake for everyone else.*
greedy – greedier – greediest
greedily [*adv*] *The children rushed to the table and started eating greedily.*

pig /pɪg/ [n C] SPOKEN INFORMAL a rude word for describing someone who eats too much: *What a pig! He ate that whole box of chocolates himself.*

glutton /ˈglʌtn/ [n C] FORMAL someone who enjoys eating, and who eats too much: *I didn't want to appear to be a glutton.*

EDGE

the part of something that is furthest from its centre

➡ see also SIDE, MIDDLE

edge /edʒ/ [n C] the part of something that is nearest to its outside or end: *The plates had blue lines around the edges.*
+of *She eventually reached a path along the edge of the cliff.*
on the edge (of sth) *They live in a little house on the edge of town.*

side /saɪd/ [n C] the part of an object that is near its left or right edge: *The stage was lit from the side.*
left-hand/right-hand side of sth (=on the left or right) *Roy's seat was on the left-hand side of the plane.*

> ⚠ The **edge** of an object is where it ends or begins. The **side** of an object is along one of its lengths.

> ⚠ Use **the edge of the road/pool/lake etc** about activities that happen near the road, pool, lake etc but not in it: *We stood at the edge of the lake and watched the sunset.* Use **the side of the road/pool/lake etc** about things that happen in the road, pool, lake etc, but close to the edge of it: *She swam to the side of the pool.*

the outskirts /ði: ˈaʊtskɜːʰts/ [n plural] the areas of a city furthest away from the centre
+of *By the time we reached the outskirts of the city it was already dark.*
on the outskirts (of sth) *Her parents lived in a big house on the outskirts of Seoul.*

boundary /ˈbaʊndəri/ [n C] the official line that marks the edge of an area of land, for example a farm or part of a country
+of *She had never gone beyond the boundaries of the city.* | *The farmer put up a high fence to mark the boundary of his land.*
+between *The Mississippi River forms the boundary between Tennessee and Arkansas.*
plural **boundaries**

margin /ˈmɑːʰdʒən/ [n C] the part where nothing is written or printed at the side of a page: *Leave a two centimetre margin on the left side of the page.*

EDUCATION

➡ see Word Banks section

EFFECT

a change caused by something that happens or by something that someone does

➡ see also RESULT, CHANGE

1   an effect

effect /ɪˈfekt/ [n C/U] a change that is caused by something that happens or by something that someone does
+of *the harmful effects of smoking* | *Gail was still recovering from the effects of her operation.*
the effect of sth on sth *the effect of fertilizers on the size of crops*
without much effect (=having almost no effect) *I tried using detergent to remove the stain, but without much effect.*
feel the effects of sth *By now we were feeling the effects of lack of sleep.*
side effects (=unwanted effects of a drug or medicine) *One of the possible side effects of the drug is loss of memory.*

> ⚠ Don't confuse **effect** (a noun) and **affect** (a verb – see Section 2).

impact /ˈɪmpækt/ [n singular/U] the big and permanent changes that happen as a result of something important

the impact of sth on sth *the impact of computers on people's lives*

have a great/enormous impact on sth *Einstein's work had an enormous impact on the way physics developed.*

have little impact on sth *At first, the revolution had little impact on the lives of ordinary people.*

influence /ˈɪnfluəns/ [n singular/U] the continuing effects that something has on the way that people think or behave, or on the way that things develop

+of *The Chinese authorities were worried about the influence of western films and TV programmes.*

the influence of sth on sth *a book about the influence of feminist ideas on American society*

2 to have an effect on someone or something

have an effect /ˌhæv ən ɪˈfekt/ to make someone or something change in some way, for example by changing the way that things are done or by changing someone's attitudes: *For some patients, the treatment has an immediate effect.*

+on *What you eat when you are pregnant can have an effect on your baby.*

have a serious/significant/dramatic etc effect (=make something change in a big way) *The war had a significant effect on the economy of the country.*

have little/no effect *The tobacco companies say their advertisements have little effect on people's behaviour.*

have an influence /ˌhæv ən ˈɪnfluəns/ to have a continuing effect on the way that people think or behave, or on the way that things develop

+on *Clearly, the cost of fuel has an influence on ticket prices.*

have a great/important/profound influence on sth *Descartes' ideas have had a profound influence on modern science.*

affect /əˈfekt/ [v T] to produce a change, for example in the way that something develops or in someone's situation: *The new tax law doesn't affect students.* | *The rate at which plants grow is affected by the amount of sunlight they receive.*

badly / seriously / severely affect *Smoking when pregnant can seriously affect the health of your baby.*

> ⚠ Don't confuse **affect** (a verb) and **effect** (a noun – see Section 1).

influence /ˈɪnfluəns/ [v T] to affect someone's opinions or behaviour: *Don't let anything he says influence your decision.* | *How much does TV advertising influence what people buy?*

○ do sth to sth /ˈduː (sth) tuː (sth)/ [phrasal verb T] ESPECIALLY SPOKEN to affect someone or something in a harmful way: *Do you ever think about what those cigarettes must be doing to your lungs?* | *Look what the storm has done to the flowers.*

be good for/be bad for /biː ˈɡʊd fɔːʳ, biː ˈbæd fɔːʳ/ to have a good or bad effect on something or someone: *Eating plenty of fruit is good for your health.* | *Changing schools too often is bad for a child's development.*

it's good/bad for sb to do sth *It'll be good for her to meet some new people.* | *I think it's bad for children to always get what they want.*

EMBARRASSED

feeling uncomfortable and nervous about what people think of you

➡ see also **ASHAMED**

> ⚠ Don't confuse **embarrassed** and **ashamed**. If you are **embarrassed**, you worry about what other people think of you. If you are **ashamed**, you feel guilty and bad about yourself, because you have done something that you know is wrong. **Ashamed** is a much stronger word.

1 embarrassed

embarrassed /ɪmˈbærəst/ [adj] feeling uncomfortable and worrying about what people think of you, for example because you have made a stupid mistake or because you have to talk about your feelings, about sex etc: *When we got to the car and it wouldn't start, I was so embarrassed!*

get embarrassed *She gets embarrassed if we ask her to sing.*

embarrassed to do sth *Most of the children are too embarrassed to talk to their teacher about sex.*

+about *I got very drunk at the party, and I feel really embarrassed about it.*

+by/at *Marlon was embarrassed by his lack of education.*

self-conscious /self 'kɒnʃəs‖-'kɑːn-/ [adj] shy and embarrassed about your body, or about the way you look or talk: *I always feel really self-conscious in a bikini.*

+about *Teenagers can feel very self-conscious about their appearance.*

uncomfortable /ʌn'kʌmftəbəl, -'kʌmfət-‖-'kʌmfərt-, -'kʌmft-/ [adj] feeling embarrassed because you cannot relax with the people around you: *All this talk about love and romance was making me uncomfortable.* | *Jim always felt uncomfortable on such formal occasions.* | *an uncomfortable silence*

uncomfortably [adv] *Rhys shuffled his feet uncomfortably, trying to think of an excuse to leave.*

awkward /'ɔːkwəʳd/ [adj] feeling so shy, nervous, and embarrassed that you cannot behave in a natural way: *I didn't know anyone at the party and I felt really awkward at first.*

2 to make someone feel embarrassed

embarrassing /ɪm'bærəsɪŋ/ [adj] an **embarrassing** situation makes you feel embarrassed: *"She got locked in a public toilet and couldn't get out!" "How embarrassing!"* | *The doctor asked me a lot of embarrassing questions about my sex life.*

embarrass /ɪm'bærəs/ [v T] to make someone feel embarrassed: *I hope I didn't embarrass you in front of your friends.* | *I chose my words carefully, in order to avoid embarrassing anyone.*

3 the feeling you have when you are embarrassed

embarrassment /ɪm'bærəsmənt/ [n U] *He looked down at the floor in an attempt to hide his embarrassment.*

die of embarrassment SPOKEN (=a humorous way of saying you feel very embarrassed about something) *She read my poem out to the whole class – I almost died of embarrassment!*

4 when your face goes red because you are embarrassed

blush/go red /blʌʃ, gəʊ 'red/ [v I] if you **blush** or **go red**, your face becomes red because you are embarrassed: *When he asked her to dance she just blushed and giggled.* | *Just mention sex and watch Dad's face go red.*

EMPHASIZE

to say that you think that something is especially important

➡ see also **IMPORTANT/NOT IMPORTANT**

emphasize/stress /'emfəsazz, stres/ [v T] *Mann stressed the need to educate people about the risks of AIDS.* | *She said smoking was not permitted anywhere in the school – emphasizing the word 'anywhere'.*

+that *She emphasized that Bosnia would need international assistance to recover from the war.*

Don't say 'emphasize on something'. Say **emphasize something**.

In British English, **emphasize** can also be spelled **emphasise**.

overemphasize (also **overemphasise** BRITISH) /ˌəʊvəʳ'emfəsazz/ [v T] to emphasize something too much: *I think the book overemphasizes the importance of religion in the history of the US.*

emphasis /'emfəsɪs/ [n U] special attention that is given to a particular activity, subject etc, because it is believed to be more important than other things

+on *There is a greater emphasis on environmental issues nowadays.*

put emphasis on sth *The school puts a lot of emphasis on discipline and respect for authority.*

with the emphasis on sth *an exciting new French course for beginners, with the emphasis on fun as well as learning*

EMPTY

→ opposite **FULL**

1 container/bottle/glass

empty /'empti/ [*adj*] a container, bottle, or glass that is **empty** has nothing inside it: *There were two empty bottles on the table.* | *I noticed her glass was empty, and offered her some more wine.* | *There's an empty box under the stairs if you need it.*

2 place/room/seat

empty /'empti/ [*adj*] a room, building, town, or place that is **empty** has nothing or no one in it: *It was Sunday, and the streets were empty.* | *My footsteps echoed across the empty room.*

free /fri:/ [*adj*] usually not before noun] ESPECIALLY SPOKEN a seat, space, or room that is **free** is not being used, and no one has arranged to use it: *You'll have to wait till there's a meeting-room free.* | *I think that table in the corner is free.* | *There were a few free seats near the door.*

vacant /'veɪkənt/ [*adj*] a seat, building, room, or piece of land that is **vacant** has no one or nothing in it and is available for someone to use: *The flat upstairs is vacant at the moment.* | *There's very little vacant land left in the city.*

bare /beəʳ/ [*adj*] a room that is **bare** has very little furniture or other things in it; a wall or floor that is **bare** is not covered with anything – use this when you think the room or wall or floor would be nicer if there were more things there: *The little church was bare and cold.* | *Fiona looked sadly at the bare walls where pictures of her family used to hang.*

deserted /dɪ'zɜːʳtɪ̣d/ [*adj*] a place or building that is **deserted** is empty and quiet, because the people who are usually there have left: *The village seemed to be completely deserted.* | *We ran along the deserted beach.*

uninhabited /ˌʌnɪn'hæbɪ̣tɪ̣d◂/ [*adj*] ESPECIALLY WRITTEN an area or place that is **uninhabited** has no people living in it: *Most of the islands in Clear Bay are uninhabited.* | *The castle is now uninhabited.*

3 paper/tape/screen

blank /blæŋk/ [*adj*] a **blank** screen, tape, or piece of paper has nothing written or recorded on it: *I want to record the film. Do we have any blank video cassettes?* | *Ian stared at the blank sheet of paper in front of him.*

space /speɪs/ [*n C*] a place that has been left empty in a piece of writing, especially so that you can write something in it: *There's a space for you to sign your name.*

4 to make a place or container empty

empty /'empti/ [*v T*] to make something empty by removing what was in it: *The garbage cans are emptied once a week.* | *"See you," he called, emptying his glass and making for the door.*

emptying – emptied – have emptied

clear out /ˌklɪəʳ 'aʊt/ [*phrasal verb T*] to empty a building, room, cupboard etc, especially because you no longer want the things that are in it

clear out sth *I found a pile of old letters while I was clearing out my desk.*

clear sth out *We must clear the garage out this weekend.*

When you see **EC**, go to the **ESSENTIAL COMMUNICATION** section.

END

➡ look here for ...
- the end of a period of time, film, book etc
- the end of an object, the street etc

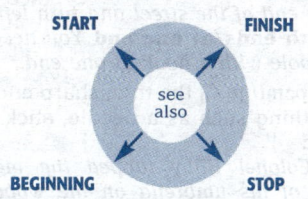

1 the last part of a period of time, event, film, book etc

the end /ði 'end/ [n singular]
+of *The end of the game was really exciting.*
at/before/until the end *Sam left New York at the end of December.* | *It was such a terrible movie, half of the audience walked out before the end.*
the very end (=the last moment, sentence etc) *You don't find out who the murderer is until the very end of the book.*

ending /'endɪŋ/ [n C] the things that happen at the end of a story or film: *In the Spanish version of this story, the ending is completely different.*
happy ending (=an ending in which everyone is happy) *I love those old Hollywood movies with happy endings.*

finale /fɪ'nɑːli‖fɪ'næli/ [n C usually singular] the exciting or impressive last part of a piece of music, show, ceremony etc
+of *the finale of Beethoven's ninth symphony*
the grand finale (=the very impressive finale) *For the grand finale there was a marching band and fireworks.*

2 to end

end /end/ [v I] if an event, story, situation, or period of time **ends**, it finishes: *World War II ended in 1945.* | *How does the story end?*
end in sth (=end in a particular way, especially a bad way) *Their marriage*

finally ended in divorce three years later. | *a school trip that ended in tragedy when three children were killed in an accident*

finish /'fɪnɪʃ/ [v I] to end – use this especially to say what time something ends: *What time does your class finish?* | *The celebrations didn't finish till after midnight.*

> ⚠ **Finish** can often be used instead of **end**, but don't use it to talk about stories, films etc, or about periods of time. It is mostly used about organized events, such as a meeting, a class, or a party.

stop /stɒp‖stɑːp/ [v I] if something that has been happening continuously until now **stops**, it does not continue: *When do you think the rain will stop?* | *As soon as she walked in the room, the conversation stopped.* | *I just wanted the pressure on me to stop.*
stopping – stopped – have stopped

be over /biː 'əʊvəʳ/ if an event or activity **is over**, it has ended, and nothing more is going to happen: *By the time we arrived, the party was already over.*
be all over (=have completely finished) *The game should be all over by 5 o'clock.*

come to an end /ˌkʌm tʊ ən 'end/ to finally end – use this about a period of time, a situation, or an activity that has continued for a long time: *When this job comes to an end, I'll be unemployed again.* | *It was already September, and our stay in Zurich was coming to an end.*

3 happening at the end

at the end /ət ði 'end/ during the last part of an event or period of time: *I enjoyed the film, but it was really sad when the little girl died at the end.*
+of *There will be time for questions at the end of the meeting.*

> ⚠ Don't confuse **at the end** (=during the last part of something) and **in the end** (=after a period of time).

final /'faɪnl/ [adj only before noun] happening at the end of an event, book, or film: *the final stages of the project* | *the book's final chapter*

E

closing /ˈkləʊzɪŋ/ [adj only before noun] FORMAL

closing remarks/speech/ceremony etc remarks etc which come at the end of an event, meeting, or book: *By the time he made his closing remarks, I was almost asleep.*

end with sth /ˈend wɪð (sth)/ [phrasal verb T] if an event, book, or film **ends with** something, that particular thing happens at the end of the event, book etc: *The concert ended with a laser light show.* | *The advertisement ends with the usual appeal for people to give money.*

4 happening at the end of a long period of time

finally/eventually/in the end /ˈfaɪnəli, ɪˈventʃuəli, ɪn ði ˈend/ [adv] after a long period of time, especially after a lot of difficulties or after a long delay: *After a lot of questioning, James finally admitted he had broken the window.* | *The plane eventually arrived three hours late.* | *In the end, I decided to ask Billy for help.*

> ⚠ You can use **eventually** or **in the end** by itself to answer a question: *"Did you find the book you wanted?" "Yes, eventually."* Don't use **finally** like this.

at last /ət ˈlɑːstǁ-ˈlæst/ use this when something good happens after you have waited for it for a long time: *I'm really glad that Ken's found a job at last.* | *At last the rain stopped and the players came back on the field.*

at long last (=after a very long time) *At long last he was able to see his family again.*

end up /ˌend ˈʌp/ [phrasal verb I] If you **end up** in a situation, you get into that situation at the end of a series of events which you did not plan: *Forbes ended up in a French prison for drug dealing.*

end up doing sth *We were going to go into town for a meal, but ended up staying at home and watching TV.*

5 the part or point at the end of an object

end /end/ [n C] *Stop chewing the end of your pen!*

the end of the road/street/passage etc (=the furthest part at the end) *Go to the end of the street and turn left.*

at both ends/at one end *You need a long pole with a hook at one end.*

point /pɔɪnt/ [n C] the thin, sharp end of something such as a needle, stick, or sword

+of *Colonel Bilby tapped the metal point of his umbrella on the wooden floor.* | *the point of a knife*

tip /tɪp/ [n C] the narrow part at the end of something such as a finger, a branch, or a piece of land

+of *Dr Gordon felt my neck with the tips of his fingers.* | *The village is on the southern tip of the island.*

ENJOY

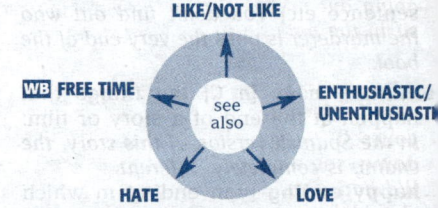

LIKE/NOT LIKE

WB FREE TIME

see also

ENTHUSIASTIC/ UNENTHUSIASTIC

HATE

LOVE

1 to get pleasure from doing something

enjoy /ɪnˈdʒɔɪ/ [v T] *Did you enjoy the party?*

enjoy doing sth *My father enjoys playing golf at weekends.*

enjoy yourself (=have fun and feel happy when you are doing something) *The park was full of people enjoying themselves in the sunshine.*

enjoy every minute/moment (of sth) *I enjoyed every minute of the holiday.*

> Don't say 'I enjoy to do it'. Say **I enjoy doing it**.

> ⚠ Don't say 'I very enjoy it'. Say **I enjoy it very much** or (in spoken English) **I really enjoy it**: We enjoyed the meal very much – thank you for inviting us.

like /laɪk/ [v T] to enjoy doing something, especially something that you do regularly or for a long time
like doing sth/like to do sth Do you like travelling by train? | I like to relax and read a book in the evenings.

> ⚠ Usually it doesn't matter whether you say **like doing sth** or **like to do sth**. But when you mean someone likes the situation or place they are in, you must use **like doing sth**: I like living in London (not 'I like to live in London').

> ⚠ Don't say 'I like very much watching TV'. Say **I really like watching TV**.

Q **love** /lʌv/ [v T] ESPECIALLY SPOKEN to enjoy doing something very much and get a lot of pleasure from it: Cassie loves her job.
love doing sth/love to do sth I love going out in the snow. | She loved to sit in the park and feed the ducks.

Q **have a good time/have a great time** /hæv ə ˌgʊd ˈtaɪm, hæv ə ˌgreɪt ˈtaɪm/ ESPECIALLY SPOKEN to enjoy yourself very much when you are doing something with other people: We had a great time last night – you should have come. | Did you have a good time at the beach?

Q **have fun** /ˌhæv ˈfʌn/ ESPECIALLY SPOKEN to enjoy yourself with other people, for example by relaxing, talking, or laughing with them: I was having so much fun I forgot how late it was.
have fun doing sth We had fun trying to guess who Mike's new girlfriend was.

2 experiences and activities that you enjoy

enjoyable /ɪnˈdʒɔɪəbəl/ [adj] an **enjoyable** activity, especially something you do with other people, is pleasant and interesting: We spent an enjoyable evening playing cards. | I try to make my lessons more enjoyable by using games.

Q **fun** /fʌn/ [n U] ESPECIALLY SPOKEN if something is **fun**, you enjoy it because you do so interesting and exciting things: "How was your weekend?" "It was fun."
it is fun to do sth/it is fun doing sth It's fun to play in the pool. | It'll be fun seeing all my old friends again.
great/good fun (=very enjoyable) Have you ever been windsurfing? It's really good fun.

> ⚠ Don't say 'it is a fun'. Say **it is fun**.

> ⚠ Don't confuse **fun** (something you enjoy) and **funny** (used to describe something that makes you laugh).

3 the feeling you get when you enjoy something

pleasure /ˈpleʒəʳ/ [n U] the happy feeling you get when you are enjoying something
get pleasure from sth My father always got a lot of pleasure from being with his grandchildren.
do sth for pleasure (=because it gives you pleasure) I don't very often read for pleasure.
give/bring pleasure (=make people happy) Her singing has given so much pleasure to so many people over the years.

enjoyment /ɪnˈdʒɔɪmənt/ [n U] the feeling you get when you enjoy doing something
get enjoyment out of sth I get a lot of enjoyment out of working with young children.
+of The bad weather didn't spoil our enjoyment of the vacation.

thrill /θrɪl/ [n C] a strong feeling of excitement and pleasure that you get from doing something
the thrill of (doing) sth the thrill of driving a very fast car
get a thrill out of doing sth I've been acting for years, and I still get a thrill out of going on stage.

satisfaction /ˌsætɪsˈfækʃən/ [n U] the feeling of happiness or pleasure that you get when you do something well or get what you want

+**from/out of** *She gets great satisfaction from her job*
with satisfaction *Jo walked into the room, grinning with satisfaction.*

4 someone that people enjoy being with

be good company /biː ˌɡʊd ˈkʌmpəni/ if someone **is good company**, people enjoy spending time with them: *I like sharing a room with Kathy – she's good company.*

○ **be fun** /biː ˈfʌn/ SPOKEN use this about people who are always cheerful, interesting, and amusing: *Let's invite Margy – she's always fun.*

5 to enjoy something that most people would not enjoy

revel in sth /ˈrevəl ɪn (sth)/ [phrasal verb T] to enjoy something very much, especially something that other people would think difficult or unpleasant: *Her job is very stressful, but she seems to revel in it.*
revelling – revelled – have revelled
BRITISH
reveling – reveled – have reveled
AMERICAN

take pleasure in doing sth /ˌteɪk ˈpleʒər ɪn duːɪŋ (sth)/ to enjoy doing something that upsets or annoys someone: *Her husband seemed to take pleasure in pointing out her mistakes. | Mr Broadbent took great pleasure in telling me I was fired.*

ENOUGH/NOT ENOUGH

➡ see also **FULL**

1 when there is a large enough amount of something that you need

enough /ɪˈnʌf/ [quantifier] *Here's $20. Is that enough? | Make sure you take enough water with you. | Have the children had enough to eat?*

enough money/space/work etc for sb/sth *I made loads of food, so there should be enough for everyone. | Will there be enough room for Joey in the car?*
more than enough (=more than you need, but not too much or too many) *I've given you more than enough time to make up your mind.*
I've had enough BRITISH (=say this when you have eaten enough food) *"Would you like some more pizza?" "No thanks, I've had enough."*

⚠ Don't say 'the food wasn't enough'. Say **there wasn't enough food. Enough** usually goes before a noun.

plenty /ˈplenti/ [quantifier] more than enough – use this when you do not need any more of something: *"Do you need any more paper?" "Oh, no thanks. I have plenty here."*
+**of** *There's plenty of food, so don't buy any more. | Don't worry, we've plenty of time.*

sufficient /səˈfɪʃənt/ [adj] FORMAL enough: *Does a vegetarian diet provide sufficient protein?*
+**for** *Seven hours sleep is sufficient for most people.*

adequate /ˈædɪkwət/ [adj] FORMAL enough in amount, and good enough in quality: *None of his workers received adequate safety training.*
+**for** *The computer has 16 megabytes of memory, which should be adequate for most users.*

last /lɑːst‖læst/ [v I] if an amount of food or money **lasts** for a period of time, there is enough of it for that period
+**until/till** *I still have $100, but that won't last till the end of the vacation.*
last (sb) 2 years/3 days etc *We set off up the mountain, carrying equipment, tents, and enough food to last five days.*
last sb 4 years/3 months etc *£50? That won't last you a day in London!*

2 to have enough time or money to do what you want

have enough time/money /ˌhæv ɪnʌf ˈtaɪm, ˈmʌni/ to have enough time or enough money to do what you want:

I'll come and see you if I have enough time.
have enough time/money to do sth
Do we have enough money to go on vacation this year?

have the time/have the money /ˌhæv ðə ˈtaɪm, ˌhæv ðə ˈmʌni/ to have time or enough money to do something: *I know I should take some exercise, but I just never seem to have the time.* | *If I had the money, I'd buy a sports car.*

have the time/money to do sth *Now that he's retired, he's got the time to travel.*

can afford /kən əˈfɔːrd/ to have enough money to do something or to buy something: *I love the apartment, but I don't think we can afford the rent.*

can afford to do sth *They can afford to go on vacation in the Caribbean every year.*

> ⚠ Don't say 'can afford doing something'.
> Say **can afford to do something**.

3 big enough/old enough/strong enough etc

enough /ɪˈnʌf/ [adv]
big enough/old enough/strong enough etc *Will that box be big enough?*

+for *The road was just wide enough for the truck to get through.*

+to do sth *Liz is old enough to look after herself.*

> ⚠ Don't say 'she's enough old to drive a car'. Say **she's old enough to drive a car. Enough** comes after the adjective.

4 when you have done something enough or when something has happened enough

enough /ɪˈnʌf/ [adv] *I think we've talked about this enough.* | *If it rains enough this month, the harvest will be a good one.*

5 not enough

not enough /nɒt ɪˈnʌf/ not enough for what you need: *I gave her $200, but she said it wasn't enough.* | *There won't be enough chairs.* | *I don't think you're getting enough sleep.*

+for *One bottle of wine won't be enough for everyone.*

not enough to do sth *There aren't enough people to make a full team.*

not have enough to do/eat/drink etc *There are people in the camps who haven't got enough to eat.*

not old/strong etc enough *She wanted to see the movie, but she wasn't old enough.* | *Could you get that book down for me? I'm not tall enough.*

too little/too few /tuː ˈlɪtl, tuː ˈfjuː/ [quantifier] less than you need or fewer than you need – use this especially when you are criticizing or complaining about something

too few roads/doctors/hotels etc *Too many patients and too few doctors – that's the problem!*

too little time/money/food etc *There's too little time to do everything that needs to be done.*

too little/too few to do sth *There were some police officers there, but too few to control the crowd.*

far too little/few (=much too little or few) *Most of us eat far too little fresh fruit.*

> ⚠ Use **too few** with plural nouns like 'books', 'shops', and 'students': *The school had to close because there were too few students.* Use **too little** with uncountable nouns like 'time', 'money', and 'food': *The government has paid too little attention to the needs of disabled people.*

> **Formal or informal?**
> In informal spoken English, it is more usual to say **not enough** than to say **too little** or **too few**.

shortage /ˈʃɔːrtɪdʒ/ [n C] a situation in which there is not enough of something very basic and important that people need in order to live or work

water/food/housing etc shortage *Parts of Britain are suffering water* *shortages after the unusually dry summer.*

+of *There is a shortage of nurses and doctors in the area.*

acute/severe shortage (=a very bad shortage) *There is an acute shortage of housing in South Africa's urban areas.*

be short of /biː ˈʃɔːᵊt ɒv/ to not have enough of something basic that you need: *I was short of money, so I had to ask George for $20.*

scarce /skeəᵊs/ [adj] ESPECIALLY WRITTEN if something is **scarce**, there is not enough of it, so it is very difficult to get or buy: *During the war, things like clothes and shoes were scarce.* | *Jobs are scarce, and a lot of people are unemployed.* | *scarce resources*

> **Formal or informal?**
> **Scarce** is used more in formal written English.

lack of /ˈlæk ɒv/ [n singular/U] if there is a **lack of** something, there is not enough of it, or there is none of it at all: *There is a lack of trust between the management and the union.*

lack of sleep/time/money etc *Fernando's eyes were red through lack of sleep.* | *Most of our problems are caused by lack of money.*

lack of enthusiasm/confidence/ interest etc *It's lack of confidence, not lack of ability, that makes most people fail.*

ENTER

➡ see also **LEAVE**

1 to enter a place

go in/go into /ˌgəʊ ˈɪn, ˌgəʊ ˈɪntuː/ [phrasal verb I/T] to go into a room, building etc: *It was getting cold, so we went in.* | *They won't let you go in unless you leave your bag outside.*

go into sth *Everyone showed their tickets as they went into the hall.*

enter /ˈentəᵊ/ [v T] FORMAL to go or come into a room, building, country etc: *The army entered the city from the north.* | *As soon as he entered the room, he knew there was something wrong.*

> Don't say 'enter in a room' or 'enter to a room'. Say **enter a room**.

come in /ˌkʌm ˈɪn/ [phrasal verb I] if someone **comes in**, they enter a room or building that you are in: *As soon as Adrian came in, everyone stopped talking.* | *That must be Nina coming in right now.*

come into sth *Come into the house and get warm.*

get in /ˌget ˈɪn/ [phrasal verb I] to succeed in entering a room, building, or area that is difficult to enter, especially by finding an unusual way in: *How did you get in? I thought the door was locked.*

get into sth *The burglars got into the apartments by pretending to be electricians.*

burst in /ˌbɜːᵊst ˈɪn/ [phrasal verb I] to suddenly enter a room making a lot of noise: *Two men with guns burst in and told us to lie on the floor.*

burst into sth *Lotty burst into the room waving a letter in the air.*

2 to use force to enter a place

force your way in /ˌfɔːᵊs jɔːᵊ weɪ ˈɪn/ to enter a building or room by using force, especially when someone is trying to stop you: *The door was locked, but we managed to force our way in.*

force your way into sth *Police eventually forced their way into the building and arrested the gunman.*

break in /ˌbreɪk ˈɪn/ [phrasal verb I] to enter a building by using force, in order to steal something: *If anyone tries to break in, the alarm will go off.*

break into sth *Vandals broke into the school last night.*

3 to tell someone to enter your room or house

◯ **come in** /ˌkʌm ˈɪn/ SPOKEN say **come in** when you want someone to come into your room, home, or office: *There was a knock at the door. 'Come in,' she called.* | *Come in and sit down. I'll be ready in a minute.*

ask sb in /ˌɑːsk (sb) ˈɪn‖ˌæsk-/ INFORMAL to ask someone if they want to come into your home: *Stella didn't know whether to ask him in or not.*

4 to allow someone to enter a place

let sb in /ˌlet (sb) 'ɪn/ [phrasal verb T] *Let me in! It's freezing out here.* | *There's Ryan at the door. Let him in, would you?*

admit /əd'mɪt/ [v T] FORMAL to allow someone to enter a public place to watch a game, performance etc: *Children under 14 are not admitted without an adult.*
admit sb to/into sth *Only ticket-holders will be admitted into the stadium.*
admitting – admitted – have admitted

> **Formal or informal?**
> **Admit** is used mainly in writing and is very formal in spoken English.

5 to not allow someone to enter a place

keep out /ˌkiːp 'aʊt/ [phrasal verb T] to prevent someone from entering a room
keep sb out/keep out sb *His house has a security system to keep out intruders.*
keep sb out of sth *We've got to keep Bill out of the kitchen – his birthday present's in there!*

turn sb away /ˌtɜːʳn (sb) ə'weɪ/ [phrasal verb T] to refuse to let someone into a place where a public event is happening, especially because it is full: *The club's so popular we have to turn people away every night.* | *Hundreds of disappointed fans were turned away at the gates.*

lock sb out /ˌlɒk (sb) 'aʊt‖ˌlɑːk-/ [phrasal verb T] to stop someone entering a room or building by locking the door: *My girlfriend locked me out of the house.*

6 a door or space that you use to enter a place

entrance (also **entry**) /'entrəns, 'entri/ [n C] a door or space that you go through to enter a place: *Simpson used a side entrance to avoid the waiting reporters.*
+to *the main entrance to the school*

way in /ˌweɪ 'ɪn/ [n C] the place where you can enter a large public building: *We walked all the way around the museum, looking for the way in.*

ENTHUSIASTIC/ UNENTHUSIASTIC

➡ see also **EXCITING/EXCITED, LIKE/ NOT LIKE, ENJOY, DON'T CARE**

1 enthusiastic

enthusiastic /ɪnˌθjuːziˈæstɪk‹ ‖-ˌθuː-/ [adj] behaving in a way that shows that you like, enjoy, or approve of something a lot: *A small but enthusiastic crowd cheered as we ran onto the field.* | *Several enthusiastic young teachers have just started working at the school.*
+about *He's still really enthusiastic about his new school.*
enthusiastically [adv] *The public has responded very enthusiastically to our appeal.*

keen /kiːn/ [adj] BRITISH very enthusiastic about an activity or job: *She hasn't much experience but she's very keen.*
+on *Alex has always been keen on athletics.*
a keen golfer/photographer/gardener etc *Chris is a keen photographer – he's won several competitions.*
keen to do sth *Mark was keen to make a good impression on the new French teacher.*

eager /'iːgəʳ/ [adj] ESPECIALLY WRITTEN very enthusiastic and excited about something that is going to happen or about something that you are going to do: *A crowd of eager fans waited outside the hotel.*

eager to do sth *She hurried home from college, eager to hear Tom's news.*
eagerness [n U] very enthusiastic and excited feelings or behaviour
eagerness to do sth *He tripped over the cat in his eagerness to get to the phone.*
enthusiasm /ɪn'θjuːziæzəm‖-'θuː-/ [n U] enthusiastic feelings or behaviour
+for *I'd forgotten about Jim's enthusiasm for going on 20-mile walks.*
be full of enthusiasm (=be very enthusiastic) *Greta was full of enthusiasm for the plan.*

2 not enthusiastic

unenthusiastic / not enthusiastic /ˌʌnɪnθjuːziˈæstɪk, nɒt ɪnˌθjuːziˈæstɪk‖ -ˌθuː-/ [adj] *Are you sure you want to see the movie? You don't sound very enthusiastic.*
+about *She had never been very enthusiastic about her job.* | *The teachers were distinctly unenthusiastic about the whole idea*
half-hearted /ˌhɑːf 'hɑːʳtɪd◂ ‖ˌhæf-/ [adj]
half-hearted attempt / response / measure etc an attempt etc that is made without much enthusiasm or effort: *Yves had made a half-hearted attempt to be friendly.*

ENVIRONMENT

➡ see Word Banks section

EQUIPMENT

things you use for doing something

➡ see also **MACHINE, COMPUTERS**

equipment /ɪ'kwɪpmənt/ [n U] the special machines or tools that you use for doing something: *a shop that sold camping equipment*
computer/electrical/video etc equipment *Thieves stole all the video equipment from the college.* | *a room full of expensive electronic equipment*

office equipment *The ministry placed a large order for new office equipment.*
a piece of equipment *a small but important piece of equipment*

> ⚠ Don't say 'equipments' or 'an equipment'. **Equipment** is an uncountable noun.

○ **things** /θɪŋz/ [n plural] SPOKEN the special clothes and other equipment that you need for a sport or similar activity: *Now, have you got all your things ready?*
swimming / painting / sewing etc things *She keeps all her sewing things in a small basket.*
gear /gɪəʳ/ [n U] INFORMAL the equipment and special clothes that you need to do something, especially an activity that you do in your free time: *Mike's crazy about photography – he's got all the gear.*
camping / fishing / skiing etc gear *Did you remember to pack your fishing gear?*
kit /kɪt/ [n C]
shaving/sewing/repair etc kit a set of small things that you use to do something: *The sewing kit contained needles, pins, cotton, and a pair of scissors.*
○ **stuff** /stʌf/ [n U] SPOKEN INFORMAL the equipment that you use to do something
camping / cleaning / painting etc stuff *The cleaning stuff's in the cupboard under the stairs.*

> When you see **WB**, go to the **WORD BANKS** section.

ESCAPE

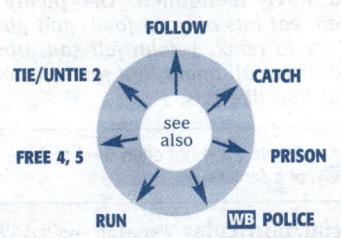

FOLLOW

TIE/UNTIE 2   CATCH

see
also

FREE 4, 5   PRISON

RUN   **WB** POLICE

1 from a place/person/prison/dangerous situation

escape /ɪ'skeɪp/ [v I] to succeed in leaving a dangerous place or situation, or a place that someone is trying to stop you from leaving: *Anyone trying to escape will be shot.* | *Only four people managed to escape before the roof collapsed.*
+from *Josie managed to escape from her attacker and call the police.* | *Two men escaped from Durham Jail last night.*
+over/into/through etc *Some refugees managed to escape over the border into Tanzania.*

get out /ˌget 'aʊt/ [phrasal verb I] to escape from a place that is difficult to escape from, or where there is danger: *How could the dog get out when the gate was shut?*
+of *No-one's gotten out of the Kansas county jail in 50 years.*
get out alive *We were lucky to get out alive – the whole building was on fire.*

> **Formal or informal?**
> **Get out** is more informal than **escape**.

get away /ˌget ə'weɪ/ [phrasal verb I] to escape from someone who is chasing you, so they do not catch you: *The gunmen got away in a stolen car.*
get away from *Thousands of civilians are trying to get away from the advancing army.*

run away/run off /ˌrʌn ə'weɪ, ˌrʌn 'ɒf‖ -'ɔːf/ [phrasal verb I] to try to escape from someone by running away: *Don't run away – I'm not going to hurt you.*
+into/down/across etc *He jumped out of the car and ran off into the woods.*
+from *If you run away from the bull, it's almost certain to attack you.*

break out /ˌbreɪk 'aʊt/ [phrasal verb I] to escape from a prison: *Some of the men were planning to break out.*
+of *his attempt to break out of a maximum security prison*

on the run /ˌɒn ðə 'rʌn/ someone who is **on the run** is trying to hide or escape from someone who is chasing them, especially the police: *After the train robbery he spent three years on the run.*
+from *Dean was a drug addict who was constantly on the run from the police.*

2 from a difficult/embarrassing/boring situation

escape/get away /ɪ'skeɪp, ˌget ə'weɪ/ [v I] to succeed in leaving a place or to successfully avoid being with someone, especially because you are bored or embarrassed: *He decided to tell me all about his trip to Majorca, and I just couldn't get away.* | *Let's see if we can escape before the speeches start.*

3 when someone escapes

escape /ɪ'skeɪp/ [n C] when someone escapes from prison, from danger, or from someone who is chasing them: *They had planned their escape very carefully.* | *Police described it as a very daring escape.*
+from *her escape from a group of kidnappers*
make your escape (=succeed in escaping) *They made their escape in a small boat they had built themselves.*
a narrow escape (=when you only just escape from danger) *The two firemen had a narrow escape when the roof collapsed.*

4 unable to escape

can't escape/can't get out /ˌkɑːnt ɪ'skeɪp, ˌkɑːnt get 'aʊt‖ˌkænt-/ *I've* locked all the doors and windows – he can't get out. | Two of the children couldn't escape, and died in the fire.

trapped /træpt/ [adj] unable to escape from a dangerous place or an unpleasant situation: The miners have been trapped underground for three days. | He was beginning to feel trapped in his job.

be stuck /biː 'stʌk/ ESPECIALLY SPOKEN to be unable to escape from an unpleasant or boring situation
+in/with/here I don't want to be stuck in an office all my life. | I'm tired of being stuck here with the kids all day.

ESPECIALLY

more than usual or more than others

especially / particularly /ɪ'speʃəli, pəˈtɪkjʊləˈli/ [adv] use this to emphasize that something is more important than other things, or that something happens more with one particular thing than with any others: This disease mostly affects women, particularly women over 50. | Paris is always full of tourists, especially during the summer months. | It's very worrying, especially if you have young children.
especially good/important/difficult etc This sauce is especially good with fish.

> ⚠ Don't use **especially** or **particularly** at the beginning of a sentence. Don't say 'Especially I like tennis'. Say **I like a lot of sports, especially tennis**.

in particular /ɪn pəˈtɪkjʊləˈ/ use **in particular** to mention one person or thing that is more important or more interesting than all similar things: Mary loves most classical music, in particular Bach and Vivaldi. | We enjoyed visiting Britain and thought that Scotland in particular was very beautiful.
anything / anyone / anywhere in particular Was there anything in particular that you wanted to talk about?

above all /ə,bʌv 'ɔːl/ use **above all** to emphasize that something is more important than all the other things you have mentioned: Get plenty of sleep, eat lots of good food, and above all try to relax. | John felt sad, upset, and above all angry that his wife could treat him like this.

> ⚠ **Above all** is not often used at the end of a sentence.

special/particular /'speʃəl, pəˈtɪkjʊləˈ/ [adj only before noun] if you give **special** or **particular** care or attention to something, you give it more attention than usual, or more attention that you give anything else
+care/attention You should pay particular attention to spelling. | Take special care on the roads tonight – it's icy.

EVERYWHERE

in or to every place

everywhere /'evriweəˈ/ [adv] in every place, or in every part of a place: I can't find my keys – I've looked everywhere for them. | There was water everywhere. | There are health clubs everywhere these days. | Poverty affects children everywhere – in Europe as well as Africa.
everywhere else (=in every other place) We deliver goods by 10 a.m. in the UK and by midday everywhere else.

every place /'evri pleɪs/ [adv] AMERICAN SPOKEN INFORMAL everywhere: They go every place together.

all over /ɔːl 'əʊvəˈ/ [preposition/adv] in every part of a place or surface
all over the world/country etc a bank with branches all over the country | competing teams from all over the world
all over the floor/wall/your face etc Katie's toys were spread out all over the floor. | There was jam all over her face.
all over We had a great holiday in America – we travelled all over. | After a couple of hours of exercise, my body ached all over.

🔍 **wherever you go** /weər,evə^r juː 'gəʊ/ ESPECIALLY SPOKEN if you see or do something **wherever you go**, you see it or do it in a lot of different places: *Wherever you go there are people asking for money.*

widespread /'waɪdspred/ [*adj*] happening in many places – use this especially about problems or bad situations that affect many areas or many countries: *There has been widespread flooding in Germany, and the rivers are still rising.* | *Diseases such as typhoid are widespread in the region.*

worldwide /ˌwɜːrld'waɪd‹/ [*adj* only before noun] in every part of the world: *There has been a worldwide increase in cases of AIDS.* | *Campaigners are calling for a worldwide ban on whale hunting.* | *A worldwide TV audience of over a billion people*
worldwide [*adv*] *The company employs about 20,000 people worldwide.* | *On the Internet, people can communicate worldwide in seconds.*

nationwide /ˌneɪʃən'waɪd‹/ [*adj* only before noun] in every part of a country
nationwide search/hunt/manhunt *A nationwide hunt was launched yesterday for the killer of 13-year-old Nicola Jones.*
nationwide study/survey/poll etc *Recent nationwide polls show that 9 out of 10 African Americans will vote Democrat.*
nationwide strike *Workers in Spain held nationwide strikes.*
nationwide [*adv*] *We have a total of 96 stores nationwide.*

EXACT

1 an exact number/amount/time

exact /ɪg'zækt/ [*adj* usually before noun] an **exact** number, amount, or time is completely correct and is no more and no less than it should be: *"Can you tell me the exact time?" "It's 6.37."* | *The exact weight of the baby at birth was 3.2 kg.*
to be exact SPOKEN (=used after a number when giving an exact answer, statement etc) *It took her about an hour – 58 minutes to be exact.*

exactly /ɪg'zæktli/ [*adv*] use this to emphasize that the number, amount, or time that you are mentioning is completely correct: *It's exactly 5 o'clock.* | *The bill came to exactly $1000.*

precise /prɪ'saɪs/ [*adj* usually before noun] **precise** information is based on clear and exact measurements, especially when it is important that no mistakes are made: *We need to know your precise location.* | *Each plane has to follow a precise route.*
be precise (=give precise information or figures) *It's difficult to be precise about the number of deaths caused by smoking.*
precisely [*adv*] exactly – use this before or after a time: *At precisely 3 o'clock the ceremony began.*

> **Formal or informal?**
> **Precise** is more formal than **exact**.

on the dot /ɒn ðə 'dɒt‖-'dɑːt/ INFORMAL if something happens at a particular time **on the dot**, it happens at exactly that time: *The doors of the museum closed at six o'clock on the dot.*

2 an exact description/ translation/copy

accurate /'ækjʊrət/ [*adj*] **accurate** information, descriptions, reports etc are completely correct because all the details are true: *Keep an accurate*

EXAMPLE 240

record of everything you eat for one day. | The witness tried to give an accurate description of what she had seen.

exact /ɪgˈzækt/ [adj] an **exact** copy, model etc of something is like it in every possible way: 'Eavesdrop' means to listen secretly outside someone's door, but there is no exact equivalent in Spanish. | It's not an exact copy, but most people wouldn't notice the difference.

literal /ˈlɪtərəl/ [adj only before noun] a **literal** translation gives the exact meaning of each single word instead of translating whole sentences in a natural way: You can't give a literal translation of most poetry.

literally [adv] 'Vino di tavola' literally means 'table wine' in Italian. | The French word for 'bat' is 'chauve-souris', which literally means 'bald mouse'.

word for word /ˌwɜːʳd fəʳ ˈwɜːʳd/ if you repeat, copy, or translate something **word for word**, you use the exact words that are in it: He asked me to repeat word for word the instructions he'd just given me.

3 exactly how, what, where etc

exactly /ɪgˈzæktli/ [adv] use this when you are giving or asking for exact details or information: Glue the pieces together, exactly as shown in the diagram.
exactly who/what/where etc The police want to know exactly when you left the building. | The doctors can't say exactly what's wrong with my mother, but she's very ill.
who/what/where exactly? Where exactly are you from? | Who exactly did you want to see?

precisely /prɪˈsaɪsli/ [adv] exactly – use this when it is important to describe something very carefully or to get very exact information
precisely what/where/who etc We need to know precisely how much this is going to cost.
where/what/who precisely? What precisely do you mean by relativity?

> **Formal or informal?**
> **Precisely** is more formal than **exactly**.

4 exactly the right thing

exactly /ɪgˈzæktli/ [adv] use this to emphasize that something is the particular thing that you want or mean: This is exactly the kind of job that computers are good at.
exactly what The earrings are beautiful! They're exactly what I wanted.

precisely /prɪˈsaɪsli/ [adv] exactly – use this to emphasize exactly what the situation is, exactly what happened, exactly what you meant etc: "But none of us can speak French." "That's precisely the problem." | There have been a lot of burglaries, and we installed an alarm system for precisely this reason.

> **Formal or informal?**
> **Precisely** is more formal than **exactly**.

5 not exact

➡ see also **ABOUT**

rough /rʌf/ [adj only before noun] not exact, or not containing exact details: a rough estimate of the number of people without jobs | Tim drew me a rough plan of the farmhouse.

roughly [adv] Roughly how many people are you expecting?

approximate /əˈprɒksɪmət ‖ ɪgˈzæm-/ [adj] FORMAL an **approximate** number, amount, or time is close to the true number, amount, or time but does not need to be completely correct: Our approximate time of arrival will be 10:20. | What's the approximate value of your car?

approximately [adv] We should arrive at approximately 3 o'clock.

EXAMPLE

1 a typical example of something

example /ɪgˈzɑːmpəl ‖ ɪgˈzæm-/ [n C] something that you mention because it is typical of the kind of thing that you are talking about: There are many ways in which technology has changed our lives. The car is an obvious example.

+of The church is an interesting example of the Gothic style.

give an example Attitude problems? Can you give me an example?

good/typical example This painting is a typical example of Picasso's work in his Blue Period. | Korea and Vietnam are good examples of the fast-growing economies of South-East Asia.

case /keɪs/ [n C] an example of something that has happened, especially something bad

+of There have been some cases of women employees being fired because they are pregnant.

in one case/in some cases/in every case In one case a man was charged $2000 for a simple medical check-up.

instance /'ɪnstəns/ [n C] FORMAL an example of a particular kind of situation: Some users of Ecstasy have actually died, but such instances are very rare.

+of several instances of bad management that have led to serious problems

2 what you say when you give an example

for example/for instance /fər ɪg'zɑːmpəl, fər 'ɪnstəns‖-'zæm-/ use this when you are giving an example: There are lots of famous buildings in Kyoto, for example the Golden Pavilion and Ryoanyi Temple. | Car prices can vary a lot. For example, in Belgium the VW Golf costs £1000 less than in Britain.

eg/e.g. /ˌiː 'dʒiː/ use this in written English when you are giving an example or a series of examples: Make sure you eat foods that contain protein, e.g. meat, cheese, fish, milk or eggs. | This course includes a study of basic language skills (e.g. speaking and listening).

> ⚠ In British English, people usually write **eg**; in American English, people usually write **e.g.** Don't use **eg/e.g.** at the beginning of a sentence.

such as /'sʌtʃ æz/ [preposition] ESPECIALLY WRITTEN use this directly after a plural noun to give one or two examples of

the things you have just mentioned: It is difficult to get even basic foods such as sugar and bread. | Clint Eastwood is most famous for his tough-guy police movies, such as 'The Enforcer'.

⊙ **like** /laɪk/ [preposition] ESPECIALLY SPOKEN use this when you are giving one or two examples: We could cook something easy, like pasta. | There are a few problems we still haven't settled, like who is going to be in charge while I'm away.

> **Formal or informal?**
>
> **Like** is used a lot in spoken English, but is also used in writing, especially informal writing.

EXCEPT

➡ see also **EC** LINKING WORDS

1 not including someone or something

except/except for /ɪk'sept, ɪk'sept fɔːʳ/ [preposition] not including the person or thing that you have mentioned: Everyone's going except Donald. | The house was silent except for a clock ticking in the living room.

> ⚠ Don't say 'except of' or 'except from'. Say **except** or **except for**.

> ⚠ At the beginning of a sentence, always use **except for**, not just the word **except** on its own: Except for a couple of old chairs, the room was empty.

except /ɪk'sept/ [conjunction] use this when you say that something is true but then you want to introduce a fact that does not match what you have said

except (that) Celia looks just like her sister, except that her sister has shorter hair. | It's similar to Paris, except the people look a lot poorer.

except do sth a computer that can do everything except talk (=that is the only thing it cannot do)

> ⚠ Don't begin a sentence with **except**.

apart from (also **aside from** AMERICAN) /ə'pɑːˈt frɒm, ə'saɪd frɒm/ [*preposition*] use this when you mention one or two facts that do not fit into the main thing that you are saying: *This is an excellent piece of work, apart from a couple of spelling mistakes. | Aside from a toothbrush, she took no baggage with her.*

apart from doing sth *Apart from going swimming occasionally, I don't get much exercise.*

with the exception of /wɪð ði ɪk'sepʃən ɒv/ FORMAL not including the thing, person, or group mentioned: *The whole school, with the exception of the youngest class, had to attend the ceremony.*

with the possible exception of (=but possibly not that person or thing) *I think they should all pass the test, with the possible exception of Fauzi.*

2 someone or something that is not included

exception /ɪk'sepʃən/ [*n C*] someone or something that is not included in a general rule, or does not do what most others in the same situation do: *Most of the students did well, though there were one or two exceptions.*

notable exception (=one that is very famous or special) *Women do not usually get to the top in politics, but there have been a few notable exceptions.*

major/minor exception (=an important/not very important one) *With a few minor exceptions, the legal system in the two countries is very similar.*

EXCITING/EXCITED

➡ see also **ENJOY, ENTHUSIASTIC/ UNENTHUSIASTIC, HAPPY**

1 feeling excited about something

excited /ɪk'saɪtⁱd/ [*adj*] feeling happy and full of energy, especially about something good that has happened or is going to happen: *Steve's coming home tomorrow – we're all really excited. | crowds of excited football fans*

+about *How can you be so excited about a stupid computer game?*

get excited (=start becoming excited) *Maria's getting pretty excited about her wedding.*

+by *Doctors are very excited by the discovery.*

be excited to do sth *You must be really excited to be chosen out of all those other people.*

> ⚠ Be careful not to confuse **excited** (=the way you feel) and **exciting** (=making you feel excited) *We were all* **excited**. | *The movie was very* **exciting**.

look forward to /lʊk 'fɔːˈwəˈd tuː/ [*phrasal verb T*] to feel excited about something good that is going to happen and to think about it a lot: *The kids are looking forward to their vacation.*

look forward to doing sth *She's really looking forward to getting her own flat.*

🔍 **can't wait /can hardly wait** /ˌkɑːnt 'weɪt, kən ˌhɑːˈdli 'weɪtǁˌkænt-/ SPOKEN if you **can't wait** for something to happen, you want it to happen soon because you are very excited about it

+for *I can't wait for him to walk in and find we're all already here.*

can't wait to do sth *He couldn't wait to get home and tell Dean the news.*

thrilled /θrɪld/ [*adj* not before noun] very excited, happy, and pleased

be thrilled to do sth *I'm thrilled to be back in this country again.*

+with *Chester's absolutely thrilled with his baby daughter.*

+at/by *Gemma's parents were thrilled by the enormous response to their appeal.*

🔍 **be thrilled to bits** BRITISH SPOKEN **be thrilled to pieces** AMERICAN SPOKEN (=be very thrilled) *It's a dream come true for me, and I'm thrilled to bits.*

be on the edge of your seat /biː ɒn ði ˌedʒ əv jɔːˈ 'siːt/ INFORMAL to be excited and slightly nervous when you are watching something because you do not know what will happen next: *This is a movie that will keep you on the edge of your seat till the final seconds.*

2 when something makes you feel excited

exciting /ɪkˈsaɪtɪŋ/ [adj] making you feel excited: *I've got some exciting news for you.* | *Hockey is a fast, exciting game to watch.*
find sth exciting *Stuart found life in Paris enormously exciting.*

> ⚠ Be careful not to confuse **exciting** (= making you feel excited) and **excited** (=the way you feel) *The movie was very* **exciting** | *We were all* **excited**

thrilling /ˈθrɪlɪŋ/ [adj] making you feel very excited and slightly nervous: *The helicopter trip over the mountains was a thrilling end to a fantastic holiday.* | *a really thrilling game won by a last-minute goal*

gripping /ˈɡrɪpɪŋ/ [adj] use this about books or films that are so exciting that you cannot stop reading or watching them: *a gripping detective story*

exhilarating /ɪɡˈzɪləreɪtɪŋ/ [adj] an **exhilarating** experience or activity makes you feel excited and full of energy: *Surfing is a demanding and exhilarating sport.*

> **Formal or informal?**
> **Exhilarating** is not used in very informal spoken English and is not used much by young people.

dramatic /drəˈmætɪk/ [adj] a **dramatic** part of a story, film etc has a lot of exciting and unexpected things happening in it: *The movie starts with a dramatic car chase across the desert.*

3 feeling too excited

overexcited /ˌəʊvərɪkˈsaɪtɪd/ [adj] someone, especially a child, who is **overexcited** has become too excited to behave calmly: *If the kids become overexcited, they won't go to sleep.*

hysterical /hɪˈsterɪkəl/ [adj] unable to stop shouting, crying etc because you are extremely excited: *Hysterical fans tried to stop Damon's car at the airport.*
get/go hysterical (=become hysterical) *The crowd went hysterical as*

Juventus scored in the last minute of the game.

4 the most exciting part of something

climax /ˈklaɪmæks/ [n C usually singular] the most exciting or important part of a story or event, usually near the end
+of *A parade through the streets marks the climax of the festival.*
reach a climax *The opera reaches its climax with Violetta's death in the third act.*

highlight /ˈhaɪlaɪt/ [n C] the part of an activity such as a holiday or game that is the most exciting or enjoyable
+of *The week in New York was definitely the highlight of our trip.* | *Highlights of the ball game will be shown later.*

5 the feeling of being excited

excitement /ɪkˈsaɪtmənt/ [n U] *If you're looking for excitement, you won't find it here.*
in/with excitement (=in an excited way) *Louise began jumping up and down in excitement.*
great/tremendous excitement (=a lot of excitement) *There's an atmosphere of tremendous excitement here in the stadium.*

thrill /θrɪl/ [n C usually singular] a sudden very strong feeling of excitement and sometimes fear: *Some people enjoy the thrill of hunting dangerous animals.*
get a thrill out of doing sth *I used to get a thrill out of riding a motorbike at high speed.*

exhilaration /ɪɡˌzɪləˈreɪʃən/ [n U] a feeling of excitement and energy that you get from an activity
the exhilaration of doing sth *the exhilaration of riding a horse along the empty beach*

> **Formal or informal?**
> **Exhilaration** is not used in very informal spoken English and is not used much by young people.

EXERCISE

➡ see Word Banks section

EXIST

➡ see also **ALIVE, DEAD**

1 to exist

exist /ɪgˈzɪst/ [v I] to happen or be present in a place, or to be real and living: *politicians who behave as if poverty didn't exist* | *The Earth has existed for more than four thousand million years.* | *Do you think ghosts really exist?*

> ⚠ Don't say 'it is existing', 'they are existing' etc. Say **it exists**, **they exist** etc.

there is /ˈðeər ɪz/ if you say **there is** something, you mean that it exists: *Is there life on other planets?* | *There's no evidence to prove that Gray is the murderer.*

be found /biː ˈfaʊnd/ to exist in a particular place, or inside a particular thing: *Vitamin C is found in green vegetables and fresh fruit.* | *Otters are still found in some parts of Britain.*

existence /ɪgˈzɪstəns/ [n U] when something exists
the existence of sth *For the first time she began to doubt the existence of God.*
be in existence *The club has been in existence since 1990.* (=has existed since 1990)

2 to not exist

non-existent /ˌnɒn ɪgˈzɪstənt◂ ‖ ˌnɑːn-/ [adj] something that is **non-existent** does not exist: *In rural parts of Japan, crime is virtually non-existent.*

◯ there's no such thing /ˌðeəʳz ˌnəʊ ˌsʌtʃ ˈθɪŋ/ SPOKEN use **there's no such thing** to tell someone that you are sure something does not exist: *I don't believe in witchcraft – there's no such thing.*

+as *I've come to the conclusion that there's no such thing as perfect happiness.*

3 when something that used to exist no longer exists

extinct /ɪkˈstɪŋkt/ [adj] if a type of animal is **extinct**, none of them are alive any more: *The white rhino is now almost extinct.*
become extinct *Why did the dinosaurs become extinct?*

die out /ˌdaɪ ˈaʊt/ [phrasal verb I] if something such as a type of plant or animal **dies out**, there are fewer and fewer of them until finally there are none left: *Unless we do something now, hundreds of plant and animal species will die out.* | *Many of the old village traditions are dying out.*

disappear /ˌdɪsəˈpɪəʳ/ [v I] if something **disappears**, it stops existing and can no longer be seen or felt: *Thousands of miles of rainforest are disappearing every year.* | *When I got my first job I felt as if all my worries had disappeared.*

> ⚠ Don't say 'is disappeared' or 'was disappeared'. Say **has disappeared**.

EXPECT

➡ see also **HOPE, SURPRISING/ SURPRISED**

1 to expect something

expect /ɪkˈspekt/ [v T] if you **expect** something to happen, you think it will happen or is likely to happen, especially because it is planned: *I'm expecting a fax from Korea. Has anything arrived yet?* | *Drivers should expect long delays on all roads out of town today.*
expect to do sth *I expected to find him in the bar, but he wasn't there.*

expect sb/sth to do sth *No-one really expected the President to resign.* | *Economists expect the economy to grow by 5% next year.*
+(that) *We all expected she'd get the job – it was a real shock when she didn't.*

> ⚠ Don't confuse **expect** and **wait for**: *She stood outside the hotel, waiting for a taxi.* (=waiting until a taxi came past) | *I'm expecting a taxi.* (=I think a taxi will come because I ordered one)

think /θɪŋk/ [v T] to believe that something is likely to happen
+(that) *Do you think that she'll win an Oscar for the movie?* | *I never thought her business would do so well.*
think sth is likely *The builders said the job would be finished tomorrow, but I don't think that's likely.*

be due /biː ˈdjuː‖-ˈduː/ if something **is due** at a particular time, you expect it to happen or arrive at that time: *When's your baby due?*
be due in an hour/in three months/at 5 o'clock etc *The flight from New York is due at 10.30.* | *You'd better clean up this mess – Clarrie's due back in half an hour.*

2   what you say when you expect something to happen

🔍 **I expect** /aɪ ɪkˈspekt/ SPOKEN say this when you think something will probably happen: *Don't worry – they'll be here soon, I expect.*
+(that) *I expect the tickets will be sold out by now.*
I expect so BRITISH (=used to say 'yes', but not in a confident way, when someone asks you if you think something is going to happen) *"Do you think he'll lend us the money?" "I expect so."*

🔍 **I bet** /aɪ ˈbet/ SPOKEN INFORMAL say this when you are almost certain something will happen, because of what you know about a person or situation
+(that) *I bet you'll miss your boyfriend when he goes to university.* | *She promised to arrive early, but I bet she doesn't.*

> ⚠ You can use 'will' or the present tense after **I bet**: *I bet she'll win.* | *I bet she wins.*

🔍 **I wouldn't be surprised** /aɪ ˌwʊdnt biː səˈpraɪzd/ SPOKEN say this when you think that something may happen, even though other people may think it is unlikely: *"Do you think they'll get married?" "I wouldn't be surprised."*
+if *You know, I wouldn't be surprised if Warren ends up running the whole company.*

3   expecting something good to happen

optimistic /ˌɒptɪˈmɪstɪk◂ ‖ˌɑːp-/ [adj] someone who is **optimistic** expects good things to happen: *In spite of all her problems she manages to remain optimistic.* | *an optimistic economic forecast*
+about *I'm pretty optimistic about our chances of winning here today.*
+that *Are you still optimistic that the climbers can be rescued?*

optimist /ˈɒptɪmɪst‖ˈɑːp-/ [n C] someone who always expects good things to happen: *Optimists still believe we can resolve the problem without going to war.*

4   expecting something bad to happen

pessimistic /ˌpesɪˈmɪstɪk◂/ [adj] someone who is **pessimistic** always expects bad things to happen: *I think that the banks are being too pessimistic.* | *his pessimistic attitude*
+about *He's quite pessimistic about his chances of getting another job.*

pessimist /ˈpesɪmɪst/ [n C] someone who always expects bad things to happen: *Don't be such a pessimist – I'm sure you'll pass your driving test!*

5 when things happen in the way that you expected

as expected /əz ɪk'spektɪd/ if something happens **as expected**, it happens in the way that you expected it to happen: *As expected, the Democrats won the majority of seats in Congress.* | *The parcel arrived the next day, as expected.*

it is no surprise /ɪt ɪz ˌnəʊ səˈpraɪz/ if something that happens **is no surprise**, it is exactly what you expected, so you are not surprised by it
+that *It's no surprise that Jeff and his wife are getting divorced.*
it is no surprise to hear/discover/find etc *It was no surprise to hear that Joel had messed the whole thing up again.*

predictable /prɪ'dɪktəbəl/ [adj] happening exactly as you expect – use this especially about someone's behaviour, when you think they are boring or stupid because they always do exactly what you expect: *My dad's so predictable – every evening he comes home, has exactly two beers, and falls asleep in front of the TV.* | *His resignation had a predictable effect on the company's share price.*

predictably [sentence adverb] as you would expect: *Predictably, all the political parties are claiming the credit for rising living standards.*

> **Formal or informal?**
> **Predictably** is used in written English and in formal spoken English.

6 when something happens that you did not expect

unexpected /ˌʌnɪk'spektɪd/ [adj] something that is **unexpected** surprises you because you did not expect it: *The experiment produced some unexpected results.*
completely/totally unexpected *Bobby's decision to leave the band was totally unexpected.*

unexpectedly [adv] *His father died unexpectedly last week.*

out of the blue /ˌaʊt əv ðə 'bluː/ INFORMAL if something happens **out of the blue**, you did not expect it, and you are very surprised or shocked by it: *One evening, Angela phoned me out of the blue and said she was in trouble.*

EXPENSIVE

➡ opposite **CHEAP**

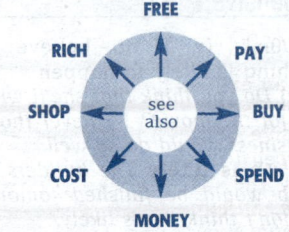

FREE
RICH • PAY
SHOP • see also • BUY
COST • SPEND
MONEY

1 expensive

expensive /ɪk'spensɪv/ [adj] something that is **expensive** costs a lot of money, more than other things of the same type: *She spends most of her money on expensive clothes.* | *Things tend to be much more expensive in the cities.*
expensive to make/run/buy etc *Cadillacs are beautiful cars, but they're very expensive to run.*

> ⚠ Don't say 'prices, costs, taxes etc are expensive'. Say **prices, costs etc are high**.

cost a lot (of money) /ˌkɒst ə ˌlɒt əv 'mʌniǁˌkɔːst ə ˌlɑːt-/ if something **costs a lot (of money)**, it is expensive: *They had a big party at the Waldorf, and that must have cost a lot.*
it costs a lot to do sth *It costs quite a lot to fly to Ireland, but it's worth it.*

high /haɪ/ [adj] if the price or cost of something is **high**, it costs a lot
high prices/costs/fees/rents *The cost of living is higher in Denmark than in Germany.* | *Rents in central London are very high.*

cost a fortune /ˌkɒst ə 'fɔːtʃənǁˌkɔːst-/ INFORMAL, ESPECIALLY SPOKEN if something **costs a fortune**, it is very expensive cost sb a fortune *We had to eat out every night – it ended up costing us a fortune.*

it costs a fortune to do sth *It'll cost a fortune to get that old car of his repaired.*

dear /dɪəʳ/ [*adj* not before noun] BRITISH expensive – use this especially about things you buy in shops: *The blue jacket is slightly dearer, but it's much better material.*

2 expensive and fashionable

expensive /ɪk'spensɪv/ [*adj* only before noun] an **expensive** hotel, restaurant, area etc is very fashionable and it is expensive to stay, eat, or live there: *an expensive Chinese restaurant in town* | *The house is on West Boston Avenue, Detroit's most expensive residential area.*

exclusive /ɪk'skluːsɪv/ [*adj*] an **exclusive** area, school, shop, club etc is very expensive, and only a few very rich people have enough money to live there or use it: *They live in Bel Air, an exclusive suburb of Los Angeles.* | *He's been invited to join the exclusive Millionaire's Club.*

luxurious /lʌg'zjuəriəs, ləg'ʒuəriəs‖ əg'ʒuəriəs/ [*adj*] a **luxurious** building or room is large, very comfortable, and has expensive decorations and furniture: *a room in a luxurious New York hotel* | *a luxurious bathroom*

posh /pɒʃ‖pɑːʃ/ [*adj*] INFORMAL, ESPECIALLY BRITISH a **posh** restaurant, house, car etc is expensive and looks as if it is used or owned by rich people: *When I'm famous I'm going to stay in a posh hotel and drink champagne all day.* | *She goes to a posh girls' school near Brighton.*

fancy /'fænsi/ [*adj*] INFORMAL, ESPECIALLY AMERICAN a **fancy** house, car, hotel, restaurant etc is expensive and fashionable: *eating in fancy restaurants*

fancy – fancier – fanciest

3 too expensive

can't afford /ˌkɑːnt ə'fɔːʳd‖ˌkænt-/ if you **can't afford** something, you do not have enough money to pay for it: *I really need a new coat, but I can't afford one.*

can't afford to do sth *We couldn't afford to go on vacation last year.*

can't afford it *Hiring a lawyer would be expensive, and she just couldn't afford it.*

exorbitant /ɪg'zɔːʳbɪtənt/ [*adj*] FORMAL **exorbitant** prices, charges, rents etc are very much higher than they should be and you think they are unfair: *The rents in this part of town are exorbitant.* | *They charge exorbitant prices for very ordinary food.*

○ **a rip-off** /ə 'rɪp ɒf/ SPOKEN INFORMAL you say something is **a rip-off** when you think someone is unfairly charging too much money for it: *$80 for a pair of jeans? What a rip off!*

a complete/total rip-off *Don't go to that new restaurant – it's a complete rip-off.*

4 worth a lot of money

valuable /'væljuəbəl, -ljᵿbəl/ [*adj*] use this about things that are expensive to replace such as jewellery or cameras, or things that are old and rare such as paintings, furniture, and books: *The museum has a valuable collection of old books and manuscripts.* | *a valuable porcelain vase*

be worth a lot (of money) /biː ˌwɜːʳθ ə ˌlɒt əv 'mʌnɪl-ˌlɑːt-/ if something **is worth a lot**, you can get a lot of money if you sell it: *You should look after those old dolls – one day they could be worth a lot.*

be worth a fortune /biː ˌwɜːʳθ ə 'fɔːʳtʃən/ INFORMAL if something **is worth a fortune**, it is worth a very large amount of money: *He was very poor when he died, but now his paintings are worth a fortune.*

precious /'preʃəs/ [*adj* only before noun]

precious metal/stone a metal such as gold or a jewel such as a diamond that is very valuable

priceless /'praɪsləs/ [*adj*] worth so much money that it is impossible to calculate the price – use this about objects that are old and rare such as paintings, furniture, or jewellery: *The house was full of priceless antiques.* | *a priceless oil painting*

EXPERIENCE

➡ look here for ...
• something that happens to you
• when you know a lot about something

1 something that happens to you

experience /ɪk'spɪəriəns/ [n C] something that happens to you or something that you do, especially something unusual or important that you remember and learn from: *Hannah later wrote a book about her experiences as a war reporter.*
+of *Tonight on Channel 1, young people will be discussing their experiences of racism.*
have an experience *During her trip she had several frightening experiences.*
good/bad experience *Living alone has been a good experience for her.*

adventure /əd'ventʃəʳ/ [n C/U] a situation in which exciting and dangerous things happen to you: *My grandfather used to tell us about his adventures as a sea captain during the war.* | *As a young man he went off to Africa, looking for adventure.*

2 something bad that happens to you

bad experience /ˌbæd ɪk'spɪəriəns/ [n C] something that happens to you that is unpleasant, frightening, or dangerous: *Don't let one bad experience put you off travelling altogether.* | *She described childbirth as the worst experience of her life.*

nightmare /'naɪtmeəʳ/ [n singular] a very unpleasant or very frightening experience: *Starting school can be a real nightmare for some children.* | *She describes the war years as 'one long nightmare'.*

ordeal /ɔː'diːl, 'ɔːʳdiːl/ [n C] a painful, frightening, or worrying experience, especially one that continues for a

long time: *The hostages have now been released, and are recovering from their ordeal in a military hospital.*

3 when something happens to you

happen to sb /'hæpən tuː (sb)/ [phrasal verb T] if something **happens to** you, it affects you and you are involved in it, but you did not do anything to make it happen: *The crash wasn't your fault. It could have happened to anyone.* | *Meeting Penny was the best thing that ever happened to me.*

experience /ɪk'spɪəriəns/ [v T] if you **experience** something, especially a physical feeling or an unpleasant situation, it happens to you: *When you first tried a cigarette, you probably experienced a feeling of dizziness.* | *help for people who are experiencing financial difficulties* | *It was the first time she had ever experienced real poverty.*

go through sth /'gəʊ θruː (sth)/ [phrasal verb T] to live through a difficult or unhappy period: *Clare's been through a lot lately, so we should all try to help her.*
🔾 **go through hell** SPOKEN (=have a very unpleasant time) *He's been going through hell in the two years since his daughter died.*

4 when you know a lot about something because you have done it before

➡ see also **JOB, WORK, GOOD 5, 6**

experience /ɪk'spɪəriəns/ [n U] the knowledge and skill you get from doing something, especially a job, for a long time
have experience *She's very bright and ambitious but she doesn't have much experience.*
experience of (doing) sth *She has plenty of experience of dealing with difficult situations.*
teaching/secretarial/political etc experience *Only people with five years' secretarial experience can apply for the job.*

E

previous experience (=experience you have gained already in a previous job) *Have you any previous experience of working in a restaurant?*

gain experience (=get experience) *Fran is gaining valuable experience working for her father's firm.*

> ⚠ Remember that in this meaning **experience** is uncountable. Don't say things like 'I have an experience as a teacher' or 'I have experiences as a teacher'.

experienced /ɪkˈspɪəriənst/ [adj] someone who is **experienced** knows a lot about a job or activity because they have done it for a long time: *Ms Carter is one of our most experienced teachers.*

experienced in (doing) sth *This job would suit someone experienced in dealing with the public.*

highly experienced (=very experienced) *Dr Blake is highly experienced in microsurgery.*

5 when you have not done something before

inexperienced /ˌɪnɪkˈspɪəriənst◂/ [adj] someone who is **inexperienced** does not know much about a job or activity, either because they have not done it at all or because they have done it for only a short time: *Inexperienced managers often have problems with their staff.* | *There are a lot of young, inexperienced players on the team.*

be new to sth /biː ˈnjuː tuː (sth)‖-ˈnuː-/ if you **are new to** a job or activity, you do not have much experience of doing it because you have only just started it: *As you are new to the job, we don't expect you to work as fast as the others.*

lack experience /ˌlæk ɪkˈspɪəriəns/ if you **lack experience**, you have not done a job or activity before, or you have not done it enough to be very good at it yet: *People in their twenties often lack experience.*

+in *Johnson lacked experience in foreign affairs.*

lack of experience /ˌlæk əv ɪkˈspɪəriəns/ when you have not done a particular job or activity before, or you have not done it enough to be very good at it

yet: *My main problem was a lack of experience.* | *They decided to offer him the job, despite his lack of experience.*

EXPLAIN

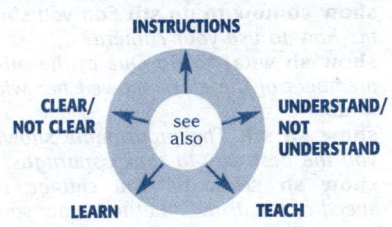

1 to explain something

explain /ɪkˈspleɪn/ [v I/T] to give someone the information they need to understand something: *It's very simple really – I'll try to explain.* | *We listened carefully while Pam explained the process.*

explain sth to sb *Could you explain the rules of the game to me, please?* | *I'll explain it to you later.*

+how/what/which etc *Can anyone really explain how the universe started?* | *Let me explain exactly what this drug is doing to your body.*

> ⚠ Don't say 'explain me the rules' or 'I explained her the rules' etc. Say **explain the rules to me**.

> ⚠ Don't say 'explain me how/what etc'. Say **explain how/what** etc: *Can you explain what I need to do?*

tell /tel/ [v T] ESPECIALLY SPOKEN to explain to someone how something works or how to do something

tell sb how/what etc *Can you tell me how to log on to the computer?* | *The leaflet tells you what to do if you get malaria.*

telling – told – have told

> ⚠ Don't say 'tell to someone'. Say **tell** **someone**.

⚠ Don't say 'please teach me' when you are asking someone to explain something to you. Say **please tell me**.

show /ʃəʊ/ [v T] to explain to someone how to do something by doing it while they watch you

show sb how to do sth *Can you show me how to use your camera?*

show sb what to do *One of the other members of the class showed her what to do.*

show sb sth *The programme showed you the best way to cook asparagus.*

show sb *"How do you change the speed of the drill?" "Let me show you."*

demonstrate /'demənstreɪt/ [v I/T] to show someone how to do something by doing it while they watch you, especially as part of your job: *The ski instructor began by demonstrating the correct way to turn.*

+how *He's here to demonstrate how the new computer system works.*

go through sth /ˌgəʊ 'θruː (sth)/ [phrasal verb T] to explain all the details about something in the right order, to help someone understand it: *I'll go through the instructions once more in case you missed anything.*

2 what you say when you are going to explain something

🗨 **you see** /juː 'siː/ SPOKEN say this when you are explaining something to someone, and you want to check that they are listening and that they understand you: *This fits on here, you see, where the arrow is. | Simon's car broke down, you see, and neither of us knew how to fix it.*

in other words /ɪn ˌʌðəʳ 'wɜːʳdz/ use this when you are saying something in a different way in order to explain it more clearly: *What we need is an efficient transport system, in other words, more buses and trains, and fewer cars.*

that is /ðæt ɪz/ ESPECIALLY WRITTEN use this when you are explaining the meaning of the previous word or phrase by giving more information about it: *The fare is reduced for children, that is, anyone under 16 years old. | Make sure you practise all*

four language skills, that is, reading, writing, listening, and speaking.

🗨 **what I mean is** /wɒt aɪ 'miːn ɪz/ SPOKEN say this when you are explaining something that you have just said: *When I say Joe likes to win, what I mean is, I don't think he'll play for our team if we keep losing.*

🗨 **let me explain** /ˌlet miː ɪk'spleɪn/ SPOKEN say this when you want to explain something to someone because you think they have not understood it: *I can see you're getting confused. Let me explain.*

3 the words you write or say to explain something

explanation /ˌekspləˈneɪʃən/ [n C] something that you say or write in order to make something clearer or to explain why something happened: *Each diagram is followed by a simple explanation.*

give (sb) an explanation *Can you give us a quick explanation of how it works? | He left suddenly, without giving any explanation.*

+for *Did they give any explanation for their decision?*

instructions /ɪn'strʌkʃənz/ [n plural] written or spoken information that explains exactly how to do something: *The cooking instructions are on the back of the box. | Make sure you read the instructions carefully first.*

give (sb) instructions *They gave us detailed instructions explaining how to get to their house.*

follow instructions (=do what they tell you) *If you had followed my instructions, none of this would have happened.*

4 to explain why something happened

say why/tell sb why /ˌseɪ 'waɪ, ˌtel (sb) 'waɪ/ to tell someone the reasons why something happened: *Did he say why he needed the money? | My aunt never told us why she got divorced.*

explain /ɪk'spleɪn/ [v I/T] to tell someone the reasons why something happened, so that they can understand the situation completely:

Don't get angry – I can explain everything.
+why *Can you explain why you're so late?*

EXPLODE

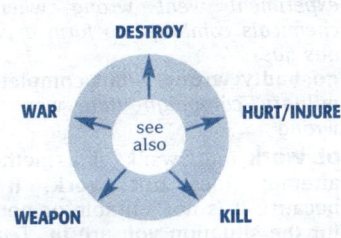

1 a bomb explodes

explode/go off /ɪkˈspləʊd, ˌɡəʊ ˈɒf‖-ˈɔːf/ [v I] if a bomb **explodes** or **goes off**, it bursts suddenly and violently with a loud noise, causing a lot of damage: *A bomb exploded in a crowded Metro station this morning, killing five people.* | *The bomb went off as people were still leaving the building.*

set off /ˌset ˈɒf‖-ˈɔːf/ [phrasal verb T] to make a bomb explode, either deliberately or accidentally
set off sth *Any slight movement could have set off the device and blown us all up.*
set sth off *the skill needed to remove a mine without setting it off*

detonate /ˈdetəneɪt/ [v T] to make a bomb explode, especially by using special equipment: *Army experts detonated the bomb safely in a nearby field.* | *The 200 kg bomb was detonated by terrorists using a remote-control device.*

Formal or informal?

Detonate is a more formal and technical word than **set off**.

2 a building/plane etc explodes

blow up /ˌbləʊ ˈʌp/ [v I] if a building, car, plane etc **blows up**, it bursts suddenly and violently into pieces, causing a lot of damage: *The plane blew up in mid-air, killing all the passengers and crew.*

explode /ɪkˈspləʊd/ [v I] if a container of chemicals, oil, or gas **explodes**, it bursts suddenly and violently into pieces: *The car crashed and its fuel tank exploded a few seconds later.*

3 to destroy something using a bomb

bomb /bɒm‖bɑːm/ [v T] to attack a building, town, country etc in order to destroy it or cause a lot of damage, either by dropping bombs from a plane or by leaving a bomb there: *Enemy warplanes bombed the capital every night for a week.* | *The church was bombed in the Second World War.*

blow up sth /ˌbləʊ ˈʌp (sth)/ [phrasal verb T] to destroy a building, car, plane etc using a bomb: *Terrorists blew up a government building in the city centre.* | *Two of the ships were blown up while they were still in the harbour.*

4 an explosion

explosion /ɪkˈspləʊʒən/ [n C] the loud noise and violent force that is produced when something explodes: *The noise of the explosion could be heard all over the city.*

blast /blɑːst‖blæst/ [n C] an explosion – used especially in news reports: *Twelve people were injured in a bomb blast in the city centre.* | *Every window in the building had been shattered by the force of the blast.*

F, f

FAIL

1 when you do not succeed

➡ opposite **SUCCEED**

fail /feɪl/ [v I] if you **fail**, you do not succeed in doing or achieving something that you have tried to do: *We tried to make her change her mind, but we failed.*
fail to do sth *So far, scientists have failed to find a cure for the disease.*

not succeed /nɒt sək'siːd/ to fail to do something, or not be completely successful: *Simon had tried several times to get a job in TV, but he never succeeded.*
not succeed in doing sth *I didn't really succeed in convincing her that I was telling the truth.*

2 when a plan or attempt does not succeed

➡ opposite **SUCCEED**

fail /feɪl/ [v I] if a plan or attempt **fails**, it does not achieve what you want it to achieve: *Try changing the spark plugs, but if that fails take the car to a mechanic.* | *They said the latest space mission was bound to fail.*
fail to do sth *The investigation failed to establish the cause of the accident.*

failure [n U] lack of success: *an attempt to climb Everest that ended in failure*
+of *the failure of the peace negotiations*

unsuccessful /ˌʌnsək'sesfəl◄/ [adj] an **unsuccessful** attempt to do something does not have the result that you wanted: *The army made an unsuccessful attempt to end the rebellion.* | *I regret to inform you that your application was unsuccessful.*

be a failure /biː ə 'feɪljəʳ/ to be unsuccessful – use this especially about something that fails even though it was very carefully planned: *The*

government's expensive election campaign had been a failure.
be a complete/total failure *There was a 5-year plan to modernize the economy, but it was a complete failure.*

go wrong /ˌgəʊ 'rɒŋǁ-'rɔːŋ/ if something that you are trying to do **goes wrong**, it fails after it has started well: *The experiment went wrong when the chemicals combined to form a poisonous gas.*
go badly wrong (=fail completely) *a military campaign that went badly wrong*

not work /nɒt 'wɜːʳk/ if a method or attempt does **not work**, it fails because it is not suitable or not right for the situation you are in: *Teaching methods that work with adults do not always work with children.* | *I tried to fix it with glue, but that didn't work.*

3 when you fail an exam or test

➡ opposite **PASS**
➡ see also **TEST,** **DRIVE**

fail /feɪl/ [v I/T] to not succeed in an examination or test: *Jonathan failed his law exams at the end of the year. If I fail my driving test again, I'm going to give up.* | *We expected her to pass easily, but she failed by 15 marks.*

⚠ Don't say 'he failed in the exam'. Say **he failed the exam** or just **he failed**.

flunk /flʌŋk/ [v I/T] AMERICAN INFORMAL to fail an examination or test: *Tony flunked chemistry.* | *I flunked, and had to do the test again.*

4 when something seems certain to fail

pointless /'pɔɪntləs/ [adj] something that is **pointless** is unlikely to have a very useful or successful result, so it would be better not to do it or try it: *The argument was completely pointless.* | *a pointless waste of money*
it is pointless doing sth *It's pointless trying to speak to the boss – she's always too busy.*

🔍 **there's no point/what's the point?** /ðeəʳz ˌnəʊ 'pɔɪnt, ˌwɒts ðə 'pɔɪnt/ SPOKEN say this when you think that you will not achieve anything useful by doing something, and so do not want to do it: *"Why don't you try to explain things to him?" "There's no point, he never listens to anything I say."*

there's no point (in) doing sth
There's no point in going shopping now – the stores will all be shut in half an hour.

what's the point of doing sth?
What's the point of taking the exam if you know you're going to fail?

be a waste of time /biː ə ˌweɪst əv 'taɪm/ ESPECIALLY SPOKEN something that is a **waste of time** is unlikely to achieve any useful result, so you would be wasting your time if you tried to do it

a complete waste of time *These meetings are a complete waste of time. Nothing ever gets decided.*

it is a waste of time doing sth *It's a waste of time going to the doctor – he'll just tell you to get plenty of rest.*

5 when a company, shop, or business fails

➡ opposite **SUCCEED 4**
➡ see also **BUSINESS, COMPANY, SHOP**

close down /ˌkləʊz 'daʊn/ [phrasal verb I] if a shop, factory, or business **closes down**, it stops making or selling things because it is no longer making a profit: *If the factory closes down, 600 people will lose their jobs. | A lot of small shops had to close down during the recession.*

go out of business /ˌgəʊ ˌaʊt əv 'bɪznɪs/ if a company **goes out of business**, it stops existing because it is no longer making a profit: *Many small farms are going out of business.*

go bankrupt /ˌgəʊ 'bæŋkrʌpt/ if a person or company **goes bankrupt**, they cannot pay their debts, so they have to sell all their property and goods: *The family grocery business went bankrupt last year.*

go bust /ˌgəʊ 'bʌst/ INFORMAL if a business or company **goes bust**, it has to close because it does not have enough money: *More and more small businesses are going bust each year.*

FAIR/UNFAIR

➡ see also **CRUEL**

1 fair

fair /feəʳ/ [adj] treating everyone equally, or treating people in a way that most people think is right: *The old system seemed much fairer. | a fair way of dividing up the profits | He will get a fair trial.*

it is fair that *Do you think it's fair that she gets paid more money than me?*

it's only fair (that) SPOKEN (=say this when you think that something would make a situation more fair) *Her husband should help take care of the baby – it's only fair. | It's only fair that you should pay tax on that money too.*

be fair to sb (=treat them in a fair way) *In order to be fair to everyone, ticket sales are limited to two for each person.*

to be fair SPOKEN (=say this when you are giving a reason why someone should not be criticized too strongly) *He really should have called you – though to be fair he's been very busy.*

fairly [adv] *Her job is to make sure that the money is distributed fairly.*

fairness [n U] *I wasn't sure about the fairness of the judge's decision.*

reasonable /'riːzənəbəl/ [adj] behaving fairly and sensibly, for example by not asking someone to do too much or not criticizing them unfairly: *I don't know why she reacted like that – it was a perfectly reasonable request.*

it is reasonable to do sth *Do you think it's reasonable to expect people to work more than 60 hours a week?*

just /dʒʌst/ [adj] FORMAL if something that people do or the way it is done is **just**, it is morally right and fair: *Many people do not think it is a just war. | What is a just punishment for murder?*

2 when all people have the same rights and are treated fairly

equal /'iːkwəl/ [adj] people who are **equal** have the same rights as each other and are treated the same way

F

as each other; if people get **equal** treatment, pay etc, they are all treated in the same way or get paid the same money: *The constitution states that all citizens are equal.* | *The women are demanding equal pay.*

equal rights (=the idea that all types of people in society should have the same rights and should be treated fairly and equally) *Black Americans campaigned for equal rights throughout the 1960s.*

equally [*adv*] *People should be treated equally, regardless of their race or sex.*

equality /ɪˈkwɒlɪtiǁɪˈkwɑː-/ [*n* U] when all people have the same rights and opportunities in society and are treated equally: *Greater equality was one of the aims of the post-war government.*

racial/sexual equality *the movement towards sexual equality*

3 unfair

unfair/not fair /ˌʌnˈfeəʳ◂, nɒt ˈfeəʳ/ [*adj*] not treating everyone equally, or not treating people in a way that most people think is right: *an unfair law* | *The present welfare system is very unfair.*

Q **it's not fair** SPOKEN *Why do I always have to do the laundry? It's not fair!*

it is unfair/not fair that *It seems very unfair that she was blamed for the accident.*

it is unfair/not fair to do sth *It's not fair to keep pets locked up in the house all day.*

+to *The law is unfair to people who have no permanent home.*

unreasonable /ʌnˈriːzənəbəl/ [*adj*] behaving in a way that is not fair or sensible, especially by asking someone to do too much or criticizing them unfairly: *My parents say I should stay in and do homework every night – I think they're being very unreasonable.* | *an unreasonable demand*

it is unreasonable to do sth *It's unreasonable to expect people to pay for something they haven't even seen yet.*

biased /ˈbaɪəst/ [*adj*] unfairly treating one person or group better or worse than another person or group – use this especially about newspapers, laws etc that should treat everyone fairly and equally: *accusations of biased reporting*

+against *The Socialists claim that the newspapers are biased against them.*

biased in favour of sb (=unfairly treating someone better just because you like them better) *Do you think the law courts are biased in favour of white people?*

favouritism BRITISH **favoritism** AMERICAN /ˈfeɪvərɪtɪzəm/ [*n* U] when a teacher, parent, or manager treats one person in a much better way than the others because they like that person, not because that person deserves it: *If I give Paul the job, I'll be accused of favoritism.*

bias /ˈbaɪəs/ [*n* singular/U] an opinion about a person, group, or idea which makes you treat them unfairly or differently

political/racial/gender etc bias *He claimed that his dismissal was due to racial bias.*

+against/towards/in favour of *Employers may have some bias against people over 50.* | *In those days people often showed a bias towards their sons.*

4 when people are treated unfairly because of their race, sex, age etc

discrimination /dɪˌskrɪmɪˈneɪʃən/ [*n* U] when people are treated unfairly because of their race, sex, age etc

+against *discrimination against women*

racial discrimination (=because of someone's race) *tough new laws against racial discrimination*

sex discrimination (=because of someone's sex)

 Don't say 'discriminations'. **Discrimination** is uncountable.

discriminate against sb /dɪˈskrɪmɪneɪt əˌgenst (sb)/ [*phrasal verb* T] to treat someone unfairly because of their race, sex, age etc – use this especially about companies, the police, judges etc: *Shaun says he has definitely been discriminated against because he's black.* | *Why do so many companies* *think that it's OK to discriminate against older people?*

prejudice /ˈpredʒədʒs/ [n C/U] when people do not like or trust someone who is different, for example because they belong to a different race, country, or religion
+against *There's still a lot of prejudice against gay men.*
racial prejudice (=because of someone's race) *the problem of racial prejudice in the police force*

inequality /ˌɪnɪˈkwɒlɪtɪll-ˈkwɑː-/ [n C/U] when people do not have the same rights or opportunities in their education, their jobs etc, because of their sex, race, or social class: *The report looks at inequality in education.*
+between *There are still a lot of inequalities between men and women.*
social/sexual/racial etc inequality *Social inequality tended to increase in the 1980s.*

FALL

➡ look here for ...
- when someone or something falls
- when you make someone fall
- when you drop something
➡ see also **ACCIDENT, HURT/INJURE, STAND 2**

1   when someone falls accidentally

fall /fɔːl/ [v I] to accidentally fall onto the ground or towards the ground: *She was taken to the hospital after falling and hitting her head on the side of the table.*
+off/out of/down *"How did you break your arm?" "I fell off my bike."* | *The police say he fell out of the window, but I think he was pushed.*
falling – fell – have fallen

fall over/fall down /ˌfɔːl ˈəʊvəʳ, ˌfɔːl ˈdaʊn/ [phrasal verb I] to fall onto the ground from a standing position: *Don't run so fast – you'll fall over.* | *He tried to stand up, but immediately fell down again.*

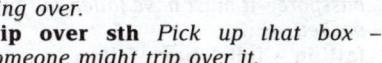

trip/trip over /trɪp, ˌtrɪp ˈəʊvəʳ/ [v I] to accidentally hit something with your foot when you are walking or running, so that you fall or nearly fall: *I didn't push him – he tripped.* | *She'd had quite a lot to drink and kept tripping over.*
trip over sth *Pick up that box – someone might trip over it.*
trip on sth *She tripped on the stairs and broke her wrist in the fall.*
tripping – tripped – have tripped

slip /slɪp/ [v I] to accidentally slide on a wet or smooth surface, so that you fall or nearly fall: *Be careful you don't slip – I've just washed the floor.*
+on *She slipped on the icy sidewalk and grabbed Will's arm to steady herself.*
slipping – slipped – have slipped

stumble /ˈstʌmbəl/ [v I] to nearly fall down when you are walking or running, because you do not put your foot down carefully or because something is in the way: *In her hurry, Eva stumbled and dropped the tray she was carrying.*
+on/over *Mason headed towards the house, stumbling on the rough ground.*

lose your balance /ˌluːz jɔːʳ ˈbæləns/ to fall or nearly fall, when you are doing something that needs balance, for example standing on a ladder or riding a bicycle: *I tried to help Gina up, but I lost my balance and we both fell into the stream.*

2 when an object, building, wall etc falls

fall /fɔːl/ [v I] to fall from a higher place to a lower place
+across/onto/on top of *A tree had fallen across the road and blocked it.*
+off/out of/from *The days were getting shorter and the leaves had started falling from the trees. | I can't find my passport – it must have fallen out of my pocket.*
falling – fell – have fallen

fall over /ˌfɔːl ˈəʊvəʳ/ [phrasal verb I] if a tall object **falls over**, it falls onto its side from an upright position: *That bookcase looks as if it's about to fall over.*

fall down /ˌfɔːl ˈdaʊn/ [phrasal verb I] if a building, wall, or fence **falls down**, part or all of it falls to the ground, because it is in bad condition or because it has been damaged: *A boy was injured yesterday when part of a wall fell down near to where he was playing.*

collapse /kəˈlæps/ [v I] if a building, wall etc **collapses**, it suddenly falls down, especially because it has been damaged by the weather or an explosion: *Our tent collapsed in the middle of the night. | The building was badly damaged in the explosion, and rescue workers are worried that it may collapse.*

topple /ˈtɒpəlǁˈtɑː-/ [v I] ESPECIALLY WRITTEN if a tall object, tree etc **topples**, it becomes unsteady and then falls over: *The pile of plates toppled and fell to the floor.*
+over *Many of the older trees eventually topple over with age.*

3 to make someone fall

➡ see also **HIT**

knock sb over/knock sb down /ˌnɒk (sb) ˈəʊvəʳ, ˌnɒk (sb) ˈdaʊnǁˌnɑːk-/ [phrasal verb T] to push or hit someone hard, so that they fall to the ground: *He was knocked down and kicked in the stomach by a gang of kids. | Careful where you're going! You nearly knocked me over!*

trip (also **trip up** BRITISH) /trɪp, ˌtrɪp ˈʌp/ [v T] to make someone fall or almost fall by putting your foot or another object in their way: *One of the athletes claimed she had been tripped.*
trip sb up *One man tripped me up and the other one grabbed my handbag.*
tripping – tripped – have tripped

push sb over /ˌpʊʃ (sb) ˈəʊvəʳ/ [phrasal verb T] to make someone fall to the ground by pushing them: *One of the bigger boys had pushed him over in the playground.*

send sb flying /ˌsend (sb) ˈflaɪ-ɪŋ/ to hit someone or crash into them with such force that they fall over very quickly: *Mark aimed a blow at the guy's chest and managed to send him flying. | The two players collided and sent each other flying.*

4 to let something fall or make something fall

drop /drɒpǁdrɑːp/ [v T] to stop holding something so that it falls, especially accidentally: *Watch you don't drop that box – it's very heavy. | Her hands shake constantly and she keeps dropping things.*

drop

dropping – dropped – have dropped

knock over /ˌnɒk ˈəʊvəʳǁˌnɑːk-/ [phrasal verb T] to hit something so that it falls onto its side from an upright position, especially when you do this accidentally

knock over

knock sth over *Be careful or you'll knock the vase over.*
knock over sth *He bumped into the table and knocked over the candle.*

spill

spill /spɪl/ [v T] to accidentally allow liquid or powder to fall onto a surface **spill sth down/all over/onto** *"How was the party?" "OK, but some idiot spilled wine all over my new dress."*
spilling – spilt – have spilt BRITISH
spilling – spilled – have spilled AMERICAN

FALSE

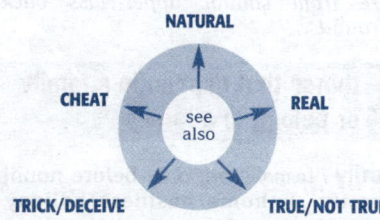

NATURAL

CHEAT   see   REAL
              also

TRICK/DECEIVE   TRUE/NOT TRUE

1 made to look real or natural

artificial /ˌɑːrtɪˈfɪʃəl/ [adj] something that is **artificial** is not real or natural, but is made to look real or to do the job of something real: *It was hard to tell whether the flowers were real or artificial.* | *an electric fire with artificial logs*
artificial hip/leg/limb *My grandfather has an artificial hip.*

false /fɔːls/ [adj only before noun] not real – use this about teeth, nails, eyelashes etc that are made to look real: *She was wearing a sixties-style wig and false eyelashes.* | *Nearly a third of adults in the UK have false teeth.*

imitation /ˌɪmɪˈteɪʃən/ [adj usually before noun] use this about materials that look like something valuable, but are actually made of something less expensive
imitation leather/gold/diamonds/ fur *an armchair made of imitation leather* | *She wore a woollen coat with an imitation fur collar.*

2 made to look real for dishonest purposes

false /fɔːls/ [adj only before noun] not real, but intended to seem real in order to trick someone or cheat them: *The man had given a false name and address.* | *Her suitcase had a false bottom, containing 2 kilos of heroin.*

fake /feɪk/ [adj only before noun] use this about objects or documents that are not real, but are intended to look like something more important or valuable: *They were selling fake Rolex watches on the market stall.* | *a fake driver's license*
fake [n C] a copy of a valuable object or painting that is intended to make people think it is real: *Is the vase a genuine antique or a fake?*

forged /fɔːrdʒd/ [adj] a **forged** official document or bank note has been illegally made to look like a real one: *He came into the country using a forged visa.* | *a forged £50 note*

forgery /ˈfɔːrdʒəri/ [n C] a copy of a document, painting, or bank note that is made to look real for dishonest purposes: *The painting, believed to be by Renoir, turned out to be a very clever forgery.*
plural **forgeries**

3 feelings or opinions that are not real

false /fɔːls/ [adj] ESPECIALLY WRITTEN emotions or feelings that are **false** are not honest or sincere, and you are only pretending to feel them: *"Merry Christmas," she said with false cheerfulness.* | *The politician greeted them with a false smile.*

insincere /ˌɪnsɪnˈsɪər/ [adj] pretending to like someone or to care about them when you do not really care: *"It's so good to see you again," she said, with an insincere smile.* | *an insincere* compliment | *He always praised everyone, so it was difficult to tell if he was being insincere or not.*

hypocritical /ˌhɪpə'krɪtɪkəl/ [adj] pretending to be morally good or to have beliefs that you do not really have: *I think it's a little hypocritical to get married in a church when you don't believe in God.* | *Politicians are so hypocritical – they preach about 'family values' while they all seem to be having affairs.*

hypocrite /'hɪpəkrɪt/ [n C] someone who is hypocritical: *My dad is such a hypocrite – he tells me off for smoking but he smokes 20 a day.*

FAMILY

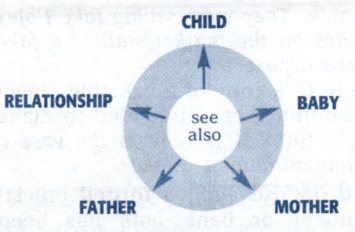

CHILD

RELATIONSHIP — see also — BABY

FATHER — MOTHER

1 a group of people who are related to each other

family /'fæməli/ [n C] a group of people who are related to each other, especially a mother, father, and their children all living together: *He comes from a family of eight children.* | *A lot of the families living in this area are very poor.*
member of the family *Only members of the family were allowed in to see her.*
the Armstrong/Mitchell/Jones family (=the family with this name) *Various members of the Kennedy family were at the funeral.*
nuclear family (=a typical family consisting of a mother, a father, and their children)
extended family (=including cousins, grandparents etc as well as parents and children)
one-parent family (=a family in which there is only one parent)
plural **families**

⚠ In British English, you can use **family** with a singular or plural verb: *The family now lives/live in London.* In American English, always use a singular verb: *The family now lives in California.*

⚠ **Family** usually means a group of close relatives who live together: *The average family spends $120 a week on food.* But it can also mean all the other people you are related to, such as your cousins and grandparents: *It was a big wedding, and the whole family was there.*

parents /'peərənts/ [n plural] someone's mother and father: *Do you get on well with your parents?* | *It's natural for parents to worry about their children.*

background /'bækgraʊnd/ [n C] the kind of family and social class that you grew up in: *The teachers try to know something about each child's background.*
working-class/middle-class/upper-class background *Most of his friends are from similar upper-class backgrounds.*

2 things that happen in a family or belong to a family

family /'fæməli/ [adj only before noun]
family home/business/holiday/ argument etc something that belongs to a family or happens in a family: *Dino's family home is in Palm Springs.* | *I stopped going on family holidays when I was 15.* | *a big family celebration*

domestic /də'mestɪk/ [adj only before noun] FORMAL relating to families and the things that happen in a family
domestic life *His domestic life isn't very happy.*
domestic violence (=violence in a family, especially by a husband to his wife) *Victims of domestic violence are often too frightened to tell the police.*

3 someone that belongs to your family

relative/relation /'relətɪv, rɪ'leɪʃən/ [n C] someone who is a member of your family – use this about your aunts, cousins etc, but not about your parents or your brothers or sisters: *Over 100 friends and relatives came to the funeral.*

close relative/relation (=someone who is closely related to you)

distant relative/relation (=someone who is not closely related to you) *We have some distant relations in Australia who we've never met.*

be a relative/relation of sb *She's a relative of the Queen, you know.*

> ⚠ Use **relatives** and **relations** to talk about members of your family who do not live with you in the same house. The people you live with (your parents, sisters etc) are your **family**, not your **relatives** or **relations**.

4 to belong to the same family as someone

be related /biː rɪˈleɪtɪd/ if two people **are related**, they are both members of the same family – use this about cousins, grandparents etc, but not about your parents or your brothers and sisters: *I didn't know you and Ted were related.*

+to *John told me he was related to Mel Gibson – is it true?*

be descended from sb /biː dɪˈsendɪd frɒm (sb)/ to be related to someone who lived a long time ago, especially someone famous or important: *She is descended from the Duke of Marlborough.*

5 people who are related to you because of marriage

mother-in-law/son-in-law etc /ˈmʌðər ɪn lɔː, ˈsʌn ɪn lɔː (etc)/ [n C] someone who is related to you by marriage; for example, your **mother-in-law** is the mother of your wife or husband, and your **sister-in-law** is the sister of your wife or husband or the wife of your brother

plural **mothers-in-law, sons-in-law** etc

stepmother/stepson etc /ˈstepmʌðər, ˈstepsʌn (etc)/ [n C] **stepmother/ stepfather/stepsister stepbrother/ stepson/stepdaughter** someone who becomes your mother, sister, son etc

when you or a person that you are related to marries for a second time: *I have two stepsisters.*

half-brother/half-sister /ˈhɑːf brʌðər, ˈhɑːf sɪstər‖ˈhæf-/ [n C] if one of your parents marries a second time and has a child, that child is your **half-brother** or **half-sister**

by marriage /baɪ ˈmærɪdʒ/ if you are related to someone **by marriage**, they are married to someone in your family or you are married to someone in their family: *John's my cousin by marriage.* (=he is the cousin of my wife or husband)

in-laws /ˈɪn lɔːz/ [n plural] INFORMAL the parents of your husband or wife: *We lived with my in-laws until we had enough money to buy a house.*

6 people who were in the same family as you a long time ago

ancestor /ˈænsəstər, -ses-‖-ses-/ [n C] a member of your family who lived a long time ago, especially hundreds of years ago: *My ancestors originally came from Ireland.* | *Tom's interested in finding out more about his ancestors.*

family /ˈfæməli/ [n C] people that you are related to who lived many years ago: *Her family came to America from Scotland in about 1750.*

plural **families**

descendant /dɪˈsendənt/ [n C] someone who is a relative of a person who lived and died a long time ago, especially a famous or important person

+of *a descendant of King Charles I*

> When you see **EC**, go to the **ESSENTIAL COMMUNICATION** section.

FAMOUS

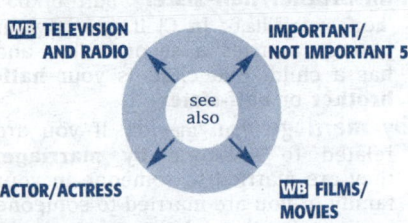

WB TELEVISION AND RADIO

IMPORTANT/ NOT IMPORTANT 5

see also

ACTOR/ACTRESS

WB FILMS/ MOVIES

1 famous

famous /'feɪməs/ [adj] **famous** people, places, books etc are known about and talked about by many people in many places: *famous stars, like Keanu Reeves and Demi Moore | Sydney's famous Opera House | 'David Copperfield' is one of Dickens' most famous books.*
+for *Manchester is famous for its nightlife and for its football teams.*
world-famous (=famous all over the world) *Rio's world-famous carnival*
the rich and famous (=people who are rich and famous) *a nightclub that is popular with the rich and famous*

well-known/well known /ˌwel 'nəʊn◂/ [adj] fairly famous, especially in a particular place or among a particular group of people: *She works in local radio, and is quite well known in the Houston area. | a well-known engineering company*
best-known *one of the best-known names in the music business*
+for *Hawking is well known for his work on the theory of black holes.*
well-known – better-known – best-known

legendary /'ledʒəndəriǁ-deri/ [adj] someone or something that is **legendary** is famous for being very special or interesting, and people like to talk or read about them: *The studio was owned by Sam Goldwyn, the legendary Hollywood producer. | the legendary wealth of John D Rockefeller | The album was recorded at the legendary Abbey Road studios.*

notorious /nəʊ'tɔːriəs/ [adj] well known because of something bad: *One of the country's most notorious criminals has escaped from prison.*

+for *a part of the city that is notorious for violence and prostitution*
notoriously [adv] *a notoriously inefficient company*

fame /feɪm/ [n U] the success and attention people get when they are famous: *She came to Hollywood in search of fame.*
achieve fame/win fame (as) *Streisand first won fame as a singer before becoming an actress.*
at the height of your fame *The Beatles were at the height of their fame in 1965.*

2 to become famous

become famous /bɪˌkʌm 'feɪməs/ *She dreamed of becoming really famous.*
become famous overnight (=very suddenly) *With the success of their first record, they became famous overnight.*
make your name /ˌmeɪk jɔːʳ 'neɪm/ to become well known, especially as a result of hard work: *Clint Eastwood first made his name in the TV series 'Rawhide'.*
+as *By the time he was 30, Evans had made his name as the editor of the 'Sunday Times'.*
make a name for yourself *She is beginning to make a name for herself as a fashion designer.*

3 a famous person

star /staːʳ/ [n C] a very famous and successful film actor, entertainer, or sports player: *Tilda's latest movie role could make her a big star.*
movie/rock/tennis etc star *Bruce Willis is one of my favourite movie stars. | She was once married to a well-known football star.*
celebrity (also **celeb** INFORMAL /sə'lebrəti, sə'leb/ [n C] someone who is well known, for example as an entertainer or sports player, and who is often seen on television or is written about in the newspapers: *Several celebs were at the party.*
TV/show business/Hollywood celebrity *The club is popular with TV celebrities and footballers. | The event was attended by various Hollywood celebrities.*
plural **celebrities**

superstar /'suːpəˈstɑːʳ, ˈsjuː-‖ˈsuː-/ [n C] an actor, musician, or sports player who is famous all over the world: *This was the movie that made Brando an international superstar.* | *footballing superstar, David Beckham*

4   not famous

unknown /ˌʌnˈnəʊn◂/ [adj] not at all famous: *Gorbachev was virtually unknown in the West when he first came to power.* | *As an unknown author, it isn't easy to get your work published.*

a nobody /ə ˈnəʊbədi/ [n singular] INFORMAL someone who is very ordinary and not at all famous or important: *Six months ago she was a nobody, and now she's a superstar.*

FAR

➡ opposite **NEAR**

1   a long distance

far /fɑːʳ/ [adv] a long distance – use this especially in negatives and questions: *Have you driven far?* | *Since I changed jobs, I have to travel farther to get to work.* | *Let's see who can jump the farthest.*
far away (=a very long way from where you are) *The ship was so far away that we could hardly see it.*
+from *We were sitting too far from the stage to hear what the actors were saying.* | *The beach isn't far from here.*
+above/below/behind *They lay on the hillside with the sea far below them.*
far – farther – farthest (or **far – further – furthest**)

> ⚠ Don't say 'the school is far'. Say **the school is a long way away** or **it's a long way to the school**. **Far** is usually only used in questions and negative sentences.

> ⚠ You can use **farther/further** or **farthest/furthest** in any kind of sentence, and you can use phrases such as **far away**, **far enough** or **too far** in any kind of sentence.

> ⚠ Don't say 'he lives far' or 'he lives 10 miles far from here'. Say **he lives far away/a long way away** or **he lives 10 miles away**.

a long way /ə ˌlɒŋ ˈweɪ‖-ˌlɔːŋ-/ a long distance: *You must be tired, you've come a long way.*
+from *The farm is a long way from the highway.*
a long way away/a long way off (=a long way from where you are now or from the place you are talking about) *We could hear them shouting from a long way away.* | *From the map, it looked like the lake was still a long way off.*
+ahead/below/behind etc *A long way below me, a man was riding his horse across the plain.*

miles /maɪlz/ [n plural] INFORMAL a very long way: *We walked miles yesterday.* | *When we got to the top, we could see for miles.*
+away *I don't see Jane much any more – she lives miles away.*
+from *The hotel is miles from the station – I'll come and get you.*
miles from anywhere (=a long way from the nearest town) *They live up in the mountains, miles from anywhere.*

nowhere near /ˌnəʊweəʳ ˈnɪəʳ/ [preposition] a very long way from somewhere: *West says he was nowhere near the cliff when his wife was killed.* | *After 8 hours' climbing, we were still nowhere near the top of the mountain.*

> ⚠ Use **nowhere near** to emphasize that someone is not at or near a place.

2   when something you can see or hear is far away

in the distance /ɪn ðə ˈdɪstəns/ ESPECIALLY WRITTEN if you can see or hear something **in the distance**, it is a long way from where you are, so it looks small or does not sound loud:

In the distance, he could see the tall chimneys of the factory. | *There was the sound of church bells in the distance.*

distant /'dɪstənt/ [*adj* only before noun] WRITTEN very far away, so that it looks small or sounds quiet: *distant thunder* | *By now, the plane was just a distant speck in the sky.*

 Use **distant** when you are writing stories or descriptions.

on the horizon /ɒn ðə hə'raɪzən/ ESPECIALLY WRITTEN at the place far away where the land or sea seems to meet the sky: *Another ship appeared on the horizon.*

from a distance /frəm ə 'dɪstəns/ ESPECIALLY WRITTEN from a place that is a long way away: *From a distance, we could hear the faint sound of drums beating.* | *Until then I had only seen the castle from a distance.*

3 far away from other places

distant/far-off /'dɪstənt, 'fɑːr ɒf/ [*adj* only before noun] WRITTEN a **distant** or **far-off** town or country is far away from where you are: *The travellers told us stories about distant lands.* | *Many years ago, in a far-off city, there lived a wise old man.*

 Use **distant** and **far-off** when you are writing stories or descriptions.

remote /rɪ'məʊt/ [*adj*] **remote** places are far away from other places or people, and very few people go there: *They moved to a remote farmhouse in North Wales.* | *The helicopter crashed in a remote desert area.*

in the middle of nowhere /ɪn ðə ˌmɪdl əv 'nəʊweər/ INFORMAL in a lonely place a long way from towns or villages, where you do not expect to find any houses: *I don't want to live in the middle of nowhere!*

4 how far

how far /ˌhaʊ 'fɑːr/ use this to ask what the distance is between where you

are and another place: *"How far is it to Newark?" "It's about 200 miles."* | *God knows how far it is to the next gas station.*

from /frəm, *strong* frɒm‖frəm, *strong* frʌm, frɑːm/ [*preposition*] if one place is 10 kilometres/30 miles/20 minutes etc **from** another place, that is the distance between the two places, or the time it takes to get from one to the other: *Seattle is about 100 miles from the Canadian border.* | *The junior high school is five minutes from our house.* | *She was standing just a couple of metres from the edge of the cliff.*

away /ə'weɪ/ [*adv*] if a place or person is 10 kilometres/30 miles/20 minutes etc **away**, they are that distance from where you are, or it takes that amount of time to travel there: *The nearest village was about 20 miles away.* | *Toronto's only about an hour and a half away by car.*

distance /'dɪstəns/ [*n* C/U] how far it is from one place to another
the distance from sth to sth *What is the distance from Freeport to Miami?*
the distance between sth and sth *Measure the distance between the window and the door.*

FASHIONABLE/ UNFASHIONABLE

➡ see also **CLOTHES,** WB **MUSIC**

1 fashionable

fashionable /'fæʃənəbəl/ [*adj*] clothes, styles, ideas etc that are **fashionable** are popular at the present time, but will probably only be popular for a short time: *The store sells fashionable clothes at prices you can afford.* | *a style of painting that was fashionable in the 1930s*
fashionable restaurant/resort/area etc (=a place that a lot of people want to go to or live, especially rich people, because it is fashionable) *a fashionable skiing resort*

trendy /'trendi/ [*adj*] INFORMAL very fashionable and exciting – use this about things people do, places they

go etc in order to show how modern and fashionable they are: *a trendy club* | *Parents and teachers are worried that some drugs are considered very trendy among teenagers.*
trendy – trendier – trendiest

stylish /'staɪlɪʃ/ [adj] well designed, and attractive in a fashionable way: *She was wearing a stylish black woollen dress.* | *stylish modern furniture*

designer /dɪ'zaɪnəʳ/ [adj only before noun] **designer jeans/watch/label/ clothing etc** use this about clothes, watches etc that are made by a well-known and fashionable designer and are usually very expensive: *She was wearing a designer dress.*

in fashion /ɪn 'fæʃən/ fashionable at the present time – use this especially about clothes: *Long skirts are back in fashion.* (=are fashionable again)

in /ɪn/ [adj] INFORMAL fashionable at the present time – use this especially about clothes: *Purple is in this year.*

2 fashionable people

fashionable /'fæʃənəbəl/ [adj] someone who is **fashionable** wears fashionable clothes, has fashionable things, and goes to fashionable places: *the style of hat worn by fashionable women in Milan*

trendy /'trendi/ [adj] INFORMAL someone who is **trendy** likes to show how fashionable and modern they are by the way they behave, dress, and decorate their home: *a trendy young photographer* | *She only talks like that because she wants to sound trendy.*
trendy – trendier – trendiest

> ⚠ **Trendy** is sometimes used in a negative way to say that someone has modern ideas that are fashionable but not good: *trendy politicians* | *The school's bad exam results are being blamed on trendy teaching methods.*

sophisticated /sə'fɪstɪ̣keɪtɪ̣d/ [adj] someone who is **sophisticated** knows a lot about fashionable things and feels confident about being with fashionable people: *a sophisticated woman whose friends included many rich and famous people* | *a play that will appeal to a sophisticated audience*

3 a fashionable activity, product, style etc

fashion /'fæʃən/ [n C] a style of clothes, hair, behaviour etc that is fashionable
latest fashion *the latest Paris fashions*
fashion in clothes/music etc *changing fashions in popular music*
fashion for doing sth *Who started this fashion for wearing old army clothes?*

trend /trend/ [n C] a way of doing something or a way of thinking that is becoming fashionable
+in *the latest trend in kitchen design*
set/start a trend (for sth) *'Rambo' set the trend for a whole wave of violent action movies.*

craze/fad /kreɪz, fæd/ [n C] a fashion, activity, type of music etc that suddenly becomes very popular, but only remains popular for a short time: *The break-dancing craze soon passed, as most fads do.* | *a craze for wearing underwear outside your clothes*

4 the business of making and selling fashionable clothes

fashion /'fæʃən/ [n U] *He's one of the best-known designers in the world of fashion.*

> ⚠ **Fashion** is usually used before a noun, like an adjective: *a top-selling fashion magazine* | *She works for a well-known fashion designer.* | *the fashion industry*

5 not fashionable

out of fashion /,aʊt əv 'fæʃən/ no longer fashionable – use this especially about clothes and music: *Shoulder pads are definitely out of fashion now.*
go out of fashion *Rock'n'Roll began in the fifties and has never really gone out of fashion.*

unfashionable /ʌn'fæʃənəbəl/ [adj] not fashionable – use this especially about people's ideas, beliefs, and way of life: *formal language-teaching methods that were unfashionable in the 60s and 70s* | *She lived in an unfashionable part of West London.*

dated /'deɪtɪd/ [adj] not fashionable any more – use this especially about the way something looks or the style of something: *He turned up in a very dated old suit.*

look dated *Some of the old TV series look incredibly dated now.*

out /aʊt/ [adj not before noun] INFORMAL no longer fashionable – use this especially about clothes: *Coloured tights are out.*

FAST

➡ opposite **SLOW**

➡ see also **HURRY, RUN**

1 moving fast

fast /fɑːst‖fæst/ [adv] *Don't drive so fast – there's ice on the road.* | *The new fighter aircraft flies almost twice as fast as the old one.* | *Pat walked faster and faster as the footsteps behind her got closer.*

as fast as you can *He ran home as fast as he could.*

fast [adj] able to go fast: *the fastest runner in the world* | *Dean always loved fast cars and expensive clothes.*

quickly /'kwɪkli/ [adv] use this to talk about someone moving fast, especially for a short distance: *Richard ran quickly down the stairs.* | *If you hear the alarm, leave the building quickly and calmly.* | *Tell the doctor to come quickly.*

> ⚠ **Fast** and **quickly** both mean 'at high speed', but you use **quickly** especially to talk about someone who is going only a short distance, especially because they are in a hurry.

at high speed /ət ˌhaɪ 'spiːd/ ESPECIALLY WRITTEN very fast – use this about cars, trains, machines etc: *Two cars raced past him at high speed.* | *a metal disc revolving at high speed*

high-speed [adj only before noun] *You can travel by high-speed train from Paris to Brussels.* | *a high-speed drill*

at top speed /ət ˌtɒp 'spiːd‖-ˌtɑːp-/ ESPECIALLY WRITTEN if someone is driving, running etc **at top speed**, they are moving as fast as they can: *Carson drove to the hospital at top speed.*

flat out /ˌflæt 'aʊt/ INFORMAL if someone or something is going, running, driving etc **flat out**, they are moving as fast as possible: *A motorcycle passed us, going flat out.* | *He increased his speed gradually until he was running flat out.*

2 doing things quickly or happening quickly

quickly /'kwɪkli/ [adv] quickly, without taking much time – use this about actions and events: *She undressed quickly and got into bed.* | *It's important to realize how quickly this disease can spread.* | *You fry the onions quickly, then add the meat.*

quick /kwɪk/ [adj] a **quick** movement or action is one that you do quickly or one that only takes a short time: *I'll just take a quick shower.* | *That was quick! Have you finished already?* | *I had to make a quick decision.*

🔍 **be quick** SPOKEN (=use this when you are telling someone to hurry) *You'll have to be quick – we don't have much time.*

fast /fɑːst‖fæst/ [adv] if you work, talk, or write **fast**, you do it quickly: *Don't talk so fast – I can't understand what you're saying.* | *We're working as fast as we can.*

rapid /'ræpɪd/ [adj usually before noun] a **rapid** change, increase, or improvement is one that happens much more quickly than usual: *a rapid increase in the population* | *In China, it was a period of rapid change.* | *She made a rapid recovery after her operation.* (=she got better very quickly)

rapidly [adv] *the rapidly changing world of computer technology*

> **Formal or informal?**
> **Rapid** and **rapidly** are used in writing and in formal spoken English such as news reports.

prompt /prɒmpt‖prɑːmpt/ [adj] doing things quickly and without delay, especially when you have to deal with a problem

prompt action / reply / delivery *A major disaster was prevented by the prompt action of the police.* | *We guarantee prompt delivery of the goods you have ordered.*

promptly [*adv*] *Sanders raised objections to the plan, and was promptly sacked.*

3 how fast

speed /spi:d/ [*n* C/U] how fast something or someone moves: *Police are advising drivers to reduce their speed because of thick fog.*
at a speed of 70 mph/40 kph etc *a truck travelling at a speed of 50 mph*
at a constant/steady speed (=keeping the same speed all the time) *The planet revolves at a constant speed.*

rate /reɪt/ [*n* C] how fast things happen, change, or develop
rate of growth/increase/change/development *China's economy is experiencing a very high rate of growth.*
at a faster/slower/different rate *Children learn to read at different rates.* | *The population is increasing at a faster rate than ever before.*

pace /peɪs/ [*n* singular] how fast someone walks or runs, or how fast they work or do things
at a brisk/steady/gentle etc pace (=going at a fast, regular, or slow speed) *soldiers marching at a steady pace*
pace of work/life *The whole pace of life seems a lot slower there.*

4 to go somewhere fast

⚠ All these verbs must be used with a preposition (such as **to**, **across**, **through**, or **into**), or with an adverb (such as **away**, **out**, or **there**).

race /reɪs/ [*v* I] to go somewhere as fast as you can, especially because you have to deal with a dangerous situation
+across/back/ahead etc *Hearing the children's screams, she raced back into the house.* | *A police car came racing down the road.*

rush /rʌʃ/ [*v* I] to go somewhere very quickly because you are in a hurry
+out/around/into etc *Everyone rushed out into the street to see what was happening.* | *People were rushing past me on their way to work.*

dash /dæʃ/ [*v* I] to run somewhere very fast, especially only a short distance
+into/around/to etc *Pam dashed into the room, grabbed her bag and ran out again.* | *He was dashing across the road to catch a bus.*

speed /spi:d/ [*v* I] ESPECIALLY WRITTEN to move very fast – use this about cars, trains, or buses, or about people travelling in them
+along/past/across etc *Soon we were speeding across the desert.* | *An ambulance sped past on its way to the accident.*
speeding – sped – have sped

⚠ Use **speed** especially when you are writing stories or descriptions.

hurtle /'hɜ:ʳtl/ [*v* I] to go somewhere very fast, especially in a dangerous or careless way – use this about cars, trucks etc or people
+past/along/through etc *A black car hurtled past, travelling at over 90 mph.* | *Two of the boys hurtled around the corner, straight into the head teacher.*

5 to move or work faster

faster /ˌgəʊ 'fɑ:stəʳ‖-'fæs-/
go/move/work etc faster *Could you go a little faster? We don't want to miss our plane.* | *You'll have to work a lot faster than this.*
faster and faster (=more and more quickly) *I could feel my heart beating faster and faster.*

speed up /ˌspi:d 'ʌp/ [*phrasal verb* T] to make something happen more quickly, especially a job or process
speed up sth/speed sth up *Certain herbs were thought to speed up the healing process.* | *I'll phone the manager and get them to speed things up.*

accelerate /əkˈseləreɪt/ [*v* I] to go faster – use this about a car, bus etc, or about the person driving it: *They were* all thrown backwards as Josef suddenly accelerated. | The Ferrari Mondial can accelerate from zero to 60 mph in 6.3 seconds.

6 to move as fast as someone else

keep up with sb /ˌkiːp 'ʌp wɪð (sb)/ [phrasal verb T] to move as fast as someone else who is walking, running, or driving in the same direction: Slow down, I can't keep up with you. | She walked so fast that Charlie had to run to keep up with her.

keep pace with sb /ˌkiːp 'peɪs wɪð (sb)/ to move as fast as someone else who is going somewhere with you: Dad used to get annoyed if I couldn't keep pace with him. | You should stop now and then, to allow the slowest walkers to keep pace with you.

> **Formal or informal?**
>
> **Keep pace with sb** is more formal than **keep up with sb**.

FASTEN/UNFASTEN

to join together the two sides of a piece of clothing, bag, belt etc, so that it is closed

➡ see also **TIE/UNTIE, CLOTHES**

1 to fasten something

fasten /ˈfɑːsən‖ˈfæ-/ [v T] Fasten your coat – it's cold outside. | We will shortly be landing in Athens. Please fasten your seatbelts. | I can't fasten my suitcase.
fastened [adj not before noun] Is your safety belt fastened?
button/button up /ˈbʌtn, ˌbʌtn 'ʌp/ [v T] to fasten the buttons on a piece of clothing: He began buttoning his shirt.
button up sth/button sth up He buttoned up his jacket and straightened his tie. | Button your coat up – it's raining.
zip up /ˌzɪp 'ʌp/ [phrasal verb T] to fasten clothes, bags etc with a zip
zip up sth I can't zip up these jeans – they're too tight!

zip sth up She took some money out of her purse and zipped it up again quickly.
do up /ˌduː 'ʌp/ [phrasal verb T] ESPECIALLY SPOKEN to fasten clothes, or the buttons, zips etc on clothes
do up sth Come on then, do up your coat and let's go.
do sth up I can't do this zip up – it's stuck. | Are your shoelaces done up properly?
tie /taɪ/ [v T] to fasten something by making a knot
tie shoelaces/a scarf etc Don't forget to tie your shoelaces. | She tied a scarf around her head.
tying – tied – have tied

2 to unfasten something

unfasten /ʌnˈfɑːsən‖-ˈfæ-/ [v T] to open the two sides of a piece of clothing, bag, belt etc: It was hot in the waiting-room, so I unfastened my coat. | Jack unfastened his seatbelt and stepped out of the car.
unfastened [adj not before noun] The back of her dress was unfastened.
undo /ʌnˈduː/ [v T] to unfasten clothes, or unfasten the buttons, zips etc on clothes: My fingers were so cold that I couldn't undo the buttons. | Rosie undid the necklace and gave it back to him.
undoing – undid – have undone
undone /ʌnˈdʌn/ [adj not before noun] Your zip's undone!
come undone (=become unfastened) One of his shoelaces had come undone.
unbutton /ʌnˈbʌtn/ [v T] to unfasten the buttons on a piece of clothing: She unbuttoned her uniform and changed into her normal clothes.
unbuttoned [adj not before noun] His trousers were unbuttoned and his shirt was hanging out.
unzip /ʌnˈzɪp/ [v T] to unfasten clothes, bags etc by unfastening a zip: She unzipped the case and took out a thick file.
unzipping – unzipped – have unzipped
untie /ʌnˈtaɪ/ [v T] to unfasten the knot that fastens shoes, a tie, a scarf etc: Amy untied her apron and folded it neatly on the chair.
untying – untied – have untied

loosen /'luːsən/ [v T] to unfasten clothes a little, in order to make yourself more comfortable: *I'd eaten so much that I had to loosen my belt.* | *Lay the patient on his side and loosen any tight clothing.*

FAT

➡ opposite **THIN**

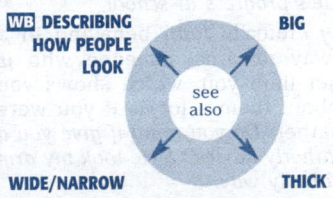

WB DESCRIBING HOW PEOPLE LOOK

see also

BIG

WIDE/NARROW

THICK

1 someone who is fat

fat /fæt/ [adj] *Do I look fat in this dress?* | *Clare's on a diet because she thinks she's too fat.*
get fat *I'm getting too fat for these jeans.*
fat – fatter – fattest

⚠ We usually use **fat** only to talk about ourselves. It is rude to say that someone else is **fat**. It is more polite to say that they are **large** or **overweight**, or that they **have put on weight**.

overweight /ˌəʊvəˈweɪt◂/ [adj] a little fatter or heavier than you should be: *Many teenagers are overweight because they don't get enough exercise.*
5 kilos/10 pounds etc overweight *I was ten kilos overweight and smoked 40 cigarettes a day.* | *a nation of overweight people*

plump /plʌmp/ [adj] fat in a fairly pleasant way – use this when you want to avoid saying that someone is fat: *Her mother was a small, plump woman.*

chubby /'tʃʌbi/ [adj] a **chubby** child is a little fat in a pleasant, healthy-looking way: *a nice chubby baby* | *Who's that chubby little girl with dark hair?*
chubby – chubbier – chubbiest

large /lɑːrdʒ/ [adj] use this as a polite way of saying that someone is fat: *fashionable clothes for the larger woman* | *I was squashed between two*

rather large men for most of the journey.
large – larger – largest

obese /əʊˈbiːs/ [adj] much too fat, in a way that is dangerous to your health: *30% of the women on the island are obese.*
obesity [n U] the medical problem of being much too fat in a way that is dangerous to your health: *Doctors have recommended the diet as a treatment for obesity.*

Formal or informal?
Obese is used especially in formal medical writing.

2 part of the body

fat /fæt/ [adj] *I hate going swimming. I don't like people seeing my fat legs.*
fat – fatter – fattest

flabby /'flæbi/ [adj] having unattractive soft loose flesh rather than strong muscles: *Her body was getting old and flabby.* | *my flabby stomach*
flabby – flabbier – flabbiest

chubby /'tʃʌbi/ [adj] **chubby** arms, cheeks, legs etc are slightly fat in a pleasant attractive way: *a little girl of about three, with blonde hair and chubby arms*
chubby – chubbier – chubbiest

thick /θɪk/ [adj] fat – use this about people's necks, legs, ankles, wrists, or arms that have a lot of muscles or a lot of flesh on them: *a big heavy man with a thick neck and a broad red face*

3 to become fatter

get fatter /get 'fætər/ *Steve has got a lot fatter since I last saw him.*

put on weight /ˌpʊt ɒn 'weɪt/ *John's put on a lot of weight recently, hasn't he?*
put on 5 kilos/2 pounds etc (=become 5 kilos/2 pounds etc heavier than you were before) *I put on several pounds over Christmas.*

⚠ It is more polite to say someone **has put on weight** than to say they **have got fatter**.

4 food that makes you fat

fattening /ˈfætnɪŋ/ [adj] food that is **fattening** makes you fat: *Try to avoid fattening foods.* | *Grilled fish tastes better and is less fattening than fried fish.*

FATHER

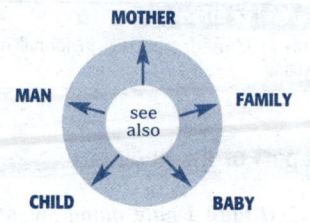

MOTHER
MAN
see also
FAMILY
CHILD
BABY

father /ˈfɑːðəʳ/ [n C] *My father's a doctor.* | *Like most fathers, I felt anxious when my son got his first motorcycle.* | *Larry Blake, a father of three children, was shot dead outside his home last night.*

⚲ **dad** /dæd/ [n C] SPOKEN a name you use to talk to your father or to talk informally about him or someone else's father: *Was your dad angry when you got home?* | *Can I borrow your car, Dad?* | *My dad retired ten years ago.*

⚲ **daddy** /ˈdædi/ [n C] SPOKEN a name for your father – used especially by young children or when you are talking to young children: *Daddy, can I have a drink, please?* | *Go and ask Daddy if he'll play with you.*

⚲ **pop** /pɒpǁpɑːp/ [n singular] AMERICAN SPOKEN a name for your father: *Pop and I went for a walk along the beach.*

When you see **WB**, go to the **WORD BANKS** section.

2 like a father

 The words in this section are used when talking about men, not women.

paternal /pəˈtɜːʳnl/ [adj] FORMAL **paternal** feelings are like the feelings that a good father has for his children: *Although he had no children of his own, he took a paternal interest in Katie's progress at school.*

fatherly /ˈfɑːðəʳli/ [adj] behaving in a kind way towards someone who is younger than you, which shows you care about them a lot as if you were their father: *Do you mind if give you a little fatherly advice?* | *He took my arm in a fatherly way.*

FAVOURITE/ FAVORITE

the one you like better than any others

➡ see also **LIKE/NOT LIKE, BEST**

favourite BRITISH **favorite** AMERICAN /ˈfeɪvərɪt/ [adj only before noun] **sb's favourite colour/food/teacher etc** the colour, food etc that someone likes better than any other colour, food etc: *My favourite colour is purple.* | *Who is your favorite singer?* | *We're going to her favourite restaurant for a meal.*

⚲ **like best** /ˌlaɪk ˈbest/ ESPECIALLY SPOKEN to like something better than other things – use this especially when you are asking someone to choose or when you are choosing: *Which of these dresses do you like best?*
like sth best *I think I like the red one best.*

favourite BRITISH **favorite** AMERICAN /ˈfeɪvərɪt/ [n C] something that you like more than other things of the same kind: *I like all her books, but this one's my favourite.* | *Oh great! Chocolate ice-cream – my favourite!*

teacher's pet /ˌtiːtʃəʳz ˈpet/ [n singular] INFORMAL someone who is their teacher's favourite student, and who the other students do not like because of this: *Some of the kids teased her and called her 'teacher's pet'.*

FEEL

➡ see also **TOUCH**

1 to feel hot/tired/hungry etc

feel/be /fiːl, biː/ [v]
feel/be tired/hot/hungry etc *I was very tired and I just wanted to sleep.* | *If you feel hungry between meals, have a piece of fruit.* | *Stop the car – Ben feels sick!* | *You'll be cold if you don't wear a coat.*
feel well/better *"How do you feel?" "I feel much better now I've had some sleep."*
feeling – felt – have felt
being – was – have been

experience /ɪk'spɪəriəns/ [v T] FORMAL to have a feeling of pain, sickness etc: *Most women experience some nausea when they are pregnant.* | *He said that he had never experienced such pain before.*

sensitive /'sensɪtɪv/ [adj] a part of your body that is **sensitive** feels pain, cold, heat etc more than is usual
sensitive to heat/light/cold etc *Blue eyes tend to be more sensitive to light.*
sensitive teeth/skin/eyes (=easily affected or damaged by cold, light etc) *a special toothpaste for sensitive teeth*

2 a physical feeling

feeling /'fiːlɪŋ/ [n C] a physical feeling of heat, cold, tiredness etc: *When he woke up there was a horrible tight feeling in his chest.*
+of *One symptom of this illness is a general feeling of ill-health and tiredness.*

sensation /sen'seɪʃən/ [n C] a physical feeling, especially one that is unclear or difficult to describe exactly: *I had a strange sensation in my stomach.*
+of *the sensation of being in love*

> **Formal or informal?**
> **Sensation** is more formal than **feeling**.

3 how something feels when you touch it

feel /fiːl/ [v] if something **feels** hot, soft, wet etc, this is the feeling it gives you when you touch it
feel hot/cold/soft etc *Your forehead feels very hot – let's check your temperature.* | *The marble felt cold and smooth against her cheek.*
feel like sth (=feel the same as) *The material feels just like silk.*
feeling – felt – have felt

4 when you cannot feel anything in part of your body

numb /nʌm/ [adj] if part of your body is **numb**, it does not feel anything, for example because it is very cold or because your blood is not reaching it: *My left hand was completely numb.*
go numb (=become numb) *It was so cold my fingers had gone numb.*

5 to feel happy/frightened/bored etc

feel/be /fiːl, biː/ [v]
be happy/frightened/bored etc *Most people are nervous about speaking to a large audience.*
feel happy/frightened/bored etc *I couldn't help feeling a little sad when he left.* | *You shouldn't feel guilty – it wasn't your fault.*
feeling – felt – have felt
being – was – have been

mood /muːd/ [n C] the way someone feels at a particular time, for example sad, happy, or angry: *She's a strange girl – her moods change very quickly.*
be in a good/bad etc mood (=be happy, angry etc at the present time) *Bill's in a good mood tonight, isn't he?*
put sb in a good/bad etc mood (=make someone feel happy, angry etc) *I was stuck in the traffic for hours, which put me in a bad mood all morning.*

state of mind /ˌsteɪt əv ˈmaɪnd/ [n singular] the way someone feels and thinks at a particular time, especially when they are upset or confused and this affects the way they behave: *Try to imagine this woman's state of mind at the time she committed the crime.*

6 a feeling of happiness, anger, fear etc

feeling /ˈfiːlɪŋ/ [n C] *It was a wonderful feeling to be home again.* | *Many men find it hard to express their feelings.*
a feeling of horror/sadness/rage etc *With a feeling of relief, I heard him coming home at last.* | *feelings of helplessness and terror*

emotion /ɪˈməʊʃən/ [n C/U] a strong feeling such as love, hate, or anger that is often difficult to control: *She stared at him, overcome by emotion.* | *Parents feel a mixture of emotions when their first child starts school.*

> ⚠️ Don't say 'an emotion of anger/love etc'. Say **a feeling of anger/love etc**.

a sense of /ə ˈsens ɒv/ a good or bad feeling, for example of loneliness or peace, that stays with you for a long time: *Children need to be given a sense of security.* | *After his wife died, he had a terrible sense of emptiness.*

7 someone who has strong feelings

emotional /ɪˈməʊʃənəl/ [adj] someone who is **emotional** has strong feelings and is not afraid to show them: *In an emotional speech, Nicky thanked everyone for helping her to win.*
get/become emotional *George got very emotional when it was time for us to leave.*

passionate /ˈpæʃənɪt/ [adj] use this about people who express very strong feelings of sexual love, or about their behaviour and relationships: *a passionate and beautiful woman* | *He pulled her to him in a passionate embrace.* | *a passionate love affair*
passionately [adv] *She kissed him passionately.*

8 something that makes you have strong feelings

moving /ˈmuːvɪŋ/ [adj] a **moving** experience or event makes you feel strong emotions such as sadness or sympathy: *She told a moving story of life in the refugee camp.* | *I found the funeral ceremony very moving.*

emotional /ɪˈməʊʃənəl/ [adj] an **emotional** situation or event makes people show strong feelings of sadness, happiness, anger etc: *It was a very emotional moment for all of us.*

sentimental /ˌsentɪˈmentl/ [adj] a **sentimental** story, film, song etc is intended to make you feel emotions of love or sadness, but it is too emotional and seems silly and false: *a sentimental children's story about a little orphan girl in 19th century London*

9 to feel that you know something

feel /fiːl/ [v T] to feel that you know something, but without understanding why you feel this
+(that) *She felt that something terrible was about to happen.* | *"What do you mean?" he asked, feeling that she wasn't telling him the whole truth.*
feeling – felt – have felt

instinct /ˈɪnstɪŋkt/ [n C/U] a natural ability to know what you should do without having to learn it or be told it: *Some instinct told her that she couldn't trust him.*
+for *Even a young animal has a strong instinct for self-preservation.*

intuition /ˌɪntjuˈɪʃən‖-tu-, -tju-/ [n U] the ability to understand or know things by using your feelings instead of considering the facts: *If you feel there's something odd about him you should trust your intuition.*

feeling /ˈfiːlɪŋ/ [n C] if you have a **feeling** that something is true or that something will happen, you feel sure about it, even though you do not know why
have a feeling (that) *I had a strange feeling that we would meet again.*
gut feeling INFORMAL (=a feeling that you are sure is right, even though

you cannot prove it) *Her gut feeling was that he was lying.*

FESTIVALS AND SPECIAL DAYS

➡ see Word Banks section

FEW

➡ see also **LITTLE/NOT MUCH, ONLY, LOT**

1 a small number

a few /ə 'fjuː/ [quantifier] a small number of people, things, or places etc: *Most of the trees were destroyed by fire, but a few survived.*
a few people/days/things/places etc *She's gone to stay with her father for a few days.* | *At that time of night, there were only a few cars on the road.* | *I invited a few friends around on Saturday night.*
a few of (=a small number from a larger group) *I've read a few of his books.* | *Only a few of the students can afford computers.*

⚠ Don't use **a few** with uncountable nouns like 'money', 'food', or 'water'. Use **a little**: *Would you like a little milk in your coffee?*

⚠ Don't confuse **few** (=not many or hardly any) and **a few** (=a small number): *He was a horrible man and he had few friends.* | *Let's invite a few friends for dinner.*

Formal or informal?
In formal English, **a few** may seem too vague or casual. You can use **a small number** instead: *A small number of the children have learning difficulties.*

Q one or two /ˌwʌn ɔːʳ 'tuː◂/ [quantifier] ESPECIALLY SPOKEN a small number of people or things: *"Do you have any R.E.M. records?" "Yes, one or two."*
one or two people/places/questions etc *We've had one or two*

problems with the car, but nothing serious. | There are one or two things I'd like to ask you about.*
+of *One or two of the girls started arguing with the teacher.*

rare /reəʳ/ [adj] something that is **rare** is not common and not many of them exist: *The library contains some of the rarest books in Europe.* | *a new law to prevent the export of rare birds*

a minority /ə maɪˈnɒrɪ̩till-mə̩ˈnɔː-/ [quantifier] a small number of the people within a larger group
+of *Nowadays only a minority of people leaving school have jobs to go to.*
a tiny/small minority *The Gaelic language is still spoken in Ireland, but only by a tiny minority.*

Q a couple /ə 'kʌpəl/ [quantifier] ESPECIALLY SPOKEN a small number, usually only two or three
+of *A couple of kids were playing in the street.* | *I saw her a couple of days ago.*

⚠ In British English **a couple** usually means 'two', but in American English it can mean any small number.

2 a very small number

few/very few /fjuː, ˌveri 'fjuː/ [quantifier] a very small number of people, things, or places etc: *At that time, few people had televisions.* | *Very few companies have women directors.*
+of *Very few of the students we asked said they were interested in politics.*

Formal or informal?
We usually say **very few**. On its own, **few** is formal.

not many /nɒt 'meni/ [quantifier] a smaller number than you expect or want: *"Were there many people in town?" "No, not many."*
not many people/places etc *There weren't many people at the party, but it was still fun.* | *Not many restaurants stay open after midnight.*
+of *Not many of my friends play musical instruments.*

hardly any /ˌhɑːʳdli 'eni/ [quantifier] almost no people or things – use this especially to show that you are surprised or disappointed by how few there are

hardly anyone/anything etc *We thought there would be lots of places to see, but there were hardly any.* | *Hardly anyone came to my party.*
+of *Hardly any of the people there even spoke to me.*

FIGHT

➡ look here for ...
• when people fight each other
• when you try hard to change something

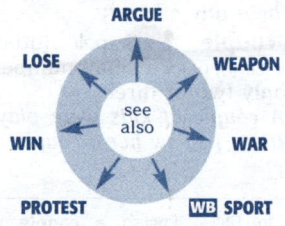

ARGUE
LOSE
WEAPON
see also
WIN
WAR
PROTEST
 SPORT

1 when people hit each other

fight /faɪt/ [v I/T] if people **fight**, or if one person **fights** another, they hit or kick each other in order to hurt each other: *Two men were fighting in the street outside.* | *Grant fought the other boy and won.*
+with *Billy had been fighting with some kids from another school.*
fight over sth (=fight because you disagree about something or because you both want to get something) *Two men in the bar began fighting over a game of cards.*
fighting – fought – have fought

fight /faɪt/ [n C] when people fight each other: *There was a fight after school yesterday – one of my friends got badly hurt.*
have a fight (with sb) *I didn't want to have a fight with him – he was much bigger than me.*
be in a fight *You look terrible – have you been in a fight?*
get into a fight (=become involved in a fight, often without intending to) *David was always getting into fights at school.*

start a fight/pick a fight (with sb) (=deliberately try to make someone fight you, by arguing with them or insulting them) *I walked into a bar, and this drunk tried to pick a fight with me.*

fighting /ˈfaɪtɪŋ/ [n U] when a lot of people fight each other in a public place: *There was fighting on the streets of Paris yesterday when police and demonstrators clashed.*
+between *Fighting between rival gangs resulted in the death of a teenage boy.*
fighting breaks out (=it starts suddenly) *Fighting broke out between English and Dutch football fans after the game.*

riot /ˈraɪət/ [n C] a violent fight in a public place, in which a lot of people attack the police and damage shops, cars etc, for example when they are protesting against the government or against a new law: *Their store got burned down in the LA riots.*

rioting [n U] when there are riots happening, especially for a long period: *Days of rioting left the city in chaos.*

rioter [n C] someone who takes part in a riot: *Police began shooting at the rioters.*

punch-up /ˈpʌntʃ ʌp/ [n C] BRITISH INFORMAL a fight between two or more people, especially because of an argument: *There was a big punch-up outside the club last night.*
get into a punch-up *They got into a punch-up over a girl.*
plural **punch-ups**

brawl /brɔːl/ [n C] a fight between a group of people in a public place, especially when they are drunk: *Several people were injured in a street brawl.* | *a drunken brawl*

> ⚠ **Brawl** is used especially in written English.

2 when people fight each other as a sport

fight /faɪt/ [v T] to take part in a sport in which you hit your opponent or try to throw him onto the ground: *Tyson*

fought Lewis for the World Heavyweight Championship. | *The two wrestlers have fought each other many times before.*
fighting – fought – have fought

fight /faɪt/ [*n* C] a game in which two people hit each other or try to throw each other onto the ground: *Are you going to watch the big fight tonight?*
+between *the fight between Joe Louis and Rocky Marciano*

boxing /ˈbɒksɪŋǁˈbɑːk-/ [*n* U] a sport in which two people wearing special thick gloves on their hands hit each other and try to make the other person fall onto the ground
boxing match (=a sporting event involving boxing)
boxer [*n* C] someone who does boxing

wrestling /ˈreslɪŋ/ [*n* U] a sport in which two people hold each other and try to throw each other onto the ground
wrestling match (=a sporting event involving wrestling)
wrestler [*n* C] someone who does wrestling

martial art /ˌmɑːʳʃəl ˈɑːʳt/ [*n* C] one of several sports that developed in Eastern Asia, in which you fight with your hands and feet: *Japanese martial arts such as Judo and Karate*

3 when soldiers try to kill other soldiers

➡ see also **WAR**

fight /faɪt/ [*v* I/T] if soldiers **fight**, they try to kill other soldiers in a war or battle
fight in a war/battle/campaign (=be a soldier in a war etc) *As a young man, he fought in the Spanish Civil War.*
fight for sb/sth (=fight to defend your country or ruler) *He died fighting for his country.*
+against *Your grandfather fought against the Russians on the Eastern Front.*
fighting – fought – have fought

> ⚠ Only use **fight** as a transitive verb [*v* T] when talking about two countries or armies that fight against each other: *The British and German armies fought each other in Northern France.*

fighting /ˈfaɪtɪŋ/ [*n* U] when soldiers fight during a war or battle: *There has been fighting in the capital, and around 1000 people have been killed.* | *The road was full of refugees trying to escape the fighting in Sudan.*

battle /ˈbætl/ [*n* C] a fight between two armies in one place: *After a long battle, the rebels were defeated.*
the Battle of Waterloo/Stalingrad etc *The Battle of the Somme started on the first of July, 1916.*

combat /ˈkɒmbæt, kəmˈbætǁkəmˈbæt, ˈkɑːmbæt/ [*n* U] FORMAL organized fighting between soldiers during a war
in combat *Her husband was killed in combat.*
unarmed combat (=without any weapons)

4 to try hard to stop something happening or to make something happen

fight /faɪt/ [*v* I/T] to try hard for a long time to stop something bad from happening or to make something good happen
fight sth (=fight to stop it from happening) *We are determined to fight drug abuse in schools.*
fight for freedom/independence/your rights etc (=fight in order to achieve something good) *Freedom of speech is something worth fighting for.*
fight to do sth *Local people have been fighting to save the forest.*
fight against terrorism/injustice/poverty (=fight to stop it from happening) *Amnesty is an organization that fights against torture and injustice.*
fighting – fought – have fought

campaign /kæmˈpeɪn/ [*v* I] to do things, such as writing to the government and organizing public meetings, because you want to change society or stop something bad from happening
+against *Greenpeace campaigned against nuclear weapons tests in the Pacific.*
+for *Disabled people have been campaigning for equal rights for years.*
campaign to do sth *The animal rights movement is campaigning to stop experiments on live animals.*

F

fight /faɪt/ [n singular] when people try hard for a long time to stop something bad from happening or to make something good happen
+**against** *New laws have been passed to help the police in their fight against organized crime.*
+**for** *women's fight for equality*

battle /'bætl/ [n C usually singular] when a person or group tries hard for a long time to change a bad situation, or deal with a problem in society
+**against** *her long battle against cancer* | *The President is fully committed to the battle against the drug traffickers.*

struggle /'strʌɡəl/ [n C usually singular] when people try for many years to get freedom, independence, or equal rights, and a lot of people suffer, are killed, or are put in prison
+**for** *Nkrumah led the people in their struggle for independence.*
+**against** *He devoted his life to the struggle against fascism and oppression.*

FILMS/MOVIES

➡ see Word Banks section

FIND

➡ see also **LOOK FOR**

1 to find someone or something that is lost

➡ opposite **LOSE**

find /faɪnd/ [v T] to find someone or something that you have lost: *I've looked everywhere but I can't find my sunglasses.* | *Have you found your passport yet?* | *The murder weapon was found in bushes nearby.*
finding – found – have found

🔍 **turn up** /ˌtɜːrn 'ʌp/ [phrasal verb I] ESPECIALLY SPOKEN if something that is lost **turns up**, someone finds it later in a place where they did not expect it to be: *Don't worry about your earrings – I'm sure they'll turn up.* | *Have those files turned up yet?*

trace /treɪs/ [v T] to find someone or something by a careful process of asking a lot of people for information *Police are anxious to trace the owner of a red Ford, which was seen near the crime scene.* | *Mr Philips is trying to trace his daughter, who has been missing for two months.*

2 to find something that you need or want

➡ opposite **LOSE 5**

find /faɪnd/ [v T] to find something that you need, such as a job or a place to live: *I'm only working here until I find something better to do.* | *It took us ages to find somewhere to park.* | *We need to find a new team coach.*
be easy/difficult/hard to find *Apartments like this one are hard to find.*
finding – found – have found

3 to find a place that you are trying to go to

find /faɪnd/ [v T] to find a place that you are trying to go to: *Did you manage to find the house OK?*
be difficult/easy/hard to find *The hotel is easy to find, and is situated right in the centre of the city.*
find your way (=find the right way to go) *The building was so big, I couldn't find my way out.* | *It was my first visit to New York, but I managed to find my way to the studio.*
finding – found – have found

4 to find something new and important

find /faɪnd/ [v T] to find important information, or think of a new way of doing something, after trying to do this for a long time: *Medical researchers are determined to find a cure for cancer.* | *They are trying to find cleaner ways of generating electricity.*
finding – found – have found

discover /dɪs'kʌvər/ [v T] to find an object, a substance, a place, information etc, which is important and which no one knew about before: *The planet Pluto was discovered in 1930.*

FIND OUT

to get information about something

➡ see also **SECRET**

1 to find out about something

find out /ˌfaɪnd ˈaʊt/ [*phrasal verb* I/T] to get information about something, either by chance or by deliberately trying to get it: *"Do you have these shoes in a size 39?" "I'm not sure – I'll just go and find out."*
find out what/where/whether etc *I'll go and find out which platform the train leaves from.* | *Dad was really mad at me when he found out where I'd been.*
+about *He's trying to find out about Japanese classes.* | *If she ever finds out about this, she'll kill me!*
find out sth/find sth out *Could you find out his address for me, please?* | *"John's been married twice." "How did you find that out?"*
+(that) *She found out that her husband was having an affair.*

discover /dɪsˈkʌvəʳ/ [*v* T] to find something out, especially something that is surprising or something that is difficult to find out: *Fire officers are still trying to discover the cause of the fire.*
+(that) *I began to learn the guitar, and discovered that I was pretty good at it.* | *She discovered there was over £1000 missing from the cash box.*
discover how/why/what etc *They never discovered who the murderer was.*

> **Formal or informal?**
> **Discover** is more formal than **find out** and is used more in writing than in speech. For example, you would usually say **I'll find out where the meeting is**, not '*I'll discover where the meeting is*'.

see /siː/ [*v* I/T] to get the information that you want by going somewhere to look, or by doing something and watching what happens: *"Is he ready yet?" "I don't know – I'll go and see."*
see if/whether *Sharon, see if there's any beer in the fridge.*

see how/where/what etc *Can you just see who's at the door?* | *Let's see what happens if we add some oil.*
seeing – saw – have seen

> **Formal or informal?**
> **See** is not used in formal scientific writing.

hear /hɪəʳ/ [*v* I/T] to be told about something: *"Nina quit her job." "Yes, so I heard."*
+about *He had heard about the accident from Helen.*
+(that) *We heard there was a party at Bill's place, so we all went over there.*
hear what/how/whether etc *When will you hear whether you've got the job?*
hearing – heard – have heard

> ⚠ You can say **I hear (that)** when you mean **I have heard (that)**: *I hear you're moving to Toronto.* (=someone told me that you are moving).

find /faɪnd/ [*v* T] to find out a fact or find out that something is true, especially by asking questions
+that *The survey found that more than 50% of teenagers had been offered drugs.*
finding – found – have found

2 to try to find out about a crime, accident etc

investigate /ɪnˈvestɪɡeɪt/ [*v* I/T] to try to find out the truth about a crime, an accident, or a problem, especially by using careful and thorough methods: *Police are investigating an explosion at a city store.* | *We sent our reporter, Michael Gore, to investigate.*

> ⚠ Don't say '*investigate into the problem*'. Say **investigate the problem**.

look into sth /ˌlʊk ˈɪntuː (sth)/ [*phrasal verb* T] if someone in an official position **looks into** a problem or bad situation, they try to find out more about it so that the situation can be improved: *The manager promised to look into my complaint.* | *Police are looking into the possibility that the bomb warning was a hoax.*

solve /sɒlv‖sɑːlv, sɔːlv/ [v T] if someone **solves** a crime or a mystery, they get all the information they need so that they can explain exactly what happened: *Detectives are trying to solve the murder of a young girl.*

3 the process of finding out about a crime, accident etc

investigation /ɪnˌvestɪˈgeɪʃən/ [n C] a process by which the police or other official organizations try to find out the truth about a crime or accident: *Following a major police investigation, two men have been arrested.*
+into *The investigation into the cause of the air crash is continuing.*
carry out an investigation (=investigate) *Prison officials are carrying out a full investigation after two prisoners escaped from a prison vehicle.*

inquiry (also **enquiry** BRITISH) /ɪnˈkwaɪəri‖ɪnˈkwaɪəri, ˈɪŋkwəri/ [n C] a series of official meetings at which people try to find out why something happened
+into *Local people are calling for an inquiry into the accident.*
hold an inquiry (=have an inquiry) *An inquiry will be held to discover why the school's educational record is so bad.*
plural **inquiries**

inquest /ˈɪŋkwest/ [n C] a legal process to find out the cause of someone's death: *The inquest heard that Mr Bovary was found hanging by a rope in his bedroom.*
+into *an inquest into the death of a 54-year-old woman*
hold an inquest (=have an inquest) *An inquest will be held into the actor's death.*

FINISH

➡ look here for ...
• to finish doing something
• when you have used all of something
➡ see also **STOP, END, READY/NOT READY**

1 to finish doing something or making something

finish /ˈfɪnɪʃ/ [v I/T] *Have you finished your homework yet?* | *After we had finished our lunch, we went out for a walk.* | *The builders say they will have finished by Friday.*
finish doing sth *Give me a call when you've finished unpacking.*
finish with sth (=stop using something so someone else can use it) *Can I have a look at your newspaper when you've finished with it?*

have done /həv ˈdʌn/ ESPECIALLY SPOKEN if you **have done** a piece of work, you have finished doing it: *Ask Jane if she's done that essay yet.* | *I've done all the dishes.*

complete /kəmˈpliːt/ [v T] to finish making something, writing something, or doing something that takes a long time to finish: *The building is likely to be completed in two years' time.* | *Students who have completed the course usually find it fairly easy to find jobs.*

finalize (also **finalise** BRITISH) /ˈfaɪnəlaɪz/ [v T] to finish arranging a plan, a business deal etc, by doing the last few things that need to be done: *Mr Samuels is flying to Detroit to finalize the details and sign the contract.* | *We still haven't finalized all the arrangements for the wedding.*

get it over with /get ɪt ˈəʊvəʳ wɪð/ SPOKEN to do something that you have to do but do not want to do, so that you will not have to worry about it any more: *I hate going to the dentist, but I suppose I'd better go and get it over with.*

2 something that is finished

finished /ˈfɪnɪʃt/ [adj] something that is **finished** has all been done, made, or completed in the way you wanted: *Can I read your assignment when it's finished?*
finished product/version (=finished and containing all its final details or features) *Looking at the finished product, you wouldn't know it was made from recycled paper.*

be over /biː ˈəʊvəʳ/ if an event or activity **is over**, it has completely ended and nothing more is going to happen: *By the time we arrived, the party was already over.*
be all over *The game should be all over by 5 o'clock.*

◯ **be done** /biː ˈdʌn/ ESPECIALLY SPOKEN if something **is done**, you have finished doing it: *We'll send you a bill when the repairs are done.*

complete /kəmˈpliːt/ [adj] not before noun] use this about plans, arrangements, or activities with several different stages that are now all finished: *Building work should be complete in 20 weeks.* | *When your training is complete you will receive a special certificate.*

come to an end /ˌkʌm tu ən ˈend/ to finally end – use this about a period of time, a situation, or an activity that has continued for a long time: *It seemed as though the winter would never come to an end.* | *We both knew really that our marriage had come to an end.*

be at an end /biː ət ən ˈend/ FORMAL if a meeting, conversation etc **is at an end**, it has ended because someone wanted it to end: *She got up to indicate that the interview was at an end.* | *"I think this conversation is at an end," he said.*

3 something that is not finished

not finished/unfinished /nɒt ˈfɪnɪʃt, ʌnˈfɪnɪʃt/ [adj] *On the desk was an unfinished letter to his mother.* | *The new swimming pool wasn't finished last time I drove past.*

incomplete /ˌɪnkəmˈpliːt/ [adj] not finished, because not all of the work has been done on something, or

because it does not have all the parts that it should have: *The excavation of the tunnel is still incomplete.* | *incomplete sentences*

> **Formal or informal?**
>
> **Incomplete** and **unfinished** are more formal than **not finished**.

4 to finish a performance/lesson/ speech etc

finish/end /ˈfɪnɪʃ, end/ [v T] to finish a performance, lesson, speech etc that you are giving: *I finished my speech and sat down.* | *Our history teacher never ends her classes on time.*
finish/end sth with sth *He finished his lecture with a quotation from Shakespeare.*
finish/end sth by doing sth *I thought we'd end the evening by singing that old Irish favourite 'Danny Boy'.*

round off /ˌraʊnd ˈɒf‖-ˈɔːf/ [phrasal verb T] to do something as a way of ending what you are doing in a special or suitable way
round off sth *To round off National Peace Week, a concert was organized in the park.*
round sth off with sth *They rounded the day off with a barbecue on the beach.*

5 to use all of something

finish /ˈfɪnɪʃ/ [v T] to eat or drink all of something, so that there is none left: *The kids have finished all the ice-cream.*
◯ **be finished** ESPECIALLY SPOKEN (=when all of something has been used) *The butter's all finished. Can you buy some more?*

use up /ˌjuːz ˈʌp/ [phrasal verb T] to use all of something, especially when it is difficult or impossible to get more of it
use up sth *By 2100 we will probably have used up all our supplies of natural gas.*
use sth up *He'd used all his savings up, and had to sell his house.*

◯ **be all gone** /biː ˌɔːl ˈɡɒn‖-ˈɡɔːn/ ESPECIALLY SPOKEN if something **is all**

gone, there is none of it left: *"Are there any cookies left?" "No, they're all gone."*

run out /ˌrʌn 'aʊt/ [*phrasal verb* I] if something that you need **runs out**, there is none of it left because it has all been used; if you **run out of** something that you need, there is none of it left: *I was in a phone box and my money ran out before I'd finished.* | *We ran out of gas on the freeway last night.*

FIRE

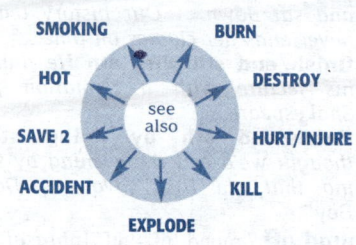

SMOKING
BURN
HOT
DESTROY
see also
SAVE 2
HURT/INJURE
ACCIDENT
KILL
EXPLODE

 Don't say 'do you have fire?' if you want to light a cigarette. Say **do you have a light?**

1 a fire that damages a building, forest etc

fire /faɪəʳ/ [*n* C/U] *30 people died in a fire in Chicago last night.* | *The fire quickly spread throughout the building.* | *a raging fire* (=continuing with great force)
fire breaks out (=it starts suddenly) *A fire broke out in the hotel kitchen.*
start a fire *The fire was started by an electrical fault.*
forest fire *A huge forest fire is burning out of control in the south of France.*

blaze /bleɪz/ [*n* singular] a large and dangerous fire that burns very strongly: *Firefighters struggled to control the blaze at a huge chemical plant.* | *The church was completely destroyed in the blaze.*

⚠ **Blaze** is used especially in news reports.

flames /fleɪmz/ [*n* plural] the bright parts of a fire that you see burning in the air: *I saw flames coming from the engine.*

2 when something is burning and being damaged by fire

be on fire /biː ɒn 'faɪəʳ/ if something **is on fire**, it is burning and being damaged by fire: *One of the plane's engines was on fire.* | *I can smell smoke. Something must be on fire.*

be in flames/be ablaze /biː ɪn 'fleɪmz, biː əˈbleɪz/ if something **is in flames** or **is ablaze**, it is burning strongly and being very badly damaged by fire: *The ship was ablaze.* | *Within minutes the whole school was in flames.*

⚠ **Be in flames** and **be ablaze** are used especially in stories and news reports.

3 a fire for making you warm, for cooking, or for burning unwanted things

fire /faɪəʳ/ [*n* C] *She sat down in front of the fire and read a book.*
log/coal fire *There's something very comforting about a real log fire.*
make a fire (=collect things you need for a fire) *The children collected some wood to make a fire.*
light a fire (=make a fire start burning) *Where are the matches? I need to light the fire.*

bonfire /ˈbɒnfaɪəʳ‖ˈbɑːn-/ [*n* C] a large outdoor fire for burning dead leaves, wood, or things you do not need
build/make a bonfire *They piled up all the branches and made a big bonfire.*

campfire /ˈkæmpfaɪəʳ/
[n C] a fire that
people make out-
doors when they are
camping, for keeping
warm and for cook-
ing: *In the evening,
we all sat around the
campfire telling
stories.*

campfire

4 to make something start burning

set fire to sth /set ˈfaɪəʳ tuː (sth)/ to
make something start to burn, so that
it gets damaged: *Vandals set fire to a
disused warehouse near the docks last
night.* | *Don't put up the barbecue
there – you'll set fire to the trees.*

light /laɪt/ [v T]
light a cigarette/fire/candle etc to
make a cigarette, fire etc start to
burn: *Ricky sat down and lit a
cigarette.* | *We searched around for
twigs and fallen branches, so we could
light a fire.*
lighting – lit – have lit

arson /ˈɑːʳsən/ [n U] the crime of
deliberately starting a fire in order to
damage a building: *Police are treating
the fire as a case of arson.*

5 to stop a fire

put out /ˌpʊt ˈaʊt/ [phrasal verb T] to
make a fire stop burning
put out the fire/the blaze *It took
firefighters four hours to put out the
blaze.*
put sth out *She threw sand on the fire
to put it out.*

extinguish /ɪkˈstɪŋgwɪʃ/ [v T] FORMAL to
stop a fire burning: *He managed to
extinguish the flames with his coat.*

blow out /ˌbləʊ ˈaʊt/ [phrasal verb T] to
make a flame or fire stop burning by
blowing on it
blow out a candle/a match/a fire
*He blew out the candle and went to
sleep.*
blow sth out *We tried to light a fire
but the wind kept blowing it out.*

6 people whose job is to stop fires

firefighter /ˈfaɪəʳˌfaɪtəʳ/ [n C] someone
whose job is to stop fires burning:
*Firefighters rescued the children, who
were trapped in an upstairs room.*

fireman /ˈfaɪəʳmən/ [n C] a man whose
job is to stop fires burning
plural **firemen**

the fire brigade BRITISH **the fire
department** AMERICAN /ðə ˈfaɪəʳ
brɪˌgeɪd, ðə ˈfaɪəʳ dɪˌpɑːʳtmənt/ [n
singular] the organization in a town
or area that works to prevent fires
and to stop fires burning: *The City
Fire Department recommends that
every home should have a smoke
alarm.*

fire engine (also **fire truck** AMERICAN)
/ˈfaɪər ˌendʒən, ˈfaɪəʳ trʌk/ [n C] a
special vehicle that carries firefighters and their equipment, including
the equipment used to shoot water at
a fire

FIRST

➡ opposite **LAST**
➡ see also **BEGINNING, START**

1 before other things or people

first /fɜːʳst/ [adj] before everyone or
everything else: *Laurie's name was
first on the list.* | *I still remember my
first day of school.* | *She had her first
baby in 1984.* | *I only read the first
chapter.* | *The first thing I noticed was
that the front door was open.*
the first person to do sth *Yuri
Gagarin was the first man to travel into
space.*

first /fɜːʳst/ [adv] before you do any
other things, or before anything else
happens: *I always read the sports page
of the newspaper first.* | *Shall we go
out now, or do you want to eat first?* |
*He's had a bad year. First he lost his
job, then his girlfriend left him.*
first of all (=first, before a lot of
other things) *First of all, fry the
onions.*

be first/come first /biː ˈfɜːᵣst, ˌkʌm ˈfɜːᵣst/ to be the person who wins a race or a competition: *Joyner came first in the 200 metres.*

original /əˈrɪdʒɪnəl, -dʒənəl/ [adj only before noun] before all the others – use this about something that existed at the beginning, especially before a lot of things were changed: *The house still has its original stone floors.* | *Our original plan had been to go camping, but it was pouring with rain.*

initial /ɪˈnɪʃəl/ [adj only before noun] use this to talk about what happened at the beginning or how someone felt at the beginning, especially when this changes later
initial reaction/response/feeling *My initial reaction was one of complete disbelief.*
initial difficulties/problems/set-backs *Initial difficulties with the computer system were soon fixed.*

> **Formal or informal?**
> **Initial** is used in writing and in formal spoken English.

2 to do something for the first time

first /fɜːᵣst/ [adv] for the first time – use this before a verb: *I first met Mari in 1975.* | *Howard first went to Egypt when he was a student.*

the first time /ðə ˌfɜːᵣst ˈtaɪm/ use this to say what happened when you did something that you had never done before
+(that) *The first time I went on a plane I was really nervous.* | *It was the first time that she had seen her mother cry.*

3 the first thing you want to say or ask

firstly/first/first of all /ˈfɜːᵣstli, fɜːᵣst, ˌfɜːᵣst əv ˈɔːl/ [adv] used to say that the fact or reason that you are going to mention is the first one and will be followed by others: *First of all I'd like to thank you very much for all the lovely presents.* | *I wanted to change schools, firstly because I didn't like the*

teacher and secondly because it was too far away.

FLAT/NOT FLAT

1 flat

flat /flæt/ [adj] a place that is **flat** has no hills or mountains; a surface that is **flat** is not sloping or has no raised parts: *The countryside around Cambridge is very flat and you can see for miles.* | *The houses all had flat roofs.* | *The plant's broad, flat leaves are used for serving food.* | *We could see the moon's reflection in the perfectly flat surface of the lake.*
flat – flatter – flattest

level /ˈlevəl/ [adj] a surface or area that is **level** does not slope in any direction, so every part of it is at the same height: *He looked for a strip of level ground where he could land the plane.* | *Make sure the shelves are level.*

smooth /smuːð/ [adj] a **smooth** surface feels completely flat and has no rough or raised parts, especially in a way that is pleasant and attractive: *The marble table felt smooth and cold against her arm.* | *She's got lovely smooth skin.*

even /ˈiːvən/ [adj] a surface such as a floor or road that is **even** is completely flat and all of it is the same level: *You need an even surface to work on.* | *The floor must be completely even before we lay the tiles.*

horizontal /ˌhɒrɪˈzɒntl‖ˌhɑːrɪˈzɑːntl/ [adj] a **horizontal** line, position, or surface is straight, flat, and not sloping: *a T-shirt with red and blue horizontal stripes* | *horizontal layers of rock* | *The wine bottles should be kept in a horizontal position.*

2 to make something flat

roll sth flat/press sth flat/squash sth flat etc /ˌrəʊl (sth) ˈflæt, ˌpres (sth) ˈflæt, ˌskwɒʃ (sth) ˈflæt‖-ˌskwɔːʃ-/ to make something flat by rolling it, pressing it etc: *Roll the pastry flat and cut out two 8-inch circles.* | *A car ran over the ball and squashed it flat.*

flatten /ˈflætn/ [v T] to make something flat, especially something that is not usually flat: *The wind and rain had flattened the crops.* | *You'll need to flatten the ground before you plant seeds.*

3 not flat

rough /rʌf/ [adj] not flat – use this about roads, walls, areas of land etc where the surface is not smooth because there are a lot of stones or small raised parts: *A rough dirt track led up to the farm.* | *rough mountain paths* | *the rough stone walls of the old castle*

bumpy /ˈbʌmpi/ [adj] a **bumpy** road, path, or area of land has a lot of holes and raised parts in it: *Neal drove the last mile down the bumpy road towards the highway.* | *The field was too bumpy to play football on.*
bumpy – bumpier – bumpiest

bump /bʌmp/ [n C] a small raised area that sticks up from the surface of something such as a road or piece of land: *The car rattled as we went over another bump in the road.*

uneven /ʌnˈiːvən/ [adj] an **uneven** surface has areas that are not flat or not all at the same level: *Be careful here – the sidewalk's very uneven.* | *His teeth were yellow and uneven.*

sloping /ˈsləʊpɪŋ/ [adj] something that is **sloping** is higher at one end than at the other: *A gently sloping bank led down to the stream.* | *houses with sloping roofs*

FOLD

to bend paper, cloth etc so that one part covers another

1 to fold something

fold /fəʊld/ [v T] to bend a piece of paper or cloth, so that one part of it covers another: *She folded her clothes and put them on the chair.*
fold sth in two/in half (=across the middle) *I folded the letter in half and slipped it into an envelope.*
fold sth into a square/triangle (=so

that it has the shape of a square or triangle) *The napkins were folded into neat triangles.*
folded [adj] *She was carrying a pile of folded towels.*

fold up /ˌfəʊld ˈʌp/ [phrasal verb T] to fold something, usually several times, in order to make it into a smaller or neater shape
fold up sth *The boy was having great trouble folding up his map.*
fold sth up *Don't just leave your clothes on the floor like that – fold them up.*

folding /ˈfəʊldɪŋ/ [adj only before noun] a **folding** bed, knife, bicycle etc is one that is specially designed so that it can be folded up and easily carried or stored: *I had to sleep on a folding bed in the living room.*

2 to open something that is folded

unfold /ʌnˈfəʊld/ [v T] *He unfolded the blanket and placed it around her shoulders.* | *We watched as she took out the letter and slowly unfolded it.*

FOLLOW

➡ if you mean 'happening after something else', go to **AFTER**

follow /ˈfɒləʊ‖ˈfɑː-/ [v I/T] to walk, drive, run etc behind someone else, going in the same direction as them: *Follow me and I'll show you where the library is.* | *You drive on ahead and I'll follow.* | *I had a horrible feeling that I was being followed.*
follow sb around (=follow someone wherever they go) *Journalists followed the couple around everywhere.*
followed by sb *The woman entered the room, followed by three little children.*
follow sb out/down/across etc *She didn't notice that Jack had followed her into the kitchen.*

run after sb/go after sb /ˌrʌn ˈɑːftər (sb), ˌgəʊ ˈɑːftər (sb)‖-ˈæf-/ [phrasal verb T] to run or walk quickly behind someone who is moving away from you, in order to catch them or talk to them: *A group of little boys ran after him to ask for his autograph.*

chase

chase /tʃeɪs/ [v I/T] to run after someone who is trying to escape from you, in order to catch them
chase sb across/up/down etc *The farmer chased the children across the field.*
+after *Two men chased after the robbers but they managed to escape.*

pursue /pəˈsjuː‖-ˈsuː/ [v T] FORMAL to follow someone in a very determined way in order to catch them: *Police pursued the gunman into an abandoned building.* | *Kim pursued him down the street, but he had already gone.*

> ⚠ **Pursue** is used especially in stories and news reports.

tail

tail /teɪl/ [v T] INFORMAL to secretly follow someone in order to find out where they are going or what they are doing: *He hired a private detective to tail her.* | *Do you think that police car is tailing us?*

FOOD

➡ see Word Banks section

FORBID

to tell someone that they must not do something

➡ opposite **LET**

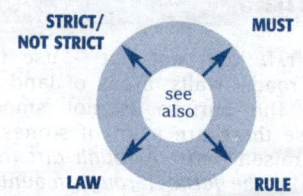

1   to forbid something

not let/not allow /nɒt ˈlet, nɒt əˈlaʊ/ to say that someone must not do something, and to stop them doing it
not let sb do sth *My parents won't let me stay out after 11 o'clock.*
not allow sb to do sth *They do not allow anyone to enter the country without a visa.*
not allow sth *Joan and Bill don't allow smoking in their house.*

> **Formal or informal?**
> **Not allow** is more formal than **not let**.

tell sb not to do sth /ˌtel (sb)nɒt tə ˈduː (sth)/ to tell someone that they should not do something, especially because it is dangerous or harmful: *My mother always told us not to talk to strangers.* | *His doctor told him not to drink any alcohol for six weeks.*

forbid /fəˈbɪd/ [v T] FORMAL if a person or rule **forbids** something, they state clearly and firmly that it must not be done: *Their religion forbids the eating of pork.*
forbid sb to do sth *As part of his punishment, he was forbidden to leave the house.*
forbidding – forbade – have forbidden

ban /bæn/ [v T] to officially forbid something – use this about activities that are forbidden by laws or agreements, especially because they are dangerous: *Many doctors now say that boxing should be banned.* | *a new* *international treaty banning all nuclear tests*

banning – banned – have banned

ban /bæn/ [n C] an official order or rule that forbids something, based on a law or a government decision

+on *a ban on smoking in restaurants*

a total/complete ban *The government is considering a total ban on the sale of handguns.*

impose a ban (=ban something) *A ban has been imposed on the hunting and killing of whales.*

lift a ban (=stop having a ban) *The school refused to lift the ban on pupils wearing jewellery.*

2 to forbid someone to take part in an activity or sport

suspend /sə'spend/ [v T] to remove someone from their job or their school for a limited period of time because they have done something wrong: *Martinez was suspended for a week because he attacked another student.*

suspend sb for doing sth *Three police officers have been suspended for accepting bribes.*

ban /bæn/ [v T] to officially state that someone is not allowed to do something, especially as a punishment for something bad they have done

ban sb from doing sth *She was banned from driving for 6 months.* | *For many years, the Olympic Committee banned South Africans from taking part in the Games.*

banning – banned – have banned

disqualify /dɪs'kwɒlᵻfaɪ‖-'kwɑː-/ [v T] to officially state that someone is no longer allowed to take part in a competition or activity, because they have broken a rule

disqualify sb from sth *Three athletes were disqualified from the championships after failing drugs tests.*

disqualify sb from doing sth *He was fined £500, and disqualified from holding any political office.*

disqualifying – disqualified – have disqualified

3 when you are not allowed to do something

not allowed /nɒt ə'laʊd/ [adj not before noun] if someone is **not allowed** to do something, a person or rule says that they must not do it

sb is not allowed to do sth *We're not allowed to wear jewellery at school.* | *She wasn't allowed to go out with boys until she was 16.*

sth is not allowed *Smoking is not allowed anywhere in the building.*

forbidden /fə'bɪdn/ [adj] if something is **forbidden** or someone is **forbidden** to do something, there is a rule which says that they must not do it

sth is forbidden *The use of calculators in the examination room is forbidden.*

sb is forbidden to do sth *Prisoners were forbidden to speak to each other while they were working.*

strictly forbidden *Drinking alcohol is strictly forbidden in Muslim countries.*

> **Formal or informal?**
> **Forbidden** is more formal than **not allowed**.

can't /kɑːnt‖kænt/ ESPECIALLY SPOKEN if you **can't** do something, you are not allowed to do it: *You can't park here.* | *My dad says I can't go out tonight.*

no smoking/no parking etc /nəʊ 'sməʊkɪŋ, nəʊ 'pɑː'kɪŋ (etc)/ WRITTEN used on signs and notices to say that you are not allowed to smoke, park your car etc: *There were 'no smoking' signs in every room.* | *Beside the lake was a large notice saying 'No Fishing'.*

prohibited /prə'hɪbᵻtᵻd‖prəʊ-/ [adj] ESPECIALLY WRITTEN something that is **prohibited** is forbidden by a law or rule – used especially on official notices and warnings: *Cars are prohibited in the city centre.* | *Cameras are prohibited inside the cathedral.*

FORCE SB TO DO STH

to make someone do something that they do not want to do

➡ see also **MUST**

force /fɔːʳs/ [*v* T] *You didn't have to come with us – nobody forced you.*
force sb to do sth *Government troops forced the rebels to surrender.*
force sb into doing sth *Her parents are trying to force her into marrying him.*

make /meɪk/ [*v* T] to force someone to do something: *I didn't want to go but my dad made me.*
make sb do sth *She made me promise never to mention the subject again.*
be made to do sth *We were made to work really hard.*
making – made – have made

Formal or informal?
Make is less formal than **force**.

put pressure on sb /ˌpʊt ˈpreʃər ɒn (sb)/ to keep trying to persuade someone to do something, for example by saying that it is their duty or that it will help other people
put pressure on sb to do sth *Our parents keep putting pressure on us to get married.*

compel /kəmˈpel/ [*v* T] FORMAL to make someone do something by using force or official power
compel sb to do sth *The law compels companies to provide health insurance.*
compelling – compelled – have compelled

pressure (also **pressurize/pressurise** BRITISH) /ˈpreʃəʳ, ˈpreʃəraɪz/ [*v* T] to make someone do something by persuading them very strongly and making them feel that they ought to do it
pressure/pressurize sb into doing sth *Don't let them pressure you into buying something you don't need.* | *Many children are pressurized into studying subjects that they are not interested in.*

FOREIGN

➡ see also **FROM, COUNTRY**

1 not from your own country

foreign /ˈfɒrɪ̆n‖ˈfɔː-, ˈfɑː-/ [*adj*] not from your own country or connected with your own country: *They are learning English as a Foreign Language.* | *Britain's car industry faces a lot of competition from foreign companies.*
foreign currency (=the money a foreign country uses) *The bank can provide you with enough foreign currency for the trip.*

⚠ It is not polite to call people 'foreign'. It is better to say they are **from abroad** or to say which country they are from.

overseas /ˌəʊvəʳˈsiːz◂/ [*adj* only before noun] from or connected with a foreign country, especially one that is a long way away
overseas student/visitor etc *The university has a lot of overseas students.* | *He was one of the first overseas players to join an English club.*
overseas trade/travel/trip/business *There has been an increase in overseas trade during the last year.*

from abroad /frəm əˈbrɔːd/ from another country or from other countries: *A lot of the doctors here are from abroad.* | *goods imported from abroad*

2 someone from a different country

foreigner /ˈfɒrɪ̆nəʳ‖ˈfɔː-, ˈfɑː-/ [*n* C] someone who comes from another country: *Any foreigner wishing to work in this country must have a work permit.* | *Saleem felt that people were suspicious of him because he was a foreigner.*

⚠ Many people think it is rude to call someone a **foreigner**, because this can sometimes mean they are strange or not welcome in your country.

immigrant /'ɪmⁱgrənt/ [n C] someone who has left their own country and now lives permanently in another: *Many of the immigrants in France come from North Africa.*
illegal immigrant (=someone who does not have official permission to live and work in another country)

expatriate /eksˈpætriət, -trieɪt‖eksˈpeɪ-/ [n C] someone who lives in a country they were not born in, for example because they have a job there or enjoy living there: *British expatriates living in Spain*

> You can also use **expatriate** before a noun, like an adjective: *There are a lot of expatriate workers living in Dubai.*

3 in or to a different country

abroad /əˈbrɔːd/ [adv] in or to a foreign country: *Katya will make her first trip abroad next month, to Japan.*
go/live/work etc abroad *Mike is planning on studying abroad for a year.*
be abroad *Mr Harris is abroad on business this week.*

> Don't say 'he's gone to abroad'. Just say **he's gone abroad**.

overseas /ˌəʊvəʳˈsiːz◂/ [adv] in or to a foreign country, especially a country that is a long distance across an ocean from your own: *The wood is shipped overseas from ports in the north west.*
go/work/travel etc overseas *Douglas travelled overseas a lot when he was in the army.*

> Don't say 'to overseas'. Just say **overseas**.

emigrate /'emⁱgreɪt/ [v I] to leave your own country in order to live permanently in another country
+to *Jenny and Tim emigrated to Australia in 1958.*

FORGET

➡ opposite **REMEMBER**

1 to forget something

forget /fəʳˈget/ [v I/T] to no longer remember information, something that happened in the past, or something that you must do: *I'm sorry, I've forgotten your name.* | *It was an experience she would never forget.* | *It's his birthday tomorrow. I hope you haven't forgotten.*
forget what/where/how etc *She's forgotten where she parked the car.*
+(that) *We forgot that it was Sunday and the banks would be closed.*
forget to do sth (=not do something because you forget) *I forgot to ask her for her phone number.*
+about *Tom had forgotten about Tanya coming to stay.*
completely forget *I completely forgot about the meeting.*
I forget (=I have forgotten) *She had this boyfriend – I forget his name – who was an actor.*
forgetting – forgot – have forgotten

don't remember/can't remember /ˌdəʊnt rɪˈmembəʳ, ˌkɑːnt rɪˈmembəʳ‖ ˌkænt-/ [v I/T] to not be able to remember something that you want to remember: *"How did you get home after the party?" " I can't remember."* | *I was going to phone you, but I couldn't remember your number.*
not remember doing sth *I don't remember inviting her.*
+what/where/how etc *I don't remember exactly what happened.*

○ **it's on the tip of my tongue** /ɪts ɒn ðə ˌtɪp əv maɪ ˈtʌŋ/ SPOKEN use this to say that you know a name or word, but you are having difficulty remembering it at that moment: *That place we visited in Paris, what's it called? It's on the tip of my tongue...Oh yes, La Geode.*

your mind goes blank /jɔːʳ ˌmaɪnd gəʊz ˈblæŋk/ INFORMAL if **your mind goes blank**, you are suddenly unable to remember something at a time when you need to: *That's... Oh, my mind's* *gone blank – I can't remember her name. | When she saw the questions in the test her mind just went totally blank.*

2 to forget to bring something

forget /fər'get/ [v T] to not bring something that you intended to bring, because you did not think of it: *Michael was at the airport before he realized he'd forgotten his passport. | How stupid of me! I forgot your photos – I must have left them on my desk.*
forgetting – forgot – have forgotten

leave /liːv/ [v T] to forget to take something with you when you leave: *I can't find my coat – I must have left it at work.*
leave sth behind *Oh hell! I think I left my credit card behind at the restaurant.*

3 to try to forget something

put sth out of your mind /ˌpʊt (sth) aʊt əv jɔːr 'maɪnd/ to make yourself stop thinking about something that makes you angry or sad: *She tried to put all thoughts of revenge out of her mind. | It's time to put her out of your mind and find a new girlfriend.*

take your mind off sth /ˌteɪk jɔːr 'maɪnd ɒf (sth)/ if an activity **takes your mind off** a worrying problem, it makes you forget about it for a short time: *Joe suggested a game of cards to take my mind off things. | I need something to take my mind off work.*

4 someone who often forgets things

have a bad memory /hæv ə ˌbæd 'meməri/ to not be good at remembering facts or information: *"We've met once before. At David's place." "Oh, I'm sorry – I have such a bad memory."* **+for** *I have a bad memory for names.*

forgetful /fər'getfəl/ [adj] someone who is **forgetful** often forgets things, especially things that they have to do: *My grandfather's getting so forgetful – I have to remind him to take his medication. | Some forgetful person had left the door unlocked.*

absent-minded /ˌæbsənt 'maɪndɪd/ [adj] someone who is **absent-minded** often forgets things because they are thinking about other things: *He's a brilliant scientist but hopelessly absent-minded.*

have a memory like a sieve /hæv ə ˌmeməri laɪk ə 'sɪv/ INFORMAL to not be able to remember facts or information, even for a short time: *You'd better remind him about the party – he has a memory like a sieve!*

FORGIVE

to stop being angry with someone for something bad they have done

➡ see also **SORRY**

1 to forgive someone

forgive /fər'gɪv/ [v I/T] to stop being angry with someone for something bad they have done, especially when they have upset you or done something unkind: *Try to forgive him – he didn't mean to hurt you. | Hugh found his wife's behaviour hard to forgive.*
forgive sb for sth *He had lied to me, and I couldn't forgive him for that.*
forgive and forget (=forgive someone for something, and behave as if they had never done it) *He's the type of person who finds it hard to forgive and forget.*
forgiving – forgave – have forgiven

> ⚠ Don't say 'I am forgiving you'. Say **I forgive you**.

excuse /ɪk'skjuːz/ [v T] to forgive something that someone has done, usually something that is not seriously wrong: *Please excuse my handwriting – I'm in a hurry. | He's always late, and I don't see why we should excuse it.*

> ⚠ You can politely ask a visitor to **excuse** something such as the state of your room when it is not quite the way it should be: *Come in – and please excuse the mess.*

2 what you say to tell someone that you forgive them

○ **that's all right/that's OK** /,ðæts ɔːl
'raɪt, ,ðæts əʊ'keɪ/ SPOKEN say this when
someone says they are sorry for
something they did: *"Sorry I didn't
phone you last week." "That's OK – I
know how busy you've been." | "I must
apologize for keeping you waiting so
long." "That's all right."*

○ **forget it** /fəˈget ɪt/ SPOKEN INFORMAL
say this to tell someone that you do
not blame them for something, and
you do not want them to mention it
again: *"I feel so bad about upsetting
your plans." "Oh, forget it, it really
doesn't matter."*

> **Formal or informal?**
> **That's OK** and **forget it** are more informal
> than **that's all right**.

3 when something is too bad to be forgiven

unforgivable/unforgiveable
/,ʌnfəˈgɪvəbəl◂/ [adj] behaviour that is
unforgivable is so bad that you cannot forgive it: *I think the way she
spoke to her mother was unforgivable.*

4 to refuse to forgive someone

never forgive /,nevəʳ fəˈgɪv/ to refuse
to forgive someone, because they
have done something very bad
never forgive sb for sth *She never
really forgave Roy for what he said.*
never forgive yourself *I'd never
forgive myself if anything happened to
the children while I was out.*

bear a grudge /,beər ə 'grʌdʒ/ to
continue to feel angry with someone
for a long time because they treated
you badly in the past
+against *Can you think of anyone who
might bear a grudge against you?*

hold it against sb /,həʊld ɪt əˈgenst (sb)/
to dislike someone because of
something they did in the past, even
though it is no longer important:
*Look, he made one mistake – you can't
hold it against him for the rest of his
life.*

FREE

1 something that costs no money

➡ look here for ...
　• not costing any money
　• able to do what you want
　• not in prison

free /friː/ [adj] something that is **free**
does not cost any money: *Parking is
free after 6 p.m. | "How much is it to
get into the concert?" "Oh, I think it's
free." | There's a free gift with this
month's magazine.*

cost nothing/not cost anything /,kɒst
'nʌθɪŋ, ,nɒt kɒst 'eniθɪŋǁ,kɔːst-/ to be
free, especially when this is unusual:
*Luckily I was insured, so the treatment
didn't cost anything. | It costs nothing
to call the emergency number.*

freebie /'friːbi/ [n C] INFORMAL
something that a company gives free
with its products or services, or gives
to the people it employs: *The kids love
going on planes because of all the
freebies they get.*
on a freebie (=a free trip somewhere
or a free holiday that you are given)
*The company paid for us all to go on a
freebie!*

2 when you can do something or get something without paying

free /friː/ [adv] if you do or get
something free, you do not have to
pay: *If you buy one pair of glasses,
we'll give you another pair completely
free. | You can get into EuroDisney free
with this special voucher.*

for nothing/for free /fəʳ 'nʌθɪŋ, fəʳ 'friː/
INFORMAL without having to pay for
something that you would normally
have to pay for, or without asking for

payment: *My Dad owns the club, so we can get in for nothing.* (=without paying) | *I got lots of extra software for free with my new computer.* (=without paying) | *He offered to fix the car for nothing.* (=without being paid)

free of charge /ˌfriː əv ˈtʃɑːᵈdʒ/ free – used especially in advertisements or written information telling you that something is free: *The leaflets are available free of charge at the tourist office.* | *When you've chosen your gift, we will wrap it for you free of charge.*

no charge /ˌnəʊ ˈtʃɑːᵈdʒ/ if there is **no charge** for a service that someone provides, you do not have to pay for it: *You can leave your car at the hotel – there's no charge.*
+for *There is no charge for cashing these traveller's cheques.*

3 allowed to do what you want

free /friː/ [*adj*] allowed to do whatever you want, without being controlled or restricted: *I had just left home, and was enjoying the feeling of being free and independent at last.* | *Bulgaria's first free elections were held in 1990.*
free to do sth *You are free to come and go as you like.*
free speech (=the right to say or write what you want without the police or government stopping you) *All Americans have the right to free speech.*
a free press (=when newspapers are not controlled by the government)

freedom /ˈfriːdəm/ [*n* U] the right to do what you want without being controlled or restricted: *There was a huge party at the Berlin Wall as East Germans celebrated their freedom.*
freedom to do sth *People here have the freedom to practise whatever religion they like.*
freedom of speech/expression (=the right to say or write what you want without the police or government stopping you)

liberty /ˈlɪbəᵈti/ [*n* U] FORMAL a person's legal right to do what they want, without being unfairly controlled by the government: *They were fighting for liberty and equality.* | *I think forcing people to carry identity cards is a threat to personal liberty.*

freely /ˈfriːli/ [*adv*] if you can speak **freely**, travel **freely** etc, you can say what you like, go where you like etc, and no one will try to prevent you: *For most of the year farmers allow the sheep to roam freely on the hillside.* | *At last Jim could talk freely and frankly about being gay.*

4 not in prison

➡ see also **PRISON, ESCAPE**

free /friː/ [*adj* not usually before noun] not in prison, or not being kept somewhere by force: *He was free again, after 10 long years in jail.* | *The hostages are now free after their five-day ordeal.*

out /aʊt/ [*adv*] no longer in prison, because the punishment is over: *Peters could be out in as little as 3 years.* | *Her husband gets out of jail next week.*

5 to let someone leave prison

➡ see also **PRISON, ESCAPE**

release /rɪˈliːs/ [*v* T] *McKay moved to Newcastle after being released from prison.* | *They released ten political prisoners last year.*

let sb out /ˌlet (sb) ˈaʊt/ [*phrasal verb* T] to let someone leave a place where they are being kept, especially a prison: *He's in a high security prison and may never be let out.*
+of *She was let out of prison to attend her daughter's funeral.*

> **Formal or informal?**
> **Let sb out** is more informal than **release**.

set sb free /ˌset (sb) ˈfriː/ to let someone leave a place where they are being kept by force: *The American hostages were set free last night.*

FREE TIME

➡ see Word Banks section

FRIEND

➡ see also **FRIENDLY/UNFRIENDLY, GIRLFRIEND/BOYFRIEND, RELATIONSHIP**

1 a friend

friend /frend/ [n C] someone who you know well and enjoy spending time with, but who is not a member of your family: *Martha went to London with some friends.*
a friend of mine (=one of my friends) *I'm going out for a drink with a friend of mine.*
good/close friend (=someone you know very well and like very much) *Rob is one of my closest friends.*
best friend *Even my best friend didn't know my secret.*
old friend (=someone you have known well for a long time) *We spent the weekend with our old friends, Bill and Judy.*

mate BRITISH **buddy** AMERICAN /meɪt, 'bʌdi/ [n C] INFORMAL a friend: *I always go to the pub with my mates on Friday night.*
a mate/buddy of mine (=one of my friends) *Terry's an old buddy of mine.*
plural **buddies**

pal /pæl/ [n C] INFORMAL a friend: *Thanks, Frankie. You're a real pal.*
a pal of mine *Nick was a pal of mine at school.*

> **Pal** is a little old-fashioned.

acquaintance /ə'kweɪntəns/ [n C] someone that you know and sometimes see, but who is not one of your close friends: *She's just an acquaintance – I sometimes see her at aerobics.*

2 a group of friends

circle of friends /ˌsɜːˈkəl əv 'frendz/ [n singular] all the people that you know well and often meet in social situations: *In New York, Marcia introduced him to her large circle of friends.*

the gang /ðə 'gæŋ/ [n singular] SPOKEN a small group of close friends who often do things together: *I usually go out with the gang on Saturday nights.*

the boys/the girls /ðə 'bɔɪz, ðə 'gɜːˈlz/ [n plural] SPOKEN a group of male friends who often do things together or a group of female friends who often do things together: *Sally's having a night out with the girls from the office.*

3 to be someone's friend

be friends /biː 'frendz/ if two people **are friends**, they like each other and they enjoy doing things together: *Bill and I used to be good friends but we don't see each other much now.*
+with *I've been friends with Andrea for about 10 years.*

get along (also **get on** BRITISH) /ˌget ə'lɒŋ, ˌget 'ɒnǁə'lɔːŋ, -'ɑːn/ [phrasal verb I] if two or more people **get along** or **get on**, they find it easy to talk and agree with each other, and so they feel relaxed when they spend time together
+with *I used to argue a lot with my parents, but now we get along very well. | I like Julie, but I don't really get on with her brother. | He's a nice boy – very easy to get along with.*

be friendly with sb /biː 'frendli wɪð (sb)/ to have a good relationship with someone, even though you may not spend a lot of time together: *We're quite friendly with our neighbours, Mr and Mrs Webb. | I used to be very friendly with a girl from Boston.*

4 to become someone's friend

make friends /ˌmeɪk 'frendz/ to start to be someone's friend, especially when you make an effort to do this: *Caroline didn't find it easy to make friends.*
+with *The children soon made friends with the kids next door.*

become friends /bɪˌkʌm 'frendz/ if two people **become friends**, they begin to be friends, often after knowing each other for a long time: *I'd known Nancy for years but we only became friends when we joined the same company.*

hit it off /ˌhɪt ɪt ˈɒf‖-ˈɔːf/ INFORMAL if two people **hit it off**, they immediately become friends when they meet for the first time: *I knew you and Mark would hit it off!*

5 a friendly relationship with someone

friendship /ˈfrendʃɪp/ [n C/U] *They first met when they were at college, and it was the start of a long friendship.*
+with *I got to know Helen through her friendship with my sister.*

6 to stop being friends with someone

➡ see also **ARGUE**

fall out /ˌfɔːl ˈaʊt/ [phrasal verb I] to stop being friends because you have an argument: *It was the first time Bill and I had fallen out.*
+with *It can be difficult if you fall out with someone you work with.*
+over *Come on, there's no point in falling out over a silly game.*

FRIENDLY/ UNFRIENDLY

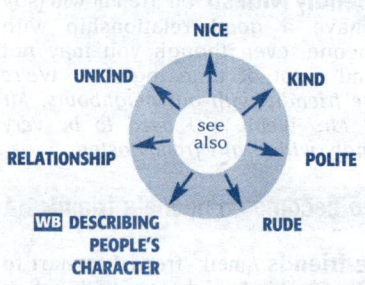

NICE
UNKIND   KIND
see also
RELATIONSHIP   POLITE
WB DESCRIBING   RUDE
PEOPLE'S
CHARACTER

1 person

friendly /ˈfrendli/ [adj] behaving towards other people in a way that shows that you like them, you enjoy being with them, or you are pleased to see them: *The staff at the hotel are always polite and friendly.* | *She gave him a friendly smile.*

+to/towards *The local people are generally friendly towards tourists.*
friendly – friendlier – friendliest

> ⚠ **Friendly** is an adjective, not an adverb, so don't say 'they treated me friendly'. Say **they treated me in a friendly way** or **they were friendly to me**.

nice/pleasant /naɪs, ˈplezənt/ [adj] friendly and kind: *He's a really nice man.* | *I enjoyed my visit to Ireland – everyone I met there was so pleasant.* | *Ralph's new girlfriend seems nice.*

easy to get on with BRITISH **easy to get along with** AMERICAN /ˌiːzi tə get ˈɒn wɪð, ˌiːzi tə get əˈlɒŋ wɪð‖-əˈlɔːŋ-/ friendly, relaxed, and easy to work with or live with: *Fortunately my boss is fairly easy to get on with.* | *I have to admit, Tom isn't exactly easy to get along with.*

sociable /ˈsəʊʃəbəl/ [adj] someone who is **sociable** enjoys being with other people and talking to them: *Why don't you invite Chris for a drink? He seems a sociable kind of guy.*

hospitable /ˈhɒspɪtəbəl, hɒˈspɪ-‖haːˈspɪ-, ˈhaːspɪ-/ [adj] someone who is **hospitable** is friendly and generous to you when you visit their home or their country: *Most of the people I met in Scotland were very hospitable and kind.*
hospitality /ˌhɒspɪˈtælɪti‖ˌhaːs-/ [n U] FORMAL someone's friendly, generous behaviour towards you when you visit their home or their country: *You must write to John and his family to thank them for their hospitality.*

2 situation/place/relationship

friendly /ˈfrendli/ [adj] a **friendly** situation, place, or relationship is one in which people behave in a friendly way: *You're lucky to work in such a friendly office.* | *The local bar had a really friendly atmosphere.*
friendly – friendlier – friendliest

welcoming /ˈwelkəmɪŋ/ [adj] a **welcoming** place or room makes you feel relaxed and happy to be there: *The fire burning in the grate made the room look bright and welcoming.*

amicable /ˈæmɪkəbəl/ [adj] FORMAL an **amicable** arrangement or solution is

one when people who do not agree with each other are able to solve their problems in a friendly way: *The meeting between the two leaders was very amicable.*
amicable arrangement/divorce/ solution *Both sides must try to find an amicable solution to the dispute.*

3 not friendly

unfriendly /ʌnˈfrendli/ [adj] *It's very difficult to work with Lindsay because she's so unfriendly.* | *Big cities can be very unfriendly places.*
+to/towards *The other girls weren't openly unfriendly towards her, but they never invited her along with them.*

cold /kəʊld/ [adj] behaving towards other people as if you do not like them or care about them: *His manner all evening was cold and unfriendly.* | *Next time she saw Harry he wasn't rude to her, just very cold and polite.*
coldly [adv] WRITTEN *She coldly asked him to leave her house.*

anti-social /ˌænti ˈsəʊʃəl◂/ [adj] someone who is **anti-social** does not enjoy being with other people and tries to avoid meeting them or talking to them: *Not everyone who likes playing computer games is an anti-social loner.*

hostile /ˈhɒstaɪl‖ˈhɑːstl, ˈhɑːstaɪl/ [adj] very unfriendly, and ready to argue with someone or criticize them in a rude and angry way: *There was a crowd of hostile demonstrators waiting outside the embassy.*
+to/towards *He's always had a very hostile attitude towards anyone in authority.*

When you see **EC**, go to the **ESSENTIAL COMMUNICATION** section.

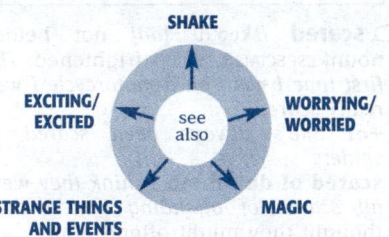

FRIGHTENING/ FRIGHTENED

SHAKE

EXCITING/ EXCITED

see also

WORRYING/ WORRIED

STRANGE THINGS AND EVENTS

MAGIC

1 frightened of something or someone

frightened /ˈfraɪtnd/ [adj] feeling very nervous and afraid of someone or something, because you think something bad is going to happen to you because of them: *Don't be frightened. No-one's going to hurt you.* | *Two frightened children were hiding in a corner of the room.*
+of *A lot of people are frightened of the dentist.* | *Are you frightened of the dark?*
frightened of doing sth *He was frightened of making mistakes.*
+that *I was frightened that my parents would get divorced.*
frightened to do sth *She was frightened to go home.*

> ⚠ Don't confuse **frightened** (=feeling afraid) and **frightening** (=making you feel afraid). Don't say 'I am frightening' when you mean 'I am frightened'.

afraid /əˈfreɪd/ [adj not before noun] frightened
+of *He had a terrible temper, and everyone was afraid of him.*
afraid of doing sth *I didn't tell anyone because I was afraid of being punished.* (=I thought I might be punished if I told anyone)
+(that) *Kerry was afraid that he was going to hit her.*
afraid to do sth *Many old people are afraid to go out at night.*

> ⚠️ **Afraid** means the same as **frightened**, but **afraid** is usually followed by **of**, **that**, or the infinitive (to + verb), except in negative sentences like 'Don't be afraid' and 'I'm not afraid'.

🔍 **scared** /skeə^rd/ [adj not before noun] ESPECIALLY SPOKEN frightened: *The first time I went on a motorcycle I was really scared.*
+of *She's always been scared of spiders.*
scared of doing sth *I think they were all scared of offending him.* (=they thought they might offend him)
+that *I hate reading out my work in class – I'm scared that people are going to laugh at me.*
scared to do sth *Don't be scared to experiment.*
scared stiff/scared to death (=very scared) *He was scared stiff at the thought of losing his job.*

terrified /'terₔfaɪd/ [adj] extremely frightened: *At first, Anna was too terrified to speak.* | *the terrified faces of the refugees*
+of *He's absolutely terrified of snakes.* | *I'm terrified of heights.*
terrified of doing sth *My mother's terrified of flying.*
+(that) *I was terrified that my father would find out I had lied to him.*

> ⚠️ Don't say 'very terrified'. Say **absolutely terrified**.

dread /dred/ [v T] to feel worried and frightened about something that you have to do, or about something that you know is going to happen: *I have to go to the dentist's tomorrow, and I'm dreading it.*
dread doing sth *I dreaded having to tell Sam his dog had died.*

2 suddenly frightened

get a fright /ˌget ə 'fraɪt/ INFORMAL to be suddenly frightened by something that happens: *She got a terrible fright when the dog jumped out at her.*
get the fright of your life (=be suddenly very frightened) *I got the fright of my life when he suddenly spoke from out of the darkness.*

panic /'pænɪk/ [v I] if you **panic** in a dangerous situation, you start behaving in a way that is not sensible, because you are very frightened and you cannot think clearly: *Keep calm and don't panic.* | *As the fire raged through the ship, some passengers panicked and jumped into the sea.*
panicking – panicked – have panicked

3 something that makes you frightened

frightening /'fraɪtnɪŋ/ [adj] something that is **frightening** makes you feel frightened: *It was the most frightening experience of my life.* | *Driving in big cities can be pretty frightening for many people.*

terrifying /'terₔfaɪ-ɪŋ/ [adj] very frightening: *They stopped me, and they had a gun. It was terrifying.* | *There was a terrifying crash, and the house seemed to shake.*

> ⚠️ Don't say 'very terrifying'. Just say **terrifying**.

🔍 **scary** /'skeəri/ [adj] ESPECIALLY SPOKEN frightening – use this especially about stories, films, or situations in which strange and frightening things happen: *She didn't like the film. It was too scary for her.* | *I had a really scary dream last night.* | *a big scary monster*
scary – scarier – scariest

spooky /'spuːki/ [adj] INFORMAL a place that is **spooky** is strange or frightening because it makes you think of ghosts: *The hotel was kind of spooky – big, dark, and empty.*
spooky – spookier – spookiest

4 a film or story that is intended to make you frightened

horror /'hɒrə^r||'hɔː-, 'hɑː-/ [adj only before noun] **horror film/movie/ story** a film or story that is intended to make you feel frightened: *The movie is based on a horror story by Stephen King.*

thriller /'θrɪlə^r/ [n C] a film or book that is intended to be exciting and frightening because you do not know what will happen next: *'Psycho' is Hitchcock's greatest psychological thriller.*

5 to make someone feel frightened

frighten /'fraɪtn/ [v T] to make someone feel frightened: *Don't shout like that – you'll frighten the baby.* | *I don't care how tough he is – he doesn't frighten me.*
frighten sb into doing sth (=make someone do something by frightening them) *Their lawyers tried to frighten us into signing the contract.*
frighten sb off/frighten off sb (=frighten someone so that they go away or stop trying to do something) *He pulled out a gun and managed to frighten off his attackers.*
scare /skeə^r/ [v T] ESPECIALLY SPOKEN to make someone feel frightened or very nervous: *There was a pale, white face at the window. It really scared me.*
scare the hell out of sb INFORMAL (=make someone feel very frightened) *The way he drives scares the hell out of me.*

Formal or informal?
Scare is more informal than **frighten** and you usually use it in spoken English.

terrify /'terₛfaɪ/ [v T] to make someone feel very frightened: *The idea of going down into the caves terrified her.*
terrifying – terrified – have terrified
startle /'stɑː^rtl/ [v T] if someone or something **startles** you, they frighten you because you see them suddenly or hear them when you are not expecting them: *I'm sorry. I didn't mean to startle you.*
gives me the creeps /ˌɡɪvz miː ðə 'kriːps/ SPOKEN INFORMAL if a person or place **gives you the creeps**, they make you feel slightly frightened and nervous because they seem strange: *I hate this house. It gives me the creeps.*

6 the feeling of being frightened

fear /fɪə^r/ [n C/U] the feeling you have when you are very frightened, or the

thought that something very unpleasant will happen: *Her hands were shaking with fear.* (=because she was frightened)
+of *fear of flying* | *fears of another war in Europe*
+that *There was always the fear that he might never return.*

terror /'terə^r/ [n U] a very strong feeling of fear when you think that something very bad is going to happen to you, especially that you will be killed
in terror (=because you are very frightened) *Shots were fired, and the children screamed in terror.*
sheer terror (=very great terror) *I'll never forget the look of sheer terror on her face.*

horror /'hɒrə^r‖'hɔː-, 'hɑː-/ [n U] a strong feeling of shock and fear, which you have when you see something terrible happen, or when you think of something terrible
in horror *The crowd watched in horror as the plane hit the ground and burst into flames.*
to sb's horror (=making someone feel very frightened) *He suddenly realized to his horror that the brakes weren't working.*

panic /'pænɪk/ [n singular/U] a sudden, strong feeling of fear when you are in a dangerous situation, which makes you do things that are not sensible because you cannot think clearly: *There was a sudden panic and everyone started rushing towards the door.*

FROM

to come from a place or to come from something else

➡ see also **COUNTRY, TOWN, LIVE**

1 when someone was born in a place or has lived there a long time

come from/be from /'kʌm frɒm, biː 'frɒm/ [phrasal verb T] if you **come from** or **are from** a particular place, that is where you were born or where you lived for a long time: *Where are you from?* | *She comes from Japan.* |

When we were on vacation, we met some people who came from the same town as us.

2   when something has developed from something that existed before

come from sth /'kʌm frɒm (sth)/ [phrasal verb T] use this to say that something which exists now developed from something else that existed before: *Martial arts such as judo and karate come from Asia. | Many modern stories come from ancient Greek and Roman myths.*

be based on sth /biː 'beɪst ɒn (sth)/ if a film, story, idea, or plan **is based on** something else, that is where its basic ideas or facts come from: *The movie is based on the novel, but the ending is not the same. | His theory was based on years of psychological studies.*

origin/origins /'ɒrɪdʒɪn(z)‖'ɔː-, 'ɑː-/ [n C] the situation, ideas, events etc that something else developed from, especially when this helps to explain why something has developed
+of *a TV programme about the origin of the universe | No one really knows what the origins of this tradition are.*

> ⚠ **Origin** and **origins** often mean the same, but use **origins** especially about something that has many different parts or stages: *the origins of the modern novel.* Use **origin** especially about something that developed from a single thing, cause, or situation: *Doctors are still not sure what the origin of the infection is.*

FULL

when nothing more can fit into a container, room, or space

➡ opposite **EMPTY**

1   full

full /fʊl/ [adj] if a container, room, or space is **full**, nothing more can go into it: *The train was completely full. |*

All the parking spaces were full. | We started with a full tank of petrol.
+of *We found a box full of old letters.*

> Don't say 'full with something'. Say **full of something**.

filled with sth /'fɪld wɪð (sth)/ ESPECIALLY WRITTEN full of something – use this about a container when a lot of things have been put into it: *an enormous vase filled with flowers | Pour the mixture into a tall glass filled with ice.*

packed /pækt/ [adj] completely full of people – use this about a room, theatre, train, bus etc: "*Were there many people on the bus?*" "*Oh, it was packed!*" | *a packed theatre*
+with *On the day of the funeral, the church was packed with friends and relatives.*

crammed with sth /'kræmd wɪð (sth)/ completely full of things or people, so that they are all pressed together: *Security guards discovered a bag crammed with explosives. | a shelf crammed with books*

overflowing /ˌəʊvəˈfləʊɪŋ◂/ [adj] a container that is **overflowing** is so full that the liquid or things inside it come out over the top: *The bath's overflowing! Who forgot to turn off the water? | The tables were covered with dirty coffee cups and overflowing ashtrays.*
+with *a trashcan overflowing with garbage*

overloaded /ˌəʊvəˈləʊdɪd/ if a vehicle or ship is **overloaded**, too many things have been put in it, so it is carrying too much: *The truck was so overloaded that things had started to fall off the back. | an overloaded bus*

2   to become full

fill up /ˌfɪl 'ʌp/ [phrasal verb I] to gradually become full: *About half an hour before the performance, the theatre starts to fill up. | In the rainy season, the reservoirs soon fill up again.*

3   to make something full

fill /fɪl/ [v T] to put enough of something into a container to make it full: *Can you fill this jug, please?*

fill sth with sth *For £2 you can fill your bowl with as much salad as you like.* | *He had a notebook which he had filled with stories and poems.*

fill up /ˌfɪl ˈʌp/ [phrasal verb T] to fill a container that already has a small amount of something in it
fill up sth *Harold went around filling up everyone's glasses.*
fill sth up *If the tank is less than half full, tell them to fill it up.*
fill up sth with sth *I've filled up the freezer with fruit and vegetables.*

cram/jam /kræm, dʒæm/ [v T] to push too many things into a container or space, so that they are all pressed together
cram/jam sth into sth *I crammed all my clothes into a suitcase and called a taxi.*
cramming – crammed – have crammed
jamming – jammed – have jammed

stuff /stʌf/ [v T] to quickly fill something such as a bag or pocket by pushing things into it tightly
stuff sth into sth *She hurriedly stuffed some things into an overnight bag and left immediately.*
stuff sth with sth *The thieves had stuffed their pockets with $100 bills.*

refill /ˌriːˈfɪl/ [v T] to fill something again, after what was inside it has been used: *Can I refill anyone's glass?*
refill sth with sth *The bottles are emptied, cleaned, and refilled with fresh water.*

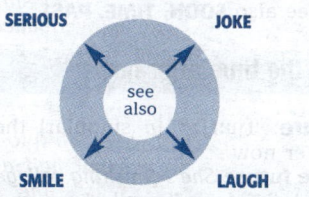

FUNNY

SERIOUS → JOKE
see also
SMILE → LAUGH

1 when something or someone makes you laugh

funny /ˈfʌni/ [adj] something or someone that is **funny** makes you laugh: *It was the funniest story I'd ever heard.* | *He can be pretty funny when he's had a few drinks.*
very/really/so funny *You look really funny in that hat.*
it is funny *It was funny when the dog came on the stage.*
find sth/sb funny *I don't find that kind of joke funny.*
funny – funnier – funniest

make sb laugh /ˌmeɪk (sb) ˈlɑːfǁˈlæf/ to make someone laugh, for example by telling a joke or doing something funny: *I must tell Jerry what you said – it'll make him laugh.*

amusing /əˈmjuːzɪŋ/ [adj] funny and entertaining enough to make you smile: *an amusing article in the newspaper* | *His speech was amusing at first, but it was too long.*
find sth/sb amusing *He's one of those comedians that everyone finds amusing.*
very/highly amusing *My mother was embarrassed, but I found the situation highly amusing.*

> **Formal or informal?**
> **Amusing** is more formal than **funny**.

witty /ˈwɪti/ [adj] a person, speech, play, or remark that is **witty** uses words in a clever and amusing way: *Sam is intelligent, witty, and great fun to be with.* | *Men adored her for her lively conversation and witty remarks.*
witty – wittier – wittiest

humorous /ˈhjuːmərəsǁˈhjuː-, ˈjuː-/ [adj] ESPECIALLY WRITTEN intended to be amusing – use this especially about stories, descriptions, letters, and other things that people write: *a book of humorous poems* | *a humorous account of a young man's travels in South America* | *humorous birthday cards*

hilarious /hɪˈleəriəs/ [adj] extremely funny – use this about situations, jokes, and stories, but not about people: *one of the hilarious scenes in a Marx Brothers film* | *The dancing was absolutely hilarious – we all kept tripping over each other.*

> Don't say 'very hilarious'. Say **really hilarious** or **absolutely hilarious**.

F

2 something that is said or written to make people laugh

joke /dʒəʊk/ [n C] something that you say to make people laugh, especially a short funny story: *There are a lot of jokes about policemen.*
make/tell a joke *It annoys me when people make jokes about women drivers.*
hear a joke (=be told a joke) *Have you heard any good jokes lately?*
get/see the joke (=understand a joke) *Everyone laughed except Henry, who didn't see the joke.*
dirty joke (=a joke about sex)
sick joke (=a joke about something very unpleasant)

comedy /'kɒmədi‖'kɑː-/ [n C] a film, play, TV programme etc that is intended to entertain people and make them laugh: *a new romantic comedy starring Hugh Grant*
plural **comedies**

> ⚠ You can also use **comedy** before a noun, like an adjective: *the best comedy performance of the year* | *the TV comedy series 'Friends'*

3 someone whose job is to make people laugh

comedian/comic /kə'miːdiən, 'kɒmɪk‖ 'kɑː-/ [n C] someone whose job is to tell jokes and make people laugh

clown /klaʊn/ [n C] someone who entertains people by dressing in funny clothes and by doing silly things, especially in a circus

4 how you feel when you think something is funny

amused /ə'mjuːzd/ [adj] if you are **amused** by something, you think it is funny and it makes you smile: *When I told him what had happened, he sounded amused rather than annoyed.*
+by/at *They seemed amused at his embarrassment.*
amused expression/smile/grin *She stood watching them with an amused expression on her face.*

amusement /ə'mjuːzmənt/ [n U] ESPECIALLY WRITTEN the feeling that you have when you think something is funny: *Larry's new haircut caused great amusement among his friends.*
watch/listen/notice etc with amusement *Everyone was watching the little dog with interest and amusement.*
in amusement *Her lips curved in amusement.*
(much) to sb's amusement (=making them feel very amused) *Suddenly, the teacher's chair collapsed, much to everyone's amusement.*

5 the ability to realize when something is funny

sense of humour BRITISH **sense of humor** AMERICAN /ˌsens əv 'hjuːmə‖ -'hjuː-, -'juː-/ [n C usually singular] your ability to understand and enjoy jokes, funny situations etc: *I like Ann – she has such a good sense of humour.* | *Maybe I'm losing my sense of humor but I didn't find that show at all funny.*

🔍 **can take a joke** /kən ˌteɪk ə 'dʒəʊk/ ESPECIALLY SPOKEN to be able to laugh and not get angry or upset when other people make jokes about you or do something that makes you look stupid: *If you're in the army, you have to be able to take a joke.*

FUTURE

➡ if you want to know how to form the future, go to **ESSENTIAL GRAMMAR** (Section 5)
➡ see also **SOON, TIME, PAST**

1 the time after now

future /'fjuːtʃər/ [n singular] the time after now
the future *She's finishing college soon, and she doesn't really have any plans for the future.*
of the future (=that will exist in the future) *The car of the future may run on solar-powered batteries.*
sb's future (=what will happen to someone in their job, their life etc) *I*

had a meeting with the boss to discuss my future.

have a great future (=be likely to be very successful in the future) *She's a very talented musician, and we think she has a great future.*

future [*adj* only before noun]
a future leader/president/prime minister etc (=someone who will be a leader/president etc in the future) *He is regarded by many as a future president.*
a future date/time FORMAL *We agreed to consider the matter again at a future date.*

the outlook /ði ˈaʊtlʊk/ [*n* singular] a general idea of what people expect to happen in the future, and whether they expect things to go well or badly: *The economic outlook is better than it has been for several years.*
+for *With drought conditions continuing, the outlook for farmers is not very good.*

> ⚠️ **The outlook** is used especially in news reports.

from now /frəm ˈnaʊ/
an hour/10 years/2 weeks etc from now an hour, 10 years etc from the time when you are speaking: *A couple of months from now, you'll probably have forgotten all about him.* | *There may be no rainforest left in 30 years from now.*

⌕ from now on /frəm ˌnaʊ ˈɒn/ ESPECIALLY SPOKEN use this to say that something will always happen in the future, starting from now: *From now on, I'm not letting anyone borrow my car.* | *From now on, you kids will have to make your own lunch.*

2 at some time in the future

in the future /ɪn ðə ˈfjuːtʃəʳ/ at some time in the future, but you do not know exactly when: *Global warming could become a major problem in the future.*
in the near future (=soon) *The new software will be available in the UK in the near future.*

⌕ some time /ˌsʌm ˈtaɪm/ ESPECIALLY SPOKEN at a time in the future, which has not been arranged yet: *Come over and see us some time.* | *Would you like to go out for a meal some time next week?*

one day/some day /ˌwʌn ˈdeɪ, ˌsʌm ˈdeɪ/ at some time in the future, especially a long time from now: *One day, I'd like to visit the Grand Canyon.* | *She always knew that some day he would leave her.*

then /ðen/ [*adv*] at a time in the future, which has just been mentioned: *"I'll come round at about seven." "OK, I'll see you then."*
until then *School starts in September, and until then I'll be staying with friends.*

G, g

GAMBLING

**when you try to win money by
guessing the result of a race,
competition etc**

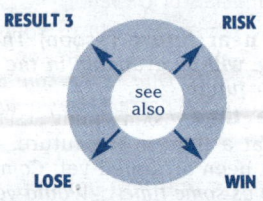

RESULT 3   RISK

see also

LOSE   WIN

1 to gamble

gambling /'gæmblɪŋ/ [n U] when you try
to win money, for example by playing
cards or guessing which horse will
win a race: *Is gambling legal here?* |
*He lost all his money through
gambling.* | *The TV star admitted he
was addicted to drugs and gambling.*

gamble /'gæmbəl/ [v I/T] to try to win
money, for example by playing cards
or guessing which horse will win a
race: *Eddie loved to gamble, and
would spend most evenings at the
roulette table.*

gamble away sth/gamble sth away
(=waste a lot of money by gambling)
*Roger gambled away all his money in a
Las Vegas casino.* | *She inherited
$50,000 but gambled it away.*

bet/have a bet /bet, ˌhæv ə 'bet/ [v I] to
try to win money by guessing who
will win a race or game: *I don't bet
very often.*

bet on sth/have a bet on sth
(=gamble money on the result of a
race or game) *We usually have a bet
on the Grand Prix.*

bet £10/$100 etc on sth *He bet
$1000 on a horse race last week.*

put £10/$20 etc on sth /pʊt £10, etc)
ɒn (sth)/ to gamble £10, $20 etc on
the horse or team that you think will
win a race or competition: *I put $20
on the Cowboys to win.*

put/place a bet on sth (=gamble on
a horse, game etc) *I think I'll put a bet
on the next race.*

2 someone who gambles

gambler /'gæmblər/ [n C] someone who
gambles, especially someone who
gambles a lot and cannot stop: *All his
life, Jack was a drinker and gambler.*
heavy gambler (=who gambles a lot)

3 ways of gambling

go to a casino /ˌgəʊ tʊ ə kə'siːnəʊ/ to go
to a place where people try to win
money by playing card games or
games like roulette (=a game in
which a ball falls into a hole with a
number on it): *Did you go to the casino
while you were in Monte Carlo?*

do the lottery BRITISH **play the lottery**
AMERICAN /ˌduː ðə 'lɒtəri, ˌpleɪ ðə 'lɒtərɪ‖
-'lɑː-/ to buy a ticket with numbers on
it, so that you will win a lot of money
if your numbers are chosen:
*Thousands of people do the lottery
every week.*

go to the races /ˌgəʊ tə ðə 'reɪsɪz/ to go
to watch horses racing, and often try
to win money by guessing which one
will win

play cards/poker/roulette /pleɪ 'kɑːrdz,
'pəʊkər, ruː'let/ to play a game in order
to try to win money: *Miles and his
friends used to sit up all night, drinking
and playing poker.*

lose money on sth /luːz 'mʌni ɒn (sth)/
to lose money by not guessing correctly the result of a game, race, or
competition: *He claims that he lost all
his money on a dice game.*

win money on sth /wɪn 'mʌni ɒn (sth)/
to win money by correctly guessing
the result of a game, race, or
competition: *He won a lot of money on
the horses last week.*

GAME

WB SPORT

GAMBLING **TAKE PART**

see also

LOSE **COMPETITION**

WIN

1 a game

game /geɪm/ [n C] an activity which you do for enjoyment which you play according to a set of rules: *Chess is such a difficult game.* | *Do you all understand the rules of the game?*
computer game *Some children spend hours each day playing computer games.*
card game (=a game you play using a set of cards with numbers or pictures on them) *I'm not very good at card games. I always lose.*
board game (=a game played on a board with pieces of wood, plastic etc that you move around) *board games like Monopoly and Ludo*

> ⚠ You can also use **game** to mean a single occasion when you play a game: *We played three games of chess, and she beat me every time.*

2 to play a game

play /pleɪ/ [v I/T] to take part in a game: *Have you played backgammon before?* | *We're having a game of Monopoly. Does anyone else want to play?*
play a game (of sth) *We were about to play a game of tennis.*
◯ have a game /ˌhæv ə ˈgeɪm/ ESPECIALLY SPOKEN to play one game of something – use this especially when asking someone to play a game
+of *Do you want to have a game of cards?*

3 someone who plays a game

player /ˈpleɪəʳ/ [n C] someone who plays a game: *Bridge is a game for 4 players.* | *The other players were much more experienced than I was.*

opponent /əˈpəʊnənt/ [n C] the person or team who is playing against you in a game: *Sharapova was surprised by the strength of her opponent.* | *Arsenal's next opponents in the cup will be Manchester United.*

contestant /kənˈtestənt/ [n C] someone who takes part in a game on television or radio: *One lucky contestant will win tonight's star prize, a luxury car.*

4 the points that you get in a game

point /pɔɪnt/ [n C] a unit used for measuring how well you are doing in a game: *The first player to get a hundred points wins the game.*

score /skɔːʳ/ [n C] the number of points that one player or all the players have at the end of a game: *What's your highest ever score?* | *The final score was 4 all.* (=both players had 4 points)

GET

➡ see also **HAVE/NOT HAVE, OWN**

1 to get something

get /get/ [v T not in passive] to get something by buying it, asking for it, or working for it: *I got a really nice coat at Browns.* | *Where did he get the money for a new car?* | *I don't feel like cooking, let's go get a pizza.* | *I still haven't gotten a birthday present for Sherri.*
get sth from sb/sth *I wonder where they got those costumes from?*
get a job *Did you hear? Stuart got a new job.*
getting – got – have got BRITISH
have gotten AMERICAN

obtain /əbˈteɪn/ [v T] FORMAL to get something: *Maps and guides can be obtained at the tourist office.*

obtain sth from sb/sth *You will need to obtain permission from the Principal.*

get hold of /get 'həʊld ɒv/ INFORMAL to get something that is difficult to get, for example by finding it or borrowing it: *I haven't been able to get hold of that book anywhere.* | *Somehow Scott had got hold of a gun.*

earn /ɜːʳn/ [v T] to get money for your work: *He was earning more than seven million dollars a year.* | *Kate earns more than her husband.*
earn £25,000 per year/$15 an hour etc *Alan earns $30,000 a year.*

gain /geɪn/ [v T] FORMAL to gradually get more of a useful skill or a good quality. Use **gain** with words like **experience**, **confidence**, **support**, **popularity**, **acceptance**: *Our training courses will help you gain confidence in communication and management skills.* | *The programme enables students to gain practical experience of the world of work.* | *His ideas are gaining a lot of support (=more and more people are supporting them).*

acquire /əˈkwaɪəʳ/ [v T] FORMAL to get something very big or expensive, or to get more knowledge or skills: *It took him a long time to acquire the skills he needed to become a professional artist.* | *The Boston Museum of Fine Arts has recently acquired several paintings by Salvador Dali.*

2 to be given something

get /get/ [v T not in passive] to be given something without having to ask for it or pay for it: *What did you get for your birthday?* | *You get a free CD with this magazine.*
get sth from sb *Here's the card I got from Jane.*
getting – got – have got BRITISH
have gotten AMERICAN

receive /rɪˈsiːv/ [v T] to be given something, especially officially: *You will receive your new credit card in approximately two weeks.* | *We receive over 100 complaints a month about aircraft noise.*
receive sth from sb/sth *She received an honorary degree from Harvard in 1990.*

be given sth /biː ˈɡɪvən (sth)/ to be given something, especially by someone in an important or powerful position: *He was given a 10 year jail sentence.* | *New employees are given a complete medical check-up.* | *I'm just so grateful to have been given this opportunity.*

be awarded sth /biː əˈwɔːʳdᵻd (sth)/ to be given a prize, especially by an important organization, for something that you have achieved: *The restaurant was awarded four stars in the 'Good Food Guide'.* | *Yasunari Kawabata was the first Japanese writer to be awarded the Nobel Prize.*

inherit /ɪnˈherᵻt/ [v T] to be given someone's money or property after they die: *Who will inherit the house when he dies?*
inherit sth from sb *She inherited the money from her mother.*

3 to get a letter, telephone call, or message

get/receive /get, rɪˈsiːv/ [v T] *Did you get my e-mail?* | *I'm sorry I didn't reply earlier, but I've only just received your letter.*
getting – got – have got BRITISH
have gotten AMERICAN

4 to get a point or result in a game, test etc

get /get/ [v T] to get a result in a test or examination: *I only got 35% in my history test.* | *Pam's really smart. She got straight A's at high school.*
getting – got – have got BRITISH
have gotten AMERICAN

score /skɔːʳ/ [v T] to get a number of points in a sports game, or in a test or examination: *The test was difficult, and no-one scored more than 45%.*

score a goal/point/run *AC Milan scored a record number of goals this season.*

5 to get back something that you had before

get sth back /,get (sth) 'bæk/ [*phrasal verb* T not in passive] to get back something that you had before, especially something that belongs to you: *The airline lost my baggage and I didn't get it back.*
+from *We never got our money back from the landlord.*

recover /rɪ'kʌvə^r/ [v T] FORMAL to get back something such as an ability that you have lost, or something that has been stolen from you: *Four paintings stolen from the gallery have been recovered.* | *She nearly fell, but somehow recovered her balance and continued running.*

retrieve /rɪ'triːv/ [v T] to get back something after you have put it somewhere: *I had left my bag at the railroad station and went back to retrieve it.*
retrieve sth from sth *She bent down and retrieved the map from under the car seat.*

> **Formal or informal?**
> **Retrieve** is formal but is used in spoken English as well as written English.

6 the person, place, company etc that you get something from

source /sɔː^rs/ [n C] the person, place, or thing that you get something from: *They get their information from various sources.*
+of *Beans and lentils are a very good source of protein.*

supplier /sə'plaɪə^r/ [n C] the person, company, or country that you regularly get a product from: *Eggs are much fresher if you buy them from a local supplier.*
+of *the UK's largest supplier of office equipment*

GET RID OF

to remove a thing or person that you do not need or want any more

➡ see also **RUBBISH**

1 to get rid of an object, a piece of furniture or clothing etc

get rid of sth /,get 'rɪd ɒv (sth)/ to remove something that you do not want or do not use any more, for example by giving it to someone else or throwing it away: *Let's get rid of some of these old books.* | *I hate these chairs. I wish we could get rid of them.*

throw away /,θrəʊ ə'weɪ/ [*phrasal verb* T] to get rid of something by putting it in the bin (=container where you put unwanted things so they can be taken away)
throw away sth *Don't throw away those boxes – they might be useful.*
throw sth away *That bread is about two weeks old! You'd better throw it away.*

> ⚠ Don't confuse **throw** (=when you throw something through the air) and **throw away**.

throw out /,θrəʊ 'aʊt/ [*phrasal verb* T] to get rid of something, especially when you are trying to make a place more tidy or to make space for new things
throw out sth *They were throwing out some old filing cabinets, so I asked if I could have one.*
throw sth out *You never wear these shoes – why don't you throw them out?*

dispose of sth /dɪs'pəʊz ɒv (sth)/ [*phrasal verb* T] FORMAL to get rid of something that is difficult or unpleasant to get rid of: *What is the best way to dispose of toxic waste?* | *Kent had disposed of his victims' bodies in the cellar.*

> ⚠ Don't say 'he disposed the body'. Say **he disposed of the body**.

dump /dʌmp/ [v T] to throw away something unpleasant or dangerous by leaving it in a place where it should not be: *Some people even dump their garbage in the woods.* | *Dangerous chemicals are being dumped in the ocean.*

discard /dɪsˈkɑːrd/ [v T] FORMAL to throw away something that you no longer need, especially by dropping it on the ground or leaving it somewhere you should not: *People who discard their litter in the street should have to pay heavy fines.*

discarded [adj only before noun] *The police believe that the fire was started by a discarded cigarette.*

scrap /skræp/ [v T] to get rid of an old machine, vehicle etc, and use its parts in some other way: *The navy's biggest aircraft carrier is being scrapped this year.*

disposable /dɪˈspəʊzəbəl/ [adj] something that is **disposable** is designed to be used once and then thrown away: *She bought some disposable cups for the party.* | *disposable paper towels*

2   to get rid of a person

➡ see also **LEAVE 10**

get rid of sb /ˌget ˈrɪd ɒv (sb)/ INFORMAL to make someone leave because you do not want them or because they are causing problems: *He's not a very good teacher. I think they should get rid of him.* | *She stayed here talking for over three hours – I couldn't get rid of her!* | *The company has announced that it will get rid of another 500 workers.*

dump /dʌmp/ [v T] INFORMAL to end a relationship with a boyfriend or girlfriend: *"Why did he dump her?" "He met someone else."*

3   to get rid of a system, law, plan etc

abolish /əˈbɒlɪʃ‖əˈbɑː-/ [v T] to officially end a law, legal right, or system, especially one that has existed for a long time: *The death penalty was abolished in 1965.* | *Wilberforce campaigned to abolish slavery.*

abolition /ˌæbəˈlɪʃən/ [n U] when something is abolished: *The group is fighting for the abolition of the death penalty.*

scrap /skræp/ [v T] to end a system, law etc, or to decide not to use a plan that you were intending to use: *Plans to build a new airport have been scrapped because of lack of money.* | *It is likely that the parking restrictions will be scrapped next year.*

scrapping – **scrapped** – **have scrapped**

4   to get rid of a problem or illness

get rid of sth /ˌget ˈrɪd ɒv (sth)/ to remove or deal with something that is causing you trouble, such as an illness or a problem: *I've had a cold for two weeks, and I just can't get rid of it.* | *Do you know how I can get rid of this stain on the carpet?*

GIRLFRIEND/ BOYFRIEND

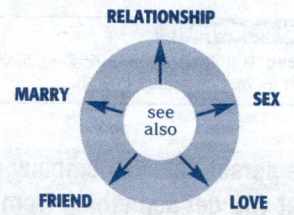

1   a person that you have a romantic or sexual relationship with

girlfriend /ˈgɜːrlfrend/ [n C] a girl or woman that you have a romantic relationship with, especially for a fairly long time: *Sam and his girlfriend have been together for over a year.*

ex-girlfriend (=someone who used to be your girlfriend) *His ex-girlfriend keeps calling him all the time.*

boyfriend /ˈbɔɪfrend/ [n C] a boy or man that you have a romantic relationship with, especially for a fairly long time: *Josh was my first boyfriend.*

ex-boyfriend (=someone who used to be your boyfriend) *Oh, my God! I've just seen Alex, my ex-boyfriend.*

partner /'pɑːˈtnəʳ/ [n C] someone that you have a romantic and sexual relationship with, especially someone that you live with: *Partners are welcome at the office Christmas party. | We run a counselling service for anyone whose partner has died.*

> ⚠ Use **partner** about a man or woman who has had a relationship with someone for a long time, especially when they live together, or when you do not know whether they are male or female.

lover /'lʌvəʳ/ [n C] someone, especially a man, that you have a sexual relationship with but are not married to: *The woman was attacked by a former lover.*

be lovers (=have a sexual relationship with each other) *They claimed that they were not lovers, just good friends.*

> **Formal or informal?**
> **Lover** is used especially in news reports, magazines, and books. You would not usually refer to your own boyfriend as your **lover**.

mistress /'mɪstrɪ̇s/ [n C] a woman who has a sexual relationship with a man who is married to someone else
have a mistress *She suspected her husband had a mistress.*
plural **mistresses**

> ⚠ The word **mistress** is a little old-fashioned, but it is often used when talking about famous people, or about people in history or literature.

2 to have a girlfriend or boyfriend

have a girlfriend/boyfriend /ˌhæv ə 'gɜːˈlfrend, 'bɔɪfrend/ *By 18 or 19, many young people will have a girlfriend or boyfriend.*

go out with sb /ˌgəʊ 'aʊt wɪð (sb)/ [phrasal verb T] to have someone as your girlfriend or boyfriend: *She's going out with that guy who works at the gas station.*

be going out together *Mark and I have been going out together for four years.*

be seeing sb /biː 'siːɪŋ (sb)/ to have a romantic or sexual relationship with someone, especially a relationship that is not very serious and does not last very long: *Do you know if Tanya's seeing anyone at the moment? | A couple of years after they got married, he started seeing other women.*

3 a romantic or sexual relationship

relationship /rɪˈleɪʃənʃɪp/ [n C] when two people spend time together or live together because they are romantically or sexually attracted to each other
have a relationship *Did Myra and Danny have a relationship?*
+with *I was determined not to start a relationship with a married man.*

affair /əˈfeəʳ/ [n C] a secret sexual relationship between two people, when one or both of them is married to someone else: *The affair had been going on for years before her husband found out.*
have an affair with sb *I'd kill my husband if he had an affair with anyone!*

fling /flɪŋ/ [n C] INFORMAL a short and not very serious relationship: *Yes, I did go out with him, but it was just a fling.*
have a fling *They had a fling years ago.*

4 to end a relationship

split up/break up /ˌsplɪt 'ʌp, ˌbreɪk 'ʌp/ [phrasal verb I] if two people **split up** or **break up**, they stop having a relationship with each other: *Tim and I have split up.*
+with *David has just broken up with his girlfriend. He's really upset.*

leave /liːv/ [v T] to end a serious relationship with someone you live with, especially your husband or wife: *His wife left him after 30 years of marriage.*
leaving – left – have left

finish with sb /ˈfɪnɪʃ wɪð (sb)/ [*phrasal verb* T] BRITISH to end your relationship with your boyfriend or girlfriend: *Frank? I finished with him years ago!*

dump /dʌmp/ [*v* T] INFORMAL to end a relationship with a boyfriend or girlfriend: *"Why did she dump him?" "She met someone else."*

GIVE

➡ see also **GET, PROVIDE, TAKE/BRING**

➡ if you mean 'give something to someone when they will give it back later', go to **LEND**

1 to give something to someone

give /gɪv/ [*v* T]
give sb sth *I gave him $10. | Why don't we give her some flowers for her birthday? | Let me give you some advice.*
give sth to sb *Would you give this letter to your uncle when you see him? | Russell was accused of giving secret information to the enemy.*
giving – gave – have given

> ⚠ Don't say 'give to her the book'. Say **give her the book** or **give the book to her**.

> ⚠ In the passive, you can say either **I was given it** or **it was given to me**: *I was given this ring by my mother. | This ring was given to me by my mother.*

pass /pɑːs‖pæs/ [*v* T] to give something to someone by putting it in their hand or putting it near them, especially because they cannot reach it themselves: *Could you pass the salt, please?*
pass sb sth *Can you pass me that box of books next?*
pass sth to sb *The boys at the back of the class were passing notes to each other under their desks.*

> ⚠ It is more polite to say **pass** than **give** when you are asking for something that you can see but cannot reach: *Could you pass me that book, please?*

hand /hænd/ [*v* T] to give something to someone by putting it into their hand
hand sb sth *"Here you are," he said, handing her the key.*
hand sth to sb *Please hand your tickets to the man at the door.*

let sb have sth /ˌlet (sb) ˈhæv (sth)/ to give something to someone, especially something they have asked for or something they need: *If you could let me have your suggestions, it would be very helpful. | She lets her kids have anything they want.*

give away /ˌgɪv əˈweɪ/ [*phrasal verb* T] to give something that you own to someone else, especially because you do not want it or need it
give away sth *I gave away most of my old furniture because I didn't have room for it in my new apartment.*
give sth away *He decided to give all his money away and become a monk.*
give sth away to sb *If you have any clothes you don't need, give them away to a thrift shop.*

provide /prəˈvaɪd/ [*v* T] to give something to someone or make it available to them, because they need it or want it: *The sports hall was built on land provided by the city authorities.*
provide sb with sth *The hotel had kindly provided her with a local map.*
provide sth to/for sb *A new leisure centre will provide a service to the whole community. | Jobs in bars provide a useful source of income for college students.*

> **Formal or informal?**
> **Provide** is used in writing and in formal spoken English.

present /prɪˈzent/ [*v* T] to give someone something at an official ceremony: *Who's going to present the prizes this year?*
present sb with sth *On his retirement, the school presented him with a gold watch.*
present sth to sb *A little girl presented a basket of flowers to the President.*
be presented with sth *She was presented with a gold medal for bravery.*

hand in/give in /ˌhænd ˈɪn, ˌgɪv ˈɪn/ [*phrasal verb* T] to give something to someone in authority, for example to the police or a teacher

hand/give in sth *When you leave the hotel please hand in your keys.*
hand/give sth in *Have you given your English assignment in yet?* | *Luckily someone found her purse and gave it in to the police.*

2 to give something to everyone in a group

hand out

hand out/give out /ˌhænd ˈaʊt, ˌɡɪv ˈaʊt/ [*phrasal verb* T] to give something to all the people in a group: *The princess will be handing out gifts at a children's hospital tomorrow.* | *Don't start the test until I've finished giving out the question papers.*
hand/give out sth to sb *Outside the embassy, students were handing out leaflets to everyone who walked past.*
hand/give sth out *I need some volunteers to hand programs out tonight.*

pass around (also **pass round** BRITISH) /ˌpɑːs (ə)ˈraʊnd‖ˌpæs-/ [*phrasal verb* T] if a group of people **passes** something **around**, one person takes it and gives it to the next person, who then gives it to the next person
pass around sth *They passed around a list and we each had to sign our name.*
pass sth around *Don't keep all the chocolates to yourself – pass them around!*

distribute /dɪˈstrɪbjuːt/ [*v* T] to give things out to a large number of people, especially in an organized way: *Anti-war protesters were distributing leaflets in the street.*
distribute sth to sb *The Red Cross has started distributing food and blankets to people in the flood area.*

distribute sth among sb *Medical supplies have been distributed among families affected by the epidemic.*

> **Formal or informal?**
> **Distribute** is used in writing and in formal spoken English.

share out /ˌʃeər ˈaʊt/ [*phrasal verb* T] to divide something into equal parts and give a part to each person
share out sth *As long as they share out the profits fairly, everyone will be happy.*
share sth out *Bill shared the pizza out.*
share out sth among/between sb *More than £1.7 million has been shared out among victims of the disaster.*

serve /sɜːʳv/ [*v* T] to give food and drinks to someone, for example in a restaurant or hotel, or at a party: *Dinner is served between 7 and 9.* | *Don't forget to serve the guests first.*
serve sth to sb *We don't serve alcohol to anyone under 21.*

> **Formal or informal?**
> **Serve** is used in writing and in formal spoken English.

3 to give money, food etc to help people who need it

give /ɡɪv/ [*v* I/T] to give money to an organization that will use it to help people who are poor, sick, in trouble etc: *We would be grateful for any donation that you are prepared to give.*
give sth to sb *Local people have given over $100,000 to our Help a Child appeal.*
give sb sth *The British give animal welfare organizations over £200 million per year.*
give generously (=give a lot of money) *Please give generously, these children need your help.*
giving – gave – have given

donate /dəʊˈneɪt‖ˈdəʊneɪt/ [*v* T] to give money, or something useful or valuable, in order to help people – use this especially about things that are given by companies or organizations:

The school books were donated by a local publishing company.
donate sth to sth *The concert organizers say they will donate all profits to charity.*

make a donation /ˌmeɪk ə dəʊ'neɪʃən/ to give an amount of money, to an organization that will use it to help people: *We're collecting money to build a hostel for homeless people. Would you like to make a donation?*
+to *The company has made several large donations to charity appeals.*

charity /'tʃærɟti/ [n C/U] an organization that collects money or goods from people who give them, and uses them to help people who need help
give/donate sth to charity *He donated £9,000 to his favourite charities.*
go to charity (=be given to help a charity) *All profits from the show will go to charity.*
do sth for charity *They aim to walk 30 miles to raise money for charity.*
plural **charities**

> ⚠ You can also use **charity** before a noun, like an adjective, to describe an event that makes money for charity: *a charity lunch | a charity dance*

---

4 something you give someone on a special occasion, or in order to thank them

present /'prezənt/ [n C] something that you give to a friend or to someone in your family on a special occasion
get a present *Did you get some nice presents for your birthday?*
+from *The watch was a present from my mother.*
Christmas/birthday/anniversary etc present *We can't afford to spend much on Christmas presents this year.*

gift /gɪft/ [n C] something that you give to someone on a special occasion
+of *He gave me a very generous gift of $200.*
+from *The earrings were a gift from my aunt.*
a wedding/Christmas/birthday gift

> ⚠ You can also use **gift** before a noun, like an adjective: *a gift shop | gift vouchers*

> ⚠ **Gift** and **present** usually mean the same, but in American English **gift** is more common than **present**, and in British English **present** is more common than **gift**. In British English, **gift** usually means something attractive rather than useful, and is used especially by people who make and sell such things.

reward /rɪ'wɔːʳd/ [n C] something that you give someone because they have done something good or helpful
+for *Employees may be promoted as a reward for outstanding service.*
offer a reward (=to offer money to people in order to get information, especially in order to deal with a crime) *The owners offered a reward of £10,000 for information leading to the return of the jewels.*

---

5 to give something to someone, and receive a similar thing from them

exchange /ɪks'tʃeɪndʒ/ [v T] *We exchanged addresses and phone numbers.*
exchange sth with sb *The workshops enable students to exchange ideas with each other.*

> **Formal or informal?**
> **Exchange** is used in writing and in formal spoken English.

swap /swɒp‖swɑːp/ [v I/T] to give something to someone that you know well and receive a similar thing from them, so that you each get something that you want: *My sister and I often swap clothes. | When we finish our books, shall we swap?*
swap sth for sth *I'll swap this CD for one of your computer games.*

> **Formal or informal?**
> **Swap** is much more informal than exchange.

trade /treɪd/ [v I/T] ESPECIALLY AMERICAN to exchange something that you have for something that someone else has:

She liked my T-shirt and I liked hers, so we traded.

trade sth for sth *The report concluded that North had traded weapons for hostages.*

in exchange/in return /ɪn ɪks'tʃeɪndʒ, ɪn rɪ'tɜːʳn/ if you give something or do something **in exchange** or **in return** for something else, you give it in order to get something else back: *They work at the hospital two hours a day and get free meals in return.*

+for *Some executives had given bribes to tax police in exchange for favorable treatment.*

6   to arrange for something to be given to someone after you die

leave /liːv/ [v T] to arrange for something to be given to someone after you die

leave sth to sb *He left £1000 to each of the nurses who had looked after him.*

leave sb sth *My aunt died last year and left me some of her furniture.*

leaving – left – have left

will /wɪl/ [n C] an official document that says who your money and possessions will be given to after you die

in sb's will *Mrs Williams left her daughter $200,000 in her will.*

make a will (=write a will) *He made a will just hours before he died.*

be handed down /biː ˌhændɪd 'daʊn/ if something **is handed down**, it is given to a younger person in the same family: *a ring that had been handed down from her grandmother*

7   to give something to someone who had it before

give back /ˌgɪv 'bæk/ [phrasal verb T] to give something to the person who gave it to you

give sth back *Don't forget to give my pen back when you've finished with it.*

give sth back to sb *He still hasn't given that book back to me.*

give sb sth back *If the show's cancelled, do they give the audience their money back?*

return /rɪ'tɜːʳn/ [v T] FORMAL to give or send something to the person or organization that gave or sent it to

you: *You must return all your library books before the end of the year.*

return sth to sb *Please return your application form to us in the envelope provided.*

8   when several people give money in order to pay for something

contribute /kən'trɪbjuːt/ [v I/T] to give some of the money that is needed to pay for something

+to *I'd like to thank all of you who contributed to the hospital appeal.*

contribute sth to/towards sth *My parents said they would contribute something towards the cost of my driving lessons.*

make a contribution /ˌmeɪk ə kɒntrɪ'bjuːʃən‖-kɑːn-/ to give an amount of money which, when added to money given by other people, can be used to pay for something useful: *If we all make a contribution, we'll be able to get her something really nice.*

+to/towards *Thousands of people have already made contributions towards the relief fund.*

have/make a collection /ˌhæv, ˌmeɪk ə kə'lekʃən/ to collect money from each of the people in a group, especially in order to buy something for someone: *They had a collection in the office and raised over $80.*

+for *His team mates have already made a collection for him.*

chip in /ˌtʃɪp 'ɪn/ [phrasal verb T] INFORMAL if everyone in a group **chips in**, they each give an amount of money so that they can pay for something together: *We all chipped in to pay for the food and wine.*

chip in with $50/£10/$20 etc *Electronics firm Compol chipped in with over £20,000.*

9   to officially give someone the right to own something

hand over /ˌhænd 'əʊvəʳ/ [phrasal verb T] to give property, goods, or power to someone else so that they officially own it or control it

hand over sth *Farmers were forced to*

hand over 60% of everything they produced.

hand sth over to sb *On his retirement, he handed the business over to his son.*

transfer /træns'fɜːʳ/ [v T] FORMAL to make official arrangements so that money, property, or control of something is legally given to someone else

transfer sth to sb *In 1923 the ownership of the forest was transferred to a rich Dutch family.* | *The ageing king was preparing to transfer power to his son.*

transferring – transferred – have transferred

GO

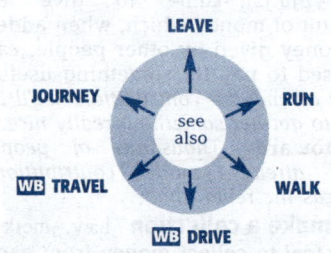

LEAVE
JOURNEY
RUN
see also
WB TRAVEL
WALK
WB DRIVE

1 to go somewhere

go /gəʊ/ [v I] to go away from where you are to another place: *We'd better go soon or we'll be late.* | *Where are you going?*

+to/into/down/there etc *"Is Allie home?" "No, she's gone to a party."* | *Does this bus go past the university?*

go home *I called her at the office but she'd already gone home.*

go for a swim/drink/walk etc (=go somewhere to have a swim, a drink etc) *We all went for a walk after dinner.*

go and do sth/go do sth AMERICAN (=go somewhere in order to do something) *I'll just go and get my coat.*

going – went – have gone

> ⚠ British speakers say **go and do sth**. American speakers usually say **go do sth**: *Do you want to go see the baseball game?*

come /kʌm/ [v I] if someone or something **comes**, they go to the place where you are already, or to the place that you are going to: *Chris called to say he can't come.* | *Look – the bus is coming.*

+to/from/here etc *Are you coming to lunch with us, Karen?* | *Come here at once!*

coming – came – have come

be off to /biː 'ɒf tuː‖-'ɔːf-/ [phrasal verb T] ESPECIALLY SPOKEN if you **are off to** a place, you are going to go there now, or you will go there very soon: *We're all off to Florida next week.* | *I'm just off to the shops. Is there anything you need?*

on your way/on the way /ˌɒn jɔːʳ 'weɪ, ˌɒn ðə 'weɪ/ if you are **on your way** somewhere, you have already left one place and you are travelling towards another

+to/from/out etc *She was attacked on the way home from a nightclub.* | *I was already on my way to work when I realized I'd forgotten my briefcase.*

head /hed/ [v I] to travel towards a place, especially when the journey is long or difficult

+towards/for *The ship was heading for Cuba.*

head north/west etc *Keep heading south until you reach the river.*

make your way /ˌmeɪk jɔːʳ 'weɪ/ ESPECIALLY WRITTEN to go somewhere slowly, carefully, or with difficulty

+to/through/there *It took us ages to make our way through the crowds.* | *After escaping from the prison camp, he made his way to the border.*

> Use **make your way** especially in stories or descriptions of past events.

cross /krɒs‖krɔːs/ [v I/T] to go from one side of something to the other, for example across a river or road, or across a field or room: *How are we going to cross the river?* | *Before you cross, make sure there are no cars coming.* | *I crossed the hall and went towards the exit.*

2 to use a car, bus, train etc as a way of going somewhere

go by sth /'gəʊ baɪ (sth)/ [phrasal verb T]
go by car/bus/train/plane/boat to go to a place in a car, bus etc: *"Are you driving there?" "No we're going by bus."*

take /teɪk/ [v T]
take a taxi/bus/train to pay to go somewhere in a taxi, bus, or train: *It was too far to walk, so we decided to take a taxi.*
taking – took – have taken

3 to go somewhere with someone

go with sb /'gəʊ wɪð (sb)/ [phrasal verb T] *One of his friends went with him to the hospital.* | *She had a spare ticket so I decided to go with her.*

come with sb /'kʌm wɪð (sb)/ [phrasal verb T] if you **come with** someone, you go with them to the same place that they are going: *We're going to the mall – do you want to come with us?* | *Sorry I'm late – I came with Phil and his car broke down.*

come along /ˌkʌm ə'lɒŋǁ-ə'lɔːŋ/ [phrasal verb I] to go with other people to a party, restaurant, film etc which they have already arranged to go to: *We're going clubbing later – you're welcome to come along.* | *We went to the beach, and Jo came along too.*

accompany /ə'kʌmpəni/ [v T often passive] FORMAL to go somewhere with someone, especially in order to give them protection or support: *A bodyguard accompanies her wherever she goes.*
be accompanied by sb (=have sb with you) *Children under the age of 14 must be accompanied by an adult.* | *The President was accompanied by his wife.*
accompanying – accompanied – have accompanied

> Don't say 'accompanied with someone'. Say **accompanied by someone**.

4 to go to a meeting, party, concert etc

go /gəʊ/ [v I] to go to a party, game, concert, meeting etc: *She invited me to her wedding, but I couldn't go.*
+to *Did you go to the baseball game last weekend?* | *I have to go to a meeting this afternoon.*
going – went – have gone

come /kʌm/ [v I] to go to a game, concert, meeting, party etc, either at the home of the person who invites you, or with someone who is also going there
+to *Can you come to my party?* | *You should have come to the concert, it was really good.*
coming – came – have come

attend /ə'tend/ [v I/T] FORMAL to go to an event such as a meeting or religious service: *Several people were unable to attend because of the storm.*
attend a meeting/service/interview/conference *If you wish to attend the memorial service, please put your name on this list.*

> Don't use **attend** for talking about things that you go to for pleasure, such as parties or concerts.

5 to regularly go to a school, church etc

go to /'gəʊ tuː/ [phrasal verb T] *As a child I used to hate going to church.* | *He's been going to Spanish lessons for months and he still can't ask for directions.*

attend /ə'tend/ [v T] FORMAL to regularly go to a church, school, class etc: *Both children attend Westwood Junior High.*

be at /'biː æt/ [phrasal verb T] if you **are at** a school, college, or university, you study there: *I'm at Belton School. What about you?*
be at school/college (=be a student) *My husband and I met when we were both at college.*

be in /'biː ɪn/ [phrasal verb T] AMERICAN if you **are in** a school or college, you study there: *We can't afford to retire* *while Jessie and Joely are still in school.* | *We had the wildest parties when we were in school.*

GOOD

➡ opposite **BAD**

BETTER
WORKING
BEST
SUITABLE/
UNSUITABLE
PERFECT
PRAISE
see
also
BEAUTIFUL
IMPROVE
CONVENIENT/
NOT CONVENIENT
ENTHUSIASTIC/
UNENTHUSIASTIC

1 something you like or enjoy very much

good /gʊd/ [adj] *Did you have a good weekend?* | *It was the best party I've ever been to.* | *That smells good. What are you cooking?*
very/really good *We enjoyed our trip to Canada. It was really good.*
good – better – best

nice /naɪs/ [adj] pleasant or enjoyable: *I hope you have a nice vacation.* | *Come over on Saturday. It would be nice to see you.*
very/really nice *She made us a really nice dinner.*

> **Formal or informal?**
> **Nice** is rather an informal word. Use it in conversation and in letters to friends, but do not use it too much in your written work.

○ **great** /greɪt/ [adj] ESPECIALLY SPOKEN very good or very enjoyable: *Thanks for a great day on Saturday.* | *It would be great if you could teach me to ski.*
really great *"What was the concert like?" "It was great, really great."*

> Don't say 'very great'. Say **really great**.

excellent /'eksələnt/ [adj] extremely good: *There are excellent beaches close to the hotel.* | *"Was it a good trip?" "Yes, it was excellent."*

> Don't say 'very excellent'. Just say **excellent**.

> **Formal or informal?**
> **Excellent** sounds rather formal in spoken English.

marvellous/wonderful/fantastic /'maːʳvələs, 'wʌndəʳfəl, fæn'tæstɪk/ [adj] very good in a way that makes you feel happy or excited: *The kids had a marvellous time at the carnival.* | *You get a wonderful view of the mountains from here.*

> Don't say 'very marvellous/wonderful/ fantastic'. Say **absolutely marvellous/ wonderful/fantastic**.

amazing/incredible /ə'meɪzɪŋ, ɪn'kredˌbəl/ [adj] very good in a surprising and exciting way: *Standing there on top of Mount Fuji was an amazing experience.* | *What a goal! That was incredible!*

> Don't say 'very amazing/incredible'. Say **absolutely amazing/incredible**.

○ **brilliant** /'brɪljənt/ [adj] BRITISH SPOKEN extremely good: *You should come to the new sports centre – it's brilliant.*

> Don't say 'very brilliant'. Say **really brilliant** or **absolutely brilliant**.

○ **neat** /niːt/ [adj] AMERICAN SPOKEN very good or enjoyable: *That's such a neat car.*
really neat *The fireworks over Golden Gate Park were really neat.*

2 something that is of a high standard or good quality

good /gʊd/ [adj] *It's a good car, but it is expensive.* | *Lisa's work has been much better recently.*
very good *There are one or two very good restaurants around here.*
good – better – best

well /wel/ [adv] if you do something **well**, you do it with care and skill, so that what you do or produce is of a

G

high standard: *Jean's playing much better since you gave her some lessons.* | *It's one of the best designed websites I've ever seen.*
very well *Both books are very well written and enjoyable to read.*
do well (=achieve a high standard and be successful) *Don't worry about the test – I'm sure you'll do well.*
well – better – best

excellent /'eksələnt/ [adj] extremely good: *The bank provides an excellent service for its customers.* | *They told me my English was excellent.*

> Don't say 'very excellent'. Just say **excellent**.

good quality/high quality /ˌgʊd 'kwɒlɪti, ˌhaɪ 'kwɒlɪtiǁ-'kwɑː-/ [adj only before noun] well made from good materials: *If you buy good quality shoes, they last longer.* | *We only use the highest quality ingredients for our pizzas.*
of good/high quality *handmade carpets of the highest quality*

impressive /ɪm'presɪv/ [adj] something that is **impressive** is of a very high standard and you admire it: *The school's examination results were very impressive.* | *an impressive achievement*

impressed /ɪm'prest/ [adj not before noun] if you are **impressed** by something, you think it is a very high standard, and so you admire it and feel pleased about it: *When I saw the computer facilities at the college, I was really impressed.*
+by/with *Everyone was very impressed by Kaori's English – she made almost no mistakes.*

outstanding /aʊt'stændɪŋ/ [adj] an **outstanding** performance or achievement is extremely good, and much better than that of other people: *an outstanding performance by a talented young actor* | *Her work has been outstanding all year.*

> **Formal or informal?**
> **Outstanding** is used especially in news reports, advertisements, and formal speeches and is not usually used in ordinary informal conversation.

3 in good condition

in good condition /ɪn ˌgʊd kən'dɪʃən/ something that is in **good condition** is not broken and has no marks or other things wrong with it: *The car's only two years old, and is in very good condition.*

as good as new/like new /əz ˌgʊd əz 'njuː, laɪk 'njuːǁ-'nuː/ ESPECIALLY SPOKEN something that is **as good as new** or is **like new** is almost as good as when it was new – use this about things that have recently been cleaned or repaired: *Within three weeks, the schoolroom looked as good as new.* | *Craig had polished the motorcycle until it looked like new.*

4 a good idea, suggestion, plan etc

good /gʊd/ [adj] *A good way of dealing with the problem is to talk about it.* | *That's the best suggestion anyone's made all day.*
good idea *"Why don't we hire a van?" "That's a good idea."*
good – better – best

excellent /'eksələnt/ [adj] extremely good: *We've been given some excellent financial advice.* | *That sounds like an excellent idea to me.*

great /greɪt/ [adj] ESPECIALLY SPOKEN a **great** idea is one that you like very much: *"Let's have a barbecue." "That's a great idea."*
great! *"Do you want to go the beach instead?" "Yeah, great! Why not!"*

fantastic /fæn'tæstɪk/ [adj] extremely good, in a way that makes you feel happy or excited: *What a fantastic idea!*

brilliant /'brɪljənt/ [adj] very clever and likely to succeed: *I think that's a brilliant suggestion – let's try it.* | *Hugh thought of a brilliant idea for a book.*

5 someone who is good at doing something

good /gʊd/ [adj] able to do something well: *You should see him play tennis – he's pretty good.*

+at *Ruth had always been good at languages.*

good at doing sth *You're much better at dealing with people than I am.*

a good singer/teacher/actor etc *Lindy is probably the best dancer in the class. | I think Robbie's a really good pianist.*

good with sth/sb (=good at dealing with them) *Mrs Hill is very good with children. | I've never been much good with money.*

good – better – best

well [adv] *Dave plays the guitar very well.*

> ⚠ Don't say 'he's good in football'. Say **he's good at football**.

brilliant /'brɪljənt/ [adj] extremely good at doing something: *Paganini was a brilliant violinist. | Have you heard her sing? She's absolutely brilliant.*

skilful BRITISH **skillful** AMERICAN /'skɪlfəl/ [adj] someone who is **skilful** does something very well using their ability to do it and their training: *He's one of the most skilful players in professional tennis. | the artist's skillful use of colour | Success in business depends on skilful management.*

skilfully/skillfully [adv] *Ben steered the boat skilfully through the narrow channel. | a skilfully worded question*

skilled /skɪld/ [adj] someone who is **skilled** at a particular job has the training and experience to do it well

skilled worker/engineer/craftsman etc *There is a demand for carpenters, and other skilled craftsmen.*

skilled at doing sth *Our advisers are skilled at dealing with financial problems.*

highly skilled (=very skilled) *A highly skilled chef can earn a lot of money.*

expert /'ekspɜːᵗt/ [n C] someone who is extremely skilful at doing something because they have gained a lot of knowledge or experience of this particular subject or activity over a period of time

+in/on *an expert in French history*

medical/legal/financial etc expert *Legal experts are calling for a change in the law.*

expert [adj] extremely skilful at doing something because you have gained a lot of knowledge or experience: *Students learn to cook French food with the help of expert chefs.*

+at/in *Politicians are usually expert at turning a crisis to their advantage.*

expert help/advice/opinion etc *Tennis coaches will be available to provide expert advice.*

genius /'dʒiːniəs/ [n C] someone who has an unusually high level of intelligence, mental skill, or ability

a genius at (doing) sth *My father was a genius at storytelling.*

musical/comic/mathematical etc genius *the greatest musical genius who ever lived*

outstanding/exceptional /aʊt'stændɪŋ, ɪk'sepʃənəl/ [adj] very good at doing something, so that people notice that you are much better than others: *At Harvard Law School he was an outstanding student. | Sarah was quite a good artist, but not an exceptional one.*

talented /'tæləntᵻd/ [adj] very good at doing something because you have a lot of natural ability

talented actor/musician/player etc *I remember Hugh as a talented actor when we were at school together.*

highly talented (=very talented) *The Brazilian team includes some highly talented young players.*

advanced /əd'vɑːnst‖əd'vænst/ [adj only before noun] someone who is **advanced** has reached a high level in a subject that they are studying: *This is an exercise for more advanced students. | The college has elementary, intermediate and advanced classes in French and Spanish.*

promising /'prɒmᵻsɪŋ‖'prɑː-/ [adj] good at something, and likely to become very good in the future – use this about young people: *a promising young footballer | The most promising students were selected for special training.*

> **Formal or informal?**
> **Promising** is used in formal writing and news reports, and by teachers and sports coaches.

6 the ability to do something well

skill /skɪl/ [n C/U] the ability to do something well because you have learned it or practised it: *You will be* taught the skills you need to become a successful journalist. | The Australians played with great skill and determination.

computer / management / language etc skills You need good communication skills for this job.

+in On the course you will develop skills in business management.

ability /ə'bɪlɪti/ [n U] being able to do something well

ability to do sth Paper 3 tests the student's ability to write in English.

talent /'tælənt/ [n C/U] a natural ability to do something very well: Her good looks and natural talent brought her immediate success in Hollywood.

musical/theatrical/artistic etc talent The boy's musical talents were first recognised by his teacher.

+for She has a talent for languages.

---

7   morally good people or behaviour

good /gʊd/ [adj] kind, honest, and helpful: Jean's a very good person – she's always ready to help. | He had always tried to lead a good life.

good – better – best

decent /'diːsənt/ [adj] someone who is **decent** is good and honest according to the normal standards of society: Decent citizens have nothing to fear from the police. | a decent, honest, hard-working woman

 Decent is a slightly old-fashioned word.

respectable /rɪ'spektəbəl/ [adj] behaving and living your life in a way that is considered morally correct by society, especially because of the family you come from: Tony was always in trouble with the police when he was young, but now he's a respectable married man. | The girls in the school all come from very respectable families.

ethical /'eθɪkəl/ [adj] morally correct according to the rules of behaviour in a particular job: It would not be ethical for me, as a doctor, to talk about my patients.

---

8   good enough, but not very good

good enough /'gʊd ɪ,nʌf/ If the weather's good enough we'll go camping.

+for It's just a cheap wine but it's good enough for a picnic.

good enough to do sth Do you think she is good enough to be in the team?

not bad /nɒt 'bæd/ SPOKEN use this to say that something is fairly good, and better than you expected: "What was the food like?" "Oh, not bad – better than last time." | You know, that's not a bad idea.

not too bad "How was your test?" "Oh, not too bad. I think I passed."

be all right/be okay /biː ,ɔːl 'raɪt, biː əʊ'keɪ/ SPOKEN to be good enough, although not especially good: "What did you think of the movie?" "Oh, it was OK – nothing special." | The children made the cakes. I hope they're all right.

+for This book is okay for beginners but it's not really suitable for more advanced students.

satisfactory /,sætɪs'fæktəri/ [adj] FORMAL something that is **satisfactory** reaches the expected standard, so it is good enough to be accepted: You won't get paid unless your work is satisfactory. | Lynne got satisfactory grades and was offered a place at university.

satisfactorily [adv] The ship's disappearance has never been satisfactorily explained.

acceptable /ək'septəbəl/ [adj] good enough to be able to be used for a particular purpose: Some low-fat cheeses have quite an acceptable flavour, but some taste like rubber.

+to an agreement which is acceptable to both sides

Formal or informal?

Acceptable is used in writing and in formal spoken English.

will do /wɪl 'duː/ SPOKEN you say that something **will do** when you think that it is good enough to use, although it is not exactly the right thing: *Don't worry if you haven't got any butter. Margarine will do.* | *This paint isn't quite the right colour but I suppose it'll do.*

GOVERNMENT/ POLITICS

➡ see Word Banks section

GROUP

➡ if you mean 'a group of people who play music together', go to WB **MUSIC**

➡ see also **CROWD, TYPE**

1 a group of people together in one place

group /gruːp/ [*n* C] several people who are together in the same place
+of *Outside the school, little groups of friends were talking to each other.* | *an old photograph of a group of soldiers sitting on the ground*
in groups (=forming separate groups) *Men stood in groups on street corners.*
get into a group (=make a group with other people so that you can do something together) *The teacher told us to get into groups of three.*

crowd /kraʊd/ [*n* C] a large number of people who are all together in the same place: *a football crowd* | *A huge crowd had gathered to hear the President speak.*
+of *A crowd of reporters was waiting for her at the airport.*

> ⚠ In British English, you can use **crowd** with a singular or plural verb: *The crowd was/were becoming impatient.* In American English, always use a singular verb: *The crowd was becoming impatient.*

> ⚠ You can say **crowds** of people when you mean a lot of people very close together: *Crowds of tourists were trying to get into the cathedral.*

2 a group of people who do things together

party /ˈpɑːʳti/ [*n* C] a group of people that someone has organized in order to go somewhere or do something: *Admission is free for school parties.*
+of *John was taking a party of tourists around the museum.*
a search/rescue party (=a group of people trying to find and help someone who is in danger)
plural **parties**

bunch/crowd /bʌntʃ, kraʊd/ [*n* singular] INFORMAL ESPECIALLY SPOKEN a group of people who do things together or spend time together: *The people on my French course are a really friendly bunch.*
+of *We were a very mixed bunch of women.*

gang /gæŋ/ [*n* C] a group of young people who spend time together, especially a group that causes trouble, fights with other groups etc
gang of youths/kids *There are always gangs of kids standing around the shopping mall.*
rival gang (=a gang that fights with another gang) *Fighting broke out between two rival gangs.*

3 a group of people who are similar in some way or have similar ideas

group /gruːp/ [*n* C] a number of people who are similar in some way, or who have the same ideas and aims: *a left-wing terrorist group*
+of *The factory was burned down by a group of animal-rights activists.*
age group/income group etc (=all the people of about the same age, with about the same income etc) *Road accidents are very common among this age group.*
ethnic group/racial group (=all the people of the same race, nation, or tribe) *Ten of the workers were members of the Hutu ethnic group.*

movement /ˈmuːvmənt/ [*n* C] a large group of people who share the same ideas and beliefs, and who work

together to achieve something important
+for *the movement for independence*
the peace/environmental/women's etc movement *one of the leaders of the pro-democracy movement*

4 a group of people who work with each other

> ⚠ In British English, you can use these words with a singular or plural verb: *A team of police divers is/are searching the lake.* In American English, always use a singular verb: *A team of police divers is searching the lake.*

team /tiːm/ [*n* C] a group of people who work together to do a job: *There will be a meeting for all members of the team next Wednesday.*
+of *The coins were discovered by a team of archaeologists.*
research/medical team *Dr Gaultier and his medical team worked in the refugee camps for over a year.*

crew /kruː/ [*n* C] the people who work together on a ship or plane: *The captain and crew would like to welcome you on board Flight 381 to Geneva.*

committee /kəˈmɪti/ [*n* C] a small group of people in an organization, company, or club who have been chosen to make decisions that affect everyone in the organization: *Bill Dean has been elected chairman of the committee.*
finance/health/housing committee *The finance committee has decided to raise membership fees for next season. | the Senate Committee on Foreign Relations*
be on a committee (=be a member of a committee) *She's been on the Church committee for 20 years.*

> ⚠ You can also use **committee** before a noun, like an adjective: *We have three new committee members this year. | a committee meeting*

5 a group of things together in one place or connected in some way

group /gruːp/ [*n* C] several things that are together in one place or connected in some way
+of *The house was hidden behind a tall group of trees. | a group of islands off the north coast*
in groups *Dolphins travel in small groups.*

set /set/ [*n* C] a group of similar things that are used together, or a group of connected ideas, facts etc: *a chess set*
+of *I gave an extra set of house keys to my neighbours. | a set of rules | We started the meeting by agreeing on a set of objectives.*

set
a chess set

collection /kəˈlekʃən/ [*n* C] a group of similar things that have been put together because they are interesting or attractive
+of *The museum has a superb collection of Mexican pottery.*
art/stamp/postcard collection *Have you seen her CD collection – it's enormous!*

collection
a stamp collection

bundle /ˈbʌndl/ [*n* C] several things of the same kind, such as papers, clothes, or sticks, that are fastened or tied together: *She keeps all his old letters, tied up in bundles.*
+of *a bundle of twigs*

bundle
a bundle of letters

bunch /bʌntʃ/ [n C] a **bunch** of flowers or keys is a group of flowers or keys tied together; a **bunch** of fruit is several pieces of fruit which grow together and which you buy as one piece: *a small girl carrying a huge bunch of roses* | *I bought some apples and a bunch of grapes.* | *He produced a bunch of keys from his pocket.*
plural **bunches**

bunch

6 a group of things on top of each other

pile /paɪl/ [n C] several things of the same kind placed one on top of the other
+of *Greg carried the pile of ironed shirts upstairs.*
in piles *All the books were arranged in neat piles on her desk.*

pile

heap /hiːp/ [n C] a lot of things lying one on top of the other in an untidy way
+of *There was a huge heap of blankets and pillows on the bed.*
in a heap *The children had left all their wet towels in a heap on the bathroom floor.*

heap

mound /maʊnd/ [n C] a large pile of something
+of *There's a mound of papers on my desk.*

7 to put things or people into groups

sort /sɔːʳt/ [v T] to arrange a large number of things by putting them in different groups, so that you can deal with each group separately: *It takes a couple of hours to sort the mail in the morning.*

sort sth into sth *We sorted all the clothes into two piles.*

categorize (also **categorise** BRITISH) /ˈkætɪɡəraɪz/ [v T] to decide which group something should belong to, when there is a clear system of several groups
categorize sth according to sth *The hotels are categorized according to the standard of the rooms and services they offer.*
categorize sth as sth (=put something in a particular group) *These books are categorized as 'Modern Classics'.*

classify /ˈklæsɪfaɪ/ [v T] to decide what group plants, animals, people etc belong to according to an official or scientific system: *Scientists have discovered a new type of butterfly which has not yet been classified.*
classify sth as sth *They are classified as manual workers.*
classifying – classified – have classified

be grouped /biː ˈɡruːpt/ [v] if people or things **are grouped**, they are put together into separate groups according to a system
+according to *For insurance purposes, the vehicles are grouped according to engine size.*
+together *Non-fiction books are grouped together under different subject areas.*
+into *Most European languages can be grouped into two main families.*

GROW

➡ if you mean 'when a number or amount gets bigger', go to **INCREASE**
➡ see also **BIG**

1 when people, animals, or plants get bigger

grow /ɡrəʊ/ [v I] to become bigger or taller over a period of time: *Tom has really grown since I last saw him.*
+to *Sunflowers can grow to a height of ten feet.*
grow one metre/two centimetres/six inches etc *Amy grew 9 inches last year.*

+into *Within a few years, these saplings will grow into tall trees.*
growing – grew – have grown

develop /dɪ'veləp/ [v I] if a child, plant, or animal **develops**, it gradually changes into the form it will have as an adult: *The baby develops very quickly during the first few weeks of pregnancy.*
+into *In less than 12 weeks the chicks will develop into adult birds.*

> **Formal or informal?**
> **Develop** is used in technical and formal medical contexts.

get taller/get bigger /ˌget 'tɔːlər, ˌget 'bɪgər/ to grow and become taller, especially in a short period of time: *Eleanor's got much bigger since I last saw her.* | *The grass got taller and taller over the summer.*

mature /mə'tʃʊər/ [v I] if a plant **matures**, it grows to its full size: *A tree takes many years to mature.*

2 to make plants or vegetables grow

grow /grəʊ/ [v T] to look after plants, vegetables, or crops so that they develop and grow: *Farmers in this area grow mainly wheat.* | *It's very satisfying growing your own vegetables.*
growing – grew – have grown

cultivate /'kʌltɪ̯veɪt/ [v T] to grow vegetables and other crops, especially in order to sell them: *Nearer the coast, huge areas of land are used for cultivating tomatoes.*
cultivate the land (=use the land to grow crops) *The settlers in the new colony began cultivating the land.*

plant /plɑːnt‖plænt/ [v T] to put seeds or young plants into the soil so that they will grow: *Plant the seeds outside in late spring.* | *They planted an oak tree in the middle of the field.*

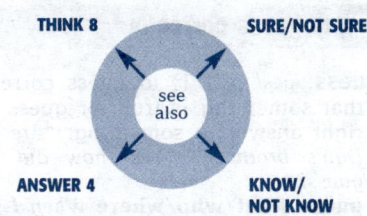

GUESS

THINK 8   SURE/NOT SURE

see also

ANSWER 4   KNOW/ NOT KNOW

1 to guess something

guess /ges/ [v I/T] to give an answer or decide that something is probably true, when you do not know enough to be sure: *Are you sure Linda's pregnant, or are you just guessing?* | *I didn't know all the answers, so I just had to guess some of them.*
guess what/how/who etc *Listen to the voices of these famous people and try to guess who they are.*
+(that) *Detectives guessed that her attacker was someone she knew.* | *From the way he looked, I guessed he'd been drinking.*

◯ **have a guess** BRITISH **take a guess** ESPECIALLY AMERICAN (also **make a guess**) ESPECIALLY SPOKEN /ˌhæv ə 'ges, ˌteɪk ə 'ges, ˌmeɪk ə 'ges/ to guess an answer, amount, or number: *"How much rent do you pay for your apartment?" "Take a guess."*
+at *Have a guess at the answer, then check it with your calculator.*

estimate /'estɪ̯meɪt/ [v T] to say how much something will cost, or how many of something there are etc, partly by calculating and partly by guessing
+that *Organizers estimated that over 10,000 people took part in the demonstration.*
estimate sth at $350/£400 etc *The mechanic estimated the cost of repairs at $350.*
estimate what/where/how much etc *Can you estimate how much fabric you will need for the curtains?*

◯ **my guess is...** /maɪ 'ges ɪz/ SPOKEN say this when you are telling someone what you think has probably happened or will probably happen

+**(that)** *My guess is she'll move back to the States.* | *My guess is that they've been delayed in a traffic jam.*

2 to guess correctly

guess /ges/ [v I/T] to guess correctly that something is true, or guess the right answer to something: *"Are you Dan's brother?" "Yes, how did you guess?"*
guess what/who/where *When I saw how upset she was, I guessed immediately what had happened.*
+**(that)** *No one would have guessed that she was French.*
guess the truth *They had already guessed the truth about their son's disappearance.*
guess right *She could tell by his face that she had guessed right.*

3 to guess incorrectly

guess wrong /ˌges 'rɒŋ‖-'rɔːŋ/ *I guessed she was over sixteen, but I guessed wrong.*
overestimate /ˌəʊvər'estɪ̩meɪt/ [v T] to guess wrongly, by thinking that the amount, level, or cost of something is greater than it really is: *People overestimated the risk of catching the disease.*
underestimate /ˌʌndər'estɪ̩meɪt/ [v T] to guess wrongly, by thinking that the amount, level, or cost of something is less than it really is: *They underestimated the amount of time it would take to finish the work.*

4 an attempt to guess something

guess /ges/ [n C] an attempt to guess something: *It'll probably take about 10 hours to get there, but that's just a guess.*
◯ **have / take / make a guess** ESPECIALLY SPOKEN (=try to guess something) *Have another guess.* | *I don't know why she left him, but I think I can make a reasonable guess.*
◯ **good guess** ESPECIALLY SPOKEN *"When was the house built – about 1600?" "Good guess – it was 1624."*
rough guess (=one that is not intended to be exact) *We think there are about 5 million users on the*

Internet, but this is only a rough guess.
guesswork /ˈgeswɜːʳk/ [n U] when you try to understand something or find the answer to something by guessing, because you do not have all the information you need: *Some of the conclusions were based largely on guesswork.*
speculation /ˌspekjʊ̩'leɪʃən/ [n U] when a lot of people, especially in newspapers and on television, try to guess what is happening or what will happen because they do not have much definite information
+**about** *There has been a lot of speculation about the date of the next election.*
+**that** *A further defeat for the government led to increasing speculation that the Prime Minister would resign.*

Formal or informal?

Speculation is used especially in writing, news reports, and formal speeches.

estimate /ˈestɪ̩mɪt/ [n C] an opinion about the value, size, speed etc of something that is formed partly by calculating and partly by guessing: *According to some estimates, almost two thirds of the city has been destroyed by the earthquake.*
rough estimate (=an estimate that is not intended to be exact) *These are the figures, but they're only a rough estimate.*
at/as a rough estimate (=making a rough estimate) *At a rough estimate, staff are recycling less than a quarter of the paper we buy.*

When you see **EC**, go to the **ESSENTIAL COMMUNICATION** section.

GUILTY/ NOT GUILTY

responsible for a crime or for doing something bad

➡ look here for ...
  • guilty of a crime or mistake
  • feeling bad because you have done something wrong
➡ if you mean 'think or say that someone is responsible for a mistake or something bad', go to **BLAME**

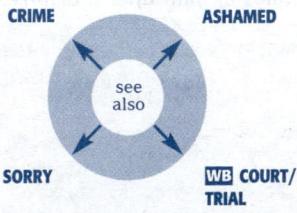

1 guilty

guilty /'gɪlti/ [adj] if someone is **guilty** of a crime, he or she is the person that did it
find sb guilty (=decide in a law court that someone is guilty) *The jury found Sewell guilty and he was sent to prison.*
guilty of murder/rape/a crime etc *A 23-year-old woman was found guilty of murder in the Central Court yesterday.*
plead guilty (=say in a law court that you are guilty of a crime) *Roberts pleaded guilty to driving without insurance.*

responsible /rɪ'spɒnsɪbəl‖rɪ'spɑːn-/ [adj] if someone is **responsible** for a crime, accident, or mistake, they did it or made it happen: *The other driver was responsible for the accident, and he should pay for the damage.*
+for *Police believe a local gang is responsible for the recent burglaries.* | *Mrs Williams says that the hospital was responsible for her husband's death.*

⚠ Use **responsible** especially to talk about accidents and mistakes caused by carelessness, or when no one knows for certain who did it.

2 not guilty

innocent /'ɪnəsənt/ [adj] if someone is **innocent** of a crime, they did not do it – use this especially about someone that other people think is guilty: *Throughout the trial, Bates had claimed he was innocent.*
+of *The report concluded that he was innocent of any wrongdoing.*
innocence [n U] when you are not guilty of a crime: *Her parents were convinced of her innocence.* | *Even after ten years in jail, he still protests his innocence.* (=insists he is innocent)

not guilty /nɒt 'gɪlti/ if someone is **not guilty** of a crime, they did not do it – use this especially when a court has decided that someone did not do a crime
find sb not guilty (of sth) (=decide in a law court that someone is not guilty) *The two women were found not guilty of drug-trafficking.*

be acquitted /bi: ə'kwɪtɪd/ if someone **is acquitted** by a law court, they are officially told that they are not guilty of a crime
+of *McQuade was acquitted of attempted murder.*

3 when you feel ashamed about doing something bad

feel guilty /ˌfiːl 'gɪlti/ to feel worried and unhappy because you have done something wrong or because you have upset someone: *I felt really guilty after spending all that money.* | *Are you feeling guilty because you didn't help her?*
+about *Ed felt guilty about leaving work so early.*

be/feel ashamed /ˌbiː, ˌfiːl ə'ʃeɪmd/ to feel very guilty and disappointed with yourself because you have done something wrong or behaved in an unpleasant or embarrassing way: *She felt thoroughly ashamed when she remembered how drunk she'd been.*
+of *I hope you are ashamed of what you did.*
be/feel ashamed to say/admit/think etc sth *I'm ashamed to admit it, but I wasn't really sorry when he died.*
be/feel ashamed of yourself (=feel very guilty about something that you

have done) *You should be ashamed of yourself, being so rude to your grand-mother.*

feel responsible /ˌfiːl rɪˈspɒns̩bəl‖-ˈspɑːn-/ to feel that you made something bad happen, especially because you were careless or you could have prevented it from happening
+for *For a long time afterwards I felt responsible for his death.*

○ **feel bad** /ˌfiːl ˈbæd/ ESPECIALLY SPOKEN to feel very sorry because you have upset someone or done something that you should not have done
+that *I should have told Helen I was sorry. I feel really bad that I didn't.*

+about *She feels bad about hitting the kids but she just can't stop.*

have a guilty conscience /hæv ə ˌgɪlti ˈkɒnʃəns‖-ˈkɑːn-/ to feel worried and unhappy for a long time because you know that you are doing or have done something wrong, especially something that other people do not know about: *For a long time, he'd had a guilty conscience about his feelings for the girl.*

guilt /gɪlt/ [n U] the feeling you have when you know you have done something that you know is wrong
feeling of guilt *People often have feelings of guilt after a divorce.*

H, h

HAIR

➡ see also **SHINE, DESCRIBING PEOPLE**

> ⚠ Don't say 'she has dark hairs'. Say **she has dark hair**. Never use 'hairs' to talk about all the hair on your head.

> ⚠ Don't say 'she has blonde long hair'. Say **she has long blonde hair**. **Long, short**, and **thick** always come before the colour of hair, not after it.

1   how long someone's hair is, or how much hair they have

short /ʃɔːʳt/ [adj] a pretty girl with short black hair

long /lɒŋǁlɔːŋ/ [adj] That's my sister – the one with long blonde hair. | Jim's hair used to be quite long.

shoulder-length /ˈʃəʊldəʳ leŋθ/ [adj] **shoulder-length** hair is long enough to reach your shoulders: She has blue eyes and shoulder-length fair hair.

down to /ˈdaʊn tuː/ if someone's hair is **down to** their waist, shoulders etc, it is long enough to reach their waist, their shoulders etc: When Gran was young, she had beautiful black hair down to her waist. | "I used to have hair down to here," said Valerie indicating her shoulder.

bald /bɔːld/ someone who is **bald** has little or no hair on their head: a short bald man in a dark suit
go bald (=lose your hair) My father started going bald in his twenties.

thick /θɪk/ [adj] if someone's hair is **thick**, they have a lot of hair growing closely together: He ran his fingers through his thick dark hair.

in a bob/bobbed /ɪn ə ˈbɒb, bɒbdǁ -ˈbɑːb, bɑːbd/ if a woman's hair is **in a bob** or is **bobbed**, it is cut to the same length all around, except above her eyes where it is shorter, and it ends at about the level of her chin

ponytail /ˈpəʊniˌteɪl/ [n C] long hair tied together at the back of your head and hanging down like a tail: Who's that guy over there with the ponytail?
in a ponytail Kathryn always wears her hair in a ponytail.

2   how straight or curly someone's hair is

straight /streɪt/ [adj] **straight** hair does not have any curls: Yuri's straight black hair was thick and shiny.

wavy /ˈweɪvi/ [adj] **wavy** hair is not straight or curly, but has smooth curves in it: Her wavy brown hair was tied back with a red ribbon.
wavy – wavier – waviest

wavy

curly /ˈkɜːʳli/ [adj] **curly** hair has tight curls: a chubby baby with blond curly hair | long dark curly hair
curly – curlier – curliest

curly

frizzy /ˈfrɪzi/ [adj] **frizzy** hair is full of stiff curls going in all directions, and looks as if it is difficult to control

frizzy

spiky /ˈspaɪki/ [adj] **spiky** hair is stiff and stands up on top of your head
spiky – spikier – spikiest

3   what colour someone's hair is

dark /dɑːʳk/ [adj] **dark** hair is black or brown: The attacker is described as 5ft 9ins tall, with short dark hair. | Her husband is tall and dark. (=he has dark hair)

fair /feəʳ/ [adj] **fair** hair is light brown or yellow: a little boy with fair hair and blue eyes

blonde/blond /blɒndǁblɑːnd/ [adj] **blonde** hair is very light brown or yellow – use **blonde** about women,

H

and **blond** about men: *Janet's got beautiful long blonde hair.* | *Nicola has dark hair but her brother is blond.* (=he has blond hair)

ginger/red /'dʒɪndʒə^r, red/ [adj] **ginger** or **red** hair is an orange-brown colour: *Ruth's the one with red hair.*

grey BRITISH **gray** AMERICAN /greɪ/ [adj] **grey** or **gray** hair is the colour between black and white, which most people's hair is when they are older: *a middle-aged businessman with grey hair and a grey suit*

black /blæk/ [adj] **black** hair is the darkest colour
jet black (=very dark) *jet black hair*

brown /braʊn/ [adj] **brown** hair is the colour of earth, wood, or coffee: *dark brown hair*

mousy /mousey /'maʊsi/ [adj] **mousy** hair is a dull brown colour

auburn /'ɔːbə^rn/ [adj] **auburn** hair is a reddish-brown colour

highlights/streaks /'haɪlaɪts, striːks/ [n plural] parts of your hair that have been made a lighter colour than the rest: *She has brown hair with blonde highlights.*

-haired /heə^rd/ **dark-haired/fair-haired/red-haired etc** having dark hair, fair hair etc: *a tall, fair-haired guy* | *Two grey-haired ladies got on the bus.*

4 the way your hair is cut

hairstyle /'heə^rstaɪl/ [n C] the style in which your hair is cut or shaped: *I think it's time I changed my hairstyle.* | *You can get magazines that show you all the latest hairstyles.*

haircut /'heə^rkʌt/ [n C] the way someone's hair has been cut – use this either when someone's hair has just been cut, or to talk about a particular style of haircut: *I like your new haircut, Helen!* | *Her short, neat haircut and dark suit made her look rather serious.*

5 to have your hair cut or treated

have your hair cut /ˌhæv jɔː^r 'heə^r kʌt/ to go to a shop where they cut your hair: *Where do you have your hair cut?*

have your hair cut short *Lee had his hair cut really short.*

haircut /'heə^rkʌt/ [n C] when you have your hair cut: *I really need a haircut.*

hairdresser (also **hairdresser's** BRITISH) /'heə^rˌdresə^r(z)/ [n C] the shop where you go to have your hair cut and styled: *I'm going to the hairdresser's – see you later.*

hairdresser [n C] someone whose job is to cut and treat hair: *Teresa used to be a hairdresser.*

dye /daɪ/ [v T] to change the colour of someone's hair using chemicals: *Peter's hair is so black – I'm sure he dyes it.*

dye sb's hair blond/black etc *When she was fifteen she dyed her hair bright pink.*

dyed [adj] *Do you think his hair is dyed?*

perm /pɜː^rm/ [n C] when straight hair is made curly by using a chemical treatment
have a perm *Your hair would look thicker if you had a perm.*

permed [adj] *permed hair*

6 to wash and brush your hair

wash /wɒʃǁwɔːʃ, waːʃ/ [v T] to make your hair clean by using water and shampoo: *Do you wash your hair every day?*

shampoo /ʃæm'puː/ [n C/U] special liquid soap that you use to wash your hair
shampoo [v T] to wash your hair with special liquid soap

brush /brʌʃ/ [v T] to make your hair smooth and tidy using a brush: *She brushed her hair until it shone.*
brush/hairbrush [n C] the thing you use to brush your hair: *"Where's my hairbrush?" "I think it's in the bathroom."*

comb /kəʊm/ [v T] to make your hair tidy by using a flat piece of plastic or metal with a row of thin teeth along one side: *Just give me a minute to comb my hair.*
comb [n C] the thing you use to comb your hair: *Can I borrow your comb?*

blow-dry /'bləʊ draɪ/ [v T] to dry hair and shape it after washing it, using a hairdryer

HAPPEN

➡ see also **START, FINISH**

1 to happen

happen /'hæpən/ [v I] use this especially about things that have not been planned to happen or that people do not expect: *The accident happened at 2 pm yesterday.* | *What's happened? Why are you crying?* | *Before I knew what was happening, the man grabbed my bag and ran.* | *There's something happening in the street – come and look!*

take place /ˌteɪk 'pleɪs/ to happen – use this especially about events, performances, ceremonies and other things that have been planned to happen: *The wedding will take place on 23rd August.* | *Police are trying to prevent the demonstration taking place.*

> **Formal or informal?**
> **Take place** is more formal than **happen**.

there is /ðeər ɪz/ if **there is** an event, accident, change etc, it happens: *There has been a serious accident on the Santa Monica Freeway.* | *You should see a doctor if there is any change in your condition.* | *There's a concert at the school next Saturday.*

be going on /biː ˌgəʊɪŋ 'ɒn/ ESPECIALLY SPOKEN to be happening – use this especially about something that you think is bad or that you are unable to control: *The kids are being very quiet. I'd better see what's going on!* | *There seemed to be some sort of argument going on.*

occur /ə'kɜːʳ/ [v I] FORMAL to happen – use this especially about changes, chemical reactions, and other things that happen naturally: *Major earthquakes like this occur very rarely.* | *The disease occurs most frequently in young children.* | *Death occurred at approximately 12.30.*
occurring – **occurred** – **have occurred**

come about /ˌkʌm ə'baʊt/ [phrasal verb I] to happen, especially as a result of earlier events or decisions: *Our problems came about because we ignored the advice of experts.*

come true /ˌkʌm 'truː/ if a wish or a dream **comes true**, it really happens, especially after you have wanted it to happen for a long time: *Patterson's dream came true when he won the Boston marathon on his first attempt.*

2 something that happens

event /ɪ'vent/ [n C] something that happens, especially something important or interesting, or something that has been organized and involves a lot of people: *the events leading up to the President's resignation* | *It's one of the country's major sporting events.*
annual event (=an event held every year) *The beer festival is an annual event.*
the course of events (=the way that events happen) *Nothing you could have done would have changed the course of events.*

incident /'ɪnsᵻdənt/ [n C] FORMAL something that happens, especially something involving trouble or a crime: *A man has been charged with murder following an incident at a house in North London.*
without incident (=without any problems or trouble) *The fans were well behaved, and the game passed without incident.*

occasion /ə'keɪʒən/ [n C] an important social event or celebration: *It's Mark's 21st birthday and we're having a party to celebrate the occasion.* | *The President is only seen on important state occasions.*
special occasion *The hotel caters for weddings, birthdays, and other special occasions.*

affair /ə'feəʳ/ [n C] something that happens in politics or public life, especially something shocking or illegal, which is talked about in the newspapers and on television: *the government's embarrassment over the affair* | *President Nixon was forced to resign after the Watergate affair.*

3 when something happens to someone or something

happen to sb/sth /'hæpən tu: (sb/sth)/ [phrasal verb T] if something **happens to** someone or something, it happens and has an effect on them: *What's happened to Dave? He should have been here by now.* | *A lot of people don't really understand what is happening to the environment.*

experience /ɪk'spɪəriəns/ [v T] FORMAL if a person or organization **experiences** a problem, change etc, it happens to them: *We're experiencing a few problems with our website.* | *Some local companies have been experiencing financial difficulties.*

HAPPY

➡ opposite **SAD**

1 feeling happy

happy /'hæpi/ [adj] someone who is **happy** seems relaxed and satisfied, and feels that their life is good, especially because they are in a situation, job, or relationship that they enjoy: *For the first five years of their marriage, they were extremely happy.* | *Liz seems a lot happier now that she's got a new job.* | *the children's happy faces*
happy doing sth *I was happy working in that office. The people were all really friendly.*
a happy time/childhood/life/marriage (=a time when you are happy) *That year was the happiest time of my life.*
happy – happier – happiest

cheerful /'tʃɪəfəl/ [adj] someone who is **cheerful** seems to be always happy,

smiling, and friendly: *Ed's a very cheerful, friendly person.*
a cheerful voice/smile/manner *"My name's Rosie," she said with a cheerful smile.*

be in a good mood /bi: ɪn ə ˌgʊd 'mu:d/ to feel happy and behave in a happy, friendly way – use this about someone who does not always seem so happy: *Why are you in such a good mood this morning?* | *Don't ask Dad now – wait till he's in a good mood.*

cheery /'tʃɪəri/ [adj usually before noun] happy – use this when someone's behaviour and the way they talk seems happy
cheery smile *She gave me a cheery smile.*

2 happy because something good has happened

happy /'hæpi/ [adj] feeling happy because something good has happened to you or is going to happen: *They came home from their vacation feeling happy and relaxed.*
+about *Is she happy about being pregnant?*
+(that) *We're happy that the treatment seems to be working.*
happy to be/see/hear/learn etc *I'm just happy to be safely home again.*
happy – happier – happiest

pleased /pli:zd/ [adj not before noun] happy and satisfied with something that has happened, especially something that has happened to someone else or something good they have done: *"Did you know that Barbara's had a baby girl?" "Oh, I am pleased."*
+with *Amanda's teachers seem very pleased with her progress.*
pleased to hear/see/say etc *You'll be pleased to hear that your application has been successful.*
+(that) *I'm very pleased that so many people have agreed to help us.*

> ⚠ If someone tells you about something good that has happened, don't say 'I am happy'. Say **I am pleased** or **I'm delighted**.

glad /glæd/ [adj not before noun] pleased about a situation, especially because it has improved or because it is not as bad as it could have been: *Everyone was glad when it was time to go home.*

glad to be/hear/say/see *I was very glad to see him looking so much better.*
+(that) *We're all really glad you were able to come.* | *When I saw the other guests, I was glad I'd decided to wear my best clothes.*

delighted /dɪˈlaɪt̬d/ [*adj* not before noun] extremely happy because something very good has happened: *She's been offered a job in Japan, and she's delighted of course.*
+(that) *He was really delighted that she had invited him.*
+with/by/at *Wesley said he was delighted with the court's decision.*
delighted to be/hear/see etc *We're absolutely delighted to hear that you're getting engaged.*

> Don't say 'very delighted'. Say **absolutely delighted**.

> **Formal or informal?**
> **Delighted** is more formal than pleased.

thrilled /θrɪld/ [*adj* not before noun] very happy and excited about something that has happened
+with *Louise is thrilled with the changes she has seen in her son's behavior.*
+at/by *She was thrilled at the prospect of being sent to Europe.*
+(that) *My mother's thrilled that the new house is so close to the park.*
+to do sth *She was thrilled to have her photo taken with Mel Gibson.*

satisfied /ˈsæt̬sfaɪd/ [*adj*] pleased because something has happened in the way you want it to, or because something is as good as you expect it to be
+with *Everyone seemed satisfied with the way the meeting went.*
satisfied look / expression / smile *Blake leaned back with a satisfied smile.*

3 a happy feeling

happiness /ˈhæpɪn̬s/ [*n* U] the feeling you have when you are happy: *They say that money doesn't buy you happiness.*

find happiness (=become happy) *She eventually married and found true happiness.*

pleasure /ˈpleʒəʳ/ [*n* U] the feeling of happiness, enjoyment, or satisfaction that you get from doing something you enjoy or from a good experience
get pleasure from sth *She always got a lot of pleasure from her garden.*
give/bring pleasure to sb *His music has brought pleasure to people all over the world.*
for pleasure (=when you do something just for enjoyment, not because you have to) *Are you here in Rome for business or for pleasure?*

satisfaction /ˌsæt̬sˈfækʃən/ [*n* U] the feeling of happiness you get when you do a job well, or when you do something that you feel is useful: *It was working with children that gave Diana the most satisfaction.*
great/deep satisfaction *Golding said that writing was hard work but it gave him great satisfaction.*
get satisfaction from sth *She gets a lot of satisfaction from seeing her designs turned into actual products.*
job satisfaction (=the feeling you have when you enjoy your job)

joy /dʒɔɪ/ [*n* U] ESPECIALLY WRITTEN a feeling of very great happiness: *It's hard to describe the joy we felt, seeing each other again after so many years.*
with/for joy *He leapt into the air with joy.*

4 happy because you are no longer worried about something

relieved /rɪˈliːvd/ [*adj*] happy because you are no longer worried about something, especially because something bad did not happen or something unpleasant has ended: *Kate looked relieved when she saw her husband walk through the door.*
relieved to see/know/hear etc *We were so relieved to hear that nobody was hurt in the accident.*
+(that) *The hostages were clearly relieved that their ordeal was over.*

relief /rɪˈliːf/ [*n* singular/U] the feeling you have when you are no longer worried about something
it is a relief to do sth *It was a relief to get home after that terrible journey.*

H

with relief *He watched with relief as all the passengers climbed out unhurt.*
to sb's relief (=making someone feel relieved) *To his relief, Martin found his wallet was still on the table.*

5 to make someone feel happy

make sb happy /ˌmeɪk (sb) ˈhæpi/ to make someone feel happy: *Would winning ten million dollars really make you happy? | Nothing I did ever seemed to make him happy.*

please /pliːz/ [v T] to make someone happy by doing what they want you to do: *I only got married to please my parents. | Tony will do anything to please the boss.*

satisfying /ˈsætⅰsfaɪ-ɪŋ/ [adj] a **satisfying** job, activity, or experience is one that you enjoy, especially because you feel you are doing something good and useful: *Growing your own food can be very satisfying.*

cheer up /ˌtʃɪər ˈʌp/ [phrasal verb T] to make someone feel happy again after they have been unhappy
cheer up sb *What can we do to cheer up Simon?*
cheer sb up *I'm taking Angie out to a restaurant to cheer her up.*

6 to feel happy again after feeling sad

cheer up /ˌtʃɪər ˈʌp/ [phrasal verb I] to feel happy again after you have been unhappy: *Matt soon cheered up when I offered to take him to the ball game. | Cheer up, Jenny! Things aren't so bad.*

brighten up /ˌbraɪtn ˈʌp/ [phrasal verb I] WRITTEN to start to look happy again: *Mrs Verity brightened up at the news.*

 Use **brighten up** especially when you are writing stories.

HARD

➡ opposite **SOFT**
➡ if you mean 'hard to do or understand', go to **DIFFICULT**

1 something that does not bend or change its shape

hard /hɑːʳd/ [adj] something that is **hard** does not change its shape when you press on it: *a hard stone floor | I couldn't sleep because the bed was so hard. | During the night the ground had become frozen and hard.*
rock-hard (=very hard) *The bread was rock-hard and dry as a biscuit.*

solid /ˈsɒlɪd‖ˈsɑː-/ [adj] something that is **solid** is made of thick hard material, is not hollow, and is difficult to damage or break: *a solid oak door | Do you think the table is solid enough to take the weight?*
frozen solid *In the winter, the lake was sometimes frozen solid.*

firm /fɜːʳm/ [adj] not completely hard, but not changing shape much when you press it – use this about things that are sometimes soft, such as fruit, muscles, or the ground: *exercises to make your stomach muscles nice and firm | You will need about six firm tomatoes.*

stiff /stɪf/ [adj] not easy to bend – use this about things like paper or cloth: *He stuck the photos onto a sheet of stiff card. | The collar of his shirt felt stiff and uncomfortable.*

rigid /ˈrɪdʒɪd/ [adj] a material that is **rigid** is difficult or impossible to bend, and is often used to support something else: *Spoon the ice-cream into a rigid plastic container and freeze.*

Formal or informal?
Rigid is a more formal and technical word than **stiff**.

tough /tʌf/ [adj] meat that is **tough** is difficult to eat because it is not soft enough; materials that are **tough** are strong and difficult to break or damage: *My steak's really tough – how's yours? | walking boots with tough rubber soles*

2 to become hard or to make something hard

harden /'hɑːʳdn/ [v I/T] to become hard or to make something hard: *The glue needs about 24 hours to harden.* | *Steel is hardened by heating it to a very high temperature.*

set /set/ [v I] if a liquid substance **sets**, it becomes harder – use this to talk about something that slowly becomes harder after it is mixed with water, for example food or building materials: *How long does it take for cement to set?*

setting – set – have set

HATE

1 to hate someone or something

➡ see also **LOVE, LIKE/NOT LIKE,** **📖 OPINIONS**

hate /heɪt/ [v T] to dislike someone or something very much: *"Go away!" she screamed. "I hate you!"* | *Why do you hate school so much?*
hate doing sth *Like most people, Sally hated being unemployed.*

can't stand/can't bear /ˌkɑːnt 'stænd, ˌkɑːnt 'beəʳ‖ˌkænt-/ ESPECIALLY SPOKEN to dislike a person or a situation very much so that you want to avoid them completely: *I'm not inviting Tony. I can't stand him.* | *When I was pregnant, I couldn't bear the smell of meat cooking.*
can't stand/bear doing sth *She couldn't bear seeing him in so much pain.*
can't stand/bear sb doing sth *I can't stand people smoking while I'm eating.*
can't stand the sight of sb/sth *Jerry can't stand the sight of blood.*

detest/loathe /dɪ'test, ləʊð/ [v T] to hate someone or something very much, especially because they make you feel very angry: *He is exactly the kind of selfish, inconsiderate man I detest.* | *I detest any form of cruelty toward animals.*
detest/loathe doing sth *Even after many years as an MP, he still loathed making public speeches.*

Formal or informal?
Detest is more formal than **loathe**.

2 a feeling of hating someone or something

hatred /'heɪtrɪd/ [n singular/U] an extremely strong feeling of hating someone or something: *I could see the jealousy and hatred in Jeff's eyes.*
+of *Tom had a hatred of any kind of authority.*
+for/towards (use this about a feeling of hate for people, not things) *His crimes were probably motivated by his hatred for women.*

loathing /'ləʊðɪŋ/ [n U] WRITTEN a very strong feeling of hatred for someone or something that you think is extremely unpleasant
+for/of *I felt nothing but loathing for him after the way he'd treated me.*

3 someone who hates you and wants to harm you

➡ opposite **FRIEND**

enemy /'enəmi/ [n C] *The detective asked her if her husband had had any enemies.*
make a lot of enemies (=make a lot of people hate you and want to harm you) *He made a lot of enemies while he was working as a police officer.*
plural enemies

HAVE/NOT HAVE

➡ see also **OWN, GET**

1 to have a particular feature, quality, or skill

➡ see also **📖 DESCRIBING PEOPLE'S CHARACTER**

have /hæv/ [v T] *He's a very good dad and he has a lot of patience.* | *The city has plenty of good hotels and restaurants.* | *The jacket also has two inside pockets.* | *Her teachers all say that she has a lot of talent.*
having – had – have had

> ⚠ Don't say 'I am having', 'he is having' etc. Say **I have**, **he has** etc: *She has blue eyes.*

have got /həv ˈgɒt‖-ˈgɑːt/ [v T] ESPECIALLY BRITISH *My sister's got blonde hair and blue eyes.* | *Our new car's got a sun roof and CD player.* | *She's got a lot of experience with computers.*

> **Formal or informal?**
> In spoken British English **have got** is more common than **have**.

> ⚠ **Have got** and **had got** are usually used in their short forms: **I've got**, **she's got**, **we'd got** etc.

with /wɪð, wɪθ/ [*preposition*] use this after a noun to mention the qualities, physical features etc that someone or something has: *Police are looking for a young man with a scar on his forehead.* | *The company needs more people with management experience.* | *a red shirt with a white collar*

there is/there are /ðeər ɪz, ðeər ɑːr/ use this to mention the things that a place has: *It's a big house – there are five bedrooms and 2 bathrooms.* | *Kyoto's a great place to visit. There are lots of fascinating old temples and gardens.*

possess /pəˈzes/ [v T] FORMAL to have a quality or skill, especially one that is very good or special: *All of Barbara's children possess an amazing musical ability.* | *Brown had always possessed great energy and ambition.*

> **Formal or informal?**
> **Possess** is more formal than **have** or **with**.

> ⚠ Don't use **possess** for describing what people look like. Don't say 'He possesses dark hair and brown eyes'. Say **He has dark hair and brown eyes.**

2 to own something such as a television, a car, or a house

have (also **have got** ESPECIALLY BRITISH) /hæv, həv ˈgɒt‖-ˈgɑːt/ [v T] to have something because you have bought it or someone has given it to you:

Over 25% of families in this country have two or more cars. | *Jake's got a beautiful house.* | *Do you have a fax machine?* | *Have you got a dishwasher at home?*

having – had – have had

> ⚠ Don't say 'I am having', 'she is having' etc. Say **I have**, **she has** etc: *She has a new car.*

with /wɪð, wɪθ/ [*preposition*] use this after a noun to say what someone owns: *a wealthy family with a big house in the country* | *Only people with a lot of money can afford to stay at this hotel.*

own /əʊn/ [v T] if you **own** something, especially something valuable such as a car, a house, or a company, it belongs to you legally: *Andy and his wife own a villa in Spain.* | *Do you know who owns this car?* | *The company was previously owned by the French government.*

3 to have something with you or near you, so that you can use it

have (also **have got** ESPECIALLY BRITISH) /hæv, həv ˈgɒt‖-ˈgɑːt/ [v T] to have something with you or near you, for example in your pocket or bag or on your desk: *Do you have any change for the parking meter?* | *I have the tickets in my purse.* | *Have you got a pen I could borrow?* | *Wait a minute. I think I've got a street map.*

having – had – have had

> ⚠ Don't say 'I am having', 'he is having' etc. Say **I have**, **he has** etc: *Don't worry, I have the passports.*

have sth on you /ˌhæv (sth) ˈɒn juː/ ESPECIALLY SPOKEN to have something in your pocket, bag etc, so that you can use it or let someone else use it: *Do you have a calculator on you?* | *I realized I didn't have any money on me.*

have sth with you /ˌhæv (sth) ˈwɪð juː/ to have something useful in your pocket, bag etc when you are away from the place where you usually live or work: *You should have your identity card with you at all times.* | *Unfortunately, I didn't have her phone number with me.*

4 to not have something

don't have /ˌdəʊnt 'hæv/ *My parents still don't have a computer.* | *Joe's family didn't really have much interest in his school work.*

haven't got /ˌhævənt 'ɡɒt‖-'ɡɑːt/ ESPECIALLY BRITISH *She hasn't got much patience.* | *I'd love to come with you, but I haven't got the money at the moment.*

 Be careful not to say 'I don't have got'. Say **I haven't got**, **she hasn't got** etc.

without /wɪð'aʊt/ [preposition] use this after a noun to say that someone or something does not have or own something: *a house without a garden* | *There are so many people without jobs.*
be without sth (=not have basic things that you need) *Some families in the region are still without running water.*

be missing /biː 'mɪsɪŋ/ ESPECIALLY WRITTEN if something **is missing**, you no longer have it, for example because you have lost it or it has been removed: *When I put my hand in my pocket, I realized my passport was missing.* | *Two of his front teeth were missing.*

lack /læk/ [v T] FORMAL to not have something important or something that you need: *Some schools lack even the basic equipment such as pens, pencils, and books.*
lack confidence/ability/experience *Tom has always lacked confidence.*

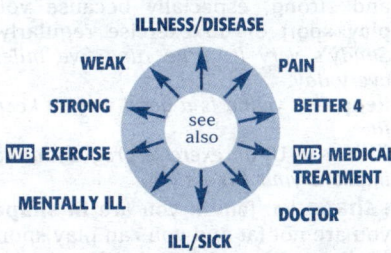

HEALTHY/ UNHEALTHY

ILLNESS/DISEASE
WEAK
PAIN
STRONG
see also
BETTER 4
WB EXERCISE
WB MEDICAL TREATMENT
MENTALLY ILL
DOCTOR
ILL/SICK

1 not ill

healthy /'helθi/ [adj] someone who is **healthy** is not often ill and has nothing physically wrong with them: *I feel much healthier since I stopped smoking.* | *Eating plenty of fresh fruit and vegetables will help you to stay healthy.* | *She's always been such a healthy child.*
healthy – healthier – healthiest

well /wel/ [adj not before noun] healthy – use this to say that someone feels or looks healthy, or that they are healthy again after an illness: *How's the family – are they all well?* | *Take plenty of rest and you'll soon be feeling well.*
look well *You're looking well. Have you been on holiday?*

fine /faɪn/ [adj not before noun] ESPECIALLY SPOKEN well – use this when someone has asked you how you or your family are: *"How are you?" "I'm fine, thanks."* | *"Is Ted all right?" "Yes, he's fine."*

 Don't say 'I'm very fine'. Just say **I'm fine**.

better /'betər/ [adj not before noun] if someone is **better**, they are well again after being ill: *"How's your father now?" "Oh, he's much better, thanks."*
feel better *After a couple of days' rest, she felt a lot better.*

2 healthy and strong because you often do physical exercise

fit /fɪt/ [adj] ESPECIALLY BRITISH healthy and strong, especially because you play sport or do exercise regularly: *Sandy's very fit – he runs five miles every day.*
keep fit *Cycling is a good way to keep fit.*
fitness [n U] *an exercise programme to improve your fitness*

in shape /ɪn 'ʃeɪp/ if you are **in shape** you are not fat and you can play sport or do exercise without getting tired
stay in shape/keep in shape *Walking to work and back helps me to stay in shape.*
in good shape *Both women played well and looked in good shape.*

3 how healthy/unhealthy someone is

health /helθ/ [n U] *Smoking can affect the unborn baby's health.*
be in good/poor health (=be healthy/unhealthy) FORMAL *Despite her age, your mother seems to be in good health.*

4 not healthy or fit

unhealthy /ʌn'helθi/ [adj] not healthy, and often ill: *James was a pale, unhealthy child.*

unfit /ʌn'fɪt/ [adj] BRITISH someone who is **unfit** gets tired very easily when they do physical activities, for example because they eat or drink too much, or they do not get enough exercise: *I'm so unfit, I can't even run to the top of the stairs! | A lot of businessmen are overweight and unfit.*

out of shape/out of condition /ˌaʊt əv 'ʃeɪp, ˌaʊt əv kən'dɪʃən/ if someone is **out of shape** or **out of condition**, they get tired easily when they do sport or exercise, because they do it less often than they used to: *He used to play squash every day but now he's really out of condition.*

5 something that is good for your health

be good for you /bi 'gʊd fər juː/ if a particular kind of food or activity **is good for you**, it helps you to stay healthy: *Citrus fruits such as oranges and lemons are very good for you. | Any kind of exercise is good for you.*

healthy /'helθi/ [adj usually before noun] **healthy** food or a **healthy** way of living helps you to stay healthy: *I'm trying to eat a healthier diet now, with less fat and sugar.*
healthy – healthier – healthiest

wholesome /'həʊlsəm/ [adj] food that is **wholesome** helps you stay healthy because it has nothing unhealthy added to it and is usually prepared very simply: *'Rosie's Pantry' is a small restaurant that serves good wholesome food.*

nutritious /njuː'trɪʃəs‖nuː-/ [adj] food that is **nutritious** contains the natural substances that your body needs in order to stay healthy or to grow: *Brown bread is more nutritious than white. | Nuts and fruit make nutritious snacks.*

Formal or informal?

Nutritious is not used much in ordinary spoken English, and is more common in formal written English.

nourishing /'nʌrɪʃɪŋ‖'nɜː-, 'nʌ-/ [adj] food that is **nourishing** helps your body to grow or to stay healthy and also gives you energy: *A simple chicken soup is both nourishing and delicious.*

6 something that is bad for your health

be bad for your health/be bad for you /bi ˌbæd fər jɔːr 'helθ, bi 'bæd fər juː/ if a particular kind of food or activity is **bad for your health** or **bad for you**, it is likely to make you ill or less healthy: *Smoking is bad for your health. | Too much sun can be bad for you and can damage your skin.*

unhealthy /ʌn'helθi/ [adj] **unhealthy** foods, places, situations etc are likely to make you ill or less healthy: *An* unhealthy diet may make your headaches worse. | A lot of young people have an unhealthy lifestyle, drinking too much and eating the wrong foods.

harmful /ˈhɑːʳmfəl/ [adj] if something is **harmful**, it has a bad effect on your health: harmful bacteria

+to The sun's rays can be very harmful to the skin.

> **Formal or informal?**
> **Harmful** is a slightly formal word that is not used in conversation.

HEAR

➡ see also **LISTEN**
➡ see also **SOUND, LOUD, QUIET**

> ⚠ Don't confuse **hear** and **listen**. If you **hear** something, a sound comes into your ears: I heard loud music coming from the next room. If you **listen** to something, you want to hear it and you pay attention to what you hear: I enjoy listening to music.

1 to hear something or someone

hear /hɪəʳ/ [v I/T] Did you hear that noise? | Suddenly we heard a knock at the door. | She called my name but I pretended not to hear.
hear sb/sth doing sth We often hear our neighbours shouting at their children. | I thought I heard the phone ringing.
hear sb/sth do sth She ran out and I heard the front door slam behind her. | Did you hear them call your name?
hearing – heard – have heard

> ⚠ Don't say 'I am hearing', 'are you hearing?' etc. You can say either **I hear**, **do you hear** etc, or (especially in British English) **I can hear**, **can you hear** etc, and it means the same: I hear footsteps on the stairs | I can hear footsteps on the stairs. But don't use 'can hear' when you are talking about something that you hear often or regularly: We often hear them arguing (not 'we can often hear them arguing'). When talking about the past, you can say **I could hear** and it usually means the same as **I heard**: We could hear footsteps on the stairs. (=We heard footsteps on the stairs.)

overhear /ˌəʊvəʳˈhɪəʳ/ [v T] to accidentally hear what someone is saying, when they do not realize that you can hear them: Claire overheard their conversation on the bus.
overhear sb saying/talking/arguing etc We overheard Jenny and her friends talking about their boyfriends last night.
overhearing – overheard – have overheard

2 the ability to hear

hearing /ˈhɪərɪŋ/ [n U]
my/her/his etc hearing My hearing's not very good – can you speak a little louder please?
sense of hearing Cats have a very good sense of hearing.
loss of hearing Years of playing in a rock band resulted in a loss of hearing.
hearing test (=a test to find out how good or bad your hearing is)

3 when you cannot hear

can't hear /ˌkɑːnt ˈhɪəʳǁˌkænt-/ use this when you mean that you want to hear something but you are unable to hear it, for example because it is too quiet or there is too much other noise: Can you turn the radio up – I can't hear the news. | The music was so loud that I couldn't hear what she was saying.

didn't hear /ˌdɪdnt ˈhɪəʳ/ use this when you mean that you did not hear something at all, especially when you did not realize there was anything to hear: I was outside in the yard, so I didn't hear the phone.
didn't hear sb/sth do sth What time

> When you see **EC**, go to the **ESSENTIAL COMMUNICATION** section.

did you get back last night? I didn't hear you come in.

didn't hear sb/sth doing sth *She didn't hear the car pulling up outside the house.*

◯ **didn't catch sth** /ˌdɪdnt ˈkætʃ (sth)/ SPOKEN use this when you mean that you did not hear what someone said, because they were speaking too quietly or because you were not listening carefully: *I'm sorry, I didn't catch your name. | We were sitting at the back and didn't catch everything he said.*

deaf /def/ [adj] someone who is **deaf** cannot hear well or cannot hear at all: *A lot of deaf children have additional problems in learning to speak. | She's partially deaf.*

hard of hearing /ˌhɑːʳd əv ˈhɪərɪŋ/ someone who is **hard of hearing** cannot hear well: *My grandfather's a little hard of hearing, so he always has the TV on very loud.*

HEAVY

➡ opposite **LIGHT 5**

1 something that weighs a lot

heavy /ˈhevi/ [adj] something that is **heavy** weighs a lot or weighs more than you expect: *That table's too heavy for you to move on your own. | Boys are usually slightly heavier than girls at birth. | a truck carrying a heavy load*

heavy – heavier – heaviest

◯ **weigh a ton** /ˌweɪ ə ˈtʌn/ INFORMAL, ESPECIALLY SPOKEN if something **weighs a ton**, it is very heavy and difficult to lift: *This box weighs a ton! Can you help me carry it?*

2 how heavy someone or something is

weigh /weɪ/ [v] to be a particular weight

weigh 50 kilos/30 tons etc *She weighs about 58 kg. | Each whale was about 40 feet long and weighed 45 tonnes.*

how much sb/sth weighs *How much does this parcel weigh?*

◯ **what sb weighs** SPOKEN (say this to ask or talk about how much someone weighs) *Guess what the baby weighs now!*

weight /weɪt/ [n U] the amount that someone or something weighs: *Your weight is about right for someone of your height.*
+of *The cost of postage depends on the weight of the package.*

◯ **how heavy** /haʊ ˈhevi/ ESPECIALLY SPOKEN use this to ask or say how much something weighs, especially something that is very heavy: *Well, how heavy is the piano? | You'd be surprised how heavy these sacks are.*

3 to find out how heavy someone or something is

weigh /weɪ/ [v T] to measure the weight of a person or thing: *Have you weighed yourself lately? | a special machine that weighs each truck and its cargo*

scales BRITISH [n plural] **scale** AMERICAN /skeɪl(z)/ [n singular] a piece of equipment for measuring the weight of people or things: *The scales showed I'd gained ten pounds in a week.*
kitchen scales (=for measuring the weight of food)
bathroom scales (=for measuring the weight of people)

HELP

➡ see also **EXPLAIN, ADVANTAGE/ DISADVANTAGE**

1 to help someone

help /help/ [v I/T] to make it easier for someone to do something, by doing part of their work, showing them what to do, or giving them something they need: *I'm not busy right now, so can I help? | Dad, I can't do my homework. Will you help me? | When you're looking for a job, your knowledge of French and Spanish should help.*

help sb to do sth *Steve helped me to clean up the mess.*
help sb do sth *Can you help me lift this box?*
help (sb) with sth *Gavin usually helps with the housework.* | *Do you want me to help you with those bags?*
help sb across/down/along etc (=help someone to go somewhere) *The nurse helped him down the stairs.*
help sb out (=help someone who has problems and needs help) *Dad's helped us out on several occasions by sending us money.*

○ **give sb a hand/lend (sb) a hand** /ˌɡɪv (sb) ə ˈhænd, ˌlend (sb) ə ˈhænd/ ESPECIALLY SPOKEN to help someone to do something, especially by carrying or lifting things: *Dave wants to paint the kitchen and I promised I'd give him a hand.*
+with *Could you lend a hand with the shopping?*

assist /əˈsɪst/ [v I/T] FORMAL to help someone by doing part of their work for them, especially the less important things
assist sb with/in sth *I was employed to assist the manager in his duties.*
+with/in *You may be asked to assist with the research.*

> ⚠ Don't say 'I assist him to do his work'. Say **I assist him with his work**.

○ **do sb a favour** BRITISH **do sb a favor** AMERICAN /ˌduː (sb) ə ˈfeɪvəʳ/ ESPECIALLY SPOKEN to do something to help someone, especially a close friend or someone you know well: *Could you do me a favour and post these letters?*
do sb a big favour (=help someone a lot) *Simon did us a big favor by lending us his car.*

do sth for sb /ˈduː (sth) fɔːʳ (sb)/ [phrasal verb T] to help someone by doing something that they would normally do: *I'll do the shopping for you if you're feeling tired.* | *Judith's always doing her brother's homework for him.*

2 to make someone feel more confident and less worried

encourage /ɪnˈkʌrɪdʒ‖ɪnˈkɜːr-/ [v T] to say or do something that helps someone feel confident enough to do something: *She was always looking for ways to encourage her students.*
encourage sb to do sth *I was encouraged to try for university by my uncle.*

be supportive /biː səˈpɔːʳtɪv/ to make someone feel less worried and more confident, talking to them in a sympathetic way and giving them practical help: *My family has been very supportive throughout the divorce.*

3 to help something to happen

help /help/ [v T] to make it easier for something good to happen
help do sth *Going to Spain for a month should help improve her Spanish.*
help to do sth *A massage will help to relax your mind and your body.*
help sb (to) do sth *All this arguing isn't going to help us win the election.*

encourage /ɪnˈkʌrɪdʒ‖ɪnˈkɜː-/ [v T] to make people more likely to want to do something, or make something more likely to happen: *Do you think that violence on TV encourages crime?*
encourage sb to do sth *If we had a better rail system, it would encourage people to leave their cars at home.*

promote /prəˈməʊt/ [v T] FORMAL to help something good to happen or develop and increase: *The aim of the meeting is to promote trade between the two countries.* | *A balanced diet promotes good health and normal development.*

aid /eɪd/ [v T] FORMAL to help something get better, develop, grow etc: *The country's economic recovery has been aided by increased international trade.*

4 when someone or something helps you

helpful /ˈhelpfəl/ [adj] someone or something that is **helpful** gives you help or makes it easier for you to do something: *Thanks, Sam. You've been very helpful.* | *A helpful woman at the tourist office showed me where to go.*

it is helpful to do sth *It's helpful to prepare a list of questions before going to an interview.*

helpful advice/idea/suggestion *Does anyone have any helpful suggestions?* | *She gave us some helpful advice about renting apartments.*

> ⚠ Don't write 'helpfull'. The correct spelling is **helpful**.

be a help /biː ə 'help/ ESPECIALLY SPOKEN if someone or something **is a help**, they make it easier for you to do something that you are trying to do: *For schools in inner cities, better sports facilities would be a help.*

be a big/great/real help *Thanks for looking after the children. You've been a real help.*

5 someone who helps another person

assistant /ə'sɪstənt/ [n C] someone whose job is to help another person who has a more important job, by doing things for them: *the dentist's assistant*

assistant to sb *Janet is the assistant to the Director of Finance.*

> ⚠ You can also use **assistant** before a noun, like an adjective: *the assistant manager* | *Peter is an assistant editor on a news programme.*

helper /'helpəʳ/ [n C] someone who helps other people, especially because they want to do it and not in order to earn money: *Ella works at the hospital once a week as a voluntary helper.*

accomplice /ə'kʌmplɪs‖ə'kɑːm,-, ə'kʌm-/ [n C] FORMAL someone who helps another person in a crime: *Evans could not have carried out the robbery without an accomplice.* | *One man held the gun while his accomplice took the money.*

6 something that someone does in order to help

help /help/ [n U] something that someone does in order to help: *If I need any help I'll call you.* | *Please don't hesitate to ask me for help.*

+with *Do you need any help with those suitcases?*

help doing sth *I wouldn't mind some help making the dinner tonight.*

with the help of sb/sth *Ian pushed the car as far as the garage with the help of some friends.*

get help (=find someone to help you) *You wait here. I'll go and get help.*

> ⚠ Don't say 'a help' in this meaning. Just say **help** or **some help**, **any help** etc.

assistance /ə'sɪstəns/ [n U] FORMAL help given to someone who needs it, often in the form of money, advice, or information: *The Association gives advice and practical assistance to motorists.*

financial assistance *Students receive very little financial assistance from the government.*

be of assistance (=help someone) *Our tour guides will be pleased to be of assistance if you have any problems.*

support /sə'pɔːʳt/ [n U] equipment, money, or help from other people that is available for you to use when you need it: *I'd like to thank you all for your support in the upcoming election.* | *Our two company lawyers provide all the legal support we need.*

aid /eɪd/ [n U] food, money, medicine, and other kinds of help that are given to countries or people who need them, because they are very poor or have serious problems: *Aid is still not getting through to the refugees.* | *Each year the US sends more than $1.8 billion in aid to sub-Saharan Africa.*

> ⚠ Don't use **aid** in the plural. **Aid** is an uncountable noun.

> ⚠ You can also use **aid** before a noun, like an adjective: *aid agencies* | *the federal aid budget*

7 not giving any help

not helpful/unhelpful /nɒt ˈhelpfəl, ʌnˈhelpfəl/ not giving someone the help they need, especially when they have asked for help: *I found the sales assistants most unhelpful.* | *The police were not at all helpful when we reported the incident.*

be no help/not be any help/not be much help /biː nəʊ ˈhelp, nɒt biː eni ˈhelp, nɒt biː mʌtʃ ˈhelp/ if something or someone **is no help**, they do not help you do something or get something: *Clarissa was no help – she just sat around and watched TV.* | *That map isn't much help.*

○ **useless** /ˈjuːsləs/ [adj] ESPECIALLY SPOKEN not giving any help – use this when you are annoyed with someone or something because they should help you but they do not: *Those useless people in the tax office gave me all the wrong advice.*
completely/absolutely useless *It's no good reading the instructions – they're completely useless.*

HERE

➡ see also **PLACE**

1 here

here /hɪəʳ/ [adv] in, to, or from the place where you are: *Were you born here?* | *I'll stay here and wait for the others.* | *I really love it here in Italy.*
be here *Check the names off the list to make sure everyone's here.*
come/get/arrive etc here (=come to this place) *What time did you get here?* | *We moved here about two years ago.*
around/near here (=near this place) *Do you live around here?*
right here (=in this exact place) *I put my keys right here in the drawer.*
from here (=from this place) *I know a really good Spanish restaurant not far from here.*
down/in/up here *"Hey, guys," she called up to us, "I'm down here in the basement."*

⚠ Don't say 'come to here', 'arrive to here' etc. Say **come here**, **arrive here**: *We came here by bus.*

⚠ Don't say 'here the weather is nice'. Say **the weather is nice here**. Don't put **here** at the beginning of a sentence.

○ **be in** /biː ˈɪn/ [phrasal verb I] ESPECIALLY SPOKEN to be in your home or at the place where you work: *Hello, Susan. Is Richard in?* (=at home) | *Sonia's not well so she won't be in today.* (=at work)

○ **be around** /biː əˈraʊnd/ [phrasal verb I] SPOKEN if someone or something **is around**, they are here or somewhere near here, especially when you need them: *Yesterday's newspaper must be around somewhere.* | *Are you going to be around at Christmas, or are you going away?*

be present /biː ˈprezənt/ FORMAL to be here – use this especially about people being at official meetings or ceremonies: *Unfortunately, the President is unable to be present here today.*

2 not here

not be here /nɒt biː ˈhɪəʳ/ *I don't know exactly what happened because I wasn't here.* | *He hasn't been here long, but he's made a lot of changes already.*

○ **not be around** /nɒt biː əˈraʊnd/ SPOKEN if someone or something **is not around**, they are not here or near here, especially when you need them: *There's never a police officer around when you need one.* | *If Julie isn't around, maybe Maria could help you.*

○ **be out/not be in** /biː ˈaʊt, nɒt biː ˈɪn/ [phrasal verb I] ESPECIALLY SPOKEN to not be in your home or at the place where you work, especially when someone wants to see you: *Mr Newton called while you were out – he'll call back later.* | *I'm afraid I have a doctor's appointment so I won't be in tomorrow.* (=won't be at work)

be away /biː əˈweɪ/ [phrasal verb I] to not be at home or work for several days or weeks because you are travelling somewhere else, or to not be at school or work because you are ill or on holiday: *She's going to be away for at least a week.*

be away on business *I'm sorry, Mr Hyam is away on business right now.*

be away from home/work/school *Because of her job, she is sometimes away from home for weeks at a time.*

be absent /biː ˈæbsənt/ if someone **is absent**, they are not at school or at the place where they work, especially because they are ill or on holiday

+from *James was absent from school again today.*

> **Formal or informal?**
> **Be absent** is more formal than **be away**.

missing /ˈmɪsɪŋ/ [adj] something or someone that is **missing** is not in the place where you expect them to be, and it is difficult or impossible to find them: *The missing files were eventually found in Slater's apartment.* | *Two crew members survived, but two are still missing.*

+from *Oh no! The last page is missing from this book!*

HIDE

➡ see also **SECRET, SHOW**

1 to hide things

hide /haɪd/ [v T] to make something difficult to see or find, for example by putting it somewhere secret, or by covering it: *Where have you hidden the gun?* | *She put up a hand to hide her face from the cameras.*

hide sth in/behind/under etc sth *He hid the money under his bed.*

hide sth from sb (=make sure someone cannot see or find something) *We'll have to hide the Christmas presents from the kids.*

hiding – hid – have hidden

hidden [adj] *a hidden microphone.*

conceal /kənˈsiːl/ [v T] to hide something, especially by covering it: *Several kilos of drugs were concealed in the back of the truck.*

concealed [adj] *a man carrying a concealed weapon*

> **Formal or informal?**
> **Conceal** is more formal than **hide**, and is often used when you are talking about things that are hidden for dishonest or criminal reasons.

cover /ˈkʌvəʳ/ [v T] if you **cover** something, you put something over it or on top of it so that it cannot be seen: *He reached for a towel to cover his naked body.*

cover sth with sth *Jane covered her face with her hands and started to cry.*

cover up sth/cover sth up *I guess I'll have to cover up this stain with a rug.*

bury /ˈberi/ [v T] to put something in a hole in the ground and cover it with earth or sand in order to hide it: *Snakes usually bury their eggs.*

bury sth in/under etc sth *He murdered his wife and buried her body in a field.*

burying – buried – have buried

2 to hide yourself

hide /haɪd/ [v I] to go somewhere where people cannot easily see you or find you: *Dad's coming! Quick – hide!*

+under/in/behind etc *I hid in a doorway until the man had gone.* | *Ben and I hid behind a hedge and waited.*

+from *Are you trying to hide from me?*

hiding – hid – have hidden

go into hiding /ˌgəʊ ɪntə ˈhaɪdɪŋ/ to go to a place where you can hide for a long time, because you are in danger or because the police are looking for you: *It is thought that the terrorists have now gone into hiding.*

3 to hide your feelings

hide /haɪd/ [v T] to deliberately not show your real feelings: *I couldn't hide my annoyance any longer.*

hide sth from sb *"That's OK," she said, trying to hide her disappointment from him.*

hiding – hid – have hidden

disguise /dɪsˈgaɪz/ [v T] ESPECIALLY WRITTEN to not show your real feelings, by pretending to feel something else: *Kate gave a cheerful smile, somehow* *managing to disguise her embarrassment.* | *He didn't even attempt to disguise his amazement.*

4 to hide information

conceal /kənˈsiːl/ [v T] to hide information from people by not telling them all the facts, or by not telling them the truth about a situation: *He managed to conceal the fact that he had been in prison, and got a job as a security officer.*
conceal sth from sb *For years, Anna had concealed her true identity from everyone.*

> **Formal or informal?**
> **Conceal** is more formal than **hide**.

hide /haɪd/ [v T] to hide a fact or hide the truth: *I think he's hiding something.* | *Of course I'll talk to you. I have nothing to hide.* | *Jenna saw no reason to hide the truth.*

cover up [phrasal verb T] to try to stop people from finding out about someone's mistakes or crimes
cover up sth *Lewis asked his wife to lie in an attempt to cover up the murder.*
cover sth up *He's made some big mistakes, and he won't be able to cover them up for long.*
cover-up /ˈkʌvər ʌp/ [n C] when an organization, for example the government or the police, tries to stop people from finding out the truth about something: *Some people suspected that the government was involved in a cover-up.*

5 places to hide

hiding-place /ˈhaɪdɪŋ pleɪs/ [n C] a place where someone can hide, or a place where you can hide something: *I've found a good hiding-place for the money.*

hideout (also **hideaway**) /ˈhaɪdaʊt, ˈhaɪdəweɪ/ [n C] a place where someone goes to hide from the police or from someone dangerous: *The kidnappers used an abandoned farmhouse as their hideout.*

HIGH

➡ opposite **LOW**
➡ look here for ...
  • a high building, mountain, tree etc
  • a high sound or voice
  • a high temperature, level etc

> Don't use **high** to talk about people. Use **tall**.

1 a high building/mountain/tree

high /haɪ/ [adj] measuring a long distance from the bottom to the top – use this especially about mountains, walls, or buildings: *The castle was surrounded by high walls.* | *Mount Everest is the highest mountain in the world.* | *a high fence*

tall /tɔːl/ [adj] high and not wide or long – use this especially about trees and plants or about buildings and parts of buildings: *The main square was surrounded by tall grey buildings.* | *Two tall marble columns stood at either side of the entrance.* | *A cat was hiding in the tall grass.*

> Don't use **tall** about mountains or walls.

skyscraper /ˈskaɪˌskreɪpər/ [n C] a very tall modern city building, especially one used for offices: *the skyscrapers of Manhattan*

high-rise /ˈhaɪ raɪz/ [adj only before noun] a **high-rise** building is a tall modern building, used either for apartments or for offices: *a high-rise apartment block*

2 a long distance above the ground

high /haɪ/ [adj/adv] *a large dining-room with a high ceiling* | *The shelf was too high for me to reach.*
+in/into/above *The plane flew high above their heads.* | *Lava from the volcano was sent high into the air.*
+up *The house was high up on a hill.*

H

3 how high something is

how high /ˌhaʊ ˈhaɪ/ use this to ask or say what the height of something is: *"How high is Mount Fuji?" "It's almost 4000 metres."* | *I'm not sure how high the ceiling is.*

30 m/100 ft etc high /(30 m etc) ˈhaɪ/ if a building or mountain is **30 m, 100 ft etc high**, the distance from top to bottom is 30 m, 100 ft etc: *Scotland's highest mountain is over 4000 ft high.* | *a 5 m high wall*

height /haɪt/ [n C/U] the distance between the top and the bottom of something, or the distance that something is above the ground
+of *What's the height of that building?*
200 ft/30 m etc in height *Some of the pyramids are over 200 feet in height.*
a height of 25 m/100 ft etc *One of the climbers fell from a height of 25 m.*

level /ˈlevəl/ [n C] the height of something, especially in relation to something else: *Hold your arms out at the same level as your shoulder.*
+of *We hung the painting just above the level of the window.*
sea level (=the height of the surface of the sea, used when measuring the height of mountains, hills etc) *The village is about 1500 metres above sea level.*
eye level (=a height equal to the level of your eyes) *Your screen should be at eye level.*

altitude /ˈæltɪˌtjuːdǁ-tuːd/ [n C] the distance that something is above the ground – use this especially to talk about planes or about places in mountainous areas
at an altitude of 10,000 metres/ 30,000 feet etc *The plane is now flying at an altitude of 30,000 ft.*
at high altitudes *At high altitudes it is often difficult to breathe.*

> **Formal or informal?**
> **Altitude** is a more formal and technical word than **height**.

4 a high sound/voice/musical note

➡ see also **SOUND**

high /haɪ/ [adj] near the top of the range of sounds that humans can hear – use this about sounds, voices, or musical notes: *Most people can't sing such high notes.*

high-pitched /ˌhaɪ ˈpɪtʃt◂/ [adj] a **high-pitched** voice or sound is very high and is often unpleasant to listen to: *I could hear high-pitched laughter coming from the girls' room.*

piercing /ˈpɪərsɪŋ/ [adj usually before noun] WRITTEN very high and loud, in a way that is painful or unpleasant to listen to: *Sammy put his fingers in his mouth and gave a piercing whistle.*
piercing shriek/scream/cry (=the loud high noise someone makes when they are frightened or in pain) *Maggie let out a piercing scream as she saw the truck speeding towards her.*

shrill /ʃrɪl/ [adj] WRITTEN very high, loud, and unexpectedly sharp, often giving the person who hears it a shock: *I was suddenly woken up by the shrill ringing of the telephone.* | *As Sophie became angry her voice got shriller.*

5 a high temperature/level/ rate/cost

high /haɪ/ [adj] *In summer, temperatures can be as high as 40°C.* | *The city has one of the highest crime rates in the world.* | *the high level of pollution in Britain's rivers*

HIT

PUNISH

VIOLENT   ACCIDENT

KILL   BREAK

see also

HURT/INJURE   ACCIDENTALLY

ATTACK   DELIBERATELY

WB DRIVE

1 to hit someone deliberately

hit /hɪt/ [v T] to deliberately hit someone with your hand, or with something that you are holding in your hand: *I was so mad I just wanted to hit her.*
hit sb with sth *Cathy turned around and hit the man with her umbrella.*
hit sb in the eye/on the nose/over the head *He hit a waiter over the head with a bottle during a drunken fight.*
hitting – hit – have hit

punch /pʌntʃ/ [v T] to hit someone hard with your closed hand, especially during a fight: *Steve swung around and punched Rick, knocking him to the ground.*
punch sb on the nose/in the eye/in the face *He punched her in the stomach and pushed her against a wall.*

slap /slæp/ [v T] to hit someone quickly with the flat part of your hand making a loud sound: *Liz got really angry with her daughter and slapped her.*
slap sb across the face *He was so rude, I felt like slapping him across the face.*
slapping – slapped – have slapped

beat up /ˌbiːt ˈʌp/ [phrasal verb T] to hurt someone badly by hitting them again and again
beat sb up *Everyone knew that Bob sometimes got drunk and beat his wife up.*
beat up sb *The gang would beat up old women and steal their money.*

beat up on sb /ˌbiːt ˈʌp ɒn (sb)‖-ɑːn-/ [phrasal verb T] AMERICAN to hurt someone younger and weaker than

yourself by hitting them again and again: *Wayne used to beat up on other kids in the class.*

strike /straɪk/ [v T] FORMAL to hit someone, with your hand or a weapon: *Her husband had never struck her before.*
strike sth with sth *Police officers struck him with their batons.*
strike sb on the head/in the stomach etc *Jack went to help, and was struck on the head with a bottle.*

thump /θʌmp/ [v T] to hit someone hard with your closed hand, especially on their body rather than on their face or head: *The other players thumped him on the back in congratulations.*

2 to hit someone or something by accident

hit /hɪt/ [v T] to hit someone or something without intending to: *Be careful with that stick! You nearly hit me with it. | The bus ran off the road and hit a tree.*
hit sb on the head/in the face etc *A ball flew across the field and hit me in the mouth.*
hit your head/knee/elbow etc *He fell, hitting his head on the side of the desk.*
hitting – hit – have hit

bump into sb/sth /ˈbʌmp ɪntuː (sb/sth)/ [phrasal verb T] to accidentally hit someone or something with part of your body when you are walking or running, because you are not paying attention or you cannot see properly: *Mark ran around the corner and bumped into his teacher. | The room was so dark that I bumped into a table.*

crash into sb/sth /ˈkræʃ ɪntuː (sb/sth)/ [phrasal verb T] to accidentally hit someone or something when you are moving very fast, especially in a vehicle, causing a lot of damage and making a lot of noise: *The car crashed straight into a tree. | Eric came running down the corridor and crashed into me.*

bang /bæŋ/ [v T] to accidentally make part of your body, or something you are carrying, hit hard against something else, often hurting yourself or damaging something

H

bang your head/knee/elbow etc
Bend down so you don't bang your head.

bang sth on/against sth *They kept banging the piano against the wall as they carried it downstairs.*

collide /kə'laɪd/ [v I] if people or vehicles **collide**, they accidentally hit each other when they are moving in different directions: *Two planes collided in mid-air.*
+with *He ran out of the door, almost colliding with Sally as she was coming in.*

Formal or informal?
Collide is a formal word, and is used mostly in writing and news reports.

knock /nɒk‖nɑːk/ [v I/T] to hit someone or something with a short quick movement
+against *The bag knocked against his hip with every step.*
+into *She turned and ran, knocking into bystanders as she went.*
knock sth against/into sth *One of the men knocked the sofa against the door frame.*

3 to hit someone as a punishment

beat /biːt/ [v T] to hit someone many times with your hand or with a stick, gun etc in order to punish them: *The guards dragged him out of his cell and beat him.*
beat sb with sth *Two of the soldiers began beating her with rifles.*
beating – beat – have beaten

smack/spank/slap /smæk, spæŋk, slæp/ [v T] to hit a child who you think is behaving badly, using your hand: *Dad would sometimes shout at us, but he never smacked us.* | *Do you think that parents should be allowed to slap their children?*
slapping – slapped – have slapped
smack/spank/slap [n singular] *Stop being so naughty or you'll get a smack!*

corporal punishment /ˌkɔːrpərəl 'pʌnɪʃmənt/ [n U] FORMAL when people, especially children in schools, are punished by being hit: *Corporal punishment was abolished in Britain in 1986.*

4 to hit a ball when playing a sport

hit /hɪt/ [v T] to hit a ball in a sport, usually with a bat, racket, or other piece of equipment: *I still don't always manage to hit the ball over the net.*
hit sth hard *He swung the bat into the air and hit the ball as hard as he could.*
hitting – hit – have hit

5 to hit a door, table, or window in order to get attention

knock /nɒk‖nɑːk/ [v I] to hit a door or window several times, especially with your closed hand, in order to attract the attention of the people inside: *Please knock before you enter.* | *We kept knocking, but no-one opened the door.*

knock

knock on/at the door *Was that someone knocking at the door?*
knock on/at the window *Ella knocked lightly on the car window to try and wake him up.*
knock [n singular] *There was a knock on the door.*

⚠ Don't say 'knock the door'. Say **knock on the door** or **knock at the door**.

bang /bæŋ/ [v I] to keep hitting a door, window, table etc, making a loud noise

bang

bang on the door/window/table etc *Mum was banging on his bedroom door, screaming at him to turn the music down.* | *The students started banging on their desks.*

hammer /'hæmə'/ [v I] to keep hitting a door or window loudly, especially because you are angry or impatient
hammer on/at the door *We were woken by the sound of the police hammering at the door.*

hammer **on/at the window** *Phil hammered on the window, hoping that someone would hear him.*

tap /tæp/ [v I/T] to hit a door, window, or table gently in order to make people notice you: *Mr Norton tapped his desk with a ruler until everyone was silent.*

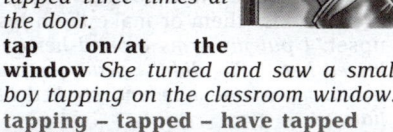

tap

tap on/at the door *I tapped three times at the door.*

tap on/at the window *She turned and saw a small boy tapping on the classroom window.*

tapping – tapped – have tapped

6 to make someone or something fall down by hitting them

knock out /ˌnɒk ˈaʊt‖ˌnɑːk-/ [*phrasal verb* T] to hit someone so hard that they fall down and become unconscious

knock sb out *He hit Colin hard with his fist, knocking him out.*

knock out sb *He knocked out his opponent with a tremendous punch.*

knock over/knock down /ˌnɒk ˈəʊvəʳ, ˌnɒk ˈdaʊn‖ˌnɑːk-/ [*phrasal verb* T] to accidentally hit someone or something that is standing, and make them fall: *A truck went out of control and knocked down a traffic light. | I bumped into Anna and almost knocked her over.*

get knocked over/down *As the crowd rushed towards the gate, several people got knocked over.*

run over /ˌrʌn ˈəʊvəʳ/ [*phrasal verb* T] to hit someone when you are driving a car, truck etc, and injure them or kill them

run sb over *A little boy stepped out in the street, and I almost ran him over.*

get run over *Get off the road! You'll get run over!*

HOLD

➡ look here for ...
  • hold something or someone
  • drop something
➡ if you mean 'have something inside', go to **CONTAIN**
➡ see also **LIFT, CARRY, TAKE/BRING**

1 to have something in your hand

hold /həʊld/ [v T] *The photo showed a young boy holding a flag. | Can you hold my coat while I try on this sweater?*

holding – held – have held

in your hand /ɪn jɔːʳ ˈhænd/ if something is **in your hand**, you are holding it: *What's that in your hand? | He already had a glass in his hand when we arrived.*

handle /ˈhændl/ [v T] to touch or hold something – use this especially about things that you must be careful with, such as weapons, food, or things that break easily: *It was the first time I had ever handled a gun. | Staff who handle food should have special training. | A sign on the box said 'Fragile. Handle with care.'*

2 to hold something tightly

grip /grɪp/ [v T] ESPECIALLY WRITTEN *I gripped the handrail and looked over the edge at the people below.*

grip sth tightly *Gripping her arm tightly, Max pulled her away from the road.*

gripping – gripped – have gripped

clutch /klʌtʃ/ [v T] ESPECIALLY WRITTEN to hold something very tightly, especially because you are frightened or nervous or because you do not want to lose what you are holding: *I could feel his little hand clutching my arm.*

clutch sth tightly *It was dark by now and Maria clutched her bag tightly.*

hold on /ˌhəʊld ˈɒn‖-ˈɑːn/ [*phrasal verb* I] to hold something tightly because you are afraid that you will fall or that you will lose what you are holding

+to *Mum was holding on to her hat to stop it blowing away.*

H

hold on tight *I just fastened my safety belt, shut my eyes, and held on tight.*

grasp /grɑːsp‖græsp/ [v T] WRITTEN to take and hold something firmly in your hand: *Helen grasped his arm tightly.*

3   to start to hold something

get hold of sth/take hold of sth /ˌget ˈhəʊld ɒv (sth), ˌteɪk ˈhəʊld ɒv (sth)/ to take something and hold it in your hand: *I took hold of the door handle and pulled as hard as I could.* | *Try and get hold of the rope and pull yourself up.*

grab /græb/ [v T] to quickly and roughly take something and hold it: *She tried to grab the knife from him.* | *Suddenly, a police officer grabbed my arm.*
grab hold of sth *The boy grabbed hold of my bag and disappeared into the crowd.*
grabbing – grabbed – have grabbed

4   to hold someone

hold /həʊld/ [v T] to put your arms around someone and hold them close to you, especially in order to make them feel less worried or upset: *I held him until he went to sleep.*
hold sb tight (=close to your body) *He held her tight and let her cry.*
hold sb in your arms *Jessie held the little girl in her arms and tried to reassure her.*
holding – held – have held

hug /hʌg/ [v T] to put your arms around someone and hold them for a short time, especially in a friendly or loving way: *My father hugged me affectionately when I got home.*

hugging – hugged – have hugged

hug [n C] *Come and give me a hug.*

cuddle /ˈkʌdl/ [v I/T] to hold someone in your arms for a long time, especially a child, a small animal, or someone you love: *She had fallen asleep in her chair, cuddling a little teddy bear.*

kiss and cuddle (=when two people hold each other and kiss each other) *They were kissing and cuddling on the sofa.*

cuddle

cuddle [n C] when you cuddle someone: *She was giving the baby a cuddle.*

put your arms around sb /ˌpʊt jɔːr ˈɑːrmz əraʊnd (sb)/ ESPECIALLY WRITTEN to hold someone in a loving way, in order to kiss them or make them less upset: *I put my arms around her and kissed her.* | *She didn't speak, just put her arms around him and stroked his hair.*

> ⚠ **Put your arms around sb** is used especially in stories.

hold sb's hand /ˌhəʊld (sb's) ˈhænd/ to hold someone's hand as a sign of love or to make sure they are safe: *Come and hold my hand to cross the road, Billy.*
hold hands (=when two or more people hold each other's hands) *Two lovers were walking along the beach, holding hands.*

5   to stop holding something

let go /ˌlet ˈgəʊ/ to stop holding something or someone: *Let go! You're hurting me.*
+of *She wouldn't let go of the letter.*

drop /drɒp‖drɑːp/ [v T] to stop holding something suddenly, especially by accident, so that it falls to the ground: *Be careful not to drop any of those plates.* | *As soon as she saw him she dropped her suitcases and ran towards him.*
dropping – dropped – have dropped

HOLE

1 a hole that goes through something

hole /həʊl/ [n C] an empty space that goes right through something, especially one that should not be there: *These socks are full of holes.*
+in *We could see the sky through a hole in the roof.* | *You can't wear that shirt if it has a hole in it.*

leak /liːk/ [n C] a small hole or crack where something has been damaged, which lets liquid or gas flow out of it when it should not
+in *There's a leak in the water tank.*

puncture BRITISH **flat tire** AMERICAN /'pʌŋktʃəʳ, ˌflæt 'taɪəʳ/ [n C] a hole in a tyre, which allows air to get out and makes the tyre unsafe: *Do you know how to mend a puncture?*
get a puncture/flat tire *I got a flat tire and I was late for work.*

gap /gæp/ [n C] a space in the middle of something, for example in a wall or a fence, where a part of it is missing
+in *The cows had escaped through a gap in the hedge.*

opening /'əʊpənɪŋ/ [n C] a hole that something can pass through or that you can see through, especially one which is at the entrance or top of something: *Bees come and go through a small opening at the bottom of the hive.*

2 a hole in the ground or in the surface of something

hole /həʊl/ [n C] an empty space in the ground or in the surface of something
+in *There were several huge holes in the road.*
make a hole *These holes in the tree trunk are made by tiny insects.*

dig /dɪg/ [v I/T] to make a hole in the ground, using a spade (=a tool for digging), a large machine, or your hands: *The prisoners escaped through a tunnel they had dug under the wall.* | *A big black dog was digging in the sand.*

dig a hole *The workmen began digging a hole in the middle of the road.*
dig for sth (=in order to find something) *Some fishermen were on the beach digging for worms.*
digging – dug – have dug

pothole /'pɒthəʊl‖'pɑːt-/ [n C] a hole in the surface of a road, caused by traffic or bad weather, that makes driving difficult or dangerous: *The bumps and potholes on the city's streets make driving more difficult.*

crater /'kreɪtəʳ/ [n C] a round hole in the ground, made by something that has fallen on it or by an explosion: *the craters on the moon*

HOLIDAY/ VACATION

➡ see Word Banks section

HOME

➡ if you mean that 'someone was born in a place or has lived there a long time', go to **FROM 1**

WB HOUSES/WHERE PEOPLE LIVE

RETURN → see also → LIVE

CHANGE 6 → → LEAVE 6

1 where you live

home /həʊm/ [n C/U] the place where you live: *Buying your first home is a very important step.* | *After three weeks in hospital, Ruth was glad to be back in her own home.*
at home *Some students live at college during the week and at home on weekends.*

⚠ Don't say 'I'm going to home', 'he drove to home' etc. Say **I'm going home**, **he drove home** etc.

○ **Helen's/my friend's/the Carters' etc** ESPECIALLY SPOKEN the place where Helen, my friend, the Carter family etc live: *There's a party at Helen's on Saturday night.* | *I'm going to my friend's for a drink and a chat.* | *We're meeting up at the Carters' so we can share cars.*

○ **place** /pleɪs/ [n singular] ESPECIALLY SPOKEN someone's house, apartment, or room: *They've got a beautiful place in the countryside, not far from Oxford.* **my place/your place/our place etc** *Let's meet at my place at 8 o'clock.* | *Barbara and Les have invited us over to their place for a meal.*

address /ə'dres‖'ædres/ [n C] the number of the house or building, and the name of the road and town where someone lives: *Can you give me your address and telephone number?* **change of address** (=when you move to a different address) *Please inform the bank of any change of address.*

2 | places for people to live

housing /'haʊzɪŋ/ [n U] houses or apartments in an area – use this to talk about how many houses are available, what they cost, and whether they are good or bad: *There is a shortage of good, inexpensive housing.* **poor housing** (=housing that is in bad condition) *health problems caused by poor housing*

> ⚠ **Housing** is used especially in political and economic contexts.

> ⚠ You can also use **housing** before a noun, like an adjective: *excellent housing conditions* | *an increase in housing costs*

somewhere to live/a place to live /ˌsʌmweəʳ tə 'lɪv, ə ˌpleɪs tə 'lɪv/ a house, apartment, or room – use this to talk about the problems of getting a place where you can live: *It's difficult to find somewhere to live if you're poor and unemployed.* | *I was starting college and I needed a place to live.*

accommodation /əˌkɒmə'deɪʃən‖əˌkɑː-/ [n U] FORMAL, ESPECIALLY BRITISH any place, such as a house, apartment, or hotel, where people can live or stay: *The tourist office can help you look for accommodation.* **rented accommodation** (=a house, apartment, or room that you rent)

> ⚠ Don't say 'look for an accommodation' or 'look for accommodations'. Say **look for accommodation**.

> ⚠ Don't write 'accomodation' or 'acommodation'. The correct spelling is **accommodation**.

> ⚠ In American English, there is a plural noun **accommodations**, which means a place where you can stay for a short time, for example when you are on holiday: *We called the office in Rome, but they said there were no accommodations available.*

3 | things for using at home

domestic /də'mestɪk/ [adj only before noun] **domestic appliance/equipment/fuel etc** designed to be used at home, not in a factory or office: *domestic appliances such as microwaves and dishwashers* | *Solar energy panels can provide domestic hot water.*

> **Formal or informal?**
> **Domestic** is used especially by people who make and sell things to be used at home, and in formal or technical writing.

home /həʊm/ [adj only before noun] used at home or done at home: *a home computer* **home shopping/schooling/banking** (use this about things you can do at home, which are usually done in other places) *home shopping through mail-order catalogues*

4 | to be in your home

be at home/be home /biː ət 'həʊm, biː 'həʊm/ to be in your home: *We kept trying to call her, but she was never home.* | *I hated being at home with the kids all day.*

○ **be in** /biː 'ɪn/ [phrasal verb I] ESPECIALLY SPOKEN if someone **is in**, they are at home, and you can talk to them or visit them: *Hi, Mrs Jones. Is Sally in?*

stay in /ˌsteɪ ˈɪn/ [*phrasal verb* I] BRITISH to spend the evening at home rather than go out: *I was tired, so I decided to stay in.*

5 to not be in your home

🔍 **be out** /biː ˈaʊt/ [*phrasal verb*] ESPECIALLY SPOKEN to not be in your home for a short period: *"Can I speak to Frank?" "I'm sorry, he's out right now, but he'll be back soon."* | *While they were out, someone broke in and stole the TV.*

be away /biː əˈweɪ/ [*phrasal verb* I] to not be in your home for several days, weeks, or months: *Who's going to look after your cats while you're away?*
+from *Jack worked as a pilot and was often away from home.*

6 to have no home

not have anywhere to live /nɒt hæv ˌeniweəʳ tə ˈlɪv/ to not have a house, apartment, or room: *Paul's staying with us at the moment because he doesn't have anywhere to live.*

homeless /ˈhəʊmləs/ [*adj*] someone who is **homeless** has no home to live in, especially because they are very poor or because their home has been destroyed: *There has been a big increase in the number of homeless people.* | *The earthquake left thousands of people homeless.*
the homeless (=people who are homeless) *We distribute food and blankets to the homeless every evening.*

be/live on the streets /biː, ˌlɪv ɒn ðə ˈstriːts/ to sleep outdoors in a city because you do not have anywhere to live: *Many of the people have ended up living on the streets in the capital city.* | *If my grandparents hadn't been able to help, our whole family would have been out on the streets.*

tramp BRITISH **vagrant** AMERICAN /træmp, ˈveɪgrənt/ [*n C*] someone, especially a man, who has no home or job and who begs for money on the streets: *An old tramp was asleep under the bridge.*

HONEST

➡ opposite **DISHONEST**

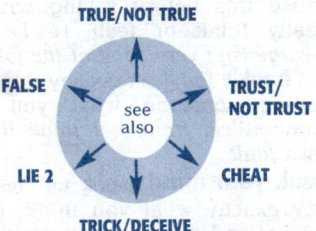

1 someone who does not lie, steal, or cheat

honest /ˈɒnɪ̩st‖ˈɑːn-/ [*adj*] someone who is **honest** does not lie, steal, or cheat and can be trusted: *I think he's one of the few honest politicians left in government.* | *As a manager, you soon learn to judge whether people are honest or not.*

can trust /kən ˈtrʌst/ if you **can trust** someone, you are sure that they are honest and that you can depend on them: *Beth's an honest hardworking girl who I can trust.*
can trust sb to do sth *I knew I could trust Neil to look after the money.*

2 honest about telling people what you really think

honest /ˈɒnɪ̩st‖ˈɑːn-/ [*adj*] if you are **honest**, you tell people what you really think or what is really happening, without hiding the truth
+about *Do you think he's being completely honest about the situation?*
+with *Parents should always try to be honest with their children.*
your honest opinion (=what you really think) *If you want my honest opinion, I don't think she should marry him.*
🔍 **to be (perfectly/quite) honest** SPOKEN (=use this when saying what you really think or feel) *To be honest, I don't really like babies.*
honestly [*adv*] *Tell me honestly, do I look fat in this dress?*

frank /fræŋk/ [*adj*] someone who is **frank** talks in an honest and direct way, especially about subjects that are difficult to talk about

+with *The doctor was very frank with me about my illness.*

🔍 **to be (perfectly) frank** SPOKEN (=use this before saying what you really think or feel) *To be frank, George isn't very good at the job.*

🔍 **frankly** [adv] SPOKEN say this before telling someone what you really think: *Well, frankly, I think it's your own fault.*

speak your mind /ˌspiːk jɔːʳ 'maɪnd/ to say exactly what you think, even if you offend people by doing this: *Liz wasn't afraid to speak her mind, even in front of the boss.*

sincere /sɪn'sɪəʳ/ [adj] someone who is **sincere** shows their true feelings and says what they really believe, and is not pretending: *She said she'd love to come, but I'm not sure if she was being sincere.*

🔍 **straight** /streɪt/ [adj] ESPECIALLY SPOKEN honest and likely to tell people exactly what you think or what is happening, without trying to hide anything

be straight with sb *We just have to trust them to be straight with us.*

a straight answer *It seemed like a simple question, but no one would give us a straight answer.*

3 an honest way of behaving

honesty /'ɒnɪstiǀ'ɑːn-/ [n U] an honest way of talking or behaving, so you tell the truth, and do not try to cheat people or hide information from them: *Honesty is important in any relationship.* | *Will talked about his experience of HIV with courage and honesty.*

HOPE

➡ see also **WANT**

1 to hope that something will happen or that something is true

hope /həʊp/ [v I/T] to want something to happen or to be true, and think

that this is possible: *See you soon, I hope!*

+(that) *Let's hope no-one saw us leaving.* | *We're hoping that more women will apply for the course.*

hope to do sth *After school, he's hoping to go to Africa for a year.*

+for *I'm hoping for a better salary when I get my next job.*

🔍 **I hope so** SPOKEN (=when you hope that what was mentioned will actually happen) *"Is Laura coming to the party?" "I hope so."*

🔍 **I hope not** SPOKEN (=when you hope that what was mentioned will not actually happen) *"Do you think it's going to rain?" "I hope not."*

> ⚠ Don't say 'I hope him to come'. Say **I hope (that) he will come**.

> ⚠ Don't say 'I don't hope it rains'. Say **I hope it doesn't rain**.

hopefully /'həʊpfəli/ [adv] use **hopefully** when you hope that what you are saying will happen or is true: *Hopefully, these problems can be solved quite quickly.* | *Karen should be feeling better by next week, hopefully.*

> ⚠ This use of **hopefully** is very common in both spoken and written English, but there are some people who think that **hopefully** should only be used to mean 'in a hopeful way', as in this example: *I waited hopefully for news.*

in the hope that (also **in hopes that** AMERICAN) /ɪn ðə 'həʊp ðət, ɪn 'həʊps ðət/ if you do something **in the hope that** something good will happen, you do it because this is the result you want: *I waited and waited in the hope that he might call.*

be hopeful /biː 'həʊpfəl/ if you **are hopeful** about a situation, you think it will probably have a good result in the end, even though it may be worrying at the moment

+(that) *Both sides are hopeful that they will reach an agreement.*

+about *After talking to the management, we felt a little more hopeful about the company's future.*

🔍 **keep your fingers crossed** /ˌkiːp jɔːʳ 'fɪŋgəʳz ˌkrɒstǀ-ˌkrɔːst/ SPOKEN used to say that you are hoping for good luck so that something will happen in the way that you want: *"Have you heard whether you got the job or not?" "No, but I'm keeping my fingers crossed."*

hope for the best /ˌhəʊp fəʳ ðə ˈbest/ ESPECIALLY SPOKEN to hope that a situation will end well, when it is possible that something might go wrong: *You practise as hard as you can and hope for the best on the day of the game.*

2 the feeling that things will happen in the way that you hope

hope /həʊp/ [n U] the feeling you have when you think that something good may happen or is likely to happen: *This discovery will give new hope to cancer sufferers.*
full of hope *We set off on our travels full of hope and excitement.*
+for *Most of these youths have no jobs and no hope for the future.*

optimistic /ˌɒptɪˈmɪstɪk‖ˌɑːp-/ [adj] someone who is **optimistic** believes that things will happen in the way they want or that good things will happen in the future: *Most of the players were in an optimistic mood before the game.*
+about *Senator Crosman, are you optimistic about the election results?*
optimistically [adv] *They had promised, rather optimistically, to finish the job in three days.*

optimism /ˈɒptɪmɪzəm‖ˈɑːp-/ [n U] the feeling that things will happen in the way you want or that good things will happen in the future: *There is a mood of optimism among our supporters tonight. | the optimism of the post-war period*

optimist /ˈɒptɪmɪst‖ˈɑːp-/ [n C] someone who always thinks good things will happen in the future

3 something that you hope will happen

hope /həʊp/ [n C] something that you hope will happen: *My one hope was that I would see my family again one day. | Politicians don't always*

understand the hopes and fears of ordinary people.
have high hopes (=want and expect someone or something to be very successful) *When we first got married we had such high hopes.*

4 something that makes you feel hopeful

encouraging /ɪnˈkʌrɪdʒɪŋ‖-ˈkɜːr-/ [adj] **encouraging** signs, remarks, news etc make you feel more confident that things will improve or happen in the way you want: *The medical test results were very encouraging. | There are encouraging signs that the economy is recovering. | His teacher made one or two encouraging comments.*

promising /ˈprɒmɪsɪŋ‖ˈprɑː-/ [adj] something that is **promising** seems likely to be good or successful in the future: *His promising career was cut short when he was killed in a plane crash.*
get off to/make a promising start (=do very well at the beginning of something) *The team got off to a promising start, winning their first three games.*

5 to stop hoping

give up hope/lose hope /ˌgɪv ʌp ˈhəʊp, ˌluːz ˈhəʊp/ to stop hoping that something good will happen or that things will get better: *Just when they had almost given up hope, Jenny became pregnant.*
give up/lose hope of doing sth *After the accident, he had given up hope of ever walking again.*
+that *We never lost hope that one day we would see our son again.*

 Don't say 'give up the hope' or 'lose the hope'. Say **give up hope** or **lose hope**.

despair /dɪˈspeəʳ/ [n U] ESPECIALLY WRITTEN the feeling that things are so bad that there is nothing you can do to make the situation any better: *She felt nothing but despair for weeks after her daughter's death.*
in despair *She turned to him in despair, with tears running down her cheeks.*

HORRIBLE/ UNPLEASANT

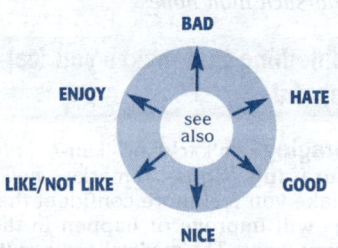

 1 horrible person/behaviour

horrible /'hɒrᵻbəl‖'hɔː-, 'hɑː-/ [adj] behaving in a very rude, unkind, or annoying way, especially towards people that you know well: *Her husband was a horrible man – lazy and always drunk.*
be horrible to sb *Why are you being so horrible to me?*

> Don't say 'very horrible'. Say **really horrible** or just **horrible**.

nasty /'nɑːsti‖'næsti/ [adj] deliberately very unkind – used especially by children or when you are talking to children: *The other boys played a nasty trick on him.*
be nasty to sb *Stop being so nasty to your sister!*

unpleasant /ʌn'plezənt/ [adj] rude or unfriendly in the way you talk to people or answer their questions: *That man in the grocery store is always so unpleasant.*
be unpleasant to sb *You shouldn't have been so unpleasant to her. She was only trying to help.*

○ **not very nice** /nɒt veri 'naɪs/ SPOKEN unkind or unfriendly – use this especially about things people say or do: *They completely ignored me, which wasn't very nice.*
not very nice of sb *It wasn't very nice of them to tease her like that.*

mean /miːn/ [adj] someone who is **mean** behaves in a rude, unkind, and sometimes cruel way: *Danny was a pretty mean character, and we were all scared of him.*
be mean to sb *Don't be so mean to her!*

2 a horrible feeling/experience/ accident

horrible /'hɒrᵻbəl‖'hɔː-,'hɑː-/ [adj] a **horrible** experience or feeling is one that makes you feel very worried and upset: *It was really horrible coming home and finding all our things had been stolen.* | *There was a horrible moment when she thought she had left all her files on the train.*

> Don't say 'very horrible'. Say **really horrible**.

nasty /'nɑːsti‖'næsti/ [adj] horrible – use this especially about events where there is violence, injury, or death: *There was a nasty accident on the freeway and seven people were killed.* | *a particularly nasty murder case* | *The news of his death came as a nasty shock.*

unpleasant /ʌn'plezənt/ [adj] an **unpleasant** situation is one that makes you feel slightly worried, uncomfortable, or embarrassed: *I had an unpleasant feeling that someone was following me.* | *Phil and Jane argued the whole time, so it was a pretty unpleasant evening.*

○ **not very nice** /nɒt veri 'naɪs/ SPOKEN unpleasant: *It's not very nice being stuck in an elevator for an hour.* | *Divorce is not very nice for anyone involved.*

> People often use **not very nice** to describe something that is in fact extremely unpleasant.

nightmare /'naɪtmeəʳ/ [n singular] a very unpleasant or frightening experience: *We were stuck in a traffic jam for four hours – it was a nightmare.*
turn into a nightmare (=become very unpleasant) *The couple's honeymoon turned into a nightmare when Martin suddenly became very ill.*

> ⚠ You can also use **nightmare** before a noun, like an adjective: *a nightmare journey*

3 a horrible taste/smell/sight etc

horrible/disgusting/revolting

/'hɒrɪbəl, dɪs'gʌstɪŋ, rɪ'vəʊltɪŋ‖'hɔː-, 'hɑː-/ [adj] very bad – use this especially to talk about things that taste or smell or look really bad: *It was the most disgusting meal I've ever eaten!* | *His teeth were a revolting yellow color.* | *What a horrible smell!* | *I couldn't eat the stew. It looked and smelled revolting.*

> ⚠ Don't say 'very horrible/disgusting/ revolting'. Say **really horrible/ disgusting/revolting**.

foul /faʊl/ [adj] ESPECIALLY WRITTEN a **foul** smell or taste is extremely bad, and is caused especially by things decaying: *There was a foul smell coming up from the river.*

Q gross /grəʊs/ [adj not before noun] SPOKEN, ESPECIALLY AMERICAN very unpleasant – use this to talk about food, smells, or things people do that you dislike very much: *Ooh, gross! I hate spinach!* | *Brad threw up on the floor at the party. It was really gross.*

HOT

➡ if you mean 'food that has a hot taste', go to **TASTE 7**
➡ opposite **COLD**
➡ see also **WEATHER**

1 object/liquid/surface

hot /hɒt‖hɑːt/ [adj] *Eat your dinner while it's hot.* | *Each room has hot and cold running water.* | *Be careful – that pan's still very hot.*
red hot (=extremely hot – used mainly about things that are burning) *The coals in the fire were glowing and red hot.*
hot – hotter – hottest

boiling/boiling hot /'bɔɪlɪŋ, ˌbɔɪlɪŋ 'hɒt◄ ‖-'hɑːt◄/ [adj] a liquid that is **boiling** or **boiling hot** is extremely hot: *Don't drink the tea yet. It's boiling!* | *Boiling hot water poured out of the radiator.*

scalding/scalding hot /'skɔːldɪŋ, ˌskɔːldɪŋ 'hɒt◄ ‖-'hɑːt◄/ [adj] ESPECIALLY WRITTEN a liquid or drink that is **scalding** or **scalding hot** is extremely hot, so that it burns you if you touch it or drink it: *She handed me a mug of scalding hot soup.*

2 room/place/weather

hot /hɒt‖hɑːt/ [adj] *It was a hot summer's day.* | *The Gobi Desert is one of the hottest places on earth.*
it's hot (=when the weather is hot or a room is hot) *It's hot in here. Shall I open the window?* | *It was too hot to play volleyball.*
hot – hotter – hottest

the heat /ðə 'hiːt/ [n U] when the temperature is hot: *In the desert, the heat of the day is soon lost when the sun goes down.* | *The heat from the fire was almost unbearable.*
in the heat *Several of her plants had died in the heat.*

Q boiling/boiling hot /'bɔɪlɪŋ, ˌbɔɪlɪŋ 'hɒt◄ ‖-'hɑːt◄/ [adj] SPOKEN very hot: *a boiling hot day in August*
it's boiling/boiling hot *Inside the car it was absolutely boiling.*

Q broiling /'brɔɪlɪŋ/ [adj] AMERICAN, ESPECIALLY SPOKEN weather that is **broiling** is very hot and makes you feel uncomfortable: *It's broiling out here.* | *the broiling heat of a Mississippi summer*

Q baking/baking hot /'beɪkɪŋ, ˌbeɪkɪŋ 'hɒt‖-'hɑːt◄/ [adj] SPOKEN very hot and dry: *The desert here is baking hot in summer.*

sweltering/sweltering hot /'sweltərɪŋ, ˌsweltərɪŋ 'hɒt‖-'hɑːt◄/ [adj] weather that is **sweltering** is very hot and makes you feel tired and uncomfortable: *the sweltering summer of 1995* | *a sweltering hot afternoon*

heatwave /'hiːtweɪv/ [n C] a period of time when the weather is much hotter than usual: *The heatwave continued throughout August and into September.*

muggy/humid /'mʌgi, 'hjuːmɪ̯d/ [*adj*] weather that is **muggy** or **humid** makes you feel uncomfortable because the air feels wet, warm, and heavy: *It was a hot, humid summer night.*

it's muggy/humid *It's really muggy in Florida at this time of year.*

> **Formal or informal?**
> **Humid** is more formal than **muggy**, which is used more often in spoken English.

3 warm, but not hot

warm /wɔːʳm/ [*adj*] a little hot, but not very hot, especially in a way that is pleasant: *I didn't want to get out of my warm bed.* | *It's nice and warm in the kitchen.* | *a warm day* | *These plants only grow in warm climates.*

warmth [*n* U] when an object, the weather, a place etc is warm: *The warmth of the sun was making them all sleepy.*

lukewarm /ˌluːkˈwɔːʳm◂/ [*adj*] food or drinks that are **lukewarm** are slightly warm, and not as hot or as cold as they should be: *The bartender handed me a mug of lukewarm beer.* | *The coffee was only lukewarm.*

4 when you feel hot

hot /hɒt‖hɑːt/ [*adj* not before noun] feeling hot, especially when this makes you uncomfortable: *I'm too hot – could you open the window?* | *The travellers were hot, tired, and thirsty.*

warm /wɔːʳm/ [*adj* not usually before noun] feeling warm in a way that is pleasant and comfortable, especially when you are in a cold place: *Are you warm enough?*

keep warm (=make yourself stay warm) *We stamped our feet in order to keep warm.*

warm coat / boots / clothes etc (=which keep you warm when the weather is cold) *Put on some warm clothes if you're going out in the snow.*

boiling /'bɔɪlɪŋ/ [*adj* not before noun] SPOKEN feeling very hot: *I'd like a cold drink – I'm boiling!*

have a temperature /ˌhæv ə 'tempərətʃəʳ/ if you **have a temperature**, your body is hotter than usual because you are ill: *If you have a temperature, go to bed and have plenty to drink.*

feverish /'fiːvərɪʃ/ [*adj* not usually before noun] feeling very hot and ill because you have a high temperature: *Her son was flushed and feverish.*

5 when your body becomes wet because you are hot

sweat /swet/ [*v* I] if you **sweat**, small drops of liquid come from the surface of your skin because you are hot: *I was sweating after the long climb.*

sweat [*n* U] the liquid that forms on your skin when you are hot: *Ian came off the squash court covered in sweat.*

sweaty /'sweti/ [*adj*] covered with sweat: *Joe felt hot and sweaty, and decided to go for a swim.*

6 how hot something is

how hot /hau 'hɒt‖-'hɑːt/ *How hot is it outside?* | *She couldn't believe how hot it was in the car.*

temperature /'tempərətʃəʳ/ [*n* C] a measurement of how hot or cold something is: *Test the temperature of the water to make sure it's not too hot.*

high/low temperature (=hot or cold) *Steel can only be produced at a very high temperature.* | *Expect low temperatures in the mountain regions tonight.*

a temperature of 30/70/100 etc degrees *Heat the oven to a temperature of 200 degrees.*

7 to become hot or warm

get hot/warm /ˌget 'hɒt, 'wɔːʳm‖-'hɑːt-/ to become hot or warm: *You'd better switch the engine off – it's getting very hot.* | *As the weather gets warmer, birds begin to return from their winter nesting places.*

it gets hot/warm (=the weather gets hot) *It got hotter and hotter as the afternoon went on.*

warm up /ˌwɔːʳm 'ʌp/ [*phrasal verb* I] to gradually get warmer, especially so that a place reaches a more comfortable temperature: *Rick lit a fire and the room began to warm up.* | *Once the weather warms up, you can move the plants outdoors.*

overheat /ˌəʊvəˈrhiːt/ [v I] if an engine or machine **overheats**, it gets too hot so that it does not work properly: *There's a special cooling system that stops the engine from overheating.*

---

8 · to make someone or something hot or warm

heat /hiːt/ [v T] to make something hot or warm using a fire, a heating system, or a cooker: *She heated the water in a small pan.* | *It's very expensive to heat a big house like this.*

heat up /ˌhiːt ˈʌp/ [phrasal verb T] to make food hot, especially food that has been cooked already and has gone cold
heat up sth *I usually just heat up some soup for my lunch.*
heat sth up *It only takes a few minutes to heat a meal up in the microwave.*

warm up /ˌwɔːrm ˈʌp/ [phrasal verb T] to make a place warmer or make yourself warmer, especially so that you feel more comfortable
warm sth/sb up *Here, have a glass of brandy. That'll warm you up.*
warm up sth *Dad lit the fire to warm up the living-room.*

turn up /ˌtɜːrn ˈʌp/ [phrasal verb T] to make something such as a heater or cooker produce more heat
turn up sth *How do you turn up this heater?*
turn sth up *After an hour, turn the oven up to 220°.*

HOUSES/WHERE PEOPLE LIVE

➡ see Word Banks section

HUNGRY

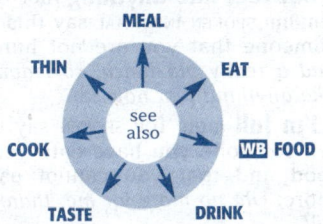

---

1 · when you want to eat

hungry /ˈhʌngri/ [adj] if you are **hungry**, you feel that you need something to eat: *Are you hungry? I can make you a sandwich.* | *We all felt really hungry after our long walk.* | *Have something before you go out, or you'll get hungry later.*

> ⚠ Don't say 'I have hunger'. Say **I'm hungry**.

◯ **starving / ravenous** /ˈstɑːrvɪŋ, ˈrævənəs/ [adj not before noun] ESPECIALLY SPOKEN very hungry: *Can we stop for lunch? I'm absolutely starving.* | *The boys always come home from school ravenous.*

> ⚠ Don't say 'very starving/ravenous'. Say **absolutely starving/ravenous** or just say **starving** or **ravenous**.

peckish /ˈpekɪʃ/ [adj not before noun] BRITISH INFORMAL if you feel **peckish**, you feel a little hungry: *By now we were all feeling a bit peckish.*

◯ **feel like something to eat** /ˌfiːl laɪk sʌmθɪŋ tu ˈiːt/ SPOKEN if you **feel like something to eat**, you want to eat something: *It's 12 o'clock – do you feel like something to eat?*

---

2 · not hungry

not hungry /nɒt ˈhʌngri/ if you are **not hungry**, you do not feel that you need to eat anything: *"How about something to eat?" "No thanks, I'm not hungry."*

lose your appetite /ˌluːz jɔːr ˈæpᵻtaɪt/ to not want to eat anything, for example because you are ill or worried: *She isn't sleeping very well and she's lost her appetite.*

◯ **not feel like anything** /nɒt fiːl laɪk ˈeniθɪŋ/ SPOKEN INFORMAL say this to tell someone that you are not hungry: *I had a really big lunch, so I don't feel like anything just now.*

◯ **I'm full** /aɪm ˈfʊl/ SPOKEN say this to tell someone you have eaten enough food and that you cannot eat any more: *Oh, no more for me, thanks. I'm full.*

3 the feeling you have when you are hungry

appetite /ˈæpɪˌtaɪt/ [n C/U] the normal feeling of wanting to eat when you have not eaten for some time: *The medicine might affect your appetite.* (=make you want to eat more or less than normal)
give sb an appetite (=make them feel hungry) *All that exercise has given me an appetite.*
have a good/big/healthy appetite (=want to eat a lot and enjoy eating) *Healthy, growing children should have a good appetite.*

hunger /ˈhʌŋɡəʳ/ [n U] the feeling you have when you have eaten very little food: *By the end of the day, I was feeling weak with hunger.*

4 when people are ill or dying because they do not have enough to eat

starving /ˈstɑːʳvɪŋ/ [adj] someone who is **starving** has not had enough food for a long time and will die soon if they do not eat: *terrible pictures of starving children* | *People in the West waste food while millions of others are starving.*

starve /stɑːʳv/ [v I] to have so little food to eat that you become ill or die: *Without more food aid, thousands of people will starve.*
starve to death (=die because of lack of food) *There were reports that whole villages had starved to death.*

starvation /stɑːʳˈveɪʃən/ [n U] when you become ill or die because you do not have enough to eat: *The climbers were close to starvation when they were rescued.* | *Thousands of people could die of cold and starvation.*

malnutrition /ˌmælnjʊˈtrɪʃən‖-nʊ-/ [n U] a serious health problem caused by not eating enough healthy food for a long time, which makes your body weak: *Children from poor families suffered from malnutrition.* | *Disease and malnutrition are widespread.*

> **Formal or informal?**
> **Malnutrition** is a formal and technical word.

famine /ˈfæmɪn/ [n C/U] a situation in which many people in a place are very hungry and die, especially because the food they planted did not grow: *Millions of people continue to die because of war and famine.* | *The drought caused famine across the country.*

HURRY

➡ see also **FAST, SLOW, RUN**

1 to go somewhere or do something as quickly as you can

hurry /ˈhʌri‖ˈhɜːri/ [v I/T] to go somewhere or do something quickly, especially because you do not have much time: *If we don't hurry, we'll miss the beginning of the movie.* | *I hate having to hurry a meal.*
+across/along/away/to etc *The station was already full of people hurrying to work.* | *Des always seemed to hurry away when he saw me coming.*
hurry to do sth *Anna was hurrying to finish her essay before lunchtime.*
hurrying – hurried – have hurried

in a hurry /ɪn ə ˈhʌri‖-ˈhɜːri/ if you do something **in a hurry**, you do it very quickly because you do not have much time, so you often make mistakes or forget things: *I bought this jacket in a hurry. Do you think it's OK?*
be in a hurry (=when you have to hurry) *Sorry, I can't stop, I'm in a hurry.*

be in a hurry to do sth *When I called, he was in a hurry to get to a lecture.*

 Don't say 'I'm in hurry'. Say **I'm in a hurry**.

rush/dash /rʌʃ, dæʃ/ [*v* I] to go somewhere or run somewhere very quickly, for example because you have to do something urgently, or because someone is in danger
+across/off/out/into etc *Everyone rushed into the street to see what had happened.* | *The boys all dashed across the playground after the ball.*
rush/dash to do sth *I dashed downstairs to answer the phone.* | *A kind man rushed across to see if I was hurt.*

hurriedly /'hʌrɪdli‖'hɜːr-/ [*adv*] WRITTEN if you do something **hurriedly**, you do it quickly because you do not have much time: *He dressed hurriedly and went to answer the door.*

 Use **hurriedly** in stories and written descriptions.

2 | what you say to tell someone to hurry

○ **hurry up/come on** /ˌhʌri 'ʌp, ˌkʌm 'ɒn‖'hɜːri-/ SPOKEN say this to tell someone to hurry, especially when you are impatient with them for being too slow: *Hurry up or we'll be late for school!* | *Come on – you should have finished packing by now!*

○ **get a move on** ESPECIALLY BRITISH **get moving** ESPECIALLY AMERICAN /ˌget ə 'muːv ɒn, get 'muːvɪŋ/ SPOKEN say this when you want someone to start to do something or go somewhere more quickly than before: *You'd better get moving or you'll miss the bus.* | *Come on, Sally, get a move on!*

3 | something that you do quickly because you are hurrying

quick /kwɪk/ [*adj* only before noun] a **quick** look, meal, visit, decision etc is done very quickly, because you do not have much time: *Mary went upstairs for a quick shower.* | *Could I just make a quick phone call?*

quick look/glance (=when you look at something or read something very quickly) *I had a quick glance at the newspaper before going to work.*
quick drink/lunch/coffee *Have we got time for a quick drink?*

hasty /'heɪsti/ [*adj* only before noun] a **hasty** decision or action is done very quickly, without planning it or thinking carefully about the results: *The army was forced to make a hasty retreat.*
hasty decision *Don't make any hasty decisions that you might regret.*
hasty – hastier – hastiest

hurried /'hʌrɪd‖'hɜː-/ [*adj* usually before noun] ESPECIALLY WRITTEN done very quickly because you are in a hurry: *his hurried departure from Paris*
a hurried lunch/dinner/meal *We ate a hurried dinner and rushed out.*

frantic /'fræntɪk/ [*adj* only before noun] ESPECIALLY WRITTEN
frantic activity/rush/search/effort when people are moving, working etc as fast as possible, especially because they are worried that they will not have enough time to finish or achieve something: *The night before the wedding, the house was a scene of frantic activity.* | *a frantic search for the missing children*
frantically [*adv*] *The library was full of students, frantically trying to finish their final essays.*

rush /rʌʃ/ [*n* singular] a situation in which you have to hurry or work very fast
a rush to do sth *There was a rush to get everything arranged for the party.*
do sth in a rush *It was clear that the men had left the hotel in a rush.*

4 | to make someone hurry

hurry sb up /ˌhʌri (sb) 'ʌp‖ˌhɜːri-/ [*phrasal verb* T] to make someone do something more quickly because they are taking too long: *Can you try and hurry the kids up? We're leaving in ten minutes.*

rush/hurry /rʌʃ, 'hʌri‖-'hɜːri/ [*v* T] to make someone do something more quickly, in an impatient way that makes them feel nervous or confused:

Don't rush me. I'll only make a mistake. | *It's an important decision, so don't let them hurry you.*

hurrying – hurried – have hurried

5 what you say to tell someone not to hurry

○ **there's no hurry/there's no rush** /ðeə^rz ˌnəʊ ˈhʌri, ðeə^rz ˌnəʊ ˈrʌʃ‖-ˈhɜːri/ SPOKEN say this to tell someone that they do not have to hurry or do something soon: *You can pay me for the ticket next week. There's no rush.*

○ **take your time** /ˌteɪk jɔː^r ˈtaɪm/ SPOKEN say this to tell someone to do something without hurrying, because it is important to do it carefully and correctly: *Take your time before you answer the question.*

○ **what's the hurry?/what's the rush?** /ˌwɒts ðə ˈhʌri, ˌwɒts ðə ˈrʌʃ‖ -ˈhɜːri/ SPOKEN say this to someone who is hurrying or trying to make you hurry, to emphasize that there is plenty of time: *The party doesn't start till eight, so what's the hurry?*

HURT/INJURE

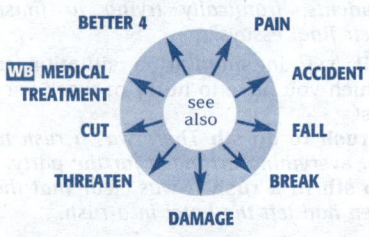

BETTER 4 **PAIN**
WB MEDICAL TREATMENT **ACCIDENT**
see also
CUT **FALL**
THREATEN **BREAK**
DAMAGE

1 be hurt or injured in an accident, fight etc

be injured/be hurt /biː ˈɪndʒə^rd‖biː ˈhɜː^rt/ if someone **is hurt** or **is injured**, part of their body is damaged, especially in an accident or fight: *Four people have been injured in a road accident.* | *Do they know yet if anyone's been hurt?*

badly/seriously injured *One man died, and another was seriously injured when a wall collapsed on a construction site.*

badly/seriously hurt *Fortunately the driver was not badly hurt.*

slightly injured/hurt *A fireman was slightly injured, but all the people in the house were saved.*

get hurt *There were riots and demonstrations and a lot of people got hurt.*

> ⚠️ Don't use the word 'damage' to talk about people. Cars, buildings, or equipment can get damaged, but people get **hurt** or **injured**.

Formal or informal?
Be **injured** is more formal than be **hurt**.

be wounded /biː ˈwuːndəd/ to be injured in a war, a fight etc, by a weapon such as a knife, gun, or bomb: *Two police officers were wounded in the attack.*

badly/seriously wounded *My father was badly wounded in the war.*

be wounded in the leg/chest etc *One soldier was slightly wounded in the leg.*

2 to hurt a part of your body

hurt /hɜː^rt/ [v T] if you **hurt** a part of your body in an accident, a fight etc, you damage it so that it feels painful or you cannot move it easily: *Nick's hurt his back, and the doctor says he'll have to rest for a few weeks.* | *I can't go running this week – I've hurt my foot.*

hurt yourself *That's a sharp knife so be careful you don't hurt yourself.*

hurting – hurt – have hurt

injure /ˈɪndʒə^r/ [v T] to hurt a part of your body, especially seriously and in a way that takes a long time to get better: *Tom injured his shoulder playing tennis.*

injure yourself *She'd fallen heavily and injured herself.*

bruise /bruːz/ [v T] to hurt a part of your body when you fall or are hit, so that a dark, painful mark appears on your skin: *Look, Mum, I've bruised my knee!*

bruised [adj] *My arm was badly bruised, but not broken.*

sprain /spreɪn/ [v T] to injure your knee, your ankle, or another place where two bones are joined, by twisting or pulling it suddenly: *I sprained my ankle while I was playing basketball.*

sprained [*adj*] *He had a sprained wrist.*

break /breɪk/ [*v T*] to break a bone in your body: *Nicola broke her leg the first time she went skiing.*

breaking – broke – have broken

broken /ˈbrəʊkən/ [*adj*] *I had three broken ribs and a broken arm.*

twist /twɪst/ [*v T*] to hurt your knee or another joint, by turning it too suddenly or strongly when you are moving: *I twisted my ankle playing basketball.*

twisted [*adj*] *a twisted ankle*

pull /pʊl/ [*v T*]

pull a muscle to injure a muscle by stretching it too much: *Valdez won't be playing as he pulled a muscle in training.*

pulled [*adj*] *a pulled muscle*

dislocate /ˈdɪsləkeɪt/ [*v T*] to injure your shoulder, knee, finger etc, so that one of the bones is moved out of its normal position: *He dislocated his shoulder in a riding accident.*

dislocated [*adj*] *The accident left her with bruises and a dislocated hip.*

damage /ˈdæmɪdʒ/ [*v T*] to injure a part of your body fairly seriously, especially in a way that means it will take a long time to get better or will never get better: *She was running in a 10k race when she damaged her knee.*

damaged [*adj*] *He will have surgery to repair his damaged right shoulder.*

> ⚠️ **Damage** is mainly used in news reports.

3 to hurt someone

hurt /hɜːʳt/ [*v T*] to cause pain or injury to someone's body, especially by hitting them: *Let go of my arm! You're hurting me! | I began to be afraid that he might hurt one of the children.*

injure /ˈɪndʒəʳ/ [*v T*] to cause physical harm to someone, for example in an accident or fight: *The bomb killed eleven people and injured 55.*

badly / seriously / critically injure *The truck hit a car, seriously injuring the driver.*

> **Formal or informal?**
> **Injure** is more formal than **hurt**.

wound /wuːnd/ [*v T*] to injure someone with a weapon such as a knife or gun: *A police officer began shooting, wounding one of the robbers.*

4 damage to part of your body

injury /ˈɪndʒəri/ [*n C/U*] physical damage done to someone's body in an accident, a fight etc: *The glass roof collapsed onto the crowd, causing horrific injuries.*

serious injury *Wearing a helmet may protect you from serious injury.*

leg/back etc injury *He was forced to withdraw from the game because of a leg injury.*

suffer an injury (=be injured) *He suffered serious injuries in a car crash, and died on the way to the hospital.*

plural **injuries**

> **Formal or informal?**
> In formal conversation, don't say 'he suffered serious injuries'. Say **he was badly/seriously injured** or **he was badly/seriously hurt**.

wound /wuːnd/ [*n C*] an injury caused by a weapon such as a knife, gun, or bomb

deep wound *The wound was deep and needed 18 stitches.*

bullet/stab/gunshot wound *Barratt was taken to the hospital with stab wounds to his chest and neck.*

bruise /bruːz/ [*n C*] a dark, painful mark on your skin where you have fallen or been hit: *Her arms were covered in cuts and bruises.*

5 someone who is injured

injured /ˈɪndʒəʳd/ [*adj*] hurt in an accident, fight etc: *Firefighters had to cut off the roof of the car, so that the injured man could be lifted out.*

the injured (=people who are injured) *The injured were rushed to St Thomas' Hospital.*

wounded /ˈwuːndɪd/ [*adj*] injured by a weapon such as a knife, gun, or bomb: *a wounded soldier | There are*

over 4000 refugees in the camp, many
of them wounded.

the wounded (=people who are
wounded) Helicopters have been sent
in to rescue the wounded from the war
zone.

paralysed BRITISH (also **paralyzed**
AMERICAN) /ˈpærəlaɪzd/ [adj] unable to
move part or all of your body because
of a serious injury or illness

leave sb paralysed The accident left
him permanently paralysed.

casualty /ˈkæʒuəlti/ [n C usually plural]
someone who has been injured or
killed in a war, attack, or accident:
The bomb caused serious damage to
the building, but there were no
casualties.

suffer casualties Indian troops suffered more than 1200 casualties.

Formal or informal?

Casualty is used especially in news reports
and in formal writing.

---

6 | not injured

unhurt /ʌnˈhɜːrt/ [adj not before noun]
if you are **unhurt**, you are not hurt,
even though you have been in an
accident or have been attacked: The
driver of the car was unhurt, but his
passenger was killed.

escape unhurt A man escaped unhurt
from a fire in Bromborough.

unharmed /ʌnˈhɑːrmd/ [adj not before
noun] if you are **unharmed**, you have
not been harmed, even though you
have been in a dangerous situation:
The boy was cold and hungry but
otherwise unharmed. | All the hostages
were released unharmed some time
afterwards.

I, i

IDEA

➡ see also **THINK, INVENT, IMAGINE**

1 a plan or suggestion that you think of

idea /aɪ'dɪə/ [n C] something that you think of, such as a plan of what to do or a suggestion
good/great/fantastic etc idea (=used especially to say that you like someone's idea) *"We could go and see a movie." "That's a good idea!"*
have an idea *We're trying to think of a name for the book. Does anyone have any ideas?*
+for *an idea for a new TV game show | Here are some new ideas for quick meals that taste great.*
it was sb's idea (=they thought of it – use this especially when you want to blame someone) *I didn't want to go to Spain – it was Sue's idea. | Whose idea was it to ask him to the party?*
get an idea from sb/sth *She got the idea from a picture in a magazine.*

thought /θɔːt/ [n C] an idea – use this especially when you have not yet considered it carefully or you are not sure if it is a good idea
have a thought *I've just had a thought – do you think Nadia would like to come with us?*
thoughts on sth *Mail me if you have any further thoughts on this.*
sb's thoughts about sth *What are your thoughts about the baby's name?*
⚲ **(it was) just/only a thought** SPOKEN (say this when someone seems to disagree with an idea you suggested) *"I'm not sure that's a good time of year to go to India." "True. It was just a thought."*

2 an idea that explains something about life or the world

theory /'θɪəri/ [n C/U] a set of ideas that explains why something happens or why something is true, especially in science
+about *There have been a lot of theories about the meaning of dreams.*
sb's theory of sth (used in the names of important scientific theories) *Darwin's Theory of Evolution | Einstein's theory of relativity*
+that *There's a theory that Kennedy was killed by the CIA.*
plural **theories**

idea /aɪ'dɪə/ [n C] something that people believe in or think may be true about life, society etc: *Ideas and customs have changed dramatically in modern times.*
+about *our ideas about the origins of the universe*
+that *the idea that there is life after death*
religious/political etc ideas

belief /bɪ'liːf/ [n C] an idea that you believe to be true, especially one that forms part of a system of ideas: *She has strong religious beliefs. | Several members of the party hold very right-wing beliefs.*

3 good at thinking of new ideas

creative /kri'eɪtɪv/ [adj] someone who is **creative** is good at thinking of new ideas, designs, or ways of doing things, especially in art, music, literature etc: *Tarantino is one of Hollywood's most creative directors.*

full of ideas /ˌfʊl əv aɪ'dɪəz/ INFORMAL someone who is **full of ideas** has a lot of good new ideas and wants to tell other people about them: *Roy was full of ideas for the new show.*

imaginative /ɪ'mædʒɪnətɪv/ [adj] an **imaginative** plan, design, or way of doing something uses new and interesting ideas: *an imaginative solution to the city's crime problem | The film uses computer graphics in a highly imaginative way.*

ILLNESS/DISEASE

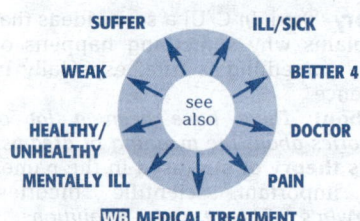

SUFFER   ILL/SICK

WEAK   BETTER 4

see also

HEALTHY/ UNHEALTHY   DOCTOR

MENTALLY ILL   PAIN

WB MEDICAL TREATMENT

1   an illness

illness /'ɪlnɪ̈s/ [n C/U] a problem with your health that makes you feel ill, especially one that makes it difficult for you to work, have a normal life etc: *She died at the age of 82, after a long illness.* | *How many days off work have you had because of illness?*
mental illness (=an illness that affects your mind) *drugs that are used to treat mental illness*
serious illness (=one that makes you very ill) *In 1985, a serious illness ended her acting career.*
minor illness (=one that does not make you very ill) *a succession of minor illnesses*
recover from an illness *She's gone away for a few weeks to recover from her illness.*

> ⚠ Don't use **illness** to talk about less serious problems such as headaches or colds.

disease /dɪ'ziːz/ [n C/U] a particular kind of illness, especially one that spreads from one person to another, or one that affects a particular part of your body: *Measles is a disease that is common among young children.* | *Mosquitoes spread diseases such as malaria.*
heart/lung/kidney disease *Smoking is a major cause of heart disease.*
catch a disease (from sb) (=get a disease from another person) *He caught the disease from one of his patients.*
suffer from a disease (=have a disease) *She suffers from a rare blood disease.*

infectious disease (=one that spreads from one person to another)

> ⚠ **Disease** can also be used to mean a lot of different diseases: *Thousands of refugees are dying of hunger and disease.*

infection /ɪn'fekʃən/ [n C] an illness that affects part of your body such as your eye, ear, or throat and that can sometimes spread from one person to another: *The doctor said I have a slight infection, and she gave me some antibiotics.*
ear / eye / throat / chest infection *Richard's not at school because he has an ear infection.*

bug /bʌg/ [n C] INFORMAL a disease that is not serious, which spreads from one person to another, for example in the air or in food, and which a lot of people get: *There's an unpleasant bug going round at school at the moment.*
stomach/tummy bug (=illness affecting the stomach) *Pete's been off work with a stomach bug.*
pick up a bug (=get a bug) *I think I picked up a bug while I was on vacation.*

problem /'prɒbləm‖'prɑː-/ [n C] when a part of your body has something wrong with it, for example when it is painful or it does not work properly
+with *Simon started to have problems with his back.*
back/chest/skin etc problems *A lot of people have skin problems when they are young.*

condition /kən'dɪʃən/ [n C] a serious problem that affects someone's health permanently or for a very long time: *High blood pressure is a condition that affects many elderly people.*
heart condition *Frank suffers from a rare heart condition.*

2   to have an illness

have (also **have got** BRITISH) /hæv, həv 'gɒt‖-'gɑːt/ [v T] *Beth has an awful cold.* | *I had all the usual childhood illnesses.* | *Have you ever had pneumonia?*

suffer from /'sʌfəʳ frɒm‖-frʌm/ [phrasal verb T] to have a particular kind of illness or health problem, especially one that is serious or one that you have often: *Dewey had been in hospital for several weeks suffering from malaria.* | *She suffers from asthma attacks.*

Formal or informal?

Suffer from is more formal than **have**.

there's something wrong with /ðeə^rz ˌsʌmθɪŋ 'rɒŋ wɪðll-'rɔːŋ-/ INFORMAL use this to say that you have a medical problem affecting part of your body, but you are not sure exactly what it is: *There's something wrong with my back and it hurts when I walk.* | *We thought there might be something wrong with her hearing.*

with /wɪð, wɪθ/ [*preposition*] use this before the name of a disease, to say that someone has this disease: *"Where's Helen?" "She's in bed with flu."* | *The charity provides support for people with AIDS.*

3 to start to have an illness

get /get/ [*v* T] to start to have an illness: *I feel all hot – I think I'm getting flu.* | *Smoking increases the risk of getting cancer.*
get sth from/off sb (=get an infectious disease from someone else) *He thinks he got the cold from someone in the office.*

catch /kætʃ/ [*v* T] to get a disease from someone else: *So far, around half the kids in the class have caught the virus.*
catch sth from/off sb *I think I must have caught the flu from Sarah.*
catching – caught – have caught

go down with sth /ˌgəʊ 'daʊn wɪð (sth)/ [*phrasal verb* T] INFORMAL to start to have an illness, especially one that is not serious: *I always go down with some bug or other in the winter.*

4 when a lot of people have an illness

outbreak /'aʊtbreɪk/ [*n* C] when a lot of people suddenly start to get an illness at the same time
+of *Doctors are very concerned about an outbreak of tuberculosis in an East London school.*

epidemic /ˌepə'demɪk/ [*n* C] when a large number of people in an area or country get a disease, and it spreads very quickly
a flu/measles/cholera etc epidemic *We have been warned that a flu epidemic may be on the way.*

5 when an illness is serious

serious /'sɪəriəs/ [*adj*] a **serious** illness or condition is very bad and may be dangerous: *In February he suffered a serious heart attack.* | *Listeriosis is not usually a serious disease among healthy adults.*
something/anything serious *Do you think it could be something serious?*
seriously [*adv*] *Her mother is seriously ill with pneumonia.*

bad /bæd/ [*adj*]
bad cold/flu/fever/cough/stomach ache etc a cold etc that makes you feel very uncomfortable or that is very painful: *She has a bad cold.* | *a bad attack of bronchitis*
get worse *His cough seems to be getting worse.*
bad – worse – worst

terminal /'tɜː^rmɪnəl/ [*adj*] a **terminal** illness cannot be cured, so the person who has it will die from it, usually after quite a long period: *a patient suffering from terminal cancer* | *Should doctors tell patients that they have a terminal illness?*

fatal /'feɪtl/ [*adj*] a **fatal** illness makes the person who has it die: *The disease is almost always fatal.* | *The former president suffered a fatal heart attack this morning.*

Formal or informal?

Fatal is not usually used in informal conversation.

6 when an illness is not serious

not serious /nɒt 'sɪəriəs/ [*adj*] *Don't worry, it's not serious. It's only a cold.*
nothing serious *The doctor told me it was nothing serious.*

slight /slaɪt/ [*adj* only before noun]
slight cold/cough/fever/headache etc a cold etc that is not at all serious

and does not make you feel very ill: *I've got a slight cold.* | *The virus sometimes causes a slight fever.*

minor /'maɪnə^r/ [*adj*] a **minor** illness is not serious: *Most of these minor illnesses only last a few days or a week.*

 Don't use **minor** with the names of diseases.

ILL/SICK

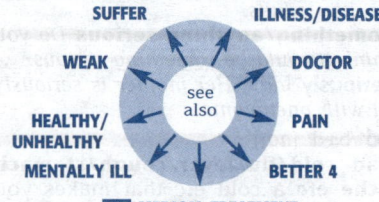

SUFFER

ILLNESS/DISEASE

WEAK

DOCTOR

see also

HEALTHY/
UNHEALTHY

PAIN

MENTALLY ILL

BETTER 4

WB MEDICAL TREATMENT

1 ill

 Ill is more common than **sick** in British English. **Sick** is more common than **ill** in American English.

 To **be sick** can also mean 'to vomit' (=bring up food from your stomach), especially in British English. And to **feel sick** can mean 'to feel that you are going to vomit'. See Section 5.

ill /ɪl/ [*adj* not before noun] someone who is **ill** has an illness or does not feel well: *I was so ill that I just had to stay in bed.*
feel ill *I felt ill for a week after I got back from Bolivia.*
get ill *It's horrible when you get ill on holiday.*
seriously ill (=very ill) *His wife is seriously ill and they think it might be cancer.*
critically ill (=so ill that you may die)
be taken ill (=suddenly become ill) *She was taken ill in the night.*

 Don't use **ill** about part of your body. Don't say 'my head is ill'. Say **I have a headache** or **my head aches/hurts**. See also **PAIN**.

 Don't say 'more ill' or 'iller'. Say **worse**: *The next morning she was even worse.*

sick /sɪk/ [*adj*] ill: *Where's Sheila today? Is she sick?* | *Anna spent months looking after her sick mother.*
+with *I've been sick with flu.*
be off sick (=not at work or school because of illness) *Les phoned to say that he's off sick.*
get/fall sick AMERICAN (=become sick)
sick pay (=money you get from your employer when you cannot work because of illness)

 Don't use **sick** about part of your body. Don't say 'my leg is sick' or 'my head is sick'. See also **PAIN**.

○ **not very well** /ˌnɒt veri 'wel/ ESPECIALLY SPOKEN ill, but not seriously ill: *Sarah's not very well – she has a throat infection.*

○ **under the weather** /ˌʌndə^r ðə 'weðə^r/ SPOKEN if you feel **under the weather**, you feel slightly ill: *Mike's been feeling a little under the weather, so he stayed home tonight.*

unwell /ʌn'wel/ [*adj* not before noun] FORMAL, ESPECIALLY BRITISH ill, especially for a short time: *Her face was pale and she seemed unwell.*

poorly /'pʊə^rli/ [*adj* not before noun] BRITISH INFORMAL ill: *My nan has been very poorly this winter.*

2 to become healthy again after being ill

get better /ˌget 'betə^r/ if you **get better**, you become healthy again after an illness, operation, or injury; if a pain or an injury **gets better**, it stops hurting and you feel healthy again: *If you don't get better soon, you'd better go to the doctor.* | *I hope your headache gets better soon.*

recover /rɪ'kʌvə^r/ [*v* I] to become healthy again after a serious illness, operation, or injury: *Survivors of the fire are recovering in the city hospital.* **+from** *My father never really recovered from his first heart attack.*

Formal or informal?
Recover is more formal than **get better**, and is used especially about serious illnesses or injuries.

get well soon /ˌget wel ˈsuːn/ you say or write this to someone who is ill, to tell them that you hope they will soon get better: *Get well soon – we all miss you!*

3 someone who is ill

patient /ˈpeɪʃənt/ [n C] someone who is looked after by a doctor or nurse because they are ill: *The hospital treats thousands of patients a year.* | *Dr Cobb is seeing a patient just now – could you wait ten minutes?*

invalid /ˈɪnvəliːd, -lɪd‖-lɪd/ [n C] someone who is permanently ill and cannot look after themselves, especially someone who has to stay in bed: *His wife was an invalid and needed constant care.*

the sick /ðə ˈsɪk/ [n plural] people who are ill: *She spent her life caring for the sick and needy.*

⚠ **The sick** is slightly old-fashioned and is used especially when talking about the past.

sickly /ˈsɪkli/ [adj] a **sickly** child is often ill: *Burns was sickly as a boy.* | *a single mother who has a sickly daughter*

4 someone who often imagines they are ill

hypochondriac /ˌhaɪpəˈkɒndriæk‖-ˈkɑːn-/ [n C] someone who worries a lot about their health, and often thinks they are ill when they are not: *He's such a hypochondriac. Every time he has a headache he thinks he's dying.*

5 when food comes up from your stomach and out of your mouth

vomit /ˈvɒmɪt‖ˈvɑː-/ [v I] if you **vomit**, food comes up from your stomach and out through your mouth, because you are ill or drunk: *If a child keeps vomiting, he or she must see a doctor.* **vomit** [n U] food that has come out of your mouth because you are ill or drunk

Formal or informal?
Vomit is more formal than **throw up** or **be sick** and is used especially by doctors and in formal written English.

 throw up /ˌθrəʊ ˈʌp/ [phrasal verb I] ESPECIALLY SPOKEN to vomit: *He was so drunk that he threw up in the street.*

Formal or informal?
Throw up is less formal than **vomit** and is used in ordinary conversation.

be sick /biː ˈsɪk/ ESPECIALLY BRITISH to vomit: *Kelly ran into the bathroom and was violently sick.*

Formal or informal?
Be sick is used in both formal written and in spoken English.

feel sick /ˌfiːl ˈsɪk/ ESPECIALLY BRITISH to have the feeling that you are going to vomit: *Stop the car – I feel sick!* | *When I was pregnant the smell of coffee made me feel sick.*

nausea /ˈnɔːziə, -siə‖-ziə, -ʃə/ [n U] the feeling that you have when you think you are going to vomit: *The treatment sometimes causes headaches and nausea.*

Formal or informal?
Nausea is a formal and technical word, and is not used in informal conversation.

IMAGINE

➡ look here for ...
• have a picture in your mind
• think that something is happening when it is not
➡ see also **REAL 2, THINK, IDEA**

1 to have a picture or idea of something in your mind

imagine /ɪˈmædʒɪn/ [v T not in passive] to have a picture or idea in your mind about something that you have never seen or experienced: *Australia was exactly how I had imagined it.*
+(that) *Imagine that you have just won a million pounds.*
+what/how/where etc *I'm trying to imagine how the house will look when it's finished.*
imagine doing sth *Can you imagine having to spend the rest of your life in jail?*
imagine sb doing sth *I can't imagine him ever winning a general election.* (=because it seems so unlikely)

> ⚠ Don't say 'imagine to do something'. Say **imagine doing something**: *Can you imagine having nowhere to live?*

picture /ˈpɪktʃəʳ/ [v T not in passive] to form a clear picture in your mind of a person, place, or situation: *Picture it – you and me, lying on a beach in the sun.*
picture sb/sth as sth *I had never met Graham, but I pictured him as tall and dark-haired.*
picture sb doing sth *I can't really picture him taking care of a baby.*
◯ **can see** /kən ˈsiː/ ESPECIALLY SPOKEN to be able to imagine something, because you think it is likely to happen
can see sb doing sth *Jimmy's gone skiing and I can just see him coming home with a broken leg.*
can see sb as sth *I can't really see her as a nurse.*
dream of /ˈdriːm ɒv/ [phrasal verb T] to often think about something pleasant that you would like to do or that you wish would happen

dream of doing sth *When I was young, I used to dream of becoming a famous writer.*
dream of sth *They dreamed of a society where everyone was equal.*

2 to wrongly think that something is happening

imagine /ɪˈmædʒɪn/ [v T] to wrongly think that something is happening when it is not really happening: *I think he really likes me. Unless I'm just imagining it.*
+(that) *He always imagines that people are talking about him behind his back.*
◯ **be seeing things/be hearing things/be imagining things** /biː ˈsiːɪŋ θɪŋz, biː ˈhɪərɪŋ θɪŋz, biː ɪˈmædʒɪnɪŋ θɪŋz/ ESPECIALLY SPOKEN to think that you might have seen or heard something, although really you have not: *Did someone call my name just then – or am I hearing things? | There's no one there – you must be seeing things.*

3 something that you imagine

imaginary /ɪˈmædʒɪnəri‖-neri/ [adj] not real, but existing only as a picture or idea in your mind: *When Linda was a child, she had an imaginary friend called Booboo. | He held up an imaginary gun and pretended to shoot me.*
fantasy /ˈfæntəsi/ [n C] an exciting or enjoyable experience which you imagine happening to you, but which will probably never happen: *He's always talking about buying a beach house in Malibu, but it's just a fantasy. | sexual fantasies*
plural **fantasies**

> When you see **EC**, go to the **ESSENTIAL COMMUNICATION** section.

daydream

daydream /ˈdeɪdriːm/ [*n* C] pleasant thoughts that you have when you are awake, that make you forget what you are doing: *She sat in the back of the class, lost in a daydream.*

4 your ability to imagine things

imagination /ɪˌmædʒəˈneɪʃən/ [*n* C/U] *Reading is a good way to develop a child's imagination.*

use your imagination *You don't have to use your imagination when you're watching television.*

a vivid imagination (=when someone is very good at imagining unusual and exciting things) *Her stories show a particularly vivid imagination.*

> ⚠ Don't confuse **fantasy** and **imagination**. A **fantasy** is something that you imagine, but your **imagination** is your ability to imagine things.

IMMEDIATELY

➡ opposite **LATER/AT A LATER TIME**

immediately /ɪˈmiːdiətli/ [*adv*] quickly and without any delay: *If there's an accident in the school, you must report it immediately.* | *When I saw her face, I knew immediately that something was wrong.* | *I immediately replied to her email.*

+after/afterwards *We left immediately after breakfast.* | *She was admitted to the hospital at 10 o'clock, and died almost immediately afterwards.*

immediate [*adj* usually before noun] happening or done immediately: *My immediate reaction was one of disappointment.* | *The baby had a fever, and needed immediate medical attention.*

> **Formal or informal?**
> **Immediately** is used especially in writing and in formal spoken English.

at once/right away (also **straightaway** BRITISH) /ət ˈwʌns, ˌraɪt əˈweɪ, ˌstreɪtəˈweɪ/ if you do something **at once**, **right away**, or **straightaway**, you do it immediately, especially because it is urgent: *The principal wants to see you at once.* | *Moira phoned and I came straightaway.* | *If they offered me the job, I could start right away.*

> **Formal or informal?**
> **Right away** and **straightaway** are less formal than **at once**, and are used especially in conversation.

this minute/right now /ˌðɪs ˈmɪnət, ˌraɪt ˈnaʊ/ SPOKEN say this when you are telling someone to do something immediately, especially in an angry way: *Tell him I want him in my office, right now!* | *You'd better go upstairs this minute and get into bed.*

as soon as /əz ˈsuːn əz/ [*conjunction*] immediately after something has happened, or immediately after you have done something: *As soon as he felt well enough, he returned to work.*

> ⚠ When talking about the future, don't use the future tense after **as soon as**. Use the present tense: *I'll call you as soon as I get home* (not 'as soon as I will get home').

as soon as possible/as soon as you can /əz ˌsuːn əz ˈpɒsəbəl, əz ˌsuːn əz juː ˈkæn‖-ˈpɑːs-/ as soon as it is possible for you to do something: *Several other students need this book, so please return it as soon as possible.* | *We came back as soon as we could.*

instantly /ˈɪnstəntli/ [*adv*] immediately – use this when something happens at almost the same time as something else: *It was a head-on crash, and both drivers died instantly.* | *You just press a button and the information's there almost instantly.*

at a glance /ət ə ˈglɑːns‖-ˈglæns/ **can see/know/tell sth at a glance** to know or realize something immediately, after only looking for a very short time: *I could see at a glance that the situation was serious.* | *An expert can tell at a glance whether a diamond is real or a fake.*

IMPORTANT/NOT IMPORTANT

➡ see also **DON'T CARE, FAMOUS, SERIOUS**

1 something that is important

important /ɪm'pɔː'tənt/ [*adj*] something that is **important** has a big effect on people's lives and on the way things happen in the future: *Next Thursday's game is very important – if Italy lose they will be out of the World Cup.* | *I have an important announcement to make, so please listen carefully.* | *Choosing a home is probably one of the most important decisions of your life.*
importance [*n* U] how important something is
+of *the importance of this election*

significant /sɪg'nɪfɪkənt/ [*adj*] **significant** events, changes etc are important enough to be noticed and considered or talked about: *In this country, there has been a significant change in people's religious attitudes.* | *Winning the award was a significant achievement.*
highly significant *The result of this election will be highly significant.*

> **Formal or informal?**
> **Significant** in used in writing and in formal spoken English.

big /bɪg/ [*adj* only before noun]
big decision/event/occasion/day/moment an important decision, event etc, especially one that will affect the rest of your life: *This is a big decision – you'll have to give me time to think.* | *Graduation Day is one of those big occasions when everyone wants a souvenir photograph.*
○ **the big day** ESPECIALLY SPOKEN (=a very important day in someone's life) *I hear you're getting married – when's the big day?*

> **Formal or informal?**
> **Big** is more informal than **important**.

key /kiː/ [*adj*] having an extremely important effect on the way something develops
key factor/issue/point etc *Education is one of the key issues in this election campaign.*
key role/player/figure etc *He has had a key role in the team's success.*

> **Formal or informal?**
> **Key** is not used in informal conversation.

historic /hɪ'stɒrɪkǁ-'stɔː-, -'stɑː-/ [*adj* only before noun] a **historic** event, moment etc is remembered as a part of history because it brings important changes or is the start of something completely new: *In his book, Churchill describes that historic first meeting with Roosevelt.*
historic moment *the historic moment when man first walked on the moon*

2 important and necessary

important /ɪm'pɔː'tənt/ [*adj*] something that is **important** should be given special attention because it is very necessary: *A healthy diet is very important for young children.*
it is important to do sth *It is important to read the instructions carefully before you start.*
it is important that *It is important that everyone understands the risks involved in this plan.*
importance [*n* U] how important and necessary something is
+of *Most people realize the importance of getting enough sleep.*

vital /'vaɪtl/ [*adj*] something that is **vital** is very important and necessary, and if it is not done or dealt with correctly with there could be serious problems: *Nurses and other health workers provide vital services.*
+to *His evidence was vital to the defence case.*
it is vital that *It is vital that leaking gas pipes are fixed immediately.*

crucial /'kruːʃəl/ [*adj*] something that is **crucial** is extremely important because everything that happens afterwards depends on it: *Evans*

scored two crucial points just before the end of the game.
+to *The result of these talks will be crucial to the future of the company.*

> ⚠️ Don't say 'very crucial'. Say **absolutely crucial**.

essential /ɪˈsenʃəl/ [*adj*] extremely important to the existence, health, safety etc of someone or something: *Computers are now an essential tool in business.*
+to *A good diet is essential to your health.*
it is essential that *It is essential that you wear protective clothing in this area.*

3 more important than anything else

the most important /ðə ˌməʊst ɪmˈpɔːʳtənt/ *the most important scientific discovery of the 20th century | For Muslims, this is the most important day of the year.*
the most important thing *If there is a fire, the most important thing is to get everyone out of the building immediately.*
main/chief/principal /meɪn, tʃiːf, ˈprɪnsɪpəl/ [*adj only before noun*] more important than all the other reasons, ideas, or things of the same kind: *What was the main purpose of your visit? | Our chief concern is for the safety of the children. | Coffee is the country's principal export.*

> **Formal or informal?**
> **Main**, **chief**, and **principal** mean the same thing, but **main** is much more common than **chief** or **principal**. **Chief** and **principal** are used especially in written or formal spoken English.

biggest /ˈbɪɡɪst/ [*adj only before noun*] the **biggest** decision, problem, event etc is the most important or serious one: *Getting married was the biggest mistake of my life. | This music festival is the biggest thing that's ever happened in Knoxville.*

> **Formal or informal?**
> **Biggest** is more informal than **most important**, **main** etc.

major /ˈmeɪdʒəʳ/ [*adj only before noun*] one of the most important or serious things – use this especially when there is a small number of really important things, and a lot of less important things: *Smoking is a major cause of heart disease. | All the world's major sporting events can be seen on HHS TV. | It's the Chief Executive who makes all the major decisions.*

> **Formal or informal?**
> **Major** is not used in informal conversation.

basic /ˈbeɪsɪk/ [*adj only before noun*] use this about something that you need more than anything else in order to do something or in order to live: *This book gives you the basic information about choosing a college course. | People's basic needs are food, housing, and health care.*
above all /əˌbʌv ˈɔːl/ use this to emphasize that what you are going to say is more important than the other things you have mentioned: *He's hard-working, cheerful, and above all honest. | Above all, she will be remembered for all the work she did in the community.*

> **Formal or informal?**
> Use **above all** in writing or in formal spoken English.

priority /praɪˈɒrɪti‖-ˈɔːr-/ [*n C/U*] the most important thing, which needs to be dealt with before anything else or given more attention than anything else: *First, let's decide what our priorities are.*
sb's priority is to do sth *My main priority is get through all my exams.*
first/top/number one priority *Safety has always been our number one priority.*
give priority to sth (=decide that something is very important, and deal with it urgently) *The President promised to give priority to reducing unemployment.*
plural **priorities**

4 someone or something that you care a lot about

important /ɪm'pɔː'tənt/ [adj] if something is **important** to you, you care a lot about it, and it has an important influence on the way you think and behave: *Which is more important – your family or your career?*
be important to sb *While I was a student, my parents' support and encouragement were very important to me.*
the important thing (=the only important thing) *At least the children are safe – that's the important thing.*

 Don't say 'money is important for me'. Say **money is important to me**.

○ **mean a lot to sb** /,miːn ə 'lɒt tuː (sb)‖-'lɑːt-/ ESPECIALLY SPOKEN if someone or something **means a lot to** you, you care about them or worry about them a lot, and your happiness depends on them: *I really hope Kate gets the job – it means a lot to her.*
mean everything to sb (=be more important than anything else) *Winning the gold medal meant everything to Luke.*

Formal or informal?
Mean a lot to sb is more informal than **important**.

5 an important person

important /ɪm'pɔː'tənt/ [adj] an **important** person has a lot of power or influence: *The school is having some very important visitors next week. | Some guys like big fast cars because it makes them feel important.*

leading /'liːdɪŋ/ [adj only before noun] a **leading** politician, scientist, doctor etc is well known and successful, and usually has a lot of influence: *a leading member of the government's environmental committee | a leading expert on heart disease*
play a leading part/role (=do a lot to help something important be successful) *Sanders played a leading role in the design of the building.*

Formal or informal?
Leading is not used in informal conversation.

VIP /,viː aɪ 'piː/ [n C] a very important, famous, or powerful person who is treated in a special way: *Many VIPs and celebrities will be attending the celebrations at Buckingham Palace.*

 You can also use **VIP** before a noun, like an adjective: *VIP guests | the VIP lounge at the airport*

6 not important

not important/unimportant /nɒt ɪm'pɔː'tənt, ,ʌnɪm'pɔː'tənt◂/ [adj] *"I forgot to buy the milk." "Don't worry, it's not important." | I don't want to waste time arguing about unimportant details.*

Formal or informal?
Unimportant is more formal than **not important**.

minor /'maɪnə'/ [adj usually before noun] **minor** problems, changes, injuries etc are only small, and therefore not important or worrying: *She suffered only minor injuries in the accident. | There have been some minor changes to the design. | Most of the problems we've had so far have been relatively minor.*

small /smɔːl/ [adj usually before noun] INFORMAL a **small** problem, detail, or thing to discuss is not important and will not take long to deal with: *Don't worry. It's only a small problem. | There were a couple of small things I wanted to talk to you about.*

○ **it doesn't matter** /ɪt ,dʌzənt 'mætə'/ SPOKEN say this to tell someone that something is not important and does not cause serious problems, even though it may seem bad: *"Oh no! We've missed the train." "It doesn't matter, there's another one in 10 minutes."*
+if/whether/when/what *It doesn't matter what other people say. Do what you think is best.*

trivial /'trɪviəl/ [adj] something that is **trivial** is very unimportant and you do not really need to worry about it or waste time on it: *I'm sorry to bother you with such a trivial question.* | *My problems seem quite trivial compared with Suzie's.*

petty /'peti/ [adj usually before noun] relating to unimportant things – use this about rules, arguments, or things people do that annoy you: *I'm sick of having petty arguments over money.* | *My new school doesn't have as many petty rules as the old one.*

IMPOSSIBLE

➡ opposite **POSSIBLE**
➡ see also **CAN/CAN'T**

impossible /ɪm'pɒsɪbəl‖ɪm'pɑː-/ [adj] something that is **impossible** cannot be done: *an impossible task* | *We're supposed to do all this work by tomorrow, but it's impossible.*
it is impossible to do sth *The twins are so alike that it's impossible to tell them apart.*
it is impossible for sb to do sth *The street was narrow, and it was impossible for the two trucks to pass.*
make it impossible *Her back injury made it impossible for her to play tennis anymore.*
find it impossible (=discover that you cannot do something) *When people leave prison, they often find it impossible to get a job.*

not possible /nɒt 'pɒsɪbəl‖-'pɑː-/ [adj] impossible or very difficult to do – use this when the situation that you are in makes something extremely difficult to do: *We can't buy a new computer for every student – it's just not possible.*
it is not possible to do sth *It is not possible in a book this size to cover every aspect of the subject.*
it is not possible for sb to do sth *She's in a meeting, so I'm afraid it's not possible for you to see her now.*

◯ **there's no way** /ðeəʳz ˌnəʊ 'weɪ/ SPOKEN say this when you strongly believe that something is impossible: *There's no way we can get to the airport in less than an hour.*

out of the question /ˌaʊt əv ðə 'kwestʃən/ if an idea or suggestion is **out of the question**, it is completely

impossible or it cannot be allowed: *The cost would be over $5000, which is quite out of the question.* | *You can't go out the night before your exams – it's out of the question.*

◯ **can't possibly** /ˌkɑːnt 'pɒsɪbli‖ˌkænt 'pɑː-/ ESPECIALLY SPOKEN say that you **can't possibly** do something in order to emphasize that you think it is impossible and that you are surprised someone thinks it is possible: *I can't possibly eat all that!* | *We couldn't possibly afford the flight.*

IMPROVE

➡ see also **BETTER**

1 **to get better**

get better /get 'betəʳ/ *I hope the weather gets better soon.*
get a lot better *Yuri's English is getting a lot better.*
things get better (=a situation gets better) *David has a new job, so things are getting better.*
get better and better (=continue to get better, in a way that makes you feel pleased) *Paula's teacher says that her schoolwork is getting better and better.*

> **Formal or informal?**
> **Get better** is used in informal spoken English more than in written English.

improve /ɪm'pruːv/ [v I] to become better: *In the weeks that followed, his health continued to improve.*
improve dramatically (=improve a lot) *Conditions in prisons have improved dramatically in the last 20 years.*

> **Formal or informal?**
> **Improve** is more formal than **get better**. It is used mostly in written English or in formal spoken situations, and not usually in ordinary conversation.

◯ **things are looking up** /ˌθɪŋz əʳ ˌlʊkɪŋ 'ʌp/ SPOKEN say this when good things have started to happen to you, and your life seems much better than it was: *Things are looking up – I've got a new job and a new boyfriend.*

pick up /ˌpɪk ˈʌp/ [*phrasal verb* I] INFORMAL if business or the economy **picks up**, it improves after a period without much activity: *The economy should start picking up early next year.*

be on the up /biː ɒn ði ˈʌp/ BRITISH INFORMAL to be improving or increasing: *After a good performance, his career was once again on the up.*

2 to make something better

improve /ɪmˈpruːv/ [*v* T] *I wanted to improve my French, so I got a job in Paris.* | *More money should be put towards improving our hospitals.* | *In this way, our quality of life can be improved.*

make sth better /ˌmeɪk (sth) ˈbetəʳ/ to improve a situation or improve someone's life: *Instead of making the traffic situation better, the new road has just made things worse.*
make things better *You won't make things any better by worrying about them.*
make life better for sb *Have computers really made life better for everyone?*

make improvements /ˌmeɪk ɪmˈpruːvmənts/ to make changes to something or add things to it in order to make it better, more useful, or more effective
+to *Several improvements have been made to the original designs.* | *We decided to use the money to make some improvements to the house.* (=for example by adding a new room or putting in a new heating system)

upgrade /ʌpˈɡreɪd/ [*v* T] to improve something such as machinery, a building, or a system by making it more modern, effective, and successful: *The company decided to upgrade its computer system.*

⌕ **brush up sth/brush up on sth** /ˌbrʌʃ ˈʌp (sth), ˌbrʌʃ ˈʌp ɒn (sth)/ [*phrasal verb* T] ESPECIALLY SPOKEN to practise doing something that you have not done for a long time, in order to try to improve it – use this especially about speaking foreign languages: *I'd like to brush up my Italian before our trip.*

3 a change that makes something better

improvement /ɪmˈpruːvmənt/ [*n* C/U] a change that makes something become better
+in *Have you noticed any improvement in his work?* | *Accidents have become less frequent, thanks to recent improvements in our safety checks.*
big/great/tremendous improvement *There's been a great improvement in the team's performance over the last three games.*

advance /ədˈvɑːnsǁ-ˈvæns/ [*n* C often plural] an important new idea or way of doing something, especially in science
+in *Advances in medical science may make it possible for people to live for 150 years.*
big/enormous/major advance *The last 20 years have seen enormous advances in computer technology.*

Formal or informal?
Advance is not used in informal conversation.

IN CHARGE OF

to be the person who controls a person, organization, or activity

➡ see also **MANAGER, POWER, CONTROL**

be in charge /biː ɪn ˈtʃɑːʳdʒ/ if you **are in charge** of an activity or a group of people, you are the person who has the power to control what happens, to tell other people what to do etc: *Who's in charge around here?*
+of *the officer in charge of the investigation*
be in charge of doing sth *As senior supervisor, she is in charge of training new employees.*
put sb in charge *David Hughes has been put in charge of the school play this year.*

run /rʌn/ [*v* T] if you **run** a business or organization, you are the person who makes the important decisions about

what will happen: *She runs a company called Sunshine Holidays.* | *Libra is a drug counselling service that is run by ex-addicts.*
running – ran – have run

be responsible for sth/sb /bɪː rɪˈspɒnsɪ̱bəl fɔːʳ (sth/sb)‖-ˈspɑːn-/ if you **are responsible for** doing something, you have to make sure that everything is done correctly and that problems are dealt with; if you **are responsible for** someone, you have to make sure that they behave well and that they are safe: *Teachers are responsible for the children while they are in their care.* | *Who is responsible for Health and Safety in this department?*
be responsible for doing sth *Janine is responsible for organizing the travel arrangements.*

responsibility /rɪˌspɒnsɪ̱ˈbɪlɪ̱ti‖rɪˌspɑːn-/ [n C/U] a duty that you have when you are in charge, for example making sure that problems are dealt with or that people are safe: *He sometimes felt weighed down by his responsibilities.*
have responsibility for (doing) sth *In the past, it was usually the mother who had responsibility for child care.*
be sb's responsibility *Garbage collection is the responsibility of the city council.*
it is sb's responsibility to do sth *It's your responsibility to ensure that the passengers in your car are wearing seatbelts.*
plural **responsibilities**

lead /liːd/ [v I/T] to be in charge of a group of people, especially a political party, a group of soldiers, or a team of workers: *He led the party successfully for over 20 years.* | *The murder investigation will be led by Inspector Scarfe.* | *a man who was born to lead*
leading – led – have led

supervise /ˈsuːpəʳvaɪz, ˈsjuː-‖ˈsuː-/ [v T] if you **supervise** an activity or a group of people, your job is to make sure that everything is done properly, especially by giving instructions or answering questions: *At work, she supervises a team of fifteen.* | *All volunteers are supervised by a qualified nurse.*

supervision /ˌsuːpəʳˈvɪʒən, ˌsjuː-‖ˌsuː-/ [n U] the activity of supervising people

or activities: *The child needs constant supervision.*
under the supervision of sb (=while being supervised by someone) *You can try sailing or rock-climbing under the supervision of experienced instructors.*

leadership /ˈliːdəʳʃɪp/ [n U] the position of being in charge of a group or organization
+of *Who is most likely to take over the leadership of the party?*

INCLUDE/ NOT INCLUDE

➡ see also **HAVE/NOT HAVE, CONTAIN**

1   to include someone or something

include /ɪnˈkluːd/ [v T] if a group of people, things, ideas etc **includes** someone or something, they are in the group, but there are other people, things etc in it as well: *Our tour party included several young families.* | *Symptoms of the disease include tiredness and loss of memory.* | *Today's programme will include a workshop on language learning games.*

> Don't say 'it is including these things'. Say **it includes these things**.

including /ɪnˈkluːdɪŋ/ [preposition] use this to say that someone or something is in the group that you have just mentioned: *Everyone in the class passed the test, including me.* | *You can play all kinds of games here, including tennis, basketball, and squash.*

consist of sth/be made up of sth /kənˈsɪst ɒv (sth), biː ˌmeɪd ˈʌp ɒv (sth)/ [phrasal verb T] use this when you are mentioning all of the parts in something: *The US government consists of the Congress, the Judiciary, and the President.* | *Each hair is made up of three layers.* | *For the first three or four months, a baby's diet consists only of milk.*

> ⚠ Don't say 'it is consisted of these things'.
> Say **it consists of these things**.

> ⚠ Don't confuse **include** and **consist of**.
> Use **include** to mention only *some* of
> the things in something, but use **consist of**
> to mention *all* of the things in something: *The
> Romance family of languages includes French
> and Spanish.* | *The Romance family of
> languages consists of French, Spanish, Italian,
> and several other languages.*

Formal or informal?

Consist of sth is more formal than **be made
up of sth**.

contain /kən'teɪn/ [v T] to include
particular ideas, images, or information – use this about things like
books, films, or reports: *The film
contains some very unpleasant scenes
of violence.* | *Her report contained
some interesting suggestions.*

cover /'kʌvəʳ/ [v T] to include or deal
with a particular subject area or
period – use this about a book, TV
programme, class etc: *His book on
European politics covers the period
from 1914 to 1989.* | *Does your French
course cover modern French literature?*

range from sth to sth /'reɪndʒ frɒm
(sth) tə (sth)/ if prices, ages, amounts
etc **range from** a low number or
amount **to** a higher one, they include
both these amounts and other
amounts in between them: *My
students' ages ranged from 20 to 55.* |
*Prices for a week in one of our villas
range from £350 to £900.*

2 when a number, total, or price includes something

include /ɪn'kluːd/ [v T] *The price of the
computer includes £500 worth of free
software.* | *"It's $50 per night." "Does
that include breakfast?"*
be included in sth *Your flights are
included in the price of your holiday.*

including /ɪn'kluːdɪŋ/ [preposition] use
this to say that something is included
in a number, total, or price: *The cost
of the meal was $60, including a 10%
service charge.* | *The phone costs £68,
including batteries.*

come with sth /'kʌm wɪð (sth)/ [phrasal
verb T] if something that you buy
comes with something else, the
second thing is included when you
buy the first, and you do not have to
pay any more for it: *All the dishes on
the menu come with either French fries
or salad.* | *The carpets came with the
house.*

with /wɪð, wɪθ/ [preposition] including a
number or amount that is added to
make a total: *With tax, the hotel bill
came to $400.*

3 to not include someone or something

leave out /ˌliːv 'aʊt/ [phrasal verb T] to
not include someone or something,
either deliberately or accidentally
leave sb/sth out of sth *Fans were
shocked that Giggs had been left out of
the team.*
leave out sb/sth *You've left out a zero
in this phone number.*

exclude /ɪk'skluːd/ [v T] to deliberately
not include someone or something,
especially in a way that seems wrong
or unfair: *The new law protects most
workers, but excludes those on part-
time contracts.*
exclude sb/sth from sth *She felt they
were deliberately excluding her from
their plans.*

omit /əʊ'mɪt, ə-/ [v T] FORMAL to not
include something, especially a piece
of information, either deliberately or
because you forget: *When you are
giving evidence, try not to omit any
details.*
omit sth from sth *Sara's name had
been omitted from the list of
employees.*
omitting – omitted – have omitted

miss out /ˌmɪs 'aʊt/ [phrasal verb T]
BRITISH to not include someone or
something that should be included,
often by mistake
miss out sb/sth *You missed out
several important facts.*
miss sb/sth out *Here's a list of the
people I'm inviting. Did I miss anyone
out?*

4 when a number, total, or price does not include something

not include /nɒt ɪnˈkluːd/ *The price does not include sales tax.*

not including *He used to earn about £300 a week, not including bonuses. | There were about 50 people on the plane, not including the crew.*

excluding /ɪkˈskluːdɪŋ/ [*preposition*] not including – use this especially when you are talking about prices or taxes: *The computer costs £1500, excluding VAT. | Car rental charges are $50 a day, excluding the cost of gasoline.*

not counting /nɒt ˈkaʊntɪŋ/ ESPECIALLY SPOKEN use this to make it clear exactly which people or things you do not want to include in a total: *We're having ten people to dinner, not counting ourselves. | I get 25 days' holiday a year, not counting public holidays.*

INCREASE

➡ see also **GROW, BIG, MORE**

➡ look here for ...
 • when a number or amount gets bigger
 • when a feeling gets stronger
 • when something happens more often

1 when a number or amount gets bigger

increase /ɪnˈkriːs/ [*v* I] to become larger in number, amount, price, value etc: *Gradually the noise and traffic increased as they approached the city.*

increase by 10%/$100/2 million etc (=become 10% etc greater) *The price of cigarettes has increased by 30% in the last two years.*

increase to $1000/2 million etc (=reach a total of $1000 etc) *Wind speeds are expected to increase to 60 mph.*

increase in number/value *Are houses in the north continuing to increase in value?*

increase considerably / greatly / enormously *Our profits increased considerably in the second half of the year.*

increasing /ɪnˈkriːsɪŋ/ [*adj* only before noun] *An increasing range and variety of health foods are now available.*

an increasing number of/increasing numbers of *Increasing numbers of North American trees are being damaged by acid rain.*

> ⚠ Don't use **increase** about the standard of something. Use **rise** or **go up**: *The standard of living has risen* (not 'increased').

go up/rise /ˌɡəʊ ˈʌp, raɪz/ [*v* I] to increase – use this about numbers, prices, temperatures etc, or about the standard of something: *My rent's gone up again. It's £100 a week now. | Spending on education has risen rapidly in recent years. | With more and more cars on the road, pollution levels are rising steadily.*

+by 10%/$500 etc (=become 10% etc greater) *House prices went up by 20% last year. | Computer sales rose by 70% just before Christmas.*

+to $1000/10 million etc (=reach a total of $1000 etc) *In summer, temperatures often rise to 40°. | The average price of a loaf of bread has gone up from 45p to 80p.*

rising – rose – have risen

> **Formal or informal?**
> **Go up** is more common in informal spoken English than **increase** or **rise**.

> ⚠ Don't confuse **raise** (=make something rise) with **rise** (=become more).

rising /ˈraɪzɪŋ/ [*adj* only before noun] increasing – use this about prices, numbers etc, or about the standard of something: *Rising student numbers have caused a crisis in funding. | the country's rising standard of living*

rising unemployment/crime/inflation (=increasing and become more serious) *a period of economic difficulty and rising unemployment*

grow /ɡrəʊ/ [*v* I] to increase gradually over a period of time – use this about numbers or amounts, or about the total amount of business activity or trade: *Sales of new cars have grown steadily since 1990.* | *China's economic output continues to grow at a remarkable annual rate.*

grow by 10%/5000 etc (=become 10% etc greater) *Last year, our profits grew by £50,000.*

growing – grew – have grown

growing /'grəʊɪŋ/ [*adj* only before noun] *Growing numbers of women are choosing to give birth at home.*

double /'dʌbəl/ [*v* I] to become twice as big: *Divorce rates doubled in the 1970s.*

double in size/value *In 30 years, San Francisco doubled in size.*

shoot up /ˌʃuːt 'ʌp/ [*phrasal verb* I] INFORMAL to increase quickly and suddenly – use this especially about prices, costs, or amounts of money: *Interest rates shot up, bringing misery to many homeowners.*

+from ... to ... *Profits shot up from $4000 to $34,000 last year.*

2 when a feeling gets stronger

growing /'grəʊɪŋ/ [*adj* only before noun] **growing doubts/fears/interest/opposition etc** doubts, fears etc that are gradually becoming stronger: *women's growing interest in football* | *I listened to his story with growing disbelief.*

> **Formal or informal?**
>
> **Growing** is used in formal writing and in news reports.

grow /grəʊ/ [*v* I] if a feeling **grows**, it gradually becomes stronger: *Fears are growing for the safety of the missing children.* | *Her confidence grew, and soon she was able to go out driving on her own.*

growing – grew – have grown

increase /ɪn'kriːs/ [*v* I] to become stronger – use this especially about a feeling that a lot of people have: *Excitement is increasing inside the stadium as we wait for the teams to come out onto the field.* | *The President's popularity has increased enormously in recent months.*

increasing [*adj* only before noun] *There is increasing uncertainty about the company's future.*

build up /ˌbɪld 'ʌp/ [*phrasal verb* I] if a bad feeling such as anger **builds up**, it gradually increases, until it makes you decide to do something: *I could feel the anger building up inside me.* | *The pressure built up over the year, and eventually I had to leave my job.*

mounting /'maʊntɪŋ/ [*adj* only before noun] **mounting anger/excitement/concern** anger, excitement etc that is quickly increasing and becoming very strong: *There is mounting concern about gun crime in the city.*

> **Formal or informal?**
>
> **Mounting** is used in formal writing and in news reports.

3 when something happens more often

increase /ɪn'kriːs/ [*v* I] if an activity **increases**, it happens more often, and so it affects more and more people or situations: *Smoking is increasing among teenage girls.*

be on the increase /biː ˌɒn ði 'ɪŋkriːs/ if a problem in society **is on the increase**, it is happening more and more often: *Drug taking is on the increase.* | *Poverty and homelessness seem to be on the increase again.*

4 to make something increase

increase /ɪn'kriːs/ [*v* T] to make something increase: *We must increase the amount of money that we spend on education.* | *Smoking increases the risk of getting lung cancer.* | *Training in new skills should increase your chances of employment.*

+from ... to ... *The company is increasing its workforce from 350 to 500.*

put up /ˌpʊt 'ʌp/ [*phrasal verb* T] to increase the prices, taxes, or rents people have to pay

put up sth *If the landlord puts up the rent again, we may have to move out.*

put sth up *This used to be quite a cheap restaurant, but they've put their prices up recently.*

raise /reɪz/ [*v* T] to increase prices taxes etc, or to make certain feelings stronger: *Before the election the President promised not to raise taxes.* | *Oil companies are planning to raise prices.*

raise hopes/expectations (=make people more hopeful)

raise awareness (=make people more aware of something)

> **Formal or informal?**
> **Raise** is more formal than **put up**.

add to sth /'æd tuː (sth)/ [*phrasal verb* T] ESPECIALLY WRITTEN to increase an amount that is already large, or increase problems, worries etc that are already serious: *His bad exam results had added to his worries.*

add sth to sth *The delay added over an hour to our journey.*

double /'dʌbəl/ [*v* T] to increase a number or amount so that it is twice as big

+from ... to ... *The government doubled the tax on cigarettes from 20% to 40%.*

turn up /ˌtɜːˤn 'ʌp/ [*phrasal verb* T] if you **turn up** a television, radio etc, you make it louder; if you **turn up** something used for heating or cooking, you make it produce more heat

turn up sth *He turned up the TV to listen to the news.*

turn sth up *Hey, turn the radio up. I like this song.* | *Shall I turn the heating up? It's cold in here.*

5   an increase in an amount or number

increase /'ɪŋkriːs/ [*n* C]

+in *The company announced a 5% increase in profits.* | *an increase in the number of part-time workers*

pay/price/tax/rent increase *Large tax increases are expected if there is a change of government.*

a sharp/dramatic/marked increase (=a big and sudden increase) *There has been a dramatic increase in the use of guns.*

> ⚠ Don't say 'an increase of tax/profits' etc. Say **an increase in tax/profits** etc.

rise /raɪz/ [*n* singular] an increase in numbers, prices, taxes etc, or an

increase in the level of something

+in *The police have been unable to stop the rise in crime.* | *a sudden rise in temperature*

a sharp/dramatic rise (=a big and sudden increase) *In January there was a sharp rise in cases of the virus.*

gain /geɪn/ [*n* C/U] an increase in the amount or level of something, especially money

+of *Sales showed a gain of 0.4%.*

+in *There were sharp gains in stock prices.* | *We hope to see a gain in the factory's weekly output.*

> **Formal or informal?**
> **Gain** is used especially in formal writing about business.

growth /grəʊθ/ [*n* U] a gradual increase over a period of time, especially in the amount of business activity and trade

+in *the steady growth in trade between the US and China*

+of *The growth of the tourist industry has provided around 5000 jobs in the region.*

rapid growth (=very quick growth) *The rapid growth in the world's population is partly due to improved medical services.*

economic/population growth

pay rise BRITISH **raise** AMERICAN /'peɪ raɪz, reɪz/ [*n* C] an increase in the amount of money that you are paid: *It's time I had a pay rise.* | *The city simply can't afford to give all teachers a raise.*

build-up /'bɪld ʌp/ [*n* singular] a gradual increase in the level of something harmful, dangerous, or worrying

+of *the build-up of harmful gases such as carbon dioxide in the atmosphere* | *a build-up of tension between the two countries*

> When you see , go to the **WORD BANKS** section.

INDEPENDENT

➡ Look here for ...
- when a country is not ruled by another country
- when someone does not need help or money from other people

1 country

➡ see also **COUNTRY,**
WB GOVERNMENT/POLITICS, FREE 3

independent /ˌɪndɪ'pendənt◂/ [adj] an **independent** country is not ruled by another country and has its own government: *Many Scottish people want Scotland to be an independent country.*

become independent *India became independent in 1947.*

independence /ˌɪndɪ'pendəns/ [n U] when a country is not ruled by another country, but has its own government: *Mexico achieved independence from Spain in 1821.* | *the Irish people's fight for independence*

2 person

➡ see also **CONFIDENT/NOT CONFI-DENT, DESCRIBING PEOPLE**

independent /ˌɪndɪ'pendənt◂/ [adj] an **independent** person can make their own decisions, organize their own life, and pay for the things they need, without help or advice from other people: *I've become much more independent since I started living on my own.* | *a magazine for young independent professional women*

financially independent (=when you don't need money from other people) *It's great being financially independent now I've started a job.*

○ **can take care of yourself** (also **can look after yourself** BRITISH) /kən teɪk ˌkeər əv jɔː'self, kən lʊk ˌɑːftə' jɔː'ˈself/ ESPECIALLY SPOKEN if you **can take care of yourself** or **can look after yourself**, you do not need other people to do things for you or tell you what to do: *Stop worrying about the kids – they can take care of themselves.*

stand on your own two feet /ˌstænd ɒn jɔː' ˌəʊn tuː 'fiːt/ INFORMAL if you can **stand on your own two feet**, you can deal with difficulties and situations alone and you do not expect other people to do things for you: *I had to learn to stand on my own two feet when my husband left me.*

self-reliant /ˌself rɪ'laɪənt◂/ [adj] able to do things for yourself and solve problems by yourself: *Parents want their children to become independent, self-reliant adults.*

self-sufficient /ˌself sə'fɪʃənt/ [adj] able to live happily on your own, without needing a lot of friends or spending a lot of time with other people: *My mother grew up on a farm, in a close-knit, self-sufficient family.*

3 not independent

dependent /dɪ'pendənt/ [adj] unable to live or do things on your own, because you need the support or help of someone else: *My grandmother has become much more dependent since her illness.*

+on *The refugees are totally dependent on foreign aid.*

financially dependent (=when you need money from someone in order to live) *Anne had never worked and was financially dependent on her husband.*

dependent on sb/sth for sth *Young children are dependent on their parents for love and emotional support.*

When you see **EC**, go to the **ESSENTIAL COMMUNICATION** section.

INFORMATION

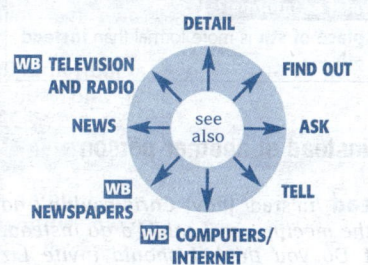

DETAIL

WB TELEVISION AND RADIO

NEWS

WB NEWSPAPERS

FIND OUT

see also

ASK

TELL

WB COMPUTERS/ INTERNET

1 information

information /ˌɪnfəˈrmeɪʃən/ [n U] facts or details that tell you about a situation, event, person, place etc
+about/on *Do you have any information on how to find a job in Europe?*
give/provide information *The tourist office will be able to give you the information you need.* | *an organization that provides information about AIDS*
further information FORMAL (=more information) *For further information, please write to the following address.*
piece of information *a useful piece of information*
detailed information (=containing a lot of facts) *The guidebook has detailed information about the hotels in the area.*

> Don't say 'informations'. Say **information**.

> Don't say 'an information'. Say **a piece of information** or **some information**.

fact /fækt/ [n C usually plural] a piece of information that is known to be true: *I'm not interested in your opinions – I just want to know the facts.*
+about *It's important that young people learn the facts about drugs.* | *The book is full of interesting facts about plant life.*
+that *He's never tried to hide the fact that he's spent time in jail.*

details /ˈdiːteɪlz‖dɪˈteɪlz/ [n plural] all the small pieces of information that

you need to know about something which you already know about in a general way
give/provide details *There's a big jazz festival in May. I'll give you the details if you want.*
+of *Please send us details of your bank account.*
further details FORMAL (=more details) *For further details, contact the conference organizer.*
full details (=all the details) *The prospectus provides full details of the courses we offer.*

data /ˈdeɪtə, ˈdɑːtə/ [n U] facts, numbers, and other information that has been collected and stored, especially on a computer: *All our data is stored on computer.*
+on *Scientists have been collecting data on air pollution levels.*

2 a collection of information

file /faɪl/ [n C] a collection of information, about a person, subject etc which is kept by an organization such as a school, a company, or the police: *Only a few people are allowed to see these files.*
+on *Could you bring me the file on the West murder case?*
keep a file *The FBI keeps files on all suspected terrorists.*
keep sth on file *Your job application will be kept on file.*

record /ˈrekɔːd‖-ərd/ [n C usually plural] information that is collected gradually over a long period of time, so that it can be looked at when necessary: *I've checked the student records, and I can't find any mention of her name.* | *medical records*
+of *the official records of births, marriages, and deaths*
keep a record (=write down details of things as they happen) *Keep a record of all your expenses during the trip.*

database /ˈdeɪtəbeɪs/ [n C] a very large collection of information kept on a computer: *I can check our database to see whether that book is in stock.*
+of *a database of car-owners in the UK*

3 to write down information

record /rɪ'kɔːᵗd/ [v T] to write down information or store it on a computer, so that it can be looked at later, especially official information about numbers or amounts: *Only 13 cases of this disease have ever been recorded.* | *The meteorological office recorded the lowest rainfall in 10 years.*

make/take notes /ˌmeɪk, ˌteɪk 'nəʊts/ to write down information during a meeting, lesson, lecture etc or while reading: *I read the first three chapters and made notes.* | *Rolland's secretary took notes during the meeting.*

INSTEAD

1 instead of another thing, place, or time

instead /ɪn'sted/ [adv] *We didn't have enough money to go to a movie, so we went to the park instead.* | *I can't manage Thursday. Can we meet on Friday instead?*
+of *Could I have tuna instead of ham?*
instead of doing sth *You should talk to your teacher instead of just complaining to me about it.*

> ⚠ Don't say 'instead of it' or 'instead of that'. Just say **instead**: *We didn't go for a walk in the end. We stayed at home instead.*

> ⚠ Don't say 'instead of to go' or 'instead to go'. Say **instead of going**.

rather than /'rɑːðəᵗ ðən‖'ræ-/ if you do one thing **rather than** another, you do the first thing because it seems better or more suitable: *A lot of young people are renting rather than buying their own houses.* | *Rather than waiting for the bus, Larry decided to take a taxi.*

in place of sth /ɪn 'pleɪs ɒv (sth)/ if one thing is used **in place of** another, it is used instead of it or put in the place where the other thing used to be: *If you want, you can use olive oil in place of butter.*

in its place/in their place *The factory was demolished, and an office block was built in its place.*

> **Formal or informal?**
> **In place of sth** is more formal than **instead of sth**.

2 instead of another person

instead /ɪn'sted/ [adv] *Chris couldn't go to the meeting, so I said I'd go instead.*
+of *Do you think I should invite Liz instead of Gemma?*

for /fəᵗ strong fɔːᵗ/ [preposition] if you do something **for** someone, you do it instead of them, especially in order to help them: *Let me carry that shopping for you.* | *Pat wasn't feeling well, so I said I'd take care of the children for her.*

in sb's place /ɪn (sb's) 'pleɪs/ if you do something or go somewhere **in someone's place**, you do it or go there instead of them: *It was decided that the Chief Secretary would go in his place.*
in place of sb *Steve played in the second half in place of Kerry.*

> **Formal or informal?**
> **In place of sb** is more formal than **instead of sb**.

on behalf of sb /ɒn bɪ'hɑːf ɒv (sb)‖ -'hæf-/ if you do something **on behalf of** someone, such as giving a speech or making an official decision, you do it instead of them because they have asked you to be their representative: *On behalf of everyone here, I'd like to wish you a long and happy retirement.*
on sb's behalf *Richardson's lawyer agreed to speak to journalists on his behalf.*

3 to do something instead of someone or something else

take the place of/replace /ˌteɪk ðə 'pleɪs ɒv, rɪ'pleɪs/ [v T] to do a job or do work that used to be done by someone or something else: *Computers very quickly replaced typewriters in most offices.* | *One 'smart' card can* now take the place of cash, cheques, and credit cards. | It won't be easy to find someone to replace Sue on the team.

take over /ˌteɪk 'əʊvəʳ/ [phrasal verb I/T] to start doing a job, especially an important job, that someone else used to do: Perryman has agreed to take over until the club can find a new coach.

take over sth John took over the chairman's position in 2003.

+from My father always expected me to take over from him and run the family business.

stand in for sb /ˌstænd 'ɪn fɔːʳ (sb)/ [phrasal verb T] to do someone's job for them for a short time: Can you stand in for Meg while she's on vacation?

replacement /rɪ'pleɪsmənt/ [n C] a person, machine, system etc that does a job or does work instead of someone or something else: When Steve announced he was leaving, the coach started looking around for a replacement.

+for We urgently need to find a replacement for fossil fuels.

INSTRUCTIONS

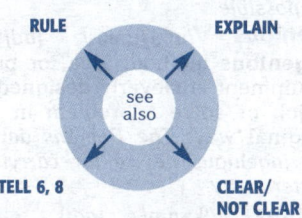

RULE

EXPLAIN

see also

TELL 6, 8

CLEAR/ NOT CLEAR

1 information about how to use something or what to do

instructions /ɪn'strʌkʃənz/ [n plural] written or spoken information telling someone what you want them to do or how something should be done: Always wash clothes according to the instructions on the label.

give sb instructions With any task, children need to be given very clear instructions.

follow instructions (=do what the instructions tell you) I've followed the

instructions, but the computer still isn't working.

+about/on Have you read the instructions about what to do if there's a fire?

have instructions to do sth (=when someone has given you instructions) The guards had strict instructions not to let anyone in.

⚠ Remember to use **instructions** in the plural. Don't say 'You didn't follow my instruction'.

directions /dɪ'rekʃənz, daɪ-/ [n plural] instructions about how to go to a place

give sb directions I've never been to his house before. Can you give me directions?

follow sb's directions (=go where someone tells you to go) You can't possibly get lost if you follow my directions.

+to Do you want me to give you directions to the restaurant?

guidelines /'gaɪdlaɪnz/ [n plural] rules or instructions about the best way to do something: a set of guidelines covering safety procedures

+for new guidelines for police

+on The department produced guidelines on diet, recommending that people eat less fat.

follow guidelines Children are given simple guidelines to follow about how to behave at school.

recipe /'resɪpi/ [n C] instructions on how to make a particular kind of food: This soup is really good – you must give me the recipe.

+for I've found a great recipe for barbecue sauce.

2 a book or document with instructions

manual /'mænjuəl/ [n C] a book that contains detailed instructions for using a complicated machine or doing a particular job or activity: Before you use the camera, read the manual carefully. | a computer manual

training manual a training manual for police officers

+on a manual on food hygiene

handbook /'hændbʊk/ [n C] a book containing useful information on a

subject and advice for a group of people who need it: *The students' handbook gives information on how to find accommodation.*
+for *a health and safety handbook for all staff*
+on *a handbook on basic psychology*
cookbook (also **recipe book** BRITISH) /'kʊkbʊk, 'resɪpi bʊk/ [n C] a book that has instructions about how to cook different kinds of food

INTELLIGENT

➡ opposite **STUPID**
➡ if you mean 'behaving in a way that is reasonable and not stupid', go to **SENSIBLE**
➡ see also **GOOD 5**

1 good at learning, thinking, and understanding ideas

intelligent /ɪn'telɪdʒənt/ [adj] someone who is **intelligent** has a high level of mental ability and is good at learning, thinking, and understanding ideas: *Natalie was very charming and extremely intelligent.* | *He's probably the most intelligent student in the class.*
highly intelligent (=very intelligent) *a highly intelligent young man*
clever ESPECIALLY BRITISH **smart** ESPECIALLY AMERICAN /'klevə', smɑːʳt/ [adj] someone who is **clever** or **smart** is good at learning or understanding things quickly and at thinking of how to solve problems: *You're so clever! How did you think of that?* | *Laura's smart and she has plenty of ambition.* | *My sister's much smarter than I am.*
bright /braɪt/ [adj] children and young people who are **bright** are intelligent and likely to be successful at school or in their jobs: *She's one of the brightest kids in her class.* | *Tom was a model employee – bright and hard-working.*
brainy /'breɪni/ [adj] INFORMAL someone who is **brainy** is very intelligent and good at studying: *At school, Kathy was always one of the brainy ones.*
brainy – brainier – brainiest

2 extremely intelligent

genius /'dʒiːniəs/ [n C] someone with a very high level of intelligence, which only a few people have, especially someone who has original and important ideas: *Einstein was probably the greatest mathematical genius of all time.*
brilliant /'brɪljənt/ [adj] a **brilliant** scientist, student, teacher etc is extremely intelligent and does very good or important work which people admire them for: *the brilliant physicist, Stephen Hawking* | *a brilliant historian*
gifted /'gɪftɪd/ [adj] a child who is **gifted** is much more intelligent and quicker at learning than most other children: *a special program for gifted children in the school*

3 clever ideas, plans, or ways of doing things

clever /'klevəʳ/ [adj] ESPECIALLY BRITISH a **clever** idea, plan, or way of doing something is good and works well: *Mark had lots of clever ideas for making money.*
cleverly [adv] *The building has been cleverly designed to use as little energy as possible.*
ingenious /ɪn'dʒiːniəs/ [adj] an **ingenious** method, idea, or piece of equipment is cleverly designed to do a job or solve a problem in a very original way: *The Romans developed an ingenious device for carrying the water away.*
cunning /'kʌnɪŋ/ [adj] carefully planned, clever, and often intended to deceive people: *They use all kinds of cunning tricks to make people give them money.* | *a cunning advertising campaign*

4 the ability to learn well

intelligence /ɪn'telɪdʒəns/ [n U] the ability to learn quickly, think clearly, and understand ideas well: *Most of the children at the school are of above average intelligence.*
brains /breɪnz/ [n plural] INFORMAL the ability to think quickly, study well,

and remember a lot of facts: *With his brains, he'll easily get into university.*

5 an annoying person who thinks he or she is very clever

know-it-all (also **know-all** BRITISH) /'nəʊ ɪt ɔːl, 'nəʊ ɔːl/ [n C] INFORMAL someone who annoys you because they always think that they know more than other people: *All right then, know-it-all, tell us what the answer is.*

6 good at getting advantages for yourself

clever ESPECIALLY BRITISH **smart** ESPECIALLY AMERICAN /'klevəʳ, smaːʳt/ [adj] someone who is **clever** or **smart** is good at getting advantages for themselves or other people by using their intelligence, sometimes in a dishonest way: *Some smart lawyer got him out of prison.* | *He's a clever politician but I don't trust him at all.*
cleverly [adv] *He cleverly avoided answering the question directly.*

cunning /'kʌnɪŋ/ [adj] someone who is **cunning** gets what they want by thinking carefully about it and making secret plans or deceiving people: *As a leader, he was cunning and manipulative.* | *Their father's reputation had been ruined by a cunning competitor.*
cunningly [adv] *A video camera was cunningly hidden behind the mirror.*

shrewd /ʃruːd/ [adj] a **shrewd** person, especially a business person, is good at deciding what people, situations etc are really like, so that it is difficult to deceive them: *Watson is a shrewd and realistic businessman.* | *She was a shrewd judge of character.*
shrewdly [adv] *He shrewdly guessed that she wouldn't do as she'd promised.*

streetwise /'striːtwaɪz/ [adj] someone who is **streetwise** has a lot of experience of life in big cities, so they know what to do in difficult or dangerous situations: *The kids around here are streetwise at an early age.*

INTEND

1 to intend to do something

➡ see also **ORGANIZE/ARRANGE, PREPARE**

intend to do sth /ɪnˌtend tə 'duː (sth)/ if you **intend to do** something, you have decided that you want to do it at some time in the future: *I don't know who did this, but I intend to find out.* | *Do you think Jones really intended to kill his wife?*

> **Formal or informal?**
> **Intend to do sth** is more formal than **mean to do sth**.

⚲ **mean to do sth** /ˌmiːn tə 'duː (sth)/ ESPECIALLY SPOKEN to intend to do something – use this especially when you forgot to do something or did not have the chance to do it: *I meant to tell you about it, but I forgot.* | *I've been meaning to phone Anne for ages.*
meaning – meant – have meant

⚲ **be going to do sth** /biː ˌɡəʊɪŋ tə 'duː (sth)/ ESPECIALLY SPOKEN if you **are going to do** something, you have arranged to do it at a particular time – use this to talk about definite arrangements: *Ruth and Al are going to open their own restaurant.* | *I'm going to go to the hospital tomorrow.*

plan to do sth /ˌplæn tə 'duː (sth)/ to intend to do something – use this especially when you have thought carefully about when and how you will do something: *Josie's planning to return to work after she's had the baby.* | *We're planning to go on vacation in October.*

set out to do sth /ˌset aʊt tə 'duː (sth)/ ESPECIALLY WRITTEN to decide to do something and make plans for how you will achieve it, especially in a determined way: *He set out to make Newcastle the best football team in the country.* | *When Amy was 18, she set out to find her father.*

2 to not intend to do something

➡ see also **ACCIDENTALLY, MISTAKE**

not intend to do sth /nɒt ɪnˌtend tə ˈduː (sth)/ if you **do not intend to do** something, you have decided that you will not do it: *I don't intend to stay in this job for the rest of my life.* | *He said he didn't intend to take legal action.*

have no intention of doing sth /hæv ˌnəʊ ɪnˌtenʃən əv ˈduːɪŋ (sth)/ if you **have no intention of doing** something, you have firmly decided that you will definitely not do it: *She has no intention of going back to her husband.* | *Mr Birt announced that he had no intention of resigning.*

have no plans to do sth /hæv nəʊ ˌplænz tə ˈduː (sth)/ if you **have no plans to do** something, you have not made a decision to do it, although you may decide to do it at a later time: *At the moment, Hugh and his girlfriend have no plans to get married.*

◯ **not mean to do sth** /nɒt ˌmiːn tə ˈduː (sth)/ ESPECIALLY SPOKEN use this to say that, although someone did something, they did not do it deliberately: *Look, I'm sorry. I didn't mean to upset you.* | *I'm sure they didn't mean to stay out so late.*

3 something that you intend to do

intention /ɪnˈtenʃən/ [n C] *I'm not sure what his intentions are.*
    with the intention of doing sth *She went to the States with the intention of getting a job at a university.*
    intention to do sth *He has announced his intention to run for president at the next election.*

> **Formal or informal?**
> **Intention** is not used in informal conversation.

4 when something is intended to do something

be intended to /bi ɪnˈtendɪd tuː/ to be done or made to achieve a particular purpose or effect: *His speech was clearly intended to reassure us.* | *The restaurant was intended to be typically Moroccan.*

be meant to/be supposed to /bi ˈment tuː, bi səˈpəʊzd tuː/ to be intended to have a particular result or effect – use this especially when the result or effect is not achieved: *This film was obviously meant to shock, but it was just boring.* | *The new laws are supposed to prevent tax fraud.*

INTERESTING/ INTERESTED

➡ opposite **BORING/BORED**
➡ see also **EXCITING/EXCITED**

> ⚠ Don't confuse **interesting** (used about a subject, book, person etc that makes you want to pay attention) and **interested** (=how you feel when you want to find out more about something).

1 something that makes you feel interested

interesting /ˈɪntrɪ̩stɪŋ/ [adj] if something is **interesting**, you give it your attention, because it is unusual or exciting or because it provides information that you want to know about: *an interesting film about African wildlife.* | *He's the most interesting person I've ever met.* | *We spent an interesting afternoon looking around the old part of the city.*
    find sth interesting (=think something is interesting) *I found the talk very interesting.*
    it is interesting to see/know/ compare *It would be interesting to know what the hotel's prices are.* | *It will be interesting to see what he does after college.*
    it is interesting that (use this about a fact that is interesting because it is unexpected or difficult to explain) *It's interesting that no one remembers seeing him that day.*
    look/sound interesting *Susan's new job sounds really interesting.*

Don't say 'I am interesting in this.' Say **I am interested in this**.

interest /'ɪntrɪst/ [v T] if something **interests** you, it makes you feel interested: *There's a film about bears on the TV tonight. It might interest the children.*

 Don't say 'It is interesting me'. Say **it interests me**.

fascinating /'fæsɪneɪtɪŋ/ [adj] extremely interesting: *Istanbul is a fascinating city.* | *a fascinating story of mystery and adventure*

 Don't say 'very fascinating'. Say **absolutely fascinating**.

fascinate /'fæsɪneɪt/ [v T] if something **fascinates** you, it makes you feel extremely interested: *The idea of travelling to other planets fascinates me.*

intriguing /ɪn'triːgɪŋ/ [adj] if something is **intriguing**, you want to know more about it because it is strange or difficult to understand: *an intriguing question that continues to puzzle scientists* | *When I got home there was an intriguing message on my answerphone.*

stimulating /'stɪmjʊleɪtɪŋ/ [adj] something that is **stimulating** is interesting and enjoyable because it gives you new ideas to think about: *Professor Buchner's lectures were always stimulating.* | *It was a stimulating experience, working among people from so many different countries.*

absorbing /əb'sɔːbɪŋ, -'zɔːr-/ [adj] something that is **absorbing** holds your attention for a long time because it is very interesting and enjoyable: *The book is an absorbing read.* | *The game contains puzzles that are well-designed and absorbing.*

🔍 **I couldn't put it down** /aɪ ˌkʊdnt pʊt ɪt 'daʊn/ SPOKEN say this about a book which was so enjoyable that you did not want to stop reading it: *What an amazing book! I just couldn't put it down.*

2 feeling interested in something

interested /'ɪntrɪstɪd/ [adj not before noun] if you are **interested** in something, you give it your attention because you want to know more about it or because you enjoy it: *The children seemed very interested when I showed them my photographs.*
+in *I've never really been interested in politics.* | *All the boys I know are only interested in sport.*
interested to know/hear/see/learn *I'd be very interested to hear your opinion about this.*

find sth interesting /ˌfaɪnd (sth) 'ɪntrɪstɪŋ/ if you **find something interesting**, you feel very interested when you see it, read it, or hear about it, because it is the type of thing that you like to know about: *It's a book about travelling in India. I think you'll find it interesting.*

with interest /wɪð 'ɪntrɪst/ ESPECIALLY WRITTEN if you watch, listen, or read with interest, you watch etc with a lot of attention because you are interested: *Richard listened with interest to the conversation at the next table.*
with great interest *I read your letter with great interest.*

show interest/express interest /ˌʃəʊ 'ɪntrɪst, ɪkˌspres 'ɪntrɪst/ to say something to show that you are interested, especially in a suggestion or plan: *I suggested going camping, but none of my friends showed any interest.*
+in *Several companies have already expressed interest in our research.*

curious /'kjʊəriəs/ [adj] eager to find out more about something because you are interested but do not know much about it yet: *The visitors were surrounded by a crowd of curious children.*
+about *People have always been curious about how life on Earth began.*
curious to know/learn/find out etc *I was curious to know what she'd said.*
curiously [adv] *Ron looked at her curiously, wondering what she meant.*

inquisitive /ɪn'kwɪzɪtɪv/ [adj] FORMAL someone who is **inquisitive** is interested in a lot of different things and wants to find out more about them: *a bright, inquisitive little boy* | *The tour group was impressed and inquisitive.*

○ **be into sth** /biː ˈɪntuː (sth)/ [*phrasal verb* T] INFORMAL, ESPECIALLY SPOKEN to be very interested in a subject or activity, and to spend a lot of time on it because you enjoy it: *Both the boys are into computer games at the moment, and nothing else!*
be into doing sth *Lisa's into keeping fit – she goes to the gym every day.*
get into sth (=become more interested in it) *I never used to like jazz, but I've been getting into it recently.*

3 to feel extremely interested in something

fascinated /ˈfæsɪneɪtɪd/ [*adj* not before noun] extremely interested in something that you are watching or listening to: *She watched fascinated as the gorillas came closer and closer.*
+by *I was fascinated by her stories of her childhood in Africa.*

be absorbed in sth /biː əbˈsɔːbd ɪn (sth)/ to be so interested in something that you give it all your attention: *She's totally absorbed in her work.* | *The children were so absorbed in their game that they didn't notice us.*

gripped/riveted /grɪpt, ˈrɪvɪtɪd/ [*adj* not before noun] extremely interested by a book, film, event etc or by what someone is saying, so that you cannot stop reading, watching, listening etc: *I was completely gripped by his account of the journey.* | *We sat riveted by the events unfolding before us.*

be obsessed with sth /biː əbˈsest wɪð (sth)/ to be too interested in something, so that you cannot stop thinking about it: *You're obsessed with sex – that's your problem.*
be obsessed with doing sth *He became obsessed with the idea of making a lot of money.*

obsession /əbˈseʃən/ [*n* C] when you think too much about one particular thing: *Mario's interest in fast cars had become a dangerous obsession.*
+with *the poet's obsession with death*

4 when you are not interested in something

➡ see also **BORING/BORED**

not interested /nɒt ˈɪntrɪstɪd/ *I started telling them about my vacation, but they weren't very interested.*
+in *He's not particularly interested in sport.*

not interest sb /nɒt ˈɪntrɪst (sb)/ if a subject or activity **does not interest** you, you do not want to know about it or learn about it: *To be honest, politics doesn't interest me at all.*

lose interest /ˌluːz ˈɪntrɪst/ to stop being interested in something that you were interested in before: *I used to go to photography classes every week, but then I just lost interest.*
+in *Jenny seems to have lost all interest in her work.*

show/express no interest /ˌʃəʊ, ɪkˌspres nəʊ ˈɪntrɪst/ to show by your behaviour that you are not at all interested in something: *She doesn't show any interest in my work at all.* | *Few parents have expressed any interest in helping the school with the project.*

INTERFERE

to try to influence a situation that you should not be involved in

➡ see also **STOP 6**

1 to interfere

interfere /ˌɪntəˈfɪər/ [*v* I] to try to influence a situation that you should not be involved in, for example by telling someone what to do or giving them advice which they do not want: *Mum, stop interfering!* | *I don't mean to interfere, but don't you think you should tell John about this?*
+in *You shouldn't really have interfered in their argument.* | *The US was accused of interfering in China's internal affairs.*

interference [*n* U] when someone interferes in a situation: *The Internet should be allowed to develop without any interference from the government.*

interfering [*adj* only before noun] an **interfering** person annoys you because they keep interfering in things that they should not be involved in: *an interfering old woman*

meddle /'medl/ [*v* I] to interfere in a situation that you do not understand or know enough about, and which someone else is responsible for dealing with
+in *In my opinion, Church leaders shouldn't meddle in politics.*

○ **poke your nose into sth** /,pəʊk jɔːʳ 'nəʊz ɪntuː (sth)/ INFORMAL, ESPECIALLY SPOKEN to ask questions about someone else's private life in a way that annoys them: *Just stop poking your nose into my private affairs.*

busybody /'bɪzi,bɒdill-,bɑːdi/ [*n* C] INFORMAL someone who always wants to know about or get involved in other people's private activities: *I can't stand busybodies like her.*
plural **busybodies**

2 to not interfere

○ **mind your own business** /,maɪnd jɔːr əʊn 'bɪznɹ̩s/ SPOKEN say this when you want someone to stop interfering or asking questions about something that is private: *"Where are you two going?" "Mind your own business!"* | *He asked me how much money I earned, and I told him to mind his own business.*

○ **stay out of it** /,steɪ 'aʊt əv ɪt/ SPOKEN INFORMAL to not get involved in a fight or an argument between other people: *It's their problem and if I were you I'd stay out of it.*

INVENT

➡ if you mean 'think of an explanation, reason, etc that is untrue', go to **TRUE/NOT TRUE 3**

⚠ Don't confuse **invent** (=think of something that did not exist before) and **discover** (=find something that people did not know about before).

1 to think of a new idea, design, or name for something

➡ see also **FIND 4, IDEA**

invent /ɪn'vent/ [*v* T] to think of an idea for a new product, machine etc for the first time, and design it and make it: *Alexander Graham Bell invented the telephone.* | *Television was invented in the 1920s.*
invention [*n* U] when someone has invented a new product: *a discovery that led to the invention of the nuclear bomb*

create /kri'eɪt/ [*v* T] to make something new in art, literature, fashion etc: *Agatha Christie created the character Hercule Poirot.* | *Mary Quant created a whole new look for women's clothes in the 1960s.*

think up/come up with /,θɪŋk 'ʌp, ,kʌm 'ʌp wɪð/ [*phrasal verb* T] INFORMAL to produce a new idea, name, method etc by thinking carefully about it
think up sth/come up with sth *See if you can come up with a better name for the book.* | *We need to think up some new ideas for the Christmas show.*
think sth up *What a brilliant idea! I wonder who thought that up.*

devise /dɪ'vaɪz/ [*v* T] to invent a way of doing something, especially one that is clever and complicated: *The exercise program was devised by a leading health expert.* | *Scientists have devised a test that shows who is most likely to get the disease.*

Formal or informal?
Devise is a formal word.

2 someone who invents things

inventor /ɪn'ventəʳ/ [*n* C] someone who invents things, especially machines
+of *Marconi, the inventor of radio*

creator /kri'eɪtəʳ/ [*n* C] the writer, artist, or designer who first produced a well-known story, character, fashion etc
+of *Walt Disney, the creator of Mickey Mouse*

3 something that someone has invented

invention /ɪnˈvenʃən/ [n C] something that someone has invented: *The light bulb was Edison's most famous invention.*

INVITE

➡ see also **PARTY**

1 to invite someone

invite/ask /ɪnˈvaɪt, ɑːskǁæsk/ [v T] to ask someone to come to a party, wedding, meal etc: *It's going to be a big wedding – they've invited over a hundred people.* | *"Are you going to Emma's party?" "No, I haven't been asked."*
invite/ask sb to a party/wedding etc *Are you going to invite Stephanie to the school disco?*
invite/ask sb to do sth *Jane's parents have asked me to come and stay with them for a couple of weeks.*
invite/ask sb for lunch/dinner *Madeline has invited us for dinner on Saturday.*
invite/ask sb in (=invite a visitor into your home) *He invited me in for a cup of coffee.*

> ⚠ Don't say 'she invited/asked me in her party'. Say **she invited/asked me to her party**.

> **Formal or informal?**
> You can use **invite** in written or spoken English. **Ask** is more informal, and is usually used in spoken English.

ask sb out /ˌɑːsk (sb) ˈaʊtǁˌæsk-/ [phrasal verb T] to ask someone to go to a restaurant, a film etc with you because you want to start a romantic relationship with them: *Why don't you ask her out? Or are you too shy?*

◔ **have sb over** /ˌhæv (sb) ˈəʊvəʳ/ [phrasal verb T] ESPECIALLY SPOKEN if you **have someone over**, they come to your home to have a meal or to spend time with you because you have invited them: *"What did you do last night?" "We had some friends over and we played cards."*
have sb over for drinks/dinner etc *We had Nick's parents over for dinner on Saturday.*

2 a message inviting someone

invitation /ˌɪnvɪˈteɪʃən/ [n C] a message inviting someone to a party, wedding etc: *Thanks for your invitation. I'd love to come.* | *a wedding invitation*
+to *Did you get an invitation to the party?*

3 someone who you invite

guest /gest/ [n C] someone who is staying at your home, or who has come to your party, wedding etc because you invited them: *the wedding guests* | *We have guests staying with us this week.*

> **Formal or informal?**
> **Guest** is used in writing and in formal spoken English.

J, j

JEALOUS

1 because someone loves another person

➡ see also **GIRLFRIEND/BOYFRIEND, LOVE, RELATIONSHIP**

jealous /'dʒeləs/ [adj] angry and unhappy because you think your husband, girlfriend etc loves someone else more than they love you

get jealous (=become jealous) *My girlfriend gets jealous if I even look at another woman.*

make sb jealous *He was talking to Nina all evening, just to make me jealous.*

jealous husband/wife/lover etc *It's a story about a woman who is killed by her jealous lover.*

jealously [adv] *He watched jealously as Rose danced with his brother.*

possessive /pə'zesɪv/ [adj] someone who is **possessive** wants their husband, wife, children, or friends to love only them, and does not like them spending time with other people: *Her mother is very possessive.*

+of/about *He loves his wife, but is very possessive of her.*

jealousy /'dʒeləsi/ [n U] the angry, unhappy feeling you have when you think your husband, girlfriend etc loves someone else more than they love you: *Morgan stabbed his girlfriend in a fit of jealousy.*

2 because you want something that someone else has

➡ see also **WANT**

jealous /'dʒeləs/ [adj] you feel **jealous** when someone has something that you want, and you are annoyed that they have it and you do not: *Maybe he's jealous because I got the job and he didn't.*

+of *I felt jealous of Katie with her new baby.*

envious /'enviəs/ [adj] ESPECIALLY WRITTEN you feel **envious** when someone has something nice or special, and you wish that you had it too: *He cast an envious look at Simon's shiny red sports car.*

+of *I was envious of her family, her house, and her whole lifestyle.*

enviously [adv] *She glanced enviously at Emma's slim figure.*

envy /'envi/ [v T] to wish that you had the same abilities, possessions etc as someone else: *I wish I could play the piano like that – I really envy you!*

envy sb for sth *He always envied his brother for the way he made friends so easily.*

envying – envied – have envied

envy /'envi/ [n U] the feeling you have when you want something that someone else has: *It was difficult to hide my envy as Jim described his new job in Hawaii.*

green with envy (=very envious) *Tom will be green with envy when he sees your new computer.*

jealousy /'dʒeləsi/ [n U] the feeling of wanting something that someone else has, especially when this makes you angry or unhappy: *Jealousy is a very negative emotion.* | *the problems of professional jealousy in the workplace*

JOB

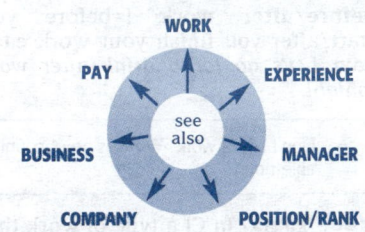

1 a job

job /dʒɒb‖dʒɑːb/ [n C] the work that you do regularly in order to earn money, especially when you work for a company or a public organization: *My first job was in a record store.* | *Daniel starts his new job on Monday.* | *She* has a well-paid job in the tax department.

get/find a job *Her son still hasn't been able to find a job.* | *Ted got a job as a bartender.*

look for a job (=try to get one) *She's looking for a job in the music business.*

apply for a job *I've applied for a job in the police.*

part-time job (=when you work less than the usual number of hours each week) *I had a part-time job while I was at college.*

job losses/job cuts (=when a lot of people lose their jobs)

> ⚠ Don't say 'What is your job?' or 'What is your work?' when you want to know what someone does to earn money. Say **What do you do?** or **What do you do for a living?**: *"What does your mother do?" "She's a doctor."*

work /wɜːʳk/ [n U] anything that you do to earn money: *My father started work when he was 14 years old.*

look for work (=try to find any job that you can) *Lena graduated from college six months ago and is still looking for work.*

find work *Mario was hoping to find work in a hotel or a restaurant.*

go back to work/return to work (=start working again) *A lot of women return to work when their children start school.*

to/at work (=to or at the place where you work) *He's marrying someone he met at work.* | *What time do you go to work?*

before/after work (=before you start/after you finish your work each day) *Let's go for a drink after work tonight.*

> ⚠ Don't say 'a work'. **Work** is an uncountable noun.

career /kəˈrɪəʳ/ [n C] a type of work that you are trained for and that you often do for most of your working life: *Have you thought about your future career?*

a teaching/political/military etc career *I'm interested in a teaching career.*

+in *a career in medicine*

+as *He'd had a successful career as an engineer.*

profession /prəˈfeʃən/ [n C] an area of work such as law, medicine, or teaching, for which you need special training and education

the teaching/medical/legal profession *There are now a lot more women in the legal profession.*

go into/enter a profession *There was a big demand for accountants in the 1980s, and many graduates entered the profession at that time.*

occupation /ˌɒkjʊˈpeɪʃənǁˌɑːk-/ [n C] the type of work that someone usually does: *Please state your age, address, and occupation in the space below.* | *low-paid occupations*

> **Formal or informal?**
>
> **Occupation** is used especially on official forms or in formal writing about the types of job that people do. Don't use **occupation** to talk about your own job.

trade /treɪd/ [n C] a skilled job in which you use your hands to do things, such as building houses, making furniture, or repairing cars

learn a trade *Young people who don't want to go to college can learn a trade.*

be a bricklayer/carpenter etc by trade (=used to say that this is someone's job) *His father had been a plumber by trade.*

post/position /pəʊst, pəˈzɪʃən/ [n C] FORMAL an important job in a company or organization

+of *He was offered the post of ambassador to Mexico.*

hold a post/position (=have an important job in an organization) *She was the first woman ever to hold the position of Prime Minister.*

vacancy /ˈveɪkənsi/ [n C] a job that is available: *We'll contact you if we have any vacancies.*

+for *Do you have any vacancies for sales staff?*

plural **vacancies**

professional /prəˈfeʃənəl/ [adj] a **professional** musician, sports player, photographer etc earns money by playing music, doing a sport etc, rather than doing it just for enjoyment: *Professional basketball players can earn a lot of money.*

turn professional (=become professional) *He had been a successful* amateur boxer before he turned professional in 1988.

professional [n C] *It's a big golf tournament, with many of the world's top professionals taking part.*

2 to give someone a job

take on /ˌteɪk ˈɒn‖-ˈɑːn/ [phrasal verb T] if a company **takes** someone **on**, it gives them a job
take on sb *The store always takes on extra sales assistants for the Christmas period.*
take sb on *They've agreed to take me on for a year after I finish college.*

hire /haɪəʳ/ [v T] ESPECIALLY AMERICAN if a company **hires** someone, it gives them a job: *She was hired in April this year. | They're not hiring any new people at the moment.*

appoint /əˈpɔɪnt/ [v T] to choose someone for an important job: *The President has appointed a new Minister of Culture.*
appoint sb director/manager/principal etc *In 1989 he was appointed managing director.*
appoint sb to a job/position/post *This is the first time a woman has been appointed to such a senior position.*

recruit /rɪˈkruːt/ [v T] to find new people to work for a company, organization, or military force: *The police department is trying to recruit more black officers. | It's getting more and more difficult to recruit experienced staff.*

promote /prəˈməʊt/ [v T often passive] to give someone who works in an organization a more important job than the one they had before
be promoted *Did you hear that David's been promoted?*
be promoted to *She was promoted to Assistant Principal.*
promotion [n C/U] when someone is given a more important job in an organization: *What are my chances of promotion if I stay here? (=am I likely to be promoted?) | Darren has had two promotions since he joined the BBC in 1998.*

3 to take away someone's job

fire (also **dismiss** FORMAL) /faɪəʳ, dɪsˈmɪs/ [v T] to make someone leave their job, because they have done something wrong or because their work is not satisfactory: *She kept arriving late, and in the end they fired her. | You're fired! | An employer is entitled to dismiss an employee for misconduct.*
fire/dismiss sb for (doing) sth *He was fired for being drunk at work.*

> **Formal or informal?**
> **Fire** is more informal than **dismiss** and is used especially in American English.

dismissal [n C/U] *He is seeking compensation for unfair dismissal.*

sack sb/give sb the sack /sæk (sb), ˌgɪv (sb) ðə ˈsæk/ BRITISH INFORMAL to make someone leave their job, because they have done something wrong or because their work is not satisfactory: *They sacked the coach after the team lost 10 games in a row.*
+for *She was given the sack for trying to organize a trade union.*

lose your job /ˌluːz jɔːʳ ˈdʒɒb‖-ˈdʒɑːb/ if you **lose your job**, your job is taken away from you: *Things have been really difficult since Terry lost his job. | Thousands of workers lost their jobs when the car factory closed.*

get the sack /ˌget ðə ˈsæk/ BRITISH INFORMAL if you **get the sack**, your job is taken away from you, especially because you have done something wrong or your work is not satisfactory: *He got the sack after he was caught stealing money.*

lay sb off/make sb redundant /ˌleɪ (sb) ˈɒf, ˌmeɪk (sb) rɪˈdʌndənt/ if a company **lays** someone **off** or **makes** them **redundant**, it stops employing them because it does not need them any more: *If sales keep falling, we'll have to lay off even more people. | The two banks merged to form a single company, and hundreds of workers were made redundant.*

> ⚠ **Lay sb off** is used in both British and American English, and it can mean either that someone loses their job permanently, or that they lose it for a short period. **Make sb redundant** is used only in British English and means that someone loses their job permanently.

redundancy /rɪ'dʌndənsi/ [n C/U] BRITISH when a company takes away someone's job because it does not need them any more: *The decline in car sales led to many redundancies.*
redundancy pay/money (=money you receive from a company when you lose your job) *He used his redundancy money to buy a boat.*
plural **redundancies**

4 to ask for a job

apply /ə'plaɪ/ [v I] to formally ask to be considered for a job that has been advertised, especially by writing a letter or answering the questions on a form: *I applied in September, but I didn't hear from them till the following January.*
apply for a job/post/position *Dear Sir, I am writing to apply for the post of Training Officer.*
applying – applied – have applied

application /ˌæplɪ'keɪʃən/ [n C] a formal written request to be considered for a job, often consisting of a form on which you have to answer questions about your education, your work experience etc
+for *Ben's just sent off an application for a job in Dubai.*
application form (=a piece of paper on which you have to answer questions about yourself when you apply for a job) *You have to give details of your previous work experience on the application form.*
job application *She filled out hundreds of job applications before she got the job she wanted.*

applicant/candidate /'æplɪkənt, 'kændɪdət‖-deɪt, -dət/ [n C] someone who is being considered for a job: *We're interviewing applicants all week.*
+for *How many candidates are there for the job?*

CV BRITISH **resumé** AMERICAN /ˌsiː 'viː, 'rezjumeɪ‖'reɪ-, ˌrezʊ'meɪ/ [n C] a written statement giving details of your education, the examinations you have passed, your previous jobs etc, which you send to an organization when you are trying to get a new job

5 when someone is asked questions to find out if they are suitable for a job

interview /'ɪntəˈvjuː/ [n C] a formal meeting at which someone is asked questions in order to find out whether they are suitable for a job: *I've got a job interview tomorrow.*
+for *She has an interview on Thursday for a job at MTV.*
interview /'ɪntəˈvjuː/ [v T] to meet someone and ask them a lot of questions so that you can decide whether they are suitable for a job
interview sb for sth *We're interviewing two candidates for the job today.*

6 when someone does not have a job

unemployed /ˌʌnɪm'plɔɪd◂/ [adj] someone who is **unemployed** does not have a job: *a poor neighbourhood where 50 per cent of the men are unemployed*
the unemployed (=people who are unemployed) *government help for the unemployed*

unemployment /ˌʌnɪm'plɔɪmənt/ [n U] when people do not have jobs: *Unemployment increased by more than 30,000 last month.* | *The survey found that people's biggest worries were about crime and unemployment.*
high unemployment (=when a lot of people are unemployed) *The North-East is an area of high unemployment.*
unemployment benefit BRITISH (=money paid by the government to people who have no job)

out of work (also **on the dole** BRITISH) /ˌaʊt əv 'wɜːˈk, ɒn ðə 'dəʊl/ someone who is **out of work** does not have a job – use this especially when they have not had a job for a long time: *My husband has been out of work for two years now.*

> ⚠ **Out of work** is spelled with hyphens when it comes before a noun: *an out-of-work actor*. **On the dole** is not used before a noun.

JOIN

➡ look here for ...
- join two things together
- when roads or rivers join together
- when people or countries join together
- join a club or organization

➡ if you mean 'join in', go to **TAKE PART**

➡ if you mean 'join two sides of a piece of clothing', go to **FASTEN/ UNFASTEN**

➡ see also **CONNECTED/NOT CONNECTED, TOGETHER, SEPARATE**

1 to join things together

join /dʒɔɪn/ [v T] to join two things together, for example by using glue or a piece of wood or metal: *Join the two pieces of wood using a strong glue.*
join sth together *Doctors had to use a metal rod to join the two pieces of bone together. | Join the sleeve and the shoulder of the jacket together with strong thread.*

fix /fɪks/ [v T] to join one thing firmly to another, using screws, nails, or glue, so that it stays there permanently
fix sth to sth *Now all I have to do is fix it to the ceiling.*
be fixed to sth *The chairs and tables were fixed to the floor.*

attach /əˈtætʃ/ [v T] to join one thing to another, so that it stays in position but can be removed later
attach sth to sth *It took a couple of minutes to attach the trailer to the back of the truck. | The doctor attached a tiny monitor to the baby's head.*
be attached to sth *Make sure your baggage tag is firmly attached to your suitcase.*

fasten /ˈfɑːsən‖ˈfæ-/ [v T] to fix one thing firmly to another, using string, wire, or tape, in a way that makes it easy to remove later

fasten sth to sth *Claire carefully fastened the brooch to her dress.*
be fastened to sth *Our bags were fastened to the roof of the car with thick ropes.*

connect /kəˈnekt/ [v T] to join two pieces of equipment together with a wire or a pipe, so that electricity, water, gas etc can pass from one to the other
connect sth to sth *Have you connected the speakers to the amplifier? | I don't know how to connect the DVD player to the TV.*
be connected to sth *We're waiting for our house to be connected to the city water supply.*

link /lɪŋk/ [v T] to connect two computers, machines, or systems so that electronic signals can pass from one to the other: *The two TV stations are linked by satellite.*
link sth to sth *We'll link your computer to our system via your modem.*

2 when something forms a connection between two places, two machines etc

connect /kəˈnekt/ [v T] if a pipe, wire, bridge etc **connects** two things or places, it forms a connection between them
connect sth to/with sth *This wire connects the TV to the video recorder. | The Golden Gate Bridge connects San Francisco with Marin County.*
be connected by sth *The two lakes are connected by a narrow canal.*

link /lɪŋk/ [v T] if a road, a railway, a plane service etc **links** two places, it connects them so that people can easily travel between them: *a new high-speed railway linking the two capitals*
link sth with sth *The Channel Tunnel has linked Britain with mainland Europe for the first time.*
link sth and sth *Interstate 5 links Los Angeles and San Diego.*

connection /kəˈnekʃən/ [n C] a wire or piece of metal that joins two parts of a machine or electrical system: *Carefully check all the electrical connections.*
loose connection (=one that is not

joined properly) *There must be a loose connection somewhere – the phone isn't working.*

link /lɪŋk/ [n C] something that joins two places that are far apart, so that people can travel between them or communicate between them: *two TV stations joined by a satellite link*
road/rail link *a high speed rail link from London to Paris*
+between *Rebels bombed the Beira railroad, a vital link between the capital and the port.* | *a telephone link between the two presidents*

3 when roads, rivers etc come together and join

join /dʒɔɪn/ [v I/T] if two roads, rivers, pipes etc **join**, or if one **joins** another, they come together: *The two rivers join down in the valley.* | *Sometimes you get leaks where the pipes join.* | *The M1 motorway joins the M62 just outside Leeds.*

4 when people, countries etc join together

unite /juːˈnaɪt/ [v I] ESPECIALLY WRITTEN if people, organizations, or countries **unite**, they decide to work together or join together as a single unit, for example because they have the same aims as each other
unite to do sth *In 1960, the two areas united to form Somalia.* | *Various political and religious groups united to oppose the law.*
+against *Police chiefs called on the local people to unite against the drug dealers.*

get together /ˌget təˈgeðəʳ/ [phrasal verb I] if people or organizations **get together**, they work together in order to do something that would be difficult to do alone: *A group of parents got together and set up a youth club.*
get together to do sth *Several local stores got together to organize the festival.*

Formal or informal?
Get together is more informal than **unite**.

team up /ˌtiːm ˈʌp/ [phrasal verb I] if two or more people **team up**, they

agree to work together, especially in business, music, theatre etc
+with *I teamed up with a local journalist, and we worked on the story together.*
team up to do sth *It all started when Paul McCartney and John Lennon teamed up to form a band.*

Formal or informal?
Team up is more informal than **unite**.

merge /mɜːʳdʒ/ [v I] if two companies or organizations **merge**, they join to form a single company or organization: *The two banks are going to merge next year.*
+with *The Liberal Party merged with the Social Democrats.*

alliance /əˈlaɪəns/ [n C] an agreement between two or more countries or groups of people to work together in order to achieve something: *the Anglo-Canadian alliance*
+between *the possibility of a political alliance between the two parties*

5 to join a club, organization, or military force

➡ see also **MEMBER**

join /dʒɔɪn/ [v I/T] to join a club, company, organization, or military force: *Do you think we should join the union?* | *She joined the Conservative Party in 1952.* | *William joined IBM in 1979 as a programmer.* | *A lot of people want to join, so there's a big waiting list.*
join the army/navy/air force *Paul joined the army when he was 16.*

 Don't say 'join in a club'. Say **join a club**.

 Don't use **join** about going to a school or college. Say **she wants to go to Harvard** (not 'she wants to join Harvard').

become a member /bɪˌkʌm ə ˈmembəʳ/ to join a club, organization, or political group, but not a company or a military force: *You have to be eighteen before you can become a member.*

+of *I was hoping to become a member of the tennis club.* | *Several other countries had applied to become members of NATO.*

enlist/join up /ɪnˈlɪst, ˌdʒɔɪn ˈʌp/ [v I] to join the army, navy, or air force: *My grandfather went to join up on the day war broke out.*

enlist in the army/navy/air force *Josie enlisted in the air force and eventually became a pilot.*

JOKE

➡ see also **FUNNY, LAUGH, SERIOUS**

1   funny story

joke /dʒəʊk/ [n C] something you say or do to make people laugh, especially a funny story: *Do you know any good jokes?*

tell a joke *Tony told me a really funny joke last night, but I've forgotten it.*

> ⚠ Don't say 'say a joke'. Say **tell a joke**.

comedian/comic /kəˈmiːdiən, ˈkɒmɪk‖ ˈkɑː-/ [n C] someone whose job is to tell jokes and make people laugh: *Sandra Bernhard is an actor, singer, comedian, and a regular guest on the David Letterman show.*

2   when you pretend that something is true as a joke

○ **be joking/be kidding** /biː ˈdʒəʊkɪŋ, biː ˈkɪdɪŋ/ INFORMAL, ESPECIALLY SPOKEN to say something that is not true, as a joke: *When he asked me to marry him, I thought he was joking!* | *Don't get mad – I was only kidding!*

○ **pull sb's leg** /ˌpʊl (sb's) ˈleg/ INFORMAL, ESPECIALLY SPOKEN to try to make someone believe something that is not true, as a joke: *He isn't really related to Madonna – he was only pulling your leg.*

3   to make someone seem stupid by making jokes about them

make fun of sb/sth /ˌmeɪk ˈfʌn ɒv (sb/sth)/ *Stop making fun of me.* | *The other children at school are always making fun of Tom's clothes.*

> ⚠ Don't confuse **make fun of** and **have fun** (=enjoy yourself).

tease /tiːz/ [v I/T] to make jokes about someone, either in an unkind way, or in a friendly way that shows you like them: *The kids at school used to tease Sam because he was overweight.* | *Don't get upset, Stuart, she's only teasing.*

tease sb about sth *Kevin's always teasing me about my cooking.*

JOURNEY

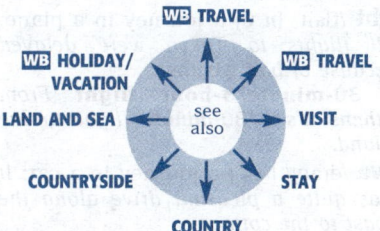

journey /ˈdʒɜːˢni/ [n C] the time during which you travel from one place to another, especially when you go a long way: *I've made us some sandwiches to eat on the journey.* | *We had an awful journey – there was heavy snow and the car broke down.*

bus/train/car journey *the long train journey to St Petersburg*

a two-hour/five-mile journey *They arrived in Nice after an eight-hour journey by car.*

make a journey *These birds make an incredible 10,000-kilometre journey to Africa every winter.*

plural **journeys**

> ⚠ Don't say 'do a journey'. Say **make a journey**.

⚠ Don't say 'Good journey' to someone who is about to make a journey. Say **Have a good journey** or **Have a safe journey**.

trip /trɪp/ [n C] a journey in which you go to a place, stay there for a while, and then come back: *We had a lovely trip – the flight was fine and the hotel was fantastic.*
take a trip *They decided to take a trip to Paris.*
business/school/skiing trip *a school trip to the zoo*
on a trip (=taking a trip) *My husband's away on a business trip in China.*
a day trip (=when you go and come back on the same day) *a day trip to Oxford*

tour /tʊəʳ/ [n C] an organized journey that someone makes, either for a holiday or for their work
+of *a coach tour of Scotland | The President left Washington today for a tour of the Middle East.*

flight /flaɪt/ [n C] a journey in a plane: *All flights to Tokyo were delayed because of bad weather.*
a 30-minute/3-hour flight *From Athens it's a 30-minute flight to the island.*

drive /draɪv/ [n C] a journey in a car: *It was quite a pleasant drive along the coast to the cottage.*
a 12-hour/15-minute drive *It's about a 20-minute drive into the city from here.*

crossing /ˈkrɒsɪŋǁˈkrɔː-/ [n C] a short journey in a boat or ship from one side of a lake, river, or sea to the other: *The crossing from Dover to Calais can be very rough.*

voyage /ˈvɔɪ-ɪdʒ/ [n C] a long journey in a boat or ship: *In those days, the voyage to Australia was long and dangerous.*

⚠ Use **voyage** especially when you are writing stories or describing events in the past.

commute /kəˈmjuːt/ [n C] someone's journey to work every day: *My commute to work takes about an hour.*

JUMP

➡ see also **RUN, DANCE, FALL**

jump /dʒʌmp/ [v I] to push yourself off the ground using your legs: *How high can you jump?*
+into/off/over *I bet you can't jump over that wall. | Boys were diving and jumping off the bridge.*
+up/down *Jump down and I'll catch you.*
jump up and down (=jump several times, while staying in the same place) *Excited fans were jumping up and down and screaming.*
jump [n C] *Aziz won the event with a jump of 2.35 metres.*

jump

leap

leap /liːp/ [v I/T] ESPECIALLY WRITTEN to jump suddenly as far as you can
+over/through/across *The barman leapt over the bar and tried to stop the fight.*
leaping – leapt – have leapt BRITISH
leaping – leaped – have leaped AMERICAN

⚠ Use **leap** especially when you are writing stories or describing events in the past.

K, k

KEEP

➡ see also **GET RID OF, INFORMATION**

1 to keep something in a place

keep /kiːp/ [v T] to keep something in a place, especially so that you can find it and use it when you need it: *Can you remember where she keeps her keys?*
keep sth in/on/under sth *Do you keep your car in a garage? | I keep a torch in the boot of the car.*
keeping – kept – have kept

> ⚠ Don't say 'I am keeping', 'she is keeping' etc. Say **I keep, she keeps** etc.

store /stɔːʳ/ [v T] to keep something in a place or container where it will not be damaged or lost, especially when you intend to keep it for a long time: *The warehouse is being used to store food and clothes for the refugees. | Medicine should be stored in a cool dry place.*

2 to keep information

keep /kiːp/ [v T] to keep many different pieces of information together in one place, so that you can find them when you need them: *The police keep detailed information about everyone who has committed a crime. | Records of all births and deaths in the country are kept in London.*
keeping – kept – have kept

> ⚠ Don't say 'I am keeping', 'they are keeping' etc. Say **I keep, they keep** etc.

store /stɔːʳ/ [v T] to keep information in a computer: *Data regarding employees' salaries is stored on the computer at our main office.*
file /faɪl/ [v T] to keep written records and documents together using an organized system, so that everything

is easy to find: *The students' records are filed alphabetically.*
file sth away (=put it in the correct file)

3 to keep something, and not sell it, give it away etc

keep /kiːp/ [v T] to keep something because you have decided not to sell it, give it away, or throw it away: *My mother kept all the love letters my father wrote. | I've decided to keep the car even though it's getting old. | Surely you don't want to keep all these old magazines!*
keeping – kept – have kept

4 to keep something for someone to use later

save /seɪv/ [v T] to keep something that you would normally use or throw away, so that someone else can use it later
save sth for sb *Let's save some of this pizza for Jill. | I save all Polly's old clothes for my sister's baby.*
reserve /rɪˈzɜːʳv/ [v T] to arrange for a place in a hotel, restaurant, plane etc to be kept for you to use at a particular time in the future: *I'm sorry Madam. All the tables have already been reserved.*
reserve sth for sb *I'll ask if they can reserve a room for us on December 22nd.*
keep /kiːp/ [v T] if a shop **keeps** something for someone, they do not sell it or give it to anyone else
keep sth for sb *If you want the necklace, we can keep it for you until Tuesday.*
keeping – kept – have kept

5 to keep things such as stamps, pictures, or coins because you are interested in them and you enjoy owning them

collect /kəˈlekt/ [v T] *My mother collects old china. | I used to collect shells when I was a kid.*
collector [n C] someone who collects

things such as stamps, pictures, or coins

collection /kə'lekʃən/ [n C] a set of stamps, pictures, coins etc that someone keeps because it is interesting or attractive: *Daniel has a fantastic stamp collection.*
+of *a collection of fine china*

6 an amount that you are keeping to use later

supply /sə'plaɪ/ [n C] an amount of something that you keep so that there is always some available when you need it: *Food supplies were already running out.*
+of *The hospital keeps a large supply of blood for use in emergencies.*
plural **supplies**

stock /stɒk‖stɑːk/ [n C] an amount of something that a shop keeps in order to sell: *Our stock of Italian wine is selling fast.* | *Buy now, while stocks last!*

KICK

to hit someone or something with your foot

➡ see also **HIT, ATTACK, HURT/INJURE**

kick /kɪk/ [v I/T] *The boy behind me kept kicking my chair.* | *He was dragged kicking and screaming to a waiting police car.*
kick sth along/over/around etc *Who kicked the ball over the fence?*
kick sb in the head/stomach etc *One of the gang kicked him in the stomach.*
kick [n C] a kicking action or movement: *A savage kick from his attacker just missed his knee.*

give sth a kick /ˌgɪv (sth) ə 'kɪk/ to kick something once: *If the door won't open, just give it a good hard kick.*

KILL

DIE
THREATEN · ACCIDENT
SHOOT · ILLNESS/DISEASE
WEAPON · see also · WAR
VIOLENT · EXPLODE
CRIME

1 to kill someone

kill /kɪl/ [v I/T] to make someone die, usually violently: *He claims that he didn't mean to kill his wife.* | *The explosion killed 32 people.* | *Many people do not realize that these drugs are dangerous and can kill.* | *The disease has already killed more than 2000 people in Latin America.*
be killed in a crash/accident etc *James Dean was killed in a car crash in 1955.*

murder /'mɜːrdər/ [v T] to deliberately kill someone, especially after planning to do it: *Wilson is accused of murdering his daughter and her boyfriend.* | *One of the country's top judges has been murdered by the Mafia.*

murder /'mɜːrdər/ [n C/U] the crime of deliberately killing someone: *He was convicted of murder and jailed for life.*
commit a murder (=murder someone) *The gun was found five miles from where the murder was committed.*

> ⚠ Don't confuse **murder** (=the crime of killing someone) and **murderer** (=the person who murders someone).

assassinate /ə'sæsɪneɪt‖-səneɪt/ [v T] to murder an important person, especially for political reasons: *President Lincoln was assassinated by John Wilkes Booth.* | *an attempt to assassinate the Pope*
assassination /əˌsæsɪ'neɪʃən‖-sən'eɪ-/ [n C/U]
+of *The assassination of Indira Gandhi caused a crisis in India.*

massacre /'mæsəkə^r/ [v T] to violently kill a large number of people who cannot defend themselves: *Hundreds of civilians were massacred during a peaceful protest.*

massacre [n C/U] *The whole world was shocked by the massacre in Rwanda.*

beat/kick/stab sb to death /ˌbiːt, ˌkɪk, ˌstæb (sb) tə 'deθ/ to kill someone by beating them, kicking them, or attacking them with a knife: *He beat his wife to death in a drunken argument.* | *A social worker was found stabbed to death in her office last night.*

---

2 to deliberately kill yourself

kill yourself /'kɪl jɔː^{r}self/ *He killed himself by taking an overdose of painkillers.* | *She had tried to kill herself several times before.*

suicide /'suːɪˌsaɪd, 'sjuː-‖'suː-/ [n C/U] when someone deliberately kills himself or herself: *Police think the man's death was suicide.* | *A record number of teenage suicides were reported last year.*

commit suicide (=kill yourself) *We were devastated when we heard the news that Kurt Cobain had committed suicide.*

suicide attempt (=when you try to commit suicide) *Stephen was rushed to the hospital after his suicide attempt.*

suicidal /ˌsuːɪˈsaɪdl◂, ˌsjuː-‖ˌsuː-/ [adj] wanting to kill yourself because you are very unhappy or upset: *He became suicidal after his wife left him.*

---

3 someone who kills someone else

murderer /'mɜː^{r}dərə^r/ [n C] someone who has deliberately killed another person: *A convicted murderer escaped from Dartmoor prison last night.*

sb's murderer (=the person who murdered someone) *She was determined to find her brother's murderer.*

mass murderer (=someone who murders a lot of people)

killer /'kɪlə^r/ [n C] someone who has deliberately killed another person – used especially in newspapers and news reports

+of *The police are searching for the killer of a nine-year-old child.* | *The couple's killers have never been found.*

serial killer (=someone who has killed several people over a long period of time) *a serial killer who is targeting gay men in the area*

assassin /ə'sæsɪn/ [n C] someone who has killed an important person, especially because they have been paid to do it or for political reasons: *His killer, a hired assassin, was later jailed for life.*

sb's assassin (=the person who killed someone important) *The king's assassin was never caught.*

---

4 when someone is killed as a punishment

be executed /biː 'eksɪˌkjuːtɪd/ to be legally killed by the government as punishment for a crime: *The leader of the rebels was caught and publicly executed.*

capital punishment /ˌkæpɪtl 'pʌnɪʃmənt/ [n U] the system of killing criminals as a legal punishment: *I don't believe that bringing back capital punishment would reduce crime.* | *Most people that we questioned were in favour of capital punishment.*

> ⚠ Use **capital punishment** especially when you are talking about whether it is a good or a bad thing.

the death penalty /ðə 'deθ ˌpenlti/ [n singular] the legal punishment of being killed for a crime: *The death penalty does not exist in Britain.* | *In many countries, drug dealing carries the death penalty.* (=the punishment is death)

be on death row /biː ɒn ˌdeθ 'rəʊ/ if someone **is on death row**, they are in prison for a period of time before they are killed as punishment for a crime: *Some prisoners have spent more than ten years on death row.*

---

5 when someone is killed because they are very ill

euthanasia /ˌjuːθə'neɪziə‖-'neɪʒə/ [n U] when people who are very ill or old are killed in a painless way in order to stop them suffering – use this especially to talk about whether this is moral or legal: *Is it true that euthanasia is legal in the Netherlands?*

mercy killing /ˈmɜːˌʳsi ˌkɪlɪŋ/ [n C/U] when someone who is very ill is killed in a painless way in order to stop them suffering any longer: *The court decided that his death had been a mercy killing. | Should the law allow mercy killing?*

6 something that can kill you

fatal /ˈfeɪtl/ [adj] a **fatal** accident, illness, or injury is one that causes death: *He suffered a fatal injury to the neck.*

be/prove fatal (to sb) *A sudden shock could be fatal to anyone with a weak heart. | If the infection reaches the brain, it could prove fatal.*

fatally [adv] *The bank manager was fatally wounded during the robbery.*

> **Formal or informal?**
> **Fatal** is not usually used in informal conversation.

lethal/deadly /ˈliːθəl, ˈdedli/ [adj] likely or able to kill people – use this especially about weapons or poisons: *Any knife can be a deadly weapon. | a lethal dose of drugs*

> ⚠ **Deadly** is sometimes also used about illnesses (but **lethal** is not): *a deadly form of skin cancer | the deadly AIDS virus*

> **Formal or informal?**
> **Lethal** and **deadly** are used especially in formal writing and news reports.

7 to kill an animal

kill /kɪl/ [v T] *You shouldn't kill spiders just because you are scared of them. | I'm a vegetarian because I don't believe in killing animals.*

slaughter /ˈslɔːtəʳ/ [v T] to kill farm animals, either for their meat or skins, or because they are ill: *Farmers*

have been told to slaughter all flocks infected with the disease. | Hundreds of baby seals are slaughtered for their fur every year.*

have sth put down /ˌhæv (sth) pʊt ˈdaʊn/ to painlessly kill an animal, especially a pet, because it is very old, very ill, or badly injured: *Our cat was hit by a car, so we had to have her put down.*

KIND

➡ if you mean a kind of person or thing, go to **TYPE**
➡ opposite **UNKIND**

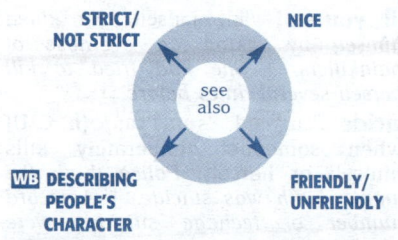

WB DESCRIBING PEOPLE'S CHARACTER

1 kind

kind /kaɪnd/ [adj] someone who is **kind** tries to help people and make them happy or comfortable, and shows that they care about them: *The nurses were all very kind. | Luckily a kind man helped me with my bags. | It was a very kind thing to do.*

+to *The people I lived with in France were really kind to me.*

it is kind of sb (to do sth) *Wasn't it kind of Ross to lend us his car?*

> ⚠ Don't say 'they were kind with me' or 'they were kind for me'. Say **they were kind to me**.

kindness /ˈkaɪndnᵻs/ [n U] kind behaviour: *I'd like to thank you for all your kindness.*

considerate /kənˈsɪdərᵻt/ [adj] someone who is **considerate** thinks about other people's feelings, and is careful not to make them unhappy or cause problems for them: *Louis was always considerate and sympathetic to others.*

it is considerate of sb (to do sth) *My boss gave me some time off when my mother died, which was very considerate of him.*

> ⚠ You often use **considerate** when complaining that someone is not considerate enough and should care more about other people's feelings: *I wish he would try and be a little more considerate.*

generous /'dʒenərəs/ [adj] someone who is **generous** often gives other people money or presents: *My sister's really generous. She's always buying things for the children.*
it is generous of sb (to do sth) *My dad offered to pay my plane fare, which was very generous of him.*
generosity /ˌdʒenə'rɒsɪtɪ‖-'rɑː-/ [n U] generous behaviour: *The Prince is famous for his generosity to his friends.*
generously [adv] *These children need your help. Please give generously.*
○ **it's nice of sb (to do sth)** /ɪts 'naɪs əv (sb)(to do sth)/ SPOKEN say this when someone has helped you or pleased you by doing something kind: *It was nice of her to let you use her car.* | *"I've brought that book you wanted." "Oh, thanks – that's really nice of you."*

2 **kind to people who have problems and difficulties**

sympathetic /ˌsɪmpə'θetɪk◂/ [adj] if someone is **sympathetic** to you when you are having problems, they say kind things to you and show that they feel sad about your situation: *Everybody was very sympathetic when they heard I'd failed my test.* | *She gave him a sympathetic look.*
sympathetically [adv] *He listened sympathetically to her story.*
understanding /ˌʌndər'stændɪŋ/ [adj] an **understanding** person is kind and patient when someone has a problem, and does not get angry with them or criticize them: *I've missed a lot of work through illness – fortunately I have a very understanding boss.*
+about *Thank you for being so understanding about all this.*
good /gʊd/ [adj not before noun] if someone is **good** to you, they help you and give you what you need,

especially when you are having problems
+to *My parents have been very good to me since I lost my job.*
it is good of sb (to do sth) *It was good of you to come and see me.*

3 **to treat someone too kindly**

spoil /spɔɪl/ [v T] to treat a child too kindly and give them everything they want, often with the result that they behave badly: *Because he was their only son, his parents spoiled him.*
spoiling – spoiled (also **spoilt** BRITISH) – **have spoiled** (also **have spoilt** BRITISH)

KNOW/NOT KNOW

➡ look here for ...
 • know a fact
 • know a person

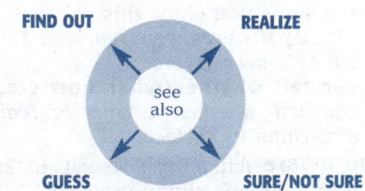

FIND OUT   REALIZE
see also
GUESS   SURE/NOT SURE

1 **to know a fact or piece of information**

know /nəʊ/ [v I/T] *This is a famous painting – do you know the name of the artist?* | *Jack's leaving. Didn't you know?* | *The instructions should tell you everything you need to know.*
+(that) *I knew he was ill, but I didn't realize he had cancer.*
know how/what/where etc *Do you know where Andy is?*
+about *We've known about the problem for some time.*
know of sth (=know that something exists) *I know of one company where members of staff get their meals free.*
know a lot about sth *Keith knows a lot about computers.*
knowing – knew – have known

K

> ⚠ Don't say 'I am knowing', 'she was knowing' etc. Say **I know**, **she knew** etc.

realize (also **realise** BRITISH) /'rɪəlaɪz/ [v I/T] to know that a situation exists, and especially to know how important or serious it is: *None of us realized the danger we were in.* | *"The reason that she hasn't been in school is that she's pregnant." "Oh, really? I didn't realize."*
+(that) *I realize that you are very busy, but could I talk to you for a few minutes?*
realize how/what/why *Do you think he realizes how much trouble he has caused?*

> ⚠ Don't say 'I am realizing', 'she was realizing' etc. Say **I realize**, **she realized** etc.

can tell /kən 'tel/ to know that something is true because you can see signs that show this
+(that) *His eyes were red, and I could tell he'd been crying.*
can tell whether/what/how etc *You can tell whether a coin is real by scratching its surface.*
be aware /biː ə'weəʳ/ FORMAL to know that a serious situation exists
+of *We are aware of the problems faced by homeless people and are trying to deal with them.*
+that *The question is, was the Chief of Police aware that so much corruption existed within the police department?*

2 someone who knows a lot about something

expert /'ekspɜːʳt/ [n C] someone who knows a lot about a subject: *Our team of experts includes psychiatrists, psychologists and social workers.*
+in/on *an expert in French history*
medical/legal/financial etc expert *Get advice from a financial expert first.*

> ⚠ You can also use **expert** before a noun, like an adjective: *expert advice* (=advice from an expert) | *expert opinions*

specialist /'speʃəlɪst/ [n C] someone who has studied a very specific subject for a long time and knows much more about it than other people: *You really need a specialist for this job.*
+in *Professor Williams teaches English Literature and is a specialist in the novels of George Orwell.*
computer/marketing/engine etc specialist *The Health Department is seeing the advice of a team of tropical disease specialists.*

knowledgeable /'nɒlɪdʒəbəl‖'nɑː-/ [adj] someone who is **knowledgeable** knows a lot of different facts, especially about a particular subject or activity: *Talk to Mr Carew – he's knowledgeable and extremely helpful.*
+about *He's very knowledgeable about garden plants.*

3 when most people know something

🔾 **everyone knows** /,evriwʌn 'nəʊz/ ESPECIALLY SPOKEN say this when you think most people know something and you would be surprised if someone did not know it: *Haven't you heard Anja's pregnant? I thought everyone knew.*
+(that) *Everyone knows Andy and Lynn are having an affair.*
everyone knows how/what/why etc *Surely everyone knows how to change a light bulb!*

well known /,wel 'nəʊn/ [adj] use this about facts and ideas that most people know about: *The Party's views on Europe are well known.*
it is well known that *It is well known that people who smoke are more likely to get lung diseases.*

> ⚠ **Well known** is spelled with a hyphen when it comes before a noun: *It is a well-known fact that most violent crimes are committed by men.*

4 facts and information that you know

knowledge /'nɒlɪdʒ‖'nɑː-/ [n singular/ U] facts and information that you

know: *He doesn't have the skills or knowledge needed to do the job.*
+of *Paula has a good knowledge of Japanese.* | *He had acquired some knowledge of this topic.*
scientific/medical/technical knowledge *the growth of scientific knowledge*

> ⚠ **Knowledge** is most commonly used as an uncountable noun but it can be used as a singular noun when it is followed by 'of'.

> ⚠ Don't use **knowledge** in expressions like 'get more knowledge' or 'increase my knowledge'. It is better to use words like **learn** and **find out**: *I'd like to learn/find out more about using the Internet.*

5 to know a person

know /nəʊ/ [v T] if you **know** someone, you have met them before and you know things about them, such as where they live or what their job is: *Yes, I know Clive. I used to work with him.* | *Do you know anyone who could babysit tonight?*
know sb well *I know Paul very well – we were at college together.*
knowing – knew – have known

> ⚠ Don't say 'I am knowing', 'she was knowing' etc. Say **I know**, **she knew** etc.

get to know /ˌget tə ˈnəʊ/ to start to have a friendly relationship with someone by spending time with them and talking to them: *When you move to a new place, it can take a long time to get to know people.* | *I got to know Jenny when we worked together at IBM.*

Formal or informal?
Don't use **get to know** in formal writing.

acquaintance /əˈkweɪntəns/ [n C] someone you know, although you do not know them well, and they are not one of your friends: *She is just a casual acquaintance of my mother's really – I've only met her a couple of times.*

Formal or informal?
Acquaintance is not used in informal conversation.

6 to know a book, place, piece of music etc

know /nəʊ/ [v T] if you **know** a place, you have been there before and spent time there; if you **know** a book, song, film etc you have read it, heard it, or seen it before: *"Do you know Boston at all?" "Yes, I went to college there."* | *I didn't know any of the songs they were singing.* | *Do you know that Hitchcock movie about a man who is being chased? What's it called?*
know sth by heart (=know every word of a song, poem etc) *I've heard that poem so often that I know it by heart.*
know somewhere like the back of your hand INFORMAL (=know a place very well) *Tony had spent a lot of time in Tokyo and knew the place like the back of his hand.*
knowing – knew – have known

> ⚠ Don't say 'I am knowing', 'she was knowing' etc. Say **I know**, **she knew** etc.

be familiar with sth /biː fəˈmɪliəʳ wɪð (sth)/ FORMAL to know something well because you have seen it, read it, or used it before: *Anyone applying for the job should be familiar with using a spreadsheet.* | *Are you familiar with the works of George Eliot?*

7 when you have seen someone or something before

recognize (also **recognise** BRITISH) /ˈrekəgnaɪz, ˈrekən-/ [v T] to know who someone is or what something is, because you have seen them before: *I didn't recognize him when he shaved his beard off.* | *Do you recognize this picture?*

> ⚠ Don't say 'I am recognizing', 'she was recognizing' etc. Say **I recognize**, **she recognized** etc.

know /nəʊ/ [v T] to recognize someone or something, especially when you have not seen them for a long time: *You'll know him when you see him. He hasn't changed at all.* | *The town has changed so much, I hardly know it any more.*

know sb by sight (=be able to recognize someone although, you do not know their name) *I've never spoken to her, but I know her by sight.*

knowing – knew – have known

> ⚠ Don't say 'I am knowing', 'she was knowing' etc. Say **I know, she knew** etc.

familiar /fə'mɪliəʳ/ [adj] someone or something that is **familiar** is easy to recognize because you have heard or seen them many times before: *a familiar tune* | *It was good to see all the old familiar faces again.*

look/sound familiar *The voice on the phone sounded familiar.*

8   to not know something or someone

not know /nɒt 'nəʊ/ *"What time's the meeting?" "Sorry, I don't know."* | *I've met Tom a few times, but I don't know his sister.*

not know how/what/why etc *I don't know why they're so angry.*

unfamiliar/not familiar /,ʌnfə'mɪliəʳ◂, nɒt fə'mɪliəʳ/ [adj] ESPECIALLY WRITTEN if something is **unfamiliar** or **not familiar**, you have not seen it, heard it, or experienced it before: *It took me a long time to get used to the unfamiliar surroundings.*

+to *He was speaking a language that was not familiar to me.*

be unaware/not be aware /biː ,ʌnə'weəʳ, nɒt biː ə'weəʳ/ FORMAL to not know about a situation or about something that is happening, especially when you should know about it

+of *She was not aware of the man who had come quietly into the room.* | *The child was clearly unaware of the danger.*

+that *His parents weren't aware that he smoked.*

ignorant /'ɪgnərənt/ [adj] someone who is **ignorant** does not know facts or information that they should know

ignorant of sth (=not knowing about a fact or situation) *She remained ignorant of the real truth about her parents.*

ignorant about sth (=not knowing about a subject) *I'm very ignorant about politics.*

ignorance /'ɪgnərəns/ [n U] when someone does not know facts or information that they should know: *a mistake that was the result of their ignorance*

+of *He showed complete ignorance of the most basic historical facts.*

9   what you say when you do not know the answer to a question

◯ **I don't know** /aɪ ,dəʊnt 'nəʊ/ SPOKEN say this when you do not know the answer to a question: *"What time is it?" "I don't know. I don't have a watch."*

◯ **I have no idea** /aɪ hæv ,nəʊ aɪ'dɪə/ SPOKEN say this when you do not know the answer to a question, and cannot even guess the answer: *"How long will it take to get there?" "I've no idea."*

◯ **who knows** /,huː 'nəʊz/ SPOKEN say this when you think it is impossible for anyone to know the answer to a question: *The world might end tomorrow. Who knows?*

who knows what/when etc *Who knows what could happen in the future?*

◯ **don't ask me/how should I know** /,dəʊnt ɑːsk 'miː, ,haʊ ʃʊd 'aɪ nəʊ‖-æsk-/ SPOKEN INFORMAL say this when it is impossible for you to know the answer to a question, and you are annoyed or surprised that someone has asked you: *"Why's Sharon in such a bad mood?" "How should I know, she never tells me anything."* | *"How do these modem things actually work?" "Don't ask me!"*

L, l

LAND AND SEA

➡ if you mean 'an area of land with its own government, eg Japan, Germany', go to **COUNTRY**

➡ if you mean 'land where there are trees and fields and not many buildings', go to **COUNTRYSIDE**

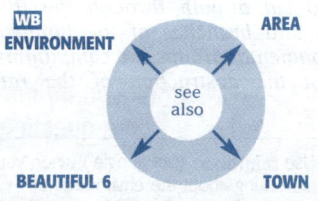

WB
ENVIRONMENT　　　　**AREA**

see also

BEAUTIFUL 6　　　　**TOWN**

1 land that is owned by someone or is used for something

land /lænd/ [n U] land that is owned by someone or that can be used for farming or building houses: *They moved to the country and bought some land.* | *There was some empty land behind the office which had been turned into a parking lot.*
piece of land *Each family was given a small piece of land where they could grow food for themselves.*
farm land/ building land (=land that can be used for farming, or for building houses, offices etc)
agricultural/arable land (=land that is used for farming, especially growing crops)
private land/sb's land (=land owned by someone) *Get off my land.*

territory /'terɪtəriǁ-tɔːri/ [n U] land that belongs to a country or that is controlled by a country during a war: *Miller had accidentally crossed into Iraqi territory and was arrested for spying.*
enemy territory (=land controlled by an enemy) *His plane was shot down over enemy territory.*

field /fiːld/ [n C] an area of land that is part of a farm, or that is used for playing sports: *cows grazing in the fields* | *a football field*
+of *a field of wheat*
playing field BRITISH (=a field where sports are played) *We went out onto the school playing fields to watch a game of football.*

the grounds /ðə 'graundz/ [n plural] the gardens and land around a big building such as a castle, school, or hospital: *Have you ever been to Penryn Castle? The grounds are beautiful.*
the palace/school/hospital grounds *The nurse said I could go for a short walk around the hospital grounds.*

2 what you see in an area of land

landscape /'lændskeɪp/ [n C usually singular] the land that you see all around you, in the countryside or in the city, with its hills, fields, buildings etc: *the beauty of the New England landscape in the fall*
rural/industrial/urban landscape *Brad's apartment looked out on the industrial landscape of Detroit.*

scenery /'siːnəri/ [n U] all the mountains, rivers, forests etc that you see around you, especially when these are beautiful: *a peaceful Alpine village surrounded by magnificent scenery*

3 the substance that forms the surface of the land

the ground /ðə 'graund/ [n singular] the surface of the land: *The ground was covered in snow.* | *There was a big hole in the ground.*

> ⚠ Don't confuse **the ground** (=the surface of the land, outside a building) and **the floor** (=the surface you walk on inside a building): *The kitchen floor needs sweeping.* | *I sat down on the ground under a tree.*

earth /ɜːʳθ/ [n U] the substance that the ground is made of: *Thousands of tons of earth were moved to build the dam.* | *Outside, the sun beat down on the red baked earth of Provence.*

soil /sɔɪl/ [n U] the earth that plants grow in: *Roses grow best in a well-drained, slightly acid soil.*

L

fertile soil (=soil that plants grow well in) *The fertile soil of southern Italy is perfect for growing grapes and olives.*

dirt /dɜːʳt/ [n U] ESPECIALLY AMERICAN loose dry earth: *The kids were playing in the yard, digging in the dirt.*

4   the land, compared with the sea or the air

land /lænd/ [n U] the land, not the sea: *After sailing across the ocean for 21 days we sighted land.* | *pollution of the sea and the land*
on land *The sea turtle lays its eggs on land.*

the ground /ðə ˈɡraʊnd/ [n singular] the land, not the air – use this to talk about planes: *Our plane was flying only 100 feet above the ground.* | *Spectators watched in horror as the aircraft plunged to the ground.*

5   hills and mountains

mountain /ˈmaʊntn̩/ [n C] a very high piece of land with steep sides: *the Rocky Mountains* | *One day she wants to climb Mount Everest, the highest mountain in the world.*

hill /hɪl/ [n C] an area of land that is higher than the land around it, like a mountain but smaller: *A rough track led over the hill to the village.*

valley /ˈvæli/ [n C] an area of low land between two hills or mountains, often with a river flowing through it: *the Welsh valleys* | *Carrie turned off the main road into a narrow valley.*

6   flat land

plain /pleɪn/ [n C] a large area of flat land: *the vast plains of central China*

7   land covered with trees

forest /ˈfɒrɪst‖ˈfɔː-, ˈfɑː-/ [n C/U] a large area of land that is covered with trees: *the thick forests of central Europe* | *Five hundred years ago, most of England was covered in forest.*

wood /wʊd/ [n C] an area of land with a lot of trees growing close together,

like a forest but smaller: *There was a little wood at the bottom of the valley.*

> You can also use **the woods** to mean an area covered with trees: *a walk through the woods* | *a story about two children who got lost in the woods.* In American English, the plural is generally used, rather than 'a wood'.

rainforest/jungle /ˈreɪnˌfɒrɪst, ˈdʒʌŋɡəl‖-ˌfɔː-, -ˌfɑː-/ [n C/U] a tropical forest with many large plants and tall trees growing close together, in an area where there is a lot of rain: *They had to cut a path through the thick leaves and branches of the jungle.* | *Environmental groups are campaigning against the destruction of the rainforest.*

> Use **rainforest** (not 'jungle') when you are talking about the environment.

8   dry land

desert /ˈdezəʳt/ [n C/U] a large area of land in a hot place, where there is very little rain and very few plants or trees: *the Sahara Desert* | *Mauritania is a poor country and most of it is desert.*

9   rivers

river /ˈrɪvəʳ/ [n C] a natural and continuous flow of water in a long line across land and into the sea: *the River Danube* | *Let's go for a swim in the river.*

stream /striːm/ [n C] a small river that is only one or two metres wide: *a mountain stream* | *We passed a couple of boys who were fishing in the stream.*

10   areas of water surrounded by land

lake /leɪk/ [n C] a large area of water surrounded by land: *There's a little island in the middle of the lake.* | *Lake Ontario*

pond /pɒnd‖pɑːnd/ [n C] a small area of water, especially one that has been made in a garden, park, or field: *The children were standing by the pond, feeding the ducks.*

pool /puːl/ [n C] a small area of water that is not moving, for example at the edge of the sea or forming part of a river: *The children hunted for crabs in the pools between the rocks.*

11 areas of land with water around them

island /ˈaɪlənd/ [n C] a piece of land completely surrounded by water: *a small island in the middle of the lake | the Hawaiian Islands | the island of Cyprus*
desert island (=a small tropical island far from other places with no-one living on it)

peninsula /pəˈnɪnsjᵿlə‖-sələ/ [n C] a long piece of land almost completely surrounded by water but joined to the rest of the land in one place: *a rocky peninsula jutting out into the Atlantic Ocean | a city near the southern tip of the Malay Peninsula*

12 the sea

the sea ESPECIALLY BRITISH **the ocean** ESPECIALLY AMERICAN /ðə ˈsiː, ði ˈəʊʃən/ [n singular] the large area of salty water that covers most of the Earth's surface: *Do you like swimming in the sea? | She sat on the beach, gazing out at the ocean. | The sea was calm and there was a gentle breeze.*

> ⚠ **The sea** is the word usually used in British English, and **the ocean** is the usual word in American English.

> ⚠ **Sea** and **ocean** are also used in the names of large areas of water. An **ocean** is one of the five very large areas of water in the world: *the Pacific Ocean | the Indian Ocean.* A **sea** is a smaller area of water which is either part of an ocean or has land all around it: *the South China Sea | the Caspian Sea.*

> ⚠ You can also use **sea** before a noun, like an adjective, in both British and American English: *sea water | sea creatures*

at sea /ət ˈsiː/ travelling on the sea far away from land: *We had been at sea for two weeks when there was a terrible storm.*

marine /məˈriːn/ [adj only before noun] **marine** plants and animals live in the sea: *She studies jellyfish and other marine life. | marine biology*

> **Formal or informal?**
> **Marine** is a formal and technical word.

13 where the sea and land meet

the coast /ðə ˈkəʊst/ [n singular] the part of a country that is close to the sea – use this when you are talking about a country or a large part of a country: *driving along the Californian coast, from San Francisco to LA*
+of *The ship slowly made its way along the west coast of Africa.*
on the coast (=on land that is close to the sea) *a little house on the coast of Brittany*
off the coast (=in the sea but close to the land) *They discovered oil off the northern coast of Scotland.*

the shore /ðə ʃɔːʳ/ [n singular] the land along the edge of the sea or along the edge of a lake: *We could see a boat about a mile from the shore.*
the shore of/the shores of *a small town on the shores of Lake Ontario*

> ⚠ You can say either **the shore of** or **the shores of**, and it means the same thing.

beach /biːtʃ/ [n C] an area of sand at the edge of the sea – use this especially to talk about a place where you go to relax and enjoy yourself: *The area has miles of unspoiled sandy beaches.*
the beach *By nine o'clock the beach was already crowded with people. | Let's go to the beach tomorrow.*

L

⚠️ You can also use **beach** before a noun, like an adjective: *a beach party* | *a beach ball*

the seaside /ðə ˈsiːsaɪd/ [*n* singular] BRITISH a place at the edge of the sea – use this especially to talk about somewhere where you go for a holiday or to enjoy yourself: *When I was little we used to go to the seaside most weekends.*

⚠️ You can also use **seaside** before a noun, like an adjective: *a seaside holiday* (=at the seaside) | *a seaside town*

by the sea /baɪ ðə ˈsiː/ on land next to the sea: *We bought a small cottage by the sea.* | *walking by the sea in the early morning*

coastline /ˈkəʊstlaɪn/ [*n* C usually singular] the land along the edge of the sea – use this especially to talk about a long length of land or the way it looks: *California's rugged coastline* | *the sandy hills along the coastline*
stretch of coastline (=long area of land) *a beautiful stretch of coastline*

14 the study of countries, rivers, oceans etc

geography /dʒiˈɒɡrəfiǁ-ˈaːɡ-/ [*n* U] the study of countries, rivers, oceans, towns etc: *She teaches geography in the high school.* | *I have to draw a map of India for my geography homework.*

LANGUAGE

➡ see also **WORD/PHRASE/SENTENCE**

1 the language used by a particular group of people

language /ˈlæŋgwɪdʒ/ [*n* C] a system of words, phrases, and grammar that is used by the people who live in a particular country for speaking and writing to each other
speak a language *"What language do they speak in Brazil?" "Portuguese."* |

She can speak four different languages – French, German, English, and Dutch.
foreign language *Children learn two foreign languages in school.*
the official language (=the language used by the government) *English is the official language here, but people also speak French and Creole.*
speak the language (=be able to speak the language of the country you are in) *It's difficult living in a country where you don't speak the language.*

⚠️ Don't say 'I'm learning the Japanese language', 'Do you speak Italian language?' etc. Say **I'm learning Japanese, Do you speak Italian?** etc.

⚠️ You can also use **language** before a noun, like an adjective: *language teaching* | *language classes*

dialect /ˈdaɪəlekt/ [*n* C] a form of a language that is spoken by the people who live in one area of a country, which is different in some ways from the standard form of the language: *The people in this part of Germany speak a dialect called 'Plattdeutsch'.* | *In some northern English dialects, people say 'nowt' instead of 'nothing'.*

slang /slæŋ/ [*n* U] very informal words used by young people or by specific groups of people, for example soldiers, prisoners, or people who take drugs: *I was totally confused by the slang that the other kids spoke.*

jargon /ˈdʒaːɡənǁ-gɑːn/ [*n* U] words used by people who do a particular job or who are interested in a particular subject, which are difficult for ordinary people to understand – use this especially when you dislike these words: *When you first learn about computers, there is a whole lot of jargon to understand.*
management / legal / medical / computer jargon *I hate all this management jargon about 'upskilling' and 'downsizing'.*

2 to change something from one language into another

translate /trænsˈleɪt, trænz-/ [*v* I/T] to change what someone has said or written from one language into another: *She has translated a number of his books.* | *Patrice doesn't speak English, so I'll have to translate.*

translate sth into Spanish/ Japanese/English *Can you translate this letter into French?*

translate from English into Japanese/from Spanish into German etc *In the second exam we have to translate from Italian into English.*

interpret /ɪnˈtɜːrprɪt/ [v I] to translate what someone is saying immediately after they say it, so that people who speak different languages can talk to each other: *No-one in the tour group spoke Spanish, so we had to ask the guide to interpret.*

+for *My boss doesn't speak any Japanese, but I interpret for her.*

translation /trænsˈleɪʃən, trænz-/ [n C/U] a piece of writing or speech that has been changed from one language into another: *I have only read the English translation of the book, not the Japanese original.*

do a translation (=translate something, especially as part of a language learning course) *I have to do a translation for homework.*

in translation (=translated into a different language) *All of Brecht's plays are available in translation.*

3 someone who translates from one language into another

translator /trænsˈleɪtər, trænz-/ [n C] someone whose job is to translate what people say or write from one language into another: *She works as a translator in Geneva.*

interpreter /ɪnˈtɜːrprɪtər/ [n C] someone whose job is to translate what has just been said, so that people who speak different languages can talk to each other: *Both Presidents were accompanied by their interpreters.*

through an interpreter (=using an interpreter) *Speaking through an interpreter, he said: "I'm afraid to go back to my own country."*

4 the language that you learn first

sb's first language /(sb's) ˌfɜːrst ˈlæŋgwɪdʒ/ the first language that you

learn as a child – use this when you are comparing someone's first language with other languages that they learn at school or later: *My first language is Dutch.*

sb's mother tongue /(sb's) ˈmʌðər ˌtʌŋ/ the first language that you learn as a child – use this especially to talk about someone who now lives in a country where a different language is spoken: *classes for students whose mother tongue is not English*

native speaker /ˌneɪtɪv ˈspiːkər/ [n C] a **native speaker** of a language is someone who was born in the country where that language is spoken: *The book is aimed at learners of English, rather than native speakers.*

5 someone who can speak more than one language

bilingual /baɪˈlɪŋgwəl/ [adj] someone who is **bilingual** can speak two languages perfectly: *Omar is bilingual in Arabic and French.*

sb's second language /(sb's) ˌsekənd ˈlæŋgwɪdʒ/ [n C] your **second language** is a language that you speak well and often use, but not the first language that you learned as a child: *Halima was born in Kenya. Her first language is Swahili, and her second language is English.*

6 the use of words to communicate

language /ˈlæŋgwɪdʒ/ [n U] the use of words, grammar etc to communicate with other people: *a fascinating study of the origins of language* | *Every child develops the natural ability to use language.*

linguistic /lɪŋˈgwɪstɪk/ [adj usually before noun] connected with people's use of language

linguistic ability/skills/studies/ development *a child's linguistic development* | *She should be able to learn Russian fairly easily – she has plenty of linguistic ability.*

Formal or informal?
Linguistic is a formal or technical word.

LAST

➡ opposite **FIRST**
➡ see also **END, FINISH**

1 coming at the end, after all the others

last /lɑːst‖læst/ [adj] happening or coming at the end, with no others after: *What time does the last train leave?* | *Could you repeat the last number for me please?* | *That was the last time I ever saw her.* (=I never saw her again) | *the last game of the football season*
the last *That lecture was the last in a series.*
the last but one (=the person or thing before the last one) *Ours was the last car but one to leave the ferry.*
last [adv] *I expect they'll interview me last because my name begins with Y.*
come last/finish last/be last /ˌkʌm ˈlɑːst, ˌfɪnɪʃ ˈlɑːst, biː ˈlɑːst‖-ˈlæst/ to finish a race or competition in the last position: *Our team came last in the gymnastics competition.* | *I don't expect to win the race, but I don't want to be last.*
final /ˈfaɪnl/ [adj only before noun] last in a series of actions, events, or parts of a story: *the final chapter of the book* | *Could I mention just one final point?*
final days/years/moments *Rooney scored the winning goal in the final moments of the game.*
final stage (=the last part of a process or activity) *The final stages of the climb were particularly tiring.*

2 when something is the last thing you want to mention

finally /ˈfaɪnəl-i/ [adv] use this when something is the last thing you want to say, especially at the end of a long speech or piece of writing: *Finally, I'd like to thank all those people who helped make the conference such a success.*

lastly /ˈlɑːstli‖ˈlæst-/ [adv] use this to say that something is the last of a list of things, or when something is the last thing you want to say: *Firstly it's too big, secondly we can't afford it, and lastly we don't really need it.* | *Lastly, I want to ask all of you to keep this information secret.*

last but not least /ˌlɑːst bət nɒt ˈliːstl‖ˌlæst-/ use this when you are mentioning the last person or thing in a list, to emphasize that they are just as important as all the others: *Last but not least, let me introduce Jane, our new accountant.*

3 most recent

last /lɑːst‖læst/ [determiner/adj only before noun] *We discussed this problem at the last meeting.*
last night/week/year/Monday etc (=the one that has just past) *Did you watch the game on TV last night?* | *We still haven't paid last month's rent.* | *Paul arrived back in England last Saturday.*
(the) last time (=the most recent occasion) *Last time I spoke to Bob he seemed happy and cheerful.* | *Do you remember the last time we came here?*
the last 10 minutes/20 years etc (=the period up to now) *Things have changed a lot in the last ten years.*
sb's last job/address/girlfriend etc (=the one they had just before this one) *Our last apartment was much smaller than this one.*
last [adv usually before verb] most recently: *When I last saw her, she was going out with an Italian student called Giovanni.*
past /pɑːst‖pæst/ [adj only before noun] use this about the period of time up until now
the past year/few days/24 hours etc *During the past year there have been eleven accidents on this stretch of road.*
previous /ˈpriːviəs/ [adj only before noun] the **previous** time, event, or thing is the one before the one you have just mentioned: *The company made more profit in the first six months of this year than it did in the whole of the previous year.*
sb's previous job/address/visit etc (=the one they had or did before the

one you have just mentioned) *She said she had left her previous job because she was unhappy.*

the day/week/year before /ðə(day, etc) bɪˈfɔːʳ/ the day, week, or year in the past before the one you have just mentioned: *Last week he was in Paris and the week before he was in Rome.*

LATE/NOT LATE

➡ look here for ...
  • arriving or happening late
  • late at night
➡ see also **EARLY**

1 arriving late

late /leɪt/ [adj/adv] arriving after the time that was arranged or after the time when you should arrive: *Cathy got there even later than I did.*
+for *She often arrives late for work.*
be late *Sorry I'm late – my car broke down.*
5 minutes/2 days/3 weeks etc late *As usual, the bus was half an hour late.*
too late *She had lost a lot of blood and, by the time the doctor arrived, it was too late.*
late arrival/departure *We apologize for the late arrival of Flight AZ709.*

not on time /nɒt ɒn ˈtaɪm/ later than the time that was arranged: *Hurry up, or you won't get to school on time! | The train is never on time.*

miss /mɪs/ [v T] to arrive too late to see an event, film etc, or too late to get on a plane, train etc: *If we don't leave soon, we'll miss the start of the show.*
miss the flight/train/bus/ferry *I missed the bus and had to wait half an hour for the next one.*

2 what you say when someone arrives late

○ **where have you been?** /ˌweəʳ həv juː ˈbiːnǁ-ˈbɪn/ SPOKEN say this when someone arrives late and you want to know why, because you are worried or annoyed: *Where have you been? You said three o'clock!*

○ **what kept you?** /wɒt ˈkept juː/ SPOKEN say this when someone arrives

late and you are annoyed: *It's nearly five already! What kept you?*

○ **about time too** /əˌbaʊt ˌtaɪm ˈtuː/ SPOKEN INFORMAL say this when someone or something arrives late, and you are annoyed because you have been waiting a long time: *"Look, the bus is coming." "And about time too!"*

3 to make someone arrive late

make sb late /ˌmeɪk (sb) ˈleɪt/ to make someone arrive somewhere later than they should arrive
+for *I don't want to make you late for work. | The car broke down again, which made her late for her meeting.*

be delayed /biː dɪˈleɪd/ if you **are delayed** by something, something unexpected happens and it makes you late
+by *Our plane was delayed by fog.*
get delayed *There was an accident on the freeway and we got delayed.*

hold up /ˌhəʊld ˈʌp/ [phrasal verb T] to make someone stop or go more slowly when they are going somewhere
hold sb up *I won't hold you up – I can see you're in a hurry.*
be/get held up by sth *On her way to the hospital she got held up by heavy traffic.*

4 when something happens later than it should or later than usual

late /leɪt/ [adv/adj] happening or done after the normal or usual time: *The library stays open late on Fridays.*
be late *The harvest was late this year because of the bad weather.*
15 minutes/3 days/6 months etc late *Tony handed in his homework a day late. | Hurry up! We're already half an hour late.*
too late *He tried to warn them of the danger, but it was too late – they had already left.*
work late (=stay at work till later than usual) *I'm afraid I'll have to work late again tomorrow.*
get up late (=get out of bed late in

the morning) *It's really nice to get up late on Saturday mornings.*

a late breakfast/lunch etc (=later than usual)

overdue /ˌəʊvəˈdjuː◂ ‖-ˈduː◂/ [adj] use this about payments that are late or library books that you give back later than you should: *I must take these books back to the library – they're overdue.*

three weeks/two months etc overdue *The rent's three weeks overdue.*

be behind with sth /bɪ bɪˈhaɪnd wɪð (sth)/ if you **are behind** with your work, you have done less of it than you should have done: *I have got to stay late tonight – I'm a little behind with my work.*

5 to make something happen later or more slowly

be delayed /bɪ dɪˈleɪd/ if an event **is delayed**, there is a problem that makes it happen later than it should, or take longer than it should: *President Chirac's visit had to be delayed because of security problems.*

be delayed for 5 hours/2 months etc *The opening of the new bridge may be delayed for several months.*

+by *The start of the game was delayed by bad weather.*

hold up /ˌhəʊld ˈʌp/ [phrasal verb T] to make something happen late, or make it happen more slowly than it should

hold up sth *Protesters held up work on the new road.*

be held up by sth *The peace talks are being held up by continued fighting on the border.*

hold sb up *They should have finished that job on Friday – what's holding them up?*

6 something that makes you late

delay /dɪˈleɪ/ [n C] a situation in which you get delayed, or the length of time that you are delayed: *There were the usual delays at the border, but otherwise we had a good journey.*

long/short etc delay *The strike is causing long delays at airports.* | *There*

will be a slight delay before passengers are allowed to board the plane.

delay in doing sth *There have been a lot of complaints about delays in issuing passports.*

hold-up /ˈhəʊld ʌp/ [n C] a delay that is unexpected but not very serious: *traffic hold-ups* | *There's been a hold-up with the builders, so the new office won't be ready until next month.*

> **Formal or informal?**
> **Hold-up** is more informal than **delay**.

7 not late

on time /ɒn ˈtaɪm/ at the time that was expected or planned: *The work must be completed on time.*

be on time (=arrive at the expected time) *Fortunately the train was on time.*

punctual /ˈpʌŋktʃuəl/ [adj] someone who is **punctual** is never late or not usually late: *I'm worried. Pat's not here yet, and she's usually so punctual.*

8 late at night

late /leɪt/ [adj/adv] *I must go home now, it's getting late.* | *I don't like coming home late to an empty house.*

stay up late (=not go to bed until late) *We usually let the children stay up late on Saturday evenings.*

have a late night (=when you go to bed very late) *I'm really tired today – I had a late night last night.*

in the middle of the night /ɪn ðə ˌmɪdl əv ðə ˈnaɪt/ late at night when most people are asleep: *I woke up in the middle of the night.*

When you see **EC**, go to the **ESSENTIAL COMMUNICATION** section.

LATER/ AT A LATER TIME

➡ if you mean 'see you later', go to **EC** **SAYING GOODBYE**
➡ see also **AFTER**

1 at a later time

later /'leɪtəʳ/ [adv] not now, or not at the time you are talking about, but some time after this: *Sorry, I'm busy right now – I'll speak to you later.* | *We heard later that he had gone back to Japan.*
a month/two weeks/three years etc later *She became ill in 1993, and died two years later.*
much later (=a long time later) *I didn't find out the truth until much later.*
later that day/month/year etc *Later that afternoon, Anna called by to see me.*
later in the day/month/year etc *I spoke to him again later in the afternoon.*
later [adj only before noun] *The meat can be frozen and used at a later date.* | *In a later speech, the Prime Minister admitted he had been wrong.*

later on /ˌleɪtər 'ɒn/ at a later time during the same period, day, week etc: *The weather was fine at first, but later on it started to rain.* | *Later on, I'll be interviewing the Vice-President, but first here is a summary of the news.*

in /ɪn/ [preposition] use this to say how far ahead in the future something will happen
in a minute/24 hours/a week etc *I'll be back in a couple of days.* | *The doctor would like to see you again in two weeks.*
in an hour's time/a few minutes' time etc *Just think, in a few hours' time we'll be in Seattle.*

from now /frəm 'naʊ/
24 hours/a week/100 years etc from now at a future time 24 hours from now, a week from now etc: *Three weeks from now the exams will be over.* | *A hundred years from now there may be no rainforest left.*

after /'ɑːftəʳ‖'æf-/ [preposition] use this when talking about a particular event or situation that happened or was done in the past, to say how much later something else happened
after two days/a week/a while etc *After a while, we got tired of waiting and went home.* | *She left the hospital in January, and the doctor saw her again after two weeks.*

2 to decide to do something later

postpone /pəʊs'pəʊn/ [v T] to change the time when something was planned to happen, and arrange for it to happen later: *They decided to postpone the wedding until Pam's mother was out of the hospital.* | *Several of today's football games have been postponed because of heavy snow.*

put off /ˌpʊt 'ɒf‖-'ɔːf/ [phrasal verb T] to decide to do something later than you planned to do it, for example because there is a problem or because you do not want to do it now
put sth off *I really should go to the dentist, but I keep putting it off.*
put off sth *The concert's been put off till next week.*
put off doing sth *The committee decided to put off making a decision until the new year.*

> **Formal or informal?**
> **Put off** is more informal than **postpone**.

delay /dɪ'leɪ/ [v T] to arrange to do something later than you planned, because you are waiting for something else to happen first or you are waiting for a more suitable time: *He decided to delay his departure until after he'd seen the Director.*
delay doing sth *The police delayed making any announcement until the girl's relatives had been contacted.*

> When you see **WB**, go to the **WORD BANKS** section.

LAUGH

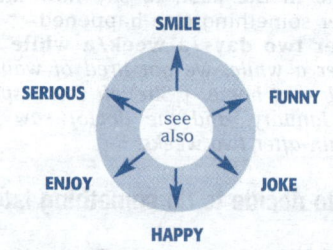

SMILE

SERIOUS ← see also → FUNNY

ENJOY ← → JOKE

HAPPY

1 to laugh because something is funny

laugh /lɑːf‖læf/ [v I] to laugh because something is funny or because you are enjoying yourself: *Jake made a funny face, and we all laughed.* | *I thought Dad would be angry, but he just laughed.*

+about *I couldn't understand what they were all laughing about.*

+at *No-one laughed at his jokes.*

burst out laughing (=suddenly laugh loudly) *We just looked at each other and burst out laughing.*

can't stop laughing (=laugh a lot because something is extremely funny) *Every time I thought about her hat, I couldn't stop laughing!*

laugh [n C] *She gave a little nervous laugh and glanced towards Robyn.*

giggle /ˈgɪgəl/ [v I] to laugh quietly in the way that children laugh, because something is funny, or because you are nervous or embarrassed: *We never learned anything in history – we just sat at the back of the class giggling.* | *Mr Brogan asked her to dance, and she blushed and giggled.*

giggle [n C] *I could hear giggles coming from my sister's bedroom.*

chuckle /ˈtʃʌkəl/ [v I] ESPECIALLY WRITTEN to laugh quietly, especially because you are thinking about something funny: *"Do you remember when Michelle fell in the river?" Morgan chuckled.* | *Simon sat reading a magazine, chuckling to himself.*

laughter /ˈlɑːftəʳ‖ˈlæf-/ [n U] the sound you make when you laugh: *We could hear laughter coming from the next room.*

roar with laughter (=laugh very loudly) *The audience roared with laughter.*

2 to laugh in a cruel or nasty way

laugh at sb /ˈlɑːf æt (sb)‖ˈlæf-/ [phrasal verb T] to laugh at someone or make unkind jokes about them, because you think they are stupid or silly: *The other children laughed at Lisa because her clothes were old-fashioned.* | *Don't laugh at me – I told you I wasn't very good at Spanish.*

snigger BRITISH **snicker** AMERICAN /ˈsnɪgəʳ, ˈsnɪkəʳ/ [v I] to laugh quietly at something that is not supposed to be funny, for example when someone is hurt or embarrassed: *As Ruth tripped and fell she could hear the boys behind her sniggering.*

+at *Some of the students starting snickering at Billy when he read out his poem.*

make fun of sb/sth /ˌmeɪk ˈfʌn ɒv (sb/sth)/ to make someone or something seem stupid by laughing at them, or by saying things that make other people laugh at them: *Stop making fun of me!* | *The other girls used to make fun of the way she spoke.*

3 to make someone laugh

make sb laugh /ˌmeɪk (sb) ˈlɑːf‖-ˈlæf/ to make someone laugh by doing or saying something funny: *Rachel used to make us all laugh by imitating the teacher.* | *Thanks for your letter. It really made me laugh.*

LAW

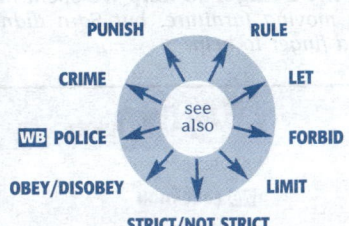

PUNISH　　　　RULE

CRIME　　　　　　　LET

WB POLICE　　see also　　FORBID

OBEY/DISOBEY　　　　LIMIT

STRICT/NOT STRICT

1 an official rule that everyone must obey

law /lɔː/ [n C] an official rule that all the citizens of a country must obey
break the law (=disobey a law) *I didn't realize I was breaking the law.*
+on *tough new laws on immigration*
+against *There is a law against cruelty to animals.*
pass a law (=make a law) *Congress passed a law that allowed women to become pilots in the Air Force.*

> ⚠ If you talk about **the law**, this often means all the laws of a country and what they say you must and must not do: *It is the job of the police to make sure that people obey the law.*

legal /'liːgəl/ [adj only before noun] connected with laws and courts: *People on a low salary can get free legal advice.*
legal battle (=a case involving a serious disagreement about something, that is judged in a court of law) *Neither side wanted a long and expensive legal battle.*
the legal profession (=use this to talk about lawyers in general) *an article in The Times criticizing the legal profession*

act /ækt/ [n C] a law made by parliament or Congress – used in the official name of a law: *the 1991 Prevention of Terrorism Act | an Act of Congress*

legislation /ˌledʒɪ'sleɪʃən/ [n U] a set of laws, especially ones that are made to control a new problem: *Parliament*

brought in legislation to ban hunting with dogs.
+on *new legislation on the sale of alcohol*

legal system /'liːgəl ˌsɪstɪm/ [n C] the laws and the way that they work in a particular country: *The Scottish legal system is different from that in England.*

2 when the law says you must do something or have the right to do it

legal /'liːgəl/ [adj only before noun] your **legal** rights, duties etc are the ones that the law says you must have: *the legal duties of parents*
legal right *Consumers have the legal right to demand their money back if a product is faulty.*
the legal owner (=the owner according to the law) *She now becomes the legal owner of the land.*

legally [adv] according to the law: *Legally, the house belongs to me. | If there is an accident, the owner of the vehicle will be legally responsible.*

by law /baɪ 'lɔː/ if something must be done **by law**, the law says that you must do it: *By law, your employer has to make sure that your working environment is safe.*

🗨 **it's the law** /ɪts ðə 'lɔː/ SPOKEN use this to tell someone that the law says that they must do something: *You have to wear a seatbelt – it's the law.*

3 allowed by law

legal /'liːgəl/ [adj] *This trade in foreign currency is perfectly legal.*
make sth legal *57% of people wanted abortion to be made legal.*
become legal *Divorce finally became legal in 1992.*
legally [adv] *Fuchs had entered the country legally on a tourist visa.*

legalize (also **legalise** BRITISH) /'liːgəlaɪz/ [T] to change the law so that something becomes legal: *a campaign to legalise cannabis*

4 not allowed by law

illegal /ɪˈliːgəl/ [adj] illegal drugs | In those days, abortion was illegal.
it is illegal to do sth It is illegal to sell tobacco to children under 16.

be against the law /biː əˌgenst ðə ˈlɔː/ if something is **against the law**, it is not allowed by law: Gambling is against the law in some countries.
it is against the law to do sth It is against the law to drive a car without insurance.
it is against the law for sb to do sth It is against the law for a teacher to hit a child.

LAZY

when someone does not like working

1 lazy

lazy /ˈleɪzi/ [adj] someone who is **lazy** does not like work or physical activity, and tries to avoid it: Marian didn't do well at school. She was intelligent, but very lazy. | Get up, you lazy thing! It's nearly lunchtime.
a lazy day/week etc (=a time when you relax and do not work hard) We spent a lazy afternoon at the beach.
lazy – lazier – laziest

○ **can't be bothered** /ˌkɑːnt biː ˈbɒðərd�‖ˌkænt biː ˈbɑː-/ BRITISH SPOKEN if you **can't be bothered** to do something, you decide not to do it because you are feeling too lazy: I was going to go shopping, but in the end I couldn't be bothered.
can't be bothered to do sth Let's go out for a meal – I can't be bothered to cook.

2 to behave in a lazy way

sit around/laze around /ˌsɪt əˈraʊnd, ˌleɪz əˈraʊnd/ [phrasal verb I] to spend time sitting and relaxing and not doing any work: We lazed around on the beach most of the day. | Why not finish your homework, instead of just sitting around doing nothing?
not lift a finger /nɒt ˌlɪft ə ˈfɪŋgər/ INFORMAL to give no help at all with work that must be done, such as cooking and cleaning: Tim doesn't lift a finger when it comes to housework.
not lift a finger to help We spent the day moving furniture, but Sara didn't lift a finger to help.

LEARN

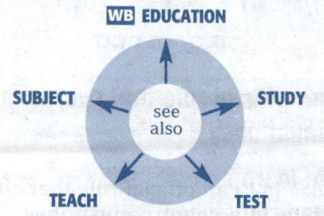

WB EDUCATION

SUBJECT — STUDY — TEACH — TEST — *see also*

1 to learn how to do something, or to learn about something

learn /lɜːʳn/ [v I/T] to learn how to do something, or to learn about a subject, especially by being taught or trained: How long have you been learning German? | Young children learn much more easily than adults.
learn to do sth His daughter's learning to drive. | William learned to read when he was four.
learn how to do sth (=learn a method or skill) On this course, you will learn how to deal with communication problems.
learning – learned (also **learnt** BRITISH) – **have learned** (also **have learnt** BRITISH)

study /ˈstʌdi/ [v I/T] to learn about a subject by reading books and going to classes at a school or university: Less than 10% of girls choose to study science at school. | She's studying music at Berkeley College in Boston.
study to be a doctor/lawyer/accountant etc He's studying to be a lawyer.
study for a test / diploma / an examination "Is Ian coming with us?" "He can't – he's studying for his exams."
studying – studied – have studied

train /treɪn/ [v I] to learn the skills and get the experience that you need in order to do a job

train to be a hairdresser/teacher/pilot/nurse *Julie is training to be a nurse.*

pick up /ˌpɪk ˈʌp/ [*phrasal verb* T] INFORMAL to learn something by watching or listening to other people, not by studying or training
pick up sth *I picked up a few words of Turkish while I was in Istanbul.*
pick sth up *The rules of the game are really easy – you'll soon pick them up.*

◯ **get the hang of sth** /ˌget ðə ˈhæŋ ɒv (sth)/ SPOKEN to learn how to do or use something that is fairly complicated: *Using the computer isn't difficult once you get the hang of it.*

2 to learn something so that you can remember it exactly

learn /lɜːʳn/ [*v* T] to learn facts, words, or numbers, especially at school, so that you can remember them exactly: *What songs have you learnt at school, then?*
learn sth by heart (=learn something so you can repeat it exactly without reading it) *We had to learn a lot of poetry by heart when we were children.*
learn your lines (=learn the words that you have to say in a play)
learning – learned (also **learnt** BRITISH) – **have learned** (also **have learnt** BRITISH)

memorize (also **memorise** BRITISH) /ˈmeməraɪz/ [*v* T] to learn numbers or words so well that you can remember them exactly: *I'm not very good at memorizing phone numbers. | I memorised the message, then destroyed it.*

3 someone who is learning something

student /ˈstjuːdənt‖ˈstuː-/ [*n* C] someone who is studying at a school, college, or university: *a student at Harvard University | There's a special price for students.*
law/medical/engineering etc student *Law students always have a lot of work to do.*
student nurse/teacher (=someone who is studying to be a nurse or a teacher)

⚠ Don't say 'a student of Oxford' or 'a student in the high school'. Say **a student at Oxford, a student at the high school** etc.

trainee /ˌtreɪˈniː◂/ [*n* C] someone who is learning a skill while working in a company or organization: *I'm a trainee in a hairdressing salon.*
trainee accountant/reporter/salesman etc *I got a job as a trainee reporter on the 'Daily Star'.*

pupil /ˈpjuːpəl/ [*n* C] ESPECIALLY BRITISH someone who is being taught at a school, especially a child: *The school has around 500 pupils between 11 and 18.*

beginner /bɪˈgɪnəʳ/ [*n* C] someone who has recently started to learn something: *Japanese classes for beginners | The tennis club welcomes beginners as well as more advanced players.*

apprentice /əˈprentɪs/ [*n* C] someone who is learning all the skills that they need in order to do a job, especially a job that they do with their hands
apprentice electrician/bricklayer/hairdresser etc *I worked as an apprentice electrician for 18 months.*

4 to learn about things by experiencing them in your life

learn /lɜːʳn/ [*v* I/T] to learn how you should behave or how to deal with situations, because of experiences you have had in your life
+(that) *I soon learned that it was best to keep quiet.*
learn to do sth *Gradually, I learned to trust her.*
learn from your mistakes (=remember mistakes you have made, and be careful not to make them again)
learn the hard way (=learn something by having an unpleasant experience) *Never lend money to your friends – that's something I learnt the hard way.*
learning – learned (also **learnt** BRITISH) – **have learned** (also **have learnt** BRITISH)

LEAST

the smallest number or amount

➡ opposite **MOST**
➡ see also **LESS**

the least /ðə 'liːst/ [quantifier] the smallest amount of something: *the engine that uses the least fuel* | *Let's buy the one that costs the least.*
the least possible *We'll try to cause the least possible disturbance.*

 Use **least** with uncountable nouns like 'money', 'food', or 'information'.

minimum /'mɪnɪ̩məm/ [adj only before noun] the **minimum** number or amount is the smallest number or amount that is possible or allowed
the minimum age/level/wage etc (=the lowest age, level, or wage that is allowed) *These workers are being paid less than the minimum wage.*
minimum [n singular]
a minimum of 20/£100/95% etc *You have to order a minimum of five CDs to get the discount.*
keep sth to a minimum (=make sure that it is as small as possible) *Costs must be kept to a minimum.*
the absolute/bare minimum (=the lowest number or amount possible) *He ate two cups of rice a day, the bare minimum needed for survival.*

the lowest /ðə 'ləʊɪ̩st/ [adj] use this about numbers, prices, wages, temperatures, or levels: *In the last election he was the candidate who got the lowest number of votes.* | *The lowest charge for a rented car is $20 a day.*
the lowest for 6 months/15 years etc *Interest rates are only 4%, the lowest for 25 years.*

the fewest /ðə 'fjuːɪ̩st/ [quantifier] the smallest number of people or things: *Drivers aged under 25 have the most accidents, those over 50 have the fewest.* | *Our team scored the fewest goals in the competition.*

 Use **fewest** with countable nouns like 'pens', 'shops', or 'students'.

LEAVE

➡ see also **RETURN, START**

1 to go away from a room or building

leave /liːv/ [v I/T not in passive] *The phone rang just as I was leaving.* | *We left before the end of the show.* | *Before you leave the house, make sure all the windows are shut.* | *The police wanted to know what time Vicky left the office.*
leaving – left – have left

 Don't say 'I left from the house'. Say **I left the house**.

go /gəʊ/ [v I] ESPECIALLY SPOKEN to leave a place to go somewhere else: *Let's go.* | *"Is Alan still here?" "No, he's just gone."*
going – went – have gone

go out /ˌgəʊ 'aʊt/ [phrasal verb I] to leave a room or building, especially when you will come back again soon: *I'm sorry, I have to go out. I won't be long.*
go out to do sth *She's just gone out to buy some cigarettes.*
+of *As he went out of the room, he slammed the door.*

go away /ˌgəʊ ə'weɪ/ [phrasal verb I] to leave your home and go to another place for a few days or weeks: *We're going away at the weekend, so could you feed the cat for us?*

walk out /ˌwɔːk 'aʊt/ [phrasal verb I] to leave angrily, for example after a quarrel: *She threw her wine in his face and then walked out.* | *Several people walked out before the end of the movie.*

slip out /ˌslɪp 'aʊt/ [phrasal verb I] to leave quietly and without anyone noticing: *No-one saw her slip out through the back door.* | *He just slipped out for a moment to speak with the principal.*

sneak out/sneak off /ˌsniːk 'aʊt, ˌsniːk 'ɒfǁ-'ɔːf/ [phrasal verb I] INFORMAL to leave secretly, taking care that no one sees you, because you should not leave: *I managed to sneak out while they were all busy talking.* | *The teacher caught Ron sneaking off early.*

sneaking – sneaked (also **snuck** AMERICAN) – have sneaked (also **have snuck** AMERICAN)

2   to leave at the start of a journey

leave /liːv/ [v I/T not in passive] to leave a place when you are going on a journey: *I'm leaving early in the morning to catch the train to Toronto.* | *When we got to Calais our boat had just left.*
leave London/New York/Singapore etc *Her plane leaves Hong Kong at 10:15.*
leave for London/Paris/Chicago etc (=in order to go to London etc) *Mr Mitchell's leaving for Paris tomorrow.*
leaving – left – have left

> Don't say 'I left from London'. Say **I left London**.

 go /gəʊ/ [v I] ESPECIALLY SPOKEN to leave at the start of a journey: *What time does the next bus go?* | *We've packed all our bags and we're ready to go.*
going – went – have gone

set off /ˌset 'ɒfǁ-'ɔːf/ [phrasal verb I] to leave at the start of a journey, especially an important, exciting, or difficult journey: *As the sun came up, we set off up the mountain.*
set off for London/Paris/Chicago etc (=in order to go to London etc) *When he received the news that his sister was sick, he set off at once for London.*

> **Set off** is used especially in the past tense, in stories or reports of past events.

take off /ˌteɪk 'ɒfǁ-'ɔːf/ [phrasal verb I] if a plane **takes off**, it leaves the ground at the beginning of a flight: *What time did your plane take off?*

depart /dɪ'pɑːʳt/ [v I] FORMAL to leave, especially on a journey – often used in official information about when and where trains, planes, buses etc start a journey: *The Ambassador departed the next day.*

+from *All trains to London depart from platform 1.*
+for *The ship departed for Africa on April 26th.*

3   to leave suddenly without telling anyone where you are going

disappear /ˌdɪsə'pɪəʳ/ [v I] to leave a place suddenly without telling anyone, so that no one knows where you have gone: *After the concert I looked around and tried to find her, but she had disappeared.*

4   what you say when you are leaving

➡ see also **EG SAYING GOODBYE**

 I have to go (also **I must go** BRITISH) /aɪ ˌhæv tə 'gəʊ, aɪ ˌmʌst 'gəʊ/ SPOKEN say this when you are leaving, because it is time to go or because you have to go somewhere else: *Sorry, I have to go or I'll miss my bus.* | *We must go – it's getting late.*

 I'm off /aɪm 'ɒf/ SPOKEN INFORMAL say this when you are leaving: *I'm off, Pete. See you tomorrow.* | *We're off now – thanks for everything.*

5   ways of telling someone angrily to go away

> These phrases are not polite. Only use them if you intend to be rude.

 go away /ˌgəʊ ə'weɪ/ SPOKEN INFORMAL say this when you want someone to leave: *I wish you'd all just go away and leave me alone.* | *"Go away!" she shouted.*

 get lost /ˌget 'lɒstǁ-'lɔːst/ SPOKEN INFORMAL say this when you want someone to leave because they are annoying you: *Get lost! I've told you already, I'm not interested.*

> **Get lost** is ruder than **go away**.

⚲ **get out** /ˌget ˈaʊt/ SPOKEN say this to tell someone to leave your house, room etc, because you are very angry with them: *Get out! I never want to see you again!*
+of *Give me back my money and get out of my house.*

6 to permanently leave the place where you live

leave /liːv/ [v I/T not in passive] to leave your home or the area where you live: *We've been so happy living here. I'll be really sorry to leave.* | *She was excited about leaving the village and going to live in London.*
leaving – left – have left

move /muːv/ [v I] to leave your house and go to live in another one: *When are you moving?* | *I've moved – here's my new address.*
+to *We're looking forward to moving to Paris.*
move house BRITISH (=go to live in another house) *They moved house three times in five years.*

move out /ˌmuːv ˈaʊt/ [phrasal verb I] to permanently leave the house where you live, especially because there are problems that make it difficult for you to stay: *We'll have to move out if the landlord increases the rent again.* | *They quarrelled, and Anna moved out.*
+of *Why do you want to move out of such a fantastic apartment?*

leave home /ˌliːv ˈhəʊm/ if a young person **leaves home**, he or she leaves their parents' house and goes to live somewhere else: *She left home when she was 18.* | *Now that the children have left home, I have more time for writing.*

run away /ˌrʌn əˈweɪ/ [phrasal verb I] if a young person **runs away**, he or she secretly leave their parents' house or the place where they are living, because they are unhappy there: *When he was 15 he ran away and got a job on a ship.*

emigrate /ˈemᵻgreɪt/ [v I] to leave your own country and go to live in another country: *His business failed, so he decided to emigrate.*
+to *My parents emigrated to Australia in 1955.*

7 to make someone leave a place

throw sb out/kick sb out /ˌθrəʊ (sb) ˈaʊt, ˌkɪk (sb) ˈaʊt/ [phrasal verb T] INFORMAL to make someone leave the house or place where they live, especially because you are angry with them: *In the end her father threw her out.*
+of *They can't just kick you out of the apartment for no reason.* | *Several foreign diplomats were kicked out of Russia for spying.*

evict /ɪˈvɪkt/ [v T] to legally force someone to leave the house where they live, either because they should not be there, or because they have not paid their rent: *If they evict us, we have nowhere else to go.*
be evicted from sth *The previous tenants were evicted from the house for not paying their rent.*

deport /dɪˈpɔːrt/ [v T] if the government of a country **deports** a foreign person who is living there, they force them to leave the country
deport sb from/to sth *He was deported from the UK when his visa ran out.*

8 to permanently leave a job or organization

leave /liːv/ [v I/T not in passive] to stop doing a job, or stop belonging to an organization: *Why did you leave your last job?* | *I had enjoyed teaching, and was sorry to leave.* | *Several leading Republicans are threatening to leave the party.*
leaving – left – have left

resign /rɪˈzaɪn/ [v I] to officially leave your job, especially because you are unhappy with it or because you have done something wrong: *I wanted to resign, but my boss persuaded me to stay.*
+from *Three more directors have just resigned from the board.*
resignation /ˌrezɪɡˈneɪʃən/ [n C/U] when someone officially leaves their job: *Hundreds of people wrote to the company, demanding the resignation of its chairman.*

retire /rɪˈtaɪər/ [v I] to permanently leave your job, because you have reached the age when most people stop working: *In the UK, men usually retire at 65, and women at 60.*

quit /kwɪt/ [v I/T not in passive] INFORMAL to leave your job, school etc because you are not happy there: *I'd had enough of college and decided to quit.* | *He quit politics in '94 and went into banking.*

quitting – quit – have quit

9 to permanently leave your school or college

leave /liːv/ [v I/T not in passive] *I hated school and was glad when I could leave.*

leave school/college/university *When he first left college, he worked in an office.*

leaving – left – have left

graduate /'grædʒueɪt/ [v I] to successfully finish studying at a school or university: *What are you going to do after you graduate?* | *When I graduate I want to go to law school in New York.*
+from *He graduated from Cambridge in 1979.*

> ⚠ In British English, you use **graduate** only to talk about leaving university. In American English, you can use **graduate** to talk about leaving high school or leaving university.

drop out /ˌdrɒp 'aʊt‖ˌdrɑːp-/ [phrasal verb I] to leave school, college, or university before you have finished studying: *One-third of the students drop out at the end of the first year.*
+of *When he was 15, he dropped out of school and joined a band.*

flunk out /ˌflʌŋk 'aʊt/ [phrasal verb I] AMERICAN INFORMAL to have to leave school or college because your work is not good enough
+of *Bart messed around and flunked out of college.*

10 to make someone leave a job, school, or organization

fire (also **dismiss** FORMAL) /faɪəʳ, dɪsˈmɪs/ [v T] to make someone leave their job, especially because they have done something wrong: *His boss fired him for being drunk.* | *The hospital dismissed him for gross misconduct.*

> **Formal or informal?**
> **Fire** is rather informal and is used especially in American English.

dismissal [n C/U] *the dismissal of the Minister for Energy*

sack sb/give sb the sack /ˈsæk (sb), ˌgɪv (sb) ðə ˈsæk/ [v T] BRITISH INFORMAL to make someone leave their job, especially because they have done something wrong: *The company has sacked three of its senior managers.* | *If I'd known what she was doing, I would have given her the sack long ago.*

kick sb out/throw sb out /ˌkɪk (sb) 'aʊt, ˌθrəʊ (sb) 'aʊt/ [phrasal verb T] INFORMAL to make someone leave a school, college, club etc, because they have done something wrong: *I said I'd kick them out if I caught them smoking again.*
+of *Nick failed his exams and was thrown out of school.*

expel /ɪkˈspel/ [v T] to make someone permanently leave a school or college, because they have behaved very badly: *The principal is expelling three boys who were caught taking drugs.*
get expelled (from/for) *She got expelled from her school for hitting one of the teachers.*
expelling – expelled – have expelled

suspend /səˈspend/ [v T] to make someone leave their school, job, or an organization for a period of time, because they have disobeyed rules or behaved badly: *Several police officers have been suspended for taking bribes.*

11 to be forced to leave your job

lose your job /ˌluːz jɔːʳ 'dʒɒb‖-'dʒɑːb/ to be forced to leave your job: *Terry lost his job just before Christmas – it was terrible.* | *People don't complain because they're frightened of losing their jobs.*

be fired (also **be dismissed** FORMAL) /biː 'faɪəʳd, biː dɪsˈmɪst/ to be forced to leave your job, especially because you have done something wrong: *Did he resign or was he fired?*

Formal or informal?

Be fired is rather informal and is used especially in American English.

be sacked/get the sack /biː ˈsækt, ˌget ðə ˈsæk/ BRITISH INFORMAL to be forced to leave your job, especially because you have done something wrong: *If you keep coming in late, you'll get the sack.*

be laid off (also **be made redundant** BRITISH) /biː ˌleɪd ˈɒf, biː ˌmeɪd rɪˈdʌndənt/ to lose your job, because your company does not need you any more: *Dad was laid off after 32 years in the steelworks. | 250 people will be made redundant when the factory closes.*

redundancy /rɪˈdʌndənsi/ [n C/U] BRITISH when someone has to leave their job, because the company does not need them any more: *The men were offered shorter working hours as an alternative to redundancy. | more redundancies in the banking industry*
plural **redundancies**

LEND

to let someone use something that they will give back to you later

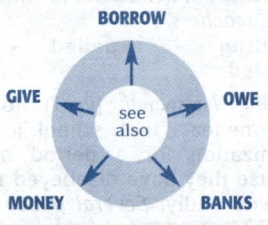

BORROW

GIVE   see also   OWE

MONEY   BANKS

> ⚠ Don't confuse **lend** and **borrow**. You **lend** something **to** someone (=you let them have it), but you **borrow** something **from** someone (=they let you have it).

1   to lend something to someone

lend (also **loan** AMERICAN) /lend, ləʊn/ [v T] to let someone have money which they will pay back later or let them use something that is yours, which they will give back to you later

lend/loan sb sth *Can you lend me $20? | I wish I'd never lent him my car. | I could loan you $100 if you need it.*
lend/loan sth to sb *Did you lend that book to Mike? | The camera had been loaned to him by his cousin.*
lending – lent – have lent

> ⚠ You **lend** or **loan** things that can be moved, but you **let someone use** a room, building etc.

let sb use sth /ˌlet (sb) ˈjuːz (sth)/ to let someone use something that belongs to you, for a short time, especially something such as a room, a house, or a piece of land: *Some friends are letting us use their house while they are on vacation. | Bob won't let me use his computer.*

on loan /ɒn ˈləʊn/ something that is **on loan**, especially a library book or a painting, has been lent to a person or organization: *I couldn't get that book from the library – all the copies are out on loan.*
+from *The museum has an exhibition of paintings on loan from the Louvre.*

2   to lend houses, land, machines etc for money

rent out /ˌrent ˈaʊt/ [phrasal verb T] to allow someone to use a house, piece of land, or vehicle that belongs to you, in exchange for money
rent sth out *If you can't sell your house, why don't you rent it out?*
rent out sth *They rent out boats for pleasure cruises.*
rent sth out to sb *The field at the back of the house is rented out to a local farmer.*

lease /liːs/ [v T] to allow a company, organization etc to use buildings, land, or equipment for a fixed period of time, in exchange for money
lease sth to sb *The aircraft had been leased to a Nigerian airline.*

let BRITISH **rent** AMERICAN /let, rent/ [v T] to allow someone to use a room, house, or office in exchange for money
let/rent sth to sb *I've let my spare room to a Japanese student. | We*

usually rent our house to someone over the long vacation.
To Let BRITISH **For Rent** AMERICAN (written on a sign to show that a room, house, or office is empty and can be rented)
letting – let – have let

3 money that is lent to someone

loan /ləʊn/ [n C] an amount of money that someone has borrowed: *The bank offered him a loan of £15,000 to set up a business.*

LESS

➡ opposite **MORE**
➡ see also **LEAST**
➡ if you want to know about using adjectives for comparing things, go to the **ESSENTIAL GRAMMAR** (Section 14)

1 a smaller amount or number

less /les/ [quantifier] a smaller amount of something: *You ought to eat less meat.* | *It'll cost about $50 – maybe less.*
+than *Harry knows even less than I do about this business.*
+of *I'd like to spend less of my time at work.*
much less/a lot less *There is much less traffic at weekends.*
less and less (=when an amount keeps getting smaller as time passes) *As the drought became worse, there was less and less food available.*

> ⚠ Use **less** with uncountable nouns like 'money', 'food', or 'information'. In formal writing it is incorrect to use **less** with countable nouns like 'pens', 'shops', or 'students'. But in ordinary conversation, **less** is often used in this way instead of **fewer**.

fewer /'fjuːəʳ/ [quantifier] a smaller number of people or things: *There are fewer jobs available nowadays.*
+than *Women are having fewer children than they used to.*
far fewer (=a lot fewer) *Far fewer people go to church these days.*

> ⚠ Use **fewer** with countable nouns like 'pens', 'shops' or 'students', and never with uncountable nouns.

not as much /ˌnɒt əz 'mʌtʃ/ less than a particular amount
+as *The Chinese don't eat as much meat as the Americans.* | *Let's rent an apartment – it won't cost as much as a hotel.*

> ⚠ Use **not as much** with uncountable nouns, like 'time', 'money', or 'food', but never with countable nouns. Use **not as many** with countable nouns.

not as many /ˌnɒt əz 'meni/ fewer than a particular number of people or things
+as *There weren't as many people there this year as last year.* | *I have quite a few CDs, but not as many as Becky has.*

> ⚠ Use **not as many** with countable nouns, like 'pens', 'shops', or 'students', but never with uncountable nouns.

lower /'ləʊəʳ/ [adj] less than another number or level – use this about prices, temperatures, marks for schoolwork, and other things that can be measured on a scale from high to low: *Foreign workers have fewer rights and get lower wages.* | *In the mountains the temperature is much lower.*
+than *I got lower grades than the other students in my class.*

2 less than a particular number or amount

less than /'les ðən/ *Some of the miners were earning less than $2 an hour.* | *They've built another hotel less than a mile from here.*
under /'ʌndəʳ/ [preposition] less than a particular age, price, amount, or number: *It's illegal to sell cigarettes to children under 16.* | *Where can you get a meal for under $5?*
just under (=slightly less than) *The baby weighed just under three kilos.*
below /bɪ'ləʊ/ [preposition] less than a particular temperature, speed, limit,

or level: *At night the temperature is often below freezing.*

fall below (=become less than) *The rate of inflation has fallen below 3%.*

3 less interesting, expensive, difficult, exciting etc

not as /'nɒt əz/ *Their first album sold over a million copies, but the second one wasn't as popular.*

not as...as *It's not as cold as it was yesterday.* | *Our house isn't as big as yours.* | *"How was the test?" "Not as bad as I expected."*

less /les/ [*adv*] *The dentist gave me an injection to make it less painful.*

less...than *I want something less formal than a traditional wedding dress.*

much less/a lot less *This disease is now much less common.*

> ⚠ Don't use **less** with very short words. Don't say 'less good/bad/tall etc'. Say **not as good**, **not as bad**, **not as tall** etc. In spoken English, **not as** is more common than **less**.

4 when something happens less than before

less /les/ [*adv*]

+than *This type of problem still occurs, but less than it did in the past.*

much less/a lot less *Since we got the car, we walk a lot less than we used to.*

less and less (=when something happens or is done less as time passes) *He seemed to care less and less about the band, and eventually decided to leave.*

not as much /nɒt əz 'mʌtʃ/ *She used to really hate her job, but she doesn't seem to complain as much now.*

+as *"Do you still go swimming?" "Not as much as I used to."*

> **Formal or informal?**
>
> **Not as much** is more common than **less** in informal spoken English.

5 when prices, numbers etc become less

go down/come down /ˌɡəʊ 'daʊn, ˌkʌm 'daʊn/ [*phrasal verb* I] to become less: *The suicide rate has gone down in the last few years.* | *I'm hoping the price will come down if I wait a while.*

fall/drop /fɔːl, drɒp‖drɑːp/ [*v* I] to become less, especially by a large amount: *Airfares to Hong Kong have fallen dramatically because of increased competition.*

+to *At night, the temperature drops to −20 °C.*

fall/drop from sth to sth *Profits fell from £98.5 million to £76 million.*

falling – fell – have fallen

dropping – dropped – have dropped

> **Formal or informal?**
>
> **Fall** and **drop** are mostly used in written English. In informal spoken English, **go down** and **come down** are more common.

decrease /dɪˈkriːs/ [*v* I] FORMAL to become less – used especially when writing or talking about business or technical subjects: *Average house prices decreased by 1% in the first month of this year.*

+to *The speed of rotation gradually decreases to zero.*

decreasing [*adj* only before noun] *The company has been hit by decreasing demand for its product.*

6 to make something less

reduce /rɪˈdjuːs‖rɪˈduːs/ [*v* T] to make something less in amount or level: *Try to reduce the amount of fat in your diet.* | *I was hoping they would reduce the price a little.* | *Yoga and meditation can help to reduce stress.*

reduce sth by half/10%/2 years etc *The new road will reduce traffic through the town by 30%.*

reduced [*adj*] *Most airlines offer reduced rates for children.*

lower /ˈləʊəʳ/ [*v* T] to reduce an amount, limit, or level – used especially when writing or talking about business or technical subjects: *After 20 minutes, lower the temperature to 200 degrees.* | *The*

Bundesbank came under pressure to lower interest rates.

turn down /ˌtɜːʳn ˈdaʊn/ [*phrasal verb* T] to reduce the level of sound, heat, or light, by turning a control
turn sth down *Could you turn the TV down a little?*
turn down sth *The weather wasn't as cold, so we decided to turn down the central heating.*

cut down /ˌkʌt ˈdaʊn/ [*phrasal verb* I] to reduce the amount of food that you eat, alcohol that you drink, or cigarettes that you smoke: *If you can't give up smoking, at least try to cut down.*
+on *I've cut down on the amount of meat I eat.*

> **Formal or informal?**
> **Cut down** is more informal than **reduce**.

lessen /ˈlesən/ [*v* T] FORMAL to make a pain less severe, or make an unpleasant feeling less bad: *Drugs can be used to lessen the pain.* | *We tried to be sympathetic, but nothing could lessen his disappointment.*

7 a reduction in numbers, prices, levels etc

reduction /rɪˈdʌkʃən/ [*n* C] when a price, level etc is reduced – use this when something is reduced deliberately: *We offer a reduction for groups of 10 or more.*
+in *Cleaner fuel has contributed to a reduction in air pollution.* | *a reduction in working hours*
reduction of £10/$5/25% etc (=a reduction by a particular amount) *There were reductions of up to 50% in some stores.*

decrease /ˈdiːkriːs/ [*n* C] when something happens less than it used to
+in *There has been a 15% decrease in violent crime.* (=it has gone down by 15%)
a significant / marked decrease (=when something happens much less than it used to) *a significant decrease in the number of deaths from heart disease*

> **Formal or informal?**
> **Decrease** is more formal than **drop** and **fall**, and is used especially in writing and news reports.

drop/fall /drɒp, fɔːl‖drɑːp/ [*n* singular] when a number or amount goes down suddenly or by a large amount
+in *Charities have reported a 25% fall in donations during the past year.* (=donations have gone down by 25%) | *a sudden drop in the number of student nurses*
a sharp fall/drop (=when an amount goes down very suddenly) *a sharp fall in profits*

> ⚠ Don't say 'a drop of the birthrate' or 'a fall of the birthrate'. Say **a drop in the birthrate** or **a fall in the birthrate**.

cut /kʌt/ [*n* C] a reduction in the amount or size of something made by a government or large organization – use this especially for talking about politics or business
+in *Cuts in the education budget have led to fewer teachers and larger classes.*
pay/job/tax cuts (=cuts in wages, number of jobs, or taxes) *Nurses are protesting about further pay cuts.* | *The new management has promised that there will be no further job cuts.*

LET

➡ see also **CAN/CAN'T** ⓔⒸ **PERMISSION,** ⓔⒸ **SUGGESTIONS**

1 to let someone do something

let /let/ [*v* T not in passive] *We wanted to go camping, but our parents wouldn't let us.*
let sb do sth *Sue never lets her children eat candy.* | *Thank you for letting me borrow your car.*
let sb in/out (=let someone go in or out of a place) *Let me in! It's cold out here!*
letting – let – have let

> ⚠ Don't say 'he let me to borrow his car' or 'he let me borrowing his car'. Say **he let me borrow his car**.

allow /əˈlaʊ/ [v T] if someone such as a teacher, official, or parent **allows** you to do something, they let you do it
allow sb to do sth *We do not allow people to smoke anywhere in the building.* | *What time was he allowed to go home?*
allow sb sth (=allow them to have it) *We allow passengers one item of hand luggage each.*
allow sb/sth somewhere (=allow someone to be in a place or something to happen in a place) *The manager doesn't allow children in the bar.* | *I don't allow smoking in my house.*

> **Formal or informal?**
> **Allow** is more formal than **let** and is used more in writing than in spoken English. For example, in ordinary conversation it is better to say **let me explain**, not 'allow me to explain'.

🔍 **say sb can do sth** /ˌseɪ (sb) kən ˈduː (sth)/ ESPECIALLY SPOKEN to tell someone that you will allow them to do something: *Mum says I can go to the party.* | *I thought you said we could use this room.*

give permission /ˌgɪv pəˈmɪʃən/ if someone such as an official, teacher, or manager **gives permission**, they say that someone is officially allowed to do something
give sb permission to do sth *Who gave you permission to leave class early?* | *The pilot was given permission to land at Rome airport.*
+for *The police have refused to give permission for a peace march through the centre of town.*

> ⚠ Don't say 'she gave us a permission' or 'she gave us the permission'. Just say **she gave us permission**.

agree to sth /əˈgriː tuː (sth)/ [phrasal verb T] to decide to allow someone to do something because you have been persuaded to allow it: *I'd like to go on holiday with my boyfriend but my parents would never agree to it.*

2 to be allowed to do something

can /kən strong kæn/ [modal verb] Now that you're seventeen, you can learn to drive. | *Can Jean stay at our house tonight?* | *You can't park there.*

> ⚠ Don't say 'you can to park here'. Say **you can park here**.

> ⚠ Use **can** in the present tense, even when you are referring to the future: *Can I borrow that book when you've finished?* You can use **will be able to** to talk about having official permission in the future: *When you're 18, you'll be able to vote.* If you want to say that someone was allowed to do something on one occasion in the past, use **be allowed**: *After being questioned by the police, he was allowed to leave.* You can use **could** when reporting what someone asked to do or was allowed to do, or talking about what was generally allowed: *They said I could go.* | *Students could leave at any time they liked.*

be allowed /biː əˈlaʊd/ to be allowed to do something, especially because a rule or law says you can do it
be allowed to do sth *Are we allowed to use calculators in the test?*
sth is allowed *Swimming is only allowed in the roped-off area of the lake.*
be allowed in/out/off/on etc (=be allowed to go in, out, off etc) *No-one was allowed off the plane at Harare.*

> ⚠ When talking about something that someone was allowed to do on one occasion in the past, use **was allowed to**, not 'could'. Don't say 'he could leave at 10'. Say **he was allowed to leave at 10**.

be permitted /biː pəˈmɪtəd/ FORMAL to be allowed to do something by an official order, rule, or law
be permitted to do sth *Orlov was arrested by the Soviet authorities, but his wife was permitted to leave.*
sth is permitted *Smoking is only permitted in the public lounge.*

may /meɪ/ [modal verb] FORMAL to be allowed to do something: *Thank you Mrs Prynn, you may go now.* | *Only authorized personnel may use this entrance.*

Don't say 'you may to go'. Say **you may go**.

 Only use **may** in the present tense. When talking about the past, use **could** or **was allowed**: *He said I could park in front of his house.* | *Only authorized personnel were allowed to use the entrance.*

3 official permission to do something

permission /pəˈmɪʃən/ [n U] when someone officially allows you to do something
permission to do sth *I had to get official permission to visit the prison.*
with/without sb's permission *We're not allowed to camp here without the farmer's permission.* | *The changes to the book were all made with the author's permission.*

permit /ˈpɜːˈmɪt/ [n C] an official document that gives you permission to do something, for example permission to work somewhere or visit somewhere: *You can't park here unless you have a permit.*
work permit (=a permit to work in a particular country)

licence BRITISH **license** AMERICAN /ˈlaɪsəns/ [n C] an official document that allows you to do something, for example to drive a car or to own a gun: *Do you have a licence for that gun?*
driving licence BRITISH **driver's license** AMERICAN *Do you have any ID? Like your driver's license?*

consent /kənˈsent/ [n U] FORMAL formal permission from someone to do something important
with/without sb's consent *They had to get married without their parents' consent.*
give your consent (=say that you allow something to happen) *She refused to give her consent for the operation because of her religious beliefs.*

4 to let someone do something that is not usually allowed

bend the rules /ˌbend ðə ˈruːlz/ INFORMAL to let someone do something that is slightly different from what is usually allowed: *No-one is allowed in before six, but I suppose I could bend the rules a little.*

make an exception /ˌmeɪk ən ɪkˈsepʃən/ to allow someone to do something that is not usually allowed: *I'll make an exception this time, but next time you hand in an essay late I won't accept it.*

5 to let something happen by not stopping it

let /let/ [v T] to let something bad happen, especially by not trying to stop it
let sb/sth do sth *You shouldn't let your husband treat you like that.* | *I've been so busy, I've let the house get terribly untidy over the past few weeks.*
letting – let – have let

 Don't say 'they let it to happen'. Say **they let it happen**.

allow /əˈlaʊ/ [v T] to let a situation continue or develop without doing anything to stop it or improve it
allow sb/sth to do sth *Allow the meat to defrost at room temperature.* | *The government has allowed the situation to get completely out of control.*

Formal or informal?
Allow is more formal than **let**.

When you see **EC**, go to the **ESSENTIAL COMMUNICATION** section.

LIE

→ look here for ...
  • lie on a bed or on the floor
  • say something that is not true

1 to lie on a bed or on the floor

→ see also **SIT, STAND**

lie /laɪ/ [v I] to lie flat on a bed or on the floor, or to get into this position: *In the next room, the old man lay dying.*
+on *She switched off the light and lay on the bed.*
lie on your back *Jones was lying on his back smoking a cigarette.*
lying – lay – have lain

> ⚠ Don't confuse these three verbs: **lie** (past tense **lay**) =be flat on a bed; **lie** (past tense **lied**) =say something that is untrue; **lay** (past tense **laid**) =put something down.

lie down /ˌlaɪ ˈdaʊn/ [phrasal verb I] to put yourself into a flat position on a bed or the floor, in order to relax or go to sleep: *You look really tired. Why don't you go and lie down?*
+on *Hannah lay down on the grass and closed her eyes.*

stretch out /ˌstretʃ ˈaʊt/ [phrasal verb I] to lie or sit with your legs and body straight, in order to rest and relax
+on *He likes to stretch out on the sofa and watch TV.*
stretched out (=lying with your legs and body straight) *Celia's dog lay stretched out on the rug.*

2 to say something that is not true

→ see also **DISHONEST, CHEAT, TRICK/ DECEIVE, TRUE/NOT TRUE, TRUST/ NOT TRUST**

lie /laɪ/ [v I] to deliberately tell someone something that is not true: *I looked at her face and I knew she was lying.*
+about *Movie stars always lie about their age.*
+to *Don't lie to me! I know you weren't working late last night.*
lying – lied – have lied

tell a lie /ˌtel ə ˈlaɪ/ to lie: *I told a lie and said that I hadn't seen him.* | *Children may tell lies to avoid being punished.*
tell sb a lie *Of course it's true. I wouldn't tell you a lie.*

lie /laɪ/ [n C] something that you say which you know is not true: *Jim said he hadn't done it, but I knew it was a lie.* | *How can the newspapers print all these lies about her private life?*
a pack of lies INFORMAL (=so many lies that you feel shocked or angry) *I couldn't believe it! They just stood up in court and told a pack of lies!*

liar /ˈlaɪəʳ/ [n C] someone who often tells lies: *How can you trust Graham? You know he's a liar.*

mislead /mɪsˈliːd/ [v T] to make someone believe something that is not true, by giving them information that is not complete or not completely true: *He deliberately misled the Senate.* | *The court decided that customers had been misled by the company's advertising.*
misleading – misled – have misled

misleading [adj] a **misleading** statement, description etc does not give complete information or completely true information: *This tour brochure is attractive, but misleading.* | *a deliberately misleading answer*

> **Formal or informal?**
> **Mislead** is used in writing and in formal spoken English.

3 to think of an untrue explanation or excuse

make up /ˌmeɪk ˈʌp/ [phrasal verb T] to think of an explanation, excuse etc that is untrue
make up sth *If you don't want to go out with Wanda, you'll have to make up some kind of excuse.*
make sth up *When I told them why I was late, they accused me of making it up!*

invent /ɪnˈvent/ [v T] to think of an explanation or excuse that is completely untrue, in order to deceive people: *He used to invent stories about his rich lifestyle to impress the women he met.* | *I began* *to invent reasons for staying away from work.*

Formal or informal?
Invent is more formal than **make up**.

LIFE

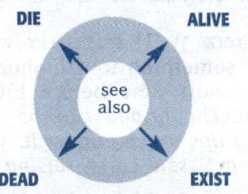

DIE   ALIVE

see
also

DEAD   EXIST

1 the time when someone is alive

life /laɪf/ [n C] *The day our daughter was born was the happiest day of my life.* | *Sutcliffe was sent to jail for the rest of his life.*
spend your life *She had spent her life moving from one town to another.*
sb's early life (=when they were young) *He knew very little about his mother's early life in Africa.*
in later life (=when you are old) *Lack of calcium can lead to bone disease in later life.*
life expectancy (=how long people are expected to live) *Women have a longer life expectancy than men.*
plural **lives**

lifetime /'laɪftaɪm/ [n singular] the time when someone is alive – use this when you are talking about how long someone lived and what happened in their life
in/during sb's lifetime *During her lifetime, my grandmother lived through two World Wars and saw the first steps on the Moon.* | *He suffered a lot of pain in his short lifetime.*
+of *The king died in 1990, after a lifetime of service to the country.*

2 the kind of life that someone has

life /laɪf/ [n C] *Having a baby completely changes your life.*

a happy/hard/exciting life *Deborah has a very busy life as a doctor.*
lead a happy/quiet/exciting life *We've led a very quiet life since Ralph retired.*
a life of crime (=when you use crime to make money instead of having a normal job) *He left school at 15, and turned to a life of crime.*
plural **lives**

lifestyle /'laɪfstaɪl/ [n C] the way a person or group of people live or behave, including the place they live in, the things they own or eat etc, and the activities they do: *Doctors are trying to persuade people to lead healthier lifestyles.* | *Her glamorous Hollywood lifestyle came to an end in 1987.*

way of life /ˌweɪ əv 'laɪf/ the way in which a person or group of people lives, and the type of things they usually do: *The modern way of life can be very stressful.* | *The tribe's traditional way of life is now under threat.*
the British/German/American etc way of life *They saw communism as a threat to the American way of life.*

3 continuing for all of someone's life

all your life /ˌɔːl jɔːʳ 'laɪf/ *My father worked hard all his life.* | *I've known her all my life.*

for life /fəʳ 'laɪf/ if something is **for life**, it will continue and not change for the rest of your life: *There's no such thing as a job for life these days.* | *As far as I'm concerned, when you're married, it's for life.*

lifelong /'laɪflɒŋǁ-lɔːŋ/ [adj only before noun] use this about beliefs, feelings, or relationships that last for the whole of your life: *It was her lifelong ambition to write a best-selling novel.* | *a lifelong friendship that started when they were at school together* | *My father was a lifelong supporter of the Democrats.*

L

LIFT

to move something into a higher position

➡ see also **CARRY, HOLD, PUT**

1 to lift a person or thing

lift

lift /lɪft/ [v T] to take something in your hands, especially something heavy, and move it upwards to another position: *After the operation, I wasn't allowed to lift anything heavy.*
lift sth onto/over etc *I tried to lift the box onto the table but it was too heavy.*
lift sb/sth up *He gently lifted the child up onto his shoulders.*
lift up sb/sth *She lifted up the smallest boy so he could see the parade.*

pick up

pick up /,pɪk 'ʌp/ [phrasal verb T] to lift something up from the ground, from a table etc, especially something small or light
pick up sth *She picked up her bag and left the room.*
pick sth up *There are papers all over the floor – could you pick them up and put them away?*

raise

"Cheers, everyone!' said Larry, raising his glass.'

raise /reɪz/ [v T] ESPECIALLY WRITTEN to move something to a higher position for a short time before lowering it again: *The bridge can be raised to allow ships to pass under it.* | *"Cheers, everyone!" said Larry, raising his glass.*

2 to lift a part of your body

raise /reɪz/ [v T] ESPECIALLY WRITTEN
raise your eyes/eyebrows/hand/arm to move or turn your eyes, head etc upwards for a short time: *She was reading a book, but raised her eyes when Paul walked in.*

lift /lɪft/ [v T]
lift your arm/leg/head etc to move your arm, leg etc upwards, especially when this is difficult to do: *I was feeling so weak that I could hardly lift my head from the pillow.*

◌ put your hand up /,pʌt jɔː ˈhænd ʌp/ ESPECIALLY SPOKEN to move your arm upwards and keep it in the air, for example because you want to speak in a class or meeting, or because you are being counted: *Put your hand up if you know the answer.* | *If you are not able to take part, please put your hand up.*

When you see WB, go to the **WORD BANKS** section.

LIGHT

➡ look here for ...
• not dark
• not heavy

1 light from the sun, a fire, an electric light etc

➡ see also **DARK, BRIGHT/NOT BRIGHT, COLOUR/COLOR**

light /laɪt/ [n U] *Light was coming into the room through a crack in the door.* | *a gas lamp that gives as much light as a 100 watt bulb*

the light (=the amount of natural light in a place) *The light was fading and I was afraid we wouldn't be home before dark.*

good/strong/bright light *The light isn't good enough to take a photograph.*

blinding / dazzling light (=very strong light that hurts your eyes) *a sudden flash of blinding light*

by the light of the moon/the fire/a candle (=with only the moon etc to give light) *She sat reading by the light of the fire.*

🔍 **it's light** /ɪts 'laɪt/ ESPECIALLY SPOKEN use this to say that there is natural daylight: *Let's go now while it's still light.* | *It's not light enough to play outside.*

daylight /'deɪlaɪt/ [n U] the natural light of day

in daylight *I'd like to look at the house again in daylight.*

daylight hours (=the time when it is light) *The park is open during daylight hours.*

sunlight /'sʌnlaɪt/ [n U] the light from the sun: *Her long blonde hair was shining in the sunlight.* | *Keep the plant out of direct sunlight.*

bright sunlight (=strong sunlight) *Maria stood blinking in the bright sunlight.*

moonlight /'muːnlaɪt/ [n U] the light from the moon: *The trees looked strangely white in the moonlight.*

glare /gleəʳ/ [n singular] a very bright and unpleasant light that makes you want to close your eyes

+of *the glare of the car's headlights*

glow /gləʊ/ [n singular] ESPECIALLY WRITTEN a soft pleasant light, especially from something that is burning: *Candles give a warm glow to the room.*

+of *the orange glow of the sunset*

2 to make a place light

light up /ˌlaɪt 'ʌp/ [phrasal verb T] to shine lights on a place so that people can see it well, or so that it looks attractive

light up sth *The fireworks lit up the sky.* | *Their garden was lit up by dozens of coloured lamps.*

light /laɪt/ [v T] to put lights in a place so that people can see what is happening there: *What are you going to use to light the stage?*

be lit by/with *The room was lit by hundreds of candles.*

lighting – lit – have lit

switch/turn/put the light(s) on /ˌswɪtʃ, ˌtɜːʳn, ˌpʊt ðə 'laɪt(s) ɒn/ to turn or press a control to make an electric light produce light: *Can you put the light on? I can't see anything!*

3 something that provides light

light /laɪt/ [n C] an electric light: *We could see the lights of Hong Kong across the bay.*

the light is on/off *There must be someone at home – the light's on in the kitchen.*

switch/turn/put the light on *It's getting dark. Can you turn the light on?*

turn/switch the light off *Don't forget to switch the lights off when you leave.*

lamp /læmp/ [n C] something that uses electricity, oil, or gas to produce light, especially a light that you can move from place to place: *There was a little oil lamp hanging from a hook in the ceiling.* | *a bedside lamp*

candle /'kændl/ [n C] a stick of wax with string through the middle that you burn to give light: *When there was a power cut, we had to use candles.* | *The cake had twelve candles on it.*

torch BRITISH **flashlight** AMERICAN /tɔːʳtʃ, 'flæʃlaɪt/ [n C] a small electric lamp that you carry in your hand: *We shone our torches around the walls of the cave.*

4 colours/hair/skin

➡ see also **DARK, HAIR**

light /laɪt/ [adj] not dark in colour: *Her hair is a lighter colour than mine.*
light brown/blue/green etc *Mike has light brown hair.* | *The walls were a horrible shade of light green.*

> Don't use **light** about the colour of people's skin. Use **fair** or **pale**.

pale /peɪl/ [adj] if someone is **pale**, their face is whiter than it usually is, especially because they are ill or frightened; a colour that is **pale** is very light: *You're very pale. Are you feeling sick?*
pale blue/green/pink etc *a pale pink dress* | *She has very pale blue eyes.*

> Don't use **pale** about the colour of someone's hair. Use **fair**, **blonde**, or **light brown**.

fair /feəʳ/ [adj] **fair** hair or skin is very light in colour: *People with fair skin should be careful when they go out in the sun.* | *Ulla has fair hair and blue eyes.*

5 not heavy

➡ opposite **HEAVY**

light /laɪt/ [adj] not heavy: *The equipment is light enough to carry around.* | *Modern tennis rackets are much lighter than the old-fashioned wooden ones.*

lightweight /'laɪt-weɪt/ [adj] **lightweight** clothes, materials, or equipment are specially made so that they weigh very little: *a lightweight summer suit* | *a lightweight bicycle*

> **Lightweight** is used especially when advertising or talking about a product that can be bought.

LIKE/NOT LIKE

➡ look here for ...
  • think someone or something is nice
  • think someone or something is not nice
➡ if you mean 'similar to someone or something else', go to **SAME**

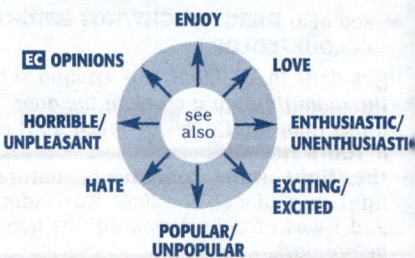

1 to like something

like /laɪk/ [v T] to think something is nice: *I like your dress – it's a beautiful colour.* | *Do you like spaghetti?*
like doing sth/like to do sth *He likes helping in the kitchen.* | *I like to see the children enjoying themselves.*
get to like sth INFORMAL (=start to like something) *At first she hated New York, but after a while she got to like it.*

> Don't say 'I am liking it', 'she is liking it' etc. Say **I like it, she likes it** etc.

> Don't say 'I like very much Paris'. Say **I like Paris very much**.

> Usually it doesn't matter whether you use **like doing sth** or **like to do sth**, but when you mean someone likes the situation or place they are in, use **like doing sth**: *I like living in London* (not 'I like to live in London').

love /lʌv/ [v T] ESPECIALLY SPOKEN to like something very much: *We had a great time at Disneyland. The kids loved it.* | *I love this song.*
love doing sth *Rachel loves driving.*

⚠ Only say 'love very much' about a person that you love. Don't use 'very much' with **love** when you are talking about a thing, place, or activity. Don't say 'I love Paris very much'. Just say **I love Paris**.

be fond of sth /biː ˈfɒnd ɒv (sth)‖ -ˈfɑːnd-/ to like something, especially something you have liked for a long time: *I know he's fond of Chinese food.* | *Gerry had always been fond of animals.*

be crazy about sth /biː ˈkreɪzi əbaʊt (sth)/ INFORMAL to be extremely interested in an activity and spend a lot of time doing it or watching it: *My kids are crazy about football.*

be into sth /biː ˈɪntuː (sth)/ SPOKEN to like doing something, watching something, reading something etc: *My brother's really into rock-climbing.*

2   to like someone

like /laɪk/ [v T] to think someone is nice: *I've always liked Sally – she's such a friendly person.* | *He's an excellent teacher, and the students really like him.*

⚠ Don't say 'I am liking her', 'he is liking her' etc. Say **I like her**, **he likes her** etc.

be fond of sb /biː ˈfɒnd ɒv (sb)‖-ˈfɑːnd-/ to like someone very much, especially when you have known them for a long time: *You're very fond of Beryl, aren't you?* | *Miss Parker was very fond of the children in her class, although she was always strict with them.*

3   to like something or someone better than others

prefer /prɪˈfɜːʳ/ [v T] to like one thing more than another thing: *Do you prefer tea or coffee?*
prefer sth to sth *I prefer classical music to rock.*
prefer to do sth *Most of my friends take the bus to school, but I prefer to walk.*
preferring – preferred – have preferred

⚠ Don't say 'I prefer coffee than tea'. Say **I prefer coffee to tea**.

like sb/sth better /laɪk (sb/sth) ˈbetəʳ/ ESPECIALLY SPOKEN to like one person or thing more than another: *Which do you like better, the red tie or the green one?*
+than *I like this new teacher much better than the one we had before.*

Formal or informal?

Like sb/sth better is more informal than **prefer**.

⚠ Don't say 'I like better summer than winter'. Say **I like summer better than winter**.

like sth best /laɪk (sth) ˈbest/ ESPECIALLY SPOKEN to like something better than anything else – use this when you are asking someone to choose or when you are choosing: *Which of these dresses do you like best?* | *I think I like the red one best.*

4   the one you like better than any others

favourite BRITISH **favorite** AMERICAN /ˈfeɪvərɪt/ [adj only before noun] your **favourite** or **favorite** colour, food, teacher etc is the one that you like better than any other colour, food etc: *My favourite colour is purple.* | *Who is your favorite singer?* | *We're going to her favourite restaurant for a meal.*

⚠ Don't say 'most favourite'. Just say **favourite**.

favourite BRITISH **favorite** AMERICAN /ˈfeɪvərɪt/ [n C] something that you like more than other things of the same kind
sb's favourite/favorite *I like all her books, but this one's my favourite.* | *Oh great! Chocolate ice-cream – my favourite!*

teacher's pet /ˌtiːtʃəʳz ˈpet/ [n singular] INFORMAL someone who is their teacher's favourite student, and who is not liked by the other students because of this

5 someone who likes something very much

fan /fæn/ [n C] someone who likes a particular sport, team, or famous entertainer very much: *Thousands of fans came to hear Oasis play.* | *a football fan*
+of *Fans of Sylvester Stallone will enjoy this movie.*

lover /'lʌvəʳ/ [n C] **music/jazz/art/animal lover** someone who likes music, art, or animals: *Every jazz lover dreams of visiting New Orleans.* | *a nation of animal lovers*

6 the kind of clothes, music etc that you like

taste /teɪst/ [n C/U] the kind of clothes, music, furniture, films etc that you like
+in *His taste in films and books is very different from mine.*
have good/bad taste (=be good or bad at deciding which things are attractive) *My grandmother's house was beautiful – she always had very good taste.*

7 to not like someone or something

➡ see also **HATE**

not like /nɒt 'laɪk/ [v T] *Why did you invite Claire? You know I don't like her.* | *I like the style of that dress, but I don't like the colour.*
not like doing sth/not like to do sth *I don't like walking home alone at night.* | *Jake didn't like to see her looking so sad.*
not like sth/sb very much (use this when the feeling is not very strong) *Mum didn't like Mark very much when she first met him.*

dislike /,dɪs'laɪk/ [v T] to think someone or something is very unpleasant: *He was a quiet person who disliked social occasions.*
dislike doing sth *Stephen dislikes having to get up early.*
dislike sb/sth intensely (=dislike them very much) *Muriel disliked Paul intensely.*

Formal or informal?

Dislike is more formal than **not like**, and is not usually used in spoken English. If you **dislike** someone or something, you feel more strongly than if you **do not like** them.

🔍 **hate** /heɪt/ [v I] ESPECIALLY SPOKEN if you **hate** something, you do not like it at all because it is very unpleasant or very annoying: *I hate those stupid talk shows on TV.* | *Don't you hate the way she interrupts you when you're talking?*
hate it when *I hate it when I'm in the shower and the phone rings.*

🔍 **don't think much of sth/sb** /,dəʊnt θɪŋk 'mʌtʃ ɒv (sth/sb)/ SPOKEN to think that something is not very good or that someone is not very good at something: *The hotel was okay but I didn't think much of the food.* | *I don't think much of that new singer, do you?*

🔍 **not be very keen on sth** /nɒt biː veri 'kiːn ɒn (sth)/ BRITISH, ESPECIALLY SPOKEN to not like something, although you do not think it is very bad or very unpleasant: *Actually, I'm not very keen on modern art.* | *I know you're not very keen on Japanese food, but try this!*

🔍 **not be sb's type** /nɒt biː (sb's) 'taɪp/ ESPECIALLY SPOKEN if someone is **not your type**, they are not the kind of person you usually like: *Vicky's friends are not my type.* | *Rob isn't her type at all.*

🔍 **go off sb/sth** /,gəʊ 'ɒf (sb/sth)ǁ-'ɔːf-/ [phrasal verb T] BRITISH SPOKEN to stop liking someone or something that you used to like: *I used to drink lots of coffee, but I've gone off it lately.*

8 to stop someone from liking a person, thing, or activity

put sb off /,pʊt (sb) 'ɒfǁ-'ɔːf/ [phrasal verb T] INFORMAL to stop someone from liking something or being interested in it: *Don't let her put you off, it's a really good movie.*
put sb off sth *That weekend put me off camping for the rest of my life!*

turn sb against sb /,tɜːʳn (sb) ə'genst (sb)/ [phrasal verb T] to deliberately change someone's feelings, so that they stop liking someone that they used to like: *My wife threw me out, and now she's trying to turn the children against me.*

LIMIT

➡ see also **CONTROL, RULE, LAW**

1 the largest amount that is allowed or possible

limit /'lɪmɪt/ [*n* singular] the highest number, speed, temperature etc that is allowed by a law or rule
+to *There's a limit to the amount of money you can take out of the country.*
time/age/speed limit *The Interstate speed limit is 65 m.p.h.*
over/above the limit (=higher than the limit) *Pollution levels in the water were found to be over the official limit.*
set a limit on sth (=decide what the limit will be) *The Education Department has set a limit on the size of classes.*
legal limit *His blood alcohol level was twice the legal limit.*

maximum /'mæksɪməm/ [*adj* only before noun] the **maximum** number or amount is the largest number or amount that is possible, normal, or allowed: *After leaving Calais, the train soon reaches its maximum speed of 300 kph.* | *40 is the maximum number of passengers this bus is allowed to carry.*
maximum [*n* singular]
the maximum *You don't have to wait long for a new passport – 3 weeks is about the maximum.*
a maximum of £10 / 50% / 30 degrees etc *The prisoners here can earn a maximum of £10 a week.*

the most /ðə 'məʊst/ [quantifier] the largest number or amount: *There are six people in the cab, and that's the most I'm allowed to take.* | *The most we can afford is $500 a month.*

2 the smallest amount that is allowed

the least /ðə 'liːst/ [quantifier] the smallest number or amount: *The least you should offer her is $10 an hour.*

minimum /'mɪnɪməm/ [*adj* only before noun] the **minimum** number or amount is the smallest number or amount that is possible or allowed: *Is there a minimum wage in your country?* | *The minimum age for joining the army is 18.*
minimum [*n* singular]
the minimum *We need at least 8 students to make the course profitable – that's the minimum.*
a minimum of £10/50%/30 degrees etc *You have to stay for a minimum of 7 days.*

3 when there are limits on what you can do

limits /'lɪmɪts/ [*n* plural] the rules or facts that control someone's freedom or their ability to do what they want
+to/on *Are there any limits on the President's power?* | *There are practical limits to the number of cases we can deal with each day.*
within limits *Within certain legal limits, you can import anything you want.*

restrictions /rɪ'strɪkʃənz/ [*n* plural] rules or laws that strictly control what you are allowed to do: *severe financial restrictions*
+on/upon sth *Are there any restrictions on changing foreign currency?* | *Because of restrictions on reporting, the newspapers were not allowed to cover the story.*
impose restrictions (=officially order that something must be limited) *New restrictions have been imposed on immigration.*

limited /'lɪmɪtɪd/ [*adj*] if something is **limited**, only a fixed amount is allowed or available: *We only have a limited amount of time in which to finish the work.*
+to *The class is limited to 20 students.*

be restricted to /bi rɪ'strɪktɪd tuː/ if something **is restricted to** a particular amount, time, group etc,

L

there are rules limiting it to that amount, time, group etc: *The sale of alcohol is restricted to people over 18. | Under the new rules, working time is restricted to 45 hours a week.*

4 to put limits on something

limit /'lɪmɪt/ [v T] to stop a number or amount from becoming too large, or stop someone from doing whatever they want: *a new law limiting the number of foreign cars that can be imported | Men hold most of the top jobs, and this limits women's opportunities for promotion.*
limit sb/sth to sth *I try to limit myself to three cups of coffee a day.*

put/set/impose a limit /,pʌt, ,set, ɪm,pəʊz ə 'lɪmɪt/ to officially control the size or amount of something by deciding what the limit will be
+on *Governments should put strict limits on tobacco advertising.*

restrict /rɪ'strɪkt/ [v T] to strictly control and limit the size, amount, or range of something: *The law restricts the sale of hand guns.*
restrict sth to sth *a population policy that restricted families to one child per couple*

5 when there is no limit

there is no limit /ðeər ɪz ,nəʊ 'lɪmɪt/ use this to say that someone can have or do as much of something as they want
+to/on *If you buy one of these tickets there's no limit to the distance you can travel. | There's no limit on the number of applications you can make.*

unlimited /ʌn'lɪmɪtɪd/ [adj] something that is **unlimited** has no fixed limit: *For £30 a month, you get unlimited access to the Internet. | They seem to have unlimited amounts of money to spend on advertising.*

LINE

1 on paper, in a pattern, or on clothes

line /laɪn/ [n C] a long thin continuous mark on a surface: *The teacher had put a red line through my work. | If the ball goes over this line, it's out of play. | You're not allowed to park on double yellow lines.*
straight line *Use your ruler to draw a straight line.*
lined [adj] paper that is **lined** has lines printed across it: *a letter written on pale blue lined paper*

stripe /straɪp/ [n C] a straight line of colour on cloth, paper etc, usually part of a pattern where the line is repeated many times: *He wore a grey suit with narrow blue stripes. | The car had green and white stripes painted along its side.*
striped [adj] clothing or material that is **striped** has stripes on it: *a yellow and white striped swimsuit*

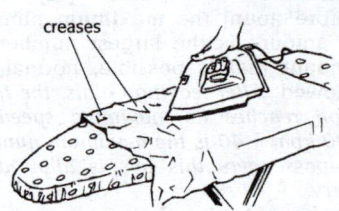

creases

crease

crease /kriːs/ [n C] a line on a piece of clothing or material where it has been folded or crushed: *She did her best to smooth the creases out of her skirt.*
creased [adj] clothes that are **creased** have a lot of creases in them: *When he unpacked his jacket, he found it was badly creased.*

2 on someone's skin

wrinkles /'rɪŋkəlz/ [n plural] deep lines on someone's face or skin, caused by growing old: *His face was old and covered in wrinkles.*

wrinkled [*adj*] if your skin is **wrinkled**, it has deep lines on it: *her wrinkled old hands*

lines /laɪnz/ [*n plural*] lines that form on someone's skin: *The deep lines on his forehead showed that he was a worried man.*

lined [*adj*] WRITTEN if your skin or face is **lined**, it has lines on it: *His forehead was deeply lined with worry.*

3 a line of writing or numbers

line /laɪn/ [*n C*] a line of writing that goes across a page: *Martin opened the letter and read the first few lines – it was bad news.* | *Start reading aloud at line 12.*
+of *a few lines of poetry*

column /ˈkɒləm‖ˈkɑː-/ [*n C*] a line of numbers, written under each other, that goes down a page: *Add up the numbers in the column on the right.*

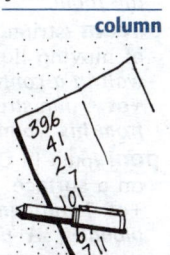

column

4 a line of people or things

line /laɪn/ [*n C*] several people, trees, hills etc standing next to each other or one behind the other
in a line (=forming a line) *The photographer asked us to stand in a line.*
+of *In front of the house there is a line of tall trees.*

row

The first two rows were empty.

row /rəʊ/ [*n C*] a line of people or things next to each other, especially one of several lines that are arranged one behind another
+of *a row of empty seats*

front/back row *Can you see me in the photo? I'm in the back row.*
row upon/after row WRITTEN (=many rows) *The beaches are packed with row upon row of sunburnt bodies.*

procession /prəˈseʃən/ [*n C*] a group of people or vehicles that move slowly along in a line, especially as part of a public ceremony: *We were held up by a long funeral procession.* | *The children were eager to take part in the carnival procession.*

5 a line of people waiting for something

queue

queue BRITISH **line** AMERICAN /kjuː, laɪn/ [*n C*] a number of people who are standing one behind another, waiting to do something: *There was a queue at the bus-stop.*
+for *The line for the movie went right around the block.*
in a queue/line *We were stuck in a queue for half an hour.*

stand in line/wait in line /ˌstænd ɪn ˈlaɪn, ˌweɪt ɪn ˈlaɪn/ ESPECIALLY AMERICAN to stand in a line of people who are waiting to do something: *Jerry joined the crowd of people waiting in line outside the stadium.*

queue /kjuː/ [*v I*] BRITISH to stand in a line of people who are waiting to do something: *We had to queue for hours in the rain.*
queue for sth (=queue to get something) *I spent so long queuing for a ticket that I nearly missed the train.*
queue to do sth *There were hundreds of football fans queuing to get in.*
queue up (=form a queue) *Every night, people queue up outside Club 49.*

queuing – queued – have queued

6 the line that separates two areas or countries

border /ˈbɔːʳdəʳ/ [n C] the official line that separates two countries, or the area close to this line: *They escaped across the border into Thailand.*
+with *Spain's border with France*
+between *The town lies on the border between Chile and Argentina.*
the German/Mexican/Swiss etc border *Strasbourg is very close to the German border.*

boundary /ˈbaʊndəri/ [n C] the official line that marks the edge of an area of land, for example a farm or one of the parts of a country: *More and more people are moving outside the city boundaries.*
+between *The Mississippi River forms the boundary between Tennessee and Arkansas.*
plural **boundaries**

LIQUID

➡ see also **MIX**

1 a liquid

liquid /ˈlɪkwɨd/ [n C/U] a substance, such as water or milk, that is not a solid and not a gas: *She screamed as the boiling liquid burned her skin.* | *Add most of the flour to the liquid and stir the mixture.*

liquid [adj usually before noun] use this about something which is a liquid, but which is usually a solid or a gas: *Treat your plants once a week with liquid fertiliser.* | *liquid soap* | *liquid oxygen*

fluid /ˈfluːɨd/ [n C/U] a liquid: *During exercise, the body loses fluid and salt.*
body/bodily fluids *blood, saliva and other bodily fluids*

> **Formal or informal?**
>
> **Fluid** is used especially in technical or scientific English.

2 an amount of liquid

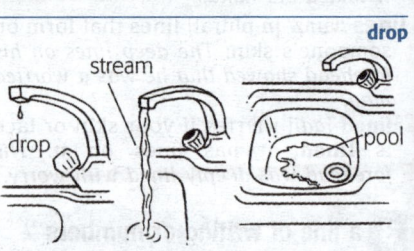

drop /drɒp‖drɑːp/ [n C] a very small amount of liquid that falls from somewhere in a round shape
+of *Big drops of rain hit the window pane.* | *A drop of wax fell onto the carpet as she carried the candle across the room.*

stream /striːm/ [n C] a continuous line of moving liquid: *Water ran down the wall in a continuous stream.*
+of *A thin stream of blood was pouring from his wound.*

pool /puːl/ [n C] an area of liquid lying on a surface
+of *Trautman was lying in a pool of blood.* | *A pool of oil had collected under the car.*

3 liquid that flows easily

thin /θɪn/ [adj] a **thin** liquid flows very easily, especially because it is not quite thick enough: *Don't make the mixture too thin or the pancakes will taste watery.*
thin – thinner – thinnest

runny /ˈrʌni/ [adj] INFORMAL food that is **runny** is liquid but should be thicker than it is: *a boiled egg with a runny yolk* | *runny custard*
runny – runnier – runniest

molten /ˈməʊltən/ [adj only before noun] **molten** rock, metal, glass etc has been made into a liquid by being heated to a very high temperature: *You can watch craftsmen make beautiful vases out of molten glass.* | *The town was buried under a river of molten lava.* | *molten wax*

4 liquid that flows slowly

thick /θɪk/ [adj] a **thick** liquid flows slowly because it is almost solid: If you want to make the sauce thicker, add flour. | The soup was thick and creamy.

lumpy /ˈlʌmpi/ [adj] a liquid that is **lumpy** contains many small solid pieces, so it is not as smooth as it should be: This gravy is lumpy. | I hate lumpy porridge.

5 to become a liquid

melt /melt/ [v I/T] if something solid **melts** or if heat **melts** it, it becomes liquid: The snow has all melted. | The chocolate had melted and was all over the inside of her pocket. | Melt the butter in a saucepan and stir in the sugar.

melted [adj only before noun] a pasta dish topped with melted cheese

dissolve /dɪˈzɒlv‖dɪˈzɑːlv/ [v I/T] if something solid **dissolves** or if you **dissolve** it, it is added to a liquid and mixed with it, so that it becomes liquid itself: The crystals dissolve in water to create a purple liquid. | Dissolve the salt in 125 ml of hot water.

6 when liquid moves or comes out of somewhere

pour /pɔːʳ/ [v I] if a liquid **pours** out of something, down something etc, large amounts of it fall in that direction

+out of/off/down Water was pouring out of the crack in the ceiling. | Tears poured down her cheeks.

flow /fləʊ/ [v I] if a liquid **flows**, it moves in a steady, continuous stream from one place to another: The river flows more slowly here and it is safe to swim.

+into/out of/over From here, factory waste flows straight into the sea.

come out /ˌkʌm ˈaʊt/ [phrasal verb I] if liquid **comes out** of a pipe, container etc, it flows out slowly and in small quantities: When I turned on the tap a brownish liquid came out.

+of There's oil coming out of your engine.

leak /liːk/ [v I] if liquid **leaks** from a container or pipe, or if a container or pipe **leaks**, the liquid comes out through a small hole or crack because the container or pipe is damaged: I think the fuel tank is leaking.

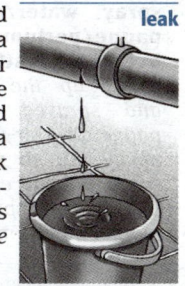

leak

+through/into/out of/from Water was leaking from a pipe in the bathroom. | Yoghurt had leaked out of my lunchbox all over my bag.

drip /drɪp/ [v I] if a liquid **drips**, it falls slowly and steadily, in drops

drip

+off/out/from/onto The blood was still dripping from the cut on his lip. | We stood under a tree, with rain dripping onto our heads.

dripping – dripped – have dripped

7 to make liquid come out of a container

pour /pɔːʳ/ [v T] to make liquid flow steadily from a container, by turning the container over or by making it lean to one side

pour sth on/into/down sth Pour the milk into a jug. | Nassim poured the whisky down the sink.

spill /spɪl/ [v T] to accidentally make liquid come out of a container

spill sth onto/over/into sth Someone had spilled red wine all over the carpet. | A tanker has spilled 6000 gallons of oil into the sea.

spilling – spilled (also **spilt** BRITISH) – **have spilled** (also **have spilt** BRITISH)

spray /spreɪ/ [v T] to force liquid out of a container so that it comes out in a stream of very small drops and covers an area

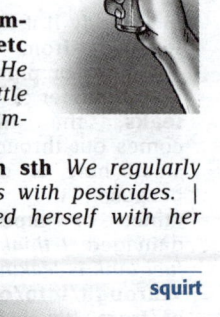

spray

spray water/cham-pagne/perfume etc over/onto sth *He shook up the bottle and sprayed champagne all over us.*

spray sth/sb with sth *We regularly spray all our crops with pesticides.* | *She quickly sprayed herself with her mother's perfume.*

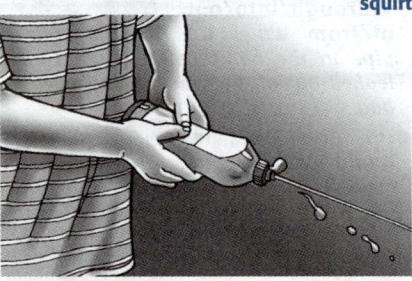

squirt

squirt /skwɜːʳt/ [v T] to make liquid come out of a container in a short thin stream, especially by pressing the sides of the container

squirt sth into/onto/over sth *Mike squirted disinfectant onto the kitchen counter and began to wipe it down.* | *Squirt a little oil into the lock to loosen it.*

LIST

1 a list

list /lɪst/ [n C] a set of names of people, places, things that you have to do etc, which are written one below the other and kept as a record

+of *a list of words that we had to learn*

be on a list *If your name isn't on the guest list, you won't get in.*

make a list *Make a list of all the people you want to send Christmas cards to.*

a waiting list (=a list of people who are waiting for something) *The*

English course is very popular so there might be a waiting list.

a shopping list (=a list of things you need to buy)

cross sth off a list (=remove it from a list) *We have plenty of eggs, so you can cross them off the list.*

register /ˈredʒɔ̰stəʳ/ [n C] an official list containing the names of all the people, organizations, or things of a particular type

+of *a register of qualified translators* | *a civil register of births, deaths, and marriages*

checklist /ˈtʃekˌlɪst/ [n C] a list that you write to make sure that you will remember all the things that you need to do or get

+of *When you go camping, it's a good idea to make a checklist of all the things you need to take with you.*

agenda /əˈdʒendə/ [n C] a list of all the things that will be discussed at a meeting: *Do you have an agenda for this morning's meeting?*

2 to provide a list

list /lɪst/ [v T] to give a written or spoken list of names, places etc: *a useful booklet, listing all the colleges that take part-time students*

be listed *The books are listed alphabetically, according to the name of the author.*

LISTEN

➡ see also **HEAR**

> ⚠ Don't confuse **listen** and **hear**. If you **listen** to something, you pay attention so that you can **hear** it well.

listen /ˈlɪsən/ [v I] to pay attention to what someone is saying or to a sound that you hear: *I didn't hear the answer because I wasn't listening when she read it out.*

+to *Gordon was lying on his bed, listening to music.*

listen carefully *They all listened carefully while she was telling them the story.*

🔍 **Listen!** SPOKEN (say this when you want to get someone's attention) *Listen! I've just had a brilliant idea.*

> Don't say 'I listen music'. Say **I listen to music**.

pay attention /ˌpeɪ əˈtenʃən/ to listen carefully to what someone is saying: *I have some important information about travel arrangements, so please pay attention.*
+to *She went on talking, but I wasn't really paying attention to what she was saying.*

eavesdrop

eavesdrop /ˈiːvzdrɒp‖-drɑːp/ [v I] to secretly listen to someone else's conversation by standing near them, hiding behind a door etc: *"How does Jake know that?" "He must have been eavesdropping."*
+on *I used to sit in cafés and eavesdrop on the conversations around me.*

listen in /ˌlɪsən ˈɪn/ [phrasal verb I] to listen to someone else's telephone conversation when they do not know that you are listening
+on *The police were listening in on their conversation.*

LITTLE/NOT MUCH

➡ if you mean 'not big', go to **SMALL**
➡ see also **FEW**

1   a small amount

a little /ə ˈlɪtl/ [quantifier] a small amount of something
a little food/time/help etc *I think I'll have a little cream in my coffee.* | *They may need a little help.*

just a little (=only a small amount) *"Do you speak Japanese?" "Just a little."*
a little more/less *I wish he'd show a little more interest in his work.*

> Don't say 'I speak a little of Spanish'. Say **I speak a little Spanish**.

a little bit (also **a bit** BRITISH) /ə ˌlɪtl ˈbɪt, ə ˈbɪt/ [quantifier] INFORMAL a small amount of something: *Don't buy a large pack – I only need a little bit.*
+of *It's a good way of making a bit of extra money.*
a little bit more/less *Tell us a little bit more about your plans.*

not much /nɒt ˈmʌtʃ/ [quantifier] only a small amount of something – use this especially when there is less than you need: *There's not much light in this room.* | *He doesn't have much experience of running a business.*
not very much *You haven't eaten very much.* | *We didn't have very much time, so we took a taxi.*

🔍 **a drop** /ə ˈdrɒp‖-ˈdrɑːp/ [quantifier] ESPECIALLY SPOKEN a small amount of something that you drink: *"Do you take cream in your coffee?" "Yes, just a drop, please."*
+of *Could I have a drop of milk in my tea?*

2   a very small amount

very little /ˌveri ˈlɪtl/ [quantifier] a very small amount of something: *"How much do you know about computers?" "Very little, I'm afraid."* | *Fish contains very little fat.* | *Changing the law will make very little difference.*

hardly any /ˌhɑːʳdli ˈeni/ [quantifier] such a small amount that there is almost none at all: *We need some more paper – there's hardly any left.* | *Ian's learning to play the guitar, but he hardly gets any time to practise.*

scarce /skeəʳs/ [adj] if something that you need is **scarce**, there is only a small amount available, and there is not enough of it: *After the war, food and clothing were scarce.* | *a waste of scarce natural resources*

3 a little tired/sad/older/bigger etc

a little /ə 'lɪtl/ [adv] *I'm feeling a little tired. I think I'll go upstairs and have a rest.* | *"Do you feel sad that you're leaving?" "Just a little."*

a little bit (also **a bit** BRITISH) /ə ˌlɪtl 'bɪt, ə 'bɪt/ [adv] INFORMAL a little: *I'm feeling a little bit better today.* | *She looked a bit surprised when she saw me.*

slightly /'slaɪtli/ [adv] very little, but not enough to be important or easy to notice: *We're almost the same age. He's slightly older than me.* | *Sean's car is a slightly different colour.*

4 when something or someone moves or changes a little

a little /ə 'lɪtl/ *His work has improved a little since he came to the school.* | *I noticed that Mrs Ewing's hand was trembling a little.*

a little bit (also **a bit** BRITISH) /ə ˌlɪtl 'bɪt, ə 'bɪt/ INFORMAL a little: *Do you mind if I open the window a little bit?* | *The centre of the town has changed a bit, but everything else is just as I remember it.*

slightly /'slaɪtli/ [adv] a little, but not enough to be important or easy to notice: *The temperature had risen slightly, but it was still very cold.*

not much /nɒt 'mʌtʃ/ only a little and not as much as you might have expected: *Things haven't changed much over the past few years.*

LIVE

➡ opposite **DIE**
➡ if you mean 'not die', go to **ALIVE**
➡ see also WB **HOUSES/WHERE PEOPLE LIVE, HOME**

1 to live in a place

live /lɪv/ [v I] to have your home in a particular place: *Where do you live?*
+in *Do you like living in Tokyo?* | *Do you live in an apartment or a house?* | *Judy lives in that nice house on the corner.*
+at *In 1905 Russell was living at 4 Ralston Street.*

> ⚠ Use **in** before the name of a country or town: *John lives in Canada/in Toronto.* Use **at** before the exact address: *John lives at 78 Clancy Street.*

> ⚠ Don't confuse **live** (=live somewhere permanently) and **stay** (=live there for a short time): *We stayed at a small hotel close to the beach.*

grow up /ˌɡrəʊ 'ʌp/ [phrasal verb I] to live in a place during the time when you are a child: *This is the place where I grew up.*
+in *Margaret Hallworth was born in Manchester, but grew up in North Wales.*

settle /'setl/ [v I] to start to live permanently in a country or city, after you have lived in several different places
+in *We lived in Thailand, then Singapore, and finally settled in Hong Kong.*

2 to live in the same house as someone else

live with sb /'lɪv wɪð (sb)/ [phrasal verb T] *I live with an old friend from college.* | *Do you still live with your parents?*

live together /'lɪv təˌɡeðəʳ/ [phrasal verb I] if two people **live together**, they live in the same house and have a sexual relationship: *These days, people often live together before getting married.*

share a house/apartment/room with sb /ˌʃeər ə ˈhaʊs, əˈpɑːˈtmənt, ˈruːm wɪð (sb)/ to live with someone who is not a member of your family and not your sexual partner: *My brother shares a house with four other students.* | *I used to share an apartment with a guy who played the drums.*

room with sb /ˈruːm wɪð (sb)/ [*phrasal verb* T] AMERICAN to live in the same room as someone at college: *Do you remember Diane? I roomed with her at college.*

flatmate BRITISH **roommate** AMERICAN /ˈflætmeɪt, ˈruːmˌmeɪt, ˈrʊm-/ [*n* C] someone that you share an apartment with, who is not a member of your family and not your sexual partner: *This is Rosalind, my flatmate.* | *You can't have a party without asking your roommate first.*

3 someone who lives in a place

> ⚠ If you want to say how many people live in a place, say **a city/country with a population of 5 million** or **a city/country with 5 million inhabitants**.

population /ˌpɒpjʊˈleɪʃən‖ˌpɑːp-/ [*n* singular/U] all the people who live in a country or town or area, or the number of people who live in it: *In Ghana 46% of the population is under 16 years of age.*
+of *The population of Singapore is almost 3 million.*
the adult/Muslim/black population (=all the people in a place who are adult, Muslim etc) *90% of the adult population is literate.*

resident /ˈrezɪdənt/ [*n* C] someone who lives in a particular area of a town, a particular street or apartment block etc: *Local residents are protesting about the new road.* | *Parking spaces are for residents only.*
+of *Residents of Glacier Bay are complaining about the pollution caused by cruise ships.*

community /kəˈmjuːnɪti/ [*n* C] all the people who live in the same area or town, considered as a group: *A library*

is very important for the local community.
serve a community (=be for all the people in an area or town) *The new health centre will serve the whole community.*
the European/Asian/Muslim etc community (=all the European etc people in an area or town)
plural **communities**

> ⚠ You can also use **community** before a noun, like an adjective: *local businesses and community groups* | *a meeting at the community centre*

inhabitant /ɪnˈhæbɪtənt/ [*n* C usually plural] ESPECIALLY WRITTEN one of the people who live in a place, especially in a town or city or in an area of a country: *Copenhagen has about 1.4 million inhabitants.* | *This is a poor rural area, with only one doctor per 10,000 inhabitants.*
+of *the inhabitants of the San Fernando Valley*

tenant /ˈtenənt/ [*n* C] someone who lives in a house, apartment, or room and regularly pays money to the person who owns it: *Tenants are not allowed to keep pets.* | *Have you found any tenants for your house yet?*

LONG

➡ look here for ...
  • long hair, a long street etc
  • a long book, list etc
  • a long time
➡ opposite **SHORT**
➡ see also **MEASURE, TALL**
➡ if you mean 'after a long time', go to **END**

1 a long object, line, space etc

long /lɒŋ‖lɔːŋ/ [*adj*] measuring a great distance from one end to the other: *The girl had long blonde hair.* | *There was a long line of people at the ticket office.* | *She led them down a long corridor, through countless swinging doors.* | *Rome has the longest shopping street in Europe.*

2 how long an object is

how long /haʊ 'lɒŋ‖-'lɔːŋ/ use this to ask or talk about how long something is: *How long is your garden?*

four inches/two metres etc long /(four inches, etc)lɒŋ‖-lɔːŋ/ use this to say exactly how long something is: *The snake was more than three metres long.* | *a mile-long tunnel*

length /leŋθ/ [n C/U] how long something is: *These fish can grow to a length of four feet.* | *We need to measure the length and width of the room.*

four inches/two metres/five miles etc in length *The hotel pool is 15 metres in length.*

3 a long book/name/list/speech etc

long /lɒŋ‖lɔːŋ/ [adj] a **long** book, speech, name etc has a lot of pages, words, or letters etc in it: *The place has a long Welsh name that I can't pronounce.* | *The principal gave a long, boring speech about discipline.* | *There was a long list of jobs that she needed to do that day.*

lengthy /'leŋθi/ [adj] FORMAL a **lengthy** book, speech, explanation, or document has a lot of words and details in it, and is often boring: *a lengthy, two-volume book on conditions in modern China* | *a lengthy financial report*

long-winded /ˌlɒŋ 'wɪndᵻd◄ ‖ˌlɔːŋ-/ [adj] boring and much longer than it needs to be: *The book begins with a rather long-winded description of the historical background to the war.* | *I had to listen to his long-winded explanation as to why he was late.*

4 a long time

a long time /ə ˌlɒŋ 'taɪm‖-ˌlɔːŋ-/

(for) a long time *He's lived here a long time.* | *The house has been empty for a long time.*

a long time ago *We met in August 1947, a long time ago.*

a very long time *We've been friends for a very long time.*

it's a long time since *It's a long time since I heard from Clive.*

a while /ə 'waɪl/ a fairly long time: *After a while people started to complain*

for a while *How's Lynn? I haven't seen her for a while.*

quite a while (=a long time) *He's been going out with her quite a while now, hasn't he?*

long /lɒŋ‖lɔːŋ/ [adv] for a long time: *Have you been waiting long?*

long before/after *Michelle was wearing platform shoes long before they came into fashion.*

ages /'eɪdʒɪz/ [n plural] SPOKEN INFORMAL, ESPECIALLY BRITISH a very long time

for ages *I haven't been out for ages.*

wait/take/spend ages *I spent ages in town trying to find something to wear for the wedding.* | *We had to wait ages for a bus.*

it's ages since *It's ages since we played this game – I'd forgotten how good you are.*

ages ago *"When did you sell the car?" "Ages ago!"*

hours/months/years /aʊəʳz, mʌnθs, jɪəʳz/ [n plural] many hours, months, or years, and a lot longer than you expected: *It was years before we found out the truth.*

for hours/months/years *I'm worried – Robin's been out for hours.*

take (sb) hours/months/years *It took us months to paint the house.*

5 continuing for a long time

long /lɒŋ‖lɔːŋ/ [adj] *The play was quite good, but it was too long.* | *He died after a long illness.* | *It's a long flight.*

long-term /ˌlɒŋ 'tɜːʳm◄ ‖ˌlɔːŋ-/ [adj only before noun] a **long-term** problem, situation, or effect is one that continues for a very long time: *Drugs such as Ecstasy may cause long-term damage to the brain.* | *long-term unemployment*

long-term relationship (=a sexual relationship that lasts for a long time) *I'm not ready for a long-term relationship right now.*

lasting /'lɑːstɪŋ‖'læs-/ [adj only before noun] strong enough or effective enough to continue for a long time a **lasting** **peace/friendship/agreement** *The people of Northern Ireland are praying for a lasting peace.*

Formal or informal?
Lasting is used in writing and in formal spoken English.

long-running /ˌlɒŋ ˈrʌnɪŋ◂ ‖ˌlɔːŋ-/ [adj only before noun]
long-running **dispute/row/debate/conflict** an argument, disagreement, or war that continues for a very long time: *The two countries have signed an agreement, ending a long-running dispute over fishing rights.*

interminable /ɪnˈtɜːˈmɪ̯nəbəl/ [adj] FORMAL something that is **interminable** continues for much too long and makes you feel impatient or annoyed: *Tuesday was always a day of interminable meetings.* | *After an interminable delay, the bus finally left the station.*

6   something that you need a lot of time to do

take a long time /ˌteɪk ə ˌlɒŋ ˈtaɪm‖ -ˌlɔːŋ-/ if something **takes a long time**, you need a lot of time to do it: *I never go to work by train because it takes such a long time.* | *Your body takes a long time to recover after an operation.*
   it takes (sb) a long time to do sth *It takes a long time to make friends when you move to a new town.* | *It took me a long time to learn how the system worked.*

take time /ˌteɪk ˌtaɪm/ if something **takes time** to do, it cannot be done quickly and you have to be patient: *Learning a new language always takes time.*
   it takes time to do sth *It takes time to get to know people.*

time-consuming /ˈtaɪm kənˌsjuːmɪŋ‖ -ˌsuː-/ [adj] an activity, process, or job that is **time-consuming** takes a very long time to do: *Checking all the calculations used to be a very time-consuming process.*

LOOK AFTER

➡ see also **CHILD, BABY**

1   to look after someone

look after sb /ˌlʊk ˈɑːftəˈ (sb)‖-ˈæf-/ [phrasal verb T] to spend time with a child or with someone who is old or sick, and make sure they are safe and have the things they need: *Can you look after the kids for me while I'm out?* | *I took a week off work to look after my mother when she had her operation.*

take care of sb /ˌteɪk ˈkeəˈ ɒv (sb)/ to look after someone, especially someone who is very young, very old, or very sick, and needs someone to help them all the time: *Taking care of young children is a full-time job.* | *My father became so ill that we couldn't take care of him at home any more.*
   take good care of sb (=look after them well) *Don't worry, I'll take good care of him.*

care for sb /ˈkeəˈ fɔːˈ (sb)/ [phrasal verb T] to look after someone who is very ill or very old by doing everything for them: *Elsie had to leave her job to care for her sick father.*

Formal or informal?
Care for sb is more formal than **look after sb** or **take care of sb**.

2   to look after children until they have grown up

bring up /ˌbrɪŋ ˈʌp/ [phrasal verb T] to look after children until they have grown up: *His parents had a lot of problems, so he was brought up by his grandparents.*
   bring up sb *I don't know how they managed to bring up six children with so little money.*
   bring sb up *I brought my son up by myself.*

raise /reɪz/ [v T often passive] ESPECIALLY AMERICAN to look after children until they have grown up: *Raising a family is one of the toughest jobs in the world.*
be raised *My brother and I were raised on a small farm in Missouri.*

3 someone who is paid to look after children

babysitter (also **sitter** INFORMAL) /ˈbeɪbiˌsɪtəʳ, ˈsɪtəʳ/ [n C] someone who is paid to look after children while their parents go out for the evening

childminder /ˈtʃaɪldˌmaɪndəʳ/ [n C] BRITISH someone who is paid to look afterchildren while their parents are at work

nanny /ˈnæni/ [n C] a woman who is paid to look after someone else's children, and who lives in the house with the family
plural **nannies**

4 to look after something

look after sth /ˌlʊk ˈɑːftəʳ (sth)‖-ˈæf-/ [phrasal verb T] to keep something in good condition and make sure that it does not get broken, damaged, or stolen: *You can have a new bike for Christmas if you promise to look after it.*
look after sth for sb *The neighbours are going to look after the house for us while we're away.*

take care of sth /ˌteɪk ˈkeəʳ ɒv (sth)/ to look after something, especially something that is expensive or easily broken, or needs a lot of attention: *That car should run for another ten years if you take care of it.*
take good care of sth (=look after it well) *The boat's previous owner had obviously taken very good care of it.*

🔍 **keep an eye on sth** /ˌkiːp ən ˈaɪ ɒn (sth)/ INFORMAL, ESPECIALLY SPOKEN to look after something that belongs to someone else for a short time, by watching it to make sure that it does not get stolen or damaged: *Tom went into the library while I kept an eye on the bikes.* | *Can you keep an eye on my bags while I go to the toilet?*

maintain /meɪnˈteɪn, mən-/ [v T] ESPECIALLY WRITTEN to make sure that a car, machine, or building is in good condition by checking it and repairing it when necessary: *Neither of his cars had been properly maintained.*

> **Formal or informal?**
> **Maintain** is a formal word that is used especially in writing.

maintenance /ˈmeɪntənəns/ [n U] the job of maintaining a car, building, or machine: *A car is quite a big expense, especially when you consider maintenance costs.* | *The landlord is responsible for the maintenance of the building.*

LOOK AT

➡ see also **SEE, WATCH**

> ⚠ Don't confuse **see**, **watch**, and **look at**. When you **see** something, you notice it with your eyes, either deliberately or accidentally: *I saw an accident on my way to school today.* You **watch** films, sports games, or other situations where there is action and movement: *Dad was watching a basketball game on TV.* When you **look at** people, scenery, pictures, and other things that are not moving, you deliberately pay attention to them: *Look at this old picture of Sally!*

1 to look at someone or something

look /lʊk/ [v I] to turn your eyes towards something so that you can see it: *Look, there are swans on the river.*
+at *"Come on, it's time to go," he said, looking at his watch.* | *Look at me when I'm talking to you.*
+into/out of/through/down etc *Helen was looking out of the window, waiting for him to arrive.* | *Janie looked into her mailbox, but there was nothing there.* | *The teacher stopped and looked around to see if there were any questions.*
look at sb/sth in amazement/ disbelief/surprise etc (=in a way that shows you are surprised or shocked) *Sean looked at her in disbelief. "Are you sure?"*
look [n C] when you turn your eyes to

look at someone or something: *Sarah needed only one look at her daughter's face to know that she was in trouble.* | *I was getting disapproving looks from the people around me.*

> Don't use **look at** when you are talking about TV programmes, games, or things that are happening. Use **watch**: *I was watching a baseball game.* | *The kids are watching a video.*

🔍 **have a look/take a look** /ˌhæv ə 'lʊk, ˌteɪk ə 'lʊk/ ESPECIALLY SPOKEN to look at something, especially something interesting or unusual
+at *We climbed to the top of the tower to have a look at the view.* | *"You'd better take a look at this," she said, passing me a letter.*

stare /steəʳ/ [v I] to look directly at someone or something for a long time, without moving your eyes
+at *Why are you staring at me like that?* | *She stared at the page for several minutes, trying to understand.*
+into/out of etc *My cat spends all day staring out of the window.*
stare back (at sb) (=stare at someone who is looking at you)
stare in amazement/horror/disbelief (=in a way that shows you are surprised or shocked) *Donna stared in horror as the man fell to the floor.*
stare [n C] WRITTEN a long direct look: *Charles didn't reply. He just gave his daughter an angry stare.*

gaze /ɡeɪz/ [v I] ESPECIALLY WRITTEN to look at someone or something for a long time, especially with a feeling of love or great pleasure
+at *I lay back on the sand and gazed at the stars above.*
+out/into/down etc *He was gazing into her eyes as he spoke.* | *Ruth gazed down at the sleeping child.*

> Use **gaze** especially when you are writing stories and descriptions.

glare /ɡleəʳ/ [v I] ESPECIALLY WRITTEN to look angrily at someone: *He sat there in silence, glaring angrily.*
+at *Sarah glared at her father. "How dare you say that!"*

> Use **glare** especially when you are writing stories and descriptions.

2 to look carefully

look carefully/closely /ˌlʌk 'keəʳfəli, 'kləʊsli/ to look carefully at something in order to see small details: *If you look carefully, you can see the artist's name in the corner of the picture.*
+at *He looked closely at the pattern on the plate. "My Grandma used to have plates like this."*

🔍 **take a look at sth/have a look at sth** /ˌteɪk ə 'lʌk æt (sth), ˌhæv ə 'lʌk æt (sth)/ ESPECIALLY SPOKEN to look carefully at something in order to find out what is wrong with it or to find out something about it: *I've asked Ken to take a look at the car – the engine's making strange noises.* | *The doctor will be here soon to have a look at your ankle.*
take/have a good look at sth (=look very carefully and thoroughly) *Take a good look at the photograph, Mr Brent. Do you recognise anyone?*

examine /ɪɡ'zæmən/ [v T] to look at something carefully and thoroughly because you want to find out more about it: *When the police examined the gun, they discovered Wright's fingerprints on it.* | *A team of divers was sent down to examine the wreck.*

> **Formal or informal?**
> **Examine** is used especially in writing and in formal spoken English.

check/inspect /tʃek, ɪn'spekt/ [v T] to look at something carefully and thoroughly to make sure that it is correct, safe, or working properly: *The factory is regularly inspected by a fire-safety officer.* | *Technicians would check the engines and replace any worn parts.*
check sth for damage/faults/cracks (=in order to find any damage) *After the explosion, they had to check the building for structural damage.*

go over sth/go through sth /ˌɡəʊ 'əʊvəʳ (sth), ˌɡəʊ 'θruː (sth)/ [phrasal verb T] to look carefully at every part of a document or plan in order to make sure that it is all correct: *I'd like* to go over last month's accounts with you. | Marion's been through your report and she hasn't found any mistakes.

examination /ɪgˌzæmᵻ'neɪʃən/ [n C/U] when you look at something carefully in order to find out more about it: *Police are continuing their examination of the scene of the crime.*

on closer examination (=when you look at something more carefully) *On closer examination the painting was found to be a clever copy.*

> **Formal or informal?**
>
> **Examination** is used in writing and in formal spoken English.

inspection /ɪn'spekʃən/ [n C] an official visit to a school, factory, prison etc by someone whose job is to make sure that everything is being done correctly
+of *There are regular inspections of the prison by government health officers.*
carry out an inspection (=make an inspection) *Admiral Naumenko personally carried out an inspection of the fleet.*

3 to look quickly or secretly

glance /glɑːnsǁglæns/ [v I] to look quickly at something or someone, and then look away
+at *Dr Morse kept glancing nervously at his watch.* | *I saw them glance at each other as if they shared a secret.*
+into/down/through etc *Glancing into Neil's room, she noticed that his suitcase was packed.*
glance [n C] a quick look: *A quick glance at the map showed that we were on the right road.*

⟠ **take a quick look/have a quick look** /teɪk ə ˌkwɪk 'lʊk, hæv ə ˌkwɪk 'lʊk/ ESPECIALLY SPOKEN to look at something quickly, especially in order to check that everything is satisfactory
+at/around/through etc *I had a quick look around the place yesterday.* | *He took a quick look in the mirror, and went out of the house.*

peep /piːp/ [v I] ESPECIALLY BRITISH to look at something quickly and secretly, especially from a place where you cannot be seen

+through / into / round We peeped through a crack in the fence, and saw her talking to a strange looking man. | Bobby peeped round the corner to see what was happening.

peep

peek/take a peek /piːk, ˌteɪk ə 'piːk/ [v I] AMERICAN to look quickly and secretly, especially from a place where you cannot be seen: *The children were peeking from behind the wall.* | *She quickly opened the door and took a peek inside.*

4 to look at things in a shop/market/area

look around/have a look around /ˌlʊk ə'raʊnd, hæv ə ˌlʊk ə'raʊnd/ [phrasal verb I] to look at the different things in a place such as a shop, market, or town etc, while you are walking around: *I think I'll just look around for a while – I'm not sure what I want.* | *You're welcome to have a look around. We have a wide range of sportswear.*

> ⚠ In British English, you can also say **look round** and **have a look round**.

browse /braʊz/ [v I] to spend time looking at things in a shop, especially books or records, without intending to buy anything: *Armando spent the afternoon browsing in Camden market.*
+through *Joanne was standing in a bookstore browsing through some magazines.*

window-shopping /'wɪndəʊ ˌʃɒpɪŋǁ-ˌʃɑːp-/ [n U] the activity of looking at goods in shop windows without intending to buy anything: *We hadn't any money but we enjoyed window-shopping in Fifth Avenue.*

⟠ **I'm just looking** /aɪm ˌdʒʌst 'lʊkɪŋ/ SPOKEN say this to tell someone who works in a shop that you are only looking at things, and you do not intend to buy anything just now: *"Can I help you?" "No thanks, I'm just looking."*

5 to stop looking at something

look away /ˌlʊk əˈweɪ/ [phrasal verb I] to turn your eyes away from something that you were looking at: *The accident was so horrible that I had to look away.*
+from *She looked away from him, unable to tell him the truth.*

look up /ˌlʊk ˈʌp/ [phrasal verb I] ESPECIALLY WRITTEN to stop looking at something and turn your face upwards, in order to see someone or talk to them: *There was a loud bang outside the classroom and we all looked up.*
+from *"Goodbye, then," she said, without even looking up from her newspaper.*

LOOK FOR

to try to find someone or something

1 to look for something you have lost or someone who is not where they should be

⇒ see also **LOSE, LOST**

look for sb/sth /ˈlʊk fɔːʳ (sb/sth)/ [phrasal verb T] to try to find something that you have lost, or someone who is not in the place where you expected them to be: *I'm looking for Simon – have you seen him?* | *I've been looking everywhere for that key! Where did you find it?*

try to find sb/sth /ˌtraɪ tə ˈfaɪnd (sb/sth)/ to look for someone or something, especially when it is difficult to find them: *Jill was up in the attic trying to find her old school books.* | *I'm trying to find my daughter – she was here five minutes ago.*

○ **have a look** /ˌhæv ə ˈlʊk/ ESPECIALLY SPOKEN to look for someone or something, especially when you do it quickly or when you only look in one place: *"I can't find my green dress." "Have a look in my bedroom."*
+for *I had a look for James but he wasn't in his office.*
have a quick look *I had a quick look but I couldn't see it.*

have a good look (=look carefully and thoroughly) *We don't have time to find it now – we'll have a good look in the morning.*

search for sb/sth /ˈsɜːʳtʃ fɔːʳ (sb/sth)/ [phrasal verb T] to look carefully and thoroughly for someone or something, especially when it is very important that you find them: *Detectives spent today searching for clues in the woods near the victim's home.* | *Friends and neighbours gathered to search for the missing boy.*

> **Formal or informal?**
> **Search for sb/sth** is used especially in formal writing and news reports.

in search of sb/sth /ɪn ˈsɜːʳtʃ ɒv (sb/sth)/ ESPECIALLY WRITTEN if you go **in search of** someone or something, you go somewhere to find them
go/set off in search of *She stayed and talked for a while, then went off in search of Flynn.*

2 to look for something or someone that you need

look for sth/sb /ˈlʊk fɔːʳ (sth/sb)/ [phrasal verb T] to try to find something or someone that you need: *Can you help me? I'm looking for a place to stay.* | *You should write to Data Corp – they're always looking for new staff.* | *I spent months looking for a job, with no luck.*

try to find sth/sb /ˌtraɪ tə ˈfaɪnd (sth/sb)/ to look for something or someone that you need, especially when it is difficult and takes a long time: *Doctors are still trying to find a cure for cancer.* | *I spent half an hour trying to find a parking space.*

in search of sth /ɪn ˈsɜːʳtʃ ɒv (sth)/ ESPECIALLY WRITTEN if you go **in search of** something that you need, you go somewhere to try to find it: *Menendez had travelled up from Mexico in search of a job.*

look up /ˌlʊk ˈʌp/ [phrasal verb T] to try to find information by looking in a book, on a list, in computer records etc
look up sth *I'll just look up her address – it's on the student database.*

look sth up *If you don't know what it means, look it up in the dictionary.*

be on the lookout for sth/sb /biː ɒn ðə ˈlʊkaʊt fɔːʳ (sth/sb)/ INFORMAL to continuously try to find something or someone that might be useful to you, and be careful to not miss any opportunities: *Maya was always on the lookout for a bargain. | The club is on the lookout for good, young players.*

3 when the police are looking for a criminal

➡ see also WB **POLICE, FOLLOW**

look for sb/search for sb /ˈlʊk fɔːʳ (sb), ˈsɜːʳtʃ fɔːʳ (sb)/ [phrasal verb T] to look for someone who has been involved in a crime or who has escaped from prison: *Police are still looking for the prisoner who escaped yesterday.*

> **Formal or informal?**
> **Search for sb** is used in news reports.

be after sb /biː ˈɑːftəʳ (sb)‖-ˈæf-/ [phrasal verb T] INFORMAL to try to find and catch someone who has done something wrong: *She said she was frightened because the police were after her. | The man we're after is one of the biggest drug-dealers in Europe.*

hunt /hʌnt/ [v I/T] to search for a criminal or for someone who has disappeared – use this when a large number of police are making an organized search over a wide area
+for *Police have been hunting for the missing woman for several days.*
hunt sb down (=search for a criminal until you find them) *The train-robbers were eventually hunted down in Australia.*

> **Formal or informal?**
> **Hunt** is used especially in formal writing and news reports.

4 when the police are looking for drugs, guns etc

➡ see also WB **POLICE, WEAPON**

search /sɜːʳtʃ/ [v T] to look in every part of a place or to look in someone's clothes or bags in order to try to find drugs, guns, stolen goods etc: *All visitors to the prison are thoroughly searched. | A team of police officers had searched the whole area, but couldn't find the murder weapon.*

go through sth /ˈgəʊ θruː (sth)/ [phrasal verb T] to carefully search all of someone's clothes, bags, or possessions to try to find things such as guns or drugs: *Customs officials went through his baggage but found nothing.*

raid /reɪd/ [v T] if the police **raid** a place, they arrive there suddenly to look for criminals, drugs, or stolen goods etc: *The Casino nightclub has been closed since it was raided last month. | The army used to raid houses in the Catholic districts in search of guns.*

frisk /frɪsk/ [v T] if the police, airport officials etc **frisk** someone, they feel the person's clothes and body looking for hidden weapons or drugs: *All the passengers were frisked before they got on the plane.*

5 an attempt to find something

search /sɜːʳtʃ/ [n C] an attempt to find someone or something, especially when this is well organized and a lot of people are doing it
+for *a search for survivors of the plane crash | Their search for gold took them west to Washington State.*
carry out a search (=search a place) *FBI agents carried out a thorough search of the building.*
search party (=an organized group of people searching for someone who is lost) *When the men did not return, the commanding officer sent out a search party.*
house-to-house search (=when every house in an area is searched) *House-to-house searches were carried out in the hope of finding the kidnapped baby.*

> **Formal or informal?**
> **Search** is used especially in formal writing and news reports.

hunt /hʌnt/ [n singular] an organized search by a lot of people, especially to find a criminal: *Police have launched a nationwide hunt for the killer.*

> **Formal or informal?**
>
> **Hunt** is used in formal writing and news reports.

raid /reɪd/ [n C] a sudden visit by the police to a building in order to look for criminals, drugs, stolen goods etc: *Two people were arrested today in a police raid on a house in South London.*

LOOSE

not fitting tightly or not firmly fixed

➡ opposite **TIGHT**

➡ see also **FASTEN/UNFASTEN**

> Don't confuse **loose** and **lose** (=to not be able to find something).

1 clothes

loose /luːs/ [adj] **loose** clothes do not fit your body tightly, so you feel comfortable when you wear them: *She wore a long, loose linen jacket.* | *In hot weather, loose cotton clothes are more comfortable.*

baggy /ˈbægi/ [adj] **baggy** clothes are designed to be big and loose and they hide the shape of your body: *Bill was wearing a polo shirt and baggy blue pants.* | *a comfortable baggy sweater*
baggy – baggier – baggiest

stretch /stretʃ/ [v I] if clothes **stretch**, they become looser and do not fit you properly any more: *Don't put that sweater in the washing machine – it'll stretch.*

loosen /ˈluːsən/ [v T] to make a piece of clothing looser and more comfortable by unfastening it: *Simon suddenly felt very hot, so he loosened his shirt and tie.* | *Loosen any tight clothing, and lay the patient on his side.*

2 rope/knot/chain

loose /luːs/ [adj] a rope, knot, chain etc that is **loose** is not tied or stretched tightly, and is not as tight as it should be: *The chain on my bicycle is loose and keeps slipping.*
come loose (=gradually become looser) *The string around the package had come loose and some of the papers had fallen out.*
loosely [adv] *a scarf tied loosely around his neck*

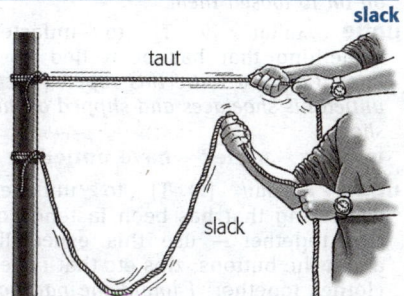

slack /slæk/ [adj] a rope or chain that is **slack** is not stretched as tightly as it can be or should be: *If the fish comes towards you, keep your line slack until it bites.*

loosen /ˈluːsən/ [v T] to make something loose when it has been pulled or fastened tightly: *She loosened the reins so that the horse could lower its head and drink.* | *Carl leaned back in his chair and loosened his belt.*

3 something that is not fixed firmly enough

loose /luːs/ [adj] something that is **loose** is not firmly fixed in the place where it should be: *Some of the floorboards are loose and they creak when you walk on them.* | *a loose tooth*
come loose (=gradually become loose) *This door handle's come loose.*
a loose connection (=when wires or electrical parts are not firmly connected)

wobbly /ˈwɒbli‖ˈwɑː-/ [adj] something that is **wobbly** shakes or moves from side to side because it is not fixed as firmly as it should be: *Don't sit on that chair – one of the legs is wobbly.* | *a wobbly ladder*

4 to make something loose that has been firmly or tightly fixed

loosen /ˈluːsən/ [v T] to make something loose in order to remove it, for example a screw or lid that has been tightly fixed: *I couldn't open the jar, so Paul loosened the top for me.* | *These screws are all rusty. Squirt some oil on to loosen them.*

untie /ʌnˈtaɪ/ [v T] to unfasten something that has been tied in a knot: *Can you untie this rope?* | *Pete untied his shoelaces and slipped off his shoes.*
untying – untied – have untied

undo /ʌnˈduː/ [v T] to unfasten something that has been fastened or tied together – use this especially about the buttons, zips etc that fasten clothes together: *I undid the package and looked inside.*
undo a button/belt/zip etc *Tony undid the buttons on his shirt.*
undo a jacket/shirt etc (=unfasten the buttons, zips etc on it)
undoing – undid – have undone

LOSE

➡ look here for ...
• when you can't find something
• not win a game, fight, or war
• lose your home, job etc
➡ If you mean 'when you do not know where you are', go to **LOST**

> ⚠ Don't confuse **lose** and **loose** (=not fitting tightly).

1 when you can't find something or someone

➡ opposite **FIND**
➡ see also **LOOK FOR, DISAPPEAR**

lose /luːz/ [v T] to be unable to find something, especially because you cannot remember where you put it: *If*

you lose your credit card, phone this number immediately.* | *Sylvia lost her keys and couldn't get into the house.*
losing – lost – have lost

can't find /ˌkɑːnt ˈfaɪndǁˌkænt-/ to be unable to find something or someone, especially after you have spent a long time looking for them: *She searched through all her pockets, but she couldn't find the tickets.* | *I don't know what's happened to Eric – I can't find him anywhere.*

2 something or someone that you cannot find

➡ see also **LOOK FOR, DISAPPER**

missing /ˈmɪsɪŋ/ [adj] a **missing** object is lost and may have been stolen; a **missing** person cannot be found and may be in danger: *Police are still searching for the missing gold.* | *She's been missing for three days now, and we're very worried.*
+from *Suddenly I realized that my passport was missing from my handbag.*
go missing (from) BRITISH (=become lost or be stolen) *Every year, hundreds of books go missing from the library.*

lost /lɒstǁlɔːst/ [adj] if something is **lost**, no one knows where it is: *Divers are searching for the plane's lost flight recorder.* | *Have you seen my calculator? I hope it isn't lost.*
get lost *I never received your parcel. It must have got lost in the mail.*

disappear /ˌdɪsəˈpɪəʳ/ [v I] if something **disappears**, it cannot be found and you think it may have been stolen; if someone **disappears**, they cannot be found and you think they may be in danger: *I left my purse here a moment ago, and now it's completely disappeared.* | *The girl was wearing a red coat when she disappeared.*

3 when you do not win in a game, argument, or war

➡ opposite **WIN**
➡ see also WB **SPORT, FIGHT, WAR**

lose /luːz/ [v I/T] to lose a game, competition, fight, or war: *I always lose when I play tennis with my sister.*
lose a game/fight/election etc

Everyone expected Truman to lose the election.

lose to sb (=be beaten by a person, team etc) *England lost to Brazil in the final.*

lose by 1 goal/10 votes/20 points etc *In the end, we only lost by one point!*

losing – lost – have lost

be beaten /biː 'biːtn/ to lose a game, competition, or race: *The Yankees were beaten yesterday in an exciting game against the Red Sox.*
+by *She reached the final, where she was beaten by Steffi Graf.*

be defeated /biː dɪ'fiːtᵻd/ to lose an important or difficult battle, election, or game: *The king's army was defeated and he was taken prisoner.*
+by *Last night England was defeated by a superior Brazilian team.*
be heavily defeated (=be very badly defeated) *Jimmy Carter was heavily defeated in the 1980 presidential election.*

> **Formal or informal?**
> **Be defeated** is more formal than **be beaten**.

defeat /dɪ'fiːt/ [n C/U] when a person, team, or army is defeated in a game, competition, election, battle etc
+of *the defeat of Napoleon at Waterloo*
a crushing/humiliating defeat (=when you are very badly defeated) *This result represents a humiliating defeat for the President.*

surrender /sə'rendəʳ/ [v I] to officially announce that you want to stop fighting in a war because you know that you cannot win: *Finally, after months of fighting, the enemy surrendered.*
+to *In May 1945, Germany surrendered to the Allied Forces.*

4 someone who loses in a game, competition etc

loser /'luːzəʳ/ [n C] the person or group that has lost a game, competition, or election: *The losers walked slowly off the field. | There was a silver cup for the winners, and medals for the losers.*

runner-up /ˌrʌnər 'ʌp/ [n C] the person or team that comes second in a game, race, or competition: *The names of the*

prizewinners and runners-up will be announced at the end of the day. | Jones was twice a runner-up in the New York City Marathon.*
plural **runners-up**

losing /'luːzɪŋ/ [adj only before noun] a losing side, team, candidate etc is one that loses in a game, competition, or election: *Nobody wants to be on the losing side. | the losing presidential candidates*

5 to no longer have something important

lose /luːz/ [v T] to stop having something important or valuable, such as your job or your home, when it is destroyed or taken away from you: *Thousands of people lost their homes in the earthquake. | I'll lose my job if the factory closes. | Another bank closed, and thousands of people lost their savings.*
losing – lost – have lost

cost /kɒst‖kɔːst/ [v T] if a mistake, accident etc **costs** you something important such as your job or your health, you lose your job or health etc because of it
cost sb sth *Another mistake like that could cost you your job. | All this delay has cost the company an important contract.*
costing – cost – have cost

LOST

when you do not know where you are

➡ see also **FIND**

1 to be lost

be lost /biː 'lɒst‖-'lɔːst/ to not know where you are, or not know the way to the place that you want to go to: *Excuse me, I'm lost. Which way is the station? | Eventually the children realized they were lost.*

not know where you are /nɒt nəʊ ˌweəʳ juː 'ɑːʳ/ if you do **not know where you are**, you do not recognize the place that you in, usually because you are not familiar with the area: *I* *really don't know where we are – let's have a look at the map.* | *He was so drunk he didn't know where he was.*

2   to become lost

get lost /ˌget ˈlɒst‖-ˈlɔːst/ *I'll give you a map so that you don't get lost.* | *Sorry we're so late. We got completely lost.*

lose your way /ˌluːz jɔːʳ ˈweɪ/ *if you* **lose your way,** *you go in the wrong direction or take the wrong road when you are trying to go somewhere:* *The climbers had lost their way in the dark.* | *If you lose your way, just stop and ask someone.*

LOT

➡ see also **ENOUGH/NOT ENOUGH, FEW, LITTLE/NOT MUCH**

1   a large number of people or things

a lot of /ə ˈlɒt ɒv‖-ˈlɑːt-/ [quantifier] *There were a lot of words that I didn't understand.* | *A lot of students have weekend jobs.*
a lot more *She has a lot more problems than you have.*
quite a lot of (=a fairly large number) *There are quite a lot of computers in the school.*
a lot *I was surprised that so few people went to the concert – I thought there'd be a lot.*

lots of /ˈlɒts ɒv‖ˈlɑːts-/ [quantifier] INFORMAL *a lot of people or things:* *I've invited lots of people.* | *We went to lots of interesting places.*

many /ˈmeni/ [quantifier] *a lot of people or things – use this especially in questions and negatives:* *Did you get many Christmas cards this year?* | *There will be rain in many parts of the country overnight.*
not many *Not many people survived the crash.*
too many *There are too many cars on the road.*
for many years *She worked as a reporter on CBS news for many years.*

many of (=many among a larger number) *Many of the houses are over 100 years old.*

plenty of /ˈplenti ɒv/ [quantifier] *a lot of people or things that you want or need, especially when there are more than enough:* *There are plenty of parking spaces further along the road.* | *The town has plenty of good bars and restaurants.* | *We have plenty of glasses, but not enough plates.*
plenty *"Are there any tickets left for tonight's show?" "Yes, plenty."*

a large number of/large numbers of /ə ˌlaːʳdʒ ˈnʌmbər ɒv, ˌlaːʳdʒ ˈnʌmbəʳz ɒv/ [quantifier] *a lot of a particular type of person or thing:* *Police seized a large number of weapons.* | *Large numbers of demonstrators were arrested during today's protest march.*
in large numbers *Japanese cars were first sold in large numbers in the 1960s* (=a lot of them were sold).

 These expressions are used especially in writing and news reports.

be full of /biː ˈfʊl ɒv/ *if something is* **full of** *people or things, there are a lot of them in it:* *In summer the town is full of tourists.* | *Her essay was full of mistakes.*

hundreds of/thousands of /ˈhʌndrɨdz ɒv, ˈθaʊzəndz ɒv/ [quantifier] *a lot of things or people – use this when you want to emphasize that you are talking about a very large number:* *Driving conditions are very bad and there have been hundreds of accidents.* | *Thousands of people came to see the carnival.*

◯ quite a few /ˌkwaɪt ə ˈfjuː/ [quantifier] SPOKEN *a fairly large number of people or things:* *I still* *have quite a few friends in Denver – I used to be in college there.*

2 a large amount of something

a lot of /ə ˈlɒt ɒv‖-ˈlɑːt-/ [quantifier] a large amount of something: *There was a lot of water on the floor.* | *a book that contains a lot of useful information* | *We spent a lot of time just lying on the beach.*
a lot *It's a big house – it must have cost a lot.*
quite a lot of (=a fairly large amount of something) *There's quite a lot of work involved, but the research is interesting.*
a lot to do/see/eat etc *There's still a lot to do before the wedding.*
a lot more/less *Ask Susan – she knows a lot more than I do.*

lots of /ˈlɒts ɒv‖ˈlɑːts-/ [quantifier] INFORMAL a large amount of something: *Don't worry – we still have lots of time.* | *It's a big apartment, so there's lots of room for all my things.*
lots to do/see/eat etc *We're never bored here – there's lots to see and do.*

much /mʌtʃ/ [quantifier] a lot of something – use this mainly in questions and negatives: *Does he speak much English?*
not much *I don't know much about cars.* | *I didn't get much help from my family.*
too much *Don't make too much noise.*
much of sth FORMAL (=a large part of it) *Much of the city was destroyed in the attack.*

> ⚠ Don't say 'he earns much money'. Say **he earns a lot of money**. Generally, use **a lot of**, not 'much', when you are talking about an amount in a positive sentence.

> ⚠ Don't say 'too much people/cars etc'. Say **too many people/cars** etc. Only use **much** with uncountable nouns: *too much work*

a great deal of /ə ˌɡreɪt ˈdiːl ɒv/ [quantifier] a large amount of something such as time, money, work, trouble, or skill: *The job requires a great deal of patience and skill.* | *The storm caused a great deal of damage.*

Formal or informal?
A great deal of is more formal than **a lot of**.

> ⚠ Don't use **a great deal of** to talk about physical objects.

plenty of /ˈplenti ɒv/ [quantifier] a large amount of something that you want or need: *There's plenty of hot water if you want a bath.* | *Don't worry – I've got plenty of money.*
plenty *No thanks, I couldn't eat any more – I've had plenty.*

be covered in sth /biː ˈkʌvəʳd ɪn (sth)/ if a person **is covered in** something, they have a lot of it on their skin, their clothes, or their hair; if an object **is covered in** something it has a lot of that thing on its surface: *My shoes are covered in mud.* | *At the end of the fight he was covered in blood.*

3 when there is a lot of something in many places

common /ˈkɒmən‖ˈkɑː-/ [adj] if an object, animal, idea etc is **common**, there is a very large number of objects, animals etc of this type in many different places: *Jones is a very common name in Britain.* | *Flatheads are a common type of fish and good to eat.*
common problem / mistake / belief etc (=one that a lot of people have or make) *You confused 'lie' and 'lay'. It's a common mistake.*

widespread /ˈwaɪdspred/ [adj usually before noun] a **widespread** feeling or attitude is one that a lot of people have in many different places; a **widespread** problem has a bad effect over a wide area
widespread opposition / support / interest etc *There was already widespread public support for women's rights.*
widespread damage / flooding / poverty etc *The bombing caused widespread damage.*

Formal or informal?
Widespread is used especially in news reports.

4 very much

➡ see also **VERY**

⌕ **a lot** /ə 'lɒt‖-'lɑːt/ [adv not before verb] ESPECIALLY SPOKEN very much: She's changed a lot since she's been here. | "How does your arm feel?" "It still hurts a lot."
a lot better/worse/bigger/more etc Your car's a lot bigger than ours. | It was a lot more interesting than I expected.

> ⚠ Don't use **a lot** before an adjective. Don't say 'a lot bigger house'. Say **a much bigger house**.

much /mʌtʃ/ [adv]
much better/worse/bigger/more etc a lot better, worse, bigger etc: You get a much better view if you stand on a chair. | a much more expensive car
much too big/old/tall etc I can't wear that coat. It's much too big! | The test was much too difficult for most of the students.

> ⚠ You can also use **much** after a verb in questions and negatives: Has he changed much? | "Did you enjoy the show?" "Not much."

> ⚠ Don't confuse **much** and **very**. Don't say 'they are much different'. Say **they are very different**.

⌕ **really** /'rɪəli/ [adv only before verb] ESPECIALLY SPOKEN very much – use this especially to talk about your feelings: I really like your dress. | What really annoys me is the way he never apologises when he's late.

very much /ˌveri 'mʌtʃ/ [adv] use this especially to talk about people's feelings: "Do you like living in Rome?" "Yes, very much."
like/admire/miss sb very much Lara enjoyed being at college, but she missed her family very much.
like/enjoy sth very much It was a wonderful show – we enjoyed it very much.

> ⚠ Don't say 'I like very much this colour'. Say **I like this colour very much**.

a good deal /ə ˌgʊd 'diːl/ [adv] FORMAL very much – use this especially to talk about changes, improvements, or differences: Her work has improved a good deal over the past year.
a good deal better/worse/bigger/more etc The situation was a good deal worse than we had first thought.

enormously /ɪ'nɔːʳməsli/ [adv] very much, especially in a good or positive way: Diana enjoyed herself enormously at the party. | The breakup of the Soviet Union was an enormously important event.

> **Formal or informal?**
> **Enormously** is more formal than the other words in this section.

LOUD

➡ opposite **QUIET**
➡ see also **SOUND**

1 loud sounds, music, machines etc

loud /laʊd/ [adj] something that is **loud** makes a lot of noise: The music's too loud. Can you turn it down? | We heard a loud explosion. | loud laughter coming from the next room
loudly [adv] Bill had dozed off in his chair, and was snoring loudly.

> **Formal or informal?**
> In informal English, you can also use **loud** as an adverb after 'as', 'so', and 'too': I wish you wouldn't talk so loud. | You're playing that music too loud. | I shouted as loud as I could.

noisy /'nɔɪzi/ [adj] use this about places where there is a lot of noise, or about people and machines that make a lot of noise, especially when this annoys you: The nightclub was crowded and noisy. | Our new neighbours are really noisy. | the truck's noisy engine
noisy – noisier – noisiest

deafening /'defənɪŋ/ [adj] a noise that is **deafening** is so loud that you cannot hear anything else: Outside there was a deafening crash of thunder. | The cheers of the crowd were deafening.

at full volume /ət ˌfʊl ˈvɒljuːm‖
-ˈvɑːljəm/ if you play music or have
the radio or television on **at full
volume**, it is as loud as it can be: *He
annoyed everyone by playing heavy
metal music at full volume.*

2 a noise

noise /nɔɪz/ [n C/U] a loud sound,
especially an unpleasant one: *Traffic
noise is a problem in inner-city areas.* |
*The noise of the machines made it hard
to talk.*
make (a) noise *Don't make too much
noise – Dad's trying to work.*

racket /ˈrækɪt/ [n singular] INFORMAL a
loud unpleasant noise: *It's impossible
to work with that racket going on.*
make a racket *I wish those kids would
stop making such a racket upstairs.*

din /dɪn/ [n singular] a loud unpleasant
noise, especially a noise made by a
large number of people
+of *We could hear the din of the crowd
in the streets below.*
make a din *All the prisoners were
making a terrible din.*

3 to make music, a radio, or a television louder

turn up /ˌtɜːˈn ˈʌp/ [phrasal verb T] to
make music, a radio etc louder by
moving a control
turn sth up *Can you turn the television
up? I can't hear the news.*
turn up sth *We turned up the music,
and we all started dancing.*

4 how loud something is

volume /ˈvɒljuːm‖ˈvɑːljəm/ [n U] how
loud a television, radio etc is: *If you
play music after ten o'clock, keep the
volume low.* | *the TV's volume control*
(=button that controls the volume)
turn the volume up/down (=make it
louder or quieter) *You can use the
remote control to turn the volume up or
down.*

LOVE

➡ opposite **HATE**

GIRLFRIEND/BOYFRIEND

LIKE/NOT LIKE   see also   MARRY

FAMILY   RELATIONSHIP

1 to love someone in a sexual way

love /lʌv/ [v T] to have a strong feeling
of liking someone, caring about them,
and being sexually attracted to them:
*My boyfriend finds it difficult to say "I
love you."* | *He was the only man she
had ever loved.*
love sb very much *We love each other
very much and we're going to get married.*

be in love /biː ɪn ˈlʌv/ to love someone
very much, so that you think about
them all the time and want to be with
them all the time: *"What's the matter
with Lois?" "She's in love."*
+with *How can you marry Adam when
you're in love with someone else?*
be madly in love/very much in love
(=very strongly in love) *We were both
seventeen and madly in love.*

fall in love /ˌfɔːl ɪn ˈlʌv/ to begin to be
in love with someone: *I suddenly realized that I'd fallen in love.*
+with *I think I'm falling in love with
your brother.*

be crazy about sb /biː ˈkreɪzi əbaʊt(sb)/
INFORMAL to love someone very much,
especially in a way that you cannot
control: *He's obviously crazy about
you. Why don't you ask him out?*

fancy /ˈfænsi/ [v T] BRITISH INFORMAL to be
sexually attracted to someone,
especially someone that you do not
know very well: *All the girls fancied
Bob.* | *My friend really fancies you.*
fancying – fancied – have fancied

2 to love your parents, children, brothers and sisters etc

love /lʌv/ [v T] to love someone in your family, so that you care a lot about what happens to them, and you want them to be happy: *When my parents got divorced I thought they didn't love me any more.* | *He loved his step-daughter as if she were his own child.*

adore /ə'dɔːʳ/ [v T] to love and admire someone very much and feel very proud of them: *Branwell Brontë adored his sister Anne.* | *She adores her grandchildren and is always buying them presents.*

close /bi:ˈkləʊs/ [adj not usually before noun] if two people are **close**, they enjoy being together and they understand each other's feelings and thoughts: *My sister and I used to argue a lot but now we're very close.* | *We have always been a close family.*
+to *He's never been close to his family.*

3 a feeling of love

love /lʌv/ [n U] a feeling of love, either for someone that you are sexually attracted to, or for a member of your family: *All children need love, attention, and encouragement.*
+for *She wrote him a letter revealing her love for him.*
love at first sight (=when you love someone in a romantic way the first time you see them) *As soon as I met Tracy it was love at first sight.*

affection /əˈfekʃən/ [n U] a gentle feeling of love for a friend or member of your family, which makes you want to be kind to them and show them that you love them: *These orphans have never been shown any affection in their lives.*
+for *Alison and I had been at school together, and I felt great affection for her.*

passion /ˈpæʃən/ [n U] a very strong and exciting feeling of love for someone you are sexually attracted to: *a thrilling story of sexual passion*
+for *He trembled with passion for her.*

4 showing love or making you feel love

affectionate /əˈfekʃənɪt/ [adj] someone who is **affectionate** shows that they like someone very much by the way they behave towards them, for example by holding or kissing them: *She was an affectionate child, always wanting to hold my hand or sit on my knee.* | *He gave me an affectionate hug and jumped onto the train.*

romantic /rəʊˈmæntɪk, rə-/ [adj] something that is **romantic** gives you a feeling of love for your boyfriend, girlfriend, husband, wife etc – use this about situations, places, or things people do or say: *We went for a romantic walk by the lake.* | *He sent me a dozen red roses – it was very romantic.*

passionate /ˈpæʃənɪt/ [adj] showing or involving very strong feelings of sexual love: *She'd had a passionate affair with an older man.*

5 a relationship between two people who love each other

relationship /rɪˈleɪʃənʃɪp/ [n C] when two people spend a lot of time together or live together because they love each other in a romantic or sexual way: *In the past his relationships had never lasted for more than a few months.* | *The relationship ended badly and they never saw each other again.*
+with *I don't want to start a relationship with him because I'm going back to South Africa.*

affair /əˈfeəʳ/ [n C] a secret sexual relationship between two people, when one of them is married to someone else, or they are both married to other people: *The affair had been going on for years before her husband found out.*
have an affair with sb *I would leave him if he had an affair with anyone.*

romance /rəʊˈmæns, rə-/ [n C] an exciting and usually short relationship between two people who are very much in love: *It was impossible for the couple to keep their romance a secret.*

holiday romance BRITISH **summer romance** AMERICAN (=while you are on holiday) *She knew it was just a holiday romance but she couldn't forget him.*

 Romance is used especially in newspapers and magazines.

6 stories, films etc about love

romance/love story /rəʊˈmæns, ˈlʌv ˌstɔːri/ [n C] a story about two people who are in love with each other: *'Romeo and Juliet' is one of the world's most famous love stories.* | *a well-known writer of popular romances* plural **love stories**

romantic /rəʊˈmæntɪk, rə-/ [adj] a **romantic** story or film is about people who are in love: *a romantic comedy in which Meg Ryan plays a single mother looking for love*

LOW

➡ look here for ...
• a low wall, table etc
• a low sound
• a low temperature, level etc
➡ opposite **HIGH**
➡ see also **DEEP/NOT DEEP, TALL**

1 not high or not far above the ground

low /ləʊ/ [adj] *A low wall surrounded the garden.* | *Some of the lowest branches were touching the ground.* | *In the middle of the room was a low table.*
low [adv] in, to, or towards a low position: *The plane flew low over the fields.* | *We had to bend down low to get through the little door.*

2 a low sound/voice/musical note

low /ləʊ/ [adj] a **low** voice or musical note is not high on the scale of musical sound: *I can't sing the low notes.* | *Her singing voice was lower than I expected.*

deep /diːp/ [adj] a **deep** voice is low, strong, and pleasant: *The men's deep voices echoed from the room below.*

3 a low temperature/level/rate/cost

low /ləʊ/ [adj] smaller than usual in level or number: *the lowest temperature ever recorded* | *Japan has a much lower crime rate than other countries.* | *the recent low level of unemployment*

LUCKY/UNLUCKY

1 a lucky person

lucky /ˈlʌki/ [adj] if you are **lucky**, good things happen to you and things go well for you, because you have good luck and not because of hard work, careful planning etc: *Isn't she lucky – she can eat what she wants and she never gets fat.* | *There are monkeys and zebra, and if you're lucky you might see a lion.*
lucky to do sth *The doctors say I'm lucky to be alive.*
+(that) *Arthur left the front door unlocked – we're lucky that nothing was stolen.*
lucky – luckier – luckiest

fortunate /ˈfɔːrtʃənət/ [adj] lucky, especially when you are luckier than other people: *David managed to escape, but the others were not so fortunate.*
fortunate to do sth *I was very fortunate to have such supportive parents.*

Formal or informal?
Fortunate is more formal than **lucky**.

with luck/with any luck /wɪð ˈlʌk, wɪð ˌeni ˈlʌk/ use this to say that you will do something or will succeed in something if you are lucky and have no problems: *With any luck, we should reach the coast before dark.*

2 a lucky thing that happens

lucky /'lʌki/ [adj] a **lucky** event happens because of good luck, and not because of hard work, careful planning etc: *"How did you know he'd be there?" "It was a lucky guess."* | *Italy got a lucky goal in the last five minutes of the game.*

it is lucky (that) *It was lucky that the weather was so nice.*

fortunate /'fɔːˈtʃənət/ [adj] lucky – use this especially about something that happens which saves you from danger or serious trouble: *a fortunate escape*

it is fortunate (for sb/sth) that *It is extremely fortunate that there was no-one in the building when the bomb went off.* | *It was fortunate for Roy that we found him so quickly – he could have drowned!*

> **Formal or informal?**
> **Fortunate** is more formal than **lucky**.

luckily/fortunately /'lʌkₐˌli, 'fɔːˈtʃənətli/ [adv] because of good luck – use this when something dangerous or unpleasant is avoided as a result of good luck: *I had forgotten my key, but luckily Ahmed was there and let me in.* | *Fortunately, there was no-one in the office when the fire started.*

+for *Luckily for us it didn't rain till the evening.*

⌕ **it's a good thing** /ɪts ə ˌgʊd 'θɪŋ/ SPOKEN say this when something lucky happens that saves you from experiencing problems or danger

+(that) *It was a good thing we brought some sandwiches, because there was no food available on the train.*

fluke /fluːk/ [n singular] INFORMAL something very surprising that only happens because of luck, not because of your skill or planning: *I'll have to win more than once, otherwise people will think it was a fluke.*

3 something that makes you have good luck

luck/good luck /lʌk, ˌgʊd 'lʌk/ [n U] the way that good things happen to someone by chance, not because of hard work, careful planning etc: *They played pretty well, but they also had a lot of good luck.*

bring sb (good) luck (=make someone have good luck) *Some people think black cats bring good luck.*

pure/sheer luck (=only luck, and nothing else) *"How did you guess the right answer?" "It was pure luck!"*

do sth for luck (=do something that you hope will bring good luck) *"I hope so," she said, crossing her fingers for luck.*

lucky /'lʌki/ [adj] something that is **lucky** seems to help you to have good luck or be successful: *My lucky number is seven.* | *I have a feeling today's going to be my lucky day.*

lucky charm (=a small object, piece of jewellery etc that someone carries with them to bring good luck)

4 to tell someone you hope they will be lucky and successful

⌕ **good luck/best of luck** /ˌgʊd 'lʌk, ˌbest əv 'lʌk/ SPOKEN say this to tell someone that you hope they will be lucky and successful: *Good luck Archie! Enjoy your new job.*

+with/in *Best of luck with your driving test.*

⌕ **keep your fingers crossed** /ˌkiːp jɔːʳ 'fɪŋgəʳz ˌkrɒst‖-ˌkrɔːst/ SPOKEN say this when you are hoping for good luck for yourself or for other people: *We're hoping Bill will be well enough to play in the next game – we're keeping our fingers crossed, anyway.*

+for *She's having her operation tomorrow, so keep your fingers crossed for her.*

wish sb luck /ˌwɪʃ (sb) 'lʌk/ to tell someone that you hope they will be lucky or successful, when they are about to do something difficult: *Wish me luck – I'll need it for this French exam.*

+in/with *Brian asked me to wish you luck in your interview.*

5 an unlucky person

unlucky /ʌn'lʌki/ [adj] if you are **unlucky**, bad things happen to you and things go badly for you, simply because you have bad luck and not for any other reason: *Val's been so unlucky recently – on Monday her car was stolen and the day after she fell and broke her arm.* | *"Were you disappointed with the team's performance?" "No, not really, I think we were just unlucky."*

unlucky to do sth *Arsenal were unlucky to lose the match.*

unfortunate /ʌnˈfɔːrtʃənət/ [adj] unlucky, especially when you are not as lucky as other people: *Some of the unfortunate victims were trapped inside the building for over 12 hours.*

unfortunate (enough) to do sth *Two drivers were unfortunate enough to be crossing the bridge when it collapsed.*

> **Formal or informal?**
> **Unfortunate** is more formal than **unlucky**.

6 an unlucky thing that happens

unlucky /ʌnˈlʌki/ [adj] an **unlucky** event happens simply because of bad luck, not because of bad planning, carelessness, stupidity etc: *The car in front braked suddenly and I went straight into it – it was just unlucky.*

it is unlucky (for sb) that *It was unlucky for Steve that the teacher walked in just at that moment.*

unfortunate /ʌnˈfɔːrtʃənət/ [adj] unlucky – use this especially about something that causes a lot of harm or problems: *Quarterback Brady Anderson was injured in an unfortunate collision with one of his teammates.* | *an unfortunate coincidence*

it is unfortunate (for sb) that *It was very unfortunate that the ambulance was held up by heavy traffic.*

> **Formal or informal?**
> **Unfortunate** is more formal than **unlucky**.

unfortunately /ʌnˈfɔːrtʃənətli/ [adv] because of bad luck – use this when something annoying, unpleasant, or dangerous happens as a result of bad luck: *I would have been here an hour ago, but unfortunately I missed the train.*

+for *Several trees were blown down and, unfortunately for us, one fell on our car.*

🔍 **just my luck** /ˌdʒʌst maɪ ˈlʌk/ SPOKEN INFORMAL say this when something bad or annoying happens to you, to show that you are not surprised because you are always unlucky: *"I'm sorry, we sold the last tickets ten minutes ago." "Just my luck."*

🔍 **it's one of those days** /ɪts ˌwʌn əv ðəʊz ˈdeɪz/ SPOKEN say this when you are annoyed because a lot of bad things have happened to you that day: *"What's the matter?" "Oh, it's been one of those days."*

7 something that makes you have bad luck

bad luck /ˌbæd ˈlʌk/ [n U] the way that bad things happen to someone by chance, not because of bad planning, carelessness, stupidity etc: *It wasn't her fault she missed the plane – it was just bad luck.* | *Tina was injured in the first five minutes of the game, which was very bad luck.*

unlucky /ʌnˈlʌki/ [adj] something that is **unlucky** makes you have bad luck: *Friday the 13th is supposed to be an unlucky day.*

it is unlucky to do sth *Some people think it's unlucky to walk under ladders.*

8 what you say when someone is unlucky

🔍 **bad luck/hard luck** /ˌbæd ˈlʌk, ˌhɑːrd ˈlʌk/ SPOKEN say this to show that you are sorry when someone has been unlucky, for example when they do not succeed in doing something: *"No, I didn't get that job, I'm afraid." "Oh, hard luck."*

9 believing in luck

superstitious /ˌsuːpəˈstɪʃəs, ˌsjuː-‖ˌsuː-/ [adj] someone who is **superstitious** believes that some objects or actions are lucky and others are unlucky: *Actors are very superstitious.*

superstition [n C/U] the belief that some objects or actions are lucky or unlucky: *primitive fears and superstitions*

M, m

MACHINE

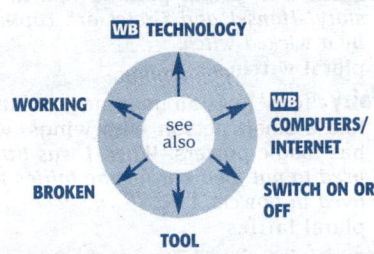

WB **TECHNOLOGY**

WORKING

WB COMPUTERS/ INTERNET

see also

BROKEN

SWITCH ON OR OFF

TOOL

1 a machine

machine /məˈʃiːn/ [n C] a piece of equipment that does a particular type of work, either in your home or in a factory, office etc, using power from an engine or from electricity: *a machine that counts coins* | *Nowadays machines do a lot of the jobs that people used to do.*
sewing / washing machine (=a machine for sewing or washing clothes)
fax machine (=a machine for sending and receiving faxes)
operate a machine (=make it work) *To operate the machine, select the drink you want and press the green button.*
by machine *The letters are sorted by machine.*

device /dɪˈvaɪs/ [n C] a piece of equipment that has been cleverly designed to do a particular job, for example one that makes measurements, records sounds or movements, or controls the operation of a machine: *An EEG is a device that records electrical activity in the brain.*
+for *a thermostatic device for controlling temperature*
listening/measuring device *a listening device that enables you to hear when your baby is crying upstairs*

appliance /əˈplaɪəns/ [n C] FORMAL a piece of electrical equipment used in your home, such as a washing machine or TV: *The store sells a range of appliances and hi-fi equipment.*

domestic/household appliance *Their kitchen has all the latest domestic appliances – microwave, dishwasher etc.*

machinery /məˈʃiːnəri/ [n U] machines in general, especially the large machines used in factories or on farms: *They are investing millions of dollars in new machinery for the factory.* | *a company that exports farm machinery*

robot /ˈrəʊbɒtǁ-bɑːt, -bət/ [n C] a machine that is controlled by a computer and can do some of the complicated jobs that humans do, such as making things in a factory: *cars built by robots*

gadget /ˈgædʒɪt/ [n C] a small useful tool or machine, especially one that is cleverly designed and slightly unusual: *a neat little gadget for sharpening knives*
kitchen gadget *Steve always bought all the latest kitchen gadgets.*

2 a thing that produces power for a machine or vehicle

engine /ˈendʒɪn/ [n C] the part of a car, aircraft etc that produces the power that makes it move: *The engine won't start.*
car/jet etc engine *The noise of the jet engines was deafening.*

motor /ˈməʊtər/ [n C] the part of a machine that makes it work or move, especially by using electrical power: *The lawnmower is powered by a small electric motor.*

3 connected with the way machines work

mechanical /mɪˈkænɪkəl/ [adj] using machines, or getting power from an engine: *They used a huge mechanical shovel to dig the foundations for the hotel.*
mechanical problem/fault/failure (=when a machine is not working properly) *Our ship had to return to port due to a mechanical problem.*
mechanically [adv] *Nowadays, the grape picking is all done mechanically.*

automatic /ˌɔːtəˈmætɪk◂/ [adj]
automatic machines, weapons etc

M

are designed to operate by themselves, without much human control or attention: *A lot of stores now have automatic doors.* | *We have an automatic time switch which makes the lights come on in the evening even when we're out.*
fully automatic (=completely automatic) *a fully automatic camera*
automatically [*adv*] *The doors open automatically when you go near them.*

MAGIC

➡ see also **STRANGE THINGS AND EVENTS**

1 magic

magic /ˈmædʒɪk/ [*n* U] a secret power to make things happen or to do things that are normally impossible, by saying special words or doing special actions: *In some villages, there were 'rainmakers', who used magic to bring rain.* | *Do you believe in magic?*
black magic (=using evil power) *Several recent murders have been linked to a group practising black magic.*
magic [*adj* only before noun] *magic powers* | *The magic potion will make him fall in love with you.*
witchcraft /ˈwɪtʃkrɑːft‖-kræft/ [*n* U] the use of magic to harm people and make bad things happen: *At that time, hundreds of women were burned at the stake for witchcraft.*
spell /spel/ [*n* C] special words or actions that are used in order to make something magic happen: *a book of spells*
put/cast a spell on sb (=make a spell that makes bad things happen to someone) *The old man threatened to put a spell on the village and make the crops fail.*
the occult /ðiː ˈɒkʌlt‖-əˈkʌlt/ the study of spirits and magic, especially when this involves communicating with evil spirits: *The major churches have always warned people against getting involved in the occult.*

2 people with magic power

witch /wɪtʃ/ [*n* C] a woman who is believed to have magic power, which she uses especially to harm people or make bad things happen; in stories, witches are usually shown dressed in black with a tall, pointed hat: *In the story, Hansel and Gretel are captured by a wicked witch.*
plural **witches**

fairy /ˈfeəri/ [*n* C] an imaginary creature like a small person with wings, who has magic powers: *When I was little I used to put food out for the fairies that lived in flowers.*
plural **fairies**

magician/wizard /məˈdʒɪʃən, ˈwɪzəʳd/ [*n* C] a man who is believed to have magic power; in stories, magicians and wizards are usually shown as having a long beard and a pointed hat with stars and moons on it: *The wizard's ring had the power to make him invisible.* | *an old legend abut King Arthur and Merlin the magician.*

3 magic done as entertainment

magic /ˈmædʒɪk/ [*n* U] the skill of doing tricks that seem like magic, as a way of entertaining people: *an evening of magic and comedy*

trick /trɪk/ [*n* C] a skilful action that makes something happen which seems impossible, performed as entertainment
magic trick/conjuring trick *She did a clever magic trick with a coin and a handkerchief.*
card trick (=a trick done with playing cards)

magician/conjuror/conjurer /məˈdʒɪʃən, ˈkʌndʒərəʳ‖ˈkɑːn-, ˈkʌn-/ [*n* C] someone who does magic tricks in order to entertain people: *The children watched in amazement as the conjurer made the rings all disappear.*

MAIL, PHONE, AND FAX

1 communicate by mail, phone, or fax

get in touch with sb /ˌget ɪn ˈtʌtʃ wɪð (sb)/ to write to someone or to speak to them on the telephone, especially someone you do not see very often or someone who is difficult to find: *I must get in touch with Lucy – I haven't spoken to her for ages.* | *They've been trying to get in touch with their daughter, but no-one knows where she is.*

contact /ˈkɒntækt‖ˈkɑːn-/ [v T] to write to, fax, e-mail, or telephone someone, in order to give or ask for important information: *If you need to contact me urgently, call me on my mobile phone.* | *Police are asking anyone who saw the accident to contact them.*

hear from sb /ˈhɪəʳ frɒm (sb)/ if you **hear from** someone, especially someone you know well, they write to you, or telephone you: *When was the last time you heard from Tina?* | *I haven't heard from her for a long time.*

 Hear from sb is usually used in questions and negative sentences.

 Don't use the word **communicate** when you are talking about writing, phoning, faxing etc a particular person. **Communicate** is usually used when you are talking generally about methods of exchanging information: *The Internet enables people to communicate with other computer users around the world.* | *How do birds communicate?*

2 phone equipment

phone (also **telephone**) /fəʊn, ˈtelɪfəʊn/ [n C] *There's a phone in the hall if you want to use it.*

mobile phone (also **mobile** BRITISH) /ˌməʊbaɪl ˈfəʊn, ˈməʊbaɪl/ [n C] a phone that you can carry with you and use anywhere

cellular phone (also **cell phone**) /ˈseljʊləʳ ˌfəʊn, ˈsel ˌfəʊn/ [n C] AMERICAN a mobile phone

phone number/telephone number /ˈfəʊn ˌnʌmbəʳ, ˈtelɪfəʊn ˌnʌmbəʳ/ [n C] the number that you use to phone a person or organization: *Do you know Rachel's phone number?*

receiver /rɪˈsiːvəʳ/ [n C] the part of the phone that you pick up and speak into

answering machine (also **answerphone** BRITISH) /ˈɑːnsərɪŋ məˌʃiːn, ˈɑːnsəʳfəʊn‖ˈæn-/ [n C] a machine that answers your phone when you are out and lets people record messages so that you can listen to them later: *Chris wasn't in, so I left a message on his answering machine.* | *When I went out, I forgot to switch the answerphone on.*

ring /rɪŋ/ [v I] if the phone **rings**, it makes a sound to show that someone is phoning you

ringtone /ˈrɪŋtəʊn/ [n C] a particular sound that a mobile phone makes when someone is phoning it. Many people have a piece of music as their ringtone.

voice mail /ˈvɔɪs meɪl/ [n U] an electronic system on your phone that lets you leave messages for people who phone you when you are not available, and lets them leave messages for you

3 contacting someone by phone

phone /fəʊn/ [v I/T] to speak to someone using the telephone: *Has Anna phoned yet?* | *I'll phone you when I get to the airport.*

 Don't say 'I phoned to Mary.' Say **I phoned Mary.**

call (also **ring** BRITISH) /kɔːl, rɪŋ/ [v I/T] to phone someone: *I'll call you tomorrow.* | *Do you need to ring your parents to tell them you'll be late?*

call/phone call /kɔːl, ˈfəʊn kɔːl/ [n C] when someone phones someone else: *Were there any calls for me while I was out?*

make a call/phone call *Can I use your phone – I need to make a quick call.*

give sb a call SPOKEN (=phone someone) *I'll give you a call at the weekend.*

call back/phone back /ˌkɔːl ˈbæk, ˌfəʊn ˈbæk/ [phrasal verb I/T] to phone someone who has phoned you earlier, especially when you were out: *Has Bill phoned back yet?*

call sb back/phone sb back *Ian called while you were out. I said you'd phone him back.*

pick up the phone /ˌpɪk ʌp ðə ˈfəʊn/ to lift up your telephone receiver

message /ˈmesɪdʒ/ [n C] a piece of information that you ask someone to give to another person, when it is not possible to speak to that person directly

leave a message (=give a message to someone who answers the phone, or to an answering machine) *"Bill called when you were out." "Oh, did he leave a message?"*

can I take a message SPOKEN (what you say when someone asks to speak to someone who is not available) *I'm afraid Martha's not home right now. Can I take a message?*

answer the phone/telephone /ˌɑːnsəʳ ðə ˈfəʊn, ˈtelɪfəʊn‖ˌæn-/ to pick up the receiver because the phone is ringing: *Could you answer the phone, Rob? I'm in the shower!*

hang up /ˌhæŋ ˈʌp/ [phrasal verb I] to finish a phone conversation by putting the receiver down or pressing a button on a mobile phone: *'I'll call you again tomorrow,' she said, and hung up.*

hang up on sb (=put the receiver down before they have finished speaking)

put the phone down /ˌpʊt ðə ˈfəʊn daʊn/ to put the receiver back onto the phone at the end of a call

busy AMERICAN **engaged** BRITISH /ˈbɪzi, ɪnˈɡeɪdʒd/ [adj] if someone's phone is **busy** or **engaged**, you cannot speak to them because they are already having a phone conversation with someone else

it is busy/engaged *Every time I call Bob, it's always busy.* | *"Did you ring*

Melissa?" "I tried, but it was engaged."*

wrong number /ˌrɒŋ ˈnʌmbəʳ‖ˌrɔːŋ-/ [n C] a number that is not the one you intended to call

get a wrong number (=call someone that you did not intend to call, because you used an incorrect number)

4 email

email /ˈiː meɪl/ [n U] a system that lets you send a message directly from your computer to someone else's computer

be on email (=have the necessary equipment to send and receive email messages) *Over half the population is on email now.*

email /ˈiːmeɪl/ [n C] a message you send using email: *"Does Glennis know about it?" "Yes, I sent her an email."*

email address /ˈiːmeɪl əˌdres‖-ˌædres/ [n C] the letters, or letters and numbers, that you type into the computer to send a message to a particular person using email: *"What's Sylvia's email address?"*

mail (also **email**) /ˈmeɪl, ˈiːmeɪl/ [v T] to send someone a message by email: *I'll mail you when I get back to the office.*

reply /rɪˈplaɪ/ [v I] to send an email to someone in reply to an email you have received from them: *The easiest way to reply is to hit the 'reply' button, then key in your message.*

reply all /rɪˌplaɪ ˈɔːl/ [n U] a way of sending a reply to an email so that everyone who got the original email receives the reply: *She accidentally did 'reply all' so her boss got to read her comments about the new software.*

cc /ˈsiː siː/ [v T] to send an email to one or more other people, as well as the person you are addressing it to: *Can you cc me on any emails you send to the design team, please?*

cc'ing – cc'd

message /ˈmesɪdʒ/ [n C] what you write and send to someone by email: *When I got back from vacation there were over 200 messages in my inbox!*

5 mail

write /raɪt/ [v I/T] to write a letter to someone: *Write and let me know how you're getting on.*
write to sb *For further information write to Sam Carter at the BBC Helpdesk.*
write sb AMERICAN *I'll write you every day I'm away.*
write sb a letter *I wrote her several letters, but she never wrote back.*
write back (=reply to someone's letter)

send /send/ [v T] to arrange for a letter or package to be taken to another place by mail: *Have you sent all your Christmas cards yet?*
send sb a card/letter/present *My grandfather sent me a check for $100.*
send a card/letter to sb *He sent a postcard to Helen while he was in France.*

the mail ESPECIALLY AMERICAN **the post** BRITISH /ðə 'meɪl, ðə 'pəʊst/ the system for carrying letters and packages from one place to another: *There must be a problem with the mail. I sent her two letters last week and she didn't get either of them.*
be in the mail/post (=when something has already been sent by mail, but has not yet arrived) *Your photos are in the mail.*
by mail/post (=using the mail system) *You can apply for a new passport by post.*

mail ESPECIALLY AMERICAN **post** BRITISH /meɪl, pəʊst/ [v T] to send a letter or package using the mail system: *Did you remember to post that letter?*
mail/post sth to sb *George mailed his résumé to over 30 companies, but none of them wrote back.*
mail/post sb sth *I posted Margaret the cheque last Friday.*

address /ə'dres‖'ædres/ [n C] the number of the building and the name of the street and town where someone lives: *"What's their address?" "3317 Ellesmere Court, Walnut Creek 94598."*

post code BRITISH **zip code** AMERICAN /'pəʊst kəʊd, 'zɪp kəʊd/ [n C] the letters or numbers that show the exact area where a house is, so that letters can be delivered more quickly: *"What's your post code?" "N4 6XJ."*

6 fax

fax /fæks/ [n C] a letter, picture etc that is sent electronically down a telephone line using a fax machine and is then printed at the place that it has been sent to
send a fax *He sent a fax to Mr McGee saying that he was resigning.*

fax /fæks/ [v T] to send someone a fax
fax sb sth *I'll fax you a map so you know how to get here.*
fax sth to sb *Can you fax these documents to the Tokyo office?*

fax machine (also **fax**) /'fæks məˌʃiːn, fæks/ [n C] a machine that sends and receives faxes
by fax *I'll send you the details by fax.*

fax number /'fæks ˌnʌmbə'/ [n C] the number that you use to fax someone

MAKE

to produce something that was not there before

➡ see also **DO, INVENT, DESIGN**
➡ if you mean 'make someone do something', go to **FORCE SB TO DO STH**
➡ if you mean 'make a meal', go to **COOK**
➡ if you mean 'build a building', go to **BUILD**

1 to make something

make /meɪk/ [v T] to produce something which did not exist before: *Diana makes all her own clothes.* | *The furniture was made by a Swedish firm.* | *They've just finished making a movie about life during the Civil War.* | *My camera was made in Japan.*
made of (=made using a particular substance or material) *a bag made of leather*
made from (=made by putting together different materials, substances, and parts) *People were living in huts made from mud, stones, and straw.*

make sth from/out of sth (=use one thing to make something different) *a children's swing made out of an old tyre*

making – made – have made

produce /prə'djuːs‖-'duːs/ [v T] to make large quantities of food, equipment, or other goods by means of industrial processes, in order to sell them: *The dairy produces over 1500 tonnes of butter every year.* | *Japan produces and exports electronic goods.* | *a factory that produces high-quality steel*

production /prə'dʌkʃən/ [n U] when food, equipment, or other goods are made in large quantities, in order to be sold: *Crude oil is used in the production of plastics.* | *a big increase in grain production*

manufacture /ˌmænjʊ'fæktʃəʳ/ [v T] to make machines, equipment, cars etc in factories: *The engines are manufactured in Portugal.* | *IBM manufactures and sells a wide range of computers.*

> **Formal or informal?**
>
> **Manufacture** is more formal than **make** or **produce**.

develop /dɪ'veləp/ [v T] to invent a new product, and gradually improve it so that it is ready to be produced and sold: *Scientists are developing new drugs to treat AIDS.* | *He helped to develop a well-known word-processing program.*

create /kri'eɪt/ [v T] to invent something new and original in art, music, fashion etc: *Picasso created a completely new style of painting.* | *This dish was created by master chef Marco Pierre White.*

generate /'dʒenəreɪt/ [v T] to produce a lot of electricity, for example by burning gas, coal, oil etc in a special large building: *France generates a large part of its electricity from nuclear power.*

publish /'pʌblɪʃ/ [v T] to print a book, newspaper, or magazine and arrange for it to be sold: *The magazine is published four times a year.* | *He couldn't persuade anyone to publish his stories.* | *Darwin's famous book was first published in 1859.*

2 a company or country that makes something

maker /'meɪkəʳ/ [n C] a company or person whose business is to make things to be sold, either by hand or using machines
+of *Makers of cars often think more about speed than safety.*
car/film/wine etc maker *The wine maker has to decide when the crop is ready for picking.*

producer /prə'djuːsəʳ‖-'duː-/ [n C] a company or country that grows food or produces goods to be sold
oil/coffee/wine etc producer *Saudi Arabia is one of the world's biggest oil producers.*
+of *She works for Toshiba, a leading producer of notebook computers.*

manufacturer /ˌmænjʊ'fæktʃərəʳ/ [n C] a company that makes machines, equipment, cars etc in a factory: *Before you use the washing machine, read the manufacturer's instructions.*
car/aircraft/shoe etc manufacturer *a major weapons manufacturer*
+of *Scantronic is a leading manufacturer of burglar alarms.*

publisher /'pʌblɪʃəʳ/ [n C] a company that makes and prints books, newspapers, or magazines: *You can't make photocopies from this book unless you have permission from the publisher.*
+of *a well-known publisher of educational books*

3 something that a company makes

product /'prɒdʌkt‖'prɑː-/ [n C] something that a company makes in large quantities in order to sell it: *a new range of skin-care products* | *The company is a maker of household paper products such as tissues and paper cups.*

4 made by a person, not a machine

homemade /ˌhəʊm'meɪd◄/ [adj] use this about food and drinks that are made at home, not in a factory: *Try one of these homemade cookies.* | *a bowl of homemade soup*

handmade /ˌhænd'meɪd◂/ [*adj*] use this about furniture, clothes etc that are made by skilled workers, not by machines in a factory: *The shoes are expensive – they're handmade.* | *a beautiful handmade rug*

5 when a natural process makes something

form /fɔːʳm/ [*v* T] if a natural process or chemical reaction **forms** something, it makes it, especially when this happens over a period of time: *Hydrogen and oxygen combine to form water.* | *These rocks were formed millions of years ago.*

produce /prə'djuːs‖-'duːs/ [*v* T] if a natural process or a part of your body **produces** a substance, it makes it, usually for a particular purpose: *The stomach produces acids which help to digest food.* | *Carbon dioxide is produced during respiration.*

6 to be made of several different parts

consist of sth/be made up of sth /kən'sɪst ɒv (sth), biː ˌmeɪd 'ʌp ɒv (sth)/ [*phrasal verb* T] if something **consists of** or is **made up of** different substances, parts, people etc, it has those things in it: *The spaghetti sauce consists of meat, onions, tomatoes, garlic, and herbs.* | *The image on a computer screen is made up of thousands of tiny dots.* | *a small committee, consisting of the principal and four teachers*

> **Formal or informal?**
>
> **Consist of sth** is more formal than **be made up of sth**.

MAN

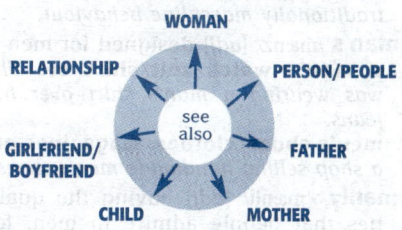

➡ if you mean 'the man someone is married to', go to **MARRY**

WOMAN

RELATIONSHIP   PERSON/PEOPLE

see also

GIRLFRIEND/   FATHER
BOYFRIEND

CHILD   MOTHER

1 a man

man /mæn/ [*n* C] an adult male person: *There were two men and a woman in the car.* | *Henry is a very rich man.* | *You wouldn't understand how she feels – you're a man!*
plural **men**

🔍 **guy** /gaɪ/ [*n* C] SPOKEN INFORMAL a man: *Dave's a really nice guy.* | *Is he the guy who used to live next door to you?*

🔍 **bloke** /bləʊk/ [*n* C] BRITISH SPOKEN INFORMAL a man: *Are you seeing this bloke again then?* | *He bought the car from a bloke at his office.*

🔍 **gentleman** /'dʒentlmən/ [*n* C] ESPECIALLY SPOKEN a man – use this as a polite way of talking about a man: *Can you serve that gentleman please, Sarah?* | *an elderly gentleman*
plural **gentlemen**

male /meɪl/ [*adj*] a **male** person is a man – use this especially when talking about jobs and work: *Most of the science teachers are male.*
male nurse/teacher/colleague etc *Salaries have increased for both male and female graduates.*

2 for men, or typical of men

male /meɪl/ [*adj*] only before noun] for men or typical of men – use this about jobs or activities that men do, or about behaviour or attitudes that are typical of men: *More women are entering traditionally male jobs like engineering.* | *male aggression*

masculine /ˈmæskjʊlən/ [adj] **masculine** behaviour or attitudes are considered to be more typical of a man than a woman: *He wanted to say he was sorry but his masculine pride wouldn't let him.* | *Violence is an extreme form of traditionally masculine behaviour.*

man's /mænz/ [adj] designed for men
a man's watch/suit/shirt etc *She was wearing a man's shirt over her jeans.*
men's shoes/clothes/magazines etc *a shop selling handmade men's shoes*

manly /ˈmænli/ [adj] having the qualities that people admire in men, for example being strong and brave: *He had a deep, manly voice.*
manly – manlier – manliest

macho /ˈmætʃəʊ‖ˈmɑː-/ [adj] INFORMAL a **macho** man behaves in a way that he thinks men are expected to behave, for example by doing dangerous things, by not showing his emotions, and by treating women as if they are not important: *He thinks he's too macho to put a sweater on, even when it's really cold.* | *macho attitudes*

MANAGER

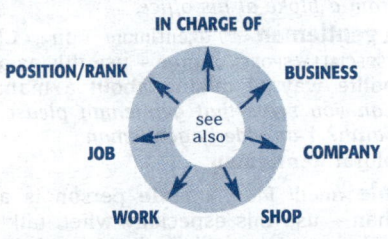

IN CHARGE OF

POSITION/RANK   BUSINESS

see also

JOB   COMPANY

WORK   SHOP

1 a manager

manager /ˈmænɪdʒəʳ/ [n C] someone whose job is to run one of the departments of a large organization, or to be in charge of a bank, shop, hotel etc: *I'd like to speak to the manager.*
bank/hotel/restaurant etc manager *He works really hard as a hotel manager.*
marketing/sales/accounts etc manager *She's one of our regional sales managers.*
+of *the advertising manager of a mail-order company*

 Don't call someone 'manager' when you are talking or writing to them.

boss /bɒs‖bɔːs/ [n C] the person who is in charge of you at work: *Does your boss know you're looking for another job?* | *There's a new guy at work who's always trying to impress the boss.*

 Boss is not an official job title.

foreman /ˈfɔːʳmən/ [n C] someone who is in charge of a group of factory workers or builders, whose job is to make sure that the workers do what the manager wants: *the construction foreman*
plural **foremen**

supervisor /ˈsuːpəʳvaɪzəʳ, ˈsjuː-‖ˈsuː-/ [n C] someone who is in charge of a group of workers, such as cleaners or secretaries, in an office, factory, airport etc, whose job is to make sure that the workers do what the manager wants: *We still need to replace the office supervisor.*

deputy /ˈdepjʊti/ [n C] someone who does the manager's job when the manager is not there
deputy director/manager/principal etc *He became the deputy head of the bank.*
plural **deputies**

2 a top manager

director /dɪˈrektəʳ, daɪ-/ [n C] one of the most important managers, especially the person who is in charge of one of the main departments: *The directors are meeting today to discuss the company's future.*
managing director BRITISH (=the person in charge of running an organization) *He's the managing director of a small printing firm.*
finance/sales/personnel etc director *Have you met the new finance director?*
+of *Dr Jane Wilde, director of the Health Promotion Agency*

chief executive (also **chief executive officer/CEO** AMERICAN) /ˌtʃiːf ɪɡˈzekjʊtɪv, ˌtʃiːf ɪɡˈzekjʊtɪv ˌɒfɪsəʳ, ˌsiː iː ˈəʊ‖ -ˌɔːf-, -ˌɑːf-/ [n C] the top manager of a

large company or organization, who is responsible for the whole business: *Universal Studios is looking for a new chief executive.*
+of *the CEO of General Motors*

> ⚠ The **chief executive** of a company makes the most important decisions, and does most of the planning. The **chairman** or **president** is responsible for the whole organization, and has the power to tell the **chief executive** what to do. Sometimes both jobs can be done by the same person: *He was the chairman and chief executive of a computer company.*

president /'prezᵻdənt/ [n C] the most important person in a large company or organization, especially in the US: *Angry shareholders called for the resignation of the company president.*
+of *the president of CBS News*

chairman /'tʃeəʳmən/ [n C] the most important person in a large company or organization, especially in Britain
+of *Brian Cuthbertson was the chairman of the Associated Life Insurance Company.*
plural **chairmen**

> ⚠ When the most important person in a company or organization is a woman, she can be called **chairman** or **chairwoman**, or sometimes **chairperson**.

head /hed/ [n C] the person in charge of an organization or department
+of *the former head of MI5, the British Intelligence Service* | *She's the head of research and development.*

> ⚠ **Head** is not usually used in official job titles.

the management /ðə 'mænɪdʒmənt/ [n singular] the people who are managers in an organization, not the ordinary workers: *Talks between the workers and the management broke down today.*

> ⚠ In British English, you can use **the management** with a singular or plural verb: *The management has worked/have worked extremely hard to improve working conditions.* In American English, always use a singular verb.

the board /ðə 'bɔːʳd/ [n singular] the group of top managers in a company who meet regularly to make the most important decisions: *Carmichael was appointed to the board in July.*
the board of directors *There are only two women on the company's board of directors.*

> ⚠ In British English, you can use **the board** with a singular or plural verb: *The board has appointed/have appointed a new Sales Director.* In American English, always use a singular verb.

3 the job of being a manager

management /'mænɪdʒmənt/ [n U] the job or skill of being a manager: *Val is looking for a job in management.*
good/bad management *The failure of many small businesses is caused by bad management.*

> ⚠ You can also use **management** before a noun, like an adjective: *a management training course*

managerial /ˌmænᵊ'dʒɪəriəl◂/ [adj only before noun] connected with being a manager – use this about the jobs that managers do or the skills that they need
managerial job/skills/ability etc *This is her first managerial job.*

MARK

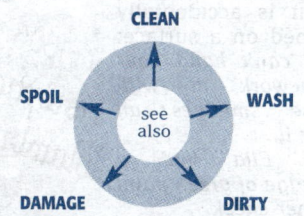

1 a mark on something that spoils its appearance

mark /mɑːʳk/ [n C] a spot or line on clothes, furniture, a wall, floor etc, for example where it has been damaged, made dirty, or where someone has dropped liquid on it: *There are marks on the door where the cat has scratched it.*

dirty/greasy/sticky mark *How did you get that dirty mark on your T-shirt?*

stain /steɪn/ [n C] a large mark that is difficult to remove, made when a liquid such as coffee or wine falls onto something: *I can't get this stain out of the carpet.*

stain

grass/coffee/wine/bl etc stain *Salt is the best remedy for a red wine stain.*

stained [adj] with a stain on it: *stained jeans*
+with *His clothes were torn and stained with blood.*

spot /spɒt‖spɑːt/ [n C] a small round mark on a surface, which is of a different colour from the rest of the surface and is made especially by drops of liquid: *There were grease spots on his shirt.*
+of *Detectives found a few spots of blood on the carpet.*

patch /pætʃ/ [n C] ESPECIALLY BRITISH an area where dirt, water, oil etc has made a mark on a floor, wall, or ceiling
greasy/dirty/damp patch *There's a damp patch under the window.*
patch of dirt/damp/grease *patches of grease on the walls*
plural **patches**

smudge /smʌdʒ/ [n C] a dirty mark made when ink or paint is accidentally rubbed on a surface: *You can't hand your homework in with those smudges all over it.*
+of *Ella had a smudge of green paint on her cheek.*

smudge

2 to make a mark

stain /steɪn/ [v T] to make a large mark on something such as cloth, which is difficult to remove: *The blackberry*

juice had stained their clothes and fingers. | *Someone had spilled their wine, staining the carpet.*

mark /mɑːᵏk/ [v T] to damage the surface of something by making a mark on it: *Don't put that hot pan down – it'll mark the table.*

leave a mark/leave a stain /ˌliːv ə 'mɑːᵏk, ˌliːv ə 'steɪn/ to make a mark or stain on something, often without realizing you have done this
+on *The children left muddy marks on the floor. | Chocolate sauce had left a stain on Andrew's shirt.*

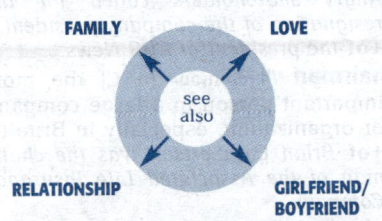

MARRY

FAMILY   LOVE

see also

RELATIONSHIP   GIRLFRIEND/BOYFRIEND

1 to get married

get married /ˌget 'mærid/ ESPECIALLY SPOKEN to officially become husband and wife: *Jenny and Tom were very young when they got married. | My daughter's getting married in July.*
+to *Is he getting married to Sophie at last?*

> ⚠ Don't say 'she got married with an Australian'. Say **she got married to an Australian**.

marry /'mæri/ [v T] to get married to someone: *Will you marry me? | She married an American guy that she met in France.*
marrying – married – have married

remarry /ˌriː'mæri/ [v I] to get married again: *My mother died when I was very young and my father never remarried.*
remarrying – remarried – have remarried

2 the relationship of marriage

marriage /'mærɪdʒ/ [n C/U] the relationship between two people who are married: *She has two children from a previous marriage.* | *Is marriage still important to young people?*
+to *Her marriage to Philip ended in divorce.*
a happy/unhappy marriage *Arnold's parents had had an unhappy marriage.*
a broken marriage (=a marriage that has ended) *It's the children who suffer in broken marriages.*

3 ceremonies, celebrations etc when people get married

wedding /'wedɪŋ/ [n C] an official ceremony at which two people get married, especially a religious ceremony: *I first met Jake at my cousin's wedding.*

> ⚠ You can also use **wedding** before a noun, like an adjective: *wedding photos* | *a lovely silk wedding dress* | *her wedding ring*

reception /rɪ'sepʃən/ [n C] an event that follows a wedding ceremony, in which there is a meal, speeches, and usually music and dancing: *We had our wedding reception in a local hotel.* | *I went to the church service, but not to the reception.*
honeymoon /'hʌnimuːn/ [n C] a holiday that two people go on when they have just got married: *We're thinking of going to Barbados for our honeymoon.*
bachelor party/stag party /'bætʃələʳ ˌpɑːʳti, 'stæg ˌpɑːʳti/ [n C] AMERICAN a party for a man and his male friends just before he gets married
stag night /'stæg ˌnaɪt/ [n C] BRITISH a party for a man and his male friends just before he gets married
bridal shower/wedding shower /'braɪdl ˌʃauəʳ, 'wedɪŋ ˌʃauəʳ/ AMERICAN a party for a woman and her female friends just before she gets married, when her friends give her gifts
hen night/hen party /'hen ˌnaɪt, 'hen ˌpɑːʳti/ [n C] BRITISH a party for a

woman and her female friends just before she gets married

4 people at a wedding

bride /braɪd/ [n C] the woman who is getting married: *Everyone turned to look at the bride.*
groom/bridegroom /gruːm, 'braɪdgruːm/ [n C] the man who is getting married: *a photo of the bride and groom together*
bridesmaid /'braɪdzmeɪd/ [n C] a woman or girl who helps the woman who is getting married on the day of her wedding: *The bridesmaids will be wearing long pink dresses.*
best man /ˌbest 'mæn/ [n singular] a male friend of the man who is getting married, who helps him on the day of his wedding: *Tony has asked me to be best man.*

5 to agree to get married

engaged /ɪn'geɪdʒd/ [adj not before noun] if two people are **engaged**, they have agreed to get married to each other at some time in the future
be engaged *Todd and Ellen have been engaged for about 3 months now.*
+to *He's engaged to Paul's sister.*
get engaged (=become engaged) *We got engaged at Christmas.*

> ⚠ Don't say 'she got engaged with him'. Say **she got engaged to him**.

engagement /ɪn'geɪdʒmənt/ [n C] an agreement by two people to get married at some time in the future
announce your engagement (=tell everyone that you are going to get married) *Glennis and John announced their engagement yesterday.*
break off your engagement (=say that you do not want to be engaged any more) *Anita broke off her engagement when she found out that Paulo had been seeing another woman.*
engagement ring *Has he bought you an engagement ring yet?*
fiancé/fiancée /fi'ɒnseɪǁˌfiːɑːn'seɪ/ [n C] the man or woman that you are going to get married to: *I'd like you to meet Janice, my fiancée.* | *She didn't know that Henry was Marie's fiancé.*

⚠ Use **fiancé** to refer to a man and **fiancée** to refer to a woman.

6 married

married /'mærid/ [adj] *Are you married or single?*
be married *Phil and I have been married for 15 years.*
+to *She's married to a famous actor.*
married man/woman *a married man with three children*

⚠ Don't say 'married with someone'. Say **married to someone**.

wife /waif/ [n C] the woman that a man is married to: *Would you and your wife like to come over for dinner on Friday? | The men had gone out for the day, leaving their wives and children at home.*
plural **wives**

husband /'hʌzbənd/ [n C] the man that a woman is married to: *I don't like Francesca's husband very much. | Brian is her second husband.*

partner /'pɑːᵊtnəᵊ/ [n C] the person that someone lives with in a romantic relationship – use this whether they are married or not: *Can people bring their partners to the office party?*

couple /'kʌpəl/ [n C] two people who are married to each other, or who are having a romantic relationship: *An elderly couple sat in total silence in the corner of the restaurant.*
married couple *a young married couple*

7 not married

not married /ˌnɒt 'mærid/ [adj] *He told her he wasn't married. | Jeff and Paula have two children, but they're not actually married.*

single /'sɪŋɡəl/ [adj] someone who is **single** is not married or is not in a romantic relationship with anyone: *a change in the tax laws for single people | I used to go out a lot more when I was single.*
single parent (=someone who has children, but who does not live with

their partner) *It is extremely difficult being a single parent.*
unmarried /ˌʌn'mærid◂/ [adj] an **unmarried** person is someone who has never been married: *She has three unmarried sons.*

⚠ You may also see the words **bachelor** (=a man who has never been married) and **spinster** (=a woman who has never been married), but these words are rather old-fashioned.

8 not married any more

divorced /dɪ'vɔːᵊst/ [adj] someone who is **divorced** has officially ended their marriage: *He's living with a divorced woman and her two children.*
be divorced *Her parents are divorced.*
get divorced (=officially end your marriage) *They got divorced only three years after they got married.*

divorce /dɪ'vɔːᵊs/ [n C/U] the legal process of ending a marriage: *She told me she wanted a divorce! | A third of all marriages in Britain end in divorce.*
get a divorce *It's much too easy to get a divorce nowadays.*

divorcee /dɪˌvɔːᵊ'siː/ [n C] someone who is divorced, especially a woman

⚠ **Divorcee** is not commonly used in ordinary conversation. It is old-fashioned in American English.

ex-husband/ex-wife /ˌeks 'hʌzbənd, ˌeks 'waif/ [n C] the man or woman that you used to be married to before getting divorced: *His ex-wife never lets him see the children.*

be separated /bi: 'sepəreɪtᵊd/ if a husband and wife **are separated**, they do not live with each other, because they are not happy together any more, but they are not divorced: *I didn't know Linda and Mike were separated.*

split up /ˌsplɪt 'ʌp/ [phrasal verb I] INFORMAL if two people **split up**, they end their marriage or they stop having a romantic relationship: *They're always arguing but I don't think they'll ever split up,*
+with *Have you heard? Katie's splitting up with Andrew!*

WORD BANKS

The WORD BANKS will help you expand your vocabulary and write correctly in English. WORD BANKS cover common topics that deal with real world language and teach vocabulary that students need at intermediate level. Model essays show how to write good essays using a wide range of vocabulary, while Writing Tips help with using the correct phrases and explain how to structure essays.

BOOKS/LITERATURE

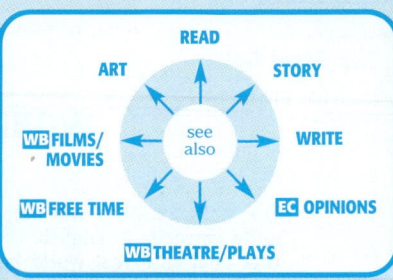

READ

ART STORY

see also

WB FILMS/ MOVIES WRITE

WB FREE TIME **EC** OPINIONS

WB THEATRE/PLAYS

Writing about your favourite book

Harry Potter

My favourite **book** is 'Harry Potter and the Philosopher's Stone'. It's about a young boy called Harry Potter, who is a wizard, although he doesn't realize this at first. He attends a special school for wizards called Hogwarts. While he's there, he learns about magic spells, and all sorts of magical things happen to him and his friends. At the end Harry has a battle with the evil Voldemort – of course Harry wins.

I read it a couple of years ago. The thing I like most about the book is that it makes the world in which the wizards live seem perfectly normal and just like ours.

Vocabulary

1 a book

book /bʊk/ [n C]
+ **by** *a book by Charles Dickens*
+ **about** *I'm reading a book about a little girl who was a slave in 19th century Atlanta.*
book on sth (=a book giving information about a particular subject) *Do you have any books on astronomy?*
paperback /ˈpeɪpəˈbæk/ [n C] a book with a cover made of stiff paper
hardback /ˈhɑːˈdbæk/ [n C] a book with a hard cover

2 books and stories about imaginary people and events

novel /ˈnɒvəlǁˈnɑː-/ [n C] a book about people and events that the writer has imagined: *Have you read any good novels recently?*
+ **by** *The movie is based on a novel by Graham Greene.*
romantic novel (=about love)
historical novel (=about people and events in the past)

fiction /ˈfɪkʃən/ [n U] books about imaginary people and events: *I mostly read fiction. | She's taking a class in Victorian fiction.*
romantic fiction (=about someone who falls in love)
historical fiction (=set in the past, often about famous events)
crime fiction (=about a crime and the criminal getting caught)
literature /ˈlɪtərətʃəʳ/ [n U] books, plays, and poems, especially famous ones that people think are important: *She's studying 19th century French literature. | He won the Nobel Prize for Literature.*
science fiction /ˌsaɪəns ˈfɪkʃən/ [n U] stories about things that happen in the future or in other parts of the universe: *a science fiction story by Douglas Adams*
detective story /dɪˈtektɪv ˌstɔːri/ [n C] a story in which someone tries to find who is responsible for a crime, especially a murder: *I like reading Sherlock Holmes and other detective stories.*
ghost story /ˈgəʊst ˌstɔːri/ [n C] a story that involves ghosts and strange events: *Ghost stories keep me awake at night.*

The Great Gatsby

F. Scott Fitzgerald's 'The Great Gatsby' is one of my favourite **books** of all time. It tells the **story** of Jay Gatsby, who is incredibly rich and successful, but always seems to have an air of sadness and mystery about him. He falls in love with a married woman called Daisy Buchanan, but he realizes that he can never marry her, and the book ends in tragedy for both of them. The book was written in the 1920s and it really gives you the feeling for the world of the "Jazz Age" and the American Dream.

I first read the book when I was at university, and it made a deep impression on me. For me, the moral of the **story** is that there's no connection between happiness and money or success.

Writing about different kinds of books

I like reading **novels**, especially by modern writers. I find **non-fiction** a bit dull. I can never remember all the facts and dates. I'd much rather read a book with a good story and interesting **characters**. I love **thrillers**, where you are always wondering what is going to happen next. **Detective stories** are good, too, although I can never manage to guess who the guilty person is. I don't really like **science fiction** stories, because they are too far from real life. My sister likes **romantic novels**, but I've never read one myself.

love story /ˈlʌv ˌstɔːri/ [n C] a story about people who fall in love: *The novel is basically a love story.*

thriller /ˈθrɪləʳ/ [n C] an exciting story, for example about a crime or war, in which surprising events happen suddenly and you never know what will happen next: *Stephen King's new psychological thriller*

short story /ˌʃɔːʳt ˈstɔːri/ [n C] a short piece of writing in which the writer tells a story: *a collection of short stories by Henry James*

3 books about real things

non-fiction /ˌnɒn ˈfɪkʃənǁˌnɑːn-/ [n U] books about real events, people, or places: *The books in the library are divided into fiction and non-fiction.*
non-fiction [adj] *non-fiction books*

4 a book about someone's life

biography /baɪˈɒgrəfiǁ-ˈɑːg-/ [n C] a book about someone's life, written by another person: *Andrew Morton's biography of Princess Diana*
plural **biographies**

autobiography /ˌɔːtəbaɪˈɒgrəfiǁ-ˈɑːg-/ [n C] a book in which someone writes about their own life: *In her autobiography, she writes about her childhood in Zimbabwe.*
plural **autobiographies**

5 books that give information

reference book /ˈrefərəns ˌbʊk/ [n C] a book that you look at in order to get information, especially a dictionary or encyclopedia: *Please do not remove reference books from the library.*

encyclopedia /ɪnˌsaɪkləˈpiːdiə/ [n C] a large book or set of books containing facts about a lot of different subjects, usually arranged in alphabetical order: *"Does anyone know when Mozart was born?" "Look it up in the encyclopedia."* | *the Encyclopedia of Science*

textbook /ˈtekstbʊk/ [n C] a book that contains information and ideas about a subject, which you use when you are studying that subject: *a geography textbook* | *The school says it doesn't have enough money to buy textbooks for every student.*

Writing tips

when you are writing about your favourite book:

✎ **say briefly what it's about**
It's about a young boy called Harry Potter …
It tells the story of Jay Gatsby …
Then give a very brief summary of the story, using the present tense.

✎ **say why you liked it**

It's a very good book
It's a brilliant book.
It's a classic story.
It's a masterpiece. (=It is an extremely good book)

It's very exciting
I couldn't put it down. (=didn't want to stop reading it until I'd finished it)
It's a real page-turner. (=it makes you always want to know what's going to happen next)
It grabs your attention right from the start.

You liked the language
It's very well written.
It's beautifully written.

You liked the atmosphere
It really gives you the feeling for the world of the "Jazz Age".
You really think you are there.

✎ **say when it was written, when you read it, or when the book is supposed to happen**
It was written in the 1920s/a long time ago/quite recently.
I read it when I was at university/a couple of years ago
I discovered it when I was at school.
The story is set in the 1950s. (=it happens in the 1950s)

✎ **say if the book has a deeper meaning, or has something important to say about people's lives, for example:**
The moral of the story is that there is no connection between happiness and money or success. (=this is the main message of the book)
The book still seems relevant today.

---

dictionary /'dɪkʃənəri‖-neri/ [n C] a book that tells you the meaning of words and lists them in alphabetical order
plural **dictionaries**
atlas /'ætləs/ [n C] a book of maps: *a road atlas of Europe*

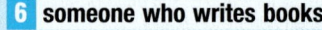 **6 someone who writes books**

writer /'raɪtəʳ/ [n C] someone who writes books, stories, or articles in magazines as a job: *When I was young I wanted to be a writer.* | *Have you read any books by American writers?* | *Greene was one of the finest writers of his generation.*

author /ˈɔːθəʳ/ [n C] someone who writes books, or who wrote a particular book: *Thomas Hardy was one of her favourite authors.* | *Who was the author of 'Catch 22'?*

novelist /ˈnɒvəlₔst‖ˈnɑː-/ [n C] someone who writes books about imaginary people or events: *the great Russian novelist, Leo Tolstoy* | *romantic novelist Barbara Cartland*

7 what happens in a book

story /ˈstɔːri/ [n C] what happens in a book: *The story begins in New York.* | *The book is the story of his travels around the world.*
a true story *I can't believe it's a true story.*

plot /plɒt‖plɑːt/ [n C] the events that happen in a book, and the way in which these events are connected: *The plot was so complicated that I kept getting lost.*

ending /ˈendɪŋ/ [n C] what happens at the end of a book: *Don't tell me the ending!*
a happy/sad ending *The book has a happy ending.*

8 the words in a book

narrative /ˈnærətɪv/ [n C/U] the series of events described in a story and the way that the writer describes them: *The narrative moves back and foward between the past and the present.* | *the book's narrative structure*
third person narrative (=telling the story using 'he' or 'she')
first person narrative (=telling the story using 'I')

dialogue /ˈdaɪəlɒg‖-lɔːg, -lɑːg/ [n C/U] the things that people in a book say to each other: *The dialogue uses a lot of slang.* | *I didn't find the dialogues very convincing.*

quotation (also **quote**) /kwəʊˈteɪʃən, kwəʊt/ [n C] a sentence or phrase from a book: *He started his speech with a quotation from Shakespeare.*

style (also **style of writing**) /staɪl, ˌstaɪl əv ˈraɪtɪŋ/ [n C] the way in which a writer uses words in order to express ideas or tell a story: *He has his own very distinctive style.*

9 the people in a book

character /ˈkærₐktəʳ/ [n C] a person in the story in a book: *The book's main character dies at the end of the story.*
a colourful character (=an interesting character) *His stories are always full of interesting characters.*
an attractive/appealing/sympathetic character *Bridget Jones is a very appealing character.*

hero /ˈhɪərəʊ/ [n C] the most important man in a story, who usually has qualities that you admire: *Winston Smith is the hero of Orwell's book '1984'.*

heroine /ˈherəʊɪn/ [n C] the most important woman in a story, who usually has qualities that you admire: *the tragic heroine of a novel by Emile Zola*

the narrator /ðə nəˈreɪtəʳ‖-ˈnæreɪtər, nəˈreɪ-/ [n singular] the person in a book who explains what happens during the course of the story: *The book's narrator describes how they escaped from the secret police.*

10 the ideas or subject of a book

be about /biː əˈbaʊt/ if a book is about a person, event, idea etc, that person, event, or idea is the main subject of the book: *The book is about growing up in Chicago in the 1920s.* | *I want to buy a book about gardening.*

be set in /biː ˈset ɪn/ if a book is set in a place or period of time, the story happens in that place or during that time: *The book is set in Paris.* | *'Brave New World' is set in the future.*

be based on /biː ˈbeɪst ɒn/ if a book is based on a story or event, the things that happen in the book are very similar to the things that really happened at that time: *The book is based on Hemingway's experiences in the Spanish Civil War.* | *The novel is based on a true story.*

theme /θiːm/ [n C] one of the main ideas that an author writes about in a book: *The main theme of the story is revenge.* | *The importance of friendship is a recurring theme in his novels.*

11 poems

poem /ˈpəʊₔm/ [n C] a piece of writing which is arranged in patterns of lines and sounds: *a poem by Sylvia Plath* | *She quoted a few lines from Eliot's famous poem 'The Waste Land'.*

poetry /ˈpəʊₔtri/ [n U] poems in general: *a book of modern poetry* | *Do you read much poetry?*

verse /vɜːʳs/ [n U] a literary word for poetry: *He had a successful career, writing both prose and verse.* | *The Faber Book of Modern Verse*

poet /ˈpəʊₔt/ [n C] someone who writes poems: *the French poet Rimbaud*

12 places where you can get books

bookshop BRITISH **bookstore** AMERICAN /ˈbʊkʃɒp, ˈbʊkstɔːʳ‖-ʃɑːp-/ [n C] a shop that sells books: *I often spend my lunch hour browsing in the local bookstore.*

library /ˈlaɪbrəri‖-breri/ [n C] a place that has a lot of books that you can borrow for a short time, usually without paying money: *the college library* | *I need to take some books back to the library.*

COMPUTERS/INTERNET

1 hard disk	**6** mouse
2 computer	**7** printer
3 monitor	**8** scanner
4 screen	**9** floppy disks
5 keyboard	**10** CD-ROM

Vocabulary

1 computers and computer equipment

computer /kəm'pjuːtə^r/ [n C] *My new computer is much faster and more powerful than my old one.* | *The information is stored on computer.*
  computer system *We've had a lot of problems with our new computer system.*

PC /ˌpiː 'siː/ [n C] a computer that is used by one person in an office, at school etc: *You can use this software on any PC.*

hardware /'hɑːʳdweəʳ/ [n U] computers and all the machinery and equipment connected with them: *a hardware problem*

screen/monitor /skriːn, 'mɒnɪ̯təʳ‖-mɑː-/ [n C] the part of a computer that looks like a television, and which shows you information, pictures, etc: *A message suddenly appeared on my screen.*

keyboard /'kiːbɔːʳd/ [n C] the set of buttons, with letters and numbers on them, that you press in order to enter information on a computer

mouse /maʊs/ [n C] a small object that you move around on a flat surface in order to give instructions to a computer. It tells the computer where on the screen you want to enter the information, and by clicking on it you can make programs start working
  plural **mouses**

modem /'məʊdem/ [n C] a piece of electronic equipment that allows information to be sent from one computer to another. They are used especially to connect a computer to the Internet using a telephone line.

floppy disk /ˌflɒpi 'dɪsk‖ˌflɑː-/ [n C] a small flat thing that you can store information from a computer on, that you can remove and use on other computers

CD-ROM /ˌsiːdiː 'rɒm‖-'rɑːm/ [n C] a small flat circular object on which large amounts of information can be stored and used on a computer. CD-ROMs hold more information than floppy disks, but less than DVDs
  on CD-ROM *a new encyclopaedia on CD-ROM*

DVD /ˌdiː viː 'diː/ [n C] a small flat circular object similar to a CD-ROM, but which can store much more information
  on DVD *The movie is available on DVD*

memory stick /'meməri stɪk/ [n C] a small piece of equipment that holds a lot of information. It

Using your computer

This morning I went to the school library, switched on the computer, **entered** my password, and waited for the machine to **start up**. I **clicked** on an **icon** and **opened** the file that I wanted to work on. I spent two hours writing an essay. Just as I was about to **save** my data, the **hard disk** made a horrible noise, the **screen froze**, the machine **crashed**, and I lost all my work. The essay I had been writing was called "The benefits of modern technology"!

The advantages of computers

It is difficult to imagine a world without computers. We use them in almost every area of our lives: at work, at school, and in our homes.

Computers have brought many advantages. They make it possible to **access** huge amounts of information very quickly and do complicated tasks in a short time. Instead of waiting inside a bank to get money from our bank accounts, we can use machines in the street 24 hours a day. People can communicate with each other instantly by **email**, and you can buy almost anything on the **Internet** without having to leave your home. Many people now work from home using a computer, and use the computer in their leisure time for playing **computer games** or just **surfing the net**. Children growing up today can't imagine what life was like before computers. They think it must have been very dull.

can be connected to a computer in order to put information onto that computer, or in order to make a copy of information that is on that computer

2 programs and other information stored on a computer

program /ˈprəʊɡræm/ [n C] a set of instructions that makes it possible for a computer to do a particular job: *a program that checks your grammar*
write a program *Students learn how to write their own programs.*
run a program (=make it operate) *My machine doesn't have enough memory to run the program.*
software /ˈsɒftweəʳ‖ˈsɔːft-/ [n U] the programs that you put into computers to make them do the job you want: *You can get special software for designing your own garden.*
icon /ˈaɪkɒn‖-kɑːn/ [n C] a small picture on a computer screen that represents a program that you can use or a job that a program will do: *Click on the icon to start the program.*

cursor /ˈkɜːʳsəʳ/ [n C] a mark that you can move round the computer screen to show you where you are working: *If you prefer, you can have your cursor in a different colour.*
file/document /faɪl, ˈdɒkjɡˌmənt‖ˈdɑːk-/ [n C] information on a computer that you store under a particular name
open/close a file/document *You can close the file by clicking on the X.*
save a file *Don't forget to save the file.*
computer game /kəmˈpjuːtəʳ ɡeɪm/ [n C] a game that you play on a computer

3 using your computer

start up (also **boot**) /ˌstɑːʳt ˈʌp, buːt/ [phrasal verb I/T] if you **start up** or **boot** a computer, you turn it on. If a computer **starts up** or **boots**, it starts working: *I waited while she started up her computer. | My computer won't boot.*
log on /ˌlɒg ˈɒn‖ˌlɔːgˈɑːn/ [phrasal verb I] to do the things that will allow you to start using a computer or computer system, for example by typing in your password: *He logged on and checked his email.*

Writing tips

✎ You work **on a computer** (not 'with a computer'). You can also say that you work **on screen**, with the same meaning. If you want to say that you work or shop using the Internet, you can say that you work or shop **online**.

✎ You always say **the Internet**, not 'Internet' on its own.

For example, don't say 'Internet is a useful source of information.' Say *The Internet is a useful source of information.*

✎ You also shop or do things **on the Internet**, not 'by the Internet' or 'in the Internet'.

✎ When talking about your computer, you often talk about your **machine**, eg *I can't get my machine to switch off.* (=I can't get my computer to switch off.)

✎ The word **computer** is a countable noun.

Don't say 'She doesn't like using computer'. Say *She doesn't like using computers.*

✎ The study of computers is usually known as **computing** or **computer science**.

Don't say 'I studied computer'. Say *I studied computing.*

open /ˈəʊpən/ [v T] to make a program or document ready to use: *Select your file from the list, and open it.*

enter /ˈentəʳ/ [v T] to put information into a computer by pressing the keys: *Have you entered the correct password?*

access /ˈækses/ [v T] if you **access** information on a computer, you use the computer to find and display the information: *The new system made it easier to access patients' medical records.*

download /ˈdaʊnləʊd/ [v T] to copy a file from the Internet onto your own computer: *You can download music from the Internet.* | *I downloaded all the software I needed from their website.*

click /klɪk/ [v I] to press a button on a mouse in order to choose something on the screen and make the computer do something: *Click here for more information.*

click on sth *Click on the left arrow if you want to go back.*

cut and paste /ˌkʌt ənd ˈpeɪst/ [v T] to remove information from one place in a computer program or document and put it in another place: *You can cut and paste the parts that you want to keep.*

save /seɪv/ [v I/T] to make a computer keep the work you have done in its memory or on a disk: *It's always best to save your work regularly.*

close /kləʊz/ [v T] to do the things that you need to do when you want to stop using a program or document: *Did you remember to press "save" before you closed the document?*

log out/off /ˌlɒg ˈaʊt, ˈɒf‖ˌlɔːg- -ˈɔːf/ [phrasal verb I] to do the actions that you have to do when you finish using a computer system: *Make sure that you log off correctly. Don't just switch the machine off.*

shut down /ˌʃʌt ˈdaʊn/ [phrasal verb I/T] if you **shut down** a computer, you turn it off. If a computer **shuts down**, it turns itself off: *I shut down my computer and went home.* | *The machine shuts down automatically after a certain period of time.*

4 computer problems

crash /kræʃ/ [v I] if a computer crashes, it suddenly stops working: *My computer crashed, and I lost a whole afternoon's work.*

freeze /friːz/ [v I] if a computer screen freezes, the computer will not accept any new instructions because of a fault, and everything remains in the same position: *I tried to exit the file, and my screen just froze.*

virus /'vaɪərəs/ [n C] a set of instructions which have secretly been put on a computer or computer program, especially from the Internet, which can change or destroy the information that is stored there: *Don't open the attachment until you're sure it doesn't contain a virus.*

bug /bʌg/ [n C] a small fault with a computer program that stops it from working properly: *The software has some kind of bug in it.*

5 the study of computers

computing (also **computer science**) /kəm'pjuːtɪŋ, kəm,pjutə^r 'saɪəns/ [n U] the study of computers: *He studied computing at college.*

IT/information technology /,aɪ 'tiː, ,ɪnfər'meɪʃən tek,nɒlədʒɪ‖-,nɑːl-/ the study or use of computers and other electronic equipment for storing, sending, and developing information: *She teaches information technology at a local school.* | *He works in IT.* | *IT support staff*

6 the Internet

the Internet/the net /ði 'ɪntər'net, ðə 'net/ a system that allows computer users around the world to send messages and information to each other: *The net is a very useful source of information.*
on the Internet *I do a lot of my shopping on the net.*
surf the net (=look at the information on the Internet in order to find something that interests you) *He spends most of his evening surfing the net.*
World Wide Web/WWW/the Web /,wɜːld waɪd 'web, ,dʌbəljuː dʌbəljuː 'dʌbəljuː, ðə 'web/ the system that connects computer users around the world

online /'ɒnlaɪn‖'ɑːn-/ [adj] using the Internet or available on the Internet: *an online bookstore* | *online banking*

online [adv] *Most of their business is done online.* | *I went online and looked for details of hotels in the area.*

website /'websaɪt/ [n C] a place on the Internet that gives you information about a particular subject or product: *Have you checked out their website?*
visit a website *More than a million people visit the company's website every week.*

web page /'web peɪdʒ/ [n C] one of the areas that you can go to on a website: *Do you want me to print off the web page for you?*

homepage /'həʊm peɪdʒ/ [n C] the first page of a website: *Click here if you want to return to the homepage.*

broadband /'brɔːdbænd/ [n U] a system of connecting to the Internet that is much faster than using an ordinary phone modem: *They charge £25 a month for the broadband connection.*

7 email

email /'iː meɪl/ [n C/U] a system that allows messages to be sent from one computer to another, or a message sent using this system: *He received 2,000 emails of support.*
by email *You can contact me by email.*
send sb an email *Send me an email when you get to New York.*
check your email (=read your email) *I checked my email as soon as I got into work.*
email address *What's your email address?*
mail (also **email**) /meɪl, 'iːmeɪl/ [v T] to send someone a message by email: *Will you email me about it?*
email sb sth/email sth to sb *I'll email you the file.* | *Can you mail it to me?*

bounce /baʊns/ [v I] if an email **bounces**, it comes back to you because there is a problem on the system and it cannot be delivered to the person you sent it to

spam /spæm/ [n U] unwanted emails which have not been asked for, sent out for example by someone trying to sell you something

DESCRIBING HOW PEOPLE LOOK

Robbers get away with half a million pounds

Robbers stole £500,000 from a bank in central London yesterday. Police are looking for a man in his late twenties, with **short dark hair**, **brown eyes**, and a **thin moustache**. He was **scruffily-dressed**, and **was wearing** a T-shirt and jeans. He has a big **scar** on his right cheek.

Police would also like to speak to a woman **in her early forties**, who was seen waiting in a red BMW outside the bank. She is **slim**, **pretty**, has **long dark hair**, and was wearing **dark glasses** and a baseball cap. If you recognize these two people or have any information about them, please contact the Serious Crime Desk on 0555 555.

HAVE YOU SEEN THIS WOMAN?

HAVE YOU SEEN THIS MAN?

Vocabulary

1 height

tall /tɔːl/ [adj] *He was tall and thin.* | *a tall handsome man*

short /ʃɔːʳt/ [adj] *His mother was a short woman with glasses.* | *Everyone in her family was short except for her brother.*

not very tall /nɒt veri ˈtɔːl/ [adj] fairly short: *My sister's not very tall.*

of average/medium height /əv ˌævərɪdʒ, ˌmiːdiəm ˈhaɪt/ [adj] neither tall nor short. This phrase is used especially in police descriptions: *The witness said that the man was of average height.*

be 6 foot tall/be 1 meter 83/be 183 cm etc *"How tall are you?" "I'm about 1 meter 80."* | *She's just under 6 foot tall.*

2 size

⚠ Be careful when referring to someone's size. It is rude to tell someone that they are **fat**, or to ask a woman how much she weighs.

fat /fæt/ [adj] *He was too fat to run.* | *a fat little boy*

overweight /ˌəʊvəʳˈweɪt◂/ [adj] a little fatter than you should be: *Many office workers are overweight because they don't get enough exercise.*

big/large /bɪg, lɑːʳdʒ/ [adj] having a big body. This does not necessarily mean that the person is fat: *He had two big bodyguards with him.* | *a large lady in her early 50s*

of medium/average build /əv ˌmiːdiəm, ˌævərɪdʒ ˈbɪld/ neither fat nor thin. This phrase is usually used in police descriptions: *The suspect is of medium build, with dark hair.*

thin /θɪn/ [adj] having very little fat on your body. This word can be used neutrally, but is often used when someone seems unhealthy: *He's very thin – is he getting enough to eat?*

slim /slɪm/ [adj] thin in a way that looks attractive: *You're looking very slim. Have you lost weight?*

skinny /ˈskɪni/ [adj] very thin, especially in a way that is unattractive: *a skinny teenager*

be/weigh 172 pounds/12 stone BRITISH **78 kilos** /biː, weɪ (172 pounds etc)/ *"How much do you weigh?" "I'm just over 65 kilos."*

Who is your ideal man?

My ideal man is incredibly **good-looking**. He's **in his 20s**, with **medium-length brown hair** and **brown eyes**, and he is **clean-shaven**. He **weighs** about **110 pounds**, and looks very strong. His **features** are slightly **rugged**, as if he spends a lot of time outdoors. He's about **6 feet tall**, and he **dresses casually**, usually in colours that match his hair and eyes.

Who is your ideal woman?

My ideal woman is probably Marilyn Monroe. She was extremely **beautiful** and with her **curly blonde hair** and bright red lips, she had the classic Hollywood look. In her movies, she often played women who were not very smart, but she was actually a very funny and intelligent actress. Her movies, such as 'Some Like It Hot' and 'The Seven Year Itch', are still popular today.

3 age

> ⚠️ Be careful when referring to someone's age. It is rude to ask a woman her age, or to tell someone that they are old or middle-aged.

old /əʊld/ [adj] She was very old and had difficulty walking.

young /jʌŋ/ [adj] A group of young boys were playing in the park.

elderly /ˈeldəˈli/ [adj] a polite word meaning 'old': An elderly lady lived next door.

middle-aged /ˌmɪdl ˈeɪdʒd◂/ [adj] neither young nor old – between about 45 and 60: a boring, middle-aged couple

be 10/15 etc (years old) "I hope you don't mind my asking, but how old are you?" "I'm 35." | I'd say she was about 40 years old.

be in your 20s/30s etc be between 20 and 29, 30 and 39 etc: I'll soon be in my 50s. | The man was in his early 20s . (=between 20 and 23) | She's in her late 30s. (=between 37 and 39) | He's in his mid-sixties. (=between 64 and 66)

be in your teens /biː ɪn jɔːʳ ˈtiːnz/ be between 12 and 19: He's in his late teens.

be thirtyish/fortyish etc INFORMAL be about 30/40 etc: She looked fortyish.

4 clothes

be wearing/be dressed in … /biː ˈweərɪŋ, biː ˈdrest ɪn/ He was wearing a T shirt and jeans. | She was dressed in her best clothes.

have sth on /hæv (sth) ˈɒn/ to be wearing something: I had my new coat on. | The boys had nothing on. (=they were not wearing any clothes) | He had on a white shirt with a red tie.

a man in …/a woman in … /ə ˈmæn ɪn, ə ˈwʊmən ɪn/ used especially in written descriptions, especially in stories, when saying what someone was wearing: The door was opened by a man in a dark suit.

well-dressed /ˌwel ˈdrest◂/ [adj] wearing good quality clothes: a well-dressed young woman

casually-dressed /ˌkæʒuəli ˈdrest◂/ [adj] wearing informal clothes such as jeans

Writing tips

✎ You can say that someone **has** *brown hair, blue eyes* etc. Another way to say this is to use **with**, for example: *a man with brown hair* or *a girl with blue eyes*

In written descriptions you can also use adjectives such as **dark-haired** or **brown-eyed**, for example: *a dark-haired man in his late 30s*

✎ Don't use too many short sentences. For example, don't write things like 'He is tall. He has dark hair and bright blue eyes. He has a small moustache.'

It sounds much more natural to link your description together into a longer sentence:
He is tall, with dark hair, bright blue eyes, and a small moustache.

✎ Don't say 'She has dark/long hairs'. Say *She has long dark hair.*

✎ Don't say 'He has black eyes'. Say *He has dark brown eyes.*

✎ In spoken British English, people often say **has got** instead of **has/have**, for example: *You've got beautiful eyes.*

In written descriptions, people usually use **has/have**. Note that when talking or writing about the past, you should always use **had**, not 'had got'.

✎ There are several ways of describing someone's age. If you know exactly, you can say, for example, *He is 22 years old.* If you are not sure, you can say *He's about 20* or *He's in his early twenties.* In more informal English you can say *He looks twentyish.*

✎ Don't say 'He is ten years'. Say *He is ten* or *He is ten years old.*

✎ When you are describing someone's clothes, you can say someone *is wearing* a *black jacket and a denim skirt*, or someone *is dressed in* a *black jacket and a denim skirt.* Another way to say this is to use **in**, for example: *a man in a black jacket.*

In more informal English, people often say that someone **has** something **on**, for example: *She had a black jacket and a denim skirt on* or *She had on a long green dress.*

---

smart/smartly-dressed /smɑːʳt, ˌsmɑːʳtli 'drestə/ [adj] BRITISH wearing clothes that are suitable for a formal occasion

scruffy/scruffily-dressed /'skrʌfi, ˌskrʌfɨli 'drestə/ [adj] wearing dirty untidy clothes

5 hair

hair /heəʳ/ [n U]

long/short hair *He had short brown hair.*
medium-length/shoulder-length hair *a girl with lovely shoulder-length hair*
dark/fair/grey/brown/red hair *a woman with long dark hair*
straight/curly hair

blonde/blond /blɒndǁblɑːnd/ [adj] **blonde** hair is very light brown or yellow – use **blonde** about women and **blond** about men: *She shook her blonde hair and smiled at him.*

bald /bɔːld/ [adj] a man who is **bald** has no hair growing on top of his head: *Her father was completely bald.*

beard /bɪəʳd/ [n C] hair on a man's chin and cheeks: *He had a pointed grey beard.*

moustache /mə'stɑːʃǁ'mʌstæʃ/ [n] hair on a man's upper lip: *a man with a thin moustache*

clean-shaven /ˌkliːn 'ʃeɪvən/ [adj] a **clean-shaven** man does not have a beard or moustache: *a clean-shaven young man*

6 face

face /feɪs/ [n C]
　long/thin face *He had rather a thin face.*
　round/oval face *a cheerful woman with a round face*

eyes /aɪz/ [n C]
　brown/blue/grey/green eyes *Her eyes are dark brown.*
　big/tiny eyes *The baby had big blue eyes.*

nose /nəʊz/ [n C] **big/small nose** *He has a really big nose.*

glasses /ˈglɑːsɪz‖ˈglæ-/ [n plural]
　wear glasses *She wore thick glasses.*
　dark glasses (=glasses that have dark coloured glass in them, to protect your eyes from the sun or to hide your eyes)

chin /tʃɪn/ [n C] the part of your face below your mouth
　have a double chin (=have a fold of fat under your chin)

feature /ˈfiːtʃəʳ/ [n usually plural] ESPECIALLY WRITTEN a part of your face, for example your eyes or your mouth: *his handsome features* | *Her eyes are her best feature.*

7 skin

skin /skɪn/ [n U] **pale/dark skin** *She had beautiful dark skin.*

freckles /ˈfrekəlz/ [n plural] small brown spots on someone's face that are made darker by the sun: *a fair-haired boy with freckles*
　freckled [adj] *a girl with red hair and a freckled face*

wrinkles /ˈrɪŋkəlz/ [n plural] lines in the skin that people get when they get older: *The old lady had wrinkles around her eyes.*
　wrinkled [adj] *a wrinkled face*

tattoo /təˈtuː, tæ-/ [n C] a picture permanently marked on someone's skin with a needle and ink: *a big man with tattoos all over his arms*

scar /skɑːʳ/ [n C] a mark left on the skin after an injury

mole /məʊl/ [n C] a permanent dark brown spot on the skin, which is higher than the skin around it

8 looks

good-looking /ˌgʊd ˈlʊkɪŋ/ [adj] use this about men or women who are attractive: *She's incredibly good-looking.* | *a good-looking guy*

pretty /ˈprɪti/ [adj] attractive – used about young women or girls: *Do you think she's pretty?*

handsome /ˈhænsəm/ [adj] attractive – used about men: *a handsome young army officer*

cute /kjuːt/ [adj] used about young men and women who look nice and are attractive. Also used about babies and children who are attractive and have a happy or amusing character: *a cute little boy* | *I think he's kind of cute.*

athletic /æθˈletɪk/ [adj] used about someone who does a lot of sport

rugged /ˈrʌgɪd/ [adj] used about a man who looks strong and handsome, does a lot of outdoor activities, but does not have perfect features

DESCRIBING PEOPLE'S CHARACTER

The signs of the zodiac

Some people believe that the time of year that you were born has an effect on your character because of the positions of the stars and the planets. They divide the year into 12 periods of time, and these are known as 'signs of the zodiac'.

People born under different signs are thought to have different characteristics.

Aquarius
20 January –
18 February
People born under the sign of Aquarius are very **loyal**, but they can be a little **insensitive** at times.

Pisces
19 February –
20 March
People with the sign of Pisces can be very **romantic**, and are always **sympathetic** if you have a problem. But they can also be extremely **pessimistic**.

Vocabulary

1 words used to describe someone's character

adventurous /əd'ventʃərəs/ [adj] always ready to try different and exciting things, even if they are dangerous: *For the more adventurous members of the group, there are activities such as rock-climbing and scuba diving.*

aggressive /ə'gresɪv/ [adj] someone who is **aggressive** behaves in an angry way and seems to want to fight or argue: *He suddenly became aggressive and started shouting.*

artistic /ɑːˈtɪstɪk/ [adj] good at painting and drawing, and at making and designing things using your skill and imagination: *She comes from a very artistic family – her mother's an interior designer and her brother's an architect.*

calm /kɑːm‖kɑːm, kɑːlm/ [adj] not getting angry or upset, even in a difficult situation: *Dr Weir answered their questions in a calm, professional manner.*
keep/stay calm *Meditation always helps me stay calm and relaxed.*

cheerful /'tʃɪəˈfəl/ [adj] always happy, smiling, and friendly: *Barbara greeted us with a cheerful smile. | The children managed to stay cheerful in spite of the bad weather.*

conceited /kən'siːtɪd/ [adj] too confident about your own abilities and achievements, in a way that annoys people: *They are an awful couple – so snobbish and conceited.*

critical /'krɪtɪkəl/ [adj] someone who is **critical** always says negative things about other people's work or the things they do and say: *Mrs Blake wasn't a popular teacher – she was too critical.*

cruel /'kruːəl/ [adj] deliberately trying to hurt or upset people, and not caring if this makes them unhappy: *'How could anyone be so cruel!' she said and burst into tears.*
+ to *Kids can sometimes be very cruel to each other.*

energetic /ˌenəˈdʒetɪk/ [adj] very active and able to work hard and do a lot of things without getting tired: *If you're feeling energetic, we could go out for a run.*

fussy /'fʌsi/ [adj] someone who is **fussy** is difficult to please because they only like a few things and will only accept exactly what they want

Aries
21 March – 19 April

People born under the sign of Aries are extremely **energetic** and **adventurous**. But they can also be **aggressive**.

Taurus
20 April – 20 May

People with the sign of Taurus are always **calm** and **patient**, but also very **materialistic**.

Gemini
21 May – 20 June

People born under the sign of Gemini are very **witty**, but they tend to be a little **impatient**.

Cancer
21 June – 22 July

People with the sign of Cancer are very **kind** and **helpful**. But they can sometimes be very **moody**.

Leo
23 July – 22 August

People born under the sign of Leo are very **sociable**, but can often be **vain** as well.

Virgo
23 August – 22 September

People born under the sign of Virgo tend to be **hard-working**, but also a little **fussy** and very **critical**.

Libra
23 September – 22 October

People born under the sign of Libra are usually **artistic**. But they also tend to be **indecisive**.

Scorpio
23 October – 21 November

People born under the sign of Scorpio are often **passionate**, but sometimes a little **cruel**.

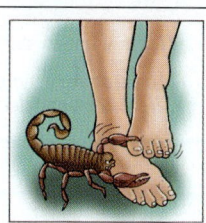

Sagittarius
22 November – 21 December

People born under the sign of Sagittarius are always **cheerful** and **optimistic**, but they often tend to be **reckless**.

Capricorn
22 December – 19 January

People with the sign of Capricorn are **sensible** and **organized**, but are sometimes **conceited**.

Writing tips

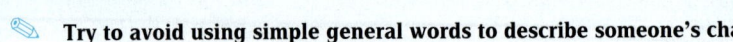

✎ **Try to avoid using simple general words to describe someone's character.**

For example, instead of saying that someone is 'kind', there are many other words that you can use, such as **considerate**, **generous**, or **sympathetic**. If you need help finding these more exact words, you can find them in your Essential Activator under the keywords KIND, HONEST, FRIENDLY, CONFIDENT etc.

✎ **It's good to give a real example of an occasion that shows that what you are saying is true.**

For example instead of just saying that someone is **helpful**, you could say: *Sue is very kind and helpful. When I first started college she made me feel at home and showed me where everything was.*

✎ Don't say things like 'Her character is very nice.' Say *She's a very nice person* or *She's very nice.*

People often also say that someone is a particular **sort/kind of person**, for example: *He always seems such a happy **sort of** person.*

✎ **If you want to say that someone does something often, and this is an important part of their character, you can say that they are always doing something.** For example:

*He's **always** complaining.*
*Margaret's very considerate – she's **always** helping people.*

✎ If you want to say that someone sometimes behaves in a particular way, you use **tend to be** or **can be**, especially when talking about negative qualities:

*She **tends to be** rather impatient.*
*He **can be** very moody at times.*

✎ If you want to say something negative about someone, you often use **not very**:

*He's **not very** sympathetic.* (=he's unsympathetic)
*She's **not very** decisive.* (=she's indecisive)

+ about *Teenagers are often very fussy about what they eat.*

hard-working /ˌhɑːᵈ ˈwɜːᵈkɪŋ◂/ [adj] always working hard in your job or schoolwork: *Jane's teachers said she was a sensible hard-working girl.*

helpful /ˈhelpfəl/ [adj] always ready to help people, for example by giving them useful advice or information: *The staff at the museum were very helpful.* | *Thanks Sasha. You've been really helpful.*

impatient /ɪmˈpeɪʃənt/ [adj] someone who is **impatient** gets annoyed if they have to wait for something: *I'm coming – don't be so impatient!*

indecisive /ˌɪndɪˈsaɪsɪv◂/ [adj] someone who is **indecisive** is not good at making decisions quickly and keeps changing their mind about what they want to do: *The President's opponents described him as weak and indecisive.*

insensitive /ɪnˈsensᵻtɪv/ [adj] not realizing that some of the things you say or do are likely to upset or offend people: *Carol's husband is an insensitive brute.*
+ to *She's insensitive to anyone's feelings but her own.*

kind /kaɪnd/ [adj] someone who is **kind** always tries to help people and make them happy or comfortable: *We'd like to thank all the doctors and*

nurses at St James's Hospital for being so kind. | *She's one of the kindest, most considerate people I ever met.*
+ to *People at work were very kind to me when my mother died.*

loyal /ˈlɔɪəl/ [*adj*] always ready to help and support your friends, family etc, especially when other people criticize or oppose them: *a loyal and devoted wife*
+ to *We'd like to thank all our fans who've been so loyal to the team.*

materialistic /məˌtɪəriəˈlɪstɪk◂/ [*adj*] thinking that money and possessions are more important than anything else: *A lot of young people nowadays are rebelling against the materialistic values of their parents.*

moody /ˈmuːdi/ [*adj*] often getting angry or annoyed, even though there seems to be no reason to feel like this: *What's wrong with Janet? She's not usually so moody.* | *After the accident, he had become increasingly moody and depressed.*

optimistic /ˌɒptɪˈmɪstɪk◂ ‖ˌɑːp-/ [*adj*] someone who is **optimistic** always expects good things to happen, and believes that they will eventually get what they want: *Donna hasn't managed to find a job yet, but she is still very optimistic.*
+ about *How optimistic are you about your chances of winning a gold medal?*

organized /ˈɔːrɡənaɪzd/ [*adj*] good at organizing your life and making plans, so you are always well prepared for the things you have to do: *You have to admire Helen – she's so organized.*

passionate /ˈpæʃənət/ [*adj*] someone who is **passionate** has strong sexual or romantic feelings: *Todd put his arms around her and gave her a passionate kiss.*

patient /ˈpeɪʃənt/ [*adj*] able to wait calmly without becoming annoyed or bored: *"Are we going now Mum?" "No, not yet, you'll just have to be patient."*
+ with *Try and be patient with her – she's doing her best.*

pessimistic /ˌpesɪˈmɪstɪk◂/ [*adj*] someone who is **pessimistic** always expects bad things to happen, and thinks that if anything can go wrong it will go wrong: *I wish you'd stop being so pessimistic!*
+ about *Experts seem pessimistic about the chances of an economic recovery.*

quiet /ˈkwaɪət/ [*adj*] someone who is **quiet** does not usually say very much: *Her husband was a quiet, sensitive man.*

reckless /ˈrekləs/ [*adj*] behaving in an irresponsible or dangerous way, and not caring whether you harm yourself or other people: *We want our leaders to be strong but not reckless.*

romantic /rəˈmæntɪk, rəʊ-/ [*adj*] someone who is **romantic** treats the person they love as someone very special, for example by buying them presents and giving them flowers: *"Phil's taking me to Paris for the weekend." "How romantic!"*

self-confident /ˌself ˈkɒnfɪdənt ‖-ˈkɑːn-/ [*adj*] someone who is **self-confident** is very confident about their abilities, and is not shy or nervous in social situations: *She always seems so self-confident when she's giving lectures.*

selfish /ˈselfɪʃ/ [*adj*] someone who is **selfish** only thinks about what they need or want, and never thinks about how other people feel: *Don't be so selfish! Leave some cake for your sister.*

sensible /ˈsensɪbəl/ [*adj*] always behaving in a responsible way, making good decisions, and not doing anything stupid or risky: *He was sensible enough to realize he wouldn't pass the exam without doing any work.* | *She's a very sensible driver.*

shy /ʃaɪ/ [*adj*] someone who is **shy** feels nervous and embarrassed about talking to other people, especially people who they do not know: *He was very shy when he was a teenager.* | *She gave a shy smile.*

sociable /ˈsəʊʃəbəl/ [*adj*] someone who is **sociable** is friendly, and enjoys being with other people and meeting new people: *Maria was a sociable and popular member of the class.*

sympathetic /ˌsɪmpəˈθetɪk◂/ [*adj*] ready to try to understand people's problems and to help them if you can: *Tell Frank how you feel – I'm sure he'll be sympathetic.*

vain /veɪn/ [*adj*] very proud of yourself, especially because you think that you look very attractive or beautiful: *The girls at school used to tease her for being so vain.*

witty /ˈwɪti/ [*adj*] someone who is **witty** always says clever and amusing things: *Edberg's witty remarks kept us all amused.*

DRIVE

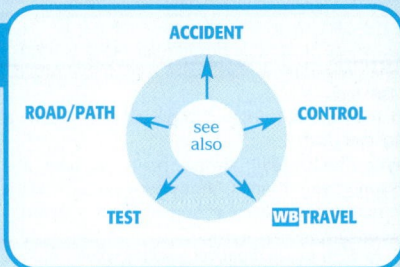

Taking your driving test

The first time I took my **driving test**, I didn't do very well. I **pulled out** into the road without looking in my mirror, and another car nearly **drove** into the back of me. Unfortunately for me, the **driver** of the other car was a police officer.

We set off again, and soon we came to a **junction**. I was **driving** too fast and the road was wet. When I **braked**, the car **skidded** and I almost crashed into a lamppost. I put the car into first **gear**, and we **drove off** again. There was a truck going very slowly in front. I **signalled** and started to **overtake**. The driving **examiner** asked me if I knew what the speed limit was. I suddenly realised that it was 30 miles an hour, and I was doing 45.

By this time the examiner was looking a bit nervous, and she asked me to stop and **park** the car. I slowly **reversed** into a **parking space**. At the last minute, I put my foot on the wrong pedal, and I bumped into the car in front. When I asked the examiner if I'd passed my test, she said: "What do you think?!"

Vocabulary

1 to drive a car or other vehicle

drive /draɪv/ [v I/T] to operate the controls on a car, bus, truck etc, so that it moves along a road: *Drive carefully – the roads are icy.* | *They drive on the left in the UK.*
drive a car/bus/truck etc *We need someone to drive the school bus.* | *"What kind of car do you drive?" "I've got a BMW."*
driving /'draɪvɪŋ/ [n U] the activity of driving a car, bus, truck etc: *Driving in central London is pretty unpleasant.* | *She was arrested for dangerous driving.*

> You can also use **driving** before a noun, like an adjective: *a driving instructor* | *driving lessons*

2 to go somewhere in a car

drive /draɪv/ [v I] to go somewhere in a car
+ to/from/into/through etc *We drove to the airport, but couldn't find anywhere to park.* | *They drove home in silence.*
+ off/away (=leave somewhere in a car) *She drove off without saying goodbye.*

drive 50 kilometres/100 miles etc *We drove 50 miles north on Interstate 75.*
drive [n C] a journey in a car: *It's a two-hour drive to Hamilton from here.*
go by car /ˌgəʊ baɪ 'kɑːʳ/ to go somewhere in a car – use this especially when you are comparing different methods of travelling: *One group went by car and the others went by train.* | *I can get to work in about 20 minutes by car.*
go for a drive (also **take a ride** AMERICAN) /ˌgəʊ fər ə 'draɪv, ˌteɪk ə 'raɪd/ to go somewhere in a car, for enjoyment: *Let's go for a nice long drive in the country.* | *We took a ride down to the ocean.*

3 to take someone somewhere

take/drive sb somewhere /ˌteɪk, ˌdraɪv (sb) 'sʌmweə/ *Could you take me to the station, please?* | *The President was driven away in a big black limousine.*
lift BRITISH **ride** AMERICAN /lɪft, raɪd/ [n C] if you give someone a **lift** or a **ride**, you take them somewhere in your car: *Dad gave me a lift to the station.*

The problems of driving in a big city

Driving in London can be a nightmare these days. The roads are always busy, and you always seem to get stuck in a **traffic jam**. No wonder there's so much **road rage**. There are **speed cameras** everywhere, and it's often impossible to find a **parking space**. If you do find one, you have to pay a fortune to park for 2 hours, after which you're likely to get a **parking ticket** or get **clamped**. The mayor is trying to encourage people to leave their cars at home and use **public transport** more. There are now special **bus lanes**, and if you want to go into central London in the week you have to pay a **congestion charge**.

Road report

There is heavy **traffic** on most Los Angeles freeways this morning. A serious **accident** on the 101/Ventura Freeway is causing long delays in both directions. There is already a five mile **tailback**, and drivers are advised to avoid the area if at all possible. Major roadworks on 4th Street have reduced the road to two **lanes**, and 5th Street remains closed in both directions following an injury accident.

Finally, severe weather conditions are expected in the next 24 hours, with many roads becoming icy overnight. Drivers are advised to use their cars tomorrow only if absolutely necessary.

+ to *Do you need a ride to school?*
a lift/ride home *I accepted her offer of a lift home.*

4 someone who drives

driver /'draɪvər/ [n C] someone who drives a car, bus, train etc: *A car and a truck crashed into each other, but both drivers were unhurt.*
a good/bad driver (=someone who is good or bad at driving) *My brother is a really good driver.*
bus/train/truck driver *Ask the bus driver where to get off.*
drunk driver *accidents caused by drunk drivers*
motorist /'məʊtərɪst/ [n C] someone who drives a car: *Some motorists ignore speed limits completely.*
motorists/the motorist (=all motorists, considered as a group) *Motorists will have to pay another £60 a year in tax.* | *Why should the countryside be destroyed for the benefit of the motorist?*

> ⚠ Use the word **motorist** when you are talking about laws, taxes, or prices that affect people who drive cars.

chauffeur /'ʃəʊfər, ʃəʊ'fɜːr/ [n C] someone whose job is to drive a car for a rich or important person: *His chauffeur held the door open for him.*

5 things you do when you drive

signal/indicate /'sɪgnəl, 'ɪndɪ̑keɪt/ [v I,T] to show the direction that you are going to turn by using the lights on a car: *He signalled that he was turning right.*
pull out /ˌpʊl 'aʊt/ [phrasal verb I] to drive onto a road after stopping at the side, or to drive onto another part of a road when there are several lines of vehicles: *Always look in your mirror before you pull out.* | *Someone pulled out right in front of me.*
overtake ESPECIALLY BRITISH **pass** ESPECIALLY AMERICAN /ˌəʊvəˈteɪk, pɑːs‖pæs/ [v I/T] to drive past another car and get in front of it: *She accelerated and overtook the truck.* | *Don't overtake now – there's a bend up ahead.*
slow down /ˌsləʊ 'daʊn/ [phrasal verb I] to drive more slowly: *You need to slow down as you approach the intersection.*

Writing tips

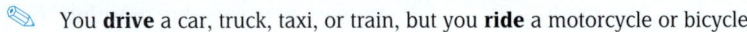

✎ You **drive** a car, truck, taxi, or train, but you **ride** a motorcycle or bicycle.

✎ Usually you don't need to say **drive a car**. Just **drive** is enough. For example, you say *He can't drive.* (not 'He can't drive a car.')

✎ Don't say 'get on a car'. Say **get in/into a car**.

✎ Don't say 'get off a car'. Say **get out of a car**.

✎ Don't say 'go drive'. Say **go for a drive**.

---

brake /breɪk/ [v I/T] to slow down or stop by using the brakes: *The man in front braked suddenly.*
brakes [n plural] the things that you use to make a car go more slowly or to make it stop
slam on your brakes (=press the brakes very hard to make your car stop suddenly)
reverse (also **back** ESPECIALLY AMERICAN) /rɪˈvɜːʳs, bæk/ [v I/T] to drive your car backwards
+ **up/along/into etc** *She reversed out of the driveway.* | *Someone backed into my car.* (=hit it when they reversed their car)
gear /ɡɪəʳ/ [n C] the **gears** are the system in a car that turns power from the engine into movement. Cars have several **gears**, and you use low gears when you are going slowly, and high gears when you are going faster: *Most cars have five gears these days.*
first/second etc gear *She put the car into first gear.*
change gear BRITISH **shift gear** AMERICAN *The car makes a funny noise when I change gear.*

6 learning to drive

driving test /ˈdraɪvɪŋ ˌtest/ [n C] a test that you must pass before you can legally drive alone
take your driving test (=do your driving test) *I'm taking my driving test on Friday – wish me luck!*
pass/fail your driving test (=be successful or unsuccessful)
driving instructor /ˈdraɪvɪŋ ɪnˌstrʌktəʳ/ [n C] someone whose job is to teach people how to drive
examiner /ɪɡˈzæmɪnəʳ/ [n C] the person who watches you drive when you take your test, and who decides whether you pass or fail
driving licence BRITISH **driver's license** AMERICAN /ˈdraɪvɪŋ ˌlaɪsəns, ˈdraɪvəʳz ˌlaɪsəns/ [n C] an official document which proves that you have the legal right to drive a car alone

7 to leave your car somewhere

park /paːʳk/ [v I/T] to put your car in a place and leave it there for a period of time: *You can park in front of the station.*
car park BRITISH **parking lot** AMERICAN /ˈkaːʳ paːʳk, ˈpaːʳkɪŋ lɒt‖-laːt/ [n C] a place where people can park their cars
multistorey car park (=a big car park that has several different levels)
parking space /ˈpaːʳkɪŋ ˌspeɪs/ [n C] a space where you can park your car, either on the street or in a car park
parking ticket /ˈpaːʳkɪŋ ˌtɪkɪt/ [n C] a notice which is put on your car, which says that you will have to pay a fine for parking illegally
clamp BRITISH /klæmp/ [v T] to put a special piece of equipment on one of the wheels of a car so that it cannot move, because it has been parked illegally. Usually you have to pay a big fine to have the clamp removed

8 to have an accident

accident /ˈæksɪdənt/ [n C] when a vehicle hits another vehicle or hits a person, tree, building etc
have an accident *Ken had an accident when he was driving to work.*
bad/serious/terrible accident *Highway Patrol reported a serious accident on Avenue 7.*
road accident/traffic accident *The number of traffic accidents has gone down.*
crash /kræʃ/ [n C] an accident in which a vehicle hits something violently and is damaged or destroyed
car crash *James Dean was killed in a car crash.*
crash into sth /ˈkræʃ ɪntuː (sth)/ [phrasal verb T] if one vehicle **crashes into** another, or into a

tree, building etc, it hits it hard and causes damage: *His car crashed into the wall outside the hotel.*

skid /skɪd/ [v I] if your car **skids**, it becomes difficult to control because the road is slippery or because you have put the brakes on too hard: *The car skidded off the road.*

swerve /swɜːᵣv/ [v I] to deliberately move sideways very quickly in order to avoid hitting something: *She swerved to avoid a cyclist.*

9 the vehicles that are on the road

traffic /ˈtræfɪk/ [n U] the vehicles that are travelling along a road: *I could hear the traffic outside the window.* | *The traffic's really bad in the rush hour.*

heavy traffic (=there are a lot of vehicles on the road) *The radio report said that there was heavy traffic on all roads out of the city.*

light traffic (=there are not many vehicles)

traffic jam (=a long line of vehicles that cannot move, or can only move very slowly) *We got stuck in a big traffic jam on the M25.*

tailback BRITISH **tie-up** AMERICAN /ˈteɪlbæk, ˈtaɪʌp/ [n C] a long line of vehicles that are not moving because the road is blocked by something

public transport BRITISH **public transportation** AMERICAN /ˌpʌblɪk ˈtrænspɔːᵣt/ [n U] vehicles such as buses and trains, which carry large numbers of people and are available for everyone to use

private cars/vehicles /ˌpraɪvᵻt ˈkɑːᵣz, ˈviːᵻkəlz/ [n plural] cars and other vehicles, which are used by individuals. This phrase is used when comparing these vehicles with public transport

10 parts of a road

lane /leɪn/ [n C] one of the parts that a wide road is divided into, usually by lines that are painted along the road

the fast/slow lane *Someone went past me in the fast lane at over 100 miles an hour.*

the inside/middle/outside lane *Stay in the middle lane till we're past the junction.*

bus lane/cycle lane (=a special part of the road which is only for buses or bicycles)

junction/intersection AMERICAN /ˈdʒʌŋkʃən, ˈɪntəᵣˌsekʃən/ [n C] a place where one road joins another: *Turn right at the next junction.*

roundabout BRITISH **traffic circle** AMERICAN /ˈraʊndəbaʊt, ˈtræfɪk ˌsɜːᵣkəl/ [n C] a circular area where three or more roads meet, which cars must drive around: *We turned left at the roundabout.*

interchange AMERICAN /ˈɪntəᵣˌtʃeɪndʒ/ [n C] a place where two or more highways or freeways meet (=large fast roads)

11 limits and controls on drivers

speed limit /ˈspiːd ˌlɪmᵻt/ [n C] the fastest speed that you are allowed to drive at on a particular part of a road

red light /ˌred ˈlaɪt/ [n C] a light in a traffic light that is red and means you must stop: *Police stopped him for failing to stop at a red light.*

congestion charging /kənˈdʒestʃən ˌtʃɑːᵣdʒɪŋ/ [n C] a system which is designed to reduce the amount of traffic in cities, in which drivers have to pay to drive at certain times of day

congestion charge /kənˈdʒestʃən ˌtʃɑːᵣdʒ/ [n singular] an amount of money that you pay in order to drive into a city at certain times of day, which is intended to reduce the amount of traffic

speed camera /ˈspiːd ˌkæmərə/ [n C] a camera that takes photographs of vehicles that are driving too quickly, so that the drivers can be fined

12 angry feelings that some drivers have

road rage /ˈrəʊd reɪdʒ/ [n U] when a driver suddenly becomes very angry and violent, and starts threatening or attacking another driver

EDUCATION

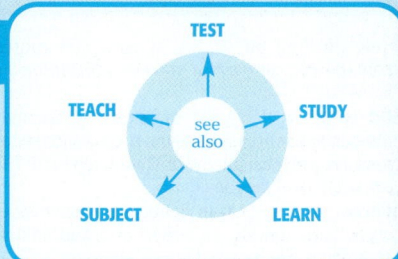

The education system in the UK and the US

class	UK school	age	US school	class
	nursery school, playgroup, or kindergarten (optional)	3 4	nursery school, pre-school (optional)	
reception class	infant school	5		kindergarten
year 1		6		first grade
year 2		7	elementary school/grade school	second grade
year 3	junior school, primary	8		third grade
year 4	school	9		fourth grade
year 5		10		fifth grade
year 6		11		sixth grade
year 7	secondary school	12	junior high school, middle school	seventh grade
year 8		13		eighth grade
year 9		14	high school	ninth grade (freshman)
year 10		15		tenth grade (sophomore)
year 11		16		eleventh grade (junior)
year 12	technical college, sixth	17		twelfth grade (senior)
year 13	form college	18	college, university	freshman
first year (fresher)	university	19		sophomore
second year		20		junior
third/final year		21		senior
postgraduate	university	22 23	graduate school (in a university)	

Vocabulary

1 school

> ⚠ Words like **school**, **nursery**, and **university** can be used as uncountable nouns, to mean the time that you spend there: *I missed a lot of school last year.* | *College starts next week.*

school /skuːl/ [n C/U] a place where children go to learn and be taught, up to the age of 18: *My mother is a teacher at the local school.* | *The nearest school was 10 miles away.*
to/from school *80% of parents take their children to school by car.*
state school BRITISH **public school** AMERICAN (=a school that is paid for by the government)

> ⚠ Be careful with the phrase **public school**: in the US, this means a school that is paid for by the government and is available to all children; in Britain, it means one of a number of expensive private schools which parents must pay for.

2 a place where children can study

nursery school /ˈnɜːˈsəri skuːl/ [n C/U] a place where children aged between three and five go for a few hours each day to play and do activities with other children
plural **nurseries**
kindergarten /ˈkɪndəˈgɑːˈtn/ [n C/U] in American English, the name of the first year of school for children aged five; in British English, another name for a **nursery school** for children aged four or five
pre-school /ˈpriː skuːl/ [n C/U] AMERICAN a school for children aged between about two and five: *a plan to provide pre-school for all children*
primary school /ˈpraɪməri ˌskuːl/ [n C/U] in Britain, a school for children aged between five and eleven; **primary schools** are usually divided into the **infant school** or **the infants** (=for children aged five to seven) and the **junior school** or **the juniors** (=for children aged seven to eleven)

In England and Wales, the education system goes from reception (the first year at primary school) to **year 12** (the final year of **sixth form college** or **secondary school**). Parents can send their children to **nursery school** between the ages of about three and five. The children spend a few hours at nursery school each day, playing and doing activities with other children. From the age of five, education is compulsory. Between five and eleven, children go to **primary school**. Primary schools are usually divided into an **infant school** (for children aged five to seven) and a **junior school** (for children aged seven to eleven). When they are 11 years old, children go to **secondary school** and take their GCSE exams at the age of 16. They can leave school when they are 16, but if they want to stay in education, they study for a further two years and take A-levels at the age of 18. They either stay at school, or go to a **sixth form college** or a **technical college**.

In the US, the education system goes from **kindergarten** (the first year of **elementary school**) to **12th grade** (the final year of **high school**). Parents can send their children to **nursery school** from the age of two or three. Children must attend school from the age of five onwards. The first year of school is called **kindergarten**. Children aged between five and eleven go to **elementary** or **grade school**. Between 12 and 14 they attend **junior high school** and between 14 and 17 they go to **high school**. **Students** in high school take examinations at the end of each **semester**. All the grades they have earned are given a number value and a grade point average (G.P.A) is calculated. Students who have passed enough courses **graduate** from high school. If they want to go to **university**, they must earn good enough grades and take a special test.

lementary school / grade school /ˌelɪˈmentəri ˌskuːl, ˈgreɪd ˌskuːl/ [n C/U] in the US, a school for children aged between five and eleven

econdary school /ˈsekəndəri ˌskuːl‖-deri-/ [n C/U] in Britain, a school for children aged between 11 and 16

unior high school/middle school /ˌdʒuːniəʳ ˈhaɪ ˌskuːl, ˈmɪdl ˌskuːl/ [n C/U] in the US, a school for children aged between 12 and 13 or 14

igh school /ˈhaɪ ˌskuːl/ [n C/U] in the US, a school for children aged between 14 and 17

ixth form college /ˈsɪksθ fɔːʳm ˌkɒlɪdʒ‖-ˌkɑː-/ [n C/U] in Britain, a college for students aged between 16 and 18

echnical college /ˈteknɪkəl ˌkɒlɪdʒ‖-ˌkɑː-/ [n C] a college where students can learn the practical skills they need to do a job, for example in computing, metalwork, or building homes.

3 a place where people over 18 can study

niversity /ˌjuːnɪˈvɜːʳsɪti/ [n C/U] a place where students study one or two subjects at a high

level, in order to get degrees: *There are many universities in Tokyo.* | *the University of Chicago*
be at university (=be a student at a university) *Both my sisters are at university.*
go to university (=become a student at a university) *She wants to go to university to study biology.*
plural **universities**

> ⚠ In British English, always use the word **university** to talk about a place where students study to get degrees. But in American English, you can also use **school** or **college** to mean this.

college /ˈkɒlɪdʒ‖ˈkɑː-/ [n C/U] in the US, a university; in Britain, a place where people can study academic subjects or practical skills after they leave secondary school, but which does not give degrees

school /skuːl/ [n C/U] AMERICAN INFORMAL a university or similar institution
go to school (=study at a college or university) *Phil gave up his job, and he's going back to school next year.*

law school/medical school/business school
/'lɔː skuːl, 'medɪkəl skuːl, 'bɪznɪ̯s skuːl/ [n C] a university or part of a university where you study law, medicine, or business

postgraduate BRITISH **graduate** AMERICAN /pəʊstˈɡrædʒuɪ̯t, 'ɡrædʒuɪ̯t/ [adj only before noun] use this about education that takes place after a student has finished a university degree, or about students who study at this level: *a postgraduate course in history | postgraduate research | We met when we were both graduate students at Berkeley.*

adult education /ˌædʌlt edjʊˈkeɪʃən‖-edʒə-/ [n U] special classes for adults, often in the evenings, either because they want to improve their skills or just for enjoyment

4 to go to a school or university to study

go to /'ɡəʊ tuː/ to go to a school or university to study: *"Which university did you go to?" "I went to Kyoto Women's University." | We both went to the same school.*

be at BRITISH **be in** AMERICAN /biː æt, biː ɪn/ if you **are at** school/college or you **are in** school/college etc, you are studying there: *My younger brother is still at school. | Eileen and I were in college together. | Sara is at Oxford, studying biology.*

> ⚠ **At school** (British) always means going to a school for children between 5 and 18 years old. **In school** (American) means attending a school, college, or university.

be educated /biː ˈedjʊkeɪtɪ̯d‖-ˈedʒə-/ to study at a particular school or university – use this especially in written descriptions of people's lives
+ at *He was educated at the King's School, Canterbury.*
Harvard-educated/Oxford-educated etc *a Harvard-educated lawyer*

5 to finish school or university

graduate /'ɡrædʒueɪt/ [v I] to successfully finish your studies – in Britain, you **graduate** from university, but in the US you can graduate either from university or from high school: *Bobby left high school without graduating.*
+ from *He graduated from Yale in 1986.*

6 someone who studies at a school, university etc

schoolboy/schoolgirl /'skuːlbɔɪ, 'skuːlɡɜːrl/ [n C] ESPECIALLY BRITISH a boy or girl who studies at school: *There was a group of schoolgirls waiting at the bus stop.*

schoolchildren /'skuːl,tʃɪldrən/ [n plural] ESPECIALLY BRITISH children who are studying at school: *Only 10% of British schoolchildren attend private schools.*

pupil /'pjuːpəl/ [n C] a child who studies at a particular school, especially a school for children under the age of 12: *With over 2000 pupils, this is one of the biggest schools in London.*

> **Formal or informal?**
> **Pupil** is formal in American English, but not in British English.

student /'stjuːdənt‖'stuː-/ [n C] someone who studies at school, university, or college: *None of my students has ever failed this exam.*
high school/college etc student (=a student at high school or college)
English/history/art etc student (=someone who is studying English, history, art etc)

class /klɑːs‖klæs/ [n C] a group of students or schoolchildren who are taught together: *Everyone in the class passed the test.*
top/bottom of the class *At the end of the year I came top of the class in French.*

first year/second year etc /'fɜːrst jɪər, 'sekənd jɪər/ [n C] BRITISH someone who is in the first year, second year etc at a school or university: *The university only provides rooms for first years.*

freshman /'freʃmən/ [n C] AMERICAN someone who is in the first year at university or high school

sophomore /'sɒfəmɔːr‖'sɑː-/ [n C] AMERICAN someone who is in the second year at university or high school

junior /'dʒuːniər/ [n C] AMERICAN someone who is in the third year at university or high school

senior /'siːniər/ [n C] AMERICAN someone who is in the fourth year at university or high school

postgraduate student BRITISH **graduate student** AMERICAN /pəʊstˈɡrædʒuɪ̯t ˌstjuːdənt, 'ɡrædʒuɪ̯t ˌstjuːdənt‖-ˌstuː-/ [n C] someone who has already taken one degree and is studying for another more advanced degree

7 what level you are at school, university etc

first/second etc grade /fɜːrst, 'sekənd (etc) ɡreɪd/ [n C] the first, second etc year of school in the US, starting from the first year of elementary school (aged six, after kindergarten)

first/second etc year /fɜːrst, 'sekənd (etc) jɪər/ [n C] the first, second etc year at university in Britain or the US

year one/two etc /jɪər ˈwʌn, 'tuː (etc)/ [n C] the first, second etc year of school in Britain, starting from the first year of primary or infant school (aged five), and ending at year thirteen (aged 18)

8 the periods into which an educational year is divided

term /tɜːʳm/ [n C] one of the three periods that the year is divided into at British schools and most British universities
autumn/spring/summer term *The main exams are at the end of the summer term.*

semester /sɪ̩'mestəʳ/ [n C] one of the two periods that the year is divided into at American schools and most American universities
first/second semester *I took five classes in the first semester and three in the second.*

the school year/the academic year /ðə ̩skuːl 'jɪəʳ, ði ̩ækədemɪk 'jɪəʳ/ [n singular] the period of the year when there are school or university classes: *In Japan the school year starts in April and ends in February or March.*

quarter /'kwɔːʳtəʳ/ [n C] one of the four main periods that the year is divided into at some American schools and universities

9 a short period in which students are taught a particular subject

class /klɑːs‖klæs/ [n C] a period of time, usually about 30 minutes to one hour, in which a teacher teaches a group of students: *Heidi fainted during the French class today!* | *Let's go – I have my first class in 10 minutes!*

lesson /'lesən/ [n C] a period in which someone teaches one person or a small number of people – use this especially about practical skills such as music, swimming, or driving: *Dominic had his first driving lesson yesterday.* | *She gives English lessons to business people.*

lecture /'lektʃəʳ/ [n C] a long talk on a subject, given by a teacher at a college or university, usually for a large number of students
+ on *a lecture on the causes of the Russian Revolution*
give a lecture *Professor Blair is giving a series of lectures on Einstein's theories.*

seminar /'semɪ̩nɑːʳ/ [n C] a class, usually at a college or university, where a teacher and a small group of students discuss a subject
+ on *Every week we have a seminar on modern political theory.*

10 work that a student does

homework /'həʊmwɜːʳk/ [n U] work that a student has to do at home
do your homework *Have you done your homework yet?*

coursework /'kɔːʳswɜːʳk/ [n U] all the work that a student has to do, apart from what they do in examinations: *Half of the marks are for the exam, and half are for coursework.*

assignment /ə'saɪnmənt/ [n C] a piece of work that a student is given to do as part of their studies: *a history assignment*

essay /'eseɪ/ [n C] a piece of writing about a particular subject by a student as part of a course of study

11 what you get when you finish a course successfully

qualification /ˌkwɒlɪ̩fɪ̩'keɪʃən‖ˌkwɑː-/ [n C often plural] you get a **qualification** when you finish a course and pass examinations at the end of it: *a two-year course, leading to a teaching qualification* | *He left school at 16, with no academic qualifications.*
sb's qualifications (=all the exams someone has passed) *List your qualifications in the space below.*

degree /dɪ'griː/ [n C] the qualification that you get when you successfully finish a course at university: *He has a degree in Chemistry.*
do a degree/take a degree BRITISH (=study in order to get one) *Maggie is doing a degree in psychology.*

Master's degree/Master's /'mɑːstəʳz dɪ̩griː, 'mɑːstəʳz‖'mæs-/ [n C] an advanced degree that you get by studying for one or two years after getting your first degree
+ in *To do this job, you need a Master's degree in Computer Science.*

doctorate/PhD /'dɒktərɪ̩t, ̩piː eɪtʃ 'diː‖'dɑːk-/ [n C] the most advanced type of degree, which you study for on your own for several years, doing work and writing a long report explaining what you have discovered
+ in *She has a PhD in industrial robotics.*

12 the process of studying and being taught

education /ˌedjʊ'keɪʃən‖ˌedʒə-/ [n U] the whole process by which people learn and develop their minds in schools, colleges, and universities: *The government should spend more on education.* | *My parents wanted me to have a good education.* | *I spent all of my life from 5 to 18 in full-time education.*
private education (=paid for by parents, not provided by the government) *Only a minority of parents can afford private education for their children.*

educational /ˌedjʊ'keɪʃənəl‖ˌedʒə-/ [adj usually before noun] connected with education: *Different children have different educational needs.* | *We offer a wide range of educational and sporting activities.*
an educational institution (=a school, a college, or university)

academic /ˌækə'demɪk◂/ [adj usually before noun] connected with education, especially at college or university level: *academic books* | *Jake was unemployed, and had no academic qualifications.*

ENVIRONMENT

What's happening to our environment?

Many people believe that the way we live our lives today is having a very damaging effect on **the environment**. Here are some examples of the kinds of problems we face, followed by some things that we can do to help protect our environment.

The Greenhouse Effect

Pollution from cars, factories, and power stations is causing harmful **greenhouse gases** to build up in the Earth's atmosphere. These gases prevent heat from escaping, and as a result our planet is getting warmer. This process is known as **global warming**.

Global warming is causing the ice at the North and South Poles to melt and **sea levels** and sea temperatures to rise, leading to serious flooding and violent storms in many parts of the world. In other places, there will be less rain and the land will be turned into desert.

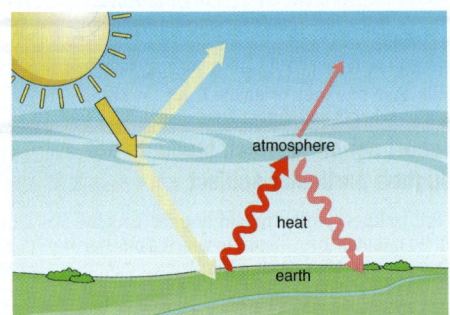

Vocabulary

1 the environment

the environment /ði ɪnˈvaɪərənmənt/ [n singular] the air, water, and land where people, animals, and plants live: *chemicals that pollute the environment* | *New laws are being introduced to protect the environment.*
environmental [adj] *an environmental catastrophe* (=a disaster for the environment)

ecology /ɪˈkɒlədʒiǁɪˈkɑː-/ [n U] the way in which plants and animals and natural features of a place affect and depend on each other: *the natural ecology of the region*
ecological [adj] relating to the environment: *Destruction of the rainforests is fast becoming an ecological disaster.*

habitat /ˈhæb¹ₜtæt/ [n U] the natural home of a plant or animal: *The gorilla's natural habitat is in Africa.*

the food chain /ðə ˈfuːd tʃeɪn/ [n singular] the natural system in which, for example, an insect eats a plant, a bird eats the insect, an animal eats the bird etc, with the result that all these different forms of life depend on each other: *the threat to life higher up the food chain*

2 signs of damage to the environment

global warming /ˌɡləʊbəl ˈwɔːrmɪŋ/ [n U] a general increase in the temperature of the world, caused by pollution from cars, factories etc: *We are already starting to see the effects of global warming.*

climate change /ˈklaɪm¹ₜt ˌtʃeɪndʒ/ [n U] changes in the weather around the world, which result in much higher or lower temperatures, violent storms, floods etc: *an international conference on climate change*

the greenhouse effect /ðə ˈɡriːnhaʊs ɪˌfekt/ [n C] the gradual warming of the Earth caused by pollution that stops heat from leaving the Earth's atmosphere

the ozone layer /ði ˈəʊzəʊn ˌleɪər/ [n C] a layer of natural gases around the Earth. The ozone layer protects the Earth from the harmful effects of the sun, but pollution is causing a hole in it: *The hole in the ozone layer is thought to be responsible for an increase in cases of skin cancer.*

sea level /ˈsiː ˌlevəl/ [n C] the natural level of the water in the world's oceans, which will rise if

Pollution from cars

The biggest **polluter** today is the car. Exhaust **fumes** are the main cause of poor air quality, which can make people feel ill and have difficulty in breathing. This problem is especially bad in cities, where the number of cars is increasing every year, causing serious **congestion** and filling the air with **smog**.

Governments try to improve the situation by encouraging people to use their cars less or buy cars that do not use as much fuel.

The destruction of animal habitats

All over the world, wildlife **habitats** are being destroyed. There are many **endangered species** that could soon become **extinct**. **Rainforests** are being cut down so that people can grow crops and feed the world's increasing population. Modern farming methods, for example using **pesticides** and **genetically modified crops**, are having a very bad effect on the **food chain**. Killing insects may be useful for growing crops, but it reduces the amount of available food for other animals and birds.

Climate change is also making conditions difficult for some animals. In the Arctic, the ice is melting, threatening the survival of animals such as polar bears.

---

global warming continues: *Scientists are predicting a substantial rise in sea levels over the next 20 years.*

rainforest /'reɪnˌfɒrɪ̯st∥-ˌfɔː-, -ˌfɑː-/ [n C] a tropical forest with tall trees growing very close together, in an area where it rains a lot. Rainforests are very important for the balance of the Earth's ecology: *Rainforests cover about 6% of the Earth's surface.* | *It is estimated that about 1% of rainforests are being cut down every year.*

deforestation /ˌdiːˌfɒrɪ̯'steɪʃən∥-ˌfɔː-, -ˌfɑː-/ [n U] a situation in which most of the trees in an area are cut down or destroyed, resulting in great damage to the environment: *the rapid pace of deforestation in Malaysia*

endangered species /ɪnˌdeɪndʒəᵊd 'spiːʃiːz/ [n C] a type of plant or animal that is likely to stop existing completely, for example because of hunting or pollution

extinct /ɪk'stɪŋkt/ [adj] if a type of animal or plant is **extinct**, it no longer exists and there are no animals or plants of that type alive: *extinct animals such as the dodo*
extinction [n C/U] *The white rhino is close to extinction.* (=there are almost none left)

3 things that can damage the environment

pollution /pə'luːʃən/ [n U] harmful chemicals, gases, or waste materials from factories, cars etc that have gone into the air, land, or water: *pollution from cars* | *air pollution* | *dangerously high pollution levels in our rivers*
polluter [n C/U] something or someone that causes pollution

greenhouse gases /'griːnhaʊs ˌgæsɪ̯z/ [n plural] gases that form a layer around the Earth and keep the heat in. These gases are produced naturally, but increasing quantities of gases are being produced from cars and factories, causing global warming

fumes /fjuːmz/ [n U] harmful gas or smoke, for example from cars or factories, which damages the environment and harms people's health: *exhaust fumes*

smog /smɒg∥smɑːg/ [n U] a mixture of smoke and fog in cities, caused by gases from cars or factories: *the smog in Los Angeles*

congestion /kən'dʒestʃən/ [n U] a situation in which there are too many cars on a road, and the

What can we do to protect our environment?

Alternative sources of energy

Burning **fossil fuels** to produce energy causes a lot of pollution. Renewable sources of energy such as **wind power**, **wave power**, and **solar power** are much cleaner. People can also easily reduce the amount of energy they use. A lot of electricity is wasted by leaving on lights, televisions, and other electrical equipment when they are not being used.

Our society produces huge amounts of waste, which end up having to be burned, buried, or taken out to sea. This waste produces **greenhouse gases**, and also spoils the environment. If we **recycle** material such as glass, paper, and metal, this will reduce the amount of waste that is produced.

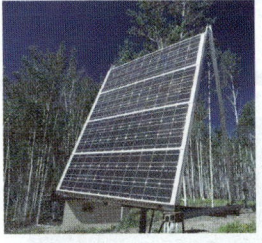

solar power

wave power

wind power

---

cars move very slowly, causing a lot of pollution: *Traffic congestion is now a major problem in many cities.*

pesticides /ˈpestɪsaɪdz/ [n plural] chemicals that are used for killing insects and animals that attack crops

GM/genetically modified /ˌdʒiː ˈem ◂ , dʒɑ̩ˌnet-ɪkli ˈmɒdɪfaɪd‖=ˈmɑː-/ [adj] **GM crops** have had their genes changed in order to make them more convenient to grow. Some people believe that they may cause damage to the environment.: *trials of GM crops in Europe* | *Many consumers don't want to eat genetically modified foods.*

toxic waste /ˌtɒksɪk ˈweɪst‖ˌtɑːk-/ [n U] very dangerous waste materials, for example from nuclear power stations or chemical factories

fossil fuels /ˈfɒsəl ˌfjuːəlz‖ˈfɑː-/ [n plural] fuels such as coal or oil. Burning these fuels causes a lot of carbon gases to be released into the atmosphere

acid rain /ˌæsɪd ˈreɪn/ [n U] rain that contains pollution from factories, power stations etc, which causes damage to forests

4 things that are good for the environment

green /griːn/ [adj] used to talk about anything that is good for the environment, or about ideas relating to protecting the environment: *The building uses green electricity from a wind turbine.* | *green sources of energy* | *information about green products* | *a discussion about green issues*

environmentally-friendly / eco-friendly /ɪnˌvaɪərənˌmentl-i ˈfrendli, ˌiːkəʊ ˈfrendli/ [adj] **environmentally-friendly** products or methods do not cause harm to the environment: *environmentally-friendly forms of transport*

clean /kliːn/ [adj] **clean** technology, electricity etc does not produce pollution and does not harm the environment: *investment in clean technology* | *clean electricity*

renewable /rɪˈnjuːəbəl‖-ˈnuː-/ [adj] **renewable sources of energy** use fuels that can be replaced naturally, and so they are never completely used up: *the switch from fossil fuels to renewable sources of energy*

organic /ɔːˈgænɪk/ [adj] **organic foods** are produced naturally, without the use of chemical

Environmentally-friendly forms of transport

If more people used public transport, this would reduce the amount of pollution. Public transport is much more **environmentally-friendly**, because buses and trains can carry large numbers of people at the same time, whereas cars often carry only one person. **Car pools** are another way of reducing the number of cars on our roads. The big car companies are also working on developing new engine technology, so that cars can run on **cleaner** fuels such as hydrogen instead of petrol. For shorter journeys cycling is a much healthier alternative to driving a car, and many towns have introduced special **cycle lanes**.

Green products

We can also help the environment by choosing to buy **green** products, for example **organic** foods that are produced without using pesticides. Not only are pesticides bad for the environment, the chemicals in them can also be harmful to humans. If we buy wood from **sustainable** sources, this will mean that our forests can be maintained for future generations.

So much of modern life is based around shopping and buying new things. Everything is out-of-date in only a few years or even months. If we stopped buying and throwing away so many things, this would help ease the pressure on the environment.

---

pesticides that have a bad effect on the environment: *organic milk* | *organic farming* (=not using harmful chemicals)

sustainable /səˈsteɪnəbəl/ [adj] **sustainable methods** of farming, fishing etc do not use up more land, natural resources etc than can be replaced naturally, and therefore do not cause harm to the environment

recycle /riːˈsaɪkəl/ [v I,T] to use materials that have already been used, in order to make new products: *Old newspapers are collected for recycling.* | *recycled glass*

alternative /ɔːlˈtɜːrnətɪv/ [adj] **alternative** methods, energy, technology etc are to do with producing electricity without using fossil fuels, in order not to cause harm to the environment: *Wind is an obvious source of alternative energy.*

solar power/wind power/wave power /ˈsəʊləʳ ˌpaʊəʳ, ˈwɪnd ˌpaʊəʳ, ˈweɪv ˌpaʊəʳ/ [n C] energy from the sun, the wind, or the movement of the sea, used to make electricity

wind farm /ˈwɪnd fɑːʳm/ [n C] a group of tall structures with blades which turn with the wind

and are used to produce electricity. These structures are called **wind turbines**.

car pool /ˈkɑːʳ puːl/ [n C] a group of car owners who agree to go in one car together, instead of all driving to work in separate cars

bus lane/cycle lane BRITISH **bycicle lane** AMERICAN /ˈbʌs leɪn, ˈsaɪkəl leɪn, ˈbaɪsɪkəl leɪn/ [n C] a special section of the road for buses or bicycles only

5 people who want to protect the environment

environmental group /ɪnˌvaɪərənˈmentl ˌgruːp/ [n C] a group of people who try to protect the environment, especially by influencing the government and large companies

green /griːn/ [adj] **green parties** and **politicians** are concerned with protecting the environment: *the Green Party* | *green politicians*

FILMS/MOVIES

Writing about your favourite film

The Matrix

One of my favourite films of all time is 'The Matrix'. The film is a **science fiction thriller**, which has a very complicated **storyline**. It **stars** Keanu Reeves who **plays** a computer expert called Neo. Neo finds out that his world has been taken over by intelligent machines. The Matrix is a computer program created by the machines, which they use to control people's minds. Neo and two other rebels (called Morpheus and Trinity) set out to try to destroy the Matrix.

What I like most about the film is the photography and the **special effects**, using **CGI** technology. These are really amazing and make it look like a computer game.

Schindler's List

'Schindler's List' is one of the best **movies** I have ever seen. It was **directed** by Steven Spielberg. It tells the story of a man called Oskar Schindler who owned a factory in Nazi Germany. He succeeded in saving the lives of thousands of Jews by giving them jobs in his factory. It is an extremely powerful movie, and is based on a true story.

One of the things I like most about the movie is the photography, because it was made almost entirely in black and white. This makes it seem ver real, even though it was filmed 50 years after the events actually happened.

Vocabulary

1 films and going to see them

film ESPECIALLY BRITISH **movie** ESPECIALLY AMERICAN (also **motion picture** FORMAL) /fɪlm, 'muːvi, ˌməʊʃən 'pɪktʃəʳ/ [n C] a story that is told using sound and moving pictures
+ about *a movie about the Vietnam War*
see a film/movie *Have you seen any good films lately?*

cinema BRITISH **movie theater** AMERICAN /'sɪnɪmə, 'muːvi ˌθɪətəʳ/ [n C] a building where you go to see films: *We went to the MGM cinema in Leicester Square.* | *They sat in the back row of the movie theater.*

multiplex /'mʌltɪpleks/ [n C] a big modern cinema where several different films are shown at the same time

go to the cinema BRITISH **go to the movies** AMERICAN /ˌgəʊ tə ðə 'sɪnɪmə, ˌgəʊ tə ðə 'muːviz/ to go to a cinema in order to see a film: *Do you want to go the movies this weekend?* | *I haven't been to the cinema for ages.*

be on ESPECIALLY BRITISH **be playing** ESPECIALLY AMERICAN /biː 'ɒn, biː 'pleɪ-ɪŋ/ if a film **is on** or **is playing**, it is being shown at a cinema: *What's on at the cinema this weekend?* | *The movie is playing in a movie theater near you.*

2 types of film

comedy /'kɒmədiǁ'kaː-/ [n C] a film that is intended to make you laugh

romantic comedy (also **rom com** INFORMAL) /rəʊˌmæntɪk 'kɒmədi, 'rɒm kɒmǁ-'kaː-, 'raːm kaːm/ [n C] an amusing film about two people who meet and have a romantic relationship

thriller /'θrɪləʳ/ [n C] a film that tells an exciting story about murder or crime

action film/action movie /'ækʃən ˌfɪlm, ˌmuːvi/ [n C] a film that has a lot of exciting events in it, for example people fighting or chasing each other in cars

horror film/horror movie /'hɒrəʳ ˌfɪlm, 'hɒrəʳ ˌmuːviǁ'hɔː-, 'haː-/ [n C] a film that is intended to make you feel frightened, in which dangerous and frightening things happen to the characters

psychological drama /ˌsaɪkəˌlɒdʒɪkəl 'drɑːməǁ-ˌlaː-/ [n C] a film about people who are experiencing strong emotions, and their relationships with each other

Going to the cinema

I usually **go to the cinema** once or twice a month, depending on what's **on**. I sometimes go to one of the big **multiplexes**, but I prefer going to our local **cinema**. I like **comedy** films or **psychological dramas**, but my best friend is a great fan of Hollywood **action films**.

Normally I sit in the front row, so that I can get as close as possible to what is happening on screen. I don't like having to sit next to people who are talking to each other or eating popcorn I also hate having to sit through lots of advertisements and **trailers**.

action film/movie

computer animated film/movie

western

war film/war movie /ˈwɔːᵣ fɪlm, ˈwɔːᵣ ˌmuːvi/ [n C] a film about people fighting a war

science fiction film/science fiction movie /ˌsaɪəns ˈfɪkʃən fɪlm, ˌsaɪəns ˈfɪkʃən ˌmuːvi/ [n C] a film about life in the future, often with people or creatures who live in other parts of the universe

cartoon /kɑːᵣˈtuːn/ [n C] a film made using drawings, which are put together to look as if they are moving

computer animated film /kəmˌpjuːtər ˌænɪ̩meɪtɪ̩d ˈfɪlm/ [n C] a film which uses images made on a computer

CGI /ˌsiː dʒiː ˈaɪ/ [n U] the use of computer images to make a film. CGI is short for "computer generated imagery".

western /ˈwestəᵣn/ [n C] a film about cowboys in the 19th century in the American West

road movie /ˈrəʊd ˌmuːvi/ [n C] a film about people who are on a long journey in a car, and the adventures they have while they are travelling

sequel /ˈsiːkwəl/ [n C] a film that continues the story of an earlier film and usually has the same characters in it: *Did they ever make a sequel to "Taxi Driver"?*

trailer /ˈtreɪləᵣ/ [n C] short parts of a new film which are shown before the main film in a cinema as an advertisement, to make people want to see it: *a trailer for the new Tom Cruise movie*

3 people in films

actor /ˈæktəᵣ/ [n C] someone who acts in films: *Who is your favourite Hollywood actor? | He began his career as an actor in the 1960s.*

> ⚠ You can use **actor** about a man or a woman. Many women prefer to be called **actors** and do not like the word **actress**.

actress /ˈæktrɪ̩s/ [n C] a woman who acts in films: *The part of Cathy will be played by the French actress Juliette Binoche.*

star/film star/movie star /stɑːᵣ, ˈfɪlm stɑːᵣ, ˈmuːvi stɑːᵣ/ [n C] a famous actor or actress

co-star /ˈkəʊ stɑːᵣ/ [n C] one of two or more famous actors who appear together as the main

Writing tips

✏️ **say who is in the film**

It **stars** Audrey Hepburn.
Harrison Ford **stars** as Indiana Jones.
Tom Cruise **plays** a fighter pilot.
The cast includes Robert de Niro and Bruce Willis.

✏️ **say who directed it, and what other films they have made**

The film **was directed** by Steven Spielberg, **who also made films such as** 'Saving Private Ryan'.

✏️ **say briefly what it's about, using the present tense**

It's about a man who keeps waking up on the same day.
It tells the story/tale of Oskar Schindler, a German factory owner.
It follows the adventures of a fish named Nemo.

✏️ **other things you can say when writing about a film:**

> **It's very good**
> It's a **classic** film/story.
> It's a **classic**.
> It's a **masterpiece**.(= it is an extremely good film)

> **It had a strong effect on you**
> It's **very/deeply moving**.
> It's a very **powerful** film.

> **It's very exciting**
> It's a **thrilling/gripping** film.(= it's very exciting)
> It's an **action-packed** adventure.(=there are lots of exciting scenes)
> I **was on the edge of my seat** all the way through.(=it was very exciting and you kept wanting to know what was going to happen next)

> **It's very original**
> It's a **ground-breaking** film.(= a very original film, which created a new type of film)

> **It's very funny**
> It's a **hilarious comedy**.(= it's a very funny comedy)
> **I couldn't stop laughing**.

> **One particular thing is especially good**
> **The thing I liked most was** the photography.
> **It's worth seeing just for** the scenery.

characters in a film: Di Caprio's co-star in the movie is British actress Kate Winslet.
the cast /ðə ˈkɑːstǁ-ˈkæst/ [n singular] all the people who act in a film: The movie has an all-British cast.

4 people who make films

director /dɔˈrektəʳ, daɪ-/ [n C] the person who is in charge of making a film, and who tells the actors what to do: The director was Martin Scorsese.

direct [v I/T] *'Psycho' was directed by Alfred Hitchcliffe.*

producer /prə'djuːsəʳ‖-'duː-/ [n C] the person in charge of making arrangements for a film, and who controls the money

film crew /'fɪlm kruː/ [n C] all the people who work to make a film, except the actors

5 to act in a film

play /pleɪ/ [v T] to act as a character in a film: *Harry Potter was played by Daniel Radcliffe.*

star /staːʳ/ [v T] if an actor **stars** in a film, or if a film **stars** an actor, he or she plays one of the most important characters in it: *The film stars Nicole Kidman and Tom Cruise.*
+ in *Elizabeth Taylor starred in 'National Velvet' when she was only ten.*
+ as *Daniel Day Lewis stars as the disabled writer, Christie Brown.*

performance /pəʳ'fɔːʳməns/ [n C] the acting that is done by an actor in a film – use this especially to say how good or bad you think the acting is: *Dustin Hoffman's performance was outstanding.*
give a wonderful/superb/moving performance *She gave a moving performance, which had most of the audience in tears.*

be in /biː ɪn/ if someone **is in** a film, they play the part of one of the characters in it: *She's been in lots of movies. | He was in 'Casablanca' and 'The Big Sleep'.*

6 the person that an actor pretends to be in a film

character /'kærɪktəʳ/ [n C] a person in the story of a film: *I didn't think the characters were very realistic. | The main character is a female detective.*

part /paːʳt/ [n C] the job of acting as a particular character in a film
+ in *She had always hoped to get a part in a movie.*
play the part of *Laurence Olivier played the part of the king.*

7 what happens in a film

story /'stɔːri/ [n C] **a love story** *The movie is basically a love story.*

plot/storyline /'plɒt, 'stɔːrɪlaɪn‖plɑːt/ [n C] the events that happen in a film, and the way in which these events are connected: *Tom Hanks was great, but I thought the plot was really boring. | The film has a great storyline.*

scene /siːn/ [n C] one part of a film: *The first scene takes place on a beach.*
a love/war/battle scene *The battle scenes were very realistic.*

special effect /ˌspeʃəl ɪ'fekt/ [n C] an unusual image or sound that is produced artificially, in order to make something that is impossible look as if it is really happening: *The special effects were amazing – the dinosaurs looked as if they were alive.*

ending /'endɪŋ/ [n C] the way that the story in a film ends: *I don't want to give away the ending of the film.*
a happy/sad ending *I like movies with a happy ending.*

twist /twɪst/ [n C] something surprising that happens in a film, which you did not expect: *The film has a twist at the end, when we discover that the detective is the murderer.*

8 the words and music in a film

soundtrack /'saʊndtræk/ [n C] the music and sounds that are played during a film

script /skrɪpt/ [n C] the words that the actors say in a film

subtitles /'sʌbtaɪtlz/ [n plural] the words that appear on the screen to translate what the actors say in a film that is in a foreign language

dubbed /dʌbd/ [adj] if a film is **dubbed**, the words spoken by the actors have been changed into another language

9 the ideas or subject of a film

be about /biː ə'baʊt/ if a film **is about** a person or idea, that person or idea is the main subject of the film: *'Back to the Future' is about a boy who travels back in time.*

be based on /biː 'beɪst ɒn/ if a film **is based on** a book, story, or real event, the things that happen in the film are very similar to the things that happened in the book, story etc: *The movie is based on his own experiences in the Vietnam War. | a film based on one of Jane Austen's novels*
be based on a true story (=be based on something that really happened) *It was supposed to be based on a true story, but it didn't seem possible to me.*

be set in /biː 'set ɪn/ if a film **is set in** a place or period of time, the story happens in that place or during that time: *The film is set in France during the First World War.*

theme /θiːm/ [n C] one of the main subjects or ideas in a film: *The themes of the movie are power and revenge.*

FOOD

see also → MEAL · THIN · EAT · FAT · RESTAURANTS/EATING AND DRINKING · HUNGRY · COOK · DRINK · TASTE

What kind of food do they eat in your country?

England

One of the most famous **English dishes** is fish and chips. Traditionally, people go to fish and chip shops where the **food** is served wrapped in paper, and they take the food away to eat either in the street or at home. It's usual to have a lot of salt and vinegar with fish and chips.

But if you ask an English person what their favourite food is, lots of people would now say curry, which has almost become England's **national dish**. **Italian**, **Chinese**, and **Thai cooking** are also very popular, and in the big cities you can eat food from just about anywhere in the world.

Some people think that the English start their day with a 'full English breakfast' of bacon, eggs, mushrooms and fried bread. In fact, people are much more likely just to have cereal or toast.

Vocabulary

1 food

food /fuːd/ [n C/U] something that you eat: *What's your favourite food?*
French/Japanese/Italian etc food *I love Italian food.*
sugary/fatty/spicy/salty food (=food with a lot of sugar, fat etc in it) *She doesn't like spicy food. | My doctors told me to avoid fatty food.*
the local food *We wanted to try the local food.*
staple food (=a basic type of food that is needed and used all the time) *Rice is a staple food in many parts of Asia and Africa.*
organic food (=food that is produced without using chemicals, for example chemicals that kill insects or weeds)
fast food (=food such as hamburgers, which is prepared and served quickly in a restaurant, and which you can take away with you)
junk food (=food that is not healthy, because it contains a lot of fat, salt, sugar etc, and does not contain the things that your body needs)
processed food (=food that has chemicals and other substances added to it, in order to preserve it for a long time, improve its colour etc)

takeaway food (=food that you buy at a restaurant, then take home to eat)

dish /dɪʃ/ [n C] a type of food, which consists of several foods cooked together in a particular way: *This dish can be eaten hot or cold. | a delicious vegetable dish with a spicy nut sauce*
Spanish/Moroccan/English etc dish *Paella is one of my favourite Spanish dishes.*
the national dish (=the most popular food in a country, especially one that you think of when you think of that country) *In Korea, the national dish is kimchi, which is a type of pickled cabbage.*
plural **dishes**

> ⚠ **Dish** is used especially by people writing or giving information about food.

accompaniment /əˈkʌmpənimənt/ [n C] FORMAL something that you eat or drink with a particular food: *Cream makes an excellent accompaniment to apple pie.*
cooking (also **cuisine** FORMAL) /ˈkʊkɪŋ, kwɪˈziːn/ [n U] a particular style of preparing food, which is typical of a country or area: *traditional country cooking*

Malaysia

The great thing about Malaysian food is the variety of different types of **cuisine**, which includes Malays, Chinese, and Indian.

A popular Malaysian **dish** is 'Nasi Lemak'. This dish consists of rice cooked in coconut milk, served with anchovies (a type of small salty fish), eggs, "sambal" (chili paste), and cucumber.

Another popular dish is 'Satay'. This consists of pieces of chicken or beef skewered on sticks, which are grilled over a charcoal fire. It is served with a delicious spicy peanut sauce, Malay traditional rice cakes, onions, and cucumber.

Japan

The Japanese diet is very healthy, and it is not surprising that Japanese people live longer than almost anyone else in the world. Japanese dishes are usually low in **fat**, and therefore very good for you. For example 'sushi' has almost no fat at all, and consists of raw fish or vegetables on boiled rice.

Japanese **meals** often include rice, pickled vegetables, and a bowl of 'miso soup', which is made using soy bean paste.

'Soba' (a type of noodle) is often eaten as a kind of fast food. People eat it quickly in noodle bars.

Chinese/Indian/Spanish etc cooking *a book on Italian cooking*
home cooking *I like my mom's home cooking the best.*

speciality BRITISH **specialty** AMERICAN /ˌspeʃiˈælɪti, ˈspeʃəlti/ [n C] a type of food that is always very good in a particular restaurant, country, or area: *The village is famous for its seafood specialities.*
local/regional speciality (=from a particular area) *Fish curry is a local speciality.*
plural **specialities/specialties**

delicacy /ˈdelɪkəsi/ [n C] a rare and expensive kind of food which people think is very good to eat, especially the people of a particular country or area: *Shark fins are a delicacy in many Asian countries. | We ordered several small dishes of Turkish delicacies.*
plural **delicacies**

2 the kind of food someone usually eats

diet /ˈdaɪət/ [n C/U] the particular combination of foods that a person or animal usually eats: *The*
doctor said there was not enough fibre in my diet. | Her diet consists mainly of hamburgers, crisps, and fizzy drinks.*
+ of *Kevin lived on a diet of peanut butter sandwiches.*
a healthy diet *If you eat a healthy diet, you don't need to take extra vitamins.*
a balanced diet (=a diet which includes a variety of different healthy foods, in the right amounts)
a low-fat/high-fibre etc diet (=when you only eat foods without much fat, with a lot of fibre etc)

3 how to make a type of food

recipe /ˈresɪpi/ [n C] a set of instructions for cooking a particular type of food: *Where can I get the recipe from?*
+ for *a recipe for chocolate cookies*
ingredient /ɪnˈgriːdiənt/ [n C] one of the foods that you use to make a particular type of food: *Mix all the ingredients together in a bowl.*

4 things in food

protein /ˈprəʊtiːn/ [n C/U] a substance found in foods such as meat, eggs, and milk, which your

Why eat organic food?

It is easy to criticize **organic food**. It is more expensive. It often doesn't taste very different from ordinary food, and it does not keep well, because it has fewer **preservatives** in it. Some people like to buy it because it is the fashionable thing to do. So why should we choose to buy organic food?

Organic food is free from harmful chemicals, for example chemicals used to control weeds and insects. Although ordinary food costs less to buy in the shops than organic food, there is another hidden cost. This cost is the damage that is caused to the environment and to people's health.

Some people say that we need to continue to produce food in large quantities using non-organic methods, in order to feed people in the developing world. In fact, the uncontrolled use of chemicals and factory farming methods in developing countries can cause the land to become useless for cultivation in only a few years.

For all these reasons, it seems better to choose organic food, so that we can protect our environment for future generations.

body needs in order to grow and be healthy: *Eggs are a good source of protein.*

fat /fæt/ [n C/U] an oily substance found in certain foods: *9 out of 10 people eat too much fat, which can cause heart disease.*

carbohydrate /ˌkɑːˈbəʊˈhaɪdreɪt, -drᵻt/ [n C/U] a substance found in foods such as sugar, bread, and potatoes, which provides the body with heat and energy: *Athletes need a diet that is high in carbohydrates.*

vitamin /ˈvɪtəmᵻn‖ˈvaɪ-/ [n C] a chemical substance found in food, which is necessary for good health.
vitamin C/A/D etc *Oranges are full of vitamin C.*

calorie /ˈkæləri/ [n C usually plural] a unit for measuring the amount of energy that a particular food will produce. If you eat food that contains too many **calories**, you will get fat: *The average person needs around 1500–2000 calories per day.*

fibre BRITISH **fiber** AMERICAN /ˈfaɪbəʳ/ [n U] parts of vegetables, fruit, or grains, which you eat, but cannot digest. Fibre helps food to move quickly through your body and keep your body healthy: *Wholemeal bread is rich in fibre.*

preservative /prɪˈzɜːʳvətɪv/ [n C] a substance that is added to food to prevent it from decaying and make it last longer: *Most sausages are full of artificial preservatives.*

additive /ˈædᵻtɪv/ [n C] a substance that is added to food to improve its taste or appearance, or to make it last longer: *Some food additives can cause allergies in children.*

colouring BRITISH **coloring** AMERICAN /ˈkʌlərɪŋ/ [n C] a substance that is added to food to make it have a particular colour: *Tinned peas only look green because of the artificial food colouring that they put in.*

5 to give someone food

serve /sɜːʳv/ [v I/T] to give someone food by putting it in front of them, especially at a restaurant or a formal meal: *Dinner will be served at eight o'clock.* | *The chef serves important guests himself.* | *We're ready to serve.*
serve sb with sth *They served us with soup and bread.*
serve sth to sb *Andrew, will you serve coffee to the visitors?*

Writing tips

✎ Food is usually used as an uncountable noun. Don't say things like 'I like Chinese foods' or 'We ate a lot of foods'. Say *I like Chinese food* OR *We ate a lot of food*.

✎ **To talk about a meal that a country is famous for, you can say:**

Paella is Spain's **national dish**.
Paella is one of Spain's most famous **traditional dishes**.

Don't say things like 'The typical food of Spain is paella'.

✎ **To talk about a meal that is eaten in a country or local area, and often not anywhere else, you can say:**

The local **specialities** *include baked salted fish and very dry white wine*.

✎ **For unusual food, which is considered to be especially tasty somewhere, you can say:**

In Japan, salmon's eggs are considered to be **a delicacy**.

✎ When you are describing food, don't say that it is 'very delicious'. Just say: that it is delicious. You can also say:

It **tastes** *really* **good**.
It's very **tasty**. | *a* **tasty** *dessert*

---

feed /fiːd/ [v T] to give food to a baby or animal: *My sister feeds the cats when we are away.* | *How often do you have to feed the baby?*
feed sb/sth on sth *Peggy feeds her dogs on raw meat and brown bread.*
feeding – fed – have fed

6 an amount of food that you get

portion /ˈpɔːrʃən/ [n C] an amount of food that is enough for one person, especially one served in a restaurant, bar etc: *We had to complain about the tiny portions we were given.*
+ of *Two portions of French fries, please.*

serving /ˈsɜːrvɪŋ/ [n C] the amount of food that is cooked or prepared for each person – used especially in recipes or on food packaging: *This recipe makes enough for six servings.* | *Rice contains about 200 calories per serving.*

helping /ˈhelpɪŋ/ [n C] an amount of food that someone takes or is given at one time: *Who wants another helping of stew?*
second helping (=another portion of food that someone takes after they have already eaten one portion)

GOVERNMENT/POLITICS

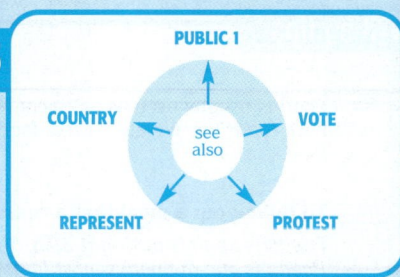

PUBLIC 1

COUNTRY — see also — VOTE

REPRESENT — PROTEST

Writing about your country's political system

The political system in the UK

The UK is a **parliamentary democracy.** The UK **parliament** is divided into two parts: the House of Commons and the House of Lords. People **vote** every 4 or 5 years to **elect** the **Member of Parliament** for their constituency. Members of Parliament sit in the House of Commons, and there are 650 of them. There are three main political parties, and the party with the biggest number of seats in parliament forms the **government**. Their leader becomes the **Prime Minister**.

The House of Lords is not elected. It can suggest changes to laws, but it does not have the power to stop them becoming law. In the end it has to accept the decisions of the House of Commons. The Queen (or King) is the official **head of state**, but she has very little real political power.

Vocabulary

1 the people who govern a country

government /ˈgʌvəmənt,   ˈgʌvənmənt‖ ˈgʌvərn-/ [n C] the people who govern a country, state, or local area, and who make all the important decisions about taxes, laws, relations with other countries etc: *The government promised to cut taxes.* | *Unemployment is a problem that faces most western governments.* | *The French government has banned the sale of British beef.* | *cuts in government spending*

the administration /ði ədˌmɪnɪ̇ˈstreɪʃən/ [n C] use this especially to talk about the national government of the United States: *The administration is trying to improve standards in health care.*

the authorities /ði ɔːˈθɒrɪ̇tiːz‖-ɔːˈθɔːr-/ [n plural] the people or organizations that have the power to decide what people are allowed to do in a country or area: *The South African authorities arrested Mandela in August 1962.*

regime /reɪˈʒiːm/ [n C] a government, especially one that was not elected fairly or that you disapprove of for some other reason: *The people want to get rid of the military regime.*

2 the people who make a country's laws

parliament /ˈpɑːrləmənt/ [n C] the group of people who are elected to make a country's laws: *Parliament will vote on the new divorce law today.* | *the European parliament*

politician /ˌpɒlɪ̇ˈtɪʃən‖ˌpɑː-/ [n C] someone who works in politics, especially a member of a parliament: *Many right-wing politicians opposed the treaty.*

MP/member of parliament /ˌem ˈpiː, ˌmembər əv ˈpɑːrləmənt/ [n C] someone who has been elected to a parliament, especially in Britain or in a country that has a similar system of government, such as India, Australia, or South Africa: *the first woman member of parliament* | *Robin Cook MP* | *the Labour MP for Birmingham South*

plural **MPs/members of parliament**

congressman/congresswoman /ˈkɒŋgrɪ̇smən, ˈkɒŋgrɪ̇sˌwʊmən‖ˈkɑːŋ-/ [n C] someone who is a member of the US Congress, especially of the House of Representatives: *a*

The political system in the US

The Federal government of the United States has three branches. The most well-known of these is the Executive branch, which is the **President** and his or her cabinet.

The Executive branch is separate from the Legislative branch, which is often called Congress. This consists of the House of Representatives and the Senate. These are like Parliament in the UK, except that all the members of Congress are elected by the people. Members of the House of Representatives are called **Congressmen** and **Congresswomen**. Members of the Senate are called **Senators**. The third part is called the Judiciary, and consists of the courts and all the judges. The highest court is the Supreme Court.

Although people think the President of the US is the most powerful person in the world, the other two branches of government can limit the President's powers. The **constitution** makes sure that no single person or group can have complete political control.

As well as the Federal government, which governs the whole country, each state has its own government. Individual states have a lot of power and can decide their own taxes and make their own laws.

Democratic Congressman from Oklahoma
plural **congressmen/congresswomen**

senator /'senətəʳ/ [n C] a member of the US Senate or a similar institution: *Senator Kennedy | The President met with a group of senators to discuss energy policy.*

3 the leader of a country

leader /'liːdəʳ/ [n C] someone, such as a president or prime minister, who is in charge of the government of a country: *World leaders are meeting in Geneva. | the French leader*

president /'prezɪdənt/ [n C] the official leader of a country that does not have a king or queen: *President Chirac | the President of Egypt*
  presidential [adj] relating to the president: *the presidential elections*

prime minister /ˌpraɪm 'mɪnɪstəʳ/ [n C] the elected leader of the government in a country that has a parliament: *The British Prime Minister lives at 10 Downing Street.*

ruler /'ruːləʳ/ [n C] someone, such as a king or queen or a military leader, who has the power to run the government of a country: *an unjust ruler | Nigeria's military rulers*

head of state /ˌhed əv 'steɪt/ [n C] the person who is officially in charge of a country, such as a king, queen, or president. Some **heads of state** are also the political leader of their country, but others are not. For instance, the Queen is the head of state in the UK, but the Prime Minister is in charge of the government.

king /kɪŋ/ [n C] a man who is the official leader of a country because he is a member of a royal family: *the King of Spain*

queen /kwiːn/ [n C] a woman who is the official leader of a country because she is a member of a royal family, or a woman who is the wife of a king: *the Queen of Sweden*

dictator /dɪk'teɪtəʳ‖'dɪkteɪ-/ [n C] a leader who has complete control over a country but was not elected by the people, and who uses their power in a cruel and unfair way: *the former Iraqi dictator*

4 different systems of government

democracy /dɪ'mɒkrəsi‖dɪ'mɑː-/ [n U] a system of government in which everyone in the country can vote to choose the government: *In 1974,*

Writing tips

 If you find it difficult to find enough things to say about the political system in your country, think about the answers to the following questions:

> **What kind of political system does your country have?**
> *Japan is a parliamentary democracy.*

> **How is the government of the country organized?**
> *The Japanese parliament is divided into two houses – the House of Representatives and the House of Councilors.*

> **How often are elections held?**
> *There are elections for The House of Representatives every 4 years. Half of the House of Councilors are elected every 3 years.*

> **Who is the head of state?**
> *The Prime Minister is in charge of the running of the country. The Emperor is considered to be the symbol of the Japanese nation, according to the Constitution.*

 Don't say *The Japanese political system is a parliamentary democracy.* It is best to omit the phrase "political system" altogether, and just say:
Japan is a parliamentary democracy.
Japan has a parliamentary democracy.

 Try to link your ideas together, and try to avoid just giving a few short sentences.

For example, instead of saying: "My country is a republic. The leader of the government is the president. My country has four main political parties. Every five years we have elections."

say: *My country is a republic which is led by a president. Presidential elections are held every five years, and voters can choose between candidates from four main political parties.*

 Make sure that you have spelt the following words right:

democracy not 'democrasy'
parliament not 'parliment'
government not 'governement'

---

democracy returned to Greece after seven years of military rule.
democracy [n C] a country in which everyone can vote to choose the government: *the democracies of Western Europe*
a parliamentary democracy (=a country that has an elected parliament)
plural **democracies**
democratic /ˌdeməˈkrætɪk◂/ [adj] a **democratic** country, government, or political system is one in which the people vote to choose the government: *a democratic society*
republic /rɪˈpʌblɪk/ [n C] a country whose leader is a president, not a king or queen: *the French Republic* | *the People's Republic of China*
monarchy /ˈmɒnəˈkiǁˈmɑːn-/ [n C/U] a system of government in which a country is ruled by a king or queen: *questions about the future of the monarchy in Britain*

a constitutional monarchy (=a country ruled by a king or queen whose powers are limited by a constitution)
plural **monarchies**

constitution /ˌkɒnstəˈtjuːʃən‖ˌkɑːnstəˈtuː-/ [n C] a formal set of rules that provides rights for all citizens, and stops governments from using power unfairly: *the US constitution*

5 a government that controls people's lives too much

dictatorship /dɪkˈteɪtəʳʃɪp/ [n C] a government in which one person or one small group has total power and uses it unfairly and cruelly: *a military dictatorship*

police state /pəˈliːs ˌsteɪt/ [n singular] a country where the police have too much power and control people's lives too much: *This is America, not a police state!*

totalitarian /təʊˌtælɪˈteəriən/ [adj usually before noun] a **totalitarian** country or system of government is one in which the government controls every part of people's lives and there is no freedom: *a writer who was imprisoned during Stalin's totalitarian rule*

oppressive /əˈpresɪv/ [adj] an **oppressive** government treats people in a cruel way, using military force to prevent any kind of opposition: *a brutal and oppressive regime*

6 government departments

department /dɪˈpɑːʳtmənt/ [n C] one of the separate parts of a government, which is responsible for a particular subject, such as health, education, or defence
the Department of Education / Health / Transport etc BRITISH *She is now head of the Department of Education.*
the Defense / Justice / Treasury Department AMERICAN

ministry /ˈmɪnɪstri/ [n C] a government department in Britain and some other countries: *She works at the Ministry of Defence.*
plural **ministries**

minister /ˈmɪnɪstəʳ/ [n C] the politician who leads a government department in Britain and some other countries: *a meeting of European finance ministers in Bonn*

7 to govern or rule a country

govern /ˈgʌvən‖-ərn/ [v I/T] if a political party or group **governs** a country, its members make all the important decisions about laws, taxes, relations with other countries etc: *The Labour Party has governed Britain for many years now.*

rule /ruːl/ [v T] if a king, queen, military leader, or a foreign government **rules** a country, they have official power over it: *The king rules the country.* | *India was ruled by the British until 1947.*

run /rʌn/ [v T] to control a country – use this especially about a powerful person or group that controls a country but has not been elected: *Who's running this country, the government or the large corporations?* | *The revolutionary council ran the country until democratic elections were held.*
running – ran – have run

be in power /biː ɪn ˈpaʊəʳ/ if a political party or a leader **is in power** at a particular time, they are the government or leader of a country at that time: *Lenin was in power for only seven years.* | *Taxes were higher when the previous government was in power.*

8 activities and ideas that are connected with governing a country

political /pəˈlɪtɪkəl/ [adj usually before noun] connected with the government of a country or local area: *There are two main political parties in the US.* | *the British political system* | *the end of his political career*

politics /ˈpɒlɪtɪks‖ˈpɑː-/ [n U] activities and ideas that are connected with governing a country or local area: *The war on terrorism is one of the biggest issues in American politics.* | *Many people aren't interested in politics.*
party politics (=when political parties are trying to get an advantage over each other)
local politics (=the politics in a town or city) *She's always been deeply involved in local politics.*
go into politics (=start working in politics as a job) *He didn't go into politics until he was over forty.*

9 when people choose a government or leader

vote /vəʊt/ [v I,T] to show which person or party you have chosen, by putting a mark on a piece of paper: *Over 60% of the people voted at the last election.*
vote for sb/sth *Did you vote for George Bush?*
vote Republican/Labour etc (=vote for a particular political party) *My parents always vote Republican.*
the vote [n singular] the right to vote: *When did women get the vote?*

elect /ɪˈlekt/ [v T] to choose a particular government or leader: *The people will have the chance to elect a new government.*

election /ɪˈlekʃən/ [n C] an occasion when people vote to choose a government or leader
hold an election *The elections will be held in May.*
a presidential election (=an election to choose a president)
a general election BRITISH (=an election to choose a government)

constituency /kənˈstɪtʃuənsi/ [n C] an area that elects a Member of Parliament, Senator etc to represent it

HOLIDAY/VACATION

An ideal place for a holiday

Last year, we **booked** a **holiday** on the island of Tioman, in Malaysia. Tioman is quite a small island (it's only 6 miles wide), just off the east coast of Malaysia. It has some of the most beautiful beaches in the world, and it is a great place for relaxing and **getting away from it all**.

Tioman is also a **paradise for** divers. The water is clear to a depth of over 30 metres and it is filled with all kinds of beautiful fish, coral, and other marine life. The colours are amazing. Apart from swimming and **lazing around** on the beach, **there are lots of** other **things to see and do**. We **went hiking** in the mountains, and we saw monkeys, flying foxes, and even a big snake.

Our **accommodation** wasn't very expensive, and you can stay in a **hotel** for as little as $30 a night. For me the best thing on the holiday was sitting outside our beach hut in the evening, looking up at the stars. It really was an unforgettable experience.

Vocabulary

1 time when you are allowed to be away from work or school

holiday /ˈhɒlɪdiǁˈhɑːlɪˌdeɪ/ [n C/U] BRITISH a period of time when you do not have to work or go to school: *I have six weeks' holiday each year.* | *What I need right now is a holiday.*
the holidays/summer holidays/school holidays (=the long periods when schools are closed) *July 20th is the first day of the summer holidays.*
in/during the holidays *Did you go away in the holidays?*
Christmas/Easter holiday *We spent the Christmas holiday at home.*

vacation /vəˈkeɪʃənǁveɪ-/ [n C/U] AMERICAN a period of time when you do not have to work or go to school: *I'll see you next time I get a vacation.* | *The company allows us 15 vacation days a year.*
summer/Christmas vacation *I spent part of the summer vacation with friends in Seattle.*

break /breɪk/ [n C] a short holiday from your work or school: *The students get a few days' break in February.*
the Easter/autumn/fall etc break *Are you going home for the Easter break?*

2 a one day holiday when shops, banks etc are closed

holiday /ˈhɒlɪdiǁˈhɑːlɪˌdeɪ/ [n C] *We'd forgotten that July 14th was a holiday in France.*
national holiday (=a holiday for the whole country) *St Patrick's Day is a national holiday.*
bank holiday/public holiday BRITISH (=an official holiday for one day when people do not have to go to work) *This shop is closed on Sundays and public holidays.* | *The roads are always busy on bank holidays.*

3 a time when you travel to another place for enjoyment

holiday BRITISH **vacation** AMERICAN /ˈhɒlɪdi, vəˈkeɪʃənǁˈhɑːlɪˌdeɪ, veɪ-/ [n C/U] a period of days or weeks that you spend in another place or country for enjoyment: *France is the ideal place for a family holiday.* | *a holiday resort*
go on holiday/vacation (=travel somewhere on holiday) *Are you going on holiday this year?*
have a holiday/vacation *Have a nice holiday, and send us a postcard.*

My holidays

I've had all sorts of holidays in the last few years. My favourite was last year when we went **camping** in Yosemite Nation Park in California. The **campsite** was near a river, and we did a lot of **hiking** to see the beautiful waterfalls.

Two years ago, I went to New York with my parents. We stayed in a really good **hotel**, and enjoyed all the restaurants and **nightlife**. We did a lot of **sightseeing** - we went to the Empire State Building, Ellis Island, and visited some interesting museums. The best part was seeing a Broadway musical!

This summer, I'm having a working **holiday** in a mountain **resort**. The resort is right next to a lake. I'll be working in one of the restaurants in the evenings, and in my time off I'll be able to go hiking and try some **watersports**.

After I finish college, I would like to go **back-packing** around South-East Asia, and probably Australia and New Zealand as well. My brother did that four years ago and had a really good time

take a holiday/vacation (=have a holiday) *I'm hoping to take a vaction at the end of July.*
be on holiday/vacation *We met when I was on vacation in Canada.*

trip /trɪp/ [n C] a holiday, especially an organized holiday that you go on, in order to take part in a particular activity or in order to see a place
take a trip *I'm taking a trip to Nepal.*
skiing/camping/fishing trip *He's in Canada on a ten day skiing trip.*
go on a trip *Angela's gone on a round-the-world trip.*

tour /tʊəʳ/ [n C] a journey for pleasure, in which you visit several different towns, areas etc
on a tour *They're on a fifteen day tour of Northern India.*

package tour/package holiday BRITISH /ˈpækɪdʒ tʊəʳ, ˈpækɪdʒ ˌhɒlɪ̩diǁ-ˌhɑːlɪ̩deɪ/ [n C] a holiday arranged by a company that includes travel, a place to stay, and sometimes meals, all for a fixed price: *The great thing about package holidays is that everything's already arranged for you.*

honeymoon /ˈhʌnimuːn/ [n C] a holiday you take just after you get married: *We went to Barbados for our honeymoon.* | *a honeymoon couple*
on honeymoon *They didn't tell anyone where they were going on honeymoon.*

backpacking /ˈbækˌpækɪŋ/ [n U] the activity of travelling for pleasure, usually with not much money, and carrying a backpack
go backpacking *We went backpacking around Europe.*

gap year /ˈgæp jɪəʳ/ [n C] BRITISH a year before starting or after finishing university, which some young people use as an opportunity to travel and get experience of working: *In her gap year she went to South America.*

4 the place where you stay on holiday

hotel /həʊˈtel/ [n C] a building where you pay to stay and eat meals: *I'm staying at the Grand Hotel.* | *a five star hotel*
check into a hotel (=to arrive at your hotel and give all the necessary information so that you can start staying there) *We'd better go and check into our hotel.*

Writing tips

 People often just say that the place they went to on holiday was 'beautiful', or they 'enjoyed it very much'.

In fact there are many other things you can say. Here are some examples:

It's a beautiful place
The island is **stunningly beautiful**. (=extremely beautiful)
There are **spectacular views**. (=very impressive views)
The countryside is **unspoiled**. (=there are no modern buildings, big roads etc)
It's a **perfect place** for a holiday.
It's a **magical** place. (=you like it very much)

It's good for doing a particular activity
It's a great place for sightseeing/shopping etc
It's a paradise for walkers/golfers etc (=very good for people who like walking, want to play golf etc)

It has a long and interesting history
There are many **historic** buildings.
The city is **rich in history**. (=lots of interesting things happened there in the past)

It's exciting
There's lots to see and do.
San Francisco is a very **lively** place.
The city has a **great nightlife**.

It's quiet and relaxing
It's very **quiet/peaceful** in the mountains.
You can get away from it all. (=it is quiet and relaxing and you can escape from the stress of modern life)

Describing where the place is
The town **is situated** close to the airport.
The village **is set on** a hill.
Their house **overlooks** the ocean. (=you can see the ocean from there)
Our hotel **is a few minutes' walk/drive from** the beach.
The resort **is within easy reach of** the coast. (=it is easy to get to the coast)

---

check out of a hotel *You must check out of the hotel before midday.*
hotel room *She spent the evening watching TV in her hotel room.*
hotel restaurant/bar/lobby etc
B&B/bed and breakfast /ˌbiː ənd ˈbiː, ˌbed ənd ˈbrekfəst/ [n C] *We stayed in a little B & B in the Lake District.*
campsite BRITISH **campground** AMERICAN /ˈkæmpsaɪt, ˈkæmpgraʊnd/ [n C] a place where you can stay in a tent for a holiday, usually with a water supply and toilets, and often with other services such as a swimming pool and a shop: *It was late Friday when we arrived at the campground.*
motel /məʊˈtel/ [n C] a hotel for people who are travelling by car, usually next to a big road
villa /ˈvɪlə/ [n C] BRITISH a house that you use or rent when you are on holiday: *We stayed at his villa in the south of France.*

apartment/condominium (also **condo** AMERI-CAN) /ə'pɑːʳtmənt, ˌkɒndə'mɪniəm, 'kɒndəʊ ‖ˌkɑːn-/ [n U] a set of rooms, for hiring or staying in, usually on one floor of a large building: *We've rented a condo in Texas.* | *a holiday apartment in Spain*

resort /rɪ'zɔːʳt/ [n C] a town where a lot of people often go for holidays
seaside/beach/mountain/ski resort *We spent four days in the seaside resort of Pattaya.*

accommodation ESPECIALLY BRITISH **accommodations** AMERICAN /əˌkɒmə'deɪʃən(z)‖əˌkɑː-/ [n U/plural] a room or other place to stay when you are away from home, for example a hotel: *The Tourist Office can help you find accommodations.* | *The accommodation was great, but the food was awful.*

5 things that you can do on holiday

sightseeing /'saɪtˌsiːɪŋ/ the activity of visiting famous or interesting places as a tourist: *I did some sightseeing while I was in Paris.*
go sightseeing *After lunch, we went sightseeing.*
see the sights /ˌsiː ðə 'saɪts/ to go and see the famous and interesting places that tourists often visit: *We spent the afternoon walking around Rome, seeing all the sights.*
excursion /ɪk'skɜːʳʃən‖-ʒən/ [n C] a short journey arranged so that tourists can visit an interesting place, especially while they are already on holiday
go on an excursion *We went on an excursion to the Pyramids.*
walking/hiking /'wɔːkɪŋ, 'haɪkɪŋ/ [n C] the activity of walking in the country or in the mountains for pleasure
go walking/hiking *We went hiking in the hills.*
camping /'kæmpɪŋ/ [n U] the activity of staying somewhere in a tent
go camping *We went camping last summer.*
watersports /'wɔːtəʳˌspɔːʳts/ [n plural] sports played on or in water. These include **scuba diving** (=diving using special breathing equipment), **snorkelling** (=shallow diving using a special tube to help you breathe), **water skiing** (=being pulled across the water by a boat, while wearing skis), and **wind surfing** (=sailing by standing on a board and holding on to a large sail)
nightlife /'naɪtlaɪf/ [n U] entertainment in the evening and night, such as bars and nightclubs: *The island is famous for its nightlife.*
laze around /ˌleɪz ə'raʊnd/ [phrasal verb I] to relax and enjoy yourself by sitting or lying down and not doing anything active like walking or swimming: *They spent the day lazing around by the pool.*
suntan /'sʌntæn/ [n C] the darker colour of your skin after you have spent time out in the sun: *He*

came back from his vacation with a great suntan.
top up your suntan (=make your skin become brown again)
get away from it all /ˌget ə'weɪ frəm ɪt 'ɔːl/ to go somewhere for a holiday which is very different from where you spend the rest of your time, so that you can forget about all the things that worry you when you are at work or at home: *I need a weekend in the mountains, just to get away from it all.*

6 arranging a holiday

book ESPECIALLY BRITISH /bʊk/ [v T] if you **book** a holiday, flight, a room etc, you arrange to travel on a plane, stay in a hotel etc at a particular time in the future: *We booked our flight on the internet.* | *I've booked us a room at the Hilton.*
reservation /ˌrezəʳ'veɪʃən/ if you make a reservation to use a hotel room, travel on a plane etc, you arrange to do this: *Do you have a reservation?*
make a reservation *I've made a reservation for us at the Holiday Inn.*
brochure /'brəʊʃəʳ, -ʃʊəʳ‖brəʊ'ʃʊər/ [n C] a book advertising the holidays that a company sells, usually printed on shiny paper and full of photographs: *The brochure said that the hotel was a few minutes' walk from the beach.*
travel agent's/travel agency /'trævəl ˌeɪ-dʒənts, 'trævəl ˌeɪdʒənsi/ [n C] a business that arranges travel and holidays

7 people on holiday

tourist /'tʊərⁱst/ [n C] someone who travels to visit a place or a country for interest and enjoyment: *In the summer, the city is full of tourists.* | *More than 3 million American tourists visit Britain each year.*
holidaymaker BRITISH **vacationer** AMERICAN /'hɒlⁱdiˌmeɪkəʳ, vəˈkeɪʃənəʳ‖'hɑːlⁱdeɪ-, veɪ-/ [n C] someone who stays in another place or country while they are having a holiday: *The beach seems deserted now that all the holidaymakers have gone home.* | *In the 1960s, the island was popular with vacationers.*

8 the business of providing holidays for people

tourism /'tʊərɪzəm/ [n U] the business of selling holidays and providing things for people to do, places for them to stay etc while they are on holiday: *The country depends on tourism for most of its income.*
mass tourism (=by large numbers of people)
the travel industry /ðə 'trævəl ˌɪndəstri/ [n singular] the companies and people that are involved in selling and providing holidays for people, considered as a single group: *She works in the travel industry.*

HOUSES/WHERE PEOPLE LIVE

Talking about where you live

Hi, I'm Paulo. I live in a small **apartment** near the centre of Lisbon. It's on the **second floor** of a modern building, just off a busy street. It's a **two-bedroomed** apartment with a small living room, a kitchen, and a bathroom. The apartment is only just around the corner from my school, and it's also very handy for the shops. We've been living there for about 8 years now.

Hi, my name's Kaori. I live with my parents and my baby sister in Kichijyoji, which is a **suburb** of Tokyo. We have a traditional Japanese-style **house**, which has three bedrooms and a small garden. The house is about 15 minutes' walk from the station. It's not very far from Inokashira Park, which is a nice place for picnics in the summer. I've lived in the house ever since I was born.

Vocabulary

1 the place where you live

house /haʊs/ [n C] the building where someone lives. You use **house** especially about a building that has more than one floor and is intended to be used by only one family: *Houses in the south of the city are very expensive.* | *He has a beautiful big house in the country.*
move house (=stop living in one house and start living in a different one) *They're planning to move house next year.*

home /həʊm/ [n C] the place where you usually live. You use **home** especially about a place where you have lived for a long time and you feel comfortable living there: *It's good to be back home again.* | *His home is in Los Angeles.* | *I've lived in New York for quite a while, but I still wouldn't call it home.*
at home *We stayed at home and watched TV.*

address /əˈdres‖ˈædres/ [n C] the exact place where you live, including your house number, the name of your street, town etc: *He wrote his name and address on a piece of paper.* | *Can I have your address?*

come from/be from /ˈkʌm frɒm, biː ˈfrɒm‖-ˈfrʌm/ if you **come from** a place, or you **are from** a place, that is where you were born, or where you usually live: *She's from Paris.* | *I come from the north of England.*

2 different types of house

terraced house BRITISH **row house** AMERICAN /ˌterɪst ˈhaʊs, ˈrəʊ haʊs/ [n C] a house that is in a row of houses that are all joined together

semi-detached house /ˌsemi dɪˌtætʃt ˈhaʊs/ [n C] BRITISH a house that is joined to another house on one side

detached house /dɪˌtætʃt ˈhaʊs/ [n C] BRITISH a house that is not joined to another house

cottage /ˈkɒtɪdʒ‖ˈkɑː-/ [n C] a small house in the country

bungalow /ˈbʌŋgələʊ/ [n C] BRITISH a small house that has all its rooms on the same level

ranch house /ˈrɑːntʃ ˌhaʊs‖ˈræntʃ-/ [n C] AMERICAN a house that has all its rooms on the same level, and a gently sloping roof

mansion /ˈmænʃən/ [n C] a very big and impressive house, owned by a very rich person

Which is better? Living in the city or living in the country?

If you live in a big city, everything is very convenient and you never have to travel far to get anything. Shops stay open until late into the evening, and some stay open 24 hours a day. There are always lots of things to do, and you can see all the latest films, exhibitions, and concerts. There are plenty of buses and taxis, and it is easy to get around.

Unfortunately, if you live in a big city you have to put up with all the traffic and the pollution. Some people don't care about their environment and throw litter everywhere, and the walls are often covered in graffiti.

Living in the country is great if you like doing outdoor activities such as walking and mountain biking. Houses are usually cheaper in the country, and people have more space. A lot of people have their own gardens. The quality of life generally is better in the country. People are friendlier and more relaxed, and there is less pollution than in the cities.

The trouble with living in the country is that it can be a little bit boring sometimes. There is not so much entertainment available, and you often have to travel a long way if you want to see a film or do the weekly shopping.

3 apartments and apartment buildings

apartment (also **flat** BRITISH) /ə'pɑːʳtmənt, flæt/ [*n* C] a set of rooms used for living in, that are usually all on the same level, and are part of a larger building

block of flats BRITISH **apartment building** AMERICAN /ˌblɒk əv 'flæts, ə'pɑːʳtmənt ˌbɪldɪŋ‖ˌblɑːk-/ [*n* C] a large building that consists of different levels and has several apartments on each level

condominium (also **condo** INFORMAL) /ˌkɒndə'mɪniəm‖ˌkɑːn-, 'kɒndəʊ‖'kɑːn-/ [*n* C] AMERICAN an apartment in a building that consists of several apartments, all of which are owned by the people who live in them

studio apartment/studio flat BRITISH /'stjuːdiəʊ əˌpɑːʳtmənt, 'stjuːdiəʊ ˌflæt‖'stuː-/ [*n* C] a small apartment with one main room, usually for only one person to live in

bedsit BRITISH /'bedsɪt/ [*n* C] a single room where one person lives and sleeps. People who live in bedsits usually share a bathroom and toilet.

hall of residence (also **hall**) BRITISH **dormitory** (also **dorm**) AMERICAN /ˌhɔːl əv 'rezɪdəns, hɔːl, 'dɔːʳmɪtəri, dɔːʳm‖-tɔːri-/ [*n* C] a large building at a college or university that consists of separate rooms where students live

4 different parts of a building

floor /flɔːʳ/ [*n* C] one of the levels in a building: *Which floor are you on?*

on the first/second etc floor *Her apartment is on the third floor.*

on the ground floor *They live in a small flat on the ground floor.*

a first-floor/second-floor etc apartment *a fifth-floor apartment with a view over the park*

> In the US, the **first floor** is on the same level as the ground, and the **second floor** is the next level above. In Britain, the part on the same level as the ground is called the **ground floor**, and the **first floor** is the next level above.

basement /'beɪsmənt/ [*n* C] the level of a building that is below the level of the ground: *Who*

Writing tips

 **Make sure that you choose the right preposition.**

You live **in** a house, apartment, city, or country, for example: *She lives **in** a small apartment in Manhattan.*

You live **on** a particular street, or floor of a building, for example. *He lives **on** Fifth Avenue.*

You live **at** an address, for example: *We live **at** Flat 2b, 23 Church Street, Oxford OX2 9JX.*

Make sure that you choose the right form of the verb.

If you say that someone **lives** in a place, you mean that this is where they normally live, for example: *She **lives** in Rome.*

If you say that someone **is living** in a place, you mean that they are only there for a short time, for example: *She's **living in** Milan at the moment, but she hopes to go back to Rome soon.*

If you want to say how long you have lived somewhere, don't say 'I am living in Paris for 5 years.' Say:

> *I **have lived** in Paris for 5 years.* OR
> *I **have been living** in Paris for 5 years.*

Don't confuse **for** and **since**. You use **for** about a period of time, for example:

*We've lived there **for** 3 years.*

You use **since** about the date when you started living there, for example:

*We've lived there **since** 2002.*

> If you want to talk about where you lived when you were a child, you can say:
>
> *I **grew up** in Tokyo.*
> *I **spent my childhood** in Tokyo.*
> *I **was brought up** in Tokyo.*
> *I **lived in Tokyo as a child/when I was young**.*

There are several ways of saying that a house or building is near another place.

*Our house is **near** the station.*
*My house is **not far from** the local supermarket.*
*His apartment is **just around the corner from** my office.*
*The flat is very **convenient/handy for** the shops.*
*We live **just off** Queen Street.* (= in a smaller street that joins Queen Street)

---

lives in the basement?
a basement flat/apartment *Carlo had a basement apartment in Grant St.*

5 the area where someone lives

area /ˈeəriə/ [n C] a particular part of a town or city: *Kensington is one of the richest areas of London.* | *They live in a quiet middle-class area.* | *It's quite a rough area.* (=the streets can be dangerous, and the housing conditions are bad) | *a peaceful residential area* (=with houses, but no offices or factories)

part of town /ˌpɑːʳt əv ˈtaʊn/ [n C usually singular] an area of a town or city: *What part of town do you live in?*

neighbourhood BRITISH **neighborhood** AMERICAN /ˈneɪbəʳhʊd/ [n C] a small area of a town or city where people live: *a nice neighborhood of Boston*

in the neighbourhood *There's only one park in the whole neighbourhood.*

suburb /'sʌbɜːʳb/ [*n C*] an area outside the centre of a city, where many people live

+ of *a quiet suburb of Los Angeles*

the suburbs *I was brought up in the suburbs.*

(housing) estate /'haʊzɪŋ ɪ'steɪt/ [*n C*] BRITISH an area where there are a lot of houses or apartments which are very similar and were all built at the same time. Many housing estates were originally built by the government to provide homes for poor families: *Conor was brought up on a big housing estate in Belfast.* | *There's a lot of crime on our estate.*

(housing) project /'haʊzɪŋ ˌprɒdʒekt‖-ˌprɑː-/ [*n C*] AMERICAN a group of houses or apartments for poor families, usually built with money from the government: *There are plans for a new housing project on the east side of town.* | *kids from the projects*

6 words for describing the size of a house or apartment

one-bedroomed/two-bedroomed etc /(one, etc) 'bedruːmd/ [*adj only before noun*] a **one-bedroomed, two-bedroomed etc** house or apartment has one bedroom, two bedrooms etc: *a one-bedroomed apartment* | *a three-bedroomed house*

three-storey/four-storey etc BRITISH **three-story/four-story etc** AMERICAN /(three, etc) 'stɔːri/ [*adj only before noun*] a **three-storey, four-storey etc** house or building has three levels, four levels etc: *a five-story apartment block*

7 the view from a house

overlook /ˌəʊvəʳ'lʊk/ [*v T*] if a building or room **overlooks** a place that is on a lower level, you see that place from it when you look out of the window: *Our apartment overlooked a small courtyard.*

a house/apartment/room etc overlooking (=which overlooks) *an 8th-floor flat overlooking Hyde Park*

view /vjuː/ [*n C*] the whole area that you see when you look out of a window, especially when this area is very large or beautiful: *She stood on the balcony admiring the view.*

+ of *The house has a spectacular view of San Francisco Bay.*

8 paying to live in a house or apartment/flat

rent /rent/ [*v I/T*] to pay money regularly to live in a house or apartment that someone else owns: *We rented for a while before buying a place of our own.*

rent sth from sb *I rent the flat from a friend's father.*

rent /rent/ [*n C/U*] the money that you pay to live in a house or apartment that someone else owns: *The rent's pretty high – about $800 a month.*

landlord/landlady /'lændlɔːʳd, 'lændˌleɪdi/ [*n C*] the man or woman that you rent a house or apartment from

mortgage /'mɔːrgɪdʒ/ [*n C*] a legal agreement in which you borrow money from a bank or other organization in order to buy a house. You usually pay back the money every month over a long period of time: *They took out a 30 year mortgage.* | *We've almost paid off our mortgage.*

MEDICAL TREATMENT

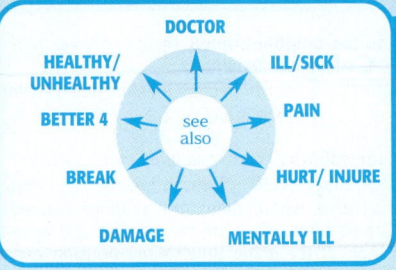

DOCTOR

HEALTHY/ UNHEALTHY   ILL/SICK

BETTER 4   see also   PAIN

BREAK   HURT/ INJURE

DAMAGE   MENTALLY ILL

Going to the doctor's

A few months ago I came home early from school because I had a really bad sore throat. I decided I had better go and see my **doctor**, and made an appointment to see her the following day. The doctor took my temperature and listened to my breathing. She told me that I had flu. She **prescribed** me some **antibiotics** and told me to go home and get plenty of rest.

I spent the next week in bed with a high temperature. I wasn't getting any better, and I was worried that it might be something more serious. My parents arranged for the doctor to come and visit me at home. She **took my temperature** again and **examined** me quite thoroughly. This time, she said it wasn't flu but glandular fever, which was a lot more serious. After a few weeks I slowly started to get better. I still have to take it really easy, and I'm not allowed to do any sport. They say it could be several months before I'm completely well again.

Vocabulary

1 the treatment of illnesses and injuries

medicine /'medsən‖'medɪ̩sən/ [n U] the science of understanding illness and injury, and the methods used for treating them: *Jane is studying medicine at Harvard.* | *The discovery of penicillin revolutionized Western medicine.*

medical /'medɪkəl/ [adj only before noun] connected with illness or injury and the methods used for treating them
  medical school (=where people train to be doctors) *Maria wants to go to medical school.*
  medical research *There have been huge advances in medical research.*
  medical attention (=treatment by doctors or nurses in a hospital) *After the accident, both drivers needed medical attention.*
  the medical profession (=doctors and nurses considered together as a group)

treatment /'triːtmənt/ [n C/U] a medical method of curing someone who is ill or injured, for example by means of drugs or an operation: *The treatment was successful.*

+ **for** *He's receiving treatment for cancer.* | *a new treatment for depression*

cure /kjʊəʳ/ [n C] a method of treating an illness, using drugs, operations etc, which makes the person with the illness completely better: *Scientists still haven't found a cure.*

+ **for** *the search for a cure for AIDS*

healthcare /'helθkeəʳ/ [n U] the medical services that are available to people in a country: *The standard of healthcare in the area is excellent.* | *the rising cost of healthcare*

conventional medicine /kən'venʃənəl ˌmedsən‖-ˌmedɪ̩sən/ [n U] the usual form of medicine used in most European and North American countries, involving the use of drugs and operations: *When patients feel that conventional medicine has failed, they may turn to other forms of treatment.*

alternative medicine / complementary medicine /ɔːl'tɜːʳnətɪv ˌmedsən, ˌkɒmplɪ̩'mentəri ˌmedsən‖ -ˌmedɪ̩sən, kɑːm-/ [n U] medical treatments based on ideas that are completely different from the ideas of conventional medicine, for example homeopathy,

Going to hospital

A three-year-old girl was recovering in **hospital** yesterday, after a series of mistakes by hospital doctors. The little girl fell down some stairs last week at her home, and said that her arm was hurting badly. Her mother immediately called an ambulance, and she was rushed to the **Accident and Emergency Department** at her local hospital. The doctor there **examined** her and sent her for an **X-ray**. The X-ray didn't show that anything was wrong, so the doctor bandaged the arm and sent her home.

After a week she was still complaining of pains in her arm, and her mother took her back to the hospital. Another doctor examined the X-rays again. He found that her arm was broken, and asked for her arm to be put **in plaster**.

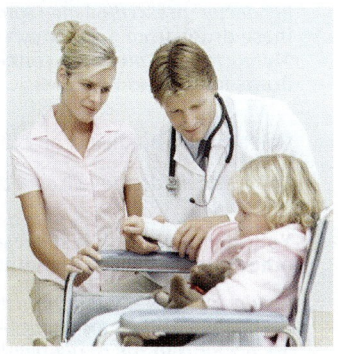

When the little girl arrived home, she was still in a lot of pain. Her mother suddenly realised that they had put the wrong arm in plaster. A spokesman for the hospital apologized for what had happened, and said that they would be carrying out a full investigation.

---

acupuncture, and herbal remedies: *The herb has been used for years in alternative medicine to treat a wide range of illnesses.* | *Complementary medicine is becoming more popular.*

2 what doctors do

treat /triːt/ [v T] to try to make someone better when they are ill or injured, for example by giving them drugs or hospital care
treat sb for sth *Doctors are treating him for cancer.*
treat sth with sth *Many common infections can be treated with antibiotics.*

examine /ɪgˈzæmɪn/ [v T] if a doctor **examines** someone who is ill, he or she looks carefully at them in order to find out what is wrong: *He was examined by three doctors, but none of them could find anything physically wrong.*
examination /ɪgˌzæmɪˈneɪʃən/ [n U] when a doctor looks at someone who is ill in order to find out what is wrong with them

3 different ways of treating someone

operation /ˌɒpəˈreɪʃən‖ˌɑːp-/ [n C] if you have an **operation**, a doctor cuts into your body to remove or repair a part that is damaged: *She's gone into hospital for an operation.*
+ on *I had an operation on my knee last year.*
perform/carry out an operation *A team of surgeons carried out an operation to remove the tumour.*

operate /ˈɒpəreɪt‖ˈɑː-/ [v I] if a doctor **operates**, he or she cuts someone open in order to remove or repair a part of their body that is damaged: *The doctors say they may have to operate.*
+ on *It can be risky to operate on very old people.* | *They had to operate on my arm because it was broken in two places.*

surgery /ˈsɜːʳdʒəri/ [n U] treatment by doctors in which they cut into someone's body to remove or repair a part that is damaged: *She needed emergency surgery after the accident.*
have/undergo surgery *Before undergoing surgery, patients can discuss their operation with a doctor.*

Writing tips

✎ **When talking about going to the doctor, you can say:**

I **went to the doctor's.** (BRITISH)/**the doctor's office.** (AMERICAN)
I **saw the doctor.**
I **made an appointment at the doctor's.** (=I arranged to see the doctor)

✎ **When saying that your doctor gave you some medicine, you can say:**

My doctor **gave me a prescription for** some antibiotics. (=wrote a note so that you can get these drugs from a pharmacy)
My doctor **prescribed (me)** some antibiotics. (=wrote a note so that you can get these drugs from a pharmacy)
My doctor **put me on a course of** antibiotics. (= said you should take these drugs for a period of time)

✎ Don't say 'eat medicine' or 'drink medicine'. Say **take medicine**, for example:

Take this medicine twice a day for the next 8 days.

✎ **Your doctor doesn't just prescribe drugs. Here are some examples of other things that the doctor may do:**

My doctor **took my temperature.** (=checked it)
My doctor **checked my pulse** (=checked to see how fast my heart was beating)
My doctor **told me to** get plenty of rest/take it easy/give up smoking.
My doctor **sent me for an X ray/a scan/some tests.**
My doctor **referred me** to a specialist. (=sent me to another doctor who has special knowledge about that type of condition)

✎ **When saying that part of your body hurts, you can say:**

My leg/shoulder/arm etc **hurts.**
I **have (got) a pain in** my leg/shoulder/arm etc.
I **have (got) a headache/a stomach ache/back ache/ear ache.**
I **was in a lot of pain.** (=part of my body hurt a lot)

---

major/minor surgery (=serious/not very serious operations) *This is a dangerous condition, and she will require major surgery.*
injection /ɪnˈdʒekʃən/ [n C] when a doctor or nurse gives someone a drug using a special needle that they push into the person's body: *I hate having injections.*
give sb an injection *The nurse gave him an injection to make him sleep.*
X-ray /ˈeks reɪ/ [n C] a medical examination that uses a beam of radiation to photograph the inside of someone's body: *The X-ray showed that he had broken his jaw.*
have an X-ray (on sth) *The doctor said I had to have a chest X-ray.*

scan /skæn/ [n C] a medical examination in which a machine produces a picture of the inside of your body: *a brain scan | The doctor sent him for a scan.*
in plaster BRITISH **in a cast** AMERICAN /ɪn ˈplɑːstəʳǁ-ˈplæs-, ɪn ə kæst/ if someone's leg, arm, or wrist is in plaster, doctors have put a stiff cover around it so that a broken bone can get better: *Her arm was in plaster for 6 weeks.*
put sb's leg/arm etc in plaster *They put his leg in plaster.*
physiotherapy /ˌfɪziəʊˈθerəpi/ [n U] treatment for people who have injured their muscles,

broken their legs etc, in which they have to do special exercises, have parts of their body rubbed and pressed etc

4 medicines

medicine /ˈmedsənǁˈmedᵻsən/ [*n* C/U] a substance used for treating illnesses, especially a liquid that you drink: *Emergency supplies of food and medicine were sent to the earthquake area.* | *Chinese herbal medicines*

take medicine *Have you taken your medicine this morning?*

drug /drʌg/ [*n* C] a chemical substance used for treating illnesses: *a drug used in the treatment of stomach cancer* | *The side effects of this drug may include fever and dizziness.* | *Morphine is a very powerful drug.*

tablet/pill /ˈtæblᵻt, pɪl/ [*n* C] a small round hard piece of medicine that you swallow

take a tablet *She took some tablets for her headache.*

be on tablets (=be taking tablets) *I'm on four tablets a day.*

sleeping tablets (=to help you sleep)

vitamin tablets (=containing vitamin C, D etc)

painkiller /ˈpeɪnˌkɪləʳ/ [*n* C] a drug used for reducing or getting rid of pain: *She gave me some painkillers for my toothache.*

medication /ˌmedɪˈkeɪʃən/ [*n* U] one or more drugs that your doctor has told you to take regularly, especially for a serious illness that you have for a long time: *Don't forget to take your medication.*

be on medication (for sth) *She's on medication for her heart.*

antibiotics /ˌæntɪbaɪˈɒtɪksǁ-ˈɑːt-/ [*n* plural] a drug that kills bacteria and is used to cure infections

dose /dəʊs/ [*n* C] the amount of a drug that you take at one time: *I think you need to increase the dose.*

+ of *She has to take massive doses of insulin.*

prescription /prɪˈskrɪpʃən/ [*n* C] a piece of paper from your doctor that says which medicine you need and allows you to get it from a pharmacy

+ for *He gave her a prescription for some sleeping tablets.*

prescribe [*v* T] to write a note saying that someone should have a particular type of medicine: *Her doctor prescribed her some tablets.*

5 places where you can get medical treatment

the doctor's BRITISH **the doctor's office** AMERICAN /ðə ˈdɒktəʳz, ðə ˈdɒktəʳz ˌɒfᵻsǁ-ˈdɑːk-, -ˌɑːf-/ the office where a doctor works, where people who are ill can go at certain times to be examined and treated: *"My leg really hurts." "You'd better go to the doctor's."* | *She went to the doctor's office the next day.* | *I've made an appointment at the doctor's.*

the dentist's BRITISH **the dentist's office** AMERICAN /ðə ˈdentᵻsts, ðə ˈdentᵻsts ˌɒfᵻsǁ-ˌɑːf-/ the place where a dentist works, where people go to have their teeth treated: *He's gone to the dentist's for a check-up.*

clinic /ˈklɪnɪk/ [*n* C] in the US, a place where several doctors have offices; in Britain, a place where people come for treatment or advice about a specific medical condition: *a clinic for people with alcohol problems* | *They're building a new dental clinic at the end of the street.*

health centre BRITISH **health center** AMERICAN /ˈhelθ ˌsentəʳ/ [*n* C] in Britain, a building where several doctors have offices, and people can go to see them for treatment; in the US a similar place in a college or university, where the students can go to see a doctor

surgery /ˈsɜːʳdʒəri/ [*n* C] BRITISH the office where a doctor works, where people can go to be examined and treated: *The waiting room at the surgery was full of people with colds and flu.*

plural **surgeries**

hospital /ˈhɒspɪtlǁˈhɑː-/ [*n* C] a large building where nurses and doctors work and where you stay while you are having medical treatment: *Dr Clark is a surgeon at a big hospital.*

in/to/from hospital BRITISH *My sister's in hospital having a baby.*

in/to/from the hospital AMERICAN *After the accident, John was rushed to the hospital.*

Accident and Emergency BRITISH **A&E** BRITISH **the emergency room** AMERICAN /ˌæksᵻdənt ənd ɪˈmɜːʳdʒənsi, ˌeɪ ənd ˈiː, ɪˈmɜːʳdʒənsi ruːm/ [*n* singular] the part of a hospital you go to for emergency treatment, for example if you have had an accident or if you suddenly become very ill: *We had to take my mother to A&E after she fell downstairs.*

6 alternative medical treatment

homeopathy /ˌhəʊmiˈɒpəθiǁ-ˈɑːp-/ [*n* U] a system of medicine in which a disease is treated by giving small amounts of the substance that causes the disease

homeopathic [adj] *a homeopathic remedy*

reflexology /ˌriːflekˈsɒlədʒiǁ-ˈsɑː-/ [*n* U] a treatment in which areas of a person's feet and hands are pressed in order to treat problems in another part of their body

aromatherapy /əˌrəʊməˈθerəpi/ [*n* U] a treatment using special oils which are used in a bath or rubbed into your skin

acupuncture /ˈækjᵿˌpʌŋktʃəʳ/ [*n* U] a treatment in which many needles are put into your skin to stop pain or cure an illness

herbal remedy /ˌhɜːbəl ˈremᵻdiǁˌɜːr-, ˌhɜːr-/ [*n* C] a medicine that is made from special plants

MUSIC

What kind of music do you like?

I'm really into **jazz**. Probably my favourite **musician** of all time is Stan Getz, an American **saxophone** player who was very big in the 1960s. He was famous for playing on records such as 'The Girl from Ipanema'. My favourite **singer** is Billie Holiday – she has such a sad voice. I have got hundreds of jazz CDs at home, but I think the best way to listen to jazz is to hear it live. There's a little jazz club not far from where we live, and I often go to **gigs** there. It's only £8 to get in, and you can sit and listen to some of the country's top jazz players.

I like all kinds of music. Like many people, I first became interested in **rock** music when I was a teenager. I used to spend a lot of money buying records and going to rock **concerts**.

At university I began listening to different kinds of music, depending on what my friends were into. That included anything from **classical music** to **jazz** or **folk**. More recently, I've been listening to **world music**. There is a lot of exciting music coming out of places like Cuba and Mali. I've just bought a brilliant new album by Ali Farke Toure, who is a guitar player from Mali. His music is truly magical, and sounds like nothing I've ever heard.

Vocabulary

1 playing music

music /ˈmjuːzɪk/ [n U] the sounds made by people singing or playing musical instruments: *What sort of music do you like?* | *I like listening to music on the radio.*
live music (=music that is not recorded) *The club has live music every Saturday night.*

> ⚠ **Music** can also mean the art and skill of writing or playing music: *He's studying music at university.| music lessons| the Royal College of Music*

play /pleɪ/ [v I/T] to make music by using a musical instrument or by singing: *Jane can play 'Yesterday' on the flute.* | *Do you play in an orchestra?*
play the piano/trumpet/drums etc *I didn't know you could play the violin.*

> ⚠ **Play** can also mean to let people hear a piece of music on the radio, on a CD player, record player etc: *The DJ played a lot of old tracks from the 1980s.*

perform /pəˈfɔːrm/ [v I/T] FORMAL to sing or play music in front of people who have come to listen: *She still gets very nervous about performing in public.* | *The orchestra will be at the Festival Hall tonight, performing a selection of works by Russian composers.*

instrument/musical instrument /ˈɪnstrʊmənt, ˌmjuːzɪkəl ˈɪnstrʊmənt/ [n C] an object such as a piano, a guitar, or a violin that you use to play music: *brass instruments* | *Do you play any instruments?*

2 types of music

classical music /ˌklæsɪkəl ˈmjuːzɪk/ [n U] music which is regarded as serious and important and has been played for a very long time, for example the music of Beethoven, Mozart, or Tchaikovsky: *a concert of classical music*

jazz /dʒæz/ [n U] music that was originally played by black Americans in the early 20th century, and which has parts in it that performers play alone, often making up new music as they play: *Do you like modern jazz?* | *a jazz band* | *a jazz singer*

Musical instruments

piano

violin

double bass

cello

drums

guitar

tuba

trombone

flute

clarinet

oboe

bassoon

trumpet

saxophone

pop /pɒpǁpɑːp/ [n U] modern music that is popular with young people and usually has simple tunes and a strong beat: *Robbie Williams is one of Britain's most successful pop singers.* | *Do you like pop music?*

rock /rɒkǁrɑːk/ [n U] a type of popular modern music with electric guitars and a strong loud beat: *rock bands such as Oasis* | *veteran rock guitarist, Eric Clapton* | *We could hear the sound of loud rock music coming from the neighbour's bedroom.*

rap /ræp/ [n U] a type of popular music in which the words of the song are spoken, not sung, in time to music that has a steady beat

dance /dɑːnsǁdæns/ [n U] a name for some types of modern music such as house, techno etc, that are made using electronic equipment and have a very fast, strong beat

folk (music) /ˈfəʊk ˌmjuːzɪk/ [n U] a type of traditional music in which people sing and play instruments without any electronic equipment: *a Russian folk group called Zabava* | *They have folk music every Tuesday evening at the club.*

country (and western) /ˌkʌntri ən ˈwestəˈn/ [n U] a type of music that originally came from the southern states of the US, which is played on guitars, violins etc: *a radio station that plays country music 24 hours a day*

world music /ˈwɜːˈld ˌmjuːzɪk/ [n U] music from places such as South America, Africa, and Asia: *World music has become very popular over the last ten years.*

3 people who play music

musician /mjuːˈzɪʃən/ [n C] someone who plays a musical instrument very well, or someone who does this as their job: *a talented young musician*

singer /ˈsɪŋəˈ/ [n C] someone who sings, especially as their job: *Rosie's a singer in a rock band.* | *an opera singer*
  lead singer (=the most important singer in a popular music group) *Justin Hawkins is the lead singer with 'The Darkness'.*

guitar/keyboard/saxophone etc player /(guitar etc) ˌpleɪəˈ/ [n C] someone who plays the guitar, keyboards, saxophone etc, especially at a concert or on a record

pop star /ˈpɒp ˌstɑːˈǁˈpɑːp-/ [n C] someone who is famous and successful as a singer or musician

Going to a concert

Last week I went with some friends to see a **singer** called Khaled. He comes from Algeria and sings in a musical style called 'rai', which is a mixture of traditional Algerian music and Western **pop music**.

The **gig** lasted about two hours. Khaled played several songs from his latest album as well as some new songs. All the **musicians** were excellent, especially the **keyboard** player. The place was packed and everyone was dancing and singing along to the music. It was a really good evening.

Do you play any musical instruments?

I started learning the **saxophone** two years ago. At first I found it difficult to remember which keys to press in order to play the different notes, but I now have a very good teacher who has helped me improve my technique. I'm still not very good, but at least I can play some simple tunes. Learning to play a musical instrument requires a lot of practice and I try to do at least half an hour a day. Eventually I hope to join a band. In the meantime, I hope the noise doesn't annoy the neighbours too much!

---

in a pop group: *My sister has pictures of pop stars all over her bedroom wall.*

band /bænd/ [n C] a group of musicians who play popular music such as jazz, rock, or pop: *a jazz band*
be in a band *When I was young, I always wanted to be in a band.*

orchestra /ˈɔːrkɪ̰strə/ [n C] a large group of people playing many different kinds of instruments, usually playing classical music, and led by a conductor: *the Berlin Philharmonic Orchestra*

conductor /kənˈdʌktər/ [n C] someone who stands in front of a group of musicians or singers and directs their playing or singing: *The orchestra always play well when Simon Rattle is the conductor.*

choir /kwaɪər/ [n C] a large group of people who sing together, often in a church or school: *The choir has been invited to sing in a concert at the Royal Festival Hall.*

4 going to see people play music

go to see /ˌɡəʊ tə ˈsiː/ to go to a performance by a particular singer or band – use this especially

about going to see modern popular musicians: *We're going to see the White Stripes at the Wembley Arena.*

concert /ˈkɒnsərt‖ˈkɑːn-/ [n C] an event at which a singer, musician, orchestra etc plays in front of a large group of people: *a pop concert | the school concert* (=when students from the school perform by singing and playing instruments)
+ of *a concert of orchestral music by Beethoven and Schubert*
go to a concert *On Friday we're going to a concert of modern African music.*

gig /ɡɪɡ/ [n C] INFORMAL a concert, especially of modern popular music or jazz
do/play a gig (=perform at a concert) *They're doing about 30 gigs on their European tour.*
go to a gig *Let's go to a gig this weekend.*

set /set/ [n C] a number of songs or pieces of music played by a singer or band in a performance at one time: *After the break, they came back and played a two-hour set.*

performance /pərˈfɔːrməns/ [n C] when a musician or group of musicians performs a piece of music
+ of *There are no tickets left for this evening's*

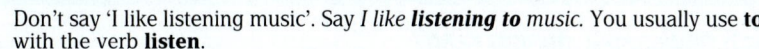

Writing tips

✎ Don't say 'I like listening music'. Say *I like **listening to** music*. You usually use **to** with the verb **listen**.

✎ Don't say 'I often listen to the music in my car.' Say *I often listen to **music** in my car*. When talking about **music** in general, don't use 'the'.

✎ **There are many ways of saying that you like a particular kind of music or singer. You can say:**

I love his music.
It's one of my favourite CDs.
***I'm into** jazz.* (= I like jazz very much) ***He's into** Bob Dylan.*
*I **love** their music. I **love** Marvin Gaye.*
***I'm a big/great fan** of the Beatles.* (=I like their music very much)
***I have her music on all the time**.* (= I listen to it a lot)

✎ **There are many ways of saying that a piece of music or a singer is very popular. You can say:**

*She is **big** in America.* (=she is popular there)
*Their first record **went** straight **to number one (in the charts)**.*(=it was the most popular record at that time)
*The song was one of the **biggest hits** of last summer.*(=it was one of the most popular records at that time)

---

performance of Mozart's Requiem.
give a performance *Eminem gave one of his best performances at Skydome.*
festival /ˈfestɪvəl/ [n C] an occasion when many different musical groups or singers perform, which happens at the same time and in the same place every year: *I first heard them play at the Pittsburgh Jazz Festival. | Are you going to the Glastonbury festival this year?*
concert hall /ˈkɒnsəʳt ˌhɔːl‖ˈkɑːn-/ [n C] a large building where concerts are performed
jazz club /ˈdʒæz ˌklʌb/ [n C] a place where you can listen to jazz bands and singers
venue /ˈvenjuː/ [n C] a place where a concert, festival etc takes place: *The club is a popular venue for folk groups.*

5 people who write music

composer /kəmˈpəʊzəʳ/ [n C] someone who writes music, especially classical music: *Henry Purcell was one of the greatest English composers.*

songwriter /ˈsɒŋˌraɪtəʳ‖ˈsɔːŋ-/ [n C] someone who writes songs: *Most of Elton John's early hits were written by songwriter Bernie Taupin.*
singer-songwriter (=someone who writes songs and sings them) *singer-songwriter Sheryl Crow*

6 writing music

compose /kəmˈpəʊz/ [v I/T] to write a piece of music, especially classical music: *a song composed by Schubert | Mozart composed his first symphony when he was still a child.*
write /raɪt/ [v I/T] to write a song or a piece of music: *an opera written by Verdi*

7 the words of a song

lyrics /ˈlɪrɪks/ [n plural] the words of a song: *John Lennon wrote the lyrics and Paul McCartney wrote the music.*

NEWSPAPERS

Which newspaper do you read?

I usually get *The Daily Mirror* on my way to work. As it's a **tabloid**, it's easy to read on the train, and the **articles** are nice and short. I like reading all the latest gossip about my favourite TV stars.

After glancing at the **headlines** on the front page, the first thing I usually read is my **horoscope**. I know it's not really true, but it's still fun to read. I also look at the **TV guide**, to see if there's anything good on television that evening. If I have time, I try to do the **crossword**.

I usually read *The Wall Street Journal*. I need to keep up with what's happening in the business world for my job. The first page I usually turn to is the share prices, to find out the latest news about the stock market.

I don't just read the **business pages**. Often I look at the **arts section** to see if there are any reviews of plays or concerts, and there's always something interesting on the **letters page**. Today, there were lots of letters about the effects of cell phones on people's health.

Vocabulary

1 newspapers

newspaper/paper /ˈnjuːsˌpeɪpəʳ, ˈpeɪpəʳ‖ˈnuːz-/ [n C] a set of large folded sheets of paper printed with news, articles, pictures etc, and sold every day or every week: *Which newspaper do you usually get?*
  in the newspaper/paper *I read it in the paper.*
  It says in the paper ... (=it is reported in the paper ...) *It says in the paper that they're getting divorced.*

Sunday paper /ˌsʌndi ˈpeɪpəʳ/ [n C] a newspaper that is sold every Sunday, and is usually bigger than papers sold on other days: *I like to sit in bed and read the Sunday papers.*

local newspaper/paper /ˌləʊkəl ˈnjuːsˌpeɪpəʳ, ˈpeɪpəʳ‖ˈnuːz-/ [n C] a newspaper that gives news mainly about the town or area where it is printed: *Did you see Dave's picture in the local paper?*

national newspaper / paper /ˌnæʃənəl ˈnjuːsˌpeɪpəʳ, ˈpeɪpəʳ‖-ˈnuːz-/ [n C] (also plural **the nationals**) a newspaper that gives news about the whole country where it is printed, and usually news about the rest of the world: *Next morning, the interview was in almost every national paper.*

the press /ðə ˈpres/ [n singular] newspapers and the people who write for them: *A spokesman later issued a statement to the press.*
  in the press *The event was widely publicized in the press.*

the media /ðə ˈmiːdiə/ [n singular] all the organizations that are involved in providing information to the public, especially newspapers, television, and radio
  in the media *Violent crime is reported daily in the media.*
  news media *The report dominated much of the news media for several days.*

tabloid /ˈtæblɔɪd/ [n C] a newspaper that does not contain much serious news, but has stories about famous people, sport, sex etc: *She'd been at school with the Prime Minister and sold a story about him to one of the tabloids.*

broadsheet BRITISH /ˈbrɔːdʃiːt/ [n C] a newspaper printed on large sheets of paper, especially a serious newspaper that has news about politics, finance, and foreign affairs: *The issue was widely reported in both the broadsheets and the popular newspapers.*

Do people still read newspapers?

A lot of people read **newspapers** when they are travelling to and from work. It's good to have something to read on the train or the bus, and newspapers are easy to carry around with you. Newspapers don't just tell you the news, they also contain a lot of other interesting information, such as film and music **reviews**, and gossip about famous people.

At the weekend, the **papers** have lots of different **sections**, for example about new ways of decorating your home, ideas for holidays, or new recipes. Many people like to read the papers while they are having breakfast on Sunday morning, because it's a relaxing thing to do.

For many people, especially young people, their main source of news is now the Internet. They can read about the latest news online as soon as it happens. They can also visit their favourite websites to look for other **stories** that might interest them. If they want they can also get the news from the television or the radio. In many ways it is surprising that newspapers are still so popular.

Nobody knows what will happen to newspapers in the future, but for the moment they are very much still part of our lives.

---

the popular press /ðə ˌpɒpjᵘləʳ 'presǁ-ˌpɑː-/ [n singular] newspapers that are read by a lot of people and generally contain articles that are entertaining rather than serious, for example stories about people on television and in sport: *There are pictures of her in the popular press nearly every day.*

copy /'kɒpiǁ'kɑːpi/ [n C] a single newspaper, especially one printed on a particular day: *How many copies does the New York Times sell?*
+ of *Do you still have a copy of Saturday's Guardian?*
plural **copies**

2 parts of a newspaper

headline /'hedlaɪn/ [n C] the words in big letters at the top of a newspaper report that tell you what the report is about: *Did you see the headlines in the Herald?*
the headline read/said *The headline read simply "THE KING IS DEAD".*

section /'sekʃən/ [n C] a separate part of a newspaper consisting of several pages folded together that deals with a particular subject area

such as sport, business, or travel: *I always read the main news section first.*
the sports/business/travel etc section *There's a good travel section in the paper on Thursdays.*

the TV/sports/business/fashion etc pages /ðə (TV, etc) ˌpeɪdʒɪz/ [n C] the pages in a newspaper that tell you about television, sport, business, the arts etc: *I usually read the business pages on the train going to work.*

the front page /ðə ˌfrʌnt 'peɪdʒ/ [n singular] the page on the front of a newspaper which has the most important news stories

the letters page /ðə 'letəʳz ˌpeɪdʒ/ [n C] the page in a newspaper where letters from readers are printed

listings /'lɪstɪŋz/ [n plural] lists of films, plays, and other events, with details of the times, dates, and places where they will happen, or lists of television programmes with their times: *movie listings | the TV listings*

horoscope /'hɒrəskəʊpǁ'hɑː-, 'hɔː-/ [n C] a description of what will happen to people in the next day or week, based on the position of the

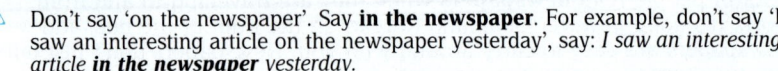

Writing tips

✎ Don't say 'on the newspaper'. Say **in the newspaper**. For example, don't say 'I saw an interesting article on the newspaper yesterday', say: *I saw an interesting article **in the newspaper** yesterday.*

But if you are talking about a particular **page** of a newspaper, you should use **on**, for example: *Her picture was **on the front page** of our local paper.*

✎ **Paper** is much more common than **newspaper**, especially in less formal situations. For example when talking about something you have read, you usually say: *I read about it in the paper,* or *I saw an advertisement in the paper.*

✎ If you want to talk about newspapers in general, you usually say **the papers**. For example: *How often do you read the papers?*

✎ If you want to mention something from a newspaper, you can use the following phrases:

It said in the paper that women are better drivers than men.
According to an article in today's/yesterday's paper, women are much better drivers than men. (more informal)

Don't say 'the paper wrote that …'

✎ Don't confuse **newspaper** and **journal**. A journal is a serious magazine on a particular subject, containing articles by university teachers, scientists, doctors etc: *the British Medical Journal | Their research was published in a scientific journal.*

---

stars, which appears in some tabloid newspapers: *It said in my horoscope that I would lose a lot of money today.*

agony column BRITISH **advice column** AMERICAN /ˈæɡəni ˌkɒləm‖ədˈvaɪs ˌkaləm/ [n C] a part of a newspaper, usually a tabloid newspaper, in which someone gives advice to readers who want help with problems they have with their personal life

crossword /ˈkrɒswɜːˈd‖ˈkrɔːs-/ [n C] a word game in which you work out the answers to questions, and then write the answers in numbered boxes. Most newspapers print a crossword every day.

3 what is written in newspapers

article /ˈɑːˈtɪkəl/ [n C] a piece of writing in a newspaper about a particular subject: *a newspaper article*
+ on/about *an article on environmental issues*
story /ˈstɔːri/ [n C] a report in a newspaper about a recent event: *a front-page story in the New York Times*
+ about *Open any newspaper and you'll see stories about shootings and muggings.*

news item /ˈnjuːz ˌaɪtə‖ˈnuːz-/ [n C] a single piece of news in a newspaper, especially a short one: *The local paper printed a small news item about the event.*

feature /ˈfiːtʃəˈ/ [n C] a special report in a newspaper about an interesting subject, place, or person: *a special feature about the lives of homeless people*

column /ˈkɒləm‖ˈkaː-/ [n C] an article on a particular subject or by a particular writer that appears regularly in a newspaper: *Clarkson writes a weekly column on motoring for The Times.*
a music/science/fashion etc column

editorial /ˌedɪˈtɔːriəl/ [n C] a piece of writing in a newspaper that gives the personal opinion of the editor about something that is in the news: *Their editorials always criticize the government, whatever the government does.*

exclusive /ɪkˈskluːsɪv/ [n C] a news story that is printed by one newspaper before any of the others know about it: *a New York Times exclusive about a secret arms deal between a US company and Iraq*
exclusive [adj] *an exclusive interview with the President's wife*

investigative   journalism / reporting
/ɪnˌvestɪɡətɪv   ˈdʒɜːˈnəlɪzəm,   rɪˈpɔːˈtɪŋ‖
-ɡeɪtɪv-/ the work that journalists do when they
try to discover and report the truth about something serious that someone else is trying to keep
secret: *The President had to resign after some
excellent investigative reporting by two Washington Post journalists.*

coverage /ˈkʌvərɪdʒ/ [n U] when a subject or
event is reported in newspapers and the way in
which it is reported
+ of *the Daily Star's coverage of the election*
media/press coverage *The allegations received
widespread media coverage.*

4 people who work for newspapers

reporter /rɪˈpɔːˈtəˈ/ [n C] someone whose job is to
find out about news stories and write about
them: *She works as a junior reporter on a local
paper.* | *A crowd of reporters were waiting outside
the house all night.*

journalist /ˈdʒɜːˈnəlɪ̹st/ [n C] someone who
writes for a newspaper: *A lot of young people
dream of working as journalists.*
journalism [n C] *a career in journalism*

correspondent /ˌkɒrɪ̹ˈspɒndənt‖ˌkɔːrɪ̹ˈspaːn-,
ˌkɑː-/ [n C] someone who writes about a particular subject, especially a serious one, for a newspaper
**political / foreign / education etc corres-
pondent** (=someone who reports news stories
about politics, what is happening in other countries, education etc) *Martin Bell worked for many
years as a BBC war correspondent.*

editor /ˈedɪtəˈ/ [n C] the person in charge of a
newspaper, whose job is to decide what subjects
are written about and how they are written: *the
editor of the New York Times*

sports/political/business etc editor /(sports,
etc) ˌedɪtəˈ/ [n C] the person who is in charge of a
particular part of a newspaper, and who decides
what is written about sport, politics, business etc:
the chief political editor of The Independent |
Morrison is the paper's senior business editor.

paparazzi /ˌpæpəˈrætsiː‖ˌpaːpəˈraː-/ [n plural]
photographers who follow famous people in

order to take photographs they can sell to
newspapers – used especially in a disapproving
way: *A crowd of paparazzi were waiting outside the
hotel.*

agony aunt BRITISH **advice columnist** AMERICAN
/ˈæɡəni ˌɑːnt‖-ˌænt, ədˈvaɪs ˌkɒləmnɪst‖ˌkɑː/
[n C] a person who writes advice in answer to
letters from readers who want help with problems they have with their personal life

5 to write for a newspaper

write /raɪt/ [v I/T] to write news reports or other
articles for a newspaper: *She writes on gardening
in one of the Sunday papers.*
+ for *He's been writing for the Evening News ever
since he left college.*

report /rɪˈpɔːˈt/ [v I/T] to find out and write about
news stories for a newspaper: *We try to report the
news as fairly as possible.*
+ on *She was sent to Sudan to report on the
situation.*
+ that *Journalists reported that seven people had
been shot.*
reporting [n U] *Press reporting of court cases
increases public awareness.*

cover /ˈkʌvəˈ/ [v T] to report the details of an
event or a series of events for a newspaper or
news programme: *Baxter had spent three weeks
covering a big murder trial.*

6 people who read newspapers

reader /ˈriːdəˈ/ [n C] someone who reads a
particular newspaper: *A majority of newspaper
readers felt that their own paper was biased.* | *The
newspaper gradually lost readers during the
1980s.*

readership /ˈriːdəˈʃɪp/ [n U] the number of
people or type of people who regularly read a
particular newspaper: *The paper has a readership
of over 1.5 million.* | *a mainly middle-class
readership*

circulation /ˌsɜːˈkjʊˈleɪʃən/ [n U] the number of
copies of a newspaper that are sold in a day, a
week, a month etc: *Since then, the paper has
increased its circulation by 10%.*

POLICE

CRIME

KILL   CATCH

STEAL   see also   PRISON

ATTACK   LAW

WB COURT/ TRIAL

Police hunt for knife attacker

Police are still **hunting for** a man who robbed six taxi drivers in South London. In one **incident**, the thief sat behind the driver and threatened him with a knife, telling him to hand over all his money. The thief then ran off with around £100. A police **detective** said: "So far there have been six attacks by the same person – four **incidents** were reported in the last month. We would advise all taxi drivers to be extra careful, and if they see anything suspicious they should **contact the police** immediately."

Man charged with knife attacks

A 30-year-old man has been **charged** with armed robbery, following a series of violent attacks on taxi drivers last month. The man, Henry Riley, is due to appear at South London Magistrates Court on Monday. Riley was **arrested** on Saturday night after a taxi driver **called the police**. Police officers took Riley down to the **police station** for **questioning**, and he has been **helping the police with their enquiries** over the weekend.

Vocabulary

1 the police

the police /ðə pəˈliːs/ [n plural] the organization and the people whose job is to catch criminals and make sure that people obey the law: *He was stopped by the police and arrested for dangerous driving.*

  call/contact the police *I heard a gunshot and called the police.* | *If you see anything suspicious you should contact the police.*

  be in trouble with the police (=get caught by the police after doing something slightly illegal) *He's never been in trouble with the police before.*

  the riot police (=a group of police officers with special equipment and special training whose job is to control large crowds of people who have become violent)

  the secret police (=a police force controlled by the government that secretly tries to defeat the political enemies of that government) *Nin was captured and tortured by the secret police.*

  a police car/van/helicopter etc *A police helicopter was circling overhead.*

  a police dog (=a dog that has been trained to help the police in their work)

  a police horse (=a horse that is ridden by a police officer, often when the purpose is to control large crowds of people)

the police force /ðə pəˈliːs fɔːʳs/ the police organization in a country or large area: *Jason joined the police force when he was 19.*

police department [n C] AMERICAN /ðə pəˈliːs dɪˌpɑːʳtmənt/ the police organization in a particular city: *the Los Angeles Police Department*

CID /ˌsiː aɪ ˈdiː/ [n singular] Criminal Investigation Department. The department of the British police that deals with very serious crimes

the FBI /ði ˌef biː ˈaɪ/ [n singular] The Federal Bureau of Investigation. The police department in the US that is controlled by central government, and that deals with crimes that break national laws rather than state laws

2 people in the police

police officer (also **officer**) /pəˈliːs ˌɒfˌɪsəʳ, ˈɒfˌɪsəʳ‖-ˌɔːr-/ [n C] a man or woman who is an official member of the police force: *He was led away by police officers.* | *Can you help me, officer?*

Have you ever been the victim of a crime?

Someone broke into our house a few months ago. They didn't take very much, just a necklace and a laptop computer. The **burglary** happened while I was out at work. As soon as I got home and realized what had happened, I phoned the **police**. A police car came almost immediately, and the **police officers** said that there had recently been a lot of burglaries in our area. They started looking for fingerprints and any other clues that might help them catch the

burglars. I read somewhere that only 12% of burglaries are ever solved, so I didn't think it was very likely that they would find the person who did it.

A few weeks later, when I was about to go out and buy another computer, I got a call from one of the police officers. He said that they had **arrested** two men. A witness had seen them breaking into a house near where I live, and they were being held **in custody** at our local **police station**. One of them had already confessed to stealing things from our house. Apparently he had **been in trouble with the police** before. I was glad that the criminals had been caught, but since the **incident** happened I always feel anxious whenever I go out of our house.

policeman / policewoman /pəˈliːsmən, pəˈliːs,wʊmən/ [n C] a male or female police officer: *Two policemen held him down while the others handcuffed him.*

detective /dɪˈtektɪv/ [n C] a police officer whose job is to find out information that will result in criminals being caught: *Detectives are hunting for any clues about the killer.*

cop (also **copper** BRITISH) /kɒp, ˈkɒpəʳ‖ˈkɑːp/ [n C] INFORMAL a police officer: *Her father had been a cop in New York before they moved to Missouri.*

plain-clothes /ˈpleɪnkləʊðz, -kləʊz/ [adj only before noun] **plain-clothes** police wear ordinary clothes, so that criminals do not know they are police officers: *A plain-clothes detective waited outside in an unmarked car.*

in uniform /ɪn ˈjuːnɪ̩fɔːʳm/ [adv] if a police officer is in uniform, he or she is wearing the usual clothes worn by the police: *A young police officer in uniform kept guard outside the door.*

3 **what the police do**

arrest /əˈrest/ [v T] if the police **arrest** someone, they take that person to a police station because

they believe that he or she has done something illegal

be/get arrested (for doing sth) *Gallagher was arrested for possessing cocaine.*

arrest [n C] **make an arrest** (=arrest someone) *Police were unable to make an arrest because they did not have enough evidence.*

catch /kætʃ/ [v T] to find a criminal and arrest him or her: *The police caught him just as he was about to get on a plane for South America.* | *The thieves have never been caught.*

investigate /ɪnˈvestɪ̩geɪt/ [v I/T] to try to find out the truth about how a crime happened and who did it: *Police are investigating the incident.*

investigation /ɪn̩vestɪˈgeɪʃən/ [n C] when the police try to find out who committed a crime, for example by asking questions and looking for evidence: *A major police investigation is under way.*

+ into *Los Angeles police are continuing their investigation into a series of armed robberies.*

carry out an investigation (=try to find out about a serious crime, especially using a lot of police officers) *The FBI is carrying out an investigation into the shootings.*

Writing tips

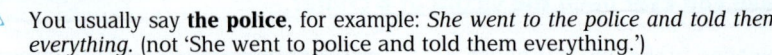

You usually say **the police**, for example: *She went to the police and told them everything.* (not 'She went to police and told them everything.')

However, in news reports, journalists often use **police** on its own without 'the' at the beginning of a sentence, when saying what the police are doing. *Police are hunting for the killer.* | *Police want to hear from anyone who was in the area.*

Police is a plural noun, and needs to be followed by plural verb, for example *The police have been interviewing her husband.* (not 'The police has been interviewing her husband.')

Don't say 'phone to the police' or 'call to the police'. Say **phone the police** or **call the police**.

When talking about a member of the police force, the usual word to use is **police officer**.

If you want to say **policeman** or **policewoman**, don't forget to write this as one word. Don't write 'police man'.

If you want to talk about crimes in general, don't say 'the crime'. Just say **crime**, for example: *Crime is increasing.* (not 'The crime is increasing.')

Also, don't say 'do a crime'. Say **commit a crime**. For example: *Women **commit** fewer crimes.* (not 'Women do fewer crimes.')

---

question /ˈkwestʃən/ [v T] to ask someone questions to find out what they know about a crime, especially someone who may have committed the crime: *He was taken to the police station for questioning.*
question sb about sth *Police questioned him for two days about the missing child.*

take sb in for questioning BRITISH **bring sb in for questioning** AMERICAN /ˌteɪk (sb) ɪn fəʳ ˈkwestʃənɪŋ, ˌbrɪŋ (sb) ɪn fəʳ ˈkwestʃənɪŋ/ to take someone to the police station, because the police think that they have done something illegal and want to get information from them: *The five suspects were taken in for questioning by the police.*

interview /ˈɪntəʳvjuː/ [v T] ESPECIALLY BRITISH to take someone to a police station and ask them questions about a crime, because they may have committed the crime: *Police want to interview him about the murder.*

interrogate /ɪnˈterəgeɪt/ [v T] to ask someone a lot of questions for a long time to find out what they know about a crime or whether they are guilty of a crime, sometimes using threats: *Following his arrest, he was interrogated at City Central police station.*

charge /tʃɑːʳdʒ/ [v T] if the police **charge** someone, they make an official statement saying that they believe that person is guilty of a crime
charge sb with murder/theft/assault etc *Roberts was arrested and charged with murder.*
be charged with doing sth *A 13-year-old boy was charged with attacking a woman.*

charge [n C] the official statement made by the police when they believe someone is guilty of a crime: *He was arrested on a charge of burglary.* | *He faces six charges of theft.*

search /sɜːʳtʃ/ [v T] to look carefully for things such as stolen goods, weapons, drugs, or evidence: *Police used dogs to search the building for any signs of drugs.* | *He was searched by customs officials.*

hunt for sb /ˈhʌnt fəʳ (sb)/ [v T] if the police are hunting for someone, they are trying to find that person, for example because they have committed a crime, or because they have disappeared and might be in danger: *Police are still hunting for the killer.*

hunt [n C usually singular] a search for a criminal or for a person who has disappeared: *Hundreds of local people offered to help in the hunt for the missing girl.*

a murder hunt (=a search for a person who has killed someone)

release /rɪˈliːs/ [v T] if the police **release** someone, they let them go free after they have questioned them in a police station: *Police took in two men for questioning, but released them five hours later.*

release sb on bail (=let someone stay out of prison until they must appear in court, after making them pay an amount of money to the court)

4 the people that the police deal with

criminal /ˈkrɪmɪnəl/ [n C] someone who has done something illegal: *Four dangerous criminals escaped from prison last night.*

petty criminal (=one who commits crimes that are not very serious) *Johnson was a petty criminal, involved in shoplifting and car theft.*

suspect /ˈsʌspekt/ [n C] someone that the police think may have committed a crime: *More than 20 suspects have been questioned.* | *Police are treating the victim's ex-wife as their main suspect.*

victim /ˈvɪktɪm/ [n C] someone who has been attacked, robbed, murdered, or harmed in some way in a crime: *The police believe that the victim knew her attacker.* | *victims of crime*

murder/rape etc victim *Many rape victims do not report the crime.*

witness /ˈwɪtnɪs/ [n C] someone who tells the police or a law court what they know about a crime or the person involved in it: *Police are appealing for witnesses after the death of a 4-year-old boy.*

5 the things that the police deal with

crime /kraɪm/ [n C/U] an action that is illegal, such as stealing something or killing someone, or these actions in general: *Where were you when the crime was committed?*

the scene of the crime (=the place where the crime happened)

incident /ˈɪnsɪdənt/ [n C] something that happens that the police need to deal with, for example because someone has been hurt or because a crime may have been committed: *An officer was badly hurt in the incident.*

evidence /ˈevɪdəns/ [n U] information that helps prove that someone is guilty of a crime

+ that *There is no evidence that he was there when the murder took place.*

collect/gather evidence (=look for and get evidence) *The police are still gathering evidence in the case.*

evidence against sb *There was a lot of evidence against him.*

clue /kluː/ [n C] an object or piece of information that helps the police solve a crime: *They are looking for clues which could help them identify the thieves.*

a vital clue (=a very important clue) *a vital clue in the hunt for the murderer*

case /keɪs/ [n C] an event that the police have to deal with in order to find out whether a crime has been committed or who committed it: *Police are investigating a case of armed robbery.* | *a famous murder case*

6 at a police station

police station /pəˈliːs ˌsteɪʃən/ [n C] the building where the police work, where you go if you want to report a crime, and where people are taken when they are arrested: *The men were taken to Paddington Green Police Station for questioning.*

in custody /ɪn ˈkʌstədi/ if someone is **in custody**, they are being kept in a police station or in prison because the police think they have done something illegal

hold sb in custody (=keep them in a police station or in prison) *A man is being held in custody in connection with the robbery.*

cell /sel/ [n C] a small room in a police station where prisoners are kept: *He had to spend the night in a police cell.*

7 telling the police what you know

report /rɪˈpɔːrt/ [v T] if you **report** a crime, you tell the police that it has happened

report sth to the police *We saw a gang fighting outside a bar, and reported it to the police.*

be helping the police with their inquiries /biː ˌhelpɪŋ ðə pəˈliːs wɪð ðeər ɪnˈkwaɪəriz/ BRITISH if someone **is helping the police with their inquiries,** the police are asking that person questions about a crime, usually because the police think they may have committed the crime – used mainly in news reports: *Police say that two men are helping them with their inquiries.*

SPORT

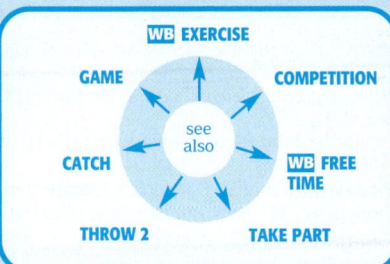

Which sports do you play?

My brother loves sports. When he was in high school he used to **play** a lot of **team games**. He was always the team **captain**. He still plays soccer sometimes on the weekend, and in winter he goes skiing or snowboarding. Recently he's started going to the **gym** three times a week in order to keep in shape.

He also likes watching sports. If there's any sport on the television – the World Series, the Olympics, or even Golf Open Championships – he'll watch it.

I used to hate sport when I was at school. We had to stand around for hours on a cold soccer **pitch**. No one ever wanted me to be on their team, and the team I was on usually lost. I never even liked to watch sport either. A lot of my friends used to go to football **matches** on Saturday afternooons, and I went with them sometimes, but only because I didn't want to feel left out. When I was at university I started **playing tennis**. I know I'm not very good at the **game**, but it's nice to get some exercise.

Vocabulary

1 sport

sport /spɔːʳt/ [n C/U] a physical activity in which people or teams play against each other and try to win: *My favourite sports are basketball and tennis.* | *He loves watching sport on television*

do sport ESPECIALLY BRITISH **play sport** ESPECIALLY AMERICAN *Do you play any sports?* | *I haven't been doing much sport lately.*

sports [adj only before noun] used for sport or connected with sport: *My son belongs to a local sports club.* | *sports equipment* | *Our school sports ground is near the station.*

> ⚠ When talking about sports in general, British people usually say **sport**, and American people usually say **sports**, for example: *He's good at sport.* (British)/ *He's good at sports* (American).

game /geɪm/ [n C] a sport that you play against another player or team, according to a set of rules: *Tennis is a popular game in the summer.*
team game *At school, we played team games such as football and hockey.*

2 an occasion when people compete against each other in a sport

game /geɪm/ [n C] a single occasion when two people or two teams compete against each other in a sport: *Barcelona beat Real Madrid 3–2 in a thrilling game.*
win/lose a game *Who won the game?*
a game of tennis/squash etc *How about a game of tennis this evening?*
a basketball/football etc game *I'm going to watch a volleyball game this Saturday.*
home game (=a game that a team plays at its own sports field) *They have won every home game this season.*
away game (=a game played at an opposing team's sports field)
match /mætʃ/ [n C] ESPECIALLY BRITISH an occasion when two people or two teams compete against each other in a sport: *Are you going to the match tomorrow?*
a football/cricket/boxing match *A cricket match was in progress on the school sports field.*

My first big match

The first **football match** I went to was a few years ago, when a friend gave me a ticket to the FA Cup Final between Arsenal and Liverpool. I had never been to such a big **stadium** before, so it was a new experience for me.

I remember being a bit nervous on the way into the ground because there were so many people everywhere. But once we had found our seats I began to relax and enjoy myself. The atmosphere was really great, and it got even better when the **teams** came out onto the **pitch**.

It turned out to be a good **game**. Both teams played well and there were lots of chances at both ends of the pitch. Arsenal scored first, only 20 minutes from the end, but Michael Owen scored twice in the last ten minutes for Liverpool. The **supporters** went crazy and when the **referee** blew the whistle for the end of the match the noise was incredible. I've been to quite a few matches since then, but none of them has been as exciting as my first Cup Final.

⚠ Don't say 'a match of tennis/football/chess etc'.

⚠ Americans never use **match** to mean a game played by two teams. They only use it for games where one person competes against another or fights with another: *a wrestling match*

race /reɪs/ [n C] a competition in which each competitor tries to run, drive, ride, swim etc faster than all the others: *More than 50 runners took part in the race.*
horse race *The Kentucky Derby is probably the most famous horse race in the US.*

3 to play a sport

play /pleɪ/ [v I/T] to take part in a sport – use this especially about games in which you try to win against another person or team: *Both teams played well.*
play football/tennis/golf/baseball etc *It's a long time since I played hockey.*
play a game (of tennis/soccer etc) *Do you want to play a game of badminton?*

+ **against** *The Rams played against the Giants twice in three weeks.*
playing – played – have played

do /duː/ [v T] use this especially with the names of sports that are not team sports: *He used to do karate, but he gave it up. | I do aerobics twice a week.*
doing – did – have done

go /gəʊ/ [v T] use this about sports whose names end in '-ing'
go climbing/swimming/running/riding etc *John goes running every morning. | I haven't been swimming for months.*
going – went – have gone

4 someone who does a sport

player /ˈpleɪəʳ/ [n C] someone who belongs to a sports team or who regularly does a sport: *One of the Arsenal players was injured.*
baseball/basketball etc player *She's probably the best tennis player in the country.*
sportsman / sportswoman /ˈspɔːʳtsmən, ˈspɔːʳts,wʊmən/ [n C] someone who is very good at sport, especially someone who does it as

Writing tips

 Don't say 'My favourite sports is football'. Say *My favourite sport is football.*

 **You use different verbs when talking about different sports:**

You **play** soccer/golf/tennis/baseball etc. but you **do** karate or judo.
You **go** swimming/running/riding etc (= sports that end with '-ing').

Don't say 'make sport(s)'. Say **play** or **do** sport(s).
*I **played** a lot of **sports** at college.*

 **Don't confuse sport and game.**

Sport includes all kinds of physical activities, for example running, hitting, or kicking a ball, climbing or fishing. Activities that do not involve much physical activity, for example chess or billiards, are **games**, not **sports**.

 **There are several ways of saying that you like a particular team.** You can say:

*I'm a Liverpool **fan**.*
*I **support** Arsenal.* (in British English)
*I'm a Chelsea **supporter**.* (in British English)

---

their job: *A special Olympic village has been built for the sportsmen and sportswomen to live in.*
plural **sportsmen/sportswomen**

athlete /ˈæθliːt/ [n C] someone who is good at sport, especially someone who does athletics (=sports such as running, throwing things, or jumping over high bars): *All athletes now have to be regularly tested for drugs.*

5 groups of people who are involved in sport

team /tiːm/ [n C] a group of people who play together against another group in a sport: *Which team do you think will win?* | *They are the top team in the league this season.*
be in a team BRITISH **be on a team** AMERICAN *We haven't decided who is going to be on the team yet.*

side /saɪd/ [n C] BRITISH one of two teams who are playing against each other: *Both sides played really well in the first half.* | *Our side lost in the final by three goals to two.*

captain /ˈkæptɪ̩n/ [n C] the main player in a team, who tells the other players what to do
+ of *the captain of the England football team*

league /liːɡ/ [n C] a number of teams who play against each other throughout a season to decide which is the best team: *There are 20 teams in the English league.* | *Beckham spent several years playing for Real Madrid in the Spanish league.*

6 a place where you do a sport

field /fiːld/ [n C] a large area of ground, usually covered in grass, where team sports are played: *The crowd cheered as the players ran onto the field.*
baseball/football/sports etc field (=a field where baseball, football etc is played) *The football field was too muddy, so the game was cancelled.*

pitch /pɪtʃ/ [n C] BRITISH a sports field: *The fans rushed onto the pitch at the end of the match.*
cricket/football etc pitch

court /kɔːˈt/ [n C] an area with lines painted on the ground, where two people or teams play a game such as tennis, badminton, basketball, or netball
tennis/basketball/squash etc court *public tennis courts* (=tennis courts that anyone can use without having to join a tennis club)

eisure centre /'leʒəʳ ˌsentəʳ‖'liː-/ [n C] BRITISH a building where you can do various different sports: *There's a really nice swimming pool at the leisure centre.*

gym /dʒɪm/ [n C] a large room where there are machines that you can use to do exercises and make your body stronger: *Are you going to the gym today?*

pool/swimming pool /puːl, 'swɪmɪŋ puːl/ [n C] a place where you can swim, consisting of a large hole in the ground that has been built and filled with water, either outdoors or inside a building: *Every morning, I swim 40 lengths of the pool.* (=swim from one end of the pool to the other 40 times)

stadium /'steɪdiəm/ [n C] a large sports field with seats all around it, where people go to watch team sports: *a baseball stadium*

ground /graund/ [n C] BRITISH a sports field, usually with seats all around it, where the sports of football, cricket, or rugby are played: *Arsenal are building a new football ground in North London*
home ground (=the ground that belongs to the team that regularly plays there)
away ground (=the ground that a team is playing on when it is not at its home ground)

7 someone who watches a sport

spectator /spek'teɪtəʳ‖'spekteɪ-/ [n C] someone who goes to a game and watches people playing a sport: *The stadium can hold over 70,000 spectators.*

fan /fæn/ [n C] someone who likes a particular team or player and often goes to watch them play: *Thousands of fans waited for over six hours to buy tickets.*

supporter /sə'pɔːʳtəʳ/ [n C] BRITISH someone who likes a particular team, especially a football team, and often goes to watch it play: *Supporters have been gathering outside the stadium all afternoon.*
Barcelona/Liverpool etc supporter (=a supporter of Barcelona/Liverpool etc)

support /sə'pɔːʳt/ [v T] BRITISH to like a particular team, and want it to win: *"Which team do you support?" "Oh, Chelsea, of course!"*

8 the person who makes sure that players obey the rules

referee/umpire /ˌrefə'riː, 'ʌmpaɪəʳ/ [n C] the person in charge of a game, who makes sure that the players obey the rules and decides who has won. Football, basketball, hockey, and boxing have a **referee**. Baseball and tennis have an **umpire**, cricket and hockey have two **umpires**: *The referee sent two players off for fighting.*

judges /'dʒʌdʒɪz/ [n plural] the people who decide which person is the best in a competition such as ice-dancing, horse-riding, or gymnastics: *The judges gave her a score of 9.5.*

9 the points you get when you are playing a sport

point /pɔɪnt/ [n C] a unit used for measuring how well you are doing in a sport or game: *Steve Jones is 15 points ahead.* | *Wales beat England by 11 points to 9 in the rugby last week.*
get/score a point *We lost the game when the Giants scored 14 points in the last quarter.*

goal /gəʊl/ [n C] the point you get when you make the ball go into the net in sports such as football or hockey: *There were no goals in the first half.*
score a goal (=get a goal) *Owen scored two goals in the last ten minutes.*

score /skɔːʳ/ [n C] the number of points that the two teams or players have in a game: *What's the score?* | *The final score was 12–18.*

10 when two teams or players have the same score

draw ESPECIALLY BRITISH **tie** ESPECIALLY AMERICAN /drɔː, taɪ/ [n C] when both players or teams have the same number of points at the end of a game: *The game ended in a draw.*

◯ **two all/four all etc** /(two etc) 'ɔːl/ SPOKEN say this when both players or teams have two points, four points etc in a game: *The score is still one all.*

TELEVISION AND RADIO

Is television a good thing or a bad thing?

98% of homes in the US have at least one **television**, and on average Americans watch about four hours every day. **Television** clearly plays an important part in most people's lives, but is this a good or a bad thing?

On the positive side, people use television as a way of entertaining themselves, especially in the evenings after work. After watching a **soap opera** or **reality TV** show, people often like to talk about it with their friends the next day. Television also provides an opportunity to keep up to date with the news, and people can increase their knowledge by watching **documentaries** and **programs** on practical subjects such as cooking.

Unfortunately, television also has many negative effects. It is not healthy for people to spend several hours on the sofa watching the screen. Sometimes people seem more interested in watching the **TV** than talking to their family. A lot of the programs which are **broadcast** are of very poor quality.

Although television can entertain and educate us, we must not let it take over our lives.

Vocabulary

1 television

television/TV /ˈtelɪˌvɪʒən, ˌtelɪˈvɪʒən, ˌtiː ˈviː/ [n U] the system of broadcasting pictures and sound, or the programmes that are broadcast in this way: *Television brings events like the Olympic Games into millions of homes.* | *the educational uses of television*
watch television/TV *She just sits there all day watching television.*
on television/TV (=shown on television) *products that you see advertised on TV*
satellite television/TV (=television programmes that are broadcast using equipment in space, which send the signal back down to earth)
digital television (=television programmes that are broadcast using a digital signal)
television/TV company (=a company that makes television programmes)
television/TV (also **television set** FORMAL) [n C] the box-shaped thing with a glass screen on which you watch programmes: *a wide-screen TV* | *He was sitting in front of the television.*

telly /ˈteli/ [n C/U] BRITISH SPOKEN INFORMAL television: *We've just bought a new telly.*
watch telly *You can watch telly after you've done your homework.*
on telly (=shown on television) *Is there anything good on telly tonight?*
the box /ðə ˈbɒks‖-ˈbɑːks/ [n singular] INFORMAL the television: *All he does is watch the box.*
on the box *What's on the box?*

2 radio

radio /ˈreɪdiəʊ/ [n U] the system of broadcasting sound, or the programmes that are broadcast in this way: *The story was specially written for radio.*
listen to the radio *In the evening, I usually watch TV or listen to the radio.*
on the radio (=broadcast on the radio) *I've often heard that song on the radio, but I can't think what it's called.*
radio [n C] the piece of electronic equipment that you listen to: *We have a radio in every room in the house.*

Is there anything good on the television tonight?

There are lots of good **programmes** on the television this evening. At 7.30, there's 'Coronation Street' on ITV, followed by 'Eastenders' on BBC1 at 8 o'clock. These two **programmes** are the most popular **soap operas** on British television. Later on at 8.30 there's 'Ground Force' on BBC1. 'Ground Force' is a garden **makeover show**, in which a team of gardeners secretly create a new garden for someone while they are away from home. After that, at 9 o'clock, 'Big Brother' is on. 'Big Brother' is a **reality TV** show, in which a group of people are filmed living together 24 hours a day. Lastly 'Newsnight' is on at 10.30 on BBC 2. 'Newsnight' is a **news programme** that deals with the main items of the day's news and has interviews with leading politicians.

But I don't think I'll be watching any of these. For me, the highlight of the evening will be on the **radio**. I'm going to listen to a live concert that's being broadcast from Milan.

---

3   when a programme is broadcast on television or radio

be on /biː ˈɒn‖-ˈɑːn/ if a programme **is on**, you can watch it on television or listen to it on the radio, especially at a particular time: *The Breakfast Show's on between 8 and 10 in the morning.*
be on television/TV/the radio *What's on TV tonight?* | *There's a good play on the radio this evening.*

show /ʃəʊ/ [v T] if a television company **shows** a particular programme, it makes the programme available for people to watch: *Highlights of the game will be shown on Channel 5.* | *They're showing a James Bond film on Saturday afternoon.*
showing – showed – have shown

broadcast /ˈbrɔːdkɑːst‖-kæst/ [v T usually passive] if a television or radio company **broadcasts** a programme, they send it out so that people can watch it on television or listen to it on the radio: *The funeral was broadcast to the whole nation.*
be broadcast live (=when an event is shown at the same time that it is happening) *The race will*

be broadcast live from Monza.
broadcasting – broadcast – have broadcast

> **Formal or informal?**
> **Broadcast** is more formal than **show**.

4   a television or radio programme

programme BRITISH   **program** AMERICAN /ˈprəʊɡræm/ [n C] a play, show, discussion etc that you can watch on television or listen to on the radio: *'The Simpsons' is one of my favourite programs.*
+ on/about *Programmes on gardening are very popular.*
TV/radio programme *a guide to this week's TV programs*
news/comedy programme
wildlife programme BRITISH
nature program AMERICAN (=a programme about wild animals or plants)

show /ʃəʊ/ [n C] a programme on television or the radio, that is intended to be entertaining or funny: *Good evening and welcome to the show.* |

Writing tips

 You usually say watch television, for example: *We stayed at home and **watched television** all evening.*

If you want to talk about watching a particular programme in the past, you can use **see** instead of **watch**, for example:
*Did you **see** the news last night?*
*Have you **seen** his new show?*

Don't say 'look at the television'.

 You usually say listen to the radio, for example: *I often **listen to** the radio when I'm driving home from work.*

If you want to talk about listening to a particular programme in the past, you use **hear**, for example:
*I **heard** a really good programme on the radio last night.*

Don't say 'listen the radio'.

 You say that a programme is on television or on the radio, for example: *There are too many sports programmes on television.*

Don't say 'in television' in this meaning.

 You can say that someone works in television (but not 'in TV'), meaning that they work for a television company, for example: *Lots of people want to **work in television** these days.*

 When talking about changing to another channel on the television, American people usually say change the channel, but British people often say turn over or switch over, for example: *Is it all right if I **turn over**?*

---

the Richard and Judy Show | She was in several TV shows in the 90s.

game/quiz show (=a show in which people play games and answer questions in order to win prizes)

talk/chat show (=a show in which famous people talk about themselves and answer questions about their lives, opinions etc)

morning/breakfast show (=a show that is broadcast early in the morning, which includes news and conversations with famous people)

makeover show (=a show in which designers decorate someone's house or change their garden, so that it looks completely different)

broadcast /'brɔːdkɑːst‖-kæst/ [n C] something that is broadcast on the radio or on television, especially a speech, discussion, or news programme: *The government banned all broadcasts by opposition parties.* | *In a nationwide TV broadcast, the President explained why the country was going to war.*

the news /ðə 'njuːz‖-'nuːz/ [n singular] a programme that is broadcast several times each day, which tells you about all the important events

that are happening in the world
on the news *His death was announced on the 6 o'clock news.*

the weather/the weather forecast /ðə 'weðə^r, ðə 'weðə^r ˌfɔː^rkɑːst‖-kæst/ [n singular] a short programme that tells you what the weather will be like

documentary /ˌdɒkjɔ'mentəri‖ˌdɑːk-/ [n C] a programme that gives you facts and information about a serious subject, such as history, science, or social problems

plural **documentaries**

soap opera/soap /'səup ˌɒpərə, səup‖-ˌɑːp-/ [n C] a television or radio story about a group of imaginary people and their lives, which is broadcast regularly for many years

sitcom /'sɪtkɒm‖-kɑːm/ [n C] an amusing programme in which there is a different story each week about the same group of people: *popular American sitcoms like 'Friends'*

drama /'drɑːmə‖'drɑːmə, 'dræmə/ [n C] an exciting but serious play on radio or television
radio/television/TV drama *a TV drama about drug-trafficking*

a police/hospital drama *an exciting police drama starring Helen Mirren*

cartoon /kɑːˈrtuːn/ [n C] a film, especially a story for children, that is made by photographing a series of drawings of people, animals etc, so that they seem to move: *The kids always watch cartoons on Saturday mornings.*

reality TV /riˌælˑti tiː ˈviː/ [n U] programmes that show real people in different situations and which do not use professional actors

phone-in (also **call-in/talk show** AMERICAN) /ˈfəʊn ɪn, ˈkɔːl ɪn, ˈtɔːk ʃəʊ/ [n C] a programme, especially on the radio, in which people telephone the programme in order to give their opinions or ask a famous person questions

5 a number of programmes about the same subject, the same people etc

series /ˈsɪəriːz/ [n C] a set of separate programmes, each of which tells the next part of a story, or deals with the same subject: *a series about the Russian Revolution* | *A new comedy series is starting next Wednesday.*

serial ESPECIALLY BRITISH **miniseries** AMERICAN /ˈsɪəriəl, ˈmɪniˌsɪriz/ [n C] a story that is broadcast in several separate parts

episode /ˈepɪˌsəʊd/ [n C] one of the parts of a story that is being broadcast in several separate parts

6 an organization that broadcasts programmes

station /ˈsteɪʃən/ [n C] an organization that broadcasts television or radio programmes: *What station are you listening to?*
television/TV/radio station *a local radio station*

channel /ˈtʃænl/ [n C] a particular set of programmes that is broadcast by one televison company; there are usually several different channels, and you can choose which one you want to watch: *the sports channel on satellite TV* | *The final episode will be shown on Channel 4 tonight.*
change channel/switch over to another channel *This is boring. Do you mind if I switch over to another channel?*

network /ˈnetwɜːrk/ [n C] a group of television or radio stations owned by the same company, which broadcasts the same programmes to different parts of a country: *The show was first broadcast on the ABC network.* | *CNN stands for 'Cable News Network'.*

the media /ðə ˈmiːdiə/ [n singular] all the organizations that provide information to the public, including television, radio, and newspapers: *The event got little attention in the media.*

7 the people on television or radio

presenter BRITISH **announcer** AMERICAN /prɪˈzentəʳ, əˈnaʊnsəʳ/ [n C] someone on a TV or radio programme who tells you what the programme will be about, and introduces the other people in it

host /həʊst/ [n C] someone who introduces the people on a TV or radio show, especially a game show or quiz show

newsreader BRITISH **anchor** AMERICAN /ˈnjuːzˌriːdəʳ, ˈæŋkəʳǁˈnuːz-/ [n C] someone who reads the news on TV or radio, and introduces news reports

commentator /ˈkɒmənteɪtəʳǁˈkɑːm-/ [n C] someone on television or radio who describes an event as it is happening, especially a sports game

DJ /ˈdiː dʒeɪ/ [n C] someone who plays records and talks to people on a music programme on the radio

contestant /kənˈtestənt/ [n C] a person who takes part in a competition on TV or the radio

guest /gest/ [n C] a famous person who is invited to appear on a show for just one programme

8 someone who watches television or listens to the radio

viewer /ˈvjuːəʳ/ [n C] someone who watches television – used especially by people in the television business: *a programme that appeals to younger viewers*

listener /ˈlɪsənəʳ/ [n C] someone who listens to the radio

THEATRE/PLAYS

The world's longest running play

Agatha Christie's famous **thriller** 'The Mousetrap' is the longest running **play** in the world. Since it first opened in 1952 there have been over 20,000 **performances**, and over 10 million people have been to see it. The play has been translated into 24 different languages and shown in 44 different countries.

In the play, eight people are staying at a hotel. One of the guests is murdered, and the detective questions each of the other guests to find out who was responsible for the murder. After every performance, audiences are always asked not to tell anyone who the murderer is.

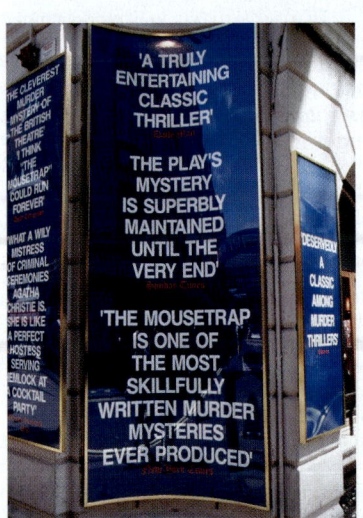

Vocabulary

1 a place where you go to watch plays

theatre ESPECIALLY BRITISH **theater** AMERICAN /ˈθɪətəʳ/ [n C] *The Old Vic is one of the oldest theatres in London.*
go to the theatre/theater (=go to a theatre to see a play) *We're going to the theatre on Saturday night.*
the house /ðə ˈhaʊs/ [n singular] the area in a theatre that contains the people who are watching the play: *They had the best seats in the house.*
full house *The show has been playing to full houses.*

2 the plays that are performed in the theatre

play /pleɪ/ [n C] a story that is written to be performed by actors in a theatre, or on the television or radio: *'The Cherry Orchard' is a famous play by Anton Chekhov.*
see a play *Have you seen the new play that's on at the Aldwych?*

a Shakespeare play/a Brecht play etc (=a play written by Shakespeare, Brecht etc)
drama /ˈdrɑːmə‖ˈdrɑːmə, ˈdræmə/ [n U] plays in general – use this especially to talk about plays as a form of literature: *Greek drama has had a big influence on modern playwrights.* | *a course in 20th century American drama*
the theatre ESPECIALLY BRITISH **the theater** AMERICAN /ðə ˈθɪətəʳ/ [n singular] plays and shows in general as a form of entertainment – use this to talk about the work of acting in plays, writing plays etc: *a Hollywood actor who began his career in the theater* | *a play on TV which was originally written for the theatre*
production /prəˈdʌkʃən/ [n C] a play, opera, or show that is produced by a director and performed in a theatre: *There's a new production of 'Private Lives' at the Apollo Theater.*
performance /pəˈfɔːʳməns/ [n C] an occasion when a play is performed: *The evening performance starts at 7.30.*
the first night /ðə ˌfɜːʳst ˈnaɪt/ [n singular] the first evening when a play is performed: *We went to see the play on the first night.*

Going to the theatre

On my birthday I went to the **theatre** with my family. We went to see the **musical** 'Les Miserables'. As it was a special occasion, we had some of the best seats in the **house**, and there was a great feeling of excitement while we were waiting for the **curtain** to go up.

'Les Miserables' is based on the novel by the French author Victor Hugo and is set in early 19th century France. It's about one man's struggle to survive in the most terrible circumstances. The **acting**, music and singing were fantastic, and there were some really memorable moments.

A review of a play – Shakespeare's 'Othello'

A new **production** of Shakespeare's famous **tragedy** 'Othello' is now on at the National Theatre in London. The play is a classic tale of love, envy, and jealousy. The play is **directed** by Sam Mendes and stars David Harewood as Othello and Simon Russell Beale as Iago.

In the play, Iago tries to makes Othello think that his beautiful wife Desdemona has betrayed him. The story ends in madness and murder. Simon Russell Beale gives a brilliant **performance** as Iago, and Claire Skinner is also very impressive as Desdemona.

---

3 types of play

comedy /'kɒmədi‖'kɑː-/ [n C/U] a play that is intended to make you laugh: *a comedy starring Julie Walters and Bob Hoskins*

tragedy /'trædʒədi/ [n C/U] a serious play that deals with the bad, violent, or harmful side of human nature, and usually ends with the death of the main character

musical /'mjuːzɪkəl/ [n C] a play in which the characters speak, sing, and dance to tell a story: *Andrew Lloyd Webber's musical 'Cats'*

thriller /'θrɪlər/ [n C] a play about a crime, and about how the police catch the person who committed it. Usually, the audience have to guess who did it because the identity of the criminal is not revealed until the very end.

opera /'ɒpərə‖'ɑːp-/ [n C] a play in which all the words are sung: *I'm going to see Verdi's opera 'La Traviata'.*

  opera singer *Luciano Pavarotti, the Italian opera singer*

show /ʃəʊ/ [n C] a performance in a theatre, especially one that includes singing and dancing or comedy: *The show was a big hit on Broadway.*

4 people involved in plays

actor /'æktər/ [n C] someone who acts in a play

actress /'æktrɪs/ [n C] a woman who acts in a play

> ⚠ You can use **actor** about a man or woman. Some women prefer to be called **actors** and do not like the word **actress**.

cast /kɑːst‖kæst/ [n singular] all the actors who act in a play: *After the play, there was a big party for the cast.*

director /dɪ'rektər, daɪ-/ [n C] the person who is in charge of a play, and who tells the actors what to do

playwright/dramatist /'pleɪraɪt, 'dræmətɪst/ [n C] someone who writes plays: *Ben Jonson was a 17th-century playwright.*

5 to perform in a play

act /ækt/ [v I/T] to perform in a play, especially as a job: *He really can't act.*

  well/badly acted (=well/badly performed by the actors) *I thought the play was very well acted.*

Writing tips

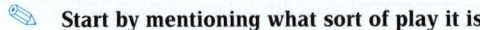

Start by mentioning what sort of play it is:

*The play is a **comedy/tragedy/thriller**.*
*We went to see the **musical** 'Les Miserables'.*

Say who is in the play, or who directs it, for example:

*David Harewood **stars as** Othello.* | *The play **stars** David Harewood **as** Othello.*
*Simon Russell Beale **plays** Iago.* | ***The part of** Iago **is played by** Simon Russell Beale.*
*The play **is directed by** Sam Mendes.*

Give the play's background:

*The play **is based on/adapted from** the novel by Victor Hugo.*
*It **is set in** France/in Chicago/in the 1920s.*

Give a brief summary of the story and the ideas in the play:

***In the play**, eight people are staying at a hotel…*
*The play **is about** one man's struggle to survive.*
*The play **is a classic tale of** love, envy and jealousy.*
***The main theme** of the play **is** the power of love.*

Say what you liked or disliked:

> *The **acting** was very good.*
> *I loved the **music**.*
> *It was very **well written**.*

> *The **plot** was a bit dull.*
> *I didn't think it was very **well acted**.*
> *I didn't find the **characters** very convincing.*
> *The first half was better than the second.*

---

acting [n U] the work or skill of performing in plays: *The acting was really good.* | *She has done some acting, but is best known as a model.*

play /pleɪ/ [v T] to say the words and do the actions of a particular character in a play: *She is currently playing Ophelia in a new production of 'Hamlet'.*
play the part of sb *I once played the part of Stella in 'A Streetcar Named Desire'.*

be in/appear in/perform in /biː ɪn, əˈpɪər ɪn, pərˈfɔːrm ɪn/ if someone **is in** a play or **appears in** or **performs in** a play, they act as one of the characters in it: *Ian Shaw is currently appearing in "Absent Friends" at the Mill Theatre.*

rehearse /rɪˈhɜːrs/ [v I/T] if actors **rehearse**, or **rehearse** a play, they practise their words and actions so they will be ready to perform: *The cast has been rehearsing all summer.*

rehearsal [n C] when actors practise what they must say and do in a play: *We're having our first rehearsal tonight.*

dress rehearsal (=a rehearsal when the actors wear the clothes that they will have to wear in the actual performance)

direct /dɪˈrekt, daɪ-/ [v I/T] to be in charge of a play and tell the actors what to do: *a famous production of 'A Midsummer Night's Dream', directed by Peter Hall*

performance /pəˈˈfɔːˈməns/ [n C] the way in which an actor plays his or her part in a play – use this especially to say how good or bad the acting is

give a powerful/stunning/magnificent performance *Julia Hunt gives a magnificent performance as Amelia, the daughter.*

audition /ɔːˈdɪʃən/ [v I] to give a short performance, usually in front of a play's director, in order to try and get a part in a play

+ for *I've auditioned for a part in 'Hamlet'.*

audition [n C] when people give a short performance in order to try to get a part in a play: *She passed the audition.* (=she was successful, and was given the part in the play)

drama /ˈdrɑːmə‖ˈdrɑːmə, ˈdræ-/ [n U] acting in general – use this when you are talking about it as an activity that people take part in: *One of my main hobbies is drama.* | *There are plenty of opportunities for drama at the school.*

6 the person that an actor pretends to be in a play

character /ˈkærˌktəˈ/ [n C] a person in the story of a play: *Many of the characters in O'Neill's plays are based on his own family.*

main character *The main character is Jerome, a poor writer living in Brooklyn.*

part /pɑːˈt/ [n C] the words and actions of one of the characters in a play: *Hamlet is the part that every young actor dreams of.*

play the part of sb *He played the part of Thomas More in 'A Man for All Seasons'.*

role /rəʊl/ [n C] a character played by an actor in a play: *It's a very difficult role to play.*

the lead role (=the most important part) *Who is in the lead role?*

7 what happens in a play

plot /plɒt‖plɑːt/ [n C] the events that happen in a play, and the way in which these events are connected: *The play has a complicated plot.*

act /ækt/ [n C] one of the main parts that a long play is divided into. An **act** is usually divided into several scenes: *The main character doesn't appear until the second act.* | *In Act 1, Macbeth decides to kill the king.*

scene /siːn/ [n C] a short part of a play in which the events all happen in one place: *The queen dies in Act 5, Scene 6.*

the opening scene/closing scene (=the first/last scene)

ending /ˈendɪŋ/ [n C] what happens at the end of a play: *a happy ending*

8 areas, objects, clothes etc that are used in the theatre

stage /steɪdʒ/ [n C/U] the raised area in a theatre which actors and singers stand on when they perform: *He walked across the stage.*

on stage (=acting on a stage) *She has a big part and is on stage for most of the show.*

scenery /ˈsiːnəri/ [n C] the wooden or cloth surfaces at the back and sides of the stage, which are painted to look like a house, garden, castle etc

the curtain /ðə ˈkɜːˈtn/ [n singular] the very large heavy piece of material that goes up or comes down at the front of a stage in a theatre at the start or end of a performance

the curtain goes up/comes down *The curtain went up and the actors came onto the stage.* | *The audience clapped and cheered as the curtain came down.*

costume /ˈkɒstjuːm‖ˈkɑːstuːm/ [n C] the clothes worn by an actor in a play

prop /prɒp‖prɑːp/ [n C] an object or piece of furniture that is used on the stage in a play

lighting /ˈlaɪtɪŋ/ [n U] the way that lights are used to light the stage and the actors in a theatre

set /set/ [n C] the whole appearance of the stage, including the scenery, the lighting, and the way things are arranged on the stage

9 the words of a play

script /skrɪpt/ [n C] the written words of a play

sb's lines /(sb's) laɪnz/ all the words that an actor has to say when he or she is playing a particular part in a play

learn your lines (=look at them for a long time until you can remember them all)

10 describing what happens in a play

be about /biː əˈbaʊt/ [phrasal verb T] if a play **is about** a person, idea, or set of events, that is the main subject of the play: *The play is about a group of kids living in Harlem.*

be set in /biː ˈset ɪn/ if a play **is set in** a place or period of time, the story happens in that place or during that time: *The play is set in South Carolina right after the Civil War.*

theme /θiːm/ [n C] one of the main ideas in a play, which the writer develops though the words and actions of the actors: *The main theme of 'Hamlet' is revenge.*

FREE TIME

DANCE

WB EXERCISE   WB SPORT

ART   WB THEATRE/PLAYS

see also

WB TELEVISION AND RADIO   WB MUSIC

WB FILMS/MOVIES   PARTY

RESTAURANTS/EATING AND DRINKING

What you do in your free time?

I don't have a lot of energy when I get home after work. Usually I just **stay in** and **watch TV** or **surf the net**. I like watching soap operas and I never miss an episode of my favourite programmes. If there's nothing on TV then I might **call** some of **my friends** for a chat. I don't **go out** very much and I'd much rather spend time at home.

I like cooking and trying out new recipes. Sometimes I'll **have friends over** for a dinner party, but I'm quite happy just relaxing in the house with a good book.

Vocabulary

1 staying at home

stay in BRITISH **stay home** AMERICAN /ˌsteɪ ˈɪn, ˌsteɪ hoʊm/ [phrasal verb I] to stay at home and not go out: *Do you want to go and see a movie tonight, or shall we stay in?* | *I usually stay in during the week, and go out on Saturday night.*

watch television/TV /ˌwɒtʃ ˈtelᵻvɪʒən, tiː ˈviːȴ, ˌwɑːtʃ-/ *"Did you go out last night?" "No, we stayed in and watched TV."*

listen to music /ˌlɪsən tə ˈmjuːzɪk/ *Sometimes I like to just sit in my room and listen to music.*

play computer games /ˌpleɪ kəmˈpjuːtər ˌɡeɪmz/ *"Where's Fran?" "She's up in her room playing computer games."*

read /riːd/ [v I/T] *I spend a lot of my free time reading.* | *She enjoys reading science fiction novels.*

surf the net /ˌsɜːrf ðə ˈnet/ to spend time looking at websites on the Internet for fun: *He usually spends his evenings surfing the net.*

download music/movies etc off the net /ˌdaʊnloʊd (music, etc) ɒf ðə ˈnet/ to get music, movies etc from the Internet using your computer: *I download a lot of music off the net so that I can listen to it later on my personal stereo.*

get a video/DVD /ˌget ə ˈvɪdiəʊ, ˌdiː viː ˈdiː/ to rent a film to watch on your own television: *Let's get a video. How about that new Johnny Depp movie?*

get a takeaway BRITISH **get takeout** AMERICAN /ˌget ə ˈteɪkəweɪ, ˌget ˈteɪkaʊt/ to buy food from a restaurant and take it home to eat: *I don't feel like cooking tonight. Let's get a takeaway.*

call your friends /ˌkɔːl jɔːr ˈfrendz/ to phone your friends and talk to them: *I like to call my friends in the evening, and catch up on all the latest gossip.*

2 going out to the cinema, a restaurant etc

go out /ˌɡəʊ ˈaʊt/ [phrasal verb I] to go out of your house and go to a restaurant, cinema, club etc: *"Did you go out last night?" "Yeah, we went to that new Mexican restaurant on 4th Avenue."*

go out to dinner/lunch (also **go out for a meal** BRITISH) /ɡəʊ ˌaʊt tə ˈdɪnər, ˈlʌntʃ, ɡəʊ ˌaʊt fər ə ˈmiːl/ to go to a restaurant and have a meal: *It was Mike's birthday, so we all went out to dinner.*

I like to **go out** and have a good time. After dinner, I usually **go to a bar** and **hang out with my friends** till 3 or 4 in the morning.

I also love **going to the movies**. If I'm in town at the weekend, I might **go to a café** with the Sunday papers, then see an exhibition or **go to a concert** in the park.

I like to keep in shape. I usually go to the gym three or four times a week. On Saturdays I often **meet up with some friends** for a game of football in the park.

When I'm on holiday, I like **going skiing** in the winter, or windsurfing in the summer. I hate being stuck at home all day – I'd rather be outdoors.

go to the cinema BRITISH **go to the movies** AMERICAN /ˌɡəʊ tə ðə ˈsɪnᵻmə, ˌɡəʊ tə ðə ˈmuːviːz/ to go and watch a film: *Do you want to go to the movies tonight?* | *We haven't been to the cinema for ages.*

go to a concert /ˌɡəʊ tʊ ə ˈkɒnsəʳt‖-ˈkɑːn-/ to go to listen to people playing music: *On Saturday, we're going to a concert of modern African music.*

go clubbing BRITISH **go to a club** /ɡəʊ ˈklʌbɪŋ, ˌɡəʊ tʊ ə ˈklʌb/ to go to a place where you can dance and drink until late at night: *Michelle always goes clubbing on Friday night.*

go to a cafe/a bar/the pub /ˌɡəʊ tʊ ə ˈkæfeɪ, ə ˈbɑːʳ, ðə ˈpʌb‖-kæˈfeɪ/ to go to a place where you can drink and talk to your friends: *On Friday we usually go to a bar after work.*

go to the theatre BRITISH **go to the theater** AMERICAN /ˌɡəʊ tə ðə ˈθɪətəʳ/ to go and watch a play being performed: *I haven't been to the theater in a long time.*

go shopping /ˌɡəʊ ˈʃɒpɪŋ‖-ˈʃɑːp-/ *We went shopping in Oxford Street.*

3 **doing outdoor activities**

go to the beach /ˌɡəʊ tə ðə ˈbiːtʃ/ *In the summer, I go to the beach every day.*

have a picnic /ˌhæv ə ˈpɪknɪk/ to take a meal to a park or the countryside to eat it: *If the weather's nice we could have a picnic.*

go to the park /ˌɡəʊ tə ðə ˈpɑːʳk/ *Jo and Tim are going to the park to play tennis.*

go for a walk /ˌɡəʊ fər ə ˈwɔːk/ to walk in a nice place for fun: *Why don't we go for a walk? It's a beautiful day.*

go for a run /ˌɡəʊ fər ə ˈrʌn/ to run somewhere, for fun or in order to get exercise: *I think I'll go for a run before it gets dark.*

take the dog for a walk /teɪk ðə ˈdɒg fər ə ˌwɔːk‖-ˈdɔːg-/ to walk somewhere with your dog, in order to exercise it: *"Where's Nick?" "He's taking the dog for a walk."*

go skiing/jogging/skateboarding etc *On Sundays I often go skateboarding with my friends.* | *We went rollerblading in Central Park.* | *I love going skiing.*

4 **spending time with your friends**

have friends over (also **have friends round** BRITISH) /hæv ˈfrendz ˌəʊvəʳ, hæv ˈfrendz ˌraʊnd/ if you have **friends over** or **round**, they come to your house because you have invited

Writing tips

 there are many different ways of saying "I like something"

> *I love* classical music
> (=I like it very much)
> *I'm fond of* her books.
> (=I've liked them for a long time and always like to read them.)

> **in an informal letter to a friend**
> *I'm crazy/mad about* soccer.
> (=I like it very much)
> *I'm into* jazz.
> (=I'm interested in it)

You can say 'My hobbies are ...' or 'My interests are ...'., but it sounds much more enthusiastic to say *I love* or *I'm really into* something. (informal)

Try to give examples and say more about what kinds of things you like. If you say you like movies, mention your favourite movie, actor, or director, and say why you like them.

Instead of saying 'I prefer...', you can say *I'd much rather* go out *than* stay at home.

If you want to suggest an example of something that you sometimes do, depending on the day, you can say *I might ...* For example:

If I'm free, I might go to the park, or I might take the dog for a walk.
I'd much rather go out than stay at home.

---

them: *We had some friends over for dinner on Friday. Sam cooked lasagne.*
go over to sb's house (also **go round to sb's house** BRITISH) /ɡəʊ ˌəʊvəʳ tə (sb's) ˈhaʊs, ɡəʊ ˌraʊnd tə (sb's) ˈhaʊs/ *We're going over to Peter's house this evening – do you want to come?*
have a party /ˌhæv ə ˈpɑːʳti/ *Steve's having a party on Saturday.*
have a barbecue /ˌhæv ə ˈbɑːʳbɪkjuː/ to have a party where you cook food outside on a special grill: *It was a warm evening, so we decided to have a barbecue.*
meet up with sb /ˌmiːt ˈʌp wɪð (sb)/ [phrasal verb T] to meet someone, at a time and place that you arranged before, so that you can do something together: *I met up with Jan and Peter outside McDonald's, and we all went shopping.*
go out with your boyfriend/girlfriend /ɡəʊ ˌaʊt wɪð jɔːʳ ˈbɔɪfrend, ˈgɜːʳlfrend/ to spend time with someone that you have a romantic relationship with: *"Is Sylvia coming tonight?" "No, she's going out with her new boyfriend."*

hang out with sb /hæŋ ˈaʊt wɪð (sb)/ [phrasal verb T] INFORMAL to spend time somewhere with your friends, not doing very much: *"What did you do today?" "Oh, I just hung out with some friends."*

5 talking about when you do things in your free time

In the evening /ɪn ði ˈiːvnɪŋ/ *In the evening, Mario usually hangs out with his friends.*
at weekends BRITISH **on weekends** AMERICAN /ət wiːkˈendz, ɒn ˈwiːkendz/ *At weekends I usually spend time relaxing in front of the TV.* | *Ben plays football on weekends.*
on Mondays/Fridays etc *On Thursdays I have my dance class.* | *We usually go to the movies on Saturdays.*
when I'm not studying/working /ˌwen aɪm nɒt ˈstʌdiɪŋ, ˈwɜːʳkɪŋ/ : *When I'm not studying, I like going for long walks with my dog.*
whenever I get the time /wenˌevər aɪ get ðə ˈtaɪm/ *Whenever they get the time, they go climbing.* | *I go to the gym whenever I get the time.*

COURT/TRIAL

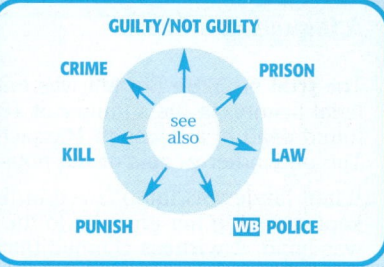

GUILTY/NOT GUILTY

CRIME   PRISON

see also

KILL   LAW

PUNISH   WB POLICE

What happens at a trial

If someone is arrested by the police and **charged** with a crime, they have to go to **court** and **stand trial**. The person who is on trial is called the **defendant**, and the trial takes place in a **courtroom**.

The defendant **pleads** either **guilty** or **not guilty**. The **prosecution** tries to prove that the defendant is guilty, and they can call **witnesses** to **give evidence against** the defendant. The defendant is represented by lawyers who are known as the **defence**, who can also call witnesses to give evidence.

The **jury** listens to all the evidence. If they are sure beyond reasonable doubt that the defendant committed the crime, they give a **verdict** of **guilty**. If they are not sure, or if they think the defendant definitely did not commit the crime, then they give a verdict of **not guilty**.

If the defendant is found guilty, the judge **passes sentence**.

Vocabulary

1 the place where crimes are judged

court /kɔːʳt/ [n C/U] a building or room where all the information concerning a crime or legal problem is publicly and officially given, so that it can be legally judged: *The court was packed.* | *Silence in court!* | *the US Supreme Court*
appear in court (=be in a court because the police think you have committed a crime or know something about a crime) *Three men appeared in court yesterday on charges of armed robbery.*
go to court (=officially ask to have a legal problem dealt with by a judge or jury in a court) *She was prepared to go to court to prove that she was unfairly dismissed from her job.*
courtroom /ˈkɔːʳtruːm, -rʊm/ [n C usually singular] the room where a trial takes place: *A group of photographers had gathered outside the courtroom.*

2 the process that takes place in a court

trial /ˈtraɪəl/ [n C] an official process in a law

court, in which people try to prove that someone is guilty of a crime
a trial is held/a trial takes place *The trial will be held next week at the Central Criminal Court.*
be on trial for sth (=if someone is on trial for a crime, a court tries to decide if they are guilty of the crime) *Jones is on trial for murder.*
stand trial (=to have to go to a trial) *Her lawyer said that she wasn't fit to stand trial.*
case (also **court case**) /keɪs, ˈkɔːʳt keɪs/ [n C] a crime or legal problem that is judged in court
win/lose your case *The men lost their case in the high court.*
murder/robbery etc case *The murder was one of the most famous cases in American legal history.*
hear a case (=if a court hears a case, they listen to the arguments and decide if someone is guilty or not)
inquest /ˈɪŋkwest/ [n C] a legal process to find out the cause of someone's death
+ into *The inquest into her death will be held next week.*

A famous court case

The **trial** of Lizzie Borden was one of the most famous cases in American legal history. In the summer of 1892, Lizzie's father and stepmother were found dead in a house in Massachusetts. They had been killed with an axe. The only other people at the house at the time were Lizzie and the maid.

When Lizzie was interviewed at the **inquest** into her parents' deaths, she kept changing her answers to the questions, and many people thought she was lying. A **witness** claimed that she saw Lizzie burning a dress three days after the murder. Lizzie said that it had paint stains on it. A local shopkeeper told the police that Lizzie had been to his shop on the day before the murder, to buy some poison.

After the **inquest**, Lizzie was arrested and charged with murdering her parents. At her **trial**, the **prosecution** said that Lizzie did not like her stepmother, and she was worried that her father was going to give her stepmother all his money, and this was why she killed them. The **defence** claimed that a mysterious stranger who was owed money might have committed the crime, and that there was no **hard evidence** that Lizzie was the murderer.

The **prosecution** asked for a **death sentence**, and for Lizzie to be executed using the electric chair, which was a new invention at the time. The **jury** took just over an hour to reach their **verdict**, which was "**not guilty**".

---

3 the people in court

judge /dʒʌdʒ/ [n C] the person in charge of a court, who knows a lot about the law, and who makes the official decision about what the punishment for a crime should be: *Everyone stood up as the judge entered the courtroom.* | *Judge Butler gave the defendant a six-month jail sentence.*

your honour BRITISH **your honor** AMERICAN /jɔːr ˈɒnərǁ-ˈɑːn-/ the official name that people use in a court when they speak to the judge

jury /ˈdʒʊəri/ [n C] a group of (usually 12) ordinary people, who listen to all the evidence about a crime, and then decide whether or not someone is guilty: *The jury was made up of seven women and five men.* | *Have you ever been on a jury?*

the court /ðə ˈkɔːrt/ [n singular] all the people in a court: *He told the court that he knew nothing about the murder.* | *The court listened in silence.*

lawyer (also **attorney** AMERICAN) /ˈlɔːjərǂ, əˈtɜːrni/ [n C] someone who is trained in the law and who represents people in court: *Everyone has the right to be represented in court by a lawyer.* | *You have to study for a long time to become a lawyer.*

defendant /dɪˈfendənt/ [n C] the person in a court who has been charged with a crime and is trying to prove that he or she did not do it: *The defendant pleaded not guilty.*

the defence BRITISH **the defense** AMERICAN /ðə dɪˈfens/ the lawyers in a court who try to show that someone is not guilty of a crime
   defence lawyer/defense lawyer (=one of the members of the defence)

the prosecution /ðə ˌprɒsɪˈkjuːʃənǁ-ˌprɑː-/ the lawyers in a court who try to prove that someone is guilty of a crime

witness /ˈwɪtnɪs/ [n C] someone who knows something about a crime, and tells the court what they know: *Would the first witness please stand up?*
   call a witness (=officially ask a witness to answer questions about a crime in a court)

4 what happens at a trial

charge /tʃɑːrdʒ/ [v T] if the police charge someone with a crime, they tell that person that they believe he or she is guilty of a crime, and that the person must appear in court so that it can be decided whether they are guilty or not

charge sb with murder/rape/theft etc *No-one has yet been charged with the murder.* | *Police have charged three men with assault.*

represent /ˌreprɪˈzent/ [v T] if a lawyer **represents** someone in a trial, they speak for that person, question witnesses for them, and try to persuade the court that they are right: *He will be represented by one of America's top attorneys.*

plead guilty/plead not guilty /ˌpliːd ˈgɪlti, ˌpliːd nɒt ˈgɪlti/ if a defendant **pleads guilty** or **not guilty**, they officially tell the court at the beginning of a trial that they did or did not commit a crime: *"How does the defendant plead?" "Not guilty, your honor."* | *If you plead guilty you might get a lighter sentence.* (=a punishment that is not as severe)

prove /pruːv/ [v T] to show that something is definitely true, so that there is no doubt
+that *The prosecution will have to prove that he was there at the time the crime was committed.*
prove a case *They failed to prove their case.*

evidence /ˈevɪdəns/ [n U] all the information, objects, documents etc that are used in a law court to help to prove what really happened during a crime
give evidence (=tell a court what you know about a crime or the people involved in it) *His former girlfriend was called to give evidence.*
give evidence against sb (=tell the court things that help to prove someone is guilty) *Husbands and wives cannot be forced to give evidence against each other.*
listen to/hear the evidence *The judges have heard all the evidence relating to the case.*
piece of evidence *The most important piece of evidence, the murder weapon, had not been found.*
hard evidence (=evidence that makes you sure about something) *There is no hard evidence against him.*

guilty /ˈgɪlti/ [adj] someone who is guilty of a crime committed that crime: *Do you think she's guilty?*

+ of *West was guilty of several robberies.*

not guilty *He said that he was not guilty of any offence.*

find sb guilty/not guilty (=when a court officially decides that someone has or has not committed a crime) *She was found guilty of attempted murder.*

innocent /ˈɪnəsənt/ [adj] someone who is innocent of a crime did not commit that crime: *Throughout their time in jail, the six men always insisted that they were innocent.*

verdict /ˈvɜːˈdɪkt/ [n C] the decision that the jury makes about whether someone is guilty of a crime or not: *What was the jury's verdict? Guilty or not guilty?*
return a verdict (=officially say whether someone is guilty or not) *The jury returned a verdict of not guilty.*

sentence /ˈsentəns/ [v T] if a judge sentences someone, he or she says what the punishment for their crime will be
sentence sb to sth *Campbell was sentenced to 42 days in jail.* | *The judge sentenced him to 100 days' community service.* (=when you have to do something that will help the people in your local area)

sentence /ˈsentəns/ [n C] the official punishment that someone is given by a judge when a court decides that they are guilty of a crime, especially a period of time in prison
a 7-year/6-month etc sentence (=when someone has to go to prison for 7 years, 6 months etc)
pass sentence (=when a judge says what the punishment will be) *Judge Evans will pass sentence on the three men tomorrow.*
life sentence (=when someone must go to prison for a very long time or for the rest of their life)
death sentence (=when the punishment is death)

FESTIVALS & SPECIAL DAYS

Christmas

Christmas is one of the most important **festivals** of the year in Britain and the US. It is the time when Christians **celebrate** the birth of Jesus Christ, and many people go to church on Christmas Eve (December 24th) or Christmas Day (December 25th). It is also a time when everyone has a holiday from school or work, and people **send cards** and **give presents** to each other.

People often spend Christmas with their families. They put **decorations** around their houses and usually have a Christmas tree, which they also **decorate** with coloured lights, shiny glass balls etc. On Christmas Day they **open their presents** and then they have a special meal. In Britain, the traditional Christmas dinner is roast turkey, followed by Christmas pudding. Later on in the day people also eat Christmas cake and mince pies. In the US people usually have roast turkey, roast beef, or ham, and often have pie or Christmas cookies for dessert.

Vocabulary

1 words meaning a festival

festival /ˈfestɪ̬vəl/ [n C] a special occasion when people traditionally celebrate something such as an important religious event or an important event in the history of their country: *For Christians, the most important religious festivals are Christmas and Easter.* | *During the festival of Ramadan, Muslims do not eat or drink between the hours of sunrise and sunset.* | *This is the time when Hindus celebrate Diwali, the festival of lights.*

national holiday/public holiday (also **bank holiday** BRITISH) /ˌnæʃənəl ˈhɒlɪ̬di, ˌpʌblɪk ˈhɒlɪ̬di, ˌbæŋk ˈhɒlɪ̬diǁ-ˈhɑːlədeɪ/ [n C] a special day when most people in a country do not have to go to work or school, because the country is celebrating an important religious or national event: *Monday is a national holiday in Japan and financial markets will be closed.* | *There are ten public holidays in a year.*

... Day /deɪ/ [noun singular] used in the names of festivals: *Today is Independence Day in Korea.* | *On Mother's Day people usually give cards and flowers.* | *Boys' Day is on May 5th.*

carnival /ˈkɑːrnɪ̬vəl/ [n C] an event in which people play music, wear special clothes, and dance in the streets: *This year's Notting Hill Carnival will be bigger and better than ever.* | *the carnival parade in Rio*

2 things people do during a festival

present (also **gift**) /ˈprezənt, ɡɪft/ [n C] something that you give someone, especially because it is a special occasion: *She bought gifts for everyone in the family.* | *He gave me a really nice present.* | *You mustn't open your present until Christmas Day.*
Christmas present *My mother wrapped the Christmas presents and put them under the tree.*

card /kɑːrd/ a folded piece of stiff paper, usually with a picture on the front and a message inside, which you send to someone on a special occasion
send sb a card *I must remember to send Amanda a card.*
Christmas card/Valentine's card/New Year's Card etc *Did you get any Valentine's cards?*

party /ˈpɑːrti/ [n C] a social event where people meet together to enjoy themselves by eating,

Thanksgiving (USA)

Thanksgiving is a **national holiday** when people in the US thank God for the harvest. It is held on the fourth Thursday in November. Traditionally, at Thanksgiving we **remember** the time in the 17th century when the first English people who came to live in America were taught to grow local crops by the Native American people, so they had enough food to live through the winter. People usually spend Thanksgiving with their families, and have a special meal of turkey and pumpkin pie.

New Year

All over the world, people **celebrate** the end of the old year and the beginning of the new year. Lots of people go to **parties** on January 31st (New Year's Eve), and round about midnight there are often **fireworks**. Cities such as London, Sydney and New York have big firework displays, and huge crowds come out to see them.

New Year is also seen as a time when people try to make improvements in their lives, for example by trying to stop smoking or to take more exercise. These plans are called "New Year resolutions".

drinking, dancing etc: *She always gets invited to lots of parties.*
have/hold a party *We're having a New Year party. Do you want to come?*
go to a party *Did you go to last year's office party?*

get together /ˌget təˈgeðəʳ/ if people get together, they meet each other and have a drink, meal etc especially in order to celebrate something: *At Christmas time the whole family gets together at our house.*

parade /pəˈreɪd/ [n C] a big public celebration when people dress up, play music, and go along the street on foot or in decorated vehicles: *We went to see the carnival parade.*
have/hold a parade *In New York they have a big parade to celebrate St Patrick's Day.*

dress up /ˌdres ˈʌp/ [v I] to wear special clothes and make-up, especially so that you look like someone or something else
+ as *Each year at the Carnival, the children dress up as butterflies and march through the town.*

decorate /ˈdekəreɪt/ [v T] to make a place, room, or thing look colourful and attractive by putting bright and pretty things everywhere
decorate sth with sth *We decorate the Christmas tree with tinsel and coloured lights.*
decorations [n plural]

fireworks /ˈfaɪəʳwɜːʳks/ things that you fire into the sky which burn and explode to produce coloured lights, noise, and smoke
a firework display (=a special event where many fireworks are lit for people to look at and enjoy) *A quarter of a million people watched the firework display over Santa Monica Bay.*

feast /fiːst/ [n C] a very big meal for a lot of people, held to celebrate a special occasion
have/hold a feast *During Diwali people have a big feast where they eat lots of delicious food.*

celebrate /ˈselᵻbreɪt/ [v I/T] to show that an event or occasion is important by doing something special
celebrate Easter/Christmas etc *What are you going to do to celebrate New Year?*
celebrate Christmas/Easter by doing sth *Jewish people celebrate Hanukkah by giving each other gifts.*

celebrations /ˌselᵻˈbreɪʃənz/ [n plural] things that people do to celebrate something: *The New Year's celebrations went on late into the night.*

remember /rɪˈmembəʳ/ [v T] to have a ceremony or do something special on a particular day because an important event happened on that day in the past: *On November 11th, we remember the end of the war, and think about those who died.*

EXERCISE

How much exercise do you do?

I do quite a lot of **exercise**. I usually go to the **gym** two or three times a week after work. When I'm at the gym I do **weight training**, because I like to stay **in shape**.

On Saturdays I go to my **yoga** class. Yoga is a fairly gentle form of exercise, but it is very good for **toning up** the muscles. In the summer, I often play tennis or go swimming at our local pool, and I try to ride my bike to work at least twice a week.

Why is exercise important?

Taking exercise on a regular basis has a number of positive effects. It can reduce the risk of heart disease and it can make you feel better about yourself. If you take regular exercise, you are likely to be healthier, and you will probably feel less stress than other people. In the 21st century, a lot of people work in offices, travel to work by car, and spend their evenings in front of the TV. So a lot of their time is spent sitting down, and many people don't **get** enough **exercise**.

Vocabulary

1 exercise

exercise /ˈeksəˈsaɪz/ [n C/U] physical activities that you do in order to stay healthy and become stronger, such as running, cycling, or lifting weights. An **exercise** is also a particular movement that you repeat many times to make a part of your body stronger: *Regular exercise makes you feel a lot healthier.* | *This exercise is good for your back.* | *a book on diet and exercise*
   do exercise (also **take exercise** BRITISH) *My doctor told me that I needed to do more exercise, and I decided to join a gym.*
   do an exercise (=do a particular movement) *You should always do some exercises to warm up before you start dancing.*
   get some exercise (=do exercise after you have not done much recently) *I'm not really in shape. I need to get some exercise.*
exercise /ˈeksəˈsaɪz/ [v I] to do sport, swim etc in order to stay healthy and become stronger: *If you exercise two or three times a week, you'll soon feel a lot healthier.*
work out /ˌwɜːˈk ˈaʊt/ [v I] to exercise in a gym or in a class using all of the important muscles in

your body, especially when you do this regularly: *Conrad works out with weights twice a week.*

2 types of exercise

aerobics /eəˈrəʊbɪks/ [n U] a type of exercise where you do a lot of very active movements to music, usually in a class: *You should try aerobics – it's a great way of getting in shape.*
   do aerobics *She does a lot of aerobics – at least five classes a week.*
   go to aerobics (=go to a class and do aerobics)
jogging /ˈdʒɒgɪŋ∥ˈdʒɑː-/ [n U] the activity of running slowly and steadily, done as a form of exercise: *A few people were already out jogging in the park.*
   go jogging *On Saturdays I usually go jogging by the river.*
running /ˈrʌnɪŋ/ [n U] the activity of running as a sport or for exercise
   go running *I don't like going to the gym, so I go running three times a week instead.*
weight training /ˈweɪt ˌtreɪnɪŋ/ [n U] a type of exercise where you lift metal weights in order to strengthen your muscles

How much exercise do we need?

Doctors recommend that we do at least 30 minutes of physical activity a day. This doesn't have to be hard physical exercise like **weight training** or **running**. Gentler forms of exercise such as cycling to work, or walking up stairs instead of taking the lift, are perfectly OK. And even doing the gardening is a surprisingly effective form of exercise.

Exercise also helps **keep your weight down**. The following chart shows how many calories you use when doing different forms of exercise for one hour.

Type of exercise	Number of calories used
walking	200–400
cycling	500–600
jogging	500–600
aerobics	400–500
walking up stairs	600–700
swimming	400–500
tennis	450–550
gardening	250–300

do weight training *More and more women are doing weight training these days.*

yoga /ˈjəʊgə/ [n U] a type of exercise in which you slowly move your body into different positions to improve its condition and to relax your mind
do yoga *She's started doing yoga, and she says she feels a lot calmer.*

Pilates /pɪˈlɑːtiz/ [n U] a type of exercise based on yoga, that you do with special equipment which makes you push, pull, and stretch, so that your body moves more easily and becomes stronger: *She's at her Pilates class.*
do Pilates *I do Pilates once a week.*

press-ups BRITISH **push-ups** AMERICAN /ˈpres ʌps, ˈpʊʃ ʌps/ [n plural] an exercise that makes your arms and chest stronger. You lie on your stomach and use your arms to push your body up.
do press-ups/push-ups *Do 16 press-ups, rest for ten seconds, then do 16 more.*

sit-ups /ˈsɪt ʌps/ [n plural] an exercise that makes your stomach muscles stronger. You lie on your back and use your stomach muscles to lift your head and shoulders off the floor.
do sit-ups *Do sit-ups every day for a flat stomach.*

warm up /ˌwɔːˈrm ˈʌp/ [phrasal verb I] to move and stretch your body gently, so that your body is prepared for more active physical exercise: *It's important to warm up before you start running.*
warm-up [n C] the part at the beginning of an exercise class when you warm up
do a warm-up *We'll do a ten-minute warm-up and then 20 minutes of aerobics.*

stretch /stretʃ/ [v I/T] to make a slow movement that straightens a part of your body so that it is at its full length: *This is a good exercise for stretching your back.* | *The teacher told us to stretch, and then relax.*

3 places where people go in order to exercise

gym /dʒɪm/ [n C] a place that has machines for doing exercises
go to the gym *How often do you go to the gym?*
join a gym (=pay money to a gym so that you can go there and use it whenever you want)

sports centre BRITISH **health club** AMERICAN /ˈspɔːrts ˌsentər, ˈhelθ klʌb/ [n C] a building where you can do lots of different types of sport,

Writing tips

 Be careful which verb you use with exercise. In ordinary conversation, you usually talk about **doing** some exercise, or doing some exercises, for example:
*How much exercise do you **do** a week?*
*We started off by **doing** some stretching exercises.*

You can also say **take some exercise** in British English. This sounds a little more formal than **do**, for example:
*My doctor told me that I needed to **take some exercise**.*
*She doesn't **take** enough exercise.*

But when you are talking about exercises in the plural, you must use 'do' and not 'take':
*We **did** some exercises to warm up before the match started.*

 Be careful also about which verb you use when talking about different sports.
You **go** running/jogging/swimming/walking/cycling etc.
You **play** tennis/ soccer/ volleyball etc.
You **do** aerobics/pilates/sit-ups etc. You also **do** weight training and gardening.
You **play** or **do** sports.

 There are a number of adjectives you can use when talking about exercise.

Exercise that involves a lot of physical effort is **hard/strenuous/vigorous exercise**. Exercise that involves less effort is **gentle exercise** (not 'mild' or 'soft' exercise).

You can also say that something **is good exercise**, meaning that it is good for exercising your body.

 When exercise is used as a verb, it is usually used with an adverb of frequency, for example:
*It's important to **exercise regularly**.*
*I **exercise twice/three times a week**.*

---

such as squash and basketball, as well as exercise classes and weight training

exercise class /'eksə^rsaɪz ˌklɑːs‖-ˌklæs/ [n C] a class where a group of people do exercises: *There's an exercise class for beginners on Thursday evenings.*

4 why people do exercise

in shape (also **fit** BRITISH) /ɪn 'ʃeɪp, fɪt/ if you are **in shape** or **fit**, your body is healthy and strong because you exercise regularly
stay in shape/keep fit *He likes to stay in shape and goes running almost every day. | I keep fit by swimming and going to the gym.*
get in shape/get fit (=become strong and healthy) *People come to exercise classes to get in shape and reduce stress.*

lose weight /ˌluːz 'weɪt/ to become thinner: *You look really good. Have you lost weight?*

keep your weight down /ˌkiːp jɔː^r 'weɪt daʊn/ to prevent yourself from becoming fat: *I find that exercising regularly helps to keep my weight down.*

burn off calories /ˌbɜː^rn ɒf 'kæləriz/ to use up the energy you get from food by doing exercise, so that your body will not turn that food energy into fat: *Walking up stairs burns off more calories than playing golf.*

tone up /ˌtəʊn 'ʌp/ [phrasal verb I/T] to make your muscles or part of your body firmer by doing exercise: *These exercises are a good way to tone up. | I'd like to tone up my stomach muscles.*

build up your muscles /ˌbɪld ʌp jɔː^r 'mʌsəlz/ to make your muscles stronger: *Use this exercise to build up your chest and arm muscles.*

TECHNOLOGY

Important discoveries and inventions

How has modern technology affected our lives?

Modern **technology** has had a great effect on our lives, both in the home and at work. **Labour-saving devices** such as washing machines, dishwashers, and microwaves have made life much easier, and mean that less time needs to be spent doing things like washing and cleaning.

Unfortunately all the **white goods** that we buy need electricity, and we are using up the earth's natural resources. Also when we throw away old fridges, microwaves etc, it can have a very bad effect on the environment.

In the office, computers, email, and photocopiers have revolutionized the way we work. People in different parts of the world can communicate with each other instantly, and business can be done much more quickly. The business world is constantly changing. The end result is that workers have to change jobs much more often and learn new skills in order to keep up with all the latest **technological advances**.

Vocabulary

1 science and technology

science /'saɪəns/ [n U] knowledge and theories about the world which are based on facts, experiments, and research: *the laws of science* | *He was good at science when he was at school.*
the wonders of science *Genetic testing is one of the wonders of modern science.*
popular science (=science that is suitable for ordinary people rather than experts, which is written about in books and magazines)
the science of sth *the science of evolution*

technology /tek'nɒlədʒiǁ-'nɑː-/ [n U] the use of scientific knowledge and discoveries to develop new machines and systems: *The plane uses the very latest technology.* | *nuclear technology* | *There have been huge advances in digital technology.*
new technology (=computers, electronic equipment etc) *At first, many businesses were slow to adapt to new technology.*

engineering /ˌendʒɪ'nɪərɪŋ/ [n U] the activity of designing and building roads, bridges, machines etc: *He studied mechanical engineering at university.* | *A US engineering firm has won the contract to build the dam.*

scientific /ˌsaɪən'tɪfɪk◂/ [adj] relating to science: *Recent scientific research suggests that animals have feelings and emotions.* | *There is no scientific evidence to support these claims.*

technological /ˌteknə'lɒdʒɪkəlǁ-'lɑː-/ [adj] relating to technology: *technological advances in communications* | *Workers are concerned that technological changes may cause them to lose their jobs.*

technical /'teknɪkəl/ [adj] relating to practical knowledge about machines, methods, and systems: *a technical adviser* | *technical knowledge* | *US companies are providing technical assistance.*

2 new science and technology

invention /ɪn'venʃən/ [n C] a new product, machine, system etc, which someone has thought of for the first time: *His greatest invention was the telephone.* | *At that time, the motor car was a relatively modern invention.*
invention [n U] the act of thinking of an idea for a new product, machine, system etc
+ of *the invention of the washing machine*

The invention of the World Wide Web

The World Wide Web was invented by an English computer **scientist** called Sir Tim Berners-Lee. While he was working at CERN (the European Organization for Nuclear Research), he and Robert Cailliau built a system called ENQUIRE. The two scientists used it to look at information stored on computers in different places. ENQUIRE contained many ideas which were later used in the Web. Berners-Lee created the world's first website in 1991. Since 1993, CERN has allowed anyone to use the World Wide Web free, and Internet use has spread across the globe extremely quickly.

The discovery of penicillin

One of the most important **breakthroughs** in the history of medical science was made by a Scottish doctor called Sir Alexander Fleming (1881–1955). He had been doing some experiments in his laboratory. One day in 1928 he was working in his **lab** when he saw something growing inside a dish, and noticed it was destroying the bacteria there. Fleming realized that it could be used as a medicine to treat infections caused by bacteria. He called this substance 'penicillin'. Penicillin saved the lives of many soldiers in World War II and is still widely used today.

---

discovery /dɪsˈkʌvəri/ [n C] a fact or thing that someone finds out about, which was not known about before: *Scientists have made some astonishing new discoveries about the origins of the universe.*
　discovery [n U] the act of finding out about something for the first time: *the discovery of radioactivity by Marie Curie*

breakthrough /ˈbreɪkθruː/ [n C] an important new discovery that is made after studying something for a long time
　+ in *Researchers have made a major breakthrough in the treatment of cancer.*

advance /ədˈvɑːns‖-ˈvæns/ [n C] when something brings progress and makes it possible for people to do things that they could not do before
　+ in *advances in the field of genetics*
　technological/scientific/medical advance *Recent medical advances have made it possible for people to survive the disease.*

the cutting edge /ðə ˌkʌtɪŋ ˈedʒ/ [n singular] the newest and most advanced point in the development of something
　at/on the cutting edge *Their work is at the cutting edge of medical research.*

cutting-edge [adj usually before noun] *cutting-edge technology*

high-tech (also **hi-tech** BRITISH) /ˌhaɪ ˈtek◂/ [adj] using the latest technology: *The recording equipment is all very hi-tech.*

3 people who are involved in science and technology

scientist /ˈsaɪəntᵻst/ [n C] someone who is trained in science, especially someone who is involved in scientific research: *Scientists are studying the effects of the drug.* | *The gene was discovered by an American research scientist.*

inventor /ɪnˈventəʳ/ [n C] the person who first invented something, or whose job is to invent things: *Stephenson was the inventor of the steam train.* | *Her father was an inventor.*

engineer /ˌendʒᵻˈnɪəʳ/ [n C] someone whose job is to design and build roads, bridges, machines etc: *the brilliant engineer who designed the bridge* | *He trained as an electrical engineer.*

technician /tekˈnɪʃən/ [n C] someone whose job is to use or check machines and equipment: *Technicians are trying to find the cause of the problem.* | *a laboratory technician*

Trevor Baylis and the clockwork radio

Trevor Baylis was born in London in 1937. After studying **engineering** at college, he became a swimming pool salesman, and worked as an **inventor** in his spare time. Many of his **inventions** were designed to help disabled people.

In 1993, he saw a programme on television about the problem of AIDS in Africa. The programme said that radio was very useful for educating people about the disease, but unfortunately many people could not afford electricity or batteries for radios. Trevor found a solution to this problem by inventing a radio that worked by clockwork. You just wind a handle and that provides the power for the radio.

Trevor's clockwork radio was shown on a science programme on British television called 'Tomorrow's World'. A South African businessman and an accountant heard about Trevor's invention and set up a company to make clockwork radios. They employed disabled people in their factory. Although it wasn't very **high-tech**, the clockwork radio was a great success. Trevor received several awards for his invention, including one from the Queen.

---

researcher /rɪˈsɜːˤtʃəˤ/ [n C] someone who studies a subject in great detail, especially in order to discover new facts or test new ideas: *a medical researcher* | *Researchers found a link between smoking and heart disease.*

techie /ˈteki/ [n C] INFORMAL someone who knows a lot about computers and electronic equipment: *The magazine is mainly for techies.*

boffin /ˈbɒfɪn‖ˈbɑː-/ [n C] BRITISH INFORMAL a scientist or a very intelligent person who knows a lot about a subject. **Boffin** is often used humorously: *Boffins are working on a car that runs on water.*

<table><tr><td>**4**</td><td>**places where people do scientific research**</td></tr></table>

laboratory (also **lab** INFORMAL) /ləˈbɒrətri, ˈlæb‖ˈlæbrətɔːri/ [n C] a room or building with special equipment, where scientists do experiments and other research work: *The samples were sent back to the laboratory for analysis.* | *the chemistry lab*

research institute /rɪˈsɜːˤtʃ ˌɪnstɪ̩tjuːt‖-tuːt/ [n C] an organization that does scientific research, or a building where scientific research is done: *a research institute that deals with artificial intelligence*

science park /ˈsaɪəns ˌpɑːˤk/ [n C] an area where there are many organizations doing scientific research, often connected to a university

<table><tr><td>**5**</td><td>**technology in the home**</td></tr></table>

appliance /əˈplaɪəns/ [n C] FORMAL a piece of equipment such as a washing machine or a refrigerator, which is used in people's homes: *Make sure that all electrical appliances are switched off.*
domestic/household/kitchen appliance

white goods /ˈwaɪt ɡʊdz/ [n plural] equipment used in the home, for example washing machines and refrigerators. **White goods** is used especially in business contexts

labour-saving device BRITISH **labor-saving device** /ˈleɪbəˤ seɪvɪŋ dɪˌvaɪs/ [n C] a machine that makes it possible for you to do something more easily and with less effort: *Modern houses have so many labour-saving devices that people no longer get exercise from doing chores.*

TRAVEL

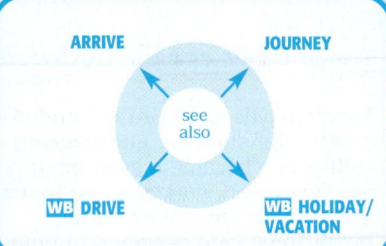

ARRIVE   JOURNEY

see also

WB DRIVE   **WB** HOLIDAY/ VACATION

How was your journey to work?

The car share

We usually **travel** into work together. We share the cost of fuel between the four of us, so it works out very cheaply. It's nice to be able to chat to each other on the way to work, and share all the latest gossip. The only problem is arranging your schedule so that everyone sets off and leaves at the same time. If anyone is late getting out of their house it means that everyone else is late. Another thing is that it's a very small car and there's only just enough room for four of us.

The bus passenger

I always take the **bus** to work. There's a **stop** right outside my house, and the buses are very frequent in **the rush hour**. Usually there's one every 5 minutes. Most days I can get a seat and read a book or newspaper. Sometimes I see someone I know on the bus, and we have a chat. One thing I don't like is all the litter. Some people just leave their food all over the floor or on the seats. Another thing is people listening to personal stereos. The noise they make can be really annoying when they have it on very loud.

Vocabulary

1 travelling from one place to another

go /gəʊ/ [v I] to go to a place that is far from where you live, especially for a holiday or for business: *We're going to Spain this summer.* | *I often go there on business.*
go abroad (=go to a different country) *My grandparents have never been abroad.*
going – went – have gone/have been

> **Have gone** and **have been** are used differently. Compare these sentences: *She's gone to Moscow.* (=she is there now) *I've been to Moscow.* (=I have visited it at some time in the past, but I'm not there now.)

travel /ˈtrævəl/ [v I/T] to make a journey from one place to another – use this either to talk about going to a place that is far away, or about a journey that you make regularly, for example to work or school: *Jack spent the summer travelling around Europe.* | *I usually travel to work by car.*
travel 50 km / 100 miles etc *Some of these people had travelled 50 miles to find food.*
travelling – travelled – have travelled BRITISH
traveling – traveled – have traveled AMERICAN

> Use **go** to talk about where you go to. Use **travel** to talk about the journey itself.

commute /kəˈmjuːt/ [v I] to travel every day to get to work: *He commutes into the city every day.*
get to /ˈget tuː/ [phrasal verb T] to arrive at the place you are travelling to: *It was dark by the time we got to Berlin.*
get from A to B /ˌget frəm ˌeɪ tə ˈbiː/ to travel from one place to another. You use this when talking generally about the most direct way: *the quickest way to get from A to B*
door-to-door /ˌdɔːʳ tə ˈdɔːʳ ◂/ [adv] from one place to another. You use this when saying exactly how long it takes to travel from one place to another: *My journey usually takes me about 30 minutes door-to-door.*
journey time BRITISH /ˈdʒɜːʳni taɪm/ [n singular] the time it takes for you to go from one place to another: *The new train service will cut the journey time from London to Paris by up to 40 minutes.*
destination /ˌdestɪˈneɪʃən/ [n C] the place that you are travelling to
reach your destination *They reached their destination in the early hours of the next morning.*

The cyclist

I use my bike because it's the quickest way to **get from A to B** in **the rush hour**. All the cars are stuck in **traffic jams**, and you can go straight past them. My journey to work usually takes about 20 minutes **door-to-door**. It's a good way of getting your daily exercise. The thing I don't like about cycling is all the pollution. I don't like breathing in exhaust fumes from cars and buses. It can also be rather dangerous, and you need to watch out for people opening car doors or coming out of junctions without looking.

The car driver

I normally go to work by car. I'd say my average **journey time** is about 50 minutes. When I'm in my car it's very comfortable, like being in my own living room. I can turn on the stereo system and listen to my favourite CDs or listen to the car radio. There are some things though that I don't like about driving. The **traffic** keeps getting worse, and other drivers sometimes behave very badly. I know I should use my car less because it is bad for the environment, but it is much more convenient than **public transport**.

2 different ways of travelling

drive /draɪv/ [v I] to travel in a car: *Jenny drove down to the coast for the weekend.*
driving – drove – have driven

fly /flaɪ/ [v I] to travel by plane: *My mother never liked flying.* | *Jerry flew to Rome last week.*
flying – flew – have flown

sail /seɪl/ [v I] to travel by any kind of boat or ship: *We sailed from Southampton on May 6th.*

cycle ESPECIALLY BRITISH **bike** ESPECIALLY AMERICAN /'saɪkəl, baɪk/ [v I] to travel by bicycle: *I usually bike to work.* | *We're going to cycle across France this summer.*

take /teɪk/ [v T] if you **take** a train, bus, or plane, you travel in it: *Do you want to take the train or drive?* **taking – took – have taken**

by car/bus/plane/train/boat /baɪ 'kɑːʳ, bʌs, 'pleɪn, 'treɪn, 'bəʊt/ travelling in a car, plane, train or boat: *Did you come by car?* | *Some of the beaches can only be reached by boat.*

on foot /ɒn 'fʊt/ if you go somewhere **on foot**, you walk there: *They took the bus to town, then came back on foot.*

by air/by sea/by land /baɪ 'eəʳ, baɪ 'siː, baɪ 'lænd/ if you travel **by air**, **by sea**, or **by land**, you travel by plane, in a boat, or on land: *It's much quicker if you go by air.*

public transport BRITISH **public transportation** AMERICAN /ˌpʌblɪk 'trænspɔːʳt, ˌpʌblɪk trænspɔː'teɪʃən‖-trænspər-/ [n U] buses, trains etc, that are available for everyone to use: *the public transportation system in New York*

3 the busiest time for travelling

the rush hour /ðə 'rʌʃ aʊəʳ/ [n singular] the time in the morning and evening when a lot of people are travelling to or from work: *The roads are extremely busy in the rush hour.* | *We got held up by rush hour traffic.*

the peak season /ðə 'piːk ˌsiːzən/ [n singular] the most popular time of year for travelling to a place on holiday: *Plane fares always go up during the peak season.*

The train passenger

I generally take the **train** to work. It's quick and convenient, and I can be in my office in about 35 minutes. In winter the service can be rather erratic, and I sometimes find myself waiting on the **platform** at the **station** in freezing cold weather, wishing I was in a nice warm car. The other thing I don't like is people in my **carriage** with mobile phones, who talk loudly and say things like "I'm on the train". The good thing about taking the train is that someone else does all the driving, and I can just relax and read my newspaper.

Travelling by plane

Last week we **flew** to London. We **took the bus** to JFK airport. When we arrived at the **terminal** we went to the **check-in desk** for our flight. We showed our passports at **passport control**, and then went through **security**. We had to wait for a while in the **departure lounge**. When our flight was called, we went through the **departure gate**, and got on our plane. After the plane had **landed** at Heathrow, we went to the **baggage reclaim** to collect our bags, then went through **immigration** and **customs**, and out into the **arrivals** area.

4 the activity of travelling

travel /'trævəl/ [n U] the activity of travelling: *Her job involves a lot of travel.*
air/space/road/rail/travel *New technology has made air travel much safer.*
travel writer (=someone who writes about travelling)
travel agent (=someone whose job is to make arrangements and sell tickets for people's holidays or long journeys)

5 someone who is travelling

passenger /'pæsɪndʒəʳ, -sən-/ [n C] someone who is travelling in a car, boat, plane, or train, but who is not the driver or pilot: *The plane can carry up to 500 passengers.* | *The driver and his passengers were all killed in the crash.*
tourist /'tʊərɪ̥st/ [n C] someone who travels around and visits places for pleasure, while they are on holiday: *Oxford is full of tourists in the summer.*

commuter /kə'mjuːtəʳ/ [n C] someone who travels to and from work every day, especially on a train: *The train was packed with rush-hour commuters.*

6 getting on and off a bus, train, plane etc

get on /ˌget 'ɒn‖-'ɑːn/ [phrasal verb I/T] to go into a bus, train etc at the beginning of a journey: *He got on the plane at Boston.*
get off /ˌget 'ɒf‖-'ɔːf/ [phrasal verb I/T] to leave a bus, train etc at the end of a journey: *I got off the train at Paddington.*
board /bɔːʳd/ FORMAL [v I/T] to get on a plane, ship, train or bus: *He was stopped by police while boarding a plane out of the country.*
catch /kætʃ/ [verb T] to get on a bus, train, or plane that is travelling somewhere, or arrive in time to get on a bus train, plane etc: *I caught the last train to York.* | *Did you catch your plane?*
change /tʃeɪndʒ/ [v I/T] to get out of one train, bus or plane and get into another in order to continue your journey

Writing tips

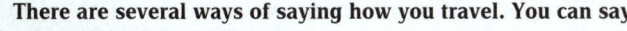

     There are several ways of saying how you travel. You can say:

> *I usually **take** the train/car/bus.*
> *I normally **go by** car/bus/train/bike.*
> *Most days I **use** my bike/my car/the bus/the train.*
> *I generally **drive/bike** to work.*

     Be careful which prepositions you use when talking about travelling.

Don't say 'with the train', 'with my car' etc. Say **by train/by car/by bike** etc.
Don't say 'by foot'. Say **on foot**.

     Be careful with phrasal verbs.

You **get on** a bus, train, plane, or ship, but you **get in** or **into** a car or taxi.
*She kissed him, then **got in** her car and drove away.*

You **get off** a bus, train, plane, or ship, but you **get out of** a car or taxi.
*Both drivers **got out of** their cars and started shouting at each other.*

     Don't say 'the travel' when you mean the journey (British) or the trip.

*It was a long **journey**.* (not 'The travel was long'.)
*Did you enjoy your **trip**?* (not 'Did you enjoy your travel?')

+ at *"Is it a direct flight?" "No, we have to change at Bangkok."*

miss /mɪs/ [v T] to be too late for your train, flight etc so that it leaves before you can catch it: *I almost missed my flight.*

7 travelling by car or by bus

traffic /ˈtræfɪk/ [n U] the vehicles moving along a road or street: *the noise of the traffic | The traffic was really bad and I was late for work.* (=there were a lot of vehicles on the road)
heavy traffic (=there are a lot of vehicles on the road) *We got stuck in heavy traffic.*
traffic jam (also **jam**) /ˈtræfɪk ˌdʒæm, dʒæm/ [n C] a long line of vehicles on a road, which cannot move, or can only move very slowly: *They got stuck in a huge traffic jam on the freeway.*
bus stop (also **stop**) /ˈbʌs stɒp, stɒpǁ-ˌstɑːp/ [n C] the place at the side of the road where buses stop for passengers

8 travelling by train

station (also **train station** ESPECIALLY AMERICAN) /ˈsteɪʃən, ˈtreɪn ˌsteɪʃən/ [n C] a place where you can go to get on a train: *Can I give you a lift to the station?*
stop /stɒpǁstɑːp/ [n C] one of the places on a railway line, where the train regularly stops for people to get on or off: *The next stop is Brighton.*
platform /ˈplætfɔːˈm/ [n C] the place beside a railway track where you get on and off a train in a station: *Your train leaves from Platform 2.*
track /træk/ [n C] the two metal lines that trains travel along
line /laɪn/ [n C] a part of a railway system, which connects a series of places, or the tracks that the trains travel along : *Oxford Circus is on the Victoria Line.*
carriage BRITISH **car** AMERICAN /ˈkærɪdʒ, kɑːˈ/ [n C] one of the vehicles that form part of a train, where the pasengers sit: *a first-class carriage*
dining car (also **buffet car** BRITISH) /ˈdaɪnɪŋ ˌkɑːˈ, ˈbʊfeɪ ˌkɑːˈǁbəˈfeɪ-/ [n C] the part of a train where you can buy food or drink

the Underground BRITISH **the subway/metro** AMERICAN /ði ˈʌndəˈɡraʊnd, ðə ˈsʌbweɪ, ˈmetrəʊ/ [n singular] the system of trains that run under the ground. The system in London is also often called 'the Tube'.

9 travelling by plane

terminal **terminal building** /ˈtɜːˈmɪ̩nəl, ˈtɜːˈmɪ̩nəl ˌbɪldɪŋ/ [n C] a large building at an airport where people begin and end their journeys: *Your plane leaves from Terminal 2.*

check in /ˌtʃek ˈɪn/ [phrasal verb I] to go to the desk at an airport to show your ticket, give them your bags and get a boarding card: *Passengers must check in at least 2 hours before departure.*

check-in desk BRITISH **check-in counter** AMERICAN /ˈtʃek ɪn ˌdesk, ˈtʃek ɪn ˌkaʊntəʳ/ [n C] the place at an airport where you check in

passport control /ˈpɑːspɔːˈt kənˌtrəʊl‖ˈpæs-/ [n U] the place where your passport is checked when you leave or enter a country

security /sɪˈkjʊərɪ̩ti/ [n U] the part of an airport where people's bags are checked for weapons, bombs, or other illegal articles

departures /dɪˈpɑːˈtʃəʳz/ [n plural] the place in an airport where you go before you get on the plane

departure lounge /dɪˈpɑːˈtʃəʳ ˌlaʊndʒ/ [n C] the place in an airport where you sit and wait just before you get on your plane

departures board /dɪˈpɑːˈtʃəʳz ˌbɔːˈd/ [n C] a large piece of equipment at an airport which shows information about which planes are leaving and at what time

gate (also **departure gate**) /ɡeɪt, dɪˈpɑːˈtʃəʳ ɡeɪt/ [n C] the place where you leave the airport building to get on a plane: *Would passengers for flight BA423 please proceed to gate 34.*

boarding card /ˈbɔːˈdɪŋ ˌkɑːˈd/ [n C] a piece of card with your name and seat number printed on it, which you have to you show before you get on a plane

take off /teɪk ˈɒf‖-ˈɔːf/ [phrasal verb I] if a plane **takes off**, it goes up into the air at the beginning of a flight: *The plane took off from Narita airport at 3pm.*

take-off [n C] when a plane leaves the ground and moves up into the sky: *The accident happened shortly after take-off.*

land/touch down /lænd, ˌtʌtʃ ˈdaʊn/ [v I] if a plane **lands** or **touches down**, it moves down onto the ground at the end of a journey: *Our plane landed in Moscow at 4 a.m.*

baggage reclaim /ˈbæɡɪdʒ ˌriːkleɪm/ [n U] the place at an airport where you collect your cases and bags after a flight

immigration /ˌɪmɪ̩ˈɡreɪʃən/ [n U] the place where officials check the passports and documents of everyone entering the country: *She got stopped at immigration because her visa had expired.*

customs /ˈkʌstəmz/ [n U] the place where your bags are checked for goods that you should not bring into a country

arrivals /əˈraɪvəlz/ [n U] the area in an airport where you go after you have been through immigration and customs

arrivals board /əˈraɪvəlz ˌbɔːˈd/ [n C] a large piece of equipment at an airport or station which shows information about which planes are arriving and at what time

flight /flaɪt/ [n C] a journey on a plane: *Did you have a good flight?*

10 tickets

ticket /ˈtɪkɪ̩t/ [n C] a small printed piece of paper that shows you have paid to travel on a train, bus, plane etc: *I showed him my ticket.*

ticket inspector (=someone whose job is to check people's tickets)

ticket office (=a place that sells tickets)

season ticket /ˈsiːzən ˌtɪkɪ̩t/ [n C] a ticket that allows you to make the same journey every day for a week, a month, or a year. Season tickets cost less than buying individual tickets for each journey: *a monthly season ticket from Leatherhead to London*

fare /feəʳ/ [n C] the amount of money you pay to travel on a bus, train, plane etc: *Last year, fares went up by 20%.*

air/rail/train/bus/taxi fare *cheap air fares to Europe*

return (ticket) BRITISH **round trip ticket** AMERICAN /rɪˌtɜːˈn ˈtɪkɪ̩t, ˌraʊnd trɪp ˈtɪkɪ̩t/ [n C] a ticket to travel to a place and back again: *a round trip ticket to Chicago* | *I'd like a return to Cambridge please.*

one-way ticket (also **single (ticket)** BRITISH) /ˌwʌn weɪ ˈtɪkɪ̩t, ˌsɪŋɡəl ˈtɪkɪ̩t/ [n C] a ticket to travel to a place, but not come back: *I'd like a one-way ticket to Madrid.*

reserve (also **book** BRITISH) /rɪˈzɜːˈv, bʊk/ [v T] to arrange for a seat on a plane, bus, or train to be kept for you to use: *We had booked our tickets months in advance.*

11 the list of times of buses and trains

timetable BRITISH **schedule** AMERICAN /ˈtaɪmteɪbəl, ˈʃedjuːl‖-ˈskedʒʊl/ [n C] a list of the times of buses or trains

widow /'wɪdəʊ/ [n C] a woman whose husband has died, and who has not got married again: *Mr Jarvis died suddenly, leaving a widow and four children.*

widower /'wɪdəʊə^r/ [n C] a man whose wife has died, and who has not got married again: *He's been a widower for eight years now.*

9 **connected with people who are married**

married life /ˌmærɪd 'laɪf/ [n U] your life as a married person: *After 30 years of married life, she couldn't imagine being on her own.*

marital /'mærɪtl/ [adj only before noun] FORMAL use this about problems that people have in their marriage
marital problems/violence/difficulties/breakdown *Their marital problems began when Martha lost her job. | Marital breakdown can have a devastating effect on the children.*

marital status /ˌmærɪtl 'steɪtəs‖-'steɪtəs, -'stæ-/ [n singular] FORMAL whether you are married, single, or divorced

> **Formal or informal?**
> **Marital status** is used especially on official forms: *Name: John Thorpe. Age: 26. Marital status: Single.*

marriage certificate /'mærɪdʒ səˈtɪfɪkət/ [n C] an official document that proves you are married

MATERIAL

any solid or liquid substance

1 **material**

substance /'sʌbstəns/ [n C] a type of solid or liquid, such as a chemical, a mineral, or something produced by a plant or tree: *Poisonous substances should be clearly labelled. | The animal's horns contain a substance called keratin. | Resin is a dark, sticky substance. | radioactive substances*

material /məˈtɪəriəl/ [n C/U] any solid substance that can be used for making things: *Steel is a stronger material than iron. | The company supplies building materials such as bricks and cement. | The wire is covered by an insulating material such as plastic.*

⊖ stuff /stʌf/ [n U] INFORMAL, ESPECIALLY SPOKEN a substance: *What's this sticky stuff on the floor? | Do you have any of that clear plastic stuff to cover food with?*

2 **material for making clothes, curtains etc**

➡ see **CLOTHES, DESIGN**

cloth /klɒθ‖klɔːθ/ [n U] the substance that clothes are made from: *fine woollen cloth for making men's suits*

material /məˈtɪəriəl/ [n C/U] cloth used for making clothes or curtains, covering furniture etc: *She was wearing a long black dress of some silky material.*
dress/curtain material *Could I have six metres of that curtain material?*

fabric /'fæbrɪk/ [n C/U] cloth – use this especially when you are talking about cloth used to make clothes: *I want to buy some fabric to make a skirt. | Man-made fabrics such as polyester are easy to wash and iron.*

textiles /'tekstaɪlz/ [n plural] cloth for making clothes, curtains etc – use this for talking about the business of producing and selling cloth: *They make most of their money by exporting textiles.*

> ⚠ You can use **textile** before a noun, like an adjective: *textile workers | a large textile industry*

> When you see **EC**, go to the **ESSENTIAL COMMUNICATION** section.

MAYBE

when you think something may happen or may be true, but you are not sure

➡ see also **SURE/NOT SURE, POSSIBLE, PROBABLY**

maybe/perhaps /'meɪbi, pə^r'hæps/ [adv] use this when you think that something may happen or may be true, but you are not sure: *"Are you going to the party?" "I don't know, maybe."* | *I wonder why she's late. Maybe she missed the train.* | *The footprints belonged to a large cat, a tiger, perhaps.* | *Perhaps it would be better if you left now.*
maybe not/perhaps not *"It wasn't her fault!" "Well, maybe not, but she should have been more careful."*

> **Formal or informal?**
> **Maybe** is more informal than **perhaps**. Use **maybe** in conversation or stories, but not in formal letters or reports.

may/might/could /meɪ, maɪt, kəd *strong* kʊd/ [modal verb] use this with other verbs, to show that something is possible or likely, but you are not sure about it: *Take your umbrella – it might rain.* | *Hundreds of workers may lose their jobs.* | *We could be home before midnight if the traffic isn't too bad.*
may/might/could have done sth *"Bruce isn't here yet." "He may have decided not to come."*

> **Formal or informal?**
> **Could** is more informal than **may** and **might**.

it is possible (that)/there is a chance (that) /ɪt ɪz 'pɒsₑbəl (ðæt), ðeə^rz ə 'tʃɑːns (ðæt)‖'pɑːs-, -'tʃæns-/ use this when you think that something may happen or may be done, but that it is not very likely: *It's possible I won't be able to come to your party.*
it is just possible (that)/there is just a chance (that) (=when something is possible, but very unlikely) *There's*

just a chance that she left her keys in the office.* | *It's just possible we'll finish the job by tonight, but it'll probably be tomorrow.*

possibly /'pɒsₑblɪ‖'pɑː-/ [adv] use this when you think that something may be true, but you do not have enough information to be sure: *"Do you think she was murdered, Inspector?" "Possibly."* | *He's playing in the US Open Golf Championships, possibly for the last time.* | *The cancer was possibly caused by exposure to asbestos.*

♀ you never know /juː ˌnevə^r 'nəʊ/ SPOKEN say this when you are not sure whether something will happen, because no one knows what will happen in the future: *"I don't think I'll ever get married." "Oh, you never know."* | *Let's buy a lottery ticket. You never know, we might win.*

MEAL

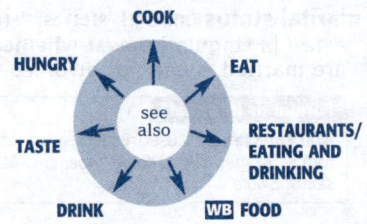

COOK
HUNGRY
EAT
see also
TASTE
RESTAURANTS/ EATING AND DRINKING
DRINK
WB FOOD

1 a meal

meal /miːl/ [n C] the food that you eat in the morning, in the middle of the day, or in the evening, either at home or in a restaurant: *The hotel was nice, and the meals were really good.* | *Miriam was silent all through the meal.* | *He hadn't had a hot meal in days.*
have a meal *We had an excellent meal in a Chinese restaurant.*
cook sb a meal *Jeff cooked us a delicious meal last night.*
go out for a meal (=go to a restaurant) *Would you like to go out for a meal sometime, Emma?*
take sb out for a meal (=take someone to a restaurant and pay for their meal) *It was Lisa's birthday so we took her out for a meal.*
main meal (=the biggest meal of the

day) *We usually have our main meal in the middle of the day.*

something to eat /ˌsʌmθɪŋ tʊ ˈiːt/ ESPECIALLY SPOKEN a meal, especially a small or quick meal: *Can I get you something to eat?*
have something to eat *We'll have something to eat, and then go out.*

snack /snæk/ [n C] something small such as an apple, some bread, or some chocolate that you eat between meals: *Yogurt is his favorite snack.*
have a snack *The children have a snack at 11 o'clock – usually some fruit and a drink.*

takeaway BRITISH [n C] **takeout** AMERICAN [n U] /ˈteɪkəweɪ, ˈteɪkaʊt/ a meal that you buy from a restaurant and then eat at home: *Dave just lives on beer and takeaways. | I don't feel like cooking tonight – let's get takeout. | a takeaway pizza*

2 a meal in the morning

breakfast /ˈbrekfəst/ [n C/U] the meal you eat when you get up in the morning: *What do you want for breakfast – cereal or toast? | After breakfast we went for a walk on the beach.*
have breakfast *George was having his breakfast when the phone rang.*

> ⚠ You can say 'eat breakfast' in American English, but in British English it is more usual to say **have breakfast**.

3 a meal in the middle of the day

lunch /lʌntʃ/ [n C/U] the meal you eat in the middle of the day: *We had an early lunch and spent the afternoon shopping. | At work we are allowed one hour for lunch. | See you after lunch.*
have lunch *Shall we have lunch before we go out?*
plural **lunches**

> ⚠ You can say 'eat lunch' in American English, but in British English it is more usual to say **have lunch**.

4 a meal in the evening

dinner /ˈdɪnəʳ/ [n C/U] the meal you eat in the evening: *What shall we have for dinner? | Sarah cooked us a really nice dinner.*
go out for dinner (=go to a restaurant or to someone else's house) *We went out for dinner at the Ritz.*
have dinner *Why don't you come and have dinner with us?*

> ⚠ You can say 'eat dinner' in American English, but in British English it is more usual to say **have dinner**.

supper /ˈsʌpəʳ/ [n C/U] the meal you eat in the evening: *After supper we watched a video. | I had my supper and went to bed.*

> ⚠ You can say 'eat supper' in American English, but in British English it is more usual to say **have supper**.

> ⚠ In British English, **supper** is usually a less formal meal than **dinner**, and you have it at home, never in a restaurant.

tea /tiː/ [n C/U] BRITISH a meal you eat at home early in the evening: *What's for tea?*
have tea *The children came home from school, had their tea, and did their homework.*

> ⚠ Don't say 'eat tea'. Say **have tea**.

dinner party /ˈdɪnəʳ ˌpɑːʳti/ [n C] a formal meal in your home when you invite friends or guests
have a dinner party *We're having a dinner party on Tuesday, would you like to come?*
plural **dinner parties**

5 a meal outside

picnic /ˈpɪknɪk/ [n C] a meal that you take with you to eat outside: *We took a picnic down to the beach.*
have a picnic *It was a beautiful day – we had a picnic by the river.*

barbecue /'bɑːˈbɪkjuː/ [n C] a party when you cook and eat food outside: *I'll get some burgers and ribs for the barbecue.*
have a barbecue *If the weather's nice, we'll have a barbecue.*

6 part of a meal

course /kɔːˈs/ [n C] one of the parts of a meal, especially in a restaurant: *The waiter brought the first course, carrot soup.*
main course (=the biggest course in a meal) *For the main course we had roast turkey with vegetables.*
a three-course meal/a five-course meal *In La Porcetta you can get a really nice three-course meal for $20.*

starter BRITISH **appetizer** AMERICAN /'stɑːˈtəˈ, 'æpɪtaɪzəˈ/ [n C] the first part of a meal in a restaurant: *What would you like for a starter – soup or garlic mushrooms?* | *a delightful appetizer of small clams*

main dish /ˌmeɪn 'dɪʃ/ [n C] the biggest part of a meal: *a hot main dish* | *Today's main dish was steak and chips.*

dessert (also **pudding/sweet** BRITISH) /dɪ'zɜːˈt, 'pʊdɪŋ, swiːt/ [n C/U] the sweet part of a meal that you have at the end: *"Would you like a dessert, Madam?" "Yes please, I'll have the cheesecake."* | *Would you like a sweet, or some cheese and biscuits?*
have sth for dessert/pudding *I had fruit salad for dessert.* | *What are we having for pudding?*

MEAN

➡ see also **WORD/PHRASE/SENTENCE, LANGUAGE**

1 to mean something

mean /miːn/ [v T] to have a particular meaning – use this about a word, sign, or statement: *What does 'abandon' mean?* | *It says 'not suitable for children', which means anyone under 16.* | *He said Sara was a very close friend, but I'm not sure what he meant.* (=he could mean she is just a

friend, or he could mean she is his girlfriend)
+(that) *The flashing light means that we're running out of gas.* | *When it makes a 'bleep', that means it's switched on.*
meaning – meant – have meant

stand for sth /'stænd fɔːˈ (sth)/ [phrasal verb T] if a letter or group of letters **stands for** a word, name, or number, it is a short way of saying or writing it: *NATO stands for the North Atlantic Treaty Organization.* | *What does the F stand for in John F. Kennedy?*

represent /ˌreprɪ'zent/ [v T] if a shape, letter, object etc **represents** something, it is used as a sign for that thing in a map, plan, calculation etc: *The red lines on the map represent railways.* | *Single letters or combinations of letters represent different phonetic sounds.*

in other words /ɪn ˌʌðəˈ 'wɜːˈdz/ use this to show that you are saying something again in a simpler way, in order to explain what it means: *If goods are faulty you are entitled to a full refund – you get your money back, in other words.* | *There are growing inequalities in the distribution of wealth – in other words, the rich are getting richer.*

2 meaning

meaning /'miːnɪŋ/ [n C/U] what a word, sign, or statement means: *The word 'spring' has several different meanings.* | *Semantics is the study of meaning.*
+of *There is a chart that explains the meaning of all the symbols on the map.*

sense /sens/ [n C] one of the meanings of a word that has several meanings
+of *In the dictionary the different senses of the word are marked by numbers.*
in the broadest/fullest sense (=in the most general meaning of the word) *I'm using the word 'education' in the broadest sense here.*

implication /ˌɪmplɪ'keɪʃən/ [n C/U] a meaning which is not directly stated, but which seems to be intended: *He didn't actually accuse me of stealing, but that was the implication.*
+that *Staff members were asked to work on Sundays, with the implication*

that they would lose their jobs if they refused.
by implication (=the intended meaning is that) *The law bans organized protests and, by implication, any form of opposition.*

> **Formal or informal?**
>
> **Implication** is used in writing and in formal spoken English.

the gist /ðə ˈdʒɪst/ [*n* singular] the main meaning of something such as a speech, report, or piece of writing, without considering all the specific details
+of *The gist of the report seems to be that safety standards need to be improved.*
get the gist (of sth) (=understand the main meaning) *Read through the article quickly to get the gist of it.*

MEASURE

to find out the size, length, or amount of something

➡ see also **LONG, SHORT, AMOUNT/ NUMBER**

to measure something

measure /ˈmeʒəʳ/ [*v* T] to find out the size or amount of something, by using a special tool, machine, or system: *Can you measure the desk to see if it'll fit into that corner? | The GNP figure measures the rate of growth in the economy. | A device for measuring the speed of a tennis ball in flight*
measurement /ˈmeʒəʳmənt/ [*n* C] a number or amount that you get when you measure something: *What are the measurements of this room?*
take a measurement *I'll just take a few measurements, then I can tell you how much paint you will need.*
waist/chest/hip etc measurement (=how much you measure around your waist, chest etc)
weigh /weɪ/ [*v* T] to find out how heavy something is by measuring its weight with special equipment: *Weigh all the ingredients carefully before mixing them together.*

time /taɪm/ [*v* T] to measure how long it takes for someone to do something or for something to happen: *We timed how long it took us to get there. | The swimming teacher always times us over 100 metres.*
take /teɪk/ [*v* T] **take sb's pulse/ temperature/blood pressure** to measure how hot someone is, how fast their heart is beating etc, as part of a medical examination: *The doctor will take your blood pressure and check your weight.*
taking – took – have taken

MEDICAL TREATMENT

➡ see Word Banks section

MEET

➡ see also **VISIT, TALK**

1 when you have arranged to meet someone

meet /miːt/ [*v* I/T] to go to the same place as someone else at a particular time, because you have arranged to see them and do something: *I'll meet you outside the theatre at 7 o'clock. | We agreed to meet again next Friday. | I used to meet her every week to discuss my work.*
meet for lunch/coffee/a drink etc *Let's meet for lunch one day next week.*
meet sb at the airport/station etc (=go to meet someone when they have just arrived somewhere) *My brother came to meet me at the airport.*
meeting – met – have met

> ⚠ If you want to say that two people meet each other, it is better just to say **they meet**: *We met outside the theatre.*

meet with sb /ˈmiːt wɪð (sb)/ [*phrasal verb* T] ESPECIALLY AMERICAN to meet someone in order to discuss something: *She's flying to New York tomorrow to meet with her agent.*

meet up/get together /ˌmiːt ˈʌp, ˌget təˈgeðəʳ/ [phrasal verb I] INFORMAL if friends **meet up** or **get together**, they meet in order to do something together, for example to have a meal or a drink: *Let's meet up after work.*
+with *I usually meet up with my friends on a Friday night and go for a drink.*
+for lunch/coffee/a drink *We must get together for lunch some time.*

2 when you meet someone by chance

meet /miːt/ [v T not in passive] to see someone by chance and talk to them: *You'll never guess who I met yesterday! | I met Jill at the bus stop this morning.*
meeting – met – have met

bump into sb/run into sb /ˌbʌmp ˈintuː (sb), ˌrʌn ˈintuː (sb)/ [phrasal verb T] INFORMAL to meet someone that you know, by chance: *I'm glad I bumped into you. I wanted to ask you about tomorrow's history test. | She's always running into friends that she knows from school.*
chance meeting /ˌtʃɑːns ˈmiːtɪŋǁˌtʃæns-/ [n C usually singular] when you meet someone by chance: *It was a chance meeting that later led to a passionate love affair.*

3 when you meet someone for the first time

meet /miːt/ [v I/T not in passive] to meet someone you have not met before: *I was 15 years old when I met Andrew. | Have you ever met his wife?*
first meet *Where did you first meet Dr Steiner? | Janet and Pete first met when they were at university.*
meeting – met – have met

> ⚠ If you want to say that two people meet each other, it is better just to say **they meet**: *I remember the day we met.*

introduce /ˌintrəˈdjuːsǁ-ˈduːs/ [v T] if you **introduce** someone to a person they have never met before, you tell them each other's names: *Oh, Bob, let me introduce Rosie Webb, our new marketing manager. | Have you two been introduced? (=to each other)*
introduce sb to sb *Tom introduced me to his sister, Gloria.*
this is /ˈðɪs ɪz/ SPOKEN say this when you are introducing someone to a person they have never met before: *"Sam, this is Julia – she's in college with me." "Hi, Julia, nice to meet you!"*

4 when a large group comes together in one place

gather /ˈgæðəʳ/ [v I] if a crowd or group of people **gathers**, they come together somewhere in order to do something or see something
+in/at/on etc *The family gathered on the porch to say goodbye. | Eager fans are already gathering outside the stadium.*
assemble /əˈsembəl/ [v I] FORMAL if a group of people **assembles**, they all come together in the same place, especially as part of an organized plan: *Prisoners must assemble in the courtyard every morning for exercise. | Foreign diplomats and their wives had assembled in the Great Hall to meet the President.*
come together /ˌkʌm təˈgeðəʳ/ [phrasal verb I] if people or groups who do not usually meet each other **come together**, they meet in order to discuss things, exchange ideas etc: *People came together from all over the country to attend the funeral. | Seminars provide an opportunity for students to come together and discuss a particular topic.*

5 a meeting

meeting /ˈmiːtɪŋ/ [n C] an occasion when people meet in order to discuss something: *I have to go to a meeting. | Peter's in London for a business meeting.*
have/hold a meeting *I think we'd better have a meeting to discuss these problems.*
attend a meeting FORMAL (=be at a meeting) *The president is attending a meeting in Prague today.*

call/arrange/organize a meeting *The principal has called a meeting for 4 o'clock.*

conference /'kɒnfərəns‖'kɑːn-/ [n C] an organized event, especially one that continues for several days, at which a lot of people meet to discuss a particular subject
+of *a conference of women business leaders*
attend a conference FORMAL (=be at a conference) *She was in Boston attending a conference on the environment.*
hold a conference *The Institute of Accountants is holding its conference in Edinburgh this year.*

convention /kən'venʃən/ [n C] a large meeting of members of a political organization or professional group for a particular purpose: *the Democratic Party convention*
+of *a convention of computer salespeople*

MEMBER

➡ see also **ORGANIZATION, JOIN**

1 a member of a club, political party etc

member /'membər/ [n C] a person or organization that belongs to a club, a political party, or a similar organization: *Members can use the bar at any time.*
+of *She's a member of the local drama society.* | *Is Switzerland a member of the European Union?*
a club/union/party member *Union members voted against the strike.*

2 to be a member of something

be a member of sth/belong to sth /biː ə 'membər ɒv (sth), bɪ'lɒŋ tuː (sth)‖-'lɔːŋ-/ *My sister's a member of the school choir.* | *Do you belong to any political party?*
join /dʒɔɪn/ [v T] to become a member of a club, a political party, a military force, or a company: *He joined the*

Marines at the age of 19, and fought in Vietnam. | *I've joined the photographic club.* | *Walters joined the company in 2002.*

> ⚠ Don't use **join** to talk about going to a school or college. Say **she went to Oxford in 1995** (not 'she joined Oxford').

be in sth /biː ɪn (sth)/ [phrasal verb T] to be a member of an organization, especially a large, well-known one: *Nina's son is in the army.* | *I used to really enjoy camping when I was in the Boy Scouts.*
be on sth /biː ɒn (sth)‖-ɔːn-/ [phrasal verb T] to be a member of a group or committee that meets to make official decisions
be on a committee/council/board/ panel *Kathryn is on the school board for the district.*

3 being a member

membership /'membərʃɪp/ [n U] being a member: *What is the cost of membership?*
+of *Membership of political parties has been increasing.* | *Canada's membership of NATO*
+in AMERICAN *Did you renew your membership in the sailing club?*

MENTALLY ILL

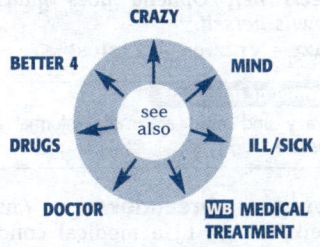

1 mentally ill

mentally ill /ˌmentəli 'ɪl/ someone who is **mentally ill** has an illness of the mind which affects the way that they behave: *Many of these homeless people have been mentally ill at some time.*

the **mentally ill** (=people who are mentally ill) *He works in a hostel for the mentally ill.*

mental illness /ˌmentl ˈɪlnᵻs/ [n C/U] illness of the mind: *Depression is a mental illness and can be treated with drugs.* | *He had a history of mental illness and alcoholism.*

mental /ˈmentl/ [adj only before noun] connected with mental illness or people who are mentally ill
mental hospital/patient/institution *a hospital ward for non-violent mental patients*
mental problem/disorder/ breakdown *We knew she had been having mental problems.*

insane /ɪnˈseɪn/ [adj] permanently and seriously mentally ill, so that you cannot have a normal life: *Powell, who has attacked 13 women, was judged to be insane.*
go insane (=become seriously mentally ill) *Sometimes I thought I was going insane.*

insanity /ɪnˈsænᵻti/ [n U] permanent and serious mental illness: *Hobbs was found not guilty by reason of insanity.*

crazy (also **mad** BRITISH) /ˈkreɪzi, mæd/ [adj] mentally ill – use this in conversations or stories, but not in formal, medical, or legal English: *Some crazy guy walked into the store and started shooting people.* | *We soon realized that the old man was completely mad.*
go crazy/mad (=become crazy) *I felt like I was going crazy.* | *After Hamlet rejects her, Ophelia goes mad and drowns herself.*
crazy – crazier – craziest

Formal or informal?
Crazy and **mad** are more informal than **insane**.

nervous breakdown /ˌnɜːrvəs ˈbreɪkdaʊn/ [n C] a medical condition in which you feel very tired, anxious, and upset, often because you have been working too hard or because of emotional problems: *After the divorce, Sonia had a nervous breakdown and had to stop work.*

2 not mentally ill

sane /seɪn/ [adj] not mentally ill, so that you are able to make sensible decisions and lead your life in a normal way: *He's as sane as I am.* | *No sane person could believe such garbage.*
perfectly sane (=completely sane) *To his neighbours, Sutcliffe appeared perfectly sane.*

sanity /ˈsænᵻti/ [n U] FORMAL when you are mentally healthy: *If you have your health and your sanity, money is not important.* | *I began to doubt Hamad's sanity as his story got stranger and stranger.*

MIDDLE

➡ see also **EDGE, SIDE**

1 the middle

the middle /ðə ˈmɪdl/ [n singular] the part of something, such as a space or area, a piece of writing, or a period of time, which is about halfway between one side and the other, or halfway between the beginning and the end: *"Did you enjoy the film?" "It was OK but I got a little bored towards the middle."*
+of *Gary rowed out towards the middle of the lake.* | *It was the middle of summer.* | *Going through the middle of Tokyo in the rush hour can be a nightmare.*

centre BRITISH **center** AMERICAN /ˈsentər/ [n C usually singular] the middle of a space, area, or object, especially the exact middle: *I love chocolates with soft centers.* | *The flower has white petals, and is deep pink at the centre.*
+of *Draw a line through the centre of the circle.*
at the centre/in the centre (of) (=exactly in the middle of something) *One child stands at the centre of the circle, and the others dance around her.*

the heart of /ðə ˈhɑːrt ɒv/ the middle of an area, town, or city: *The hotel is located in the heart of Moscow.* | *a quiet village in the heart of the English countryside*

Formal or informal?
The heart of is used mainly in written descriptions of places, to make the place sound interesting, pleasant, or very near to shops, theatres, trains etc.

2 in the middle

in the middle /ɪn ðə 'mɪdl/ *a garden with a fish-pond in the middle*
+of *Don't walk in the middle of the road!*

middle /'mɪdl/ [adj only before noun]
the middle drawer/shelf/finger etc (=the one in the middle) *You'll find the scissors in the middle drawer of my desk.* | *Jane was wearing a gold ring on her middle finger.* | *I am the middle child in a family of five.*

central /'sentrəl/ [adj] in the middle of an area, country, or town: *We are getting reports of bad weather in central Europe.* | *The houses face onto a central courtyard.* | *central London*

halfway /ˌhɑːf'weɪ◂ ‖ˌhæf-/ [adv] at the middle point between two places or the middle point of a period of time or an event
+across/between/down/up etc *Our car broke down halfway across the bridge.* | *We were halfway down the mountain when it started snowing.* | *Joe left college halfway through the year.*

mid- /mɪd/ [prefix] in or near the middle of a period of time
mid-afternoon / mid-week / mid-December / mid-18th century / mid-1990s etc *The house was built in the mid-18th century.* | *That's how people used to wear their hair in the mid-80s.*

When you see **WB**, go to the **WORD BANKS** section.

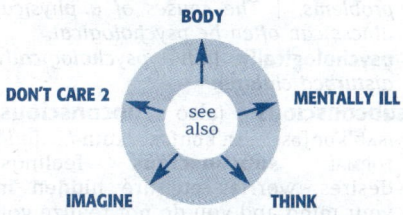

MIND

BODY

DON'T CARE 2   **MENTALLY ILL**

see also

IMAGINE   **THINK**

1 your mind

mind /maɪnd/ [n C] what you use to think and imagine things: *His mind was full of big ideas for developing the company.* | *I never know what's going on in her mind.* | *She had a picture of him in her mind – tall, blond, and handsome.* | *He tried to push these worries out of his mind.* (=tried not to think about them)

brain /breɪn/ [n C] your ability to think and the way that you think: *My brain worked fast as I tried to decide what to do.* | *She has an excellent business brain.*

head /hed/ [n C] someone's mind – use this especially when talking about the thoughts that are in someone's mind: *Dan's head was full of big ideas.*
what's going on in/inside sb's head (=what someone is thinking) *She's so quiet – you never quite know what's going on inside her head.*

2 affecting your mind

mental /'mentl/ [adj usually before noun] affecting your mind or happening in your mind: *After months of overworking, Briggs was suffering from mental and physical exhaustion.* | *It takes a lot of mental effort to understand these ideas.*
mental picture/image (=a picture that you have in your mind)
mental illness/problem/breakdown (=an illness, problem etc of your mind, not your body)
mentally [adv] *By the end of the day we were mentally and physically worn out.*

psychological /ˌsaɪkə'lɒdʒɪkəl◂ ‖-'lɑː-/ [adj] relating to the way your mind works and how this affects your behaviour – use this especially about mental problems: *She works with children who have psychological problems.* | *The causes of a physical illness can often be psychological.*

psychologically [adv] *psychologically disturbed children*

subconscious (also **unconscious**) /ˌsʌbˈkɒnʃəs, ʌnˈkɒnʃəs‖-ˈkɑːn-/ [adj] FORMAL **subconscious** feelings, desires, worries etc are hidden in your mind and you do not realize you have them: *a subconscious fear of failure*

subconsciously [adv] *Fathers are often subconsciously jealous of their sons.*

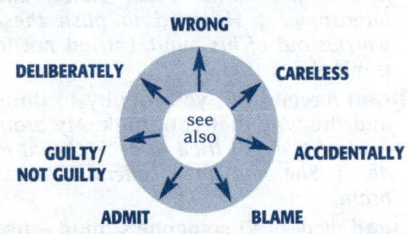

MISTAKE

WRONG

DELIBERATELY   CARELESS

see also

GUILTY/ NOT GUILTY   ACCIDENTALLY

ADMIT   BLAME

1   a mistake

mistake /mɪˈsteɪk/ [n C] something that is not correct, which you do, say, or write without intending to: *Your essay's full of mistakes.*
make a mistake *Henman was playing badly, making a lot of mistakes.*
+in *There's a mistake in the address.*
correct a mistake (=make it correct) *I hope you'll correct any mistakes I've made.*
spelling mistake (=when you spell a word wrongly) *Check your work carefully for any spelling mistakes.*

error /ˈerəʳ/ [n C/U] a mistake – use this especially to talk about mistakes in calculating or in using a language, system, or machine: *the most common errors among students of English*
+in *an error in the calculations*
human error (=when a mistake is caused by people, not by a machine) *The report decided that the accident was caused by human error.*
computer error (=a mistake caused

by a computer) *Our enormous phone bill was due to a computer error.*

Formal or informal?
Error is more formal than **mistake**.

misprint /ˈmɪs-prɪnt/ [n C] a small mistake in the way a word or number has been printed, for example a spelling mistake: *There were several misprints in the menu.*

2   a bad decision, idea etc that causes problems for you

mistake /mɪˈsteɪk/ [n C] something that you do or decide which is not at all sensible and which causes a lot of problems for you
make a mistake *My first marriage was a terrible failure. I don't want to make the same mistake again.*
it is a mistake to do sth *It was a mistake to let our credit card bill get so big.*
big/serious mistake *Buying the farm was the biggest mistake of her life.*

be a bad move /biː ə ˌbæd ˈmuːv/ INFORMAL if something you do **is a bad move**, it is a mistake because it puts you in a bad or dangerous situation: *He tried arguing with her. This was a bad move.* | *Perhaps changing jobs wasn't such a bad move after all.*
it is a bad move doing sth *It was a bad move letting him come here in the first place.*

3   to make a mistake

make a mistake /ˌmeɪk ə mɪˈsteɪk/ *My spoken Spanish was okay, but I kept making mistakes in my written work.* | *Don't worry – everyone makes mistakes.*

get sth wrong /ˌget (sth) ˈrɒŋ‖-ˈrɔːŋ/ ESPECIALLY SPOKEN to make a mistake in something that you do, say, or write, especially when this has bad or annoying results: *I've been there a year now, and my boss still gets my name wrong!* | *There was a report about it in the newspaper, but they got their facts wrong.*
get it wrong *Economists had predicted an improvement in the economy, but they got it wrong.*

M

MIX

➡ see also **CONFUSED 4**

1 mix substances/liquids

mix /mɪks/ [v T] to mix different liquids or substances together so that they become one substance that can no longer easily be separated
mix sth and sth *You can make green by mixing blue and yellow paint.*
mix sth with sth *Shake the bottle well to mix the oil with the vinegar.*
mix sth together *Concrete is made by mixing gravel, sand, cement, and water together.* | *If these two chemicals are mixed together they will explode.*

stir /stɜːʳ/ [v T] to mix things by moving them around in a container with a spoon or a stick: *He sat on the front step stirring the paint.*
stir in sth/stir sth in (=add something to a food mixture by stirring it) *When the butter has melted, stir in the soy sauce and ginger.* | *Add the grated cheese to the sauce and stir it in.*
stirring – stirred – have stirred

beat /biːt/ [v T] to mix liquids or soft substances together when you are preparing food, with quick, strong movements of a fork, spoon, or special machine: *Beat the eggs, then add the milk.*
beat sth together *In a separate bowl, beat together the oil and the flour.*
beat sth into sth *Gently beat the cream into the mixture.*
beating – beat – have beaten

blend /blend/ [v T] to mix liquids or soft substances when you are preparing food, in order to make a single smooth substance
blend sth and sth *Blend the sugar, eggs, and flour.*
blend sth together *The ingredients should be blended together until they are smooth.*

dilute /daɪˈluːt/ [v T] to make a liquid weaker by mixing it with water: *You should dilute the juice before you drink it.*

2 when feelings, ideas, styles etc are mixed with each other

be a mixture of /biː ə ˈmɪkstʃər ɒv/ to contain different features or ideas, mixed together: *The movie is a mixture of comedy and romance.* | *Her work is a mixture of classical and modern styles.*

be a cross between /biː ə ˈkrɒs bɪtwiːn‖-ˈkrɔːs-/ something that **is a cross between** one thing and another is a mixture of two different things: *The expression on Paul's face was a cross between amusement and disbelief.* | *It's difficult to describe my job. I suppose I'm a cross between a secretary and a translator.*

3 a mixture

mixture /ˈmɪkstʃəʳ/ [n C] several different things, ideas, feelings, or people mixed together
+of *The sauce is a mixture of flour, butter, milk, and cheese.* | *There was an interesting mixture of people at the party.* | *Sasha was looking at her with a mixture of admiration and curiosity.*

combination /ˌkɒmbɪˈneɪʃən‖ˌkɑːm-/ [n C] a mixture of different people working together, or different ideas, problems etc happening together, which has a particular effect
+of *Our problems were due to a combination of bad management and lack of experience.* | *Their music is an odd combination of jazz and opera.*
a good/bad/successful/disastrous etc combination *The show had the perfect combination of funny lines and good acting.*

4 not mixed with anything

pure /pjʊəʳ/ [adj] a material, substance etc that is **pure** has not been mixed with anything else: *The jacket is pure silk.* | *a necklace made of pure gold*

solid /ˈsɒlɪd‖ˈsɑː-/ [adj only before noun] not mixed with anything else – use this about wood or metals, especially expensive ones
solid gold/silver/pine/oak etc *The necklace is solid gold.* | *We bought a solid pine chest for only £50.*

M

straight (also **neat** BRITISH) /streɪt, niːt/ [adj] not mixed with anything else – use this about strong alcoholic drinks that are usually made weaker by adding something else: *Would you like your whisky neat or with water?* | *She was drinking straight vodka.*

MODERN

➡ see also **FASHIONABLE/ UNFASHIONABLE, NEW**

1 modern machines/buildings/methods

modern /ˈmɒdn‖ˈmɑːdərn/ [adj] using new methods, designs, or equipment: *Seattle has a very modern public transportation system.* | *a bright, modern office building* | *the horrors of modern warfare*
modern technology *Modern technology has made many household tasks much easier.*

the latest /ðə ˈleɪtˌəst/ [adj only before noun] **the latest** machines, computers, and methods are the newest and best ones that are available: *He was using one of the latest Japanese hand-held computers.* | *The latest model can print 15 pages every minute.*
the very latest *fast microprocessors that are produced using the very latest techniques*

up-to-date /ˌʌp tə ˈdeɪt◂/ [adj] **up-to-date** equipment, machines, or methods are very modern, and much better than the ones that many other people or organizations are still using: *This hospital has the most up-to-date equipment in Europe.* | *up-to-date training methods*

advanced /ədˈvɑːnst‖ədˈvænst/ [adj] **advanced** machines, weapons, and systems have been designed using the newest technical knowledge: *We have the most advanced security system available.* | *advanced weapons technology*

Formal or informal?
Advanced is not used in informal conversation.

high-tech/hi-tech /ˌhaɪ ˈtek◂/ [adj] using very modern electronic equipment and machines, especially computers: *a high-tech recording studio* | *the hi-tech industries of the 21st century*

2 modern art/literature/music/ fashion

modern /ˈmɒdn‖ˈmɑːdərn/ [adj] **modern** art, literature, music etc uses styles that have been developed very recently – use this especially about styles which are deliberately different from traditional styles, and which some people dislike because of this: *I like both modern dance and classical ballet.* | *Even critics of modern architecture like the new museum.*

contemporary /kənˈtempərəri, -pərɪ‖ -pəreri/ [adj only before noun] **contemporary** art, music, literature etc was produced or written recently: *Composers like Philip Glass have made contemporary music more popular.*
contemporary artist/writer/composer etc *a new exhibition of paintings by contemporary artists*

Formal or informal?
Contemporary is not used in informal conversation.

the latest /ðə ˈleɪtˌəst/ [adj only before noun] **the latest** fashion, style, or design is the one that is the most modern and the most fashionable: *Brightly colored shirts are the latest fashion.*
the latest in sth (=the most fashionable type of) *the latest in designer shoes*

3 modern ideas/ways of thinking

progressive /prəˈgresɪv/ [adj] using new methods for dealing with social problems, education, crime etc, especially when these methods are less strict than traditional ones. You can use **progressive** with these words: **methods,**

ideas, views, education, school, government, policy: *The principal has very progressive methods for dealing with young criminals*

4 to make something more modern

update /ʌpˈdeɪt/ [v I] to improve something, so that it includes the most modern equipment, methods, or information: *The school has just updated all its computer equipment.* | *Nursing staff were sent on training courses to update their skills.*

modernize (also **modernise** BRITISH) /ˈmɒdəˈnaɪz‖ˈmɑː-/ [v T] to make big changes to a place or organization, by putting in modern equipment or modern systems, and getting rid of old ones: *It was an old farmhouse that had been modernized by the previous owner.* | *attempts to modernize the prison system*

MONEY

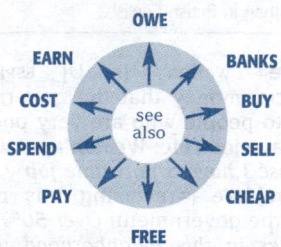

OWE

EARN   BANKS

COST   BUY

    see
    also

SPEND   SELL

PAY   CHEAP

FREE

1 money

money /ˈmʌni/ [n U] what you use to buy things, what you earn by working etc: *We don't have enough money for a vacation this year.*

money to do sth (=money you can use to pay for something) *I didn't have enough money to buy a ticket.*

spend money *I spent far too much money on Christmas presents.*

save money (=not spend much money) *"Are you coming out with us on Saturday?" "No, I'm trying to save money."*

pay money *I paid a lot of money for that coat.*

earn money *Accountants can earn a lot of money.*

make money (=earn money) *The restaurant makes a lot of money in the summer.*

lose money (=fail to make a profit in business, so that you spend more than you earn) *The state railway has been losing money for years.*

cash /kæʃ/ [n U] money, especially money that is available for you to spend: *I don't have much cash at the moment. Could I pay you next week?* | *She earns extra cash by babysitting.*

> **Formal or informal?**
> **Cash** is more informal than **money**.

a fortune /ə ˈfɔːˈtʃən/ [n singular] INFORMAL a lot of money: *That dress must have cost a fortune.*

be worth a fortune *They bought their house really cheaply but it's worth a fortune now.*

sum /sʌm/ [n C] an amount of money – use this to say how large or small an amount is: *Stars like Chaplin earned $2000 a week, which was an enormous sum in those days.*

sum of money *My uncle left me a small sum of money when he died.*

> **Formal or informal?**
> **Sum** is used in writing and in formal spoken English.

2 money in the form of notes and coins

money /ˈmʌni/ [n U] notes and coins that you use for buying things: *He counted the money carefully before putting it in his pocket.* | *The Queen never carries any money.*

cash /kæʃ/ [n U] money – use this to emphasize that you mean coins and notes, and not cheques, bank cards etc: *Thieves escaped with cash and computer equipment worth over $100,000.*

in cash (=using cash) *I'll give you £50 in cash and a cheque for the rest.*

pay (in) cash *There's a 5% discount if you pay cash.*

M

currency /ˈkʌrənsi‖ˈkɜːr-/ [n C/U] the money used in a particular country **Italian/Malaysian/Japanese etc currency** *I was carrying about £300 in Malaysian currency.*

foreign currency (=the currency of another country) *I'm taking £200 in traveller's cheques and £100 in foreign currency.*

plural **currencies**

change /tʃeɪndʒ/ [n U] money in the form of coins, or the money you get back when you pay for something with more money than it costs: *He emptied all the change out of his pockets.*

in change (=in the form of coins) *I've got a £10 note and about £5 in change.*

change for $10/£5 etc (=coins in exchange for a note) *Do you have change for a $5 bill?*

loose change (=a few coins) *I saved $20 in a month just by tossing my loose change in a jar.*

exact change (=the exact amount of money something costs) *The buses take exact change only.*

M 3 money that you receive regularly

➡ see also **EARN, PAY**

income /ˈɪŋkʌm, ˈɪn-/ [n C/U] all the money that you receive regularly, for example from your job or from the government: *Their combined income is more than £250,000 a year.* | *Most of her income comes from savings and investments.*

an income of £800/$2000 etc *The whole family lives on an income of less than $400 a month.*

be on a low/high income (=earn very little money or a lot of money) *Families on low incomes get free medical care.*

high-income/low-income *low-income workers*

annual income (=all the money you receive in a year) *His annual income is $35,000.*

disposable income (=money that you have available to spend after you have paid taxes and bills)

pension /ˈpenʃən/ [n C] an amount of money that old people receive regularly after they have stopped working: *Many elderly people find it very difficult to live on their pensions.* | *Bill gets a big pension from General Motors – he worked there for 30 years.*

Social Security /ˌsəʊʃəl sɪˈkjʊərɪti/ [n U] money that people receive from the government in the US when they have finished working at 65: *Paying the rent uses all his Social Security money.*

⚠ In British English, **Social Security** is sometimes used to mean the same as **benefit**.

benefit /ˈbenɪfɪt/ [n C/U] money that the government gives to people who are very poor, who do not have jobs etc

unemployment/sickness/maternity benefit *You cannot receive unemployment benefit unless you are looking for a job.*

on benefit (=receiving benefit) *After I became too ill to work I was forced to live on state benefit.*

Formal or informal?

In American English, you usually say **benefits** rather than **benefit**, and it is a more formal word than in British English.

welfare /ˈwelfeər/ [n U] ESPECIALLY AMERICAN money that the government pays to people who are very poor, do not have jobs etc: *We don't get welfare because I have a part-time job.*

on welfare (=receiving this money from the government) *Over 50% of the families in this neighborhood are on welfare.*

⚠ You can also use **welfare** before a noun, like an adjective: *cuts in welfare benefits* | *welfare payments* | *the welfare system*

allowance /əˈlaʊəns/ [n C] an amount of money that children get from their parents every week or every month: *My parents give me an allowance of $50 a month.*

pocket money /ˈpɒkɪt ˌmʌni‖ˈpɑː-/ [n U] BRITISH an amount of money that children get from their parents every week: *How much pocket money do you get?*

grant /grɑːnt‖grænt/ [*n* C] an amount of money that a government or other organization gives to someone to help pay for something good or useful, such as their education: *You can get a grant from the council to repair your roof.*
apply for a grant *Researchers have applied for a grant from the Carnegie Foundation.*

scholarship /ˈskɒləʳʃɪp‖ˈskɑː-/ [*n* C] money that a student receives from their school, college etc to pay for their education, especially by passing a difficult examination
win a scholarship (=because they have passed an exam) *When she was 18, she won a scholarship to study at the Conservatoire in Paris.*

4 money that you make by doing business

profit /ˈprɒfɪ̈t‖ˈprɑː-/ [*n* C/U] money that you make by doing business, for example when you sell something for more than it cost you to buy it or to produce it: *We aim to increase our profits by at least 5% every year.* | *For the first time, the company's annual profits were over $1 million.*
make/turn a profit *They made a huge profit when they sold the business.*
at a profit (=making a profit) *He sold the stocks at a profit.*

profitable /ˈprɒfɪ̈təbəl‖ˈprɑː-/ [*adj*] a **profitable** business or activity makes a profit: *We don't sell children's clothes any more – it wasn't profitable enough.*

5 money that you pay to the government

tax /tæks/ [*n* C/U] money that you have to pay to the government, especially from the money you earn or as an additional payment when you buy something: *The Republicans promised to reduce taxes.*
pay tax *families that work hard and pay their taxes*
tax on alcohol/cigarettes etc (=tax that is added to the price of alcohol, cigarettes etc)
income tax (=tax that you pay according to how much money you earn)
sales tax (=a tax added to the price of something you buy)
after tax (=after you have paid income tax) *I made over $600 a week, which was around $450 after tax.*
plural **taxes**

> You can also use **tax** before a noun, like an adjective: *a tax inspector* | *You have to fill in a tax form.*

duty /ˈdjuːti‖ˈduːti/ [*n* C/U] a tax you pay on something you buy, especially goods you have bought in another country: *You have to pay a duty on goods that you bring into the country if the value is over $500 .*
customs duty *The customs duty on luxury cars went up last month.*
plural **duties**

taxpayer /ˈtæksˌpeɪəʳ/ [*n* C] someone who pays tax
taxpayers' money (=money the government gets from taxes) *This defence project is simply a waste of taxpayers' money.*
the taxpayer (=all the people in a country who pay tax) *Bonus payments to top officials cost the taxpayer millions of pounds each year.*

6 additional money that you pay when you borrow money, or that you receive when you save money

interest /ˈɪntrɪ̈st/ [*n* U] *If you had half a million dollars you could easily live off the interest.*
+on *The interest on the loan is 16.5%.*
pay/earn interest *a savings account that earns high interest*
interest rate (=the amount of interest you pay or receive) *My bank charges really high interest rates.*
high/low interest *a high interest savings account*

M

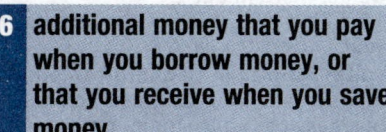

7 money that you give to someone to make them do something dishonest

bribe /braɪb/ [n C] money that someone gives to a person in an official position, in order to persuade them to do something for you that they should not do

take/accept a bribe *The judge admitted that he had accepted bribes.*

pay (sb) a bribe (=give someone a bribe) *You won't get across the border unless you pay the guards a bribe of at least $500.*

bribery [n U] when people give and accept bribes: *The inquiry showed that bribery was widespread.*

8 money for starting a business, paying for something important etc

finance /ˈfaɪnæns, fɪˈnæns‖fɪˈnæns, ˈfaɪnæns/ [n U] money that you borrow or receive in order to pay for something important and expensive, for example for starting a business: *We can't continue our research unless we get more finance.*

+for *How will you get the finance for your university course?*

capital /ˈkæpɪtl/ [n U] a large amount of money that you can use to start a business or to pay for something that will eventually produce more money: *You can make a lot of money from renting property to people, but you need capital to get started.*

raise capital FORMAL (=get the money you need, for example by borrowing from a bank) *It took him just three months to raise the capital for making the movie.*

funding /ˈfʌndɪŋ/ [n U] money that a government or large organization provides to pay for education, theatre, music etc, not for business activities: *Nowadays, schools have to find funding from private industry as well as from the Education Department. | The daycare center couldn't survive without government funding.*

+for *cuts in funding for the arts*

fund [v T] to provide money for education, music etc: *The scheme is funded by the government.*

subsidy /ˈsʌbsɪdi/ [n C] money that the government provides to help a business or industry which might not be able to operate without this additional money: *Generous subsidies are available to farmers who produce wheat. | Without state subsidies, the railways couldn't survive.*

plural **subsidies**

invest /ɪnˈvest/ [v I/T] to let a company, business, or bank use your money for a period of time, especially because you expect that you will eventually get back more money than you gave: *I want to invest the money my aunt left me.*

+in *Investing in property is no longer as safe as it used to be.*

invest money in sth *I invested £5000 in my brother's printing business.*

investor [n C] someone who invests money in a bank or business: *Most of the money came from foreign investors.*

put money into sth /ˌpʊt ˈmʌni ɪntuː (sth)/ to give money to a business to help it become successful, often in order to get back more money than you have given: *Unless they can find someone to put more money into it, the film studio will have to close. | The government ought to put more money into public transportation.*

> **Formal or informal?**
> **Put money into sth** is not used in formal writing such as official reports.

9 connected with the way that money is used

financial /fɪˈnænʃəl, faɪ-/ [adj usually before noun] connected with money – use this about the way that people and organizations use and control their money: *Joan has a lot of financial problems. | Wall Street is the financial center of the US. | The school's financial position is very healthy.*

financially [adv] *She wanted to go out to work and be financially independent.*

economic /ˌekəˈnɒmɪk◂, ˌiː-‖-ˈnɑː-/ [adj usually before noun] use this about the way that a country's money and wealth is produced, spent, and controlled: *The President's economic reforms have put a lot of people out of work.* | *a period of economic growth* | *the need for economic planning*

economically [adv] *an economically advanced country*

economy /ɪˈkɒnəmi‖ɪˈkɑː-/ [n C] the economic system of a country, including its trade and industry: *the collapse of the German economy in the 1920s* | *one of the most successful economies in Asia*

the economy (=a country's economy) *This government has ruined the economy.*

plural **economies**

10 someone who wants a lot of money or always thinks about money

greedy /ˈɡriːdi/ [adj] someone who is **greedy** wants a lot of money, even though they do not need it: *Britain has some of the greediest landlords in Europe.* | *corrupt and greedy politicians*

greedy – greedier – greediest

greed [n U] when you keep wanting more money: *No-one needs to earn that much – it's just greed!*

materialistic /məˌtɪəriəˈlɪstɪk◄/ [adj] someone who is **materialistic** thinks that money and possessions are more important than anything else: *Are today's young people more materialistic than previous generations?*

11 having no money

➡ see also **POOR**

bankrupt /ˈbæŋkrʌpt/ [adj] a company or person that is **bankrupt** does not have enough money to pay their debts, and so they have to stop doing business: *Five years ago she was a successful actress, but now she is bankrupt.*

go bankrupt (=become bankrupt) *Many small businesses will go bankrupt unless interest rates fall.*

◯ **broke** /brəʊk/ [adj not before noun] SPOKEN someone who is **broke** has no money or very little money: *"Can you lend me some money?" "Sorry, I'm broke."* | *When I was a student I was always broke.*

12 to have just enough money to live

get by INFORMAL (also **survive**) /ˌɡet ˈbaɪ, səˈvaɪv/ [phrasal verb I] to have just enough money to buy the things you need, but no more: *She does cleaning jobs in the evenings, and makes just enough to get by.*

+on *My grandmother gets by on just £50 a week.* | *They survive on very low incomes.*

make ends meet /ˌmeɪk ˌendz ˈmiːt/ INFORMAL to have just enough money to buy what you need – use this when someone has so little money that life is very difficult for them: *Many families struggle to make ends meet, especially during the winter.* | *How am I supposed to make ends meet on $150 a month?*

live on sth /ˈlɪv ɒn (sth)/ [phrasal verb T] if you **live on** a particular amount of money, this is all the money that you have to buy everything you need: *You can't live on less than $25,000 a year in New York.* | *My salary doesn't really give me enough to live on.*

MORE

➡ opposite **LESS**

➡ if you want to know about using adjectives for comparing things, go to the **ESSENTIAL GRAMMAR** (Section 14)

➡ see also **MOST, ADD, INCREASE, ANOTHER**

1 more of the same thing, or another one of the same things

more /mɔːʳ/ [quantifier] more of something in addition to what is already there: *I gave him $200 last week and he's already asking for more.* | *We have enough tables but we need more chairs.*

M

+of *I forced myself to swallow more of the medicine.* | *Do you have any more of those delicious cookies?*

three more/100 more etc *They walked for two more miles before they found a telephone.* | *Some of the students arrived today, and about 20 more of them are arriving tomorrow.*

some more/a few more/any more *Do you want any more tea?* | *You may need to buy some more books.*

another /əˈnʌðəʳ/ [*determiner/pronoun*] one more thing, person, or amount that is the same as one you already had: *Look, your glass is cracked. I'll get you another.* | *Would you like another drink?* | *Could you get another loaf of bread while you're out?*

another ten minutes/five miles/two gallons etc *Add the pasta and heat the soup for another ten minutes.*

another one *There were two cars in the driveway and another one in the garage.*

+of *Is this another of your crazy ideas for making money?*

extra /ˈekstrə/ [*adj/adv*] more of something, in addition to the usual amount or number: *You'd better get some extra milk if Steve and Richard are staying the weekend.* | *Residents can use the hotel swimming pool at no extra cost.*

an extra ten minutes/three pounds/four litres etc *I asked for an extra day to finish my assignment.*

be/cost/earn extra (=extra money) *Dinner costs $15, but wine is extra.*

additional /əˈdɪʃənəl/ [*adj* only before noun] FORMAL more than the amount that was agreed or expected at the beginning: *Our own car broke down, so we had the additional expense of renting a car.*

an additional £10/10 miles/10 minutes etc *They've extended his contract for an additional 12 months.*

further /ˈfɜːʳðəʳ/ [*adj* only before noun] more, in addition to what there is already or what has happened already: *The doctors are keeping her in the hospital to do further tests.* | *For further information, contact the help line.*

a further £10/10 miles/10 minutes *Strike action will continue for a further 24 hours.*

2 more than a number or amount

more /mɔːʳ/ [*quantifier*] more than a number or amount: *Salaries are in the region of $200,000 a year, with top executives earning even more.*

+than *I've been working here for more than ten years.* | *More than 50,000 people attended the open-air concert.*

much more/far more/a lot more *Diane earns much more than I do.*

10/100/$50 more (=more than another number) *It's a better hotel, but it costs about £50 more than the other one.*

or more *There must have been 200 people or more, all trying to crowd into the hall.*

over /ˈəʊvəʳ/ [*preposition/adv*] more than a number or amount: *I've been waiting over half an hour for you.* | *She weighs over 200 kilos.* | *The train was travelling at speeds of over 150 mph.*

just over (=slightly over) *She weighs just over 120 pounds.*

well/way over (=much more) *The US gave the country well over a million dollars in aid.*

8/10/12 etc and over *The club is for children aged 10 and over.*

above /əˈbʌv/ [*preposition/adv*] more than a number or level on a scale that can be exactly measured: *The temperature was just 2 degrees above zero.* | *Anyone earning above $80,000 will pay more tax.*

3 years/6 metres/80% etc and above *Babies of 6 months and above need to be vaccinated.*

well/way above (=much more) *The pay is well above the minimum wage.*

outnumber /aʊtˈnʌmbəʳ/ [*v T*] ESPECIALLY WRITTEN if one type of person or thing **outnumbers** another, there are more of the first type than of the second: *Women teachers outnumber their male colleagues by two to one.*

greatly/far outnumber *a city where bicycles greatly outnumber cars*

3 more than before

more /mɔːʳ/ [quantifier/adv] more than before: *The new airport will just mean more traffic, more noise, and more pollution.* | *As mobile phones got cheaper, people started using them more.*
more quickly/slowly/easily etc *I wish she'd talk more slowly.*
more expensive/important/difficult etc *Today's test was definitely more difficult than last week's.*
+than *People are travelling around more than they used to.* | *She seems more relaxed than she was last week.*
a lot more/much more/far more *There are a lot more game shows on TV than there used to be.* | *David earns far more now than he did in his old job.*
a little more/slightly more *Next time, try and be a little more patient.*
more and more /ˌmɔːr ənd 'mɔːʳ◂/ use this to say that something continues to happen more often than it did before or continues to become more difficult, more expensive etc than it was before: *More and more students are using computers to do their schoolwork.* | *As the years passed, she depended more and more on her daughter.*
more and more expensive/tired/difficult etc *The concert was very long, and I began to feel more and more bored.*
more and more slowly/quickly/clearly etc *As the gas cools, the molecules move more and more slowly.*
increasingly /ɪn'kriːsɪŋli/ [adv] use this to say that something continues to happen more often than before, or continues to become more difficult, more expensive etc than it was before: *Increasingly, it is the female students who are getting the best grades.*
increasingly difficult/common/important/complex *It is looking increasingly likely that Tarrant will resign.* | *People have become increasingly interested in environmental issues.*

Increasingly and **more and more** mean the same, but there are some differences in the way they are used. **Increasingly** is used mainly in written English, and is often used at the start of a sentence. **More and more** is used in written and spoken English, and can be used as a quantifier before a plural noun as well as like an adverb: *More and more people are choosing this kind of holiday.*

---

a growing number/an increasing number /ə ˌɡrəʊɪŋ 'nʌmbəʳ, ən ɪnˌkriːsɪŋ 'nʌmbəʳ/ use this when the number of people that are doing something is not yet very large, but is increasing all the time
+of *A growing number of refugees were entering the country.* | *Increasing numbers of elderly people are living alone.*
in growing/increasing numbers *Doctors are leaving the profession in increasing numbers.*

> ⚠ **Growing numbers** and **increasing numbers** mean the same as **a growing number** and **an increasing number**.

higher /'haɪəʳ/ [adj] use this about prices, speeds, or amounts that are bigger than they were before
higher price/proportion/level/rate *There is now a higher proportion of women in management jobs.*
+than *The cost of student accommodation is higher than it was a year ago.*
greater /'ɡreɪtəʳ/ [adj] use this about a feeling or state that is stronger or more noticeable than it was before
greater interest/need/support/freedom *After the war, the country began to enjoy greater prosperity.*
+than *The need for people with computing skills is greater than ever before.*

Greater is used in writing and in formal spoken English.

---

4 more than someone or something else

more /mɔːʳ/ [quantifier] more than another person, thing, or place: *My*

parents are both teachers, but my father earns more. | Ask Hilary. She knows more about it.
+than It's not fair. He's got more than I have. | There is more oil in the Middle East than in any other part of the world.

higher /ˈhaɪərˈ/ [adj] use this about prices, speeds, or amounts that are bigger than someone else's
+than In the 1960s, Japan achieved a higher rate of economic growth than most other countries. | Car prices in Britain are higher than in many European countries.

MOST

➡ opposite **LEAST**
➡ if you want to know about using adjectives for comparing things go to the **ESSENTIAL GRAMMAR** (Section 14)
➡ see also **MORE**

1 most of an amount, number, total, group etc

most /məʊst/ [quantifier] the largest part of something, or the largest number of people, places, things etc
most people/things/days etc What most people want is a peaceful life. | Most evenings we just stay in and watch TV.
most of the students/my friends/ her money etc (=the largest part of a group, amount, or thing) Most of the people I spoke to were very worried. | Alex spends most of his allowance on books. | Most of what Hannah told me wasn't true. | This is a poor country, and most of it is desert.

⚠ Don't say 'the most people drive to work'. Say **most people drive to work**.

⚠ Don't say 'almost Japanese people live in cities'. Say **most Japanese people live in cities**.

almost all/nearly all /ˌɔːlməʊst ˈɔːl, ˌnɪərˈli ˈɔːl/ not all, but almost all: We got nearly all our food from the farm.
+of I've read almost all of Jane Austen's novels. | Nearly all of my clothes are too small now.

mostly/mainly /ˈməʊstli, ˈmeɪnli/ [adv] use this to say that most of the people or things in a group are of the same type: A huge crowd of fans, mostly girls, waited outside the hotel. | Our customers are mainly young people interested in fashion. | She reads a lot of books, mostly science fiction stories.

the majority /ðə məˈdʒɒrɪtiˈməˈdʒɔː-, məˈdʒɑː-/ [n singular] more than half of the people or things in a large group
+of In June the majority of our students will be taking examinations.
the vast/great majority (=far more than half) an education policy that will please the vast majority of parents | The great majority of accidents in the Alps occur while climbers are coming down.
be in the majority (=be the largest part of a group) Young people were in the majority at the meeting.

Formal or informal?
The majority is used in writing and in formal spoken English.

⚠ Use a plural verb after **the majority (of)**: Some of the children go home for lunch, but the majority have their lunch in school.

2 more than anyone or anything else

most /məʊst/ more than anything else – use this especially to talk about something that you like, want, need, or dislike more than anything else: I want to study biology – that's what interests me most. | The part we enjoyed most was the trip to the Grand Canyon.
most of all (=much more than anything else) What the people here need most of all is food and clean water.

the most /ðə ˈməʊst/ a larger amount or number than anyone or anything

else: *In a fair tax system those who earn the most should pay the most.*
the most things/points/votes etc *The player who scores the most points wins.*
the most money/fuel/information etc *Choose the program that gives you the most information.*

3 the largest possible amount

the most /ðə 'məʊst/ the largest amount that is possible: *I'm afraid £500 is the most I can offer you.* | *The most you can hope to achieve is a 10% increase in production.*

maximum /'mæksɪ̩məm/ [adj only before noun] the **maximum** amount of something is the largest amount that is possible or allowed
maximum amount/number/speed *Travelling at its maximum speed of 186 mph, the train reached Paris in less than two hours.* | *We want our message to reach the maximum number of people.*
the maximum [n singular] the maximum number or amount: *Thirty students per class is the maximum.*

top /tɒp‖tɑːp/ [adj only before noun]
top speed/price/salary etc the highest speed, price etc, or the most that is possible: *The 1.6 litre sports version has a top speed of 121 mph.* | *The top price paid was $1,200,000 for a print by Degas.*

> **Formal or informal?**
> **Top** is often used in newspapers, advertisements etc. **Maximum** is more formal or more technical than **top**.

4 most often

mostly/mainly /'məʊstli, 'meɪnli/ [adv] use this to say that someone does one thing more than they do anything else: *We eat mostly Italian food.* | *She has to travel abroad a lot, mostly to Spain and France.* | *He paints mainly landscapes.*

in most cases /ɪn 'məʊst ˌkeɪsɪ̩z/ use this to say that things happen in one way more often than in any other way, in the situation that you are talking about: *In most cases the new drug is very effective.* | *The seeds will start to grow within two weeks in most cases.*

> **Formal or informal?**
> **In most cases** is used in writing and in formal spoken English.

most of the time /'məʊst əv ðə ˌtaɪm/ almost always: *Most of the time I just answer the phone and type letters.* | *This place is really busy most of the time.*

MOTHER

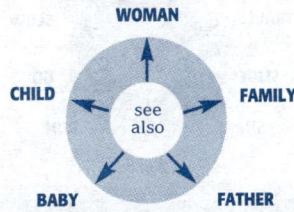

WOMAN
CHILD — see also — FAMILY
BABY — FATHER

1 mother

mother /'mʌðəʳ/ [n C] *Her mother is a teacher.* | *Like most mothers, I always felt anxious when my children came home late.* | *Terri Godwin, a mother of three, was attacked as she walked home yesterday.*

mum BRITISH **mom** AMERICAN /mʌm, mɒm‖mɑːm/ [n C] SPOKEN a name you use to talk to your mother or to talk about her: *My mum and dad are both doctors.* | *Mom, what's for dinner?*

mummy BRITISH **mommy** AMERICAN /'mʌmi, 'mɒmi‖'mɑːmi/ [n C] SPOKEN a name for your mother – used especially by young children or when you are talking to young children: *Ben, is your mommy coming to the winter concert?* | *"Goodnight, Mummy," said Sara.*
plural **mummies/mommies**

2 like a mother

maternal/motherly /mə'tɜːʳnl, 'mʌðəʳli/ [adj] caring and kind like a mother – use this about women or girls or their feelings: *Claire was very maternal towards the other children.* | *She kept a maternal eye on them all.* | *Mrs Woodrow, a good-natured motherly woman, took care of their children while they were at work.*

Formal or informal?
Motherly is less formal than **maternal**.

MOVE/NOT MOVE

➡ If you mean 'move house', go to
WB HOUSES/WHERE PEOPLE LIVE

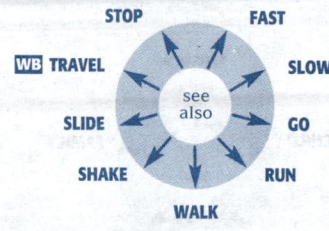

1 to move from one place or position to another

move /muːv/ [v I] to go to a different place or to change the position of your body: *Every time I move I get a pain in my shoulder.* | *Will you move so that I can come past, please?* | *Don't get off the bus while it's moving.* | *Don't move, or I'll shoot!*
+away/forward/toward etc *She moved away from the window.*
move around (=to different parts of an area) *I can hear someone moving around downstairs!*

movement /'muːvmənt/ [n C/U] when something or someone moves: *the dancer's graceful movements* | *Any movement will set off the alarm.*
+of *Tourists come to see the mass movement of these animals across the plains of Africa.*

moving /'muːvɪŋ/ [adj only before noun] not staying still, but changing position or going from one place to another: *This photograph was taken from the window of a moving vehicle.* | *All the moving parts of the engine must be kept well oiled.*

2 to move something from one place or position to another

move /muːv/ [v T] to take something to a different place or change the position of something: *Will you move your car, please – it's blocking the road.* | *I think my hand is broken. I can't move my fingers.*
move sth to/into sth *We'll have to move the table into the hall.*

transfer /trænsˈfɜːʳ/ [v T] to move something and put it in a different place or container
transfer sth (from sth) to sth *Transfer the cookies to a wire rack to cool.* | *Information can be transferred from one computer to another.*
transferring – transferred – have transferred

Formal or informal?
Transfer is more formal than **move**.

3 to keep moving your body

fidget /'fɪdʒɪt/ [v I] to keep moving or playing with your fingers, hands, feet etc, because you are bored or nervous: *Stop fidgeting!*
+with *Diana started fidgeting with her pencil.*

can't keep still /ˌkɑːnt kiːp 'stɪl‖ˌkænt-/ (also **can't sit/stand still**) if you **can't keep still**, you keep moving your body because you are excited or nervous and you cannot relax: *I was so excited that I couldn't keep still all morning!* | *It was the morning before his first game, and Hansen couldn't sit still.*

twitch /twɪtʃ/ [v I] if part of your body **twitches**, it makes small movements that you cannot control: *My eyelid won't stop twitching.*

4 something that you can move from one place to another

portable /'pɔːʳtəbəl/ [adj] a **portable** machine or piece of equipment is designed to be carried or moved easily: *We only have a little portable TV.* | *portable toilets*

5 | unable to move or impossible to move

can't move /ˌkɑːnt ˈmuːvǁˌkænt-/ if you **can't move**, you are unable to move, for example because you are frightened or injured: *I was so frightened that I couldn't move.*
can't move sth *I can't move my leg – I think it's broken.*

stuck /stʌk/ [*adj* not before noun] something that is **stuck** is fixed or trapped in a particular position or place and it cannot be moved: *I can't open the window – it's stuck.* | *The elevator's stuck again.*
+in *Our bus was stuck in a traffic jam for three hours!*
get stuck (=become stuck) *They tried to drive through the snow, but the car got stuck.*

jammed /dʒæmd/ [*adj* not before noun] something that is **jammed** cannot be moved because it is trapped between two surfaces or trapped between parts of a machine: *This drawer's jammed.*
+in/under/between etc *The paper has got jammed in the printer again.*

stiff /stɪf/ [*adj*] if your fingers, back, neck, legs etc are **stiff**, it is difficult and usually painful for you to move them: *His back was stiff.* | *I was so stiff the next day!*
stiff neck/back/arm *I woke up with a stiff neck.*

paralysed BRITISH **paralyzed** AMERICAN /ˈpærəlaɪzd/ [*adj*] someone who is **paralysed** or **paralyzed** cannot move, either because of an injury or because of fear, shock, etc: *A car crash in 1989 left him completely paralysed.*
+by/with *His father had been partially paralyzed by the fall.* | *She stood at the side of the stage, paralysed with fear.*

6 | not moving

still /stɪl/ [*adj* not before noun] not moving – use this especially about people who are not moving or about places where there is no wind: *There was no wind and the trees were completely still.* | *Anna looked out across the still water of the lake.*

keep/stand/sit still *Keep still while I tie your shoes.* | *I want you all to sit still and listen to the story.*

stationary /ˈsteɪʃənəriǁ-neri/ [*adj*] FORMAL
stationary car/vehicle/truck/traffic a car, vehicle etc that is not moving: *The truck swerved and hit a stationary vehicle.* | *a four-mile queue of stationary traffic*

at a standstill /ət ə ˈstændstɪl/ if traffic or a vehicle is **at a standstill**, it is not moving, especially when this is annoying: *Traffic was at a standstill on the motorway.*

> **Formal or informal?**
> **At a standstill** is used in formal writing and in news reports.

MUSIC

➡ see Word Banks section

MUST

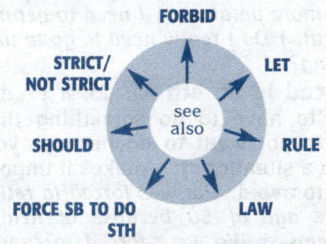

1 | when you have to do something

must /mʌst/ [*modal verb*] to have to do something, especially because you feel that you should do it or because there is a rule that says you have to do it
must do sth *All passengers must wear seatbelts.* | *I must go and do my homework.* | *Accidents must be reported to the safety officer.*
must sb do sth? FORMAL *Must you leave so soon?*

> Don't say 'we must to go'. Say **we must go**.

M

⚠ Only use **must** in the present tense. When talking about the past, use **had to**: *At my old school, we had to wear a uniform.* When talking about the future, use **will have to**: *If you fail the test, you will have to take it again.*

⚠ You can say **I must** do something to mean that you feel you really should do it because it is important or urgent: *I must write to my mother.* | *I really must try to stop smoking.*

have to do sth /ˌhæv tuː ˈduː (sth)/ if you **have to do something**, you must do it, especially because the situation that you are in makes it necessary or because there is a rule that says you must do it: *I have to stay late today.* | *She had to leave early.* | *The doctor said I would have to have an operation.* | *Do we have to take our passports with us?*
have got to do sth BRITISH *I've got to return my library books today.*

need to do sth /ˌniːd tə ˈduː (sth)/ to have to do something because you think it is necessary or someone else thinks it is necessary: *We need to buy some more potatoes.* | *I need to get my hair cut.* | *Do I really need to go to this meeting?*

be forced to do sth /biː ˈfɔːʳst tə ˈduː (sth)/ to have to do something that you do not want to do because you are in a situation that makes it impossible to avoid: *She was forced to retire at the age of 50 because of health problems.* | *We were forced to cancel the party.*

feel obliged to do sth /ˌfiːl əˌblaɪdʒd tə ˈduː (sth)/ FORMAL to feel that you should do something because other people expect you to do it and will be disappointed or upset if you do not: *I felt obliged to invite them all.*

Formal or informal?

Feel obliged to do something is formal, so in conversation use **feel I have to do something**: *I felt I had to invite them all.*

have no alternative /ˌhæv ˌnəʊ ɔːlˈtɜːʳnətɪv/ to have to do something, even though you do not want to, because there is nothing else you can possibly do in the situation: *The police*

say they had no alternative: *the man was armed and they had to shoot him.*
have no alternative but to do sth *He had no alternative but to resign.*

2 when you must not do something

➡ see also **FORBID**

must not/mustn't /ˈmʌst nɒt, ˈmʌsənt/ use this to tell or order someone not to do something: *This book must not be removed from the library.*
must not/mustn't do sth *Remember, you mustn't tell Pat about this.*

⚠ Don't say 'you mustn't to go'. Say **you mustn't go**.

⚠ Only use **must not/mustn't** in the present tense. When talking about the past, use **couldn't** or **wasn't/weren't allowed to**: *He couldn't stay in the US because he didn't have a green card.* | *The children were not allowed to watch horror movies.* When talking about the future use **will not be allowed to**: *Under the new rules, employees will not be allowed to smoke in the office.*

⚠ Don't confuse **must not do something** (=when you are not allowed to do it) and **not have to do something** (=when you can do it, but you do not need to).

🔍 **can't** /kɑːnt‖kænt/ ESPECIALLY SPOKEN use this to say that someone is not allowed to do something: *"Ben wants to borrow the car." "Well, tell him he can't."*
can't do sth *I'm sorry, but you know I can't discuss my work.*

⚠ Only use **can't** in the present tense. When talking about the past, use **couldn't** or **wasn't/weren't allowed to**. When talking about the future, use **will not be allowed to**.

⚠ Don't say 'you can't to go'. Say **you can't go**.

not be allowed /ˌnɒt biː əˈlaʊd/ if something **is not allowed**, there is a

rule that forbids it: *Smoking is not allowed on the train.*
sb is not allowed to do sth *You are not allowed to use a dictionary during the test.*

3 something that must be done

compulsory /kəm'pʌlsəri/ [*adj*] FORMAL something that is **compulsory** must be done because of a rule or law: *Compulsory education* (=when all children have to go to school) *was introduced in 1870.*
it is compulsory for sb to do sth *It's compulsory for all drivers to have insurance.*

necessary /'nesəsərill-seri/ [*adj*] if something is **necessary**, there are very good reasons why it should be done, and it would not be sensible to avoid doing it: *If any changes are necessary, you can make them.*
it is necessary to do sth *Is it really necessary to keep all the doors locked?*
it is necessary for sb to do sth *The doctor says it may be necessary for me to have an operation.*
make it necessary to do sth *The heavy rain made it necessary to close several roads.*

essential/vital /ɪ'senʃəl, 'vaɪtl/ [*adj*] if something is **essential** or **vital**, it is very important to do it, and there could be serious problems if it is not done: *Choosing the right equipment is vital.*
absolutely essential *In cases of heart attack, immediate medical help is absolutely essential.*
it is essential/vital to do sth *It is vital to take precautions before handling toxic substances.*
it is essential/vital that *It is essential that you finish the job before Christmas.* | *It is vital that you keep accurate records of what you spend.*

4 when you do not have to do something

not have to do sth /nɒt hæv tə 'duː (sth)/ if you do **not have to do something**, you can do it if you want, but you are not forced to do it by a rule, another person, or the situation

you are in: *Paola came from a wealthy family and didn't have to work.* | *You don't have to go if you don't want to.*

> ⚠ Don't confuse **not have to do something** (=when you are not forced to do it) and **must not do something** (=when you are not allowed to do it).

there is no need to do sth /ðeər ɪz ˌnəʊ 'niːd tə ˌduː (sth)/ SPOKEN say this to tell someone that it is not necessary for them to do something: *There's no need to do the dishes – I'll do them in the morning.* | *There's no need to bring a towel.*

unnecessary/not necessary
/ʌn'nesəsəri, nɒt 'nesəsərill-seri/ [*adj*] if something is **unnecessary** or **not necessary**, is it not needed or there is no good reason for you to do it: *Building another shopping mall here is completely unnecessary.*
+to do sth *It's not necessary to oil your bike every day.*

not need to do sth (also **needn't do sth** BRITISH) /ˌnɒt 'niːd tə duː (sth), 'niːdnt duː (sth)/ to not have to do something because it is not necessary and there will not be any problems if you do not do it: *You don't need to tell Sandy.* | *You needn't come with me – I'll be fine.* | *Marian had a rich husband and did not need to work.*

> ⚠ Don't say 'you needn't to pay now'. Say **you needn't pay now** or **you don't need to pay now**.

> ⚠ Don't confuse **not need to do something** (=when something is not necessary) and **must not do something** (=when something is not allowed).

optional /'ɒpʃənəlll'ɑːp-/ [*adj*] if something is **optional**, you do not have to do it or use it but you can if you want to: *We all had to study English, but Spanish was optional.*

> **Formal or informal?**
> **Optional** is used in writing and in formal spoken English.

voluntary /'vɒləntərill'vɑːlənteri/ [*adj*] a **voluntary** activity is one that you do because you want to do it, especially because you believe it is useful or will help other people, and not because you have to: *I do voluntary work at a young mothers' centre.* | *We get all our money from voluntary contributions.*

5 to say that someone must do something

insist /ɪnˈsɪst/ [v I/T] to say firmly that someone must do something or that something must happen, and not let anyone refuse: *"You must stay," he insisted.*
insist (that) sb do sth *They insisted that we paid for the damage before we left.*
insist on doing sth (=say that you must be allowed to do something) *I insist on speaking to the manager.*

MYSELF/YOURSELF

➡ see also **ALONE**

1 when you do something yourself, instead of someone else doing it for you

yourself/myself etc [*pronoun*] if you do something **yourself**, no one else does it for you: *I made these curtains myself.* | *Why can't your boyfriend cook lunch himself?* | *"Could you pass me that book?" "Get it yourself!"*
(all) by yourself/myself etc (=without help from anyone else) *The girls made these cookies all by themselves.*

personally /ˈpɜːrsənəli/ [*adv*] if an important person does something **personally**, they do it, although you

would normally expect someone else to do it for them: *The chairman wrote to us personally to thank us for our hard work.*

> **Formal or informal?**
> **Personally** is used in writing and in formal spoken English.

in person /ɪn ˈpɜːrsən/ if you do something **in person**, you do it by going somewhere yourself, instead of writing, telephoning, or asking someone else to do it: *He delivered the document in person to Friedman's house.* | *Do I have to come and get it in person?*

first-hand /ˌfɜːrst ˈhænd◄/ [*adj* only before noun] **first-hand experience/knowledge/account etc** experience, knowledge etc that you get by doing or seeing something yourself, not by reading about it or hearing about it from someone else: *She has first-hand experience of the French education system, having taught there for five years.* | *a first-hand account of the robbery*

2 when someone only thinks about himself or herself

selfish /ˈselfɪʃ/ [*adj*] someone who is **selfish** only thinks about what they need or want, and never thinks about how other people feel: *Amy, don't be so selfish! Let the others have a turn.* | *a selfish old man* | *selfish motives*
selfishly [*adv*] *She selfishly refused to give us any of the food.*
selfishness [*n* U] when someone behaves in a selfish way: *a political philosophy based on selfishness and greed*

N, n

NAME

1 a person's name

name /neɪm/ [n C] *What's your name? | I'm not very good at remembering people's names. | His name is Raymond Ford.*
full name (=all your names) *Ayrton Senna's full name was Ayrton Senna da Silva.*
surname/last name /'sɜːʳneɪm, 'lɑːst ˌneɪmǁ'læst-/ [n C] your last name, which is the same as your parents' or husband's name: *Smith is the most common English surname.*

> ⚠ Until recently, women always took their husband's **surname** or **last name** when they got married, but many women no longer do this.

first name /'fɜːʳst ˌneɪm/ [n C] the name that your parents choose for you when you are born, which in western countries comes at the beginning of your full name: *Her first name is Liz. I don't know her surname.*
maiden name /'meɪdn ˌneɪm/ [n C] the surname that a woman had before she was married: *My mother kept her maiden name when she got married.* (=did not change her name to her husband's name)
initials /ɪ'nɪʃəlz/ [n plural] the first letters of your names: *a suitcase marked with the initials JR*
title /'taɪtl/ [n C] a word such as Mrs, Miss, Ms, Mr, Dr, or Professor that you put before your name: *The title 'Ms' became much more popular in the 1980s.*

2 your name when you write it on a cheque, at the end of a letter etc

signature /'sɪgnətʃəʳ/ [n C] your name as you usually write it, especially when you write it on an important document, a cheque, or a letter: *I can't read the signature on this letter. | We got more than 4000 signatures on our petition to save the park.*
autograph /'ɔːtəgrɑːfǁ-græf/ [n C] a famous person's name that they write and give to someone who admires them: *Can I have your autograph? | I'd be too shy to ask for his autograph.*

3 a name that is not your real name

nickname /'nɪkneɪm/ [n C] a name given to someone by their friends or family, which is not their real name and is often chosen because of something about their appearance or behaviour: *At school, her nickname was Carrots because of her red hair.*
false name /ˌfɔːls 'neɪm/ [n C] a name that someone uses instead of their real name, so that people will not find out who they really are: *It is illegal to give a false name to your employer. | They used a false name to hire a car.*
stage name /'steɪdʒ ˌneɪm/ [n C] the name used by an actor, singer etc instead of their real name: *Greta Garbo was the stage name of Greta Gustavson, born in Stockholm in 1905.*

4 the name of a place, object etc

name /neɪm/ [n C] *I've forgotten the name of the street where she lives.*
the Chinese/French etc name for sth *The Chinese name for this plant means 'cat's ears'.*
brand name /'brænd ˌneɪm/ [n C] the name given to a product by the company that makes it, often including the name of the company itself: *Our customers prefer goods with brand names, such as Levi's or Adidas.*

5 to have a particular name

sb's name is /(sb's) 'neɪm ɪz/ *Hi! My name's Ted.* | *"Who's that man over there?" "His name is Lucio Mannonetti and he owns the company."*

be called /bi: 'kɔːld/ to have a particular name – use this about a person, thing, or place: *There's someone called Russell on the phone for you.* | *What's the new teacher called?* | *They are in favour of what is called 'sustainable development'.*

be named /bi: 'neɪmd/ ESPECIALLY AMERICAN someone who **is named** Paul, Jane etc has the name Paul, Jane etc: *Their new baby is named Caroline.* | *She went to the movies with some guy named Rudi.*

> ⚠ Don't say 'what's their son named?' Say **what's their son called?** or **what's their son's name?** Don't use **be named** in questions, use **be called**.

be known as /bi: 'nəʊn æz/ if someone or something **is known as** a particular name, that is the name that people call them, although it is not their real name: *He was known as Rambo to his friends.* | *This area is known as Little Odessa because there are a lot of Russians living here.*

6 to give a name to someone or something

call /kɔːl/ [v T] to give a name to someone or something
call sb Paul/Jane etc *My mother wanted to call me Yuri.* | *Guidebooks call Chicago 'The Windy City'.* | *This is what psychologists call 'body language'.*

name /neɪm/ [v T] ESPECIALLY AMERICAN to officially give someone or something a name: *Have they named the baby yet?*
name sb Paul/Jane etc *We named our daughter Sarah.*
name sb/sth after (also **name sb/sth for** AMERICAN) *Bill was named after his father.* | *The new college is going to be named for John F. Kennedy.*

christen /'krɪsən/ [v T] to give a baby its name at a Christian religious ceremony
christen sb Paul etc *They christened him Patrick John.* | *She was christened Jessica, but everyone calls her Jess.*

rename /riːˈneɪm/ [v T] to change something's name: *New Amsterdam was renamed New York in the 17th century.*

7 to publicly announce the name of someone

name /neɪm/ [v T] to publicly say who someone is, by telling people his or her name: *She refused to name the father of her child.*
name sb as *Police have named the dead woman as Annabel Tomms.*

identify /aɪˈdentɪfaɪ/ [v T] to officially recognize someone and say that you know who they are, for example in order to help the police: *The victim identified her attacker in court.* | *Greg had to identify the body of his wife.*
identifying – identified – have identified

8 what you call someone or something when you cannot remember their name

🔍 **what's his name/what's her name** /'wɒts hɪz neɪm, 'wɒts hərˈ neɪm/ SPOKEN INFORMAL use this when you cannot remember someone's name: *I saw Guy with what's her name in town yesterday.*

🔍 **what's its name/whatsit/ whatchamacallit** (also **thingy** BRITISH) /'wɒts ɪts neɪm, 'wɒtʃəməkɔːlɪt, 'wɒtsɪt, 'θɪŋɪlˈwɑːt-/ [n C] SPOKEN INFORMAL use this when you cannot remember the name of something: *"Can I have the whatsit for the TV?" "You mean the remote control?"*

NATURAL

not made by humans or changed by humans

➡ if you mean 'land where there are trees and fields and not many buildings', go to **COUNTRYSIDE**

➡ see also **LAND AND SEA,** **WB ENVIRONMENT**

1 plants/animals/places/substances

natural /'nætʃərəl/ [adj usually before noun] not made, caused, or changed by humans: *The river had worn away the rock to form a natural bridge.* | *elephants in their natural environment* | *a pipeline carrying natural gas from under the sea*

wild /waɪld/ [adj usually before noun] **wild flowers/plants/animals/birds** flowers, plants, and animals that are in their natural state and have not been changed or controlled by humans: *There were lots of wild flowers growing by the roadside.* | *Wild horses were running down the canyon.* **grow wild** *There were banana trees growing wild on the edge of the forest.*

2 food/drink

natural /'nætʃərəl/ [adj usually before noun] produced without using chemicals: *The manufacturers claim that only natural ingredients are used in their products.* | *Consumers like drinks that contain natural flavourings.*

organic /ɔːˈɡænɪk/ [adj] **organic fruit/vegetables/produce** fruit, vegetables etc that have been grown without using chemicals to help them grow: *Most supermarkets now sell organic produce.* | *Organic fruit is generally more expensive.*

pure /pjʊəʳ/ [adj only before noun] **pure** food or drink has not had anything added to it: *pure orange juice* | *The burgers are made of 100% pure beef.*

3 not natural

➡ opposite **REAL 1**
➡ see also **FALSE**

artificial /ˌɑːˈtɪ̥ˈfɪʃəl/ [adj] not made of natural materials or substances: *The food contains no artificial colours or flavourings.* | *a football pitch with artificial grass*

man-made /ˌmæn ˈmeɪd/ [adj] made by humans, but similar to something that is natural: *The Badesee is a man-made lake which is popular with swimmers.* | *a coat made of 80% wool and 20% man-made fibres*

> ⚠ **Artificial** and **man-made** are similar in meaning, but you can use **artificial** to give the idea that something is bad because it is not natural: *I don't like these artificial flowers, do you?*

synthetic /sɪnˈθetɪk/ [adj] **synthetic** materials, cloth, or substances are similar to natural ones but are made by a chemical process: *Her dress was made of some shiny synthetic material.* | *synthetic rubber*

processed /'prəʊsest‖'prɑː-/ [adj only before noun] **processed** food has been treated with chemicals in order to make it stay in good condition or to make it look good: *processed cheese* | *Processed food may lack the vitamins found in fresh food.*

NEAR

➡ opposite **FAR**

1 not far away

near /nɪəʳ/ [preposition/adv/adj] only a short distance from a person, place, or thing: *Bob was standing near enough to hear what they were saying.* **near sth/sb** *We camped near a large lake.* | *Don't go near the fire.* | *Have you ever been to Versailles? It's near Paris.* **nearer to/nearest to** *If we moved to Dallas we'd be nearer to my parents.* **near here** *The accident happened near here.*

somewhere / nowhere / anywhere near *I'm sure the restaurant is somewhere near here.*

close /kləus/ [*adj/adv*] very near to something or someone, or almost touching them: *As we approached Abbeville, the gunfire sounded very close.*

+to *Don't drive too close to the edge of the road.*

close together *The houses were built very close together.*

+behind/beside *Suddenly we heard footsteps close behind us.* | *Nancy sat down close beside me.*

close by (=near where you are) *Is there a gas station close by?*

not far /nɒt 'faːʳ/ not a very long distance away – use this about somewhere that is near enough to be easy to get to: *"How far's the station?" "Oh, not far – about ten minutes by car."*

+from *Asti is not far from the French border.*

not far away *Our hotel was in the centre of town but the beach wasn't far away.*

nearby /ˌnɪəˈbaɪ◂/ [*adv*] near the place where you are or the place you are talking about: *Dave, who was sitting nearby, laughed.* | *A lot of my friends live nearby.*

nearby [*adj* only before noun] ESPECIALLY WRITTEN *Lucy was staying with her aunt in the nearby town of Hamilton.*

neighbouring BRITISH **neighboring** AMERICAN /'neɪbərɪŋ/ [*adj* only before noun]

neighbouring country/town/area etc a country, town etc that is near the place where you are or the place you are talking about: *The fire quickly spread to the neighbouring areas.*

> **Formal or informal?**
>
> **Neighbouring** is used in formal writing and news reports.

local /'ləukəl/ [*adj* only before noun]

local store/hospital/school etc a store, hospital etc that is in the area where you live and that you are most likely to use: *We spent the summer evenings in the local park.*

sb's local school/cinema etc *You can find all these books in your local library.*

locally [*adv*] in the area near where you live or work: *We prefer to do all our shopping locally.* | *Do you live locally?*

within walking distance /wɪðɪn 'wɔːkɪŋ ˌdɪstəns/ when a place is not far away, and you can walk there easily: *There are several good restaurants within walking distance.*

+of *Dr Goldthorpe lived within walking distance of the University.*

2 the nearest house/shop/station etc

the nearest /ðə 'nɪərɪst/

the nearest shop/station/bank etc the shop, station etc that is closest to where you are: *Excuse me, where's the nearest subway station?*

the next /ðə 'nekst/

the next house/street/room etc the house, street etc that is closest to the one you are in or the one you are talking about: *The people in the next apartment were making a lot of noise.*

3 convenient because it is near

convenient for (also **handy for** INFORMAL) /kən'viːniənt fɔːʳ, 'hændi fɔːʳ/ BRITISH if your home, office etc is **convenient for** or **handy for** a particular place, that place is near it and easy to reach: *The place where we live now is very convenient for the school.* | *Our flat is on the High Street, so it's very handy for the shops.*

4 near enough to pick up or touch

handy /'hændi/ [*adj*] INFORMAL if something is **handy**, it is near enough for you to pick it up and use it quickly and easily

keep/have sth handy *Keep a pen and paper handy, because we'll be giving our phone number in a moment.* | *Make sure you have the manual handy when you install the new software.*

handy – handier – handiest

within reach /wɪðˌɪn 'riːtʃ/ if something is **within reach**, it is near enough for you to take hold of it when you stretch out your hand: *As soon as she was within reach, he grabbed her wrist.*

5 to get nearer

get near/get close /ˌget 'nɪəʳ, ˌget 'kləʊs/ to go or come nearer to a person, place, or thing: *As Kay got near the house she began to feel nervous.*
+**to** *Don't get too close to the microphone.*

approach /əˈprəʊtʃ/ [v I/T] ESPECIALLY WRITTEN to move gradually closer to a person, place, or thing: *The train slowed down as it started to approach the station.* | *We could hear footsteps approaching down the corridor.*

 Don't say 'he approached to the place'. Say **he approached the place**.

Formal or informal?
Approach is a fairly formal word and is used mostly in writing rather than in informal conversation.

catch up/be catching up /ˌkætʃ 'ʌp, biː ˌkætʃɪŋ 'ʌp/ to gradually get closer to a moving person or vehicle in front of you, by moving faster than they move: *Schumacher is still in front but the other Ferrari is catching up.*
+**with** *I could see that the other walkers were catching up with us.*

NEED/NOT NEED

➡ see also **MUST, IMPORTANT/NOT IMPORTANT**

1 to need something

need /niːd/ [v T] if you **need** something, you must have it, because you cannot live, succeed, or do something without it: *It's cold outside – you'll need a coat.* | *I need time to think.* | *I think she might need a doctor.*
need sth for sth *He needs the information for an article he's writing.*
need to do sth (=when it is necessary for someone to do something) *That*

cat looks as if she needs to go to the vet.
need sb to do sth *We need more volunteers to help clean up after the party.*
need cleaning / washing / mending etc (=need to be cleaned etc) *The plants need watering at least once a week.*
badly/desperately/urgently need sth (=need something very much) *The refugees desperately need food and clean water.*

 Don't say 'I am needing', 'he is needing', etc. Say **I need, he needs** etc.

require /rɪˈkwaɪəʳ/ [v T] FORMAL to need something: *Is there anything further you require, sir?* | *Guests who require special diets should inform the catering manager.*
be required for sth *I regret that you do not have the qualifications required for this job.*

 Don't say 'I am requiring', 'she is requiring' etc. Say **I require, she requires** etc.

🔍 **could do with sth/could use sth** /kʊd 'duː wɪð (sth), kʊd 'juːz (sth)/ SPOKEN INFORMAL say that you **could do with** something or **could use** something, when you feel that you need it and that it would improve things for you: *"Let's stop for a minute." "Sure, I could do with a rest."* | *I could use some help around here.*

be desperate for sth /biː 'despərət fɔːʳ (sth)/ to urgently need something and want it very much: *He was desperate for money to pay for medical care.* | *The heat was unbearable, and we were desperate for water and rest.*

2 when you cannot live without someone or something

🔍 **can't do without sb/sth** /ˌkɑːnt duː wɪð'aʊt (sb/sth)‖ˌkænt-/ ESPECIALLY SPOKEN to be unable to do the things that you have to do without someone who usually helps you or without something that you usually use: *He* *always says he couldn't do without his mobile phone. | My secretary's so efficient that I just can't do without her.*

depend on/be dependent on /dɪ'pend ɒn, biː dɪ'pendənt ɒnǁ-ɑːn-/ [phrasal verb T] ESPECIALLY WRITTEN to be unable to live, exist, or continue normally without something or someone, because they provide you with what you need: *Since becoming blind she had been totally dependent on her husband. | Our research program depends entirely on gifts of money from private individuals.*

depend heavily/be heavily dependent on sth (=be very dependent on it) *Japan is heavily dependent on oil imports from the Middle East.*

depend/be dependent on sb/sth for sth *All young mammals depend on their parents for food and shelter.*

3 something you need

necessary /'nesǁsəriǁ-seri/ [adj] if something is **necessary**, you need to have it or do it: *Make sure you have all the necessary documents for your trip.*

if necessary (=if it is necessary) *If necessary, we will employ some extra people to finish the work.*

+for *Fats in our diet are necessary for both heat and energy.*

it is necessary (for sb) to do sth FORMAL *It will be necessary to close the pool while the repairs take place. | The doctor says it may be necessary for me to have an operation.*

absolutely/really necessary *The police will not use force unless it is absolutely necessary.*

essential /ɪ'senʃəl/ [adj] if something is **essential**, you need it because you cannot be successful, healthy, safe etc without it: *Computers form an essential part of any business nowadays.*

+for *Calcium is essential for the development of healthy teeth and bones.*

it is essential to do sth *It is essential to read any document carefully before you sign it.*

it is essential that *It is essential that the oil is checked every 10,000 km.*

vital /'vaɪtl/ [adj] if something is **vital**, it is extremely important and you will have serious problems if you do not have it or do it: *One vital piece of*

evidence is missing – the murder weapon. | In this job, the ability to remain calm is vital.

+for *Efficient food production was vital for such a highly-populated country.*

it is vital that *It is vital that you keep accurate records.*

sb's needs/the needs of sb /(sb's) 'niːdz, ðə 'niːdz ɒv (sb)/ the things that someone must have in order to live a normal, healthy, and comfortable life: *In designing new buildings we must consider the needs of disabled visitors.*

meet/satisfy sb's needs (=provide what someone needs) *Schools should try to meet the educational needs of every child.*

> **Formal or informal?**
> **Sb's needs** is not usually used in informal conversation.

necessity /nɪ'sesǁti/ [n C] something that you need to have in order to live or to do your job: *Most Americans consider a phone a necessity rather than a luxury.*

an absolute necessity *A car is an absolute necessity for this job.*

the bare necessities (=the basic things that you must have, such as food and clothes) *Their wages are so low that they cannot even afford the bare necessities.*

plural **necessities**

> **Formal or informal?**
> **Necessity** is rather a formal word. In conversation it is more natural to say **this is something we really need** (not 'this is a necessity').

4 the fact that something is needed

need /niːd/ [n singular] if there is a **need** for something, that thing is needed

+for *the need for stricter safety regulations | Some politicians now believe there is a need for more discipline in schools.*

feel the need to do sth (=feel that you need to do something) *Don't you ever feel the need to take a vacation?*

5 to not need something

don't need /ˌdəʊnt ˈniːd/ to not need something or someone: *I'm going to give these books away. I don't need them any more.*

> ⚠ Don't say 'I am not needing', 'he is not needing' etc. Say **I don't need, he doesn't need** etc.

unnecessary/not necessary

/ʌnˈnesəsəri, nɒt ˈnesəsəri‖-seri/ [adj] if something is **unnecessary** or **not necessary**, you do not need to have it or do it: *Don't fill your report with unnecessary information.* | *The journey had been totally unnecessary.*
it is not necessary to do sth *It's not necessary to spend a lot of money on clothes to look good.*
unnecessarily [adv] *I think you're worrying unnecessarily.*

hardly necessary /ˌhɑːʳdli ˈnesəsəri‖ -seri/ not necessary at all – use this when you are surprised that someone thinks something is necessary: *They asked to see my passport, my driver's licence, and my bank card, which was hardly necessary.*

spare /speəʳ/ [adj usually before noun] use this about something which you do not need now, but which is available so that you can use it later or let someone else use it: *I always keep a spare can of oil in the garage.* | *We have two spare tickets for the game – do you want to come?* | *Do you have a spare pair of gloves I could borrow?*

can do without sb/sth /kən ˌduː wɪðˈaʊt (sb/sth)/ to not need someone or something, because you can live normally or do what you want to do without them: *The country now has a strong economy and can do without western aid.* | *He felt he could do without other people and was happy to live on his own.*

NEVER

➡ opposite **ALWAYS**
➡ see also **OFTEN, USUALLY, SOMETIMES**

1 never

never /ˈnevəʳ/ [adv] not once, or not at any time: *"Have you ever been to Paris?" "No, never."* | *The countryside was beautiful – I'll never forget it.* | *Ali had never seen snow before.* | *He never even says 'hello'.*

> ⚠ Don't use **never** with negative words like 'nobody', 'no one', and 'nothing'. Use **ever**: *Nobody will ever find me here.* You can use **never** with words like 'anybody', 'anything', and 'anywhere': *I'll never tell anyone.*

> ⚠ **Never** usually comes before the main verb: *He never told me.* If there is a modal or auxiliary verb (**will, should, have** etc), **never** comes after this verb and before the main verb: *You must never speak to strangers.*

🗣 **never ever/never, never** /ˌnevər ˈevəʳ, ˌnevəʳ ˈnevəʳ/ SPOKEN say this when you want to emphasize strongly that something has never happened or will never happen: *You must never ever tell anyone what you heard tonight.* | *I'll never, never stop loving you.*

🗣 **not in a million years** /nɒt ɪn ə ˌmɪljən ˈjɪəʳz/ SPOKEN INFORMAL say this when you think it is completely impossible that something could ever happen: *You'll never get Kieran to give you that money – not in a million years!*

not once /nɒt ˈwʌns/ say this when you are surprised or annoyed because someone never did something, although they often had the opportunity to do it: *She's never said thank you – not once!* | *He hasn't once come here to see us.*

2 almost never

hardly ever /ˌhɑːʳdli 'evəʳ/ almost never: *"How's Dorothy?" "I don't know. I hardly ever see her these days." | My grandmother hardly ever goes out of the house.*

> ⚠ **Hardly ever** is much more common in spoken English than **rarely** and **seldom**.

rarely/seldom /'reəʳli, 'seldəm/ [*adv*] ESPECIALLY WRITTEN almost never: *Mr Gluck rarely went to bed before midnight. | She seldom talked about her personal life.*

> ⚠ Don't say 'I go there rarely/seldom'. Say **I rarely/seldom go there**. Use **rarely** and **seldom** before the main verb, unless the main verb is 'be': *The disease is rarely fatal.*

rare /reəʳ/ [*adj*] something that is **rare** does not happen often: *The disease is rare, but very dangerous. | On the rare occasions when I do go to the theatre, I really enjoy it.*

NEW

➡ opposite **OLD**
➡ see also **MODERN, SHINE 2**

1 recently made or produced

new /njuː‖nuː/ [*adj*] recently made, produced, or bought: *Do you like my new dress? | That's a nice bag – is it new? | the city's new hospital*
brand new (=completely new and almost unused) *Larry was very proud of his brand new BMW.*
buy sth new *My dad bought this car new in 1986.*

latest /'leɪtₔst/ [*adj* only before noun]
the latest film/book/model/fashion etc the film, book etc that has been produced or made most recently: *Have you seen Spielberg's latest movie? | the latest fashions from the Paris catwalks*

be just out /biː ˌdʒʌst 'aʊt/ if a book, record, or film **is just out**, it has only

recently arrived in the shops, cinemas etc: *Their new album is just out.*

fresh /freʃ/ [*adj*] **fresh** food has been recently made, killed, or picked, and it still tastes good: *Make sure that the fish is fresh.*
fresh from the oven/sea/garden *The vegetables are picked fresh from the garden every day.*
freshly [*adv*] *These strawberries were freshly picked this morning. | freshly baked bread*

> ⚠ You can also use **fresh** to describe food that has not been frozen, dried, or put in cans: *fresh peas | fresh pasta*

2 instead of the one that you had before

new /njuː‖nuː/ [*adj* only before noun] your **new** job, home etc is the one you got most recently, and is different from the one you had before: *Are you enjoying your new job? | Have you met Keith's new girlfriend? | After the divorce, she went off to Canada to start a new life.*

another /ə'nʌðəʳ/ [*determiner*] if you want **another** job, **another** system etc, you want it instead of the one that you have now: *I decided to look for another job. | If you don't like one doctor, you can ask to see another one.*

replace /rɪ'pleɪs/ [*v T*] if you **replace** something that is old or damaged, you put a new one in its place to be used instead of it: *The roof needed to be completely replaced.*
replace sth with sth *They're replacing the old windows with modern ones.*

3 new ideas/methods/information

new /njuː‖nuː/ [*adj*] **new** ideas, methods, or information did not exist before, or were not known about before: *important new scientific discoveries | Her lawyers have found new evidence that may prove her innocence. | the company's new non-smoking policy*

original /ə'rɪdʒɪnəl, -dʒənəl/ [*adj*] completely different from anything that has been thought of before original **idea/design/style** *a jazz musician with a completely original style* | *My job is to think up creative and original advertising ideas.*

revolutionary /ˌrevəˈluːʃənəriǁ-ʃəneri/ [*adj*] a **revolutionary** idea, method, or invention is completely different from anything that existed before, and is likely to bring important changes or improvements: *revolutionary technology for producing cheap, pollution-free energy* | *a revolutionary new treatment for cancer*

4 a new government/company

new /njuːǁnuː/ [*adj*] a **new** organization, government etc has only existed for a short time: *Within weeks of the election, the new government announced big tax cuts.* | *Thousands of new businesses are set up each year.* | *one of Europe's newest TV stations*

5 someone who has just started a new job, school etc

new /njuːǁnuː/ [*adj*] someone who is **new** has only recently arrived in a place, or has only recently started working in a job: *You're new here, aren't you?* | *All new employees are given training.*
+to *Children who are new to the school may need extra help.*

newcomer /ˈnjuːkʌməʳǁˈnuː-/ [*n* C] someone who has only recently arrived in a place or has only recently started a job, sport, or other activity: *The villagers are very suspicious of newcomers.* | *The team includes some familiar faces as well as a few newcomers.*
+to *Although she's a newcomer to the sport, she's already very successful.*

NEWS

➡ see also **INFORMATION, NEWSPAPERS AND MAGAZINES,** **WB TELEVISION AND RADIO**

1 news that people tell each other

news /njuːzǁnuːz/ [*n* U] information about something that happened recently

+of *There hasn't been any news of him since he left home.*
+that *He brought the news that their father was seriously ill.*
your/my/her news (=what you have been doing recently) *Sit down and tell me all your news.*
have good/bad news for sb *I'm afraid I have some bad news for you.*
hear news *Have you heard the news? Sara's going to have a baby.*
good/bad news *Good news! Ian passed his driving test!*
the latest news *The NBA site has all the latest news about players, games, and teams.*

> ⚠ Don't say 'a news'. Say **a piece of news** or **some news**: *I heard an interesting piece of news yesterday.*

the latest /ðə ˈleɪtɪst/ SPOKEN the most recent news: *Have you heard the latest? Phil's going out with Judy!*
+on *What's the latest on the election?*

scandal /ˈskændl/ [*n* C/U] when shocking facts about someone's behaviour become publicly known: *a sex scandal involving senior politicians* | *the public's interest in scandal and gossip*

2 on television or in a newspaper

news /njuːzǁnuːz/ [*n* U] reports about recent events, printed in newspapers or given on television or radio: *I always read the sports news first.* | *It's a local paper, so most of the news is about local events.*
+of *Later on, we'll bring you all the news of today's football games.*
the news (=a news programme on television or radio) *Do you want to watch the news?* | *the nine o'clock news*
on the news (=in a television or radio news programme) *I heard it on the news this morning.*

> ⚠ You can also use **news** before a noun, like an adjective: *a news broadcast* | *a news item*

newsflash BRITISH **news bulletin** AMERICAN /ˈnjuːzflæʃ, ˈnjuːz ˌbʊlɪtɪnǁ-ˈnuːz-/ [*n* C] a piece of news that is so important that it is broadcast

immediately, often in the middle of another programme: *We interrupt this programme to bring you a newsflash.*
plural **newsflashes**

the headlines /ðə ˈhedlaɪnz/ [*n plural*] the important points of the news, printed in big letters on the front page of a newspaper or read at the beginning of a news broadcast: *I stopped to read the front page headlines: 'KILLER ESCAPES FROM JAIL'.* | *This is the six o'clock news. First, the headlines ...*

NEWSPAPERS

➡ see Word Banks section

NICE

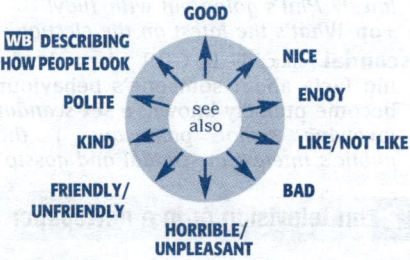

WB DESCRIBING HOW PEOPLE LOOK

GOOD
NICE
ENJOY
LIKE/NOT LIKE
BAD
HORRIBLE/UNPLEASANT
FRIENDLY/UNFRIENDLY
KIND
POLITE

see also

1 nice person

🔍 **nice** /naɪs/ ESPECIALLY SPOKEN [*adj*] friendly and kind: *He's one of the nicest people I know.* | *Claire's really nice, isn't she?*
+to *He's only nice to me when he wants something.*
it is nice of sb to do sth *It was nice of you to help me.*
nice – nicer – nicest

pleasant /ˈplezənt/ [*adj*] friendly, polite, and easy to talk to – use this especially about someone you do not know well: *I thought she was a quiet, pleasant girl.* | *The Ambassador and his wife were surprisingly pleasant.*

> **Formal or informal?**
> **Pleasant** is more formal than **nice**.

likeable /ˈlaɪkəbəl/ [*adj*] nice, and easy to like: *The only likeable character in the whole movie is Judge White.*

lovely /ˈlʌvli/ [*adj*] BRITISH INFORMAL very nice, kind, and friendly: *Old Dr Macintosh was a lovely man.*
lovely – lovelier – loveliest

sweet /swiːt/ [*adj*] INFORMAL someone who is **sweet** is kind and gentle, and tries to make other people happy: *He's a really sweet guy but I couldn't date him.*
it is sweet of sb to do sth *It was very sweet of you to buy me those flowers.*

2 something you like or enjoy

🔍 **nice** /naɪs/ [*adj*] ESPECIALLY SPOKEN *That's a nice jacket. Is it new?* | *Have a nice day!*
nice to do sth *It's really nice to see you again.*
+for *It's much nicer for the kids when they have other kids to play with.*
look/taste/smell nice *You look really nice in that dress.*
nice big/quiet/long etc *I got a nice long letter from Andreas this morning.* | *a nice hot bath*
nice and hot/long/cosy etc *The rooms were nice and warm.*
nice – nicer – nicest

lovely /ˈlʌvli/ [*adj*] BRITISH INFORMAL very nice: *We had a lovely time at the beach.* | *Thank you for the lovely birthday present.*
it is lovely to do sth *It would be lovely to see you.*
look/taste/smell lovely *Anna's perfume smells lovely.*
lovely big/long etc *They've got a lovely big house.*
lovely – lovelier – loveliest

pleasant /ˈplezənt/ [*adj*] a **pleasant** place, occasion, or activity is one that you like, especially because it is peaceful, attractive, or relaxing: *We spent a very pleasant evening chatting.* | *Relax in the peaceful and pleasant surroundings of our hotel.* | *a pleasant little town*
pleasantly [*adv*] *It was pleasantly cool by the river.*

Formal or informal?
Pleasant is more formal than **nice**.

enjoyable /ɪn'dʒɔɪəbəl/ [adj] an **enjoyable** experience or activity is one that you enjoy, because it is interesting, exciting etc: *We hope you will have an enjoyable trip.* | *I find aerobics more enjoyable than jogging.* | *an enjoyable day at the Carnival*

great/fantastic/wonderful /greɪt, fæn'tæstɪk, 'wʌndəˈfəl/ [adj] extremely enjoyable – use this about holidays, parties, films, and other experiences that you enjoy very much: *I went to a fantastic party last night.* | *We had a wonderful month in Italy.* | *I think it's a great movie.*

Formal or informal?
Great and **fantastic** are more informal than **wonderful**, and should not be used in written English, except in personal letters.

 Don't use 'very' with any of these words.

NONE/NOTHING

➡ see also **NEVER**

1 when there isn't any of something

none /nʌn/ [pronoun] not any of something, or no people or things: *I was going to offer you some cake, but there's none left.* | *"Coffee?" "None for me, thanks."*
+of *None of her friends ever came to see her.* | *None of the equipment was actually working.*
none at all *"Do you have any objections to the plan?" "None at all."*

In spoken English, if **none of** is followed by a plural noun or pronoun, you can use it with a plural verb: *I invited some friends, but none of them were interested.* But in written English it is better to use a singular verb: *None of them was interested.*

not any /nɒt 'eni/ [determiner/pronoun] none: *If you're looking for bread, you won't find any. I haven't been shopping yet.*
not any time/money/food etc *There won't be any time for questions after the lecture.*
not any shops/clothes/books etc *There aren't any good book stores in our town.*
+of *I haven't read any of Henry Miller's novels.*

no /nəʊ/ [determiner] not any or not one
no time/money/milk etc *Do you mind having black coffee? There's no milk.* | *We've had no rain for three months.*
no cars/houses/dogs etc *There are no buses today.* | *a very plain room, with no pictures on the wall*
no reason/reply/intention etc *I knocked on the door, but there was no reply.* | *He just started hitting her for no reason.*
no more *There are no more classes until Monday.*

nothing/not anything /'nʌθɪŋ, nɒt 'eniθɪŋ/ [pronoun] *There's nothing in this box.* | *These people don't know anything about computers.* | *I switched the TV on, but nothing happened.* | *"What are you doing?" "Nothing."*
nothing new/serious/exciting etc *Nothing exciting ever happens in this place!*
nothing to eat/say/do etc *There was nothing to do, so we just watched TV.* | *She hasn't had anything to eat all day.*
nothing at all *"Do you know anything about fixing cars?" "No, nothing at all."*

2 the number that means none

zero /'zɪərəʊ‖'zi:rəʊ/ [number] the number 0

Formal or informal?

In American English, **zero** is used more than in British English as a way of saying the number '0': *I think her phone number is two zero five three zero.* In British English, the usual way of saying '0' is **nought**, and **zero** is mostly used in scientific or technical language: *The pressure increases from zero to maximum in 25 seconds.*

nil /nɪl/ [*number*] none or nothing: *The new machine has reduced our labour costs to almost nil.* | *The chances of finding them alive are virtually nil.*

⚠ In British English, **nil** is also used when talking about sports results: *United won the game three nil.*

◌ **nought** /nɔːt/ [*number*] BRITISH SPOKEN the number 0: *The interest rate on this account is only nought point seven five per cent.* (=0.75%)

◌ **o** /əʊ/ [*number*] SPOKEN the number 0: *All Manchester numbers start with o-one-six-one.* | *You'll be in room two-o-four.*

⚠ **o** is used especially when saying a telephone number, address, or room number, or a number after a decimal point.

NORMAL/ ORDINARY

➡ opposite **UNUSUAL**

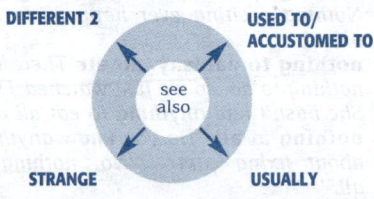

DIFFERENT 2

USED TO/
ACCUSTOMED TO

see
also

STRANGE

USUALLY

1 ordinary, not special

ordinary /'ɔːᵣdᵊnɪrɪ‖-neri/ [*adj*] **ordinary** things are not special or unusual; **ordinary** people are not famous or powerful, and are not especially rich or clever: *It's just an ordinary house in an ordinary street.* | *Politicians don't seem to care about ordinary people.* |

Can you get connected to the Internet through an ordinary telephone line?

average /'ævərɪdʒ/ [*adj* only before noun] an **average** person or thing is a typical example of a person or of a particular type of thing: *How much does the average family spend each week on food?* | *In an average week I watch about 20 hours of TV.* | *Foreign affairs do not usually interest the average voter.*

normal /'nɔːᵣməl/ [*adj*] something that is **normal** is just as you expect it to be, because it is not special or different: *It looks like a perfectly normal car, but it uses hydrogen instead of petrol.* | *January 2nd is a public holiday in Scotland, but in England it is a normal working day.*

normally [*adv*] *Now the strike is over, and trains are running normally.*

standard /'stændəᵣd/ [*adj* usually before noun] normal – use this especially about products or methods that are the most usual type, without any special features
standard model/size/shape/pattern (=not special) *We make shoes in all standard sizes.* | *The standard model costs $4000 less than the luxury model.*
standard practice/procedure (=the way a job is usually done) *It is standard practice to x-ray all hand baggage at international airports.*
standard English/pronunciation/spelling (=normally accepted as correct)

routine /ˌruː'tiːn◂/ [*adj* only before noun] use this about something that is done regularly as part of the normal system and not because of any special problem
routine check/inspection/examination etc *The fault was discovered during a routine check of the plane.* | *a routine visit to the dentist*

conventional /kən'venʃənəl/ [*adj* only before noun] a **conventional** method, piece of equipment, weapon etc is of the normal type that has been used for a long time – use this especially when you are comparing these things with something that is new or different: *A microwave cooks food much faster than a conventional oven.* | *conventional weapons* (=not nuclear weapons) | *The hospital provides both* conventional and alternative medical treatments.

Formal or informal?

Conventional is not usually used in informal conversation.

---

day-to-day /'deɪ tə deɪ/ [adj only before noun] use this about the ordinary work, activities, and problems that happen every day: As Managing Director, I am responsible for the day-to-day running of the company.

regular /'regjʊləʳ/ [adj only before noun] ESPECIALLY AMERICAN not special in any way, but good enough for a particular purpose: Even though the dye is quite strong, a regular shampoo will remove it.

2 normal behaviour or feelings

normal /'nɔːʳməl/ [adj] if a person is **normal**, or if their behaviour or feelings are **normal**, there is nothing strange about them, and they are mentally and physically healthy: Her breathing was normal, but she had a very high temperature.
it is normal (for sb) to do sth It is quite normal for children to be afraid of the dark.
perfectly normal (=completely normal) Lisa seems a perfectly normal little girl.
normally [adv] His family say that the day before he disappeared, he seemed to be behaving quite normally.

natural /'nætʃərəl/ [adj] feelings that are **natural** are what you would normally expect in a particular situation, so there is no need to feel worried or embarrassed about them: Anger is a natural reaction when you lose your job.
it is natural (for sb) to do sth I suppose it's natural for a mother to feel sad when her children leave home. | It isn't natural for a child to be so quiet.
perfectly/quite natural (=completely natural) Boys need to know that sometimes it's perfectly natural to cry.
🔍 **it's only natural** SPOKEN Of course Jean misses her boyfriend – it's only natural.

conventional /kən'venʃənəl/ [adj] **conventional** people, behaviour, and opinions are the kind that most people in society think are normal and socially acceptable, although some people think they are boring and old-fashioned: My parents were so conventional with their smart house and two cars. | a young man with conventional tastes in clothes and music
conventionally [adv] She was dressed very conventionally in a dull grey suit.

3 not ordinary/not normal

special /'speʃəl/ [adj] not ordinary, but more important, interesting, or impressive than usual: Tomorrow is a special day for us – it's our first wedding anniversary. | Students are not allowed to change to a different class unless there is a special reason. | She had a special talent for learning languages.
🔍 **something/anything/nothing special** SPOKEN "Are you doing anything this weekend?" "No, nothing special."
special occasion (=an important social event or celebration) I only wear this suit on special occasions, like weddings.

abnormal /æb'nɔːʳməl/ [adj] very different from what is normal, in a way that is strange, worrying, or dangerous: Abnormal behaviour may be a sign of mental illness. | an abnormal chest x-ray
it is abnormal (for sb) to do sth My parents thought it was abnormal for a boy to be interested in ballet.
abnormally [adv] abnormally low blood pressure | She seems abnormally fascinated by death.

no ordinary /nəʊ 'ɔːʳdənrɪ‖-neri/
no ordinary dog/party/car etc a dog, party, car etc that is not at all ordinary, but is very unusual, very impressive etc: As soon as I got there, I realized that this was no ordinary family gathering. | It was no ordinary birthday cake – it was massive!

4 when something becomes normal again

get back to normal/return to normal /get ˌbæk tə 'nɔːʳməl, rɪˌtɜːʳn tə 'nɔːʳməl/ if a situation **gets back to normal** or returns to normal, it becomes normal again after a period when it was not normal: *After the war it took a long time for things to get back to normal.* | *The strike has caused serious problems, but we hope bus services will quickly return to normal.*

Formal or informal?
Return to normal is more formal than **get back to normal**.

NOT

➡ see also **EC** SAYING NO

1 not

not /nɒt‖nɑːt/ [adv] "*Why don't you go to bed?*" "*I'm not tired.*" | *He told me not to worry.* | *He's not my boyfriend – he's just someone I work with.* | *Jo and Dan aren't here yet.*

Formal or informal?
In spoken informal English, we usually use **-n't** (the short form of **not**): *Don't worry, I won't hurt you.* However, use **not** after 'I'm', 'she's' etc: *I'm not ready yet.*

⚠ Don't use another negative word, for example 'nothing', 'nobody', or 'nowhere', in the same sentence as **not**. Use 'anything', 'anybody', 'anywhere' etc instead: *We didn't see anything.* | *They do not know anybody.*

neither /ˈnaɪðəʳ‖ˈniː-/ [adv] use this to say that a negative statement that has just been made about someone is also true about someone else
neither am I/neither does she/ neither have we etc "*I've never been to Australia.*" "*No, neither have I.*" | *Tom didn't believe a word she said, and neither did the police.*

⚠ **Neither** can only be followed by these words: 'be', 'have', 'do', 'can', 'could', 'will', 'would', 'shall', 'should'.

not very/not particularly /nɒt ˈveri, nɒt pəʳˈtɪkjʊ̩ləʳli/ not very or not very much: *The roads were not very busy.* |

I'm not particularly interested in soccer, but I did enjoy the World Cup. | *I don't particularly want to go out tonight.*

⚠ **Not very** and **not particularly** are often used as an indirect or polite way of expressing a strong idea: *She wasn't very pleased when she found out.* (=she was angry) | *The film wasn't particularly good.* (=it was fairly bad)

not at all /ˌnɒt ət ˈɔːl/ use this to emphasize that something is definitely not true: *She's not at all happy about the situation.* | *No, that's not at all what I meant.*

not quite /nɒt ˈkwaɪt/ not completely, but almost: *The measurements are not quite accurate.* | *We haven't quite finished yet.*

not exactly /nɒt ɪɡˈzæktli/ not very or completely: *She's not exactly fat, but she is slightly overweight.*

hardly /ˈhɑːʳdli/ [adv] use this to emphasize that something is definitely not true, and if someone thinks it is true they are being a little stupid: *They only won 1–0 – hardly a great victory!* | *It's hardly surprising he's upset, considering the way you've treated him!*

by no means/not by any means /baɪ ˈnəʊ miːnz, nɒt baɪ ˈeni miːnz/
by no means certain/clear/impossible etc FORMAL not at all certain, clear etc – use this especially when other people think that something is certain, is clear etc, and you think they are wrong: *It is by no means certain that King Arthur ever existed.* | *It's difficult, but not by any means impossible.*

in no way /ɪn ˈnəʊ weɪ/ FORMAL if something is **in no way** affected by something else, it is definitely not affected by it in any way: *This will in no way influence our original decision.* | *The damage is very slight and in no way reduces the value of the painting.*

2 not one thing and not the other

neither /ˈnaɪðəʳ‖ˈniː-/ [determiner/ pronoun] use this to emphasize that you are talking about both of two

people or things when you make a negative statement about them
+of *Neither of us enjoys cooking very much.*
neither thing/person/place etc *The problem is worse when neither parent is employed.*

neither ... nor /naɪðə^r ... nɔː^r/ use this when you want to make a negative statement about two people, things, actions etc: *He neither drinks nor smokes.* (=he does not drink, and he does not smoke) | *Neither the President nor his advisers knew anything about the plan.* | *She felt neither sad nor happy when she heard the news.*

 Don't use 'or' after **neither**. Always use **nor**.

Formal or informal?

Neither ... nor is fairly formal. In spoken English or less formal written English, we express the same idea in a different way, for example: *He doesn't drink or smoke.* | *Reagan didn't know anything about the plan, and neither did his advisers.*

NOTICE

to see, hear, or feel something

➡ if you mean 'a sign that tells people something', go to **SIGN**
➡ see also **REALIZE, SEE, SHOW 5**

1 to notice someone or something

notice /'nəʊtɪs/ [v I/T] to realize that something is there or that something is happening, because you see it, hear it, or feel it: *"Julie's home." "Yes, I noticed her bicycle outside." | Dominic took a huge slice of cake, hoping no-one would notice.*
+(that) *I was driving home when I noticed that the engine was making a strange noise.*
notice how/when/where etc *Did you notice what he was wearing?*
notice sb doing sth *I was about to leave when I noticed someone coming up the driveway.*

⚠ Don't use 'can' with **notice**. Don't say 'we can notice an improvement'. Say **we notice an improvement** or **we can see an improvement**.

can see/can tell /kən 'siː, kən 'tel/ to know that something is true, because you notice signs that show you this
+(that) *We could tell that she had been crying.* | *I can see you're not really enjoying this.*

I see (that) /aɪ 'siː ðət/ SPOKEN say this to mention something that you have noticed: *I see Pete's had his hair cut again.* | *I see that you two have met each other before.*

spot /spɒt‖spɑːt/ [v T] to see something that is difficult to notice, or something that no one else notices: *I'm glad you spotted that mistake before it was too late.*
spot sb doing sth *She spotted him getting into a white Fiesta.*
spotting – spotted – have spotted

become aware of sth /bɪˌkʌm ə'weər ɒv (sth)/ ESPECIALLY WRITTEN to gradually begin to notice something: *When did you first become aware of the problem?*
become aware of sb doing sth *As he was reading, he became aware of someone watching him.*

catch sb's eye /ˌkætʃ (sb's) 'aɪ/ if something **catches your eye**, you notice it because it is unusual, interesting, or attractive: *I was walking through the market when a beautiful dress caught my eye.* | *At the station, a newspaper headline caught his eye.*

note /nəʊt/ [v T] WRITTEN to notice a fact or detail and remember it, because it tells you about a person or because it might be useful to you in the future: *I noted her habit of looking at the floor whenever I asked her a question.*
+how/when etc *He chatted to her, noting how her face reddened every time that Ian's name was mentioned.*
+that *She noted that he wasn't wearing a wedding ring.*

⚠ **Note** is often used in the imperative to draw someone's attention to something: *Note the poet's use of adjectives.*

observe /əb'zɜːrv/ [v T] FORMAL to notice something as a result of watching or studying it closely: *I didn't observe anything unusual about her behaviour that day.*

+that *Psychologists observed that the mice became more aggressive when they were put in smaller cages.*

perceive /pə'siːv/ [v T] FORMAL to notice something, especially something that is difficult to notice: *That morning he perceived a change in Louise's mood.*

(+that) *The prime minister will only resign if he perceives there is no other way out of the crisis.*

2 to not notice something

not notice /nɒt 'nəʊtʃəs/ *"Does Alex like your new hairstyle?" "He didn't even notice."* | *I saw Mike in town but he didn't notice me.*

not notice how/who/what etc *We were so busy we didn't notice how late it was.*

miss /mɪs/ [v T] to not notice something because it is difficult to see: *Jo spotted a mistake that everyone else had missed.* | *It's easy to miss the entrance – there's no sign outside.*

overlook /ˌəʊvə'lʊk/ [v T] to not notice something because you have not been careful enough: *They found some important evidence that the police had overlooked.*

fail to notice /ˌfeɪl tə 'nəʊtʃəs/ WRITTEN to not notice something, especially when this could have a serious result: *Atkinson failed to notice the car ahead of him was parked and drove straight into the back of it.*

3 good at noticing things

observant /əb'zɜːrvənt/ [adj] good at noticing things: *Men aren't very observant about things like hair and clothes.* | *An observant reader has pointed out a mistake on page 26.*

perceptive /pə'septɪv/ [adj] good at noticing things and understanding situations or people's feelings: *I like her novels – she's so perceptive about people's relationships.* | *A perceptive teacher noticed that Val was having problems.*

Formal or informal?
Perceptive is a formal word.

🔍 **not miss much** /nɒt 'mɪs mʌtʃ/ SPOKEN if you do **not miss much**, you notice a lot about what is happening and what other people are doing or feeling: *Grandad might be getting old but he doesn't miss much.*

4 something that is easy to notice

obvious /'ɒbviəs‖'ɑːb-/ [adj] a fact that is **obvious** is easy to see or realize: *She tried not to show it, but her disappointment was obvious.*

it is obvious (to sb) that *It's obvious that Paul is in love with Liz.* | *It was obvious to everyone that Gina was lying.*

noticeable /'nəʊtʃəsəbəl/ [adj] easy to notice: *After two days, there was a noticeable improvement in his health.* | *The new supermarket has had a noticeable effect on people's shopping habits.*

it is noticeable that *It was noticeable that she deliberately avoided answering the question.*

conspicuous /kən'spɪkjuəs/ [adj] FORMAL someone or something that is **conspicuous** is very easy to notice, because they look very different from everyone or everything around them: *It was a small country town, and Lauren looked very conspicuous in her fashionable New York clothes.*

eye-catching /'aɪ ˌkætʃɪŋ/ **eye-catching** colours, designs, patterns etc are bright, attractive, and unusual, so everyone notices them: *The posters come in several eye-catching designs.* | *Larger patterns tend to be more eye-catching.*

stand out /ˌstænd 'aʊt/ [phrasal verb I] if something **stands out**, it is easy to notice because it looks very different from everything around it: *A yellow background will make the black lettering stand out.*

+against *The dark shapes of the trees stood out against the evening sky.*

🔍 **you can't miss it** /juː ˌkɑːnt 'mɪs ɪt‖-ˌkænt-/ SPOKEN say this when you are telling someone how to get to a place that is very easy to find or notice: *Their house has a pink door. You can't miss it.*

5　to make people notice you

get attention/attract attention /ˌget
ə'tenʃən, əˌtrækt ə'tenʃən/ to try to
make someone notice you, by doing
something that they will notice:
*Young children sometimes behave
badly simply in order to get attention.*
get/attract sb's attention *Phil was
trying to attract the waiter's attention.*

NOW

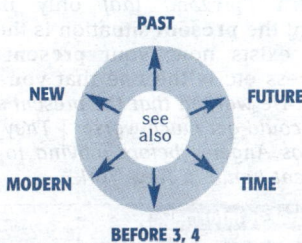

PAST

NEW　　　　　　　FUTURE

see
also

MODERN　　　　　TIME

BEFORE 3, 4

1　now, at this moment or at this time

now /naʊ/ [adv] *If we leave now, we'll be
there before dark.* | *It's not raining
now, but they said it might rain later.* |
Where do you go to school now?

already /ɔːl'redi/ [adv] if something is
already happening or already true, it
began to happen or be true before
now: *He's only three and he's already
reading.* | *"Should I tell Kay?" "She
already knows."* | *The show has
already started.*

> ⚠ **Already** usually comes immediately
> before the main verb: *She already knows
> about it.* | *Some cars can already run on this
> new petrol.* However, it comes after the main
> verb 'be': *The book is already out of date.* You
> can also use **already** at the end of a
> sentence to emphasize that something has
> happened sooner than you expected: *Is the
> taxi here already?*

currently /'kʌrəntli‖'kɜːr-/ [adv] now –
use this when you are describing
what the situation is at this time: *The
firm currently employs 113 people.* |
*Peterson is currently writing a book
about his travels.*

> **Formal or informal?**
> **Currently** is used especially in newspapers,
> official reports, and formal meetings. It is not
> usually used in ordinary conversation.

at present/at the moment (also
presently AMERICAN) /ət 'prezənt, ət ðə
'məʊmənt, 'prezəntli/ now – use this
especially to say that something is
happening now but you do not expect
it to continue for a long time: *I'm
working in a restaurant at the moment.*
| *The item you want is out of stock at
present.* | *She's presently working on
her own talk show on TV.*

> **Formal or informal?**
> **At present** is more formal than **at the
> moment** or **presently**.

🔍 **right now** /ˌraɪt 'naʊ/ SPOKEN at this
moment or at this time

> ⚠ In American English, **right now** means
> 'at this time', and is often used about a
> situation which you expect to change: *Right
> now, we're living with my mother.* | *I want to pay
> her back, but I don't have the money right now.*
> In British English, **right now** is usually used to
> emphasize that something is very urgent: *I
> want to see the manager, right now!*

🔍 **just now** /ˌdʒʌst 'naʊ/ BRITISH SPOKEN
at this exact moment – use this
especially to say that you cannot do
something immediately: *Sorry, I'm
busy just now – can I call you later?*

at this time /ət ˌðɪs 'taɪm/ AMERICAN
FORMAL at this particular time: *"Do you
have any health insurance?" "Not at
this time."* | *I have no further questions
at this time, your honor.*

2　now, not in the past

now /naʊ/ [adv] use this when you are
comparing the present situation with
what happened in the past: *We used
to be good friends, but I don't see her
much now.* | *Julie has moved to a new
school and she's much happier now.*

nowadays/these days /'naʊədeɪz, 'ðiːz
ˌdeɪz/ use this when you are describing how life or the way you live now
is different from the way it was in the
past: *It isn't safe for children to play in
the street these days.* | *Nowadays*

divorce is more common. | I don't go to London much these days. | More people nowadays are aware of the importance of a healthy diet.

today /tə'deɪ/ [adv] at the present time, especially when compared with the past: Cars are the biggest cause of pollution in the world today. | Today, only a few of these beautiful animals survive.

> **Formal or informal?**
>
> **Today** is used especially in news reports and articles, and formal speeches.

3   until now

so far /ˌsəʊ 'fɑːʳ/ until now – use this when you are talking about a situation that will continue or develop after this time: There haven't been any problems so far. | This is the hottest day we've had so far this summer. | "How many people say they will come to the party?" "About 20 so far."

still /stɪl/ [adv] use this to say that a situation which started in the past continues to exist now, especially when this is surprising: He's been studying French for five years, but he still can't speak it well. | Are you still working at that restaurant?

> ⚠ **Still** usually comes immediately before the main verb: He still loves her. | I can still remember it. However, it comes after the main verb 'be': She's still on holiday. **Still** usually comes before any negative word or before 'do not': We still don't know. | They still aren't ready.

yet /jet/ [adv] use this in questions or negative statements to talk or ask about things that you expected to happen before now: Has the new washing machine arrived yet? | We are 30 minutes into the game, and neither team has scored yet. | "Have you finished your homework?" "Not yet."

> ⚠ In British English, use the present perfect with **yet**: Have you read that book yet? In American English, you can use the simple past or the present perfect: Did you read that book yet?

up to now/until now /ˌʌp tə 'naʊ, ən,tɪl 'naʊ/ use this about a situation which has existed until now, but which has started to change or will change in the future: The house has been fine up to now, but when we have kids we'd like to move somewhere bigger. | Until now, there has been no effective treatment for this disease.

4   things or situations that exist now

➡ see also **MODERN**

present /'prezənt/ [adj only before noun] the **present** situation is the one that exists now; your **present** job, address etc is the one that you have now: He warned that the present situation could get much worse. | They lived in Los Angeles before moving to their present home in New York.

> **Formal or informal?**
>
> **Present** is not used in informal conversation.

current /'kʌrənt‖'kɜːr-/ [adj only before noun] use this about a situation or activity which is happening now, but which is not expected to continue for a long time: the current economic situation | Coca-Cola's current advertising campaign
current level/rate/price The current rate for the job is $15 an hour.

> **Formal or informal?**
>
> **Current** is used especially in newspapers, official reports, and formal meetings.

existing /ɪg'zɪstɪŋ/ [adj only before noun] use this about things or situations that exist now, when you think they may be changed in the future: The existing building is too small, and there are plans to replace it within the next five years. | Despite pressure for reform, the existing system still has its supporters.

> **Formal or informal?**
>
> **Existing** is not used in informal conversation.

today's/of today /tə'deɪz, əv tə'deɪ/ [adj] use this about social, economic, or political conditions and attitudes that exist now, when you are comparing them with those that existed in the past: *The first computers were extremely slow by today's standards.* | *The teenagers of today have a different attitude to sex.*

> ⚠ **Today's** and **of today** are used especially in news reports and articles.

5 happening now, but likely to change

for now/for the time being /fəʳ 'naʊ, fəʳ ðə ˌtaɪm 'biːɪŋ/ for a short time, but not permanently – use this about a temporary arrangement or way of dealing with a situation: *You'll have to use the other car for now.* | *Economists say that interest rates will remain stable for the time being.*

◌ **for the moment** /fəʳ ðə 'məʊmənt/ ESPECIALLY SPOKEN use this to say that something is true or happening now, but may change soon: *For the moment the city seems quiet, but the fighting could start again at any time.* | *"How's your apartment?" "It's fine for the moment, but I'd rather live nearer town."*

for the present /fəʳ ðə 'prezənt/ FORMAL use this to say that a situation will continue for a while, though it may change in the future: *It is assumed, for the present, that the meeting will go ahead.*

(in the) meanwhile/in the meantime /ɪn ðə 'miːnwaɪl, ɪn ðə 'miːntaɪm/ between now and some time in the future, for example until a situation changes: *Payday is not until next week, but if you need any money in the meantime, let me know.* | *The flight will be announced soon. Meanwhile, please remain seated.*

6 when something does not happen now, but used to happen

no longer/not any more /nəʊ 'lɒŋgəʳ, nɒt eni 'mɔːʳ‖-'lɔːŋ-/ use this to say that a situation that existed until recently

does not exist now: *Alice doesn't live here any more.* | *He no longer felt sure that he was right.*

no longer possible/necessary/ available etc *The bridge had collapsed, and it was no longer possible to cross the river.*

> **Formal or informal?**
>
> **No longer** is more formal than **not any more**, and it always comes before the verb or adjective: *She no longer loved him.* **Any more** comes after the verb or adjective: *She didn't love him any more.*

◌ **not now** /nɒt 'naʊ/ ESPECIALLY SPOKEN use this to say that something happened in the past, but it does not happen now: *When I was younger I could stay up all night having fun, but not now.* | *People used to respect teachers, but they don't now.*

NUMBER

➡ see also **COUNT/CALCULATE, TOTAL**

1 a written number

number /'nʌmbəʳ/ [n C] a word or sign that represents a quantity, which is used for example for counting or for showing the position of something in a series: *Choose a number between 1 and 10.* | *Football shirts usually have a number on the back.*

number 12/20/4 etc *She lives at number 853 Ocean Boulevard.*

even number (=2,4,6,8,10 etc) *Write down all the even numbers between 2 and 20.*

odd number (=1,3,5,7,9 etc) *All the doors on this side of the street have odd numbers.*

phone/passport/registration/licence number *What's your phone number?*

numbered [adj] having a number: *The report is organized in numbered paragraphs.*

figure /'fɪgəʳ‖'fɪgjər/ [n C] a number written as a sign, not as a word: *Write the amount in words and in figures.*

double figures (=more than 9 and less than 100) *Temperatures reached double figures yesterday, going as high as 14 degrees.*

single figures (=less than 10) *The*

inflation rate was still in single figures. (=less than 10%)

five-figure/six-figure etc (=consisting of five/six numbers etc) *The chief executive earns a six-figure salary.*

digit /ˈdɪdʒɪt/ [n C] a single number between 0 and 9, for example 1, 5, or 8 – used especially in formal or technical contexts: *French telephone numbers have six digits.*

double-digit (=more than 9 and less than 100) *The nation has not experienced double-digit inflation for many years.*

2 a number used in calculating

number /ˈnʌmbəʳ/ [n singular] the number of people or things in a group: *There have been several cases of tuberculosis, and the number is rising.*

+of *The number of cars on the roads increased by 22% last year.* | *The regulations limit the number of students in each class.*

figures /ˈfɪgəz‖ˈfɪgjərz/ [n plural] a set of numbers that are regularly calculated by a government, a company etc, especially in order to show how much something has increased or decreased: *Government figures show that unemployment is rising again.*

sales figures *Our sales figures have been steady this month.*

statistics /stəˈtɪstɪks/ [n plural] information about financial matters, social changes etc, which is shown in the form of numbers: *Statistics show that 50% of new businesses fail in their first year.* | *According to the latest government statistics, 2 million people retired last year.*

O, o

OBEY/DISOBEY

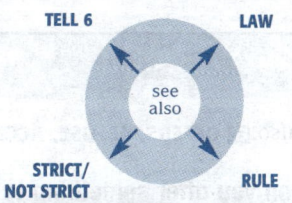

TELL 6   LAW

see also

STRICT/ NOT STRICT   RULE

1 to obey a person, rule, or law

obey /əʊ'beɪ, ə-/ [v I/T] to do what someone tells you to do, or do what a law or rule says you must do: *Soldiers must always obey their commanding officer.* | *I knew that if I didn't obey, I would be shot.*
obey an order/command *You can teach most dogs to obey simple commands.*

> Don't say 'he obeyed to the officer'. Say **he obeyed the officer**.

> **Formal or informal?**
> **Obey** is rather formal, and is used especially to talk about obeying the law or obeying military orders. **Do as you are told** is the usual expression for talking about children doing what their parents or teachers ask them to do.

follow /'fɒləʊ‖'fɑː-/ [v T] to do what someone tells you to do, wants you to do, or thinks you should do
follow orders/instructions *He was a military man, and therefore used to following orders.* | *I followed your instructions exactly.*
follow sb's advice *He followed the doctor's advice and had no further trouble.*
follow sb's orders/instructions etc to the letter (=do exactly what someone tells you) *You'll have a perfect cake if you follow these instructions to the letter.*

◯ **do as you are told** /ˌduː əz juː ɑːˈr ˈtəʊld/ ESPECIALLY SPOKEN to obey

without asking any questions – used especially by parents or teachers when they are telling children to do something, especially in a slightly angry way: *Don't ask why, just do as you're told.* | *Do as you're told and read your book.*

comply with sth /kəmˈplaɪ wɪð (sth)/ [phrasal verb T] FORMAL if you **comply with** a law or a decision, you do what it says you must do: *Companies must comply with European employment laws.* | *Failure to comply with these conditions could result in prosecution.*
complying – complied – have complied

keep to sth /'kiːp tuː (sth)/ [phrasal verb T] to always obey the law or rules closely and not ignore them: *If you keep to the rules, nothing can go wrong.* | *Do you always keep to the speed limit when you're driving?*

observe /əbˈzɜːʳv/ [v T] FORMAL to take notice of and obey rules, laws, customs etc: *You can avoid danger by observing these simple rules.* | *employers who fail to observe safety regulations*

2 to not obey a person, rule, or law

disobey /ˌdɪsəˈbeɪ, ˌdɪsəʊ-/ [v I/T] to refuse to do what someone tells you to do, or what a rule or law says you must do: *No one dared to disobey the captain.* | *If anyone disobeyed, they were severely punished.*
disobey an order *Around 1,000 soldiers had disobeyed orders and surrendered.*

> **Formal or informal?**
> **Disobey** is rather formal, and is used especially to talk about disobeying military orders.

break a rule/break the law /ˌbreɪk ə 'ruːl, ˌbreɪk ðə 'lɔː/ to not do what a rule or law says you must do: *Students who continue to break the rules may be asked to leave.* | *If you don't buy a ticket before you get on the train, you are breaking the law.*

ignore /ɪgˈnɔːʳ/ [v T] to pay no attention to a law or rule, or to what someone has told you to do, and behave as if it does not affect you: *Many cyclists ignore the law and ride around at night without lights.* | *I tell her to come home by 11 o'clock, but she just ignores me.*

🔍 **not pay any attention** (also **not take any notice** BRITISH) /nɒt peɪ ˌeni əˈtenʃən, nɒt teɪk ˌeni ˈnəʊtɪs/ ESPECIALLY SPOKEN to not do what someone has told you to do, in a way that annoys them: *I told him to book tickets early but he didn't pay any attention.* | *My kids never take any notice when I tell them to do their homework.*

rebel /rɪˈbel/ [v I] to deliberately behave in a way that is completely different from the way that your parents and people in general expect you to behave: *Her parents wanted her to go to university, but she rebelled and left school at 17.*
+against *Teenagers tend to rebel against people in authority.*
rebelling – rebelled – have rebelled

3 always doing what you are told to do

obedient /əˈbiːdiənt, əʊ-/ [adj] ESPECIALLY WRITTEN someone who is **obedient** always does what their parents, teachers, or people in authority tell them to do – use this especially about children: *Bruno was a quiet and obedient little boy.* | *I wish my children were more obedient.*
obedience [n U] obedient behaviour: *The General demanded absolute obedience from his men.*

law-abiding /ˈlɔː əˌbaɪdɪŋ/ [adj]
law-abiding people/citizens etc people who always obey the law and never break rules or do anything bad: *The majority of people round here are decent, law-abiding citizens.*

4 refusing to obey

disobedient /ˌdɪsəˈbiːdiənt◂, ˌdɪsəʊ-/ [adj] ESPECIALLY WRITTEN someone who is **disobedient** refuses to do what their parents, teachers, or people in authority tell them to do – use this especially about children: *As a small child, he was noisy and disobedient.*
disobedience [n U] disobedient

behaviour: *I've had enough of your disobedience.*

rebellious /rɪˈbeljəs/ [adj] someone who is **rebellious** deliberately behaves in a way that their parents or teachers disapprove of – use this about older children or young adults: *At sixteen, she became very rebellious.* | *rebellious teenagers*

OFFER

➡ see also EC **OFFERS, REFUSE, ACCEPT**

1 when you offer something to someone

offer /ˈɒfərǁˈɔː-, ˈɑː-/ [v T] to ask someone if they would like to have something or to say that they can have it if they want it
offer sb sth *She didn't even offer me a cup of tea.* | *I've been offered the job!*
offer sth to sb *Unfortunately, they offered the contract to someone else.*

🔍 **would you like....?** /ˌwʊd juː ˈlaɪk/ SPOKEN say this as a polite way of offering something to someone: *We have some maps of the city – would you like one?*

🔍 **can I get you.....?** /ˌkæn aɪ ˈget juː/ SPOKEN say this when you are offering someone a drink or food, for example at a party: *Can I get you some coffee?* | *What can I get you? There's beer or wine.*

🔍 **help yourself** /ˌhelp jɔːrˈself/ SPOKEN say this to tell someone they can take anything they want from the food and drink that is available: *There's plenty of food, so help yourselves.*
+to *Help yourself to some salad.*

🔍 **have** /hæv/ SPOKEN INFORMAL say this to persuade someone to take some food or drink that you are offering: *Have a piece of cake – my Mum made it.* | *Go on, have another beer.*

2 when you offer to help

offer /ˈɒfərǁˈɔː-, ˈɑː-/ [v I/T] to say that you will do something in order to help someone: *We hope that the meeting will encourage people to offer help and ideas.* | *"Do you want me to look*

after the children next week?" "No, but thanks for offering."
offer to do sth *I offered to give her a ride into town.*

> ⚠ Don't say 'I offered him to do it'. Say **I offered to do it**.

volunteer /ˌvɒlənˈtɪə^rǁˌvɑː-/ [v I] to offer to do something, especially something difficult or unpleasant: *Someone has to clean up all this mess. Who'll volunteer?*
volunteer to do sth *Jill has volunteered to go with me to the hospital.*
+for *No one volunteered for night duty.*

◯ **can I/would you like me to** (also **shall I** BRITISH) /ˈkæn aɪ, wʊd juː ˈlaɪk miː tuː, ˈʃæl aɪ/ SPOKEN say this when you are offering to do something for someone: *Can I take your bag – it looks heavy. | Would you like me to mail that letter for you? | Shall I make a copy for you?*

◯ **let me** /ˈlet miː/ SPOKEN say this when you are offering to help someone, especially when you want to be kind or friendly to them: *Let me drive you to the station. | Why don't you let me cook dinner tonight?*

3 to offer money for something

offer /ˈɒfə^rǁˈɔː-, ˈɑː-/ [v T] to say that you will pay someone a particular amount of money in exchange for something
offer sb sth *Chaldon was offered a huge salary to become team manager.*
offer (sb) sth for sth *Police are offering a reward for information about the robbery. | They said that they couldn't offer us more than £2000 for the car.*
make an offer /ˌmeɪk ən ˈɒfə^rǁ-ˈɔː-/ to offer a particular amount of money in order to buy a house, car etc
+for *Has anyone made an offer for the house yet?*
make sb an offer *I'm prepared to make you a very generous offer.*
bid /bɪd/ [v I/T] to offer to pay a particular amount of money for something you want to buy, in competition with other people

bid $10/£20 etc for sth *I bid £5 for a vase I saw on Ebay. | How much did you bid for the wardrobe?*
bidding – bid – have bid

4 something that you offer

offer /ˈɒfə^rǁˈɔː-, ˈɑː-/ [n C] something that someone has offered to give you or do for you, such as money, help, or advice: *I'll sell the car if I get an offer over $5000.*
+of *They received several offers of help.*
accept an offer (=say yes) *He would never accept any offers of help with the gardening.*
refuse an offer (=say no) *How could you refuse such a fantastic offer?*

OFFEN

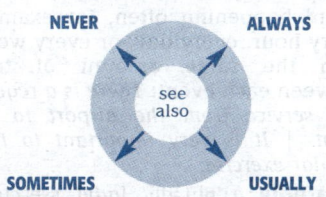

1 when something happens many times

often /ˈɒfən, ˈɒftənǁˈɔːf-/ [adv] *Rosi often works till 7 or 8 o'clock in the evening. | I often see her walking past with the children. | You should come and visit us more often.*
not very often *I have a mobile phone, but I don't use it very often.*
how often *"How often do you see your parents?" "Only two or three times a year."*

> ⚠ **Often** usually comes immediately before the main verb: *He often plays tennis in the evening. | You can often buy cheap tickets.* However, it comes after the main verb 'be': *In summer the beach is often so crowded that you cannot find space to sit down.*

◯ **a lot** /ə ˈlɒtǁ-ˈlɑːt/ [adv] SPOKEN if you do something **a lot**, you often do it:

It's nice to meet you. Wendy's talked about you a lot.

quite a lot BRITISH *She goes abroad on business quite a lot.*

tend to do sth /ˌtend tə ˈduː (sth)/ if something **tends to** happen, it often happens and it is likely to happen: *Studies show that girls tend to be better at languages than boys.*

frequently /ˈfriːkwəntli/ [adv] FORMAL often: *Passengers complain that trains are frequently cancelled.* | *Heat the sauce gently, stirring frequently.*

frequent /ˈfriːkwənt/ [adj] FORMAL happening often: *His job involved making frequent trips to Saudi Arabia.* | *The treatment was effective, and her headaches became less frequent.*

regularly /ˈregjʊlərli/ [adv] often and at regular times, for example every day, every week, or every month: *I used to go to church regularly.* | *Dave likes to keep fit, and he plays squash regularly.*

regular /ˈregjʊlər/ [adj usually before noun] happening often, for example every hour, every day, or every week, with the same amount of time between each event: *There is a regular bus service from the airport to the town.* | *It is very important to take regular exercise.*

repeatedly /rɪˈpiːtɪdli/ [adv] ESPECIALLY WRITTEN use this to emphasize that someone did something many times: *Graham's doctor had repeatedly warned him not to work so hard.* | *The boy had been punched and kicked repeatedly.*

again and again /əˌgen ənd əˈgen/ many times, much more often than you would expect: *I've told you again and again what his name is.* | *Again and again, the boat was almost smashed against the rocks.*

2 very often, in a way that makes you annoyed

keep (on) doing sth /ˌkiːp ɒn ˈduːɪŋ (sth)/ ESPECIALLY SPOKEN to do something many times, in a way that is annoying: *Dad, Bobby keeps hitting me.* | *How can I explain if you keep on interrupting?* | *I keep forgetting to mail this letter.*

always/all the time /ˈɔːlweɪz, -wɪz, ˌɔːlˈð ə ˈtaɪm/ [adv] very often, in a way that is annoying: *She just complains all the time and never tries to help*

be always doing sth *I'm sick of Harold – he's always telling me what to do.*

> ⚠ **Always** comes immediately before the main verb, unless the main verb is 'be': *He always forgets to bring his pen.* | *She's always late.*

time and time again /ˌtaɪm ənd taɪm əˈgen/ use this to say that something has been done many times, but without any effect: *I've told you time and time again not to play with matches.*

continually/constantly /kənˈtɪnjuəli, ˈkɒnstəntli‖ˈkɑːn-/ [adv] use this when you are annoyed because something seems to keep happening over a long period of time: *They seemed to be continually arguing.* | *I wish you'd clean up your room without having to be constantly reminded.*

continual/constant [adj only before noun] *It's impossible to work with these constant interruptions.* | *We've had continual problems with the computer system ever since it was installed.*

> **Formal or informal?**
> **Continually** and **constantly** are not usually used in informal conversation.

When you see **EC**, go to the **ESSENTIAL COMMUNICATION** section.

OLD

→ look here for ...
  • someone or something that is old
  • something that has been used before
→ if you want to talk about exactly how old someone or something is, go to **AGE**

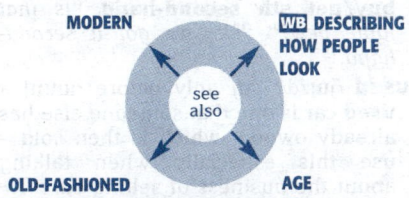

MODERN

WB DESCRIBING HOW PEOPLE LOOK

see also

OLD-FASHIONED   AGE

1 things

→ opposite **NEW**

old /əʊld/ [adj] They live in a big old house. | She was wearing jeans and an old blue jacket. | This is one of the oldest hotels in Venice. | How old is your car? | That's a really old joke – I've heard it lots of times.

ancient /'eɪnʃənt/ [adj] very old – use this about buildings, cities, countries, languages, or customs that existed many hundreds of years ago: Rome is famous for its ancient monuments. | the Pyramids of ancient Egypt | Very few schools still teach ancient Greek. (=the language spoken in Greece hundreds of years ago, which is different from modern Greek)
the ancient Egyptians/Chinese/Greeks etc (=the people who lived in Egypt etc many hundreds of years ago)

antique /ˌæn'tiːk◂/ [adj only before noun] **antique** furniture, jewellery, clocks etc are old and valuable, and often beautiful to look at: a lovely antique desk

antique /ˌæn'tiːk/ [n C often plural] something such as a piece of furniture or a beautiful object that is old and valuable: The house is full of valuable antiques.
antique shop/dealer/market (=one that sells antiques)

2 people

→ opposite **YOUNG**

old /əʊld/ [adj] The old lady was rather deaf. | Nowadays you're not considered old at sixty. | You shouldn't marry him – he's much too old for you.
get old (=become old) Dad's always worrying about getting old.
the old (=old people) hospital care for the old and sick

> ⚠ Be careful about using **old** to talk about people. It is more polite to use **elderly**.

elderly /'eldəʳli/ [adj] old – use this as a polite way of talking about old people: I was sitting next to a very nice elderly lady.
the elderly (=old people) a retirement home for the elderly

elder /'eldəʳ/ [adj only before noun] **elder brother/sister** someone's older brother or sister: My elder brother's an actor.

> ⚠ Don't say 'elder people', 'elder students' etc. Only use **elder** to talk about members of the same family.

eldest /'eldɪst/ [adj] **eldest brother/sister/son/daughter** someone's oldest brother, sister, son, or daughter: Her eldest son is in college. | I shared a bedroom with my eldest sister.
the eldest (=the oldest) Rosie was the eldest of four daughters.

senior citizen (also **senior** AMERICAN) /ˌsiːniəʳ 'sɪtɪzən, 'siːniəʳ/ [n C] someone who is above the age of 60 – use this to talk about older people as a group, and their particular interests, rights etc: There are special prices for senior citizens. | Many seniors have very active lives.

pensioner/old age pensioner /'penʃənəʳ, ˌəʊld eɪdʒ 'penʃənəʳ/ [n C] BRITISH an old person who has stopped working and receives money from the government: Many pensioners cannot afford to heat their homes in winter. | Old age pensioners can travel free on the buses.

3 food and drink

stale /steɪl/ [*adj*] **stale** bread or cake is hard, dry, and unpleasant to eat because it is no longer fresh: *There was only a bit of stale cake in the tin.*
go stale (=become stale) *The bread's gone stale – you'd better throw it away.*

mouldy BRITISH **moldy** AMERICAN /'məʊldi/ [*adj*] **mouldy** cheese, bread etc has a soft green or black substance growing on it because it has been kept too long: *I threw away the mouldy bread and cheese.*
go mouldy (=become mouldy) *a disgusting piece of pizza that had gone mouldy*
mouldy – mouldier – mouldiest

rotten /'rɒtn‖'rɑːtn/ [*adj*] **rotten** food, especially eggs or fruit, has been kept too long and smells bad: *At the back of the cupboard was a bag of rotten apples.* | *Some of the tomatoes were rotten.*

off /ɒf‖ɔːf/ [*adj* not before noun] food that is **off** is no longer fresh enough to eat: *Ugh! The milk's off!*
go off *Do you think the meat's gone off?*

vintage /'vɪntɪdʒ/ [*adj* only before noun] **vintage** wine is good quality wine made in a particular year

mature /mə'tʃʊə^r/ [*adj*] **mature** cheese, wine etc has a good strong taste which has developed during a long period of time: *mature cheddar*

4 the time when someone is old

old age /ˌəʊld 'eɪdʒ/ [*n* U] the time in someone's life when they are old: *the problems of old age*
in his/her old age (=when he/she is old) *Her grandfather's getting a bit forgetful in his old age.*

5 when something has been used before

old /əʊld/ [*adj* only before noun] **old** clothes, books, chairs etc have already been worn or used a lot by someone else: *My dad just bought a new TV, and he's giving me the old one.* | *I was the youngest in the family,* so I had to wear all my brothers' old clothes. | *Do you have any old magazines the kids can cut up?*

second-hand /ˌsekənd 'hænd◂/ [*adj*] **second-hand** books, clothes, cars etc have already been owned by someone else and are then sold: *Do you know where I can buy a second-hand bicycle?* | *Max spent a whole afternoon looking around a second-hand book store.*
buy/get sth second-hand *"Is that table new?" "No, we got it second-hand."*

used /juːzd/ [*adj* only before noun] a **used** car is one that someone else has already owned, which is then sold – use this especially when talking about the business of selling cars: *He made his money buying and selling used cars.*

OLD-FASHIONED

not modern, or not suitable for the present time

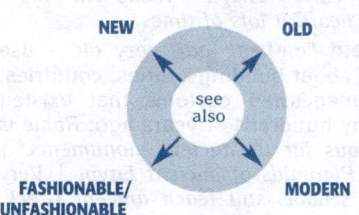

1 clothes/styles/words

old-fashioned /ˌəʊld 'fæʃənd◂/ [*adj*] **old-fashioned** clothes, styles, words etc are no longer considered modern or fashionable, although some people still wear them or still use them: *My cupboard's full of old-fashioned clothes that I never wear.* | *The word 'disco' sounds really old-fashioned now.*

dated /'deɪtɪd/ [*adj* not usually before noun] use this about clothes or styles that used to be fashionable, especially until recently, but now seem old-fashioned: *Just look at the hairstyles in this photo – they're so dated.* | *Pine furniture was popular not long ago, but now it looks a bit dated.*

2 ideas/methods/systems/people

old-fashioned /ˌəʊld ˈfæʃənd◂/ [adj]
old-fashioned ideas and ways of living were common in the past, but are not the way most people think and behave now: *He still has some very old-fashioned ideas about women.* | *That style of teaching now seems very old-fashioned.*

⚠ You can also use this about people who have old-fashioned opinions: *Her parents were very old-fashioned and wouldn't let her go out with boys.*

outdated /ˌaʊtˈdeɪtɪd◂/ [adj] **outdated** ideas, methods, or systems are not suitable for modern times and need to be changed and made more modern: *The British legal system is hopelessly outdated.* | *the outdated concepts of the sixties and seventies*

traditional /trəˈdɪʃənəl/ [adj]
traditional ideas, methods, or customs have existed for a long time, and are usually very different from more modern ideas, methods etc: *The local people still use traditional farming methods.* | *traditional ideas about how boys and girls should behave* | *Tom went to a very traditional all-boys school.* (=a school using traditional methods)

⚠ **Outdated** is always used in a negative way, but **old-fashioned** and **traditional** are sometimes used in a positive way when you approve of an old idea, method etc: *old-fashioned family values* | *They want to bring back traditional teaching methods.*

3 machines/equipment

old-fashioned /ˌəʊld ˈfæʃənd◂/ [adj]
old-fashioned machines and equipment have a design that is no longer modern: *He rides one of those old-fashioned bikes with high handlebars.* | *A lot of the machines at the factory are very old-fashioned.*

outdated /ˌaʊtˈdeɪtɪd◂/ [adj] use this about machines or equipment that use old-fashioned designs, and should be replaced with more

modern ones: *You can't run a business with outdated equipment.* | *The replacement of outdated computer hardware is long overdue.*

obsolete /ˈɒbsəliːt‖ˌɑːbsəˈliːt/ [adj] use this about machines and equipment that are no longer being produced, and that seem old-fashioned because newer machines have been invented, which can do the same job much better: *The old 5½ inch floppy disks are now obsolete.*
make sth obsolete *New anti-tank missiles are making battle tanks obsolete.*

Formal or informal?
Obsolete is used in writing and in formal spoken English.

4 books/information

out of date /ˌaʊt əv ˈdeɪt/ [adj] use this about books, maps etc that do not contain the most recent information, or about information that is no longer right because the facts have changed: *The map we had with us was completely out of date.*

⚠ **Out of date** is written with hyphens when it comes before a noun, but without hyphens when it comes after a noun: *out-of-date medical records* | *Your medical records are out of date.*

5 old-fashioned in a pleasant way

old-fashioned /ˌəʊld ˈfæʃənd◂/ [adj]
old-fashioned in a way that reminds you of nice things in the past: *good old-fashioned home cooking* | *The town has a lovely old-fashioned charm about it.*

quaint /kweɪnt/ [adj] old-fashioned and unusual, but attractive and interesting – use this about small buildings or places, or about customs and beliefs: *We stayed in a quaint little fishing village.* | *quaint country cottages*

ONE

➡ see also **ALONE**

1 one person or thing

one /wʌn/ [*number*] *I have four sisters and one brother.* | *Turn to page one.* | *one thousand pounds*
+of *One of your friends called.*
one-legged/one-eyed/one-armed etc (=having only one leg, one eye etc) *a one-eyed cat*

> ⚠ Don't say **one** when you should say **a** or **an**. Say 'he offered me a cigarette' (not 'one cigarette'). Use **one** to emphasize that you really mean only one, and not a larger number. Compare: *In the middle of the room there was a big table.* | *There were five small tables and one big table.*

> ⚠ With measurements (like month, mile, metre etc), it is more usual to say **a** than **one**: *I saw her a week ago.* | *It's about a mile from here.* | *a hundred litres of water*

single /'sɪŋɡəl/ [*adj* only before noun] only one – use this especially when it is surprising that there is only one: *They won the game by a single point.* | *These dealers can earn $10,000 in a single day.*
not a single (=not even one) *It was 3 a.m. and there wasn't a single car on the road.*

solo /'səʊləʊ/ [*adj* only before noun] use this about something that one person does alone, but which is usually done by several people together: *a solo attempt to climb Mount Everest* | *Ridgeway's solo voyage across the Atlantic* | *This is his first solo album.* (=he made the record on his own, not with a band)
solo [*adv*] *When did you first fly solo?*

2 one time

once /wʌns/ [*adv*] one time or on one occasion: *I've only met her once.* | *He rang the bell once, then waited.*
once a day/week/month (=once every day, week etc) *Staff meetings take place once a week.* | *This is a*

desert region, where it only rains once or twice a year.
once more (=one more time) *I checked my reflection once more in the mirror.*

ONLY

➡ if you mean 'the largest or smallest amount that is allowed', go to **LIMIT**
➡ see also **FEW**

1 only one, or only a small number

only /'əʊnli/ [*adj/adv*] only one person or thing, or only a small number of people or things, and not anyone or anything else: *There was only one dress that she really liked.* | *Only rich people were able to travel abroad in those days.* | *You can only take one piece of hand baggage onto the plane.* | *Today there are only a few cotton mills left.*
the only person/thing/place etc *She's the only woman I've ever loved.*
be only for sb (=only one person or group can use something) *These seats are only for first class passengers.*

just /dʒʌst/ [*adv*] ESPECIALLY SPOKEN only one person, thing, type, or group, especially when this is surprising: *"Were there a lot of people there?" "No, just me and David."* | *At first, the shop sold just prints and posters.* | *"Does everyone have to wear uniform?" "No, just the first-year students."*

the one /ðə 'wʌn/ **the one thing/person/time/problem etc** the only person, thing etc and no others – use this to emphasize that there really is only one person or thing of this type etc: *She was the one friend that I could trust.* | *The one thing I don't like about my car is the colour.* | *The one disadvantage of Internet banking is that it may not be secure.*

all /ɔːl/ [*pronoun*] the only thing or things, especially when this is disappointing, annoying, or surprising: *All Kevin ever talks about is football.* | *We were so hungry, but all we could find was some stale bread.* | *All I wanted was a bit of sympathy.*

nothing but /'nʌθɪŋ bʌt/ only – use this especially when you feel disappointed, annoyed, or surprised that this is the only thing there is or the only thing someone does: *They did nothing but argue for the whole journey.* | *She answered the door wearing nothing but a towel.*

sole /səʊl/ [*adj* only before noun] FORMAL the only person, thing etc, especially when you would expect there to be more or expect it to be different
the sole person/thing etc *In many households, the woman is the sole breadwinner.* (=the only person who has a job)
with the sole intention/objective/ aim of doing sth *I think he came here with the sole intention of causing trouble.*
sb's sole concern/objective etc *NASA's sole concern was the safety of the astronauts.*

---

2 a surprisingly small price/number/amount etc

only /'əʊnli/ [*adv*] use this to say that a number, amount, price, size etc is surprisingly small: *I got these four chairs for only $99.* | *We only have a very small garden.* | "Is it far?" "No, it's only a mile away." | *She was only 17 when she got married.*

just /dʒʌst/ [*adv*] only a small amount, number, period of time etc, especially when this is surprising and good: *There is a beautiful park just 300 metres from the busiest shopping street.* | *It took the firefighters just three minutes to arrive.* | *His car hit a wall, but he escaped with just cuts and bruises.*

◌ **just a little** (also **just a bit** BRITISH) SPOKEN (=only a small amount, number etc) "Do you take milk?" "Just a little, please."

◌ **is that all?** /ɪz ðæt 'ɔːl/ SPOKEN say this when you are surprised because you expected a number, price etc to be higher: "The tickets are $10." "Is that all?"

no more than /nəʊ 'mɔːʳ ðən/ use this to emphasize that something is small, unimportant, difficult to notice etc: *We were standing no more than 10*

yards away from the scene of the crime and we didn't realize it.

---

3 for only one reason, and no others

only /'əʊnli/ [*adv*] for only one reason or purpose, and not for any others – use this especially when explaining why someone does something: *She only married him for his money.* | *The woman said she had only started stealing because her children were hungry.*

◌ **just** /dʒʌst/ [*adv*] ESPECIALLY SPOKEN only – use this when explaining why someone does something: *I think she just wanted someone to talk to.* | *I didn't mean to interfere – I was just trying to help.*
just because *My brother thinks he can tell me what to do, just because he's older than me.*

merely /'mɪəʳli/ [*adv*] FORMAL use this to emphasize that you are doing something only for the reason you say, and not for any other reason, especially when someone seems annoyed or upset: *The committee does not blame any individual; we are merely trying to find out how the accident happened.*

---

4 someone or something that is not important, special, or interesting

only/just /'əʊnli, dʒʌst / [*adv*] use this to emphasize that someone or something is not particularly important, special, or interesting: *Don't ask me – I'm only the cleaner.* | "What's for dinner?" "Just pasta."
only another/just another *It's just another of those daytime talk shows.*

> **Formal or informal?**
> **Just** is used especially in informal spoken English.

merely /'mɪəʳli/ [*adv*] FORMAL use this to emphasize that someone or something is not really important or special, although they may seem to be: *The President's position is merely ceremonial; it is the Chancellor who holds real power.*

O

OPEN

➡ opposite **SHUT/CLOSE**
➡ see also **FASTEN/UNFASTEN, TIE/ UNTIE**

1 to open a door, window, drawer etc

open /'əupən/ [v T] *It's very hot in here. Do you mind if I open the window? | The drawer was stuck, but Tom eventually managed to open it.*

unlock /ʌnˈlɒkǁ-ˈlɑːk/ [v T] to turn a key in the lock on a door, drawer, cupboard etc so that you can open it: *Unlock the door! We can't get out! | Which of these keys unlocks the cupboard?*

force open

force open /ˌfɔːʳs ˈəupən/ to open a door, window, cupboard etc by using force, often with a tool
force sth open *If the door's stuck, we'll just have to force it open.*
force open sth *The burglars had forced open the window with an iron bar.*

break open /ˌbreɪk ˈəupən/ to open a container by using force, so that it is damaged
break open sth *We managed to break open the wooden box with an axe.*
break sth open *There's no key for the suitcase – we'll have to break it open.*

break the door down /ˌbreɪk ðə ˈdɔːʳ daʊn/ to hit or push a locked door very hard so that the lock breaks and the door opens or falls down: *Firefighters had to break the door down.*

wind down the window BRITISH **roll down the window** AMERICAN /ˌwaɪnd daʊn ðə ˈwɪndəu, ˌrəul daʊn ðə ˈwɪndəu/ to open a car window, especially by turning a handle: *The driver wound down his window and asked us the way to the stadium. | Mom, will you roll down your window a little?*

2 when a door or window opens

open /'əupən/ [v I] if a door or window **opens**, it moves so that it is no longer shut: *The door opened and Dr Neil came in. | I can't get this window to open.*

burst open/fly open /ˌbɜːʳst ˈəupən, ˌflaɪ ˈəupən/ WRITTEN to open very suddenly: *Suddenly the door flew open with a bang. | The door burst open and Flora came running in.*

 Use **burst open** or **fly open** in stories or written descriptions of events.

3 an open door or window

open /'əupən/ [adj] *Carrie stood in front of the open window. | The office door was open, and I could hear everything they said.*
wide open (=open as much as possible) *Do you know you left the kitchen window wide open all night?*

ajar /əˈdʒɑːʳ/ [adj not before noun] WRITTEN a door that is **ajar** is slightly open: *She had left her bedroom door ajar and could hear her parents talking downstairs.*

 Use **ajar** in stories and written descriptions of events.

4 to open a container

open /'əupən/ [v T] to open a bottle, box, or other container by removing or lifting its top or lid: *I'll ask the waiter to open another bottle of champagne. | Jonah opened his tool* box and pulled out a hammer. | It's a little gadget that helps you to open jars.

unscrew /ʌnˈskruː/ [v T] to remove the top or lid of a bottle or container by turning it: I can't unscrew this lid. Can you try?

5 to open a packet or something that is folded

open /ˈəʊpən/ [v T] to remove or partly remove the outside covering of something so that you can reach what is inside it: Aren't you going to open your letter? | Judy opened another pack of cigarettes.

unwrap /ʌnˈræp/ [v T] to open a package by removing the paper that is wrapped around it: I just love unwrapping Christmas presents! | Sarah sat down and unwrapped her sandwiches.
unwrapping – unwrapped – have unwrapped

unfold /ʌnˈfəʊld/ [v T] to open something that was folded, such as a piece of paper or cloth: They unfolded the tablecloth and set out the picnic. | The wind was so strong that it was impossible to unfold the map.

6 to open your eyes or mouth

open your eyes/open your mouth /ˌəʊpən jɔːr ˈaɪz, ˌəʊpən jɔːr ˈmaʊθ/ She opened her eyes and sat up in bed. | The dentist told me to open my mouth a little wider.

open /ˈəʊpən/ [adj not usually before noun] when your mouth or eyes are open
keep your eyes open (=stay awake) I was so tired I could hardly keep my eyes open.
wide open (=open as much as possible) Ben was staring at her with his mouth wide open.

7 when a shop, bank, restaurant etc opens

open /ˈəʊpən/ [v I] if a shop, bank, restaurant etc **opens** at a particular time in the day, people can use it

from that time: "What time does the bank open?" "9.30." | On Saturdays, the restaurant opens at 7 p.m.

> ⚠ You can also use **open** to say that a new shop, bank, restaurant etc starts to be available for people to use: A new McDonalds has opened in St Petersburg. | The store first opened in 1976. You can also say that someone **opens** a shop, bank, restaurant etc, meaning that they make it available for people to use: They plan to open a huge new superstore on the edge of town.

open /ˈəʊpən/ [adj not before noun] if a shop, bank, restaurant etc is **open**, it is available for people to use: The World Café is open from 10 a.m. till 11 p.m.
stay open In some places, the bars stay open all night.

OPINION

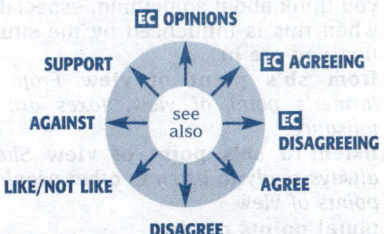

EC OPINIONS
SUPPORT
EC AGREEING
AGAINST   see also   EC DISAGREEING
LIKE/NOT LIKE
AGREE
DISAGREE

1 what you think about something

opinion /əˈpɪnjən/ [n C]
my/your/her etc opinion If you want my opinion, I don't think the colour really suits you.
in my/your/her etc opinion In my opinion, most lawyers are overpaid. | This is, in the opinion of the critics, their best record for years.
+about/on Can I ask your opinion about something, Michael?
give your opinion (=say what you think) Do you think it's a good essay? Give me your honest opinion.

○ **what you think of/about sth** /ˌwɒt juː ˈθɪŋk ɒv, əˈbaʊt (sth)/ ESPECIALLY SPOKEN your opinion about something, especially whether you think it is good or bad: *What do you think of their new album? | Tell me what you think about the design.*

view /vjuː/ [n C] your opinion about something, especially about a serious or important subject: *Children often have very different views from their parents.*
+that *I don't agree with the view that longer prison sentences stop people from committing crime.*
in my/his/John's view *In Freud's view, people's dreams often reveal their unconscious fears.*
+on *She has strong views on environmental issues.*

attitude /ˈætₔtjuːd‖-tuːd/ [n C] what you think and feel about something or someone, especially when this is shown in the way that you behave: *I don't understand your attitude. Why don't you like her?*
+to/towards *He had a very serious attitude to life.*

point of view /ˌpɔɪnt əv ˈvjuː/ [n C] what you think about something, especially when this is influenced by the situation you are in
from sb's point of view *From a farmer's point of view, foxes are a nuisance.*
listen to sb's point of view *She's always ready to listen to other people's points of view.*
plural **points of view**

public opinion /ˌpʌblɪk əˈpɪnjən/ [n U] what most people in a country think about a particular subject, idea, government etc: *The government responded to public opinion and introduced new controls on guns. | Public opinion was turning against the President.*

position /pəˈzɪʃən/ [n singular] what a government, political party, or person has decided is their official opinion
+on *What is the Republican position on welfare?*

Formal or informal?

Position is used in writing and news reports, and in formal spoken English.

line /laɪn/ [n C usually singular] the publicly stated opinion of a political party, government etc, which all their members are supposed to agree with
the party/government/official etc

line *He found it hard to accept the party line on every issue.*

2 what other people think about you

reputation /ˌrepj˳ˈteɪʃən/ [n C] someone's **reputation** is the general opinion that other people have about them, for example whether they are good or bad
excellent/good/bad reputation *No parent wants to send their child to a school with a bad reputation.*
+as *She has a reputation as a very efficient worker.*
+for *a car with a reputation for reliability*
damage sb's reputation *A series of scandals had damaged the reputation of the Royal Family.*

image /ˈɪmɪdʒ/ [n singular] the idea that people have about a well-known person, company, or product – use this especially about an idea that is created through television, newspaper stories, advertising etc: *his image as a Hollywood tough guy*
be bad/good for sb's image *The President's advisers said it would be bad for his image to be photographed with union leaders.*
improve sb's/sth's image *If the company doesn't improve its image, it will go out of business.*

name /neɪm/ [n singular] the reputation a person or an organization has because of something they do or because of the quality of what they produce, usually when this is good
good/bad name *He didn't want to do anything to damage the good name of the company.*
have a name for doing sth *Jack Brown has a name for making tough business deals.*

OPPOSITE

➡ look here for ...
• when two things are completely different
• in the opposite direction
• when two people or things are facing each other
➡ see also **DIFFERENT, SAME**

1 when two things or people are completely different

opposite /'ɒpəzɪ̯t‖-'ɑːp-/ [adj] as different as possible from something or someone else: *John and I have opposite opinions on almost everything.* | *The medicine was supposed to make him sleep, but it had the opposite effect.*
+to *In every way he was opposite to his timid little mother.*

the opposite /ði 'ɒpəzɪ̯t‖-'ɑːp-/ [n singular] a person or thing that is as different as possible from someone or something else, or a word whose meaning is as different as possible from the meaning of another word: *They asked for our advice, and then did exactly the opposite!*
+of *'Hard' is the opposite of 'soft'.*
just the opposite (=exactly the opposite) *Larry is friendly and outgoing, but his brother is just the opposite.*

◌ **the other way around** (also **the other way round** BRITISH) /ði ˌʌðəʳ weɪ (ə)'raʊnd/ SPOKEN if a situation is **the other way around**, it is the opposite of what you thought or of what someone has just said: *Pete's the doctor and Steve's the lawyer, or is it the other way round?* (=is Steve the doctor and Pete the lawyer?) | *I thought he was the boss and she was his secretary, but in fact it was the other way around.*

2 in or from the opposite direction

the other way /ði ˌʌðəʳ 'weɪ/ *She didn't see me – she was looking the other way.* | *Their car hit a truck which was coming the other way.*

Formal or informal?
The other way is more informal than **in the opposite direction**.

in the opposite direction/in the other direction /ɪn ði ˌɒpəzɪ̯t dʒ'rekʃən, ɪn ði ˌʌðəʳ dʒ'rekʃən‖-ˌɑːp-/ *I saw him and hurried away in the opposite direction.* | *The road is very narrow, so slow down if you meet a car coming in the other direction.*

in opposite directions *Two trains travelling in opposite directions had collided.*

3 when two people or things directly face each other

opposite /'ɒpəzɪ̯t‖-'ɑːp-/ [adj/adv/preposition] something that is **opposite** something else is facing it, for example on the other side of the street or on the other side of a table: *When you get off the bus, you'll see a grocery store on the opposite side of the street.* | *She recognized the man who was sitting opposite.*
be opposite sb/sth *The bathroom is opposite the bedroom.*
directly opposite (=exactly opposite) *The entrance to the park is directly opposite our house.*

> ⚠ Don't say 'the cinema is opposite of the station'. Say **the cinema is opposite the station**.

across /ə'krɒs‖ə'krɔːs/ [preposition]
across the street/river/table etc opposite where you are, and on the other side of the street, river etc: *She lives across the road.* | *From the hotel you can see the pretty villages across the bay.*
across the street/table etc from sb/sth *Across the street from the hotel was a little park.*

on the other side /ɒn ði ˌʌðəʳ 'saɪd/ on the opposite side of a road, river etc: *If you look across the lake, you can see Ruskin's house on the other side.*
+of *You can park on the other side of the road.*

face /feɪs/ [v T] to be opposite someone or something or to be looking or pointing in their direction: *Rita's apartment faces the harbour.* | *The seat facing mine was empty.* | *They stood facing each other for a few minutes.*

face to face /ˌfeɪs tə 'feɪs/ if two people are **face to face**, they are sitting or standing opposite each other, and they are very close: *The two men stood face to face, glaring at each other.* | *We sat face to face across the table.*

O

ORDER

**the order in which things are
arranged, or the order in which things
happen**

➡ if you mean 'order someone to do
something', go to **TELL**

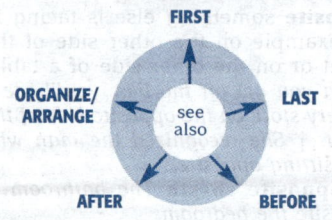

FIRST

ORGANIZE/
ARRANGE — see also — LAST

AFTER — BEFORE

1 order

order /'ɔːʳdəʳ/ [n C/U] the way that
events happen or that information is
arranged, with one thing first,
another thing second, and so on
in this/that/what/any order *Safety
checks must be carried out in the cor-
rect order.* | *It doesn't matter which
order you answer the questions in.*
+of *We were given a printed sheet
showing the order of events for the day.*
**in order of importance/difficulty/
size etc** (=when the most important
thing is first, then the next most
important etc) *Their main exports, in
order of importance, are copper, coal,
and maize.* | *The subjects that students
enjoyed most were, in order of popular-
ity, music, history, and art.*
in alphabetical order (=with 'a' first,
then 'b', then 'c' etc) *Our names were
listed in alphabetical order.*

sequence /'siːkwəns/ [n C] a number of
events, actions, or pieces of information that follow one another in a
particular order
+of *Police are not sure of the exact
sequence of events that led to the riot.* |
*The dance is basically a sequence of
steps that you repeat over and over
again.* | *Basic computer code consists
of sequences of ones and zeros.*

> **Formal or informal?**
> **Sequence** is a fairly formal word.

pattern /'pætənǁ'pætərn/ [n C] the order
in which things usually happen or

someone usually does something,
which you notice because it seems to
be regular: *It's a common pattern:
failure at school and unemployment,
leading to a life of crime.*
+of *the normal pattern of development
for a child*
follow a pattern (=happen in the
same way) *Police say that each of the
murders follows the same pattern.*

2 in the correct order

in the right order /ɪn ðə ˌraɪt 'ɔːʳdəʳ/ if a
set of things, actions, or events is **in
the right order**, it is correctly
arranged or it happens in the correct
order: *Have you put all the pages in
the right order?* | *It is important to add
each ingredient in the right order.*

3 in the wrong order

in the wrong order /ɪn ðə ˌrɒŋ 'ɔːʳdəʳǁ
-ˌrɔːŋ-/ if a set of things, actions, or
events is **in the wrong order**, it is not
correctly arranged: *All the files were in
the wrong order, so it took me hours to
find her letter.* | *If you give commands
in the wrong order, the computer will
not respond.*

mixed up /ˌmɪkst 'ʌp◂/ [adj not before
noun] in the wrong order, especially
when this has been done deliberately:
*In this exercise, the sentences are all
mixed up and you have to put them in
the right order.*

backwards /'bækwəʳdz/ [adv] starting at
the end and finishing at the beginning:
Can you say the alphabet backwards?

ORGANIZATION

**a group of people who do something
together, or who work for a particular
purpose**

➡ see also **MEMBER, COMPANY, JOIN**

organization (also **organisation** BRIT-
ISH) /ˌɔːʳgənaɪ'zeɪʃənǁ-gənə-/ [n C] a
large group of people who work
together in business, politics, education, sport etc: *Greenpeace is an international organization that works to*

protect the environment. | Most big organizations employ their own legal experts. | the World Health Organization

institution /ˌɪnstᵻˈtjuːʃən‖-ˈtuː-/ [n C] an organization that does educational, scientific, or financial work, especially a large and important organization that has existed for a long time
financial/educational/medical institution More money is needed for higher educational institutions. | banks, insurance companies, and other financial institutions | A major study of women and heart disease is being carried out by the Johns Hopkins Medical Institution.

party /ˈpɑːʳti/ [n C] an organization of people who all have the same political ideas, which you can vote for in elections: The Republican Party now has a majority in Congress.
political party There are three main political parties in Britain.
join a party He joined the Communist Party when he was a student.
plural **parties**

> ⚠ You can also use **party** before a noun, like an adjective: Party leaders met today to discuss the crisis. | This is not party policy. | party members

> ⚠ In British English, you can use **party** with a singular or plural verb: The Labour Party is likely/are likely to oppose any change in the law. In American English, always use a singular verb.

club /klʌb/ [n C] a group of people who meet regularly in their free time to do something that they are all interested in, especially a particular sport or activity
tennis/photography etc club He's a member of the local tennis club.
join a club How much does it cost to join the golf club?
belong to a club (=be a member of a club) She belongs to the college chess club.

society /səˈsaɪᵻti/ [n C] an organization for people who have the same interest or aim, especially a large official

organization: The Royal Society for the Protection of Birds | the university film society | the president of the American Historical Society
plural **societies**

> ⚠ **Clubs** are usually for sport and other activities that people do in their free time, such as photography or gardening. **Societies** are interested in subjects like art, literature, and science, or in working to help people or animals.

association /əˌsəʊsiˈeɪʃən, əˌsəʊʃi-/ [n C] an important organization for people in a particular sport, profession, activity etc, which officially represents its members and has the power to make rules: The new health care proposals have been criticized by the British Medical Association. | The National Basketball Association negotiates TV rights for important games.

> ⚠ The word **association** is almost always used in the name of an organization.

union /ˈjuːnjən/ [n C] an organization formed by workers to protect their rights and improve their pay and working conditions: the National Union of Teachers | As you know, our union supports a free press.
trade union BRITISH **labor union** AMERICAN (=union) The President could not rely on the support of the labor unions.
join a union Some workers refused to join the union.

> ⚠ You can also use **union** before a noun, like an adjective: Union members have voted against a strike. | a union official

> ⚠ In British English, you can use **union** with a singular or plural verb: The union has rejected/have rejected the latest pay offer. In American English, always use a singular verb.

O

ORGANIZE/ ARRANGE

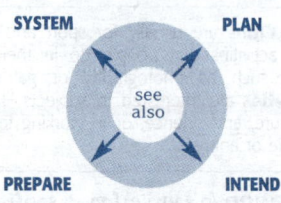

SYSTEM   PLAN

see also

PREPARE   INTEND

1 to make preparations for something to happen

arrange /ə'reɪndʒ/ [v I/T] to make preparations for a meeting, party, journey etc, for example by choosing a suitable time and place and telling people about it: *Ann's arranging a surprise party for Russell's birthday.*
arrange to do sth *They arranged to meet the following day.*
arrange for sb to do sth *He arranged for her to leave on the next flight home.*
🔍 **it's all arranged** SPOKEN (=all the preparations have been made) *We're going on Friday – it's all arranged.*
it was arranged that *It was arranged that our visitors should stay at a nearby hotel.*

organize (also **organise** BRITISH) /'ɔːˤgənaɪz/ [v T] to make preparations for an event, especially a big public event that needs a lot of preparation and planning: *I've been asked to organize this year's Summer Carnival. | an exhibition organised by the local camera club*

organizer (also **organiser** BRITISH) [n C] someone who organizes a large public event: *the organizers of the music festival | a conference organizer*

make   arrangements /ˌmeɪk ə'reɪndʒmənts/ to arrange all the details of an event that you have planned such as the dates, times, and places
+for *Rita and Howard are busy making arrangements for their wedding.*

set up /ˌset 'ʌp/ [phrasal verb T] to make all the arrangements that are necessary so that a meeting can happen or a system can start working

set up sth *I'll get my secretary to set up a meeting for all of the sales executives. | We need to set up emergency procedures to deal with this sort of problem.*
set sth up *There will be an inquiry into the accident, and Judge Mather has been asked to set it up.*

fix up /ˌfɪks 'ʌp/ [phrasal verb I/T] BRITISH INFORMAL to arrange a meeting, a visit, a journey etc
fix up sth *Let's fix up a date to have lunch together.*
fix up to do sth *I've fixed up to go to the airport with Bill.*
fix up for sb to do sth *He fixed up for her to go and see Dr Graham.*

2 plans and preparations for an event

arrangements /ə'reɪndʒmənts/ [n plural] all the preparations that must be made for an event, a journey etc to happen successfully
+for *Who is in charge of the arrangements for the President's visit?*
make arrangements *Her nephew has made all the funeral arrangements.*
travel / seating / sleeping arrangements *Lena wasn't very happy about the travel arrangements.*

plans /plænz/ [n plural] things that you have planned to do and arranged to do: *The weather spoiled our plans for a picnic.*
+for *What are your plans for the weekend?*

appointment /ə'pɔɪntmənt/ [n C] an arrangement to meet someone such as a doctor, a lawyer, or a business person at a particular time and place: *What time is your appointment at the hospital?*
have an appointment with sb *I have an appointment with the dentist on Monday afternoon.*
make an appointment *If you want to see the manager, you'll have to make an appointment.*

3 something that is well organized

well-organized (also **well-organised** BRITISH) /ˌwel 'ɔːˤgənaɪzd/ [adj] organized in a careful and thorough way, and therefore likely to be good or successful: *The exhibition was very well-organized.* | *a clear, well-organized report* | *a well-organized political campaign*

efficient /ɪˈfɪʃənt/ [*adj*] use this about an organization, method, or system in which all the parts work well together and good results are achieved without any money or time being wasted: *The passport office is very efficient – I got a new passport in just 48 hours.* | *We need more efficient methods of transporting goods.*

well-run /ˌwel ˈrʌn◂/ [*adj*] use this about an organization or business that is successful because the people in charge organize it well: *a comfortable, well-run hotel*

organized (also **organised** BRITISH) /ˈɔːrgənaɪzd/ [*adj*] organized in a way that is effective and likely to be successful: *Tonight after supper we want to have a more organized discussion.* | *Organized networks of thieves are stealing cattle.*

4   someone who organizes things well, and gets good results

well-organized (also **well-organised** BRITISH) /ˌwel ˈɔːrgənaɪzd/ [*adj*] someone who is **well-organized** plans things well so that they achieve what they want to achieve: *As a personal assistant, you need to be well-organized.* | *Well-organized rebel forces have succeeded in recapturing the town.*

efficient /ɪˈfɪʃənt/ [*adj*] someone who is **efficient** works well and does what needs to be done without wasting time: *Friendly and efficient staff are essential.*

businesslike /ˈbɪznəˌslaɪk/ [*adj*] someone who is **businesslike** deals with people effectively and does not waste time on things that are not important: *Ted was brisk and businesslike and very much in charge.* | *"Sign here, please," she said in a businesslike way.*

5   something that is badly organized

badly organized (also **badly organised** BRITISH) /ˌbædli ˈɔːrgənaɪzd/ [*adj*] use this about events or activities that are not successful, because they have not been planned well: *The festival was very badly organized, and nobody seemed to know what they were doing.*

badly run /ˌbædli ˈrʌn◂/ [*adj*] a business or organization that is **badly run** produces bad results because it is badly managed or organized: *The company is not badly run, but it still has not made a profit.*

disorganized (also **disorganised** BRITISH) /dɪsˈɔːrgənaɪzd/ [*adj*] not organized or arranged in a careful and thorough way, and therefore not likely to be successful or easy to manage: *The rescue effort was totally disorganized.* | *A disorganized desk is a sign of a disorganized mind.*

chaos /ˈkeɪ-ɒsǁ-ɑːs/ [*n* U] a very confused situation in which nothing seems to be organized, especially when something bad has happened unexpectedly: *The floods have caused widespread chaos.*
in chaos *The country was in chaos following the death of the President.*
chaotic /keɪˈɒtɪkǁ-ˈɑːt-/ [*adj*] use this about situations in which everything seems confused and nothing seems organized: *The traffic in the city centre is chaotic.*

confusion /kənˈfjuːʒən/ [*n* U] a situation in which no one is sure what is happening and there is a lot of noise and activity: *The bombers escaped in the confusion that followed the explosion.*

be a mess/be a shambles /biː ə ˈmes, biː ə ˈʃæmbəlz/ INFORMAL if a situation or event **is a mess** or **a shambles**, no one seems to be in control and nothing good or useful is being achieved: *The country's economy is a shambles.* | *My life seems to be a mess at the moment.*

6 to put things or people in a particular order

arrange /əˈreɪndʒ/ [v T] to put a group of things or people into a particular order or position, according to a plan or design: *Nina arranged the roses in a tall vase.* | *A photographer was arranging the children for the school photograph.*
arrange sth in a circle/in rows etc *The chairs had been arranged in a circle around the piano.*

organize (also **organise** BRITISH) /ˈɔːˈɡənaɪz/ to arrange information, ideas etc in order according to a system, so that they will be more effective or easier to use: *Organize your notes very carefully before giving a speech.*
organize sth into piles/groups etc *The book is organized into three sections.*

set out /ˌset ˈaʊt/ [phrasal verb T] to arrange a group of things on the floor, on a table, on a shelf etc for people to use, take, or look at
set out sth *Let's set out the chairs so they'll be ready for tonight's meeting.*
set sth out *A waiter brought drinks and sandwiches, and set them out on a table beside the pool.*

rearrange /ˌriːəˈreɪndʒ/ [v T] to arrange things in a different order or position from the way they were arranged before: *Who's been rearranging the furniture?* | *With a word processor you can easily rearrange the paragraphs when you've finished writing.*

7 to put things into the correct order

put sth in order /ˌpʊt (sth) ɪn ˈɔːˈdə/ to arrange things so that they are in the correct order: *Collect all the pages together, put them in order, and file them.*
put sth in alphabetical/numerical order *We need to put all the names in alphabetical order.*

sort out /ˌsɔːt ˈaʊt/ [phrasal verb T] to organize something that is untidy or unclear, so that it is tidier and easier to use

sort out sth *I spent most of the morning sorting out my desk.*
sort sth out *Sort the files out, and throw away any we don't need.*

8 the way that things are arranged

arrangement /əˈreɪndʒmənt/ [n C] a group of things that are arranged according to a pattern or in a way that makes them look attractive
+of *a simple design consisting of an arrangement of circles and rectangles*
flower arrangement (=flowers that have been cut and arranged attractively)

layout /ˈleɪaʊt/ [n C] the way that a building, town, garden, book etc is arranged according to a plan, so that it looks attractive or works well
+of *the architects who had planned the layout of our hospital*
page layout (=the way in which writing and pictures are arranged on a page) *On a computer, it's easy to change the page layout.*

OWE

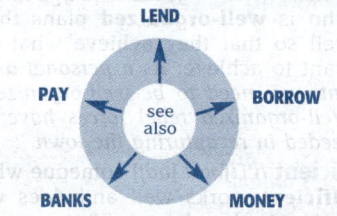

1 to owe money to someone

owe /əʊ/ [v T] if you **owe** someone money, you have to pay them, either because you borrowed money from them or because you got something from them and have not yet paid for it
owe money/$50 etc *The business collapsed, owing $50 million.*
owe sb sth *I owe him £5.*
owe sth to sb *How much money do you owe to the bank?*
owe sb sth for sth *They still owe us money for the car.*

be in debt /biː ɪn 'det/ if you **are in debt**, you owe a lot of money and you have difficulty paying it: *The helpline offers financial advice to people who are in debt.*

get into debt (=start being in debt) *We got into debt when my wife lost her job.*

be £1000/$2000 etc in debt (=owe that amount) *The report showed that most students were over £5000 in debt.*

be heavily in debt (=owe a very large amount of money) *Several companies were heavily in debt by the end of the 1980s.*

be overdrawn /biː ˌəʊvəʳ'drɔːn/ to owe money to your bank because you have spent more than you had in your bank account: *I was overdrawn at the end of last month.*

be $100/£200 etc overdrawn *The bank wrote to tell us we were $500 overdrawn.*

be in the red /biː ɪn ðə 'red/ INFORMAL if you **are in the red**, you owe more money than you have: *I'm always in the red by the middle of the month.*

be £100/$500 etc in the red (=owe that amount) *At the end of the war, Britain was about $50 million in the red.*

2 money that you owe

debt /det/ [n C/U] money that you owe, especially a large amount: *Debt is one of the main social problems of our time.*

+of *The government now has debts of $2.5 billion.*

pay off/repay a debt (=pay all the money that you owe) *It took us three years to pay off all our debts.*

overdraft /'əʊvəʳdrɑːftǁ-dræft/ [n C] an amount of money that you owe to your bank when you have spent more money than you had in your bank account

have an overdraft *I've already got an enormous overdraft.*

a £100/$1500 etc overdraft *When he left college, he had a $3000 overdraft.*

3 to not owe any money

be in credit /biː ɪn 'kredɟt/ if your bank account **is in credit**, there is money in it, and you do not owe the bank anything: *We offer free banking for customers whose accounts remain in credit.*

be in the black /biː ɪn ðə 'blæk/ INFORMAL if someone is **in the black**, they have earned more than they have spent: *After three years of problems, we're now back in the black.*

OWN

➡ if you mean 'on your own', go to **ALONE**

➡ see also **HAVE/NOT HAVE**, **GET**

1 to own something

own /əʊn/ [v T] if you **own** something, especially something big like a house, a car, or a company, it is your property and you have the legal right to have it: *We don't own the apartment, we're just renting it.* | *Clark owns about 40 companies in northern Europe.* | *The horse is owned by an Italian businessman.*

> ⚠ Don't say 'I am owning this house'. Say **I own this house**.

have (also **have got** ESPECIALLY BRITISH) /hæv, həv 'gɒtǁ-'gɑːt/ [v T] to own something, especially something that ordinary people are likely to own: *What kind of car has she got?* | *We don't have a TV.* | *Most of our students have a computer.*

having – had – have had

> ⚠ Don't say 'he is having a car'. Say **he has a car**.

 be mine/yours/John's etc /biː (mine, etc)/ ESPECIALLY SPOKEN if something **is mine**, **yours**, **John's** etc, it belongs to me, you, John etc: *Is this book yours?* | *"Whose bike is that?" "It's Martin's."*

possess /pə'zes/ [v T] FORMAL to own something – use this especially in negative sentences to say that someone does not own something that most people own: *Very few families in this area possess a telephone.* | *He never wore a suit – I don't think he possessed one.* | *They lost everything they possessed in the earthquake.*

⚠ Don't say 'everything that they are possessing'. Say **everything that they possess**.

belong to sb /bɪ'lɒŋ tuː (sb)‖-'lɔːŋ-/ [phrasal verb T] if something **belongs to** someone, they own it: *This watch belonged to my grandfather.* | *Who does this jacket belong to?*

⚠ Don't say 'Who is this bag belonging to?'. Say **Who does this bag belong to?**

my own/your own etc /maɪ 'əʊn, jɔːr 'əʊn (etc)/ if something is **your own**, it belongs to you and not anyone else: *You can rent skis or you can bring your own.* | *Joe left the company to set up his own business.*
a room/car/house etc of your own *When we move to the new house, I'm going to have a room of my own.*

2 the person who owns something

owner /'əʊnər/ [n C] the person who owns something: *The previous owner painted the outside of the house yellow.*
+of *The owners of the company live abroad.*
home/car/dog etc owner *Car owners are facing a 10% rise in the price of gasoline.*

landlord/landlady /'lændlɔːrd, 'lændleɪdi/ [n C] someone who owns a building and is paid money by the people who live in it or use it: *Our landlord has promised to fix the heating by Tuesday.*
plural **landladies**

3 the things that someone owns

property /'prɒpərti‖'prɑː-/ [n U] things that someone owns, especially large, expensive things such as buildings, land, or cars: *Some of the stolen property was discovered in an empty warehouse.* | *The boys have been charged with damaging school property.*

private property (=something that is owned by a person, organization etc) *Most of the land around here is private property.*

personal property (=the small things that someone owns) *Your insurance policy will cover all your personal property.*

⚠ Don't say 'properties' when you mean the things that someone owns.

Formal or informal?
Property is not usually used in informal conversation.

possessions /pə'zeʃənz/ [n plural] FORMAL all the things that a person owns, which they keep in their home or carry with them: *They lost all their possessions in the floods.* | *This book is one of my most treasured possessions.*

 things /θɪŋz/ [n plural] SPOKEN things such as clothes, records, and books that you own: *She always leaves her things all over the floor.*

stuff /stʌf/ [n U] SPOKEN INFORMAL your clothes, furniture, plates, pans etc: *I don't know how I'm going to fit all my stuff into the new apartment.*

belongings /bɪ'lɒŋɪŋz‖bɪ'lɔːŋ-/ [n plural] things you own such as clothes, equipment, bags etc, especially things you take with you when you are travelling somewhere: *Please keep your belongings with you at all times.* | *They packed all their belongings into the car and left the city that night.*

valuables /'væljuəbəlz, -jͧbəlz‖ 'væljͧbəlz/ [n plural] small valuable things, such as jewellery or cameras, which may get stolen if you do not look after them: *The hotel management advises guests not to leave any valuables in their rooms.*

Formal or informal?
Valuables is used in writing and in formal spoken English.

P,p

PAIN

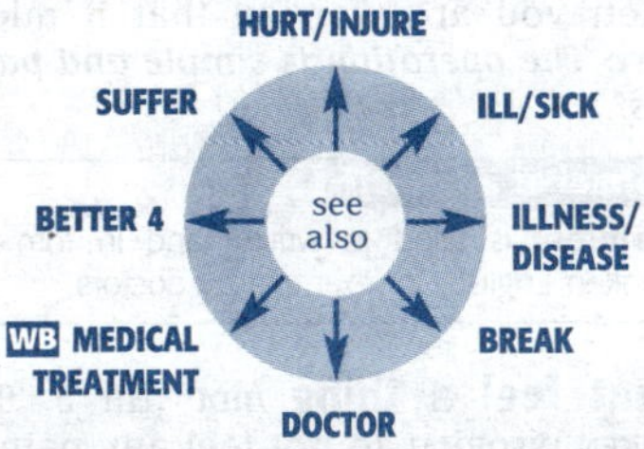
HURT/INJURE
SUFFER
ILL/SICK
see also
BETTER 4
ILLNESS/ DISEASE
WB MEDICAL TREATMENT
BREAK
DOCTOR

1 when part of your body hurts

hurt /hɜː^{r}t/ [*v* I] if a part of your body **hurts**, you feel pain in it, for example because you have hit it or cut it, or because you are ill: *My neck felt stiff and my shoulder hurt.* | *I fell and banged my knee, and it really hurts.*
it hurts SPOKEN (say this when part of your body hurts) *It hurts when I move my arm.*
hurting – hurt – have hurt

painful /ˈpeɪnfəl/ [*adj*] a **painful** injury or apart of your body that is **painful** makes you feel pain: *Jim's knee was still painful where he had fallen on it.* | *a painful back injury*

> Don't say 'she is painful'. Say **she is in pain**. Don't say 'I am painful'. Say **my leg/back etc hurts**.

ache /eɪk/ [*v* I] if a part of your body **aches**, you feel a pain in it that is continuous but not very strong – use this about pains in your arms, legs, or back, or in your head or stomach: *My arms ached from carrying all the groceries.* | *She felt hot and her head was beginning to ache.* | *I went to dance class last week and I've been aching ever since.*

sore /sɔː^r/ [*adj*] if a part of your body is **sore**, it hurts when you touch it or use it – use this about painful areas of your skin, for example where you have cut yourself: *My shoes had been rubbing and my feet were sore.* | *I cut my finger last week, and it's still sore.*
sore throat (=when the inside of your throat is sore, especially because you have a cold) *Honey is very good for a sore throat.*

tender /ˈtendə^r/ [*adj*] a part of the body that is **tender** is painful when it is touched: *My mouth was tender and swollen where he had hit me.*

sting /stɪŋ/ [*v* I] to hurt with a sudden sharp pain for a short time – use this about your eyes or your skin: *The smoke made our eyes sting.*
stinging – stung – have stung

throb /θrɒb||θrɑːb/ [*v* I] if a part of your body **throbs**, you feel pain that seems to get stronger and weaker in a regular repeated pattern: *By late afternoon my head was throbbing, and I couldn't see straight.*
throbbing – throbbed – have throbbed

stiff /stɪf/ [*adj*] if a part of your body is **stiff**, the muscles hurt when you move them, for example because you have been using the muscles too much or you have been in an uncomfortable position: *"How do you feel?" "My legs are a little stiff, but otherwise I'm fine."*
stiff neck/leg/back etc *The next day I woke up with a stiff neck.*

2 when something or someone hurts you

hurt /hɜː^{r}t/ [*v* I/T] if something or someone **hurts** you, they make you feel pain: *Don't do that. It hurts.* | *Stop it – you're hurting me.*
hurting – hurt – have hurt

sting /stɪŋ/ [*v* I/T] to cause a sudden sharp pain on your skin or in your eyes for a short time: *The antiseptic might sting a little.* | *The smoke stung my eyes.*
stinging – stung – have stung

P

3 the feeling you have when part of your body hurts

pain /peɪn/ [n C/U] the feeling you have when part of your body hurts: *The pain is getting worse.* | *You won't feel any pain during the operation.*
chest/back/neck etc pain *He told the doctor he was suffering from chest pains.*
a pain in your chest/leg/back etc *I have a terrible pain in my left arm.*
be in pain (=be feeling pain) *The old man looked white and was obviously in pain.*
be in great pain/be in a lot of pain *She's in a lot of pain with her back.*
severe pain (=very bad pain) *A slipped disc can cause severe back pain.*
ease/relieve the pain (=make a pain hurt less) *These pills should help to ease the pain.*

ache /eɪk/ [n C] a pain that continues for a long time but is not very sharp: *The ache in my shoulder seemed to be getting worse.*
dull ache (=a continuous annoying ache) *Lisa felt a dull ache in one of her teeth.*

be in agony /bi: ɪn ˈæɡəni/ to have a lot of severe pain: *Yves lay in agony on the slope. He was sure that he had broken his leg.*

headache/toothache/backache/ stomach ache /ˈhedeɪk, ˈtuːθeɪk, ˈbækeɪk, ˈstʌmək eɪk/ [n C/U] a continuous pain in a part of your body: *Is your backache any better?*
have/get a headache/toothache etc *I always get a headache when I've been using the computer.* | *She came home from school with a really bad stomach ache.*
have toothache/backache/stomach ache BRITISH *A lot of people start to have backache as they get older.*
a splitting headache (=a very bad headache)

⚠ Don't say 'I have headache' or 'it gives me headache'. Say **I have a headache** or **it gives me a headache**.

4 when something does not hurt

not hurt /nɒt ˈhɜːᶜt/ if something **does not hurt**, it is not painful: *This won't hurt at all. Just sit still while I remove the bandage.*

painless /ˈpeɪnləs/ [adj] something that is **painless** does not hurt, especially when you are worried that it might hurt: *The operation is simple and painless.*

> **Formal or informal?**
>
> **Painless** is used in writing and in formal spoken English, for example by doctors.

◯ **not feel a thing** /nɒt ˌfiːl ə ˈθɪŋ/ SPOKEN INFORMAL to not feel any pain at all: *Don't worry about the injection – you won't feel a thing.*

PAINT

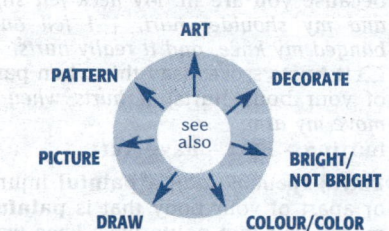

ART
PATTERN
DECORATE
see also
PICTURE
BRIGHT/ NOT BRIGHT
DRAW
COLOUR/COLOR

1 to paint pictures

paint /peɪnt/ [v T] to make a picture of something or someone, by putting paint onto a surface with a brush: *Gerry was sitting on the beach, painting the seagulls and the fishing boats.*
paint a picture (of sth/sb) *I'm going to paint a picture of the church.* | *a picture painted by Monet*
painting [n U] the activity of painting pictures: *I'm not very good at painting.* | *a painting class*

painter /ˈpeɪntəʳ/ [n C] someone who paints pictures: *This is by the great Spanish painter, Goya.*
portrait painter (=someone who paints pictures of people)
landscape painter (=someone who paints pictures of places, the countryside etc)

artist /ˈɑːᵗtɪ̯st/ [n C] someone who produces works of art, especially paintings or drawings: *an exhibition of works by local artists* | *the artists of the Italian Renaissance*

2 to paint walls/doors/rooms

paint /peɪnt/ [v I/T] to put paint on walls, doors, pieces of furniture etc: *I'm going to paint the bathroom tomorrow.*
paint sth blue/red/white etc *She painted the walls yellow.* | *What colour did you paint the doors?*

decorate /ˈdekəreɪt/ [v I/T] ESPECIALLY BRITISH to paint the inside of a house or put paper on the walls: *They've just finished decorating the kitchen.* | *We spent all weekend decorating.*
have sth decorated (=pay someone to decorate it) *Mum had the whole house decorated before she moved in.*

painter /ˈpeɪntəʳ/ [n C] someone who paints houses, walls etc as their job

PART

➡ see also **PIECE**

1 part of an object/area

part /pɑːʳt/ [n C] *When you have filled in the form, keep the top part and send the other part to the bank.*
+of *The front part of the car was badly damaged.* | *Malaria is still common in many parts of Africa.*

◯ **bit** /bɪt/ [n C] SPOKEN, ESPECIALLY BRITISH a small part of an object or area: *The bit you've painted looks really nice.*
+of *that bit of the garden where the fruit trees are*
a little bit *"Would you like some cake?" "Just a little bit, please."*

piece /piːs/ [n C] one of several different parts that must be joined together to make something: *a 1000-piece jigsaw puzzle*
in pieces (=as separate pieces) *The equipment had to be taken apart and transported in pieces.*

section /ˈsekʃən/ one of several parts that a place, shop, container etc is

divided into and that is clearly different or separate from the rest: *You'll find her books in the 'English classics' section.*
+of *The spoons go in the front section of the drawer.* | *the non-smoking section of the plane*

2 part of a story/book/film/play etc

part /pɑːʳt/ [n C] *The novel was adapted for radio in six parts.*
+of *The first part of the story takes place in Crete.*
Part One/Part Two etc (=one of the main parts that a play, TV story etc is divided into) *Part One ends with the death of the old King.*

◯ **bit** /bɪt/ [n C] SPOKEN, ESPECIALLY BRITISH a small part of a story or film: *I liked the bit with the car chase best.*
+of *Some bits of the film were really boring.*

episode /ˈepɪ̯səʊd/ [n C] part of a story on radio or television that is told in separate parts, usually weekly: *Brad Pitt made a guest appearance in last week's episode.*
+of *an early episode of Star Trek.*

chapter /ˈtʃæptəʳ/ [n C] one of the parts that a book is divided into: *Read the first two chapters before next week's class.*
Chapter One/Chapter Two etc *I've only read as far as Chapter 6.*

instalment BRITISH **installment** AMERICAN /ɪnˈstɔːlmənt/ [n C] part of a story that is told in several parts which are printed regularly in a magazine or newspaper over a period of time: *the first instalment of a science fiction trilogy*
weekly/monthly instalments *Dickens wrote his novels in weekly instalments for a magazine.*

scene /siːn/ [n C] one of the parts that a play or film is divided into: *The ghost appears in the first scene.* | *a love scene*

clip /klɪp/ [n C] a short part of a film or other recording that is taken and used in another film or in a television programme: *The police have released a video clip of the attack.*
+from *I saw a clip from the new Michael Douglas film on TV last night.*

trailer /ˈtreɪləʳ/ [n C] an advertisement for a new film in which a small part of the film is shown: *a trailer for the new James Bond film*

3 part of an organization

branch /brɑːntʃǁbræntʃ/ [n C] a shop, office, or bank in a particular area that is part of a larger organization: *Our store has branches all over the country.*
+of *Which branch of the bank do you use?*

> ⚠ You can also use **branch** before a noun, like an adjective: *He was appointed Branch Manager.* | *a branch office*

department /dɪˈpɑːʳtmənt/ [n C] a **department** of a large organization, such as a company, a school, or a hospital, is a part of it that is responsible for a particular kind of work: *Our department deals mainly with exports.*
Sales/Accounts/Planning etc Department (=in a company or large organization) *Melissa is in charge of the Marketing Department.*
Art/History/Science etc Department (=in a school or university)

division /dɪˈvɪʒən/ [n C] a large part of an organization, especially a company, which often includes several smaller parts: *The sales and advertising departments are both parts of the marketing division.*
+of *the Japanese division of American Express*

section /ˈsekʃən/ [n C] a part of an organization, especially a part of a company or a political group, that is responsible for a special area of its work: *The party's Young Conservative section is growing fast.*
+of *We had to go to the 'late payments' section of the Financial Aid office.*

4 part of an activity/job/period of time

part /pɑːʳt/ [n C] *Organizing the party was easy – the hardest part was getting my parents to agree to it.*

+of *Which part of your job do you enjoy most?* | *She spent the early part of her life in Barcelona.* | *Part of the research program involved interviewing teenagers in inner-city areas.*

bit /bɪt/ [n C] SPOKEN, ESPECIALLY BRITISH a part of an activity, plan, or job: *Filling in the application form is the easy bit. It's the interview I find stressful.*
+of *The last bit of the climb was really difficult because it started to snow.*

stage /steɪdʒ/ [n C] one of several parts of a long process, which happen one after another
+of *The early stages of pregnancy are usually the worst.*
+in *Safety checks are carried out at every stage in the production process.*
at this stage *At this stage of the election campaign, it is impossible to say who will win.*

phase /feɪz/ [n C] a separate part in the development or growth of something
+in *There are three phases in the life of a butterfly.*
initial/final phase (=the first or last part) *The initial phase of the project should take about three months.*

> **Formal or informal?**
> **Phase** is a more formal and technical word than **stage**.

5 part of a situation/subject/someone's character

aspect /ˈæspekt/ [n C] one of the many parts of a situation or subject, which can each be considered separately: *The book describes the post-war period in all its aspects – social, political, and economic.*
+of *Drug addiction affects all aspects of a person's life.* | *There are aspects of the problem that we haven't discussed.*

> **Formal or informal?**
> **Aspect** is not used in informal conversation.

side /saɪd/ [n C] one part of a situation or of someone's character – use this especially when you are comparing one part with another: *I'm in charge of*

production, and Martha takes care of the marketing side. | I had never seen his awkward side before. (=the awkward part of his character)
+of Many people seem to forget the religious side of Christmas. | Try to see the funny side of the situation.

feature /ˈfiːtʃəʳ/ [n C] a part of something that you notice because it seems important, interesting, or typical: Air bags are a standard feature in most new cars.
+of An important feature of Van Gogh's paintings is their bright colours.
common feature These trees are a common feature of the landscape.

6 of an amount/number

➡ see also **AMOUNT/NUMBER**

proportion /prəˈpɔːʳʃən/ [n C] a part of an amount or number – use this when you are comparing the part with the whole amount or number
+of What proportion of your income do you spend on food?
high/large proportion A high proportion of women with children have jobs.
small proportion We get a small proportion of our funding from the government.

> **Formal or informal?**
> **Proportion** is a formal word. In ordinary conversation, don't say 'What proportion of the work has been completed?' Say **How much of the work has been completed?**

fraction /ˈfrækʃən/ [n C] a small part of an amount or number, especially a very small part
+of Employees' salaries are only a fraction of the total cost of the project.
a small fraction This problem affects only a small fraction of the total population.

percentage /pəˈsentɪdʒ/ [n C] an amount or number that is expressed as part of a total which is 100
+of What percentage of our students passed the exam? | The percentage of company profit from this department is less than 20%.
high/large percentage A high percentage of the coffee they produce goes to the US.

small percentage Only a small percentage of the population has private medical insurance.

PARTLY

➡ for words meaning the opposite, go to **COMPLETELY**

partly /ˈpɑːʳtli/ [adv] The road was partly blocked by a fallen tree. | What he told us was only partly true.
partly because The accident happened partly because we were having an argument in the car.

partially /ˈpɑːʳʃəli/ [adv] FORMAL if something is **partially** done, it has not been completely done or does not include all of something: The house was partially destroyed by the explosion. | By the morning, the ice and snow had partially melted.
partially successful Our advertising campaign was only partially successful.

half /hɑːf‖hæf/ [adv]
half-eaten / half-dressed / half-finished etc partly eaten, partly dressed etc: I found him sitting on his bed, half-dressed. | a half-smoked cigarette in the ashtray | The houses were half-submerged by flood water.

to some extent /tə ˈsʌm ɪkˌstent/ use this when you want to say that something is partly true but not completely true: Doing well in examinations is to some extent a matter of luck. | To some extent it was our own fault that we lost the contract.

> **Formal or informal?**
> **To some extent** is used in writing and in formal spoken English.

> When you see **EC**, go to the **ESSENTIAL COMMUNICATION** section.

PARTY

INVITE
WB MUSIC
ENJOY
DANCE
WB FREE TIME
see also
DRUNK
FESTIVALS AND SPECIAL DAYS
DRINK
MARRY
WB FOOD

1 a party

party /ˈpɑːʳti/ [*n* C] a social event, especially in someone's house, when people talk, drink, eat, and dance: *Are you going to Susie's birthday party? | I really enjoyed your party last night.*
have a party *We're having a party next Saturday. Would you like to come?*
throw a party (=have a big party, with lots of food and drink etc) *Ed's parents threw a big party for his 21st birthday.*
invite sb to a party *I've been invited to a party at Dave's tonight.*
dinner party (=a party at someone's house in the evening, when people have a meal)
office party (=a party for people who work together)
fancy-dress party BRITISH **costume party** AMERICAN (=a party where people wear strange, funny, or historical clothes)
plural **parties**

> ⚠ You can also use **party** before a noun, like an adjective: *party games | a party invitation*

celebration /ˌseləˈbreɪʃən/ [*n* C] a party or other enjoyable event that is organized because something good has happened or because it is a special day: *We had a big family celebration for our wedding anniversary. | New Year celebrations in Scotland go on for three days. | celebrations to mark the 50th anniversary of the country's independence*

> ⚠ The plural form, **celebrations**, is used especially to talk about big public events that take place to celebrate important occasions, such as New Year. The singular form, **celebration**, is used especially to talk about a party to celebrate a personal or family event such as a birthday.

celebrate /ˈseləbreɪt/ [*v* I/T] to show that a happy event or occasion is important by doing something enjoyable, for example by having a party or going to a restaurant: *Congratulations on your new job – we must go out and celebrate. | We all went to a club to celebrate the end of the school year.*
celebrate by doing sth *Why don't we celebrate by going out for a meal?*
celebrate sth with sth *She celebrated her election victory with a party at the Hilton Hotel.*

2 people at a party

host /həʊst/ [*n* C] the person who invites people to a party and provides them with food and drink: *Our host greeted us at the door.*

hostess /ˈhəʊstəs/ [*n* C] a woman who invites people to a party and provides them with food and drink: *Pam was a wonderful hostess – everyone enjoyed her parties.*

guest /gest/ [*n* C] someone who goes to a party: *There were 100 guests at the garden party.*

> **Formal or informal?**
> **Host**, **hostess**, and **guest** are all rather formal words, used when talking about formal parties.

> When you see WB, go to the **WORD BANKS** section.

PASS

➡ look here for ...
- be successful in an examination
- go past a person or place
- when time passes

1 to be successful in a test or examination

➡ see also **TEST,** WB **DRIVE,**
WB **EDUCATION**

pass /pɑːsǁpæs/ [v I/T] to reach a high enough standard to succeed in an examination or test: *Did you pass your driving test?* | *You'll never pass the exam if you don't work!*

> ⚠ Don't say 'pass in an exam'. Say **pass an exam**.

qualify /ˈkwɒlɪfaɪǁˈkwɑː-/ [v I] to pass all the examinations that you need in order to become a doctor, lawyer, engineer etc: *After qualifying, doctors spend at least two years working in hospitals.*
+as *I decided to return to college and qualify as a teacher.*
qualifying – qualified – have qualified

graduate /ˈgrædʒueɪt/ [v I] to pass all your final examinations at university or college, and get a degree
graduate from Oxford/Stanford etc *Mitch graduated from Stanford in 1993 with a degree in Law.*
graduate in history/French/medicine etc *She graduated in modern languages and now works as an interpreter.*

> ⚠ In American English, **graduate** also means to successfully complete your high school education: *Jerry will be graduating from high school this year.*

scrape through /ˌskreɪp ˈθruː/ [phrasal verb I/T] INFORMAL to pass an examination, but with difficulty, because you get only a few marks more than are necessary: *I might scrape through if I'm lucky.* | *Daniel only just scraped through the entrance exam.*

sail through/breeze through /ˈseɪl θruː, ˈbriːz θruː/ [phrasal verb I/T] INFORMAL to pass a test or examination very easily: *"How did his exams go?" "He breezed through – no trouble at all."* | *She sailed through her driving test first time.*

2 to go past a place or person

➡ see also WB **DRIVE, WALK, RUN**

past /pɑːstǁpæst/ [adv/preposition]
walk/drive/rush/run past *An ambulance rushed past on its way to the accident.* | *Will you be going past the library on your way home?* | *He walked straight past her without even looking at her.*

by /baɪ/ [adv] ESPECIALLY WRITTEN going past, especially not very quickly
go/pass/walk/sail by *I lay on the grass and watched the clouds floating by.*

pass /pɑːsǁpæs/ [v I/T] to go past a place or person: *Could you get me some aspirin if you pass a chemist's?* | *They kept quiet until the soldiers had passed.* | *A big Cadillac passed us as we walked up the hill.*
passing [adj only before noun] going past: *the noise and fumes from the passing traffic*

overtake /ˌəʊvəˈteɪk/ [v I/T] ESPECIALLY BRITISH to pass a moving vehicle and the people in it in order to go in front of them: *Before you start to overtake, make sure the road ahead is clear.* | *A couple of police cars overtook us, going at top speed.*
overtaking – overtook – have overtaken

3 when time passes

go by/pass /ˌgəʊ ˈbaɪ, pɑːsǁpæs/ [v I] *Several years passed before she learned the truth.* | *The days passed slowly.* | *As you get older, time seems to go by more quickly.*

go quickly /ˌgəʊ ˈkwɪkli/ if time **goes quickly**, it seems to pass quickly: *The last few days of the holiday went far too quickly.*

○ **time flies** /ˌtaɪm ˈflaɪz/ SPOKEN say this when you are surprised at how quickly the time has passed: *Is Martin eight already? How time flies!* | *Time flies when you're having fun!*

go slowly /ˌɡəʊ ˈsləʊli/ if time **goes slowly**, it seems to pass slowly: *Time always goes slowly when you're bored.*

PAST

➡ if you want to know how to form the past, go to the **ESSENTIAL GRAMMAR** (Section 4)

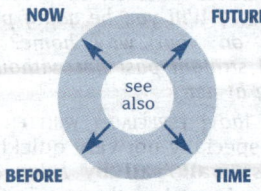

NOW   FUTURE

see also

BEFORE   TIME

1 the past

the past /ðə ˈpɑːst‖-ˈpæst/ [*n* singular] the time that existed before the present time: *My grandfather enjoys talking about the past.*
in the past (=during the time before now) *I decided to ask Anna, as she had always been very helpful in the past.* | *In the past, there were far fewer roads and less traffic.*
a thing of the past (=something that used to happen or exist but does not any more) *For many people, a relaxing weekend has become a thing of the past.*

past /pɑːst‖pæst/ [*adj* only before noun] **past** events, experiences etc happened before now: *He's learned a lot from his past experience.* | *Judging by her past performance, Rowena will do very well in her exams*
the past 10 years/2 weeks etc (=the 10 years, 2 weeks etc before now) *The past few months had been very difficult for Mary.* | *For the past two weeks, I've been doing my boss's job while she's away on business.* | *the enormous changes of the past 30 years*

history /ˈhɪstəri/ [*n* singular] all the things that have happened in the past, especially to a country, a town, or an organization
the history of sth/sth's history *a*

book about the history of the United Nations | *India has been invaded several times in its history.*

sb's past /(sb's) ˈpɑːst‖-ˈpæst/ all the things that have happened to someone in the past: *Greg didn't like to talk about his past.*

2 when something happened in the past, but does not happen now

used to /ˈjuːst tuː/ [*modal verb*] if you **used to** do something, you did it for a period of time in the past, or you did it regularly in the past, but you do not do it now: *"Do you smoke?" "No, but I used to."*
used to do sth *We used to live in Glasgow when I was young.*
there used to be *There used to be a market in the town.*
○ **didn't use to (do sth)** SPOKEN *I was surprised to see her driving – she didn't use to.* | *I didn't use to be as fat as this.*
never used to (do sth) *You never used to swear.*
used not to do sth BRITISH *Even ten years ago, people used not to eat so much junk food.*

once/at one time /wʌns, ət ˌwʌn ˈtaɪm/ [*adv*] during a period of time in the past, but not now – use this when it is not important to say exactly when this period was: *Apparently, he once worked for the FBI.* | *It is a big city now, but at one time the population was only 50,000.* | *a sports car once owned by Paul McCartney*

Formal or informal?

Once is more formal than **at one time** and is used more in writing.

then/at that time /ðen, ət ðæt ˈtaɪm/ [*adv*] during a particular period of time in the past – use this when you are comparing that period with the present: *I was a student in the 1950s, and things were very different then.* | *We were married before the war, and at that time most married women stayed at home.*

in the past /ɪn ðə ˈpɑːst‖-ˈpæst/ use this to talk about a situation that existed before, especially a long time ago, but does not exist now: *In the past, only around 8% of people went to university.* | *There were very few roads in the past, and villages were isolated.*

in those days/in the old days /ɪn 'ðəʊz deɪz, ɪn ði 'əʊld deɪz/ use this to talk about a time long ago in your life, or in your parents' or grandparents' lives, when things were different: *He was paid £5 a week, which was a lot of money in those days.* | *In the old days there was no bridge over the river, and we crossed it by boat.*

in the good old days (=at a time when you think that things were better than now) *In the good old days people showed more respect to the older generation.*

formerly /'fɔːᵊməˡli/ [*adv*] WRITTEN in the past, before the present situation existed: *The school was formerly a hospital.* | *Peru was formerly ruled by the Spanish.*

<h2>3   on one occasion in the past</h2>

once /wʌns/ [*adv*] *She once called me a liar and I've never forgiven her.* | *Once, when I was a little boy, I found a gold watch on the beach.*

one time /'wʌn ˌtaɪm/ INFORMAL on one occasion in the past: *One time we went out fishing on the lake at night.*

one day / one morning / one afternoon /wʌn 'deɪ, wʌn 'mɔːˡnɪŋ, wʌn ˌɑːftəˡnuːn‖-ˌæf-/ on a day, morning, or afternoon in the past – use this when you are telling a story and it is not important to say exactly which day you mean: *One day he went away and never came back.* | *I was having my breakfast one morning when the telephone rang.*

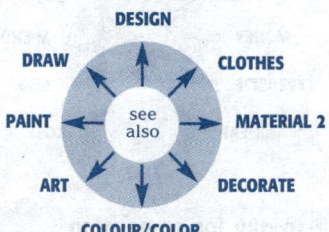

PATTERN

a regular arrangement of shapes, colours, or lines

pattern /'pætən‖'pætərn/ [*n* C] a regular arrangement of shapes, colours, or lines on a surface, especially one that is used to decorate paper, cloth, plates etc: *Do you have any wallpaper with the same pattern but a different colour?*
+of *a blue skirt with a pattern of black and white dots*

design /dɪ'zaɪn/ [*n* C] a pattern which is used to decorate a surface such as cloth or paper: *This design is very common on Turkish carpets.* | *curtains with an attractive floral design*

markings /'mɑːˡkɪŋz/ [*n* plural] the natural patterns on the skin, fur, or feathers of animals or birds: *The bird is easy to recognize, with its unusual red and yellow markings.*

patterned /'pætənd‖'pætərnd/ [*adj*] **patterned** clothes, materials etc have patterns on them: *The shops are full of brightly patterned summer dresses.* | *an old-fashioned patterned carpet*

When you see **EC**, go to the **ESSENTIAL COMMUNICATION** section.

When you see **WB**, go to the **WORD BANKS** section.

PAY

EARN
OWE   BUY
MONEY   SPEND
EXPENSIVE   *see also*   SHOP
CHEAP   COST
FREE

1   to pay for something

pay /peɪ/ [v I/T] to give money in exchange for goods or services: *Please pay at the desk.* | *Several fans tried to get in without paying.*
+for *Have you paid for the tickets?*
pay £20/$40 etc for sth *She paid $5000 for three nights in a hotel in New York.*
pay a bill/the rent *He hardly earns enough to pay the rent.* | *I thought you already paid the phone bill.*
pay cash (=pay using coins, notes etc) *You get a 5% discount if you pay cash.*
pay by cheque/pay by credit card etc
paying – paid – have paid

payment /'peɪmənt/ [n C] an amount of money that you pay for something, especially when it is only one part of the total amount you have to pay: *Your first payment is due on 16th July.* | *mortgage payments*
make a payment *He makes monthly payments into his ex-wife's bank account.*

on credit /ɒn 'kredᵻt/ **buy/get sth on credit** to buy something and pay for it later, usually by making small regular payments: *In 2001, 56% of new cars were bought on credit.*

2   to pay for someone else's food, drink, ticket etc

pay /peɪ/ [v I] to pay for someone else, for example for their meal, drink, or ticket: *Come out for a pizza – I'll pay.*

+for *If you go to the conference, the company will pay for you.* | *Did your parents pay for your driving lessons?*
paying – paid – have paid

treat /triːt/ [v T] to buy something such as a meal or theatre ticket for someone, because you like them or you want to celebrate: *As it's your birthday, I thought I'd treat you.*
treat sb to sth *We treated Sally to lunch at the Savoy.*

buy a round /ˌbaɪ ə 'raʊnd/ to buy drinks for the people you are with in a bar: *Joe bought a round of drinks for everyone.*

3   to be able to pay for something

can afford /kən ə'fɔːʳd/ if you **can afford** something, you have enough money to pay for it: *I'd love to visit Australia, but I just can't afford it.*
can afford to do sth *How can you afford to eat in restaurants all the time?*

4   to pay someone to do something

pay /peɪ/ [v T] to pay someone for work
pay sb for (doing) sth *They still haven't paid her for the work she did last year.* | *Did she pay you for taking care of her kids?*
be/get paid *We get paid at the end of every month.*
pay sb £100/$200 etc *The agency pays drivers around £6 an hour.* | *How much do they pay you?*
well/highly paid (=paid a lot) *He has a very well-paid job in finance.* | *a highly paid executive*
badly paid (=not paid much) *It's hard physical work, and it's very badly paid.*
paying – paid – have paid

bribe /braɪb/ [v T] to give money to someone in an official position, in order to persuade them to do something dishonest that they should not do: *He was accused of bribing tax inspectors two years ago.*
bribe sb to do sth *He bribed a guard to smuggle a note out of the prison.*
bribe [n C] money that you give someone to bribe them: *The judge was accused of accepting bribes.*

bribery [n U] when people are being bribed

bribery and corruption (=bribery and dishonest behaviour) *There was widespread bribery and corruption in the police department.*

5 to provide money to help someone do something

subsidize (also **subsidise** BRITISH) /'sʌbsɨdaɪz/ [v T] if a government or other organization **subsidizes** something, it pays part of the cost of it: *Many companies subsidize meals for their workers.* | *a government-subsidized health service* | *The city council subsidizes the local orchestra.*

sponsor /'spɒnsəʳǁ'spɑːn-/ [v T] if a company **sponsors** something such as a sports event, a theatre, or an art show, it provides some of the money that is needed, often as a form of advertising: *The event was sponsored by British Airways.* | *Sotheby's is sponsoring an exhibition of 16th century drawings.*

fund /fʌnd/ [v T] to provide all the money needed to pay for something, especially an important or expensive plan: *Government and industry will both be involved in funding the new training projects.*

6 to give money back to someone

pay back /ˌpeɪ 'bæk/ [phrasal verb T] to give back the money that you have borrowed from a person or organization

pay sb back *I'll pay you back tomorrow.*

pay back sth/pay sth back *How are you going to pay back all that money?*

repay /rɪ'peɪ/ [v T] to pay a large amount of money that you owe, especially to a bank or other organization: *The loan has to be repaid within two years.*

repaying – repaid – have repaid

> **Formal or informal?**
> **Repay** is more formal than **pay back**.

pay off /ˌpeɪ 'ɒfǁ-'ɔːf/ [phrasal verb T] to finish paying back an amount of money that you have borrowed

pay off a debt/loan/mortgage *Twenty years later they still hadn't paid off their mortgage.*

pay a debt/loan/mortgage off *We're hoping to pay all our debts off by 2010.*

give sb their money back/give sb a refund /ˌgɪv (sb) ðeəʳ 'mʌni ˌbæk, ˌgɪv (sb) ə 'riːfʌnd/ to give back to a customer the money that they paid for something, especially because they are not satisfied with what they bought: *We'll give you a refund if you're not entirely satisfied.* | *I don't really like the colour. Do you think they'll give me my money back?*

refund [n C] the money you get when someone gives you a refund: *You can have a refund if you still have the receipt.*

7 a piece of paper that shows how much you must pay

bill /bɪl/ [n C] a piece of paper that tells you how much you must pay for services you have received or for work that has been done for you: *We've just had a huge telephone bill.*

pay a bill *They left the hotel without paying the bill.*

a bill for £50/$100 etc *The garage sent me a bill for $400.*

> ⚠ In British English, you can also use **bill** when you are talking about paying in a restaurant: *Ask the waiter for the bill.*

check /tʃek/ [n C] AMERICAN a piece of paper that tells you how much you must pay in a restaurant: *A waiter came over and handed me the check.*

pay the check *Let me pay the check.*

invoice /'ɪnvɔɪs/ [n C] a piece of paper that a company sends you to tell you how much money you owe them for goods or for work they have done: *My accountant sends me an invoice twice a year.*

8 paid/not paid for doing a job, activity or sport

professional /prə'feʃənəl/ [adj only before noun] a **professional** sports player, musician, actor etc gets paid for playing, acting etc, and they do it as their job: *Professional basketball players can earn millions of dollars.*

professional [n C] someone who gets paid for doing a job, sport, or activity that most people do for enjoyment: *I learned to play golf by watching the professionals on TV.*

amateur /'æmətəʳ, -tʃʊəʳ, -tʃəʳ, ˌæmə'tɜːʳ/ [adj only before noun] an **amateur** sports player, musician, actor etc plays, acts etc for enjoyment and does not get paid for it: *A group of amateur actors were performing 'Romeo and Juliet'.* | *an amateur photographer*

amateur [n C] someone who does an activity or sport for enjoyment, and does not get paid for doing it: *The orchestra is made up entirely of amateurs.*

voluntary /'vɒləntəriǁ'vɑːlənteri/ [adj usually before noun] **voluntary** work is done by people who offer to do it because they believe it is useful, and who do not expect to be paid for their work: *Many students spend a year after school doing voluntary work overseas.*

PEACE

when there is no war

➡ opposite **WAR**

1 when there is no war

peace /piːs/ [n U] when there is no war: *There has been peace in the region for six years now.*

world peace *It is a dangerous situation that threatens world peace.*

peace talks/negotiations (=when enemies meet and talk, to try and achieve peace) *the Middle East peace talks*

the peace process (=a continuing attempt, over a long period, to achieve peace between enemies)

> Don't say 'a peace'. **Peace** is uncountable.

peacetime /'piːstaɪm/ [n U] a period when a country is not fighting a war – use this when comparing this period with a time when there is war: *A country's army may be quite small during peacetime.* | *In peacetime the Hercules aircraft has been used for distributing food to famine areas.*

peaceful /'piːsfəl/ [adj] use this about changes or events that happen without war or fighting: *a peaceful solution to the troubles in the region* | *Political change must be achieved by peaceful and democratic means.*

peacefully [adv] *Can they win their independence peacefully?*

2 when two countries agree to stop fighting

ceasefire /'siːsfaɪəʳ/ [n C] an agreement to stop fighting for a limited period, especially in order to talk about making peace: *The ceasefire won't last unless both sides are prepared to compromise.*

ceasefire agreement *The ceasefire agreement ended at midnight.*

truce /truːs/ [n C] an agreement to stop fighting for a short time, especially in order to discuss making peace: *The rebels have ended a 17-month truce and could strike at any time.*

+between *a truce between the two rival forces*

call/negotiate/secure etc a truce *The two sides agreed to call a truce.*

peace treaty /'piːs ˌtriːti/ [n C] a written agreement between enemies saying that they agree to end the war: *Both countries agreed to work towards a peace treaty.* | *The peace treaty was finally signed in 1919.*

plural **peace treaties**

make peace /ˌmeɪk 'piːs/ if two countries **make peace**, they stop fighting and agree to end the war: *France and Spain made peace in 1659 after a war lasting 25 years.*

+with *The two armies made peace with each other in 1918.*

Formal or informal?
Make peace is used in writing and in formal spoken English.

3 someone who is against war

pacifist /'pæsɪfɪ̣st/ [n C] someone who believes that all war and violence is wrong: *Bergson was imprisoned as a pacifist during World War I.*

anti-war /ˌænti 'wɔːʳ◂/ [adj only before noun] strongly against war, especially a war that your country is fighting at the present time
anti-war protest/demonstration/campaigner *Several big anti-war demonstrations took place at the weekend. | People's anti-war feeling increased the longer the war went on.*

PERFECT

➡ see also **BEST, GOOD, SUITABLE/UNSUITABLE**

1 very good, with nothing wrong

perfect /'pɜːʳfɪkt/ [adj] someone or something that is **perfect** is good in every way and could not be any better: *We had a wonderful vacation and the weather was perfect. | It's an old car, but it's in perfect condition.*
absolutely perfect *The meal was absolutely perfect.*
the perfect husband/secretary/couple etc *Beth and Martin always seemed to be the perfect couple.*
perfectly [adv] *It's a beautiful dress, and it fits perfectly.*

flawless/faultless /'flɔːləs, 'fɔːltləs/ [adj] FORMAL completely perfect, with no mistakes or faults at all: *Hiroshi's English was flawless. | He gave a faultless performance as Julius Caesar.*

model /'mɒdlǁ'mɑːdl/ [adj only before noun]
a model husband/wife/student etc someone who has all the qualities that a husband, wife, student etc should have: *Karen was a model student; hardworking, intelligent and enthusiastic.*

2 the best and most suitable person or thing

ideal /ˌaɪˈdɪəl◂/ [adj] an **ideal** person or thing is very suitable and is exactly what you want: *The house was a little too small, so it was not ideal.*
+for *Our hotel was ideal for families with young children.*
my ideal man/woman/job/house etc (=one that has all the qualities you like best) *My ideal man would be kind and considerate with a good sense of humour.*

perfect /'pɜːʳfɪkt/ [adj] completely suitable for a person or situation: *A dry white wine is perfect with any fish dish.*
+for *This dress will be perfect for the summer party. | perfect weather for a picnic*
the perfect place/time/job etc *That sounds like the perfect job for you.*

just right /ˌdʒʌst 'raɪt/ SPOKEN suitable in every way: *"Do these curtains look OK?" "Yes, they're just right."*
+for *I'm glad they're getting married – they're just right for each other.*

be just the thing (also **be just the job** BRITISH) /biː ˌdʒʌst ðə 'θɪŋ, biː ˌdʒʌst ðə 'dʒɒbǁ-'dʒɑːb/ INFORMAL to be exactly what is needed: *Cold lemonade is just the thing on a hot day.*

PERSON/PEOPLE

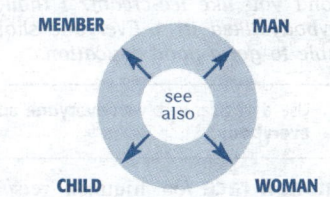

1 a person

person /'pɜːʳsən/ [n C] *Sue's a really nice person. | He's the only person I know who can speak Chinese. | There were over 200 people at the meeting. | I like the people I work with.*
plural **people**

someone / somebody /'sʌmwʌn, 'sʌmbɒdi, -bədɪll-,bɑːdi, -bədi/ [*pronoun*] a person – use this when you do not know who the person is, or when it is not important to say who it is: *Someone phoned you, but I didn't get their name.* | *What would you do if somebody tried to rob you in the street?*
someone else/somebody else (=another person) *Can't you get someone else to look after the kids that day?*

human being/human /,hjuːmən 'biːɪŋ, 'hjuːmən/ [*n C*] a person – use this when you are comparing people with animals or machines: *Chimpanzees are closely related to human beings.* | *Computers have replaced humans in many factories.*

2 people in general

people /'piːpəl/ [*n plural*] *People are very worried about rising crime.* | *I don't want people to feel sorry for me.*
most people *Most people hate writing essays, but I quite like it.*

> ⚠ Don't say 'peoples'. **People** is a plural noun.

❑ **everyone/everybody** /'evriwʌn, 'evri,bɒdɪll-,bɑːdi/ [*pronoun*] ESPECIALLY SPOKEN all people – use this to make general statements about how people behave, what people like etc: *Everyone knows that smoking is bad for you.* | *Don't you like ice-cream? I thought everybody liked it!* | *Everyone should be able to get a good education.*

> ⚠ Use a singular verb with **everyone** and **everybody**

the human race /ðə ,hjuːmən 'reɪs/ all the people in the world, considered as one group: *Pollution is threatening the future of the human race.* | *the history of the human race*

mankind/humankind /mæn'kaɪnd, ,hjuːmən'kaɪnd/ [*n U*] people in general – used especially when talking about their history and development, or how something affects their continued existence: *Global warming*

could prove a disaster for mankind.* | *Poverty is the greatest threat to humankind.*

> ⚠ **Humankind** is less common than **mankind** and is used by people who think that the word **mankind** does not seem to include women.

man /mæn/ [*n U*] people in general – use this when you are comparing humans with other living things: *Man has the power of speech.*
known to man *This is one of the worst diseases known to man.*

> ⚠ Some people do not use **man** because they think it does not seem to include women.

society /sə'saɪ̯ti/ [*n U*] people in general – use this to talk about people as an organized group with a system of laws and accepted behaviour: *attitudes to religion in modern society* | *The judge described Smith as 'a danger to society'.*
member of society *We want our students to become useful and responsible members of society.*

social /'səʊʃəl/ [*adj* only before noun] use this about conditions, problems, and changes that affect all the people in society: *Rising unemployment led to even more social problems.* | *During this period there were some important economic and social changes.*

the public /ðə 'pʌblɪk/ [*n singular*] ordinary people who do not belong to the government, the police etc, and do not have any special rights: *The castle is open to the public during the summer.* | *The public ought to know how the money from taxes is being spent.*
members of the public *Some politicians rarely meet ordinary members of the public.*
the general public *The movie was never allowed to be shown to the general public.*
public [*adj* only before noun] use this about the actions or feelings of ordinary people: *The plan cannot succeed without public support.* | *The decision caused a public outcry.*

In British English, you can use **the public** with a singular or plural verb: *The public is always/are always interested in stories about the Royal Family.* In American English, always use a singular verb: *The public isn't interested in foreign affairs.*

3 all the people in a group, town, or country

community /kə'mjuːnɪ̩ti/ [*n* C] a group of people who live in the same area, especially when they all belong to the same religious group or race: *The local community was shocked by the murder.*
the Jewish/Muslim/Greek etc community *New York's Jewish community*
plural **communities**

◯ **everyone/everybody** /'evriwʌn, 'evri,bɒdɪll-,baːdi/ [*pronoun*] ESPECIALLY SPOKEN all the people in a group or in a place: *There's plenty of food for everybody.* | *It's the sort of place where everyone knows everyone else.*

 Use a singular verb with **everyone** and **everybody**.

population /,pɒpjᵿ'leɪʃən‖,paː-/ [*n* singular] all the people who live in a town or country – use this when saying how many people live there, or giving some facts about them
the population of Tokyo/Greece etc *In 1966 the population of Lima was about two million.*
a population of five million/twenty million etc *New Jersey has a population of around 7.6 million.*
the black/Catholic/male population (=all the black people, Catholic people etc in a place) *30% of the male population suffers from heart disease.*

Formal or informal?
Population is used in writing and in formal spoken English.

the people /ðə 'piːpəl/ [*n* plural] all the people who live in a particular place
the people of Paris/China etc *The people of Hong Kong feel very strongly about this matter.*
the British/Korean/Nigerian etc people *the suffering of the Iraqi people*

4 about people, not animals or machines

human /'hjuːmən/ [*adj* usually before noun] use this about people's abilities, character, or behaviour, when you are comparing people with animals or machines: *Bacteria cannot be seen with the human eye.* | *the effects of global warming on the human and animal population*

5 for each person

per person /pəʳ 'pɜːʳsən/
$500/two pieces etc per person (=$500, two pieces etc for each person) *There were only two pieces of bread per person.* | *The annual income per person is less than $250.*

each /iːtʃ/ [*adv*] use this to say what every member of a group of two or more people gets or has: *You get two cookies each.*

a head /ə 'hed/ use this to say how much something costs for each person
$10/£5 etc a head *We paid £10 a head for our Christmas dinner.*

6 no people

no-one/no one/nobody /'nəʊ wʌn, 'nəʊbədi/ [*pronoun*] no person or people: *No-one was home, so I left a note.* | *He explained what had happened but nobody believed him.*

PERSUADE

➡ see also **ADVERTISING**

1 to persuade someone to do something

persuade /pəʳ'sweɪd/ [*v* T] to make someone agree to do something, by giving them reasons why they should do it: *Neil didn't want to come at first, but we persuaded him.*
persuade sb to do sth *I persuaded Tom to lend me his car.*

get sb to do sth /ˌget (sb) tə ˈduː (sth)/ INFORMAL to make someone do what you want them to do, especially by persuading them over a long time: *I finally got Eddie to cut the grass.* | *My girlfriend's always trying to get me to stop smoking.*

influence /ˈɪnfluəns/ [v T] to affect what someone decides to do, but without directly persuading them: *I admired my father and I suppose he influenced me a lot.* | *Young people are greatly influenced by their friends' behaviour.*

> ⚠ Don't say 'TV influences on children'. Say **TV influences children**.

encourage /ɪnˈkʌrɪdʒ‖ɪnˈkɜːr-/ [v T] to try to persuade someone to do something, because you think it is a good idea
encourage sb to do sth *Patricia encouraged me to apply for the job.* | *We want to encourage more children to use the library.*

talk sb into sth /ˌtɔːk (sb) ˈɪntuː (sth)/ [phrasal verb T] INFORMAL to persuade someone to do something that they do not want to do
talk sb into doing sth *I managed to talk the agency into paying me more money.*
talk sb into it *I didn't really want to go to the party, but Dave talked me into it.*

urge /ɜːʳdʒ/ [v T] to strongly advise someone to do something because it is very important
urge sb to do sth *Police are urging drivers to avoid the city centre this weekend.*
+that *He urged everybody to read the report.*

> **Formal or informal?**
> **Urge** is used in writing and in formal spoken English.

2 **to persuade someone not to do something**

persuade sb not to do sth /pəʳˌsweɪd (sb) nɒt tə ˈduː (sth)/ to make someone decide not to do something, by giving

them reasons why they should not do it: *Catherine persuaded him not to resign.*

talk sb out of sth /ˌtɔːk (sb) ˈaʊt ɒv (sth)‖-ɑːv-/ [phrasal verb T] INFORMAL to persuade someone not to do something that they were planning to do
talk sb out of doing sth *Everyone tried to talk me out of buying such an old car.*
talk sb out of it *I nearly cancelled the wedding, but my best friend talked me out of it.*

discourage /dɪsˈkʌrɪdʒ‖-ˈkɜːr-/ [v T] to stop someone wanting to do something, by making them think that it will be difficult or unpleasant: *We need to discourage the use of cars.*
discourage sb from doing sth *Girls at my school were discouraged from studying engineering or physics.*

deter /dɪˈtɜːʳ/ [v T] to make someone decide not to do something by making them realize that it will be difficult or dangerous or will have unpleasant results: *The new alarm system should deter car thieves.*
deter sb from (doing) sth *The security camera was installed to deter people from stealing.*

> **Formal or informal?**
> **Deter** is a formal word.

deterrent /dɪˈterənt‖-ˈtɜːr-/ [n C] FORMAL something that is intended to stop people from wanting to do something: *Prison is supposed to be a deterrent.*
+to *Window locks are a cheap and effective deterrent to burglars.*

3 **to persuade someone that something is true or right**

convince /kənˈvɪns/ [v T] to make someone believe that something is true, especially when they doubted it before: *You still don't believe me, do you? What do I have to do to convince you?*
convince sb that *It took him a long time to convince the police that he was telling the truth.*

persuade /pəʳˈsweɪd/ [v T] to make someone believe that something is

true or right, by telling them things that seem to prove it
persuade sb that *I managed to persuade my parents that I'd be fine on my own for the weekend.*

4 something that persuades you

persuasion /pəˈsweɪʒən/ [n U] things that you say in order to persuade someone to do something: *It took a lot of persuasion to get Dad to agree to the idea.* | *We'd prefer to end the conflict using persuasion rather than threats.*

convincing /kənˈvɪnsɪŋ/ [adj] a **convincing** reason, explanation, or excuse makes you believe that something is true or right: *That's not a very convincing excuse for being late!* | *There is convincing evidence that smoking causes heart disease.*

persuasive /pəˈsweɪsɪv/ [adj] good at persuading people to agree or to do something: *Ben can be very persuasive if he wants something.* | *The salesman had a smooth persuasive manner.*

PICTURE

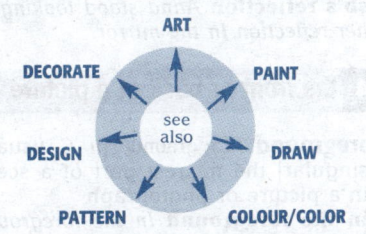

see also

ART
PAINT
DRAW
COLOUR/COLOR
PATTERN
DESIGN
DECORATE

1 a picture that you paint or draw

picture /ˈpɪktʃər/ [n C] a painting or drawing: *Van Gogh's 'Sunflowers' is one of the most famous pictures in the world.*
+of *There was a picture of a windmill on the bedroom wall.*
sb's picture (=a painting or drawing of someone) *The house belonged to the Duke of Wellington, and his picture hangs in the hall.*
draw/paint a picture *She drew some beautiful pictures of the church.*

do a picture INFORMAL (=draw or paint a picture) *Jamie loves doing pictures of cats.*

painting /ˈpeɪntɪŋ/ [n C] a picture that someone has painted: *an exhibition of paintings by French artists*
+of *a painting of the Grand Canal in Venice*
do a painting *She enjoys doing paintings of wild flowers.*

drawing /ˈdrɔːɪŋ/ [n C] a picture that someone has drawn using a pen or pencil: *Sylvia's teacher was very impressed by her drawings.*
+of *The walls of the caves were covered with drawings of animals.*
do a drawing *He did a series of drawings of his wife.*

sketch /sketʃ/ [n C] a picture consisting of a few lines drawn quickly with a pen or pencil
+of *I thought your sketches of the garden were very attractive.*
do a sketch *The architect did a sketch of how the building will look when it's finished.*
quick/rough sketch (=a sketch done very quickly) *Gail did a quick sketch of her baby daughter.*
plural **sketches**

illustration /ˌɪləˈstreɪʃən/ [n C] a picture in a book, which shows people or events that have been mentioned in the book: *The new encyclopedia is full of colour illustrations and photographs.* | *Who did the illustrations for the book? They're beautiful.*

cartoon /kɑːˈtuːn/ [n C] a funny drawing in a newspaper or magazine, often with a joke written under it: *a very funny cartoon of the President dressed as Superman*

poster /ˈpəʊstər/ [n C] a very large picture or photograph printed on paper, which you put on a wall for decoration
+of *Anna's bedroom wall was covered in posters of Elvis.*

portrait /ˈpɔːtrɪt/ [n C] a painting, drawing, or photograph of a person
+of *A portrait of the Queen hung on the wall.*
paint a portrait *He has painted the portraits of a lot of famous people.*

P

self-portrait (=a picture of the artist that is done by the artist himself or herself)

landscape /'lændskeɪp/ [n C] a painting showing an area of countryside

2 a photograph

photograph /'fəʊtəɡrɑːf‖-ɡræf/ [n C] a picture made using a camera: *an exhibition of war photographs*
+of *a beautiful book full of photographs of Kenya*
take a photograph *Visitors are not allowed to take photographs inside the museum.*
sb's photograph (=a photograph of someone) *I hate having my photograph taken.*
wedding/passport/school photograph *Do you want to see their wedding photographs?*
photograph album (=a book that you put photographs in)

> **Formal or informal?**
> **Photograph** is more formal than **photo** or **picture**

photo/picture /'fəʊtəʊ, 'pɪktʃəʳ/ [n C] a photograph – use this especially to talk about photographs of you, your friends or family, or places you have visited: *Who's that woman in the picture? She looks familiar.*
+of *That's an awful photo of me!*
take a photo/picture *Frank took lots of photos of the children.*
sb's photo/picture (=a photo of someone) *Shall I take your photo in that dress?* | *We saw her picture in the local paper.*
wedding/passport/school photo *I must remember to get some passport photos.*

> ⚠ You can also use **photo** before a noun, like an adjective: *a photo album* | *a silver photo frame*

snap ESPECIALLY BRITISH **snapshot** ESPECIALLY AMERICAN /snæp, 'snæpʃɒt‖ -ʃɑːt/ [n C] INFORMAL a photograph which you take yourself, for example of your family or on holiday, not one that is taken by a professional photographer

take a snap/snapshot *Did you take any snaps in Greece?*
+of *She showed me a snapshot of her three children.*
holiday snaps *Patrick was showing his holiday snaps to everyone in the office.*

mug shot /'mʌgʃɒt‖-ʃɑːt/ [n C] INFORMAL a photograph of a criminal's face, taken by police: *The police showed me some mug shots, and I had to say if any of them looked like the man who attacked me.*

photography /fə'tɒɡrəfi‖-'tɑː-/ [n U] the art or profession of taking photographs: *Chris is studying photography at night school.*

3 what you see in a mirror, on a screen, or on water

image /'ɪmɪdʒ/ [n C] a picture on the screen of a television, cinema, or computer: *The images on a computer screen are made up of thousands of tiny dots.* | *the flickering images of an old silent movie*

reflection /rɪ'flekʃən/ [n C] what you see when you look in a mirror or at the surface of water: *the reflection of the moon on the surface of the lake*
sb's reflection *Anna stood looking at her reflection in the mirror.*

4 the front or back of a picture

foreground /'fɔːʳɡraʊnd/ [n C usually singular] the nearest part of a scene in a picture or photograph
in the foreground *In the foreground of the painting were three dark figures.*
background /'bækɡraʊnd/ [n C usually singular] the area behind something or someone in a picture or photograph
in the background *It was a photo of everyone in my class, with the school building in the background.*

PIECE

➡ see also **PART, CUT**

1 part of something that has been separated from the rest

piece /piːs/ [n C] an amount of something that has been broken, cut, or separated from something larger: *I've just made a cake. Would you like a piece?* | *a pack of chicken pieces* (=the wings, legs etc separated from the rest)
cut/divide etc sth into pieces *Chop the apples into three or four pieces.*
+of *There were pieces of broken glass all over the road.* | *a simple boat made from a few pieces of wood*
in pieces (=broken into many pieces) *The vase lay in pieces on the floor.*

bit /bɪt/ [n C] ESPECIALLY BRITISH a small piece of something: *"Do you want some of this pie?" "Yes, I'll try a bit."*
+of *I used a bit of cloth to try and stop the bleeding.*
little/small/tiny bits *There were little bits of food all over the carpet.*

scrap /skræp/ [n C] a small piece of paper, material, or food that is left after you have used the main part

+of *I wrote down her address on a scrap of paper.* | *She made a lovely bedcover out of scraps of old material.*

slice /slaɪs/ [n C] a thin flat piece of food that you cut from a larger piece
+of *Have a slice of bread and butter.*
cut/carve sth into slices *We had beef, carved into very thin slices, and salad.*

2 a piece that has a regular shape

block /blɒk‖blɑːk/ [n C] a large solid piece of wood, stone, or ice that has straight sides: *a building made out of concrete blocks*
+of *The fish were lying on huge blocks of ice to keep them cold.*

cube /kjuːb/ [n C] a solid object with six equal square sides: *Cut the cheese into small cubes.*
ice/sugar cube *I dropped a couple of ice cubes into my cocktail.*
+of *a cube of sugar*

slab /slæb/ [n C] a heavy piece of stone or rock, which is long and wide but not very thick
stone/concrete/marble slab *The floor was made out of stone slabs.*
+of *His grave is covered by a huge slab of marble.*

P

piece

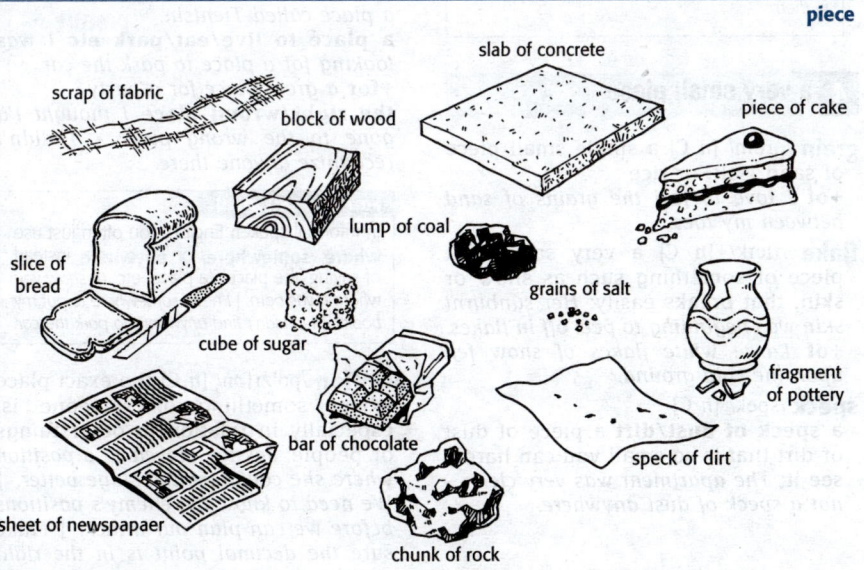

slab of concrete

scrap of fabric

block of wood

piece of cake

lump of coal

slice of bread

grains of salt

cube of sugar

fragment of pottery

bar of chocolate

speck of dirt

sheet of newspapaer

chunk of rock

P

sheet /ʃiːt/ [n C] a thin flat piece of glass, paper, metal etc: *Wrapping paper is sold in sheets or rolls.*
sheet of glass/paper/steel/metal *She took a sheet of paper and began to write.* | *The roof is made of sheets of corrugated iron.*

bar /bɑːʳ/ [n C] a piece of soap, chocolate, or metal that has a long shape with straight sides: *The gold bars were transported in a security vehicle.*
+of *a bar of chocolate*

3 a piece that does not have a regular shape

chunk /tʃʌŋk/ [n C] a piece of something solid that does not have a regular shape: *Cut the potatoes into chunks and boil them for 15 minutes.*
+of *A large chunk of plaster had fallen from the ceiling.* | *The lions were eating a huge chunk of red meat.*

lump /lʌmp/ [n C] a small piece of something solid that does not have a regular shape
+of *He threw some more lumps of coal onto the fire.* | *I was almost hit by a lump of rock that fell from the cliff.*

> ⚠ When **lump** is used to talk about a piece of food, it is usually unpleasant food: *The sausages had lumps of fat and gristle in them.*

4 a very small piece

grain /greɪn/ [n C] a single small piece of sand, salt, or rice
+of *I love to feel the grains of sand between my toes.*

flake /fleɪk/ [n C] a very small, flat piece of something such as snow or skin, that breaks easily: *Her sunburnt skin was beginning to peel off in flakes.*
+of *Large white flakes of snow fell upon the cold ground.*

speck /spek/ [n C]
a speck of dust/dirt a piece of dust or dirt that is so small you can hardly see it: *The apartment was very clean – not a speck of dust anywhere.*

crumbs /krʌmz/ [n plural] very small pieces of food such as bread or cake: *The tablecloth was covered in crumbs.*
breadcrumbs *She brushed the breadcrumbs off her skirt.*

fragment /ˈfrægmənt/ [n C] FORMAL a very small piece that has been broken or torn from something bigger
+of *The doctor removed some fragments of glass from the wound.* | *A fragment of cloth, caught on a nail, showed that someone had been that way.*

PLACE

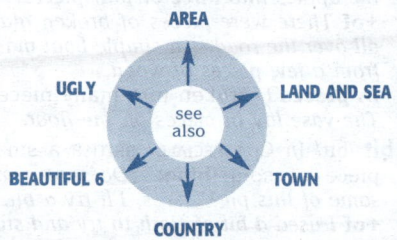

AREA

UGLY   LAND AND SEA

see also

BEAUTIFUL 6   TOWN

COUNTRY

1 a place

place /pleɪs/ [n C] *Have you put your passport in a safe place?* | *This is the place where the accident happened.* | *the coldest place on earth* | *She lives in a place called Tientsin.*
a place to live/eat/park etc *I was looking for a place to park the car.*
+for *a great place for a party*
the right/wrong place *I thought I'd gone to the wrong place – I didn't recognize anyone there.*

> **Formal or informal?**
> In informal spoken English, you often just use **where**, **somewhere**, or **anywhere** instead of saying 'the place', 'a place' etc: *I'll show you where I was born.* | *I need somewhere to put my books.* | *I couldn't find anywhere to park the car.*

position /pəˈzɪʃən/ [n C] the exact place where something or someone is, especially in relation to other things or people: *Jessica moved to a position where she could see the stage better.* | *We need to know the enemy's positions before we can plan our attack.* | *Make sure the decimal point is in the right position.*

+of *From the position of the sun, I guessed that it was about two o' clock.*

spot /spɒt‖spɑːt/ [n C] INFORMAL a place where something happened, or a pleasant place where people go to relax: *People had left flowers at the spot where the police officer was killed. | We camped in a pleasant, shady spot beside the river.*
+for *a favourite spot for picnics*
beauty spot (=a place that is famous for being beautiful) *We spent the afternoon at a local beauty spot.*

location /ləʊ'keɪʃən/ [n C] FORMAL the place where an office, shop, hotel, or house is built: *a hotel in an extremely attractive location*
+for *This is the ideal location for the company's new head office.*

 Location is used especially in advertisements and in business English.

site /saɪt/ [n C] an area of ground where something is going to be built, or where something important or interesting happened or existed in the past: *an archaeological site* (=a place were people examine what remains of ancient cities, graves etc)
+of *the site of the Battle of Waterloo | A home for the elderly will be built on the site of the old hospital.*
building site BRITISH **construction site** AMERICAN (=place where a new building is being built)

point /pɔɪnt/ [n C] an exact place or position: *At this point the river is half a mile wide. | We reached a point where the road divided. | the distance between two points on the map*

surroundings /sə'raʊndɪŋz/ [n plural] ESPECIALLY WRITTEN all the objects, buildings, and natural things that are in the place where you are – use this to say whether a place is pleasant, unpleasant etc: *The hotel is in beautiful surroundings on the edge of a lake. | We had the chance to watch great football in comfortable surroundings. | Sara felt nervous in the unfamiliar surroundings of her new school.*

be /bi, *strong* biː/ [v I] *Where are my keys?*

+in/on/near/there etc *Egypt is in North Africa. | There's a bank on the corner.*
being – was – have been

stand /stænd/ [v I] ESPECIALLY WRITTEN use this about buildings, furniture, trees, or tall objects: *There is a parking lot now where the old school once stood.*
+in/near/on there etc *The house stood next to a church. | A single tall candle was standing in the middle of the table.*
standing – stood – have stood

 Use **stand** especially when you are writing descriptions and stories.

lie /laɪ/ [v I] use this about paper, clothes, books, or other things that have been placed flat on a surface
+in/on/near etc *His letter was lying on the table. | The children's clothes lay on the bed, ready to be put on.*
lying – lay – have lain

Don't confuse **lie** (past tense **lay**) meaning 'to be flat on a surface' and **lay** (past tense **laid**) meaning 'to put something down in a flat position'.

be situated/be located /biː 'sɪtʃueɪtɪd, biː ləʊ'keɪtɪd‖-'ləʊkeɪtɪd/ FORMAL use this about towns, buildings, offices etc
+in/on/near *Soweto is an African township situated to the south west of Johannesburg. | The company's offices are located in downtown Manhattan.*
conveniently / pleasantly / ideally situated *a new hotel, conveniently situated close to the airport*

be based /biː 'beɪst/ if a company or organization **is based** in a place, its main offices are there
+in/at *The United Nations is based in New York.*
London-based/Tokyo-based etc *a London-based insurance company*

go/belong /gəʊ, bɪ'lɒŋ‖-'lɔːŋ/ [v I] ESPECIALLY SPOKEN if something **goes** or **belongs** in a place, it should always be put there when it is not being

P

used: *Put those books back where they belong.*
+in/on/under etc *"Where do these plates go?" "They go in the cupboard above the sink."*

4 not in any place

nowhere/not anywhere /'nəʊweə^r, nɒt 'enɪweə^r/ [*adv*] not in any place or to any place: *Where's Nick? I can't find him anywhere.* | *I'm not going anywhere tonight.* | *a path that seems to lead nowhere*
nowhere else/not anywhere else (=no other place) *They're staying here because there's nowhere else they can go.*
nowhere to live/sit/stay *The room was already full, and there was nowhere to sit.*

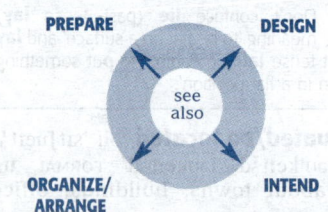

PLAN

PREPARE   DESIGN

see also

ORGANIZE/ ARRANGE   INTEND

1 a plan to do something

plan /plæn/ [*n C*] something that you have decided to do, and the methods you will use to do it: *Her plan is to finish her degree and then go and teach in Japan.* | *You can't start a new company if you don't have a good business plan.*
+for *NASA has announced plans for a new space mission to Mars.*
plan to do sth *The school has plans to build a computer centre.*
go according to plan (=when things happen exactly as you intended) *Everything went according to plan, and we all crossed the river safely.*

strategy /'strætɪdʒi/ [*n C* usually singular] a carefully designed plan for achieving something that is difficult and may take a long time: *the*

President's long-term economic strategy
+for *We need a new strategy for increasing our sales in Europe.* | *Murdoch bought several TV stations, as part of his strategy for building a media empire.*
plural **strategies**

programme BRITISH **program** AMERICAN /'prəʊgræm/ [*n C*] a series of activities, organized by a government or other large organization, that is designed to achieve something important and will continue for a long time
+of *The irrigation project is part of a programme of aid to West Africa.*
training/research/space etc programme *a major research program, aimed at developing cheaper fuels*

2 a plan to do something bad

plot /plɒt‖plɑːt/ [*n C*] a secret plan to do something bad, especially to the members of a government
plot to do sth *a plot to assassinate the President*

conspiracy /kən'spɪrəsi/ [*n C/U*] FORMAL a secret and usually complicated plan made by two or more people to do something bad or illegal together
conspiracy to do sth *a conspiracy to defraud the company of millions of dollars* | *They were charged with conspiracy to murder.*
+against *Members of the Secret Service were involved in a conspiracy against the elected government.*
plural **conspiracies**

Formal or informal?

Conspiracy is the formal name of the crime of planning to do something illegal with other people.

---

3 a plan of the times when things will happen

timetable BRITISH **schedule** AMERICAN /'taɪm,teɪbəl, 'ʃedjuːl‖'skedʒʊl, -dʒəl/ [*n C*] a written list that shows the exact times when something will happen, for example when planes or buses leave, or when classes at school take place

school/railway/rail/bus timetable *The winter bus timetable is available now.*
+of *I want a schedule of flights from Boston to New York.*

schedule /'ʃedjuːl‖'skedʒʊl, -dʒəl/ [n C] a detailed plan of what someone is going to do and when they will do it, especially someone important: *The President's schedule includes a two-day visit to St Petersburg.*
busy/tight schedule (=when you plan to do a lot of things in a short time) *She has a pretty tight schedule, but she may be able to meet you for lunch.*

programme BRITISH **program** AMERICAN /'prəʊgræm/ [n C] a plan that shows the order of activities at a ceremony, sports meeting, public event etc: *The next race on today's program is the women's 1000 metres.* | *Who is organizing the conference programme?*

4 to make plans

➡ see also **ORGANIZE/ARRANGE**

plan /plæn/ [v I/T] to think carefully about something you are going to do, and decide how you will do it: *Sue spent months planning her trip.* | *The burglary had obviously been very carefully planned.*
plan ahead (=make plans for the future) *Now that you're pregnant, you'll have to plan ahead.*
planning – planned – have planned

planning [n U] the activity of deciding how you will do something that you intend to do: *financial planning* | *After weeks of planning, the big day finally arrived.*

make plans /ˌmeɪk 'plænz/ to think about and talk about something that you intend to do, especially something that needs to be carefully planned: *We sat around the table, talking, laughing, and making plans.*
+for *I've already started to make plans for the wedding – there's so much to do.*

> ⚠ If you **make plans** for something, you think about it in a general way. If you organize times, travel etc in detail, you **make arrangements**.

plot /plɒt‖plɑːt/ [v I/T] to make secret plans to harm a person or organization: *The girls were in the kitchen, plotting their revenge.*
plot to do sth *She was accused of plotting to murder her boss.*
+against *Plotting against the government was punishable by death.*
plotting – plotted – have plotted

5 not planned

unplanned /ˌʌn'plænd◂/ [adj] *On the way to Denver, we made an unplanned visit to my mother's.* | *More than 4 out of every 10 pregnancies are unplanned.*

spontaneous /spɒn'teɪniəs‖spɑːn-/ [adj] something that is **spontaneous** is done because you suddenly feel you want to do it, not because you have arranged to do it or been asked to do it: *The crowd gave a spontaneous cheer when the news was announced.* | *His spontaneous reaction was to run away.*
spontaneously [adv] *Quite spontaneously, members of the audience started leaving the theatre.*

POLICE

➡ see Word Banks section

POLITE

behaving in a way that is socially correct and shows respect for other people

➡ opposite **RUDE**
➡ see also **FRIENDLY/UNFRIENDLY, KIND, NICE**

polite /pə'laɪt/ [adj] *He seemed a very polite young man.* | *a polite request*
it is polite to do sth *We left the party as soon as it was polite to do so.*
politely [adv] *"I hope your mother is well?" he asked politely.*
politeness [n U] when people are polite: *During my stay in Japan, I was treated with great politeness by everyone I met.*

good manners /ˌgʊd 'mænəʳz/ [n plural] someone who has **good manners**

P

knows how to behave politely in social situations, for example, when to say 'please' and 'thank you': *My mother was impressed with Tony's good manners.* | *At least she had the good manners to let us know she would be late.*

well-behaved /,wel bɪ'heɪvd◂/ [adj] a **well-behaved** child is polite and does not cause trouble or make noise: *His older brother was quieter and far better-behaved.*

well-behaved – better-behaved – best-behaved

tactful /'tæktfəl/ [adj] careful not to mention something that might embarrass or upset someone: *I wish you'd learn to be more tactful.*

it is tactful of sb to do sth *It wasn't very tactful of you to ask whether she'd put on weight.*

tactfully [adv] *Claire tactfully changed the subject when someone mentioned the war.*

tact [n U] when people are tactful: *This job requires tact and patience.*

POOR

➡ opposite **RICH**

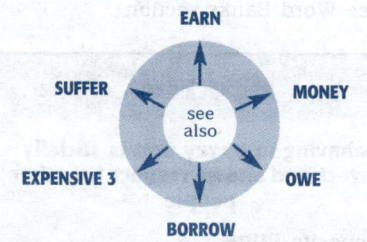

1 having very little money

poor /pʊəʳ/ [adj] *They were so poor they couldn't afford to buy shoes for their children.* | *Ethiopia is one of the poorest countries in the world.*

the poor (=poor people) *the growing gap between the rich and the poor*

be broke/be hard up /biː 'brəʊk, biː ,hɑːʳd 'ʌp/ ESPECIALLY SPOKEN to have very little money, either permanently or just at the present time: *Most*

students are too hard up to spend much money on clothes.* | *We're always broke at the end of the month.* | *I'm a little hard up just now – can I pay you back next week?*

poverty /'pɒvəʳtiǀ'pɑː-/ [n U] when people have very little money: *Charles was shocked by the poverty he saw in India.* | *Poverty and unemployment are two of the biggest causes of crime.*

live in poverty *Old people should not have to live in poverty.*

> **Formal or informal?**
> **Poverty** is not usually used in informal conversation.

2 an area where poor people live

slum /slʌm/ [n C] a house in bad condition in a poor area of a city: *Maria lives with her eight children in a slum outside Montevideo.*

the slums (=an area where there are a lot of slums) *He grew up in the slums of East London.*

> ⚠ You can also use **slum** before a noun, like an adjective: *a slum area* | *slum dwellers*

inner city /,ɪnəʳ 'sɪti/ [n C] the part near the middle of a city where the buildings are in bad condition and where a lot of poor people live: *the problems of Britain's inner cities*

plural **inner cities**

inner-city [adj] *inner-city schools*

ghetto /'getəʊ/ [n C] a poor and crowded part of a city, where people live separately from the rest of the population, especially people of one race or from one country: *a novel about life in the ghettos of New York*

plural **ghettos (or ghettoes)**

POPULAR/ UNPOPULAR

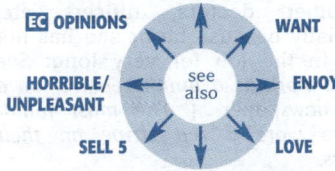

LIKE/NOT LIKE

EC OPINIONS

WANT

HORRIBLE/ UNPLEASANT

see also

ENJOY

SELL 5

LOVE

ENTHUSIASTIC/UNENTHUSIASTIC

1 people/places/activities that a lot of people like

popular /'pɒpjələʳ‖'pɑː-/ [adj] if things or people are **popular**, a lot of people like them: *Lisa's one of the most popular girls in class.* | *a popular holiday resort* | *Is baseball America's most popular sport?*
+with *The London Eye is very popular with tourists.*

2 a popular book/film/song

bestseller /ˌbest'seləʳ/ [n C] a book that a lot of people buy: *Jackie Collins' latest book is certain to be a bestseller.*

blockbuster /'blɒkˌbʌstəʳ‖'blɑːk-/ [n C] INFORMAL a film that a lot of people watch and that makes a lot of money, especially a film with a lot of exciting action: *Bruce Willis's new blockbuster took $10.6 million in its first weekend.*

hit /hɪt/ [n C] a record, song, or play that a lot of people buy, listen to, or watch: *When I first heard the song I knew it would be a hit.*
hit song/single/musical *a new hit single from Janet Jackson* | *the hit musical 'Cats'*
big hit *The album was a big hit in the States.*

3 when something becomes popular again

revival /rɪ'vaɪvəl/ [n C] when something or someone becomes popular and fashionable again, for example, a kind of music, a style of clothes, a writer, or a singer: *Sixties pop music enjoyed a big revival in the mid-90s.* | *There's been something of a Raymond Chandler revival recently.*

4 not popular

unpopular /ʌn'pɒpjələʳ‖-'pɑː-/ [adj] if things or people are **unpopular**, a lot of people do not like them: *The government is more unpopular now than it has been for years.* | *Mr Venables must be the most unpopular teacher in the school.*
+with *The new uniforms were extremely unpopular with the students.*

POSITION/RANK

your position in an organization, company etc, which shows how important you are

➡ see also **CLASS IN SOCIETY**

1 your position or rank

position /pə'zɪʃən/ [n C] your job in an organization, company, or profession – use this to talk about how important someone is and how much responsibility they have: *Because of her position in the company, she is responsible for the major financial decisions.* | *He eventually became Lord Chancellor, the most powerful position in the British legal system.*
hold a position (=have a position) *Thorn holds one of the most senior positions in the Federal Bank.*

level /'levəl/ [n C] all the jobs in an organization that are similar in importance and that pay the same amount of money: *We provide training for staff at all levels in the company.* | *There are not many part-time workers in the middle and higher levels of management.*

rank /ræŋk/ [n C] someone's position in an organization such as the army or police force: *He joined the Los Angeles police department and was quickly promoted to the rank of lieutenant.*

> ⚠ Don't use **rank** about someone who works in a company, a school etc.

status /'steɪtəs‖'steɪtəs, 'stæ-/ [n U] someone's position within an organization or within society, based on how important they are considered to be: *the president's status as a world leader*
low/high status *In the Middle Ages, priests and other religious figures had a very high status.*
gain/lose status *She gained celebrity status with her publication of 'Mastering the Art of French Cooking'.*

2 someone who has a high position

senior /'siːniə'/ [adj only before noun] a **senior** manager, official etc is one who has an important position in an organization or company: *He's a senior executive at Volkswagen.* | *a job in senior management* | *one of the country's most senior judges*

top /tɒp‖tɑːp/ [adj only before noun]
top manager/lawyer/executive etc someone who has one of the most powerful jobs in business, or one of the most important jobs in a profession: *The President met with top Korean businessmen.* | *There are still not many women in top jobs.* | *a top fashion designer*

high-ranking /ˌhaɪ 'ræŋkɪŋ◂/ [adj only before noun]
high-ranking officer/official/member etc someone who has a high position in an organization like the police or army, or in a government department, but not in business: *A high-ranking State Department official was accused of selling secret information.* | *a high-ranking officer in the air force*

Formal or informal?
High-ranking is used especially in formal writing and news reports.

3 someone who has a lower position than someone else

junior /'dʒuːniə'/ [adj only before noun] a **junior** doctor, officer etc does not have as much power or responsibility as other doctors, officers etc, especially because he or she has not been in the job for very long: *She started work as a junior reporter on a local newspaper.* | *The most junior officers wore a red stripe on their sleeves.*

assistant /ə'sɪstənt/ [adj only before noun]
assistant manager/editor/director etc someone whose job is just below the position of a manager etc: *My mother is assistant principal at a school in Washington.*

POSSIBLE

→ opposite **IMPOSSIBLE**

1 when something can be done

possible /'pɒsɪbəl‖'pɑː-/ [adj] if something is **possible**, it can be done: *Travel to other planets may soon be possible.* | *The only possible way of getting your money back is to go to the police.* | *Detectives can now check every criminal's records, which wouldn't be possible without computers.*
it is possible to do sth *Is it possible to find a room in a good hotel for less than $100?*
if possible (=if it is possible to do it) *I want to get back by 5 o'clock if possible.*
as soon/quickly as possible *Please let me know your answer as soon as possible.* (=as soon as you can) | *We must get her to the hospital as quickly as possible.*
everything possible (=everything that can possibly be done) *The doctors did everything possible to save her life.*

can be done /kən biː 'dʌn/ if something **can be done**, it is possible to do it:

The job can be done by Friday if we all make an effort. | *I'm sure that more could be done to help the homeless.* | *Val got her MA while she was working full-time, so it can be done, you see.*

possibility /ˌpɒsəˈbɪləti‖ˌpɑː-/ [n C] one of the things that you could try to do: *One possibility is that we could offer him more money.* | *Beth decided that she wanted to start her own business, and began to explore the possibilities.*

consider/discuss the possibility of doing sth (=consider whether you could do it) *We are considering the possibility of providing a new class for advanced students.*

2 when something can happen

possible /ˈpɒsəbəl‖ˈpɑː-/ [adj] if something is **possible**, there is a chance that it may happen or it may be true: *Accidents are always possible in heavy industries like mining.* | *"I think I saw Jack in the street yesterday." "That's not possible! He's in Kenya at the moment."* | *climate change and its possible effect on our lives*

it is possible for *It is possible for more than one person to win the competition.*

it is possible that *It is possible that the children are still alive.*

possibly [adv] *He could possibly be released from prison within three years.*

possibility /ˌpɒsəˈbɪləti‖ˌpɑː-/ [n C] something that can happen or may happen: *A Republican victory in next month's elections now seems to be a real possibility.*

+of *We could not ignore the possibility of an enemy attack.*

a distinct possibility (=something that is likely to happen) *There's a distinct possibility that there will be another earthquake.*

can /kən, *strong* kæn/ [modal verb] if something **can** happen, it is possible for it to happen at some time: *Anyone can make a mistake.* | *A lot can happen in two years.*

> ⚠ Don't say 'it can to happen'. Say **it can happen.**

potential /pəˈtenʃəl/ [adj only before noun] a **potential** problem, advantage, effect etc is not a problem, advantage etc now, but it may become one in the future: *Why was the chemical factory built so close to the town? Didn't people realize the potential risks?*

potential customer/buyer/student etc (=someone who may become a customer, buyer etc in the future) *ways of attracting potential customers*

> **Formal or informal?**
> **Potential** is not used in informal conversation.

there is a chance/there is a possibility /ˌðeər ɪz ə ˈtʃɑːns, ˌðeər ɪz ə ˌpɒsəˈbɪləti‖-ˈtʃæns, -ˌpɑː-/ use this to say that it is possible that something will happen

+of *On the northern hills there is always the possibility of a snow shower, even in June.*

+that *Is there any chance that he will recover from his injury in time for the race?*

3 to make something possible

make sth possible /ˌmeɪk (sth) ˈpɒsəbəl‖-ˈpɑː-/

make sth possible *We are grateful to Mr. Johnson, who made this event possible by letting us use his land.*

make it possible for sb to do sth *Satellite broadcasting made it possible for people all over the world to watch the 1960 Olympic Games.*

allow/enable /əˈlaʊ, ɪˈneɪbəl/ [v T] ESPECIALLY WRITTEN to make it possible for someone to do something that they want to do

allow/enable sb to do sth *The Internet allows people to send messages all over the world.* | *The money from her aunt enabled Maxine to buy a small restaurant.*

POWER

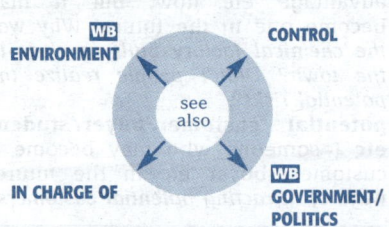

ENVIRONMENT WB

CONTROL

see also

IN CHARGE OF

GOVERNMENT/ POLITICS WB

1 the ability to control people and events

power /'paʊə'/ [n U] the ability or the right to control other people and make decisions that affect them: *Do you think the police have too much power?* | *Stalin's desire for power*

great/enormous power *the enormous economic power of the United States*

+over *The big Hollywood studios have a lot of power over what kind of films get made.*

have the power to do sth *Only Parliament has the power to make new laws.*

> Don't say 'he wanted the power'. Say **he wanted power**.

influence /'ɪnfluəns/ [n U] if someone has **influence**, they can use their important social position or their wealth to persuade other people to do things: *The Catholic Church has always had a lot of influence in Polish politics.*
+over *The banks had too much influence over government policy.*

authority /ɔː'θɒrɪ̯ti, ə-‖ə'θɑː, ə'θɔː-/ [n U] the right to make decisions and control people, which a person has because of their job or official position: *No one dared to question the principal's authority.*
+over *In the British system, the mayor has no authority over the local police.*
the authority to do sth *Every manager has the authority to dismiss employees.*

> Use **authority** to talk about the rights and power that people have, but not to talk about the power that countries have.

2 someone who has a lot of power

powerful /'paʊə'fəl/ [adj] a **powerful** person, organization, or country has a lot of power, and can control people and influence events: *Parliament had become more powerful than the King.* | *one of the most powerful men in US politics* | *Berlusconi was the owner of a powerful media empire.*

influential /,ɪnflu'enʃəl◂/ [adj] someone who is **influential** can influence events, because they are rich, important, or greatly respected, and therefore people pay attention to what they say: *Her uncle is a rich and influential businessman.* | *She is probably the most influential member of the finance committee.* | *an influential film critic*

highly influential (=very influential) *Galbraith was a highly influential writer on economic affairs.*

strong /strɒŋ‖strɔːŋ/ [adj] powerful – use this about a political group that is supported by a lot of people: *There has been a strong anti-nuclear movement in Japan for many years.* | *The Democrat Party has traditionally been very strong in the northeast of the country.*

dominant /'dɒmɪ̯nənt‖'dɑː-/ [adj] more powerful than other people, groups, countries etc: *Gradually, Microsoft became the dominant company in the software business.* | *At that time Portugal was the dominant naval power in the Mediterranean.*

> **Formal or informal?**
> **Dominant** is used in writing and in formal spoken English.

3 to have official power

in power /ɪn 'paʊə'/ a person or political group that is **in power** has political control of a country or government: *The Socialists have been in power since the 1965 revolution.* | *The king could not remain in power without the support of the army.*

in authority /ɪn ɔː'θɒrɪ̯ti‖-ə'θɑː, ə'θɔː-/ someone **in authority** has a job or position that gives them the right to tell other people what to do: *I want to speak to someone in authority. | Problems arise when people in authority can't keep discipline.*

rule /ruːl/ [v I/T] to have the power to control what happens in a country – use this especially about a person or group that has not been elected: *In 1860, Italy was a collection of small states ruled by princes and dukes.*
+over *The Romans ruled over a large empire.*
rule [n U] when a person or group rules a country: *British rule in India came to an end in 1947.*
ruling [adj only before noun]
the ruling party/class/group the political party, social class, or group of people that has most power in a country: *Australia's ruling Labor Party | the struggle between the workers and the ruling class*

come to power /ˌkʌm tə ˈpaʊəʳ/ to take political control of a country, especially by being elected: *De Gaulle came to power in 1958.*

4 someone who has no power

powerless /ˈpaʊəʳləs/ [adj not before noun] FORMAL someone who is **powerless** has no power to control or influence what happens: *Blocked by the Republicans in Congress, the President seemed powerless.*
+against *When their forces attacked, we were powerless against them.*
powerless to do sth *The UN was powerless to prevent the war spreading.*

weak /wiːk/ [adj] someone who is **weak** does not have much power because they cannot make other people respect them or obey them: *These policies failed because the government was weak and ineffective. | a weak, indecisive principal*
weakness [n U] *The king's mercy towards the rebels was regarded as a sign of weakness.*

PRACTISE/PRACTICE

to do something a lot in order to improve your skill at it

➡ see also **IMPROVE, BETTER, GOOD 5, 6**

1 to practise for a competition, test, or performance

practise BRITISH **practice** AMERICAN /ˈpræktɪs/ [v I/T] to do an activity a lot in order to improve your skill: *I'm learning to play the piano, and I practise every day. | We're going to Paris for a few days, so that Bill can practice his French.*
practise doing sth *Now let's practise speaking slowly and clearly.*

> ⚠ Don't use **practise** about sports. For example, don't say 'I practise tennis/golf every weekend'. Say **I play tennis/golf every weekend**. But you can use **practise** about doing a particular movement in a sport many times in order to improve it. For example, you can say: *I need to practise my backhand.*

train /treɪn/ [v I] to prepare for a race or game by exercising and practising: *If you're really going to run in the marathon, you need to start training now.*
+for *Lewis is training for the big fight next week.*

rehearse /rɪˈhɜːʳs/ [v I/T] to practise a speech, play, or concert so that you will be ready to perform it: *The producer made us rehearse the last scene again. | His band has been rehearsing at the TV studio all day.*

2 activities people do in order to practise

practice /ˈpræktɪs/ [n U] things you do regularly in order to improve your skill at something: *She's playing pretty well now – she just needs a little more practice.*
piano/football/choir etc practice (=time that you spend practising the piano etc) *I scored two goals at hockey practice tonight. | Anna never misses her violin practice.*

training /'treɪnɪŋ/ [n U] time that you spend practising and doing exercise in order to improve your skill at a sport: *The team captain got a knee injury during training.*
a training course / session / programme *I have to go to the weekly training session at the gym.*

> ⚠ Don't say 'a training' or 'trainings'. **Training** is an uncountable noun.

rehearsal /rɪ'hɜːʳsəl/ [n C] an occasion when all the people in a play, concert etc practise it before performing it in public
+of *We're having our first rehearsal of 'Hamlet' tonight.*

3 when you have not practised something for a long time

be out of practice /biː ˌaʊt əv 'præktɪs/ if you are **out of practice**, you have not done something for a long time, so that you are not able to do it as well as you could in the past: *I'm a little out of practice, but I'll play if you need me.*

rusty /'rʌsti/ [adj] INFORMAL if your skill at something is **rusty**, it is not as good as it used to be because you have not used it for a long time: *My Spanish is very rusty these days.*
rusty – rustier – rustiest

> When you see **EC**, go to the **ESSENTIAL COMMUNICATION** section.

PRAISE

to say that you admire or approve of someone or something

➡ opposite **CRITICIZE**

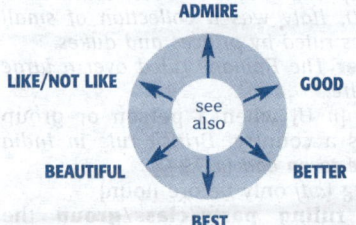

1 to praise someone or something

praise /preɪz/ [v T] to say that you admire someone or approve of something good that they have done: *Fire chiefs praised a 10-year-old girl who saved her brother's life yesterday. | The play was widely praised when it first appeared on Broadway.*
praise sb for sth *Local people were praised for their calm response to the crisis.*

> **Formal or informal?**
> **Praise** is used especially in formal writing and news reports.

congratulate /kən'grætʃʊleɪt/ [v T] to tell someone that you are pleased because they have achieved something special or because something good has happened to them: *She got the job? I must go and congratulate her.*
congratulate sb on doing sth *We all congratulated him on winning the title.*

> ⚠ Don't say 'congratulate someone for something'. Say **congratulate someone on something**.

compliment /'kɒmplɪmənt‖'kɑːm-/ [v T] to tell someone that you like the way they look or that you are pleased with something that they have done
compliment sb on sth *He complimented her on the perfume she was wearing. | Everyone complimented me on my new hairstyle.*

flatter /'flætə^r/ [v T] to say nice things that you do not mean about someone, especially in order to get something from them: *Flatter her a little – tell her she's beautiful.*

2 what you say when you praise someone

◯ **well done** BRITISH **good job** AMERICAN /ˌwel 'dʌn, ˌgʊd 'dʒɒbǁ-'dʒɑːb/ SPOKEN say this to someone when they have done something well or succeeded in doing something difficult: *Well done! You got all the answers right. | Good job, John! That was a great shot.*

congratulations /kənˌgrætʃʊ'leɪʃənz/ say or write this: *Congratulations! Is it a girl or a boy?*
+on *Congratulations on your new job, Jenny.*
congratulations on doing sth *Congratulations on passing your driving test.*

> ⚠ Don't say 'congratulation'. **Congratulations** is always plural.

◯ **way to go** /ˌweɪ tə 'gəʊ/ AMERICAN SPOKEN INFORMAL use this to praise someone who has just done something very good or impressive: *"I got accepted at Stanford." "Way to go!" | Way to go, Sam! Good hit!*

3 remarks that praise someone

praise /preɪz/ [n U] things you say to someone to show that you admire them or approve of what they have done
+for *The police deserve a lot of praise for the way they handled the situation.*
be full of praise for sb/sth (=praise someone a lot) *Most parents are full of praise for the school.*
win/earn praise FORMAL (=be praised for something) *The charity has earned widespread praise for its work.*

compliment /'kɒmplɪ̰mənt ǁ'kɑːm-/ [n C] something you say to someone, telling them they look nice or they have done something well: *He said my English was almost as good as his, but I don't know if he really meant it as a compliment!*

pay sb a compliment (=give someone a compliment) *He's always paying her compliments and buying her flowers.*

flattery /'flætəri/ [n U] nice things that you say about someone, which may not be true, in order to get something that you want from them: *She used a mixture of persuasion and flattery to get what she wanted.*

PREPARE

➡ if you mean 'make food', go to **COOK**
➡ if you mean 'ready to do something' or 'ready to be used', go to **READY**
➡ if you mean 'organize a meeting, party etc', go to **ORGANIZE/ARRANGE**

1 to make something ready to be used

prepare /prɪ'peə^r/ [v T] *Before you start painting, prepare the walls by cleaning them and filling any cracks.*
prepare sth for sth *We have a team of mechanics who prepare the car for the race.*
prepare a talk/presentation/speech/ lesson *Teachers spend a long time preparing lessons.*

get sth ready /ˌget (sth) 'redi/ to make sure a room, building, or piece of equipment is ready to be used
+for *I spent the afternoon getting everything ready for the party. | Blake was down at the marina, getting his boat ready for the trip.*

> **Formal or informal?**
> **Get sth ready** is more informal than **prepare**.

set up /ˌset 'ʌp/ [phrasal verb T] to make a piece of equipment ready to work, by putting all the pieces of it together and putting it in the right place
set up sth *Ask Keith to set up your computer for you.*
set sth up *It'll take me a few minutes to set the camera up.*

P

2 to prepare for something that will happen soon

prepare /prɪ'peəʳ/ [v I] to do things so that you will be ready for something that is going to happen soon: *I'm worried about tomorrow's interview – I haven't had enough time to prepare.*
+for *Captain Harper told the flight crew to prepare for take-off.*
prepare to do sth *Jane was busy preparing to go abroad.*

get ready /,get 'redi/ to do the things you need to do so that you will be ready to go somewhere, such as getting washed and changing your clothes: *You'd better go and get ready – it's nearly 7 o'clock.*
+for *John took ages getting ready for the party.*
get ready to do sth *I was just getting ready to go out when Tim arrived.*

make preparations /meɪk ,prepə'reɪʃənz/ to do all the things you need to do so that you will be ready for an important event
+for *We started to make preparations for the wedding over a year ago.*

train /treɪn/ [v I] to prepare for a race or game by exercising and practising: *The team is training at a secret location in Hampshire.*
+for *She's training for next month's marathon.*

be in training for sth /beɪ ɪn 'treɪnɪŋ fɔːʳ(sth)/ to be doing physical exercises in order to prepare for a competition: *She's in training for the Olympics.*

be prepared /biː prɪ'peəʳd/ if you **are prepared** for something unpleasant or difficult that might happen, you expect it and you have made yourself ready for it
+for *The children were sea-sick last time, so this time we'll be prepared for it.*
be well prepared *When the hurricane came, we made sure we were well prepared.*

3 things you do to prepare for something

preparation /,prepə'reɪʃən/ [n U] the time and work that is needed to prepare for something: *Months of preparation have gone into organizing the festival.*

in preparation for sth (=in order to prepare for something) *The hospital was being repainted in preparation for the Queen's visit.*

preparations /,prepə'reɪʃənz/ [n plural] all the things you have to do so that you will be ready for an important event
+for *She's busy with preparations for the school concert.*

make preparations *Belgium is making preparations for next year's centenary celebrations.*

PRESS

➡ see also **PUSH, PULL**

1 to push something firmly, especially with your fingers

press /pres/ [v T] to push something firmly with your fingers or with your feet: *The doctor gently pressed her stomach.* | *I pressed the brake pedal, but nothing happened.*
press sth down *Press the lid down hard to seal the tin.*
press a button/bell/key (=in order to make a machine work, a bell ring etc) *Which key do I press to delete it?* | *If you need the nurse, just press the green button.*

squeeze /skwiːz/ [v T] to push something firmly inwards with your hands or fingers: *I squeezed the toothpaste tube, but nothing came out.* | *squeezing a damp cloth to get the water out*

squeeze

squeeze sb's arm/hand (=as a sign of love or friendship) *Alice squeezed my arm affectionately, and said goodbye.*

pinch /pɪntʃ/ [v T] to press someone's skin tightly between your fingers and thumb, so that it hurts: *Dad! Katy just pinched me!*

touch /tʌtʃ/ [v T] AMERICAN to press a button, for example on a telephone or a computer screen, in order to make a choice, get information, or make something work – used especially in instructions: *For room service, touch button 9.*

2 to press something so hard that it breaks or becomes flat

squash /skwɒʃ‖skwɑːʃ, skwɔːʃ/ [v T] to damage something, especially something soft, by pressing it and making it flat: *Someone sat on my hat and squashed it.* | *Careful you don't squash those peaches.*
squashed [adj] *a squashed tomato*

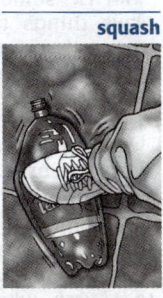
squash

crush /krʌʃ/ [v T] to press something so hard that it gets damaged or broken into pieces: *His leg was crushed in the accident.* | *a machine for crushing rocks*
crushed [adj] *The path was made of crushed shells.*

crush

mash /mæʃ/ [v T] to press fruit or cooked vegetables with a fork or similar tool, until they are soft and smooth: *Mash the bananas and add them to the mixture.*
mashed [adj] *pie and mashed potatoes*

mash

grind /graɪnd/ [v T] to break something such as corn or coffee beans into powder, using a machine or special tool: *Grind some black pepper over the salad.*
grinding – ground – have ground
ground [adj] *freshly-ground coffee*

grind

roll/roll out /rəʊl, ˌrəʊl ˈaʊt/ [v T] to make something flat using a tool or machine shaped like a tube: *Roll the pastry as thin as you can.*
roll out sth/roll sth out *Roll the dough out to a thickness of four centimetres.*

PRETEND

➡ if you mean 'pretend to have a feeling or opinion', go to **FALSE 3**

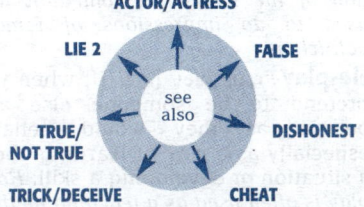

ACTOR/ACTRESS
LIE 2   FALSE
see also
TRUE/   DISHONEST
NOT TRUE
TRICK/DECEIVE   CHEAT

1 to pretend that something is true

pretend /prɪˈtend/ [v I/T] to behave as though something is true when you know that it is not: *We thought he had really hurt himself, but he was just pretending.*
+(that) *The kids were pretending that they were in a space rocket.*
pretend to do sth *She pretended to listen, but I could tell she was thinking about something else.*

🔾 **put it on/be putting it on** /ˌpʊt ɪt ˈɒn, biː ˌpʊtɪŋ ɪt ˈɒn/ SPOKEN to pretend to be ill, upset, injured etc, because you want to avoid doing something or you want people to feel sorry for you: *Kelly's not really ill – she's just putting it on because she doesn't want to go to school.*

2 to pretend to be someone else

pretend /prɪˈtend/ [v T] to behave as if you are someone else and try to make other people believe this
pretend to be sb *We pretended to be students and went along to the party too!*
+(that) *They got into the house by pretending they worked for the electricity company.*

P

impersonate /ɪmˈpɜːʳsəneɪt/ [v T] to behave as though you are someone with official power or someone famous, either for dishonest reasons or in order to entertain people: *It's illegal to impersonate a police officer. | I got home to find him impersonating Elvis Presley in front of the mirror.*

do an impersonation/do an impression /duː ən ɪmˌpɜːʳsəˈneɪʃən, duː ən ɪmˈpreʃən/ to speak, walk, or behave like someone else, in order to make people laugh
+of *Stuart did a brilliant impersonation of the boss. | a comedian who used to do impressions of famous politicians*

role-play /ˈrəʊl ˌpleɪ/ [n C/U] when you pretend to be someone else and behave as they would behave, especially as a way of learning about a situation or developing a skill: *Role-play is often used as a teaching method in language classes.*

3 **to pretend not to notice someone or something**

pretend not to see/hear/notice /prɪˌtend nɒt tə ˈsiː, ˈhɪəʳ, ˈnəʊtᵻs/ *She winked at me, but I pretended not to notice. | She pretended not to see the look of surprise on Karen's face.*
pretend (that) you have not noticed/seen/heard *I called out his name, but he pretended that he hadn't heard me.*

ignore /ɪgˈnɔːʳ/ [v T] if you **ignore** someone, you rudely pretend you have not seen them or heard them; if you **ignore** something, you pretend you have not noticed it, especially because it does not seem important: *John totally ignored her and went on talking to his new girlfriend. | Someone made a rude noise, which the teacher decided to ignore.*

○ **not take any notice** BRITISH **not pay any attention** AMERICAN /nɒt ˌteɪk eni ˈnəʊtᵻs, nɒt ˌpeɪ eni əˈtenʃən/ ESPECIALLY SPOKEN to not let someone's words or behaviour affect what you do or affect the way you feel: *I keep telling them to turn the music down, but they don't take any notice. | We complained to the school about it, but no one pays attention.*

not take any notice of/not pay any attention to *Don't take any notice of him – he's just jealous.*

4 **pretending to have feelings you do not have**

insincere /ˌɪnsɪnˈsɪəʳ/ [adj] ESPECIALLY WRITTEN someone who is **insincere** says things that they do not really mean, for example when they praise you or say something friendly: *an insincere smile | an insincere apology | He always praised everyone, so it was difficult to tell if he was being insincere or not.*

hypocritical /ˌhɪpəˈkrɪtɪkəl/ [adj] pretending to be morally good or to have beliefs that you do not really have: *It's hypocritical to get married in a church when you don't believe in God. | Politicians are so hypocritical – they preach about 'family values' while they all seem to be having affairs.*
hypocrite [n C] someone who pretends to have strong opinions about how people should behave, but who does not behave like this themselves: *My dad is such a hypocrite – he says I shouldn't smoke, but he smokes 20 a day.*

false /fɔːls/ [adj] ESPECIALLY WRITTEN emotions or feelings that are **false** are not real, and you are only pretending to feel them: *"Merry Christmas," she said, with false cheerfulness. | The politician greeted them with a false smile.*

When you see **WB**, go to the **WORD BANKS** section.

PRISON

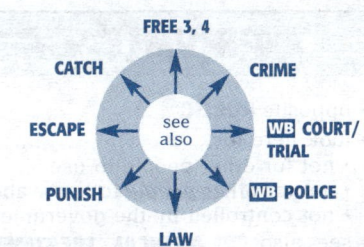

FREE 3, 4

CATCH · CRIME

ESCAPE ← see also → **WB** COURT/ TRIAL

PUNISH · **WB** POLICE

LAW

 You can also use **jail** before a noun, like an adjective: *a jail sentence*

cell /sel/ [n C] a small room in a prison or police station, where someone is kept as a punishment: *The prisoners spend most of the day locked in their cells.* | *a prison cell*

1 a place where people are kept as a punishment

prison /'prɪzən/ [n C/U] a building where people are kept as a punishment for a crime: *Conditions in the prison were appalling.* | *a maximum security prison*
in prison *She's been in prison for eight years.*
be sent to prison *Davis was sent to prison for selling drugs.*
be released from prison (=be allowed to leave) *Forbes will be released from prison next week.*

> ⚠ You can also use **prison** before a noun, like an adjective: *a long prison sentence* | *prison officers*

Formal or informal?

Prison and **jail** mean the same, and both words can be used in many situations. But **prison** is the usual word in more formal or official contexts.

> ⚠ Don't use 'a' or 'the' with **prison** if you are talking about the punishment of being kept in a prison: *He spent half his life in prison* (not 'in the prison'). | *She was sent to prison.*

jail /dʒeɪl/ [n C/U] a prison where criminals are kept as part of their punishment, or where people who have been charged with a crime are kept before they are judged in a law court: *Los Angeles County jail*
in jail *She was released after just three days in jail.*

2 someone who is kept in prison

prisoner /'prɪzənəʳ/ [n C] someone who is kept in prison as a punishment: *The prisoners are allowed an hour's exercise every day.*

convict /'kɒnvɪkt‖'kɑːn-/ [n C] someone who has been proved guilty of a crime and has been sent to prison: *an escaped convict* | *Stubbs was an ex-convict who got a job as a security guard.*

> ⚠ **Convict** is used especially in news reports.

hostage /'hɒstɪdʒ‖'hɑːs-/ [n C] someone who is kept as a prisoner by an enemy or a group of criminals, and is threatened with death or injury if their government, their family etc does not do what the enemy or criminals want: *They say they will kill the hostages if we don't agree to their demands.*

3 to put someone in prison

put sb in prison/send sb to prison /ˌpʊt (sb) ɪn 'prɪzən, ˌsend (sb) tə 'prɪzən/ to officially order someone to be taken to a prison and kept there: *Eventually, her attacker was caught and put in prison.* | *The judge sent him to prison for seven years.*
🔍 **lock up** /ˌlɒk 'ʌp‖ˌlɑːk-/ [phrasal verb T] ESPECIALLY SPOKEN to put someone in prison
lock sb up/lock up sb *Rapists deserve to be locked up for the rest of their lives.* | *a new law allowing the courts to lock up very young criminals*

> ⚠ Use **lock up** especially when you mean that someone deserves to be in prison because they are very bad or dangerous.

imprison /ɪmˈprɪzən/ [v T] to put someone in prison, especially when you think this is wrong or unfair: *The government has arrested and imprisoned all opposition leaders.* | *Mandela and Sobukwe were imprisoned on Robben Island.*

imprisonment [n U] when someone is put in prison, or the time that someone spends in prison: *The maximum penalty is three years' imprisonment.* | *His confession led to the arrest and imprisonment of several gang members.*

> ⚠ **Imprison** is used especially in writing and news reports.

4 to force someone to stay in a place as a prisoner

keep /kiːp/ [v T] to force someone to stay in a place, as if they were a prisoner
keep sb in sth *West had abducted a young girl and kept her in his basement for 10 days.*
keep sb prisoner *The rebels kidnapped her and kept her prisoner for three months.*

take sb hostage /ˌteɪk (sb) ˈhɒstɪdʒ‖ -ˈhɑːs-/ if an enemy or group of criminals **takes** someone **hostage**, they make that person their prisoner, and threaten to kill or injure them unless they get what they want: *The Ambassador and his wife have been taken hostage by terrorists.*

> ⚠ Don't say 'take someone as a hostage'. Say **take someone hostage**.

hold /həʊld/ [v T] to keep someone in a place and not allow them to leave – used especially in news reports: *Police are holding two men in connection with the robbery.*
hold sb prisoner/hostage/captive *Several tourists were being held captive by rebels in Kashmir.*
holding – held – have held

be imprisoned /biː ɪmˈprɪzənd/ to be kept somewhere and prevented from leaving: *the castle where Mary Queen of Scots was once imprisoned* | *Many*

old people are too frightened to go out, and feel as if they are imprisoned in their own homes.

PRIVATE

➡ opposite **PUBLIC**
➡ look here for ...
  • not for other people to use
  • not for other people to know about
  • not controlled by the government
➡ see also 🔲 **MEDICAL TREATMENT,** 🔲 **EDUCATION**

1 not for other people to use

private /ˈpraɪvɪt/ [adj] a **private** room, piece of land etc can only be used by one person or group, and is not for everyone: *All the rooms have a private bathroom.* | *The hotel has its own private beach.* | *Private property. No entry!*

2 not for other people to know about

private /ˈpraɪvɪt/ [adj] someone's **private** feelings, discussions, letters etc concern themselves or their family and friends, and are not for other people to know about: *You shouldn't be listening to a private conversation!* | *The book contains extracts from his diary and private letters.*
sb's private life (=things they do that are not connected with their work) *The newspapers are full of stories about the private lives of famous people.*

personal /ˈpɜːrsənəl/ [adj] someone's **personal** problems, relationships, letters etc are connected with their private life, not with their work: *There is a letter marked 'personal' for you.* | *I'd like to talk to you about a personal matter.* | *Are we allowed to make personal calls on the office phone?*

secret /ˈsiːkrɪt/ [adj only before noun] someone's **secret** thoughts and feelings are ones that they never tell anyone else about: *The diaries reveal all his secret hopes and fears.* | *a secret ambition*

secretly [adv] *He told her not to worry, but secretly he still blamed her for the accident.*

○ **be none of sb's business** /bi: ,nʌn əv (sb's) 'bɪznɪ̣s/ ESPECIALLY SPOKEN use this when you think someone has no right to ask about something, because it is private: *What I do at the weekend is none of your business! | Why should I tell Dan who I'm seeing? It's none of his business.*

○ **mind your own business** /,maɪnd jɔːr əʊn 'bɪznɪ̣s/ SPOKEN say this when you are annoyed because someone is asking questions that you do not want to answer: *"Where did you sleep last night?" "Mind your own business." | I wish you'd stop interfering and mind your own business.*

3 | **not controlled by the government**

private /'praɪvɪ̣t/ [adj usually before noun] **private school/hospital/education etc** a place or service that is not owned or provided by the government and that you must pay to use: *Do you think the teaching in private schools is better than in state schools?*

privately [adv] *He was privately educated.* (=at a private school)

commercial /kə'mɜːᵣʃəl/ [adj only before noun] **commercial TV/radio/channel** a television or radio company that is not paid for by the government, but gets its money from advertising: *the most popular commercial radio station in London*

PROBABLY

when it is likely that something will happen, or that something is true, but it is not definite

➡ see also **MAYBE, SURE/NOT SURE, POSSIBLE**

1 | **probably**

probably /'prɒbəbli‖'prɑː-/ [adv] when something will probably happen or is

probably true: *"Are you going to Lucy's party?" "Yes, probably." | We're probably going to move to New York next year. | Archaeologists think the temple was probably built in the 3rd century AD. | He wrote dozens of books, but this is probably his best-known novel.*

⚠ **Probably** usually comes immediately before the main verb: *She probably left the car at home. | We will probably be late.* But it comes after the main verb 'be': *It was probably an accident.*

likely /'laɪkli/ [adj] something that is **likely** will probably happen or is probably true: *A peace settlement now seems likely. | The most likely reason for the crash is that the car was travelling too fast.*
likely to do sth *Men are more likely to die from heart attacks than women. | The price of books is likely to rise again this year.*
it is likely that *It is likely that the murdered girl knew her killer.*
very likely (=almost certain) *There will be a lot of cloud tomorrow, and rain is very likely.*
likely – likelier – likeliest

probable /'prɒbəbl‖'prɑː-/ [adj] FORMAL likely to be true or likely to happen: *This seems the most probable explanation. | The probable result of global warming will be a rise in sea levels.*
it is probable that *It is probable that they would have won the war if they had continued fighting.*
probable cause *The report states that the probable cause of death was a heart attack.*
highly probable (=when something will almost certainly happen) *A victory for the Communist Party now seems highly probable.*

○ **I suppose** (also **I should think** BRITISH) **I guess** AMERICAN /aɪ sə'pəʊz, aɪ ʃʊd 'θɪŋk, aɪ 'ges/ SPOKEN say this when you think something is likely to be true or likely to happen: *She's a year or two older than you, I should think.*
+(that) *There's no light on in the house, so I suppose they are all out. | I should think you must be tired after your journey. | I guess Kathy will want to bring her boyfriend.*

P

I **suppose so/I should think so/I guess so** (=use this to say 'yes' to a question) *"Is Bill coming too?" "Yes, I suppose so."*

⊂ **it looks as if/it looks like** /ɪt 'lʊks əz ɪf, ɪt 'lʊks laɪk/ SPOKEN say this when you think that something is very likely to happen, based on what you know about a situation: *It's almost 11, so it looks as if Fred isn't coming tonight. | I can't see any buses – it looks like we'll have to take a taxi.*

⊂ **I wouldn't be surprised if** /aɪ ˌwʊdnt biː səˈprraɪzd ɪf/ SPOKEN say this when you think that something which seems unlikely is in fact quite likely to happen: *You know, I wouldn't be surprised if they decided to get married.*

2 how likely it is that something will happen

likelihood /'laɪklihʊd/ [n U] how likely it is that something will happen
+of *What's the likelihood of the war ending this year? | As you get older, the likelihood of illness increases.*
+that *There is little likelihood that the number of college places will go up this year.*

chances /'tʃɑːnsᵻz‖'tʃæn-/ [n plural] how likely it is that something you hope for will actually happen
chances of sth/of doing sth *The new treatment will increase her chances of survival. | For these men the chances of getting another job are not very high.*

probability /ˌprɒbə'bɪlᵻtiː‖ˌprɑː-/ [n U] how likely it is that something will happen – use this especially when you can calculate fairly accurately how likely it is for something to happen
+of *The probability of catching the disease from your partner is extremely low.*
+that *There is a 90% probability that the hurricane will hit the coast of Florida later today.*

3 probably not

probably not /ˌprɒbəbli 'nɒt‖ˌprɑː-/ *Her parents probably won't let her go. | I'll* come and see you again, but probably not before Christmas. | *"Do you think they'll offer you the job?" "Probably not."*

 Probably comes before 'won't', 'isn't', 'don't' etc: *It probably won't work.*

unlikely /ʌn'laɪkli/ [adj] something that is **unlikely** will probably not happen or is probably not true: *She might let you borrow the car, but it's very unlikely.*
unlikely to do sth *The police are unlikely to find the attacker before dark.*
it is unlikely (that) *It is unlikely that anyone saw the attack.*

doubtful /'daʊtfəl/ [adj] very unlikely
it is doubtful whether/that *It seems doubtful whether the terrorists will ever be found.*

Formal or informal?

Doubtful is not used in informal conversation.

PROBLEM

➡ see also **DEAL WITH**

1 something that causes difficulties and must be dealt with

problem /'prɒbləm‖'prɑː-/ [n C] a bad situation that must be dealt with, because it is causing harm or difficulties, or because it is stopping you from doing what you want to do
big/serious problem *Our biggest problem is lack of money. | Teenage crime is a serious problem.*
have a problem *If you have any problems, give me a call.*
+with *Sue's had a lot of problems with her neighbours recently.*
cause/create problems *The new traffic system is causing problems for everyone.*
solve a problem (=find a way to deal with it) *Scientists still have not solved the problem of what to do with nuclear waste.*

the drug/crime etc problem *efforts to combat the drug problem*
 the problem of sth *the problem of industrial pollution*

> ⚠ Don't say 'an important problem'. Say **a serious problem** or **a big problem**.

trouble /'trʌbəl/ [n U] problems that someone or something is causing you, especially when this makes you worried or annoyed
have trouble with sth *We've had a lot of trouble with our bank.*
cause trouble *She seems to cause trouble wherever she goes.*
have trouble doing sth (=when something is difficult and causes problems) *We had a lot of trouble borrowing the money we needed.*

> ⚠ Don't say 'troubles' or 'a trouble'. **Trouble** is uncountable in this meaning.

difficulty/difficulties /'dɪfɪkəlti, 'dɪfɪ̱kəltiz/ [n U/plural] problems that make it difficult to do what you want to do
face / experience difficulty (=have difficult problems that you must deal with) *Without more rain, the farmers will face serious difficulties.* | *Some parents experienced difficulty when they tried to move their children to other schools.*
run into difficulty / difficulties (=start to have difficulties, especially about money) *The magazine ran into difficulties after only a few months.*
be in difficulty/difficulties (=experiencing problems) *Manchester United won easily, and they never seemed to be in any difficulty.*

setback /'setbæk/ [n C] something that happens which stops you making progress, or which makes things worse than they were before
have/suffer a setback *The peace talks have suffered a series of setbacks.*
+for *This latest scandal is a major setback for the President's election campaign.*

snag /snæg/ [n C] a problem which seems small or not very serious, but which spoils your plans or causes you difficulties: *That's a great idea – the only snag is that we don't have enough money.*

 hassle /'hæsəl/ [n C/U] INFORMAL, ESPECIALLY SPOKEN an annoying problem that causes difficulties or a lot of extra work for you, especially when you are already trying to do something: *the hassles of getting a visa*
it's too much hassle (=there are too many things to do) *I don't want to organize a big party – it's too much hassle.*

2 something wrong with a machine, system, plan etc

problem /'prɒbləm‖'prɑː-/ [n C] something that stops a machine or system from working normally
have problems *Please call 5326 if you have any computer problems.*
+with *There's a problem with the heater.*

trouble /'trʌbəl/ [n U] something that is wrong with a machine, car etc – use this especially when you do not know exactly what is causing the problem: *engine trouble*
+with *We've had trouble with the air conditioning.*
the trouble (=the specific thing causing the problem) *I think we've found out what the trouble is.*

fault /fɔːlt/ [n C] something that is wrong with one of the parts of a machine, which prevents it from working
+in *There's a fault in one of the loudspeakers.*
electrical / mechanical / technical fault *The rocket launch was delayed because of a technical fault.*

defect /'diːfekt, dɪˈfekt/ [n C] something that is wrong with a product or machine, caused by a mistake in the way it was made or designed: *All the computers are checked for defects before they leave the factory.*
+in *Investigators found a defect in the design of the ship.*

flaw/weakness /flɔː, 'wiːknɪ̱s/ [n C] something that is wrong with a plan or set of ideas, which may make the whole plan or set of ideas useless or not effective

P

+**in** *There are several obvious flaws in his argument.* | *One major weakness in the study is that it is based on a very small sample.*

3 something that makes you feel worried and unhappy

problem /'prɒbləm‖'prɑː-/ [n C often plural] something that happens in your life that makes you feel worried and unhappy

have a problem *Bill isn't sleeping well – I think he's having problems at school.*

personal/emotional problems *He's had a lot of personal problems ever since his mother died when he was eight years old.*

troubles /'trʌbəlz/ [n plural] things that make you feel worried and unhappy, especially problems that have continued for a long time: *It's nice to have someone to talk to about your troubles.* | *family troubles*

4 to have a lot of problems

be in trouble /bɪ ɪn 'trʌbəl/ to be in a difficult situation and have a lot of problems

be in deep/serious/big trouble *Their marriage was in serious trouble.*

get into trouble (=start to have problems) *A lot of people get into trouble when they borrow money.*

be (in) a mess /bɪ ɪn ə 'mes/ INFORMAL if something is **in a mess**, there are so many problems that there is not much hope that things will get better: *The economy is in a complete mess.*

get into a mess *How did you manage to get into this mess in the first place?*

sb's life is a mess (=they have a lot of problems and seem unable to deal with them) *Her boyfriend left her and she lost her job – her life is just a mess at the moment.*

5 what you say when you are explaining about a problem

⌕ **the trouble is/the problem is** /ðə 'trʌbəl ɪz, ðə 'prɒbləm ɪz‖-'prɑː-/ SPOKEN say this when you are explaining why

something is difficult or what is causing problems: *The trouble is, there's no-one here who really understands computers.*

+**that** *The problem is that we can't really afford the plane fare.*

the trouble/problem with sth is *The trouble with using credit cards is that it's so easy to get into debt.*

⌕ **the thing is** /ðə 'θɪŋ ɪz/ SPOKEN INFORMAL say this when you are explaining to a friend why you cannot do what they want: *The thing is, I have an important exam next week.*

6 what you say to ask someone about a problem

⌕ **what's wrong?/what's the matter?** /ˌwɒts 'rɒŋ, ˌwɒts ðə 'mætə‖-'rɔːŋ-/ SPOKEN say this when you are asking someone what is causing a problem, for example why they are upset, or why a machine will not work: *What's the matter? You look as if you've been crying.*

+**with** *What's wrong with the TV?*

⌕ **what's up?** /ˌwɒts 'ʌp/ SPOKEN INFORMAL say this when you are asking someone if there is a problem that they want to talk about: *"Karen, can I talk to you for a minute?" "What's up?"*

what's up with sb? (=say this when someone seems to have a problem) *What's up with Larry today?*

⌕ **what's the problem?** /ˌwɒts ðə 'prɒbləm‖-'prɑː-/ SPOKEN say this when you are asking why someone cannot do something or why something will not work: *"I can't finish the last question." "Why? What's the problem?"*

+**with** *What's the problem with the coffee machine this time?*

7 someone who causes a lot of problems

troublemaker /'trʌbəlˌmeɪkə^r/ [n C] someone who deliberately causes problems, especially by complaining a lot or trying to make people fight or argue: *The violence was started by a small group of troublemakers.*

difficult/awkward /'dɪfɪkəlt, 'ɔːkwəʳd/ [adj] someone who is **difficult** or **awkward** causes a lot of problems, because they behave in an unreasonable or unhelpful way: *Darren's always been such a difficult child.*
+**about** *She's being really awkward about the divorce.*

PROMISE

to tell someone that you will definitely do something or that something will definitely happen

➡ see also **AGREE 4**

1 to promise something

promise /'prɒmɪs‖'prɑː-/ [v I/T] to tell someone that you will definitely do something that they want you to do or expect you to do: *"I can't take you to the beach today." "But you promised!"*
+**(that)** *Hurry up, we promised we wouldn't be late.* | *He promised that he wouldn't tell anyone about our secret.*
promise to do sth *The government has promised to investigate why the accident happened.*
promise sb (that) *Harper promised her he would get the money somehow.*

assure /ə'ʃʊəʳ/ [v T] to tell someone that something will definitely happen or is definitely true, so that they are less worried
assure sb (that) *The doctor assured me that I wouldn't feel any pain.* | *The airline has assured travellers there will be no further delays.*

Formal or informal?

Assure is used in writing and in formal spoken English.

give sb your word /ˌgɪv (sb) jɔːʳ 'wɜːʳd/ to promise someone very seriously and sincerely that you will do something: *I have to go and meet her. I've given her my word.*
+**(that)** *Phil gave me his word that he wouldn't ever take drugs again.*

guarantee /ˌgærən'tiː/ [v T] to say that something will definitely happen, or will definitely be provided, especially when you feel very certain about this

+**(that)** *Can you guarantee that there won't be any job losses when the company is taken over?* | *It's a great movie – I guarantee you'll enjoy it.*
guarantee sth *The authorities could not guarantee the safety of UN observers.* | *Companies can no longer guarantee 'jobs for life'.*
guarantee sb sth *Have you been guaranteed a place in the team?*

swear /sweəʳ/ [v T] make a very serious promise, especially publicly or in a law court
+**(that)** *During the ceremony you swear that you will serve the country loyally.*
swear to sb (that) *Swear to me that you will never mention it again.*
swear to do sth *Do you swear to tell the truth?*
swearing – swore – have sworn

2 a promise

promise /'prɒmɪs‖'prɑː-/ [n C] a statement telling someone that you will definitely do something that they want you to do
+**of** *The refugees are relying on promises of food and aid from the West.*
make a promise *I made a promise to help her, and that's what I'm going to do.*
promise to do sth *She seemed to have forgotten her promise to drive us to the airport.*
+**that** *He left with a promise that he would be back before six.*
keep a promise (=do what you have promised) *I said I would take her out, so I have to keep my promise.*
break a promise (=not do what you have promised) *She never forgave her father for breaking his promise.*

3 what you say when you promise something

◔ **I promise** /aɪ 'prɒmɪs‖-'prɑː-/ SPOKEN *"Promise me you'll write to me." "I promise."*
+**(that)** *I promise I won't forget.*

◔ **I give you my word** /aɪ ˌgɪv juː maɪ 'wɜːʳd/ SPOKEN say this when you want to make a very serious and sincere

promise: *You won't regret this – I give you my word.*
+(that) *I give you my word that I'll do everything I can.*

4 when a company makes a promise about its products

guarantee /ˌgærən'tiː/ [n C] a formal written promise by a company to repair or replace a product free if it has a fault within a fixed period: *The VCR comes with a two-year guarantee.*
be under guarantee (=be protected by guarantee) *Your watch will be repaired free if it is still under guarantee.*

be guaranteed /biː ˌgærən'tiːd/ if a product **is guaranteed**, the company that made it has formally promised to repair or replace it free if it has a fault within a fixed period of time: *All our computers are fully guaranteed for two years.*

PROTECT

to prevent someone or something from being harmed or damaged

➡ see also **DEFEND, LOOK AFTER**

1 to protect someone or something

protect /prə'tekt/ [v T] to keep someone or something safe from harm, injury, damage, or illness: *laws to protect the environment* | *The painting is protected by thick glass.* | *He came towards me with a knife, and I put my arm up to protect myself.*
protect sb/sth from sth *Try to protect your skin from the sun.*
protect sb/sth against sth *Garlic was once thought to protect people against evil spirits.*

guard /gɑːʳd/ [v T] to stay close to a person, a valuable object etc and watch them carefully, in order to make sure that they do not escape, get stolen, or get attacked: *They took turns to guard the prisoner during the night.*
guard sb/sth against sth *Soldiers*

have been called in to guard the embassy against further attacks.

shield /ʃiːld/ [v T] ESPECIALLY WRITTEN to protect someone from something harmful or unpleasant, especially by putting yourself or something else between them and the cause of the harm: *Wilson shielded the baby with his body when he realized the bomb was going to explode.*
shield sb/sth from sth *He held up his hands, shielding his eyes from the sun.*

shelter /'ʃeltəʳ/ [v T] ESPECIALLY WRITTEN to provide a place where someone or something is protected, especially from danger or bad weather
shelter sb/sth from sth *A low hill sheltered us from enemy gunfire.* | *Plant roses next to a wall to shelter them from the wind.*
sheltered [adj] protected from wind, rain etc: *We found a sheltered beach where we could sunbathe.*

2 someone who protects a person or place

guard /gɑːʳd/ [n C] someone whose job is to watch a place, person, or valuable object, in order to protect them or stop them escaping: *There were guards on all the gates of the castle.*
security guard (=someone whose job is to guard a building) *Two men overpowered the security guard and stole $20,000.*
armed guard (=with guns) *The captain put armed guards all around the camp.*

bodyguard /'bɒdigɑːʳd‖'bɑː-/ [n C/U] a person, or a group of people working together, whose job is to protect someone important: *The President arrived, surrounded by bodyguards.* | *a member of the Emperor's bodyguard*

bouncer /'baʊnsəʳ/ [n C] someone whose job is to stand at the door of a club, bar etc and stop unwanted people coming in, or make people leave if they are behaving badly: *a nightclub bouncer* | *The bouncer checked me out for weapons at the door.*

night watchman /ˌnaɪt'wɒtʃmən‖-'waːtʃ-, -'wɔːtʃ-/ [n C] someone whose job is to guard a building at night

3 something that protects a person, animal etc

protection /prə'tekʃən/ [n U] something that protects you against harm or damage
+against *Their light summer clothes were no protection against the bitter cold.*
give/provide protection (=protect someone) *Vitamin C provides some protection against minor illnesses.*
+from *At the moment, the law gives women very little protection from violent husbands.*

shield /ʃiːld/ [n C] an object or material that protects someone or something from harm or damage: *Suncream acts as a kind of shield against the sun's harmful ultraviolet rays.* | *The spacecraft is covered in a material that acts as a heat shield.* | *Before operating this machine, make sure the safety shield is in place.*

shelter /'ʃeltər/ [n U] a place where you will be protected from danger or from bad weather: *It began to rain and we all ran for shelter.*
the shelter of sth *William hurried towards the shelter of the old cowshed.*
take shelter (=find a safe place) *When the bombing started, we took shelter in the basement.*

protective /prə'tektɪv/ [adj only before noun] ESPECIALLY WRITTEN **protective** clothes, covers, substances etc protect someone or something from being hurt or damaged: *a tortoise's protective shell* | *Remove the hard disk from its protective packaging.*
protective clothing *Always wear protective clothing when you are working in the laboratory.*

4 someone who wants to protect people

protective /prə'tektɪv/ [adj] someone who is **protective** wants to protect someone else from harm: *Philip noticed Maggie's protective attitude to the girl.*
+towards *It is normal for parents to feel protective towards their children.*

overprotective /ˌəʊvəˈprəˈtektɪv / [adj] someone who is **overprotective** tries

too hard to protect someone else, in a way that restricts their freedom: *Maria's father was an overprotective man who wouldn't let her meet any boys.*

PROTEST

when people show publicly that they do not agree with something

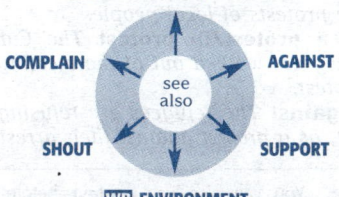

1 to protest about something

protest /prə'test/ [v I/T] if people **protest** about something, they show that they think it is wrong or unfair, for example by holding public meetings or writing letters to politicians: *When the army took power, huge crowds gathered in the capital to protest.*
+about/against *Prisoners had climbed onto the roof to protest about conditions in the jail.*
protest sth AMERICAN *Crowds gathered to protest the war in Iraq.*

demonstrate /'demənstreɪt/ [v I] to protest about something in an organized way, by having a large outdoor meeting or by marching through the streets: *Police arrested 120 people who were demonstrating outside an army base.*
+against *a large crowd demonstrating against US arms exports*

march /mɑːrtʃ/ [v I] to walk with a large group of people from one place to another, in order to show that you do not agree with something
+through/to *Over three hundred farmers marched through Brussels to protest against the new tax.*

boycott /'bɔɪkɒt‖-kɑːt/ [v T] to not buy something, not go somewhere, or not take part in an event, in order to protest about the actions of a country or company: *We are asking people to boycott stores that sell furniture made from rainforest wood.* | *Several countries have said they may boycott next year's Olympic Games.*

2 things that people do in order to protest

protest /'prəʊtest/ [n C/U] anything that you do to protest about something: *The hospital was closed down, despite the protests of local people.*
as a protest/in protest *The Cuban delegates walked out of the meeting in protest.*
+against *The refugees are refusing to eat, as a protest against their arrest.*

> ⚠ You can also use **protest** before a noun, like an adjective: *a big protest meeting*

demonstration (also **demo** BRITISH INFORMAL) /ˌdemən'streɪʃən, 'deməʊ/ [n C] an organized event at which a large number of people come to the same place, often marching through the streets together to get there, in order to protest about something: *The police had to break up yesterday's animal rights demonstration.*
+against *a huge demonstration against the French nuclear tests*

march /mɑːrtʃ/ [n C] an organized event in which a large group of people walk together from one place to another in order to protest about something: *The march ended in front of the White House.*
protest march *I went on a lot of protest marches when I was a student.*

boycott /'bɔɪkɒtǁ-kɑːt/ [n C] when people protest against the actions of a country or company, for example by not buying its products, not attending its events etc
+of *The international boycott of South African products led to the release of Nelson Mandela.* | *a boycott of the peace talks*

3 people who protest

protester /prə'testər/ [n C usually plural] someone who takes part in a public event with other people to protest about something: *Some of the protesters climbed onto the roof of the police station and refused to leave.*

demonstrator /'demənstreɪtər/ [n C usually plural] someone who takes part in an organized event, such as a march or an outdoor meeting, to protest about something: *Thirteen demonstrators were killed when soldiers started shooting.*

marcher /'mɑːrtʃər/ [n C] someone who takes part in an organized walk though an area in order to protest against something: *The Rev. Jesse Jackson led 1000 marchers through downtown Detroit to protest state welfare cuts.*

PROUD

pleased with your achievements, abilities etc

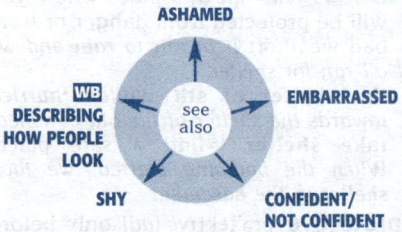

ASHAMED

WB
DESCRIBING HOW PEOPLE LOOK

see also

EMBARRASSED

SHY

CONFIDENT/NOT CONFIDENT

1 to feel proud

proud /praʊd/ [adj] someone who is **proud** of their achievements, their school, their family, or something they own etc is very pleased with them and feels that they are very good or special: *I felt so proud when my son went up to collect his medal.* | *the proud parents with their new baby*
+of *Jane's very proud of her new car.* | *My students have worked hard, and I'm proud of them.*
proud to be/do sth *Morris was proud to be part of such a brilliant team.*
+that *He's very proud that his work has finally been published.*

proudly [adv] *She turned to the crowd, proudly holding up the silver cup.*

pride /praɪd/ [n U] the feeling of being proud because of something special you have achieved, someone special

you are connected with etc: *a sense of national pride*
do sth with pride *He talked with great pride about his father's work.*
bursting with pride (=feeling extremely proud) *Bursting with pride, she stood up to receive her prize.*

take pride in sth /ˌteɪk 'praɪd ɪn (sth)/ to feel proud of your work, your appearance etc, and always try to keep them at a high standard: *The people of the Basque country take great pride in their local cuisine.*
take pride in doing sth *The owners of the hotel take pride in offering an excellent service.*

> **Formal or informal?**
> **Take pride in sth** is used in writing and in formal spoken Englsih.

2 too proud, in a way that other people think is rude

conceited/big-headed /kən'siːtɪd, ˌbɪg'hedɪd◄/ [*adj*] someone who is **conceited** or **big-headed** is too proud of their own achievements or abilities, in a way that annoys other people: *You're the most conceited, selfish person I've ever met! | I know this sounds big-headed, but I think these photos of mine are really good.*

> **Formal or informal?**
> **Big-headed** is more informal than **conceited**.

arrogant /'ærəgənt/ [*adj*] someone who is **arrogant** behaves as if their opinions are more important than other people's, and thinks that they are always right: *a rude and arrogant young man | his arrogant disregard for other people's opinions*
arrogantly [*adv*] *They arrogantly assumed that their form of democracy was better than anyone else's.*
arrogance [*n* U] when someone behaves as if their opinions are more important than other people's and thinks that they are always right: *She was amazed at the arrogance of her landlord who totally ignored her request.*
vain /veɪn/ [*adj*] someone who is **vain** thinks they are very good-looking,

special, or intelligent: *Men can be just as vain as women.*

be pleased with yourself /bi 'pliːzd wɪð jɔːʳˌself/ to feel very satisfied because of something you have achieved – use this especially about someone who seems too satisfied: *Ed walked out of the examination room looking very pleased with himself. | He's a nice young man, I suppose, but perhaps a little too pleased with himself.*

3 someone who thinks they are better than other people

snob /snɒbǁsnɑːb/ [*n* C] someone who thinks that they are better than people from a lower social class: *My mother was a real snob – she wouldn't let me play with the local children.*
snobbish [*adj*] like a snob: *Don't be so snobbish! | snobbish attitudes*

stuck-up /ˌstʌk 'ʌp◄/ [*adj*] INFORMAL someone who is **stuck-up** thinks that they are better than people from a lower social class, and behaves in a proud, unfriendly way: *The children who go to that school are so stuck-up.*

pompous /'pɒmpəsǁ'pɑːm-/ [*adj*] someone who is **pompous** tries to sound important, especially by using very long or formal words: *The headteacher gave a pompous speech about 'the values of learning'.*

look down on sb /ˌlʊk 'daʊn ɒn (sb)ǁ -ɑːn-/ [*phrasal verb* T] if you **look down on** other people, you think you are better or more important than them: *He looks down on anyone who hasn't had a college education.*

4 to talk too proudly about yourself

boast /bəʊst/ [*v* I/T] to talk too proudly about your achievements or possessions, because you want people to admire you: *"I can do better than any of them," she boasted.*
+about *He's always boasting about how many girlfriends he's had.*
+that *She liked to boast that she could speak six languages fluently.*

show off /ˌʃəʊ 'ɒfǁ-'ɔːf/ [*phrasal verb* I] to keep doing things and saying things to show people how clever you are, how brave or strong you are etc, and make them admire you: *Ben was at the pool, showing off to the girls.* | *"I can say it in French, Spanish, Japanese, and Greek." "Oh, stop showing off!"*

show-off /ˈʃəʊ ɒf‖-ɔːf/ [n C] INFORMAL someone who is always doing or saying things to make people admire them: *Don't be such a show-off!*

---

5 a feeling of respect for yourself

self-respect /ˌself rɪˈspekt/ [n U] a feeling of respect and confidence in yourself and in your abilities: *It is difficult to keep your self-respect when you have been unemployed for a long time.* | *Serious illness often results in a loss of confidence and self-respect.*

dignity /ˈdɪgnɨti/ [n U] the ability to behave in a calm way that shows that you respect yourself, even in difficult situations
 do sth with dignity *Very sick people should be allowed to die with dignity.*
 lose your dignity *She lost her home and all her money, but she never lost her dignity.*

pride /praɪd/ [n U] the feeling that you deserve to be respected by other people – use this especially when someone finds it difficult to admit they need help or that they are wrong: *He has too much pride to say he's sorry.* | *Her pride would not allow her to ask for help.*
 hurt sb's pride *Don't offer her money – you'll hurt her pride.*

dignified /ˈdɪgnɨfaɪd/ [adj] ESPECIALLY WRITTEN behaving in a calm way, even in a difficult situation, that makes other people respect and admire you: *She was a quiet, dignified old lady.* | *Jo listened to their criticisms in dignified silence.*

---

6 when someone does not talk proudly about themselves

modest /ˈmɒdɨst‖ˈmɑː-/ [adj] someone who is **modest** never talks proudly about their abilities and achievements: *Fame didn't affect him – he remained a charming and modest man.*

| *She was too modest to tell you that she got top marks in the test.*
 +about *He's really modest about his talent.*

modestly [adv] *"It was really brave of you." "Oh, it was nothing," he replied modestly.*

modesty /ˈmɒdɨsti‖ˈmɑː-/ [n U] a modest way of talking or behaving: *"I couldn't have done it without the rest of the team," he said, with typical modesty.*

PROVE

to show that something is true or correct

➡ see also WB **COURT/TRIAL, TRUE/NOT TRUE**

---

1 to prove something

prove /pruːv/ [v T] to show that something is definitely true, by providing facts or information
 +(that) *Can you prove that you were at home at the time of the attack?* | *He wanted to prove that he was right.*
 prove sb wrong/innocent/guilty *I would love to prove him wrong.*
 prove sth to sb *I'm telling the truth, and I can prove it to you.*
 proving – proved – have proved (also **have proven** ESPECIALLY AMERICAN)

show /ʃəʊ/ [v T] if facts or actions **show** that something is true, they prove that it is true: *The Prime Minister's comments show his ignorance of people's feelings.*
 +(that) *Her record shows that Graf is one of the best players of all time.*
 show how/what *These figures show how serious the company's problems are.*
 showing – showed – have shown

 People or things can **prove** something, but only things can **show** something.

demonstrate /ˈdemənstreɪt/ [v T] to do something or provide information which makes it very clear to people that something is true: *The studies demonstrate a clear link between smoking and heart disease.*

+that *The President is anxious to demonstrate that he has a strong foreign policy.*

Formal or informal?
Demonstrate is more formal than **show**.

confirm /kənˈfɜːʳm/ [v T] if a piece of new information **confirms** an idea or belief that people already have, it shows that it is definitely true: *Police have found new evidence that confirms his story.*
+that *The discovery seems to confirm that people lived here over 10,000 years ago.*

2 to prove that something is wrong or not true

disprove /dɪsˈpruːv/ [v T] *She was able to produce figures that disproved Smith's argument.*
disproving – **disproved** – **have disproved** (also **have disproven** ESPECIALLY AMERICAN)

3 the information that proves something

proof /pruːf/ [n U] information or facts that prove that something is true: *He was the only person in the room when the money disappeared – what more proof do you want? | The police knew she was guilty, but they had no proof.*
+of *You can't drink in bars without some proof of your age.*
+that *There is no proof that he did it.*

 Don't say 'proofs' or 'a proof'. **Proof** is an uncountable noun.

evidence /ˈevɪdəns/ [n U] information that helps to prove whether something is true or not: *The police did not have enough evidence to charge anybody with the murder.*
+that *There is some evidence that a small amount of alcohol is good for you.*
+of/for *evidence of life on other planets*
medical/scientific evidence *There is no scientific evidence to support this theory.*

 Don't say 'an evidence'. Say **a piece of evidence**.

PROVIDE

to make something available for someone who needs it or wants it

➡ see also **GIVE, MONEY 8**

provide /prəˈvaɪd/ [v T] if a person or organization **provides** something, they make it available for someone who needs it or wants it: *They provide free legal advice.*
provide sth for sb *Free parking is provided for hotel guests. | The university should provide more facilities for disabled students.*
provide sb with sth *The money will be used to provide the school with new computer equipment.*

supply /səˈplaɪ/ [v T] to provide things for people, especially regularly and over a long period of time
supply sth to sb *The company supplies beauty products to several major stores.*
supply sb with sth *The US government supplied the rebels with weapons.*
supplying – **supplied** – **have supplied**

supplier /səˈplaɪəʳ/ [n C] a company or country that supplies things to people
+of *one of the world's biggest suppliers of defense equipment*

PUBLIC

➡ opposite **PRIVATE**
➡ look here for ...
  • for everyone to use
  • controlled by the government
  • when a lot of people can see you
➡ if you mean 'people in general', go to **PERSON/PEOPLE 2**
➡ see also **WB** **GOVERNMENT/POLITICS**

1 for everyone to use

public /ˈpʌblɪk/ [adj only before noun] a **public** place or **public** service is one that anyone can use, not one that is only for a particular person or group: *a public telephone | proposals to ban smoking in public places | Is this a public beach? | public toilets*

public transport BRITISH **public transportation** AMERICAN (=buses, trains etc, not cars) *If more people used public transport, there would be less pollution.*

2 owned or controlled by the government

public /'pʌblɪk/ [adj only before noun] **public** libraries, hospitals etc are provided and paid for by the government, not by private companies: *a public library | garbage collection and other public services | We need to raise taxes to pay for better public healthcare.*

public spending/expenditure (=money spent by the government to provide public services) *a big increase in public spending*

publicly owned [adj] owned by the government, not by private companies: *Until the 1980s, industries like electricity and telecommunications were publicly owned.*

> ⚠ In the US and other countries, a **public** school is one that is run by the government, but in Britain a **public** school is the same as a private school and is not run by the government.

state /steɪt/ [adj only before noun] owned, controlled, or paid for by the government: *the state education system | State aid has been promised for the victims of the flood. | state schools*

> ⚠ When you are talking about the US, Canada, or Australia, **state** has a different meaning. A **state** is one of the separate parts of the country which has its own government. So in these countries, a 'state university', for example, is one that is run and paid for by one of the states.

nationalized (also **nationalised** BRITISH) /'næʃənəlaɪzd/ [adj only before noun] **nationalized industry/company etc** an industry or company that used to be private but is now owned

and run by the government: *The government is trying to sell off as many nationalized industries as it can.*

3 when a lot of people can see you or know about what is happening

in public /ɪn 'pʌblɪk/ if you do something **in public**, you do it in a place where a lot of people can see or hear you: *Most people feel nervous about speaking in public. | Her husband was always very nice to her in public, but not at home.*

appear in public (use this to say that a famous person is seen in public by ordinary people) *The Prince has not appeared in public since the announcement.*

publicly /'pʌblɪkli/ [adv] if you do or say something **publicly**, you do or say it so that everyone knows about it, and you do not try to keep it secret: *He was put in prison after publicly criticizing the military government. | They plan to announce their engagement publicly in the New Year.*

public /'pʌblɪk/ [adj only before noun] **public** statements, meetings, or events happen in places where everyone can see them or know about them: *In a public statement, Jackson and his wife announced their intention to get divorced. | a country where they still hold public executions*

openly /'əʊpənli/ [adv] if you do something **openly**, you do it in a public place and without being embarrassed or trying to hide what you are doing: *He was the first person to talk openly on TV about having AIDS. | Drugs are sold openly on the city streets.*

> **Formal or informal?**
> **Openly** is used especially in formal writing and news reports.

PULL

➡ see also **PUSH, PRESS**

1 to pull something with your hands

pull /pʊl/ [v I/T] to hold something and make it move towards you by moving your arms: *You need to pull this lever to start the machine.*
pull sth up/towards/away etc *He pulled her towards him and kissed her.* | *Pull the chair nearer to the fire.*
pull hard (=pull using a lot of effort) *Take hold of the rope and pull hard.*

tug /tʌg/ [v I/T] to pull something using short quick movements: *Mandy was tugging my sleeve.*
+at *I tugged at the dog's collar but he wouldn't move.*
tugging – tugged – have tugged

yank /jæŋk/ [v T] INFORMAL to pull something with a sudden, strong movement
yank sth off/out/from etc *I picked up the box and yanked the lid off.*
yank sth open *Bruno rushed to the door and yanked it open.*

2 to pull something heavy

pull /pʊl/ [v T] to make a vehicle or piece of machinery move along behind you – use this especially about animals or heavy vehicles pulling things: *a tractor pulling a plough* | *The Queen's carriage was pulled by two white horses.*

drag

drag /dræg/ [v T] to pull something along the ground, especially because it is too heavy to carry

drag sth along/over/away etc *They dragged the boat out of the water and up the beach.* | *Pick up your chair. Don't drag it along the floor.*
dragging – dragged – have dragged

haul /hɔːl/ [v T] ESPECIALLY WRITTEN to pull something heavy, with a strong continuous movement, often using a rope
haul sth along/out/away etc *Andrew helped them haul the cart from the ditch.*
haul sth in (=pull it towards you) *We watched the fishermen hauling their nets in.*

tow

tow /təʊ/ [v T] if a vehicle or boat **tows** something, it pulls it behind it: *What's the speed limit for cars towing trailers?*
tow sth to/from/away etc *The damaged ship was towed to the nearest port.* | *The police had towed his car away because it was blocking the road.*

heave /hiːv/ [v I/T] to pull something very heavy with one great effort: *Everyone pull together now. Are you ready? Heave!*
heave sth onto/into/over etc *He heaved the sack onto his shoulder.*

When you see **EC**, go to the
ESSENTIAL COMMUNICATION section.

PUNISH

to do something unpleasant to someone because they have done something wrong

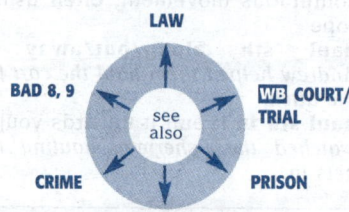

LAW

BAD 8, 9   see also   **WB** COURT/TRIAL

CRIME   PRISON

STRICT/NOT STRICT

sheep-stealing, the usual punishment was hanging.
+for Billy was sent to bed early as a punishment for his bad behaviour.
capital punishment (=the system of punishing people by killing them) Some people are demanding the return of capital punishment for murder.
corporal punishment (=punishing people, especially children, by hitting them) Do you agree with corporal punishment?

> ⚠ Don't say a punishment is 'big', 'heavy', or 'strict'. Use **harsh** or **severe**: Losing a day's pay seems quite a severe punishment for being 10 minutes late!

1 to punish someone

punish /'pʌnɪʃ/ [v T] to do something unpleasant to someone because they have done something wrong, for example by putting them in prison, or making them do something that they do not want to do: We had a teacher who used to punish us by twisting our ears.
punish sb for sth We don't punish people for crimes if they are insane.
punish sb for doing sth He wanted to punish her for deceiving him.

fine /faɪn/ [v T] to make someone pay money as a punishment: Inspectors can fine any passenger travelling without a ticket.
be fined £10/$100 etc She was fined $50 for careless driving.

sentence /'sentəns/ [v T] to announce officially in a court what punishment someone will be given for a crime
sentence sb to 20 years'/life imprisonment etc The judge sentenced her to a year in jail. | Lund was sentenced to eight years' imprisonment for the murder.
sentence sb to death (=say officially that someone will be killed as a punishment) 60 prisoners have been sentenced to death.

2 a way of punishing someone

punishment /'pʌnɪʃmənt/ [n C/U] something that is done to someone in order to punish them: In cases of

penalty /'penlti/ [n C] an official punishment for someone who breaks a law, rule, or legal agreement
+for The penalty for treason was always death.
the death penalty (=being officially killed as a punishment) Drug smugglers face the death penalty if they are caught.
a heavy/severe/stiff penalty The contract includes stiff financial penalties for failure to complete the work on time.
plural **penalties**

fine /faɪn/ [n C] an amount of money that you are ordered to pay as a punishment
get a fine (=be told to pay a fine) I got a £40 fine for speeding.
a heavy fine (=a large fine) There are heavy fines for drink-driving.

sentence /'sentəns/ [n C] a punishment given by a judge in a court
a prison sentence He got a 10-year prison sentence.
the death sentence (=when someone is punished by being killed) The victim's family are demanding the death sentence for his attacker.
a life sentence (=a very long time in prison)
a heavy/light sentence (=a long/short time in prison) Evans was given a light sentence because he had given information to the police.

3 **to be punished for something bad you have done**

be punished /biː ˈpʌnɪʃt/ to be punished for something bad that you have done: *If you commit a crime you must expect to be punished.*
+for *Ellen was punished for being rude to her teacher.*
be severely punished *Anyone who disobeyed his orders was severely punished.*

get/be given /get, biː ˈgɪvən/ to be officially given a punishment: *He deserves to get at least 10 years in prison.* | *You'll probably just get a fine.* | *McLean was given a life sentence for his part in the bombing.*

◯ **be in trouble** /biː ɪn ˈtrʌbəl/ ESPECIALLY SPOKEN if you **are in trouble**, you are likely to be punished because you have done something bad: *You'll be in trouble if they catch you cheating!*
be in trouble with the police/the authorities *My sister's in trouble with the police again.*
get into trouble *I'll get into trouble if my parents see me smoking.*

4 **to punish someone because they harmed you**

get revenge/take revenge /get rɪˈvendʒ, teɪk rɪˈvendʒ/ to do something to punish someone who has harmed you, your family, or your friends
+on *She took revenge on her husband by cutting up all his best clothes.*
+for *Flavio was determined to get revenge for the murder of his sister.*

get your own back/get back at sb /get jɔːr ˈəʊn bæk, get ˈbæk æt (sb)/ INFORMAL to do something which causes problems for someone, because they have done something that causes problems for you: *Okay, she made me look stupid, but I'll get my own back!* | *He wanted to get back at his supervisor for criticizing him in public.*
get your own back on sb *He kept looking for a chance to get his own back on Freddie.*

5 **when someone is not punished**

escape punishment/avoid punishment /ɪˌskeɪp ˈpʌnɪʃmənt, əˌvɔɪd ˈpʌnɪʃmənt/ to avoid being punished for something wrong that you have done: *He managed to escape punishment by saying that he was mentally ill.*

get away with sth /get əˈweɪ wɪð (sth)/ [phrasal verb T] to not be punished for something bad you have done
get away with doing sth *How does he manage to get away with being so cheeky to the teacher?*
get away with it *You're not supposed to park here, but you'll probably get away with it.*

> **Formal or informal?**
> **Get away with sth** is more informal than **escape punishment** or **avoid punishment**.

let sb off /ˌlet (sb) ˈɒf‖-ˈɔːf/ [phrasal verb T] to not punish someone, or give them a less severe punishment than they deserve: *I'll let you off this time, but don't do it again!*
let sb off with a warning/a fine etc (=only give them a warning etc, although they deserve a worse punishment) *The police let him off with a warning.*

PURE

not mixed with anything else

pure /pjʊər/ [adj usually before noun] a **pure** substance or material contains only one substance and is not mixed with anything else: *pure cotton* | *Our burgers are made from pure beef.*

> ⚠ Water or air that is **pure** is very clean and does not contain any harmful substances or chemicals: *The water in the stream was pure enough to drink.*

solid /ˈsɒlɪd‖ˈsɑː-/ [adj only before noun] **solid gold/silver/pine etc** gold, silver, pine etc that has not been mixed with any other metal or wood: *My parents gave me a solid gold necklace for my 18th birthday.* | *a table made of solid oak*

100% /ˌhʌndrᵊd pəˈsent◂/ if food or material is **100%** beef, **100%** cotton etc, it is made only from beef, cotton etc, and has no other food or material added to it: *The label said '100% wool'.*

neat/straight /niːt, streɪt/ [adj] if you have a strong alcoholic drink **neat** or **straight**, you do not mix it with another drink or with water: *He always drinks his whisky neat.* | *I'll have a straight vodka please.*

PURPOSE

what an event or action is supposed to achieve

➡ if you mean 'on purpose', go to **DELIBERATELY**
➡ see also **REASON**

purpose /ˈpɜːˈpəs/ [n C] the thing that you want to achieve, when you do something or make a plan
+of *The purpose of the study is to find out if people will buy the product.*
the main purpose (=the most important purpose) *The main purpose of the meeting is to discuss who will be in the team.*
sb's purpose in doing sth *My purpose in writing this book was to draw attention to the problem of global warming.*
for this/that purpose *Clifford intended to buy a restaurant, and he had borrowed the money for this purpose.*

> **Formal or informal?**
> **Purpose** is a fairly formal word, so in ordinary conversation it is better to say something like 'why did you do it?' (not 'what was your purpose?') or 'I did it because ...' (not 'my purpose was ...').

aim /eɪm/ [n C] the thing that someone hopes to achieve: *Their aims may be difficult to achieve.*
+of *The aim of the bombers was to destroy public property and get maximum publicity.*
sb's/sth's aim *The organization's aims are to provide food for homeless people and help them find somewhere to live.*

with the aim of doing sth *He started going to the gym, with the aim of improving his fitness.*

> ⚠ Don't say 'with the aim to do something'. Say **with the aim of doing something**.

the point /ðə ˈpɔɪnt/ [n singular] the purpose of something that you are doing or planning – use this especially when someone does not understand what the purpose is
+of *The point of the experiment is to show how this chemical reacts with water.*
the whole point (=exactly the purpose of doing something) *Of course it'll annoy Dad – that's the whole point!*
see the point of sth (=understand why someone does something) *I can't see the point of travelling all that way and then only staying for one day.*

the idea /ði aɪˈdɪə/ [n singular] the effect or result that you hope to achieve by doing something – use this especially when you are doubtful whether that effect or result can be achieved: *We make toys that are both fun and educational – at least that's the idea.*
the idea is to do sth *The idea of the centre was to provide a place where old people could go during the day.*

objective /əbˈdʒektɪv/ [n C] FORMAL the thing that someone is trying to achieve in business or politics: *The President believes that all military objectives have been achieved.*

PUSH

to make someone or something move away from you by pressing against them

➡ see also **PRESS, PULL**

1 to push someone or something

push /pʊʃ/ [v I/T] to make something or someone move away from you, by putting your hands or your shoulder against them and pressing them hard:

We kept pushing but we couldn't get the door open. | *Stop pushing me!*
push sb into/away/back etc *I was pushed into the car with my hands tied behind my back.* | *She tried to kiss him but he pushed her away.* | *We pushed the chairs back against the wall and rolled up the carpet.*
pushing and shoving (=when people in a crowd keep pushing each other) *There was a lot of pushing and shoving as we all tried to get nearer the stage.*

give sth/sb a push /ˌgɪv (sth/sb) ə ˈpʊʃ/ to push something or someone, with a single firm movement: *Suddenly, someone gave him a push from behind.* | *If the door is stuck, just give it a push.*

nudge

nudge /nʌdʒ/ [v T] ESPECIALLY WRITTEN to gently push someone with your elbow to get their attention, especially when you do not want anyone else to notice: *Toby nudged my arm. "That's the guy I told you about," he whispered.*

poke

poke /pəʊk/ [v T] to push someone or something with your finger or with something sharp: *I poked the fish with my finger to see if it was still alive.*
poke sb in the eye/side/ribs *Careful with that stick! You nearly poked me in the eye with it.*

shove /ʃʌv/ [v T] to push someone or something roughly, without caring if you hurt them
shove sb into/aside/against etc *He was shoved into a van, which then drove off at high speed.* | *The police were shoving people aside to make way for the President's car.*

2 to push something so that it keeps moving

push /pʊʃ/ [v T]
push a cart/trolley/car/pram etc to push something that has wheels on it so that it moves along: *Bert was pushing a wheelbarrow loaded with sand.*
push sth along/around/into/up etc *Three men helped push the car into a side-street.*

roll /rəʊl/ [v T] to push a round object so that it keeps turning and moves forward
roll sth along/across/down/up etc *We had to roll the barrels up the slope and through the back door.* | *The kids were rolling an enormous snowball along the ground.*

3 to push something into a small space or into something soft

stick /stɪk/ [v T] to push a sharp object into something soft, or push something into a small space
stick sth into/up/inside etc sth *They stuck pins into a map to show where the enemy camps were.* | *The doctor had to stick a tube down my throat in order to examine my stomach.*
sticking – stuck – have stuck

force /fɔːʳs/ [v T] to push something into a small space using a lot of strength
force sth into/through/down sth *She tried to force her feet into the shoes but they were too small.* | *The burglar must have forced his hand through the window bars and reached the lock inside.*

stuff/shove /stʌf, ʃʌv/ [v T] INFORMAL to push something quickly and carelessly into a pocket, or bag, or a small space

stuff/shove sth into/up/down sth *I rolled up the money and shoved it into my back pocket.* | *Just before his mother came in, Jamie stuffed the letter down the side of the sofa.*

4 | to push something to operate a machine

push/press /puʃ, pres/ [v T]
push/press a button to push something that makes a machine operate: *To send a fax, put the paper in here, then push the red button.* | *It's a very easy camera to use – just point it in the right direction and press the shutter.*

PUT

➡ see also LIFT, MOVE 2, SPREAD 5

1 | to put something somewhere

put /put/ [v T] to move something to a place or position and leave it there
put sth in/on/there etc *Just put the bags on the table.* | *I can't remember where I put my keys.*
put sth back (=put it in the place where it was before or where it should be) *Can you remember to put everything back when you've finished? | I put the letter back in the envelope.*
put sth away (=put it where it is usually kept) *Could you put your books away now, please?*
put sth down/put down sth (=put something that you were holding onto a surface) *I'll have to put them down for a minute – I'm exhausted!*
put sth up/put up sth (=fasten something to a wall, ceiling, or in a high position) *I'm not allowed to put up any posters in my bedroom. | They asked him to put some shelves up in the kitchen.*
putting – put – have put

🔍 **stick** /stɪk/ [v T] SPOKEN to put something somewhere, especially quickly or carelessly
stick sth on/in/over sth *"Where shall I put these groceries?" "Oh just stick them on the table."*

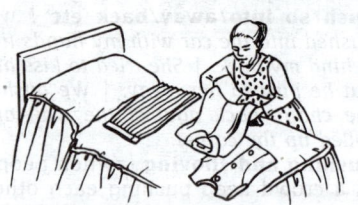
lay

lay /leɪ/ [v T] to put something on a surface so that it is flat
lay sth on/across sth *She unfolded the map and laid it on the table.*
lay sth out/lay out sth (=arrange something carefully on a surface) *Before you start packing, lay out all the clothes on the bed.*
laying – laid – have laid

⚠ Don't confuse **lay** (past tense **laid**) meaning 'to put something on a surface so that it is flat' and **lie** (past tense **lay**) meaning 'to be flat on a surface'.

lean /liːn/ [v T] to put something in a sloping position against something such as a wall, fence, or tree
lean sth against sth *She leaned the ladder against the wall and climbed up.*
leaning – leaned (also **leant** BRITISH) – **have leaned** (also **have leant** BRITISH)

lean

hang /hæŋ/ [v T] if you **hang** clothes somewhere you put them up on a hook, door etc; if you **hang** a picture you put it on a hook or nail on the wall
hang sth on/over/in sth *The room would look better if you hung a few pictures on the walls. | Hang your coat over the back of the chair.*
hang sth up/hang up sth *Take off your wet clothes and hang them up to dry.*
hanging – hung – have hung

hang

2 to put several things on top of each other

pile /paɪl/ [v T] to put a lot of things on top of each other, especially in an untidy way
pile sth on/onto/there etc *Don't pile so much food onto your plate!* | *We piled all the furniture into the middle of the room.*

stack /stæk/ [v T] to put things neatly on top of each other: *I'll start stacking the chairs.*
stack sth against/in/on sth *Unload the boxes and stack them in that corner.*
stack sth up (=put a lot of things on top of each other in a tall pile) *The plates were stacked up in the sink.*

3 to put one thing onto another, so that they are joined

attach /ə'tætʃ/ [v T] to put one thing onto another and join them using pins, glue, thread etc
attach sth to sth *Attach a recent photograph to your application form.*

fix /fɪks/ [v T] to join one thing to another so that it will stay there permanently
fix sth to sth *It took me hours to fix the shelf to the wall.*
fix sth on (=join one thing onto another) *I managed to fix the top on with some glue.*

fasten /'fɑːsən‖'fæ-/ [v T] to join one thing to another, using a pin, string, rope etc, in a way that lets you remove it easily when you need to
fasten sth to sth *She fastened the badge to her dress.* | *You have to fasten the rope to a tree.*

4 to put things into a bag, box, car etc before taking them somewhere

pack /pæk/ [v I/T] to put things into cases, bags, boxes etc so that you can take them sòmewhere: *We're going to Greece tomorrow, and I haven't started packing yet!* | *Did you remember to pack the suntan lotion?*
pack a bag/suitcase (=put things

pack

into a bag etc) *She packed her suitcase and set off for the airport.*
pack sth into sth *We packed all our books into boxes.*

load

load /ləʊd/ [v T] to put goods, furniture, or other large objects into a large vehicle so that they can be taken somewhere
load sth into/onto sth *I'll start loading the boxes into the truck.*

5 to put equipment in a place and make it ready to be used

put in /ˌpʊt 'ɪn/ [phrasal verb T] to put a new piece of machinery or equipment into a room or building
put in sth *The landlord has promised to put in a new heating system.*
put sth in *The workmen are coming to put the new windows in today.*
putting – put – have put

install /ɪn'stɔːl/ [v T] to put a new piece of machinery or equipment into a room or building, and connect it to the electricity supply, water supply etc: *Crime has dropped since the video cameras were installed in the shopping mall.* | *The company is installing a new computer system.*

Formal or informal?

Install is more formal than **put in**.

fit /fɪt/ [v T] to put a new part or piece of equipment into or onto something such as a machine or car: *I had to fit new locks after the burglary.*
fit sth with sth *All the new cars are fitted with alarms.*
fit sth to sth *We decided to fit bars to the ground-floor windows.*
fitting – fitted (or fit) – have fitted

6 to put seeds or plants in the ground

plant /plɑːntǁplænt/ [v T] to put plants or seeds in the ground so that they can grow: *We've planted some new rose bushes in the yard this year.*

sow /səʊ/ [v T] to put seeds in the ground so that they can grow: *The seeds should be sown in spring.*
sowing – sowed – have sown

7 to put something under the ground

bury /ˈberi/ [v T often passive] if you **bury** something, you put it in a hole in the ground and put soil over it: *The bodies were buried in a nearby field.* | *Police found guns and ammunition buried in the yard.*
burying – buried – have buried

Q, q

QUIET

➡ opposite **LOUD**
➡ if you mean 'someone who does not talk much', go to **TALK 8**
➡ see also **SOUND**

 Don't spell this as 'quite'. The correct spelling is **quiet**.

1 when a place is quiet

quiet /'kwaɪət/ [adj] if a place is **quiet**, there is not much noise there: *Inside the church it was quiet and peaceful.* | *David and I found a quiet corner where we could talk.*

quiet [n U] when there is little or no noise: *There was a moment of quiet before the shouting started again.*

silent /'saɪlənt/ [adj] WRITTEN if a place is **silent**, there is no noise at all: *The streets of the city were silent in the moonlight.* | *Apart from the humming of the bees, all was silent and still.*

 Don't say 'very silent'. Say **completely silent**.

 Use **silent** in stories or descriptions.

peaceful /'piːsfəl/ [adj] if a place is **peaceful**, it makes you feel calm and relaxed because there is no unpleasant noise or activity: *It was so peaceful in the garden that Philip almost forgot about his problems.* | *a quiet peaceful valley*

silence /'saɪləns/ [n C/U] ESPECIALLY WRITTEN when there are no sounds at all: *Nothing disturbed the silence of the night.* | *There was a long silence before anyone answered.*

peace /piːs/ [n U] when there is no unpleasant noise or activity, so you can feel calm and relaxed: *The square was a little oasis of peace, only minutes from the heart of the city.*

peace and quiet *I'm going to my room for a bit of peace and quiet.*

2 when sounds, music, or voices are quiet

quiet /'kwaɪət/ [adj] a **quiet** sound, voice, or music is not loud: *He spoke in a quiet yet confident voice.* | *There was a quiet knock at the door.*

quietly [adv] *We were talking quietly so as not to wake the baby.*

low /ləʊ/ [adj] a **low** voice or sound is quiet and deep: *A low humming noise was coming from the refrigerator.*

in a low voice (=speaking quietly) *"Take care," he said in a low voice.*

soft /sɒft‖sɔːft/ [adj] ESPECIALLY WRITTEN a **soft** sound, voice, or music is quiet, gentle, and pleasant: *He spoke with a soft Irish accent.* | *a whisper so soft that I could scarcely hear it*

softly [adv] *Music was playing softly in the background.*

3 when people or machines are quiet

quiet /'kwaɪət/ [adj] if someone or something is **quiet**, they make little or no noise: *I want you all to be very quiet and listen carefully.* | *Our new washing machine is much quieter than the old one.*

quietly [adv] *The children were reading quietly at their desks.*

silent /'saɪlənt/ [adj] ESPECIALLY WRITTEN not making any sound at all: *The engine is almost silent.* | *The children remained silent and watchful as the police questioned their parents.*

fall silent (=stop talking) *The crowd fell silent as he stood up to speak.*

silently [adv] *Silently, the mist crept closer.*

 Use **silent** especially in stories or descriptions.

in silence /ɪn 'saɪləns/ ESPECIALLY WRITTEN if you do something **in silence**, you do it without speaking: *Thousands of* protesters stood in silence outside the prison gates. | We drank our coffee in silence.

in total/complete silence The two of them walked all the way to Matilda's house in complete silence.

> ⚠ Use **in silence** especially in stories or descriptions of events.

not make a sound /nɒt ˌmeɪk ə 'saʊnd/ to not make any noise at all: *Sit still and don't make a sound.*

without making a sound *She managed to get into the house without making a sound.*

4 to become quieter

go quiet /ˌgəʊ 'kwaɪət/ to stop speaking or making any noise at all, for example because you are shocked or embarrassed: *Laurie went very quiet after Jo told him how she felt.*

fade away /ˌfeɪd ə'weɪ/ [phrasal verb I] ESPECIALLY WRITTEN if a sound **fades away**, it gradually becomes quieter until you cannot hear it any more: *The sound of a police siren was slowly fading away into the distance.*

lower your voice /ˌləʊəʳ jɔːʳ 'vɔɪs/ ESPECIALLY WRITTEN to speak more quietly because you do not want other people to hear what you are saying: *Kath lowered her voice so that Mike wouldn't hear.*

5 to make someone or something quieter

quieten sb down BRITISH **quiet sb down** AMERICAN /ˌkwaɪətn (sb) 'daʊn, ˌkwaɪət (sb) 'daʊn/ [phrasal verb T] to make someone quieter and calmer, when they are making a lot of noise because they are angry or upset: *I spent half the lesson trying to quieten them down.* | *Sue managed to quiet us both down and stop us arguing.*

silence /'saɪləns/ [v T] WRITTEN to make someone suddenly stop speaking: *Mrs Talbot silenced me with an angry look.*

> ⚠ Use **silence** when you are writing stories.

shut sb up /ˌʃʌt (sb) 'ʌp/ [phrasal verb T] INFORMAL to make someone stop talking, especially by speaking to them rudely or angrily: *Can't you shut those kids up? | The only way to shut her up is to give her something to eat.*

6 what you say to someone to tell them to be quiet

 ssh /ʃ/ SPOKEN say **ssh** when you want someone to speak more quietly or make less noise: *Ssh, keep the noise down, Timmy's asleep.*

 shut up /ˌʃʌt 'ʌp/ SPOKEN INFORMAL a rude way of telling someone to stop talking: *Just shut up, will you?*

> ⚠ Only use **shut up** with people you know very well. It is not polite.

be quiet /biː 'kwaɪət/ SPOKEN say **be quiet** to tell someone to stop talking or to make less noise, especially when you are annoyed with them: *"Be quiet, James!" she snapped.*

R, r

RACE

one of the main groups of people in the world, who have the same colour of skin and physical appearance

➡ if you mean 'a sports race', go to **SPORT 2**

1 race

race /reɪs/ [n C/U] one of the main groups of people in the world, who have the same colour of skin and physical appearance as each other: *People should be treated equally, regardless of their race, age, or sex.* | *people of all races and religions*
race relations (=the relationship between people of different races) *The group is working to improve race relations in our cities.*

> ⚠ Use **race** to talk about people of the same colour and physical type. To talk about people who have the same history, language, customs etc, use **nation**.

ethnic /'eθnɪk/ [adj only before noun]
ethnic group/community/minority a group from one race or country living in a place where many of the people are different from them: *There are hundreds of different ethnic groups living in London.*
ethnic origin/background (=the ethnic group that someone belongs to) *people from different ethnic backgrounds*

2 when people are treated badly because of their race

racism /'reɪsɪzəm/ [n U] unfair treatment of people because of their race: *The company has been accused of racism after firing three Algerian workers.* | *the struggle against racism in our society*

racial /'reɪʃəl/ [adj only before noun]
racial discrimination / prejudice / violence/attack when people are treated unfairly or attacked because of their race: *Some people complained of racial discrimination in the way housing was allocated.* | *Racial attacks are becoming more common.*

racist /'reɪsɪst/ [adj] **racist** statements, jokes, behaviour, or opinions are based on a dislike of people from other races and a feeling that your race is better than others: *racist attitudes* | *a comedian well known for his racist and sexist jokes*
racist [n C] someone who has racist opinions: *Kamal had been attacked by a gang of white racists.*

3 including people from several races

multiracial/multicultural
/ˌmʌltiˈreɪʃəl◂ , ˌmʌltiˈkʌltʃərəl◂ / [adj only before noun] **multiracial society/school/community** etc a society, school etc where people from several different races live together or work together, especially in a friendly way: *In Britain we live in a multicultural society.* | *a multiracial neighbourhood*

REACH

1 when something is long or high enough to reach something

reach /riːtʃ/ [v I/T] to be long enough, high enough, or deep enough to get to a particular place or point: *The snow was very deep and it almost reached my knees.* | *You see, the paint doesn't quite reach the edge of the paper.* | *a long ladder reaching as high as the 3rd floor*

stretch /stretʃ/ [v I] ESPECIALLY WRITTEN if a river, road, or area of land **stretches** to a place that is far away, it continues as far as that place
+into/to *The highway stretched into the distance.*
+as far as *There were poppy fields stretching as far as the eye could see.*

Stretch is used especially in stories and descriptions.

2 when a number reaches a particular level

reach /riːtʃ/ [v T] if a number or amount **reaches** a particular level, it increases or decreases until it gets to that level: *Gold prices have reached their lowest level for 15 years.* | *Inflation continued to rise, reaching a peak of 28%.*
reach $500/100 mph etc *a car which can reach 140 mph*

hit /hɪt/ [v T] to reach a very high or very low level: *The temperature hit 40° C in parts of the country yesterday.* | *As oil production increased, prices hit an all-time low.*
hitting – hit – have hit

Hit is used especially in news reports.

3 when someone can reach something

reach /riːtʃ/ [v I/T] to be able to touch something or take hold of it, by stretching your arm or moving your body: *Can you get that cup down for me? I can't reach.* | *She can reach the top shelf if she stands on a chair.*

4 to reach a place that you are travelling to

➡ see also **ARRIVE,** ᴡʙ **TRAVEL, JOURNEY**
reach /riːtʃ/ [v T] to arrive at a place, especially after a long or difficult journey: *We didn't reach the hotel until midnight.* | *In winter, some parts of Northern Canada can only be reached by plane.*

Don't say 'we reached at the hotel' or 'we reached to Paris'. Say **we reached the hotel** or **we reached Paris.**

○ **get** /get/ [v I] ESPECIALLY SPOKEN if you **get** to a place, you reach it

+to *By the time we got to York, it was pouring with rain.*
+home/here/there *What time did you get home?*
+as far as *We only got as far as the end of the road, then the car broke down.*
getting – got – have got BRITISH **have gotten** AMERICAN

○ **make it** /'meɪk ɪt/ ESPECIALLY SPOKEN to arrive at a place, especially when you were not sure that you would be able to get there: *The weather looked so bad that I wasn't sure we would make it.* | *If we run, we should be able to make it before the bus leaves.*
+to/across/home etc *He couldn't swim, but somehow he managed to make it to the side of the pool.*

READ

➡ see also ᴡʙ **BOOKS/LITERATURE, NEWSPAPERS AND MAGAZINES**

1 to read something

read /riːd/ [v I/T] *Read the instructions carefully before you start.* | *Have you read 'A Tale of Two Cities'?* | *Don't believe everything you read in the newspapers.*
+about *Did you read about that terrible car crash?*
read to sb/read sb a story (=read something aloud, so that people can listen) *Our mother used to read to us every evening.*
+that *Steve was amazed when he read that his sister had won a prize*
reading – read – have read

reading [n U] the skill or activity of reading: *Children are taught reading and writing in their first years at school.* | *I like to do a lot of reading when I'm on vacation.*

reader [n C] someone who reads books, newspapers, or magazines: *The newspaper is trying to attract more women readers.*

read out /ˌriːd 'aʊt/ [phrasal verb T] to read something and say the words so that people can hear it, especially the words or numbers that are written in a message, list etc

read out sth *He opened the envelope and read out the name of the winner.*
read sth out *Read the numbers out and I'll write them down.*
read sth out to sb *Sarah left a message – I'll read it out to you.*
browse through sth /'braʊz θruː (sth)/ [*phrasal verb* T] to turn the pages of a magazine or book, stopping to read parts that interest you: *I was browsing through the magazines at the station bookstall when I noticed Susan.*
read through/read over /'riːd θruː, 'riːd əʊvəʳ/ [*phrasal verb* T] to read something carefully from beginning to end, in order to check details or find mistakes
read through/over sth *Always read through what you have written before you leave the exam room.*
read sth through/over *Before you sign the contract, read it through carefully.*

2 to be able to read

can read /kən 'riːd/ *Tom is only four and he can read already.* | *Two hundred years ago, few ordinary people could read or write.*
literate /'lɪtərɪt/ [*adj*] FORMAL someone who is **literate** can read and write – use this about adults or older children: *People have become healthier, more literate, and better educated.* | *Every student should be literate by the time he or she leaves primary school.*
literacy [*n* U] the ability to read and write: *a program to improve standards of literacy*

3 to not be able to read

can't read /,kɑːnt 'riːd‖,kænt-/ *We run courses to help adults who can't read.* | *Of course she can't read – she's only 3!*
illiterate /ɪ'lɪtərɪt/ [*adj*] someone who is **illiterate** cannot read or write – use this about adults or older children: *an illiterate farm worker* | *If 70% of the population is illiterate, how do people know who they are voting for?*

4 writing that is easy to read

legible /'ledʒəbəl/ [*adj*] written clearly enough for you to read: *Is the date on the coin still legible?* | *Her writing was so tiny that it was barely legible.*

5 writing that is impossible to read

can't read sth /,kɑːnt 'riːd (sth)‖,kænt-/ *I can't read your handwriting – it's so messy.*
illegible /ɪ'ledʒəbəl/ [*adj*] writing that is **illegible** is impossible to read because it is not clear: *I don't know what this note says – Dad's handwriting is totally illegible!* | *The label had got wet and was now illegible.*

READY

➡ see also **PREPARE, HURRY**

1 when you are ready to do something

ready /'redi/ [*adj* not before noun] if you are **ready** for something, you have done everything that needs to be done in order to prepare for it: *Are you ready? The taxi's here.* | *When everyone is ready, I will give the signal to start.*
ready to do sth *Everything is packed and we're ready to leave.*
+for *I don't want to take the test until I'm ready for it.*
get ready (=prepare yourself to do something) *We have to leave in 10 minutes, so you'd better go and get ready.* | *We've spent the last few days getting ready for Christmas.* | *Why does it take you so long to get ready to go out?*

> ⚠ We often use **get ready** to mean 'get washed and dressed in the right clothes': *I got ready for bed.* | *She's getting ready to go out.*

prepared /prɪ'peəʳd/ [*adj* not before noun] ready to deal with a situation, because you were expecting it or because you have made careful preparations

+for *The police were prepared for trouble.* | *I was not prepared for all those questions.*

well prepared *When the storm came, we were well prepared.*

2 ready to be used or eaten

ready /'redi/ [adj not before noun] if something is **ready**, you can use it or eat it immediately: *I'll let you know when lunch is ready.* | *When the pasta is ready, add the sauce.* | *Your suit will be ready on Wednesday, sir.* | *I'm sorry, your car isn't ready yet.*

ready to use/eat etc (=ready to be used, be eaten etc) *The computer is all set up and ready to use.*

+for *Is everything ready for the party?*

get sth ready (=prepare it) *They were getting the boat ready for a long voyage.*

ripe /raɪp/ [adj] ready to eat – use this about fruit that has been on the plant for long enough: *The apples were ripe and juicy.* | *Is this melon ripe enough to eat?*

REAL

➡ see also **FALSE, NATURAL, IMAGINE**

1 not false or artificial

real /rɪəl/ [adj] *That's a nice watch – is it real gold?* | *Are those flowers real or artificial?* | *Sinbad's not his real name.*

genuine /'dʒenjuɪn/ [adj] real, not just seeming to be real or pretending to be real: *For years people thought the picture was a genuine Van Gogh, but in fact it's a fake.* | *a system for dealing with genuine refugees*

authentic /ɔː'θentɪk/ [adj] **authentic** food, music, clothes etc are correct for the place or the period in history that they are supposed to be from: *a friendly restaurant offering authentic Greek food* | *They play music on authentic medieval instruments.*

2 not imagined or invented

real /rɪəl/ [adj only before noun] actually existing, and not just imagined or invented: *There are some real advantages to the system.* | *Children often think that fairies are real.*

in real life (=not in a story, film, or your imagination) *Many great comic actors are anxious and depressed in real life.*

actual /'æktʃuəl/ [adj] real – use this especially to compare how something really is with what you expected it to be or intended it to be: *How does the actual cost compare with the original estimate?* | *The actual number of people without jobs is much higher than the government claims.*

actually [adv] *He looks quite young, but he's actually about 50.*

3 when someone really feels something

really /'rɪəli/ [adv] when you **really** feel something, **really** want something etc, you are not just pretending to feel or want it: *Do you think she's really sorry?* | *Do you really want to come with us? It'll be very boring for you.* | *He talks about wanting equality, but I don't think he really believes it himself.*

sincere /sɪn'sɪəʳ/ [adj] if you are **sincere**, you really mean or believe what you say, and your feelings are honest: *a sincere wish for peace*

+in *They seemed to be sincere in their concern for the children's welfare.*

sincere thanks/apologies FORMAL *I would like to express my sincere thanks to all those who helped us.*

sincerely [adv] *I believe they sincerely want to find a peaceful solution to the dispute.*

genuine /'dʒenjuɪn/ [adj] **genuine** feelings are real and not pretended – use this especially when you are surprised that someone has these feelings: *I'm not sure if her sympathy was really genuine.* | *a genuine attempt to improve relations between the two countries*

genuinely [adv] *He seemed genuinely interested in our work.*

4 pictures/books that make things seem real

realistic /rɪə'lɪstɪk/ [adj] use this about books, pictures, and films that show or describe things as they really are: *I loved the drawings, they were so realistic.* | *The documentary gave a very realistic account of the war.*

lifelike /'laɪflaɪk/ [adj] use this about pictures and models that look very like the real person or thing: *a very lifelike statue*

REALIZE

to notice or understand something that you did not notice or understand before

➡ see also **UNDERSTAND/NOT UNDERSTAND, NOTICE, KNOW/NOT KNOW**

realize (also **realise** BRITISH) /'rɪəlaɪz/ [v I/T] *Tim only realized his mistake the next day.* | *Without realising it, we had gone the wrong way.* | *Oh, is that your chair? Sorry, I didn't realize.*
+(that) *She woke up and realised that there was someone moving around downstairs* | *I never realized you were from Rome!*
realize how/what/why etc *I'm sorry, I didn't realize how upset you were about all this.*

occur to sb /ə'kɜːʳ tu: (sb)/ [phrasal verb T] if something **occurs to you**, you suddenly realize that it may be true
it occurs to sb that *It suddenly occurred to me that maybe she was lying.* | *Didn't it ever occur to you that they would probably like to be alone together?*
occurring – **occurred** – **have occurred**

become aware /bɪ,kʌm ə'weəʳ/ ESPECIALLY WRITTEN to gradually begin to realize that something is happening or is true
+of *I was slowly becoming aware of how much Melissa was suffering.*
+that *He became aware that the man sitting opposite was staring at him intently.*

sink in /,sɪŋk 'ɪn/ [phrasal verb I] if a new piece of information **sinks in**, you gradually understand it and realize how important, serious, or good it is: *The news of the President's assassination had only just begun to sink in.* | *"How do you feel about winning this award?" "It hasn't really sunk in yet."*

dawn on sb /'dɔːn ɒn (sb)‖-ɑːn-/ [phrasal verb T] if a fact **dawns on you**, you slowly begin to realize it, especially something that you should have realized before: *The awful truth only dawned on me later.*
it dawns on sb that *It slowly dawned on her that they were all making fun of the way she spoke.*

REASON

➡ see also **CAUSE, PURPOSE**

1 why something happens or why someone does something

reason /'riːzən/ [n C] what makes something happen, or what makes someone do something: *"Why didn't Mike come to the party?" "I don't know, but there must be a reason."*
+for *The reason for the price rise was the increase in the cost of materials.*
reason for doing sth *What was your reason for leaving your last job?*
reason why *There's no reason why Johnnie can't come with us.*
+(that) *The only reason she didn't win was that she had injured her knee.*
for personal/health/business etc reasons *For security reasons, there were video cameras at the school entrance.*
🔍 **for some reason** ESPECIALLY SPOKEN (=for a reason that you do not know or understand) *No, he isn't here – he had to go back to Poland for some reason.*

 Don't say 'the reason of something'. Say **the reason for something**: *What was the reason for her strange behaviour?*

explanation /,eksplə'neɪʃən/ [n C] a fact, statement, or idea that helps you to understand why something has happened: *I don't know where your bike is.*

The only explanation I can think of is that someone borrowed it.
+for *What is the explanation for these changes in climate?*

motive /'məutɪv/ [n C] the reason that makes someone decide to do something, especially something bad or dishonest
+for *Police believe the motive for the murder was jealousy.*
motive for doing sth *What was her real motive for phoning me?*

2 | why something is right or should be done

reason /'riːzən/ [n C/U] a fact that makes it right or fair for someone to do something
reason why *The reason why we need these laws is to protect children from violent adults.*
reason to do sth *I can think of lots of reasons to get married.*
with good reason (=when it is right or fair that someone does something) *The school is proud of its record, and with good reason.*
that's no reason to do sth *I know I'm late but that's no reason to shout at me.*

argument /'ɑːʳgjʊ̩mənt/ [n C] one of the reasons that someone uses to try to persuade someone to agree with them
+that *the argument that violence on TV makes people behave violently*
+for/against (=a reason why something should or should not be done) *What are the arguments for the legalization of cannabis?*
argument for/against doing sth *The main argument against smoking is that it's bad for your health.*

justification /ˌdʒʌstɪ̩fɪ̩'keɪʃən/ [n C/U] a reason that someone gives for doing something that seems wrong to most people: *She had her residence permit taken away, without any justification.*
+for *There's no justification for cruelty.*
justification for doing sth *What justification can there be for paying women lower wages?*

3 | a reason explaining why you did something wrong

excuse /ɪk'skjuːs/ [n C] something that you say to try to explain why you did something bad, so that people will forgive you: *Oh shut up Bill, I'm tired of listening to your excuses.*
excuse for doing sth *"What's your excuse for being late?" "My alarm clock didn't go off, so I overslept."*

explanation /ˌeksplə'neɪʃən/ [n C/U] the reasons you give for why you did something wrong: *This work should have been finished a week ago. What's your explanation?*
+for *He gave no explanation for his absence from the previous day's meeting.*

4 | to tell someone the reason for something

say why/tell sb why /ˌseɪ 'waɪ, ˌtel (sb) 'waɪ/ ESPECIALLY SPOKEN to tell someone why something happened: *I knew she was annoyed, but she wouldn't say why.* | *Can anyone tell us why there are no buses today?*

explain /ɪk'spleɪn/ [v I/T] to tell someone the reason for something, so that they understand the situation better: *She just doesn't like me. How else can you explain her behaviour?* | *I don't have time to explain now – just come with me quickly!*
explain why/how/what etc *Doctors are unable to explain why the disease spread so quickly.*
+that *Sarah explained that she hadn't been feeling well recently.*
+to *It was difficult explaining to the children why their father was leaving home.*

> ⚠ Don't say 'he explained me it', 'he explained me why he left' etc. Say **he explained it to me**, **he explained to me why he left** etc.

give a reason /ˌgɪv ə 'riːzən/ to tell someone why you are doing something, especially something surprising: *"He says he's not coming." "Oh, did he give a reason?"*

give sb a reason *The landlord told us we had to go, but we were never given any reason.*

5 to be the reason why something happened

be the reason /bi: ðə 'ri:zən/ to be the reason why something happened or why someone did something
+for *Nick's teachers think that problems at home are the reason for his poor school work.*
be the reason why/(that) *He borrowed too much money, and that's the main reason why his business failed.*

explain /ɪk'spleɪn/ [v T] if a fact or situation **explains** something, it helps you to understand why it happened: *We were all puzzled: what could explain his sudden change of mind?*
explain why / what / how *Mark couldn't sleep last night, which explains why he was in such a bad mood this morning.*

account for sth /ə'kaʊnt fɔːʳ (sth)/ [*phrasal verb* T] FORMAL to be the reason that explains why something strange or surprising happened: *If it's true that he was taking drugs, that would account for his strange mood swings.*

RECENTLY

➡ see also **GRAMMAR 6**

1 a short time ago

recently /'ri:səntli/ [*adv*] if something happened **recently**, it happened a short time before now, especially a few days or weeks ago: *The President has recently returned from a five-day tour of South America.*
only recently *I only recently started eating meat again.*
until recently *He lived in Boston until quite recently.*
very recently *"When did she go back to Italy?" "Oh, very recently – just a couple of days ago."*
recently discovered / completed / built etc *a recently published textbook*

just /dʒʌst/ [*adv*] very recently, for example only a few minutes, hours, or days ago: *I've just heard that Julie's getting married.*
only just *You haven't missed much of the show – it's only just started.*
🔍 **just this minute** SPOKEN (=a moment ago) *"Where's Karen?" "I saw her leaving the building just this minute."*

> ⚠ In British English, use the present perfect tense with **just**: *They have just arrived.* Notice that **just** comes between 'have' and the main verb. In American English, use the simple past tense with **just**: *They just arrived.*

not long ago /nɒt 'lɒŋ əgəʊ‖-'lɔːŋ-/ use this especially about something that seems quite recent, although it actually happened quite a long time ago: *Now the French are saying they oppose nuclear testing, but not long ago they were carrying out tests themselves.*
not so long ago/not very long ago *Not so long ago, India and Pakistan were one country.*
🔍 **a minute ago/a moment ago** /ə 'mɪnɪt əgəʊ, ə 'məʊmənt əgəʊ/ SPOKEN a few minutes ago: *Michael was looking for you a moment ago. | What did I do with my glasses? I had them in my hand a minute ago.*

2 when something has been happening during the recent period

recently /'ri:səntli/ [*adv*] use this to say that something has been happening for a few weeks or months, and it is still happening now: *Her schoolwork has been much better recently.*
🔍 **just recently** ESPECIALLY SPOKEN *Just recently I've been thinking about changing my job.*

lately /'leɪtli/ [*adv*] recently – used especially in questions and negative sentences: *Have you done any painting lately?*
🔍 **just lately** BRITISH, ESPECIALLY SPOKEN *Gerry hasn't been feeling very well just lately.*

R

Formal or informal?

Lately is more informal than **recently**.

in the last few days/weeks/months/years

/ɪn ðə 'lɑːst fjuː (days etc)‖-'læst-/ during the days, weeks, months, or years closest to now: *We've had very little rain in the last few months.* | *Crimes against elderly people have risen sharply in the last few years.*

3 something that happened recently

recent /'riːsənt/ [*adj*] use this about something that happened recently, especially a few days or weeks ago: *He hadn't completely recovered from his recent illness.* | *A recent report said that small amounts of alcohol were good for the health.*

in recent weeks/months/years *She's had a lot of problems at school, but in recent weeks things have improved.*

Formal or informal?

Recent is not used much in informal conversation.

latest /'leɪtɪst/ [*adj* only before noun] someone's **latest** book, record, film etc is the one produced most recently; the latest news is the newest information: *In her latest movie she plays an LA cop.*

the latest news *What's the latest news from home?*

REFUSE

➡ look here for ...
  • refuse to do something
  • say no when someone offers you something
  • not accept someone for a job or course
➡ see also **EC SAYING NO**

1 to say that you will not do something

➡ opposite **AGREE**

refuse /rɪ'fjuːz/ [*v* I/T] to tell someone firmly that you will not do what they asked you to do: *I'm sure if you ask her to help you, she won't refuse.*

refuse to do sth *If they refuse to leave, call the police.*

flatly refuse (=refuse very firmly) *Mother flatly refused to see the doctor.*

refuse sb sth (=refuse to give them something) *The US authorities refused him a visa.*

refusal /rɪ'fjuːzəl/ [*n* C/U] when someone refuses to do something that they have been asked to do: *He was upset by her refusal.*

refusal to do sth *his stubborn refusal to admit that he was wrong* | *Refusal to do military service was a criminal offence.*

 Don't say 'refusal of doing something'. Say **refusal to do something**.

Q **say no** /ˌseɪ 'nəʊ/ ESPECIALLY SPOKEN to tell someone that you will not do what they asked you to do: *I asked Dad to lend me some money, but he said no.*

+to *They asked me so nicely, I couldn't really say no to them.*

Q **will not/won't** /ˌwɪl 'nɒt, wəʊnt/ ESPECIALLY SPOKEN if someone **will not** or **won't** do something that they have been asked to do or told to do, they are determined not to do it: *He's so naughty – he won't do what I tell him.* | *I simply will not sign the contract unless they offer me more money.*

 Will not is stronger and more definite than **won't**.

Q **not prepared to do sth** /nɒt prɪˌpeəʳd tə 'duː (sth)/ ESPECIALLY SPOKEN use this to emphasize that you refuse to do something, and that you think it is wrong or unfair that anyone expects you to do it: *I'm not prepared to help her if she just criticizes me all the time.* | *Our landlord says that he is not prepared to pay for the repairs.*

2 **to say no when someone makes an offer or suggestion**

➡ opposite **ACCEPT**

refuse /rɪˈfjuːz/ [v T] to say you do not want something that you have been offered: *Their offer is too good to refuse.* | *He never refuses a drink, does he?*

not accept sth /nɒt əkˈsept (sth)/ to say no to an offer or invitation, because you think it would not be right to accept it: *She's given us all this stuff and she won't accept any money for it.* | *I decided not to accept their invitation.*

🔍 **say no** /ˌseɪ ˈnəʊ/ ESPECIALLY SPOKEN to say no when someone makes an offer or suggestion: *I asked him if he wanted a drink, but he said no.* | *I'll offer to buy it from her, but I expect she'll say no.*
+to *John's so unhelpful – he just says no to everything I suggest.*

reject /rɪˈdʒekt/ [v T] to say no very firmly to an offer or suggestion, especially in a way that seems rude or unhelpful: *Sarah rejected her parents' offer of financial help.* | *The government has rejected the latest ceasefire proposals from the rebels.*

> **Formal or informal?**
> **Reject** is more formal than **turn down**.

turn down /ˌtɜːʳn ˈdaʊn/ [phrasal verb T] to say no to an offer – use this especially when someone refuses a good offer or opportunity, and this is surprising
turn sth/sb down *They offered her a really good job, but she turned it down.*
turn down sth/sb *If you turn down the opportunity to go to college, you'll always regret it.*

3 **to refuse to give someone a job, a chance to study etc**

reject/turn down /rɪˈdʒekt, ˌtɜːʳn ˈdaʊn/ [v T] to officially tell someone that you will not offer them the job or the chance to study at college which they asked for: *Ian was rejected by the army because of his bad eyesight.*

turn sb down *I applied to six different colleges but they all turned me down.*
turn down sb *We turn down any candidate who makes a spelling mistake on their application.*

> **Formal or informal?**
> **Reject** is more formal than **turn down**.

rejection /rɪˈdʒekʃən/ [n C/U] when a company, college etc tells someone they cannot have the job or the chance to study which they asked for: *You'll have to expect a lot of rejections if you want to work in TV.*

REGULAR

➡ see also **USUALLY, SOMETIMES, OFTEN**

1 **when you do something regularly, or something happens regularly**

regularly /ˈreɡjʊləʳli/ [adv] if you do something **regularly**, you do it on many different occasions, usually with the same amount of time in between: *Bryan and Martha regularly play golf together, about twice a month.* | *Don't forget to take your medicine regularly.*

regular /ˈreɡjʊləʳ/ [adj usually before noun] a **regular** event or activity happens every hour, every week, every month etc, usually with the same amount of time in between: *It's important to visit your dentist for regular check-ups.* | *The Parent-Teacher Association has regular meetings – usually one every month.* | *She needs regular injections of insulin.*
on a regular basis (=regularly) *We give our students tests on a regular basis.*
at regular intervals (=with equal amounts of time between) *The prison is inspected at regular intervals by government health officers.*

every day/every week/every year etc /evri (day etc)/ *Marilyn cycles to work every day.* | *Every Sunday we go to my mother's for lunch.* | *They bring* *out a new record about every six months.*

> Don't use the spelling 'everyday'. The correct spelling is as two separate words (**every day**): *I phoned her every day.*

hourly/daily/weekly/monthly   etc
[*adj* only before noun] happening every hour, every day etc: *There are daily flights to Frankfurt.* | *a weekly current affairs TV show* | *a monthly magazine*
hourly/daily etc [*adv*] *The news is broadcast hourly on Network Five.* | *Do you get paid monthly or weekly?*

every 5 miles/every 3 kilometres etc
/ˌevri (5 miles, etc)/ regularly, after a particular distance: *You should change the oil every 7000 kilometres.* | *After every 100 yards, Grandpa had to stop and sit down.*

2 not regularly

every now and then/every so often
/ˌevri ˌnaʊ ənd ˈðen, ˌevri səʊ ˈɒfn‖ -ˈɔːfən/ sometimes, but not very often and not regularly: *Chris goes to visit his mother in Paris every now and then.* | *Every so often the silence was broken by the sound of gunfire.*

○ **on and off** /ˌɒn ənd ˈɒf‖ˌɑːn ənd ˈɔːf/ ESPECIALLY SPOKEN if you do something **on and off** during a long period, you do it for short periods but not regularly: *I've been trying to learn Spanish on and off for the past five years.*

> When you see ▣, go to the **ESSENTIAL COMMUNICATION** section.

the way that people or groups behave and feel towards each other

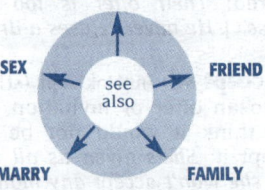

GIRLFRIEND/BOYFRIEND

SEX   see also   FRIEND

MARRY   FAMILY

1 the relationship between two people or groups

relationship /rɪˈleɪʃənʃɪp/ [*n* C] the way that two people or groups feel about each other and behave towards each other
+with *His relationship with his parents had never been very good.*
+between *the relationship between doctor and patient*
a close relationship (=when you know someone very well and like them a lot) *They'd known each other for years and had a very close relationship.*

> Don't say 'relationship to someone'. Say **relationship with someone**.

relations /rɪˈleɪʃənz/ [*n* plural] the public relationship between groups, organizations, or countries, especially when this affects how well they work together
+between *Relations between management and workers have improved.*
+with *Will this dispute damage our relations with the United States?*
race relations (=between people of different races)
diplomatic relations (=between the governments of two countries) *New Zealand broke off diplomatic relations with France because of the nuclear tests.*
industrial relations BRITISH **labor relations** AMERICAN (=between workers and managers)

2 when you have a good relationship

have a good relationship /hæv ə ˌgʊd rɪˈleɪʃənʃɪp/ when two people or groups are friendly towards each other and work well together: *My boss and I have a very good relationship.*
+with *It's important that the school has a good relationship with the students' parents.*

get along (also **get on** BRITISH) /get əˈlɒŋ, get ˈɒn‖-əˈlɔːŋ, -ˈɑːn/ [phrasal verb I] if people **get along** or **get on**, they have a friendly relationship with each other: *We all get on really well, so we're going to share a flat next year.*
+with *He's very easy to get along with.*

> **Formal or informal?**
> **Get along** and **get on** are more informal than **have a good relationship**.

be on good terms /bi: ɒn gʊd ˈtɜːrmz/ if people are **on good terms**, they have a polite relationship and they can work well together, but they are not close friends: *The members of the band were on good terms, but they never spent much time together socially.*
+with *We're on good terms with all our neighbours.*

close /kləʊs/ [adj] if two or more people are **close**, they like each other very much, and can talk to each other about their feelings, their problems etc: *Dad and I have always been very close.* | *close friends from my schooldays*
+to *She was never very close to her stepmother.*

3 when you have a bad relationship

not get along (also **not get on** BRITISH) /nɒt get əˈlɒŋ, nɒt get ˈɒn‖-əˈlɔːŋ, -ˈɑːn/ if people do **not get along** or do **not get on**, they have a bad relationship and they often argue and disagree with each other: *Barney and I just don't get along.*
+with *He's not getting on very well with his new boss.*

fall out /ˌfɔːl ˈaʊt/ [phrasal verb I] BRITISH if friends or relatives **fall out**, they have an argument and stop being friendly with each other: *They fell out last year, and they won't even speak to each other now.*
+with *He's fallen out with his girlfriend again.*

4 when a relationship ends

split up /ˌsplɪt ˈʌp/ [phrasal verb I] INFORMAL if people who are married or having a romantic relationship **split up**, they end their relationship: *Steve's parents split up when he was four.*
+with *Have you heard? Tim's split up with his girlfriend.*

separate /ˈsepəreɪt/ [v I] if people who are married **separate**, they stop living together: *It's the children who suffer when their parents separate.*
separation /ˌsepəˈreɪʃən/ [n C/U] when a husband and wife agree to live apart: *So many marriages end in separation or divorce.*

get divorced /ˌget dɪˈvɔːrst/ if people who are married **get divorced**, they officially end their marriage by means of a legal process: *They got divorced only two years after they were married.*
divorce [n C/U] the legal process of ending a marriage: *About a third of marriages in Britain end in divorce.*

breakup /ˈbreɪkʌp/ [n C/U] when a marriage or romantic relationship ends: *the effects of marital breakup on children*

RELAX

➡ see also **REST, WORRYING**

1 to make yourself feel calmer and more comfortable

relax /rɪˈlæks/ [v I] to make yourself feel calmer, more comfortable, and less worried, by resting or doing something enjoyable: *Just wait! In two weeks' time I'll be relaxing on a beach in Greece.* | *Trained staff will look after your children, so that you*

can relax and enjoy yourself. | *Relax!
It'll be okay.*

> ⚠ Don't say 'relax yourself'. Just say **relax**

unwind /ʌnˈwaɪnd/ [v I] to gradually
relax after you have been working
hard or worrying a lot: *A hot bath is a
pleasant way to unwind.* | *I need a
drink to help me unwind.*

**unwinding – unwound – have
unwound**

chill out /ˌtʃɪl ˈaʊt/ [phrasal verb I]
INFORMAL to relax and calm down,
especially after doing something
exciting: *I spent the afternoon chilling
out in front of the TV.* | *The main
reason I'm going to Jamaica is so that I
can lie on the beach and chill out.*

2 feeling calm and comfortable

relaxed /rɪˈlækst/ [adj] feeling calm,
comfortable, and not worried or
annoyed: *How can you be so relaxed
when you have an interview tomorrow?*
| *Gail was lying in the sun looking very
relaxed.*

laid-back /ˌleɪd ˈbæk◄/ [adj] INFORMAL
someone who is **laid-back** always
seems relaxed, and does not easily
get worried or annoyed: *My parents
are pretty laid-back and don't mind me
staying out late.* | *She seems to have a
fairly laid-back attitude to life.*

3 making you feel calm and comfortable

relaxing /rɪˈlæksɪŋ/ [adj] making you
feel calm, comfortable, and not worried: *We had a lovely holiday – it was
very relaxing.* | *a relaxing massage*

RELIGION

1 a religion or a religious group

religion /rɪˈlɪdʒən/ [n C] a set of beliefs
that a group of people has about a
god, and the ceremonies, customs,
and rules that go with these beliefs: *a*
*book about the religion of ancient
Egypt* | *"What religion are you?" "I'm
a Christian."* | *one of the great world
religions*

faith /feɪθ/ [n C] a religion, especially
one of the large important world
religions: *People of all faiths are
welcome to come to our church.*
**the Jewish/Christian/Islamic/Hindu
faith** *Most of the island's population
belong to the Islamic faith.*

sect /sekt/ [n C] a religious group that
is part of a larger religious group,
and has its own beliefs and
ceremonies: *Islam has two main sects:
the Sunnis and the Shias.* | *The Quak-
ers are a Christian religious sect who
strongly oppose violence and war.*

church /tʃɜːtʃ/ [n C] a religious group
that is part of the Christian religion:
Which church do you belong to? | *a
meeting of church leaders* | *The Pope
is the head of the Catholic Church.*

cult /kʌlt/ [n C] a small religious group
which is not part of one of the main
world religions, especially a group
that has very unusual ideas which
they believe very strongly: *The cult
has several thousand followers in
Europe, and many more in Africa.*

2 religions in general

religion /rɪˈlɪdʒən/ [n U] religions and
religious beliefs and activities in
general, for example as a subject that
people talk about or study: *They spent
hours discussing politics and religion.* |
*Discrimination on the grounds of
religion is strictly forbidden by law.*

> When you are talking about religions in
> general, don't say 'the religion'. Just say
> **religion**.

3 things that you believe because of your religion

beliefs /bɔˈliːfs/ [n plural] all the ideas
that someone believes because of
their religion: *They were persecuted
because of their religious beliefs.* |
*people with very traditional Christian
beliefs*

faith /feɪθ/ [n U] a strong belief in a particular god or religion: *When her husband died, she found great comfort in her faith.*
+in *Nothing could shake his faith in God.*

4 connected with religion

religious /rɪˈlɪdʒəs/ [adj only before noun] connected with religion: *Kusbu doesn't eat meat for religious reasons. | Religious education is compulsory in British schools.* (=students have to learn about religion) | *a religious ceremony*

holy /ˈhəʊli/ [adj usually before noun] a **holy** place, person, or object is one that people think is special because it is connected with God and religion: *Jerusalem is a holy city for Jews, Christians, and Muslims. | holy water | Criminals were not allowed to be buried in holy ground.*
holy – holier – holiest

spiritual /ˈspɪrɪtʃuəl/ [adj] your **spiritual** feelings and ideas are your most private feelings about religion, the meaning of life, and other things that are not connected with the ordinary experiences of daily life: *He seems to have no interest in spiritual matters. | The materialism of the 1980s failed to satisfy people's spiritual needs.*

5 someone who believes in a religion

religious /rɪˈlɪdʒəs/ [adj] someone who is **religious** believes strongly in a particular religion: *He was raised as a Catholic, but he isn't very religious.*
deeply religious (=very religious) *Her father was a deeply religious man who spent hours praying each day.*

practising BRITISH **practicing** AMERICAN /ˈpræktɪsɪŋ/ [adj only before noun] a **practising** Catholic, Muslim etc does not just say they are a Catholic, Muslim etc, but regularly goes to religious ceremonies and lives according to the rules of their religion

devout /dɪˈvaʊt/ [adj] a **devout** Catholic, Muslim etc is someone who has strong and sincere religious beliefs, and who carefully obeys all the rules of their religion: *Devout Muslims pray to Allah five times a day.*

fundamentalist /ˌfʌndəˈmentəl-ɪst/ [n C] someone who has a strong belief that the laws of their religion must be followed very strictly: *Fundamentalists believed that women should not be educated. | a campaign that was funded by Christian fundamentalists*

6 things that people do as part of their religion

pray /preɪ/ [v I] to speak to God, silently or aloud, especially in order to ask for help or to thank him for something: *He got down on his knees and began to pray.*
+to *Abdullah prayed to God to help him.*
pray for sb (=ask God to help someone) *The minister asked us to pray for the dead girl's family.*
pray for sth (=ask God to make something happen) *Let us pray for peace.*

prayer /preər/ [n C] words that you say when you are praying: *a prayer for the dead*
say a prayer (=say a fixed set of words) *An old lady was kneeling in front of the statue, saying a prayer.*
say your prayers (=say prayers as a duty you regularly have to do) *Make sure the children say their prayers before they go to bed.*

worship /ˈwɜːrʃɪp/ [v I/T] FORMAL to pray, sing, or take part in a religious ceremony, in order to show your love of God: *Muslims come to worship and study at the mosque. | The Ancient Egyptians worshipped many gods.*
worshipping – worshipped – have worshipped (also **worshiping – worshiped – have worshiped** AMERICAN)
worship [n U] when you worship: *The building has been used for worship for centuries.*

hymn /hɪm/ [n C] a song praising God sung in a church or at a religious ceremony: *a well-known Christian hymn*
sing hymns *They gather on Sundays to pray and sing hymns.*

R

fast /fɑːst‖fæst/ [v I] to eat no food for a period of time, for religious reasons: *Muslims fast during Ramadan.*

meditate /ˈmedɪ̩teɪt/ [v I] to sit quietly and think deeply or to make your mind completely empty, as a form of religious training: *The monks spend hours every day meditating.*

meditation /ˌmedɪ̩ˈteɪʃən/ [n U] when you sit quietly and calmly, and try to make your mind completely empty

7 someone who does not believe in God

atheist /ˈeɪθi-ɪ̩st/ [n C] someone who believes that there are no gods: *Dr Conan has been an atheist all her adult life.*

agnostic /ægˈnɒstɪk, əg-‖-ˈnɑː-/ [n C] someone who thinks it is impossible to know whether God exists or not: *Though brought up in the Jewish faith, he became an agnostic in later life.*

8 not connected with religion

secular /ˈsekjʊ̩lər/ [adj] not connected with any religious belief or organization – use this especially when comparing religious and non-religious institutions, ideas etc: *The choir sang a mixture of secular and religious music.* | *Unlike the UK, France is actually a secular state.*

9 buildings for religion

church /tʃɜːrtʃ/ a holy building where Christians go to pray and to have their religious ceremonies

chapel /ˈtʃæpəl/ a small church, or a church where particular Christian groups go to pray and to have their religious ceremonies: *There's a Methodist Chapel opposite the library.*

temple /ˈtempəl/ a holy building where people pray and religious ceremonies take place, in religions such as Buddhism, Hinduism, Sikhism, and Shinto: *the Buddhist Temple in Ladakh*

mosque /mɒsk‖mɑːsk/ a holy building where Muslims go to pray and to have their religious ceremonies: *the Great Mosque of Damascus*

synagogue /ˈsɪnəgɒg‖-gɑːg/ a holy building where Jews go to pray and to have their religious ceremonies

REMAIN

to still exist after everything else has gone

➡ if you mean 'continue to be the same', go to **CONTINUE 3**

1 to remain

left /left/ [adj not before noun] if something or someone is **left**, they are still there after everything or everyone else has gone or has been used: *Is there any milk left?* | *By 5 o'clock there was no one left in the office.* | *If Tracey leaves, I'll be the only girl left in the class.*
have sth left *How much time do we have left to finish this?*

be left over /biː left ˈəʊvər/ something that **is left over**, especially money or food, is still there after you have used everything that you need: *I pay all the bills and save any money that is left over.*
+from *Was there any food left over from the party?*

remain /rɪˈmeɪn/ [v I] FORMAL if something **remains**, it still exists or is still available after everything else has gone, or been used, or been dealt with: *Not much of the house remained after the fire.* | *We have dealt with most things, but a few small problems remain.* | *Some elements of the old class system still remain.*
remain to be done *A few problems remain to be discussed.*

2 someone or something that remains

the rest /ðə ˈrest/ [n singular or plural] what is left after everything or everyone else has gone, or been used, or been dealt with: *You carry these two bags and I'll bring the rest.* | *Four of the attackers were killed, the rest escaped.*

+of *What will you do with the rest of the money?* | *He'll be in a wheelchair for the rest of his life.*

the remains /ðə rɪ'meɪnz/ [n plural] **the remains** of something are the small parts of it that are left after most of it has been destroyed or has disappeared
+of *Archaeologists have discovered the remains of an ancient Roman village.*

remaining /rɪ'meɪnɪŋ/ [adj only before noun] ESPECIALLY WRITTEN the **remaining** people or things are the ones that are left when all the others have gone, or been used or dealt with: *The few remaining guests were in the kitchen finishing off the wine.* | *The only remaining question is whether we can borrow the money.* | *the Navy's one remaining aircraft-carrier*

what is left of sth /wɒt ɪz 'left ɒv (sth)/ the small amount that remains after everything else has gone or been used: *As the noise of the explosion died away, he looked up at what was left of his roof.* | *At last she went, and I settled down to enjoy what was left of the afternoon.*

leftovers /'leftəʊvəʳz/ [n plural] food that has not been eaten at the end of a meal: *We used the leftovers to make soup the next day.*

REMEMBER

➡ opposite **FORGET**

1 to remember something from the past

remember /rɪ'membəʳ/ [v I/T] if you **remember** something that happened, something you did, or something you used to know, the thought of it comes back into your mind: *Do you remember your first day at school?* | *I couldn't remember her name.* | *Where are my keys? Oh, I remember, I left them in the kitchen.*
remember who/what/where/how *I can't remember where I put my bag.*
+(that) *Suddenly I remembered that I'd left the iron on!*
remember doing sth *He remembered meeting her at a party once.*

remember sth well/vividly *That was a wonderful Christmas – I remember it well.*

 Don't say 'I am remembering that day'. Say **I remember that day** or **I can remember that day**.

 Don't say 'I remember to have seen him'. Say **I remember seeing him**.

I will never forget /aɪ wɪl ˌnevəʳ fəʳ'get/ ESPECIALLY SPOKEN use this to say that you will remember something for a long time because it was very shocking, very enjoyable, very frightening etc: *I'll never forget the sight of him lying there in the hospital.* | *I can promise you an experience you will never forget!*

think back/look back /ˌθɪŋk 'bæk, ˌlʊk 'bæk/ [phrasal verb I] to think about something that happened in the past because you want to remember it: *She tried to think back and remember exactly what Jim had said.*
+to *Thinking back to when I was first married, I realize now that I made a lot of mistakes.*
look back on *When I look back on those days, it always makes me sad.*

reminisce /ˌremə'nɪs/ [v I] to talk about pleasant events, people, experiences etc from the past, because you want to remember them or enjoy talking about them: *At club meetings, we like to reminisce, remembering old times.*
+about *I used to spend hours listening to my grandfather reminisce about life in the army.*

memory /'meməri/ [n C usually plural] something that you remember from the past about a person, place, or experience
+of *I have lots of happy memories of my time in Japan.*
bring back memories (=when something makes you think of a happy time in the past) *Those old songs bring back memories!*
plural **memories**

nostalgia /nɒ'stældʒəllnɑː-/ [n U] the slightly sad feeling you have when you remember happy things from the past: *There's a mood of nostalgia throughout the whole book.*

+for *nostalgia for the 'good old days' of steam trains*

nostalgic [*adj*] *Finding the old school photograph had made me feel quite nostalgic.*

2   to remember something that you must do

remember /rɪ'membə^r/ [*v* I/T] to think of something that you must do, get, or bring, and not forget about it: *I hope he remembered the wine.* | *Just remember, I want you to be home before midnight.*

remember to do sth *Remember to close the windows before you go out.*

not forget /,nɒt fə^r'get/ to remember something you must do – use this especially when it seems likely that you will not remember something: *Don't worry, I won't forget.*

not forget to do sth *I hope he doesn't forget to water the plants.*

+(that) *I might be home a little late, but I haven't forgotten that we're going out.*

3   to learn something so that you can remember it

memorize (also **memorise** BRITISH) /'meməraɪz/ [*v* T] to learn facts, numbers, lines from a play or poem etc, so that you can remember them later: *I memorised huge lists of names and dates before the exam.* | *You have to memorize this number – don't write it down!*

learn sth by heart /,lɜː'n (sth) baɪ 'hɑː^rt/ to learn lines from a play or poem etc so that you can remember them exactly later: *Actors have to learn their lines by heart.*

4   to make someone remember something they must do

remind /rɪ'maɪnd/ [*v* T] to make someone remember something they must do or something they need to know: *I must pay the gas bill – I'll put it here to remind me myself.*

remind sb about sth *Pauline phoned to remind you about the party.*

remind sb to do sth *Remind me to buy some batteries for my Walkman.*

remind sb (that) *I just want to remind you that your assignments must be completed by Friday.*

remind sb how/what/when *I made a few notes to remind myself what I wanted to say*

reminder /rɪ'maɪndə^r/ [*n* C] a spoken or written message to help you remember something that you might forget: *When your next check-up is due, the dentist will send you a reminder.* | *Finally, a reminder that the school concert will be on 17 December.*

 don't forget /,dəʊnt fə^r'get/ SPOKEN say this to tell someone to remember something that you think they might forget: *Don't forget your keys.*

don't forget to do sth *Don't forget to mail that letter, will you?*

+(that) *Don't forget that we're going out on Friday evening.*

5   when something makes you remember something from the past

remind /rɪ'maɪnd/ [*v* T] if something **reminds** you of a person, thing, or time from the past, it makes you remember them

remind sb of sb/sth *The perfume always reminded him of his mother.* | *It's horrible! It reminds me of the lumpy custard we had at school!*

> ⚠ Don't say 'it reminds me her'. Say **it reminds me of her**.

> ⚠ Don't use **remind** (=make you remember) when you mean **remember**.

make sb think of sth /,meɪk (sb) 'θɪŋk ɒv (sth)/ to remind you of something that you experienced in the past: *I hate that smell – it makes me think of hospitals.*

6   something that is easy to remember

memorable /'memərəbəl/ [*adj*] a **memorable** event or occasion is so good, so enjoyable, or so unusual that you remember it for a long time: *that memorable day when we won 5–0 | She gave a memorable performance as Lady Macbeth.*

unforgettable /ˌʌnfəˈɡetəbəl/ [adj] an **unforgettable** experience, sight, etc affects you so strongly that you will never forget it: *A visit to India is a truly unforgettable experience. | those awful unforgettable images of starving children*

7 **the ability to remember things**

memory /ˈmeməri/ [n singular] your ability to remember things: *I had a good memory, and usually did well in tests. | You know what your memory's like – you're sure to forget!*
have a good/bad memory for sth (=be good/bad at remembering something) *I have a terrible memory for names.*

REMOVE

to take something away from the place where it is

➡ if you mean 'take off your clothes', go to **CLOTHES**

1 **to remove something from inside something**

take out /ˌteɪk ˈaʊt/ [phrasal verb T] to take something from inside a container, space, room etc
take out sth *She opened her briefcase and took out a letter. | We'll have to take out the engine to fix the gearbox.*
take sth out *Roland reached inside his jacket and took his passport out.*
take sth out of sth *Take that bicycle out of the house!*

remove /rɪˈmuːv/ [v T] to take something from inside something: *Cut the fruit in half and remove the stones.*
  remove sth from sth *Someone had removed an important document from the file.*

get sth out /ˌget (sth) ˈaʊt/ [phrasal verb T] to remove something that is deep inside something else, especially when this is difficult to do: *My keys fell down a drain, but I got them out with a piece of wire.*
+of *Did you manage to get all the glass out of the wound?*

pull out /ˌpʊl ˈaʊt/ [phrasal verb T] to suddenly take something out from a place where it cannot be seen, for example from a pocket, bag etc
pull out sth *The man pulled out a gun and fired three shots.*
pull sth out *He opened his wallet, pulled a note out, and put it down on the table.*

2 **to remove something from a surface**

➡ see also **CLEAN**

take off /ˌteɪk ˈɒf‖-ˈɔːf/ [phrasal verb T] to remove something that is on a surface, or that covers a surface
take off sth *You will be able to take off the bandages in about a week.*
take sth off sth *Take the sheets off your bed and I'll wash them. | Could you take all those things off the table?*

remove /rɪˈmuːv/ [v T] to take something off the surface of something else, especially dirt, marks, or something that should not be there: *You can use lemon juice to remove the grease. | A waiter came and removed the empty bottles.*
remove sth from sth *Remove any dirt from the negative before printing the photograph.*

wipe off /ˌwaɪp ˈɒf‖-ˈɔːf/ [phrasal verb T] to remove something such as dirt, paint, or liquid from a surface by moving a cloth over it
wipe off sth *Make sure you wipe off all those marks.*
wipe sth off *Angela wiped her lipstick off and washed her face.*

wipe sth off sth *Werner sat down, wiping the sweat off his forehead with a handkerchief.*

rub off /ˌrʌb ˈɒfǁ-ˈɔːf/ [*phrasal verb* T] to remove dirt, marks etc from a surface by rubbing it hard with a cloth or brush

rub sth off sth *I tried to rub the dirt off my shoes with a tissue.*

rub off sth *I managed to rub off most of the mud, but my coat was still filthy.*

scrape off /ˌskreɪp ˈɒfǁ-ˈɔːf/ [*phrasal verb* T] to remove something from a surface, using a knife or sharp tool

scrape off sth *We started by scraping off the old wallpaper.*

scrape sth off sth *Kevin was scraping some burnt food off the bottom of a pan.*

3 to remove something that is fixed or joined to something else

take off /ˌteɪk ˈɒfǁ-ˈɔːf/ [*phrasal verb* T] to remove something that is fixed to something else or that fits on something else

take sth off *I took the lid off and tasted the soup.*

take off sth *We had to take off the handles to get it through the door.*

remove /rɪˈmuːv/ [*v* T] to take off something that forms a piece or part of something else or that fits on something else: *Remove all the fat, then cut the meat into cubes.*

remove sth from sth *She was in the hospital, having a lump removed from her breast.* | *After 30 minutes, remove the lid from the pan and let it cool down.*

> **Formal or informal?**
>
> **Remove** is more formal than **take off** and is used especially in writing.

break off /ˌbreɪk ˈɒfǁ-ˈɔːf/ [*phrasal verb* T] to remove a part of something by breaking it

break off sth *She broke off a piece of chocolate and gave it to me.*

break sth off sth *George broke a branch off the tree and threw it on the fire.*

cut off /ˌkʌt ˈɒfǁ-ˈɔːf/ [*phrasal verb* T] to remove a part of something by cutting it with a knife or with scissors

cut off sth *At the end of the play, he cuts off Macbeth's head.*

cut sth off *Do you want me to cut the label off?*

chop off /ˌtʃɒp ˈɒfǁˌtʃɑːp ˈɔːf/ [*phrasal verb* T] to remove something by hitting or pressing it with a sharp tool

chop off sth *Chop off the tops of the carrots.*

chop sth off *Careful you don't chop your fingers off!*

tear off /ˈteər ˈɒfǁ-ˈɔːf/ [*phrasal verb* T] to remove part of a piece of paper or cloth, by pulling it so that it tears

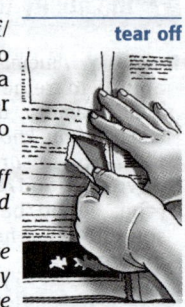
tear off

tear off sth *Tear off the coupon and send it to this address.*

tear sth off sth *I tore the corner off my newspaper and wrote her phone number on it.*

4 to remove writing, film, or music from paper, a tape, a computer etc

delete /dɪˈliːt/ [*v* T] to remove part or all of a document in a computer, so that it no longer exists: *I think you should delete the second paragraph.* | *The computer automatically deletes any files that you have not saved.*

rub out BRITISH **erase** AMERICAN /ˌrʌb ˈaʊt, ɪˈreɪzǁɪˈreɪs/ [*v* T] to remove writing or pictures from paper by rubbing with a piece of rubber, or to remove writing or pictures from a board by rubbing with a cloth: *Use a pencil, so that you can erase your mistakes.*

rub sth out/rub out sth *I had to rub the whole thing out and start again.*

cross out /ˌkrɒs ˈaʊtǁˌkrɔːs-/ [*phrasal verb* T] to draw a line through a word to show that it was a mistake or that you want to change what you have written

cross out sth *Someone had crossed out my name.*

cross sth out *That's not right. Cross it out and start again.*

erase /ɪ'reɪz‖ɪ'reɪs/ [v T] to remove writing, film, or music that has been recorded on a machine: *You can erase what you have recorded by pressing this button.* | *I accidentally erased the movie I had recorded before I had a chance to watch it.*

5 the process of removing something

removal /rɪ'muːvəl/ [n U]
+**of** *Police arranged for the removal of the wreckage.* | *the removal of Russian troops from the area* | *an operation for the removal of her appendix*

REPAIR

➡ see also **BROKEN, DAMAGE**

1 to repair something that is broken or damaged

repair /rɪ'peər/ [v T] if you **repair** something that is broken or not working properly, you work on it so that it is in good condition again: *The builders are coming to repair the roof today.* | *The plane was too badly damaged to be repaired.*
get/have sth repaired (=pay someone else to repair it) *How much will it cost to have the TV repaired?*

fix /fɪks/ [v T] to repair something that is broken or not working properly, especially a machine: *The radio isn't working – can you fix it?*
get/have sth fixed (=pay someone else to fix it) *I must get my camera fixed before we go to France.*

> **Formal or informal?**
> **Fix** is less formal than **repair** and is used especially in spoken English.

mend /mend/ [v T] to repair something that is broken or not working, or something that has a hole in it: *When are you going to mend the fence?* | *a gang of workers mending the road*

> **Formal or informal?**
> **Mend** is less formal than **repair**.

> ⚠ In American English, **mend** is only used to talk about repairing holes in things, especially clothes.

service /'sɜːˑʳvɪ̩s/ [v T] to look at a vehicle or machine in order to make sure that it is working properly, and repair it if necessary: *Has the heating system been serviced recently?*
have/get sth serviced (=pay someone else to service it) *I'm having the car serviced next week.*

2 work done to repair something

repairs /rɪ'peəʳz/ [n plural] work done to repair something: *The roof repairs cost £650.*
carry out repairs/do repairs *We will send workmen to carry out emergency repairs.*
+**to** *$8000 for repairs to the church roof*

maintenance /'meɪntənəns/ [n U] regular work done to check and repair something so that it stays in good condition
routine maintenance (=checks or repairs that are done regularly in order to keep something in good condition) *Smoke detectors require routine maintenance.*
+**of** *The department is responsible for the maintenance of roads and bridges.*

> ⚠ You can also use **maintenance** before a noun, like an adjective: *maintenance work* | *maintenance costs*

REPRESENT

to officially speak or do things for another person, group, or organization

➡ see also **WB GOVERNMENT/POLITICS, WB COURT/TRIAL**

1 to represent a person or group

represent /ˌreprɪ'zent/ [v T] if you **represent** a person or organization at a meeting or in a law court or parliament, you give their opinions and take action for them; if you **represent**

a country, school etc in a competition, you have been chosen to compete for that country or school: *Who will be representing the UK in the next round of peace talks?* | *Students will elect two people to represent them on the School Council.* | *the athletes representing China in this year's Olympic Games*

be represented by sb *Wilson was represented in court by a top criminal lawyer.*

on behalf of /ɒn bɪˈhɑːf ɒv‖-ˈhæf-/ if you do something **on behalf of** someone, you do it because they want you to or have asked you to: *On behalf of everyone here, I'd like to wish Ted a long and happy retirement.* | *The woman who bought the painting said she was acting on behalf of a New York art gallery.*

on sb's behalf *The letter had been signed on the manager's behalf by his assistant.*

speak for sb/act for sb /ˈspiːk fɔːʳ (sb), ˈækt fɔːʳ (sb)/ to represent someone by speaking for them in an official discussion or court, or by making legal decisions for them: *Mr Knight, speaking for the unions, said that the strike would go ahead on Monday.* | *The family has instructed me to act for them in this case.*

2   someone who represents a group

representative /ˌreprɪˈzentətɪv/ [n C] someone who has been chosen to represent an organization or country: *Japan, Britain, and the US are all sending representatives to the talks in Geneva.* | *John Kohorn is the company's representative in Prague.*

When you see **WB**, go to the **WORD BANKS** section.

REST

➡ if you mean 'spend time in a place', go to **STAY**

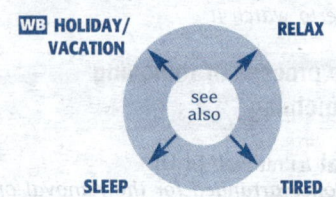

WB HOLIDAY/VACATION   RELAX

see also

SLEEP   TIRED

1   to rest

rest /rest/ [v I] to stop working or stop being active, and sit down or lie down so that you become less tired: *If you're tired, we'll stop and rest for a while.* | *The doctor told me to take some time off work and try to rest.*

have a rest/take a rest /ˌhæv ə ˈrest, ˌteɪk ə ˈrest/ to stop doing something for a short time because you are tired and need to rest: *Halfway up the mountain we stopped to have a rest.*

Formal or informal?

Have/take a rest is less formal than **rest**.

---

have a break/take a break /ˌhæv ə ˈbreɪk, ˌteɪk ə ˈbreɪk/ to stop working for a short time, so that you can rest: *Let's take a break and have some coffee.* | *Is it all right if we have a break at about 10:30?*

relax /rɪˈlæks/ [v I] to do something that makes you feel calm and comfortable and helps you to forget about your work and problems: *relaxing on the beach after a hard week's work* | *Try to relax at lunchtime, perhaps go for a walk.*

 Don't say 'relax yourself'. Just say **relax**.

---

2   a period when you rest

rest /rest/ [n C/U] a period of time when you do not have to do anything tiring or active, and you can relax or sleep: *We painted the walls and then* stopped for a rest. | She will need plenty of rest after the operation.

a good rest (=one that makes you feel completely relaxed) Make sure you have a good rest at the weekend.

break /breɪk/ [n C] a short time when you stop working so that you can rest or eat: OK, let's run through it again straight after the break.

without a break (=not stopping to rest or eat) Harry had worked for eight hours without a break.

coffee/tea/lunch break I'll phone you during my lunch break.

recess AMERICAN **break** BRITISH /rɪ'ses, breɪk‖'riːses/ [n U] a time between classes when the children in a school can go outside and play: The children played kickball during recess. | Come and see me at break, Tom.

RESTAURANTS/ EATING AND DRINKING

1 places to eat

restaurant /'restərɒnt‖-rənt, -rɑːnt/ [n C] a place where you buy and eat a meal, which is usually brought to your table, especially a place that you go to with other people as a social event: Have you ever been to 'Peking Palace'? It's a really nice restaurant.

a Chinese/Italian/Mexican/etc restaurant A new Japanese restaurant just opened on Upper Street.

café/cafe /'kæfeɪ‖kæ'feɪ, kə-/ [n C] a place where you can drink coffee or tea and sometimes alcoholic drinks, and eat cakes or small meals: We found a small café just off the main street.

canteen BRITISH **cafeteria** AMERICAN /kæn'tiːn, ˌkæfə'tɪəriə/ [n C] a place in a school, factory, or company building where the students or workers can buy and eat meals: I usually eat in the college canteen.

fast food restaurant /'fɑːst fuːd ˌrestərɒnt‖'fæst-, -rənt/ [n C] a place where you can buy and eat small meals such as hamburgers that are

ready to eat so that you do not have to wait for them: Fast food restaurants such as McDonald's and Burger King can be found in almost every country in the world.

diner /'daɪnəʳ/ [n C] AMERICAN a small restaurant where you can buy cheap meals: They stopped for breakfast at a roadside diner.

deli /'deli/ [n C] a shop that sells cheese, salads, cooked meats etc, and where you can also buy small meals and sandwiches

sandwich bar /'sænwɪdʒ ˌbɑːʳ‖-'sænwɪtʃ-/ [n C] a place where you can buy sandwiches and drinks that you can take away to eat or drink somewhere else

takeaway /'teɪkəweɪ/ [n C] BRITISH a place that sells complete meals that you take away to eat at home, or one of the meals it sells: a Chinese takeaway | Shall we get a takeaway tonight?

2 places to drink

bar /bɑːʳ/ [n C] a place where you can buy and drink alcoholic drinks: I met her in a bar in Manhattan.

pub /pʌb/ [n C] a place, especially in Britain or Ireland, where people meet their friends and drink alcoholic drinks: We had a few drinks in a local pub.

go down the pub BRITISH (=go to the pub) Mike's gone down the pub.

wine bar /'waɪn ˌbɑːʳ/ [n C] a fashionable, fairly expensive place that serves many different types of wine and small meals: a trendy wine bar in Islington

coffee shop /'kɒfi ʃɒp‖'kɔːfi ʃɑːp/ [n C] a small café where you drink coffee, tea, and other non-alcoholic drinks, and which also sells cakes, sandwiches etc: He was sitting in a coffee shop reading the local paper.

microbrewery /'maɪkrəʊˌbruːəri/ [n C] a place in the US where you can buy meals and drink beer that is made by the bar's owners: The number of microbreweries has increased dramatically in recent years.

R

R

3 to go somewhere to eat or drink

eat out /ˌiːt ˈaʊt/ [phrasal verb I] to have a meal in a restaurant, not at home: *I don't feel like cooking tonight – let's eat out.*

go out to dinner/lunch /gəʊ aʊt tə ˈdɪnəʳ, ˈlʌntʃ/ (also **go out for a meal** /gəʊ aʊt fəʳ ə ˈmiːl/ BRITISH) to go to a restaurant and have a meal: *They went out to dinner as a celebration.* | *When was the last time we went out for a meal?*

go out for a drink /gəʊ ˌaʊt fəʳ ə ˈdrɪŋk/ to go to a bar, pub etc in order to meet your friends and drink alcoholic drinks: *Would you like to go out for a drink sometime?*

4 the people who serve food in a restaurant

waiter /ˈweɪtəʳ/ [n C] a man who serves food and drink at the tables in a restaurant: *I called the waiter over and asked for the bill.*

waitress /ˈweɪtrɪ̥s/ [n C] a woman who serves food and drink at the tables in a restaurant: *She worked as a waitress in a fancy restaurant.*

> In American English, **waitperson** is sometimes used instead of **waiter** or **waitress**.

5 the list of food or drink in a restaurant

menu /ˈmenjuː/ [n C] a list of all the meals that a restaurant serves: *The woman sat down at a table and asked the waiter for the menu.*
set menu (=a complete meal that you pay a fixed price for, instead of ordering and paying for the different parts separately) *The restaurant offers a three course set menu for under $30.*
on the menu (=available and included on the list of food or drink that a restaurant serves) *Are there any vegetarian dishes on the menu?*

wine list /ˈwaɪn lɪst/ [n C] a list of all the alcoholic drinks that a restaurant serves

6 asking for a table in a restaurant

book a table BRITISH **make a reservation** AMERICAN /ˌbʊk ə ˈteɪbəl, ˌmeɪk ə rezəʳˈveɪʃən/ [v I/T] to tell the restaurant that you want to eat there, usually on the phone, so that they do not give your table to someone else: *We've booked a table in the name of "Baxter".*
Do you have a reservation? SPOKEN (=said when asking if someone has made a reservation)

a table for two/three etc /ə ˈteɪbəl fɔːʳ (two, etc)/ say this to the waiter or waitress when you arrive, so that they know how many people are with you: *We'd like a table for four, please.*

7 ordering your meal

order /ˈɔːʳdəʳ/ [v I/T] to tell the waiter or waitress what you want to eat or drink: *Are you ready to order, sir?* | *They ordered a huge plate of French fries.*
order [n C] details of the food and drink that you want to eat, which the waiter writes down: *I think they've lost our order.*
take sb's order (=if a waiter takes your order, they write down what you want to eat) *Can I take your order?*

I'll have... We'll have ... /ˈaɪl hæv, ˈwiːl hæv/ SPOKEN say this to tell the waiter or waitress what you want to eat: *I'll have the Greek salad please.* | *We'll have the house wine.*

8 paying for your meal

bill BRITISH **check** AMERICAN /bɪl, tʃek/ [n C] a piece of paper with a list of what you have had and how much you must pay: *Can we have the bill?* | *Check please!* | *They left without paying their bill.*

tip /tɪp/ [n C] money that you give to the waiter or waitress, as a way of showing your thanks, in addition to the money you pay for your meal
leave a tip (=put a tip on the table when you leave) *He left a big tip.*

service /ˈsɜːʳvɪ̥s/ [n U] the charge for serving your food, which you pay in addition to the cost of the food: *Service is not included.*

It's on me! My treat! /ɪts ɒn 'miː, 'maɪ triːt/ SPOKEN you say this when offering to pay for the meal or the drinks: *Don't worry about the bill. It's on me. | The drinks are on me!*

RESULT

1 something that happens or exists because of something else

➡ see also **CAUSE, REASON**

result /rɪ'zʌlt/ [n C] something that happens because of someone's actions or because of something else that happened before
+of *Her constant cough was the result of many years of smoking.*
with the result that *Chemicals escaped from the factory, with the result that the river became polluted.*
as a result *Jobs are hard to get and, as a result, more young people want to continue their education.*
a direct result of sth (=caused by only one thing even if people think there may be other causes) *Her parents believe that her death was a direct result of medical errors.*

effect /ɪ'fekt/ [n C] the way that a person or situation is changed by something that happens or something that someone does
+of *the harmful effects of radiation*
have an effect *My efforts to persuade them were beginning to have an effect.*
+on *The death of a parent can have very serious and long-lasting effects on a child.*
have a bad/good effect (on) *Any increase in fuel costs could have a bad effect on business.*
side effects (=unwanted effects of a drug or medicine) *The side effects of the drug can include headaches and tiredness.*

⚠ Don't confuse **effect** and **affect**. **Effect** is a noun and **affect** is a verb.

outcome /'aʊtkʌm/ [n C] the situation that exists at the end of a meeting, activity, or series of events, especially when no one knows what this will be until it actually happens: *Whatever the outcome, I hope we remain friends. | The government is hoping for a successful outcome to the talks.*
+of *the final outcome of the dispute*

Formal or informal?
Outcome is not used in informal conversation.

consequence /'kɒnsɪ̯kwəns‖ 'kɑːnsɪ̯kwens/ [n C usually plural] the **consequences** of an action, decision etc are the things that happen as a result of it, which are usually bad: *Safety procedures had been ignored, with tragic consequences.*
+of *The environmental consequences of the oil leak were horrific.*

Formal or informal?
Consequence is more formal than **result** or **effect**.

2 when one thing happens because of another

➡ see also **CAUSE, REASON**

because of /bɪ'kɒz əv‖bɪ'kɔːz-/ if something happens **because of** an earlier problem, event etc, it happens as a result of the problem, event etc: *Beckham didn't play because of an injury. | Because of problems with the fuel system, the launch has been put back a week. | She was chosen for the Peace Prize because of her courageous fight for democracy.*

be the result of sth /biː ðə rɪ'zʌlt ɒv (sth)/ to happen because of something else that happened or was done: *Our success is the result of a great deal of hard work. | The big population increase in the US was partly the result of immigration.*

as a result of sth /əz ə rɪ'zʌlt ɒv (sth)/ because of something else: *He died as a result of cold and exhaustion. | Over 60 drugs have been removed from sale as a result of recent tests.*

resulting /rɪ'zʌltɪŋ/ [adj only before noun] ESPECIALLY WRITTEN happening or

R

existing because of something else that happened before: *During the storm the dam collapsed. The resulting floods caused several deaths.*

3 the result of a game, competition, or election

➡ see also **WB** **SPORT, VOTE, TEST**

result /rɪ'zʌlt/ [n C usually plural] the final number of points, votes etc at the end of a competition, election etc: *These are excellent results for the Christian Democratic Party.*
+of *And now, the results of last week's competition.*

> ⚠ In British English, you can also use **result** to talk about sport. *Turn to BBC1 for the latest football results.* In American English, use **score**.

score /skɔːʳ/ [n C] the number of points that each team or person has at the end of a game: *What was the score? | The final score was 2–1 to Juventus. | listening to the baseball scores on the radio*

4 the result of a test, exam etc

grade /greɪd/ [n C] ESPECIALLY AMERICAN a letter that is put on a student's work or on an exam to show how good or bad it is: *I wasn't very happy with the grade on my essay.*
good/bad grade *I need a really good grade on the final exam to pass the class.*
get a grade *If he gets good enough grades, he'll get a scholarship to Michigan State University.*
mark /mɑːʳk/ [n C] ESPECIALLY BRITISH the number or letter that is put on a student's work to show how good or bad it is: *His mark on the last test gave him a final average of 88%.*
get a mark *"What mark did you get?" "B."*
good/high mark *She came out with the second highest marks in the class.*
bad/low/poor mark *You have to do the course again if you get low marks.*
results /rɪ'zʌlts/ [n plural] BRITISH all the marks that a student gets in a set of tests or examinations, that show

whether he or she has been successful or not: *The school's GCSE results had been much better the previous year.*
get good results *Ceri got better results than she expected.*
exam results *David had terrible exam results at school despite his obvious intelligence.*

score /skɔːʳ/ [n C] AMERICAN a number which shows how well or badly a student has done in an examination, especially an important exam taken by a lot of students
high/low score *Students at King Elementary School generally have the highest test scores in the city.*
+on *Scores on these tests have been steadily falling over the past ten years.*

pass /pɑːs‖pæs/ [v I/T] to reach a high enough standard to succeed in an examination or test: *"I'm taking my driving test today." "Do you think you'll pass?"*
pass with flying colours BRITISH / **colors** AMERICAN (=pass a test or examination with very high marks) *She was so nervous about her examination results, but in fact she passed with flying colours.*

fail /feɪl/ [v I/T] to not reach a high enough standard to succeed in a test or exam: *She failed her history class and had to take it again. | "How did Chris do in his driving test?" "He failed."*

5 to decide how well a student has done in a test etc

➡ see also **TEST**

mark (also **grade** AMERICAN) /mɑːʳk, greɪd/ [v T] to look at students' work or examination papers and put numbers or letters on them to show how good they are: *Mrs Parry, have you marked our tests yet? | I have 48 English papers to grade this evening.*

RETURN

to go back to the place where you were before

➡ see also **GO**

go back /ˌgəʊ 'bæk/ [*phrasal verb* I] to go back to the place you just came from, or to a place you have been to before: *I've had my treatment, but I have to go back next week for a check-up.*
+to *When will you be going back to Japan?*
+there/inside/downstairs etc *It's cold out here, let's go back indoors.*
go back for sth (=go back in order to get something) *Richard forgot his wallet and had to go back for it.*

 If someone goes back to visit a place where they were before and then comes back here, you can say they **have been back**: *He left Germany in 1950 and he's only been back there once.*

come back /ˌkʌm 'bæk/ [*phrasal verb* I] if someone **comes back**, they return to the place where you are: *Rachel's left me, and I don't think she'll ever come back.*
+to/from *When will you be coming back to London? | He's just come back from a vacation in Miami.*

return /rɪ'tɜːᵊn/ [*v* I] to go back or come back to the place where you were before, especially to your home or your country: *I left early, but promised to return the next day.*
+to/from *He had to return to India to look after his mother. | Alastair returned from the office late that night.*

 Don't say 'return back'. Just say **return**.

Formal or informal?
Return is used in writing, news reports, and formal spoken English.

return /rɪ'tɜːᵊn/ [*n* singular] the time when someone returns to a place: *We eagerly await your return.*
on sb's return (=after they return) *On*

her return to Washington, she immediately went to the French Embassy.

Formal or informal?
Return is used in writing, news reports, and formal spoken English.

go home /ˌgəʊ 'həʊm/ to return to your home or to the country where you were born: *It's late, I should be going home. | John used to go home once a month when he was at college.*
+to *Isabelle is going home to France on Saturday.*

 Don't say 'go to home'. Just say **go home**.

Ϙ **be back** /biː 'bæk/ [*phrasal verb* I] ESPECIALLY SPOKEN to be in the place where you lived or worked before you went away: *Don't worry, I'll be back soon. | Jane, what a surprise! How long have you been back?*

RICH

➡ opposite **POOR**
➡ see also **MONEY, EXPENSIVE, EARN**

1 **rich people**

rich /rɪtʃ/ [*adj*] someone who is **rich** has a lot of money: *He's marrying the daughter of a rich lawyer. | If I was rich I'd buy a Ferrari. | Bill Gates is one of the richest men in the world.*
the rich (=rich people) *the wide gap between the rich and the poor*

wealthy /'welθi/ [*adj*] rich – use this especially about someone whose family has owned a lot of land or property for a long time: *a wealthy landowner | She came from one of Boston's wealthiest families.*
wealthy – wealthier – wealthiest

wealth /welθ/ [*n* U] FORMAL the large amount of money and property that makes someone rich: *His Hollywood films brought him wealth and fame.*

well off /ˌwel 'ɒf◄ ‖-'ɔːf◄/ [*adj*] not very rich, but with enough money to have a comfortable life and do the things that you want to do: *a relatively well-off family* (=richer than most people) | *They were sufficiently well off to buy their own apartment.*

better off (=having more money than before or more than someone else) *Most families will be better off when the tax changes are introduced.*

millionaire /ˌmɪljəˈneəʳ/ [*n* C] someone who is extremely rich and has at least a million pounds or a million dollars: *He had his own company at 25 and was a millionaire by 30.* | *You'd have to be a millionaire to afford a place like that.*

2 rich countries

rich /rɪtʃ/ [*adj*] a **rich** country has a lot of money so most of the people living there have comfortable lives: *Many of the former Soviet republics have received aid from their richer neighbours.*

developed /dɪˈveləpt/ [*adj* only before noun]

developed country/nation a country that is rich and has modern industrial, health, and education systems: *These diseases are no longer a serious problem in developed countries.*

the developed world (=all the developed countries, considered as a whole) *Britain is one of the biggest consumers of sugar in the developed world.*

3 to become rich

get rich /ˌget ˈrɪtʃ/ ESPECIALLY SPOKEN to become rich, especially to make a lot of money quickly: *Roger got rich selling second-hand cars.*

make a fortune /ˌmeɪk ə ˈfɔːʳtʃən/ INFORMAL to become rich by earning or winning a lot of money: *A good salesman can make a fortune if he works hard.*

make a fortune doing sth *He had made a fortune gambling in Las Vegas.*

RIGHT

➡ look here for ....
- correct and without any mistakes
- when someone's behaviour is reasonable
- morally right
- legal rights and rights in society

➡ opposite **WRONG**

➡ see also **SUITABLE/UNSUITABLE, GOOD**

1 correct and with no mistakes

right /raɪt/ [*adj*] something that is **right** is true, or has no mistakes in it, or is the way that it should be: *Yes, that's the right answer.* | *Is that the right time?* | *Make sure you use the right amounts of flour and sugar.* | *Put the words in the right order to make a sentence.*

sb is right ESPECIALLY SPOKEN (=what they say is right) *I think you're right – there's not going to be enough food for everyone.*

that's right SPOKEN (use this to emphasize that what someone has said is true) *"Your mother's a teacher isn't she?" "Yes, that's right."*

be right about sb/sth (=have the right opinion about someone or something) *You're right about Tara. You can't trust her.*

get sth right (=be right in what you say or write) *Make sure you get people's names right when you're sending out the invitations.*

correct /kəˈrekt/ [*adj*] **correct** answers, facts, methods etc are right, for example because they contain no mistakes or they break no rules: *The first ten correct answers will win a prize.* | *This information is no longer correct.* | *Did the police use the correct procedure when they interrogated him?*

> **Formal or informal?**
> **Correct** is more formal than **right**.

> Don't use **correct** about people. Use **right**: *You're right, Maria.*

accurate /'ækjᵿrət/ [adj] information, measurements, descriptions etc that are **accurate** are completely correct and all the details are true: *She managed to give the police an accurate description of her attacker.* | *It is vital that our measurements are accurate.*

2 in the right way

⚲ **right** /raɪt/ [adv] ESPECIALLY SPOKEN if you do something **right**, you do it without making any mistakes: *Have I spelled your name right?* | *Most people can't do it right the first time.*

correctly /kə'rektli/ [adv] if you do something **correctly**, you do it in the way that it should be done and without making any mistakes: *The drug is quite safe if used correctly.* | *You're not holding the racket correctly.*

> **Formal or informal?**
> **Correctly** is more formal than **right**.

properly /'prɒpə'li||'prɑː-/ [adv] ESPECIALLY BRITISH if you do something **properly**, you do it in a satisfactory way or in the way that it should be done: *Make sure you put the lid on properly.* | *He accused me of not doing my job properly.*

3 to make something correct

correct /kə'rekt/ [v T] to change something wrong that someone has said or written, and make it right: *We read through the first version, correcting the errors.* | *It's a program that lets you say a sentence, then corrects you if it's wrong.*

correction /kə'rekʃən/ [n C] a mark or note that corrects something in a piece of writing: *My homework was covered with corrections.*
make a correction *I still have a few last-minute corrections to make.*

4 when you think it is right to do something

right /raɪt/ [adj] use this to say that you agree with what someone has done because it was fair or reasonable
be right to do sth *You were right to*

complain – *the waiter was rude and the food was awful.*
the right thing to do *Believe me, it's the right thing to do. You can't let him treat you like this.*

justified /'dʒʌstɪ̰faɪd/ [adj] if you say that someone is **justified** or that something they do is **justified**, you believe they have good reasons for what they do, based on what you know about the situation: *I don't think Colin's criticisms were really justified.*
be/feel justified in doing sth *The government feels justified in using military force to protect its own citizens.* | *Do you think the principal was justified in expelling those students?*

> **Formal or informal?**
> **Justified** is more formal than **right**.

reasonable /'riːzənəbəl/ [adj] if someone does something **reasonable**, they are behaving in a fair and sensible way: *The police say they only used 'reasonable force' to break up the demonstration.*
it is reasonable to assume/expect/ suppose *It is reasonable to assume that about half of the students will pass.*

⚲ **I don't blame you/her etc** /aɪ ˌdəʊnt 'bleɪm (you, etc)/ SPOKEN INFORMAL say this when you can understand why someone has behaved in a particular way, and you think they were right: *"Sheila's left her husband." "Well, I don't blame her!"*
+for (doing) sth *I don't blame you for losing your temper with Ann – she was being so annoying.*

justify /'dʒʌstɪ̰faɪ/ [v T] to show that there are good reasons for doing something that seems wrong to most people: *How can you justify a 200% pay rise!* | *a desperate attempt to justify his decision*
justify doing sth *I don't think anyone can justify spending so much money on weapons.*
justifying – justified – have justified

rightly /'raɪtli/ [adv] if someone says or does something **rightly**, you believe that they are right to say it or do it: *His opponents point out, quite rightly,* *that government money is really tax-payers' money.*

> **Formal or informal?**
>
> **Rightly** is used in writing and in formal spoken English.

5 your beliefs about what is right and wrong

conscience /'kɒnʃəns‖'kɑːn-/ [*n* singular] the part of your mind that tells you what is right or wrong, and makes you feel guilty if you do something wrong: *My conscience told me that I shouldn't accept the money.*
guilty conscience (=a guilty feeling because you know you have done something wrong) *Paul couldn't sleep: 'A sign of a guilty conscience,' he thought.*
with a clear conscience (=when you feel sure you have not done anything wrong) *Ben had treated her so badly, she felt she could leave him with a clear conscience.*

principles /'prɪnsₐpəlz/ [*n* plural] your beliefs about what is morally right or wrong, which help you to decide what you should or should not do: *Some politicians are only interested in power, and don't seem to have any principles at all!*
against sb's principles (=not morally acceptable to them) *I never borrow money – it's against my principles.*

6 to think that something is morally right

right /raɪt/ [*adj*] if you think something is **right**, you believe that there are good reasons for doing it, or that it is not morally wrong: *I don't think they should test drugs on animals. It's not right.*
it is right to do sth *Do you think it is ever right to lie to someone?*

approve /ə'pruːv/ [*v* I] if you **approve** of what someone does, you think it is morally good or not morally wrong; if you **approve** of someone, you like them because you think they are sensible, honest etc: *Martha wants to get a motorcycle but her parents don't approve.*

+of *Most people approve of the changes in the gun laws.* | *Tom's mother doesn't approve of his new girlfriend.*
approve of sb doing sth *Would you approve of your teenage son smoking?*

> Don't say 'I approve it'. Say **I approve of it**

agree with sth /ə'griː wɪð (sth)/ [*phrasal verb* T] to think that an action, decision, or type of behaviour is the right thing to do – used especially in questions or negative sentences: *I do not agree with the use of violence.* | *Do you agree with the administration's immigration policy?*

> Don't say 'I agree this decision'. Say **I agree with this decision**.

> Don't confuse **agree with sth** (=think that something is right) and **agree to do sth** (=say that you will do it): *He agreed to meet me after work.*

 believe in sth /bₐ'liːv ɪn (sth)/ [*phrasal verb* T] ESPECIALLY SPOKEN to think that a type of behaviour is morally right or is a sensible thing to do: *Hilary doesn't believe in sex before marriage.* | *I don't believe in all these silly diets.*
believe in doing sth *We've always believed in letting the children have plenty of freedom.*

be in favour of sth BRITISH **be in favor of sth** AMERICAN /biː ɪn 'feɪvər ɒv (sth)/ if you are **in favour of** something, especially something that affects a lot of people, such as a government plan or policy, you strongly support it because you think it is the right thing to do: *Are you in favour of the death penalty?*
be in favour of doing sth *80% of those interviewed were in favour of banning nuclear weapons.*

approval /ə'pruːvəl/ [*n* U] ESPECIALLY WRITTEN the feeling that something is good, right, or sensible: *When the awards were announced there was general public approval.* | *shouts of approval from the crowd*

7 the legal right to do something

right /raɪt/ [n singular] something that you are legally or officially allowed to do

the right to do sth *Women fought very hard for the right to vote.*

have the right to sth *Everyone should have the right to a decent education.*

give sb the right to do sth *Having a European passport gives you the right to travel and work anywhere in the European Union.*

> ⚠ Don't say 'the right of something' or 'the right of doing something'. Say **the right to something** or **the right to do something**.

rights /raɪts/ [n plural] the political and social freedom that everyone in a country should have: *laws that have gradually taken away workers' rights*

human rights (=the basic rights that all people should have, including the right to be treated fairly and without cruelty by their government) *The country has a bad record on human rights.*

equal rights (=the right of everyone to be treated fairly and equally) *equal rights for women*

be entitled to sth /biː ɪnˈtaɪtld tuː (sth)/ to be legally allowed to have something or do something: *You may be entitled to compensation for loss of earnings.*

be entitled to do sth *If she marries him, will she be entitled to live in this country?*

RISK

the possibility that something bad might happen

➡ see also **DANGEROUS, GAMBLING**

1 a risk

risk /rɪsk/ [n C/U] the possibility that something harmful or unpleasant might happen: *There are a lot of risks involved when you start your own business.*

+of *People continue to smoke, despite all the risks of heart disease, cancer etc.*

reduce/increase the risk of *Clean the wound thoroughly to reduce the risk of infection.*

risk of doing sth *Drivers often break the speed limit, and there's little risk of getting caught.*

+that *There is always the risk that share prices could fall in value.*

danger /ˈdeɪndʒəʳ/ [n singular/U] the possibility that something dangerous or very unpleasant might happen

+of *Is there any danger of Grant being sent to prison? | Cover your head and drink plenty of fluids, to reduce the danger of sunstroke.*

+that *There's a real danger that Britain's forests may disappear completely within the next 50 years.*

threat /θret/ [n singular] a strong possibility that something very bad will happen, especially something that affects many people

+of *Once again the people of Sudan face the threat of famine.*

2 actions or situations that are full of risk

risky /ˈrɪski/ [adj] a **risky** action or situation is one that involves the risk that something harmful or unpleasant might happen: *It's always risky leaving your car out in the street all night. | a risky investment*

risky – riskier – riskiest

dangerous /ˈdeɪndʒərəs/ [adj] involving risks that are not necessary and that could cause harm or serious problems: *Using humor in a job interview is a dangerous thing – you never know how the interviewer will react.*

it is dangerous to do sth *It is dangerous to assume that share prices will continue to rise.*

R

3 to do something even though there is a risk

take a risk /ˌteɪk ə 'rɪsk/ to decide to do something, even though you know that something bad might happen: *I knew we were taking a risk when we lent him the money.* | *Sometimes it's worth taking a few risks to get what you want.*

take a chance /ˌteɪk ə 'tʃɑːns‖-'tʃæns/ to decide to do something even though there is a risk, because you think that you will succeed: *I was offered a job in Hong Kong and decided to take a chance.*
take chances *You can trust them if you like, but I'm not taking any chances!*

risk /rɪsk/ [v T] if you **risk** doing something, you do it even though you know it is risky
risk doing sth *He couldn't risk going through the hall in case his boss saw him leaving early.*
risk it (=risk doing something in spite of possible problems or danger) *They said the snow was too deep for cars to travel, but we decided to risk it.*

⚠ Don't say 'risk to do something'. Say **risk doing something**.

4 to be in a situation where there are risks

risk /rɪsk/ [v T] to get into a situation where something very unpleasant might happen to you
risk death/punishment/defeat etc (=do something that might result in you being killed, punished etc) *They are prepared to risk death or imprisonment for what they believe.*
risk doing sth *I don't want to risk offending your parents.*
risk your life (=risk dying) *She risked her life trying to rescue a cat from a blazing building.*

be in danger /biː ɪn 'deɪndʒəʳ/ to be in a situation in which something very dangerous might happen: *It was a terrible storm, and the little ship was in danger.* | *With the rise of the fascist*

movement, democracy itself was in danger.
+of *Thousands of refugees are now in danger of starvation.*
be in danger of doing sth *The island's traditional culture is in danger of being destroyed.*

> **Formal or informal?**
> **Be in danger** is not used in informal conversation.

threaten /'θretn/ [v T] if actions or events **threaten** something, they cause danger for it and make it likely to be harmed or destroyed: *Severe droughts often threaten the rice crop.* | *According to some scientists, global warming threatens the survival of the whole human race.*

> **Formal or informal?**
> **Threaten** is used especially in news reports.

put sb/sth at risk /ˌpʊt (sb/sth) ət 'rɪsk/ to do something that makes it more likely that someone or something will be harmed: *The pilot has been accused of putting his passengers' lives at risk.* | *Your stupid behaviour could put your whole future at risk.*

ROAD/PATH

➡ see also WB **DRIVE, WALK**

1 in a town

road /rəʊd/ [n C] a long area of ground with a hard, flat surface, for cars, buses, bicycles etc to travel on: *They're building a new road around the city centre.*
along/down/up the road *The boys go to the school down the road.* | *The park is just along the road from our house.*
across/over the road (=on the other side of the road) *Who lives in that house across the road?*
main road (=a large road with a lot of traffic) *It's very noisy living on a main road.*
cross the road (=walk to the other side) *Stop, look, and listen before you cross the road.*

busy road (=a road with a lot of traffic) *It's a busy road, so be careful when you cross.*

street /striːt/ [n C] a road close to the centre of a town, with houses, shops, or offices, and a path down each side for people to walk on: *There were stores on both sides of the street.*

side street (=a small quiet street) *You can park in one of the side streets.*

in a street BRITISH **on a street** AMERICAN *Meg lived in the same London street all her life.* | *We used to have an apartment on 23rd Street.*

one-way street (=where you can only drive in one direction) *You can't turn here, it's a one-way street.*

high street BRITISH **main street** AMERICAN /ˈhaɪ striːt, ˈmeɪn striːt/ [n C] the main street in the middle of a town where most of the shops, hotels, and offices are: *Our bank used to have a branch in every high street.* | *the bars and restaurants that line the town's main street*

alley /ˈæli/ [n C] a very narrow street or path between buildings in a town, especially one that is dirty, dark, or unpleasant: *homeless people sleeping in alleys* plural **alleys**

alley

2 outside a town

road /rəʊd/ [n C] a road that connects towns or cities: *Route 66 used to be one of the main roads across the States.* | *I like driving on French roads – they're so straight, and there isn't much traffic.*

+to *As you leave the city, turn right and take the road to Madrid.*

lane /leɪn/ [n C] a narrow road in the countryside, connecting villages or farms: *We rode our bicycles along pretty country lanes.*

track /træk/ [n C] a narrow road, usually without a hard surface, leading to a farm or field: *The track was only wide enough for one car.* | *A dirt track led up to the cottage.*

3 a road for travelling quickly

motorway BRITISH **freeway** AMERICAN /ˈməʊtərweɪ, ˈfriːweɪ/ [n C] a wide road connecting cities and towns, on which cars can travel fast for long distances: *The speed limit on motorways is 70 mph.* | *We headed east on the Pasadena Freeway.*

> ⚠ When talking about particular motorways, people say 'the M1', 'the M62' etc: *Take the M4 to Swindon.* | *There is heavy traffic on the M6, especially between junctions 6 and 9.*

highway /ˈhaɪweɪ/ [n C] AMERICAN a wide fast road that connects cities and towns: *I got onto the highway and drove as fast as I could.*

Highway 61/70 etc *There's a rest stop somewhere on Highway 61.*

freeway/expressway /ˈfriːweɪ, ɪkˈspresweɪ/ [n C] AMERICAN a wide fast road that takes traffic into and out of a big city: *They took the expressway to the airport.*

bypass /ˈbaɪpɑːs‖-pæs/ [n C] BRITISH a road that goes around a town, so that people can avoid driving through the town

4 an area for people to walk on

path /pɑːθ‖pæθ/ [n C] a long, narrow piece of ground for people to walk along: *A narrow path took us down to the river.* | *a path though the woods*

pavement BRITISH **sidewalk** AMERICAN /ˈpeɪvmənt, ˈsaɪdwɔːk/ [n C] a path built along the side of a street for people to walk on

footpath /ˈfʊtpɑːθ‖-pæθ/ [n C] BRITISH a public path for people to walk on in the countryside: *They followed the coastal footpath into the village.*

trail /treɪl/ [n C] AMERICAN a path in the mountains or in the forest: *hiking trails* | *The trail follows the river most of the way to Avalanche Lake.*

5 a place where roads or paths join

junction /'dʒʌŋkʃən/ [n C] ESPECIALLY BRIT-ISH a place where two or more roads cross or join: *Kerry slowed down as she approached the junction.*
+of *Turn left at the junction of Abbots Road and Church Street.*

intersection /'ɪntərˌsekʃən/ [n C] ESPECIALLY AMERICAN a place, especially in a city, where two or more roads cross each other: *The accident happened at a busy intersection downtown.*

crossroads /'krɒsrəʊdz‖'krɔːs-/ [n C] a place where two small roads or streets cross each other: *Go straight on at the crossroads.*
plural **crossroads**

RUBBISH

things that you throw away because you do not want them

➡ see also **GET RID OF**

rubbish /'rʌbɪʃ/ [n U] BRITISH all the paper, empty bottles, cans, pieces of food etc that you throw away: *The dustmen collect the rubbish on Wednesdays.*
rubbish bin (=a container for rubbish)
rubbish dump (=a large open area where people's rubbish is taken after it is collected)

garbage/trash /'gɑːrbɪdʒ, træʃ/ [n U] AMERICAN all the paper, empty bottles, cans, pieces of food etc that you throw away: *There were piles of trash in the backyard.* | *Empty the wastebaskets and take out the garbage.*
garbage/trash can (=a container for garbage)
garbage dump (=a large open area where people's rubbish is taken after it is collected)

litter /'lɪtər/ [n U] empty bottles, packets, and pieces of paper that people have dropped on the street or in a park: *You can be fined £100 for dropping litter.*

litter bin BRITISH **litter basket** AMERICAN (=a container for people to put litter in)

refuse /'refjuːs/ [n U] FORMAL all the things that are regularly thrown away from the houses, shops, factories etc in an area: *the weekly refuse collection*

waste /weɪst/ [n U] useless materials which are left over, especially after an industrial process, and which must be thrown away: *Too much waste has been dumped into the North Sea.* | *We've been trying to recycle our household waste.*
industrial/toxic/nuclear waste *Industrial waste had leaked into the water supply.*

RUDE

➡ opposite **POLITE**
➡ see also **FRIENDLY/UNFRIENDLY, DESCRIBING PEOPLE**

1 not polite, and likely to upset people or make them angry

rude /ruːd/ [adj] someone who is **rude** upsets or offends people by not following the rules of good social behaviour: *He's so rude! I was talking to him and he just walked away!* | *I heard her making rude remarks about your furniture.*
be rude to sb *My mother doesn't like my boyfriend because he was rude to her once.*
be rude about sth *My French friends are always rude about English food.*
it is rude to do sth *It's rude to interrupt people when they are speaking.*
it is rude of sb to do sth *I thought it was very rude of her not to answer my letter.*
rudely [adv] *Blair rudely pushed his way to the front of the line.*

impolite/not polite /ˌɪmpə'laɪt, nɒt pə'laɪt/ [adj] not following the rules of good social behaviour, especially when someone does this without realizing it: *I was tired, but I thought it might not be polite to leave so early.* | *In Senegal it is considered impolite if you do not share your food.*

offensive /ə'fensɪv/ [adj] **offensive** words, jokes, or actions make people angry, because they show no respect for people's moral or religious beliefs: *His racist jokes are really offensive.*
find sth offensive (=think it is offensive) *Some viewers may find the language in this film offensive.*

insulting /ɪn'sʌltɪŋ/ [adj] something that you say or do that is **insulting** criticizes or insults someone in an offensive and rude way: *He kept making insulting remarks about women drivers.* | *She talks to me as if I'm stupid. It's so insulting.*

tactless /'tæktləs/ [adj] someone who is **tactless** upsets or embarrasses someone else without intending to, by mentioning something that it would be better not to talk about: *I wanted to know about her divorce, but I thought it would be tactless to ask.* | *It's so tactless of him to keep complaining about his job when Sam is unemployed.* | *tactless remarks*

cheeky /'tʃiːki/ [adj] BRITISH use this about a child who says something rude to a parent or teacher: *Stop being so cheeky.*
cheeky – cheekier – cheekiest

bad manners /ˌbæd 'mænəᵉz/ [n plural] someone who has **bad manners** does not behave politely in social situations, for example by not saying 'please' and 'thank you': *Marilyn apologized for her husband's bad manners.*
it is bad manners to do sth *It's bad manners to talk with your mouth full.*

2 to say or do something rude

insult /ɪn'sʌlt/ [v T] to be very rude and unpleasant to someone, either by saying rude things to them or by making them feel stupid or unimportant: *Jarvis was fired for insulting a customer.* | *They offered me $20 for a whole day's work – I felt really insulted.*

offend /ə'fend/ [v T] to make someone angry or upset by doing something that they think is socially or morally unacceptable: *I think I offended Kevin by not inviting him to the party.* | *Many people are offended by sex scenes on television.*

swear /sweəʳ/ [v I] to deliberately use words that shock people because they are considered to be very rude, especially words about sex or religion: *Don't swear in front of the children.*
+at *The other driver got out of his car and started swearing and shouting at me!*
swearing – swore – have sworn

3 rude things that people say

insult /'ɪnsʌlt/ [n C] something that someone says to someone else, which is very rude because it criticizes their intelligence, character, or appearance: *Outside the bar, a drunk was shouting insults at everyone who came past.*

bad language /ˌbæd 'læŋgwɪdʒ/ [n U] words that are considered to be very rude, especially words about sex or religion: *My mother is coming to stay, so no smoking, no drinking, and no bad language.* | *There were hundreds of complaints about the bad language in the film.*

RULE

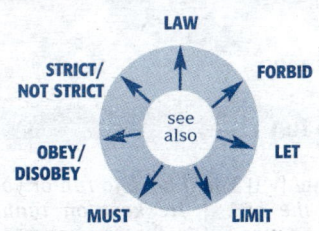

LAW

STRICT/
NOT STRICT   FORBID

see
also

OBEY/
DISOBEY   LET

MUST   LIMIT

rule /ruːl/ [n C often plural] an instruction that says what people are allowed to do or not allowed to do, for example in a game, or in a school or organization: *Do you want me to explain the rules of the game?* | *It says* in the rules that every child has to wear school uniform.

break a rule (=not obey it) *Anyone breaking the rules will be punished.* | *If you put a plural verb with a singular noun, you're breaking a basic rule of grammar.*

rules and regulations (use this when you think there are too many official rules) *Businessmen are tired of all these rules and regulations.*

be against the rules (=not be allowed by the rules) *It's against the rules to run in the corridors.*

regulation /ˌregjʊ'leɪʃən/ [n C usually plural] an official rule made by a government or organization, which is part of a set of rules: *health and safety regulations* | *The new regulations are very strict about what you can and cannot bring into the country.*

bureaucracy /bjʊə'rɒkrəsi‖-'rɑː-/ [n U] a complicated official system which has a lot of unnecessary rules, so that it takes a long time to do anything: *We wanted to film the scene in the European Parliament building but there was too much bureaucracy involved.*

RUN

➡ if you mean 'be in charge of an organization', go to **IN CHARGE OF**

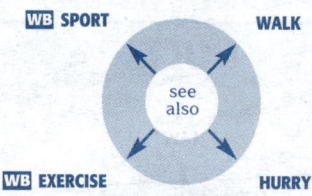

SPORT **WALK**

see also

EXERCISE **HURRY**

1 to run

run /rʌn/ [v I] *You'll have to run or you'll miss the bus.* | *He kept on running until he was out in the open country.*

+across/through/along/out etc *A dog ran straight out in front of my car.* | *She ran upstairs and slammed her bedroom door.*

run for the bus/train (=in order to catch it) *Just running for the bus leaves me out of breath.*

run away/off (=run fast in order to leave a place) *They grabbed her purse and then ran off towards the subway.*

run after sb/sth (=chase someone) *I ran after Karen, calling her name as loudly as I could.*

running – ran – have run

dash /dæʃ/ [v I] to run very quickly for a short distance, because you have to do something urgently

+around/into/across etc *He dashed forward and pulled the child away from the road.*

dash [n singular]

make a dash for sth (=run quickly towards something) *She got up and made a dash for the door.*

sprint /sprɪnt/ [v I] to run as fast as you can over a short distance: *A man sprinted past, then five seconds later two policemen came running after him.*

trot /trɒt‖trɑːt/ [v I] ESPECIALLY WRITTEN to run fairly slowly, taking short steps

trot along/back/off *Paul walked quickly, with his little dog trotting along behind.*

trotting – trotted – have trotted

2 to run as a sport or for exercise

run /rʌn/ [v I/T] to run in a race or for exercise: *Omar's running the marathon this year.*

go running/go for a run (=go out and run for exercise) *I usually go running on Saturday afternoons.*

run 2 miles/400 metres etc *She runs a couple of miles twice a week.*

running – ran – have run

runner [n C] someone who runs, especially in a race: *a long-distance runner*

jog /dʒɒg‖dʒɑːg/ [v I] to run fairly slowly for a long distance, for exercise: *I started jogging to lose a little weight.*

jog along/down/past etc *When I lived in Washington I jogged along the river every morning.*

go jogging/go for a jog (=go out and jog) *Sharon goes for a jog every evening after work.*

jogging – jogged – have jogged

jogger [n C] someone who jogs for exercise: *The park is full of joggers in the summer.*

S, s

SAD

➡ opposite **HAPPY**
➡ see also **SATISFIED/DISSATISFIED, CRY**

1 feeling sad or unhappy about something

sad /sæd/ [adj not usually before noun] not happy, especially because a happy time has ended, or because you feel sorry about someone else's unhappiness: *She felt sad as she waved goodbye.* | *Why is Sandra looking so sad?*
sad to see/hear/learn/leave/go etc *We were very sad to hear about your father's death.*
+about *I was glad to be going home, but sad about leaving all my friends.*
sad look / expression / voice / face *There was such a sad look in her eyes.*
sad – sadder – saddest
sadly [adv] *She shook her head sadly and sighed.*

unhappy /ʌnˈhæpi/ [adj] not happy, because you are in a situation, job, or relationship that you do not enjoy at all, and it seems likely to continue for a long time: *He was very unhappy at school.* | *Her parents' divorce left her feeling confused and unhappy.*
desperately/deeply unhappy (=very unhappy) *I was desperately unhappy after Sean left me.*
unhappy – unhappier – unhappiest
unhappily [adv] *"What a fool I've been," said James, unhappily.*

upset /ʌpˈset/ [adj not before noun] unhappy because something very unpleasant or disappointing has happened, so that you feel shocked or you want to cry: *Miss Hurley is too upset to speak to anyone at the moment.* | *The children were very upset when we told them that we wouldn't be going to Disneyland.*
+about *She's still upset about her uncle's death.*

miserable /ˈmɪzərəbəl/ [adj] extremely unhappy because of the situation you are in, especially because you are lonely, hungry, cold etc: *He sat all alone in his room, thoroughly miserable.* | *The poor miserable animals were starving, dirty, and wet.* | *All the staff seemed to look miserable and the atmosphere was not at all pleasant.*

depressed /dɪˈprest/ [adj not before noun] very unhappy for a long time, and feeling that your life will never get any better: *Her husband's been very depressed since he lost his job.*
+about *Gretta gets depressed about her weight.*

> ⚠ **Depressed** can also be used about someone who is suffering from a serious medical condition in which they feel so unhappy that they cannot lead a normal life.

feeling sorry for yourself /ˌfiːlɪŋ ˈsɒri fəʳ jɔːʳˈself‖-ˈsɑːri-/ ESPECIALLY SPOKEN spending all your time thinking about how unlucky you are or how unfairly you have been treated, and not doing anything to improve the situation: *You've got to stop feeling sorry for yourself and try to find a job.*

homesick /ˈhəʊmˌsɪk/ [adj] unhappy because you are a long way from your home, your family, and your friends, and you wish you were back there: *My sister was very homesick when she first went to college.*

2 unhappy because someone has been unkind to you

upset /ʌpˈset/ [adj not before noun] unhappy because someone has been unkind to you, so that you want to cry: *She's upset because Dan didn't invite her to his party.*
get upset (about) *It was an awful thing for him to say, but there's no point in getting upset about it.*
+that *She was very upset that Matthew hadn't told her he was leaving.*

hurt /hɜːʳt/ [adj not before noun] upset and shocked because someone has been unkind to you, especially someone that you trusted and thought was a friend: *Bill felt very hurt when he realized she had lied to him.*

deeply hurt (=extremely hurt) *Jackson was said to be 'deeply hurt' by the newspaper reports about him.*

offended /əˈfendɪd/ [adj not before noun] upset and angry because you think someone has treated you rudely or without respect: *She'll be offended if you don't thank her for her help.*
get offended *He gets very offended if you criticize his work.*

3 something that makes you feel sad

sad /sæd/ [adj usually before noun] use this about a story, piece of music, period of time etc that makes you feel sad
sad time/day/moment/occasion etc *The day her son left home was one of the saddest days of her life.*
sad news / story / song / film etc *Fairuz sang a sad song that made us all homesick.* | *I don't like movies with sad endings.*
it is sad that *It's very sad that she died before her children grew up.*
sad – sadder – saddest

unhappy /ʌnˈhæpi/ [adj] not happy because you are in a difficult or unpleasant situation that you do not enjoy at all
unhappy childhood/marriage/year etc *Phil was married for three unhappy years.* | *That photo always brings back unhappy memories.* | *an unhappy love affair*
unhappy – unhappier – unhappiest

depressing /dɪˈpresɪŋ/ [adj] a **depressing** experience, story, place, piece of news etc makes you feel that there is nothing to be happy about and not much hope for the future: *What a depressing novel!* | *It's such a depressing town – there's nothing to do here!* | *the depressing news that violent crime has increased again*

⚠ Don't say **depressive** when you mean **depressing**. **Depressive** is a technical word used to describe the mental illness of depression.

upsetting /ʌpˈsetɪŋ/ [adj] an **upsetting** experience or event has a strong emotional effect on you, and makes you want to cry: *She can't talk about*

her son's death – she finds it too upsetting. | *Being burgled can be a very upsetting experience.*

4 to make someone sad

make sb sad/make sb unhappy /ˌmeɪk (sb) ˈsæd, ˌmeɪk (sb) ʌnˈhæpi/ *Something at school is making her unhappy, but she won't talk about it.* | *It made me sad to see her looking so old and ill.*

upset /ʌpˈset/ [v T] if something **upsets** you, it makes you feel as if you want to cry, especially because someone has been unkind to you or because you have had a very unpleasant experience: *I'm sorry if I upset you – I didn't mean to.*
it upsets sb to see/hear/think sth *Her parents got divorced when she was 10, and it still upsets her to think about it.*
upsetting – upset – have upset

hurt /hɜːʳt/ [v T] to make someone feel upset by being unkind to them or not thinking enough about their feelings, especially someone who trusts you and thinks you are their friend: *I would never do anything to hurt her.*
hurt sb's feelings *I didn't really like her boyfriend, but I couldn't tell her that – I didn't want to hurt her feelings.*
it hurts sb to see/hear/learn etc *It hurt me to think that Jane had lied to me.*
hurting – hurt – have hurt

get sb down /ˌget (sb) ˈdaʊn/ [phrasal verb T] INFORMAL if something **gets you down**, it makes you feel unhappy and tired because it has continued for too long: *I know it's a boring job, but don't let it get you down.* | *The endless rain was beginning to get him down.*

5 a sad feeling

sadness /ˈsædnɪs/ [n U] a sad feeling, especially when a happy time is ending, or when you feel sorry about someone else's unhappiness: *Her eyes were full of sadness.*
with (great) sadness *I remembered with great sadness all the friends I had left behind.*

unhappiness /ʌnˈhæpinɪs/ [n U] the unhappy feeling you have when you are in a very difficult or unpleasant situation: *After years of unhappiness, she finally decided to leave him.*

grief /griːf/ [n U] ESPECIALLY WRITTEN great sadness that you feel when someone that you love has died: *He was overcome with grief when his wife died.*

depression /dɪ'preʃən/ [n U] a mental illness that makes someone feel so unhappy that they have no energy or hope for the future, and they cannot live a normal life

severe depression *My father had suffered from severe depression for many years.*

6 to make someone feel less sad

cheer sb up /ˌtʃɪəʳ (sb) 'ʌp/ [phrasal verb T] to make someone feel happier when they are disappointed or sad about something: *She failed her test, so I'm taking her out to cheer her up.*

comfort /'kʌmfəʳt/ [v T] ESPECIALLY WRITTEN to make someone feel less upset by being kind to them and telling them not to worry: *Bill stroked her hair gently, trying to comfort her.* | *We did our best to comfort him, but he was obviously very upset.*

cheer up /ˌtʃɪər 'ʌp/ SPOKEN say this to tell someone to stop feeling disappointed or sad and try to be more cheerful: *Cheer up, Phil! It's only a game, and you can't win every time.*

it's all right/it's OK /ɪts 'ɔːl raɪt, ɪts 'əʊkeɪ/ SPOKEN say this to make someone feel calmer or make them stop crying, when they are very upset and worried about something: *It's all right, honey, I'm here now.*

SAFE

➡ opposite **DANGEROUS**
➡ see also **RISK**

1 when you are not in danger

safe /seɪf/ [adj not before noun] not in danger of being harmed or attacked: *Will she be safe in the house on her own?* | *I feel safer in London than I do in New York.*

+from *The ants live in underground*

nests where they are safe from birds and lizards.

safe and sound (=safe and unharmed after being in danger) *We're praying that she will come back safe and sound.*

safely /'seɪfli/ [adv] without being harmed: *Did you get home safely last night?* | *The pilot managed to land the plane safely.*

safety /'seɪfti/ [n U] when you are safe from danger, harm, or accidents: *I worry about the children's safety if they are late home from school.*

in safety (=without any danger) *From behind a glass screen, we could watch the experiment in complete safety.*

for your own safety (=in order to make sure you are safe) *Embassy staff were advised to leave the country for their own safety.*

> ⚠ **Safety** is a noun, not an adjective. Use **safe** (not 'safety') in sentences like this: *She's a very safe driver.* | *We always feel safe here.*

be out of danger /biː ˌaʊt əv 'deɪndʒəʳ/ to be safe, after being in danger of dying or of being harmed or attacked: *The patient is out of danger, but he's still very weak.* | *We're not out of danger yet – they're still following us.*

2 something that will not cause harm

safe /seɪf/ [adj] not likely to cause any injury or harm: *That bridge doesn't look very safe.* | *a safe driver* (=someone who drives carefully and does not cause accidents)

it is safe to do sth *Is it safe to swim in the water here?*

+for *We want the streets to be safe for our children.*

safely [adv] *The nuclear waste is safely buried in the deepest part of the ocean.*

harmless /'hɑːʳmləs/ [adj] an animal or chemical that is **harmless** will not harm or injure anyone, even though it may seem dangerous: *Our dog makes a lot of noise, but he's perfectly harmless.* | *Barnes claims that cannabis is a relatively harmless drug.*

3 when something will not get lost, stolen, or damaged

safe /seɪf/ [adj] Your money will be safer in the bank.
in a safe place Keep your keys in a safe place.
it is safe to do sth Would it be safer to park my car in the driveway?
keep sth safe Leave your necklace with me – I'll keep it safe.

secure /sɪˈkjʊəʳ/ [adj] safe, especially from thieves or other criminals: Make sure the building is completely secure before you leave. | If your password is known by other people, your data may not be secure.
+from Doors to restricted areas should be kept secure from unauthorized entry.

4 a place where someone or something is safe

safety /ˈseɪfti/ [n U] a place where you are safe from danger: By the time the men reached safety, they were exhausted and half starved.
in/to/from the safety of sth She rushed back to the safety of her own house.
carry/lead/take sb to safety The firefighters carried the children to safety.

refuge /ˈrefjuːdʒ/ [n C/U] a place that you go to in order to escape from a dangerous or unpleasant situation
+from The basement provided us with a refuge from the fighting.
take refuge (=go somewhere that is safe) During the flooding, people took refuge in the hills.
seek refuge from sth (=try to find a safe place, to escape from a dangerous situation) Thousands of families came here seeking refuge from the civil war.

> **Formal or informal?**
> **Refuge** is not used in informal conversation.

out of harm's way /aʊt əv ˌhɑːʳmz ˈweɪ/ if someone or something is **out of harm's way**, they are in a place where they cannot be hurt or damaged: Keep all medicines out of harm's way, where children cannot reach them. | She put the glass vases on the top shelf, out of harm's way.

5 things done to make people and places safer

security /sɪˈkjʊərɪti/ [n U] things that are done to make sure that someone does not get attacked or robbed: They need to improve security here – anyone could just walk in.
tight security (=very careful security) There is tight security at the airport and all baggage is being searched.

> ⚠ You can also use **security** before a noun, like an adjective: Strict security measures were in force during the President's visit. | a security guard (=someone whose job is to protect a person or building)

safety /ˈseɪfti/ [n U] ways of preventing dangerous accidents: the importance of safety in the workplace
road safety (=rules and methods for using roads safely) The children are all given advice on road safety.

> ⚠ You can also use **safety** before a noun, like an adjective: Unless safety standards are improved, there could be a major accident. | Read the safety instructions first.

SAME

➡ if you mean 'have the same score as another team', go to **SPORT 10**
➡ look here for ...
  • the same thing or person
  • similar to another thing or person
➡ see also **DIFFERENT, ANOTHER, CONTINUE 3**

> ⚠ **The same** can be used in two different ways. Compare these sentences: She's so rich, she never wears the same dress twice (=when you are talking about one dress). | I saw someone wearing the same dress as me (=when you are talking about two dresses that look the same).

1 the same one

the same /ðə 'seɪm/ [adj only before noun] the same place, person, or thing, not a different one: *My friend and I went to the same school.* | *They are both in love with the same woman.*
the same ... as *She was born on the same day as me.* | *I was staying in the same hotel as Bill Clinton. Can you believe it!*

 Don't use 'same' on its own. Always say **the same**.

 Don't say 'the same with' or 'the same like'. Say **the same as**.

2 exactly like another one

the same /ðə 'seɪm/ [adj] the same as another thing, place, situation etc: *They were both wearing the same shoes.*
look/sound/taste etc the same *The houses here all look the same.*
just the same/exactly the same (=not different in any way) *I tried three different types of wine, but they all tasted just the same to me.*
the same ... as *They were doing the same jobs as the men, but being paid less.*
do the same *We've opened up stores in the UK and we hope to do the same in the rest of Europe.*
◯ **it's the same** SPOKEN (=say this when you mean that another situation is the same) *"We always get up late on Saturdays." "It's the same in our house."*

 Don't use 'same' on its own. Always say **the same**.

 Don't say 'the same like' or 'the same with'. Say **the same as**.

just like/exactly like /'dʒʌst laɪk, ɪg'zæktli laɪk/ if someone or something is **just like** or **exactly like** someone or something else, there is very little difference between them: *Clare looks just like her mother.* | *This song sounds exactly like that one by The Beatles.*

identical /aɪ'dentɪkəl/ [adj] two or more things that are **identical** are exactly the same in every way: *To me the two patterns looked identical.*
+to *The picture is identical to the one in the Museum of Modern Art in New York.*

◯ **can't tell the difference** /ˌkɑːnt tel ðə 'dɪfərəns‖ˌkænt-/ ESPECIALLY SPOKEN if you **can't tell the difference** between two things or people, they seem exactly the same to you: *The twins were so alike that I really couldn't tell the difference.*
+between *People who are colour-blind can't tell the difference between red and green.*

be no different from sth /biː nəʊ 'dɪfərənt frɒm (stʰ)/ use this especially when you expect something or someone to be different from another thing or person, but in fact they are the same: *People think that movie stars are so special, but really they're no different from anybody else.* | *Life on the island is no different from life on the mainland.*

3 the same height/age/amount etc

the same /ðə 'seɪm/ [adj only before noun] *Both stores are charging the same price for CD players.*
the same height/age etc as *Her sister is the same age as me.*
exactly the same *We're both exactly the same height.*

 Don't use 'same' on its own. Always say **the same**.

 Don't say 'the same with' or 'the same like'. Say **the same as**.

be as old/long/strong etc as /biː əz (old etc) əz/ to be the same age, length etc as someone or something else: *At 14, Richard was already as tall as his father.*

equal /'iːkwəl/ [adj] two or more amounts, totals, levels etc that are **equal** are the same as each other: *Try*

to spend an equal amount of time on each question in the test.
+to *A pint is equal to about half a litre.*

equally /ˈiːkwəli/ [*adv*]
equally good/bad/difficult etc (=as good, bad etc as something else) *Both schools seem equally good.*
divide/share sth equally (=so that everyone has the same amount) *The money was divided equally between their three children.*

4 the same as before

the same /ðə ˈseɪm/ [*adj*] *I hadn't seen John for ages, but he was still the same.*
the same as ever *School's the same as ever – too much work and not enough time to do what I really want!*
just the same/exactly the same (=not changed in any way) *We went to the office Christmas party, but it was just the same as last year's.*

hasn't changed /ˌhæzənt ˈtʃeɪndʒd/ ESPECIALLY SPOKEN if someone or something **hasn't changed**, they are the same as they were before, even though you have not seen them for a long time: *I went back to my old school and it hadn't changed.*
hasn't changed at all (also **hasn't changed a bit** BRITISH) *He hasn't changed at all – he's still crazy about football.*

5 always the same

stay the same /ˌsteɪ ðə ˈseɪm/ to continue to be the same and not change: *Tamara lived in a government apartment, and the rent stayed the same for five years.*

constant /ˈkɒnstənt‖ˈkɑːn-/ [*adj*] an amount, temperature, speed etc that is **constant**, stays the same and does not change: *The number of deaths from road accidents has remained constant over the last five years. | It is important to store wine at a constant temperature.*

Formal or informal?
Constant is often used in scientific writing.

6 similar to someone or something else

like /laɪk/ [*preposition*] similar to or almost the same as something or someone else: *It has teeth like sharp knives.*
be like *The houses here are like the ones in Northern France. | I can't describe the taste – it was like vanilla but not quite.*
look/sound/feel etc like *It looks and tastes like meat, but it's actually made from vegetable protein. | What lovely material – it feels like velvet.*

similar /ˈsɪmələ(r), ˈsɪmɪlə(r)/ [*adj*] if one thing is **similar** to another, or if two or more things are **similar**, they are like each other but not exactly the same: *We have similar tastes in music.*
+to *The cars have blue flashing lights on the roof, very similar to police cars.*
similar in size/appearance/style etc *The two dresses were similar in style.*

alike /əˈlaɪk/ [*adv*] if two people are **alike**, they look like each other or they have a similar character: *My mother and I are very alike.*
look alike *A lot of couples look alike.*

remind you of sb/sth /rɪˈmaɪnd juː ɒv (sb/sth)‖-ɑːv-/ [*phrasal verb* T] to be similar to another person, thing, or event, and make you think of them: *My brother really reminds me of my father sometimes. | The restaurant reminded her of one she used to go to in Paris.*

take after sb /ˈteɪk ɑːftə(r) (sb)‖-æf-/ [*phrasal verb* T] to be like your mother, father, grandmother etc, because you look like them or you have a similar character, similar abilities etc: *Neil takes after his father. | Jennie's good at languages. She takes after her grandmother in that way.*

have a lot in common /hæv ə ˌlɒt ɪn ˈkɒmən‖-ˌlɑːt ɪn ˈkɑːmən/ if two or more people **have a lot in common,** they have the same interests, opinions, experiences etc, so they are likely to have a good relationship: *You'll like Paul. I think the two of you have a lot in common.*
+with *I had nothing in common with her, and didn't know what to talk about.*

7 ways in which people or things are similar

similarity /ˌsɪmɪ̩ˈlærɪ̩ti/ [n C/U] a way in which people, things, or events are similar
+between *Detectives said there were similarities between the two murders.*
+with/to *The English language has certain similarities with German.*
striking similarity (=one that is very easy to notice) *There are some striking similarities between the two stories.*
plural **similarities**

resemblance /rɪˈzembləns/ [n C/U] ESPECIALLY WRITTEN if there is a **resemblance** between two people or things, they look like each other
+between *The resemblance between him and Andy was remarkable.*
bear a strong/striking/close resemblance to ESPECIALLY WRITTEN (=look very like someone or something else) *The two paintings bore a striking resemblance to each other.*

SATISFIED/ DISSATISFIED

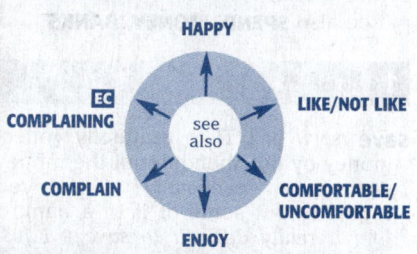

HAPPY

EC COMPLAINING

LIKE/NOT LIKE

see also

COMPLAIN

COMFORTABLE/ UNCOMFORTABLE

ENJOY

1 when you think that something is good enough

satisfied /ˈsætɪ̩sfaɪd/ [adj] how you feel when you think that something is as good as it should be, for example someone's work or something you buy: *I did the whole essay again, but she still wasn't satisfied.*
+with *His boss seems satisfied with his work.* | *95% of passengers say they are satisfied with the bus service.*

 Don't say 'I'm satisfied of it'. Say **I'm satisfied with it**.

be happy with sth /biː ˈhæpi wɪð (sth)/ to be satisfied with a situation, decision, or arrangement: *The doctor said he was happy with the way the operation had gone.*
be perfectly happy with sth *Until now she·seemed perfectly happy with the arrangement.*

Formal or informal?
Be happy with sth is less formal than **satisfied**.

satisfactory /ˌsætɪ̩sˈfæktəriˑ/ [adj] FORMAL something that is **satisfactory** is good enough because it is of a high enough standard or it gives you what you need: *You can only take the advanced class if your work is of a satisfactory standard.* | *I wrote and complained, but I still haven't had a satisfactory answer.*

pleased /pliːzd/ [adj] how you feel when you think something is very good and you feel very satisfied with it: *Were you pleased when you saw the results?*
+with *Tom's teacher was pleased with his progress, and gave him an 'A' on his report card.* | *"How's your new car?" "It's great – I'm really pleased with it."*

2 when you have what you want in your life, your job etc

satisfied/happy /ˈsætɪ̩sfaɪd, ˈhæpi/ [adj not before noun] happy because you have what you want and you do not want anything more or anything different
+with *I'd be quite happy with a part-time job, so long as the money's OK.* | *I don't really want a bigger house – I'm satisfied with what I have.*
keep sb satisfied/happy *They have to make bigger and bigger profits to keep the bosses happy.*

Formal or informal?
Happy is more informal and more common in spoken English than **satisfied**.

content /kən'tent/ [adj not before noun] ESPECIALLY WRITTEN happy and satisfied with everything in your life, so that you do not want to change anything
+with Although Lawrence was poor, he was basically content with life.
content to do sth At present he seems content to just sit at home and watch TV.

3 the feeling you have when you are satisfied

satisfaction /ˌsætɪs'fækʃən/ [n U] the feeling of being satisfied, especially because you have achieved something good or useful: She finished her essay, and read it through with satisfaction.
get satisfaction from sth He enjoys coaching the hockey team, and gets a lot of satisfaction from it.
express satisfaction FORMAL (=say you are satisfied) Most users have expressed satisfaction with the new system.

4 not satisfied

not satisfied / dissatisfied /nɒt 'sætɪsfaɪd, dɪ'sætɪsfaɪd/ how you feel when something is not as good as you want it to be or expect it to be: The Arsenal coach was not entirely satisfied with his team's performance against Chelsea.
+with The teacher told James that she wasn't satisfied with his work. | Paul had become increasingly dissatisfied with his job and his marriage.

> **Formal or informal?**
> **Dissatisfied** is more formal than **not satisfied**.

not be happy with sth /nɒt biː 'hæpi wɪð (sth)/ to feel dissatisfied or disappointed because something has not been done well enough, or because you have not achieved what you wanted: If you are not happy with the service that you get from your bank, you should consider moving your account.

> **Formal or informal?**
> **Not be happy with sth** is less formal than **not satisfied**.

5 the feeling you have when you are not satisfied

dissatisfaction /dɪˌsætɪs'fækʃən/ the feeling you have when you are not satisfied: Teaching standards are low and there is widespread dissatisfaction among the students.
+with Opinion polls show increasing dissatisfaction with the way the country is being governed.

> **Formal or informal?**
> **Dissatisfaction** is used especially in formal writing and news reports.

SAVE

➡ look here for ...
  • to save money
  • to save someone from a dangerous situation
  • to keep something so that you can use it later
➡ see also **SPEND, MONEY, BANKS**

1 to save money

save /seɪv/ [v I/T] to gradually collect money by not spending all the money you have, especially when you regularly put some of it in a bank: I find it really difficult to save – I just spend everything I get.
save money/£500/$400 etc He's managed to save $800 so far. | I try to save a little money each month.
+for She starts saving for Christmas in the middle of July!

save up /ˌseɪv 'ʌp/ [phrasal verb I/T] to save money in order to buy something or do something special: I'm trying to save up enough money to buy a computer.
save up to do sth We're saving up to go to the Caribbean next year.
+for If you want a new bike, you'll have to save up for it.

savings /'seɪvɪŋz/ [n plural] the money that you have saved: *I'm paying for my Spanish classes out of my savings.*
life savings (=all the money you have saved in your life) *My parents spent their life savings on a retirement home in Florida.*

2 to save someone from danger or from an unpleasant situation

➡ see also **FIRE, ACCIDENT**

save /seɪv/ [v T] to prevent someone from being killed or badly hurt: *He almost fell off the cliff, but she put out her arm and saved him.*
save sb from sth *His cycling helmet saved him from serious injury.*
save sb from doing sth *A lifeguard dived into the pool and saved her from drowning.*
save sb's life *Wearing a seat belt can save your life.*
rescue /'reskjuː/ [v T] if you **rescue** someone, you take them away from a dangerous situation, so that they do not get killed or badly hurt: *Paramedics and firefighters worked for hours to rescue people who were trapped in the bus.*
rescue sb from sth *The couple were rescued from the burning building by neighbours.*

3 to save something to use later

save/keep /seɪv, kiːp/ [v T] to keep something and not use it now, so that you can use it later: *Save some of the cheese to sprinkle on top of the dish.*
save/keep sth for sth *He got out the bottle of champagne that he'd been saving for this occasion.*
save/keep sth for later *We can keep the rest of the food for later.*
keeping – kept – have kept

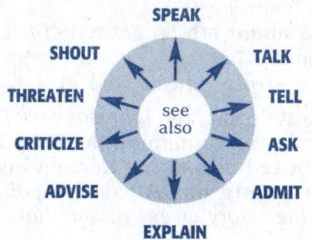

SAY

SPEAK

SHOUT   TALK

THREATEN   TELL

see
also

CRITICIZE   ASK

ADVISE   ADMIT

EXPLAIN

> ⚠ Don't confuse **say**, **tell**, **talk**, and **speak**. You **say** words to someone. You **tell** someone facts or information about something. You **talk** to someone about a subject. You **speak** (=you say words) or you **speak** a language.

1 to say something

say /seɪ/ [v I/T] to say something using spoken or written words: *"I must be going," she said.* | *"Where's Pam going?" "I don't know. She didn't say."*
+(that) *James wrote to the bank and said we needed a loan.* | *It says in today's paper that gas prices are going up again.*
say what/where/why etc *The doctor didn't say how long the operation would take.*
say hello/sorry/yes etc (to sb) *Lauren came over to say goodbye to us.* | *I asked Dad if he'd lend me some money, but he said no.*
say sth to sb *What did you say to her?*
saying – said – have said

> ⚠ Don't say 'say someone that ...'. Say **say that ...** or **tell someone that ...**: *She said that she was going home.* | *She told me that she was going home.*

> ⚠ **Say**, not 'tell', is the word most commonly used when reporting someone's actual words: *"I'm going home," she said.*

tell /tel/ [v T] to give someone information, using spoken or written words
tell sb (that) *Rosie told me that she might be late.*

S

tell sb sth *He refused to tell me his name.*

tell sb who/what/where etc *There are signs telling you where the exits are.*

tell sb about sth *Sit down and tell me all about it.*

telling – told – have told

point out /ˌpɔɪnt ˈaʊt/ [*phrasal verb* T] to tell someone something that they had not noticed or had not thought about **as sb points out** *As Sharon pointed out, the story was rather hard to believe.*

point out sth *Barnett pointed out several practical problems with the idea.*

+that *It's worth pointing out that very few people ever die of this disease.*

mention /ˈmenʃən/ [*v* T] to talk about someone or something, but without giving details or saying very much about them: *He mentioned something about a party, but he didn't say when it was.* | *When I mentioned her name, he looked embarrassed.*

+(that) *I forgot to mention that I won't be in tomorrow.*

> ⚠ Don't say 'mention about something'.
> Say **mention something**.

add /æd/ [*v* T] to say something more, after what has already been said or written: *Is there anything you'd like to add, Peter?* | *"Finally," she added, "I would like to thank my family for their support."*

+that *I should add that I do not agree with Dr Mitchell.*

put it /ˈpʊt ɪt/ to express an idea in a particular way, choosing your words carefully to explain what you mean simply and clearly: *When they looked at him blankly, he tried to put it another way.*

🗨 put it this way SPOKEN (use this when you are trying to say something in the clearest possible way) *Put it this way: if we don't make a profit, we're out of a job.*

express /ɪkˈspres/ [*v* T] to let someone know your feelings, by putting them into words: *Ollie found it hard to express his feelings.*

express concern/satisfaction/annoyance etc (=say that you are worried, satisfied etc) *Many people wrote to her to express their sympathy.*

express concern etc about sth *Parents have expressed concern about the amount of violence in some children's shows.*

express yourself (=make people understand what you are thinking or feeling) *Young children often find it difficult to express themselves in words.*

> **Formal or informal?**
> **Express** is not used in informal conversation.

2 publicly or officially

say /seɪ/ [*v* T] to say something publicly or officially, using spoken or written words

+(that) *The President said he had no intention of resigning.* | *The sports club rules say that sports shoes must be worn in the gym at all times.*

say what/how/who/when etc *Did they say who will take over as Chairman?*

saying – said – have said

announce /əˈnaʊns/ [*v* T] to officially tell people what has happened or what will happen, in a written or spoken public statement: *The company announced profits of $400 million.*

+(that) *The Prime Minister has just announced there is to be a General Election next month.*

state /steɪt/ [*v* T] FORMAL to say something publicly or officially in clear, definite language

+that *The law states that you are innocent until proved guilty.* | *Justice Cohen stated clearly that no further action would be taken.*

confirm /kənˈfɜːrm/ [*v* T] if you **confirm** something that other people have already said is true, you say publicly that it is definitely true: *Mr Eastwood refused to confirm or deny the rumour.*

+that *Police have confirmed that they are questioning a woman about the murder.*

make a statement /ˌmeɪk ə ˈsteɪtmənt/ say or write something publicly in order to tell people what you intend to do, what your opinion is etc – use this about politicians, business leaders, and other important people: *The President is expected to make a statement on the crisis later this afternoon.*

3   quietly or unclearly

whisper /ˈwɪspəʳ/ [v T] to say something very quietly, using your breath rather than your voice: *"Don't wake the baby," whispered Cecilia.* | *Fran whispered something in her sister's ear.*

mutter /ˈmʌtəʳ/ [v T] to say something quietly, especially when you are annoyed but do not want someone else to hear you complaining: *"Why do I have to do all the work?" she muttered.* | *Grant muttered something about having to see a client.*

mumble /ˈmʌmbəl/ [v T] to say something quietly without pronouncing the words clearly, so that it is difficult to understand: *He mumbled something I didn't hear.* | *Kaye mumbled an apology.*

4   in an indirect way

imply /ɪmˈplaɪ/ [v T] to say one thing which seems to show that another thing is true, but without saying the other thing directly
+(that) *Michael did imply that I could have the job if I wanted it.* | *The article implied that unemployed people are lazy.*
implying – implied – have implied

suggest /səˈdʒest‖səg-/ [v T] to say something in an indirect way, especially something bad that you prefer not to say directly: *What are you suggesting? Do you think I'm a thief?*
+(that) *His letter seemed to suggest that he wasn't satisfied with my work.*

hint /hɪnt/ [v I/T] to say something in a very indirect way, but so that other people can guess what you really

mean
+(that) *Ralston hinted that the painting might be a fake.*
+at *The President hinted at the possibility of military action.*

hint [n C] something that you say in a very indirect way, but so that other people can guess what you really mean
drop a hint (=say something very indirectly) *He kept dropping hints about what he wanted for Christmas.*

5   to say that something is definitely true or not true

claim /kleɪm/ [v T] to say that something is true, even though it has not been proved and people may not believe it
+(that) *Martin claimed that he was with friends at the time of his wife's murder.*
claim to be/do sth *Doctors claim to have discovered a cure for the disease.*

swear /sweəʳ/ [v T] to say very strongly that something is definitely true
swear (that) *Vic swears he saw a ghost standing at the end of his bed.* | *Una swore that she hadn't stolen the money.*
swearing – swore – have sworn

deny /dɪˈnaɪ/ [v T] to say that you have not done something bad that people say you have done: *Bowlam denies all charges of selling drugs to children.*
+(that) *Muller denied that he was driving the car at the time of the crash.*
deny doing sth *Joanna denied ever having lied to me.*
flatly/categorically deny (=deny very strongly) *Leeman categorically denied any involvement in the robbery.*
denying – denied – have denied

> ⚠ Don't confuse **deny** (=say you have not done something) and **refuse** (=say you will not do something): *He denied that he had given her the gun.* | *He refused to give her the gun.*

S

S

insist /ɪn'sɪst/ [v T] to keep saying that something is true, especially when a lot of people say it is not true
+(that) *Barker insisted that he was the legal owner of the car.* | *Miller insisted he had never had an affair with the actress.*

6 to say that someone has done something bad or illegal

accuse /ə'kjuːz/ [v T] to say or write that someone is guilty of a crime or of doing something bad
accuse sb of doing sth *Are you accusing me of cheating?*
accuse sb of sth *The article accused the company of sex discrimination.*
accusation /ˌækjʊ'zeɪʃən/ [n C] a statement saying that someone is guilty of a crime or of doing something bad
make an accusation *You can't go around making accusations without proof.*
+of *There have been accusations of racism in the Los Angeles police department.*
+against *The accusations against Dr Jones were found to be false.*
allege /ə'ledʒ/ [v T] to say publicly that someone has done something bad or illegal, even though this has not been proved
+(that) *Mrs Taylor alleges that she lost her job because she was pregnant.*
be alleged to have done sth *He was alleged to have planted a bomb in the parliament building.*
the alleged murderer/rapist/attacker etc (=the person someone alleges is a murderer etc) *The alleged terrorists are in the custody of the German police.*

 Allege is used especially in news reports.

allegation /ˌælɪ'geɪʃən/ [n C usually plural] a public statement saying that someone has done something bad or illegal, but giving no proof
make an allegation *He has made*

some serious allegations concerning the company's financial dealings.
+of *There were allegations of corruption in the police department.*
+about *allegations about the senator's private life*
+that *The newspaper printed allegations that politicians had been accepting bribes.*
deny an allegation (=say it is false) *Weimar denied allegations of financial mismanagement.*

 Allegation is used especially in news reports.

say /seɪ/ [v T] ESPECIALLY SPOKEN to say or write that someone has done something bad or illegal
+(that) *Are you saying I'm a liar?* | *His ex-wife says that he used to beat her.*
saying – said – have said

7 to say something again

repeat /rɪ'piːt/ [v T] to say something again, for example because someone did not hear you or understand you: *Could you please repeat the question?*
+that *She repeated that anyone who really needed help would get it.*
repeat yourself (=say something again, without realizing it) *Have I told you this before? Please stop me if I'm repeating myself.*
say sth again /ˌseɪ (sth) ə'gen/ ESPECIALLY SPOKEN to say something again, either because someone did not hear you or because you want to emphasize it: *Sorry, would you say that again?* | *I've said it before and I'll say it again: I never trusted that man.*

8 how you ask someone to say something again

sorry?/pardon? (also **excuse me?** AMERICAN) /'sɒri, 'pɑːrdn, ɪk'skjuːz miːll'sɑːri, 'sɔːri/ SPOKEN say this when you want to ask someone politely to repeat what they just said because you did not hear it: *"It's hot today, isn't it?" "Pardon?"*

what?/what did you say? /wɒt, ˌwɒt dɪd juː 'seɪ/ SPOKEN INFORMAL say this when you did not hear what someone said, or when you are surprised by what they said: *"Are you going to the bar?" "What? Oh, yes, I suppose so."* | *"Oh shut up!" "What did you say?"*

⚠ Some people think it is rude to say **what?**

9 to say something that someone else has said

quote /kwəʊt/ [v I/T] to repeat exactly something that someone else has said or written, especially someone famous: *He was always quoting clever sayings from Oscar Wilde's plays.*
+from *Let me quote from the report: "6000 children die each day from curable diseases."* | *Phil can quote from any Shakespeare play you mention.*

quotation /kwəʊˈteɪʃən/ [n C] a sentence or phrase from a book, poem etc, which you repeat because it is interesting or funny, or because it supports what you are saying
+from *Spencer began his speech with a quotation from Karl Marx.*

10 to say what will happen in the future

predict /prɪˈdɪkt/ [v T] to say what you think will happen in the future: *Most of the papers are predicting an easy victory for the Dallas Cowboys.* | *a major earthquake that no-one had predicted*
+that *Some experts predict that the Earth's temperature will rise by as much as 5°C over the next 20 years.*
predict what/whether/how etc *Even experts cannot predict what the stock market will do tomorrow.*

prediction /prɪˈdɪkʃən/ [n C] a statement saying what you think will happen in the future: *Despite their confident predictions, sales of the new car have not been very good.*
make a prediction *It's too early to make any predictions about the election results.*

forecast /ˈfɔːˈkɑːst‖-kæst/ [v T] to publicly say what will happen in the future with the weather or with the

economic or political situation, especially when you have special or technical knowledge: *Economists are forecasting a rise in unemployment.*
forecast rain/fine weather/snow etc *Rain is forecast for southern England tomorrow.*
+that *Hardly anyone had forecast that the drought would last so long.*
forecasting – forecast (or forecasted) – have forecast (or have forecasted)

forecast /ˈfɔːˈkɑːst‖-kæst/ [n C] a public statement saying what is likely to happen with the weather or with the economic or political situation, based on special or technical knowledge
the weather forecast (=a statement in a newspaper, or on the TV or radio, saying what the weather will be like during the next few days) *According to the weather forecast, it's going to stay hot for the rest of the week.*
give/make a forecast *It is impossible to give an accurate forecast of company sales 10 years from now.*
sales/earnings/growth etc forecast *the company's annual sales forecast*

11 something that someone says

remark /rɪˈmɑːˈk/ [n C] something that you say, for example an opinion or something you have noticed: *I ignored his rude remarks about my clothes.*
make a remark (=say something) *Mr Hill made a few remarks about the weather.*

comment /ˈkɒment‖ˈkɑː-/ [n C/U] something that you say or write, especially to give an opinion or explanation: *OK, does anyone have any comments?*
+on/about *She had written some useful comments on my essay.*
make a comment *Jill made some interesting comments about the movie.*
🗪 **no comment** SPOKEN (=used by politicians, business leaders etc when they do not want to publicly answer a question) *"What is your view of the affair, Prime Minister?" "No comment."*

🗪 **thing to say** /θɪŋ tə ˈseɪ/ ESPECIALLY SPOKEN **a strange/stupid/horrible etc thing to say** a remark that is strange, stupid etc: *What an awful thing to say about your mother!* | *It was a silly thing to say.*

point /pɔɪnt/ [n C] something that you say, which people had not thought about or discussed until you mentioned it: *That's a good point, and we should take it into consideration.*

make a point (=say something in a discussion, which people had not thought of before) *Marks made the point that far more people died from smoking tobacco than from taking drugs.*

prove a point (=show that what you say is right) *These examples help to prove my point.*

announcement /ə'naʊnsmənt/ [n C] a public or official statement telling people what has happened or what will happen: *The announcement was heard by millions of radio listeners this morning.*

+of/about *I read the announcement of her death.*

make an announcement *The principal made an announcement.*

statement /'steɪtmənt/ [n C] something that someone says or writes publicly in order to tell people what they intend to do, what their opinion is etc: *In a statement, the BBC admitted that it had given incorrect information.*

make a statement (=say something publicly) *The President will make a statement to the press this afternoon.*

12 what people say about something

according to /ə'kɔːʳdɪŋ tuː/ use this to tell someone what someone else has said or written

according to John/my sister/the newspaper etc *According to the paper, 20 people died in the fire.* | *Rob's got a new girlfriend, according to Janine.*

they say/people say /ðeɪ 'seɪ, ˌpiːpəl 'seɪ/ SPOKEN use this to say what a lot of people believe and are talking about

+(that) *They say her husband's in prison.*

so they say (=when you are not sure whether something is true) *The test isn't difficult, or so they say.*

apparently /ə'pærəntli/ [adv] use this to say what you have read or been told, although you do not know about it yourself: *It's going to be hot this weekend, apparently.* | *Apparently, Jim's a really good tennis player.*

rumour BRITISH **rumor** AMERICAN /'ruːməʳ/ [n C/U] a story that is passed from one person to another among a lot of people, and which may or may not be true

+about *Have you heard the rumor about him and his secretary?*

+that *There are rumors that the band may be splitting up.*

spread a rumour (=tell other people a rumour) *Someone's been spreading nasty rumours about me.*

gossip /'ɡɒsɪp‖'ɡɑː-/ [n U] things people tell each other about other people's private lives, which may or may not be true: *I was eager to hear all the latest gossip.*

juicy gossip (=interesting gossip) *some juicy gossip about the neighbors*

> Don't say 'gossips'. **Gossip** is uncountable in this meaning.

13 not saying anything

➡ see also **QUIET**

silent /'saɪlənt/ [adj] ESPECIALLY WRITTEN not speaking: *She was silent for a moment as she tried to think.*

fall silent (=become silent) *The crowd fell silent as the President stood up to speak.*

> Use **silent** especially in stories or descriptions of events.

I didn't/don't know what to say /aɪ ˌdɪdnt, ˌdəʊnt nəʊ wɒt tə 'seɪ/ SPOKEN say this when you are suddenly surprised or embarrassed about something, and you cannot think of anything suitable to say: *I didn't know what to say. It was such a wonderful present.*

speechless /'spiːtʃləs/ [adj not before noun] unable to say anything because you are very angry, surprised, or upset: *Anna was speechless. She had never seen such luxury before.*

speechless with anger/rage/horror
etc *Laura stared at him, absolutely
speechless with rage.*

SECRET

**when only a few people know about
something, and they do not tell
anyone else**

➡ see also **PRIVATE, TELL, HIDE**

1 information/plans/places/ meetings

secret /'si:krₔt/ [*adj*] if something is
secret, not many people know about
it, and they agree not to tell anyone
else about it: *The tunnel had a secret
entrance.* | *The decision was made at a
secret meeting yesterday.*
top secret (=when an official document is very secret) *top secret plans
for a new fighter plane*
secretly [*adv*] without anyone else
knowing: *They were secretly married
last week.*

secret /'si:krₔt/ [*n* C] something that
you do not want other people to know
about: *Her exact age remained a
secret.*
○ **be a secret** ESPECIALLY SPOKEN *Don't
tell anyone. It's a secret.* | *The recipe is
a family secret.*
tell sb a secret *I'll tell you a secret if
you promise not to tell anyone else.*
keep a secret (=not tell anyone a
secret) *Can you keep a secret?*
state secret (=information that a
government keeps secret from other
countries) *Burgess was accused of giving away state secrets to the Russians.*

confidential /ˌkɒnfₔ'denʃₔl ‖ˌkɑːn-/ [*adj*]
confidential information is known
only by a few official people, and
must not be told to anyone else, for
example because it contains military
secrets or private details about
people: *We can't give out confidential
information about our patients.* |
confidential records on each employee
highly confidential (=very confidential) *This is a highly confidential
matter.*

confidentially [*adv*] *She spoke
confidentially to a reporter.*

> **Formal or informal?**
> **Confidential** is used in writing and in formal
> spoken English.

in secret /ɪn 'si:krₔt/ if you do
something **in secret**, you do it
secretly, especially because other
people do not want you to do it: *They
planned the attack in secret.* | *Church
services were held in secret, because
they were not officially allowed.*

in private /ɪn 'praɪvₔt/ if you talk to
someone or discuss something **in
private**, you do it where other people
cannot see you or hear you: *I'd like to
talk to you in private.* | *The judge
heard the case in private.*

undercover /ˌʌndəˈkʌvəʳ/ [*adj* only
before noun] working secretly – use
this about the activities of the police,
the army etc
**undercover agent/detective/police
officer** *The bomb was found by an
undercover detective.*
undercover operation/investigation
*Six drug smugglers were arrested after
an undercover police operation.*

2 thoughts/feelings

secret /'si:krₔt/ [*adj*] ESPECIALLY WRITTEN
secret thoughts and feelings are ones
that you do not tell anyone else
about: *Her secret ambition was to be a
dancer.* | *He kept a secret diary for
fifteen years.*
secretly [*adv*] *He was secretly ashamed
of his family.*

private /'praɪvₔt/ [*adj*] **private** thoughts
and feelings are about you, your fam-
ily, and your friends, and you do not
think other people should know about
them: *She wrote her most private
thoughts in a special diary.* | *I don't
want to discuss it with you – it's
private.*

3 to not tell other people about a secret

not tell sb /nɒt 'tel (sb)/ to not tell
someone about something: *I didn't tell
my parents in case they got worried.*

+about *Vinny didn't tell the police about his visit to Mahoney's apartment.*

+(that) *She didn't tell anyone she was leaving.*

keep sth secret /ˌkiːp (sth) ˈsiːkrᵻt/ to not tell other people something, because you want it to remain a secret: *They tried to keep their relationship secret.*

+from *Many of Stalin's actions were kept secret from the world until after his death.*

keep sth from sb /ˈkiːp (sth) frɒm (sb)/ [*phrasal verb* T] to deliberately not tell someone about something, especially because you think they would be upset if they knew the truth: *Edward never told anyone about his illness. He even tried to keep it from his wife.*

keep quiet /ˌkiːp ˈkwaɪət/ to deliberately not talk about something in public, especially something you are ashamed or embarrassed about:

+about *Roberts advised her to keep quiet about the affair.*

keep sth quiet (=keep something secret) *Some officials would have preferred to keep the incident quiet.*

SEE

➡ if you mean 'see someone doing something wrong', go to **CATCH 4**

➡ see also **WATCH, LOOK AT, NOTICE**

⚠ Don't confuse **see**, **watch**, and **look at**. When you **see** something, you notice it with your eyes, either deliberately or accidentally: *I saw an accident on my way to school today.* You **watch** films, sports games, or other situations where there is action and movement: *Dad was watching a basketball game on TV.* When you **look at** people, scenery, pictures, and other things that are not moving, you deliberately pay attention to them: *Look at this old picture of Sally!*

1 to see someone or something

see /siː/ [v T] *I saw your brother in town this morning.* | *Have you seen my pen anywhere?*

see sb doing sth *I saw Matt coming out of the cinema with Jane.*

see sb do sth *Did you see Jim leave?*

see who/what/where *It was too dark to see who the woman was.*

see (that) *I came out of the house and saw that my car was gone.*

can see sb/sth *Shh! I can see someone moving in the bushes.*

seeing – saw – have seen

⚠ When talking about the present, don't say 'I am seeing', 'are you seeing' etc. Say **I can see**, **can you see** etc.

catch sight of/catch a glimpse of /ˌkætʃ ˈsaɪt ɒv, ˌkætʃ ə ˈɡlɪmps ɒv/ ESPECIALLY WRITTEN to see someone or something for only a second, and not very clearly: *Rick caught sight of the driver's face as the car raced past.* | *Lynn caught a brief glimpse of herself in the mirror.*

see

She was blindfolded so she couldn't see.

She enjoyed looking at her friend's photographs.

He was watching television.

spot /spɒt‖spɑːt/ [v T] to suddenly see someone or something that you have been looking for, or something interesting or unusual: *Yates was spotted by police as he drove through the centre of Manchester.* | *I was just browsing through the job adverts when I spotted it.*
spotting – spotted – have spotted

witness /'wɪtn̩s/ [v T] to see something happen, especially an accident, a crime, or an important event: *Police are appealing for information from anyone who witnessed the attack.* | *The crash was witnessed by millions of viewers who were watching the race on TV.*

> **Formal or informal?**
> **Witness** is a more formal or official word than **see**, and is not usually used in normal conversation.

make out /ˌmeɪk 'aʊt/ [phrasal verb T] to see someone or something, but only with difficulty
make out sth *It was dark, and Patrick could just make out the shape of a woman in front of him.*
make out what/where/who *It was difficult to make out where the rocks ended and the sea began.*

2 something that you see

sight /saɪt/ [n C] something that you see: *Sunrise over the Himalayas is a magnificent sight.*
the sight of sth (=when you see something) *I can't stand the sight of blood.*
a familiar sight (=something that you often see) *Homeless kids are now a familiar sight on London's streets.*
the sights (=the interesting things for tourists to see in a place) *Klaus took me around Munich and showed me the sights.*
sights and sounds (=all the things you see and hear) *the sights and sounds of the forest*

view /vjuː/ [n C] the whole area that you see from somewhere, for example when you look out of a window or down from a hill and see a beautiful place

get/have a view (=be able to see all of it) *She had a great view from her window across the park.*
+of *a view of the sea*

scene /siːn/ [n C often plural] what you see in a place, especially when you are describing a place where something unusual or shocking is happening: *Reporters described the horrific scenes which followed the bombing.*
scenes of confusion/suffering/violence etc *There are scenes of confusion here as refugees pour out of the city.*

> ⚠ **Scene** is used in writing and news reports.

3 when something can be seen

visible /'vɪzɪ̩bəl/ [adj] ESPECIALLY WRITTEN if something is **visible**, it can be seen: *I examined the animal, but there were no visible signs of injury.*
clearly visible *The bullet-marks are still clearly visible in the walls.*
+to *Yellow jackets make cyclists more visible to drivers.*

in sight /ɪn 'saɪt/ if someone or something is **in sight**, you can see them from where you are: *The only building in sight was a small wooden cabin.* | *Meredith looked around – there was no one in sight.*

show /ʃəʊ/ [v I] if something **shows**, people can see it, especially when you do not want them to: *Don't worry about that mark – it won't show.* | *Your vest is showing through your shirt.*
showing – showed – have shown

appear /ə'pɪəʳ/ [v I] if someone or something **appears**, you begin to see them or you suddenly see them
+at/in/on etc *At that moment, Kenny appeared in the doorway.*
+from behind/under *A man suddenly appeared from behind the bushes.*

in front of sb /ɪn 'frʌnt ɒv (sb)/ if something happens **in front of** someone, it happens where they can see it, especially when it is something shocking or unpleasant: *The man was* *shot in front of his wife and three children.*

right in front of sb (use this to emphasize how shocking something is) *He lit up a cigarette right in front of the head teacher!*

come into view /ˌkʌm ɪntə ˈvjuː/ WRITTEN if someone or something **comes into view**, you start to see them as you get nearer to them or as they come closer: *As we turned the corner, the house came into view.*

> **Come into view** is used in stories and written descriptions.

4 when something cannot be seen

invisible /ɪnˈvɪzɪbəl/ [adj] if something is **invisible**, it cannot be seen: *The gas is invisible but highly dangerous.*

out of sight /ˌaʊt əv ˈsaɪt/ if someone or something is **out of sight**, you cannot see them because they are too far away, or because they are behind something else: *Jim waved until the car was out of sight.*

5 someone who cannot see

blind /blaɪnd/ [adj] someone who is **blind** cannot see at all: *Her grandfather is now almost blind.*
go blind (=become blind) *Helena went blind at the age of 30.*
the blind (=people who are blind) *a radio programme specially for the blind*

> Don't say 'become blind'. Say **go blind**.

blind [v T often passive] to make someone unable to see, either for a short time or permanently: *As I came out of the tunnel, I was blinded by the sun.* | *A riding accident left her blinded in one eye.* (=she can still see with the other one)

can't see /ˌkɑːnt ˈsiː‖ˌkænt-/ ESPECIALLY SPOKEN if you **can't see**, you are unable to see things, either because there is something wrong with your eyes, or because something

is preventing you seeing clearly: *My mother can't see very well.* | *When I woke up, I found I couldn't see.*

6 the ability to see

sight /saɪt/ [n U] the ability to see: *There are five senses: sight, smell, hearing, taste, and touch.*
lose your sight (=become unable to see) *He lost his sight in an accident.*

eyesight /ˈaɪsaɪt/ [n U] the ability to see – use this to talk about how well or badly someone can see: *My eyesight's got a lot worse over the last few years.* | *William has perfect eyesight.*

can see /kən ˈsiː/ if you **can see**, you are able to see things, especially after you have been unable to: *Thanks to a new operation, Ann can see for the first time in her life.* | *Turn the light on so we can see!*

7 something that you can see through

clear /klɪəʳ/ [adj] if water, air, or glass is **clear**, you can easily see through it: *The lake was so clear that you could see the plants on the bottom.* | *On a clear day, you can see Mount Fuji from Tokyo.*

transparent /trænˈspærənt/ [adj] use this about objects or materials that you can see through, especially things made of plastic: *The box has a transparent plastic lid.*

see-through /ˈsiː θruː/ [adj usually before noun] **see-through** clothes are made of thin material that you can see through: *a see-through blouse*

8 things that help you to see

glasses (also **spectacles** FORMAL) /ˈglɑːsɪz‖ˈglæ-, ˈspektəkəlz/ [n plural] something that you wear in front of your eyes in order to see more clearly, consisting of two pieces of glass in a frame

sunglasses /ˈsʌnˌglɑːsɪz‖-ˌglæ-/ [n plural] dark glasses that you wear to protect your eyes when the sun is very bright

contact lenses /ˈkɒntækt ˌlenzɪz‖ˈkɑːn-/ [n plural] two small round pieces of plastic that you wear on the surface of your eyes in order to see more clearly

telescope /ˈtelɪˌskəʊp/ [n C] a piece of equipment like a tube that you look through in order to see things that are very far away

microscope /ˈmaɪkrəskəʊp/ [n C] a piece of scientific equipment that you look through in order to see extremely small things

SEEM

⇒ see also **SHOW 5**

1   to seem

seem /siːm/ [v] if someone or something **seems** to be happy, dishonest, true etc, that is what you think they are, even though you are not completely certain
seem nice / worried / honest / unfair etc She seemed happy at her new school.
sth seems strange/unfair/important etc (to sb) The whole situation seems very strange to me.
seem to be/do sth Lack of money seems to be the main problem. | At first the crowd didn't seem to notice him.
it seems (that)/it seems to sb (that) (use this to say what you think about a situation) It seems that someone forgot to lock the door. | It seemed to Jim that Amy was worried about something.
🔍 **seem like sth** ESPECIALLY SPOKEN (=seem to be) Kevin seems like a nice guy.
there seems to be There seems to be something wrong with the TV.
it seems as if There were so many delays – it seemed as if we would never get home.
it seems likely/possible/probable (that) It seems likely that they will release the hostages soon.

 Don't say 'she is seeming', 'it was seeming' etc. Say **she seems**, **it seemed** etc.

appear /əˈpɪəʳ/ [v] to seem
appear to be/appear to do sth My father appeared to be in good health. | His statement appeared to contradict what he said last week.
appear calm/rude/angry etc It's difficult to ask someone their age without appearing rude.
it appears that It appeared that no-one was at home.

> **Formal or informal?**
> **Appear** is more formal than **seem**.

look /lʊk/ [v] if someone or something **looks** good, bad, tired etc, that is how they seem to you when you look at them
look good / happy / tired etc That book looks interesting. | Warren looked tired after his long drive.
look like sth The burglar was holding what looked like a shotgun.
look as if You look as if you haven't slept all night.
it looks as if (use this to say how a situation seems to you) It looks as if we are going to need more help.

 Don't say 'she looked like excited'. Say **she looked excited**.

sound /saʊnd/ [v] if someone or something **sounds** good, bad, strange, angry etc, that is how they seem to you when you hear about them or read about them
sound good/bad/awful/angry etc Istanbul sounds really exciting. | He sounds a pretty strange person.
sound like sth Serge's idea for a party sounded like fun.
it sounds (to me) as if (use this to say how a situation seems to you when you hear about it) It sounds to me as if he needs to see a doctor.

strike sb as sth /ˈstraɪk (sb) əz (sth)/ [phrasal verb T] if a person or a situation **strikes** you **as** strange, interesting, unusual etc, this is your opinion of how they seem: What strikes me as odd is the fact that she didn't report the burglary to the police. | Clare didn't strike me as the type who would want to be a teacher.
strike sb as being/having He never struck me as being very interested in politics.

2 when a feeling or situation seems to be real

apparent /ə'pærənt/ [adj only before noun] ESPECIALLY WRITTEN **apparent**-abilities, feelings etc seem to be real, but you cannot be sure if they are real: *She was upset by her father-in-law's apparent dislike of her.* | *What shocked me was the parents' apparent lack of interest in their child.*
apparently [adv] *He walked away from the crash, apparently unhurt.*

on the surface /ɒn ðə 'sɜːʳfˈɪˢs/ if a person, place, or situation is pleasant, normal, calm etc **on the surface**, they seem that way until you know them better: *On the surface, life seemed normal at that time.* | *Mike seemed quite serious on the surface, but he could be very funny.*

3 the way something seems

appearance /ə'pɪərəns/ [n C/U] if someone or something has the **appearance** of being a particular kind of person or thing, they seem to be like that, but in fact they may not be
give the appearance of (=seem like) *Karen gives the appearance of being confident, but she isn't really.*
to all appearances (=it seems to everyone) *To all appearances, Ken and Gina were a happily married couple.*

impression /ɪm'preʃən/ [n C] your **impression** of someone or something is the way they seem to you
+of *What's your impression of Frank as a boss?*
get the impression (that) (=think something is a fact, because it seems true) *We got the impression that Sally wasn't very pleased to see us.* | *She got the impression that you didn't like her.*
give (sb) the impression that (=make people believe something, by making it appear to be true) *In her book, she gives the impression that she was a close friend of the Prince, but in fact she only met him twice.*
first impression (=how someone or something seems to you the first time

you see them) *My first impression of England was of a grey and rainy place.*

> ⚠ Don't say 'what's your impression about him?' Say **what's your impression of him?**

SELL

BUY

MONEY · SHOP

ADVERTISING · see also · BUSINESS

COST · CHEAP

EXPENSIVE

1 to sell something

sell /sel/ [v T] to give something to someone in exchange for money: *Tom's thinking of selling his motorcycle.* | *Postcards were being sold outside the cathedral.*
sell sb sth *The woman who sold us the house went to live in Florida.*
sell sth to sb *It is illegal to sell tobacco to anyone under the age of 18.* | *The picture was sold to an art gallery in Philadelphia.*
sell sth for £250/$50 etc *I managed to sell my old car for £2000.*
selling – sold – have sold

export /ɪk'spɔːʳt/ [v T] if a country or company **exports** its products, it sends them to another country in order to sell them: *Japanese companies export televisions all over the world.*
export sth to sb *In 1986 they exported 210,000 cases of wine to the UK.*
exporter [n C] *Saudi Arabia is one of the world's leading exporters of oil.*

deal in sth /'diːl ɪn (sth)/ [phrasal verb T] to buy and sell products for business purposes, but usually not in a shop – use this especially about valuable things like paintings or gold, about farm products, or about stolen or illegal goods: *a wholesale commodity firm dealing in cotton and corn* | *Slater dealt in stolen car radios.*

bring out sth /ˌbrɪŋ ˈaʊt (sth)/ [*phrasal verb* T] if a company **brings out** a new product, they produce it and make it available for people to buy: *The publisher will soon be bringing out a new edition of the dictionary.* | *Ford has brought out a new sports car.*

the sale of sth /ðə ˈseɪl ɒv (sth)/ the business of selling something: *The sale of marijuana is illegal in Britain.* | *They make most of their profits from the sale of farm machinery.*

2   available for people to buy

for sale /fəʳ ˈseɪl/ if something is **for sale**, the person who owns it wants to sell it: *There are several houses for sale in our street.* | *"For Sale: Black and White Kittens".*

on sale /ɒn ˈseɪl/ if a product is **on sale**, you can buy it in the shops: *These cameras are on sale in most electrical stores.*
go on sale (=begin to be available) *The new model Toyota goes on sale next month.*

on the market /ɒn ðə ˈmɑːʳkᵻt/ goods that are **on the market** are available for people to buy – use this especially when comparing products of the same general type: *It's one of the cheapest computers on the market.* | *There are so many different shampoos on the market that it's hard to know which one to buy.*

> ⚠️ Don't say 'in the market'. Say **on the market**

3   someone who sells something

sales assistant (also **shop assistant** BRITISH)   **sales clerk** AMERICAN /ˈseɪlz əˌsɪstənt, ˈʃɒp əˌsɪstənt, ˈseɪlz ˌklɑːkǁˈʃɑːp-, -ˌklɜːrk/ [*n* C] someone who deals with customers in a shop and sells them things: *Rowan worked as a sales assistant in a large department store.* | *a shop assistant in the shoe department*

> **Formal or informal?**
> **Sales assistant** is more formal than **shop assistant** or **sales clerk**.

salesman/saleswoman   /ˈseɪlzmən, ˈseɪlzˌwʊmən/ [*n* C] someone whose job is to persuade people, shops, and companies to buy their company's products: *I worked for a while as a salesman for a big computer corporation.* | *Gail has been the firm's top saleswoman for the last two years.*
plural **salesmen, saleswomen**

seller /ˈseləʳ/ [*n* C] the person who sells something to someone – use this either to talk about the buyer and seller in a business deal, or about someone who sells things to people in the street: *It was a good time for both buyers and sellers of houses.*
a fruit/flower/ice-cream/soft-drink etc seller *Outside the theatre, there was a row of flower sellers.*

dealer/pusher /ˈdiːləʳ, ˈpʊʃəʳ/ [*n* C] someone who buys and sells illegal drugs: *Dealers were selling heroin to teenagers outside the stadium.*
drug dealer/pusher *Drug pushers have been warned to stay away from the club.*

4   something that is sold

goods /gʊdz/ [*n* plural] things that are produced in order to be sold: *The store sells a wide range of goods.*
electrical/household/luxury goods *We import a lot of electrical goods from Japan.*

> **Formal or informal?**
> Don't use **goods** in ordinary conversation when talking about shopping for things. Don't say 'I need to buy some household goods'. Say **I need to buy some things for the house.**

product /ˈprɒdʌktǁˈprɑː-/ [*n* C] anything that is made, grown, or designed in order to be sold: *There is less demand now for products like coal and steel.* | *I'm allergic to dairy products, like milk and cheese.*

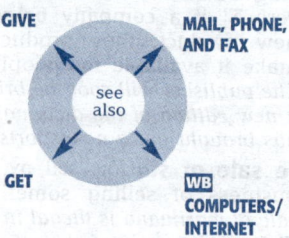

SEND

GIVE

MAIL, PHONE, AND FAX

see also

GET

WB COMPUTERS/ INTERNET

> ⚠ **Products** can be things made in factories or grown on farms, but they can also be services like insurance or holidays: *We sell pensions, life insurance, and a range of financial products.*

exports /'ekspɔːrts/ [n plural] goods that are sent to another country to be sold: *The value of China's exports to the US rose by over 50% last year.*

5 when a lot of something gets sold

sales /seɪlz/ [n plural] the number of products that a business sells, or the value of the products it sells: *A big price increase led to a fall in sales.*
+of *Sales of computer games have risen dramatically over the past five years.*
retail sales (=sales in shops) *an increase in retail sales*

> ⚠ You can also use **sales** before a noun, like an adjective: *sales figures* | *The department failed to achieve its sales target.*

sell /sel/ [v I] to be sold in large numbers: *Tickets for the concert just aren't selling.*
sell well *Rolls-Royces sell very well in the Far East.*
selling – sold – have sold

sell out /ˌsel 'aʊt/ [phrasal verb I] if a shop, ticket office etc **sells out** of goods or tickets, it has no more of that thing left to sell: *I went to the store to get some bread but they had sold out.*
+of *They opened at 8 o'clock, and by 8.30 they had sold out of tickets for the big game.*
be sold out (=when all the tickets for a performance or sports event have been sold) *The show was completely sold out.*

best-selling /ˌbest 'selɪŋ◄/ [adj only before noun] a **best-selling** product is sold in large numbers, and sells more than other products of the same kind: *Coca-Cola is the world's best-selling soft drink.* | *Stephen King has written many best-selling novels.*

1 thing/letter/message

send /send/ [v T] to send a letter, package, message, or object to another person or place: *How many Christmas cards did you send?* | *Send a cheque for £50 with your order.*
send sb sth *Could you send me a copy of the report?* | *Mary's boyfriend sent her a dozen red roses.*
send sth to sb *Diego sent a fax to the managing director telling him about his decision.*
send sth out (=send letters, messages etc to many people) *The voting forms are sent out in September.*
sending – sent – have sent

> ⚠ Don't say 'I sent to him a letter'. Say **I sent him a letter**.

post BRITISH **mail** AMERICAN /pəʊst, meɪl/ [v T] to send a letter, package etc by putting it in a letter box or taking it to the post office: *I must remember to post Joey's birthday card.* | *Her letter had been mailed from Paris.*
post/mail sth to sb *Could you mail those photographs to me?*

send off /ˌsend 'ɒf‖-'ɔːf/ [phrasal verb T] to send something somewhere so that it can be dealt with
send sth off *I must send this film off to be processed.*
send off sth *Did you send off your application form?*

send back /ˌsend 'bæk/ [phrasal verb T] to return something by sending it to the place it came from
send sth back *She sent all Patrick's letters back without opening them.*
send back sth *Complete all the details, then send back the form.*

email /ˈiːmeɪl/ [v T] to send a message directly from one computer to another computer in a different place: *You can email Richard in Sydney.*
email sb sth *A reader emailed me a question about the story.*
email sth to sb *It's so easy to email photos to friends and family.*

fax /fæks/ [v T] to send someone a message using a fax machine: *Shall I fax the report or mail it?*
fax sth to sb *The order will be faxed directly to the manufacturer.*
fax sb sth *They've agreed to fax us their proposals tomorrow.*

2 person

send /send/ [v T] to make someone go somewhere, especially so that they can do something for you
send sb to/into/there etc *I've sent Michael to the supermarket to get some wine.* | *French troops were later sent into the war zone.*
sending – sent – have sent

SENSIBLE

not behaving in a stupid or unreasonable way

➡ opposite **STUPID, CRAZY**

1 person

sensible /ˈsensɪbəl/ [adj] someone who is **sensible** is unlikely to do anything stupid, because they judge situations well and make good decisions: *Laura is a very sensible girl – she wouldn't talk to strangers.* | *I wish you'd be more sensible – you can't go out without a coat on!*
+about *People are far more sensible about what they drink now.*

> ⚠ Don't confuse **sensible** (=likely to make good decisions and not do stupid things) and **sensitive** (=good at realizing how other people feel).

reasonable /ˈriːzənəbəl/ [adj] someone who is **reasonable** makes sensible decisions that are fair to everyone:

Just talk to him. He's a reasonable man. | *Let's try and discuss this in a calm and reasonable way.*
◯ **be reasonable!** SPOKEN *Be reasonable! You can't expect her to do all the work on her own!*

responsible /rɪˈspɒnsɪbəl‖rɪˈspɑːn-/ [adj] someone who is **responsible** can be trusted to do what they ought to do and to think about the results of their actions: *If Mary was a little more responsible, I wouldn't mind lending her the car.* | *We want our children to become responsible citizens.*

mature /məˈtʃʊəʳ/ [adj] a child or young person who is **mature** behaves in a sensible way, as you would expect an older person to behave: *She's very mature for her age.* | *After two years of college, the students have a much more mature attitude.*

rational /ˈræʃənəl/ [adj] if someone is **rational**, their actions are based on a clear understanding of the facts or a situation, and are not influenced by their feelings or imagination: *He was being calm, rational, and reassuring.*
rationally [adv] *Do people behave completely rationally when they vote in elections?*

◯ **talk sense** /ˌtɔːk ˈsens/ ESPECIALLY SPOKEN if someone **talks sense**, they express sensible ideas or opinions that you agree with: *I know he's rather bigheaded, but he does talk a lot of sense.*

2 decision/plan/idea/action

sensible /ˈsensɪbəl/ [adj] a **sensible** decision, plan etc is likely to have good results because it is based on good, practical reasons and judgements: *I think that's a very sensible suggestion.* | *a sensible solution to a difficult problem*
it is sensible to do sth *It would have been more sensible to save the money.*
the sensible thing to do *The sensible thing to do would be to rest until you feel better.*
sensibly [adv] *She had sensibly decided to leave the car at home.*

reasonable /ˈriːzənəbəl/ [adj] a **reasonable** idea, request, action etc seems sensible and fair, and you can understand the reasons for it: *I thought her request was perfectly* reasonable. *I've no idea why it was refused. | You don't have to go. You have a perfectly reasonable excuse.*

it is reasonable to assume/believe/ suppose FORMAL *It's reasonable to assume that prices will rise again soon.*

◯ **make sense** /ˌmeɪk 'sens/ ESPECIALLY SPOKEN if something **makes sense**, it seems a very sensible thing to do: *You don't live here but you're still paying rent? That doesn't make sense!*
it makes sense (for sb) to do sth *It made sense for Sam to live nearer the college.*

wise /waɪz/ [adj] a **wise** decision or action is based on good judgement and on your experience of life: *So Raymond's going to retire? I think he's made a wise decision.*
it is wise (for sb) to do sth *He thought it might be wise not to tell her what had happened. | Do you think it's wise for him to travel alone?*
wise move (=a sensible decision or action) *Taking out insurance was a wise move.*

logical /'lɒdʒɪkəl‖'lɑː-/ [adj] a **logical** action or decision seems to be clearly the right thing to do, because it is based on thinking intelligently about all the facts of a situation, and not based on feelings or emotions: *As I wanted to travel to other countries, studying languages was the logical choice. | This is the logical place to build a new airport.*
it is/it seems logical to do sth *It seemed logical to start by visiting the scene of the crime.*

rational /'ræʃənəl/ [adj] **rational argument/behaviour/decision/explanation etc** a decision, way of behaving etc that is based on real facts or scientific knowledge, and not influenced by feelings or imagination: *It can't just have disappeared! I'm sure there's a perfectly rational explanation. | The doctor should give you the facts so that you can make a rational decision.*

realistic /ˌrɪə'lɪstɪk◂/ [adj] based on a good understanding of what is or is not possible and practical: *Starting my own business is not a realistic idea at the moment.*
it is realistic to do sth *It's not realistic to expect my parents to lend us any more money.*

◯ **be a good idea** /bi: ə ˌgʊd aɪ'dɪə/ ESPECIALLY SPOKEN if a plan, decision, or action **is a good idea**, it seems sensible and seems to be the right thing to do: *Yes, I think a short meeting this afternoon would be a good idea.*
it's a good idea to do sth *It's a good idea to tell a friend if you are going on a date with someone you don't know well.*

3 **the ability to make sensible decisions**

common sense /ˌkɒmən 'sens◂ ‖ˌkɑː-/ [n U] the ability to make sensible, practical decisions, based on experience: *She has a lot of common sense. | Common sense should tell you that this is not a good idea.*
◯ **use your common sense!** ESPECIALLY SPOKEN *It's not difficult to work out the answer – you just have to use your common sense.*

sense /sens/ [n U] the ability to behave in an intelligent and sensible way, and to avoid doing anything stupid
have the sense to do sth (=be sensible enough to do what is needed in order to avoid problems, danger etc) *Luckily Sheena had the sense to call the police before Baxter left the building.*
have enough/little/not much sense *I'm sure she has too much sense to give him her address.*

SEPARATE

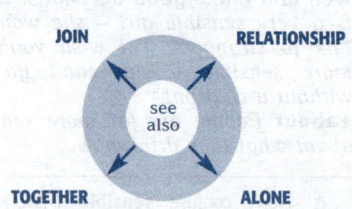

JOIN   RELATIONSHIP

see also

TOGETHER   ALONE

1 **not together**

separate /'sepərɪt/ [adj] not together: *They sleep in separate beds. | a university with three separate campuses*

+from *Their house was separate from the rest of the village.*

keep sth separate *It's safer to keep cooked and uncooked meat separate. | Keep your bank card and your PIN number separate.*

apart /ə'pɑːᵊt/ [*adv*] if people or things are **apart**, they are in different places and there is a distance between them: *Jo and Sam decided to try living apart for a while. | Since the universe began, the galaxies have gradually moved further apart.*

+from *Helen noticed one little boy standing apart from the rest of the group.*

keep sb apart *The two sets of rival fans had to be kept apart by the police.*

far apart *They have offices in countries as far apart as India and Peru.*

separately /'sepərₐtli/ [*adv*] not together, but at separate times or in separate places: *The couple arrived separately at London Airport yesterday. | Each problem should be considered separately.*

2 to separate two things, people, or groups

separate /'sepəreɪt/ [*v* T] to put people or things that were together into different places or groups: *If you two don't stop talking during class, I'll have to separate you.*

separate sth from sth *Farmers separate calves from their mothers when they are only a few days old. | Break an egg and separate the white from the yolk.*

separate sth into groups/piles/ parts etc *Sheila had separated the clothes into two piles.*

divide /dɟ'vaɪd/ [*v* T] to separate something into a number of smaller parts

divide sth into two/three etc (=into two, three etc parts or pieces) *We divided the pizza into three and had a slice each. | The country is divided into seven provinces.*

divide sth between/among sb *They divided the money equally between them.*

be divided into *Most of these big old houses have been divided into apartments.*

split /splɪt/ [*v* T] to separate something that used to be a single thing or a single group into two or more completely different parts: *Rutherford first split the atom on 3rd January 1919.*

split sth in half/in two (=so that it makes two equal parts) *Why don't you just split the money in half?*

split sth into two/three etc (=into two, three etc parts or pieces) *Split the class into three groups.*

splitting – split – have split

> **Formal or informal?**
> **Split** is less formal than **divide**.

segregate /'segrɪgeɪt/ [*v* T often passive] FORMAL to separate one group of people from others, especially because of their race, sex, religion etc: *The school system should not segregate children with disabilities.*

be segregated from *Male prisoners were strictly segregated from the females.*

segregated [*adj*]

segregated school/hotel/cinema/ housing etc (=for only one group or race, and not for others) *At that time, the beaches in South Africa were segregated.*

3 when something becomes separated into different parts

divide /dɟ'vaɪd/ [*v* I] ESPECIALLY WRITTEN to become separated into two or more parts

a road/path/river divides *They came to a point where the river divided.*

+into *The single cell divides into two identical cells.*

split /splɪt/ [*v* I] if a group of people **splits**, it becomes separated into two or more smaller groups

split into two/three etc *The former Soviet Union split into 15 independent republics. | a political party that split into three separate groups*

splitting – split – have split

SERIOUS

➡ look here for ...
• a serious problem, accident, illness, crime
• not joking
➡ see also **JOKE**

1 a serious problem/accident/illness/crime

serious /'sɪəriəs/ [adj] very bad – use this about problems, accidents, illnesses, or crimes: *There was a serious accident on the freeway.* | *serious head injuries* | *Unemployment is a serious problem.* | *Drug smuggling is a serious crime.*
seriously [adv]
seriously ill/injured/affected *Her father is seriously ill.*

bad /bæd/ [adj] serious enough to cause problems or make you feel worried – use this especially about accidents or illnesses: *I stayed home yesterday with a bad cold.* | *a bad car crash*
badly [adv]
badly injured/damaged/affected *Several people were badly injured in the attack.* | *The furniture was badly damaged by fire.*

⚠ Don't say 'her hands were burned badly'. Say **her hands were badly burned**. **Badly** comes before a past participle.

desperate /'despərₔt/ [adj] use this about a very serious or dangerous situation, especially when people will die if it does not improve: *The situation is getting desperate as the country has had no rain for months.* | *a desperate shortage of food and medical supplies*
in desperate need *They are in desperate need of help.*

◯ **nasty** /'nɑːstɪ‖'næsti/ [adj] ESPECIALLY BRITISH SPOKEN use this about small accidents or illnesses that are worse than you would normally expect them to be: *That cough sounds nasty.* | *He had a nasty cut on his head.*
nasty – nastier – nastiest

2 when you really mean what you say

be serious /biː 'sɪəriəs/ to really mean what you say, or really intend to do something: *I'm serious! I'm not lending you any money.* | *He said he was going to steal a car, but I didn't think he was serious.*
be serious about doing sth *I hope Jeff's serious about giving up smoking.*
be perfectly/absolutely serious (=be serious, even though this seems very unlikely) *The former astronaut is perfectly serious when he says people will soon be taking vacations in space.*

◯ **not joking** /nɒt 'dʒəʊkɪŋ/ ESPECIALLY SPOKEN if you are **not joking**, you really mean what you say, even though it seems surprising or unlikely: *There must have been 10 people in that car – I'm not joking.* | *She told him she'd call the police if he bothered her again, and she wasn't joking.*

◯ **seriously** /'sɪəriəsli/ [adv] SPOKEN say this to emphasize that something surprising is really true, or to ask whether something surprising is really true: *Seriously, I think you're making a big mistake.* | *"She's quit her job." "Seriously?"*

◯ **mean** /miːn/ [v T] ESPECIALLY SPOKEN if someone **means** what they say, they are being serious when they say it, and they are not pretending or lying
mean it *I mean it – I'll scream if you don't let me go.* | *She told me she loved me, but I wasn't sure if she meant it.*
mean what you say *I meant what I said – I never want to see you again.*
really mean *You don't really mean that, do you?*
meaning – meant – have meant

mean business /,miːn 'bɪznₔs/ INFORMAL if someone **means business**, it is very clear that they will definitely do what they say or what they are threatening to do: *The man had a gun. It was obvious he meant business.*

3 someone who does not tell jokes or laugh

serious /'sɪəriəs/ someone who is **serious** is quiet and sensible, and does

not seem to enjoy laughing and joking: *Friends described him as a serious and thoughtful man.*
+about *Laura was always very serious about her work.*

SHAKE

1 when things shake

shake /ʃeɪk/ [v I] if something **shakes**, it makes small quick movements from side to side or up and down: *The branches of the trees were shaking in the wind.* | *Suddenly the ground began to shake beneath my feet.* | *The floor shook as they danced.*
shaking – shook – have shaken

rattle /'rætl/ [v I] if something **rattles**, it makes a noise because it keeps shaking and hitting something else: *The windows were rattling in the storm.* | *Mike knocked against the table and made the coffee cups rattle.*

wobble /'wɒbəl‖'waː-/ [v I] if something **wobbles**, it moves from side to side because it is not steady or not well balanced: *The pile of books wobbled and almost fell.* | *I wish this desk would stop wobbling!*

vibrate /vaɪ'breɪt‖'vaɪbreɪt/ [v I] if something **vibrates**, it shakes continuously with very small, very fast movements: *When you switch on the engine, you can feel the whole car vibrate.*

> **Formal or informal?**
> **Vibrate** is a fairly formal word that is often used in technical writing.

2 when someone's body, hand etc shakes

shake /ʃeɪk/ [v I] if you **shake**, you make small quick uncontrolled movements with your body, for example because you are frightened, nervous, or angry: *My hands were shaking so much I could hardly write my name on the exam paper.*
shake with fear/anger/laughter (=shake because you are frightened,

angry etc) *The others were all shaking with laughter.*
shaking – shook – have shaken

tremble /'trembəl/ [v I] WRITTEN to shake very slightly because you are frightened or upset: *Jane's lip began to tremble and I thought she was going to cry.* | *The dog sat trembling in a corner.*
tremble with anger/excitement/ fear etc *Jack was trembling with rage.*

> Use **tremble** when you are writing stories or descriptions.

shiver /'ʃɪvəʳ/ [v I] to shake because you are cold: *Julia shivered and pulled her coat more tightly around her.* | *You're shivering! Do you want to go indoors?*

3 to make something shake

shake /ʃeɪk/ [v T] to make something move up and down or from side to side with small quick movements: *Shake the bottle before you open it.* | *She shook the blanket to get rid of all the dust.* | *a huge explosion that shook houses up to five miles away*
shaking – shook – have shaken

make sth shake /,meɪk (sth) 'ʃeɪk/ to make a place or object shake – use this especially about loud noises or strong movements or explosions: *The music was so loud that it made the floor shake.* | *The distant earthquake made all the furniture shake.*

give sth a shake /,gɪv (sth) ə 'ʃeɪk/ ESPECIALLY BRITISH to hold something and shake it a few times: *I gave the box a shake to see if there was anything inside.*

4 to shake hands as a greeting

shake hands /,ʃeɪk 'hændz/ *The two leaders shook hands and walked into the White House.*
+with *The picture shows him shaking hands with Saddam Hussein.*

SHAPE

1 the shape of something

shape /ʃeɪp/ [n C/U] the shape that something is, for example a square, a circle etc: *You can get pasta in lots of different shapes.* | *What shape is the swimming pool?*

2 to have a particular shape

be round/square/rectangular etc use this to say what shape something is: *The windows were round, like the windows on a ship.* | *"What shape is the table?" "It's rectangular."*
be round/square etc in shape WRITTEN *The dining-room was square in shape, and simply furnished.*

> ⚠ When you want to describe the shape of something, don't say 'it has a square/circular etc shape' or 'its shape is square/circular etc'. Say **it is square/circular** etc.

shaped /ʃeɪpt/ [adj] **star-shaped/heart-shaped/L-shaped etc** when something has the shape of a star, a heart, the letter L etc: *The lounge was L-shaped.* | *He gave me some heart-shaped chocolates.*
shaped like sth *Her birthday cake was shaped like a train.*
in the shape of sth /ɪn ðə ˈʃeɪp ɒv (sth)/ when something has the same shape as something else, for example a bird or animal: *a blue bowl in the shape of a flower*

SHARE

1 to use something with another person

share /ʃeər/ [v I/T] if two or more people **share** something, they all use it together: *We don't have enough books, so some of you will have to share.* | *I have my own room but we share the kitchen and bathroom.*

share sth with sb *I shared a room with Tom while I was at college.*

2 to do something with another person

share /ʃeər/ [v T] if two people **share** a job or activity, they each do part of it: *Judy and I shared the driving.*
share sth with sb *She shares the job with another woman who also has a young child.*

take turns (also **take it in turns** BRIT-ISH) /ˌteɪk ˈtɜːrnz, ˌteɪk ɪt ɪn ˈtɜːrns/ if two or more people **take turns** or **take it in turns** to do something, they do it one after the other, and each person does it several times: *If the housework is too much for one person, why don't you take it in turns?*
take turns/take it in turns to do sth *The parent birds take turns to guard the nest.*
take turns/take it in turns doing sth *The kids take turns doing the dishes.*

3 when several people each have part of something

share/share out /ʃeər, ˌʃeər ˈaʊt/ [v T] to divide something so that several people have a part of it: *We agreed that we would share the prize money if we won.*
share sth (out) among/between sb *She shared the cake between the children.* | *Profits from the sale of tickets were shared out among the members of the band.*

split /splɪt/ [v T] if a small number of people **split** something, especially money, they divide it into equal parts and take a part each: *They run the business together and split the money they make.*
split sth between sb *He said that the land should be split between his four sons.*
splitting – split – have split

divide/divide up /dɪˈvaɪd, dɪˌvaɪd ˈʌp/ [v T] to separate something into two or more parts
divide sth (up) between sb *Hitler and Stalin agreed to divide Poland between them.*

divide (up) sth between sb *We divided up the rest of the pie between us.*

4 to share the cost of something

share/split /ʃeəʳ, splɪt/ [v T] to share the cost of something so that each person pays part of it: *The two families shared the cost of the wedding. | We usually share all the bills. | The companies will split the cost of development.*

splitting – split – have split

◯ **go halves** /gəʊ 'hɑːvzǁ-'hævz/ BRITISH SPOKEN INFORMAL if two people **go halves**, they each pay half of the cost of something that they buy together

go halves with sb (on sth) *I'll go halves with you on the tickets if you like.*

5 the part of something that someone gets or owns

share /ʃeəʳ/ [n C] the part of something that one person gets or owns when something is shared between several people

+of *When Grandpa died we each got a share of his money. | Wilson's share of the business is worth $500,000.*

SHARP/NOT SHARP

➡ see also **CUT**

1 sharp

sharp /ʃɑːʳp/ [adj] something that is **sharp** can easily cut things or make holes in them, because it has a very narrow edge or point: *That knife's very sharp. | You'll need some sharp scissors.*

razor-sharp (=extremely sharp) *Sharks have razor-sharp teeth.*

pointed /'pɔɪntᵻd/ [adj] long, thin, and ending in a point: *a plant with long pointed leaves | a pointed stick used for picking up trash*

2 not sharp

blunt /blʌnt/ [adj] not sharp: *All our kitchen knives are old and blunt. | a blunt pencil | Police say the man was killed with a blunt instrument, possibly a hammer.*

dull /dʌl/ [adj] ESPECIALLY AMERICAN not sharp: *The knife-blade was dull.*

3 to make something sharp

sharpen /'ʃɑːʳpən/ [v T] to make something sharper: *I'll just sharpen my pencil. | a special stone for sharpening knives*

SHINE

➡ see also **BRIGHT/NOT BRIGHT, NEW, CLEAN**

1 when light comes from the sun, a lamp etc

shine /ʃaɪn/ [v I] if the sun, a lamp etc **shines**, it sends out bright light: *The sun was shining, so we decided to go to the beach. | She could see the lights of Hong Kong shining in the distance.*

shining – shone – have shone

glow /gləʊ/ [v I] WRITTEN to make a warm soft light that is not very bright: *The evening sun glowed in the sky. | A few lumps of coal still glowed in the fire.*

glow [n singular] *the soft glow of the candles*

> ⚠ Use **glow** when you are writing stories or descriptions.

flash /flæʃ/ [v I] to make a bright light for a very short time: *Lightning flashed across the sky. | The light on top of the police car was flashing.*

flash [n C] *There was a blinding flash of light as the bomb exploded.*

flicker /'flɪkəʳ/ [v I] use this about a weak flame or light which is unsteady and keeps going on and off: *The candle suddenly started to flicker. | The flashlight is flickering. I guess it needs a new battery.*

2 when something has a bright surface

shiny /'ʃaɪni/ [adj] something that is **shiny** has a smooth bright surface: *The little girl's shoes were black and shiny.* | *Use this shampoo for thicker, shinier hair.* | *a big shiny limousine*
shiny – shinier – shiniest

glossy /'glɒsi‖'glɔːsi, 'glɑːsi/ [adj] **glossy** hair or fur looks shiny and healthy; **glossy** magazines and books use expensive shiny paper: *She stroked the horse's glossy neck.* | *There was a stack of glossy magazines on the table.* | *glossy travel brochures*
glossy – glossier – glossiest

gleaming /'gliːmɪŋ/ [adj usually before noun] ESPECIALLY WRITTEN **gleaming** objects or vehicles are shiny because they are very new or clean: *A gleaming Porsche was parked in front of the house.* | *a gleaming white kitchen*

shine /ʃaɪn/ [v I] WRITTEN if something with a smooth surface **shines**, it is very bright and sends back any light that falls on it: *He polished the silver plates until they shone.*

sparkle /'spɑːʳkəl/ [v I] ESPECIALLY WRITTEN something that **sparkles**, such as jewellery or water, looks attractive because there are many small bright points of light on its surface: *Her diamond ring sparkled in the sunlight.* | *a sparkling mountain stream* | *The children's eyes sparkled with excitement.*

When you see **EC**, go to the **ESSENTIAL COMMUNICATION** section.

SHOOT

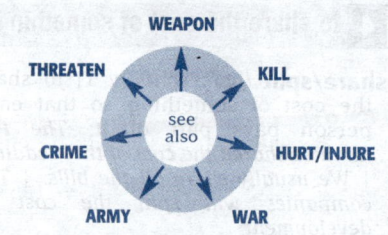

WEAPON
THREATEN
KILL
see also
CRIME
HURT/INJURE
ARMY
WAR

1 to shoot someone

shoot /ʃuːt/ [v T] to kill or injure someone by firing bullets from a gun: *Ruth Ellis shot her lover in a pub in London.* | *the news that President Kennedy had been shot*
shoot sb in the back/chest/leg etc *He had been shot in the chest but managed to crawl to safety.*
shoot sb dead (=shoot someone and kill them) *A tourist was shot dead by muggers in New Orleans last night.*
shooting – shot – have shot

be hit /biː 'hɪt/ to be injured or damaged by bullets: *I didn't realize he'd been hit until he fell to the ground.* | *One of our planes was hit.*

2 to shoot a gun or other weapon

shoot /ʃuːt/ [v I] to point a gun towards someone, and make bullets come out of it: *Don't shoot! We surrender!* | *Make sure you hold the gun steady and shoot straight.*
+at *We used to shoot at empty bottles for practice.*
shooting – shot – have shot

fire /faɪəʳ/ [v I/T] to make bullets come out of a gun, or shoot a bomb or explosive object into the air: *The police fired into the air to make the crowd break up.*
+at/on *As soon as we crossed the border, enemy troops started firing at us.*
fire a shot/bullet *Kendrick fired three shots at the car.*
fire a gun/weapon/rifle etc *The boy accidentally fired the gun.*
fire a missile/rocket *US warships began firing cruise missiles into Iraq.*

3 the sound of shooting

shot /ʃɒt‖ʃɑːt/ [n C] the noise made by a gun when it is fired: *One witness claimed she had heard eight shots.*
a shot rings out WRITTEN (=when you hear a loud shot) *Suddenly, a shot rang out.*

gunfire /ˈɡʌnfaɪəʳ/ [n U] the sound made by several guns being fired, especially in a war: *Enemy gunfire could be heard from several kilometres away.*

SHOP

➡ if you mean 'go shopping', go to
BUY

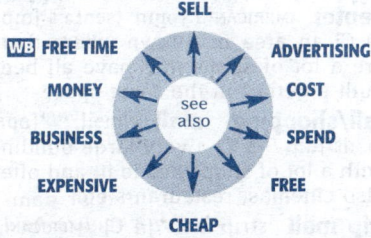

SELL
ADVERTISING
COST
SPEND
FREE
CHEAP
MONEY
BUSINESS
EXPENSIVE
WB FREE TIME
see also

1 a shop

shop ESPECIALLY BRITISH **store** ESPECIALLY AMERICAN /ʃɒp, stɔːʳ‖ʃɑːp/ [n C] a building or place where things are sold: *There's a store across the street that sells ice cream.*
clothes/record/furniture etc shop/store *Have you been to that new clothes shop on Park Road yet? | She works in a video store on Tenth Avenue.*
go to the shops BRITISH **go to the store** AMERICAN *Helen's gone down to the shops to get a few things.*

> ⚠ **Shop** is the usual word to use in British English, and **store** is the usual word to use in American English. In British English, **store** is often used in newspapers and in business reports, especially when talking about big shops: *All the big stores are open from 8am till 8pm. | High street stores are getting ready for Christmas.*

> ⚠ **Go to the shops** or **go to the store** means to go to your local shops to buy food and other small things you need. **Go shopping** means to go to look at things in shops and buy things that you do not buy regularly, such as clothes or records.

chain store /ˈtʃeɪn stɔːʳ/ [n C] one of a group of shops that have the same name and are owned by the same company: *The big chain stores have made it very difficult for smaller shops to do business.*

2 different types of shop

> ⚠ If you want to talk about a shop that sells a particular kind of thing, you usually say a **clothes shop**, **record shop**, **furniture shop** etc in British English, and a **clothes store**, **record store**, **furniture store** etc in American English. **Bookshop** (British) and **bookstore** (American) are usually written as one word.

supermarket (also **grocery store** AMERICAN) /ˈsuːpəʳˌmɑːʳkᵊt, ˈɡrəʊsəri ˌstɔːʳ/ [n C] a large shop that sells a wide range of things, especially food, cleaning materials, and other things that people buy regularly

convenience store /kənˈviːniəns ˌstɔːʳ/ [n C] AMERICAN a shop in your local area that sells food, alcohol, magazines etc and is often open 24 hours a day

corner shop /ˈkɔːʳnəʳ ʃɒp‖-ʃɑːp/ BRITISH a small local shop, usually on the corner of a street, that sells food, alcohol, magazines etc

bakery (also **baker's** BRITISH) /ˈbeɪkəri, ˈbeɪkəʳz/ [n C] a shop that sells bread and cakes, especially one that also makes the bread and cakes
plural **bakeries** (or **bakers**)

butcher's /ˈbʊtʃəʳz/ [n C] a shop that sells meat
plural **butchers**

delicatessen (also **deli** INFORMAL) /ˌdelɪkəˈtesən, ˈdeli/ [n C] a shop that sells high quality food such as cheeses and cold meats, often from different countries, and that usually sells sandwiches too

off licence BRITISH **liquor store** AMERICAN /'ɒf ˌlaɪsəns, 'lɪkəʳ ˌstɔːʳ/ [n C] a shop that sells beer, wine, and other alcoholic drinks which you drink at home

chemist's BRITISH **drugstore** AMERICAN /'keməsts, 'drʌgstɔːʳ/ [n C] a shop that sells medicines, beauty and baby products etc
plural **chemists**

pharmacy /'fɑːʳməsi/ [n C] ESPECIALLY AMERICAN a shop or part of a shop where medicines are made and sold
plural **pharmacies**

hardware store (also **hardware shop** BRITISH) /'hɑːʳdweəʳ ˌstɔːʳ, 'hɑːʳdweəʳ ˌʃɒpǁ-ˌʃɑːp/ [n C] a shop that sells equipment and tools that you can use in your home or garden

newsagent's/newsagent /'njuːzˌeɪdʒənt(s)ǁ'nuːz-/ [n C] BRITISH a shop that sells newspapers and magazines, cigarettes, chocolates etc
plural **newsagents**

newsstand /'njuːzstændǁ'nuːz-/ [n C] a small movable structure on a street, which sells newspapers and magazines

kiosk

kiosk /'kiːɒskǁ-ɑːsk/ [n C] a very small shop on a street, which has an open window where you can buy newspapers, cigarettes, chocolate etc

3 a very large shop

department store /dɪ'pɑːʳtmənt ˌstɔːʳ/ [n C] a very large shop which is divided into several big parts, each of which sells one type of thing, such as clothes, furniture, or kitchen equipment

superstore /'suːpəʳstɔːʳ, 'sjuː-ǁ'suːʳ-/ [n C] a very large modern shop, especially one that is built outside the centre of a city

DIY store BRITISH **home center/home improvement center** AMERICAN /ˌdiː aɪ 'waɪ ˌstɔːʳ, 'həʊm ˌsentəʳ, ˌhəʊm ɪm'pruːvmənt ˌsentəʳ/ [n C] a very large shop that sells equipment and tools for repairing and decorating your home

garden centre BRITISH **nursery** AMERICAN /'gɑːʳdn ˌsentəʳ, 'nɜːʳsəri/ [n C] a place that sells a wide range of plants, seeds, and things for your garden

4 a lot of shops together in one place

shopping centre BRITISH **shopping center** AMERICAN /'ʃɒpɪŋ ˌsentəʳǁ'ʃɑːp-/ [n C] an area in a town where there are a lot of shops that have all been built together in the same space

mall/shopping mall /mɔːl, 'ʃɒpɪŋ mɔːlǁ'ʃɑːp-/ [n C] a very large building with a lot of shops inside it, and often also cinemas, restaurants etc

strip mall /'strɪp mɔːl/ [n C] AMERICAN a row of shops in one long building that has space to park cars around it

parade /pə'reɪd/ [n C] BRITISH a street with a row of small shops: a parade of shops

market /'mɑːʳkət/ [n C] an area outside where people buy and sell many different types of things
market stall (=one of the tables that things are sold from in a market)
farmer's market (=a market in a town or city, once a week or once a month, where farmers sell things directly to the public)

5 people who work in a shop

sales assistant (also **shop assistant** BRITISH) **sales clerk** AMERICAN /'seɪlz əˌsɪstənt, 'ʃɒp əˌsɪstənt, 'seɪlz ˌklɑːkǁ-'ʃɑːp-, -ˌklɜːrk/ [n C] someone whose job is to serve customers and sell things in a shop, especially in a big shop such as a department store

manager /'mænɪdʒəʳ/ [n C] someone who is in charge of a shop

shopkeeper BRITISH **storekeeper** AMERICAN /'ʃɒp,kiːpəʳ, 'stɔːʳ,kiːpəʳǁ'ʃɑːp-/ [n C] someone who owns or manages a small shop

checkout assistant /'tʃekaʊt ə,sɪstənt/ [n C] someone who works at the place in a supermarket where customers pay for the things they have collected

store detective /'stɔːʳ dɪ,tektɪv/ [n C] someone whose job is to watch the customers in a large shop, to stop them from stealing things

customer services /,kʌstəməʳ 'sɜːʳvɪ̯sɪ̯z/ [n U] the part of a company or business that deals with questions, problems etc that customers have

SHORT

➡ look here for ...
  • a short distance or length
  • a short person
  • a short time

1 short in length or distance

➡ opposite **LONG**

short /ʃɔːʳt/ [adj] if something is **short**, there is only a small length or distance from one end of it to the other: *a girl with short blond hair* | *The curtains are much too short.* | *The hotel is just a short distance from the station.* | *There was a short path leading up to the house.*
short walk/drive/ride (=a short distance to walk, drive etc) *It's only a short walk to the bus stop.*

2 someone who is short in height

➡ opposite **TALL**
➡ see also **SMALL**

short /ʃɔːʳt/ [adj] not as tall as most people: *She was short and fat.* | *a short, heavy-looking man* | *Mr Haddad was several inches shorter than his wife.*

not very tall /nɒt veri 'tɔːl/ fairly short: *She's not very tall – about 1.4 metres, I'd say.*

small /smɔːl/ [adj] not as big or as tall as most people: *a small man in a dark suit*
small for his/her age (=smaller than other children of the same age) *Bobby's small for his age, but he's perfectly healthy.*

> ⚠ **Short** means 'not tall'. **Small** means 'not tall, and also not fat'. People are often described as 'short and fat', but not 'small and fat'.

3 a short time

a short time /ə ,ʃɔːʳt 'taɪm/ [n singular] *We only had a short time together.* | *How did you manage to do all this in such a short time?* | *Your friends left a short time ago.*

a while /ə 'waɪl/ [n singular] a period of time that is neither very short nor very long: *After a while, he came back.*
for a while *We lived in Seattle for a while after we got married.* | *Can you stay for a while?*
a little/short while (=a short period of time) *Bob's only been working here a short while.*

a minute/a moment /ə 'mɪnɪ̯t, ə 'məʊmənt/ [n singular] a very short time, no more than a few minutes: *Where's Charles gone? He was here a moment ago.* | *Wait a minute, I'm nearly ready.*
in a minute *I'll be back in a minute.*
for a minute *I thought for a minute before agreeing.*
a minute or two *It took me a minute or two to realize what she meant.*
just a minute (=wait a short time) *Just a minute, I'm almost done.*
take a minute (=last a very short time) *It only takes a minute to make your bed!*

a second/an instant /ə 'sekənd, ən 'ɪnstənt/ [n singular] an extremely short time, no more than a few seconds
in a second/an instant *In an instant her mood had changed from sadness to anger.*
for a second/instant *Liz hesitated, but only for a second.*

just a second (=wait a short time) *Just a second, I'm almost ready.*

take a second (=last a short time) *It'll only take a second.*

> ⚠ A **second** and an **instant** mean the same thing, but an **instant** is usually used in written stories or descriptions of events.

○ **a bit** /ə 'bɪt/ [n singular] BRITISH SPOKEN INFORMAL a short time, usually just a few minutes: *Oh, wait a bit, can't you?*

for a bit *I think I'll lie down for a bit.*

4 continuing for only a short time

short /ʃɔːʳt/ [adj] continuing for only a short time: *The meeting was shorter than I'd expected.* | *the shortest day of the year*

quick /kwɪk/ [adj only before noun] a **quick** action takes only a very short time, because you are in a hurry

quick look/drink/shower *I took a quick look at the map.* | *Do I have time for a quick shower before we go out?*

brief /briːf/ [adj] a **brief** pause, visit etc is short, especially because there is not much time available: *It was impossible to see everything during one brief visit to Paris.* | *After a brief intermission the performance continued.* | *a brief period of calm*

> **Formal or informal?**
> **Brief** is more formal than **short**, and is used in writing and in formal spoken English.

not take long /nɒt teɪk 'lɒŋǁ-'lɔːŋ/ if something does **not take long**, you do it and finish it in a short time: *Here, let me show you how. It won't take long.*

it does not take long to do sth *It didn't take long to solve the problem.*

temporary /'tempərəri, -pərɪǁ-pəreri/ [adj] something that is **temporary** is expected to continue for only a short time and will not be permanent: *Ben's found a temporary job, till November.* | *They're living in temporary accommodation at the moment.*

temporary workers/staff (=doing temporary jobs)

temporarily [adv] for a limited period of time: *The library is temporarily closed for repairs.*

short-lived /ˌʃɔːʳt 'lɪvdǁ-'laɪvd/ [adj] something that is **short-lived** ends sooner than you want it to – use this especially about a feeling, or a relationship: *We were glad to be home, but our happiness was short-lived.* | *The President's popularity may be short-lived.*

5 a short piece of writing

short /ʃɔːʳt/ [adj] a **short** piece of writing does not have many pages or words: *a book of short stories* | *a short letter from my employer* | *Your essay is too short.*

brief /briːf/ [adj] **brief note/description/comments/outline/account** a note, description etc that has been written using very few words, to give only the most important information without a lot of details: *I sent them a brief note saying what the problem was.* | *The book begins with a brief outline of the history of modern China.*

> **Formal or informal?**
> **Brief** is more formal than **short**. Don't use **brief** about a whole book or story.

6 a shorter way of saying or writing something

abbreviation /əˌbriːvi'eɪʃən/ [n C] a shorter way of writing or saying a word or phrase: *the Central Intelligence Agency, usually known by the abbreviation CIA*

+for/of *'Dr' is the written abbreviation of 'Doctor'.*

be short for sth /biː 'ʃɔːʳt fɔːʳ (sth)/ if a word, a name, or a set of letters **is short for** something, it is a shorter way of saying or writing it: *They call me Beth – it's short for Elizabeth.* | *What's 'etc' short for?*

for short /fəʳ 'ʃɔːʳt/ if you call someone or something a name **for short**, you use a shorter form of their real name: *His name's Moses – Mo for short.* | *They are chlorofluorocarbon gases, or CFCs for short.*

7 a short statement giving the main ideas and facts

summary /'sʌməri/ [n C] a short statement that gives only the main ideas and facts of something that has been written or said
+of Write a two-page summary of the results of your research. | a summary of the Secretary General's speech
news summary (=a short programme reporting the main events in the news)
plural **summaries**

outline /'aʊtlaɪn/ [n C] an **outline** of a plan or of a series of historical events is a short statement that gives only the main points and facts
+of an official statement giving a general outline of the Middle East peace plan | The book begins with an outline of the events that led to the First World War.

8 to give the main ideas or facts of something

summarize (also **summarise** BRITISH) /'sʌməraɪz/ [v T] to make a short statement giving only the main information, but not the details, of a report, plan, event etc: Your final paragraph should summarize the main points of your essay.

sum up /,sʌm 'ʌp/ [phrasal verb I/T] to make a very short statement, especially at the end of a speech, report, or discussion, giving the main ideas or facts: The chairman's job is to introduce the speakers and then sum up at the end of the discussion.
sum up sth In these few words Churchill summed up the feelings of the whole nation.
summing – summed – have summed

in short /ɪn 'ʃɔːʳt/ FORMAL use this when you have been writing or talking about something, and you want to say in a few words what the most important fact or idea is: In short, I believe that we need to change our whole attitude towards cars.

9 to make something shorter

shorten /'ʃɔːʳtn/ [v T] to make something shorter: Could you shorten the sleeves for me?
shorten sth to sth The three-year course has been shortened to two years. | Diana's name is often shortened to Di.

cut /kʌt/ [v T] to make a film or piece of writing shorter by removing parts from it: Even after it had been cut, the film was still over three hours long.
cut sth down This last paragraph is too long – you'll have to cut it down.
cutting – cut – have cut

 Use **cut something down** only about pieces of writing.

SHOULD

➡ see also **MUST, DESERVE**

1 when you should do something because it is right and it is your duty

should /ʃʊd/ [modal verb] if you **should** do something, it is your duty to do it, or it is the best thing to do because it is right, fair, or honest: I don't want to go to the meeting but I suppose I should.
should do sth I think you should tell her the truth. | He should visit his parents more often. | All accidents should be reported to the Health and Safety Officer.
should not/shouldn't do sth You shouldn't leave young children at home alone.
should have done sth (=it was the right thing to do, but someone did not do it) They should have given you your money back.
shouldn't have done sth (=it was the wrong thing to do, but someone did it) I'm sorry, I shouldn't have shouted at you.

⚠ Don't say 'you should to go'. Say **you should go**. **Should** is followed by an infinitive without 'to'.

ought to do sth /ˌɔːt tə 'duː (sth)/ use this to say that someone should do something because it is right or it is the best thing to do in a situation: *I think you ought to apologize.* | *Do you think we ought to get permission before we do this?* | *The Government ought to spend more on education.*

ought not/oughtn't to do sth *I think that animals have rights, and we ought not to use them for experiments.*

ought to have done sth (=it was the right thing to do, but someone did not do it) *It was a serious matter. They ought to have called the police.*

⚠ **Ought to** is less common than **should** in written and spoken English.

◯ **had better do sth** /həd ˌbetəʳ 'duː (sth)/ ESPECIALLY SPOKEN use this to say that you think someone should do something because it would be the correct, polite, or fair thing to do: *You had better phone Alan and tell him you're going to be late.* | *You'd better ask Dad first.*

had better not do sth *We'd better not tell anyone about this just yet.*

⚠ Don't say 'we better go' or 'we'd better to go'. Say **we'd better go**.

be supposed to do sth /biː sə,pəʊzd tə 'duː (sth)/ use this to say that someone should do something because there is a rule that says they should, because they have been told to do it, or because it is part of their job: *You're supposed to knock before you come in.* | *Put that cigarette out! You're not supposed to smoke in here.* | *I had no idea what I was supposed to do next.*

it is sb's job to do sth /ɪt ɪz (sb's) ,dʒɒb tə 'duː (sth)‖-,dʒɑːb-/ use this to say that someone is responsible for doing something, because it is officially part of their job, or because they have agreed to do it: *It's my job to check that the equipment is in good working order.* | *I thought we'd agreed it was Mike's job to send out all the invitations.*

◯ **it's up to sb to do sth** /ɪts ,ʌp tə (sb) tə 'duː (sth)/ ESPECIALLY SPOKEN say this to emphasize that a particular person is responsible for doing something: *It's up to parents to teach their children the difference between right and wrong.*

it is sb's duty to do sth /ɪt ɪz (sb's) ,djuːti tə 'duː (sth)‖-,duːti-/ FORMAL use this to say that someone should do something because it is their legal or moral duty: *It is the judge's duty to give a fair summary of both sides of the case.*

---

2 **when you should do something because it is sensible or it is good for you**

should /ʃʊd/ [modal verb] if you **should** do something, it is the best thing to do because it is good for you or it will help you: *I should give up smoking.* | *You should go to bed early if you're feeling tired.*

should not/shouldn't do sth *They shouldn't worry so much. Everything will be all right.*

should have done sth (=it was the best thing to do, but someone did not do it) *I should have spent more time studying.*

shouldn't have done sth (=it was not a sensible thing to do, but someone did it) *We shouldn't have bought such a big car.*

⚠ Don't say 'you should to go'. Say **you should go**. **Should** is followed by an infinitive without 'to'.

ought to do sth /ˌɔːt tə 'duː (sth)/ use this to say that you think someone should do something because it is good for them or will help them: *The doctor told Dan he ought to exercise more.* | *You ought to ask Eric. I'm sure he'd help.*

ought not to do sth/oughtn't to do sth *She oughtn't to drive if she's been drinking.*

⚠ **Ought to** is less common than **should** in written and spoken English.

◯ **had better do sth** /həd ˌbetə^r ˈduː (sth)/ ESPECIALLY SPOKEN use this to say that you think someone should do something because it is sensible or it will help them avoid problems: *You'd better ask your teacher for advice.* | *It was starting to snow and we thought we had better go home.*

> ⚠ Don't say 'you better go home' or 'you'd better to go home'. Say **you'd better go home**.

◯ **it's/that's a good idea** /ɪts, ðæts ə ˌɡʊd aɪˈdɪə/ ESPECIALLY SPOKEN say this to emphasize that you think an idea or suggestion will help someone or prevent problems: *"I'll check the oil before we set off." "Yes, that's a good idea."*
it's a good idea to do sth *It's a good idea to write down the serial number of your computer in case it gets stolen.*

SHOUT

to say something very loudly

shout /ʃaʊt/ [v I/T] to say something very loudly, because you want to make sure that someone hears you, or because you are angry or excited: *"Get out!" she shouted angrily.* | *There was so much noise from the engine that we had to shout to hear each other.* | *The protesters marched through the streets, shouting slogans.*
+at *I wish you'd stop shouting at the children.*
shout [n C] *As we got near the stadium, we could hear the shouts of the crowd.*

scream /skriːm/ [v I/T] to make a loud, high noise, or say something in a high, loud voice, because you are excited, frightened, angry, or in pain: *The man took out a gun and everyone started screaming.* | *"Help me!" she screamed.*
+at (=because you are angry with them) *Maria felt like screaming at her husband.*
scream with pain/delight/terror etc *She woke up screaming with terror.*

scream [n C] *We could hear screams coming from the burning building.*

yell /jel/ [v I/T] to shout very loudly, either because you are excited, angry, or in pain, or because you want to make sure that someone can hear you: *The audience was yelling and clapping.* | *"Don't touch me!" she yelled.*
+at *Children were yelling at each other across the street.*
yell [n C]
give/let out a yell (=yell once) *Thomas gave a sudden yell of excitement.*

cheer /tʃɪə^r/ [v I/T] to shout in order to show that you like or approve of a person, team, performance etc: *The crowd cheered as the President's car drove past.* | *The speaker was cheered loudly when he called for a total ban on nuclear weapons.*
cheer [n C] *There was a big cheer as the band came onto the stage.*

call out /ˌkɔːl ˈaʊt/ [phrasal verb I/T] to shout something in order to get someone's attention, for example to warn them or ask them for help: *She opened her mouth to call out, but no sound came.*
call out sth *A voice from the back of the room called out "Never!"*
call sth out *When I call your name out, put up your hand.*

cry out /ˌkraɪ ˈaʊt/ [phrasal verb I] WRITTEN to make a sudden loud noise, for example when you are suddenly hurt or afraid
cry out in fear/pain/surprise etc *Chris fell, crying out in pain.*

cry /kraɪ/ [v T] WRITTEN to shout something loudly, especially because you are feeling strong emotions such as pain or excitement: *"I can't move," Lesley cried. "I think I've broken my leg."* | *"Come and see what I've found!" Kurt cried.*

raise your voice /ˌreɪz jɔː^r ˈvɔɪs/ to speak more loudly than usual, because you are angry: *I never heard my father raise his voice.*
raised voices (=the sound of people talking loudly because they are angry) *I heard raised voices coming from the next room.*

SHOW

➡ if you mean 'show that something is true/not true or correct', go to **PROVE**

➡ if you mean 'show someone how to do something', go to **EXPLAIN**

➡ if you mean 'show off', go to **PROUD 4**

1 to let someone see something

show /ʃəʊ/ [v T] to let someone see something, especially by holding it out in front of them: *Everyone has to show their identity cards at the entrance to the building.*
show sb sth *Stephanie showed us her engagement ring.* | *Has he shown you his photos of the baby yet?*
show sth to sb *Show your ticket to the inspector, Charlie.*
showing – showed – have shown

○ **let sb see sth** /ˌlet (sb) 'siː (sth)/ ESPECIALLY SPOKEN to show something to someone, especially because they have asked to see it: *She won't let anyone see the painting until it is finished.* | *I couldn't let anyone see the house in such a mess.*

show off /ˌʃəʊ 'ɒfǁ-'ɔːf/ [phrasal verb T] to show something that you are proud of to other people, because you want them to admire it
show off sth *He couldn't wait to show off his new car.*
show sth off to sb *Rosa showed her new baby off to all her friends.*

2 to show someone where something is

show /ʃəʊ/ [v T] to show someone where something is
show sb where *The secretary showed her where to put her coat.*
show sb sth *Uncle Joe showed me the best place to go fishing.*
show sb the way (=go somewhere with someone when they do not know how to get there) *I'll show you the way to the station – it's not far.*
show sb around (=show someone all the interesting or important parts of a

place) *Jan has offered to show me around Oxford tomorrow.*
showing – showed – have shown

point /pɔɪnt/ [v I] to show someone where something is, by pointing towards it with your finger
+to *"That's your desk," he said, pointing to a table piled with files and books.*
point out sth/point sth out (=show something to someone, when there are many of the same things together) *She pointed out the house where she was born.*

3 when a machine or sign shows information or measurements

show /ʃəʊ/ [v T] to show information about something: *There was a thermometer showing the temperature of the water in the pool.*
+(that) *This light shows that the machine is switched on.*
showing – showed – have shown

○ **say** /seɪ/ [v T] ESPECIALLY SPOKEN to show a particular distance, time, or speed: *The clock said three o'clock when we left.* | *I was surprised that the fuel gauge still said half full.*
saying – said – have said

display /dɪ'spleɪ/ [v T] if a computer or sign **displays** information, it shows the information in a way that makes it easy to see or notice: *The computer displays the date in the top right corner of the screen.* | *The parking restrictions are displayed on a small yellow sign.*

> **Formal or informal?**
> **Display** is more formal than **show**.

4 paintings/art

be shown/be on show /biː 'ʃəʊn, biː ɒn 'ʃəʊ/ if a work of art **is shown** or **is on show**, it is put in a public place so that people can look at it: *Some of the artist's paintings are on show at the National Gallery.* | *This is the first time the jewels have been shown outside Russia.*

exhibition (also **exhibit** AMERICAN) /ˌeksɪ'bɪʃən, ɪg'zɪbɪt/ [n C] an event at which paintings, photographs etc are shown to the public for a period of time: *We went to see the Picasso exhibition at the Museum of Modern Art.*

5 when actions, behaviour, or events show that something is true

show /ʃəʊ/ [v T] to show that something is true
+(that) *The election results showed that people weren't satisfied with the government.* | *The case shows that women still face discrimination at work.*
show how/why/what etc *Send her flowers to show how much you care.*
showing – showed – have shown

demonstrate /'demənstreɪt/ [v T] FORMAL to show very clearly that something is true: *The Chernobyl disaster demonstrated the dangers of nuclear power.*
+that *The results of the experiment demonstrate that there is no difference between girls' and boys' abilities at this age.*

be a sign /biː ə 'saɪn/ if an event or action **is a sign** of something else, it is one of the things that shows that something is probably true
+that *When a dog shakes his tail it's a sign that he's happy.*
+of *He kept fiddling with the pen, which I thought was a sign of nervousness.*

suggest /sə'dʒest‖səg'dʒest/ [v T] to show that something is probably true, even though there is no definite proof
+(that) *There was nothing in his letter to suggest that he might be unhappy.*
strongly suggest (=show that something is very likely) *The door had not been forced open, which strongly suggests that the victim knew the killer.*

mean /miːn/ [v T] if an event or action **means** something, you can guess from it that something is true
+(that) *The lights are on – that means he must still be there.* | *Just because I asked her out for a meal, it doesn't mean that I'm madly in love with her.*
meaning – meant – have meant

indicate /'ɪndᵻkeɪt/ [v T] FORMAL if scientific facts, tests, official figures etc **indicate** something, they show

that it is likely to be true
+that *Research indicates that the drug can be harmful to pregnant women.* | *A recent survey has indicated that viewers want a wider choice of programmes on TV.*

6 to show your feelings, abilities, or attitudes

show /ʃəʊ/ [v T] to behave in a way that shows people how you feel or what your character is like
show interest/surprise/enthusiasm/ anger etc (=show that you are interested, surprised etc) *Paul didn't show much interest in the idea.*
show how angry/upset/unhappy etc you are *I was determined not to show how upset I felt.*
show courage/determination/skill/ confidence etc (=show that you are brave, determined etc) *The hostages showed great courage in a very frightening situation.*
showing – showed – have shown

express /ɪk'spres/ [v T] to tell people what you are feeling or thinking: *He finds it very hard to express his feelings.*
express anger/doubts/surprise/ concern etc FORMAL (=say you are angry, uncertain etc) *Relatives of the murdered man expressed anger that the police had done so little.*

> **Formal or informal?**
> **Express** is not used in informal conversation.

can't hide /ˌkɑːnt 'haɪd‖ˌkænt-/ if you **can't hide** a strong feeling, you cannot stop yourself from showing it: *Kris couldn't hide his delight.* | *She didn't know if she could hide her feelings for much longer.*

SHUT/CLOSE

➡ opposite **OPEN**

1 door/window/box etc

shut /ʃʌt/ [v T] to move a door, window, gate etc so that it is no

longer open: *Come in and shut the door behind you.* | *Someone had shut the gate to stop the sheep from getting out onto the road.* | *She heard Charlotte downstairs shutting the windows and locking up for the night.*
shutting – shut – have shut

close /kləʊz/ [v T] to shut something: *Do you mind if I close the window?* | *She took the necklace out of the box and closed the lid.*

> ⚠ In most situations, **shut** and **close** mean exactly the same: *She shut the door = She closed the door.* But if you want to say that someone shuts a door slowly and quietly, you usually say **close**: *She closed the door carefully behind her so as not to wake the children.*

shut/closed /ʃʌt, kləʊzd/ [adj not before noun] not open: *Make sure all the windows are shut before you go out.* | *The gates were closed, and there was no other way in.*

slam /slæm/ [v T] to shut a door quickly so that it makes a loud noise, especially because you are angry: *Jane marched out of the room, slamming the door behind her.* | *He slammed the door so hard that the glass cracked.*
slamming – slammed – have slammed

lock /lɒk‖lɑːk/ [v T] if you **lock** something, you turn a key so that people cannot open it or go into it: *Don't forget to lock the back door.* | *I can't remember if I locked the car.*
locked [adj] *I need to get my coat out of your car – is it locked?* | *Karl kept the gun in a locked drawer in his bedroom.*

draw the curtains/close the curtains /ˌdrɔː ðə ˈkɜːrtnz, ˌkləʊz ðə ˈkɜːrtnz/ to close curtains by pulling them across a window: *Draw the curtains and turn on the lights.*

2 eyes/mouth

close/shut /kləʊz, ʃʌt/ [v T] to close your eyes or mouth: *I lay down and closed my eyes.* | *He shut his eyes and listened to the music.*
shutting – shut – have shut

closed/shut [adj not before noun] *The* girl was lying on the bed with her eyes closed. | *He kept his mouth tightly shut.*

3 to become shut

close/shut /kləʊz, ʃʌt/ [v I] WRITTEN to become shut: *He walked out and the door closed behind him.* | *There was a bang as the gate shut.* | *Her eyes closed, and she fell into a deep sleep.*
shutting – shut – have shut

slam (also **slam shut**) /slæm, ˌslæm ˈʃʌt/ [v I] WRITTEN if a door **slams** or **slams shut**, it shuts quickly and makes a loud noise: *Outside in the street, car doors slammed and people were shouting.* | *She heard a door slam shut and the sound of footsteps on the path.*
slamming – slammed – have slammed

4 shop/office

shut/close /ʃʌt, kləʊz/ [v I] if a shop or office **shuts** or **closes**, it stops being open for business: *"What time does the bank shut?" "Four o'clock."* | *Most of the stores close at 6:30.*
shutting – shut – have shut

be shut/be closed /biː ˈʃʌt, biː ˈkləʊzd/ if a shop or office **is shut** or **is closed**, it is not open for business: *The ticket office was closed.* | *It was nine o'clock and all the stores were shut.*

SHY

➡ opposite **CONFIDENT/NOT CONFIDENT**

1 not confident

shy /ʃaɪ/ [adj] nervous and embarrassed about talking to other people, especially people you do not know: *David was always rather quiet and shy at school.* | *Carrie gave him a shy smile.* | *I was too shy to ask her out on a date.*
shy – shyer – shyest

shyly [adv] *"Would you like to go for a drink?" he asked shyly.*
shyness [n U] shy feelings or

behaviour: *Alan forgot his shyness and began asking them questions.*

timid /'tɪmɨd/ [adj] frightened to talk to people or to give your opinion, because you have very little confidence: *Ralph's wife was a small, timid woman who hardly ever spoke.*

timidly [adv] *"Can I go home now?" Sue asked, timidly.*

reserved /rɪ'zɜːᵊvd/ [adj] someone who is **reserved** tries not to show their feelings to other people and does not talk a lot: *English people have a reputation for being very reserved.*

SIDE

➡ see also **MIDDLE, EDGE**

1 the part of an area that is furthest from the middle

side /saɪd/ [n C] one of the parts of an area that is furthest from the middle and closest to the edge
+of *We walked along the side of the road.*
on the side of sth *There were high walls on all four sides of the prison yard.*

side

I left the book on the side of the desk.

edge /edʒ/ [n C] the part around an object or area that is furthest from its centre, or the part along its side where its surface ends
+of *The edges of the carpet were torn.* | *Keep away from the edge of the cliff.*
on the edge of sth *Just leave it on the edge of your plate.*
at the edge of sth (=next to the edge) *The house stood right at the edge of the lake.*

edge

The edges of the paper were ragged.

end /end/ [n C] the part of a long object or area that is furthest from its beginning or centre
+of *He cut a thick slice from the end of the loaf.*
at one end of sth *Mrs Deacon sat at one end of the long table and I sat at the other.*

at both ends/at each end *There are scoreboards at both ends of the stadium.* | *A dumbbell is an iron bar with a heavy weight at each end.*
opposite ends *Their offices are at opposite ends of the hallway.*
the far end (=the end furthest from you) *A man stood on the far end of the pier.*

border /'bɔːᵊdəʳ/ [n C] a line or band around the edge of something such as a picture or a piece of cloth: *a tablecloth with a brightly patterned border*
+around *The card had a blue border around it.*

margin /'mɑːᵊdʒɨn/ [n C] the empty space on the left or right side of a page: *Someone had written a note in the left-hand margin.*

margin

margin

2 one of the two areas on either side of a line, wall, river etc

side /saɪd/ [n C]
+of *This side of the fence is private property.* | *From the other side of the wall came the sounds of children playing.* | *We crossed the bridge to the north side of the river.*

bank /bæŋk/ [n C] the land along the side of a river
on the bank of/banks of sth *a new theatre on the south bank of the Thames* | *the vineyards along the banks of the Rhone*

⚠ Don't confuse **bank** (of a river or stream), **shore** (of a sea or large lake), and **coast** (the part of a country that is close to the sea).

3 not the back or front

side /saɪd/ [n C] one of the two surfaces of a building, vehicle, or boat that is not the back, front, top, or bottom

+of *A truck ran into the side of the car.*
at the side of sth *There was another entrance at the side of the building.*

> ⚠️ **Side** is also used to mean one of the two surfaces of something flat, such as a sheet of paper, a coin etc: *Write on both sides of the paper.*

4 the left or right half of an object, area, or road

side /saɪd/ [n C]
+of *The left side of the brain controls the right side of the body.* | *The dancers came on from both sides of the stage.*
on the left-hand/right-hand/other side *In Japan they drive on the left-hand side of the road.*

5 towards the side

sideways /ˈsaɪdweɪz/ [adv] towards the left or right instead of straight ahead: *The car skidded sideways off the road.*
to one side/to the side /tə ˌwʌn ˈsaɪd, tə ðə ˈsaɪd/ if someone or something moves **to one side** or **to the side**, they move from where they are to the left or to the right: *She pushed her plate to one side and leaned forward.* | *Could you move a little to the side so we can get past?*
from side to side /frəm ˌsaɪd tə ˈsaɪd/ first to one side, then to the other: *The boat rocked from side to side.*

SIGN

➝ if you mean 'write your name', go to **WRITE 2**

1 a written sign that gives instructions or information

sign /saɪn/ [n C] something with words or shapes on it, which is put in a public place to show the name of a

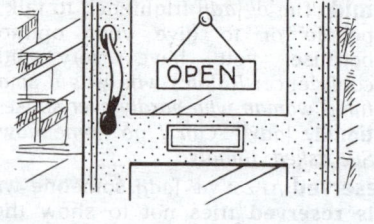

sign

building, town etc, or to give a warning or information: *The sign said 'No smoking'.* | *There was a big sign above the entrance.* | *Didn't you see the speed limit signs?*
traffic/road sign (=a sign that gives information to drivers)
the signs for (=the signs on a road that show how to go to a place) *Follow the signs for Atlanta.*

notice

notice /ˈnəʊtɪs/ [n C] a piece of paper giving instructions or information, which is put in a place where people can see it: *The details of the trip are on that notice over there.*
put up a notice (=attach it to a wall) *I'll put up a notice about the meeting.*
take down a notice (=remove it from a wall)

poster

poster /ˈpəʊstəʳ/ [n C] a large printed piece of paper which is put on a wall in a public place, and which gives information about something that is going to happen, for example a film or concert

+for *There are posters for the Van Gogh exhibition everywhere.*

election poster (=a poster that tells you to vote for a party or person in an election)

2 a picture or shape that has a special meaning

sign /saɪn/ [n C] a picture or a shape which has a particular meaning, and which is well known and often used: *You've forgotten to put the dollar sign before the total amount.* | *Where's the percentage sign on this keyboard?*

symbol /ˈsɪmbəl/ [n C] a picture, shape, or design that has a special meaning or represents an idea: *The walls were covered with magical symbols.* | *This symbol means the vegetables are organic.*

+of *The dove is a symbol of peace.*

+for *What is the mathematical symbol for 'infinity'?*

logo /ˈləʊgəʊ/ [n C] a sign that has been designed to represent an organization, company, or product: *The baseball team has a new logo.* | *bags with our company logo on them*

emblem /ˈembləm/ [n C] a picture of an object, flower, animal etc that is used to represent a country or organization: *England's national emblem is the rose.*

+of *The hammer and sickle is the emblem of the Communist Party.*

3 a movement or sound that you make to tell someone something

sign /saɪn/ [n C] a movement that you make in order to tell someone something: *He raised his hand in a sign of greeting.*

sign for sb to do sth *When the teacher puts her finger to her lips, it's a sign for us to be quiet.*

signal /ˈsɪgnəl/ [n C] a sound or movement that you make in order to tell someone to do something

give a signal *Don't start until I give the signal.*

signal to do sth *The soldiers were waiting for the signal to start firing.*

signal for sb to do sth *When I blow my whistle, that's the signal for you to start filming.*

gesture /ˈdʒestʃəʳ/ [n C] ESPECIALLY WRIT-TEN a movement of your hands, arms, or head that shows how you feel, especially when you are very worried or angry

+of *Jim raised his hands in a gesture of despair.*

make a gesture *Someone in another building started making gestures and pointing towards our kitchen.*

make a rude gesture *The fight started when one of the drivers made a rude gesture at someone.*

4 to make a movement or sound to tell someone something

make a sign /ˌmeɪk ə ˈsaɪn/ to make a movement, especially with your hand, in order to tell someone something: *I'll make a sign when I'm ready.*

make a sign to show/tell etc *The President made a sign to indicate that he wanted to leave.*

signal /ˈsɪgnəl/ [v I/T] to make a movement or sound in order to give instructions or information: *A sailor began signalling with two flags.*

+to *Capone finished his drink and signalled to the waiter.*

+that *An official signalled that it was time for the race to begin.*

signalling – signalled – have signalled BRITISH
signaling – signaled – have signaled AMERICAN

wave /weɪv/ [v I/T] to move your hand or arm from one side to the other, for example in order to get someone's attention or to tell them something

+at *Who's that waving at you?*

wave goodbye (=wave to someone who is leaving) *Her parents stood in the doorway and waved goodbye.*

wave sb through/on (=wave to show someone that they can go through or continue their journey) *At the border the customs officer just waved us through.*

wave [n C]

give sb a wave (=wave at someone in order to say hello or goodbye) *I gave him a friendly wave.*

wink /wɪŋk/ [v I] to quickly close and open one eye, in order to show that you are joking or that you share a secret with someone
+at *Ben grinned and winked at his father.*
wink [n C] when you close and open one eye quickly: *"Don't worry," he said with a wink. "I won't tell anyone about this."*

5 something that shows what is true or what is happening

sign /saɪn/ [n C] an event or fact that shows that something is true or that something is happening
+of *the first signs of the disease*
+(that) *A score of 80 or more is a sign that you are doing very well.*
be a sure sign of/(that) (=show that something is definitely true) *When Emma offers to help you it's a sure sign that she wants something from you!*
a good/hopeful/encouraging sign (=a sign that things are improving) *He ate all his food, which is a good sign.*
a clear/obvious sign *The fish are healthy, which is a clear sign that the water is clean.*
a bad sign (=a sign that things are getting worse) *The room suddenly got very quiet, which I took as a bad sign.*

evidence /ˈevɪdəns/ [n U] facts, objects etc that show that something exists or is true
+of *People have been looking for evidence of life on other planets for years.*
+that *There is no evidence that he ever worked for the company.*

> Don't say 'a lot of evidences'. Say **a lot of evidence**.

symptom /ˈsɪmptəm/ [n C] a sign that someone has an illness or that a serious problem exists: *Dr Duncan asked me what my symptoms were.*
+of *The first symptoms of hepatitis are tiredness and loss of weight.* | *The Bishop regards these crimes as a symptom of society's moral decline.*

SIMPLE

not complicated or not decorated

1 methods/systems/explanations/words

➡ opposite **DIFFICULT**

simple /ˈsɪmpəl/ [adj] not complicated, and therefore easy to understand: *All you have to do is to follow a few simple instructions.* | *The rules are simple.* | *There must be a perfectly simple explanation for what has happened.*
simple to use/operate/prepare etc *We chose a system that was simple to use.*
simply [adv] *Try to express your ideas more simply.* (=using simple language)
simplicity /sɪmˈplɪsɪti/ [n U] when something is easy to use or understand: *The simplicity of the system is its great advantage.*

easy /ˈiːzi/ [adj] not difficult to do, use, or understand: *The questions were really easy.* | *Our new computer system should make the work a lot easier.*
easy to read/use/learn etc *All the instructions are in large print to make them easy to read.*
it is easy to do sth *It is easy to see why she didn't marry him.*
easy for sb to do sth *Was it easy for you to find a job?*
find sth easy/find it easy to do sth *Susan's always found school work easy.*
easy – easier – easiest

straightforward /ˌstreɪtˈfɔːrwərd/ [adj] simple – use this especially about explanations, instructions, and methods which contain nothing difficult or unexpected: *The new accounting system is fairly straightforward.* | *The rules of the game are very straightforward.*

plain English /ˌpleɪn ˈɪŋglɪʃ/ English that ordinary people can understand, without any difficult or confusing words: *I wish they'd write in plain English, instead of all this business jargon.*

2 food/clothes/rooms designs

simple /'sɪmpəl/ [adj] **simple** food, clothes, or designs do not have a lot of decoration or unnecessary things added, but they are usually attractive or enjoyable: *a simple black dress* | *The meal was simple, but delicious.*

plain /pleɪn/ [adj] **plain** food, clothes, or designs do not have anything added or any decoration, and may be a little boring: *English food is rather plain compared to French food.* | *a plain black dress* | *The chapel was a small, plain, whitewashed building.*

basic /'beɪsɪk/ [adj] **basic** food, rooms, or designs only have the necessary features, and do not include things that make them more comfortable, more attractive etc: *Some of the hotels in the mountains are pretty basic.* | *The basic model of this car is £7000 including insurance and car tax.*

3 machines/tools

simple /'sɪmpəl/ [adj] a **simple** machine or tool has only a few parts and is not made in a complicated way: *The tribes of Central New Guinea use very simple tools such as hammers and axes.*

basic /'beɪsɪk/ [adj] **basic** machines, equipment, or tools only have the most necessary features and you cannot use them to do unusual, difficult, or complicated things: *The hospital lacked even the most basic medical equipment.* | *The basic tool-kit is good enough for most everyday repairs.*

4 to make something simpler

simplify /'sɪmpləfaɪ/ [v T] to make something simpler and easier to use or understand: *The government is planning to simplify the tax laws.*
simplifying – simplified – have simplified

simplified [adj] something that is **simplified** has been made easier to understand: *a simplified version of Jonathan Swift's novel, 'Gulliver's Travels'*

SING

→ see also **WB** **MUSIC, DANCE**

1 to sing

sing /sɪŋ/ [v I/T] to make musical sounds with your voice, especially the words of a song: *Sophie sings in the church choir.* | *I could hear someone singing downstairs.*
sing a song/tune/hymn *The kids were singing songs.* | *We sang 'Happy Birthday' as Dad came in.*
sing sb a song/tune *Come on, David, sing us a song!*
sing to sb *She sang softly to her baby.*
sing along (=sing with someone who is already singing) *Sing along if you know the words.*
singing – sang – have sung

hum /hʌm/ [v I/T] to make musical sounds with your voice, but with your mouth closed: *Carole hummed to herself as she worked.* | *He walked along, humming a tune.*
hum along to/with (=hum with a song that is playing) *Dave was humming along to the radio.*
humming – hummed – have hummed

whistle /'wɪsəl/ [v I/T] to make musical sounds by blowing air out between your lips: *Sam was painting the door, whistling softly as he worked.*
whistle a song/tune *You've been whistling that tune all day.*

2 someone who sings

singer /'sɪŋər/ [n C] someone who sings, especially as their job: *He's a really good singer.*
opera/jazz/blues/rock singer *Jodie dreamed of being a rock singer.*
lead singer (=the main singer in a pop group) *Mick Jagger, the lead singer with the Rolling Stones*

choir /kwaɪər/ [n C] a large group of singers who regularly sing in a church or school or with an orchestra (=large group of musicians): *I used to be in the school choir.*

S

3 something that you sing

song /sɒŋǁsɔːŋ/ [n C] a short piece of music with words for singing: *It's one of Bob Dylan's most famous songs.* | *an old Beatles song* | *The song was originally written by Schubert.*

hymn /hɪm/ [n C] a religious song that people sing in church

SIT

➡ see also **STAND, LIE**

1 to be sitting in a chair, on the floor etc

sit /sɪt/ [v I] to be in a chair, on the floor etc, with the weight of your body resting on your bottom, not on your feet: *It was a lovely day, and we sat outside in the sun.* | *Billy was sitting on the edge of the desk, swinging his legs.*
sit at a desk/table/bar/counter *I used to spend all day sitting at a desk.*
sit back (=sit and lean back against something) *Just sit back and relax.*
sit up (=sit with your back straight) *It's better for your back if you sit up straight.*
sit still (=sit quietly without moving) *I wish you children would sit still for 10 minutes.*
sitting – sat – have sat

> ⚠ You **sit on** something with a flat surface, such as the floor, a bed, a sofa or bench, or a plain chair or stool. You **sit in** a comfortable chair or a seat in a car, train etc. You **sit at** a desk, table, or bar (meaning that you sit facing it, for example to work or to eat a meal). And you **sit in front of** a television, computer, or fire.

sit up /ˌsɪt ˈʌp/ [phrasal verb I] to move your body so that you are sitting, after you have been lying down: *The day after the operation, he was allowed to sit up in bed.* | *Anna sat up at once, looking startled.*

2 to sit after you have been standing

sit down /ˌsɪt ˈdaʊn/ [phrasal verb I] to sit on a chair, bed, floor etc, after you have been standing: *Come in and sit down.*
+in/on/next to/beside etc *Fay sat down on the edge of the bed.*

sit /sɪt/ [v I] to sit down after you have been standing
+in/on/next to/beside etc *Come and sit next to me.* | *Let's go and sit by the window.*
sitting – sat – have sat

3 a place where you can sit

seat /siːt/ [n C] something you can sit on, especially in a bus, train, plane, theatre etc: *Our seats were right at the front of the bus.* | *He leaned back in his seat and lit a cigarette.*
back/front seat (=in a car)

place /pleɪs/ [n C] a seat – use this especially to talk about whether seats are available: *There are still some places at the back of the hall.* | *Are there any places left on tonight's flight to Rio?*

chair /tʃeəʳ/ [n C] a piece of furniture for one person to sit on: *He sat down in his favourite chair by the fireplace.*

> ⚠ You say sit **on** a chair if it is a plain piece of furniture with a hard seat. You say sit **in** a chair if it is a comfortable piece of furniture with a soft seat.

sofa/couch (also **settee** BRITISH) /ˈsəʊfə, kaʊtʃ, seˈtiː/ [n C] a comfortable piece of furniture which is big enough for two or three people to sit on: *Roy was lying on the sofa.* | *Come and sit with me on the couch.*

armchair /ˈɑːʳmtʃeəʳ, ɑːʳmˈtʃeəʳ/ [n C] a large comfortable chair with parts at the sides where you can rest your arms: *Dad was dozing in the armchair.*

bench /bentʃ/ [n C] a long hard seat made of wood or metal that several people can sit on, which does not have a back or arms

stool /stuːl/ [n C] a seat for one person, which has three or four legs and has no back or arms: *a bar stool*

4 what you say to tell someone to sit

🔍 **sit down** /ˌsɪt 'daʊn/ SPOKEN *Sit down, I have something to tell you.* | *Will you sit down and finish your breakfast!*

🔍 **have a seat/take a seat** /ˌhæv ə 'siːt, ˌteɪk ə 'siːt/ SPOKEN say this when telling someone politely to sit down: *Have a seat – the dentist won't be long.*

SITUATION

what is happening in a particular place or at a particular time

➡ see also **PLACE**

---

situation /ˌsɪtʃuˈeɪʃən/ [n C usually singular] the combination of all the things that are happening in a particular place and at a particular time, especially when this is causing problems: *With no rain for six months, the situation was becoming desperate.* | *I tried to explain the situation to my boss.*
economic/political situation *The economic situation in the US is getting better.*
difficult/awkward/tricky situation *They are working very hard to improve a difficult situation.*
be in a situation *It's good to be able to talk to other people who are in the same situation as yourself.*

circumstances /'sɜːˈkəmstænsɪz/ [n plural] the situation at a particular time, which influences what you do, what you decide, and what can happen: *TV cameras are sometimes allowed in the courts, but it depends on the circumstances.*
in some/certain circumstances *In some circumstances you may have to work on Saturdays.*
under normal circumstances *Under normal circumstances she would never have left the children alone.*
in the circumstances/under the circumstances (=use this to say that you think something should happen because of the situation now) *In the circumstances, it might be better if you took a few days off work.*

⚠ Don't say 'a circumstance' or 'the circumstance'. Say **the circumstances**.

🔍 **things** /θɪŋz/ [n plural] INFORMAL, ESPECIALLY SPOKEN the general situation that exists, especially the way it affects your life: *Don't worry! Things can't get any worse.* | *Things haven't changed much since I wrote to you last.*

position /pəˈzɪʃən/ [n C usually singular] the way things are at the present time, in a situation that is likely to change: *The position now is that the peace talks are continuing.*
in a good / bad / strong / difficult position *The party is now in a strong position in Congress.*

conditions /kənˈdɪʃənz/ [n plural] the things that make your life or your work comfortable or uncomfortable, for example whether you have enough food or money, whether the place where you are living or working is warm enough, safe enough etc: *Conditions in the city are getting worse every day.* | *How can people bring up a family in such dreadful conditions?*

⚠ Don't say 'a condition' or 'the condition'. Always say **conditions** in this meaning.

environment /ɪnˈvaɪərənmənt/ [n C] all the things that influence the way you live, work, and develop, such as the physical conditions you live in and the people around you: *Do girls learn better in an all-female environment?*
working/home environment *The company's comfortable offices and enthusiastic employees make for a pleasant working environment.*

Formal or informal?
Environment is not usually used in informal conversation.

SIZE

how big or small something is

➡ see also **BIG, SMALL, MEASURE**

size /saɪz/ [n C/U] how big or small something is: *Your piece of cake is exactly the same size as mine.* | *The price of a carpet will depend on its size and quality.*
be twice the size/be half the size (=be twice as big or half as big) *Their apartment is half the size of ours.*
of different sizes/of various sizes *There were several pieces of wood of different sizes.*
vary in size (=be of different sizes) *The American states vary enormously in size, from very large to very small.*
... the size of sth (=when something is the same size as something else) *an area of forest the size of Luxembourg*
... this/that size (=as big as this one or that one) *In a class this size, there will always be a few problems.*

> ⚠ When you are asking about someone's clothes size, you can say **what size are you?** or **what size do you take?** (British) or **what size do you wear?** (American). When you are talking about your clothes size, you say **I'm a 6/12/42 etc** or **I take a size 6/12 etc** (British), or **I wear a size 6/12 etc** (American).

how big /haʊ ˈbɪg/ use this to ask or talk about the size of something: *How big is the table?* | *We need to know how big the hall is.*

area /ˈeəriə/ [n C/U] the amount of space a flat surface such as a floor or a field covers
+of *Calculate the area of the walls and ceiling before you buy the paint.* | *Forest fires caused damage over an area of about 5000 square miles.* | *a room with a floor area of 20 square metres*

be 5 metres high/2 miles long/6 centimetres wide etc use this to say how high, how long etc something is: *The River Nile is over 6000 kilometres long.* | *In some places the path is only a couple of feet wide.*

be 10 metres by 15 metres/be 5 cm by 20 cm etc use this to say what the size of an area, object, or room is: *The kitchen is 4 metres by 2 metres.* (=4 metres long and 2 metres wide)
measure 10 m by 15 m/5 cm by 20 cm etc *The photographs should measure 3 cm by 2 cm.*

SLEEP

➡ see also **TIRED, REST, WAKE UP/GET UP**

1 to sleep

sleep /sliːp/ [v I] *The baby was sleeping peacefully.* | *I had to sleep on the floor.*
sleep well *"Did you sleep well?" "Yes, thanks."*
sleep like a log INFORMAL (=sleep very well)
sleep badly/not sleep well *I haven't been sleeping well recently.*
sleep in/late (=deliberately sleep until a later time than usual, and get up late) *We usually sleep in on Sundays.* | *I slept late that morning.*
sleep rough BRITISH (=sleep outside or in an empty building, because you have no home) *Hundreds of homeless people sleep rough every night in London.*
sleeping – slept – have slept

> ⚠ Don't confuse **sleep** (=be asleep) and **go to sleep** (=start sleeping). Don't say 'I slept at midnight'. Say **I went to sleep at midnight**.

sleep /sliːp/ [n singular/U] time when you are sleeping: *Lack of sleep can make you bad-tempered.*
in your sleep (=while you are sleeping) *Katie sometimes talks in her sleep.*
get some sleep (=spend time sleeping, especially when you are very tired and need to sleep) *I didn't get much sleep last night.*
a good night's sleep (=a long sleep at night, which makes you feel relaxed and comfortable) *What you need is a good night's sleep.*
have a sleep BRITISH (=sleep for a short time, especially in the daytime)

The baby usually has a sleep after lunch.

deep sleep (=time when you are asleep and difficult to wake) *Exhausted, she fell into a deep sleep.*

be asleep /biː əˈsliːp/ to be sleeping: *Nicky was still asleep.* | *We found Mom asleep on the sofa.*

be fast asleep (=be sleeping very well) *The kids were all fast asleep in the back of the car.*

oversleep /ˌəʊvəʳˈsliːp/ [v I] to sleep for too long, so that you are late for something: *I'm sorry I'm late – I overslept.*

oversleeping – overslept – have overslept

have a nap/take a nap /ˌhæv ə ˈnæp, ˌteɪk ə ˈnæp/ to sleep for a short time during the day: *The children have a nap every morning at about 11 o'clock.*

doze /dəʊz/ [v I] to sleep for a short time, often waking up and going back to sleep again, especially when you are not in your bed: *Grandpa was dozing by the fire.*

snooze (also **have/take a snooze**) /snuːz. ˌhæv, ˌteɪk ə ˈsnuːz/ [v I] INFORMAL to sleep for a short time, especially during the time when you do not usually sleep: *Dad was snoozing in his armchair.*

snooze [n usually singular] a short period of time when you are asleep, especially during the day: *The cat was having a snooze in its usual place next to the radiator.*

2 to start sleeping

go to sleep /ˌgəʊ tə ˈsliːp/ to start sleeping: *Shut up and go to sleep!* | *I didn't go to sleep until after midnight.* | *"I'll stay with her till she goes to sleep," said Theo.*

fall asleep /ˌfɔːl əˈsliːp/ to start sleeping, especially when you do not intend to: *The movie was so boring that I fell asleep halfway through it.* | *As usual, he had fallen asleep in front of the TV.*

doze off /ˌdəʊz ˈɒfǁ-ˈɔːf/ [phrasal verb I] to start sleeping when you do not intend to, and sleep for just a short time: *I must have dozed off for a few minutes.*

drop off /ˌdrɒp ˈɒfǁˌdrɑːp ˈɔːf/ [phrasal verb I] to go to sleep easily and peacefully, often when you do not intend to: *She nearly dropped off during the meeting.*

drop off to sleep *I must have dropped off to sleep.*

3 to get into your bed at the end of the day

go to bed /ˌgəʊ tə ˈbed/ *I usually go to bed at about eleven-thirty.* | *"Can I speak to Andrea?" "Sorry, she's already gone to bed."*

4 what you say to someone when they are going to bed

goodnight (also **night** INFORMAL) /gʊdˈnaɪt, naɪt/ SPOKEN say this when you are going to bed, or to someone else who is going to bed: *Goodnight, everyone.* | *"Night Dad." "Night Steve."*

say goodnight *I said goodnight to my parents and went up to bed.*

sleep well /ˌsliːp ˈwel/ SPOKEN say this to someone who is going to bed, especially someone in your family or a close friend: *Goodnight, Paula. Sleep well!*

5 not asleep

awake /əˈweɪk/ [adj not before noun] not sleeping: *"Are you awake?" he whispered.*

wide awake (=not asleep and not tired) *It was 3 o'clock in the morning, but Peter was still wide awake.*

lie awake (=lie in bed, but not be able to sleep) *I lay awake all night worrying about it.*

keep sb awake (=prevent someone from sleeping) *The noise of the party kept us awake for most of the night.*

stay awake (=deliberately not go to sleep) *One of us should stay awake and keep watch.*

can't get to sleep/can't sleep /ˌkɑːnt get tə ˈsliːp, ˌkɑːnt ˈsliːpǁˌkænt-/ use this to say that someone cannot sleep although they want to: *There was so* *much noise that I couldn't get to sleep till four o'clock in the morning.* | *Mum, I can't sleep.*

conscious /ˈkɒnʃəs‖ˈkɑːn-/ [*adj* not before noun] awake and able to understand what is happening around you – use this about someone who is ill or has had an accident: *The driver was still conscious but in great pain.*
fully conscious (=completely conscious)

insomnia /ɪnˈsɒmniə‖ɪnˈsɑːm-/ [*n* U] someone who has **insomnia** cannot sleep – use this when it is considered to be a health problem: *Strong coffee can cause insomnia.*

6 when someone cannot feel anything and seems to be asleep

unconscious /ʌnˈkɒnʃəs‖-ˈkɑːn-/ [*adj*] if you are **unconscious**, you cannot see, hear, or feel anything, for example because you have had an accident or been given a drug: *She was lying unconscious on the floor.*
be knocked unconscious (=become unconscious because you have been hit on the head) *There was a fight, and Mark was knocked unconscious.*

faint /feɪnt/ [*v* I] to become unconscious and fall down, for example because you are feeling very hot or hungry: *I need to go outside. I think I'm going to faint.* | *Several of the fans fainted and had to be carried out of the concert.*

in a coma /ɪn ə ˈkəʊmə/ unconscious for a long time because of a serious accident or illness: *Her father has been in a coma for six months.*
go into a coma (=start to be in a coma) *Ellen went into a coma and died soon afterwards.*

SLIDE

1 to slide

slide /slaɪd/ [*v* I] to move smoothly across a surface
+along / around / down etc *The*

slide

children were having fun sliding around on the ice. | *Several glasses slid off the tray and crashed to the floor.*
sliding – slid – have slid

slip /slɪp/ [*v* I] to accidentally slide a short distance, especially when you then fall down: *He slipped and fell – I think he's broken his arm.* | *The floor's wet – careful you don't slip!*
+on *I slipped on some ice and landed on my back.*
slipping – slipped – have slipped

skid

skid /skɪd/ [*v* I] if a vehicle **skids**, it suddenly slides to the side and it is difficult for the driver to control it: *The car rounded the bend, skidded, and crashed into a tree.*
+across/on/off etc *Nineteen people were injured today when a bus skidded off the road into a ditch.*
skidding – skidded – have skidded

2 a surface that makes you slip

slippery /ˈslɪpəri/ [*adj*] a **slippery** surface is so smooth or wet that it is difficult to stand or move safely on it: *Be careful – the floor is very slippery.* | *The track is steep and slippery.* | *slippery rocks*

icy /'aɪsi/ [adj] covered in ice and very slippery: *Be careful – the roads are very icy this morning.* | *Despite the icy ground, the children ran on ahead.*

greasy /'griːsi/ [adj] a **greasy** surface is slippery because it is covered with a mixture of rain and oil: *Police say the rain is making the roads greasy.*

SLOW

➡ opposite **FAST**

1 moving slowly or doing something slowly

slow /sləʊ/ [adj] not moving quickly or not doing something quickly: *The train was slow, noisy, and uncomfortable.* | *a slow graceful dance* | *The race got off to a fast start and the slowest runners were soon left behind.* | *My computer's really slow compared to the ones at school.*
be slow to do sth (=not do it quickly enough) *Unfortunately, many of our clients have been slow to pay their bill.*

slowly /'sləʊli/ [adv] *He got up slowly out of his chair and came towards me.* | *Can you speak more slowly? I can't understand what you're saying.* | *A big white cloud drifted slowly across the sky.*

2 happening slowly or changing slowly

slow /sləʊ/ [adj] taking a long time: *She's making a slow recovery after her illness.* | *For the first few months my progress was extremely slow.* | *Rebuilding the country's economy is likely to be a long, slow process.*

slowly /'sləʊli/ [adv] *The situation is slowly improving.* | *Slowly, prices began to fall.*

gradually/little by little /'grædʒuəli, ˌlɪtl baɪ 'lɪtl/ [adv] happening slowly by a series of small amounts or changes, over a long period of time: *Our climate is gradually becoming warmer and drier.* | *Little by little, Guy's health improved.* | *I was gradually beginning to realize the seriousness of the situation.*

 Little by little is used in written stories or descriptions of events.

gradual /'grædʒuəl/ [adj] happening or changing slowly over a long period of time – use this about a process or change, or an increase or reduction: *I had noticed a gradual improvement in her written work.* | *a gradual fall in the number of unemployed people*

take too long /ˌteɪk tuː 'lɒŋǁ-'lɔːŋ/ if something **takes too long**, it happens too slowly, or you need too much time to do it: *I won't read out the whole statement – that would take too long.*
take too long to do sth *I've changed my mind – it would take too long to explain why.*

3 to become slower or make something slower

slow down /ˌsləʊ 'daʊn/ [phrasal verb I/T] *You're driving too fast – slow down!*
slow sth/sb down *The bad weather slowed us down a lot.*

When you see **WB**, go to the **WORD BANKS** section.

SMALL

➡ if you mean 'become smaller in amount' or 'make something smaller in amount', go to **LESS**

➡ opposite **BIG**

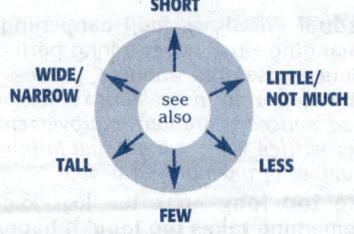

1 small in size

⚠ **Small** and **little** mean the same, but always use **small** (not 'little') when you are simply talking about the size of something or giving information about its size. Use **little** when you want to show your feelings or opinion about a small thing or person.

small /smɔːl/ [adj] His office was a small room at the top of the building. | These shoes are too small for me. | a small insect that can give you a nasty bite | Arthur was 16, but he was small for his age. | Her father owns a small printing business. | a small town in Missouri | Which is the smallest state in the US?

little /'lɪtl/ [adj only before noun] small – use this especially to show how you feel about someone or something, for example to show that you like them, dislike them, or feel sorry for them: It's just a little souvenir I brought back from Italy.

🔍 **nice little/lovely little** ESPECIALLY SPOKEN What a lovely little dog! | They've bought a nice little house in the country.

🔍 **poor little** SPOKEN (use this when you feel sorry for someone) a poor little bird with a broken wing

🔍 **silly little / horrible little etc** SPOKEN silly little coffee cups that only hold one mouthful of coffee | What a horrible little boy!

 Don't use 'very', 'more', or 'most' with **little**.

tiny /'taɪni/ [adj] very small: the baby's tiny fingers | The apartment has two bedrooms and a tiny kitchen.

🔍 **tiny little** ESPECIALLY SPOKEN The box was full of tiny little blue beads.
tiny – tinier – tiniest

minute /maɪ'njuːt‖-'nuːt/ [adj] extremely small and difficult to see: minute pieces of broken glass | Her handwriting is minute. | The problem was caused by minute particles of dust getting into the disk drive.

> **Formal or informal?**
> **Minute** is more formal or more technical than **tiny**.

cramped /kræmpt/ [adj] a room, space, or vehicle that is **cramped** is uncomfortable because there is not enough space inside it for people to move around: I hated working in that cramped little office. | Conditions on board the ship were extremely cramped.

2 small numbers/amounts

small /smɔːl/ [adj] Our drinking water contains small quantities of fluoride and calcium. | The car industry is dominated by a small number of very powerful companies.

 Don't use **little** to talk about numbers or amounts – use **small**.

 Don't use **small** about prices and wages – use **low**.

low /ləʊ/ [adj] **low** prices, wages, levels etc are less than usual or less than they should be: It's a good time to buy a computer, because prices are low. | Farm workers are complaining about long hours and low wages. | low interest rates

 Don't say 'a low amount'. Say **a small amount**.

tiny /'taɪni/ [adj usually before noun] a **tiny** amount or number is very small: *Only a tiny fraction of our profit comes from book sales.*
a tiny minority (=a very small number of a much larger group) *Millions of people buy lottery tickets, but only a tiny minority ever win anything.*
tiny – tinier – tiniest

3 small changes/differences/ problems

small /smɔːl/ [adj] *a small increase in unemployment | I want to make a few small changes to the design. | There is still one small problem that we haven't dealt with.*

slight /slaɪt/ [adj usually before noun] small and not very important or noticeable: *There has been a slight change of plan. | The doctor says there has been a slight improvement in her condition.*
the slightest change/difference (=one that is extremely small and difficult to measure) *a thermometer that can record the slightest change in temperature*

 Don't say 'slighter'.

minor /'maɪnəʳ/ [adj only before noun] use this about small changes or problems that are not important enough or serious enough to worry about
minor change/difference/problem/ injury/detail *Except for one or two minor changes, the course is the same as last year. | She fell off her horse, but suffered only minor injuries.*

4 to become smaller

➡ see also **LESS**

get smaller /ˌget 'smɔːləʳ/ *The dot got smaller and smaller, and vanished from the screen. | Am I getting fatter or is this dress getting smaller?*

shrink /ʃrɪŋk/ [v I] if clothes **shrink**, they get smaller when they are washed: *Don't wash that sweater in hot water – it'll shrink.*
shrinking – shrank – have shrunk

SMELL

➡ see also **TASTE**

1 a smell

smell /smel/ [n C] something that you notice by using your nose: *What's that smell? Is something burning? | the smells from the factory | cooking smells*
+of *There was a lovely smell of freshly-baked bread.*

> ⚠ When **smell** is used without an adjective, it usually means an unpleasant smell: *Can we open the window and get rid of the smell?*

stink /stɪŋk/ [n singular] a strong and very unpleasant smell: *The stink from the drains is almost unbearable in summer.*
+of *There was a stink of dead fish coming from the garbage can.*

odour BRITISH **odor** AMERICAN /'əʊdəʳ/ [n C] a strong and usually unpleasant smell that is easy to recognize: *Buyers will be put off by unpleasant household odours.*
+of *A strong odour of sweat filled the air.*

> **Formal or informal?**
> In British English, **odour** is more formal than **smell**, and is mostly used in writing. But in American English, **odor** is often used as another way of saying 'smell'.

aroma /ə'rəʊmə/ [n C] a pleasant smell, especially from food or coffee: *Each of these herbs has its own flavour and aroma.*
+of *the aroma of fresh coffee*

> **Formal or informal?**
> **Aroma** is more formal than **smell**.

scent/fragrance /sent, 'freɪɡrəns/ [n C] a pleasant smell, especially from flowers, plants, or fruit: *The rose has a delicate fragrance.*
+of *the scent of jasmine*

S

2 to have a particular kind of smell

have a nice/horrible/strange etc smell /hæv ə (nice etc) 'smel/ *The house was empty, and the rooms had a stale, damp smell.* | *The drink has an unusual smell, but it tastes very nice.*

smell /smel/ [v] to have a particular smell

smell nice/good/awful/sweet etc *The air smelled clean and fresh after the storm.*

smell of sth *The house still smells of paint.* | *She smelled of alcohol and was unsteady on her feet.*

smell like sth *It smells like a hospital in here.*

smelling – smelled (also **smelt** BRITISH) - **have smelled** (also **have smelt** BRITISH)

> ⚠ When **smell** is used without an adjective or preposition, it always means that something has an unpleasant smell: *Those socks really smell.*

3 to have a bad smell

smell /smel/ [v I] to have an unpleasant smell: *Does my breath smell?* | *It's time you cleaned the bird cage out – it's starting to smell.*

smell awful / terrible / disgusting *What's in this bag? It smells absolutely awful.*

smelling – smelled (also **smelt** BRITISH) – **have smelled** (also **have smelt** BRITISH)

stink /stɪŋk/ [v I] to have a strong and unpleasant smell: *How can you eat that cheese – it stinks!*

stink of sth *The house stank of cigarette smoke.*

stinking – stank – have stunk

smelly /'smeli/ [adj] something that is **smelly** has a bad smell: *smelly socks* | *The water in the pond had turned brown and smelly.*

smelly – smellier – smelliest

reek of sth /'riːk ɒv (sth)/ [phrasal verb T] ESPECIALLY WRITTEN to have a very strong smell of something unpleasant: *The whole place reeked of garlic.* |

After days of travelling in the tropical heat, their bodies reeked of sweat.

4 to smell something

smell /smel/ [v T not in passive] to notice the smell of something, especially by putting your nose near it: *Smell these roses – aren't they lovely?* | *Have you been drinking? Let me smell your breath.* | *If you smell gas, call this number immediately.*

can smell (=notice a smell) *I'm sure I can smell something burning.*

smelling – smelled (also **smelt** BRITISH) - **have smelled** (also **have smelt** BRITISH)

> ⚠ Don't say 'I am smelling gas'. Say **I can smell gas**.

sniff /snɪf/ [v I/T not in passive] to take quick breaths through your nose in order to smell something: *He opened the milk and sniffed it.* | *Before you stroke a dog, let it sniff the back of your hand.*

+at *The dog was rushing around excitedly, sniffing at the ground.*

sense of smell /ˌsens əv 'smel/ [n singular] the ability to notice smells: *Dogs have a very good sense of smell.*

5 something that you put on your body to make it smell nice

perfume (also **scent** BRITISH) /'pɜːˈfjuːm, sent/ [n C/U] a liquid that a woman puts on her neck or body to make it smell nice: *The pillow smelled of cheap perfume.*

wear perfume/scent (=have perfume on your body) *I wish she wouldn't wear that perfume to work.*

fragrance /'freɪɡrəns/ [n C] a perfume for women or for men – used mainly in advertisements: *Calvin Klein's exciting new fragrance for men – available now!*

cologne /kə'ləʊn/ [n C] a liquid that you put on your face or body to make it smell nice, similar to perfume but with a less strong smell

aftershave /'ɑːftəˈʃeɪv‖'æf-/ [n C/U] a liquid that a man puts on his face and neck to make it smell nice, especially after shaving (=cutting hair from his face)

deodorant /di'əʊdərənt/ [n C/U] a substance that you put on the skin under your arms to prevent or hide smells

SMILE

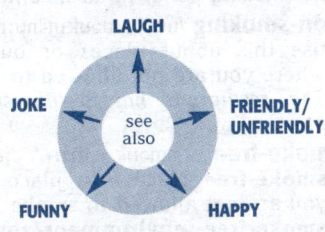

LAUGH

JOKE ← see also → FRIENDLY/ UNFRIENDLY

FUNNY ← → HAPPY

1 to smile

smile /smaɪl/ [v I] to make your mouth curve upwards, as a sign that you are happy or amused or that you want to be friendly: *She smiled and said "Good morning".* | *Rosie's such a cheerful girl – always smiling.*
+at *The twins turned and smiled at each other, sharing a private joke.*

> ⚠ Don't say 'he smiled to me'. Say **he smiled at me**.

grin /grɪn/ [v I] to give a big happy smile: *Hank was grinning with pleasure.* | *Grinning shyly, he offered her a drink.*
+at *She kept grinning at me as if we were old friends.*
grinning – grinned – have grinned

beam /biːm/ [v I] WRITTEN to smile for a long time, because you are very pleased about something or proud of something you have achieved: *Her parents stood there*

smile

grin

beaming as she went up to receive the prize.
+at *The bride and groom walked out of the church, beaming at everyone they passed.*

> Use **beam** especially in stories and descriptions of past events.

smirk /smɜːᵊk/ [v I] to smile in an unpleasant way, for example because you are pleased about someone else's bad luck or because you know something that they do not know: *She sits there smirking as if she's the only one who knows the answer.*
+at *What are you smirking at?*

sb's face lights up /(sb's) ˌfeɪs laɪts 'ʌp/ if **someone's face lights up**, they suddenly look very happy: *The children's faces lit up when we told them we were going to Disney World.*
+with joy/pleasure *Chantal's face lit up with joy as Max came towards her.*

2 a smile

smile /smaɪl/ [n C] the look on your face when you make your mouth curve upwards to show that you are happy, friendly, amused etc: *Helga has a lovely smile.*
give sb a smile (=smile at them) *Barry gave the old lady a warm smile.*
a big smile *"See you later," she said, giving us all a big smile.*
with a smile on your face *He fell asleep with a contented smile on his face.*

grin /grɪn/ [n C] a big happy smile: *That's Larry on the left of the picture, the one with the big grin on his face.*
give sb a grin (=grin at them) *William gave her a friendly grin as he walked past.*

smirk /smɜːᵊk/ [n C] ESPECIALLY WRITTEN an unpleasant, satisfied smile, for example when you are pleased about someone else's bad luck or when you think you know something that they do not know: *"You didn't pass, then?" Richard asked with a smirk.*

SMOKING

➡ see also **BURN, FIRE**

1 to smoke a cigarette, pipe etc

smoke /sməʊk/ [v I/T] *How old were you when you started smoking?* | *Do you mind if I smoke?* | *My father smokes a pipe.* | *He sat behind his desk, smoking a fat cigar.*
smoke 20/30 etc a day (=smoke 20, 30 etc cigarettes every day) *Anyone who smokes 40 a day can expect to have a lot of health problems.*
chain-smoke (=smoke cigarettes continuously) *While he was directing a movie, he would chain-smoke and drink black coffee.*

smoking /'sməʊkɪŋ/ [n U] the habit of smoking: *Smoking is bad for your health.*
passive smoking (=when you breathe in the smoke from other people's cigarettes)

puff on sth /'pʌf ɒn (sth)‖-ɑːn-/ [phrasal verb T] ESPECIALLY WRITTEN to take small amounts of smoke into your mouth from a cigarette, cigar, or pipe: *Barry was puffing on his pipe and looking thoughtful.*

smoker /'sməʊkəʳ/ [n C] someone who smokes regularly: *The survey shows that most smokers would like to stop smoking.* | *The average smoker spends about £18 a week on cigarettes.*
heavy smoker (=someone who smokes a lot) *I knew she was a heavy smoker when I saw the yellow stains on her fingers.*

2 to not smoke

don't smoke /,dəʊnt 'sməʊk/ [v T] if you **don't smoke**, you never smoke cigarettes or other tobacco products: *"Would you like a cigarette?" "No, thanks, I don't smoke."*

give up smoking ESPECIALLY BRITISH **quit smoking** ESPECIALLY AMERICAN /,gɪv ʌp 'sməʊkɪŋ, ,kwɪt 'sməʊkɪŋ/ to stop smoking, especially when you make a firm decision that you will not smoke again: *I'm trying to give up smoking, but it isn't easy.*

non-smoker /nɒn 'sməʊkəʳ‖nɑːn-/ [n C] someone who never smokes: *This part of the restaurant is reserved for non-smokers.* | *Non-smokers get cheaper health insurance.*

no-smoking /,nəʊ 'sməʊkɪŋ/ [adj only before noun] use this about rules or signs that say you must not smoke
a no-smoking sign/policy *There were big no-smoking signs on all the walls.* | *The company has a no-smoking policy in all its offices.*

non-smoking /nɒn 'sməʊkɪŋ‖nɑːn-/ [adj] use this about places or buildings where you are not allowed to smoke: *The restaurant has a non-smoking area.*

smoke-free /,sməʊk 'friː◂/ [adj] a **smoke-free** place is a place where you are not allowed to smoke
smoke-free environment/zone etc *new laws to create a smoke-free environment*

3 to light a cigarette, pipe etc

light /laɪt/ [v T] to make a cigarette, cigar, or pipe start burning: *The old man struck a match and lit his pipe.* | *I leaned forward to light her cigarette.*
lighting – lit (also **lighted**) – **have lit** (also **have lighted**)

 have you got a light? BRITISH **do you have a light?** AMERICAN /,hæv juː gɒt ə 'laɪt, ,duː juː hæv ə 'laɪt‖-gɑːt-/ SPOKEN say this to ask someone for a match or a lighter to light your cigarette: *Excuse me, do you have a light?*

> ⚠ Don't say 'have you got fire?' or 'do you have fire?'

4 to make a cigarette, pipe etc stop burning

put out /,pʊt 'aʊt/ [phrasal verb T] to make a cigarette, cigar, or pipe stop burning
put out sth/put sth out *Bill put out his pipe and stood up to leave.*

extinguish /ɪk'stɪŋgwɪʃ/ [v T] FORMAL to put out a cigarette, cigar, or pipe – often used in official notices or announcements, especially in the past: *Passengers are requested to extinguish all cigarettes when the red light goes on.*

stub out /ˌstʌb ˈaʊt/ [phrasal verb T] to put out a cigarette by pressing the end of it against something
stub out sth/stub sth out *She nervously stubbed out her cigarette, and immediately lit another one.*

SOFT

➡ opposite **HARD**

soft /sɒft‖sɔːft/ [adj] not hard, and easy to press or crush, or pleasant to touch: *I need a softer pillow. | shoes made of very soft leather | The ground was soft after all the rain.*
softness [n U] when something is not hard, and is easy to press or crush: *She loved the softness of the cat's fur.*
tender /ˈtendəʳ/ [adj] use this about meat and vegetables that are soft and easy to cut because they have been cooked well: *Fry the chicken for a further 15 minutes, until it is tender.*
smooth /smuːð/ [adj] use this about skin or fur that is soft and pleasant to touch: *Her skin was as smooth as silk.*

SOME

➡ look here for ...
• some but not many
• some but not much
• some but not all

1 **some, but not a large number**

some /səm, strong sʌm/ [determiner/pronoun] a number of people or things, but not a large number – use this when you are not saying exactly

what the number is: *There were some children playing in the street. | "Do you have any tools?" "Yes, there should be some in the back of the car."*
some more/some other *I've got some more pictures of her upstairs. | There are some other reasons besides those I have mentioned.*

⚠ Don't use **some** in negative sentences. Use **any**. Don't say 'I don't have some cigarettes'. Say **I don't have any cigarettes**.

⚠ In questions, you can use either **some** or **any**: *Do you want some chips? | Do you want any chips?* But use **some** especially when you think that the other person will answer 'yes'.

a few /ə ˈfjuː/ [quantifier] a small number of people, things, facts etc: *"Are there any chocolates left?" "Only a few." | They went to China a few years ago. | We know a few people who work in advertising. | There are a few problems I'd like to discuss with you.*

⚠ Don't confuse **a few** (=a small number) and **few** (=almost none): *She has few friends* (=almost no friends). | *She has a few friends* (=some friends).

⚠ Don't confuse **a few** (=a small number) and **a little** (=a small amount). **A few** is only used with plural nouns.

⚠ **Quite a few** means 'a fairly large number of people or things': *There were already quite a few people there.*

several /ˈsevərəl/ [quantifier] more than a few people or things, but not a large number: *The President visited several states on his tour. | Several people complained about the noise from the party. | I've been to Japan several times.*
a number of /ə ˈnʌmbər ɒv/ several: *A number of people said they had seen the gunman earlier in the day. | We have received a number of complaints about last night's television programme.*

Formal or informal?

A number of is not usually used in informal conversation.

🔍 **a couple of** /ə ˈkʌpəl ɒv/ INFORMAL, ESPECIALLY SPOKEN at least two, but not many more: *I'd just like to ask you a couple of questions before I go.* | *There wasn't much mail this morning – just a couple of bills.*

a series of /ə ˈsɪəriːz ɒv/ several things of the same kind that happen one after the other: *There has been a series of robberies in the area recently.* | *We are planning a series of concerts to raise money for charity.*

Formal or informal?

A series of is not usually used in informal conversation.

2 some, but not a large amount

some /səm, *strong* sʌm/ [*determiner/pronoun*] an amount of something, but not a large amount – use this when you are not saying exactly what the amount is: *Can I borrow some money, Dad?* | *I need some time to think about what you've said.* | *"We've run out of milk." "Do you want me to go and get some?"*
some more *Would you like some more meat?*

⚠️ Don't use **some** in negative sentences. Use **any**. Don't say 'I don't have some money'. Say **I don't have any money**.

⚠️ In questions, you can use either **some** or **any**: *Do you want some wine?* | *Do you want any wine?* But use **some** especially when you think that the other person will answer 'yes'.

a certain amount of /ə ˌsɜːˈtn əˈmaʊnt ɒv/ FORMAL a fairly large amount – use this to talk about people's feelings, abilities etc, not to talk about things: *a job that required a certain amount of intelligence and skill* | *A certain amount of stress is unavoidable in daily life.*

3 some, but not all

some/some of /sʌm, ˈsʌm ɒv/ [*quantifier*] some but not all of a number or amount: *Some students only come here because they want to have fun.* | *"Have you met Jack's friends?" "Some of them."* | *I've already spent some of the money.* | *Some trees lose their leaves in the autumn; others remain green all through the winter.*

a few of /ə ˈfjuː ɒv/ [*quantifier*] a few but not all of a number of people or things: *I'm going to the club with a few of my friends.*

several of /ˈsevərəl ɒv/ [*quantifier*] several but not all of a number of people or things: *Several of us are going on a trip to France.* | *Several of the islands have beautiful beaches.*

SOMETIMES

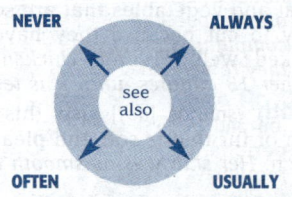

sometimes /ˈsʌmtaɪmz/ [*adv*] on some occasions, but not always: *Sometimes I drive to work and sometimes I walk.* | *Traffic noise is sometimes a problem.* | *The journey takes about an hour, sometimes even longer.*

⚠️ Don't forget the 's' at the end of **sometimes**.

occasionally /əˈkeɪʒənəli/ [*adv*] use this to talk about something that only happens a few times, and does not happen often: *Occasionally we go out to restaurants, but mostly we eat at home.*
very occasionally (=not at all often) *He lives in Australia now, so we only see him very occasionally.*
occasional [*adj*] only before noun happening a few times, but not at all

often: *Prisoners are allowed occasional visits from their relatives.*

> You can also say **the occasional ...** when you mean **an occasional ...**: *Apart from the occasional Christmas card, we never heard from her again.*

now and then/every now and then
/ˌnaʊ ənd 'ðen, ˌevri naʊ ənd 'ðen/ sometimes, but not regularly: *Now and then she would look up from her work and smile at him.* | *You see stories like this in the newspapers every now and then.*

from time to time /frəm ˌtaɪm tə 'taɪm/
sometimes, but not regularly and not often: *This is a problem that we all have from time to time.* | *It may rain from time to time.*

◯ the odd /ði 'ɒdǁ-'ɑːd/ [adj only before noun] **the odd drink/game/occasion/weekend etc** INFORMAL, ESPECIALLY SPOKEN a few drinks, games etc at various times, but not often and not regularly: *Jim and I have the odd drink together.* | *We get the odd complaint from customers, but mostly they're very satisfied.*

◯ off and on/on and off /ˌɒf ənd 'ɒn, ˌɒn ənd 'ɒf/ ESPECIALLY SPOKEN for short periods, but not continuously or regularly, over a long period of time: *We've been going out together for five years, off and on.* | *I worked in bars on and off for two years before I decided to go back to college.*

can be /'kæn biː/ sometimes – use this to talk about what may happen in a particular situation: *These dogs can be quite aggressive if they are not well trained.* | *She can be really stubborn once she has made up her mind about something.*

SOON

➡ see also **EARLY, LATER/AT A LATER TIME**

> Don't confuse **soon** (=in a short time) and **early** (=before the usual time).

1 soon

soon /suːn/ [adv] in a short time from now, or a short time after something else happens: *It'll soon be Christmas.* | *Driving in the city was hard at first, but she soon got used to it.* | *She arrived home sooner than we expected.*

as soon as possible *Please reply to this email as soon as possible.*

as soon as you can *I came as soon as I could.*

the sooner (...) the better (=when it is important that something is done very soon) *The sooner we get him to the hospital the better.* | *Hopefully, both sides will reach an agreement, and the sooner the better.*

soon after/afterwards *They set off soon after breakfast.*

before long /bɪˌfɔːʳ 'lɒŋǁ-'lɔːŋ/ if something happens **before long**, it happens after a fairly short time: *The bus will be here before long.* | *He joined the business as Sales Director, but before long he was running the whole company.*

shortly /'ʃɔːʳtli/ [adv] soon – use this especially about something that you know will happen soon: *We apologize for the delay – the train will be leaving shortly.* | *The President will shortly be on his way to Italy for a trade conference.*

shortly after/before *Her last novel was published shortly after her death.*

> **Formal or informal?**
> **Shortly** is more formal than **soon**.

in the near future /ɪn ðə ˌnɪəʳ 'fjuːtʃəʳ/ FORMAL use this to talk about something that will happen in the next few weeks or months, although you do not know exactly when: *She doesn't have a driver's licence, but is hoping to pass her test in the near future.* | *Successful candidates will be contacted in the near future.*

2 very soon

in no time /ɪn 'nəʊ taɪm/ INFORMAL use this to talk about something good that will happen very soon or that happened a very short time after

something else: *Take this medicine and you'll be feeling better in no time.*
in no time at all *In no time at all they were back together again.*

🔍 **in a minute** /ɪn ə 'mɪnɪt/ ESPECIALLY SPOKEN use this to talk about something that will happen within a few minutes, especially something you are waiting for or hoping for: *"I'm bored. Can we go now?" "OK – in a minute!"* | *Coffee will be ready in a minute.*

🔍 **any minute now** /ˌenɪ mɪnɪt 'naʊ/ SPOKEN use this to talk about something that will happen or start very soon, especially something exciting or important: *We will be bringing you the first live pictures from Jupiter any minute now.*

quickly /'kwɪkli/ [*adv*] if you do something **quickly**, you do it very soon after something else happens: *We quickly realised that something was wrong when we saw her expression.* | *Alex was knocked to the ground, but he quickly recovered.*

3 something that will happen soon

imminent /'ɪmɪnənt/ [*adj*] FORMAL an important or worrying event that is **imminent** will happen very soon: *By then, war was imminent.* | *With a general election imminent, Churchill returned to London.*
in imminent danger of sth (=when something bad is likely to happen very soon) *Whole sections of the ruined abbey are in imminent danger of collapse.*

🔍 **be coming up** /bɪ ˌkʌmɪŋ 'ʌp/ ESPECIALLY SPOKEN if something **is coming up**, it is going to happen soon: *Katie's working much harder now that her final exams are coming up.*
have sth coming up *You have a birthday coming up, don't you?*

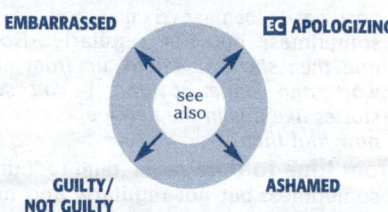

SORRY

➡ look here for ...
  • feel sorry because you have done something bad or stupid
  • feel sad for someone because they are in a bad situation

EMBARRASSED　　　　**EC APOLOGIZING**

see also

GUILTY/ NOT GUILTY　　　　**ASHAMED**

1 to tell someone you are sorry you did something

say you are sorry /ˌseɪ juː əʳ 'sɒrɪl-'sɑːri/ to tell someone you are sorry because you have upset them or done something that causes problems for them: *Sometimes it's not easy to say you are sorry.*
+(that) *She finally arrived, and said she was sorry we had been kept waiting.*

> ⚠ **Say you are sorry** is more informal than **apologize**.

🔍 **say sorry** /seɪ 'sɒrɪl-'sɑːri/ ESPECIALLY SPOKEN to tell someone that you are sorry after you have upset them or done something bad: *She says she won't see him again unless he says sorry.*
+to *Go and say sorry to your mother, Andrew.*

apologize (also **apologise** BRITISH) /ə'pɒlədʒaɪz‖ə'pɑː-/ [*v* I] to tell someone you are sorry, especially in a formal or official situation: *The hotel manager apologized and agreed to give us our money back.*
+for *British Airways apologizes for the late arrival of flight BA297.*
+to *The US has apologized to Britain for an accident in which two British soldiers were killed.*
apologize for doing sth *She apologized for causing us so much inconvenience.*

> ⚠️ Don't say 'I apologized her'. Say **I apologized to her**.

apology /ə'pɒlədʒi‖ə'pɑː-/ [n C] something that you say or write to tell someone that you are sorry: *The story was full of lies, and the paper had to print an apology.*
accept sb's apology/apologies *I hope you will accept our sincere apologies.*
demand an apology *Blake was wrongfully arrested and is now demanding an apology from the police.*
plural **apologies**

2 what you say to tell someone you are sorry

◯ **sorry/I'm sorry** /'sɒri, aɪm 'sɒri‖ -'sɑːri, 'sɔːri/ SPOKEN say this to tell someone you are sorry that you upset them or caused problems for them; you can also say this as a polite way of excusing yourself for a small mistake: *I'm sorry, I didn't mean to be rude.* | *Sorry, did I step on your foot?*
I'm very/really/terribly sorry *I'm really sorry, Joanna. I've broken one of your glasses.*
+(that) *I'm sorry that I shouted at you.* | *Sorry we're late, Shelley.*
+about *Sorry about all the noise.*
sorry to do sth *I'm sorry to disappoint you, but your application has been unsuccessful.*
(I'm) sorry to interrupt/disturb etc you (say this to interrupt someone who is working, talking etc when you want to politely ask them something) *I'm sorry to bother you, but I need to discuss my essay.*
sorry for doing sth *I'm sorry for disturbing you.*

> **Formal or informal?**
> **Sorry** is more informal than **I'm sorry**.

◯ **excuse me** /ɪk'skjuːz miː/ SPOKEN, ESPECIALLY AMERICAN say this to tell someone you are sorry because you accidentally touched them or made a small or embarrassing mistake: *Oh, excuse me, is that your bag I just stood on?* | *Excuse me – I didn't realize there was anyone in here.*

◯ **I beg your pardon** /aɪ ˌbeg jɔːʳ 'pɑːʳdn/ SPOKEN FORMAL say this when you make a small mistake and you want to say sorry politely: *"That's my pen." "Oh, I beg your pardon – I thought it was mine."*

3 to feel sorry about something you have done

be sorry/feel sorry /biː 'sɒri, ˌfiːl 'sɒri‖ -'sɑːri/ to feel sad, embarrassed, or annoyed about something bad or stupid that you have done, and wish you had not done it
+(that) *Now she felt sorry that she had never written to her parents.* | *I didn't enjoy myself and I was sorry I ever agreed to go with them.*
+for/about *I hope you're sorry for the trouble you have caused.* | *He said he was sorry about what had happened.*

regret /rɪ'gret/ [v T] to wish that you had not done something, especially because it has bad results that affect you for a long time: *I decided to leave my job – a decision which I later regretted.* | *It was a stupid thing to say, and I immediately regretted it.*
regret doing sth *I've always regretted giving up my piano lessons.*
+(that) *I think she regrets now that she never went to college.*
regretting – regretted – have regretted

> **Formal or informal?**
> **Regret** is more formal than **be/feel sorry**.

> ⚠️ Don't say 'I regret to do it' or 'I regret to have done it'. Say **I regret doing it** or **I regret that I did it**.

regret /rɪ'gret/ [n C/U] a feeling of sadness because you wish you had not done something, or you wish the situation was different: *Burgess left with a feeling of regret, knowing that he would never return.*
with great/deep regret *We have accepted her resignation with deep regret.*
have no regrets (=not regret anything) *I moved to the US ten years ago, and I have no regrets.*

S

Formal or informal?

The singular and plural forms are sometimes used in conversation, but the uncountable form is used only in writing and formal spoken English.

wish you had/wish you hadn't /'wɪʃ ju: hæd, 'wɪʃ ju: hædnt/ to feel that you have done the wrong thing, and wish that you had behaved differently: *I wish I had told him the truth.* | *She wished now that she had not agreed to marry him.*

4 to feel sorry because someone else is in a bad situation

be sorry /bi: 'sɒrɪ‖-'sɑːri/ to feel sad about something bad that has happened to someone else
+(that) *I'm sorry she didn't get the job – I think she really deserved it.*
be sorry to hear/see/read *We were all sorry to hear about your accident.*

feel sorry for sb /ˌfiːl 'sɒri fɔːʳ (sb)‖ -'sɑːri-/ to feel sad for someone because they have had very bad luck or they are in a bad situation: *He felt sorry for Tina – she seemed so lonely.* | *It's his wife I feel sorry for.*

sympathize (also **sympathise** BRITISH) /'sɪmpəθaɪz/ [v I] to feel sad for someone who is having problems, because you understand how they feel: *I know what it's like to be alone in a strange country, and I do sympathise.*
+with *They say they sympathize with people who are unemployed, but how do they know what it's like?*

sympathy /'sɪmpəθi/ [n U] the feeling you have when you feel sorry for someone who is having problems, and you understand how they feel: *She felt that their answer showed a lack of sympathy towards her situation.*
have sympathy for sb *I have a lot of sympathy for her – divorce is a very upsetting experience.*

pity /'pɪti/ [v T] to feel very sorry for someone who is in a much worse situation than you: *I pity anyone who has to feed a family on such a low income.*
pitying – pitied – have pitied

⚠ You can also use **pity** to talk in a joking way about someone whose problems are not very serious: *He spends all his time cleaning and polishing the car – I pity his poor wife!*

empathize /'empəθaɪz/ (also **empathise** BRITISH) [v I] to be able to understand someone else's feelings, problems etc, especially because you have had similar experiences
+with *My brother died last year so I can really empathize with what she's going through.*

5 what you say when you feel sorry for someone

◌ **I'm sorry** /aɪm 'sɒrɪ‖-'sɑːri/ SPOKEN say this to tell someone you are sad that something bad has happened to them: *I heard about your father's death; I'm very sorry.* | *I really am sorry. I hope Jim finds another job soon.*

◌ **bad luck** /ˌbæd 'lʌk/ SPOKEN say this to show your sympathy for someone who has tried to do something and failed: *Bad luck, Paul. I'm sure you'll pass next time.*

◌ **poor** /pʊəʳ/ [adj only before noun] ESPECIALLY SPOKEN use this when talking about someone that you feel sorry for: *The poor girl gets blamed for everything that goes wrong.*
poor old INFORMAL (used about someone you know well) *I hear poor old Steve broke his ankle.*

SOUND

➡ see also **LOUD, QUIET,** 🔲 **MUSIC**

1 a sound

sound /saʊnd/ [n C/U] something that you hear: *The only sound in the house was the ticking of the clock.* | *The TV's broken – you can see the pictures, but there's no sound.*
+of *We could hear the sound of laughter in the next room.*
a clicking/tapping/buzzing etc sound *There's a funny rattling sound coming from the back of the car.*

noise /nɔɪz/ [n C/U] a sound, especially a loud or unpleasant one: *The children are making a lot of noise.* | *street noises*
+of *The noise of the traffic kept me awake.*
a banging/scratching etc noise *What's that banging noise?* | *We heard a creaking noise, and saw the door begin to open.*

> ⚠ Don't say 'a big noise'. Say **a loud noise**.

echo /'ekəʊ/ [n C] a sound which repeats the last part of a loud sound made, for example, in a large empty room or near a high wall
+of *the faint echo of thunder in the distance*
plural **echoes**

2 to make a sound

make a sound/make a noise /,meɪk ə 'saʊnd, ,meɪk ə 'nɔɪz/ *I knew that if I made any noise, they would find me.* | *The lamb was making a sound like a baby crying.*
 go /gəʊ/ [v] ESPECIALLY SPOKEN **go bang/beep/pop etc** to make a short loud sound: *I was using the hairdryer and suddenly it went bang.*
going – went – have gone

echo /'ekəʊ/ [v I] ESPECIALLY WRITTEN if a sound **echoes**, you hear the last part of it again because it was made in a large empty room, near a high wall etc: *I heard footsteps echoing down the corridor.*
echoing – echoed – have echoed

with /wɪð, wɪθ/ [preposition] WRITTEN
with a bang/crash/thud etc making a loud sound: *The picture fell to the floor with a loud crash.*

go off /,gəʊ 'ɒf‖-'ɔːf/ [phrasal verb I] if something **goes off**, it starts to make a noise – use this about bells that warn you about danger, clocks that tell you it is time to get up etc: *My neighbour's car alarm went off three times last night.* | *Our alarm clock goes off at 7:15 every morning.*

3 to make a sound because you are in pain, are disappointed etc

groan /grəʊn/ [v I] to make a long sound in a deep voice, because you are in great pain or you are very disappointed: *Alex groaned as the pain got worse.* | *Everyone groaned when Tim walked into the room.*
groan [n C] the sound you make when you groan: *There was a loud groan from the crowd as Shearer's shot missed the goal.*

sigh /saɪ/ [v I] to breathe in and out deeply and loudly because you feel disappointed, bored, or impatient: *Pamela sighed and looked at her watch.*
sigh [n C] the sound you make when you sigh: *John gave a sigh and sat down.*

4 when a sound stops

fade away/die away /,feɪd ə'weɪ, ,daɪ ə'weɪ/ [phrasal verb I] if a sound **fades away** or **dies away**, it gradually becomes quieter and quieter until you cannot hear it any more: *The noise of the bombing died away and the town was quiet once more.*

SPACE

➡ see also **HOLE**

1 space that is available to use

space /speɪs/ [n C/U] an empty area of any size, which can be used or filled by things or people: *I wish we had more space in our office.* | *There's a space on the form where you write the name of your school.* | *parking spaces*
+for *We don't have enough space for all our furniture.*
space to do sth *I need space to work.* | *I was lucky to find a space to park.*
make/clear a space (=make a space by moving things) *She cleared a space on the desk for her computer.*

room /ruːm, rʊm/ [n U] enough space for something or someone to fit into: *I can't sit there, there isn't enough room.*
+for *Is there room for my camera in your bag?*
room to do sth *I had to back the car out of the driveway – there wasn't enough room to turn around.*
make room for sb/sth (=move people or things closer together so there is room for another person or thing) *Can you move and make room for Jerry, please?*

2 a space between things

space /speɪs/ [n C] an empty area between two things: *There was an empty space on the shelf where the book had been.*
+between *The children hid in the space between the wall and the sofa.*

gap /gæp/ [n C] a space where there should not be one, for example because something has been removed or something is missing
+in *We'll have to fix this gap in the fence.*
+between *The dentist says the gaps between her teeth may cause problems later.*

gap

gap

opening /ˈəʊpənɪŋ/ [n C] a small hole or space that you can pass through or see through
+in *The guards passed food to the prisoners through an opening in the wall.* | *The children were peeping through an opening in the curtains.*

opening

When you see **EC**, go to the **ESSENTIAL COMMUNICATION** section.

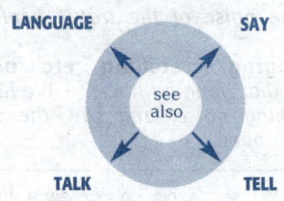

SPEAK

LANGUAGE   SAY

see also

TALK   TELL

⚠ Don't confuse **say**, **tell**, **talk**, and **speak**. You **say** words to someone. You **tell** someone facts or information about something. You **talk** to someone about a subject. You **speak** (=you say words) or you **speak** a language.

1 to speak

speak /spiːk/ [v I] to produce words with your voice: *She had a sore throat and couldn't speak.* | *How old are babies when they learn to speak?*
speak up (=speak louder) *Can you speak up? – I can't hear you.*
speaking – spoke – have spoken

talk /tɔːk/ [v I] to produce words with your voice in order to have a conversation, tell people what you think etc: *Please don't all talk at the same time.* | *You're not supposed to talk in the library.*

stammer/stutter /ˈstæməʳ, ˈstʌtəʳ/ [v I/T] to speak with difficulty because you cannot stop yourself repeating the first sound in some words: *She always used to stutter when she was nervous.* | *"I d-d-don't know," he stammered.*

whisper /ˈwɪspəʳ/ [v I] to speak very quietly, using your breath rather than your voice: *We had to whisper because Jill's mother was in the next room.* | *What are you two whispering about?*

mumble /ˈmʌmbəl/ [v I] to speak quietly and not at all clearly, so that it is difficult for people to understand you: *Don't mumble – I can't hear what you're saying.*

speech /spiːtʃ/ [n U] the ability to speak: *Only humans are capable of speech.* | *The left side of the brain controls speech.*

2 to speak a language

speak /spiːk/ [v T] to be able to speak a language: *Nadia speaks six languages.*
speak French/Japanese/Russian etc *Is there anyone here who can speak Arabic?*
speaking – spoke – have spoken

> ⚠ Don't say 'he can speak in English'. Say **he can speak English**.

> ⚠ Don't say 'he talks English', 'I talk Japanese' etc. Say **he speaks English**, **I speak Japanese** etc.

> ⚠ Don't confuse **she is speaking English** (=she is saying English words now) and **she speaks English** (=she can speak it).

fluent /ˈfluːənt/ [adj] very good at speaking a language, so that you can speak it quickly without stopping and you understand it very well
fluent in English/German etc *Danielle is fluent in Cantonese.*
fluent French/Arabic/Japanese etc *Ann speaks fluent Italian.*
fluently [adv] *Douglas speaks Hindi fluently.*

> ⚠ Use **fluent** and **fluently** about languages you have learned, not about your own first language.

bilingual /baɪˈlɪŋgwəl/ [adj] able to speak two languages very well: *Their children are completely bilingual.*
speaker /ˈspiːkəʳ/ [n C] someone who can speak a particular language
speaker of English/Russian/Arabic etc *Speakers of Cantonese often cannot understand speakers of Mandarin.*
English/Spanish/Urdu etc speaker *The hotel has two English speakers on its staff.*
native speaker (=someone who speaks a particular language as their first language, not as a second or foreign language) *All our English teachers are native speakers.*

3 the way someone speaks

pronunciation /prəˌnʌnsiˈeɪʃən/ [n singular] the way someone says the words and sounds of a language: *Gianni has problems with his grammar but his pronunciation is very good.*

> ⚠ Don't write 'pronounciation'. The correct spelling is **pronunciation**.

accent /ˈæksənt‖ˈæksent/ [n C] the way someone speaks a language, which shows which country or which part of a country they come from, and which sometimes shows which social class they come from: *She speaks Spanish with a Mexican accent.* | *I knew from his accent that he was Scottish.*
strong/broad accent (=an accent that is easy to notice) *Her companion had a strong French accent.*
upper-class accent (=typical of people from a high social class)
speech /spiːtʃ/ [n U] the way someone speaks, especially when this is affected by illness, drugs etc: *He was drunk, and his speech slow and unclear.*
speech impediment (=a permanent speech problem, which makes it difficult to pronounce certain sounds) *She was born with a slight speech impediment.*

4 spoken, not written

spoken /ˈspəʊkən/ [adj usually before noun] **spoken** language is produced with the voice, not written down: *This book will help you with both spoken and written English.*
oral /ˈɔːrəl/ [adj usually before noun] using spoken language rather than written language – use this especially about tests and exams
oral test/exam *We had a 15-minute oral exam in German.*

5 unable to speak

can't speak /ˌkɑːnt ˈspiːk‖ˌkænt-/ to be unable to speak because you are too ill, weak, frightened, or shocked: *I was so terrified, I couldn't speak*

lose your voice /ˌluːz jɔːʳ 'vɔɪs/ to become unable to speak because of illness, or because you have been using your voice too much: *All that shouting has made her lose her voice.*

dumb /dʌm/ [adj] permanently unable to speak: *Martin was born deaf and dumb.*

> **Dumb** is not used by doctors, and is often considered offensive.

SPECIAL

➡ see also **UNUSUAL, DIFFERENT, FESTI-VALS AND SPECIAL DAYS**

special

special /'speʃəl/ [adj] something that is **special** is different from other things, for example because it is better, more important, or intended for a particular purpose: *They have special meals for children.* | *United Airlines is offering a special $299 return fare to London.* | *I made a special effort to be nice to him.*
+for *Today is a very special day for her.*
special occasion (=a wedding, birthday, or other time when people celebrate something) *He has a dark suit, which he only wears on special occasions.*
something special about sb/sth (=something good about a person, place etc which makes you like them very much) *There's something special about the countryside in this part of France.*
specially /'speʃəli/
specially designed / made / built / chosen/trained/prepared etc [adv] designed, made, built etc for a special purpose: *a new range of beauty products specially designed for teenagers* | *Customs officers use specially trained dogs to search for drugs.*
particular/specific /pəʳ'tɪkjᵘləʳ, spə'sɪfɪk/ [adj only before noun] use this to say that something is clearly different or separate from other things of the same kind, or that something is more important than

other things: *Each flower has its own particular smell.* | *Is there any particular reason why you want to go back to Japan?* | *Each class will focus on one specific aspect of American culture.*
be of particular interest/ importance (=be especially interesting or important to a particular person or group) *This discovery is of particular interest to scientists studying the origins of the universe.*

unique /juː'niːk/ [adj] so special and unusual that it is the only one of its kind – use this especially about things or people that you think are extremely good: *Winning the championship five times was a unique achievement.* | *The exhibition provides a unique opportunity to see all of the artist's work.*

> Don't say 'very unique'. Just say **unique**.

SPEND

to spend money or time

➡ look here for ...
  • spend money
  • spend time

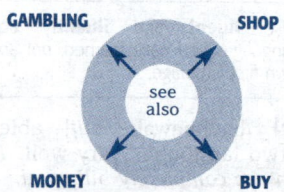

1 to use money to buy things

spend /spend/ [v T]
spend £5/$10 etc *I bought two skirts and a T-shirt and I only spent $50.*
spend £5/$10 etc on sth *We spend about £85 a week on food.* | *The government should spend more on education.* | *She spends far too much money on clothes.*
spend money on doing sth *Carrie spends most of her money on travelling to school.*
spending – spent – have spent

> ⚠ Don't say 'I spend a lot of money for clothes'. Say **I spend a lot of money on clothes**.

pay £5/$10 etc for sth /'peɪ (£5/$10 etc) fəʳ (sth)/ [phrasal verb T] to spend £5, $10 etc in order to buy something: *They paid over $100 each for tickets.* | *The set meal costs £15 but you have to pay extra for wine.*

> ⚠ Use **pay for** to talk about what you must pay for something because that is what it costs. Compare: *We pay more for food than people in America* (=because food is more expensive here). | *French people spend more on food than British people* (=they choose to spend more of their money on food).

blow /bləʊ/ [v T] INFORMAL, ESPECIALLY SPOKEN to spend a lot of money on something expensive and enjoyable, especially something that you do not really need
blow £50/$100 etc on sth *We blew $3000 on a trip to Barbados.*
blow the lot BRITISH **blow it all** AMERICAN (=spend everything) *He won £500,000 in the National Lottery, but he's blown the lot.*
blowing – blew – have blown

squander /'skwɒndəʳ‖'skwɑːn-/ [v T] to spend money on unnecessary things instead of saving it or using it sensibly: *In less than three years he had squandered the entire family fortune.* | *There was no money to pay the rent. They'd already squandered the little that they had.*
squander money on sth *Here's £50, but don't just go and squander it on beer!*

2 **to spend less money or to spend money carefully**

cut down /ˌkʌt 'daʊn/ [phrasal verb I/T] to reduce the amount of money that you regularly spend: *He's spending much more than he can afford – he'll have to cut down.*
+on *She's already cut down on going out and buying clothes, but she still doesn't have enough money.*

economize (also **economise** BRITISH) /ɪ'kɒnəmaɪz‖ɪ'kɑː-/ [v I] to spend less money by buying only what you really need, or by buying cheaper things: *Sorry, I can't come out tonight – I'm trying to economize.*
economize on sth (=spend less money on something) *Families on low incomes had to economize on food and heating costs.*

thrifty /'θrɪfti/ [adj] spending money carefully and cleverly so that nothing is wasted and you can manage with the money you have: *Mrs Jones was a very thrifty woman who never wasted anything.* | *By being thrifty and shopping wisely you can feed an entire family on $100 a week.*
thrifty – thriftier – thriftiest

careful /'keəʳfəl/ [adj] spending money only on things that are necessary or cheap, because you want your money to last as long as possible: *I wouldn't say he was mean – just careful.*
careful with money *Once you've spent your allowance there won't be any more. You must learn to be more careful with money.*

economical /ˌekə'nɒmɪkəl, ˌiː-‖-'nɑː-/ [adj] spending money carefully and sensibly, so that you do not spend more than necessary: *I'm trying to be more economical when I go out shopping.* | *Tim's a very economical person. He always looks around for the best buys.*

3 **the amount of money you spend**

spending /'spendɪŋ/ [n U] the amount of money that is spent, especially by a government
public/government spending *increases in government spending*
health/education/defence spending *In recent years the government has reduced defence spending.*

> ⚠ You can also use **spending** before a noun, like an adjective: *a survey of people's spending habits* | *big spending cuts*

costs /kɒsts‖kɔːsts/ [n plural] the money that a person or organization has to spend regularly on heating, rent, electricity etc: *What are your annual fuel costs?*
cut costs (=reduce costs) *Falling sales have forced companies to cut costs.*

running costs (=the costs of owning and using a car or machine) *I'm looking for a car with low running costs.*

expenses /ɪk'spensɪz/ [n plural] the money that you need to spend in order to buy the things you need: *John and Rachel have a new baby, so they have a lot of expenses right now.*
travel/living/medical/legal expenses *Living expenses are much higher in London.* | *The company doesn't pay my travel expenses.*

budget /'bʌdʒɪt/ [n C] the amount of money that you have planned to spend or that is available to spend on a particular thing: *I have a budget of $50 for the week's groceries.* | *Government cuts in the defence budget have meant a loss of 2000 jobs.*

4 someone who hates spending money

stingy /'stɪndʒi/ [adj] INFORMAL not generous with your money, even though you are not poor: *It's no use asking him – he's too stingy to give money to charity.*
stingy – stingier – stingiest

mean /miːn/ [adj] BRITISH someone who is **mean** does not like spending money or sharing what they have with other people: *He's so mean, he never even buys his wife a birthday present.*
+with *Marsha has always been mean with her money.*

cheap /tʃiːp/ [adj] AMERICAN, ESPECIALLY SPOKEN someone who is **cheap** does not like spending money, and always tries to avoid spending it: *She's too cheap to take a cab.*

miser /'maɪzər/ [n C] someone who hates spending money, and tries to spend as little as possible, especially someone who stores their money in a secret place: *Everyone said Mr Henny was a miser who had thousands of pounds hidden under his bed.*

5 someone who likes spending money

extravagant /ɪk'strævəgənt/ [adj] spending a lot of money on things that you do not really need: *$200 on a dress? You're so extravagant!*

throw your money around /ˌθrəʊ jɔːr 'mʌni əˌraʊnd/ INFORMAL someone who **throws their money around** has a lot of money and enjoys spending it: *a luxury skiing resort, full of rich people throwing their money around*

6 to spend time

⇒ see also **STAY**

spend /spend/ [v T] to spend time somewhere, with someone, or doing something: *I never seem to have any time to spend with the children.* | *Dani spends hours on the phone.*
spend time doing sth *Fay spent a year in Italy teaching English.*
spending – spent – have spent

pass the time /ˌpɑːs ðə 'taɪm‖ˌpæs-/ to spend time doing something unimportant, because you have nothing else to do: *I started doing a crossword to pass the time.*
pass your time *The security guards used to pass their time playing cards.*

waste /weɪst/ [v T] to use your time badly, by doing nothing or by doing something that is not useful: *Stop wasting time. We have to finish this by five o'clock.* | *I must have wasted two whole hours trying to fix this machine.*

kill /kɪl/ [v T]
kill time/a couple of hours etc INFORMAL to spend time doing something which is not important, so that time passes more quickly while you are waiting for something else: *I was early so I sat in a café, killing time.* | *The train doesn't leave till two, so we have a couple of hours to kill.*

SPOIL

to make something less attractive, less enjoyable, or less effective

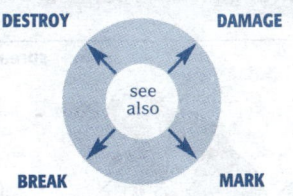

DESTROY   DAMAGE

see
also

BREAK   MARK

spoil /spɔɪl/ [v T] *That new supermarket has really spoiled the view from the house.* | *Yes, it rained a lot, but we didn't let that spoil our vacation.*
spoil sth for sb (=make it less enjoyable or exciting for them) *Don't tell me the ending of the movie – you'll spoil it for me.*
spoil everything / spoil things (=completely spoil someone's plans) *If you don't come it'll spoil everything.*
spoiling – spoiled (also **spoilt** BRITISH) – have spoiled (also **have spoilt** BRITISH)

⟲ **mess up** /ˌmes ˈʌp/ [phrasal verb T] SPOKEN INFORMAL to spoil something important or something that has been carefully planned
mess up sth *The travel agents messed up the arrangements and there was no room for us at the hotel.* | *He's messed up my whole life.*
mess sth up *We secretly organized a party for her, but then Bill messed everything up by telling her about it.*

ruin /ˈruːɪn/ [v T] to spoil something completely: *John and Sandy argued all the time, which completely ruined the evening for the rest of us.* | *My new white dress was totally ruined!* | *If the newspapers find out about this, it could ruin his career.*

wreck /rek/ [v T] to completely spoil something important so that it can never exist again or be like it was before: *The bombing was a deliberate attempt to wreck the peace talks.* | *a dreadful car crash that wrecked their lives*

SPORT

➡ see Word Banks section

SPREAD

to cover a larger area or affect a larger group of people

1   when fire/liquid etc spreads

spread /spred/ [v I] if fire, liquid, smoke etc **spreads**, it moves outwards in all directions to cover a larger area: *The fire spread quickly through the building.*
+through/across/to etc *By now the flood water had spread across 80 square miles of farmland.* | *She knocked over her glass, and a dark pool of wine spread over the tablecloth.*
spreading – spread – have spread

2   when information/ideas/feelings etc spread

spread /spred/ [v I/T] if information, an idea, or a feeling **spreads**, or if you **spread** it, more and more people begin to know about it or be affected by it: *News of the President's death spread quickly.*
+to/into/through etc *a feeling of panic that spread through the whole army*
spread lies/rumours/gossip (=deliberately tell untrue information to a lot of people) *Someone's been spreading lies about Nancy again.*
spreading – spread – have spread
spread [n singular]
the spread of sth (=when ideas, feelings etc are spread) *the spread of liberal ideas in the 19th century*

get around /ˌget əˈraʊnd/ [phrasal verb I] INFORMAL if news or information **gets around**, people tell other people, so that soon many people know about it: *News soon got around that Nick was back in town.* | *It's a small place, so news and gossip get around pretty quickly.*

S

3 when diseases spread

spread /spred/ [v I/T] if a disease **spreads**, or if it **is spread**, it is passed from one person to another, and it affects more and more people: *Some diseases are spread by insects.*
+through/to/across *Cholera is spreading through the refugee camps at an alarming rate.*
spreading – spread – have spread

spread [n singular]
the spread of sth (=when a disease spreads) *the spread of AIDS*

infectious /ɪnˈfekʃəs/ [adj] an **infectious** disease is spread by being passed from one person to another: *infectious diseases such as typhoid*
highly infectious (=very infectious) *Measles is a highly infectious illness that can be extremely serious.*

4 when people go in many directions

spread out /ˌspred ˈaʊt/ [phrasal verb I] if a group of people **spreads out**, they move apart from each other so that they cover a larger area: *The search party spread out to search the woods.* | *Small groups of survivors spread out across the plain.*

scatter /ˈskætəʳ/ [v I] ESPECIALLY WRITTEN if a group of people **scatter**, they all suddenly move in different directions, especially to avoid something dangerous: *A gun went off and the crowd scattered.* | *The rioters scattered when police vans arrived.*

5 to put butter, glue etc on a surface

spread /spred/ [v T] to put a thin layer of a soft substance, such as butter or glue, on a surface, so that it covers it
spread sth on sth *Spread the glue evenly on both surfaces.* | *He spread plaster on the walls.*

spread sth with sth *two slices of toast spread with peanut butter*
spreading – spread – have spread

6 to open something out and arrange it on a surface

spread out

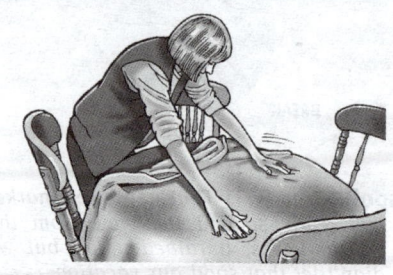

spread/spread out /ˌspred, ˌspred ˈaʊt/ [v T] to open something such as a sheet, a map, or a newspaper, and arrange it so that it lies flat on a table, the floor, or another surface
spread out sth *Jim spread out a blanket for her to sit on.*
spread sth out/over/on *He took the map and spread it out on the table.* | *I spread the towels over the radiator to dry.*

7 when things are spread over a wide area

scattered /ˈskætəʳd/ [adj] things that are **scattered** are spread over a large area in an irregular or untidy way
+about/over/among etc *Tiny cottages were scattered all over the hillside.*

spread out /ˌspred ˈaʊt/ [adj not before noun] things that are **spread out** are spread over a large area with a lot of space between them
+on/among/across etc *Diane had her papers spread out all over the floor.*

STAND

➡ if you mean 'can't stand something', go to **BAD 6**
➡ see also **SIT, LIE**

1 to be in a standing position

stand /stænd/ [v I] to be in a standing position: *I was standing next to the entrance.* | *There were no seats, so we had to stand.* | *Who's that girl standing over there?*

stand doing sth (=stand while you are doing something) *She stood watching him as he turned to go.*

stand up straight (=with your back and legs straight) *The ceilings were so low that Mark couldn't stand up straight.*

stand still (=stand without moving) *Stand still a moment while I brush your hair.*

standing – stood – have stood

be on your feet /bi: ɒn jɔːʳ 'fiːt/ to be standing, especially for a long time, with the result that you feel tired – use this especially about people who have to stand and walk a lot in their jobs: *I've been on my feet all day and I need to rest.*

on tiptoe/on tiptoes

/ɒn 'tɪptəʊ(z)/ standing on your toes, especially when you stretch your body in order to see something or reach something: *She had to stand on tiptoe to see over the fence.*

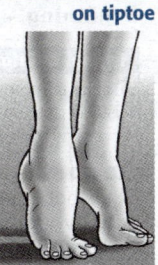
on tiptoe

lean /liːn/ [v I] to stand while resting part of your body against a wall, a table etc

+against/on *Kay was leaning against the school wall, smoking a cigarette.* | *Joe leaned on the gate and watched them drive away.*

leaning – leaned (also leant BRITISH**) – have leaned (also have leant** BRITISH**)**

lean

2 to stand after sitting or lying down

get up /ˌget 'ʌp/ [phrasal verb I] to stand after you have been sitting, bending, or lying down: *She got up and turned off the TV.*

get up from a chair/seat/sofa etc *Max got up from his chair and shook her hand.*

get up off the floor/ground/grass etc *One of her friends helped her to get up off the floor.*

get up to do sth *I was left with Maria when the others got up to dance.*

stand up /ˌstænd 'ʌp/ [phrasal verb I] to stand after you have been sitting: *"I must go now," she said, standing up.* | *Everyone stood up as the bride and her father entered the church.*

get to your feet /ˌget tə jɔːʳ 'fiːt/ ESPECIALLY WRITTEN to stand up, especially slowly or when it is difficult for you: *He got to his feet, looking pale and anxious.* | *Somehow Jenny managed to get to her feet and stumble out of the room.*

3 to put your foot down on something

stand on sth/step on sth (also **tread on sth** BRITISH) /'stænd ɒn (sth), 'step ɒn (sth), 'tred ɒn (sth)‖-ɑːn-/ [phrasal verb T] to put your foot down on something while you are standing or walking, especially accidentally: *I think I must have stood on some glass.* | *Be careful! You nearly trod on my foot.*

stamp on sth /'stæmp ɒn (sth)‖-ɑːn-/ [phrasal verb T] to deliberately put your foot down very hard on something, especially an insect, in order to hurt or kill it: *There was a big cockroach in the kitchen and Barbara stamped on it.*

START

➡ opposite **STOP, FINISH, END**
➡ see also **BEGINNING, FINISH, END**

1 to start doing something

start /stɑːʳt/ [v I/T] *We can't start until Carol gets here.* | *I'm starting a new job next week.* | *Have you started that book yet?* (=started reading it)
start doing sth *I've just started learning German.* | *If the baby starts crying, give her some milk.*
start to do sth *Has Gemma started to write that report yet?*
start by doing sth (=do something as the first part of an activity) *Start by melting the butter in the frying-pan.*
start with sth (=do something or deal with something as the first part of a long activity) *Tina wanted to paint the whole apartment, and she decided to start with the kitchen.*
get started (=start a journey, activity etc, especially one that will take a long time) *It was a fine morning, and the boys were eager to get started.*

begin /bɪˈgɪn/ [v I/T] ESPECIALLY WRITTEN to start doing something: *When the children were quiet, Martha began.* | *They began their journey in Venice.*
begin to do sth *Ann slowly began to climb the steps to the castle.* | *I began to realize that she no longer loved me.*
begin doing sth *The audience suddenly began shouting and cheering.*
begin by doing sth (=do something as the first part of an activity) *They began by asking me questions about my previous job.*
+with *The speaker began with a short introduction about the history of the town.*
beginning – began – have begun

> **Formal or informal?**
> **Begin** is more formal than **start**. It is not usually used in conversation.

get down to sth /get ˈdaʊn tuː (sth)/ [phrasal verb T] INFORMAL to finally start doing something, after you have been avoiding doing it or after something has prevented you from doing it: *Come on Bill – it's time you got down to some homework.*
get down to doing sth *Once the summer's here we must get down to painting the outside of the house.*

 get cracking /get ˈkrækɪŋ/ SPOKEN INFORMAL to start doing something immediately, because you are in a hurry or there is a lot to do: *Come on – get cracking! I want this whole house clean when I get back.* | *You'd better get cracking if you want to get to the airport by ten.*

> ⚠ Only use **get cracking** in the infinitive or in commands. Don't say 'we got cracking' etc.

2 to start doing something regularly

start/begin /stɑːʳt, bɪˈgɪn/ [v T] to start doing something which you then do regularly
start/begin doing sth *I started doing aerobics two years ago.* | *She was only 16 when she began seeing Alan, who was already married.*
start/begin to do sth *His parents got divorced last year – that's when he started to take drugs.*
beginning – began – have begun

> **Formal or informal?**
> **Begin** is more formal than **start**, and is not usually used in conversation.

take up sth /ˌteɪk ˈʌp (sth)/ [phrasal verb T] to become interested in a sport or activity, and start to spend time doing it: *When did Bryan take up golf?*

turn to sth /ˈtɜːʳn tuː (sth)/ [phrasal verb T]
turn to crime/drugs/alcohol etc to start doing something dangerous or illegal: *Hal turned to drink after his wife and kids were killed in a car crash.* | *Research shows that young people without jobs are most likely to turn to crime.*

3 when something starts happening

start/begin /stɑːʳt, bɪ'gɪn/ [v I] *Do you know what time the class starts? | My day starts at 5 or 6 o'clock, when the baby wakes up. | The movie was just beginning when Richard and James arrived. | Work on the new bridge will begin next year.*
beginning – began – have begun

> **Formal or informal?**
> **Begin** is more formal than **start**, and is not usually used in conversation.

break out /ˌbreɪk 'aʊt/ [phrasal verb I] to start happening – use this about unpleasant things like fires, wars, or diseases: *The fire broke out on the top floor of the hotel. | Fighting broke out between gangs of rival football fans.*

outbreak /'aʊtbreɪk/ [n C] if there is an **outbreak** of something unpleasant, such as a fire, war, or disease, it suddenly starts to happen
+of *There's been an outbreak of food poisoning at the hotel.*

4 to make something start happening

start /stɑːʳt/ [v T] *The referee couldn't start the game because there were fans on the field. | Don't drop your cigarette here – you could start a fire. | Jim parked in someone else's space, and that's what started the fight.*

launch /lɔːntʃ/ [v T]
launch an attack/appeal/inquiry/ campaign to start a public or military activity, when there is a clear aim that you want to achieve: *The local hospital has launched a campaign to raise money for new X-ray equipment. | Police are launching a major murder inquiry. | Rebel forces launched an attack on Kabul.*

introduce/bring in /ˌɪntrə'djuːs, ˌbrɪŋ 'ɪnǁ-'duːs/ [v T] to officially start a new system, method, or rule for the first time: *The company is thinking of introducing medical tests for all*

employees. | *New safety measures will be introduced next month. | They have promised to bring in a minimum wage if they win the election.*

> **Formal or informal?**
> **Bring in** is less formal than **introduce**.

5 to start a new business or organization

start/start up /stɑːʳt, ˌstɑːʳt 'ʌp/ [v T] *Luigi's family came here in 1966 and started up a chain of restaurants. | John decided to start his own textile business shortly after the war.*

open /'aʊpən/ [v T] to start a business that provides services to the public, such as a shop, a restaurant, or a hotel: *They just opened a new super-market on Van Nuys Boulevard.*

set up /ˌset 'ʌp/ [phrasal verb I/T] to start a new business by making all the necessary arrangements, buying equipment etc
set up sth *Bruno and his partner are setting up their own printing business.*
set up in business (=start to run your own business) *People attend the col-lege to learn how to set up in business on their own.*
set up as *Sean got a bank loan to set up as an architect in his own studio.*

found /faʊnd/ [v T] to start an organiza-tion, school, hospital etc, especially by providing the money for it – use this especially about something that was started a long time ago: *Pierpont was one of the group who founded Yale College in 1701.*
be founded *The bank was founded 60 years ago in Munich.*

6 to start doing something again

start again /ˌstɑːʳt ə'gen/ [phrasal verb I/T] to start doing something again, or to start happening again: *The Mid-dle East peace talks have started again.*
start sth again *After her vacation, Trish really didn't feel like starting work again. | She failed her degree, so she had to start her course again.*

S

start over /ˌstɑːˈʳt ˈəʊvəˈʳ/ [*phrasal verb* I] ESPECIALLY AMERICAN to start doing something again from the beginning, especially because you want to do it better: *If you make a mistake, just press 'delete' and start over.*

bring back sth /ˌbrɪŋ ˈbæk (sth)/ [*phrasal verb* T] to start using a custom, system, law etc again, which was used in the past but then stopped: *Do you think they should bring back the death penalty? | They're talking about bringing back formal grammar teaching.*

go back to sth /ˌgəʊ ˈbæk tuː (sth)/ [*phrasal verb* T] to start doing something again, after a period when you did something else: *Some mothers go back to full-time work only a few weeks after their baby is born.*

go back to doing sth *This time, Ben was determined not to go back to using drugs again.*

STAY

➡ look here for ...
- stay in a place and not leave it
- spend time in a place
- stay in someone's house or a hotel

➡ if you mean 'continue to be the same', go to **CONTINUE 3**

1 to stay in the same place, job, school etc and not leave it

➡ opposite **LEAVE**

stay /steɪ/ [*v* I] *Stay there – I want to take a photograph of you.*

+with *He stayed with the baby until she fell asleep.*

stay at home (=not have a job and be at home most of the time) *My husband wants me to stay at home and look after the children.*

stay at school BRITISH **stay in school** AMERICAN (=continue to go to school) *Most students stay at school until they are 16 or 17.*

stay in a job *Alice has never stayed in the same job for more than a year.*

stay behind (=stay somewhere after other people have left) *After the party a few of us stayed behind to help clean up.*

stay in /ˌsteɪ ˈɪn/ [*phrasal verb* I] to stay in your house and not go out, especially in the evening: *The others went out to a club, but I stayed in and watched television.*

stay on /ˌsteɪ ˈɒnǁ-ˈɑːn/ [*phrasal verb* I] to stay in a place, job, school etc for a longer time than you had planned, or after other people have left: *We've had such a great time that we're thinking of staying on here for another week.*

stay on at school/university *He stayed on at college for an extra year to do a Master's degree.*

remain /rɪˈmeɪn/ [*v* I] to stay in the same place, job, or school: *Picasso remained in Paris throughout the rest of the war.*

remain at home/at school/at work *In those days, unmarried daughters usually remained at home.*

> **Formal or informal?**
> **Remain** is more formal than **stay**. It is used especially in written English.

2 to spend some time in a place

stay /steɪ/ [*v* I] to spend a period of time in a place that is not your permanent home: *I'm planning to stay in Paris for a couple of months. | How long are you staying in New York?*

> ⚠ Don't confuse **stay** (=be somewhere temporarily, for a few days, weeks, or months) and **live** (=be somewhere all or most of the time, because it is your home).

be there /biː ˈðeəʳ/ to be staying somewhere – use this to talk about a place that has just been mentioned: *"Have you ever been to Prague?" "Yes, I was there in 1978." | While you're there you should go to the Louvre.*

3 to stay at a hotel or at someone's house

➡ see also WB **HOLIDAY/VACATION, VISIT**

stay /steɪ/ [*v* I] to spend a few days, weeks etc at someone else's house or at a hotel, but not live there permanently

stay at a hotel/at sb's house *I'm staying at my brother's house for a couple of weeks.* | *Which hotel are you staying at?*

stay with sb (=stay at their house) *You could stay with John and Anne while you're in London.*

stay the night BRITISH **stay over** AMERICAN (=sleep at someone else's house) *Is it all right if I stay the night?*

come to stay *One of Sarah's friends is coming to stay with us this summer.*

visit /ˈvɪzɪ̯t/ [v I/T] to go to the house of a friend or relative and stay there for some time, because you want to see them: *Aunt Jane usually visits us for two or three weeks in the spring.*

guest /gest/ [n C] someone who is staying with friends or relatives or at a hotel: *The hotel bar is for guests only.* | *I'm really busy – I'm expecting guests this weekend.*

> **Formal or informal?**
>
> **Guest** is rather a formal word. In spoken English, you often say **someone staying** or **someone coming to stay** instead of **guest**: *I have someone staying with me at the moment.*

4 a place where you can stay for a short time, such as a hotel

◯ **a place to stay/somewhere to stay** /ə ˌpleɪs tə ˈsteɪ, ˌsʌmweəʳ tə ˈsteɪ/ ESPECIALLY SPOKEN a place where you can stay, for example a hotel or a room in someone's house: *She needs somewhere to stay while she's at college.* | *We're going to Tokyo – do you know any good places to stay?*

accommodation (also **accommodations** AMERICAN) /əˌkɒməˈdeɪʃən(z)‖ə̯ˌkɑː-/ [n U/plural] a place where you pay money to stay, for example a hotel or a room that you rent: *The cost of rented accommodation keeps going up.* | *The travel agency will help you find accommodations.*

> **Formal or informal?**
>
> **Accommodation** is more formal than **a place to stay**, and is often used when talking in a general way about places where people can pay to stay: *a shortage of accommodation for students*

> Don't say 'an accommodation'.

5 to let someone stay in your home

◯ **put sb up** /ˌpʊt (sb) ˈʌp/ [phrasal verb T] ESPECIALLY SPOKEN to let a friend stay in your home for a short time, and provide them with a bed to sleep in: *"Where are you staying?" "Carole's putting us up for a couple of days."*

6 the time when you stay somewhere

stay /steɪ/ [n singular] the time when you stay in a place, for example when you go somewhere on holiday or for business: *I met her during my stay in Venice.* | *Did you enjoy your stay?*

visit /ˈvɪzɪ̯t/ [n C] the time when you go to stay somewhere, especially in order to see people or see a place: *It was my first visit to my wife's parents' house.*

STEAL

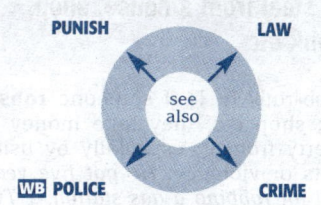

> Don't confuse **steal** and **rob**. A thief **steals** money or property, but a robber **robs** a shop, a bank, or another person (=steals money etc from them).

1 to steal something

steal /stiːl/ [v I/T] to take something that does not belong to you: *Thousands of cars get stolen every year.* | *In the end he had to steal in order to survive.*

+**from** *drug addicts who steal from their friends and families*
steal sth from sb/sth *Thieves stole paintings worth $5 million from a Paris art gallery.*

stealing – stole – have stolen

> ⚠ Don't say 'steal someone'. Say **steal something from someone**.

stolen /'stəʊlən/ [*adj*] *The three men escaped in a stolen car.*

take /teɪk/ [*v* T] to steal something, especially money or things that can be carried away: *Someone has been taking money from the cash box.* | *The burglars took our TV and stereo, but they didn't find the jewellery.*

taking – took – have taken

nick/pinch /nɪk, pɪntʃ/ [*v* T] BRITISH SPOKEN INFORMAL to steal something: *He's been arrested loads of times for nicking cars.*
nick/pinch sth from sb/sth *Jimmy was caught pinching money from his mum's purse.*

rip off /ˌrɪp 'ɒf‖-'ɔːf/ [*phrasal verb* T] SPOKEN, ESPECIALLY AMERICAN to steal something
rip off sth *The store was very crowded, and someone ripped off my purse.*

2 to steal from a house, shop, bank etc

rob /rɒb‖rɑːb/ [*v* T] if someone **robs** a bank, shop etc, they take money or property from it, especially by using threats or violence: *He got five years in jail for robbing a gas station.* | *Two men robbed the Central Bank yesterday, escaping with over $1 million.*

robbing – robbed – have robbed

burgle BRITISH **burglarize** AMERICAN /'bɜːˡgəl, 'bɜːˡgləraɪz/ [*v* T] to illegally enter a house or office and steal things: *He was caught burgling the house of a police officer.* | *Our apartment has been burglarized twice since we moved here.*

> ⚠ You can say 'we've been burgled', or 'we were burglarized', when you mean 'our house has been burgled'.

hold up sth /'həʊld ʌp (sth)/ [*phrasal verb* T] to go into a bank, shop etc with a gun and demand money: *The men who held up the store were wearing Halloween masks.*

3 to steal from someone in the street

rob /rɒb‖rɑːb/ [*v* T] if someone **robs** you, they take money or property from you, especially in a public place such as a street: *Two men tried to rob him as he left the restaurant.*

robbing – robbed – have robbed

mug /mʌg/ [*v* T usually in passive] to violently attack someone in the street and rob them: *Since she was mugged she's been scared to go out on her own.*

mugging – mugged – have mugged

4 someone who steals

thief /θiːf/ [*n* C] someone who steals things, usually secretly and without violence: *The thieves had been careful not to leave any fingerprints.*
car thief/jewel thief etc (=someone who steals cars, jewels etc)
plural **thieves**

robber /'rɒbəˡ‖'rɑː-/ [*n* C] someone who steals from banks, offices, houses etc, especially by using threats or violence: *The robbers forced bank staff to give them £4000 in cash.*
bank robber (=someone who robs a bank)
armed robber (=a robber with a gun)

burglar /'bɜːˡgləˡ/ [*n* C] someone who illegally gets into a house, office etc and steals things: *The burglar must have got in through the kitchen window.*

pickpocket /'pɪkˌpɒkɪt‖-ˌpɑːk-/ [*n* C] someone who steals from people in a public place, by taking things from their pockets or bags without them noticing: *There are a lot of pickpockets in crowded tourist areas, so look after your belongings.*

shoplifter /'ʃɒp,lɪftə^r‖'ʃɑːp-/ [n C]
someone who takes things from
shops without paying for them,
especially by hiding them in their
clothes or in a bag: *The store has
installed hidden cameras to catch
shoplifters.*

mugger /'mʌgə^r/ [n C] a thief who
violently attacks someone in the
street and robs them: *Harry suffered
serious head injuries when he was
attacked by a gang of muggers.*

5 the crime of stealing

robbery /'rɒbəri‖'rɑː-/ [n C/U] the crime
of stealing money or other things
from a bank, shop etc, especially by
using threats or violence: *He took part
in his first robbery when he was 17.*
armed robbery (=using guns) *Spencer
was jailed for eight years for armed
robbery.*
bank robbery *Police are investigating
a series of bank robberies.*
plural **robberies**

burglary /'bɜː^rgləri/ [n C/U] the crime of
illegally entering a house, office etc
and stealing things: *Call the police –
there's been a burglary.* | *Most
burglaries occur when a house or
apartment is empty.*
plural **burglaries**

theft /θeft/ [n C/U] FORMAL when
something is stolen
+of *the theft of £150 from the office*
car/bicycle theft (=when a car or
bicycle is stolen) *Bicycle theft is a
major problem in the city.*

break-in /'breɪk ɪn/ [n C] when someone
breaks a door or window in order to
enter a place and steal things: *There
was a break-in at the college last night
and they took all the computers.*
plural **break-ins**

hold-up /'həʊld ʌp/ [n C] when someone
goes into a bank or shop with a gun
and demands money: *A man was shot
dead in a hold-up at a downtown bank.*
plural **hold-ups**

mugging /'mʌgɪŋ/ [n C] a violent attack
on someone in the street in order to
rob them: *The number of muggings in
the area has doubled in the last year.*

shoplifting /'ʃɒp,lɪftɪŋ‖'ʃɑːp-/ [n U] the
crime of taking things from shops

without paying for them: *Shoplifting
cost the major stores millions of dollars
last year.* | *He's been arrested 32 times
for shoplifting.*

STICK

➡ see also **JOIN**

1 to join one thing to another thing

stick /stɪk/ [v T] to join one thing to
another thing, especially by using
glue or tape with glue on it
stick sth on/in sth *It took hours to
stick all the stamps on these letters.* |
*Stick a label on each box to say what's
inside it.*
stick sth together *We gathered up the
pieces and stuck the vase back together
again.*
sticking – stuck – have stuck

glue /gluː/ [v T] to use glue to join
things together, when you are making something or repairing something
glue sth to/onto sth *I tried to glue
the handle back onto the cup.*
glue sth together *You make the
model by cutting out these shapes and
gluing them together.*

2 when one thing sticks to another

stick /stɪk/ [v I] if something **sticks** to
something else, it becomes joined to
it when it touches it, because it has
glue or a sticky substance on it: *He
pressed down hard but the stamp
wouldn't stick properly.*
+to *Peter was very hot, and his shirt
was sticking to his back.*
be stuck together *Some of the pages
were stuck together.*
sticking – stuck – have stuck

sticky /'stɪki/ [adj] something that is
sticky sticks to other things, and
sticks to your fingers when you touch
it: *There was a horrible sticky mess on
the table.* | *Add flour to the mixture to
prevent it from becoming sticky.*
sticky – stickier – stickiest

3   a substance that you use to stick things together

glue /gluː/ [n C/U] a liquid or soft substance that you use to join things together: *Wait for the glue to dry before you paint the model.*

Sellotape BRITISH **Scotch tape** AMERICAN /'seləteɪp, ,skɒtʃ 'teɪp‖,skɑːtʃ-/ [n U] TRADEMARK transparent tape with glue on it that you use to join things together, for example when you are wrapping a present or a package: *a roll of Sellotape*

STOP

➡ look here for ...
- stop doing something
- stop something from happening
- stop moving

➡ opposite **START**

➡ see also **FINISH, END, REST**

1   to stop doing something

stop /stɒp‖stɑːp/ [v I/T] to no longer do something that you have been doing or that you used to do: *That baby is always crying – doesn't he ever stop?*
stop doing sth *Everyone stopped talking as soon as she entered the room.* | *They stopped making the 3-litre Austin-Healey sports car in 1967.*
🔍 **stop it/that** SPOKEN (say this to tell someone to stop doing something) *Stop it! You're hurting me.*
stop work *At five o'clock we stopped work and went home.*

stopping – stopped – have stopped

> Don't say 'she stopped to cry'. Say **she stopped crying.**

quit /kwɪt/ [v I/T] ESPECIALLY AMERICAN to stop doing something, especially something that is difficult or unpleasant, or something that annoys other people: *"Have you found it?" "No, and if I don't find it soon I'm going to quit."*
quit doing sth *I wish he'd quit bothering me.* | *She's trying to quit smoking.*
🔍 **quit it/that** SPOKEN (say this to tell someone to stop doing something

annoying) *Quit it, Robby, or I'll tell Mom.*

quitting – quit – have quit

give up /,gɪv 'ʌp/ [phrasal verb T] to stop doing something, especially something that you used to do regularly
give up sth *I had to give up tennis when I injured my knee.*
give up smoking/drinking/fatty food etc (=stop smoking, drinking etc because you want to be healthy) *Michelle gave up smoking three years ago.*
give up doing sth *After about 10 minutes, I gave up trying to explain it to her.*
give it up *I used to play a lot of football, but I had to give it up because of an injury.*

abandon /ə'bændən/ [v T]
abandon a plan/attempt/search/ policy etc to stop something before you finish it, especially because it is too difficult to continue or there are too many problems: *They had to abandon the search because of the bad weather.* | *We abandoned the climb after Collins fell and broke his leg.*

> **Formal or informal?**
> **Abandon** is used especially in formal writing and news reports.

2   to stop doing something for a short time

stop /stɒp‖stɑːp/ [v I] to stop doing something for a short time, before continuing again: *Can we stop for a moment – I want to look at the map.*
stop for coffee/lunch/a break etc (=stop what you are doing, so you can have coffee, lunch etc) *We'll stop for lunch at 12:30.*
stop to look/listen/watch/talk/rest etc (=stop in order to look at something etc) *We stopped to listen to a couple of boys who were playing guitars in the street.* | *I stopped to rest for a few minutes.*

stopping – stopped – have stopped

pause /pɔːz/ [v I] ESPECIALLY WRITTEN to stop speaking or stop doing something for a very short time, before starting again: *Lawrence* *paused and turned to me: "Look, if you don't think it's a good idea ..."*

pause for breath (=because you need to rest for a moment) *She talked for about twenty minutes without even pausing for breath.*

pause to do sth (=in order to do something) *We waited while Graham paused to light a cigarette.*

hesitate /ˈhezɪteɪt/ [v I] ESPECIALLY WRITTEN to stop for a moment and wait before doing something, because you feel unsure or nervous about it: *She hesitated for a moment before replying. | Barry stood at the door hesitating. Should he walk straight in or knock?*

hesitation /ˌhezɪˈteɪʃən/ [n U] when someone hesitates: *After some hesitation, one of them began to speak.*

◯ **take a break** /ˌteɪk ə ˈbreɪk/ ESPECIALLY SPOKEN to stop working for a short time in order to rest, eat etc: *We're all getting tired. Let's take a break for ten minutes.*

---

3 | **a period of time when you stop doing something**

break /breɪk/ [n C] a long or short period when you stop your work or normal activities, before continuing them again later: *She returned to her career after a six-month break.*
+from *Murray felt he needed a break from studying.*
lunch/coffee/tea break (=when you stop work to have lunch, coffee etc)

pause /pɔːz/ [n C] WRITTEN a short period of time when you stop speaking or stop doing something before starting again: *After a long pause, Barney said: "Yes, I suppose you're right."*
+in *There was a pause in the conversation as everyone turned to say hello to Paul.*

---

4 | **to stop happening**

stop /stɒpǁstɑːp/ [v I] *Let's wait until the rain stops. | The noise stopped as suddenly as it had begun.*
stopping – stopped – have stopped

end /end/ [v I] if an event, activity, or story **ends**, it finally stops when it

reaches its end: *When the war ended, there were over a million refugees. | Our journey ends on the banks of the River Ganges.*

finish /ˈfɪnɪʃ/ [v I] to end – use this about an organized event such as a meeting, party, or lesson, especially to say what time it ends: *The meeting finished at lunchtime. | What time does your Spanish class finish?*

come to an end /ˌkʌm tʊ ən ˈend/ to finally end – use this about things that have continued for a long time: *Their marriage came to an end after twenty-two years. | The war in Vietnam finally came to an end in 1975.*

fade away /ˌfeɪd əˈweɪ/ [phrasal verb I] if a sound **fades away**, it gradually gets quieter and finally stops: *He waited until the sound of the engines had faded away. | As the music faded away the audience broke into applause.*

---

5 | **to make something stop happening**

stop /stɒpǁstɑːp/ [v T] to make someone stop doing something, or make something stop happening: *The referee stopped the fight when one of the boxers was badly hurt. | A power failure stopped the concert half-way through.*
stop sb doing sth *I gave him some chocolate to stop him crying.*
stopping – stopped – have stopped

put an end to sth /ˌpʊt ən ˈend tuː (sth)/ to permanently stop something, so that it can never start again: *A broken ankle put an end to her career as a dancer. | The war put an end to their romance.*

put a stop to sth /ˌpʊt ə ˈstɒp tuː (sth)ǁ-ˈstɑːp-/ to stop something unpleasant or harmful that has been happening for a long time: *The UN commander was determined to put a stop to the fighting.*

stamp out /ˌstæmp ˈaʊt/ [phrasal verb T] to completely stop a bad or illegal activity, by making rules about it and making sure that people obey them
stamp out sth *The police are determined to stamp out street robberies.*

6 to make it impossible for someone to do what they want to do

prevent /prɪˈvent/ [v T]
prevent sb from doing sth *A leg injury may prevent Shearer from playing in tomorrow's game.* | *There were reports that some people had been prevented from voting in the election.*

stop /stɒp‖stɑːp/ [v T] to stop someone from doing something that they want to do, especially by controlling them in an unreasonable way: *I've made up my mind to leave home, and you can't stop me.*
stop sb (from) doing sth *My parents tried to stop me seeing Anna.* | *The BBC was stopped from broadcasting a programme about the Secret Service.*
stopping – stopped – have stopped

Don't say 'stop someone to do something'. Say **stop someone doing something** or **stop someone from doing something**.

get in the way of sth /ˌget ɪn ðə ˈweɪ ɒv (sth)/ if something **gets in the way of** something you want to do or something you must do, it makes you too busy to do it: *Don't let your social life get in the way of your education.*

7 to stop someone from going somewhere

stop /stɒp‖stɑːp/ [v T] to prevent someone or something from going somewhere: *We were stopped and searched when we tried to enter the building.* | *The police were stopping drivers to ask questions about the accident.*
stopping – stopped – have stopped

be in the way /biː ɪn ðə ˈweɪ/ if someone or something **is in the way**, they are in a position that stops you from going where you want to go:

There's a car in the way and I can't get out of the garage.
be in sb's way *Could you move please, Sonia? You're in my way.*

block /blɒk‖blɑːk/ [v T] if objects or people **block** a road, entrance etc, they lie or stand right across it, so that no one can pass through: *A big truck had turned over on its side, and it was blocking the road.* | *Hundreds of protesters blocked the entrance to the President's palace.*

ban /bæn/ [v T] to officially say that someone may not enter a building or area, especially because they have caused trouble or because it is dangerous for them to go there: *The pub banned Ted for starting a fight.*
ban sb from sth *We've had to ban visitors from the garden because some of the paths aren't safe.*
banning – banned – have banned

8 to make sure that something does not happen

prevent /prɪˈvent/ [v T] to make sure that something will not happen or cannot happen, especially something bad: *The rules are intended to prevent accidents.* | *Managers and union leaders are hoping to prevent the strike.*
prevent sth from doing sth *The chemical is stored in sealed tanks to prevent poisonous gases from escaping.*
prevention [n U] when something is prevented: *crime prevention*
+of *the prevention of accidents*

stop /stɒp‖stɑːp/ [v T] to make sure that something bad that is happening cannot continue and become worse: *If it can help to stop the spread of AIDS, it's worth trying.*
stop sth from doing sth *They had to stop the fire from reaching the oil storage tanks.*
stopping – stopped – have stopped

cancel /ˈkænsəl/ [v T] to change a previous arrangement, so that a meeting, concert, game etc which was planned will not happen: *We've cancelled the meeting because Wayne can't come.* | *I forgot to cancel my doctor's appointment.*

cancelling – cancelled – have cancelled BRITISH
canceling – canceled – have canceled AMERICAN

call off /ˌkɔːl ˈɒf‖-ˈɔːf/ [*phrasal verb* T] to stop a meeting or event that you have organized, just before it is going to start
call off sth *If it goes on raining, we'll have to call off the game. | Damian called off the wedding at the last moment.*
call sth off *"Will there be a train strike tomorrow?" "No, the union called it off."*

> **Formal or informal?**
> **Call off** is more informal than **cancel**.

9 to stop someone from working, paying attention etc

interrupt /ˌɪntəˈrʌpt/ [*v* I/T] to stop someone when they are working, talking, or having a meeting, especially because you want to ask a question or tell them something: *Don't interrupt – I haven't finished yet. | I'm sorry to interrupt your meeting, but I have an important announcement.*
interruption [*n* C] when someone interrupts you: *It's hard to study with so many interruptions.*
disturb /dɪˈstɜːʳb/ [*v* T] to stop someone who is busy doing something, for example by asking them a question or making a noise: *Sorry to disturb you, but could I ask you a quick question? | Try not to disturb your Dad – he's working.*
distract /dɪˈstrækt/ [*v* T] to stop someone who is trying to work, study, or read, by making them look at or listen to something else: *The couple behind us kept distracting everyone by talking during the movie.*
be distracted by sth *I was distracted by the sound of a car alarm in the street.*
put sb off /ˌpʊt (sb) ˈɒf‖-ˈɔːf/ [*phrasal verb* T] BRITISH to make it difficult for someone to do something, by preventing them from paying attention and thinking clearly about what

they are doing: *I tried to do my homework, but Jack kept on laughing and putting me off.*

10 to stop moving

stop /stɒp‖stɑːp/ [*v* I] *I stopped and picked up the coin. | What's happened? Why have all the cars stopped?*
stop to do sth (=stop in order to do something) *He stopped to buy a newspaper on the way home.*
stop dead (=stop very suddenly) *My horse stopped dead, and I was thrown forward.*
stopping – stopped – have stopped

come to a halt/come to a stop /ˌkʌm tʊ ə ˈhɔːlt, ˌkʌm tʊ ə ˈstɒp‖-ˈstɑːp/ ESPECIALLY WRITTEN to gradually slow down and then stop – use this about trains, cars etc: *As the train came to a stop he jumped off and ran away. | The bus finally came to a halt half-way up a very steep hill.*

brake /breɪk/ [*v* I] to make a car, train, bicycle etc stop or go more slowly by using the brake (=the control that reduces the speed): *I had to brake suddenly to avoid a dog that ran into the road.*

pull in/pull over /ˌpʊl ˈɪn, ˌpʊl ˈəʊvəʳ/ [*phrasal verb* I] to make your car stop at the side of the road: *If you start to feel tired on long journeys, pull in and have a rest.*

11 when a train, bus, or plane stops somewhere

stop /stɒp‖stɑːp/ [*v* I] to stop somewhere to let passengers get on or off – use this about trains or buses
+at/near/outside etc *Does this train stop at York? | The bus stops just outside my house.*
stopping – stopped – have stopped

stop /stɒp‖stɑːp/ [*n* C] a place where a bus or train regularly stops to let passengers get on or off: *Get off at the third stop.*
bus stop *We live miles from the nearest bus stop.*

call at /ˈkɔːl æt/ [*phrasal verb* T] if a train or ship **calls at** a place, it stops there while it is on the way to

S

somewhere else: *This is the 10:30 to Bristol, calling at Reading and Bath.* | *The ship calls at Madeira to collect cargo.*

direct /dɟ'rekt, daɪ-/ [adj/adv] if a journey is **direct**, or if you travel **direct**, you go straight from one place to another without stopping to change planes, trains etc: *With this ticket you can travel direct from Paris to Berlin overnight.*
direct flight/bus/train *There are no direct flights from Rochester to Cincinnati.*

non-stop /ˌnɒn 'stɒp◂ ‖ˌnɑːn 'stɑːp◂/ [adj only before noun] a **non-stop** flight, train, service etc takes people from one place to another without stopping anywhere: *There are three non-stop flights to Los Angeles every day.* | *British Airways' new non-stop service between London and Hong Kong*
non-stop [adv] *You can travel from Paris to London non-stop on Eurostar.*

STORY

a description of a series of events that is told to entertain people

➡ see also **WB** **BOOKS/LITERATURE, WB FILMS/MOVIES**

1 a story

story /'stɔːri/ [n C] *a book of short stories*
tell/read sb a story *Our teacher used to read us a story every afternoon.*
+about *Grandpa's always telling us stories about when he was a boy*
the story of (=a well-known story about someone) *the story of Cinderella*
fairy/ghost/love story (=a story about magic/ghosts/love) *We sat around the fire telling ghost stories.*
true story (=about events that really happened) *Apparently the film is based on a true story.*
plural **stories**

tale /teɪl/ [n C] an exciting story of imaginary events: *'Treasure Island' – a tale of pirates and adventure*
fairy tale (=a story for children, with magic in it) *Hans Christian Andersen's fairy tales*

myth /mɪθ/ [n C/U] a very old story, about gods and magical creatures: *The myth tells of how the gods sent fire to the earth in flashes of lightning.* | *a ballet based on a Greek myth*

legend /'ledʒənd/ [n C/U] an old story, usually about strange events or people with magic powers: *According to legend, the whole castle was washed into the sea.*
+of *the legend of Robin Hood*

anecdote /'ænɪkdəʊt/ [n C] a short funny story about something that really happened: *The book is full of amusing anecdotes about his time in the police force.*

2 a person in a story

character /'kærɪktə^r/ [n C] one of the people in a story: *The two main characters in the book are a young boy and his teacher.*

hero /'hɪərəʊ/ [n C] the man or boy who is the main character in a story, especially when he is very good, very brave etc: *At the end of the story, the hero rescues the princess and they get married.*
+of *the hero of the novel*
plural **heroes**

heroine /'herəʊ̩ɪn/ [n C] the woman or girl who is the main character in a story, especially when she is very good, very brave etc
+of *Tess is the tragic heroine of the novel.*

3 the way the events in a story are arranged

plot /plɒt‖plɑːt/ [n C] the series of events that happen in a book, play, film etc, and the way they are all connected: *The plot of 'Twin Peaks' was so complicated that I couldn't follow it.*

storyline /'stɔːrilaɪn/ [n C] the main story of a book, play, film etc: *The play has a strong storyline which will appeal to children as well as adults.* | *Anna's marriage problems form the main storyline in Episode One.*

STRAIGHT

➡ see also **BEND**

1 when lines or objects are straight

straight /streɪt/ [adj] **straight** lines, roads, edges etc have no bends or curves: First, draw two straight lines. | Her hair is blonde and very straight. | a long straight avenue
dead straight ESPECIALLY BRITISH (=completely straight) The road ran dead straight for 50 miles across the desert.

2 travelling or moving in a straight line

straight /streɪt/ [adv] Terry was so drunk he couldn't walk straight.
straight ahead/down/towards etc If you look straight ahead, you'll see the church in the distance. | The truck was heading straight towards us.
go straight on BRITISH **go straight** AMERICAN /ˌgəʊ streɪt ˈɒn, ˌgəʊ ˈstreɪt/ SPOKEN to continue travelling ahead in the same direction as before, without turning left or right – use this when you are telling people which way to go: When you get to the intersection, go straight. | Keep going straight on through the town and when you come to the school, turn left.
in a straight line /ɪn ə ˌstreɪt ˈlaɪn/ if something moves **in a straight line**, it does not turn to the left or to the right: Light always travels in a straight line. | It's difficult to walk in a straight line with your eyes closed.
direct /dɪˈrekt, daɪ-/ [adj] going straight from one place to another without changing direction
direct route/line/path/way Which is the most direct route to London from here?

3 sitting or standing straight

upright /ˈʌpraɪt/ [adv] ESPECIALLY WRITTEN sitting or standing with your back and neck straight, not bent: The roof of the cave was so low that we couldn't stand upright.
bolt upright (=sitting with your back very straight) There was a sudden noise outside, and she sat bolt upright in bed.

4 to make something straight

straighten /ˈstreɪtn/ [v T] He was standing outside the manager's office, straightening his tie.
straighten your legs/arms/back Gradually straighten your legs until you are standing upright.

STRANGE

unusual, in a way that makes you feel surprised, frightened, worried etc

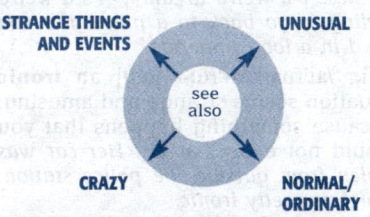

STRANGE THINGS AND EVENTS — UNUSUAL — see also — CRAZY — NORMAL/ORDINARY

1 strange object/situation/experience

strange /streɪndʒ/ [adj] very different from what you expect or from what usually happens, in a way that makes you feel a little frightened or surprised: A strange noise woke her up. | I had a strange feeling that I'd been there before.
it is strange that It's strange that you've never met him – he lives in your street.
funny/odd /ˈfʌni, ɒdǁɑːd/ [adj] ESPECIALLY BRITISH something **funny** or **odd** is a little strange and it makes you feel slightly worried, because you cannot explain it or you do not know what it is: There's a funny smell coming from the fridge.
it is odd/funny that It seems odd that no-one noticed him coming in.
that's funny/that's odd SPOKEN (say this when something seems odd)

"Your keys aren't here." "That's odd, I'm sure I left them on the table."

peculiar /pɪˈkjuːliəʳ/ [adj] strange and slightly unpleasant: *This meat tastes peculiar. | The walls were painted a very peculiar shade of green.*

mysterious /mɪˈstɪəriəs/ [adj] use this about something that people know very little about, and that is difficult to explain or understand: *His father died of a mysterious illness. | I kept getting mysterious phone calls where the caller would hang up as soon as I answered. | his mysterious disappearance*

   mysteriously [adv] *Mysteriously, no-one had noticed anyone leave or enter the room.*

weird /wɪəʳd/ [adj] a **weird** experience, feeling, sight, or sound is strange and very different from what you are used to: *She always wears really weird clothes. | a weird dream | It's a weird feeling to go back to a place that you lived in a long time ago.*

ironic /aɪˈrɒnɪk‖aɪˈrɑː-/ [adj] an **ironic** situation seems strange and amusing, because something happens that you would not expect at all: *Her car was stolen from outside the police station, which is pretty ironic.*
   it is ironic that *It's ironic that athletes are often such unhealthy people.*

2 strange person/behaviour

strange /streɪndʒ/ [adj] someone who is **strange** behaves differently from most people, and seems unusual or a little frightening: *Pearl was a strange girl who never played with the other children. | He's very strange – you never really know what he's thinking.*

strangely [adv] *Conor was acting very strangely last night – do you think he's all right?*

> ⚠ Don't confuse a **strange** person (=someone who behaves in a strange way) and a **stranger** (=someone you have never met before).

funny/odd /ˈfʌni, ɒd‖ɑːd/ [adj] ESPECIALLY BRITISH someone who is **funny** or **odd** behaves strangely and is difficult to understand: *Did Anna*

warn you that her aunt is rather ... well, rather odd? | He's a bit funny – sometimes he's very friendly, other times he just ignores you.*

mysterious /mɪˈstɪəriəs/ [adj] ESPECIALLY WRITTEN a **mysterious** person is someone that people know very little about, and who therefore seems strange or interesting: *The package had been left outside the door by a mysterious visitor.*

eccentric /ɪkˈsentrɪk/ [adj] an **eccentric** person has strange and slightly crazy habits or ideas, which people find amusing: *Our neighbour is an eccentric old lady who has about 25 cats.*

weird /wɪəʳd/ [adj] INFORMAL a **weird** person is very strange and makes you feel frightened or uncomfortable: *She's living with this really weird guy who's into witchcraft and black magic.*

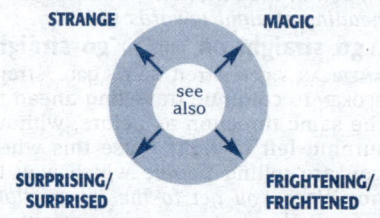

STRANGE THINGS AND EVENTS

   STRANGE   **MAGIC**

see also

SURPRISING/   **FRIGHTENING/**
SURPRISED   **FRIGHTENED**

1 things that happen which cannot be explained by science

the paranormal /ðə ˌpærəˈnɔːʳməl/ [n singular] strange things that happen or exist but cannot be explained by science: *The committee investigates the paranormal, such as events involving UFOs and poltergeists. | There seems to be a growing interest in the paranormal.*

paranormal [adj] *paranormal experiences*

supernatural /ˌsuːpəʳˈnætʃərəl◂, ˌsjuː-‖ˌsuː-/ [adj] **supernatural** powers, creatures, or events cannot be explained by science, and seem to be connected with magic or gods: *a horror movie about a little girl with supernatural powers | supernatural beings*

the supernatural [n singular] *His stories mingle realism with the super-natural.*

mystery /'mɪstəri/ [n C] something strange that no one can understand or explain: *Her disappearance still remains a mystery.*
+of *the mystery of the lost city of Atlantis*
mysterious /mɪ'stɪəriəs/ [adj] if something is **mysterious**, no one can understand it or explain it: *The newspapers reported that he had died in mysterious circumstances.*
mysteriously [adv] *Mysteriously, the food on the plates was still warm, but the ship was deserted.*

2 creatures from other parts of the universe

alien /'eɪliən/ [n C] a creature that is from another part of the universe: *Thousands of people claim to have been kidnapped by aliens from outer space.*
alien [adj] *There was a rumour going around about an alien spacecraft that had crashed into the desert.* | *creatures from an alien planet*

UFO /'juːfəʊ, ˌjuː ef 'əʊ/ [n C] a strange object in the sky that people believe is a space vehicle from another planet: *There have been several UFO sightings in this area.*

3 spirits and ghosts

spirit /'spɪrɪt/ [n C] the part of a person that, according to some people's beliefs, continues to live after they have died: *In Japan, people believe that the spirits of the dead return to earth every summer, during the Obon festival.*
evil spirits (=spirits that want to harm people) *They painted their faces to ward off evil spirits.* (=keep them away)

ghost /ɡəʊst/ [n C] the spirit of a dead person that seems to exist in a place after their death, and that some people think they see, hear, or feel there: *Do you believe in ghosts?* | *I saw a ghost at the end of my bed – a woman in a long, white dress.*

the ghost of sb *She was convinced she'd seen the ghost of King Arthur.*

poltergeist /'pɒltəˈɡaɪst‖'pəʊl-/ [n C] a type of ghost you cannot see, which moves furniture, throws things around, and makes a lot of noise: *The poltergeist had thrown books around the room and smashed plates.*

haunt /hɔːnt/ [v T] if a ghost **haunts** a place, people think that they see, hear, or feel it there: *The ghost of the murdered prince still haunts the castle.*
be haunted by sth *The wood is a spooky, secret place, said to be haunted by a headless man on a horse.*

haunted /'hɔːntɪd/ [adj] a place that is **haunted** has ghosts in it: *a haunted house* | *The people refused to go into the forest alone because they thought it was haunted.*

ghostly /'ɡəʊstli/ [adj] looking like a ghost, or making you think of ghosts
ghostly figure (=a ghost, or something that could be a ghost) *A ghostly figure hovered at the top of the stairs.*
ghostly voice/hand/footsteps *She felt the touch of a ghostly hand on her shoulder.*

spooky /'spuːki/ [adj] INFORMAL a place that is **spooky** is a little frightening because it makes you feel that there might be ghosts there: *Let's get out of here. This place is really spooky.* | *What a spooky castle! It would be a great place to make a film.*

4 when someone has mental powers that seem impossible

psychic /'saɪkɪk/ [adj] someone who is **psychic** or has **psychic** powers has very unusual mental powers that cannot be explained, and uses them to know what other people are thinking, what will happen in the future etc: *She uses her psychic abilities to help the police find people who are missing.* | *psychic healing*
psychic phenomena (=unusual things that happen because of psychic powers, such as communicating with dead people, or making people's illnesses better)

psychic /'saɪkɪk/ [n C] someone who has psychic powers: *As a psychic, she could sense when evil things had happened in a place.*

telepathic /ˌtelɪ'pæθɪk◂/ [adj] someone who is **telepathic** has the ability to know what someone else is thinking or feeling without being told, even if the other person is a long way away: *There have been many cases of identical twins who seem to be telepathic.*

telepathy /tɪ'lepəθi/ [n U] the ability to know what someone else is thinking without them telling you: *Over the years the pair had developed a kind of telepathy.*

5 when someone knows what will happen in the future

clairvoyant /kleəˈʳvɔɪent/ [n C] someone who has the ability to know what will happen in the future: *A clairvoyant predicted that something terrible would happen to the President.*

clairvoyance /kleəˈʳvɔɪens/ [n U] the ability to know what will happen in the future

fortune teller /'fɔːʳtʃən ˌteləʳ/ [n C] someone who tells people what will happen to them in the future and is paid for doing this: *I went to see a fortune teller, and she told me that I would have three children.*

see into the future /ˌsiː ɪntə ðə 'fjuːtʃəʳ/ someone who can **see into the future** has the ability to know what will happen before it happens: *Would you really want to be able to see into the future?*

predict /prɪ'dɪkt/ [v T] to correctly say what will happen in the future: *Nostradamus predicted many of the key events of the 20th century.*

prediction [n C] something that you say will happen in the future: *My prediction is that the world will run out of petrol by the year 2050.*

premonition /ˌpreməˈnɪʃən, ˌpriː-/ [n C] a strange feeling that you get, which makes you think that something bad is going to happen soon: *The night before we sailed, I had a terrible premonition of danger ahead.*

6 when someone tries to talk to the spirits of dead people

medium /'miːdiəm/ [n C] someone who claims that they can hear messages from the spirits of dead people

seance /'seɪɑːns, -ɒnsǁ-ɑːns/ [n C] a meeting where someone tries to help people to talk to the spirits of their dead friends or relatives: *Helen was a medium, and once a month she held a seance in her house.*

STRICT/NOT STRICT

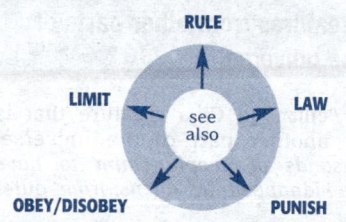

1 strict person

strict /strɪkt/ [adj] someone who is **strict** makes definite rules and expects people to obey them completely: *a strict teacher*
+**with** *I think Jill's parents are too strict with her.*
+**about** *Their boss is very strict about people getting to work on time.*
strictly [adv] *They brought their children up very strictly.*

firm /fɜːʳm/ [adj] if you are **firm** with someone, you tell them that they must accept your decision because you are not going to change it: *The principal replied with a polite but firm 'no'.*
+**with** *You'll just have to be firm with him and tell him he can't have any more money.*
firmly [adv] *"No," she said firmly, "you can't go." | Bill was firmly opposed to any change in the plans.*

tough /tʌf/ [adj] very strict, and determined that your orders will be obeyed – use this especially when you think that someone is right to be strict

+on *Ray was a baseball coach, and known for being tough on his players.* | *The government has promised to be tough on crime.*

get tough with sb (=start being very strict with them) *The police have been told to get tough with drunken teenagers in the town centre.*

> **Formal or informal?**
> **Tough** is more informal than **strict** or **firm**.

2 strict rule/law

strict /strɪkt/ [*adj* usually before noun] a **strict** rule or law is very clear and must always be obeyed: *There are strict rules about the use of dangerous chemicals.* | *He had strict instructions to return the key to me.*

strictly [*adv*] *Smoking is strictly forbidden in this area.*

harsh /hɑː^rʃ/ [*adj*] a **harsh** law or system of government has severe punishments – use this especially about something that you think is unfair and too strict: *The laws concerning alcohol are very harsh.* | *a harsh military regime*

harshly [*adv*] *Young offenders were treated very harshly.*

tough /tʌf/ [*adj*] **tough** laws or rules are very strict and do not allow much freedom: *The federal government is introducing tough new rules to control immigration.* | *The athletes had to undergo a tough training programme.*

> **Formal or informal?**
> **Tough** is more informal than **strict** or **harsh**.

3 not strict

lenient /'liːniənt/ [*adj*] not strict in the way that you punish people or control their behaviour: *The younger teachers generally had a more lenient attitude towards the students' behaviour.*

+with *The judge was criticized for being too lenient with young offenders.*

leniently [*adv*] *He asked the police to deal leniently with the boys.*

leniency (also **lenience**) [*n* U] when someone is not punished in a strict or

severe way: *The judge rejected the defendant's plea for leniency.*

lax /læks/ [*adj*] not strict enough, especially through carelessness: *The report criticizes the lax security at many prisons.*

+about *I think the school has been too lax about bad behaviour in the past.*

easy-going /ˌiːzi 'ɡəʊɪŋ◂/ [*adj*] someone who is **easy-going** is not strict, and is usually calm and relaxed: *Our parents are pretty easy-going, and don't mind if we stay out late.*

STRONG

➡ look here for ...
- a strong person or thing
- a strong government or leader
- a strong feeling or belief
- a strong taste or smell

➡ opposite **WEAK**

➡ see also **BRAVE/NOT BRAVE**

1 strong person

➡ see also **WB** **EXERCISE**, **WB** **SPORT**

strong /strɒŋ‖strɔːŋ/ [*adj*] someone who is **strong** has big muscles and can lift heavy things, do a lot of physical work etc: *It took four strong men to lift the piano.* | *strong hands*

strength /streŋθ, streŋθ/ [*n* U] the ability to lift or carry heavy things, to do a lot of physical work etc: *Bill was doing a lot of exercise to build up his strength.*

the strength to do sth *I didn't have the strength to climb any further.*

with all your strength (=as hard as you can) *Diana pulled on the rope with all her strength.*

energetic /ˌenə^r'dʒetɪk◂/ [*adj*] someone who is **energetic** likes to be active or busy, and has the ability to work hard for a long time: *With a new and energetic director, the company was soon doing well again.* | *For more energetic visitors, there are many sports and activities.*

energy /'enə^rdʒi/ [*n* U] the feeling of physical and mental strength that helps you to do a lot of things without getting tired easily: *Vitamin pills can give you extra energy.* | *I don't have the time or the energy to go out much during the week.*

powerful /'pauəᵊfəl/ [adj] ESPECIALLY WRITTEN very strong – use this about someone's body, arms, muscles etc: *a tall man with a powerful physique* | *Birds have very powerful wing muscles.* | *the crocodile's powerful jaws*

muscular /'mʌskjᵿləᵊ/ [adj] someone who is **muscular** looks strong because you can see that they have big muscles: *She liked men who were tall and muscular.* | *He had broad shoulders and muscular arms.*

athletic /æθ'letɪkǁəθ-/ [adj] ESPECIALLY WRITTEN someone who is **athletic** has a strong but fairly thin body, and looks as if they are good at sports: *She was tall, athletic, and very attractive.* | *long athletic legs*

stamina /'stæmᵻnə/ [n U] the ability to work hard, run, play sports etc for a long time without getting tired: *You need stamina to be a long-distance runner.* | *exercises to increase your strength and stamina*

2 strong government/leader/organization

➡ see also **POWER, WB GOVERNMENT/ POLITICS**

strong /strɒŋǁstrɔːŋ/ [adj] a **strong** government, leader, manager etc has clear ideas about what should be done, and takes firm control of what happens: *This country needs a strong government to solve the economic crisis.* | *The school's main problem is that it lacks strong leadership.*

powerful /'pauəᵊfəl/ [adj] a **powerful** person, group, or organization has a lot of influence over events, for example because they are very rich or they hold an important position: *The Senator has powerful allies in America's business community.* | *Murdoch controls dozens of newspapers and TV stations, and is an immensely powerful man.*

3 strong thing/material

strong /strɒŋǁstrɔːŋ/ [adj] something that is **strong** cannot be broken or destroyed easily: *The bags are made of strong black plastic.* | *You'll need a strong piece of rope for towing the car.*
strength [n U] how strong something is: *a machine for testing the strength of the steel beams*

solid /'sɒlɪdǁ'sɑː-/ [adj] a building or piece of furniture that is **solid** is strong and well made: *The table seemed solid enough, so I climbed up onto it.* | *rows of solid little houses built of local stone*

tough /tʌf/ [adj] not easily broken, cut, or damaged – use this about cloth, leather, plastic, or natural substances: *jackets made from tough waterproof cotton* | *a pair of tough leather boots* | *Before cooking the artichoke, cut off the tough outer leaves.*

4 strong feeling/belief

strong /strɒŋǁstrɔːŋ/ [adj] if you have **strong** feelings, beliefs, or opinions about something, your feelings affect you a lot and you are very serious about them: *The subject of abortion always arouses strong emotions.* | *These plans faced strong opposition from local people.* | *a strong sense of family loyalty*
strongly [adv] *If you feel very strongly about this, write to your Congressman and complain.*
strength [n U] how strong someone's feelings are: *The President could not ignore the strength of public opinion.*

intense /ɪn'tens/ [adj] ESPECIALLY WRITTEN a feeling that is **intense** is so strong that you can hardly control it: *We were waiting for the winner to be announced, and the excitement was intense.* | *intense pleasure* | *Every car was stopped and searched, which caused intense annoyance to the drivers.*
intensely [adv] *From the moment I first met him I disliked him intensely.*

deep /diːp/ [adj] usually before noun] very strong – use this especially about a feeling of love, sympathy, sadness, or disappointment: *The news*

came as a deep disappointment to us all. | the deep sorrow that we all felt when Arthur died
deeply [adv] *I was deeply offended by their remarks.*

> **Formal or informal?**
> **Deep** and **deeply** are used in writing and in formal spoken English.

extreme /ɪkˈstriːm/ [adj] **extreme** opinions or beliefs about politics, religion etc are too strong and most people regard them as unreasonable: *extreme nationalist views | an extreme left-wing party*

---

5 strong taste/smell

strong /strɒŋ‖strɔːŋ/ [adj] a **strong** smell or taste is one that you notice easily: *This cheese has a very strong taste. | There's a strong smell of gas.*
strongly [adv] *His breath smelled strongly of garlic.*
rich /rɪtʃ/ [adj] a **rich** smell or flavour is strong and pleasant: *the rich scent of the pine trees | a rich fruit cake*

---

6 to make something stronger

make sth stronger /ˌmeɪk (sth) ˈstrɒŋgəʳ‖-ˈstrɔːŋ-/ to make something physically stronger: *I've put in some extra posts to make the fence stronger.*
strengthen /ˈstreŋθən, ˈstrenθən/ [v T] to make something stronger, physically or emotionally: *The ship's decks will have to be strengthened to carry the extra weight. | Her parents' opposition only strengthened her determination to succeed. | This trade agreement will strengthen the links between our countries.*

> When you see **WB**, go to the **WORD BANKS** section.

STUDY

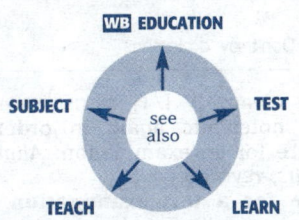

WB EDUCATION

SUBJECT · TEST · TEACH · LEARN — see also

1 to study something at school, university etc

study /ˈstʌdi/ [v I/T] to learn about a subject by reading books, going to classes, and doing work that your teacher asks you to do: *It's difficult to study when the weather's so hot. | I've been studying English for six years now.*
study to be a doctor/engineer etc *She's at business school, studying to be an accountant.*
studying – studied – have studied

take /teɪk/ [v T] to study a subject – use this to talk about subjects that you choose to study at a school or university: *In my final year, I decided to take English, French, and Economics.*
taking – took – have taken

do /duː/ [v T] BRITISH to study a subject at school or university: *I can't decide whether to do German or Spanish next year. | Did you do computing at school?*
do a course *Why not do a language course at your local college?*
doing – did – have done

> **Formal or informal?**
> **Do** is less formal than **study**.

major in sth /ˈmeɪdʒər ɪn (sth)/ [phrasal verb T not in passive] AMERICAN to study something as your main subject at university: *Diane majored in psychology at Berkeley. | What are you majoring in?*

take lessons/have lessons /ˌteɪk ˈlesənz, ˌhæv ˈlesənz/ to pay for lessons from a teacher in order to study a subject or skill in your free time: *My* *mother wants me to take violin lessons. | I'm having Spanish lessons after work.*

 Don't say 'do lessons'.

revise /rɪ'vaɪz/ [v I/T] BRITISH to read facts, notes etc again in order to prepare for an examination: *Ahmed's upstairs, revising.*
revise for a test/examination *The library was full of students revising for the final exams.*

2 to study something in order to discover new facts

study /'stʌdi/ [v T] to examine something carefully, do tests on it etc, in order to find out more about it and discover new facts: *Scientists are studying the development of the disease in children. | She spent several years studying the behaviour of gorillas in Africa.*
studying – studied – have studied

analyze (also **analyse** BRITISH) /'ænəlaɪz/ [v T] to carefully examine information, reports, the results of tests etc, in order to understand something better: *The detective's main job is to analyze all the evidence relating to a crime. | We use a special computer program to analyse all the sales figures.*

do research /duː rɪ'sɜːᵗtʃ/ to study a subject in a careful, detailed way, in order to discover new information or produce new ideas about it: *She got a degree in biology, then went to work for a drug company, doing research.*
+into/on *a team of scientists doing research into the causes of heart disease*

3 the work that you do when you study

studies /'stʌdiz/ [n plural] all the work that you do when you are a student at school or university
his/her/your etc studies *My uncle*

asked me if I was enjoying my studies. | He graduated in history at Stanford, then went to continue his studies at Harvard.

Formal or informal?
Studies is a formal word. It would not usually be used by a young person in conversation.

homework /'həʊmwɜːᵗk/ [n U] work that a school pupil is given to do during free time, not during lessons: *Did Mrs Harvey give you any homework? | homework assignments*
do your homework *I'm going to the library to do my French homework.*

 Don't say 'homeworks'. **Homework** is an uncountable noun.

 Don't say 'I made my homework'. Say **I did my homework**

coursework /'kɔːᵗswɜːᵗk/ [n U] all the work that a student has to do as part of a course of study, apart from what they do in examinations: *Half of the marks are for the exam, and half are for coursework.*

research /rɪ'sɜːᵗtʃ, 'riːsɜːᵗtʃ/ [n U] careful, detailed work that you do in order to discover new information or produce new ideas about a particular subject: *Recent research has shown that human language is much older than we previously thought.*
+into/on *More research is needed into the ways in which this virus is spread.*
medical/historical etc research *the latest scientific research*
do research *She's doing research into the connection between crime and poverty.*

 Don't say 'a research' or 'researches'. **Research** is an uncountable noun.

 Don't say 'make research'. Say **do research**.

revision /rɪ'vɪʒən/ [n U] BRITISH when you read facts, notes etc again in order to prepare for an examination: *How is your history revision going?*

do revision *I can't come out tonight – I have a lot of revision to do.*

STUPID

➡ see also **SENSIBLE, INTELLIGENT, CRAZY**

1 people who behave in a stupid way

stupid /'stjuːpɪ̑d‖'stuː-/ [*adj*] someone who is **stupid** behaves in a way that shows very bad judgement and that is likely to cause problems for themselves or for other people: *You stupid boy! I've told you never to play with matches.* | *He told me a lot of lies, and I was stupid enough to believe him.* | *If your stupid brother hadn't left the door open, we wouldn't have been robbed.*
it is stupid of sb to do sth *I should have called the police – it was stupid of me not to.*
stupidly [*adv*] *I stupidly agreed to lend him some money.*

> ⚠ You can use **stupid** about yourself, but it is rude to say someone else is **stupid**. People usually say this only when they are very annoyed with someone.

dumb /dʌm/ [*adj*] INFORMAL, ESPECIALLY AMERICAN stupid: *She told him Jeff was just a friend, and he was dumb enough to believe her.*

silly /'sɪli/ [*adj*] someone who is **silly** behaves in a way which is not at all sensible or serious, and which they may be embarrassed about later: *The children were running around and shouting and being very silly.* | *I think you're silly to worry so much about your hair.*
silly – sillier – silliest

foolish /'fuːlɪʃ/ [*adj*] FORMAL stupid and not thinking sensibly about the possible results of what you do: *Sue realized later that her behaviour had been very foolish.* | *I was young and foolish at the time.*
it is foolish (of sb) to do sth *It was a warning that she would have been foolish to ignore.*

foolishly [*adv*] *She foolishly agreed to go with them.*

crazy /'kreɪzi/ [*adj*] someone who is **crazy** behaves in a way that does not seem normal, for example because they do something very strange or very dangerous: *You're crazy to think of hitch-hiking on your own.* | *I said I enjoyed doing exams, and she looked at me as if I was crazy!*
crazy – crazier – craziest

> ⚠ Don't say 'very crazy'. Say **completely/ totally/absolutely crazy**: *Put that gun down! Are you completely crazy?*

idiot/fool /'ɪdiət, fuːl/ [*n C*] someone who does something very stupid or embarrassing: *You lost the tickets? How could you be such a fool?* | *Some idiot in a fast car was trying to overtake me.*
be a fool/idiot to do sth *I realized later that I was a fool to believe all his lies.*
make a fool of yourself (=do something that makes you seem very stupid) *Sorry I made such a fool of myself yesterday. I had far too much to drink.*

childish /'tʃaɪldɪʃ/ [*adj*] someone who is **childish** annoys you by being unreasonable and unhelpful, or by complaining and being rude, as if they were a small child: *He said he wouldn't go out with us if Jerry was going too – he's so childish!* | *It would be very childish to walk past without saying hello.*

immature /ˌɪmə'tʃʊə◂‖-'tʊər◂/ [*adj*] someone who is **immature** behaves as if they were younger than they really are, so they are not as sensible or responsible as you expect them to be: *Teenage boys are often more immature than girls.* | *I was 19 when I went to college, but still very immature.*

2 stupid things that people do or say

stupid /'stjuːpɪ̑d‖'stuː-/ [*adj*] a **stupid** question, idea, action, or situation annoys you because it shows a lack of sensible thinking or good judgement: *It's a stupid idea and it'll never work.*

a stupid question/remark/comment
Of course you have to pay! What a stupid question!

a stupid thing to do/say *You followed her home? That was a really stupid thing to do!*

it is stupid to do sth *I think it's stupid not to keep copies of your work on disk.*

dumb /dʌm/ [*adj*] INFORMAL, ESPECIALLY AMERICAN stupid: *She's always asking such dumb questions.* | *He's always doing something really dumb.*

silly /ˈsɪli/ [*adj*] **silly** behaviour, jokes, mistakes etc show that someone is not very sensible or serious or does not think carefully about what they do: *I'm tired of Paul and his silly jokes.* | *Her work is rather careless, and she keeps making the same silly mistakes.*

a silly thing to do/say *I had locked myself out, which was a silly thing to do.*

silly – sillier – silliest

crazy /ˈkreɪzi/ [*adj*] **crazy** ideas, plans, or situations make you feel annoyed or very surprised, because they are not at all sensible or reasonable: *Ian's got a crazy plan to drive all the way across Africa.* | *I don't know why I thought we'd be happy together. It was a crazy idea.* | *The farmers can make more money by not planting crops – it's crazy, isn't it?*

crazy – crazier – craziest

> ⚠ Don't say 'very crazy'. Say **completely/ totally/absolutely crazy**: *"There's only one computer for a class of 35 students." "That's absolutely crazy."*

ridiculous/absurd /rɪˈdɪkjᵿləs, əbˈsɜːʳd/ [*adj*] use this about plans, suggestions, situations etc which are so stupid that you cannot believe anyone would think of them or allow them to happen: *They're asking a ridiculous rent for that apartment.* | *What an absurd suggestion!*

it is ridiculous/absurd that *It's ridiculous that you have to wait six weeks to get the books you ordered.*

> **Formal or informal?**
> **Absurd** is more formal than **ridiculous**.

irrational /ɪˈræʃənəl/ [*adj*] FORMAL irrational actions, feelings, or beliefs are not based on clear thinking or sensible reasons: *an irrational fear of flying* | *irrational behaviour*

○ **daft** /dɑːft‖dæft/ [*adj*] BRITISH, ESPECIALLY SPOKEN stupid, but often also amusing: *Is this another one of your daft ideas?* | *What a daft thing to say!*

3 | not intelligent

not very bright/not very intelligent /nɒt veri ˈbraɪt, nɒt veri ɪnˈtelɪdʒənt/ [*adj*] someone who is **not very bright** or **not very intelligent** is unable to learn and understand things quickly and easily: *Sometimes I think that woman just isn't very bright.* | *Franco works hard but he isn't really very intelligent.*

stupid /ˈstjuːpɪd‖ˈstuː-/ [*adj*] not at all intelligent: *She talks to us as if we're completely stupid.* | *Poor Larry's too stupid to realize when you're making fun of him.*

> ⚠ It is rude to say someone is **stupid**, so usually we say that they are **not very bright** or **not very intelligent**.

dumb /dʌm/ [*adj*] INFORMAL, ESPECIALLY AMERICAN not at all intelligent: *The athletic guys were seen as 'cute but dumb'.* | *You're so dumb, Clarissa!*

thick /θɪk/ [*adj*] BRITISH INFORMAL not at all intelligent: *He's a nice boy, but he's a bit thick, isn't he?*

dim /dɪm/ [*adj*] INFORMAL very slow at learning things, and not very clever: *She's not the brightest kid in the class – in fact, she's quite dim.*

dim – dimmer -dimmest

> **When you see** ⁨EC⁩, go to the **ESSENTIAL COMMUNICATION** section.

SUBJECT

what you talk about, write about, or study

1 something that you talk about, write about etc

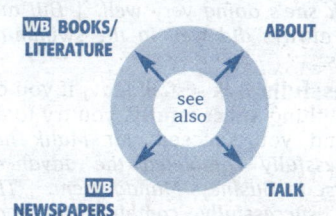

WB BOOKS/
LITERATURE

ABOUT

see
also

WB
NEWSPAPERS

TALK

subject /'sʌbdʒɪkt/ [n C] something that is talked about or written about, for example at a meeting, in an essay, or newspaper article, or in a conversation: *I read a lot of books about astronomy. It's a very interesting subject.* | *We talked about all sorts of subjects.*
the subject of crime/racism/animal rights etc (=crime etc as a subject that people write about or talk about) *Until about 20 years ago, the subject of the environment was hardly ever discussed.*
change the subject (=start talking about something different) *I could see John was embarrassed, so I changed the subject.*
thing /θɪŋ/ [n C] ESPECIALLY SPOKEN something that people talk about or think about: *The first thing we have to discuss is the price.* | *I had a lot of things to think about.*
topic /'tɒpɪk‖'tɑ:-/ [n C] a subject that people often discuss or write about, in books, newspapers, at school etc: *The rise of Islam is a popular topic these days.* | *Our teacher gave us a list of topics to choose from.*
topic of conversation (=something you talk about with other people) *Their main topic of conversation seems to be football.*
theme /θi:m/ [n C] an important idea that appears several times in a book, film etc, and slowly influences the way it develops: *One of the themes of*

the book is the relationship between humans and nature. | *The idea of duty is a favourite theme in the President's speeches.*
main/central theme (=the most important theme) *The play's central theme is greed and its corrupting effects.*
issue /'ɪʃu:, 'ɪsju:‖'ɪʃu:/ [n C] an important subject that people discuss and argue about: *Global warming is an important issue.*
+of *the issue of drugs in sports*
political/environmental/educational etc issues *a book dealing with environmental issues*
major/big/key issue (=a very important issue) *Unemployment and crime were the key issues in the election campaign.*
question /'kwestʃən/ [n C] a difficult subject or problem that has often been discussed but still needs to be solved
+of *The question of where to hold the conference has still not been settled.*
raise a question (=make people consider a problem) *These operations can save lives, but they raise difficult questions about animal rights.*
the point /ðə 'pɔɪnt/ [n singular] the main subject of a meeting, discussion, speech etc
stick to the point (=keep talking about the main subject, not about other less important things) *Just stick to the point, John – what we want to know is how much the plan will cost.*
come/get to the point (=start talking about the main subject, not about unimportant details) *Mr Bailey came straight to the point and asked me why I wanted the job.*
miss the point (=not understand the main point of what someone is saying)

2 a subject that you study at school or university

➡ see also **WB** **EDUCATION, TEST, LEARN, STUDY, TEACH**

subject /'sʌbdʒɪkt/ [n C] one of the things that you study at school or university, such as English, history, or mathematics: *English was my favourite subject at school.*

S

course (also **class** AMERICAN) /kɔːʳs, klɑːs‖klæs/ [n C] a series of lessons in one subject, often with an exam at the end: *Are you enjoying the course?* **language/computing/history etc course/class** *The college is offering three basic computer courses this year.* **+in/on** *a course in journalism* **take a course/class** (also **do a course** BRITISH) *She's taking a class in art history.*

> ⚠ Don't say 'a course/class of business studies'. Say **a course/class in business studies**.

> ⚠ Don't say 'make a course/class' or 'attend a course/class'. Say **take a course/class**.

major /ˈmeɪdʒəʳ/ [n C] AMERICAN the main subject that you study at university: *"What was your major?" "Political Science."*

SUCCEED

➡ opposite **FAIL**
➡ see also **WIN, IMPROVE**

1 to succeed in doing what you hoped to do or tried to do

succeed /səkˈsiːd/ [v I] to do something that you hoped to do, tried to do, or wanted to do: *She wanted to be the first woman to climb Mount Everest and she almost succeeded.*
succeed in doing sth *In one year we've succeeded in increasing profits by 40%.* | *If they succeed in getting across the border, the police will never catch them.*

> ⚠ Don't say 'he succeeded to do it'. Say **he succeeded in doing it**.

> **Formal or informal?**
> **Succeed** is fairly formal, and is not often used in conversation. Don't say 'I succeeded in my course/studies/exam'. It is better to say **I did well**.

do well /duː ˈwel/ ESPECIALLY SPOKEN to achieve good results at school, in your job, in a sport etc: *She's working for a record company in London, and I think she's doing very well.* | *Bill and Jim always did well in the swimming races.*

successfully /səkˈsesfəli/ [adv] if you do something **successfully**, you try to do it and you succeed: *Mr Malik has successfully completed the advanced course in Business Management.* | *The film successfully combines a good storyline with a serious political message.*

manage /ˈmænɪdʒ/ [v I/T] to succeed in doing something difficult after trying very hard, especially when you almost do not succeed: *She has to do all that work before Friday – do you think she'll manage?*
manage to do sth *He finally managed to find an apartment near his office.* | *I couldn't manage to get the bed down the stairs.*
manage it/that ESPECIALLY SPOKEN *You got him to change his mind? How did you manage that?* | *I said we'd be there by seven, but I doubt if we'll manage it.*

achieve /əˈtʃiːv/ [v T] to succeed in doing something important, especially something that other people will admire you for: *She's achieved a lot in the short time she's been with the company.* | *He hopes to achieve his dream of playing for the Red Sox.* | *When you get your MA, you really feel that you've achieved something.*

make progress /ˌmeɪk ˈprəʊgres‖-ˈprɑː-/ to gradually start to achieve something that you want to achieve, by working hard: *I'm not very good at Japanese yet, but I feel I am making progress.*
+with *At last I began to make some progress with my research.*

2 when something has the result that you want it to have

succeed /sək'siːd/ [v I] if something that you plan to do or try to do **succeeds**, you get the result that you hoped for: *If the terrorists' plan had succeeded, the bomb would have killed hundreds of people.* | *The new government's efforts to control inflation are unlikely to succeed.*

successful /sək'sesfəl/ [adj] if something that you plan to do or try to do is **successful** you get the result that you hoped for: *If the treatment is successful, she could be back at school next month.* | *successful peace negotiations*
highly successful (=very successful) *a highly successful election campaign*

work /wɜːʳk/ [v I] if a plan or method **works**, it produces the result that you want: *"I can't open the jar." "Try putting it in hot water. That sometimes works."* | *The recipe works just as well if you cook the fish in a microwave.*

go well /ˌgəʊ 'wel/ if something such as a meeting, party, or performance **goes well**, everything happens in the way you wanted and there are no problems: *Did the party go well?* | *If everything goes well, I'll have a new job by January.*

effective /ɪ'fektɪv/ [adj] a method or action that is **effective** is very good because it does exactly what it is intended to do: *the most effective way of cleaning glass* | *The ad was simple but very effective.*
effective in (doing) sth *Penicillin is effective in the treatment of many common diseases.* | *Extra police on the street have been very effective in reducing crime.*
highly effective (=very effective) *a method of teaching foreign languages that has proved highly effective*

> ⚠ Don't say 'this drug is effective to treat cancer'. Say **it is effective in treating cancer**.

3 a successful book/film/product etc

successful /sək'sesfəl/ [adj] a **successful** book, film, product etc is one that a lot of people buy or enjoy, and that makes a lot of money: *This is his most successful movie since 'Robocop'.*
highly successful (=very successful) *Harper Lee's highly successful novel sold over 11 million copies.*

do well /ˌduː 'wel/ if a product **does well**, it is successful because a lot of people buy it, especially over a long period of time: *The magazine has continued to do well despite new rivals.* | *Our perfumes and cosmetics are doing very well in Japan.*

be a success /biː ə sək'ses/ if a product, show etc **is a success**, it is very popular and it makes a lot of money: *The new sports car was launched six months ago, and looks like being a real success.*
be a great success *The musical was a great success on Broadway, though it didn't do so well in London.*

hit /hɪt/ [n C] a record, film, play etc that is very popular and successful: *It's more than 30 years since 'Love Me Do', the Beatles' first hit.* | *another big hit for Spielberg*
smash hit (=a very successful film, play etc) *the smash hit musical 'Chicago'*

4 a successful person or business

successful /sek'sesfəl/ [adj] a **successful** person achieves good results in their job, in a sport etc, and people admire them for this; a **successful** business makes a lot of money: *He has trained many of Britain's most successful athletes.* | *She retired in 1992, after a successful career in journalism.* | *a successful electronics company*

promising /'prɒmɪ̩sɪŋ‖'prɑː-/ [adj] a **promising** young player, student, manager etc is doing well and seems likely to be very successful in the future: *one of the most promising young players in the Italian league* | *Promising employees are quickly promoted.*

top /tɒp‖tɑːp/ [adj only before noun]
top player/model/designer etc one of the best and most successful players, designers etc: *All the world's top tennis players will be taking part in the tournament.* | *a conference attended by some of Europe's top scientists*

star /stɑːʳ/ [adj only before noun]
star player/performer/reporter etc one of the best players, performers etc: *Jerry Tonelli is the team's star player.*

5 something successful that you do

success /sək'ses/ [n C/U] when someone or something is successful: *Steffi says success hasn't changed her at all.* | *After her recent successes in Tokyo and New York, Bjork has returned to perform in England.*
+of *Auster was surprised at the success of his latest novel.*
success in doing sth *Did you have any success in persuading Adam to come?*
+in *Success in business depends on hard work, determination, and good ideas.*
plural **successes**

achievement /ə'tʃiːvmənt/ [n C] something important that you succeed in doing by your own efforts and that other people admire: *Winning three gold medals is a remarkable achievement.*

progress /'prəʊgres‖'prɑː-/ [n U] when you gradually get closer to the result you want to achieve: *We are very pleased with your son's progress at school.*

+in *Progress in technology has changed people's lives dramatically.*
+towards *progress towards equal status for men and women*

breakthrough /'breɪkθruː/ [n C] an important discovery or achievement, especially one which happens suddenly after people have been trying for a long time
+in *Scientists are claiming a major breakthrough in the treatment of AIDS.*
make a breakthrough *Police say they have made a breakthrough in their search for the killer of Diane Sutton.*

SUDDENLY

➡ opposite **SLOW 2**
➡ see also **FAST, SURPRISING/SURPRISED**

1 suddenly

suddenly /'sʌdnli/ [adv] if something happens **suddenly**, it happens quickly when you are not expecting it: *Robert died very suddenly last week.* | *Suddenly there was a loud bang and all the lights went out.* | *I suddenly realized that there was someone following me.*

all of a sudden /ˌɔːl əv ə 'sʌdn/ suddenly: *We waited and waited, then all of a sudden we saw a sail on the horizon.*

out of the blue /ˌaʊt əv ðə 'bluː/ INFORMAL if something happens **out of the blue**, you are not expecting it at all, and you are very surprised by it: *Do you remember Jane? Well, she phoned me yesterday, completely out of the blue.*

without warning /wɪð‚aʊt 'wɔːʳnɪŋ/ if something bad or dangerous happens **without warning**, it happens suddenly and there were no signs that it was going to happen: *The earthquake in California came without warning.* | *Without warning, the car swerved across the road and hit a tree.*

on the spur of the moment /ɒn ðə ˌspɜːr əv ðə ˈməʊmənt/ if you do something **on the spur of the moment**, you suddenly decide to do something that you had not planned to do: *I bought the car on the spur of the moment.* | *On the spur of the moment, Ian leaned across and kissed her.*

spur-of-the-moment [*adj* only before noun] *a spur-of-the-moment decision*

2 something that happens suddenly

sudden /ˈsʌdn/ [*adj*] happening suddenly: *a sudden sharp pain in my stomach* | *Rebecca's decision to leave was very sudden.* | *There was a sudden increase in the price of oil.*

dramatic /drəˈmætɪk/ [*adj*]
dramatic change/improvement/ increase/fall/rise etc a sudden very noticeable change, which makes things either much better or much worse: *a dramatic change in temperature* | *There has been a dramatic increase in homelessness over the last few years.*
dramatically [*adv*] *The sales figures improved dramatically last year.*

Formal or informal?

Dramatic is not used in informal conversation.

---

abrupt /əˈbrʌpt/ [*adj*] ESPECIALLY WRITTEN sudden, unexpected, and often unwanted
abrupt end/departure/change etc *The bus came to an abrupt stop.* | *His departure was abrupt and completely unexpected.*
abruptly [*adv*] *She turned abruptly and went back inside.*

When you see **WB** , go to the **WORD BANKS** section.

SUFFER

when something very painful or unpleasant happens to you

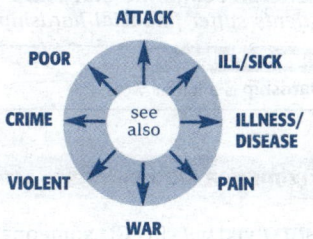

ATTACK
POOR   ILL/SICK
CRIME   see   ILLNESS/
        also   DISEASE
VIOLENT   PAIN
WAR

1 to suffer

suffer /ˈsʌfəʳ/ [*v* I/T] to experience physical or emotional pain when something bad happens to you: *Children always suffer when their parents get divorced.* | *Anne still suffers a lot of pain in her leg.*
+from *My sister has suffered from nightmares since the accident.*

endure /ɪnˈdjʊəʳ‖ɪnˈdʊər/ [*v* T] ESPECIALLY WRITTEN to experience pain or have difficult and unpleasant experiences over a long period – use this especially about people who are brave and patient: *She has endured ten years of painful back operations.* | *They were lost in the mountains for ten days, enduring hunger, thirst, and intense cold.*

go through sth /ˈgəʊ θruː (sth)/ [*phrasal verb* T] to experience a lot of problems in your life over a long period of time: *Pete had lost his job, and the family was going through a very difficult time.*

2 something painful or unpleasant that you suffer

suffering /ˈsʌfərɪŋ/ [*n* U] very unpleasant, painful, or upsetting conditions – use this especially about a situation that affects a lot of people: *The earthquake has caused massive damage and a great deal of human suffering.* | *Reporters described the suffering they had seen in Somalia.*

hardship /ˈhɑːʳdʃɪp/ [*n* C/U] when your life is difficult and uncomfortable, especially because you are very poor: *the hardships of life for the early settlers in the US*

great hardship (=serious difficulties) *Rising food prices caused great hardship for most of the population.*

financial/economic hardship *Many students suffer financial hardship.*

> **Formal or informal?**
> **Hardship** is a formal word.

3 someone who suffers

victim /'vɪktᵻm/ [n C] someone who suffers because of an illness, accident, crime etc: *Our aim is to help victims of crime.* | *Heart attack victims stand a better chance if they are treated immediately.*

casualty /'kæʒuəlti/ [n C] someone who suffers as a result of an event or situation over which they have no control – used especially in news reports

+of *Another casualty of the scandal was the Finance Minister, who was forced to resign last night.*

SUGGEST

➡ see also **EC** SUGGESTIONS, WARN

> ⚠ Compare **suggest** and **advise**. If you **suggest** something to someone, you mention something they could or should do, or something you could do together: *I suggested a walk in the park.* If you **advise** someone to do something, you tell them quite strongly that you think they should do it: *I advised her to put locks on all the windows.*

> ⚠ After **suggest that**, **propose that**, and **recommend that**, you can either use **should** or you can leave out **should**: *I suggested that we should meet for a drink.* | *I suggested that we meet for a drink.* In American English, **should** is usually left out.

1 to suggest something

suggest /sə'dʒest‖seg'dʒest/ [v T] to tell someone your ideas about what they could or should do, where they could

or should go etc, or about what you and that person should do together: *"Why don't you come with us?" Alan suggested.* | *It was a sunny afternoon, and Jim suggested a trip to the beach.*

+(that) *My Dad suggested that I should apply for the job.* | *I suggest we take a break and finish this later.*

suggest doing sth *It was raining heavily, and she suggested calling a taxi.*

> ⚠ Don't say 'he suggested me to go'. Say **he suggested that I go** or **he suggested that I should go**.

make a suggestion /ˌmeɪk ə sə'dʒestʃən‖-səg-/ to suggest something that you think will help someone or will solve a problem: *Can I just make a suggestion? I think there's an easier way to do this.*

recommend /ˌrekə'mend/ [v T] to suggest something to someone because you know that it is good and you are sure that they will like it: *Can you recommend a comfortable hotel near here?*

recommend sth to sb *Oh, that book? Karen recommended it to me.*

> ⚠ Don't say 'I recommend to read this book'. Say **I recommend this book**.

2 to make a formal suggestion in a meeting, report etc

propose /prə'pəuz/ [v T] to formally suggest that something should be done, especially at a meeting: *The Russians proposed a treaty banning all nuclear tests.*

+that *I propose that we continue the meeting tomorrow.*

> ⚠ In this meaning, don't say 'I propose to ban cars from the city centre'. Say **I propose that we ban cars from the city centre** or **I propose that cars be banned from the city centre**.

recommend /ˌrekə'mend/ [v T] to officially suggest that something should be done, after you have considered the situation carefully:

The report recommends a number of changes in the existing law.
+that *The committee recommended that the money should be given to charity.* | *It is recommended that you back up all your important files at least once a week.*

> ⚠ Don't say 'I recommend to increase the price'. Say **I recommend that we increase the price** or **I recommend that the price be increased**.

put forward /ˌpʊt ˈfɔːˈwəˈd/ [*phrasal verb* T] to suggest new plans or ideas for people to discuss and make decisions about
put forward sth *The UN has put forward a peace plan.* | *ideas put forward by environmental advisers*

nominate /ˈnɒmᵻneɪt‖ˈnɑː-/ [*v* T] to formally suggest someone for an important job or prize, especially when people will vote to make a decision
nominate sb for sth *Jane Campion was one of the people nominated for the 'Best Director' award.*
nominate sb as sth *Gorbachev unexpectedly nominated Yanayev as Vice-President.*
nomination /ˌnɒmᵻˈneɪʃən‖ˌnɑː-/ [*n* C/U] when someone is suggested for an important job or prize: *His nomination to the Supreme Court was blocked by political opponents.*

3 something that someone suggests

suggestion /səˈdʒestʃən‖səg-/ [*n* C] something that someone suggests: *That's an excellent suggestion.*
make a suggestion *She made some useful suggestions about places we could visit.*
+that *Barry ignored my suggestion that he should try phoning her again.*
have a suggestion (=want to make a suggestion) *Does anyone have any other suggestions?*

proposal /prəˈpəʊzəl/ [*n* C] a formal or official suggestion that something should be done: *They will consider our proposal at their next meeting.*
proposal to do sth *Their proposal to build a new airport has finally been rejected.*

+for *American proposals for a Middle East peace settlement*

4 what you say to suggest something

→ see also **SUGGESTIONS**

○ **I suggest** /aɪ səˈdʒest‖-səg-/ SPOKEN say this especially to suggest something that you think is a sensible or helpful thing to do
I suggest (that) sb do sth *I suggest we take a half-hour break and start again at 3.* | *If you don't know the answer, I suggest you try the encyclopedia.*

> **Formal or informal?**
> **I suggest** is more formal than all the other expressions here.

○ **let's** /lets/ **let's go/do/have/meet etc** SPOKEN say this to suggest to someone what you and they should do together: *Let's have a meal after the concert.*
let's not *Let's not argue – it's my birthday!*

○ **why don't you?/why not?** /ˈwaɪ dəʊnt juː, ˈwaɪ nɒt/ SPOKEN say this to suggest something to someone, especially to help them decide what to do: *Why not get Andreas a book for his birthday?* | *Why don't you just phone and tell them you can't come?*

○ **shall we?/shall I?** /ˈʃæl wiː, ˈʃæl aɪ/ SPOKEN, ESPECIALLY BRITISH say this to suggest what you might do, and to ask someone if they agree: *Shall I get the theatre tickets?* | *Shall we go shopping this afternoon, then?*

○ **do you want to?** /duː juː ˈwɒnt tuː‖ -ˈwɑːnt-/ SPOKEN say this to suggest something that you and someone else could do together, and to ask the other person if they agree: *Do you want to go out for a meal?*

○ **how about?/what about?** /ˈhaʊ əbaʊt, ˈwɒt əbaʊt/ SPOKEN say this to suggest something which you think is a good idea: *We need a break – how about a weekend in London?* | *Well, if the car's too small, what about renting a bigger one?*

○ **could always** SPOKEN /kʊd ˈɔːlwᵻz/ say this to suggest something that may solve a problem: *You could* *always stay with me if you miss the train.* | *I suppose I could always get Rosie some perfume for Christmas.*

SUITABLE/ UNSUITABLE

➡ see also **BEST, PERFECT, CONVENIENT/NOT CONVENIENT**

1 suitable

suitable /ˈsuːtəbəl, ˈsjuː-‖ˈsuː-/ [*adj*] something or someone that is **suitable** is the right kind of thing or person for a purpose, job, or situation: *I still haven't found a suitable job.* | *You must wear something suitable – preferably black.*
+for *The house would be suitable for a large family.* | *the type of leather that is suitable for this purpose*
suitably [*adv*] *suitably dressed for a wedding*

⚠️ Don't say 'suitable to someone/ something' or 'suitable to do something'. Say **suitable for someone/something**.

right /raɪt/ [*adj*] the **right** thing or person is exactly suitable: *I've found some curtains that are just the right colour.* | *I don't know the right word to describe it.*
+for *It's a good school, but it wasn't really right for Melissa.* | *We all agree that Carey is the right person for the job.*
just right (=completely suitable) *I moved into a small apartment close to the college – it was just right.*

proper /ˈprɒpəʳ‖ˈprɑː-/ [*adj* only before noun]
the proper equipment/clothes etc
ESPECIALLY BRITISH the equipment, clothes etc that are generally considered to be right for a particular purpose: *You can't climb a mountain without the proper equipment.* | *I must have the proper tools for the job.*
properly [*adv*] *The machine operators had not been properly trained.*

appropriate /əˈprəʊpri-ɪt/ [*adj*] FORMAL suitable for a situation or purpose – use this especially about something that has been carefully chosen for a particular situation: *Considering the warnings he's had, I think the punishment was appropriate.* | *You will be given your orders at the appropriate time.*
+for *Each member is given a special exercise routine that is appropriate for his or her needs.*
appropriately [*adv*] *a delightful place that was appropriately named Mount Pleasant*

 good /ɡʊd/ [*adj* only before noun] ESPECIALLY SPOKEN very suitable for a purpose or job – use this especially when there are several suitable people or things to choose from: *Bates would be a good person to have on the team.*
+for *The big jars are good for storing rice or pasta.*
good – better – best

ideal /aɪˈdɪəl/ [*adj*] the **ideal** thing or person is the most suitable one you can possibly choose, when there are many to choose from: *If you're setting up your own company, our Business Starter Loan would be ideal.* | *Disneyworld is an ideal place to take young children.*
+for *With its tough suspension and 4-wheel drive, it's ideal for driving in the desert.*

suit /suːt, sjuːt‖suːt/ [*v* T not in passive] something that **suits** a person, purpose, or situation is suitable for them: *Make sure you choose a computer that suits your needs.* | *a job that would suit a young science graduate* | *They found us a house close to the campus, which suited us very well.*

⚠️ Don't say 'it suits to me' or 'it suits with me'. Say **it suits me**.

2 not suitable

unsuitable/not suitable /ʌnˈsuːtəbəl, nɒt ˈsuːtəbəl, -ˈsjuː-‖-ˈsuː-/ [*adj*] *We never planted vines there because the climate was not suitable.*

+for *violent movies that are totally unsuitable for children* | *The road is not suitable for heavy vehicles.*

wrong /rɒŋ‖rɔːŋ/ [*adj*] not the right one for a particular job or purpose: *You're using the wrong spoon – this is the soup spoon.* | *This is a very important job, so we don't want to choose the wrong person.* | *I think you picked the wrong time to call her.*

inappropriate/not appropriate /ˌɪnəˈprəʊpriˈt, nɒt əˈprəʊpriˈt/ [*adj*] FORMAL not suitable for a situation or purpose – use this especially about something that has been done or chosen without enough care or thought: *I thought his remarks were quite inappropriate on such a serious occasion.* | *This is not an appropriate use of taxpayers' money.*
+for *They didn't show the movie because it was considered inappropriate for young children.*

out of place /ˌaʊt əv ˈpleɪs/ if something or someone looks or feels **out of place**, they do not seem suitable for the place or situation that they are in, especially because they look very different: *I felt completely out of place among all those rich fashionable people.* | *a large concrete building that looked out of place in such a pretty mountain village*

not cut out for sth /nɒt kʌt ˈaʊt fɔːʳ (sth)/ INFORMAL if you are **not cut out for** a type of work or way of life, you do not have the right qualities to enjoy it or to be successful in it: *Obviously, Paul was not cut out for army life.* | *I've decided I'm not cut out for teaching.*

SUPPORT

➡ look here for ...
  • agree with someone or something
  • help someone
  • stop something from falling down
➡ see also **DEFEND**

1 to support an idea, person, or political party

➡ opposite **AGAINST**
➡ see also **PROTEST, AGREE, DISAGREE**

support /səˈpɔːʳt/ [*v T*] to say that you agree with an idea, plan, political party etc, and want it to succeed: *I've always supported the Democrats.* | *75% of voters support the idea of joining the EU.*
strongly support *Plans for a new school were strongly supported by local residents.*

⚠ Don't say 'I am supporting them'. Say **I support them**.

be in favour of sth BRITISH **be in favor of sth** AMERICAN /biː ɪn ˈfeɪvər ɒv (sth)/ to support a plan or suggestion because you think it is a good idea: *Most UN delegates are in favor of the peace plan.*
be in favour of doing sth *Some teachers were in favour of retaining the existing system.*
 be all in favour of sth ESPECIALLY SPOKEN (=completely agree with it) *I'm all in favour of people having smaller cars.*

⚠ Don't say 'I'm in favour with it' or 'I'm in favour to do it'. Say **I'm in favour of it**.

pro- /prəʊ/ [*prefix*] **pro-democracy/ pro-government/ pro-independence etc** supporting democracy, the government etc: *The pro-independence group has been attacked and suppressed.* | *pro-western forces* | *The 'pro-choice' group believes in the right to abortion.*

⚠ **Pro-** is used especially in formal writing and news reports.

 be on sb's side /biː ɒn (sb's) ˈsaɪd/ ESPECIALLY SPOKEN to support one person or group against another in an argument, war etc: *Why did you keep agreeing with my parents? I thought you were on my side.* | *With most of the newspapers on their side, they have a good chance of winning.*

2 someone who supports a person, political party, idea etc

supporter /səˈpɔːʳtəʳ/ [*n C*] someone who supports a person, political

party, or idea: *a Labour Party supporter*
+of *Supporters of women's rights are protesting against the court's decision.*

follower /ˈfɒləʊəʳ‖ˈfɑː-/ [n C] someone who supports the ideas of a political or religious leader: *Marx and his followers were convinced that capitalism would not survive.*
+of *the followers of Mahatma Gandhi*

sympathizer (also **sympathiser** BRITISH) /ˈsɪmpəθaɪzəʳ/ [n C] someone who supports the ideas of a political organization but does not belong to it, especially an organization that is illegal: *His opponents accused him of being a Nazi sympathiser.* | *The group has many sympathisers in the US.*

following /ˈfɒləʊɪŋ‖ˈfɑː-/ [n singular] all the people who support a person or organization: *The civil rights movement attracted a large following in the northern cities.*

3 to support someone with money or with help

support /səˈpɔːʳt/ [v T] to give help, encouragement, money etc to someone because you want them to succeed: *The rebels were supported by the former South African government, which provided arms and money.* | *She managed to raise money from friends to support the scheme.*

in support of /ɪn səˈpɔːʳt ɒv/ if you do something **in support of** someone or something, you do it to show that you support them: *The miners were striking in support of the nurses.* | *a big demonstration in support of democratic reforms*

back /bæk/ [v T] to support a person or plan by providing money or practical help – used especially in newspapers to talk about governments or other powerful groups that support something: *Several major insurance companies have agreed to back the healthcare reforms.* | *The plans for a new shopping mall are backed by the city council.*

4 the money or help that you give when you support someone

support /səˈpɔːʳt/ [n U] the help and encouragement that you give to someone when you want them to succeed: *I couldn't have finished my degree without the support of my family.*
+for *the growing support for Greenpeace in Australia and New Zealand*
financial support (=money given to support something) *political parties that receive financial support from foreign businessmen*

backing /ˈbækɪŋ/ [n U] money or practical help given to support a person or plan, especially by a government or other powerful group: *Does this policy have government backing?*
+of *a magazine that originally started with the backing of the TV companies*

funding /ˈfʌndɪŋ/ [n U] money that a government provides to pay for education, theatre, music etc, not for business activities
+of *The President hasn't yet approved the funding of the program.*
+for *Cuts in funding for the arts have lead to the closure of several theatres.*

5 to support an object so that it does not fall down

support/hold up /səˈpɔːʳt, ˌhəʊld ˈʌp/ [v T] to hold something or someone up and stop them from falling down
support sth *The ceiling was supported by huge stone columns.*
hold sth up *The only thing holding it up is one small section of scaffolding.*
hold up sth *The poles hold up the outer part of the tent.*

> **Formal or informal?**
> **Hold up** is more informal than **support**.

prop up /ˌprɒp ˈʌp‖ˌprɑːp-/ [phrasal verb T] to stop something from falling by putting something else against it or under it
prop up sth *The builders have propped up the walls with steel beams.*
prop sth up *I sat down and propped my feet up on the edge of the desk.*

SURE/NOT SURE

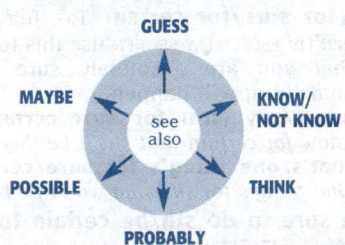

GUESS

MAYBE   KNOW/
                         NOT KNOW
            see
            also

POSSIBLE   THINK

PROBABLY

1 when you feel sure about something

sure /ʃʊəʳ/ [adj not before noun] if you are sure about something, you feel that it is almost certainly true or correct
+(that) *You've worked so hard, I'm sure you'll do well in your exams.* | *Are you quite sure that he understood your instructions?*
+about/of *I think children are influenced by these films, but it's impossible to be sure about this.*
feel sure *I'm surprised she isn't here – I felt sure she would come.*

> ⚠ Don't say 'it is sure'. Say **I'm sure**: *I'm sure that the food will be nice.*

certain /'sɜːʳtn/ [adj not before noun] completely sure that something is true
+(that) *Are you absolutely certain you didn't leave your keys at home?*
+about/of *She won't let you borrow the car – I'm certain of that.*

> ⚠ Don't say 'very certain'. Say **quite certain** or **absolutely certain**: *We're quite certain that Hayes is guilty.*

convinced /kən'vɪnst/ [adj not before noun] sure that something is true, even if you have no information to support this belief
+(that) *We've had no news of him, but we're convinced he's still alive.* | *She became convinced that her boyfriend was seeing someone else.*
+of *Brown's wife was convinced of his innocence.*

> ⚠ Don't say 'very convinced'. Say **totally/absolutely convinced**: *She seems absolutely convinced that she's going to fail.*

positive /'pɒzɪtɪv‖'pɑː-/ [adj not before noun] ESPECIALLY SPOKEN completely sure that something is true – use this especially when other people are saying it might not be true: *"Are you sure you locked the door?" "Yes, I'm positive."*
+(that) *She said she was positive the exam was next Tuesday.*

confident /'kɒnfɪdənt‖'kɑːn-/ [adj not before noun] sure that something good will happen, or that you will be able to achieve what you want: *Both leaders said they were confident about the election.*
+(that) *Doctors are confident that he'll make a full recovery.*

I bet /aɪ 'bet/ SPOKEN INFORMAL say this when you feel sure that something is true
+(that) *I bet you're tired after such a long journey.* | *I bet she hasn't told her parents about this.*

must /mʌst/ [modal verb] ESPECIALLY SPOKEN if you say that something **must** be true or **must** have happened, you think it is very likely to be true or very likely to have happened, because of the information you have: *They must be having a party next door, judging by all the cars parked outside.*
must have *Kim didn't answer when I called – she must have gone to bed.* | *The lights aren't working – there must have been a power cut.*

> ⚠ The opposite of **must** in this meaning is **can't**. Use **can't** to say you are sure that something is not true or has not happened: *She can't have gone to bed yet – it's only 8 o'clock* (=I am sure that she has not gone to bed).

2 when something is definitely true and there are no doubts at all

certainly/definitely /'sɜːʳtnli, 'defɪnɪtli, 'defənɪtli/ [adv] use this to emphasize that something is definitely true, especially when other people think

S

that it might not be: *I'm sorry if I upset you. I certainly didn't mean to.* | *We don't know exactly when the house was built, but it's certainly over 100 years old.* | *I definitely posted the cheque last week, so it should have arrived by now.*

certainly not/definitely not *"Did you see a white van outside the house?" "No, definitely not."*

◯ **surely** /'ʃʊə^rli/ [*adv*] ESPECIALLY SPOKEN use this to emphasize that you think something must be true, and you are asking someone else to agree with you: *Surely, he must have realized that the money was stolen.* | *Surely your car is worth more than £1000, isn't it?*

there is no doubt /ðeər ɪz nəʊ 'daʊt/ use this to say that, in your opinion, something is definitely true
+(that) *There is no doubt that smoking contributed to Margaret's heart attack.*
◯ **there's no doubt about it/that** ESPECIALLY SPOKEN *Paul's under a lot of stress. There's no doubt about that.*

3 when something will definitely happen

certainly/definitely /'sɜː^rtnli, 'defɪnᵻtli, 'defənᵻtli/ [*adv*] use this to say that you are completely sure that something will happen or that someone will do something: *It will certainly be expensive.* | *We'll definitely be back by 7 o'clock.* | *Beckham is injured and will definitely miss the game on Saturday.*

certain /'sɜː^rtn/ [*adj* not usually before noun] if something is **certain**, you believe it will definitely happen: *Computer prices will continue to fall – that's certain.*
it is certain (that) *It's now almost certain that the President will resign.*
certain death/failure/disaster etc ESPECIALLY WRITTEN (=when something very bad is definitely going to happen) *He was alone on the mountain, his leg broken, facing almost certain death.*

definite /'defɪnᵻt, 'defənᵻt/ [*adj*] something that is **definite** has been agreed or decided, and it is certain that it will happen: *I think I have a good chance of getting the job, but it's not definite yet.*

 Definite is used especially in questions or negative sentences.

◯ **for sure/for certain** /fə^r 'ʃʊə^r, fə^r 'sɜː^rtn/ ESPECIALLY SPOKEN use this to say that you are absolutely sure that something will happen
know/say (sth) for sure/certain *I know for certain that she'll be there.*
that's/one thing's for sure/certain *One thing's for sure, he won't be back.*

be sure to do sth/be certain to do sth /biː 'ʃʊə^r tə duː (sth), biː 'sɜː^rtn tə duː (sth)/ use this to say that you strongly believe that something will happen, because of what you know about the situation: *Drivers heading for the coast are certain to face long delays this weekend.* | *Don't talk to her about her mom. It's sure to upset her.*

Formal or informal?
Be certain to do sth is more formal than **be sure to do sth**.

be bound to do sth /biː 'baʊnd tə duː (sth)/ if you say something **is bound to** happen, you think it certainly will happen, because that is what normally happens: *Chris is bound to arrive late – he always does.* | *His new record isn't very good, but it's bound to be a hit.*

be sure of doing sth /biː 'ʃʊər əv 'duːɪŋ (sth)/ if you **are sure of doing** something, you will definitely get what you want or achieve what you want: *If they win tonight's game, they are sure of winning the championship.* | *To be sure of arriving on time, I took an earlier train.*

inevitable /ɪn'evᵻtəbəl/ [*adj*] something unpleasant that is **inevitable** will certainly happen and is impossible to prevent: *War now seems inevitable.*
inevitable result/consequence *Bread prices were doubled, with the inevitable result – food riots.*
it is inevitable (that) *It is inevitable that some people won't like the new arrangements.*
the inevitable (=a situation that is certain to happen) *One day the inevitable happened and I got a speeding ticket.*
inevitably [*adv*] *Inevitably, some*

people will lose their jobs when the two companies merge.

4 | not sure about something

not sure /nɒt ˈʃʊəʳ/ *"What time does the film start?" "I think it's 8.30, but I'm not sure."*
not sure how/whether/when etc *I'm not sure where she lives.*
+about/of *If you're not sure about the meaning of a word, look it up in a dictionary. | I'm not sure of the name of the street.*
⊂ **can't be sure** SPOKEN (when you think something is true, but you are not completely sure) *I can't be sure, but I think I saw Maggie coming out of the hospital this morning.*

not know /nɒt ˈnəʊ/ to not be at all sure what you should decide, whether something is true etc: *"How old is she?" "Oh, I don't know – fifty, fifty-five?"*
not know if/whether/how etc *He didn't know whether he should accept their offer or not. | I don't know if I really agree with that.*
⊂ **not know for sure** ESPECIALLY SPOKEN *It could be this week but it might be much later. We don't know for sure.*

doubt /daʊt/ [n C/U] a feeling of not being sure whether something is true or right
+about/as to *There are still some doubts about her suitability for the job.*
have (your) doubts (=not be sure that something is really the right thing to do) *My parents thought I should go to business school, but I had my doubts.*

5 | something that you cannot be sure about

uncertain /ʌnˈsɜːʳtn/ [adj] if a situation is **uncertain**, you cannot be sure what will happen, because nothing is definite: *Our holiday plans are still uncertain. | The company faces an uncertain future.*
it is uncertain whether *It is still uncertain whether the conference will actually take place.*

not clear /nɒt ˈklɪəʳ/ if something is **not clear**, people do not know enough or understand enough to be sure about

it: *The causes of the dispute are not entirely clear.*
it is not clear how/why/whether etc *It isn't clear how the fire started.*

be doubtful/be in doubt /biː ˈdaʊtfəl, bi ɪn ˈdaʊt/ if the success or future of something **is doubtful** or **is in doubt**, you cannot be sure what will happen, but you think it is likely to be something bad: *With more and more cuts in government spending, the school's future now looks doubtful. | After yet another injury, his football career is in doubt.*

6 | to do something in order to be sure that something else will happen

make sure /ˌmeɪk ˈʃʊəʳ/ to do something in order to be sure that something else will happen: *I think Harry knows the way, but I'll go with him just to make sure.*
+(that) *Make sure that you lock your car.*

ensure BRITISH **insure** AMERICAN /ɪnˈʃʊəʳ/ [v T] to do something in order to be sure that something else will happen
+(that) *It is the company's responsibility to ensure that everyone knows the safety rules.*

> **Formal or informal?**
>
> **Ensure** and **insure** are more formal than **make sure**.

⊂ **see that/see to it that** /ˈsiː ðət, ˈsiː tʊ ɪt ðət/ ESPECIALLY SPOKEN if you **see that** or **see to it that** something happens, you make sure that it happens, often by getting someone else to do this for you: *Don't worry. I'll see that he gets the message. | We see to it that all our guests receive a very high standard of service.*

When you see **EC**, go to the
ESSENTIAL COMMUNICATION section.

SURPRISING/ SURPRISED

➡ see also **SUDDENLY, EXPECT 6**

1 feeling surprised

surprised /səˈpraɪzd/ [adj] if you are **surprised** by something that happens, you do not expect it, so it seems strange or unusual: *I was really surprised when I passed my driving test first time.* | *Carrie looked surprised. "I didn't expect to see you here!"*
surprised to see/hear/learn etc *We were surprised to see Drew's picture in the newspaper.*
+(that) *I'm really surprised that he remembered my birthday.*
+at/by *He was surprised at how late it was.* | *Julia seemed a little surprised by my question.*

> ⚠ Don't say 'surprised for something'. Say **surprised at something** or **surprised by something**.

amazed/astonished /əˈmeɪzd, əˈstɒnɪʃtǁəˈstɑː-/ [adj] extremely surprised by something that happens, because it seems so unlikely: *Liz was amazed when she found out how much the meal had cost.*
+that *I'm amazed that the bank keeps lending him money.*
+at *Everyone was astonished at how calm and relaxed she was before her big speech.*
amazed to see/learn/find out etc *We were amazed to see John looking so well, so soon after his operation.*
astonished to see/hear/discover/ find etc *Sarah was astonished to see Neil and Beth kissing.*

startled /ˈstɑːʳtld/ [adj] ESPECIALLY WRITTEN surprised and a little frightened or worried because of something that has suddenly happened or something that someone said: *"Have we met somewhere before?" The man looked startled for a moment.*
+by *They were startled by a sudden flash in the sky.*

to my/her/their surprise /tuː (my etc) səʳˈpraɪz/ use this when you are telling a story or describing past events, to say that someone was surprised by something: *He asked her to go out with him and, to his surprise, she agreed.*

> ⚠ Don't use **to my/her/their surprise** at the end of a sentence.

 can't believe /ˌkɑːnt bɪˈliːvǁˌkænt-/ ESPECIALLY SPOKEN if you **can't believe** something, you are very surprised by it because it does not seem possible **can't believe it** *I can't believe it! Jane and Richard are getting married!*
+(that) *She was a brilliant pianist – we couldn't believe that she was only fifteen.*

taken aback /ˌteɪkən əˈbæk/ so surprised or shocked by what someone has done or said to you that for a moment you do not know what to say
be/look/seem taken aback *When I asked her to marry me, she looked rather taken aback.*
+by *Bill was taken aback by her rude and aggressive behaviour.*

speechless /ˈspiːtʃləs/ [adj] so surprised, by something very good or very bad, that you do not know what to say: *When I told her I was pregnant, she was totally speechless.*

2 surprised and upset by something very bad that has happened

shocked /ʃɒktǁʃɑːkt/ [adj] *When they heard that Janet was in hospital they were really shocked.*
+by *The whole town was shocked by the news.*
shocked to hear/learn/find *We were shocked to hear of Brian's death – he was so young.*

horrified /ˈhɒrɪfaɪdǁˈhɔː-, ˈhɑː-/ [adj] extremely shocked by something very unpleasant or frightening that has happened: *Horrified passengers saw the man fall under the train.*
+by *Sam's parents were horrified by his injuries.*
horrified to see/hear/find *They looked out of the window, and were horrified to see two men attacking each other with knives.*

stunned /stʌnd/ [adj] so shocked that you are unable to speak or do anything: *When I heard about the accident I was stunned.*
+by *Staff were stunned by the news that 200 people were to lose their jobs.*

3 to make someone surprised

surprise /səˈpraɪz/ [v T] if something **surprises** you, it makes you feel surprised: *Diana's reaction surprised him – he hadn't realized that she was so upset.* | *The exam was actually quite easy, which surprised me.*
it surprises sb that *It surprised me that he could still walk.*

amaze /əˈmeɪz/ [v T] to make someone feel extremely surprised: *Dave amazed his friends by leaving a well-paid job to travel around the world.*
it amazes sb that *It amazes me that no-one thought of the idea sooner.*

come as a surprise /ˌkʌm əz ə səˈpraɪz/ if something **comes as a surprise**, it surprises you because you were not expecting it at all
+to *Richard's marriage came as a surprise to everyone.*
come as a complete surprise *I didn't think I'd get the job, so it came as a complete surprise when they offered it to me.*

take sb by surprise /ˌteɪk (sb) baɪ səˈpraɪz/ if something **takes you by surprise**, it happens suddenly at a time when you are not expecting it: *The President's resignation took everyone by surprise.*

shock /ʃɒk‖ʃɑːk/ [v T] if something very bad or unpleasant **shocks** you, it makes you feel very surprised and upset: *What really shocked me was that no-one seemed to care about all the beggars.*
it shocks sb to see/realize/hear etc *It shocked us to see how ill she looked.*

come as a shock /ˌkʌm əz ə ˈʃɒk‖-ˈʃɑːk/ if something unpleasant **comes as a shock**, it makes you feel surprised and upset because you were not expecting it to happen: *We knew he had been ill, but Robert's death still came as a shock.*
come as a complete/terrible shock (to sb) *It came as a terrible shock to Richard when his wife told him she was seeing another man.*

make sb jump /ˌmeɪk (sb) ˈdʒʌmp/ ESPECIALLY SPOKEN to make someone feel surprised and nervous by making a sudden noise or movement, especially when they did not know you were there: *I'm sorry, I didn't mean to make you jump.*

4 when something makes you surprised

surprising /səˈpraɪzɪŋ/ [adj] something that is **surprising** makes you feel surprised: *A surprising number of 16-year-olds leave school without being able to read and write.* | *a surprising choice*
it is surprising (that) *It is surprising that so few people came to the party.*
it is surprising how/what *It was surprising how quickly we got used to the new house.*

surprisingly [adv] *The restaurant was surprisingly cheap.* | *Surprisingly, very few people complained about the delay.*

amazing /əˈmeɪzɪŋ/ [adj] very surprising – use this especially about something very good or impressive: *an amazing achievement* | *Hong Kong is an amazing city, with all those tall modern buildings.*
it is amazing how/what *It's amazing how fast these Grand Prix cars can go.*
it is amazing that *It's amazing that the inscriptions are still clear enough to read after 2000 years.*

amazingly [adv] *We were amazingly lucky to find such a nice hotel.* | *Five cars crashed into each other, but amazingly no-one was hurt.*

unexpected /ˌʌnɪkˈspektəd◂/ [adj] something **unexpected** is surprising, because you did not think that it would happen: *the unexpected success of her first novel* | *His decision to leave was completely unexpected.*

unexpectedly [adv] *Phil arrived unexpectedly while we were having lunch.*

startling /ˈstɑːˈtlɪŋ/ [adj] ESPECIALLY WRITTEN a **startling** fact is one that you would never have expected to be true: *There had been a startling* increase in the numbers of homeless people. | startling new discoveries about the way the universe began

unbelievable/incredible

/ˌʌnbɪˈliːvəbəl, ɪnˈkredɪbəl/ [adj] extremely surprising and difficult to believe: *He's so rude. It's unbelievable! | Over the next two weeks, we saw an incredible change in her character.*

it is unbelievable/incredible that *They were driving much too fast. It's incredible that no-one was hurt.*

unbelievably/incredibly [adv] *Throughout the crisis, Bill remained incredibly calm. | It was a fantastic hotel, and unbelievably cheap.*

staggering /ˈstægərɪŋ/ [adj] a **staggering** number or amount is very surprising because it is so large: *There has been a staggering rise in the number of attacks and murders in our cities. | We spend a staggering £2.4 billion a year on food for our pets.*

> **Staggering** is used especially in newspapers and on television.

5 something surprising that happens

surprise /səˈpraɪz/ [n C] something that you did not expect, especially something nice

it is a surprise *It was a real surprise when Tony walked in. We thought he was still in America. | We've got Katie a bike for her birthday, but don't tell her – it's a surprise.*

a complete surprise (=one that you did not expect at all) *The news came as a complete surprise.*

Q **what a surprise!** SPOKEN *Flowers? For me? What a lovely surprise!*

shock /ʃɒkǁʃɑːk/ [n C] something very bad or unpleasant that happens to you and that you did not expect: *"The bill came to almost £500." "That must have been a shock."*

get a shock *She got a shock when she opened the letter and saw who it was from.*

give sb a shock *It gave me a shock to realize that I had nearly been killed.*

6 when something does not make you surprised

Q **not surprising/hardly surprising** /ˌnɒt səˈpraɪzɪŋ, ˌhɑːˈdli səˈpraɪzɪŋ/ ESPECIALLY SPOKEN if something is **not surprising** or **hardly surprising**, you are not surprised by it because the situation makes it very likely to happen: *Now she's frightened to go out at night, which is hardly surprising after what happened to her.*

it is not surprising/hardly surprising (that) *It's not surprising you're tired – you've been out every night this week.*

not surprisingly [adv] *Not surprisingly, she's very annoyed* (=it is not surprising that she is annoyed) .

Q **I'm not surprised** /aɪm ˌnɒt səˈpraɪzd/ SPOKEN say this when you can clearly see why something has happened: *"I'm starving." "I'm not surprised. You haven't eaten all day."*

+(that) *I'm not surprised she's fed up with him.*

Q **no wonder** /nəʊ ˈwʌndəʳ/ SPOKEN say this when you realize the reason why something happened, so that it is not surprising any more: *No wonder my camera wasn't working – there's no battery in it!*

come as no surprise /ˌkʌm əz nəʊ səˈpraɪz/ if something **comes as no surprise**, you are not surprised when it happens, because you expected it to happen

it comes as no surprise when *It came as no surprise when President Santos announced his resignation.*

When you see **WB**, go to the **WORD BANKS** section.

SWITCH ON OR OFF

to make a light, machine, radio etc start or stop working by pressing or turning something

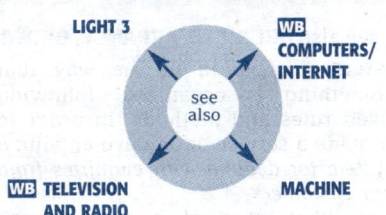

LIGHT 3

WB COMPUTERS/ INTERNET

see also

WB TELEVISION AND RADIO

MACHINE

1 to switch something on

switch on /ˌswɪtʃ ˈɒnǁ-ˈɑːn/ [phrasal verb I/T] to make something start working, for example by pressing a button – use this about things that use electricity, for example, lights, televisions, or computers

switch on sth Can you switch on the television? | I switched on the radio to listen to the news.

switch sth on Do you mind if I switch the light on?

turn on /ˌtɜːʳn ˈɒnǁ-ˈɑːn/ [phrasal verb T] to make something start working, for example by turning a tap or pressing a button – use this about things that use electricity, gas, or water

turn on sth He went into the bathroom and turned on the shower.

turn sth on Do you want me to turn the lights on?

put sth on /ˌpʊt (sth) ˈɒnǁ-ˈɑːn/ [phrasal verb T]

put the light/radio/TV/kettle etc on to make a light, radio etc start working: Eva put the kettle on to make a cup of coffee. | Put the light on, then we can see what we're doing.

start /stɑːʳt/ [v T]

start a car/engine/motor to make a car, engine, or motor start working: She started the car and backed slowly out of the garage.

2 to switch something off

switch off /ˌswɪtʃ ˈɒfǁ-ˈɔːf/ [phrasal verb I/T] to make something stop working, for example by pressing a button –

use this about things that use electricity, for example, lights, televisions, or computers

switch off sth Always switch off your computer when you've finished.

switch sth off It's OK – I switched it off before I went out.

turn off /ˌtɜːʳn ˈɒfǁ-ˈɔːf/ [phrasal verb T] to make something stop working, for example by pressing a button or turning a tap – use this about things that use electricity, gas, or water

turn off sth She got up and turned off the TV. | Could you turn off the heater before you go to bed?

turn sth off Who forgot to turn the tap off?

stop /stɒpǁstɑːp/ [v T] to make an engine or machine stop working: George stopped the engine and got out of the car. | We had to stop the pump and unblock it.

3 when something is switched on

on /ɒnǁɑːn, ɔːn/ [adj/adv not before noun] if something is **on**, it is working – use this about lights, machines, and other things that use electricity, gas, or water: Is the heating on? I'm freezing.

leave sth on Did you leave the kitchen light on?

keep sth on In the winter, I keep the gas fire on all day.

come/go on (=start working) The heating comes on automatically.

be switched on /biː ˌswɪtʃt ˈɒn/ use this about things that use electricity, for example machines, computers, or heating equipment: A green light shows that the computer is switched on. | Have you checked that the power is switched on?

be turned on /biː ˌtɜːʳnd ˈɒn/ use this about machines or about the electricity, gas, or water supply: If the boiler fails to light, first check that the gas is turned on.

be running /biː ˈrʌnɪŋ/ if an engine or a machine **is running**, it is working and its parts are moving: Do not touch the machine while it is running.

leave sth running Nick left the engine running while he ran into the house.

4 when something is switched off

off /ɒf‖ɔːf/ [adj/adv not before noun] if something is **off**, someone has switched it off to make it stop working – use this about lights, machines, and other things that use electricity, gas, or water: *Is the cooker off? I can smell gas.* | *I don't think anyone's at home. All the lights are off.*
go off (=stop working) *The heating goes off at 10:30.*

be switched off /biː ˌswɪtʃt 'ɒf/ use this about things that use electricity, for example machines, computers, or heating equipment: *Do you mean the alarm was switched off all night?*

be turned off /biː ˌtɜːʳnd 'ɒf/ use this about lights or machines, or about the electricity, gas, or water supply: *Make sure everything's turned off before you leave the house.*

go out /ˌgəʊ 'aʊt/ [phrasal verb I] if a light **goes out**, it stops shining because it has been switched off, or because there is no electricity: *I watched the house until all the lights had gone out.*

SYSTEM

the way in which something is organized

➡ see also **ORGANIZE/ARRANGE, ORDER**

system /'sɪstɪ̬m/ [n C] the way that something is organized, following fixed rules and methods, in order to provide a service or achieve an aim: *a system for dealing with enquiries from our customers*
+of *What we need is a cheap and reliable system of public transportation.* | *a democratic system of government*
education/transport/banking system *Most teachers are opposed to recent changes in the education system.* | *the French legal system*

set-up /'set ʌp/ [n singular] INFORMAL the way in which things are organized or done within a company, school etc: *My last school was quite traditional, but it's a different set-up at the new one.* | *It's a very strange set-up – everyone here earns exactly the same salary.*

network /'netwɜːʳk/ [n C] a system of lines, tubes, wires, roads etc that are connected to each other: *A 24-hour strike brought the railway network to a standstill.*
+of *A network of veins and arteries carries the blood around the body.*

T, t

TAKE/BRING

➡ if you mean 'take something out', go to **REMOVE**
➡ see also **STEAL, CARRY**

1   to take someone or something from one place to another place

take /teɪk/ [v T] to have someone or something with you when you go to another place: *Don't forget to take your keys.*
take sth to/out/into *"Where's Dan?" "He's taken the car to the garage."* | *Let's take the kids to the beach.*
take sb sth *I took Alice a cup of tea.*
take sth/sb with you *Did they take the tent with them on their holiday?*
taking – took – have taken

bring /brɪŋ/ [v T] if someone **brings** a person or thing to the place where you are, they have that person or thing with them when they come: *I brought my camera so that I could take pictures of all of you.* | *We've brought someone to see you.*
bring sth to/into/out *Will you bring your CD player to the party?*
bring sb sth *Robert asked the waiter to bring him the check.*
bring sth/sb with you *I hope he hasn't brought his brother with him.*
bringing – brought – have brought

drive /draɪv/ [v T] to take someone from one place to another in a car
drive sb to/from/away *Bill offered to drive me to the airport.* | *The man was driven away in a police van.*
driving – drove – have driven

fly /flaɪ/ [v T] to move people or goods from one place to another in a plane
fly sb to/from *His company is flying him to New York for the meeting.*
fly sth into/to/out *The Red Cross is flying emergency supplies into the earthquake zone.*
flying – flew – have flown

deliver /dɪˈlɪvəʳ/ [v T] to take letters, newspapers, goods etc to someone's home or office: *The store will deliver your new washing-machine tomorrow morning.*
deliver sth to *Unfortunately the package was delivered to the wrong address.*
delivery [n C/U] when letters, newspapers, goods etc are taken to someone's house or office: *We offer free home delivery for every purchase over $150.*

transport /trænˈspɔːʳt/ [v T] to move large quantities of goods or large numbers of people from one place to another, especially over a large distance: *It is much cheaper to transport goods by ship.* | *a large plane that is used for transporting military personnel*
transport sth to/from/across *Meat is transported across Europe in refrigerated containers.*

ship /ʃɪp/ [v T] to take goods a long distance to another place in a ship, plane, truck, or train, so that they can be used or sold
ship sth to/from/back etc *About half of the whisky produced in Scotland is shipped to Japan and the US.* | *A new engine was shipped over from Germany.*

2   to go to a place and take someone or something from there

get /get/ [v T] to go to the place where someone or something is, and bring them back, or tell them to come back: *I'll get my coat and then we can go.* | *Dinner's ready. Can you get Jo?*
get sb sth (=get something for someone) *Could you get me my keys from the kitchen?*
go and get sb/sth *Go and get your father. He's in the garden.*
getting – got – have got BRITISH **have gotten** AMERICAN

pick up /ˌpɪk ˈʌp/ [phrasal verb T] to go to a place where someone or something is waiting for you or ready for you, and take them with you
pick up sb/sth *I'll pick up the airline tickets on my way home from work.*
pick sb/sth up *Omar and Nadia are waiting for you to pick them up at the airport.*

collect /kə'lekt/ [v T] BRITISH to go to a place where someone or something is waiting for you, and bring them back: *I'm at the station. Can you come and collect me?*
collect sb/sth from *I have to go and collect a parcel from the post-office.*

fetch /fetʃ/ [v T] ESPECIALLY BRITISH to go to to get someone or something that you need and bring them back: *Can you fetch some more bread when you go to the kitchen? | Jim went off to fetch a policeman.*
fetch sb/sth from *Martha fetched a towel from the bathroom.*
fetch sb sth (=fetch something for someone) *Could you fetch me a screwdriver?*

3 to take someone or something back to the place where they came from

take back /,teɪk 'bæk/ [phrasal verb T]
take sb/sth back to *Paul asked the taxi driver to take him back to his hotel.*
take sb/sth back *The dress was too big for me so I took it back. | I'll take you back after the party.*
take back sth *Did you remember to take back all your library books?*

bring back /,brɪŋ 'bæk/ [phrasal verb T] to bring someone or something back to the place where you are now or to your home
bring sb/sth back *Mrs Ali will bring you back from school today.*
bring back sth *I've brought back the book you lent me. | They brought back some lovely cheese from France.*

return /rɪ'tɜːrn/ [v T] to bring or take something back to the place where you got it from: *Penny has still not returned the office keys.*
return sth to *If there is a problem with the computer you can return it to the store.*

Formal or informal?

Return is more formal than **take back** or **bring back**.

---

4 to take something from someone

take /teɪk/ [v T] to take something out of someone's hands: *Let me take your bags – you look exhausted.*
take sth from sb *He walked across the room and took the gun from her.*
taking – took – have taken

grab/snatch /græb, snætʃ/ [v T] to take something from someone with a sudden violent movement, for example because you are angry or you want to steal something: *A thief snatched her purse while she was walking down the street.*
grab/snatch sth from sb *Larry tried to grab the letter from me.*
grabbing – grabbed – have grabbed

take away /,teɪk ə'weɪ/ [phrasal verb T] to take something important from someone, such as a possession or a right, either as a punishment or in a way that is wrong or unfair
take away sth *a new law that would take away the rights of workers to go on strike*
take sth away from sb *Johnson failed a drugs test, and his gold medal was taken away from him.*

confiscate /'kɒnfɪˌskeɪt‖'kɑːn-/ [v T] to officially take something away from someone, either as a punishment or because they are not allowed to have it: *The teacher confiscated my Walkman. | Police will confiscate nets and rods from anyone found fishing illegally.*

5 to take something from the place where it is

take /teɪk/ [v T] *Have you taken my keys? I can't find them.*
take sth from/off/down etc *He took a dictionary down from the shelf.*
take sth away (=take something permanently from a place) *They haven't taken the garbage away for two weeks.*
taking – took – have taken

take out /,teɪk 'aʊt/ [phrasal verb T] to take something from a place where it could not be seen, for example from a pocket, drawer, or container

take out sth *He reached into his pocket and took out a handkerchief.*
take sth out *Sally opened a pack of cigarettes, took one out and lit it.*
take sth out of sth *Take that chewing gum out of your mouth!*

pull out /ˌpʊl ˈaʊt/ [phrasal verb T] to quickly take something from a place where it was hidden or could not be seen
pull out sth *He pulled out a gun and fired three shots.*
pull sth out *I saw her pull a bag out from under the seat.*

remove /rɪˈmuːv/ [v T] to take something away from the place where it is, especially something that you do not want or something that should not be there: *Please do not remove this notice.* | *She was in the hospital, having her appendix removed.*
remove sth from sth *Remove the packaging and place the pizza in a preheated oven.*

> **Formal or informal?**
> **Remove** is more formal than **take off**, **take out** etc.

6 **to take someone away using force**

take sb away /ˌteɪk (sb) əˈweɪ/ [phrasal verb T] if soldiers, the police etc **take** someone **away**, they force that person to go with them: *The soldiers took my son away and I never saw him again.* | *Our neighbour was taken away in a police car.*

kidnap /ˈkɪdnæp/ [v T] to take someone away by force and keep them as your prisoner, in order to make their family or their government give you money or other things you want: *Terrorists have kidnapped a French officer and are demanding $400,000 from the French government.*
kidnapping – kidnapped – have kidnapped

kidnapping [n C] when someone is kidnapped: *Most diplomats now travel with bodyguards, following a series of kidnappings.*

abduct /əbˈdʌkt, æb-/ [v T] to take someone away by force, especially a child or young person, often in order

to kill them or sexually attack them – used especially in news reports: *Several young women had been abducted from their villages and forced to work as prostitutes.*

take sb hostage /ˌteɪk (sb) ˈhɒstɪdʒ‖-ˈhɑː-/ to take someone and keep them as a prisoner, especially for political reasons, and threaten to kill them if their government does not do what you demand: *Rebel forces have taken five UN peacekeepers hostage.*

TAKE PART

to do something together with other people

➡ see also **WB** **SPORT, COMPETITION, GAME**

1 **to take part in an event, activity, discussion etc**

take part /ˌteɪk ˈpɑːʳt/ to do something together with other people, by joining them in an activity, discussion, event etc: *There are meetings every month, and local people are invited to take part.*
+in *She was invited to take part in a TV debate on drugs.* | *Police have arrested a number of people who took part in the riot.*

be involved /biː ɪnˈvɒlvd‖-ˈvɑːlvd/ to take part in an activity with a small number of other people, often something bad or illegal: *Choosing a school is an important decision, and both parents ought to be involved.*
+in *Mason says he wasn't involved in the kidnapping.* | *At least three politicians are involved in the scandal.*

participate /pɑːʳˈtɪsɪ̩peɪt/ [v I] FORMAL to take part in an activity, especially an organized activity: *There are regular class discussions, but some of the students never participate.*
+in *Over 300 local firms participated in the survey.* | *Members can participate in any of the trips organized by the club.*
participation /pɑːʳˌtɪsɪ̩ˈpeɪʃən/ [n U] when people participate: *The workforce want more participation in decision-making.*

2 to start taking part

join in /ˌdʒɔɪn ˈɪn/ [phrasal verb I/T] to start taking part in something that other people are already doing, especially something enjoyable such as a game, or a song: *When we get to the chorus I want everybody to join in!* | *We all wanted to join in the fun.*
+with *She was a shy girl, and wouldn't join in with the other children's games.*

get involved in sth /ˌget ɪnˈvɒlvd ɪn (sth)‖-ˈvɑːlvd-/ to start to take part in something, especially something that will cause you problems or take a lot of your time: *I don't want to get involved in their family arguments.* | *When did you first get involved in local politics?* | *The US are unwilling to get involved in another war.*

get caught up in sth /get ˌkɔːt ˈʌp ɪn (sth)/ to become involved in something dangerous, unpleasant, or illegal, without wanting or intending to: *His brother got caught up in crime when he was still at school.*

3 to take part in a competition

compete/take part /kəmˈpiːt, ˌteɪk ˈpɑːˈt/ [v I] to take part in a competition or race: *Only cars over 50 years old are allowed to compete.* | *The competition was a great success. Nearly two hundred people took part.*
+in *How many runners will be competing in the marathon?* | *Please contact Debbie if you would like to take part in the charity swim.*

enter sth/go in for sth /ˈentəˈ (sth), ˌgəʊ ˈɪn fɔːˈ (sth)/ [v T] to say that you will take part in a competition or race, for example by putting your name on a list: *You have to be under 18 to enter the painting competition.* | *Dad says he's going in for the talent contest.*

Formal or informal?
Enter is more formal than **go in for**, and **go in for** is only used in British English.

---

4 someone who takes part

competitor /kəmˈpetᵻtəˈ/ [n C] someone who takes part in a race, game, or competition: *Two of the competitors failed to turn up for the race.*

participant /pɑːˈtɪsᵻpənt/ [n C] FORMAL someone who takes part in an organized event or activity: *At the end of the conference, all the participants were given a questionnaire.*
+in *an active participant in the civil rights movement*

5 to not take part

not take part /nɒt teɪk ˈpɑːˈt/ *The President was invited to appear on the program but decided not to take part.*
+in *I noticed that Darren was not taking part in the discussion.*

pull out/drop out /ˌpʊl ˈaʊt, ˌdrɒp ˈaʊt‖ˌdrɑːp-/ [phrasal verb I] to suddenly decide not to take part in something that has already started or is about to start, especially when this causes problems: *The show was cancelled when the star guest pulled out.*
+of *Dave wants to drop out of the team.* | *It's too late to pull out of the agreement now.*

⊂ have nothing to do with sth /hæv ˌnʌθɪŋ tə ˈduː wɪð (sth)/ ESPECIALLY SPOKEN to not be involved in any way in something bad or illegal – use this especially when other people think that you were involved: *Tell the police that you had nothing to do with the robbery.* | *She had nothing to do with the break-up of my marriage.*

take no part in sth /ˌteɪk nəʊ ˈpɑːˈt ɪn (sth)/ FORMAL to deliberately not take part in something, because you disagree with it or think it is wrong: *They were pacifists and would take no part in the war.*

withdraw /wɪðˈdrɔː, wɪθ-/ [v I] to decide not to take part in a competition, race, discussion etc, which you previously agreed to take part in
+from *Clare had to withdraw from the race after injuring her knee.*
withdrawing – withdrew – have withdrawn

6 to not let someone take part

leave sb out /ˌliːv (sb) ˈaʊt/ [phrasal verb T] to not include someone in an activity or in a group: *They considered twenty candidates, but Melissa was left out.*
leave sb out of sth *It would be very unfair to leave him out of the team.*

exclude /ɪkˈskluːd/ [v T] to prevent someone from taking part in an activity, or from joining a group
exclude sb from sth *The black majority in South Africa was excluded from politics under apartheid.* | *The Church had previously excluded women from the priesthood.*

drop /drɒp‖drɑːp/ [v T often passive] to decide that someone can no longer be in a team
drop sb from sth *She was dropped from the badminton team because she missed practice too often.*

dropping – dropped – have dropped

TALK

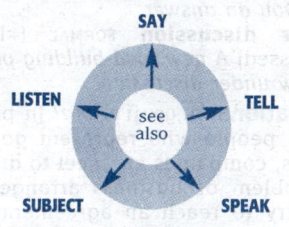

SAY

LISTEN   TELL

see also

SUBJECT   SPEAK

⚠ Don't confuse **say**, **tell**, **talk**, and **speak**. You **say** words to someone. You **tell** someone facts or information about something. You **talk** to someone about a subject. You **speak** (=you say words) or you **speak** a language.

1 to have a conversation

talk /tɔːk/ [v I] *We sat around talking for hours.* | *two friends talking on the phone*
+about *They talked about their favourite pop stars.*
+to *Danny was talking to a girl he'd just met at the bar.* | *It's been nice talking to you.*

talk with sb AMERICAN *I left Mario talking with my mother.*
get talking (=start having a conversation with someone that you do not know) *Kay got talking to a taxi-driver.*

speak to sb /ˈspiːk tuː (sb)/ [phrasal verb T] to say something to someone or have a conversation with them: *Natalie's on the phone. She wants to speak to you.* | *He hasn't spoken to me since we quarrelled.*
speaking – spoken – have spoken

chat/have a chat /tʃæt, ˌhæv ə ˈtʃæt/ [v I] to talk in a friendly and informal way, especially about things that are not very important: *The girls were sitting on the steps, chatting.* | *Just call me if you feel like having a chat.*
+about *We drank our coffee and chatted about our experiences.*
+with/to *Harry chatted to a couple of Australian tourists as we waited for the show to begin.*
chatting – chatted – have chatted

visit /ˈvɪzɪt/ [v I] AMERICAN to talk in a relaxed way to someone you know well: *Mom and Aunt Jo were sitting drinking coffee and visiting.*
+with *I don't see him that often, but I like to go and visit with him when I can.*

gossip /ˈgɒsɪp‖ˈgɑː-/ [v I] if people **gossip**, they talk about other people's behaviour and private lives, often including remarks that are unkind or untrue: *They sat in the kitchen, drinking coffee and gossiping.* | *Don't tell Bill about this. You know how he gossips.*
+about *People in small towns often gossip about each other.*
gossip [n singular/U] conversation about other people's behaviour and private lives: *There has been a lot of gossip about her divorce.* | *I stopped by at Marsha's house for a gossip.*

conversation /ˌkɒnvəˈseɪʃən‖ˌkɑːn-/ [n C/U] when people talk to each other, especially in an informal situation: *a telephone conversation* | *The noise of the traffic made conversation almost impossible.* | *They didn't realize their conversation was being recorded.*
have a conversation (with sb) *Vicky was having a long conversation with the bartender.*

get **into conversation (with sb)**
(=start talking to someone you do not
know) *While I was on the train to
Cambridge, I got into conversation with
an American.*

2 to talk to someone about a problem, plan, or serious subject

talk /tɔːk/ [v I] *I think we need to talk.*
+about *If you have a problem at
school, let's sit down and talk about it.*
+to *Gerry wants to talk to his girlfriend
before he makes a decision.*
talk with sb AMERICAN *If you need more
money you should talk with Richard.*

speak to sb (also **speak with sb**
AMERICAN) /'spiːk tuː (sb), 'spiːk wɪð (sb)/
[phrasal verb T] to talk to someone
about something that you are worried
about or annoyed about: *The King's
envoy travelled to Rome to speak to the
Pope.*
+about *I intend to speak to the
manager about the way I've been
treated.* | *Have you spoken with
Michael about your problem?*

have a word with sb /ˌhæv ə 'wɜːd
wɪð (sb)/ ESPECIALLY SPOKEN to talk to
someone alone for a short time, for
example because you need their
advice or because you want to tell
them something privately or criticize
them for something they have done
wrong: *The boss wants to have a word
with me.*
+about *Could I have a word with you
about my homework assignment?*

discuss /dɪ'skʌs/ [v T] if people **discuss**
a subject or situation, they exchange
ideas and opinions about it, so that it
is easier to make a decision or make
plans: *The two families got together to
discuss the wedding arrangements.*
discuss sth with sb *Don't make any
plans yet – I want to discuss this with
Jamie first.*
discuss what/how/where etc *We
need to discuss what kind of food we
want at the party.*

talk over /ˌtɔːk 'əʊvəʳ/ [phrasal verb T]
to talk to someone about all the
details of a serious problem or difficult situation, in order to
understand it better
talk sth over/talk over sth *If you're*

*worried about your work, come and see
me and we'll talk it over.*
talk sth over with sb *It's often useful
to talk things over with a trained
counsellor.*

negotiate /nɪ'gəʊʃieɪt/ [v I/T] to discuss
a political problem or business
arrangement in order to try to reach
an agreement – use this about political or business leaders
+with *The government refuses to
negotiate with terrorists.*
**negotiate an agreement/deal/price
etc** *Colombia and Venezuela are currently negotiating a trade agreement.*

3 a meeting where people talk seriously about something

discussion /dɪ'skʌʃən/ [n C/U] when
people exchange ideas and opinions
about something, especially in order
to make a decision
+about *a discussion about cars and
pollution*
+with *After a long discussion with her
father, she decided not to take the job.*
have a discussion *I need to have a
discussion with my boss before I can
give you an answer.*
under discussion FORMAL (=being
discussed) *A new road-building project
is now under discussion.*

negotiations /nɪˌgəʊʃi'eɪʃənz/ [n plural]
when people who represent governments, companies etc meet to discuss
a problem or business arrangement
and try to reach an agreement: *The
trade negotiations between the US and
Japan are going very well.*
+with *Negotiations with the Turkish
government are due to begin tomorrow.*

talks /tɔːks/ [n plural] a series of
discussions between political or business leaders, which may continue for
several days or weeks and are
intended to solve a difficult problem:
*the Strategic Arms Limitation Talks,
known as 'SALT'*
hold talks *The peace talks are being
held in Geneva.*
+with *The company's managers have
begun talks with union leaders.*
+between *trade talks between France
and Korea*

debate /dɪ'beɪt/ [n C] a formal public
discussion, for example in parliament

or on television, in which two or more groups of people make speeches giving different opinions about a subject, and people vote on it afterwards: *The law was passed, after a long and sometimes angry debate.*

+on/about *a televised debate on abortion*

conference /ˈkɒnfərəns‖ˈkɑːn-/ [n C] an organized event, especially one that continues for several days, at which a lot of people meet to discuss a particular subject and hear speeches about it: *Didn't you give a talk at the conference last year?*

+on *an international conference on AIDS*

attend a conference FORMAL *Baxter was in Boston attending a conference on the environment.*

hold a conference *The Institute of Accountants is holding its conference in Edinburgh this year.*

4 when someone makes a speech

speech /spiːtʃ/ [n C] a formal talk to a group of people, for example in a parliament or at an official meeting or ceremony: *She left early to write her speech for the next day.* | *an election speech*

make/give a speech *After the concert the mayor made a speech, congratulating the school.*

+about/on *a speech on the economy* plural **speeches**

talk /tɔːk/ [n C] a planned speech about a particular subject, for example at a large public meeting where people discuss subjects such as business, science, language etc: *a series of talks by well-known writers*

give a talk on/about sth *Mr. Munroe gave an interesting talk on his recent visit to Peru.*

give a talk to sb *Alice Walker has been invited to give a talk to the literary group this evening.*

> ⚠️ Compare **speech** and **talk**. **Speeches** are often about politics. **Talks** are about things like literature, science, art, or history, but not usually about politics.

speak /spiːk/ [v I] to make a speech, for example in parliament or at an official meeting or ceremony: *I've been invited to speak at the party's annual conference.*

+to *The President will speak to the nation tonight on television.*

talk /tɔːk/ [v I] to speak publicly to a group of people about a particular subject

+about *This evening Professor Welch will be talking about Shakespeare's historical plays.*

speaker /ˈspiːkəʳ/ [n C] someone who makes a speech in public: *the first speaker in tonight's debate*

public speaker *Kennedy was known as a brilliant public speaker.*

guest speaker (=someone who has been invited to come and give a speech or talk)

5 to mention someone or something when you are talking

mention /ˈmenʃən/ [v T] to say something about a person, plan, event etc during a conversation, but without giving any details or saying very much: *When you were talking to Barbara, did she mention her mother?* | *One of the students mentioned something about a party on Thursday.*

mention sth to sb *I mentioned the idea to Joan, and she seemed to like it.*

+(that) *He mentioned that he was having problems, but he didn't say what they were.*

refer to sth/sb /rɪˈfɜːʳ tuː (sth/sb)/ [phrasal verb T] to talk about a person, plan, event etc in a conversation, speech, or piece of writing: *She didn't mention any names, but everyone knew who she was referring to.* | *In his speech the President referred to the achievements of the Olympic team.*

> **Formal or informal?**
> **Refer to** is more formal than **mention**.

bring up /ˌbrɪŋ ˈʌp/ [phrasal verb T] to start to talk about a subject during a conversation or meeting

bring up sth *She wished she'd never brought up the subject of money.*

bring sth up *If you think safety is a problem, I suggest you bring it up at the next meeting.*

6 to talk when someone else is already speaking

interrupt /ˌɪntəˈrʌpt/ [v I/T] to start talking when someone else is already speaking: *I wish you wouldn't interrupt all the time.* | *She's always interrupting people before they've finished talking.*

butt in /ˌbʌt ˈɪn/ [phrasal verb I] INFORMAL to interrupt someone rudely: *Will you please stop butting in!*

7 someone who talks a lot

talkative /ˈtɔːkətɪv/ [adj] someone who is **talkative** talks a lot: *The wine was making her more relaxed and talkative.*

chatterbox /ˈtʃætəˈbɒks‖-bɑːks/ [n C] INFORMAL someone, especially a child, who talks a lot in a friendly way plural **chatterboxes**

 go on /ˌgəʊ ˈɒn‖-ˈɑːn/ [phrasal verb I] INFORMAL, ESPECIALLY SPOKEN to keep talking or complaining about something, in a way that is annoying or boring: *Doesn't she go on? She's always complaining.*
+about *I wish you'd stop going on about how expensive everything is.*
go on and on (=keep talking for a long time) *He went on and on until we were all practically falling asleep.*

8 someone who does not talk much

➡ see also **QUIET**

quiet /ˈkwaɪət/ [adj] someone who is **quiet** does not talk much: *The new girl's quiet, but nice enough.* | *Steven's a very quiet boy who loves reading.*

silent /ˈsaɪlənt/ [adj not usually before noun] ESPECIALLY WRITTEN if someone is **silent**, they do not say anything
remain silent *Alice was laughing and joking, but her sister remained silent.*
fall silent (=suddenly stop talking) *When the priest entered the room, everyone fell silent.*

Formal or informal?
Use **silent** especially in stories or descriptions of events.

9 what you say to tell someone to stop talking

➡ see also **QUIET**

 be quiet /biː ˈkwaɪət/ SPOKEN say this when you want someone to stop talking, especially when you are annoyed: *Please be quiet for a moment.*

⚠ Only say **be quiet** to children or to someone that you know well.

 shut up /ˌʃʌt ˈʌp/ SPOKEN INFORMAL a rude way of telling someone to stop talking: *Oh, shut up! I don't want to hear your excuses.*
+about *We know you won, but just shut up about it, okay?*

⚠ Only say **shut up** to people you know very well, because it is not polite.

TALL

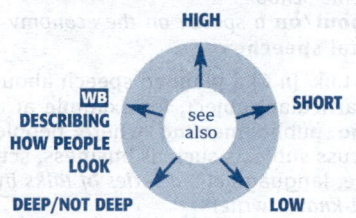

1 tall

tall /tɔːl/ [adj] a **tall** person, building, tree etc has a greater height than average: *You'll recognize him – he's very tall and thin.* | *a tall building like the Sears Tower* | *The photographer asked the tallest people to stand at the back of the group.*

> ⚠ Use **tall** about people, and about things that are high but not wide or long, such as trees or some buildings. Use **high** about things that are wide or long as well as being high, such as mountains or walls.

> ⚠ **Short** is the opposite of **tall** when you are talking about a person: *He's short and fat with grey hair.*

2   how tall someone is

how tall /ˌhaʊ ˈtɔːl/ use this to ask or talk about someone's height: *"How tall are you?" "I'm about 1 metre 65."*

6ft tall/2m tall etc /(6ft, etc) ˈtɔːl/ use this to say exactly how tall someone is: *John is 1.78 metres tall and weighs 95 kilos.*

> ⚠ Don't say 'I am tall 180 cm'. Say **I am 180 cm tall**.

height /haɪt/ [n U] how tall someone or something is: *They need to know your age, weight, and height.*
+of *What's the height of the Eiffel Tower?*
be the same height (as) *My daughter is only 14 but she is nearly the same height as me.*
of medium height ESPECIALLY WRITTEN (=someone who is not tall and not short) *a man of medium height*

TASTE

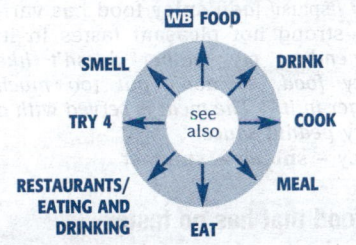

WB FOOD
SMELL — DRINK
TRY 4 — *see also* — COOK
RESTAURANTS/ EATING AND DRINKING — MEAL
EAT

1   the taste of food or drink

taste /teɪst/ [n singular] the feeling that something produces in your mouth

when you eat it or drink it: *I never drink beer, I just don't like the taste.*
+of *Have some water to take away the taste of the medicine.*

> ⚠ Don't say 'this cake is good taste'. Say **this cake tastes good**.

flavour BRITISH **flavor** AMERICAN /ˈfleɪvəʳ/ [n C/U] the interesting, pleasant, or strong taste that a type of food or drink has, which makes it different from any other food or drink: *This sauce has a really unusual flavour.* | *We have three flavors of ice-cream – strawberry, chocolate, and vanilla.* | *The wine wasn't bad, but it didn't have much flavour.*

2   when food has a particular taste

taste /teɪst/ [v I] use this to say that food has a particular taste
taste good/awful/strange/sweet etc *This milk tastes strange – do you think it's OK to drink?*
taste of sth (=have the taste of something) *The yoghurt tastes of strawberries.*
taste like sth *It's a vegetarian pie, but it tastes just like meat!*

> ⚠ Don't say 'it is tasting good/awful etc'. Say **it tastes good/awful etc**.

have a strong/sweet/unpleasant etc taste /hæv ə (strong etc) ˈteɪst/ use this when you want to describe exactly what something tastes like: *The soup had a very strong, spicy taste.*

flavoured BRITISH **flavored** AMERICAN /ˈfleɪvəʳd/ [adj] **lemon-flavoured / chocolate-flavoured etc** with the taste of lemon, chocolate etc added: *an orange-flavoured drink*

3   food that tastes good

delicious /dɪˈlɪʃəs/ [adj] something that is **delicious** tastes very good, and you enjoy eating it or drinking it: *Thank you, that was a delicious meal.* | *"What do you think of the wine?" "Mmm, delicious!"*

⚠ Don't say 'very delicious'. Say **absolutely delicious** or **quite delicious**: *The tomato soup was absolutely delicious.*

🔍 **good** (also **nice** ESPECIALLY BRITISH) /gʊd, naɪs/ [*adj*] ESPECIALLY SPOKEN pleasant to eat or drink: *This is a really good pizza. I think I'll have another slice.* | *You can get very nice bread at Walker's Bakery.*
taste good/nice *This sauce tastes nice. How did you make it?*
good – better – best

tasty /'teɪsti/ [*adj*] food that is **tasty** has a strong taste that you like: *These sausages are very tasty – where did you buy them?* | *a range of tasty snacks*

⚠ Don't confuse **tasty** (which is used about food) and **tasteful** (which is used about things such as furniture and clothes that look attractive).

mouth-watering /'maʊθ ,wɔːtərɪŋ/ [*adj* usually before noun] **mouth-watering** food makes you feel hungry because it looks or smells very good: *There was a mouth-watering selection of cakes to choose from.* | *the mouth-watering aroma of freshly made fish soup*

4 **food that tastes bad**

disgusting/revolting /dɪs'gʌstɪŋ, dɪz-, rɪ'vəʊltɪŋ/ [*adj*] food or drink that is **disgusting** or **revolting** has an extremely unpleasant taste: *This hamburger tastes disgusting – I wonder what they put in it.* | *It wasn't a bad meal, but the coffee was absolutely revolting.*

⚠ Don't say 'very disgusting' or 'very revolting'. Say **absolutely disgusting** or **absolutely revolting**.

5 **food that tastes sweet**

sweet /swiːt/ [*adj*] food or drink that is **sweet** has a taste like sugar: *Italian oranges are much sweeter than the ones we buy in Britain.* | *a cup of hot sweet tea*

sugary /'ʃʊgəri/ [*adj*] very sweet or too sweet because a lot of sugar has been added: *Eat fruit between meals, and try to avoid sugary snacks.*

6 **food that does not taste sweet**

bitter /'bɪtə'/ [*adj*] food or drink that is **bitter** has a taste like the taste of strong coffee without milk or sugar, or the taste of very dark chocolate: *The medicine tasted bitter and Jessie spat it out.*

sour /saʊə'/ [*adj*] something that is **sour**, especially fruit, has a sharp taste like a lemon: *The strawberries are a little sour – you may need to put sugar on them.*

savoury BRITISH **savory** AMERICAN /'seɪvəri/ [*adj*] **savoury** foods are not sweet but have the taste of meat, cheese, fish etc: *You can use this herb to flavour almost any savoury dish.* | *As a child I didn't like sweet things, but I loved crisps, nuts, and anything savoury.*

dry /draɪ/ [*adj*] a **dry** wine is not sweet at all: *We drank dry white wine with our fish.* | *dry sherry*
dry – drier – driest

7 **food that has a hot taste**

hot /hɒt‖hɑːt/ [*adj*] food that has a **hot** taste seems to burn your mouth, and makes you want to drink a lot of water: *Bring me the hottest curry on the menu.* | *The sauce had a hot peppery taste.*
hot – hotter – hottest

spicy /'spaɪsi/ [*adj*] **spicy** food has various strong hot pleasant tastes in it: *Remember, my mother doesn't like spicy food, so don't put too much ginger in it.* | *The meat is served with a spicy peanut sauce.*
spicy – spicier – spiciest

8 **food that has no taste**

have no taste/not taste of anything /,hæv nəʊ 'teɪst, nɒt 'teɪst əv ,eniθɪŋ/ *What's this soup supposed to be? It doesn't taste of anything to me.* | *Watermelon is refreshing on a hot day but it doesn't have much taste.*

bland/tasteless /blænd, 'teɪstləs/ [adj] use this about food or drink that has no strong noticeable taste, and is not interesting or enjoyable: *Food tastes very bland if you stop using salt.* | *a plate of tasteless, overcooked vegetables*

TEACH

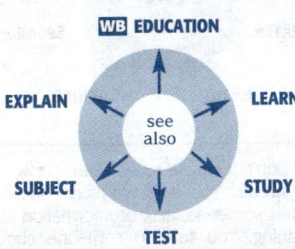

EXPLAIN — see also — LEARN

SUBJECT — STUDY

TEST

WB EDUCATION

1 to teach

teach /tiːtʃ/ [v I/T] to help someone to learn a subject or skill, by giving them lessons or instructions, especially when this is your job: *She teaches at the local high school.*
teach sth *I got a job teaching French and Spanish.* | *He was working at the technology school, teaching classes in computer programming.*
teach sb *I didn't enjoy teaching teenagers.*
teach sb sth *You remember Mr Hughes – he used to teach us history.*
teach sb to do sth/how to do sth *Who taught you to drive?* | *It was my mother that taught me how to cook.*
teaching – taught – have taught

train /treɪn/ [v T] to teach someone the practical skills and knowledge that they need to do a job: *She works at the flying school, training pilots.*
train sb to do sth *All our staff will be trained to use the new computer system.* | *They had trained the dog to detect illegal drugs.*
train sb in sth *We train people in skills such as typing and business administration.*
trained [adj] *a shortage of trained medical staff*

teaching /'tiːtʃɪŋ/ [n U] the work that a teacher does, or the job of being a teacher: *Andrea took some time off from teaching when her children were small.*
go into teaching (=become a teacher) *What made you decide to go into teaching?*

> ⚠ **Teaching** can also be used before a noun, like an adjective: *Do you have any teaching experience?* | *a teaching job*

training /'treɪnɪŋ/ [n U] the process of teaching people the skills that are needed for a job: *The equipment can only be used by people who have had special training.* | *military training*

> ⚠ **Training** can also be used before a noun, like an adjective: *a training course*

2 someone who teaches

teacher /'tiːtʃəʳ/ [n C] someone who teaches, especially someone whose job is to teach children in a school: *She's a teacher in the high school.*
English/science/chemistry etc teacher *The school doesn't have enough French teachers.*
+of *a conference for high-school teachers of Spanish*
a good/bad teacher *I gave her some driving lessons, but I'm afraid I'm not a very good teacher.*

tutor /'tjuːtəʳ‖'tuː-/ [n C] someone who gives lessons to just one student or a small group of students: *When she was ill she studied at home with a private tutor.* | *They hired a tutor to help Carlos with his English.*

instructor /ɪn'strʌktəʳ/ [n C] someone who teaches a sport or a practical skill
a swimming/driving/riding etc instructor *Do you know any good driving instructors?* | *a ski instructor*

coach /kəʊtʃ/ [n C] someone who trains a person or a team in a sport, and helps them to improve their skill
a basketball/football/tennis coach

professor /prəˈfesəʳ/ [n C] a university teacher – used in Britain to mean a teacher of the highest rank, and in the US to mean any university teacher who has a higher degree such as a PhD: *a linguistics professor*
+of *She's a professor of history at Oxford.*

> You can also use **professor** as a title: *Our guest speaker today is Professor Julius Weissman from the University of Chicago.*

> Never use **professor** to mean a school teacher.

lecturer /ˈlektʃərəʳ/ [n C] BRITISH someone who teaches at a university or college: *a chemistry lecturer*
+in *a lecturer in economics*

3 books, games etc that teach something

educational /ˌedjʊˈkeɪʃənəl‹ ‖ˌedʒə-/ [adj] **educational** books, games, television programmes etc are designed to help you to learn something: *educational toys for 7 to 11 year-olds* | *a leading publisher of educational books and software*

TECHNOLOGY

➡ see Word Banks section

TELEVISION AND RADIO

➡ see Word Banks section

When you see **EC**, go to the **ESSENTIAL COMMUNICATION** section.

TELL

➡ look here for ...
• tell someone about something
• order someone to do something

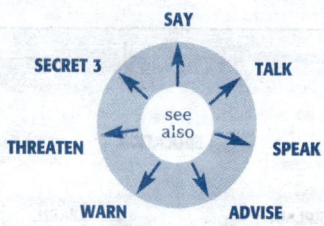

> Don't confuse **say**, **tell**, **talk**, and **speak**. You **say** words to someone. You **tell** someone facts or information about something. You **talk** to someone about a subject. You **speak** (=you say words) or you **speak** a language.

1 to give someone information

tell /tel/ [v T]
tell sb (that) *Jane told me you have a new job.* | *She wrote to tell us that she was getting married.*
tell sb sth *Let's have a cup of coffee and you can tell me all the details.*
tell sb who/what/where etc *Just tell me what happened.* | *This leaflet tells you how to apply for a driving licence.*
tell sb about sth *Have you told anyone about this?*
telling – told – have told

> You must always say who you are telling. Don't say 'he told that he was going'. Say **he told me that he was going**. Don't say 'he told about it'. Say **he told me about it**.

🔍 **let sb know** /ˌlet (sb) ˈnəʊ/ ESPECIALLY SPOKEN to tell someone something important that they need to know or want to know: *If you ever need any help, just let me know.*
+about *I said we'd let her know about the job by the end of the week.*
let sb know sth *I'll let you know our new address as soon as I have it.*
+(that) *When you get there, will you*

phone and let me know you arrived safely?

let sb know what/where/how etc
Could you let us know what time you'll be home?

inform /ɪnˈfɔːʳm/ [v T] FORMAL to officially or formally give someone information about something: *Do you think we ought to inform the police?*
inform sb of sth *You should inform your bank of any change of address.*
inform sb (that) *I am sorry to inform you that your application has been unsuccessful.*

keep sb informed /ˌkiːp (sb) ɪnˈfɔːʳmd/ to give someone regular information about decisions, events etc so that they know what is happening: *I've very concerned about this, so please keep me informed.*
+of/about *Some parents felt the school had not been keeping them informed about their children's progress.*

give /ɡɪv/ [v T] to provide information about something, especially written information
give information/details/instructions etc *Please give details of all your previous jobs.* | *The handbook gave full instructions on how to change the oil.*
give an account/description/report *The article gave a vivid account of life after the earthquake.*
give sb information/details etc *Could you give me some information on how to apply for a loan?*
giving – gave – have given

break the news /ˌbreɪk ðə ˈnjuːzǁˈnuːz/ to tell someone some bad news or something that might upset them
+to *After Jack's body was found, a policewoman had to break the news to his mother.*

communication /kəˌmjuːnᵻˈkeɪʃən/ [n U] when people exchange information and tell each other about their decisions and ideas: *Good communication is essential in a large organization.*
+between *There seems to have been a breakdown in communication between the police and the army.*

 You can also use **communication** before a noun, like an adjective: *You need good communication skills to be a teacher.* | *communication problems between managers and employees*

2 | to publicly tell a lot of people about something

announce /əˈnaʊns/ [v T] to make a public statement in order to tell people about a decision or about something important that has happened or will happen: *The winner of the award will be announced at a dinner at the Sheraton Hotel.*
+(that) *Lord McGowan has announced that he will retire at the end of the year.*

Don't say 'she announced us that ...'. Just say **she announced that ....**

report /rɪˈpɔːʳt/ [v I/T] to give people news about what is happening, in newspapers, on television, or on the radio: *The local newspaper has reported several cases of meningitis in the area.*
+(that) *Our correspondent in Rwanda reports that conditions in the refugee camps are filthy and overcrowded.*
+on *She was sent to Chechnya to report on the independence struggle.*

publicize (also **publicise** BRITISH) /ˈpʌblᵻsaɪz/ [v T] to use the newspapers, television etc to provide information about something such as a new product or a special event, because you want everyone to know about it: *She did a series of radio interviews to publicize her new book.*
well publicized (=mentioned often in newspapers or on television or radio) *The parade was well publicized and thousands came to see it.*

publicity /pʌˈblɪsᵻti/ [n U] the attention that someone or something gets from newspapers, television etc, which a lot of people hear or read about: *The judge was forced to resign because of the publicity surrounding his divorce.*
get/receive/attract publicity *The town got a lot of publicity after the new concert hall was built.*

3 to tell someone about your feelings

confide in sb /kən'faɪd ɪn (sb)/ [phrasal verb T] to tell someone you trust about personal matters which you are worried about and which you do not want anyone else to know: *Maria felt she had no-one she could confide in.*

communicate /kə'mjuːnɪkeɪt/ [v I] to make your feelings or thoughts clear to other people by talking to them: *Counselling may help married couples to start to communicate again.*
+with *She's not very good at communicating with young people.*

4 to tell something that was a secret

tell /tel/ [v T] to tell someone something that should be kept secret: *What did she say? Tell me!*
tell sb where/what/who etc *He didn't tell me where he got this information.*
tell sb about sth *Don't tell anyone about this just yet.*
tell sb a secret *I'll tell you a secret – Beth has a new boyfriend!*

reveal /rɪ'viːl/ [v T] ESPECIALLY WRITTEN to let people know about something that was previously kept secret, especially something embarrassing: *What actually happened to the gold has never been revealed.*
+(that) *Markov revealed that he had once worked for the CIA.*

leak /liːk/ [v T] to deliberately give secret government information to a newspaper or television company: *The Congressman was furious that the report had been leaked.*
leak sth to sb *The contents of the fax were leaked to the press.*
leak [n C] secret government information that someone gives to a newspaper etc: *The scandal began with a leak to 'The Times'.*

5 to tell the police about a crime or criminal

➡ see also **CRIME, WB POLICE**

report /rɪ'pɔːrt/ [v T] to tell the police or someone in authority that a crime or accident has happened: *I'd like to report a theft.*
report sth to sb *Sally was too scared to report the attack to the police.*

inform on sb /ɪn'fɔːrm ɒn (sb)‖-ɑːn-/ [phrasal verb T] to secretly tell the police that someone you know is responsible for a crime: *He informed on his brother, who was later arrested for drug-dealing.*

talk /tɔːk/ [v I] to give the police information about a crime when they ask you questions about it: *The suspect was questioned for six hours but refused to talk.*

tip off /ˌtɪp 'ɒf‖-'ɔːf/ [phrasal verb T] to secretly tell the police or other authorities about a crime that is planned, so that they can prevent it
tip off sb *Someone must have tipped off the police because they were already waiting at the house.*
tip sb off *I wonder who tipped them off.*
tip-off [n C] a piece of information secretly given to someone such as the police, about a crime that is going to happen: *Acting on a tip-off, customs officers searched the vehicle for drugs.*

informer /ɪn'fɔːrmər/ [n C] someone who is part of a criminal group but who secretly tells the police about its activities: *An informer had warned the police about the bombing.*

6 to tell someone that they must do something

tell /tel/ [v T] *"Wait here!" he told the children.*
tell sb to do sth *Tell her to come and see me as soon as possible!*
tell sb not to do sth *She told him not to phone her again.*
tell sb what to do *I'm sick of being told what to do by my parents.*
tell sb (that) *Ian's teachers keep telling him that he must work harder. | The doctor told me I should give up smoking.*

🔍 **do as you're told!** SPOKEN (used to tell children to obey) *Do as you're told and go and wash your hands!*

⚠️ Don't say 'he told to me to stop'. Say **he told me to stop**.

---

order /ˈɔːʳdəʳ/ [v T] to tell someone to do something, either officially or in an angry, threatening way: *"Don't move," he ordered.*
order sb to do sth *The judge ordered Timms to pay £20,000 in legal costs.* | *Army units have been ordered to advance towards the river.*
order sb into/out of/back etc (=order them to go somewhere) *She pointed her gun at him, ordering him out of the room.*
order sth (=give an order that something must happen) *After the plane crash, the Government ordered a full public inquiry.*

ask sb to do sth /ˌɑːsk (sb) tə ˈduː (sth)‖ˌæsk-/ to tell someone politely but firmly to do something or to stop doing something: *Mr Evans, I must ask you to come with me to the police station.*
ask sb not to do sth *Would you ask visitors not to park their cars in front of the entrance?*

give orders/give instructions /ˌgɪv ˈɔːʳdəʳz, ˌgɪv ɪnˈstrʌkʃənz/ if someone such as a leader or officer **gives orders** or **gives instructions**, they tell other people exactly what they must do
give sb orders/instructions to do sth *The General has given them orders to bomb the city.*
+that *We were given strict instructions that nobody should enter the building without a security card.*

on sb's orders/on sb's instructions /ɒn (sb's) ˈɔːʳdəʳz, ɒn (sb's) ɪnˈstrʌkʃənz/ ESPECIALLY WRITTEN if you do something **on** someone's **orders** or **on** someone's **instructions**, you do it because they have officially told you to do it: *On the instructions of the new military government, soldiers burned books and other documents.*
acting on sb's orders/instructions (=doing what someone has told you to do) *Sergeant Dean claims that he was acting on the orders of the police chief.*

---

7 to give orders in a rude, unpleasant way

order sb around (also **order sb about** BRITISH) /ˌɔːʳdəʳ (sb) əˈraʊnd, ˌɔːʳdəʳ (sb) əˈbaʊt/ [phrasal verb T] if someone **orders you around** or **orders you about**, they keep telling you what to do in an annoying or unfair way, and they seem to enjoy it: *I hate the way she's always ordering us around.* | *You have no right to order the children around like that.*

push sb around /ˌpʊʃ (sb) əˈraʊnd/ [phrasal verb T] INFORMAL to tell someone what to do in a rude or threatening way: *Tom was a bully who enjoyed pushing the younger kids around.* | *Don't let Mary push you around – she's not your boss!*

bossy /ˈbɒsi‖ˈbɔːsi/ [adj] someone who is **bossy** enjoys telling other people what to do, although they usually do not have the right to do it: *Let Simon do things his way, and stop being so bossy!*

---

8 a statement telling someone to do something

order /ˈɔːʳdəʳ/ [n C] an official statement ordering you to do something, given by someone with the power to do this, especially a military officer: *The commander's orders must be obeyed at all times.* | *We are still waiting for orders from HQ.*
order to do sth *We received an order to attack.*
give (sb) an order *The captain gave the order to fire.*
my/your/their orders (=the orders you have been given) *My orders are to give this letter to the Commissioner.*

instructions /ɪnˈstrʌkʃənz/ [n plural] a statement telling someone what they should do and how they should do it: *The coach kept shouting instructions at his team.*
follow/obey instructions *If you had followed my instructions none of this would have happened.*
instructions to do sth *Scott has just received instructions to return to Washington.*

+**on** *We were given strict instructions on what to do in an emergency.*

TEST

➡ look here for ...
• a test or examination
• a test done in order to find out about something

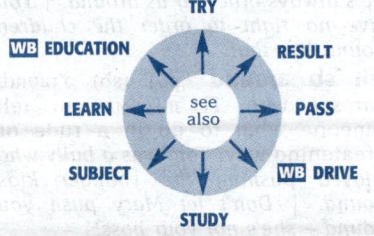

WB EDUCATION

LEARN

SUBJECT

TRY

see also

STUDY

RESULT

PASS

WB DRIVE

1 a test of your knowledge or skill

test /test/ [n C] a set of spoken or written questions or practical activities, which are intended to find out how much someone knows about a subject or skill
spelling/reading/biology etc test *Don't forget there's a chemistry test tomorrow.*
driving test *Did Lauren pass her driving test?*
+**on** *Listen carefully, because there will be a test on this next week.*

exam /ɪgˈzæm/ [n C] an important test that you do at the end of a course of study or at the end of the school year: *How did you do in your exams?*
history/French/biology etc exam *We have a biology exam tomorrow, and I haven't done any work for it yet.*
entrance exam (=an exam you must pass to enter a school or university)
midterm/final exam AMERICAN (=a test you take in the middle of a course or at the end) *Suzanne was studying for a midterm exam.*

⚠ You can also use **exam** before a noun, like an adjective: *an exam paper* (=the piece of paper that has the exam questions on it) | *When do you get your exam results?*

examination /ɪgˌzæmɪˈneɪʃən/ [n C] FORMAL an exam: *Students are not allowed to talk during the examination.*

quiz /kwɪz/ [n C] AMERICAN a quick short test that a teacher gives to a class: *Oh no, I think we're having a history quiz today.*
+**on** *Mr. Morris gave us a quiz on the chapter we'd read for homework.*
pop quiz (=a short test that the students are not expecting)
plural **quizzes**

oral exam (also **oral** BRITISH) /ˈɔːrəl ɪgˌzæm, ˈɔːrəl/ [n C] an exam in which you answer questions by speaking, instead of writing, for example to test how good you are at speaking a foreign language: *I failed the oral exam because my pronunciation was so bad.* | *Nicky got an A in her Spanish oral.*

practical /ˈpræktɪkəl/ [n C] BRITISH an exam that tests your ability to do or make things, rather than your ability to write about them, for example in subjects such as chemistry or cooking: *We've got our chemistry practical tomorrow morning.*

finals /ˈfaɪnlz/ [n plural] BRITISH the last exams that you take at the end of a university course: *During my finals, I was revising till 3 o'clock in the morning most days.*

final /ˈfaɪnl/ [n C] AMERICAN an important exam that you take at the end of a set of classes: *Robert was studying for his finals.*
chemistry/history/English etc final

midterm /ˈmɪdtɜːrm/ [n C] AMERICAN an important exam that you take during the middle of a set of classes: *We had our midterm yesterday.*
chemistry/history/English etc midterm *My Spanish midterm was really hard.*

2 to do a test or exam

take /teɪk/ [v T] to do a test or exam: *Anna will be taking her music exam in the summer.* | *I took my driving test when I was 18.*
taking – took – have taken

> ⚠ Don't confuse '**take** an exam' (=do it) and '**pass** an exam' (=be successful in it): *Only 25% of the students who took the exam passed it.*

have (also **have got** ESPECIALLY BRITISH) /hæv, həv 'gɒt‖-'gɑːt/ [v T] if you **have** an exam tomorrow, next week etc, you are going to do it then: *I have a written test in the morning, and an interview in the afternoon.* | *Lucy's got her driving test next week.*
having – had – have had

3 to be successful in a test or exam

pass /pɑːs‖pæs/ [v I/T] to achieve a good enough standard to be successful in a test or exam: *Congratulations! I hear you passed all your exams.* | *"Did you pass?" "Yeah, I got a B."*

scrape through /ˌskreɪp 'θruː/ [phrasal verb I/T] INFORMAL to only just pass a test or exam: *I didn't do very well in Biology – I just scraped through.*
scrape through sth *Jim scraped through his history paper.*

graduate /'grædʒueɪt/ [v I] to get a first degree from a university or college, or to successfully finish your studies in an American high school: *After he graduated, he got a job with a law firm.*
graduate from Harvard/high school/Manchester University etc *He graduated from Harvard with a degree in Economics in 1982.*
graduate in Law/English/History etc *She graduated in Modern Languages and got a job as an interpreter.*

qualified /'kwɒlɪfaɪd‖'kwɑː-/ [adj] ESPECIALLY BRITISH a **qualified** doctor, teacher, lawyer etc has passed all the exams needed to become a doctor, teacher, lawyer etc: *My sister's a qualified nurse.*
get qualified *How long does it take to get qualified?*
fully qualified (=when you have passed all the necessary exams) *She's training to be an accountant, but she's not fully qualified yet.*

4 the result of an examination or school test

grade /greɪd/ [n C] ESPECIALLY AMERICAN the letter that is put on a student's work to show how good or bad it is: *How were your grades last semester?*
good/bad grade *If Dan gets good enough grades he'll get a scholarship to Michigan State.*

mark /mɑːʳk/ [n C] ESPECIALLY BRITISH the number or letter that is put on a student's work to show how good or bad it is: *"What mark did you get?" "B".*
good/high mark *The highest mark in the class was 75%.*
bad/low mark *You have to do the course again if you get low marks.*
get full marks (=get the highest possible marks) *I got full marks in the history test.*

results /rɪ'zʌlts/ [n plural] BRITISH all the marks that a student gets in a set of tests or examinations, which show whether he or she has been successful or not: *His exam results weren't very good.*
get good results *Ceri got better results than she expected.*

score /skɔːʳ/ [n C] AMERICAN the number that shows how well or badly a student has done in an exam, especially an important exam: *Test scores have been falling.*
high/low score *She got a high score on the SAT.*

5 to fail a test or exam

fail /feɪl/ [v I/T] to not pass a test or exam: *I failed my Spanish exam.* | *"How did Chris do in his driving test?" "He failed."*

flunk /flʌŋk/ [v T] AMERICAN INFORMAL to fail an exam: *I thought I was going to flunk math, but I got a C.*

6 to give students a test

give sb a test /ˌgɪv (sb) ə 'test/ to make someone do a test: *The students were given the same test again, and did better.*
+on *The French teacher gave us a test on irregular verbs.*

test /test/ [*v* T] to ask someone written or spoken questions to find out what they know about a subject
test sb on sth *Tomorrow you'll be tested on the main events of the Civil War.*

7 to study in order to prepare for an exam

revise BRITISH **study** AMERICAN /rɪˈvaɪz, ˈstʌdi/ [*v* I] to spend time reading things again, making notes etc, in order to prepare for an exam: *If you want an A, you have to study!*
+for *I was up all night revising for my German literature exam.*
revision /rɪˈvɪʒən/ [*n* U] BRITISH work you do to prepare for an exam: *She tries to do four hours' revision a day.*

8 a test on something to check it or find out about it

test /test/ [*n* C] a process that is used for finding out important information about something, for example whether a machine is working properly, whether a substance is safe, or whether someone has an illness: *a simple test to show whether the alarm system is working*
carry out a test/do a test *Car designers do tests using wind tunnels.*
+on *We carry out safety tests on all our products.*
a test for sth (=to find out if something exists) *There is a simple test for diabetes.*
eye/blood/skin etc test (=when your eyes, blood etc are tested) *All our pilots have regular eye tests.*

> ⚠ Don't say 'make a test'. Say **do a test** or **carry out a test**.

experiment /ɪkˈsperɪmənt/ [*n* C] a scientific test to find out how something is affected when you do something to it
do/carry out/perform an experiment *They are doing experiments to learn more about the effects of alcohol on the brain.*
experiment on sth (=an experiment using something) *experiments on animals*

trial /ˈtraɪəl/ [*n* C] a test in which a new product, such as a drug, a weapon, or an aircraft, is used by a small number of people in order to find out if it is safe and effective
+of *Trials of a new anti-cancer drug have begun.*

9 to do a test on something in order to check it or find out about it

do a test/an experiment /ˌduː ə ˈtest, ən ɪkˈsperɪmənt/ *Today we did an experiment with magnesium.*
+on *Doctors are doing tests on Greg's heart.*

test /test/ [*v* T] to do a test on something to find out whether it works or to get more information about it: *Test your brakes to check they are working correctly.* | *testing nuclear weapons*
test sth on sb/sth *These products have not been tested on animals.*
test sth for sth (=to find out whether it has a substance in it) *The water is being tested for signs of chemical pollution.*

experiment on sth /ɪkˈsperɪment ɒn (sth)‖-ɑːn-/ [*phrasal verb* T] to use something in scientific tests in order to find out how it is affected when you do something to it: *I think it's cruel to experiment on animals.*

THANK YOU

➡ see also EC **THANKING**

1 to say thank you to someone

thank /θæŋk/ [*v* T] to tell someone that you are pleased and grateful for something they have given you or done for you: *I spent three hours helping her and she didn't even thank me.*
thank sb for sth *We must write and thank Cathy for the present.*
thank sb for doing sth *The Governor thanked the people of Arizona for supporting him during his campaign.*

thanks /θæŋks/ [*n* plural] what you say, write, or do to thank someone

letter/message of thanks *He wrote me a short letter of thanks.*
without a word of thanks (=without saying thank you) *She got up and left without a word of thanks.*

thank-you letter/thank-you note etc
/'θæŋk juː(letter etc)/ [*n C*] a letter etc that you send to someone to thank them, for example when they have given you a present or when you have stayed at their house: *We spent three days after the wedding writing thank-you letters for all the presents.*

○ **say thank you** /seɪ 'θæŋk juː/
ESPECIALLY SPOKEN to thank someone for what they have done: *This little gift is our way of saying thank you to everyone who worked so hard.*

2 when you feel that you want to thank someone

grateful /'ɡreɪtfəl/ [*adj*] feeling that you want to thank someone, especially because they have done something for you and helped you a lot: *Dr. Shah has received hundreds of letters from grateful patients.*
grateful to sb for sth *I'm really grateful to you for all your help.*
gratefully [*adv*] *We gratefully accepted her offer.*

> ⚠ Don't confuse **thankful** (=happy because something good has happened or something bad has been prevented) and **grateful** (=wanting to thank someone).

gratitude /'ɡrætᵻtjuːdǁ-tuːd/ [*n U*]
ESPECIALLY WRITTEN when you feel grateful: *I'd just like to express my gratitude for all the help I've received.*

3 when someone does not thank you

ungrateful /ʌn'ɡreɪtfəl/ [*adj*] someone who is **ungrateful** does not thank you when you do something for them, and this makes you annoyed or upset: *Kids aren't usually ungrateful, but they do take what parents do for granted.*

THEATRE/PLAYS

➡ see Word Banks section

THICK

➡ opposite **THIN**
➡ see also **WIDE/NARROW, FAT, LIQUID**

1 thick

thick /θɪk/ [*adj*] if something such as a wall, a book, or a piece of glass is **thick**, there is a large distance between its two flat surfaces: *It's an old house with very thick stone walls.* | *The ground was covered in a thick layer of snow.* | *a thick slice of bread* | *shoes with thick rubber soles*

fat /fæt/ [*adj* only before noun]
fat book/envelope/wallet/briefcase/ cigar a book, envelope etc that is thick because there is a lot in it – use this especially as a humorous way of describing something that looks very thick: *He pulled out a fat wallet stuffed with banknotes.* | *a man smoking a fat cigar* | *a big fat book*

2 how thick something is

how thick /haʊ 'θɪk/ *The price of the glass will depend on how thick it is.* | *How thick is the ice on the lake?*

2 cm thick/1 m thick etc /(2 cm etc) θɪk/ use this to say exactly how thick something is: *Cut the carrots into slices about half an inch thick.* | *In some places, the walls are over two metres thick.*

thickness /'θɪknᵻs/ [*n C/U*] the distance between the opposite surfaces of a solid object or material: *It's about the same thickness as a £1 coin.* | *steel plate in a range of different thicknesses*
+of *Just look at the thickness of those old walls.*

THIN

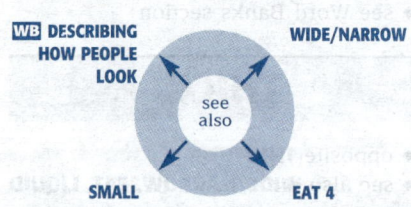

WB DESCRIBING
HOW PEOPLE
LOOK

WIDE/NARROW

see
also

SMALL   EAT 4

1 thin person

➡ opposite **FAT**

thin /θɪn/ [adj] someone who is **thin** has very little fat on their body: *She looked pale, thin, and unhealthy.* | *I wish my legs were thinner.*
thin – thinner – thinnest

slim /slɪm/ [adj] thin in a way that is attractive: *She was tall, slim, and good-looking.* | *You're looking very slim – have you lost weight?*
slim – slimmer – slimmest

skinny /'skɪni/ [adj] very thin, especially in a way that is unattractive: *I was really skinny when I was a teenager.* | *When he wore a T-shirt, you could see how skinny his arms were.*
skinny – skinnier – skinniest

emaciated /ɪ'meɪʃieɪtᵻd‖-sieɪtᵻd/ [adj] FORMAL extremely thin as a result of illness or serious lack of food: *News came of the famine, and there were pictures of emaciated children on the TV.* | *I was shocked when I saw her in the hospital – she looked so emaciated.*

2 thin object, layer etc

➡ opposite **THICK**

thin /θɪn/ [adj] if something is **thin**, there is a very small distance between its two surfaces: *The lake was covered with a thin layer of ice.* | *a box made of thin plastic* | *She was wearing a thin summer dress.*
thin – thinner – thinnest

⚠ Don't use **thin** about roads, rivers, paths etc. Use **narrow**: *a narrow street leading down to the bay*

fine /faɪn/ [adj] very thin – use this about lines, thread, wire etc: *fine lines at the corners of her eyes* | *A fine wire had been stretched across the path.* | *The pencil was sharpened to a fine point.*

3 when someone becomes thinner

lose weight /,luːz 'weɪt/ to become thinner and weigh less: *The best way to lose weight is to do lots of exercise.* | *I'm worried about my grandmother – she's lost a lot of weight recently.*
lose 5 kilos/7 pounds etc *"How's your diet going?" "Pretty well. I've lost 3 pounds this week."*

go on a diet /,ɡəʊ ɒn ə 'daɪət/ to eat less food than usual, or eat special combinations of food because you want to become thinner and weigh less: *We're both going on a diet after Christmas.*
be on a diet *"Would you like some chocolate?" "No thanks, I'm on a diet."*

THING

➡ see also **TOOL, EQUIPMENT**

1 a thing

thing /θɪŋ/ [n C] use this instead of the name of something when you do not need to say its name or when you do not know what it is called. You can use **thing** when you mean a physical object, or something such as an event, an idea, or something that someone says: *What's that thing on the kitchen table?* | *There were several things that I wanted to discuss.* | *A strange thing happened to me yesterday.* | *The first thing I noticed about him was that he seemed very nervous.*

something /'sʌmθɪŋ/ [pronoun] a thing – use this especially when you do not know what the thing is, or you have not decided yet what it will be: *I need to get something for Greg – it's his birthday tomorrow.* | *There was something floating in my coffee.*
something new/different/strange etc *She told me something really funny.* | *He wanted to get her*

something special, something expensive.

something else (=another thing) *I've just remembered something else I wanted to tell you.*

something to eat/wear/read etc *I must have something to eat before I go out.*

or something (=or something similar) *There's a stone or a nail or something stuck in my shoe.*

 Don't spell this as 'some thing'. The correct spelling is **something**.

object /'ɒbdʒɪkt‖'ɑːb-/ [n C] ESPECIALLY WRITTEN a solid thing, especially one that you can touch or hold in your hand: *His foot struck a hard object, and he fell.* | *There were many beautiful objects in the room, but the clock was really special.*

item /'aɪtəm/ [n C] one of several things in a list or group of objects, things for sale, or things to be discussed: *The most expensive item we bought was the washing machine.* | *the next item on the agenda for today's meeting*

an item of clothing/furniture/jewellery (=one piece of clothing, furniture, or jewellery) *Thieves broke into the store and stole several items of clothing.*

Formal or informal?
Item is fairly formal, and is used mostly in business or official contexts.

2   several things of different types

things /θɪŋz/ [n plural] use this when you are talking about two or more things of different types and you do not need to say what they are: *I just threw a few things into a bag and rushed to catch the train.*

my/your/their things SPOKEN (=the things that you own or that you are carrying with you) *Don't forget your things.*

all sorts of things (=a lot of different types of things) *They sell furniture, toys, cards – all sorts of things.*

stuff /stʌf/ [n U] SPOKEN INFORMAL objects or possessions of different types: *I don't know how we're going to get all this stuff into the car.*

my/your/their stuff *Someone broke in and took most of her stuff.*

camping/football/art etc stuff *Do you have all your dancing stuff in the bag?*

junk /dʒʌŋk/ [n U] ESPECIALLY SPOKEN things that are not useful and should be thrown away, for example because they are old or broken: *This cupboard is absolutely full of junk.*

odds and ends /,ɒdz ənd 'endz‖,ɑːdz-/ [n plural] several different things, especially small things that are not of much value: *In the drawer she found a photograph, an old hairbrush, and various other odds and ends.*

Formal or informal?
Odds and ends is fairly informal.

THINK

➡ look here for ...
• use your mind
• have an opinion

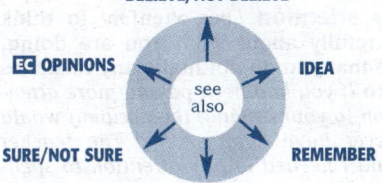

BELIEVE/NOT BELIEVE

OPINIONS   see also   IDEA

SURE/NOT SURE   REMEMBER

IMAGINE

1   to think about something

think /θɪŋk/ [v I] to use your mind in order to solve a problem, remember something, make a decision etc: *"Are you going to accept their offer?" "I'm not sure, I need more time to think."*

+about *She thought about Harry and how kind he'd been.*

think carefully *Think carefully before you answer her letter.*

think hard (=think a lot about something important) *We need to think hard about what we're going to do in the future.*

thinking – thought – have thought

consider /kən'sɪdə^r/ [v T] to think about something carefully before deciding

what to do: *Before buying a car you should consider the cost of insuring it.*
consider doing sth *Have you considered working as a journalist?*

> Don't say 'they're considering to sell their house'. Say **they're considering selling their house.**

Formal or informal?

Consider is slightly formal. In informal conversation, you can use **think about** or **think of**: *I've been thinking about becoming a teacher.*

think over /,θɪŋk ˈəʊvəʳ/ [phrasal verb T]
to think carefully about an idea, suggestion, or offer before deciding what to do
think sth over *I just need a few days to think it over before I reply.*
think over sth *I've been thinking over what you said and you're absolutely right.*

2 to think carefully about what you are doing

pay attention /,peɪ əˈtenʃən/ to think carefully about what you are doing, so that you do not make any mistakes
+to *If you had been paying more attention to your driving, the accident would never have happened.* | *The teacher said I needed to pay attention to spelling.*
concentrate /ˈkɒnsəntreɪt‖ˈkɑːn-/ [v I] to think very carefully about something that you are doing, and not allow yourself to be interrupted or to think about anything else: *Turn that music down, please – I'm trying to concentrate.*
+on *Katie was too upset to concentrate on her book.*
concentration /,kɒnsənˈtreɪʃən‖,kɑːn-/ [n U] the ability to think about something carefully for a long time: *The work requires a lot of concentration, and it's best to be in a room on your own.*
lose concentration *It's easy to lose concentration when driving for long distances.*
keep your mind on sth /,kiːp jɔːʳ ˈmaɪnd ɒn (sth)/ to keep thinking about what you are doing, even though you

want to think about something else: *Ken was worried about his daughter and found it hard to keep his mind on his work.*

3 to have a particular opinion

think /θɪŋk/ [v T]
+(that) *I didn't think that the concert was very good.* | *She thinks I'm crazy to leave this job.* | *We all thought that the new teacher was very nice.*
what do you think of sb/sth? (=what is your opinion about them?) *What do you think of my new hairstyle?*
thinking – thought – have thought

> Don't say 'I am thinking', 'he is thinking' etc. Say **I think, he thinks** etc.

believe /bɪˈliːv/ [v T] to have an opinion that you are sure is right, especially about something important such as life, religion, or politics
+(that) *Some people believe that abortion is wrong.* | *We believe the rich should pay higher taxes.*

> Don't say 'I am believing', 'we are believing' etc. Say **I believe, we believe** etc.

feel /fiːl/ [v T] to have a strong opinion, but one which is based on your feelings rather than on facts
+(that) *Liz's parents feel she isn't old enough to leave home.* | *I just feel that I should have helped him more.*
feeling – felt – have felt

> Don't say 'I am feeling', 'they are feeling' etc. Say **I feel, they feel** etc.

consider /kənˈsɪdəʳ/ [v T] FORMAL to have an opinion about something, especially after thinking about it carefully
+(that) *My client considers that she was unfairly dismissed from her job.*
consider sth important/necessary/unsuitable etc *The doctors considered it too dangerous to operate on him.*
regard/see /rɪˈɡɑːʳd, siː/ [v T] to think that someone or something is a particular kind of person or thing

be regarded/seen as sth *Forty years ago television was regarded as a luxury. | America was seen as the land of opportunity.*

regard/see sb as sth *She seemed to regard me as an enemy. | She sees herself more as an entertainer than a singer.*

seeing – saw – have seen

figure /ˈfɪɡəʳ‖ˈfɪɡjəʳ/ [v T] AMERICAN INFORMAL to form an opinion about something, after thinking about the situation
+(that) *I figured he was too drunk to drive. | Costello figured that he'd better leave before the police arrived. | We figure that they must have got in through the back window.*

 reckon /ˈrekən/ [v T] SPOKEN to have an opinion about something and say what it is: *I think it's quite a good idea – what do you reckon, Pete?*
+(that) *They reckon the French team's better than ours.*

4 to think something is true, but not be sure

think /θɪŋk/ [v T]
+(that) *I think I must have left my wallet at work. | Jim says he thinks there's something wrong with the engine.*
thinking – thought – have thought

> ⚠ Don't say 'I am thinking', 'he is thinking' etc. Say **I think, he thinks** etc.

believe /bɪˈliːv/ [v T] to feel almost sure that something is true, because you have information which makes it seem very likely
+(that) *Scientists now believe that these are the ruins of an ancient temple. | Darwin had believed that humans had evolved from apes and similar animals.*

> ⚠ Don't say 'I am believing', 'he is believing' etc. Say **I believe, he believes** etc.

suspect /səˈspekt/ [v T] to think that something is probably true, especially something bad, although you cannot prove it
+(that) *I suspect she was lying. | She suspected that he had never really loved her.*

> ⚠ Don't say 'I am suspecting', 'he is suspecting' etc. Say **I suspect, he suspects** etc.

have a feeling (that) /ˌhæv ə ˈfiːlɪŋ (ðət)/ to think that something is true, although you do not have a definite reason to think this: *He had a feeling he'd been there before. | I had a feeling that Ruby didn't really want to talk to me.*

get the impression (that) /ˌget ði ɪmˈpreʃən (ðət)/ to start to think that something is true because of what you have noticed about a situation: *I get the impression that it's a very good company to work for. | We got the impression that most of the people at the party were students.*

5 what you say when you think something is true but you are not sure

 I think/I believe /aɪ ˈθɪŋk, aɪ bɪˈliːv/ SPOKEN *Carol lives in Toronto now, I think.*
+(that) *I think that Daniel changed jobs in January. | I believe she's back in Japan now.*
I think so/I believe so (say this to answer 'yes' to a question when you are fairly sure that something is true) *"Has James gone home?" "Yes, I think so."*

 I suppose /aɪ səˈpəʊz/ SPOKEN, ESPECIALLY BRITISH say this when you think that something is probably true but are not really sure: *Having a burglar alarm makes you feel safer, I suppose.*

+**(that)** *I suppose we can pay by credit card but we'd better check first.*
I suppose so (say this to answer a question) *"Will the children be disappointed?" "Yes, I suppose so."*

🔍 **I guess** /aɪ ˈges/ SPOKEN, ESPECIALLY AMERICAN say this when you think that something is probably true or has probably happened: *I never married – I just didn't find the right girl, I guess.*
I guess so/not (say this to agree with something that someone has said) *"Looks like Danny will be leaving home soon." "I guess so."* | *"Ella wasn't happy." "I guess not."*

🔍 **I imagine** /aɪ ɪˈmædʒɪn/ SPOKEN say this when you think that something is probably true, although this is only based on your own opinion about the situation: *You'll want to leave as soon as possible, I imagine.*
+**(that)** *I imagine that she feels very lonely now the kids have left home.*

🔍 **as far as I know** /əz ˌfɑːr əz aɪ ˈnəʊ/ SPOKEN say this when you think that something is true, although you realize that you may not know all the facts: *As far as I know, the research program is going well.*

---

6 **to wrongly think that something is true when it is not true**

think /θɪŋk/ [v T]
+**(that)** *I thought you were at work. What's wrong? Are you sick?* | *She wore a lot of make-up to make them think that she was older.*
thinking – thought – have thought

be under the impression (that) /biː ˌʌndər ði ɪmˈpreʃən (ðət)/ to wrongly believe that something is true, because of something you have heard or seen: *I was under the impression that these could be recycled.* | *I had always been under the impression that all Americans were rich.*

> **Formal or informal?**
> **Be under the impression (that)** is more formal than **think**.

imagine /ɪˈmædʒɪn/ [v T] to have an idea in your mind about something, which is in fact the wrong idea
+**(that)** *Many people imagine that writers have glamorous and exciting lives.*

🔍 **you're/he's imagining it** SPOKEN *"I think she doesn't like me." "No – you're imagining it."*

---

7 **to think something is probably not true**

don't think /ˌdəʊnt ˈθɪŋk/
+**(that)** *I don't think there'll be many people at the party.*

🔍 **I don't think so** SPOKEN (say this to answer 'no' to a question) *"Is there any coffee left?" "No, I don't think so."*

doubt /daʊt/ [v T] to think that something is probably not true or will probably not happen
doubt if/whether *He doubted whether anyone would believe his story.*
+**(that)** *I doubt we'll be going on vacation this year.*

🔍 **I doubt it** SPOKEN *"Do you think Bill will have time to help us?" "I doubt it."*

> ⚠️ Don't say 'I'm doubting it'. Say **I doubt it.**

🔍 **I'd be surprised if** /aɪd biː səˈpraɪzd ɪf/ SPOKEN say this when you think that something is very unlikely to happen or to be true: *I'd be surprised if Ronnie gets the job – he just doesn't have the right experience.*

---

8 **to decide that something is true, although you have no proof**

assume /əˈsjuːm‖əˈsuːm/ [v T] to think that something is true although you have no proof
+**(that)** *I just assumed that the woman standing next to Jack was his wife.* | *I assume you all know what you're supposed to be doing today.*

take it for granted (that) /ˌteɪk ɪt fər ˈɡrɑːntɪd (ðət)‖-ˈɡræn-/ to believe that something is true without ever thinking that it might not be – use this especially when in fact you are wrong: *I'm sorry. I just took it for granted that the tickets were free.* | *Nowadays you take it for granted that everyone has a phone.*

presumably /prɪˈzjuːməbli‖-ˈzuː-/ [adv] use this to say that it is likely that something is true, based on what you know about it: *The film was presumably intended for an American audience.* | *"Where's the money for all these wonderful reforms coming from?" "The tax-payers, presumably."*

Formal or informal?
Presumably is not usually used in informal conversation.

9 to have an idea or thought in your mind

think /θɪŋk/ [v I/T] to have an idea or thought in your mind, especially one that appears suddenly: *I kept thinking, "What if someone saw me come in?"*
+of *I've just thought of a really good idea.* | *Has she thought of any names for the baby?* | *We're trying to think of a good place for a picnic.*
think (that) *I thought that I might go to see a movie tonight.*
thinking – thought – have thought

have an idea /ˌhæv ən aɪˈdɪə/ to think of an idea about something: *Mom, I have an idea. Why don't we make cookies for her?* | *Let me know if you have any good ideas.*

thought /θɔːt/ [n C] something that you think of: *She told him all her most secret thoughts.*
have a thought *I've just had a thought – why don't we ask Judith?*
+about *Have you had any thoughts about what you are going to do after university?*
the thought of doing sth *The thought of spending a weekend with Emma made him feel very excited.*
the thought (that) *He couldn't bear the thought that his wife was lying.*
sb's first thought (=the first thing that someone thinks) *My first thought was that he had been taken away by the police.*

occur to sb /əˈkɜːr tuː (sb)/ [phrasal verb T] if a thought **occurs to you**, you suddenly have that thought: *That thought had never occurred to me.*
it occurs to sb that *It occurred to Charles that he should perhaps have asked the man to wait.*
occurring – occurred – have occurred

cross sb's mind /ˌkrɒs (sb's) ˈmaɪnd‖ˌkrɔːs-/ if a thought **crosses your mind**, you think about it, but only for a short time because you do not want to believe it or think about it: *Leave him? Well, actually that thought has crossed my mind.*
it crossed sb's mind (that) *It crossed her mind that maybe Jo was right.*
it never crossed my mind *"Did you think he was lying?" "No, it never crossed my mind."*

10 to think about something too much

be obsessed /biː əbˈsest/ to keep thinking about something all the time, so that you find it difficult to think about anything else
+with/by *writers who seem obsessed with sex*

obsession /əbˈseʃən/ [n C] a very strong, continuous interest in a particular thing or person, which stops you thinking about anything else: *All they ever talk about is food – it's becoming an obsession.*
+with *the British obsession with class*

can't get sb/sth out of your mind /ˌkɑːnt get (sb/sth) aʊt əv jɔːr ˈmaɪnd‖ˌkænt-/ INFORMAL to be unable to stop thinking about someone or something, even when you do not want to think about them: *He'd only seen the girl once but he couldn't get her out of his mind.*

When you see **WB**, go to the **WORD BANKS** section.

THREATEN

to say you will harm someone if they do not do what you want

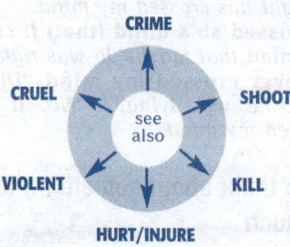

CRIME

CRUEL

see also

SHOOT

VIOLENT

KILL

HURT/INJURE

1 to threaten someone

threaten /'θretn/ [v T] to tell someone that you will hurt them or cause serious problems for them if they do not do what you want
threaten to do sth *When they found out he was an American, the soldiers threatened to kill him.* | *Every time we have a quarrel, she threatens to leave me.*
threaten sb with a knife/a gun etc *After threatening the manager with a knife, he stole £300 and ran off.*
threaten sb with violence/jail/legal action etc (=say you will hurt someone, put them in prison etc) *I was threatened with jail if I published the story.*
threaten sb *Then he started threatening me, saying that my family might get hurt.*

blackmail /'blækmeɪl/ [v T] to force someone to give you money or do what you want, by threatening to tell embarrassing secrets about them: *The information could be used to blackmail her.*
blackmail sb into doing sth *The FBI blackmailed her into informing on the other members of the gang.*

intimidate /ɪn'tɪmɪdeɪt/ [v T] to try to make someone do what you want by behaving in a way that makes them feel afraid: *He's being kept in jail until the trial so that he can't intimidate any of the witnesses.*
intimidate sb into doing sth *Some voters say they were intimidated into supporting the government.*

Formal or informal?
Intimidate is a fairly formal word.

2 words or actions that threaten someone

threat /θret/ [n C] when you tell someone that you will hurt them or cause serious problems for them if they do not do what you want
make threats against sb *Threats have been made against the judge on the case.*
death threat (=when someone threatens to kill you) *She's decided to leave Hollywood because of the death threats.*
carry out a threat (=do what you threatened to do)
receive a threat *Black families in the area have received threats from right-wing extremist groups.*

threatening /'θretnɪŋ/ [adj] **threatening** words or actions are intended to make someone feel afraid, so that they do what you want: *"You listen to me!" His voice was threatening.*
threatening letter/phone call *Before the attack I'd received several threatening phone calls.*

intimidation /ɪn,tɪmɪ'deɪʃən/ [n U] when you try to make someone do what you want by making them feel afraid: *Grugel used intimidation and violence to get money from local restaurant owners.*

Formal or informal?
Intimidation is a fairly formal word.

blackmail /'blækmeɪl/ [n U] when you force someone to give you money or do what you want, by threatening to tell embarrassing secrets about them: *They demanded $10,000 for the photos. I knew it was blackmail, but what could I do?* | *Bates got a 5-year jail sentence for blackmail.*

THROW

➡ if you mean 'throw something away because you do not need it', go to **GET RID OF**

1 to throw something

throw /θrəʊ/ [v T] to make something fly through the air by moving your arm quickly and letting it go

throw sth on/onto/across/down etc *Wallace stood on the beach, throwing stones into the waves.*

throw sth at sb (=when you want to hit them) *She was so angry that she threw the pan straight at my head.*

throw sb sth (=when you want someone to catch something) *"Got a light?" Carrie threw him a box of matches.*

throwing – threw – have thrown

toss /tɒs‖tɔːs/ [v T] to throw something, especially in a careless, relaxed way

toss sth on/into/at etc *Debbie tossed her purse onto the counter.*

toss sb sth *Could you toss me that pack of cigarettes?*

chuck /tʃʌk/ [v T] INFORMAL to throw something, especially in a careless way

chuck sth on/into/at etc *Tom took off his jacket and chucked it on the bed.*

chuck sb sth (=throw something to someone) *Could you chuck me that book?*

hurl /hɜːʳl/ [v T] to throw a heavy object in a violent way, especially because you are angry

hurl

hurl sth at sb (=when you want to hit them) *Some demonstrators began hurling bricks at the police.*

hurl sth into/out of/across etc *He picked up his chair and hurled it across the room.*

flip a coin (also **toss a coin** BRITISH) /ˌflɪp ə ˈkɔɪn, ˌtɒs ə ˈkɔɪn‖ˌtɔːs-/ to throw a coin up into the air and watch which side it falls on, so that you can make a decision about something: *We couldn't decide which movie to go to, so in the end we just flipped a coin.*

flip

2 to throw the ball in a game

➡ see also WB **SPORT**

throw /θrəʊ/ [v T] to throw a ball when you are playing a sport or game: *He threw the ball as hard as he could.*

throw the ball to sb (=so that they can catch it) *Cromartie catches the ball and throws it back to the pitcher.*

throwing – threw – have thrown

pass

pass /pɑːs‖pæs/ [v I/T] to throw the ball to another player in your team, in a game in which the ball is moved by hand

+to *Johnson passes to White, White passes to Eliot, and Eliot scores!*

pass the ball to sb *The quarterback passed the ball to Olson, who ran in for a touchdown.*

pitch

pitch /pɪtʃ/ [v I/T] to throw the ball when you are playing baseball so that someone from the other team can try to hit it with the bat: *Corgan was pitching that night.* | *Moffett pitched eight innings, allowing only 3 hits.*

bowl /bəʊl/ [v I/T] to throw the ball when you are playing cricket so that someone from the other team can try to hit it with the bat
+to *Cork is bowling to Waugh.*

TIDY

neatly arranged, with everything in the right place

➡ opposite **UNTIDY**
➡ see also **CLEAN**

1 tidy place/room

tidy /ˈtaɪdi/ [adj] ESPECIALLY BRITISH a **tidy** place, room, desk etc looks nice because everything is neatly arranged and in the right place: *Andrew's apartment is always so tidy.* | *Try and keep your bedroom a bit tidier.*
clean and tidy *We spent the morning getting the house clean and tidy.*
tidy – tidier – tidiest

tidily [adv] *She put her things away tidily in the closet.*

neat /niːt/ [adj] tidy and carefully arranged, or carefully shaped in a way that is nice to look at, with straight lines and clear edges: *He put his clothes in a neat pile on the bed.* | *Mrs Woodie cut the sandwiches in neat squares.* | *rows of white houses with neat little lawns*
neat and tidy *Be sure to leave everything neat and tidy.*
neat and clean *The apartment was small, but neat and clean.*

neatly [adv] *All the books were neatly arranged on the shelves.*

immaculate /ɪˈmækjɔlɔt/ [adj] extremely clean and tidy: *She keeps the house immaculate.*

> **Formal or informal?**
> **Immaculate** is a formal word, but it is used in spoken English as well as written English.

2 to make a place tidy

tidy /ˈtaɪdi/ [v T] ESPECIALLY BRITISH to make a room, desk, or drawer tidy, especially by putting everything back in its right place and removing things that you no longer need: *Tidy your bedroom and then you can go out.* | *I must tidy my desk before I leave.*
tidying – tidied – have tidied

tidy up /ˌtaɪdi ˈʌp/ [phrasal verb I/T] BRITISH to make a place tidy, by putting everything back in its right place and removing things that you no longer need: *I haven't had time to tidy up yet.*
tidy up sth *We have to tidy up the house before my parents come to visit.*
tidy sth up *The garden looked much better after we'd tidied it up.*

straighten/straighten up /ˈstreɪtn, ˌstreɪtn ˈʌp/ [v T] ESPECIALLY AMERICAN to make a place tidy by putting things in the right place or arranging them neatly: *I spent half an hour straightening the living room.* | *Hogan straightened the pile of papers on his desk.*

clean up /ˌkliːn ˈʌp/ [phrasal verb I/T] ESPECIALLY AMERICAN to make a place tidy and clean, by putting things away and removing dust or dirt: *It took a long time to clean up.*
clean sth up/clean up sth *Sloan said he had to clean up the house before his in-laws arrived.*
clean up after sb (=tidy a place after someone else has made it untidy) *I wish the kids would learn to clean up after themselves.*

clear up /ˌklɪər ˈʌp/ [phrasal verb I/T] BRITISH to get rid of all the things that are making a place dirty or untidy: *Who's going to clear up after the party?*
clear up sth/clear sth up *Clear up the mess you left in the kitchen!*
clear up after sb (=tidy a place after someone else has made it untidy) *I spend my life clearing up after the children.*

pick up /ˌpɪk ˈʌp/ [phrasal verb I/T] AMERICAN to tidy a room by putting everything back in its right place: *Pick up your room before you go to bed.* | *Okay, it's time to pick up.*

pick up after sb (=tidy a place after someone else has made it untidy) *I seem to spend all my time just picking up after you two!*

3 tidy person

tidy /ˈtaɪdi/ [*adj*] ESPECIALLY BRITISH someone who is **tidy** always likes to keep things neat and in their right place: *Neither she nor Nick were particularly tidy at home.* | *a tidy man who hated messy people*
tidy – tidier – tidiest

neat /niːt/ [*adj*] AMERICAN someone who is **neat** always likes to keep things in their right place: *I've never been very neat but my husband is just the opposite.*

immaculate /ɪˈmækjᵘlᵊt/ [*adj*] looking perfectly neat and clean, because you take a lot of care about your clothes, your hair etc: *Emma always looks immaculate.* | *James was wearing an immaculate white shirt.*

> **Formal or informal?**
> **Immaculate** is a formal word.

4 tidy work/writing

neat /niːt/ [*adj*] work or writing that is **neat** has been done very carefully: *Gina has very small neat handwriting.*

TIE/UNTIE

➡ see also **FASTEN/UNFASTEN**

1 to fasten things together, using rope, string etc

tie /taɪ/ [*v* T] to join one thing to another using rope, string, wire etc
tie sth to/around/onto sth *Tie this label onto your suitcase.* | *The washing line was tied to a tree.* | *Saul tied one end of the rope around a large rock and lowered himself over the cliff.*
tie a package/parcel (=keep it closed by putting string or rope around it)
tying – tied – have tied

2 to prevent someone escaping by tying rope around them

tie up /ˌtaɪ ˈʌp/ [*phrasal verb* T] to tie someone's arms and legs with rope so that they cannot move
tie sb up *The soldiers tied them up and beat them.*
be tied up *Mrs Bennett had been tied up and left in the back of a van.*

tie /taɪ/ [*v* T] to prevent someone from escaping by tying them with rope etc
tie sb to sth *The terrorists tied the hostages to their chairs.* | *Her horse was tied to a tree.*
tie sb's hands/feet together *The kidnappers had tied his hands together and blindfolded him.*
tying – tied – have tied

> Don't say 'they tied him'. Say **they tied him up** or **they tied him to the chair**.

3 to remove string or rope from something

undo /ʌnˈduː/ [*v* T] to remove the string or rope from something so that it is no longer held together: *I can't undo the string!* | *She undid the ribbon and let her hair fall over her shoulders.*
undoing – undid – have undone

untie /ʌnˈtaɪ/ [*v* T] to remove or unfasten the string or rope that joins one thing to another: *Someone had untied the boat and it floated away.* | *It was several hours before anyone found me and untied me.*
untying – untied – have untied

TIGHT

➡ opposite **LOOSE**

1 tight clothes

tight /taɪt/ [*adj*] **tight** clothes or shoes are only just big enough for you to wear, and they are often uncomfortable: *This skirt is far too tight.* | *tight shoes*

skintight /ˌskɪnˈtaɪt◂/ [adj] **skintight** clothes are very tight and fit exactly to the shape of your body, especially in a way that looks sexually attractive: *skintight jeans*

2 pulled or stretched tight

tight /taɪt/ [adj] rope, wire, cloth etc that is **tight** has been pulled or stretched as far as possible so that it is straight or it cannot move: *If the straps aren't tight enough, the saddle might slip.* | *Drive forward slowly until the towing rope is tight.*

taut /tɔːt/ [adj] WRITTEN stretched very tight – use this with these words: **rope/string/skin/muscles** *The skin of her face felt dry and taut.* | *Ron crouched, his muscles taut and ready for action.*

3 fastened tight

tight /taɪt/ [adj] a screw, lid, cover etc that is **tight** has been firmly fixed and is difficult to move: *Check that the screws are tight.* | *The lid's really tight. I can't open it.*

firmly /ˈfɜːʳmli/ [adv] if something is **firmly** closed or fixed, it has been closed or fixed so that it cannot move: *Make sure that you put the cork back firmly in the bottle.* | *The posts must be fixed firmly in the ground.*

securely /sɪˈkjʊəʳli/ [adv] ESPECIALLY WRITTEN if something is **securely** fastened or fixed, it has been carefully fastened or fixed so that it will not move or open, in order to prevent accidents: *We made sure that our bags were securely fastened to the roof of the car.*

4 to make something tight

tighten /ˈtaɪtn/ [v T] to make something tight, either by fastening it firmly so that it cannot move, or by pulling it until it is tight

tighten a screw/bolt (=by turning it) *Tighten the screws gradually until the wheel is firmly in place.*

tighten a rope/belt/string etc *You can tighten your seat belt by pulling it at this end.*

pull sth tight /ˌpʊl (sth) ˈtaɪt/ to pull a string, rope etc hard, so that it becomes tight: *Brian wrapped some string around the package and pulled it tight.* | *Pull the laces tight and tie them firmly.*

stretch /stretʃ/ [v T] to pull a piece of rope, cloth, rubber etc so that it becomes tight, making it slightly longer than it normally is: *Stretching the balloon first makes it easier to blow up.*

stretch sth over/between etc *First, stretch the canvas over the frame.*

TIME

→ if you mean 'spend time', go to **SPEND 6**

1 time that can be measured in hours, days etc

time /taɪm/ [n U] what we measure in hours, days, years etc: *How much time do we have for the test?*

spend time (=use your time doing something) *I'd like to spend more time with my family.*

time goes by/passes *The time passed very slowly when I was in prison.* | *As time went by, things started to improve.*

2 a time when something happens

time /taɪm/ [n C] a specific time when something happens or someone does something: *It's my favourite film – I've seen it five times.*

+(that) *It was the only time I saw her lose her temper.*

time when *Do you remember the time when Dad lost the car keys?*

every/each time *Every time I meet her she asks me about the children.*

next/last/this time *Give us a call next time you're in town.* | *Last time I saw him he was driving a Porsche.* | *We'll do the test again, and this time you can use a calculator.*

the first/second/third time *Is this the first time you've played pool?*

occasion /əˈkeɪʒən/ [n C] FORMAL a time
when something happens
on an occasion *Hamilton visited Paris
twice that year, and on both occasions
he stayed at the Ritz.* | *She had met
Zahid on a previous occasion.*

moment/point /ˈməʊmənt, pɔɪnt/ [n C]
an exact time when something happens, during a longer process or
series of events: *The play went well,
apart from one embarrassing moment
when I dropped my cup.* | *At several
points during the meeting, Adler
threatened to walk out.*
at this point/at that moment etc *At
that moment there was a knock on the
door.* | *At this point the surgeon real-
ized that things were going wrong.*

3 what hour of the day something happens

time /taɪm/ [n C/U] the particular
minute or hour of the day when
something happens or someone does
something
+of *a notice giving the dates and times
of the final examinations*
what time *What time did you get up
this morning?*
lunchtime/dinnertime (=the time
when you have a meal)

4 asking what time it is

**ask sb the time/ask sb what time it
is** /ˌɑːsk (sb) ðə ˈtaɪm, ˌɑːsk (sb) wɒt
ˈtaɪm ɪt ɪz‖ˌæsk-/ to ask someone to tell
you the time: *I'd forgotten my watch,
so I had to ask someone the time.* | *Go
and ask Dad what time it is.*

⌕ **what time is it?** (also **what's the
time?** BRITISH) /wɒt ˈtaɪm ɪz ɪt, ˌwɒts ðə
ˈtaɪm/ SPOKEN say this to ask someone
you are with to tell you the time

⌕ **have you got the time?** BRITISH **do
you have the time?** AMERICAN /ˌhæv juː
gɒt ðə ˈtaɪm, ˌduː juː hæv ðə ˈtaɪm‖-gɑːt-/
SPOKEN say this to ask someone the
time, when you do not know whether
they have a watch: *Excuse me, do you
have the time?*

5 telling someone the time

it's five o'clock /ɪts ˌfaɪv əˈklɒk‖-ˈklɑːk/
it's just after five /ɪts ˌdʒʌst ɑːftəʳ
ˈfaɪv‖-æf-/
it's nearly/almost five /ɪts ˌnɪəˈli,
ˌɔːlməʊst ˈfaɪv/
**it's four forty-five/it's a quarter to
five** (also **it's a quarter of five**
AMERICAN) /ɪts ˌfɔːʳ fɔːʳti ˈfaɪv, ɪts ə
ˌkwɔːʳtəʳ tə ˈfaɪv, ɪts ə ˌkwɔːʳtər əv ˈfaɪv/
it's ten past five BRITISH **it's ten after
five** AMERICAN /ɪts ˌten pɑːst ˈfaɪv, ɪts
ˌten ɑːftəʳ ˈfaɪv‖-pæst-, -æf-/
it's five thirty (also **it's half past five**
BRITISH) /ɪts ˌfaɪv ˈθɜːʳti, ɪts ˌhɑːf pɑːst
ˈfaɪv‖-hæf pæst-/

6 how to say when something happened or will happen

at /ət, *strong* æt/ [preposition] use this
with hours and minutes of the day,
special holidays, or the beginning or
end of a period of time
**at six o'clock/half-past four/mid-
night/lunchtime** *He starts work at
10, and finishes at 6:30.*
at Christmas/Easter/New Year *We
get a week's holiday at Easter.*
at the end/the beginning *Frank
joined the navy at the beginning of the
war.*

on /ɒn‖ɑːn, ɔːn/ [preposition] use this
with particular days: *We have a test
on the first day of each month.*
on Monday/Tuesday/Friday etc
We're going out to dinner on Friday.
**on Monday morning/Tuesday eve-
ning etc** *I'm flying back to London on
Monday morning.*
on August 12th/March 2nd etc *She
was born on May 12th, 1913.*
on my birthday/their wedding day
It rained on our wedding day.

in /ɪn/ [preposition] use this with parts
of the day, particular years or
particular months, and seasons of the
year
in the morning/afternoon/evening
*I'm usually too tired to cook a meal in
the evening.* | *I went to bed at 3
o'clock in the morning.*
in 1892/1997 etc *In 1996 the
Olympic Games were held in Atlanta.*

T

in January/February/the autumn etc *I came to England in the summer of 1995.*

> ⚠ Don't use **at**, **on** or **in** before these words when talking about time: **next**, **last**, **that**, **this**. Say **I'm leaving next Wednesday/this afternoon** etc (not 'on next Wednesday' etc), or **she left last January/that morning** etc (not 'in last January' etc).

> ⚠ In American English, you can say **Mondays**, **nights**, **weekends** etc, without a preposition, to mean the same as 'every Monday', 'every night' etc: *Weekends, I stay with my parents.*

ago /ə'gəʊ/ [adv] use this to say how far back in the past something happened
5 minutes/an hour/100 years ago *Michael left the office 20 minutes ago.*
a long/short time ago *I met your father once, a long time ago.*
a minute/a moment ago *I had my keys a minute ago, and now I can't find them.*

in /ɪn/ [preposition] use this to say how much time will pass before something happens
in an hour/in three days etc *Closed for lunch. Back in one hour.* | *In three days we'll be going off to Italy.*
in an hour's time/100 years' time etc (=in the future, an hour from now, a hundred years from now etc) *You'll be feeling much better in a month's time.*

7 within a period of time

during /'djʊərɪŋ‖'dʊə-/ [preposition] at one point in a period of time, or through the whole of a period of time: *Henry died during the night.* | *She has seen many changes during her life.* | *This place was used as an air-raid shelter during the war.* | *Foxes remain hidden during the day.*

> ⚠ Don't confuse **during** and **for**. Don't say 'I studied French during 5 years'. Say **I studied French for 5 years**. Use **for** to say how long something continues.

in /ɪn/ [preposition] between the beginning and end of a period of time:

They painted the whole house in a single day.
in the last few months/in the next ten minutes etc *You should get a reply in the next few weeks.*

within /wɪð'ɪn‖wɪð'ɪn, wɪθ'ɪn/ [preposition] during a period or before the end of a period – use this to emphasize that it is a short or limited period of time: *There have been five serious accidents within the last few days.* | *If we do not hear from you within 14 days, we will contact our solicitors.*

by /baɪ/ [preposition] if something happens **by** a particular time, it happens at some time before that time: *If she's not back by 10 o'clock, I'm calling the police.* | *By Christmas, our money problems had become much worse.*

8 all through a period of time

through /θruː/ [preposition] during the whole of a period of time, continuing until the end: *The party continued through the night until dawn.*

all through/throughout /ɔːl 'θruː, θruː'aʊt/ [preposition] through – use this to emphasize that something continues from the beginning to the end of a long period: *The hotel closes down all through the winter.* | *Throughout her career she has worked very hard.*

all day/all morning/all week etc /ɔːl (day etc)/ through all of the day, the morning, the week etc – use this especially when the day, morning etc has not finished yet: *We've been travelling around all week.* | *I haven't seen Sara all day – where is she?*

all the time/the whole time /,ɔːl ðə 'taɪm, ðə ,həʊl 'taɪm/ through the whole of a period of time – use this especially to talk about something unpleasant or annoying that happens **+(that)** *I was miserable all the time you were away.* | *The whole time we were there he never said thank you, not once!*

9 between two times

between /bɪ'twiːn/ [preposition] in the time between two times or events:

This house was built sometime between 1930 and 1935. | *We usually go and see Jan's parents between Christmas and the New Year.*

meanwhile/in the meantime /'miːnwaɪl, ɪn ðə 'miːntaɪm/ [adv] during the time between now and a future event, or between two events in the past: *The doctor will be here soon. In the meantime, try to relax.* | *The plane will be ready soon. Meanwhile, please wait in the departure lounge.*

---

10 | how long something continues, someone waits etc

how long /haʊ 'lɒŋ‖-'lɔːŋ/ use this to ask about or talk about how many minutes, hours, days, or years something continues for: *How long have you lived here?* | *I didn't know how long the operation would take.*

for /fər, strong fɔːʳ/ [preposition] use this to say how long something continues **for an hour/two days/a long time etc** *It rained continuously for three days.* | *We talked for a while.* | *Eggs should stay fresh for a week or two.*

> ⚠ You can leave out **for** after the verbs 'stay', 'wait', and 'last': *I waited a long time.* | *He stayed nearly three months.*

until (also **till** ESPECIALLY SPOKEN) /ʌn'tɪl, ən-, tɪl/ [preposition/conjunction] if something happens **until** or **till** a time or event, it continues and then stops at that time or event: *David worked as a teacher until 1989.* | *I'll be at home until 5:30 if you want to phone me.* | *She polished the car until it shone.* | *I didn't learn to drive until I was 31.* | *The library's only open till five on Saturdays.* | *Just wait till I've finished my coffee.*

from ... until ... /frəm ... ʌn'tɪl .../ use this to say that something starts happening at one time and continues until another time: *We worked from nine in the morning until late at night.* | *Max edited the paper from 1950 until he retired in 1989.*

from ... to ... /frəm ... tuː .../ use this to say that something starts at a particular time and stops at a later time

from May to September/from 9am to 5pm etc *The hotel is open from March to October.* | *Eisenhower was President from 1952 to 1956.*

through /θruː/ [preposition] **May through September/Monday through Friday etc** AMERICAN starting in May and continuing until September, starting on Monday and continuing until and including Friday, etc: *The store is open Monday through Saturday.*

Monday-Friday/6:00–8:00 WRITTEN starting on Monday and continuing until and including Friday, starting at 6 o'clock and continuing until 8 o'clock etc – used to give information, for example on notices: *The modern art exhibition is open every day, 9:30–6:00.* | *A special fishing licence is required for the season (May-September).*

---

11 | how long something has been happening

> ⚠ Don't confuse **for** and **since**. Use **for** with periods of time: *I've been waiting here for 25 minutes.* | *We've lived here for six years.* Use **since** with the date, time, year etc when something started: *I've been waiting here since 7 o'clock.* | *I've lived here since 1991/since my husband died.*

for /fər, strong fɔːʳ/ [preposition] during the whole of a period of time until now: *Omar's been learning English for two years now.* | *I haven't phoned my mother for over a week.*

since /sɪns/ [preposition/conjunction/adv] all the time from a time or event in the past until now: *I've had this car since 1992.* | *Graham's become a lot more confident since he finished his training.* | *I saw her this morning, but I haven't seen her since.*

since then *He arrived in Hollywood back in 1952. Since then he's appeared in over 100 movies.*

ever since (=since a time or event a long time ago) *I read that poem when I was at school, and I've remembered it ever since.* | *She's been interested in animals ever since she was a little girl.*

> ⚠ Don't say 'I lived here since 1985' or 'I live here since 1985'. Say **I've lived here since 1985**. Always use a verb in the perfect tense with **since**.

12 to happen over a period of time

last /lɑːst‖læst/ [v I] to continue happening for a period of time: *No-one knows how long the war will last.*
+for/until *The hot weather lasted for almost six weeks.* | *The trial is expected to last until Christmas.*
last 2 hours/all day/a long time etc *Each lesson lasts an hour.* | *a storm that lasted all night*
not last long *Tanya's bad mood didn't last long.*

take /teɪk/ [v T] if something **takes** two minutes, six months etc, that is the time needed to do it
take 2 hours/6 months etc *The drive takes three hours.*
it takes (sb) 2 hours/6 months etc to do sth *It often takes several months to get a visa.* | *It only took us half an hour to get here.* | *How long did it take to finish?*
taking – took – have taken

13 a period of time

period /'pɪəriəd/ [n C] ESPECIALLY WRITTEN a particular length of time with a beginning and an end: *You shouldn't sit in front of a computer screen for long periods without a break.*
period of time *The work had to be completed within a limited period of time.*
a ten-day/three-year etc period *The money can be paid back over a five-year period.*
a period of 3 weeks/2 years etc *The project will last for a period of 2 years.*

time /taɪm/ [n singular] a period of time – use this especially to talk about a period in the past, or when you are not saying whether the period was long or short: *Bill had lost his job, and it was a difficult time for him.* | *I really enjoyed my time at university.*
during that/this time *He played for Barcelona for four years, and during that time they won two major competitions.*

for a time *He chatted to us for a time, then left.*
after a time *After a time, I began to feel more relaxed.*

a while /ə 'waɪl/ a period of time – use this when you do not want to say definitely how long the period is: *You'll have to wait a while. We're very busy.*
for a while *He lived in Japan for a while.*
a little while *I spoke to Ken a little while ago and he seemed fine then.*
a long while *For a long while, she sat and stared out of the window.*

some time /ˌsʌm 'taɪm/ a period of time, especially a fairly long period: *Roach had been suffering from cancer for some time.* | *Some time later, we all met again.* | *Of course, all this happened some time ago.*

14 a long time

a long time /ə ˌlɒŋ 'taɪm‖-ˌlɔːŋ-/ *They've been married for 30 years – that's a long time.* | *The house has been empty for a long time.* | *The accident happened such a long time ago that I can't remember much about it.*
a very long time *It's well built and should last for a very long time.*

○ **ages** /'eɪdʒɪz/ [n plural] SPOKEN, ESPECIALLY BRITISH a very long time: *I've been standing here for ages.* | *It's ages since we saw Mark.* | *It takes ages to get to Glasgow by bus.*

hours/weeks/years /'aʊəˈz, wiːks, jɪəˈz/ many hours, weeks, or years and much longer than you think it should be: *My wife had to wait for hours at the hospital.* | *It'll take them years to repair all the damage.*

15 a short time

a minute/a moment /ə 'mɪnɪt, ə 'məʊmənt/ [n singular] a very short time: *Helen was here a minute ago. You've just missed her.* | *Can I show you something? It'll only take a minute.* | *Luke thought for a moment and then said: "Would you like to come too?"*

a second (also **a sec** SPOKEN INFORMAL) /ə 'sekənd, ə 'sek/ a very short time – use this especially when asking someone to wait for a short time: *Just a second – I think it's on the desk upstairs.*

not long /nɒt 'lɒŋ‖-'lɔːŋ/ a short time: *"How long will it take?" "Oh, not long – just a couple of hours."* | *His book was published not long after he died.*

🔍 **a bit** /ə 'bɪt/ [n singular] BRITISH SPOKEN a short time: *Wait a bit, I've nearly finished.* | *Do you mind looking after the kids for a bit while I go out?*

16 at the same time as something else

at the same time /ət ðə ˌseɪm 'taɪm/ *Charlie and I arrived at the same time.*
+as *I arrived at the same time as Charlie.* | *You must have been at Harvard at the same time as I was.*

at once /ət 'wʌns/ if two or more things happen **at once**, they happen at the same time, and this is annoying or it causes problems: *I can't understand what you're saying when you both talk at once.* | *The problem with my job is that I have to do several things at once.*

as /əz, strong æz/ [conjunction] ESPECIALLY WRITTEN if something happens **as** something else is happening, it happens at the same time: *As I walked towards the desk, he closed his book and stood up.*
just as (=at exactly the same time) *Just as I was getting into the shower, the phone rang.*

simultaneously /ˌsɪməl'teɪniəsli‖ˌsaɪ-/ [adv] if two or more things happen **simultaneously**, they happen at exactly the same time: *The two men fired their pistols simultaneously.* | *The system can simultaneously search up to 16 databases.*
simultaneous [adj] happening at exactly the same time: *Police carried out simultaneous drug raids on several houses in the area.*

> **Formal or informal?**
> **Simultaneously** is more formal than **at the same time**.

17 while something else is happening

while /waɪl/ [conjunction] during the same period of time that something is happening: *I bought a magazine while I was waiting for the train.* | *I'll just make a phone call while you finish the dishes.*

meanwhile /'miːnwaɪl/ [adv] while something else is happening: *Bill was upstairs, talking on the phone. Meanwhile, a burglar had broken in downstairs.*

18 not too late

on time /ɒn 'taɪm/ if you do something **on time**, you do it at the arranged time, not too late: *I'm never going to finish this work on time!*
be on time *The meeting starts at 10 a.m – try to be on time.*
right on time (=exactly at the correct time) *The train arrived right on time.*

in time /ɪn 'taɪm/ before it is too late: *If I get home in time, I'll take you swimming.*
just in time (=almost not in time) *You're just in time, Jill. We were about to leave without you.*
+for *You've arrived just in time for the start of the game.*
in time to do sth *Luckily, we still got to the airport in time to catch the plane.*

punctual /'pʌŋktʃuəl/ [adj] FORMAL someone who is **punctual** arrives at the time that was arranged, and does not come late: *It's very important to be punctual for appointments.*
punctually [adv] *The guests arrived punctually at 8 o'clock.*

19 the right or wrong time to do something

the right time /ðə ˌraɪt 'taɪm/ the best time to do something, when you are most likely to get the result that you want
the right time to do sth *It seemed like the right time to start something new.* | *I don't think it's the right time to tell Jeff .*
come at the right time (=happen at a

time when you need it) *I lost my job last month, so this offer has come at just the right time.*

the wrong time /ðə ˌrɒŋ 'taɪm‖-ˌrɔːŋ-/ a time when you should not do something, because you will probably not be successful

the wrong time to do sth *I think this is probably the wrong time to ask for a pay increase.*

come at the wrong time (=happen at a time that is likely to cause problems) *These economic problems have come at the wrong time for the Republican Party.*

a good time /ə ˌɡʊd 'taɪm/ a suitable or convenient time: *I'd like to come on Saturday – would that be a good time?*

a good time to do sth *Now is a good time to start applying for jobs. | When would be a good time to have a meeting?*

a bad time /ə ˌbæd 'taɪm/ an unsuitable or inconvenient time when there are a lot of other problems: *She called at a really bad time – the kids were screaming.*

a bad time to do sth *It's a bad time to be trying to sell your house.*

20 the time when something is planned to happen

time /taɪm/ [n C] the time when something is planned to happen

the time of sth *The letter doesn't give the time of the meeting. | This leaflet lists the dates and times of all the concerts.*

opening/closing/arrival time *The plane's estimated arrival time is 19:45.*

date /deɪt/ [n C] the day when something is planned to happen: *We need to arrange a date for the next meeting. | What date is the wedding?*

+of *June 9th is the date of the European elections.*

timetable BRITISH **schedule** AMERICAN /'taɪm ˌteɪbəl, 'ʃedjuːl‖'skedʒuːl, -dʒəl/ [n C] a list that shows the times when something will happen, for example when planes or buses leave, or when classes at school take place: *Teachers will be giving out copies of the new timetable in the first class today. | The schedule's on the bulletin board.*

+of *I want a schedule of flights from Boston to New York.*

timetable /'taɪm,teɪbəl/ [n C] a plan that shows when parts of an important and long process, especially a political one, will happen

+for *The minister announced a timetable for the discussions.*

schedule /'ʃedjuːl‖'skedʒʊl, -dʒəl/ [n C] a detailed plan of activities that have been organized, showing for example the times when someone will do something, or the times when activities will start and finish: *The President's schedule includes a two-day visit to St. Petersburg.*

+for *Do you have a schedule for the tour?*

ahead of/behind schedule (=earlier or later than was planned) *The work is already behind schedule.*

21 when you have enough time

have time /ˌhæv 'taɪm/ to have enough time to do something: *Could you go and see Jean if you have time?*

have time to do sth *We're so busy at work that I hardly have time to eat.*

+for *Do you have time for a drink?*

there is time /ðeər ɪz 'taɪm/ use this to say that there is enough time available to do something or to go somewhere: *I thought we could go to the museum, and maybe an art gallery too if there's time.*

there is time for sth/time to do sth *If we leave now, there should be time for a little shopping.*

find time/make time /ˌfaɪnd 'taɪm, ˌmeɪk 'taɪm/ to arrange your plans so that you have enough time to do something, because you think it is important

+for *I'm really busy but I try to make time for my family.*

find/make time to do sth *a nurse who always finds time to talk to her patients*

22 when you do not have enough time

not have time/have no time /nɒt hæv 'taɪm, hæv ˌnəʊ 'taɪm/ to not have enough time to do something: *I can't talk now – I don't have time.*
+to do sth *She had to leave immediately – she had no time to explain why.*
+for *She doesn't have much time for reading.*

there is no time /ðeər ɪz ˌnəʊ 'taɪm/ use this to say that there is not enough time available to do something: *We can't stop to fix it now – there's no time.*
there is no time to do sth *There was no time to say goodbye to everyone.*

run out of time /ˌrʌn aʊt əv 'taɪm/ if you **run out of time**, the time that is available ends before you have finished doing something: *I ran out of time before I finished the test.*

TIRED

➡ see also **SLEEP, BORING/BORED, WAKE UP/GET UP**

> ⚠ Don't confuse **tired** (=when you feel that you must rest) and **tiring** (=when something makes you feel tired): *I'm really tired.* | *What a tiring day!*

1 tired after exercise or work

tired /taɪəʳd/ [adj] if you are **tired**, you feel that you want to rest because you have done a lot of work, walked or travelled a long way etc: *I usually feel too tired to cook dinner after work.* | *the tired faces of the children*
get tired (=start to feel tired) *Can we stop soon? I'm getting really tired.*
tired out (=very tired) *We were tired out after a long day's skiing.*

exhausted /ɪgˈzɔːstɪd/ [adj] very tired, especially because you have been doing a sport or other hard physical activity, and you have used all your energy: *By the end of the race the runners all looked exhausted.*

completely/absolutely exhausted *We had been walking for over 20 miles, and we were completely exhausted.*

worn out /ˌwɔːʳn 'aʊt/ [adj not before noun] so tired that you cannot do anything more, especially because you have been working hard: *Come in and sit down. You look worn out.* | *She had spent the whole morning cleaning, washing, and ironing, and now she was completely worn out.*

> ⚠ Don't say 'very worn out'. Say **completely worn out**.

 knackered BRITISH **beat** AMERICAN /ˈnækəʳd, biːt/ [adj not before noun] SPOKEN INFORMAL very tired: *I've been up since four o'clock this morning – I'm absolutely knackered!* | *You look beat – what have you been doing?*

> **Formal or informal?**
> **Knackered** is very informal. Only use it when you are talking to friends, especially young people.

2 wanting to sleep

tired /taɪəʳd/ [adj] if you are **tired**, you feel that you want to sleep: *The kids were really tired, so we sent them to bed.* | *I was going to watch the late-night movie, but I was just too tired.*

sleepy /ˈsliːpi/ [adj] if you are **sleepy**, you want to sleep immediately and your eyes are starting to close: *It was 11.30, and I was starting to feel sleepy.* | *We arrived at the hotel late at night, and were too sleepy to notice how beautiful it was.*
sleepily [adv] *"What time is it?" she said sleepily.*

drowsy /ˈdraʊzi/ [adj] ESPECIALLY WRITTEN starting to sleep because you are in a warm place or because you have drunk alcohol or taken medicine: *The wine had made her drowsy.* | *Drivers who are drowsy cause many accidents.*

yawn /jɔːn/ [v I] to open your mouth very wide and breathe in very deeply through your mouth because you are tired: *I couldn't stop yawning, I was so tired.* | *Vanessa yawned. "I'm going to bed. Night!"*
yawn [n C] the movement and sound

you make when you yawn: *There was a big yawn from someone in the back row.*

3 making you feel tired

tiring /'taɪərɪŋ/ [adj] something that is **tiring** makes you feel tired: *The journey was really tiring.*
a tiring day/week *I've had such a tiring day. I just want to take a bath and go to bed.*

exhausting /ɪg'zɔːstɪŋ/ [adj] something that is **exhausting** makes you feel very weak and very tired: *I had to drive for nine hours without a break. It was exhausting.* | *The band has just finished an exhausting world tour.*

hard /hɑːʳd/ [adj] a **hard** day, journey etc is one that makes you feel very tired because you have to work very hard, travel a long distance, or deal with a lot of problems: *I've had a really hard day at the office.* | *It was a long hard walk back to the nearest town.* | *Looking after babies is hard work.*

strenuous /'strenjuəs/ [adj] **strenuous** activity, work, or exercise needs a lot of physical effort: *My doctor says I mustn't do any strenuous exercise until I'm fully recovered.*

4 the feeling of being tired

> **Formal or informal?**
> All these words are used mostly in formal written English.

exhaustion /ɪg'zɔːstʃən/ [n U] the feeling of being extremely tired and weak because you have used all your energy: *After two days marching the troops were close to exhaustion.*
from/with exhaustion (=because of exhaustion) *One of the players collapsed with exhaustion, and had to be carried off the field.*

tiredness /'taɪəʳdnɪs/ [n U] the feeling of being tired: *Tiredness and headaches are common signs of stress.*

drowsiness /'draʊzinɪs/ [n U] the feeling of wanting to sleep that you sometimes get when you are in a warm place or when you have drunk

alcohol or taken medicine: *The drug can cause drowsiness.*

TOGETHER

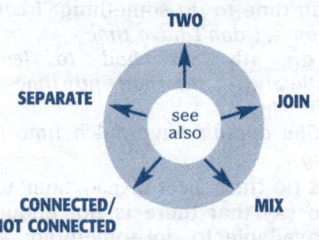

1 together in the same place

together /tə'geðəʳ/ [adv] *The whole family spent Christmas together.* | *Nicola and I were at school together.* | *I keep all my school books together in my desk.*

> Don't say 'I live together with my parents'. Say **I live with my parents**.

live side by side /lɪv ˌsaɪd baɪ 'saɪd/ if two different groups of people **live side by side**, they live together peacefully and do not fight with each other: *German and Polish peasants had lived side by side there for generations.*

2 doing things together

together /tə'geðəʳ/ [adv] when two or more people do something with each other: *"Did you build that wall yourself?" "My brother and I did it together."* | *We're thinking of going on vacation together.* | *The police and the army worked together to track down the terrorists.*

> Don't say 'I play golf together with Marie'. Say **Marie and I play golf together**.

side by side /ˌsaɪd baɪ 'saɪd/ if two different groups of people fight or work **side by side**, they fight or work together to achieve something, even though there may be big differences between them: *Communists and Nationalists fought side by side.* | *Feminists and religious groups found themselves working side by side to oppose pornography.*

in partnership with /ɪn ˈpɑːʳtnəʳʃɪp wɪð/ if people, organizations, or countries work **in partnership with** each other, they work together to do something important or useful: *The city council is working in partnership with local businesses to build new sports facilities in the area.*

> **Formal or informal?**
> **In partnership with** is used in writing and in formal spoken English.

3 things done by people working together

joint /dʒɔɪnt/ [*adj* only before noun] a **joint** decision, statement, effort, report etc is made by people or groups working together, not by just one of them: *We both wanted to move to Canada – it was a joint decision.* | *a joint declaration by Israeli and Palestinian leaders*

combined /kəmˈbaɪnd/ [*adj* only before noun] **combined** actions are done by people or groups who try to do something together which they could not do alone: *It took the combined efforts of four police officers and two paramedics to lift the driver from the wreckage.* | *a combined operation involving troops from the US and Europe*

collective /kəˈlektɪv/ [*adj* only before noun] a **collective** decision, action, or agreement is made by everyone in a group or organization, not by just one or two of its members: *The US wanted the United Nations to take collective action against Iraq.*
collective responsibility (=when everyone in a group shares responsibility for its decisions)

4 when two things are used together, or added together

together /təˈgeðəʳ/ [*adv*] *Mix the butter and the sugar together.* | *That skirt and jacket look really good together.* |

Together, these two paintings are worth more than £10,000.

combined /kəmˈbaɪnd/ [*adj* only before noun] a **combined** amount includes two or more amounts added together; the **combined** effect of two or more things is the effect that they have together: *The combined value of the investments is $5 billion.* | *Her two latest records have sold a combined total of 14 million copies.* | *He was suffering from the combined effects of heat and exhaustion.*

TOOL

a piece of equipment you use for repairing, cutting, or making things

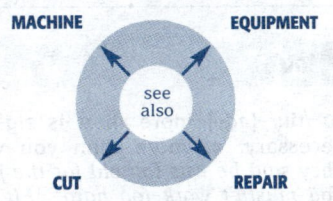

tool /tuːl/ [*n* C] a thing that you hold in your hand and use to repair, cut, or make something: *He couldn't finish repairing the engine because he didn't have the right tools.* | *I keep all my tools in the garage.* | *gardening tools*
+**for** *a tool for cutting metal*
tool kit (=a set of tools that are kept together)
tool box (=a strong box that tools are kept in)

instrument /ˈɪnstrᵿmənt/ [*n* C] a small tool used especially by doctors and scientists, for doing careful or delicate work: *I sat in the dentist's chair and looked at the row of instruments beside me.* | *the scientific instruments aboard the space shuttle*

gadget /ˈgædʒᵻt/ [*n* C] a small tool that has been designed to help you do something more easily: *a clever little gadget that lets you chop vegetables into attractive shapes* | *electronic gadgets, such as a watch that you can use as a phone*

device /dɪˈvaɪs/ [*n* C] a piece of equipment that has been designed to do a particular job, for example one that makes measurements, records sounds or movements, or controls the operation of a machine: *An EEG is a device that records electrical activity in the brain.*

+for *a thermostatic device for controlling temperature* | *The farmers there still use the 'Archimedes screw', an ancient device for raising water from a lake or well.*

TOO/TOO MUCH

⚠️ Don't confuse **too** (=more than is right, necessary, or good) and **very**. Don't say 'it's too interesting'. Say **it's very interesting** or **it's really interesting**.

1 too

too /tuː/ [*adv*] more than is right or necessary, or more than you want: *They said he was too old for the job.* | *You mustn't work too hard.* | *It's too hot in here.*

too big/small/tired etc to do sth *The car was too wide to get through the gate.* | *She's still too upset to talk about it.*

far too small/much too big etc *$200! That's far too expensive.* | *He was driving much too fast.*

too old/quick/big etc for *My room's too narrow for a king-size bed.*

⚠️ Don't say 'it's a too big house'. Say **the house is too big**. Don't use **too big, too fast, too difficult** etc before a noun.

⚠️ Don't say 'he was too much old'. Say **he was too old** or **much too old**.

2 too much or too many

too much /ˌtuː ˈmʌtʃ◂/ [*quantifier*] use this about amounts or costs: *I drank too much last night.* | *You spend too much time worrying about things.*

far too much *$200 for a room? That's far too much.*

way too much INFORMAL *I put way too much salt in the soup.*

+for *There was too much baggage for one person to carry.*

⚠️ Use **too much** before uncountable nouns, and **too many** before countable nouns. Don't say 'there are too much cars'. Say **there are too many cars**.

too many /ˌtuː ˈmeni◂/ [*quantifier*] use this about numbers of people or things: *The town doesn't need another hotel. It already has too many.* | *She can't come – she says she has too many things to do.*

far too many *Far too many people are unemployed.*

+for *There were too many bags for one person to carry.*

excessive /ɪkˈsesɪv/ [*adj*] FORMAL use this about an amount, cost, or level which is much too high, especially when you think it is wrong or unfair that it is so high: *the excessive use of chemicals in farming* | *$15 for two cups of coffee seems excessive.*

3 to do something too much

too much /ˌtuː ˈmʌtʃ/ [*adv*] if you do something **too much**, you do it more than you should: *You worry too much.* | *That kid talks too much.*

try/think/push etc too hard /(try etc) tuː ˈhɑːʳd/ to do something with too much effort, especially so that you do not get the result you want: *Don't try too hard to impress people. Just be yourself.* | *You're hitting the ball too hard.* | *I think you've been working too hard – you need a rest.*

○ **overdo it** /ˌəʊvəʳˈduː ɪt/ ESPECIALLY SPOKEN to do something too much, especially to do too much work or exercise: *You need to take more exercise, but don't overdo it.* | *The* *doctors said he's been overdoing it and needs to rest more.*

overdoing – **overdid** – **have overdone**

overreact /ˌəʊvəriˈækt/ [v I] to get too angry or too worried when something happens which is not in fact very serious: *Don't you think you're over-reacting a little? I'm only ten minutes late.*

+to *People have overreacted to the advertisement – we didn't intend to offend anyone.*

---

4 | to say something is much bigger, worse etc than it really is

exaggerate /ɪɡˈzædʒəreɪt/ [v I/T] to say that something is much bigger, better, worse, more important etc than it really is: *"He said you walked 30 miles." "Oh, no! He's exaggerating."* | *Newspapers tend to exaggerate their influence on the way people vote.*

exaggeration /ɪɡˌzædʒəˈreɪʃən/ [n C/U] when someone says that something is bigger, better, worse, more important etc than it really is: *The report says it will take thirty years to make the changes, but I think that's an exaggeration.*

it is an exaggeration to say/suggest etc sth *It would be an exaggeration to say that we never disagreed, but we certainly worked well together.*

---

5 | not too much

not too much /nɒt tuː ˈmʌtʃ/ *Not too much pizza for me please, I'm on a diet.*

not eat/drink/talk etc too much *Don't talk too much now – you need to rest.*

moderate /ˈmɒdərɪt‖ˈmɑː-/ [adj] FORMAL not too much – use this about eating, drinking, and other things that could be unhealthy if you did them too much: *Moderate exercise, such as walking and swimming, can help to prevent heart disease.* | *Some doctors*

believe that moderate drinking is good for you.

in moderation /ɪn ˌmɒdəˈreɪʃən‖-ˌmɑː-/ FORMAL if you eat or drink something **in moderation**, you do not eat or drink too much of it: *In moderation, fatty foods are not bad for you.* | *He only drinks in moderation.*

TOTAL

the number or amount that there is when everything has been counted

➡ see also **COUNT/CALCULATE NUMBER**

T

---

1 | a total

total /ˈtəʊtl/ [n C] the number or amount that there is, when everything has been counted or added together: *If you add 30 and 45, the total is 75.*

a total of *The three defendants were jailed for a total of 30 years.* | *A total of $950 million was spent on the new transportation system.*

in total *In total, these small businesses employ 71 million people.*

grand total (=a total, used especially to be humorous when the number is small) *The town has a grand total of 27 residents.*

total /ˈtəʊtl/ [adj only before noun] the **total** number or amount is the number that there is when everything has been counted. You can use **total** with these words: **number, amount, cost, value, income, earnings, population, workforce**: *The total cost was far higher than we had expected.* | *People of Chinese origin made up about 10% of the total population.*

altogether/in all /ˌɔːltəˈɡeðəʳ‹, ɪn ˈɔːl/ [adv] use this when saying or asking what the total amount is, including everything that could be included: *If you include the crew, there were 40 of us in all.* | *How much do I owe you altogether?*

2 when several numbers produce another number as a total

come to sth /ˈkʌm tu: (sth)/ [phrasal verb T] if the price of something **comes to** £50, $100 etc, this is the total amount when everything is counted: *Including wine, the bill came to $70.* | *How much does it all come to?*

reach /ri:tʃ/ [v T] if a total **reaches** 10, 50, 100 etc, it has increased until it is equal to that number: *The famine appeal has reached £45,000.* | *The city's population is expected to reach 12 million by the year 2010.*

make /meɪk/ [v T not in passive] if numbers added together **make** 10, 50, 100 etc, that is the answer or the total: *Two plus two makes four.* | *If Jane comes, that makes six of us.* | *There are also eight submarines, making a total fleet of 34 ships.*
making – made – have made

add up to sth /ˌæd ˈʌp tu: (sth)/ [phrasal verb T] if a set of several numbers **adds up to** 10, 50 etc, that is the total when you add them all together: *The numbers in each line add up to nine.* | *With the hotel, the flights, and the food, it all added up to much more than I had expected.*

TOUCH

1 to put your hand on someone or something

touch /tʌtʃ/ [v T] to put your fingers or hand onto someone or something: *Don't touch the plates – they're hot!* | *My knee still hurts if I touch it.* | *Someone's hand touched her arm.*

feel /fi:l/ [v T] to touch something in order to find out how hard, soft, hot, cold etc it is: *Just feel this material – it's so soft!* | *The nurse felt his forehead to see if he had a fever.*
feeling – felt – have felt

run your hand over/along/across/ through etc /ˌrʌn jɔːʳ ˈhænd (over, etc)/ WRITTEN to move your hand gently across the surface of something, for example to feel what it is like: *She ran*

her hand over the glossy cover of the magazines. | *Mr Roberts ran his hand across his bald head and smiled nervously.*

rub /rʌb/ [v T] to move your hands or fingers quickly backwards and forwards over a part of the body, while pressing down, especially in order to make a pain less severe: *Colin yawned and rubbed his eyes.* | *Her husband was rubbing her shoulders, which were stiff.*
rubbing – rubbed – have rubbed

scratch /skrætʃ/ [v I/T] to rub your skin with your nails, for example because it feels painful or uncomfortable: *Don't scratch. It'll make the itching worse.* | *He sat scratching his head, trying to think of the answer.* | *She was scratching her arm where the mosquito had bitten her.*

fiddle with sth/play with sth /ˈfɪdl wɪð (sth), ˈpleɪ wɪð (sth)/ [phrasal verb T] to hold something small in your hands and keep moving it around, especially because you are nervous or bored: *She fiddled nervously with her watch strap.*

2 to touch someone in a gentle or loving way

stroke /strəʊk/ [v T] to move your hand or fingers over part of someone's body in a gentle, loving way: *Tim sat beside her and began stroking her arm.* | *Every time you try to stroke the cat it bites your hand.*

stroke

pat /pæt/ [v T] to touch someone lightly several times with the flat part of your hand, in order to comfort them or to show them that you are pleased: *"Don't worry," he said, patting her hand gently.*
pat sb on the shoulder/arm/head *She bent down and patted the dog on the head.*
patting – patted – have patted

pat

pet /pet/ [v T] to touch and move your hand gently over an animal's fur: *Our cat loves being petted.*
petting – petted – have petted

tickle /'tɪkəl/ [v T] to move your fingers quickly and gently over a sensitive part of someone's body in order to make them laugh: *Stop tickling my feet!*

caress /kə'res/ [v T] WRITTEN to move your hand or fingers gently over part of someone's body in a loving, or sexual way: *Barbara lovingly caressed the baby's cheek.* | *He put his arms around her and began caressing her.*

3   when one thing touches another

touch /tʌtʃ/ [v I/T] if one thing **touches** another thing, it hits the other thing gently; if two things **are touching**, there is no space between them: *It's possible that part of the crane touched the electricity cable.* | *My head almost touched the ceiling.*
be touching *Max and Kate sat side by side, their shoulders touching.*

lean against sth /'liːn əgenst (sth)/ [phrasal verb T] if something **leans against** a wall, a fence etc, it touches the wall, fence etc and is supported by it: *There was an old bicycle leaning against the side of the shed.*

4   what something feels like when you touch it

feel /fiːl/ [v] if something **feels** cold, hot, smooth, rough etc, this is the feeling it gives you when you touch it: *When I touched his hands they felt really cold.*
feel like sth *The material feels like cotton but it's actually synthetic.*
feeling – felt – have felt

texture /'tekstʃəʳ/ [n C/U] the way a surface, material, or substance feels when you touch it, especially how rough or smooth it feels: *The wood had a lovely smooth texture.*
in texture (=in the way something feels) *The skin of the fruit is rather coarse in texture.*

> **Formal or informal?**
> **Texture** is a fairly formal word.

feel /fiːl/ [n singular] the way something feels when you touch it, especially something that feels pleasant
+of *I like the feel of soft wool against my skin.*

TOWN

➡ see also **COUNTRYSIDE, AREA,** WB **HOUSES/WHERE PEOPLE LIVE**

1   a place with houses, streets, and shops

town /taʊn/ [n C] a place with houses, streets, shops etc, which is bigger than a village and smaller than a city: *a small town in the Midwest* | *I live in a town near Paris called St Germaine-en-Laye.*
+of WRITTEN *the town of Hebron in Israel's West Bank*

city /'sɪti/ [n C] a big and important town: *You should visit San Francisco. It's a beautiful city.* | *More and more people moved to the cities, which became increasingly overcrowded.*
+of WRITTEN *The city of Barcelona is famous for its wonderful architecture.* | *the ancient city of Petra*
plural **cities**

> ⚠ You can also use **city** before a noun, like an adjective: *I don't much like city life.* | *city traffic* | *the old city walls*

village /'vɪlɪdʒ/ [n C] a place with a few houses, shops etc, which is in the countryside and is much smaller than a town: *There are some nice pubs in the villages around here.* | *Benjamas left her village in the north of Thailand and went to live in Bangkok.*

> ⚠ American people do not usually use the word **village** to talk about places in the US. They usually say **small town**.

capital /'kæpɪtl/ [n C] the city where the government of a country or state is:

Rome is one of the world's most beautiful capitals.
the capital of France/Korea etc *"What's the capital of Kenya?" "Nairobi."*
state capital (=of one of the states in a large country) *Sacramento is the state capital of California.*
capital city (=the capital) *Dublin, the capital city of Ireland*

urban /'ɜːʳbən/ [*adj* only before noun] in or relating to a city or cities – use this about places or people in cities, or about things that happen in cities or affect cities: *The problem of air pollution is especially serious in urban areas.* | *China's growing urban population* | *urban planning*
urban poverty/unemployment etc *Urban unemployment continues to rise.*

Formal or informal?
Urban is not used in informal conversation.

2 the centre of a town or city

centre BRITISH **center** AMERICAN /'sentəʳ/ [*n C*] the part of a town or city where most of the shops, banks, theatres etc are
+of *I work in the centre of London.*
city centre/city center *A bomb went off in the city center and 19 people were killed.*
town centre BRITISH *She's gone into the town centre to do some shopping.*

downtown /'dauntaun/ [*adv*] AMERICAN in or to the part of a city where most of the shops, banks, theatres etc are: *She lives in a really beautiful apartment downtown.*
go downtown *I have to go downtown later.*
downtown [*adj* only before noun] *a downtown hotel* | *Rick drove into downtown San Francisco.*

in town /ɪn 'taun/ BRITISH SPOKEN in the part of a town or city where most of the shops, theatres etc are: *I suggest we meet somewhere in town and have lunch together.*
go into town *I'm going into town. Do you want anything?*

inner city/inner-city /ˌɪnəʳ 'sɪti/ [*adj* only before noun] **inner city** areas are areas close to the centre of a big city, where many poor people live

and there are often social problems: *Crime is a big problem in inner-city areas.* | *children from inner city schools* (=schools in inner city areas)

3 the areas at the edge of a town or city

suburb /'sʌbɜːʳb/ [*n C*] an area outside the centre of a city, where many people live because it is quieter and there is more space than in the centre
the suburbs *More and more people are moving to the suburbs every year.*
a suburb of Tokyo/New York etc *They have just bought a house in Pacific Palisades, a wealthy suburb of Los Angeles.*
suburban /sə'bɜːʳbən/ [*adj*] in the suburbs: *a typical suburban house*

 Don't say 'I live in the suburb' or 'I live in suburbs'. Say **I live in the suburbs**.

the outskirts /ði: 'autskɜːʳts/ [*n plural*] the areas around the edge of a city or just outside it
the outskirts of Tokyo/London etc *By 9 o'clock we reached the outskirts of Berlin.*
on the outskirts *There are plans to build a giant shopping centre on the outskirts of Glasgow.*

 Don't say 'in the outskirts'. Say **on the outskirts**: *We live on the outskirts of town.*

out-of-town /'aut əv taun/ [*adj* only before noun] BRITISH **out-of-town** shops are built outside a town, so that people from the town have to drive to them: *an out-of-town shopping centre*

4 the town where you are from

home town /'həum taun/ [*n C*] the town where you were born or where you lived as a child, or where you live now: *Johnson lived in Seattle for ten years before returning to his home town of Cody, Wyoming.* | *Sarajevo is my home town and I did not want to leave.*

home /həʊm/ [n C/U] the place where you were born or the place where you usually live, especially if this is where you feel happy and want to live: *I've lived in Paris for many years, and it feels like home to me now.* | *Her home, she said, was in Hong Kong, but she hadn't been there since she was a child.*

TRADITION

a belief or custom that has existed among a group of people for a very long time

➡ see also **FESTIVALS AND SPECIAL DAYS, MARRY**

1 a tradition

tradition /trə'dɪʃən/ [n C] a belief, custom, or a way of doing something that has existed for a very long time in a particular country or among a particular group of people: *A lot of the old traditions are dying out.* | *We always go for a long walk on Christmas morning – it's a family tradition.*
a Jewish/American/Catholic etc tradition *The story of Dracula is based on various Eastern European traditions.*
+of *The region has a tradition of wine-making which goes back to Roman times.*
+that *the tradition that the eldest son inherits all the money*

traditional /trə'dɪʃənəl/ [adj] belonging to the traditions of a country or group of people – use this about music, food, clothes, customs etc: *They play traditional Irish music.* | *dancers wearing traditional African costume* | *the traditional British breakfast of eggs, bacon, and sausages*
it is traditional to do sth *In the US it is traditional to hang candy canes on the Christmas tree.*

traditionally [adv] *a special dish that is traditionally eaten at New Year*

custom /'kʌstəm/ [n C] a way of behaving that has existed for a long time among a group of people, and is considered normal or polite – use this especially to talk about other countries or other times: *The game teaches kids about the customs of other countries.*
an ancient/local/Jewish etc custom *an old Chinese custom*
it is the custom (for sb) to do sth *It is the custom in Japan to take your shoes off when you go into someone's house.* | *In those days it was the custom for farmers to give part of their crop to the lord of the manor.*
the custom of doing sth *The custom of sending birthday cards began in the 19th century.*

2 all the customs and beliefs of a country or group

tradition /trə'dɪʃən/ [n U] all the beliefs and ways of behaving that have existed for a very long time in a particular country or among a particular group of people: *Many Americans originated from Ireland, so there is a great respect for Irish tradition in the US.*
by tradition (=according to a tradition) *By tradition, it is the bride's parents who pay for the wedding.*

folklore /'fəʊklɔːʳ/ [n U] old stories which the people in a country or area have told each other for a very long time, and which often contain historical or religious ideas: *According to folklore, Arthur will one day return to become King of Britain.* | *In folklore the snake is often a symbol of evil.*

3 a special event that is part of a tradition

ceremony /'serɪmənɪ‖-məʊni/ [n C] a special formal event which is part of the religious or social tradition of a place, and in which there is a fixed set of words and actions: *After the ceremony we went to a reception at the bride's parents' house.*
hold a ceremony (=have a ceremony) *A ceremony is held every year to remember those who died in the war.*
plural ceremonies

ceremonial /ˌserɪˈməʊniəl◂/ [*adj*] use this about something that is part of a ceremony or that is used in a ceremony: *a ceremonial sword*

ritual /ˈrɪtʃuəl/ [*n* C/U] a set of words and actions that are always done in the same way as part of a religious ceremony: *As part of this ancient ritual, the people paint their faces blue to symbolize the ghosts of childhood.*
perform a ritual *The ritual is performed in order to thank the Sun Goddess for the rice harvest.*

TRAVEL

➡ see Word Banks section

TRICK/DECEIVE

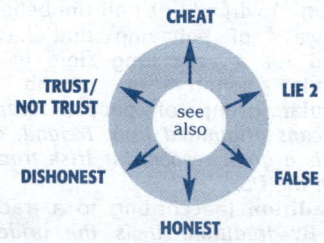

CHEAT
TRUST/ NOT TRUST
see also
LIE 2
DISHONEST
FALSE
HONEST

1 to deliberately make someone believe something that is not true

trick /trɪk/ [*v* T] to make someone believe something that is not true, in order to get something from them or make them do something: *I realized then that I had been tricked.*
trick sb into doing sth *The old man's sons had tricked him into signing the papers.*
trick sb out of sth (=take something from someone by tricking them) *They tricked her out of all her money.*

deceive /dɪˈsiːv/ [*v* T] ESPECIALLY WRITTEN to make someone who trusts you believe something that is not true because it is useful for you if they believe it: *He had been having an affair and deceiving his wife for years. | This was a deliberate attempt to deceive the public.*

fool /fuːl/ [*v* T] to make someone believe something that is not true by using a clever but simple trick: *His false moustache didn't fool anyone.*
fool sb into doing sth *They managed to fool the police into thinking they had left the country.*
◯ **you can't fool me** SPOKEN *You can't fool me with that old excuse.*

mislead /mɪsˈliːd/ [*v* T] ESPECIALLY WRITTEN to make people believe something that is not true, by deliberately not giving them all the facts or by saying something that is only partly true: *He admitted he had misled Congress. | They were accused of misleading customers about the nutritional value of their product.*
misleading – misled – have misled

misleading [*adj*] **misleading** information or statements make people believe something that is not true, especially by not giving them all the facts: *The article was misleading, and the newspaper has now apologized.*

2 something you do in order to trick someone

trick /trɪk/ [*n* C] a clever plan designed to make someone believe something that you want them to believe, or do something that you want them to do: *The phone call from the hospital was a trick to get him out of the office.*
a trick question (=a question that is cleverly designed to make someone give a wrong answer)

trap /træp/ [*n* C] a clever plan designed to harm someone, for example by making them go somewhere where they will be caught or attacked, or making them say something they did not intend to say: *Suspecting a trap, I didn't take the money with me.*
fall into a trap (=be deceived because you did not realize someone was trying to trick you) *King asked her a question about taxes, and she fell into his trap.*

TRUE/NOT TRUE

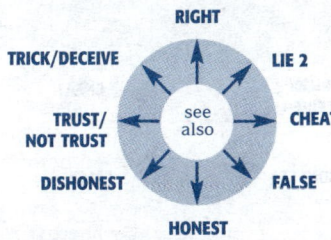

RIGHT

TRICK/DECEIVE   LIE 2

TRUST/   see   CHEAT
NOT TRUST   also

DISHONEST   FALSE

HONEST

1 true

true /truː/ [adj] something that is **true** is based on real facts and was not invented or imagined: *Everything I have told you is true.* | *The film is based on a true story.*
it is true (that) *Is it true that Tom and Lesley are getting married?*

the truth /ðə 'truːθ/ [n singular] the true facts about a situation: *It took the police a long time to find out the truth.*
+about *We may never know the truth about what really happened.*
🔍 **be the truth** SPOKEN (=be true – use this especially to persuade someone that you are not lying) *I've never seen this man before, and that's the truth.*
🔍 **the truth is (that)** SPOKEN (use this when you are explaining the true facts about something, especially when they are different from what people think) *The truth is she's worried about losing her job.*
the simple/plain/real etc truth *The simple truth is that children need their fathers.*

tell the truth /,tel ðə 'truːθ/ to say what really happened or what the true situation is: *Why won't you believe me? I'm telling the truth!*
tell sb the truth *You should have told him the truth.*

> Don't say 'she's saying the truth'. Say **she's telling the truth**.

accurate /'ækjʊ̯rət/ [adj] **accurate** information, figures, descriptions etc are based on facts that are exactly right, and do not contain mistakes: *It is important that people suffering from*

the disease get accurate information about it. | *He gave an accurate account of what had happened.*

it is a fact /ɪt ɪz ə 'fækt/ use this to emphasize that something is definitely true, especially when it is surprising or difficult to believe
+that *It is a fact that more young people die in road accidents than from any other cause.*

> **Formal or informal?**
> Use **it is a fact** especially in formal reports and discussions.

2 not true

not true/untrue /nɒt 'truː, ʌn'truː/ [adj not before noun] *"No-one ever helps me." "That's not true!"* | *There were various rumours about her private life, but they were all untrue.*
it is untrue/not true that *It is not true that all women want to go out to work.*
completely/totally   untrue   *The papers said he had beat up his wife, which was completely untrue.*

> **Formal or informal?**
> In informal spoken English, **not true** is much more common than **untrue**.

false /fɔːls/ [adj] not true or not correct – use this about statements or beliefs that are based on untrue information: *He gave a false name and address to the police.* | *This article gives a totally false impression of life in Russia today.* | *Decide whether these statements are true or false.*

not be the case /nɒt biː ðə 'keɪs/ to not be true – use this to say that something is not true even though many people believe that it is: *Recent reports suggest that violent crime is increasing, but this is simply not the case.*

> **Formal or informal?**
> **Not be the case** is fairly formal, and is used especially when writing or talking about politics or other serious subjects.

there is no truth in sth /ðeər ɪz nəʊ ˈtruːθ ɪn (sth)/ if you say that **there is no truth in** something, you mean that it is completely untrue and that people are wrong to suggest that it is true: *There is no truth in the rumour that Collins and his wife are about to divorce.* | *Someone told me the company was losing money, but Bill says there's no truth in this.*

Formal or informal?
This expression is used especially in formal or official statements.

misleading /mɪsˈliːdɪŋ/ [adj] **misleading** information or statements make people believe something that is not true, especially by not giving them all the facts: *The holiday brochure is deliberately misleading, because the hotels it shows are not the ones you actually stay in.* | *These statistics give a misleading impression of what is happening to the economy.*

3 to think of a reason, explanation etc, especially one that is untrue

make up /ˌmeɪk ˈʌp/ [phrasal verb T] to think of a reason, explanation, excuse etc that is untrue
make up sth *You're going to have to make up some kind of excuse for not going.*
make sth up *It's possible that Smith made the story up.*

invent /ɪnˈvent/ [v T] to think of a reason, explanation, or excuse that is sometimes very complicated but completely untrue: *He used to invent stories about his rich lifestyle to impress the women he met.* | *I began to invent reasons for staying away from work.*

Formal or informal?
Invent is more formal than **make up**, and is used especially in written English.

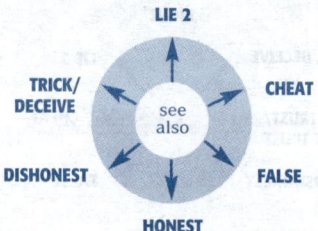

TRUST/NOT TRUST

LIE 2

TRICK/
DECEIVE   CHEAT

see
also

DISHONEST   FALSE

HONEST

1 when you think someone is honest

trust /trʌst/ [v T] to believe that someone is honest and will not tell lies, cheat you, or do anything that would harm you: *David's one of my oldest friends – I trust him completely.*
can trust sb (=you feel sure that someone is honest) *We found he had been stealing cash from the store, so how can we trust him now?* | *She needs someone she can trust to help her.*

⚠ Don't say 'I am trusting him'. Say **I trust him**.

trustworthy /ˈtrʌstˌwɜːrði/ [adj] ESPECIALLY WRITTEN if someone is **trustworthy**, you can trust them because they are completely honest: *Her school report described her as 'an intelligent and trustworthy girl'.* | *We got the information from a trustworthy source.*

dependable /dɪˈpendəbəl/ [adj] if someone is **dependable**, they can be trusted to do what you need or expect them to do: *He was described as a hard worker, dependable, and honest.* | *They are some of the Democratic Party's most dependable supporters.*

2 when you can be sure that someone will do what you want

can depend on sb/can rely on sb /kən dɪˈpend ɒn (sb), kən rɪˈlaɪ ɒn (sb)/ if you **can depend on** or **can rely on** someone, you can be sure that they will do what you want them to do or

what you have asked them to do: *"You won't tell anyone about this, will you?" "You can depend on me."*
can depend/rely on sb to do sth *We knew we could rely on Tom to bring some good records.*

reliable /rɪ'laɪəbəl/ [adj] someone who is **reliable** can be trusted to do what they say they will do and not make any mistakes: *It's strange Ben isn't here: he's usually so reliable.* | *Reliable and hardworking cleaner needed for 3 hours each week.*

responsible /rɪ'spɒnsɨbəl‖rɪ'spɑː-/ [adj] someone who is **responsible** can be trusted to behave in a sensible way, so you do not need to worry that they will do something stupid: *I don't mind leaving the kids with Nicola; she's very responsible.*

loyal /'lɔɪəl/ [adj] someone who is **loyal** can be trusted to always give help or support to their friends, their country, their political party etc: *a loyal supporter of the Green Party* | *She was described as a loyal friend of the Princess.* | *The company fired him, after 30 years of loyal service!*
+to *Most MPs remained loyal to their party leader.*

loyalty [n C/U] loyal behaviour: *The attempted coup failed, thanks to the loyalty of the army.*

> **Formal or informal?**
> **Loyal** is not usually used in informal conversation.

3 something that you can trust

reliable /rɪ'laɪəbəl/ [adj] a **reliable** machine, system etc always works well, **reliable** information, books etc do not contain mistakes and are likely to be correct: *I wish we had a more reliable computer system.* | *Do you have a reliable map of the area?*

can rely on sth/can depend on sth /kən rɪ'laɪ ɒn (sth), kən dɪ'pend ɒn (sth)/ if you **can depend on** or **can rely on** something, you can be sure that it will always work well: *You can rely on the postal service here.* | *What I need is a car I can really depend on.*

4 not trust

not trust /nɒt 'trʌst/ to not trust someone: *I don't trust these politicians, do you?*
not trust sb with sth (=when you will not let someone have something, because you think they will damage it or steal it) *I wouldn't trust him with my money.*

can't rely on sb/sth/can't trust sb/sth /ˌkɑːnt rɪ'laɪ ɒn (sb/sth), ˌkɑːnt 'trʌst (sb/sth)‖ˌkænt-/ to be unable to trust someone to do what they say they will do, or to be unable to trust a machine, system etc to work well: *You can't rely on the buses. They're often late.*
can't rely on sb/sth to do sth *That boy's hopeless – I can't rely on him to do anything.*

unreliable /ˌʌnrɪ'laɪəbəl/ [adj] if someone is **unreliable**, you cannot be sure that they will do what they say they will do; if a machine, car etc is **unreliable**, it often stops working and you cannot be sure it will work well: *I don't really want to ask the neighbours to feed the cat – they're a little unreliable.* | *My old car was becoming very unreliable.*

be suspicious of sb/sth /biː sə'spɪʃəs ɒv (sb/sth)/ to have a feeling that you should not trust someone or something, although you are not sure why: *I'm always suspicious of people who offer me money.*
deeply suspicious (=very suspicious) *Parents and teachers are deeply suspicious of the government's plans for education.*

TRY

➡ look here for ...
  • try to do something
  • try something to see if it is good
➡ see also **TEST**

1 to try to do something

try /traɪ/ [v I/T]
try to do sth *Tim tried to get another job, but he had no luck.* | *I can't come*

out tonight – I'm trying to finish all my homework before the weekend.

try not to do sth *Try not to worry – I'm sure she'll be home soon.*

try sth (=try to do something) *If you finish section one, try the exercises on page 25.*

try *"Can Larry fix the car?" "He said he'd try, but I'll probably have to take it to a garage."*

try and do sth *"What time does the game start?" "I don't know. I'll try and find out."*

trying – tried – have tried

Formal or informal?

Try and do something means the same as **try to do something**, but is less formal. Only the form **try** can be used before 'and', not 'tries', 'trying', or 'tried'.

---

attempt /əˈtempt/ [v T] to try to do something, especially something difficult, dangerous, or bad
attempt to do sth *He was attempting to climb Mount Everest without oxygen. | They were charged with attempting to overthrow the government.*
attempt sth *Bad weather conditions prevented us from attempting the jump.*

Formal or informal?

Attempt is more formal than **try**.

☖ **see if you can do sth** /ˌsiː ɪf juː kən ˈduː (sth)/ SPOKEN to try to do something – use this either to offer to do something for someone, or to ask someone to do something for you
I'll see if I can do sth *If you want to come to the show, I'll see if I can get you a ticket.*
see if you can do sth *See if you can get him to change his mind.*

☖ **have a try** (also **have a go** BRITISH) /ˌhæv ə ˈtraɪ, ˌhæv ə ˈɡəʊ/ SPOKEN to try to do something, even though you think you may not succeed: *"I can't get the lid off this jar." "Here, let me have a try." | I've never been windsurfing before, but I'll have a go.*

---

2 to try hard to do something

try hard /ˌtraɪ ˈhɑːʳd/ to make a lot of effort, because you really want to do something: *You must try harder to get all your homework done on time. | No*

matter how hard I tried, I couldn't get the window to open.

do your best/try your best /ˌduː jɔːʳ ˈbest, ˌtraɪ jɔːʳ ˈbest/ to try as hard as you can, even when the situation is difficult and you are not sure if you will succeed: *"Can you get it finished by Friday?" "We'll do our best, but we're very busy at the moment."*
do/try your best to do sth *Harry did his best to sound calm, but it was obvious that he was really annoyed.*

make an effort to do sth /ˌmeɪk ən ˈefəʳt tə duː (sth)/ to try hard to do something, especially something which you do not want to do but which you think you should do: *I made an effort to sound interested in what he was saying. | I wish you'd make an effort to be friendly to her.*

work at sth /ˈwɜːʳk æt (sth)/ [phrasal verb T] to try hard to improve the way you do something, by practising a lot: *You'll have to really work at it if you want to become a professional dancer.*

---

3 when you try to do something

attempt /əˈtempt/ [n C] when you try to do something, especially something difficult, dangerous, or bad: *After four attempts, Mike finally passed his driving test.*
attempt to do sth *another attempt to find a solution to the problem | It was a deliberate attempt to mislead the voters.*
make an attempt to do sth *The climbers will make another attempt to reach the summit today.*
in an attempt to do sth *The government built hundreds of cheap houses in an attempt to solve the homelessness crisis.*
attempt at (doing) sth *David made an attempt at a smile.*

effort /ˈefəʳt/ [n C/U] the work you do and the energy you use when you try to do something
sb's efforts to do sth *All our efforts to convince her failed.*
put a lot of effort into sth (=work very hard to do it) *Margaret had put a lot of effort into making the party a success.*

4 to eat, use, or do something to find out if it is good, if it works etc

➡ see also **TASTE**

try /traɪ/ [v T] to eat, use, or do something in order to find out if you like it or if it is successful: *Have you ever tried that chewing gum that's supposed to help you stop smoking?* | *I tried aerobics once, but I didn't really enjoy it.*

try doing sth (=do something to see if it has a successful result) *If the sauce is too thin, try adding some cream.*

trying – tried – have tried

try out /ˌtraɪ ˈaʊt/ [phrasal verb T] to use a new method, product etc, in order to find out how good it is

try out sth *I want to try out some of the recipes that I've seen on TV.*

try sth out *She had just bought a new computer, and couldn't wait to try it out.*

taste /teɪst/ [v T] to eat or drink a small amount of something to find out what it tastes like: *Come here and taste the soup. Do you think it needs more salt?*

experiment with sth /ɪkˈsperɪ̯ment wɪð (sth)/ [phrasal verb T] to try different things or methods to find out what effect they have – use this especially about drugs or about styles in art and music: *Some children start experimenting with drugs when they are 14 or 15.* | *The band has been experimenting with different styles and different instruments.*

TURN

➡ see also **BEND, AROUND**

1 to turn your head or body

turn /tɜːʳn/ [v I/T] to turn your head or body so that you are looking in a different direction: *Campbell turned and walked out of the room.* | *She turned her head to look at him.*

turn to sb (=turn to look at someone so that you can say something to them) *"What do you think we should do?" she said, turning to her husband.*

turn to do sth *She turned to face him and saw that he had been crying.*

turn away (=turn in order to avoid seeing something) *Julie turned away while the doctor put the needle in her arm.*

turn around (also **turn round** BRITISH) /ˌtɜːʳn (ə)ˈraʊnd/ [phrasal verb I] to turn your body so that you are looking in the opposite direction: *I turned round quickly to see if anyone was following me.* | *"Is my skirt too short?" "Turn around and let me see the back."*

turn over /ˌtɜːʳn ˈəʊvəʳ/ [phrasal verb I] to change the position of your body while you are lying down, so that you are facing in a different direction: *The bed squeaks every time I turn over.* | *Ray turned over onto his side.*

roll over /ˌrəʊl ˈəʊvəʳ/ [phrasal verb I/T] to turn your body over once so that you are lying in a different position, or to turn someone's body over: *John rolled over in bed.*

roll sb over *The guards rolled him over and checked his breathing.*

2 to make something turn

turn /tɜːʳn/ [v T] to make something turn by moving it with your hand: *Tim turned the handle slowly and pushed open the door.* | *The kids turned the box onto its side.*

turn sth around (=so that it is facing the opposite direction) *If we turn the table around we can fit more chairs in the room.*

turn sth over (=so that its top is facing down and its bottom is facing up) *After about two minutes, turn the pancakes over and cook the other side.*

twist /twɪst/ [v T] to turn something with a quick firm circular movement: *"I can't get the top off." "Try twisting it the other way."* | *She pushed the knife into his stomach and twisted it hard.*

twist

3 when something such as a wheel goes around

turn /tɜːʳn/ [v I] if something **turns**, it moves around a fixed central point: *Slowly, the wheels of the train began to turn.* | *We watched in terror as the handle turned and the door creaked open.*

go around (also **go round** BRITISH) /ˌgəʊ (ə)ˈraʊnd/ to move in a continuous circular movement: *When the fan goes around it moves the air and cools the room.*

go around and around (=go around many times) *The big wheel went around and around.*

spin /spɪn/ [v I] to turn around many times very quickly: *The wheels were spinning in the mud, but the car wouldn't move.*

+around *The hard disk spins around several times every second.*

spinning – spun – have spun

4 to change your direction when you are walking or driving

turn /tɜːʳn/ [v I] to change your direction when you are walking or driving: *He saw a police car up ahead, so he turned and went down a side street.*

turn left/right *Turn left at the next intersection.*

turn back (=turn and go back towards the place that you came from) *After sailing north for an hour, we had to turn back because of fog.*

turn off (=leave a street in order to go down another street) *Turn off Delaney Road just after the church.*

turn onto/into (=start going along another street after changing direction) *Turn onto South Street, then go straight for three blocks.*

change direction /ˌtʃeɪndʒ dɪ̥ˈrekʃən/ to turn while you are moving so that you start going in a different direction: *Changing direction on skis isn't difficult once you've learned the technique.*

swerve

swerve /swɜːʳv/ [v I] if a vehicle or its driver **swerves**, they change direction very suddenly, especially in order to avoid hitting something: *The driver swerved to avoid a child.*

5 when a road or river changes direction

bend /bend/ [n C] a place where a road or river curves: *The taxi went around the bend at an alarming speed.*

+in *a bend in the river*

curve /kɜːʳv/ [n C] a place where a road curves: *He lost control of the car on a sharp curve.*

> In American English, **curve** is more common than **bend** in this meaning.

turn (also **turning** BRITISH) /tɜːʳn, ˈtɜːʳnɪŋ/ [n C] a place in a road where you can turn and go onto another road: *We wanted to go toward Newark, but I think we missed the turn.* | *Take the first turning after the traffic lights.*

6 when a vehicle turns over in an accident

turn upside down /tɜːʳn ˌʌpsaɪd ˈdaʊn/ if a car, plane, boat etc **turns upside down**, it turns over so that its top is facing down and its bottom is facing up: *The plane had turned upside down and was out of control.*

turn over /ˌtɜːʳn ˈəʊvəʳ/ [phrasal verb I] if a car, train etc **turns over**, it turns upside down or falls on its side as a result of an accident: *The car turned over and burst into flames.*

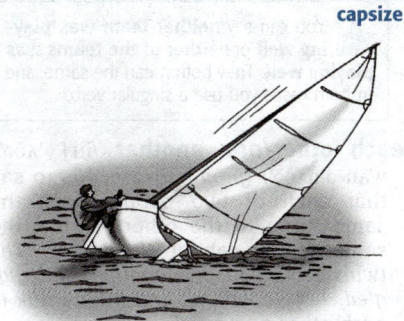

capsize

capsize /kæp'saɪz‖'kæpsaɪz/ [v I] if a boat or ship **capsizes**, it turns upside down, or falls on its side, and usually sinks: *193 passengers died when their ferry capsized in the English Channel.*

TWO

1 two

two /tuː/ [*number*] 2: *We have two dogs and three cats.* | *There used to be five churches in the town. Now there are only two.* | *It takes two hours to get there.*
+of *Two of the boys in the hockey team were sick.*

pair /peə^r/ [n C] two things of the same type that are used together
a pair of shoes/socks/gloves/ear-rings etc *I need a new pair of shoes.*

a couple /ə 'kʌpəl/ [quantifier] INFORMAL, ESPECIALLY BRITISH two: *I haven't got any stamps – could you lend me a couple?*
+of *I've got a couple of tickets for the game on Saturday.* | *She lived in Japan for a couple of years.*

> ⚠ In American English, **a couple** more usually means 'a small number'.

2 two people together

couple /'kʌpəl/ [n C] two people who are together, especially because they are married or have a sexual relationship: *The couple who live next door are always arguing.* | *a young couple walking hand in hand along the beach*
a married couple (=a couple who are married)

> ⚠ In British English, you can use **couple** with a singular or plural verb: *An old couple was sitting/were sitting at the next table.* In American English, always use a singular verb.

pair /peə^r/ [n C] two people who are doing something together, or who are similar or connected in some way
+of *a pair of dancers* | *Annie and Jane were all dressed up, and looked like a pair of movie stars.*
in pairs (=working in groups of two) *Do the next exercise in pairs.*
a strange/funny/friendly etc pair *Bill and his brother were a rather odd-looking pair.*

3 each one of two people or things

both /bəʊθ/ [*predeterminer/quantifier*] use this to talk about two people or things together: *Paul and I are both scared of spiders.* | *I can't decide which dress to buy. I like them both.* | *Both drivers were injured, but not seriously.*
both the/these/my etc *Both the robbers were wearing masks.* | *Both her parents are doctors.*
both of them/us/the dogs etc *Both of us felt sick after eating the fish.* | *Both of the windows had been broken.*
both sb/sth and sb/sth *I hope that both you and your husband will be able to join us.*

> ⚠ Don't say 'both my children goes to the same school'. Say **both my children go to the same school**. **Both** is followed by a plural verb.

> ⚠ Don't say 'I don't like both of them'. Say **I don't like either of them**. Use **either** in negative statements, not **both**.

> ⚠ When you use **both** with a noun, you can use any of these patterns, and they all have the same meaning: *The cats are both black* = *Both the cats are black* = *Both cats are black*. When you use **both** with a pronoun, you can say either *we both/they both* etc or *both of us/both of them* etc and the meaning is the same: *We both like Kung Fu movies* = *Both of us like Kung Fu movies*.

each /iːtʃ/ [*determiner/pronoun*] use this to talk about two people or things when you think of them as separate: *My wife and I each have our own bank account.*
each of them/us/the teams etc *Each of the teams can use three substitutes.*

> ⚠ **Each** is followed by a singular verb, except when it comes after a plural noun or pronoun, so we say: *Each girl has her own room.* | *Each of the girls has her own room.* But *They/The girls each have their own room.*

> ⚠ Don't say 'each boys' or 'each of boys'. Say **each boy** or **each of the boys**.

either /'aɪðəʳ‖'iː-/ [*determiner/pronoun*] use this to talk about one of two people, places, or things, especially when it does not matter which one: *"Would you like tea or coffee?" "Either – I don't mind."* | *You can operate the controls with either hand.*
either of them/you/the men etc *If you see either of these men, contact the police immediately.* | *She says she never met either of them before.*
either sth or sth *I usually drink either Coke or beer.*

neither /'naɪðəʳ‖'niː-/ [*determiner/ pronoun*] not one of two people, places, or things, and not the other: *"Do you want milk or lemon in your tea?" "Neither thanks."* | *The game wasn't very exciting, and neither team played well.*
neither of them/you/the girls etc *Luckily, neither of the passengers was hurt in the crash.*
neither sth nor sth *Neither her mother nor her father knew about her boyfriend.*

> ⚠ Don't say 'I don't like neither of them'. Say **I don't like either of them**.

> ⚠ You can say **neither team was playing well** or **neither of the teams was playing well**. They both mean the same, and in both cases you use a singular verb.

each other/one another /iːtʃ 'ʌðəʳ, wʌn ə'nʌðəʳ/ [*pronoun*] use this to say that each of two people does the same thing to the other, or has the same feeling about the other: *The twins looked at one another and giggled.* | *My boyfriend and I don't talk to each other very much.*
each other's/one another's *Ron and Joe didn't like each other's girlfriends.* (=Ron didn't like Joe's girlfriend and Joe didn't like Ron's)

4 two children born on the same day to the same mother

twin /twɪn/ [*n C*] one of two children who were born on the same day to the same mother: *She dressed the twins in the same clothes.* | *Joey's my twin.*
twin brother/sister *Bill and his twin sister got married on the same day.*
identical twins (=twins who look exactly the same)

5 intended for two people

for two /fəʳ 'tuː/
dinner/a holiday/a table etc for two dinner, a holiday etc intended for only two people: *We'd like a table for two please.* | *a romantic weekend in Paris for two*

double /'dʌbəl/ [*adj only before noun*]
double room/bed/mattress a room, bed etc intended for two people: *The room was so small, there was hardly enough space for a double bed.* | *Double rooms cost $80, single rooms are $50.*

6 when something happens two times

twice /twaɪs/ [*adv*] *The weather was great – it only rained twice in three weeks.* | *She's been married twice before.*
twice a day/month/year etc (=when something happens regularly two

times every day, month etc) *I play golf twice a week.* | *Staff meetings are held twice a month.*

7　when a number or amount is twice as big as another

twice /twaɪs/ [predeterminer/adv]
twice as big/fast/much/many etc bigger, faster etc by 100%: *This sweater would have cost twice as much if I'd bought it in England.*
twice the size/my salary/his age etc *He married a woman who was twice his age.* | *It's about twice the length of a football field.*

double /ˈdʌbəl/ [predeterminer]
double the amount/number/weight/ size/cost etc twice as much as an amount, number etc: *Over 30% of marriages end in divorce, which is double the number 20 years ago.* | *The house was now worth double the amount they paid for it.*

TYPE

1　a type of person or thing

type/kind/sort /taɪp, kaɪnd, sɔːˡt/ [n C] a group of people or things that are similar to each other in some way, or a thing or person that belongs to such a group: *I'll get you some ice-cream. What kind would you like?*
+of *The floor was made of three different types of wood.* | *What sort of fish is this?* | *There are two sorts of politician – the ones who really want to help people, and the ones who just want power.*
of this/that type etc *Accidents of this type are extremely common.* | *It's a club for writers and actors and people of that sort.*
of various/many/different types etc *They export farm machines and tools of various kinds.*
all kinds/sorts/types *a store selling all kinds of candy*
kind/sort/type of thing *The girls like to draw, paint – that kind of thing.*

Type, **kind**, and **sort** mean the same, and they can all be used in most situations. **Kind** and **sort** are more common than **type** in informal conversation. In American English, **kind** is used more often than **sort**. **Type** is the usual word to use when you are talking about technical subjects or when you are describing something in an exact way: *To do this, you need a special type of screwdriver called a Phillips screwdriver.*

⚠ You can use **type of**, **kind of**, and **sort of** before a singular or uncountable noun, but not a plural noun: *a type of flower* | *I like this kind of music* You can use **types of**, **kinds of**, and **sorts of** before a singular, plural, or uncountable noun: *different sorts of vehicle* | *all kinds of people* | *the healthiest types of food.* Don't use these words in the singular after words like 'all', 'many', or 'these': don't say 'many kind of car/food etc'. Say **many kinds of car/food** etc.

like this/like that /laɪk ˈðɪs, laɪk ˈðæt/ ESPECIALLY SPOKEN of the type that you have just been talking about: *The children need new pens and pencils and things like that.* | *People like that really annoy me.* | *I'm not sure what to do. I've never been in a situation like this before.*

category /ˈkætˡ₃gəriǁ-gɔːri/ [n C] a group that people or things of the same type are divided into for a particular purpose – use this when there are several groups and there is a clear system for deciding which group something belongs to: *Emma Thompson won the Oscar in the 'Best Actress' category that year.*
+of *Insurance companies identify six main categories of driver.* | *The novels are divided up into three categories: historical, romantic, and crime.*
plural **categories**

style /staɪl/ [n C] a particular type of building, art, literature, music etc: *The new library is a blend of various architectural styles.*
+of *a completely new style of painting*
western-style / Japanese-style etc *The room was simply furnished, Japanese-style.*

2 a type of animal or plant

species /'spiːʃiːz/ [n C] a group of animals or plants that are all similar and can produce young animals or plants of the same type
+of *There are over forty species of bird living on the island.* | *They discovered a new species of Eucalyptus tree.*
endangered species (=one that might not exist for much longer) *The giant panda is an endangered species. There are fewer than a thousand living in the wild.*
plural **species**

> **Formal or informal?**
> **Species** is a technical word for a specific type of animal or plant.

breed /briːd/ [n C] a type of animal, especially one that has been developed by humans, such as a dog, cat, or a farm animal: *Most dairy cows are Holstein or Friesian breeds.*
+of *Spaniels are my favorite breed of dog.*

3 a type of product

brand /brænd/ [n C] a type of product made by a particular company – use this about products that you use every day such as food or drink or cleaning materials
+of *Coke and Pepsi are the most popular brands of cola.* | *my favourite brand of toothpaste* | *They sell all the usual kinds of coffee, but also some less well-known brands.*

make /meɪk/ [n C] a type of product made by a particular company – use this about things such as machines, equipment, and cars, not about food or drink: *What make is your washing machine?*
+of *"What make of car was she driving?" "A Mercedes."*

model /'mɒdl‖'mɑːdl/ [n C] one particular type of car or machine from among the various types that a company produces: *"What make is the car?" "It's a Ford." "And what model?" "A Mondeo."* | *We produce a range of different computers, but this is our most popular model.*

TYPICAL

when something or someone is a good example of the type that they belong to

➡ see also **USUALLY**

1 a typical thing or person

typical /'tɪpɪkəl/ [adj] use this to say that someone or something is a normal example of a particular type of person or thing, and has all the features that you would expect: *With his camera around his neck, he looked like a typical tourist.* | *a typical middle class family* | *We had some warm weather, and quite a lot of rain – it was a typical English summer.*
+of *This painting is typical of the work that Matisse did in the 1920s.*

> ⚠ Don't say 'it's a typical restaurant', 'this house is typical' etc. You must make it clear what something is typical of, for example: *It's a typical Spanish restaurant.* | *This house is typical of the style of this region.*

be a good example /biː ə ˌgʊd ɪgˈzɑːmpəl‖-ˈzæm-/ something that **is a good example** of a type of thing is very typical of it: *There are many beautiful Norman churches in England, and Iffley church is a good example.*
+of *The fox is a good example of a wild animal that has adapted to living in towns.*

representative /ˌreprɪˈzentətɪv/ [adj] FORMAL someone or something that is **representative** is very typical of the group that they belong to and shows what everyone or everything else in the group is like
+of *Are his views representative of the other teachers at the school?*
representative group/sample/selection/cross-section (=a small group, chosen because it is typical of a larger group) *We asked a representative group of teenage girls what they thought about marriage.*

classic /'klæsɪk/ [adj usually before noun]
a classic case/example etc a very typical and very good example of something: *Tiredness, headaches and bad temper are the classic signs of stress.* | *The invention of the X-ray was a classic case of an accidental discovery.*

stereotype /'steriətaɪp/ [n C] a fixed idea which most people have in their minds about what people of a particular type or from a particular country are like, but which is not actually true: *The film is full of stereotypes: a stupid blonde, a fat American tourist, and a gay male hairdresser.*
racial stereotypes (=fixed ideas about people of certain races)
+of *the stereotype of Asian girls as quiet and hard-working*

---

2 **when someone's behaviour or character is exactly what you would expect**

typical /'tɪpɪkəl/ [adj] behaviour that is **typical** of a person is exactly what you would expect them to do – use this especially when what they do is annoying: *"Kate put the wrong address on the letter." "That's just typical!"* | *He said he was too tired to wash the dishes. Typical man!*
+of *It's typical of Ramon to waste time when we're already late.*

it's just like/that's just like /ɪts ˌdʒʌst 'laɪk, ðæts ˌdʒʌst 'laɪk/ SPOKEN say this when someone has behaved in exactly the way that you would expect them to behave: *It's just like Uncle Roy to invite us all to lunch and then forget to tell Aunt Sarah.* | *Helen stayed to help us clean up, which is just like her.*

U, u

UGLY

not nice to look at

➡ opposite **BEAUTIFUL**

1 people

unattractive /ˌʌnəˈtræktɪv◂/ [adj] ESPECIALLY WRITTEN not nice to look at and not sexually attractive: *Like many teenage girls, she was worried that she was unattractive.*

find sb unattractive (=think that someone is unattractive) *She was crazy about Carl, and couldn't understand why we found him unattractive.*

ugly /ˈʌgli/ [adj] extremely unattractive, with a face that is not at all nice to look at: *My uncle was ugly and fat and treated us cruelly.* | *An ugly little man came over and offered to buy me a drink.*

ugly – uglier – ugliest

> ⚠ In conversation, we usually avoid describing someone as **ugly** or **unattractive** because it sounds very rude.

not very good-looking/not very attractive /nɒt veri gʊd ˈlʊkɪŋ, nɒt veri əˈtræktɪv/ not nice to look at – use this as a less direct way of saying someone is unattractive: *He's a nice guy, but not very good-looking.*

plain /pleɪn/ [adj] someone who is **plain**, especially a woman, is not ugly but is not at all good-looking: *Catherine, who had been rather plain as a child, was now an attractive young woman.*

homely /ˈhəʊmli/ [adj] AMERICAN someone who is **homely** is not at all good-looking: *The waitress was a homely girl from Kansas.* | *Brad was skinny and homely.*

2 objects/buildings etc

ugly /ˈʌgli/ [adj] very unpleasant to look at: *The room was bare except for a few pieces of ugly furniture.* | *The new shopping centre is one of the ugliest buildings in the city.*

ugly – uglier – ugliest

an eyesore /ən ˈaɪsɔːʳ/ [n singular] a large and very ugly building that you cannot avoid seeing: *Critics have called the tower an eyesore.*

hideous /ˈhɪdiəs/ [adj] extremely ugly: *One of our wedding presents was a hideous clock.* | *Emma was wearing an absolutely hideous purple and orange dress.*

UNDERSTAND/NOT UNDERSTAND

➡ see also **REALIZE**

1 to understand something

understand /ˌʌndəʳˈstænd/ [v I/T] to know the meaning of what someone says, or to know why something happens or how something happens: *She spoke slowly and clearly so that everyone could understand.* | *I understand the point you're making.*

understand how / what / why etc *Scientists are beginning to understand how the universe was formed.* | *We understood why we hadn't won the election.*

fully understand (=understand completely) *Did you fully understand the choices open to you?*

easy/difficult to understand *The instructions on the packet are easy to understand.*

understanding – understood – have understood

> ⚠ Don't say 'I am understanding', 'are you understanding?' etc. Say **I understand**, **do you understand?** etc.

> ⚠ **Can understand** means the same as 'understand': *I can understand how the mistake might have happened.*

🔍 **see** /siː/ [v I/T] ESPECIALLY SPOKEN to understand the truth about a situation, or understand the reasons for something: *Don't you see? She never wanted to marry him in the first place.*
see what sb means *Yes, I see what you mean – it would be better if we didn't tell her.*
see why/how/what etc *I can see why people don't like him.*
+that *After a time, Clara saw that she had been wrong to blame Jim.*
seeing – saw – have seen

🔍 **I see** /aɪ ˈsiː/ SPOKEN say this to tell someone that you understand what they have told you: *"The door's a little stiff – just give it a push here." "Oh yes, I see."*

🔍 **I get it** /aɪ ˈget ɪt/ SPOKEN INFORMAL say this to tell someone that you understand what they have told you, especially when they have explained it more than once: *Okay, I get it now. This number is divided by this one.*

follow /ˈfɒləʊǁˈfɑː-/ [v T] to understand a story, explanation, or talk that continues for a long time: *I had difficulty following the story – there are so many different characters.*
difficult/hard/easy to follow *The lecture was very hard to follow.*

figure out/work out /ˌfɪgər ˈaʊt, ˌwɜːʳk ˈaʊtǁˌfɪgjər-/ [phrasal verb T] to think about something until you understand it, especially something complicated
+how/why/what etc *Detectives are still trying to work out what happened.*
figure/work sth out *I read the question five times, and I still couldn't figure it out.*

> **Formal or informal?**
> **Figure out** is more informal than **work out**.

2 to understand how someone feels

understand /ˌʌndəʳˈstænd/ [v I/T] to understand how someone feels, and feel sympathy for them, especially

when they are upset or have problems: *Try telling your teacher about your problem. I'm sure she'll understand. | My wife doesn't understand me.*
understand how/what/why etc *I understand how you feel, but I still think you should apologize to her.*
understanding – understood – have understood

> ⚠ Don't say 'I am understanding'. Say **I understand**.

appreciate /əˈpriːʃieɪt/ [v T] FORMAL to understand clearly how someone feels or what problems they have: *The Senator failed to appreciate the amount of anger that people felt about this issue.*
+(that) *I appreciate that it's not easy for you, but you must try to get here on time.*

🔍 **see** /siː/ [v T] ESPECIALLY SPOKEN to understand how someone feels and why they feel that way, especially because the reasons are very clear
see why/how/what *You can see why Clare was so annoyed, can't you?*
+(that) *I can see it's upsetting for you.*
seeing – saw – have seen

🔍 **know how sb feels** /ˌnəʊ haʊ (sb) ˈfiːlz/ ESPECIALLY SPOKEN to understand how someone feels, because you have had the same feelings or experiences yourself: *"My children are driving me crazy." "I know how you feel."*

3 when you cannot understand something

don't understand/can't understand /ˌdəʊnt ˌʌndəʳˈstænd, ˌkɑːnt ʌndəʳˈstændǁˌkænt-/ *They didn't understand a single word she said. | Tell me if you don't understand.*
+how/why/what etc *I really can't understand why so many people like her music.*
not fully understand (=not understand completely) *Doctors still do not fully understand the process by which the disease is transmitted.*

🔍 **don't/can't see** /ˌdəʊnt, ˌkɑːnt ˈsiːǁˌkænt-/ ESPECIALLY SPOKEN to not understand the reason for something

+why/how/what/where *I didn't see how they could sell it so cheaply.* | *All my friends liked that book, but I just can't see why.*

see no reason/not see any reason *I can't see any reason to fight.*

🔍 **not get it** /nɒt 'get ɪt/ SPOKEN INFORMAL to feel confused, and be unable to understand why something has happened or what someone has told you: *I don't get it – why would he take the money if he knew they would find out?* | *I keep telling her that Steve isn't interested in her, but she just doesn't get it.*

puzzling /'pʌzəlɪŋ/ [adj] a **puzzling** situation makes you feel confused, because you have tried to understand it or explain it, but you cannot: *There are puzzling differences in how the schools are funded.*

🔍 **it's a mystery to me/it beats me** /ɪts ə 'mɪstəri tə miː, ɪt ˌbiːts 'miː/ SPOKEN say this when you cannot understand why something happens or how someone does something, and you find it very surprising: *"Why does she stay with her husband then?" "It beats me."*

+how/what/why etc *It's a mystery to me how he can get so much work done in such a short time.*

4 **to not understand something correctly**

misunderstand /ˌmɪsʌndəʳˈstænd/ [v I/T] to think that someone means one thing when in fact they mean something else: *I think she misunderstood the question.* | *I'm sorry, I must have misunderstood you.*
misunderstanding – misunderstood – have misunderstood

miss the point /ˌmɪs ðə 'pɔɪnt/ if you **miss the point**, you think you understand what someone says or what is important about a situation, but in fact you are wrong: *I soon realised that he had completely missed the point.*

misunderstanding /ˌmɪsʌndəʳˈstændɪŋ/ [n C/U] a problem caused when someone does not understand something correctly: *There seems to have been a misunderstanding. I didn't order steak.* | *Cultural differences*

between people from different countries can sometimes lead to misunderstandings.

UNFORTUNATELY

when you wish that something had not happened or was not true

➡ see also **SORRY, LUCKY/UNLUCKY**

---

unfortunately /ʌnˈfɔːʳtʃənˌtli/ [adv] *There's nothing I can do about it, unfortunately.* | *Unfortunately, Dr Cole cannot spend as long with each patient as she would like.* | *We were supposed to arrive earlier, but unfortunately the flight was delayed.*

sadly /'sædli/ [adv] unfortunately – use this to talk about events or situations that are very sad and serious: *Alice was rushed to the hospital, but sadly she died two hours later.* | *Sadly, this fine old theatre was destroyed by fire in 2003.*

> **Formal or informal?**
> **Sadly** is more formal than **unfortunately**.

🔍 **it's a pity/it's a shame** /ɪts ə 'pɪti, ɪts ə 'ʃeɪm/ SPOKEN say this to show that you feel disappointed, sad, or annoyed about something that has happened
+(that) *It's a shame you can't come with us.* | *I don't mind you going out – it's just a pity that you didn't ask me first.*
+about *It's a shame about the weather – it was so nice yesterday.*
what a pity/what a shame! (say this to show that you feel sad or sympathetic about something) *"Janet didn't get that job." "Oh, what a pity!"*
a real/terrible shame *They've cut down all those beautiful trees. It's a terrible shame.*

🔍 **it's sad** /ɪts 'sæd/ ESPECIALLY SPOKEN use this to show that you feel upset about something sad that has happened, and you wish the situation was different
it's sad (that) *It's so sad that your father can't be here to see this.*

it's sad when *It's sad when a marriage breaks up, especially after all those years.*

it's very/terribly sad *The town centre is dying, and most of the shops have closed down. It's terribly sad.*

UNKIND

➡ opposite **KIND**
➡ see also **CRUEL**

1 treating someone unkindly

unkind /ˌʌnˈkaɪndʌ/ [*adj*] if you are **unkind** to someone, you speak to them or treat them in a way that makes them unhappy: *It is all right to correct your students' mistakes, but try not to be unkind.* | *It was a really unkind thing to say.*

+to *I'm sorry – I didn't mean to be so unkind to you yesterday.*

it is unkind (of sb) to do sth *It was very unkind of them to keep making jokes about her cooking.*

unkindly [*adv*] *He loves you, Fiona, even though you treat him so unkindly.*

cruel /ˈkruːəl/ [*adj*] someone who is **cruel** is very unkind: *He's not ugly! How can you be so cruel?*

+to *The other kids were cruel to him because he was so fat.*

it is cruel (of sb) to do sth *It was cruel of you to frighten the poor boy like that.*

cruelly [*adv*] *She wanted to leave him but, as he cruelly reminded her, she had nowhere else to go.*

⚲ **nasty** /ˈnɑːstiǁˈnæsti/ [*adj*] ESPECIALLY SPOKEN someone who is **nasty** is deliberately unkind, and seems to enjoy making people unhappy: *What a nasty thing to do!* | *He has a really nasty side to his character.*

+to *Don't be so nasty to your sister!*

nasty – nastier – nastiest

spiteful /ˈspaɪtfəl/ [*adj*] deliberately unkind to someone because you are jealous of them or angry with them: *Failure had made him bitter and spiteful.* | *That was a wicked and spiteful thing to do.*

spitefully [*adv*] *"I never liked her anyway," Rob said spitefully.*

bitchy /ˈbɪtʃi/ [*adj*] INFORMAL someone who is **bitchy** says unkind things about another person, especially about the way they look or behave

bitchy comments/remarks *She's always making bitchy comments about other people's clothes.*

+about *She was being really bitchy about Martha.*

> **Bitchy** is used especially by women when talking about other women.

2 unkind, but not deliberately unkind

thoughtless/inconsiderate /ˈθɔːtləs, ˌɪnkənˈsɪdərɪtʌ/ [*adj*] someone who is **thoughtless** or **inconsiderate** only thinks about their own situation, their own enjoyment etc, and does not think about the effects that their actions will have on other people: *A few thoughtless people spoiled the trip for everyone.* | *I have an inconsiderate neighbour who plays loud music late at night.*

it is thoughtless/inconsiderate of sb to do sth *It was thoughtless of him to mention her divorce when she's so upset.*

insensitive /ɪnˈsensɪtɪv/ [*adj*] someone who is **insensitive** does not realize that something that they do could upset other people: *I thought it was very insensitive, the way she kept talking about her new baby – she knows that Pam can't have children.* | *insensitive treatment of rape victims*

insensitive to sb's feelings/needs etc *Doctors sometimes seem insensitive to their patients' feelings.*

tactless /ˈtæktləs/ [*adj*] someone who is **tactless** says or does things that offend other people or hurt their feelings, without intending to and without realizing that they have done it: *He's not uncaring, but he is tactless.* | *Why is he wearing that hat? Or is that a tactless question?*

UNTIDY

→ opposite **TIDY**
→ see also **DIRTY**

1 place/room

untidy /ʌn'taɪdi/ [adj] if a place is **untidy**, things have been left carelessly in different parts of it instead of being neatly arranged: *Dad is always complaining that my bedroom's untidy.* | *an untidy desk* | *These drawers are so untidy – I can never find what I'm looking for.*
untidy – untidier – untidiest

be a mess/be in a mess /biː ə 'mes, biː ɪn ə 'mes/ INFORMAL if a place **is a mess** or **is in a mess**, it is very untidy and dirty: *Please sit down. Sorry everything's such a mess.* | *The whole house was in a mess, but I didn't have time to clean it up.*

messy /'mesi/ [adj] INFORMAL very untidy and dirty: *He only cleans up his room when it gets really messy.* | *She felt uncomfortable in such a messy house.*
messy – messier – messiest

cluttered /'klʌtəʳd/ [adj] untidy because there are too many things in a small space: *a cluttered little office*
+with *The room was tiny, its walls cluttered with paintings and old photographs.*

dump /dʌmp/ [n singular] SPOKEN INFORMAL a dirty and untidy place: *Why don't you do something about your room? It's a dump.*

tip /tɪp/ [n singular] BRITISH, SPOKEN INFORMAL a very untidy place: *Paul's room is an absolute tip!*

2 person/clothes/hair etc

untidy /ʌn'taɪdi/ [adj] someone who is **untidy** does not keep their house, possessions, clothes, hair etc neatly arranged: *The children are so untidy – they leave their things all over the floor.* | *Her hair was untidy and her lipstick was smudged.*

look a mess /ˌlʊk ə 'mes/ BRITISH INFORMAL to look very untidy: *When the police called, I had just got up, and my hair looked a mess.*

messy /'mesi/ [adj] AMERICAN someone who is **messy** does not keep their house or possessions tidy: *Being messy is just part of being a kid.* | *She's got to be the messiest person I know.*

scruffy /'skrʌfi/ [adj] someone who is **scruffy** is wearing old, untidy clothes: *My parents think I look scruffy in these jeans.*
scruffy clothes/jeans/sweater etc *She's wearing that scruffy old sweater again.*
scruffy – scruffier – scruffiest

3 when things are spread around in an untidy way

mess /mes/ [n singular] when things are spread around everywhere in a dirty, untidy way: *We spent the morning tidying up the mess after the party.* | *There were cups and ashtrays everywhere – what a mess!*
make a mess (=make a place dirty and untidy) *You can do some baking if you promise not to make a mess in the kitchen.*

chaos /'keɪ-ɒsǁ-ɑːs/ [n U] when everything is very untidy and there is no order or system: *We've just moved into the new office and I've no idea where anything is – it's chaos!*
in chaos (=in a state of chaos) *I arrived home to find the house in chaos.*

When you see **EC**, go to the **ESSENTIAL COMMUNICATION** section.

UNUSUAL

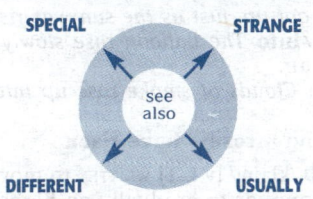

➡ opposite **NORMAL/ORDINARY**

SPECIAL   STRANGE

see
also

DIFFERENT   USUALLY

⚠ Don't confuse **unusual** (=different from what usually happens) and **strange** (=unusual, and also a little frightening, surprising, or difficult to understand).

1 not what usually happens

unusual /ʌnˈjuːʒuəl, -ʒəl/ [adj] different from what usually happens, or different from the ordinary kind: *We had snow in April, which is very unusual.* | *She had an unusual last name – Peachtree or Plumtree or something like that.*
it is unusual to do sth *It is unusual to find lakes of this size in Britain.*
it is unusual for sb to do sth *We were beginning to worry. It was unusual for Dave to be so late.*
unusually [adv] *The office was unusually quiet that morning.*

special /ˈspeʃəl/ [adj usually before noun] a **special** occasion, situation, method etc is one that is different from what normally happens, and usually better: *There were special security arrangements for the President's visit.* | *The prince said he didn't want any special treatment in his new school.*
special event/occasion *I would only buy expensive shoes for a special event such as a wedding.*
in special circumstances *Prisoners are only allowed to visit their families in special circumstances.*

extraordinary /ɪkˈstrɔːdənəri‖-dn-eri, ˌekstrəˈɔːr-/ [adj] something that is **extraordinary** is very unusual because it would normally be very unlikely to happen or exist: *His account of what happened was extraordinary.* | *At that time, $12,000 was an extraordinary amount of money.*
extraordinarily [adv] *The book has sold extraordinarily well.*

exceptional /ɪkˈsepʃənəl/ [adj] an **exceptional** situation is very unusual and happens very rarely; an **exceptional** person or quality is so good that there are very few like them: *A few of the top executives are women, but this is still exceptional.* | *a man of exceptional intelligence*
in exceptional circumstances/cases *Some people believe that doctors should be allowed to terminate their patients' lives in exceptional circumstances.*
exceptionally [adv] *This has been an exceptionally busy week.*

> **Formal or informal?**
> **Exceptional** is a more formal word than **extraordinary**.

uncommon/not common /ʌnˈkɒmən, ˌnɒt ˈkɒmən‖-ˈkɑːmən/ [adj] something that is **uncommon** or **not common** is unusual because it does not happen very often: *The disease mostly affects older people, and is not common among people under 50.*
it is uncommon/not common (for sb) to do sth *It is uncommon for small babies to sleep more than four hours without waking.*

> **Formal or informal?**
> **Uncommon/not common** is more formal than **unusual**.

🗩 **it's not like sb** /ɪts nɒt ˈlaɪk (sb)/ SPOKEN say this when you mean that someone is behaving in a way that they do not usually behave, so you think they may be ill or have some kind of problem: *Don't you want any more to eat? That's not like you.*
it's not like sb to do sth *It's not like Sally to get so upset – I think she's been working too hard.*

2 different from the way most people think or behave

unconventional /ˌʌnkənˈvenʃənəl⁴/ [adj] someone who is **unconventional** lives, behaves, or does things in ways that are very different from the way that most ordinary people live or behave: *She comes from an unconventional family.* | *unconventional teaching methods*

UP

➡ if you mean 'a price, number etc goes up', go to **INCREASE**
➡ opposite **DOWN**
➡ see also **CLIMB**

1 moving up to a higher place or level

up /ʌp/ [*preposition/adv*]
go/climb/walk etc up *There's a great view from the top – you should go up and have a look.*
up a hill/tree/wall etc *Tim had climbed up a tree to get a better view.*
+to/into/onto/over/at etc *We made our way up to the top of the mountain.* | *Don't let the cat jump up onto the table.*
straight up (=directly up) *Serena was so scared she jumped straight up in the air.*

upwards (also **upward** AMERICAN) /'ʌpwəʳd(z)/ [*adv*] towards a higher position, especially towards the sky: *Most plants grow upwards, towards the light.*
+into/above/over etc *With a loud bang, the rocket shot upward into the sky.*
upward [*adj* only before noun] *She massaged my back with a light upward movement.*

⚠ Don't say 'they walked upwards the hill'. Say **they walked up the hill**.

uphill /ˌʌp'hɪl◂/ [*adv*] going up a hill: *When I'm driving uphill the engine makes a terrible noise.* | *The bus crawled uphill for another mile.*
uphill [*adj* only before noun] *a long uphill climb through the snow*
upstairs /ˌʌp'steəʳz/ [*adv*]
go/walk/run etc upstairs to go towards a higher level in a building

by going up the stairs: *Guy ran upstairs quickly.* | *Don't go upstairs yet – Mom's still getting dressed.*

rise /raɪz/ [*v I*] WRITTEN to move straight up into the air or sky: *Hot air rises.* | *We got up, just as the sun was rising.*
+in/into *The balloon rose slowly into the air.*
+up *Clouds of smoke rose up into the air.*
rising – rose – have risen

climb /klaɪm/ [*v I/T*] WRITTEN to move up a slope, or to gradually go higher up into the sky: *The bus began to climb the steep hill out of the valley.* | *The plane climbed higher and higher until it was out of sight.*

2 looking, facing, or pointing upwards

up /ʌp/ [*adv*]
look/point/stare up *Caroline looked up and laughed.*
+at/into/towards etc *The dog just sat and stared up at me.*
straight up (=directly up) *He was pointing his rifle straight up in the air.*

upwards (also **upward** AMERICAN) /'ʌpwəʳd(z)/ [*adv*] facing or pointing up, especially towards the sky: *He held the palms of his hands upward as if he were asking forgiveness.* | *A copy of the book lay on the table, its cover facing upwards.*

vertical /'vɜːʳtɪkəl/ [*adj*] lines, walls, surfaces etc that are **vertical** go straight up: *The wallpaper had vertical pink and white stripes.* | *First, the surgeon makes a three-inch vertical cut in the abdomen.*
vertically [*adv*] *The cliffs rose vertically out of the sea.*

upright /'ʌp-raɪt/ [*adj/adv*] standing straight up: *The ceiling was so low that we couldn't stand upright.*
hold/keep sth upright *Keep the bottle upright, in case it leaks.*

3 in a higher position

upstairs /ˌʌp'steəʳz◂/ [*adv*] on a higher floor of a building, especially just

above where you are: *The bathroom is upstairs on your left.* | *Don't you think that the woman who lives upstairs is kind of strange?*
upstairs [*adj* only before noun] *The burglars got in through an upstairs window.*

> ⚠ Don't say 'she lives in upstairs'. Just say **she lives upstairs**.

up in/up on/up there etc /'ʌp ɪn, 'ʌp ɒn, ʌp 'ðeəʳ (etc)/ in a higher position than where you are: *I found some old pictures of my mother up in the attic.* | *Put the bottles up on the shelf where the baby can't reach them.* | *Are you able to see up there or do you need the flashlight?*

4 to move a part of your body up

raise /reɪz/ [*v T*] to move part of your body up: *She raised her head and looked at him.* | *If you want to ask a question, please raise your hand.*

> **Formal or informal?**
> **Raise** is used in writing, and in formal spoken instructions.

put up /ˌpʊt 'ʌp/ [*phrasal verb T*] to move your hand or arm above your head
put up your hand/arm *Put up your hand if you know the answer.*
put your hand/arm up *She put her hand up to shield her eyes from the sun.*

5 when a road or path goes towards a higher level

up /ʌp/ [*adv/preposition*] *A track continues up the hillside towards the church.*
+into/towards/over etc *The path led up into the mountains.*
go up/go uphill /ˌgəʊ 'ʌp, ˌgəʊ ʌp'hɪl/ [*phrasal verb I*] to go towards a higher level: *The road goes up from the beach into the forest.* | *The path went uphill for another two miles.*

6 when the level of water goes up

rise /raɪz/ [*v I*] *The level of water in the lake was rising fast.* | *In 2004 the river rose to a height of more than 6 metres.*
rising – rose – have risen

USE

→ see also **WASTE**

1 to use something

use /juːz/ [*v T*] to use something for a purpose: *Do you mind if I use your phone?* | *Are we allowed to use a dictionary in the test?* | *They rebuilt the church using local stone.*
use sth to do sth *Use a calculator to check your answers.*
use sth for doing sth *We use the shed for storing our firewood.*
use sth as sth *We decided to use the second bedroom as a junk room.*
with /wɪð, wɪθ/ [*preposition*] if you do something **with** a tool, piece of equipment etc, you use a tool, piece of equipment etc to do it: *Beat the egg with a fork.* | *Do you have anything I can open the bottle with?*
make use of sth /ˌmeɪk 'juːs ɒv (sth)/ to use something that is available, especially something that can help you or give you an advantage: *I made use of my old contacts to get a job when I came back from Australia.*
make good/full use of sth *Students are encouraged to make good use of all the computing facilities.*

2 to use an amount of something

use /juːz/ [*v T*] to use an amount of something such as fuel, water, or food: *Who's used all the hot water?* | *We use about six pints of milk a week.*
consume /kən'sjuːmǁ-'suːm/ [*v T*] FORMAL to use fuel, energy, water, and other natural products – use this especially to talk about the amount of fuel, energy used by people in general: *The US imports 45% of the oil that it consumes.* | *Industrialized countries consume natural resources in huge quantities.*

consumption /kənˈsʌmpʃən/ [n U] the amount of fuel, energy etc that people use: *The government is urging people to reduce their water consumption.*

3 to use something again

recycle /ˌriːˈsaɪkəl/ [v T] to put bottles, newspapers, cans etc through a process so that they can be used for making new bottles, paper etc: *New techniques for recycling plastics are being introduced.*
recycled [adj] *All our envelopes are made from recycled paper.*

reuse /ˌriːˈjuːz/ [v T] to use something more than once: *The supermarket encourages shoppers to re-use plastic bags.*

4 being used now

be in use /biː ɪn ˈjuːs/ if a room or machine **is in use**, it is being used by someone at the present time, so no one else can use it: *The meeting room is in use at the moment, so we'll have to go somewhere else.* | *All the photocopiers are in use. Could you come back later?*

◯ **be taken** /biː ˈteɪkən/ ESPECIALLY SPOKEN if a seat in a train, theatre, restaurant etc **is taken**, it is not available because someone else is already sitting there or will be soon: *Is this seat taken?* | *I'm sorry, you can't sit there. It's taken.*

5 no longer being used

unused /ˌʌnˈjuːzd/ [adj] ESPECIALLY WRITTEN something that is **unused** has not been used or has not been used for a long time: *Unused gas bottles should be stored well away from the stove.* | *His old car sat in the garage, unused.* | *Batteries which are unused for long periods may have to be recharged.*

disused /ˌdɪsˈjuːzd/ [adj only before noun] ESPECIALLY BRITISH a **disused** factory, mine, railway etc is old and not used any more: *The drugs were found in a disused warehouse.*

6 something that can be used

available /əˈveɪləbəl/ [adj] something that is **available** can be used, for example because no one else is using it or it is not being used for anything else: *This program will take up a lot of your available disk space.*
every available *Houses were being built on every available plot of land.*
whatever is available *They built the shelter using old wood and plastic – just whatever was available.*

◯ **free** /friː/ [adj] ESPECIALLY SPOKEN use this about a chair, room, table etc that you can use because no one else is using it: *The office next door is free if you need somewhere to work.* | *There's just one free table, over there in the corner.*

spare /speər/ [adj only before noun] a **spare tyre/pen/key etc** a tyre etc which you are not using at the moment, but which you keep in case the one you are using breaks, gets lost etc: *We keep a spare key in the garage.* | *Do you have a spare pen I could borrow?*

empty/vacant /ˈempti, ˈveɪkənt/ [adj] use this about buildings that no one is using: *Fire broke out in a vacant office block early this morning.* | *The house has been empty for over a year.*

> **Formal or informal?**
> **Vacant** is more formal than **empty**.

7 officially allowed to be used

valid /ˈvælɪd/ [adj] if a ticket, passport etc is **valid**, you can legally use it and it will be officially accepted: *Do you have a valid driver's license?*
+for *Your ticket is valid for travel at any time of the day.*
valid for 10 years/two months/one week etc *My passport is valid for 10 years.*

8 what something can be used for

use /juːs/ [n C often plural] a way in which something can be used: *Robots have many different uses in modern industry.* | *The land has been*

developed for tourism and other recreational uses.
+of the use of animals in scientific experiments

○**be for** /biː ˈfɔːʳ/ [phrasal verb T]
ESPECIALLY SPOKEN to be used for doing a particular job: *This cream is for removing make-up.* | *What's that switch for?*

function /ˈfʌŋkʃən/ [n C] the purpose for which something is intended or the way people use it
+of *What is the function of literature in our society?* | *The main function of the bars is to protect the driver's legs.*

> **Formal or informal?**
> **Function** is used especially in technical or formal scientific writing.

---

9 **to use something wrongly**

> **Formal or informal?**
> These words are formal and are used when talking about serious things.

misuse /mɪsˈjuːz/ [v T] to use something wrongly, for a purpose that was not intended: *Measures must be taken to prevent confidential data from being misused.* | *Politicians misused public money on entertaining their business friends.*
misuse /mɪsˈjuːs/ [n C/U] when something is used wrongly, for a purpose that was not intended: *Opponents of genetic engineering see it as a misuse of scientific knowledge.*

abuse /əˈbjuːz/ [v T] to use something for a bad purpose, especially to use a position of power or trust in order to get a personal advantage: *Local politicians abused their privileges to make themselves rich.* | *people who abuse the welfare system*
abuse /əˈbjuːs/ [n C/U] when something is used for a bad purpose: *There was widespread abuse of power.* | *drug abuse*

USED TO/ ACCUSTOMED TO

when something seems normal to you because you have often done it or experienced it before

➡ if you mean 'did something regularly in the past', go to **PAST 2**

1 **used to something**

be used to sth /biː ˈjuːst tuː (sth)/ if you are **used to** something, you have often done it or experienced it before, so it does not seem strange, new, or difficult to you
be used to doing sth *She grew up on a farm, so she's used to getting up early.*
be used to sth *At first Omar hated the rain in England, but he's used to it now.*
get used to (doing) sth *It's quite a simple system – you'll soon get used to it.* | *Mary never really got used to living on her own after her husband died.*

> ⚠ Don't say 'I am used to do this'. Say **I am used to doing this**: *I'm used to making all my own food.*

> ⚠ Don't confuse **I used to do it** (=I regularly did it in the past, but I don't do it now) and **I am used to doing it** (=I often do it, so it doesn't seem strange to me): *When I worked on a farm, I used to get up early every day.* | *I work on a farm, so I'm used to getting up early.*

be accustomed to sth /biː əˈkʌstəmd tuː (sth)/ FORMAL to be used to something, especially because it is a normal part of your life: *Zara was accustomed to a life of luxury.*
be accustomed to doing sth *They were already accustomed to waiting, so no one complained.*
become/grow accustomed to sth *After a time, she became accustomed to all the media attention.*

adjust to sth /əˈdʒʌst tuː (sth)/ [phrasal verb T] to gradually get used to a new situation, by changing your attitudes or the way you do things: *It took us a while to adjust to the tropical climate.* | *Some of the staff found it hard to adjust to all the changes in technology and working methods.*

settle in /ˌsetl 'ɪn/ [phrasal verb I] to gradually get used to a new place or a new way of life, so that you feel relaxed and confident: *Paul never really settled in at his last school.*
settle into sth *It didn't take Charlie long to settle into his new job.*

familiar /fə'mɪliə^r/ [adj] a **familiar** place, idea, situation etc is one that you are used to and that you know well: *It was good to be back in familiar surroundings.* | *the familiar sounds of home*
+to *This kind of problem will be familiar to many married couples.*

2 not used to something

not be used to sth /nɒt biː 'juːst tuː (sth)/ *I'm still not used to the new computer system.*
not be used to doing sth *Jane wasn't used to having so much money, and she didn't know what to do with it.*

be unaccustomed to sth /biː ʌnə'kʌstəmd tuː (sth)/ FORMAL to not be used to something, especially when this makes you annoyed or worried: *Curtis was a country boy, unaccustomed to city life.*
be unaccustomed to doing sth *Teachers may be unaccustomed to having their teaching methods criticised.*

unfamiliar /ˌʌnfə'mɪliə^r◂/ [adj] an **unfamiliar** place, idea, situation etc is one that you are not used to or do not know much about: *Driving on the left-hand side of the road was unfamiliar and a little frightening.* | *She needs your support even more now that she's in an unfamiliar environment.*
+to *Some of these expressions may be unfamiliar to your students.*

strange /streɪndʒ/ [adj only before noun] a **strange** country, food, custom etc is one that you are not used to because you have never been there before, experienced it before etc, and this may make you feel anxious: *She was all alone in a strange city.* | *The strange food made her ill.*

USEFUL/NOT USEFUL

⇒ see also **CONVENIENT/NOT CONVENIENT 2**

1 useful

useful /'juːsfəl/ [adj] something that is **useful** makes it easier for you to do something: *See page 35 for a list of useful addresses.* | *The bank gave us a lot of useful advice about starting our own business.* | *a useful skill*
useful for doing sth *Scotch tape is very useful for making quick repairs.*
+to *information that may be useful to the enemy*
🔍 **come in useful** SPOKEN (=be useful in a particular situation) *Take an umbrella with you – it might come in useful later.*

handy /'hændi/ [adj] INFORMAL useful and easy to use: *a handy chart for converting pounds into kilos* | *This handy booklet tells you everything you need to know about getting connected to the Internet.*
handy for doing sth *There's a special brush, which is handy for cleaning the stairs.*
🔍 **come in handy** SPOKEN (=be useful in a particular situation) *Bring a sleeping bag – it might come in handy.*

practical /'præktɪkəl/ [adj] designed to be useful rather than attractive – use this especially about clothes and things you use in your house: *a type of floor covering that is simple, practical, and cheap*
🔍 **be good for sth** /biː 'gʊd fɔː^r (sth)/ ESPECIALLY SPOKEN to be suitable and useful for a particular job or purpose: *The old table does take up a lot of space, but it's good for parties.*
be good for doing sth *The big jars are good for storing pasta.*

invaluable /ɪn'væljuəbəl,-jʊbəl‖ɪn'væljʊbəl/ [adj] FORMAL extremely useful – use this about something that you are very pleased to have because it will help you a lot, for example someone's advice or help: *Thank you, your advice has been invaluable.* | *My*

six months at IBM gave me invaluable experience of the computer business.
+to *Margaret's sensible suggestions have been invaluable to us.*

versatile /ˈvɜːsətaɪlǁˈvɜːrsətl/ [adj] ESPECIALLY WRITTEN something that is **versatile** can be used in a lot of different ways: *Few foods are as versatile as cheese.* | *a versatile work table*

2 not useful

useless /ˈjuːsləs/ [adj] not at all useful: *a piece of useless information* | *She gave me a DVD, but of course it's useless without a player.*
completely/totally/absolutely useless *I'm going to throw this old vacuum cleaner away – it's absolutely useless.*
+for *Jay's car was 20 years old, and useless for anything but a short journey to the local shops.*

pointless /ˈpɔɪntləs/ [adj] if someone does something that is **pointless**, it does not seem to have any useful purpose, and will not help anyone: *The argument was completely pointless.* | *pointless drug testing on animals*
a pointless exercise (=something that you have to do, but which does not seem to have any purpose) *We had to change the sheets daily, which always seemed to me to be a pointless exercise.*
it is pointless doing sth BRITISH *It's pointless trying to speak to the manager – she's always too busy.*

◌ **there's no point/what's the point?** /ðeəˈz ˌnəʊ ˈpɔɪnt, ˌwɒts ðə ˈpɔɪnt/ ESPECIALLY SPOKEN say this when you think that it is useless to do something because it will not achieve any useful purpose: *"Why don't you try and sort out your argument with Mike?" "There's no point – he never listens."*
there's no point (in) doing sth *There's no point in waiting any longer – she obviously isn't coming.*
what's the point of doing sth? *You've already decided so what's the point of discussing it?*

◌ **be a waste of time** /biː ə ˌweɪst əv ˈtaɪm/ ESPECIALLY SPOKEN use this when you think that someone should not

spend their time doing something because it will definitely not achieve anything
be a complete waste of time *These meetings are a complete waste of time. Nothing ever gets decided.*
be a waste of time doing sth *I told you it would be a waste of time applying for that job.*

USUALLY

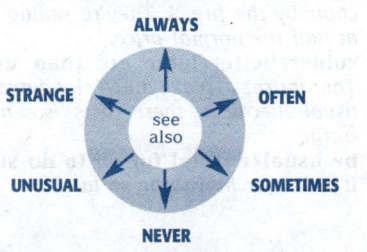

ALWAYS
STRANGE   OFFEN
see also
UNUSUAL   SOMETIMES
NEVER

1 usually

usually/normally/generally /ˈjuːʒuəli, ˈnɔːrməli, ˈdʒenərəli/ [adv] on most occasions or in most situations: *I usually get up at about 7 o'clock.* | *The journey normally takes me about 45 minutes.* | *Usually, I do all the housework and Pete does the garden.* | *The sea here is generally calm.*

> ⚠ Put **usually**, **normally**, and **generally** before the main verb in a sentence, except when the main verb is 'be': *They usually make a lot of noise.* | *They are usually very noisy.*

as usual /əz ˈjuːʒuəl/ in the same way as things usually happen: *Sam was in a bad mood as usual.* | *As usual, there was far too much food.*

> ⚠ Don't say 'as usually'. Say **as usual**.

Formal or informal?
In informal spoken English, **as usual** is often used to say that something has happened again, when it is annoying and has often happened before: *I tried to find Larry, but as usual he was outside having a cigarette.*

⌕ **nine times out of ten** /ˌnaɪn taɪmz aʊt əv 'ten/ [adv] ESPECIALLY SPOKEN almost always: *Nine times out of ten, he works late and I have to look after the kids.*

2 usual

usual/normal /'juːʒuəl, 'nɔːrməl/ [adj usually before noun] use this about something that usually happens or something that someone usually does or uses: *She was sitting in her usual chair by the fire.* | *They're selling CDs at half the normal price.*

colder/better/later etc than usual *The journey took much longer than usual because there was so much traffic.*

be usual/normal for sb to do sth *Is it usual for him to be so late?*

3 something that you usually do

habit /'hæbɪt/ [n C/U] something that you do very often and without thinking about it, because you have done it so many times before
good/bad habit *Regular exercise is a good habit for kids to develop.*
be in the habit of doing sth *She was in the habit of taking a walk in the early evening.*
get into the habit of doing sth (=start doing something regularly) *You ought to get into the habit of planning your work each morning.*

routine /ˌruːˈtiːn/ [n C/U] all the things that you usually do in the same order every day: *His routine consisted of work, dinner, then TV and bed.* | *Most babies soon develop a daily routine of eating and sleeping.*
routine [adj] a **routine** action or process is done as a normal part of a job or system: *The drugs were found during a routine check by customs officers.*

V, v

VERY

➡ see also **LOT 4, COMPLETELY, LITTLE/ NOT MUCH**

1 very

very /'veri/ [adv] We had a very good time. | The test was very difficult. | She described the scene very well. | During our time working together, I got to know her very well.

🔍 **really** /'rɪəli/ [adv] ESPECIALLY SPOKEN very – use this especially to talk about your feelings or what you think about something: It's really cold out there. | I feel really hungry. | Bob played really well.

highly /'haɪli/ [adv] very
highly successful/intelligent/effective etc He runs a highly successful company.
highly likely/unlikely The plan is highly unlikely to succeed.
highly educated/skilled a team of highly skilled engineers

> **Formal or informal?**
> **Highly** is more formal than **very**.

🔍 **real** /rɪəl/ [adv] AMERICAN SPOKEN INFORMAL very: I think he's a real smart guy. | You can take the car but be real careful. | The sidewalk was real wet and slippery.

2 even more than very

extremely /ɪk'striːmli/ [adv] use this when you want to use a stronger word than 'very': It is extremely difficult to work in these conditions. | The article contains some extremely important information. | The conference was extremely badly organized.

🔍 **absolutely** /'æbsəluːtli, ˌæbsə'luːtli/ [adv] ESPECIALLY SPOKEN as much as it is possible to imagine – use this to emphasize adjectives that already have a strong meaning

absolutely marvellous/wonderful/ delicious etc We had an absolutely marvellous day. | The cake tastes absolutely delicious – did you make it?
absolutely filthy/disgusting/awful etc When they came in from the yard, they were absolutely filthy.
absolutely terrified/exhausted/ delighted/furious etc She stood in the middle of the stage, looking absolutely terrified.

completely /kəm'pliːtli/ [adv] in every possible way: What's he doing? Has he gone completely crazy? | By Friday I'm always completely exhausted. | a place where you can feel completely relaxed

🔍 **very, very** /'veri ˌveri/ SPOKEN say this when you want to emphasize 'very': I'm very, very angry with her. | This is a very, very important decision.

🔍 **incredibly** /ɪn'kredɪbli/ [adv] ESPECIALLY SPOKEN use this when something is so good, so bad, so fast etc that you are surprised by it or you find it hard to believe: They all work incredibly hard. | Their house is incredibly cold – I don't think they heat it at all. | I've been incredibly lucky in my career.

3 less than very, but more than a little

fairly /'feəʳli/ [adv] if something is **fairly** heavy, **fairly** easy etc it is more than a little heavy or easy, but it is not very heavy or very easy: The house has a fairly big living room. | She was fairly certain that she had been there before. | Maria sings fairly well, but she needs more lessons.

quite /kwaɪt/ [adv/predeterminer] ESPECIALLY BRITISH if something is **quite** heavy, **quite** easy etc, it is more than a little heavy or easy, but it is not very heavy or very easy: The hotel was quite expensive. | Geoffrey was quite wealthy. | I quite like it here, but I'd rather live in Manchester.
quite a long way/a nice day/a good book etc It's quite a long way to the church from here. | I thought it was quite an interesting movie.
quite a lot Mick and Carla have been together quite a lot recently.

V

In American English, 'quite good', 'quite funny' etc usually means 'very good', 'very funny' etc.

pretty /'prɪti/ [adv] INFORMAL fairly: *It's pretty cold today.* | *I was pretty embarrassed when I realized that she'd been listening.* | *"Hi Beth, how are you?" "Pretty good. And you?"*

Formal or informal?
In British English, **pretty** is used mostly in informal conversation. But in American English, **pretty** is much more common, and it is the most usual way of saying **fairly**.

rather /'rɑːðəʳ‖'ræ-/ [adv/predeterminer] ESPECIALLY BRITISH fairly: *Gail seems rather unhappy today.* | *a rather annoying delay*
rather a long way/short dress etc *That's rather a large whisky; I don't think I can drink it all.*
rather a lot *She was wearing rather a lot of make-up at the party.*

VIOLENT

likely to attack or hurt people

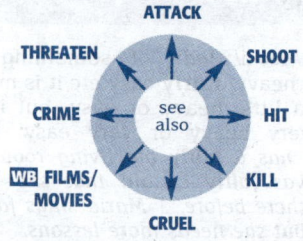

```
              ATTACK
THREATEN               SHOOT
CRIME      see         HIT
           also
WB FILMS/               KILL
   MOVIES
              CRUEL
```

1   violent person/animal/behaviour

violent /'vaɪələnt/ [adj] someone who is **violent** attacks people physically, especially because this is part of their character. A **violent** action involves physical attacks on people: *My father was a violent man who couldn't control his temper.* | *There was a violent protest outside the court, and a police officer was injured.*
violent crime *Everyone is worried about the increase in violent crime.*
turn violent (=suddenly start to behave violently) *Travellers to the*

conference have been urged to avoid large crowds, which have occasionally turned violent in the past.
violently [adv] *He was violently attacked by a gang of youths.*

aggressive /ə'gresɪv/ [adj] someone who is **aggressive** behaves in an angry way, and always seems to want to fight or argue: *Some of the crowd were very aggressive, shouting and banging on windows.* | *Kids who play video games show much more aggressive behaviour than those who don't.*
aggressively [adv] *Why do you always drive so aggressively?*

brutal /'bruːtl/ [adj] very cruel and violent, and without any pity: *Some of the prison guards were brutal and corrupt.* | *a brutal dictator*
brutal murder / attack / killing etc *Carter was jailed for the brutal murder of a young mother of three.*
brutally [adv] *Opponents of the regime were brutally tortured.*

Formal or informal?
Brutal is used especially in formal writing and news reports.

vicious /'vɪʃəs/ [adj] a **vicious** person or animal is likely to attack and injure people suddenly and for no reason: *Rottweilers are vicious dogs, far too dangerous to have as pets.*
vicious attack/assault *Stephanie was the victim of a vicious sex attack.*

fierce /fɪəʳs/ [adj] a **fierce** animal looks very frightening and is ready to attack people: *A fierce dog was standing at the gate, guarding the house.*

2   violent film/story

violent /'vaɪələnt/ [udj] **violent** films, stories, or television programmes contain a lot of fighting and killing: *I think Tarantino's films are too violent.*
gory /'gɔːri/ [adj] **gory** films, descriptions etc clearly show or describe violent injuries, blood, death etc: *a gory horror movie*

3   violent actions

violence /'vaɪələns/ [n U] fighting, killing, and other violent behaviour: *In* *some parts of the city, teachers have to deal with violence in the classroom. | complaints about sex and violence on TV*

+against *The statistics show that male violence against women is widespread.*

force /fɔːʳs/ [n U] violent action, used in order to make someone do something: *We want to end the demonstration without force.*

use force *The police do not use force when arresting people unless it's absolutely necessary.*

by force (=using force) *Her husband tried to get the children back by force.*

aggression /əˈɡreʃən/ [n U] angry feelings or behaviour that often result in fighting: *In a prison, drugs sometimes have to be used to control aggression.*

+in *Some people think aggression in children may be caused by the food they eat.*

+towards *Our dog has never shown any aggression towards other dogs.*

VISIT

to go and spend time in a place or with a person

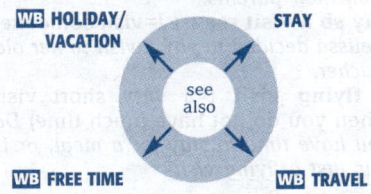

WB HOLIDAY/VACATION

STAY

see also

WB FREE TIME

WB TRAVEL

1 to visit a person

visit /ˈvɪzɪt/ [v I/T] to go and spend time with someone, especially in their home: *We're going to visit Vicky this weekend. | Paul visited her every day when she was in the hospital.*

Formal or informal?

Visit is a fairly formal word. In informal English, **go to see** is more common.

go to see /ˌɡəʊ tə ˈsiː/ to go and spend time with someone, either for enjoyment or in order to get advice or help from them: *We went to see Kim last weekend. | He goes to see his mother*

every evening. | You should go to see the doctor about that cough.

Formal or informal?

In formal spoken English, you can also say **go and see**: *Why don't you go and see your mother?* In informal American spoken English, you can also say **go see**: *You really should go see the bank manager.*

⚠ In the past tense, always say **went to see** (not 'went see'): *I went to see an accountant about my tax problems.*

stop by (also **stop in** AMERICAN) /ˌstɒp ˈbaɪ, ˌstɒp ˈɪnǁˌstɑːp-/ [phrasal verb I] to visit someone for a short time while you are on your way to somewhere else: *I just stopped by to say goodbye before I went on holiday.*

⌕ **drop in/drop by** /ˌdrɒp ˈɪn, ˌdrɒp ˈbaɪǁˌdrɑːp-/ [phrasal verb I] ESPECIALLY SPOKEN to visit someone for a short time, especially when they are not expecting you: *Lizzie said she'd drop in later to let us know what the arrangements are for tonight. | Kate dropped by this morning.*

⌕ **come by** /ˌkʌm ˈbaɪ/ [phrasal verb I] ESPECIALLY SPOKEN to visit someone in their home, especially for a short time: *Can you come by on Tuesday to pick up the keys?*

⌕ **call round/call in** /ˌkɔːl ˈraʊnd, ˌkɔːl ˈɪn/ [phrasal verb I] BRITISH, ESPECIALLY SPOKEN to visit someone in their home while you are on your way to somewhere else: *Fred calls round sometimes on his way to the sports centre. | I'll call in tomorrow then, Mum.*

see /siː/ [v T] to visit a doctor, lawyer etc at their place of work, in order to get professional help or advice: *You should see a doctor if your back doesn't get any better. | I've come to see the Planning Officer.*

seeing – saw – have seen

2 to visit a place

go to /ˈɡəʊ tuː/ [phrasal verb T] to visit a place: *We're going to Hawaii for our vacation. | I've been to Germany several times. | Have you ever been to the National Gallery in London?*

go to see /ˌgəʊ tə ˈsiː/ to visit a well-known place or building while you are in a city or country: *If you're in Paris, you must go to see the Pompidou Centre.*

> **Formal or informal?**
> In informal spoken English, you can also say **go and see**: *Let's go and see the cathedral.* In informal American spoken English, you can also say **go see**: *Why don't we go see the Statue of Liberty?*

> ⚠ In the past tense, always say **went to see** (not 'went see').

visit /ˈvɪzɪt/ [v T] to go somewhere, especially as part of your official duties: *The Ambassador last visited Hong Kong in 2002. | This afternoon the Queen will visit Great Ormond Street Children's Hospital.*

> ⚠ Don't say 'he visited to the town'. Say **he visited the town**.

> **Formal or informal?**
> In conversation and informal letters, don't say 'we visited the cinema/Disneyland etc'. Say **we went to the cinema/Disneyland** etc.

stop off /ˌstɒp ˈɒf‖ˌstɑːp ˈɔːf/ [phrasal verb I] to make a short visit to a place during a journey
+at/in *We stopped off in Boston on our way to New York. | I'll stop off at the library on the way home.*

sightseeing /ˈsaɪtˌsiːɪŋ/ [n U] the activity of visiting and travelling around a place to look at the famous and interesting places there: *We did a lot of sightseeing while we were in London.*
go sightseeing *Let's go sightseeing tomorrow. I'd like to see the Empire State Building and Central Park.*

> ⚠ Don't say 'a sightseeing'. Say **some sightseeing** or **a lot of sightseeing**.

 3 someone who visits

visitor /ˈvɪzɪtəʳ/ [n C] someone who visits a person or place: *The museum had over a million visitors last year. |*

We have visitors staying with us at the moment. | Prisoners are allowed only two visitors a week.

guest /gest/ [n C] someone that you have invited to visit you or stay with you at your house: *You're not supposed to do the dishes – you're a guest.*
have a guest *We had a couple of guests for the weekend.*

> **Formal or informal?**
> **Guest** is a rather formal word. In spoken English, it is more usual to say **visitor**, **someone visiting**, or **someone staying**: *We have some friends visiting us this weekend.*

tourist /ˈtʊərɪst/ [n C] someone who is visiting a place while they are on holiday: *Cambridge is full of tourists in the summer.*

4 a time when you visit

visit /ˈvɪzɪt/ [n C] an occasion when someone visits a person or a place: *Jenni was getting quite excited at the thought of her mother's visit.*
+to *It's the President's first visit to Moscow.*
+from *The girls were quite excited because they were expecting a visit from their parents.*
pay sb a visit FORMAL (=visit someone) *Melissa decided to pay a visit to her old teacher.*
a flying visit (=a very short visit when you do not have much time) *Do you have time to stay for a meal, or is this just a flying visit?*

VOTE

➡ see also WB **GOVERNMENT/POLITICS, REPRESENT, PROTEST**

1 to vote

vote /vəʊt/ [v I/T] to show which person you want to choose, or to show whether you agree with a plan, by putting your hand up or making a mark on a piece of paper
vote for sb/sth (=vote to support them) *I haven't decided who I'm going to vote for. | 70% of the population voted for independence.*

vote against sth (=vote to say that you do not agree with a plan or suggestion) *Only two people voted against the proposal.*
vote to do sth *Congress voted to increase spending on foreign aid.*
vote in favour of sth *The vast majority of people voted in favour of closer links with Europe.*
vote on sth (=vote in order to make a decision about something) *Teachers will be voting on a proposal to accept the 5% pay offer.*
vote *In tomorrow's election, many young people will be voting for the first time.*
vote Republican/Labour etc (=vote for a political party) *I've voted Democrat all my life.*
the vote [n singular] the right to vote: *It wasn't until 1918 that women were given the vote.*

have a vote/take a vote /ˌhæv ə ˈvəʊt, ˌteɪk ə ˈvəʊt/ if a group of people **have a vote** or **take a vote**, they each make it known which idea they agree with, as a formal way of deciding what to do: *We couldn't agree on a way forward, so we decided to have a vote.*
+on *I think we should take a vote on whether or not to accept their offer.*

elect /ɪˈlekt/ [v T] to choose a government, leader, or representative by voting: *At tonight's meeting, we will elect a new chairperson.* | *The present mayor was elected two years ago.*
elect sb leader/chairman/president etc *When was Mr Putin elected president?*

veto /ˈviːtəʊ/ [v T] if someone **vetoes** a decision that other people have agreed, they use their official power to refuse to allow it: *The president has the right to veto any piece of legislation.*
vetoing – vetoed – have vetoed

2 an occasion when people vote

election /ɪˈlekʃən/ [n C] when people vote to choose a government or leader: *It will be interesting to see what happens at the next election.*
hold an election *South Africa held its first multi-racial elections in 1994.*
presidential election (=an election to choose a president) *America is preparing for the presidential elections, which will take place in two weeks' time.*
general election BRITISH (=an election to choose a government) *Taxation will be one of the major issues at the next general election.*

referendum /ˌrefəˈrendəm/ [n C] when everyone in a country votes on a particular important political question
hold a referendum *The government has promised to hold a referendum and let the people choose.*
+on *The Irish people voted 'no' in a referendum on divorce in 1986.*

ballot /ˈbælət/ [n C] when the members of an organization decide something by marking what they want on a piece of paper, especially in order to make sure that it is secret: *The result of the ballot showed that nurses were not in favour of a strike.*
hold a ballot *It was decided to hold a ballot of all party members.*
secret ballot (=when no one knows what you voted for) *Voting will be by secret ballot.*

vote /vəʊt/ [n singular] when a group of people, especially a committee or parliament, vote to decide something: *Winterton announced that he would not be supporting the plan in Monday's vote.*

3 someone who votes

voter /ˈvəʊtər/ [n C] someone who votes in a political election: *Italian voters have shown that they are ready for a change of government.*
Republican / Labour etc voters (=people who vote for the Republican Party etc)

W, w

WAIT

➡ see also **EXPECT, STAY**

1 to wait

wait /weɪt/ [v I] to spend time not doing very much, while you are expecting something to happen or expecting someone to arrive: *Wait here until I get back.* | *Hurry up, everyone's waiting.*

wait for sb/sth (=wait until someone arrives, is ready etc) *I'll stay here and wait for Suzie.*

wait (for) a minute/two hours/a long time etc *Where have you been? I've been waiting for ages.* | *You'll have to wait a few minutes – I'm not ready yet.*

wait to do sth *Are you waiting to use the phone?*

wait for sb/sth to do sth *She waited for him to reply.*

keep sb waiting (=make someone wait, for example by arriving late) *I'm so sorry I kept you waiting.*

wait and see (=be patient until you find out) *I've sent the letter – now I'll just have to wait and see what happens.*

> Don't say 'I'll wait you', 'they waited the bus' etc. Say **I'll wait for you, they waited for the bus** etc.

> You can say **I waited an hour** or **I waited for an hour**. Both are correct.

hold on /ˌhəʊld ˈɒnǁ-ˈɑːn/ [phrasal verb I] SPOKEN to wait a little longer: *I can hold on for a few minutes if you like.*

hang around /ˌhæŋ əˈraʊnd/ [phrasal verb I] INFORMAL to wait in one place without doing anything, so that you are wasting time: *Sally hung around for over an hour, but no-one came.*

hang around for hours/ages etc *We were hanging around for hours before they opened the gates.*

keep sb hanging around *We can't keep our troops hanging around forever, doing nothing.*

2 what you say to tell someone to wait

wait /weɪt/ SPOKEN *Wait – I must phone Les before we go.*

wait a minute/second/moment *Wait a minute. I forgot to turn off the lights.*

just a minute/just a second /ˌdʒʌst ə ˈmɪnɪt, ˌdʒʌst ə ˈsekənd/ SPOKEN say this when you want someone to wait a short time: *Just a minute, I'm almost ready.*

hold on/hang on /ˌhəʊld ˈɒn, ˌhæŋ ˈɒnǁ-ˈɑːn/ SPOKEN INFORMAL say this to tell someone to wait for a short time: *Hold on – I haven't finished yet.*

+a minute/moment/second etc *Hang on a minute while I find her phone number.*

wait up /ˌweɪt ˈʌp/ AMERICAN SPOKEN say this to tell someone to stop, because you want to talk to them or go with them: *Wait up, you guys! I can't walk that fast.*

hold the line /ˌhəʊld ðə ˈlaɪn/ SPOKEN say this in a business telephone conversation to ask someone to wait for a moment: *Hold the line, please, and I'll put you through to our sales department.*

bear with me /ˈbeəʳ wɪð miː/ SPOKEN FORMAL say this to ask someone to wait patiently while you explain something or while you finish what you are doing: *If you just bear with me, I'll explain.*

3 to stand in a line of people waiting

queue/queue up /kjuː, ˌkjuː ˈʌp/ [v I] BRITISH to stand in a line of people who are all waiting for the same thing: *Students were queuing up at the bus-stop.*

queue (up) to do sth *It's worth queuing up to get the best tickets.*

queue (up) for sth *I hope we don't have to queue for tickets.*

stand in line/wait in line /ˌstænd ɪn 'laɪn, ˌweɪt ɪn 'laɪn/ AMERICAN to stand in a line of people who are all waiting for the same thing: *Go and wait in line like everyone else.*
stand/wait in line for sth *There were about 50 people standing in line for tickets outside the club.*
stand/wait in line to do sth *We stood in line for two hours to get into the stadium.*

line up /ˌlaɪn 'ʌp/ [phrasal verb I] if people **line up**, they go and stand in a line and wait to do something or be given something: *The guard ordered us to line up by the wall.*
line up to do sth *Christopher and the other children lined up to receive their awards.*

queue BRITISH **line** AMERICAN /kjuː, laɪn/ [n C] a line of people who are all waiting for the same thing: *The queue went right round the block.*
the front/back of the queue/line *After waiting an hour, we got to the front of the line.*
+for *There was a long queue for the toilets.*
join a queue/line (=start waiting in it) *I joined the queue for a taxi.*

4   able to wait quietly and calmly

patient /'peɪʃənt/ [adj] able to wait calmly without becoming annoyed or bored: *I'm sure she'll write soon. Just try to be patient.*
patiently [adv] *The audience waited patiently for the show to begin.*
patience [n U] when you can wait calmly without becoming annoyed or bored: *It's easy to grow your own plants – all you need is a little time and patience.*

5   unable to wait quietly and calmly

impatient /ɪm'peɪʃənt/ [adj] becoming annoyed because you have been waiting for a long time: *Don't be so impatient. I'm doing it as fast as I can.*
get/become/grow impatient *I could see that Max was getting impatient.*
impatiently [adv] *The customs officer waved them on impatiently.*
impatience [n U] annoyance caused

by waiting for a long time: *People were beginning to show signs of impatience.*

WAKE UP/GET UP

➡ see also **TIRED, SLEEP**

1   to stop sleeping

wake up/wake /ˌweɪk 'ʌp, weɪk/ [phrasal verb I] to stop sleeping: *She woke up early the next morning and slipped out of the house unseen.* | *Babies often wake because they are hungry.*
wake up/wake at 5 a.m./12 noon etc *I woke up at five o'clock and couldn't get back to sleep again.*
waking – woke – have woken

> **Formal or informal?**
> **Wake** is more formal than **wake up**.

be awake /biː ə'weɪk/ to not be asleep: *"Are you awake, Lucy?" she whispered.* | *I'm usually awake before anyone else.*
be wide awake (=be completely awake) *It was nearly three in the morning, but Jill was still wide awake.*
be half awake/barely awake (=be not quite awake) *He listened, only half awake, as the teacher's voice droned on.*

come round BRITISH **come around** AMERICAN /ˌkʌm (ə)'raʊnd/ [phrasal verb I] to gradually become conscious again after being given a drug or being hit on the head: *She was coming round after her operation, but she still felt dizzy and very sleepy.*

2   to make someone stop sleeping

wake/wake up /weɪk, ˌweɪk 'ʌp/ [v T] *Be quiet, or you'll wake my parents.* | *We were woken by a loud banging on the door.*
wake sb up *The alarm clock woke me up at 8 o'clock.*
wake up sb *They were making enough noise to wake up the whole street!*
wake up! (=what you say to someone

to stop them sleeping) *Come on honey, wake up! You'll be late!*
waking – woke – have woken

disturb /dɪ'stɜːʳb/ [v T] to accidentally wake someone who is sleeping, by making a noise or movement: *I got undressed in the bathroom to avoid disturbing her.* | *I hope my snoring won't disturb you too much.*

3 to get out of bed

get up /ˌget 'ʌp/ [phrasal verb I] to get out of bed, especially in the morning in order to get ready for the day: *What time do you need to get up tomorrow?*
get up at 7.00 a.m./dawn etc *Frank gets up at half past five every morning.*
get up early/late *I think we should get up early and leave before breakfast.*

be up /biː 'ʌp/ [phrasal verb I] to be out of bed and doing things: *Is Harry up yet?* | *I was up at six this morning.* | *Jake had been up since dawn.*
be up early *You're up early!*

4 to stay in bed until late in the morning

get up late /ˌget ʌp 'leɪt/ to get out of bed later than usual in the morning: *We usually get up late on Sundays.* | *Jackson's not here. He must have gotten up late again.*

have a lie in BRITISH **sleep late** AMERICAN /hæv ə 'laɪ ɪn, ˌsliːp 'leɪt/ to stay in bed longer than usual in the morning, especially because you do not need to get up: *It's Saturday tomorrow, so I can have a lovely long lie in.* | *She knows I sleep late on weekends, so she doesn't disturb me.*

stay in bed /ˌsteɪ ɪn 'bed/ to not get out of bed, even though you are not asleep: *If you're not well, you'd better stay in bed.* | *He's so lazy – he often stays in bed all day!*

oversleep /ˌəʊvəʳ'sliːp/ [v I] to accidentally sleep longer than you intended to, so that you are late for something: *Sorry I'm late – I overslept.* | *They were afraid of oversleeping and missing the plane.*
oversleeping – overslept – have overslept

WALK

➡ see also **RUN**

1 to walk

walk /wɔːk/ [v I] *Anna missed the bus, so she decided to walk.* | *How old was Daisy when she first started walking?*
+into/out of/along/back etc *He walked out of the station and got into a taxi.* | *I was walking along Main Street when I met Pierre.*
walk home *She hates walking home alone at night.*
walk two miles/100 metres etc *We must have walked about five miles today.*

on foot /ɒn 'fʊt/ if you go somewhere **on foot**, you walk instead of going by car, bus, train etc: *It's not far. It'll take you about ten minutes on foot.*
go on foot *The bus left us at the bottom of the hill, and we went the rest of the way on foot.*

wander /'wɒndəʳ‖'wɑːn-/ [v I] to walk around with no particular aim and in no particular direction, especially in a place you do not know or when you are lost
+around/about/through etc *I spent the morning wandering around the old part of the city, looking at the buildings.*

stride /straɪd/ [v I] ESPECIALLY WRITTEN to walk quickly, taking big steps, in an angry or confident way
+into/out of/towards etc *Brian strode out of the room without speaking.* | *The Principal came striding towards me, and shook my hand.*
striding – strode – have strode

 Use **stride** especially in written stories.

march

march /mɑːᵊtʃ/ [v I] if soldiers **march**, they all walk together with regular steps
+into/through/past etc *Thousands of US soldiers marched through the streets of Paris.*

wade

wade /weɪd/ [v I] to walk through deep water
+across/towards/through etc *They waded across the river.*

2 to walk for pleasure or for exercise

go for a walk /ˌɡəʊ fər ə ˈwɔːk/ to walk somewhere for pleasure or for exercise: *It's a lovely evening. Why don't we go for a walk?*
+along/through/across etc *He said he was going for a walk down by the river.*

stroll/go for a stroll /strəʊl, ˌɡəʊ fər ə ˈstrəʊl/ [v I] to walk in a slow and relaxed way, especially for pleasure
+along/through/across etc *Dave strolled along the riverbank, enjoying the evening sun. | They decided to go for a stroll along the beach.*

hiking

hiking /ˈhaɪkɪŋ/ [n U] the activity of going for long walks in the countryside
go hiking *We're going hiking in Scotland this summer.*

3 a journey that you make by walking

walk /wɔːk/ [n C] a journey you make by walking, either for pleasure or exercise, or in order to go somewhere
go for a walk (=walk for pleasure or exercise) *I love going for walks in the countryside.*
a long/short/ten-minute etc walk (=used to say how long it takes to walk somewhere) *It's a long walk from here to the nearest town. | "How far is it to the post office?" "It's not far – just a 5-minute walk."*

hike /haɪk/ [n C] a long walk in the countryside
go on a hike *We went on lots of great hikes.*

4 to walk quietly

tiptoe /ˈtɪptəʊ/ [v I] to walk on your toes because you do not want to make any noise
+into/out of/past etc *He tiptoed out of the room, trying not to wake the baby.*
tiptoeing – tiptoed – have tiptoed

W

creep

creep/sneak /kri:p, sni:k/ [v I] to walk quietly and carefully because you do not want anyone to notice you
+in/through/across/out etc *Ron unlocked the back door and crept out into the yard.* | *The thieves sneaked in while the guard had his back turned.*
creep up/sneak up behind sb (=walk quietly up behind someone in order to surprise them) *She crept up behind him and put her hands over his eyes.*
creeping – crept – have crept
sneaking – sneaked (also **snuck** AMERICAN) – **have sneaked** (also **have snuck** AMERICAN)

5 to walk slowly and with difficulty

limp /lɪmp/ [v I] to walk with difficulty because you have hurt one of your legs
+along/over/towards etc *She limped painfully over to a chair and sat down.*
a limp [n singular] a limping movement: *Josie walked with a slight limp.*
stagger /'stægər/ [v I] to walk unsteadily, with your body moving from side to side and almost falling, especially because you are injured, very tired, or drunk
+into/out of/home etc *Something hit me on the head, and I staggered across the room.* | *We staggered home from the pub.*

trudge /trʌdʒ/ [v I] to walk slowly and with heavy steps, especially because you are tired, it is difficult to walk, or you do not want to go somewhere
+through/back/along etc *She trudged back up the hill, loaded down with heavy bags of groceries.* | *The car broke down and we had to trudge back home through the snow.*

6 a single movement you make when you are walking

step /step/ [n C] the single movement that you make when you put one foot in front of the other when you are walking: *I was so breathless, I could only manage a few steps.*
take a step *Zoe took a step forward to let the man pass.*
with short/heavy/light etc steps *She walked briskly, with quick, short steps.*
footstep /'fʊtstep/ [n C usually plural] the sound of someone's foot being placed on the ground when they are walking or running: *Suddenly Rachel heard footsteps behind her in the dark street.*
pace /peɪs/ [n C] ESPECIALLY WRITTEN the distance you go when you take a single step: *He took a couple of paces forward, then stopped.*

7 someone who is walking

pedestrian /pɪ'destriən/ [n C] someone who is walking in a town, rather than travelling in a car: *Banning traffic from the shopping areas has made life much more pleasant for pedestrians.*
walker /'wɔːkər/ [n C] someone who walks long distances in the countryside for pleasure: *There's a rough track through the woods for riders and walkers.*

WANT

LIKE/NOT LIKE

INTEND — ENJOY

POPULAR/
UNPOPULAR — *see also* — LOVE

EXCITING/
EXCITED — ENTHUSIASTIC/
UNENTHUSIASTIC

DON'T CARE

1 to want something or want to do something

want /wɒnt‖wɑːnt, wɔːnt/ [v I/T]
want to do sth *What do you want to do at the weekend? | Stacey wants to be a doctor.*
want sth *Do you want milk in your coffee? | My parents moved out of London because they wanted a bigger house.*
want sb to do sth *She wants Tom to come to her party.*
what sb wants is *What we want is a car that's cheap and reliable.*

> ⚠ Don't say 'I want visit England'. Say **I want to visit England**.

> ⚠ Don't say 'I want that you do it'. Say **I want you to do it**.

> ⚠ You can use **want** by itself or just followed by 'to' in expressions like 'if you want' or 'if you want to': *You can come with us if you want to. | They are free to leave whenever they want.*

 would like /wʊd ˈlaɪk/ ESPECIALLY SPOKEN use this as a polite way of asking for something, offering something, or saying what you want to do
would like to do sth *I'd like to reserve a room for Saturday. | Would you like to borrow this book?*
would like sth *We'd like some information about flights to Chicago, please. | Would you like some more coffee?*

would like sb to do sth *We would like you to attend an interview at 3:30 on Friday.*

 feel like /ˈfiːl laɪk/ ESPECIALLY SPOKEN to want to have something or do something, because you think you would enjoy it
feel like doing sth *I feel like watching a movie tonight.*
feel like sth *I feel like a long, hot soak in the bath. | It's a lovely day – do you feel like a walk?*
if you feel like it (=if you want to) *Come and see us tomorrow if you feel like it.*

be interested in /biː ˈɪntrɪ̰stɪ̰d ɪn/ to think that you may want to do something, buy something, or get involved in something
be interested in doing sth *We're interested in buying an apartment downtown. | Would you be interested in going to the theatre with me on Friday? I have two tickets for 'Romeo and Juliet'.*
be interested in sth *Clare is interested in a career in teaching.*

I wouldn't mind /aɪ ˌwʊdnt ˈmaɪnd/ SPOKEN say this to tell someone politely that you want to do or have something, but not very strongly
I wouldn't mind sth *I wouldn't mind another cup of coffee. How about you?*
I wouldn't mind doing sth *It was a really good play. I wouldn't mind seeing it again.*

> ⚠ **I wouldn't mind** is less definite than **I want** or **I'd like**.

if you like /ɪf juː ˈlaɪk/ SPOKEN say this when you are offering to let someone do something if they want to do it: *You can stay here tonight, if you like. | If you like, I could check your essay for you.*

by choice /baɪ ˈtʃɔɪs/ if you do something **by choice**, you do it because you want to do it, and not because anyone forces you to do it: *Jim lives with his parents by choice – he could rent his own place if he wanted to.*

W

2 to want something very much

wish /wɪʃ/ [v T not in passive] to want something to happen, when it is unlikely or impossible that it will happen, or when you cannot control what will happen
+(that) *I wish I had a car like that.* | *Beth wished that she could stay there forever.*
wish sb/sth would do sth *I wish they would turn that music down.*

> ⚠ Don't confuse **wish** (=want something that is unlikely or impossible) and **hope** (=want something that is likely or possible): *I wish the weather would stay like this forever.* | *I hope the weather stays fine this weekend.*

> ⚠ Don't say 'I wish I can fly'. Say **I wish I could fly** (=but I can't). Use past tense forms after **wish (that)**: *I wish I knew.* | *I bet you wish you had a ticket!*

> ⚠ Don't say 'I wish to be rich'. Say **I want to be rich** (=it is possible) or **I wish I were rich** (=but I·am not). **Wish** is used with the infinitive only in very formal or official situations: *The President wishes to thank all his staff for their help.*

○ **would love** /wʊd ˈlʌv/ ESPECIALLY SPOKEN to want something very much, and feel that you would be happy if you had it
would love sth *I would love a cup of coffee.*
would love to do sth *She would love to have children, but she hasn't met the right man.*
would love sb to do sth *My mother would love me to come and live in New York with her.*

○ **I can't wait** /aɪ ˌkɑːnt ˈweɪt‖-ˌkænt-/ SPOKEN say this when you want something to happen as soon as possible, because you know you will enjoy it and you are very excited about it: *"You're going on holiday soon, aren't you?" "Yes, I can't wait."*
I can't wait to do sth *I can't wait to see Bill again – it's been a long time.*
+for *I can't wait for Christmas.*

○ **be dying** /biː ˈdaɪ-ɪŋ/ SPOKEN INFORMAL to want something very much, and feel that you must have it or do it immediately

be dying to do sth *I'm dying to meet Lisa's new boyfriend.*
+for *I'm dying for a drink – let's go to a bar.*

3 to want one thing more than another thing

would prefer /wʊd prɪˈfɜːʳ/ if you **would prefer** something or **would prefer** to do something, you want it or want to do it more than something else: *"Would you like a coffee?" "I'd prefer a cold drink, please."*
would prefer sb to do sth *Anna would prefer to live in Italy, but she can't find a job there.*
would much prefer (=want something much more than something else) *Jack wants to go out, but I'd much prefer to stay home and watch TV.*

○ **would rather** /aɪd ˈrɑːðəʳ‖-ˈræ-/ ESPECIALLY SPOKEN use this to say that you want to do or have something more than something else
would rather do sth *Paula said she'd rather go by car.* | *It was an experience that I'd rather forget.* | *Would you rather go swimming or play tennis?*

> **Formal or informal?**
> **Would rather** is less formal than **would prefer**.

4 to be willing to do what someone else wants you to do

be willing to do sth /biː ˌwɪlɪŋ tə ˈduː (sth)/ if you **are willing to** do something, you will agree to do it because it is necessary or because someone has asked you to do it: *He's willing to tell the police everything he knows.* | *To do well as a journalist, you have to be willing to change jobs very frequently.*
willingly [adv] *I'd willingly pay higher taxes if the money was spent on health and education.*
be ready to do sth /biː ˌredi tə ˈduː (sth)/ to be willing to do something at any time, whenever it needs to be done: *I'm always ready to help if you need me.* | *We are ready to consider any serious proposals.*

be glad/happy to do sth /bɪː ˌglæd, ˌhæpi tə 'duː (sth)/ to be very willing to do something that will help someone else: *"Could you do me a favor?" "Sure, I'd be glad to."* | *John says he'd be happy to give you a hand with the gardening.*

5 to not want to do something

not want to do sth /nɒt ˌwɒnt tə 'duː (sth)‖-ˌwɑːnt-/ *She doesn't want to see me anymore.* | *We asked him to come with us, but he said he didn't want to.*
not want sb to do sth *"Why didn't he tell me he was sick?" "He didn't want you to worry."*

⊂ **not feel like doing sth** /nɒt ˌfiːl laɪk 'duːɪŋ (sth)/ ESPECIALLY SPOKEN to not want to do something, especially because you think you would not enjoy it or because you feel too lazy: *I don't feel like writing that essay today.* | *Some days she just doesn't feel like going to work.*

⊂ **I'd rather not** /aɪd 'rɑːðər nɒt‖-'ræ-/ SPOKEN say this when you do not want to do something, especially because you think it may cause problems for you: *I could lend him the money, but to be honest, I'd rather not.*
I'd rather not do sth *I'd rather not talk about it right now.*

be unwilling to do sth /bɪː ʌn'wɪlɪŋ tə duː (sth)/ to not want to do something, even though you should do it or someone wants you to do it: *She is unwilling to admit that she was wrong.* | *Most people here are unwilling to give up their cars and use buses and trains instead.*

reluctant /rɪ'lʌktənt/ [adj] someone who is **reluctant** is not willing to do something, although they be persuaded after refusing for a while
be reluctant to do sth *Some of the older staff were reluctant to use the new equipment.*
reluctantly [adv] *We offered them $500, which they accepted rather reluctantly.*

against your will /əˌgenst jɔːr 'wɪl/ if you do something **against your will**, you do not want to do it, but someone makes you do it: *The refugees were sent back against their will.* | *No one should be forced to marry against her will.*

6 a feeling that you want to do something

desire /dɪ'zaɪər/ [n C] ESPECIALLY WRITTEN a strong feeling of wanting to have something or wanting to do something, especially something important, which makes you try very hard to have it or do it
desire to do sth *Young children have a keen desire to learn and succeed.*
+for *After so many years of war, there was a great desire for peace.*

> Don't say 'a desire of doing something'. Say **a desire to do something**.

urge /ɜːrdʒ/ [n C] a sudden strong feeling that you want to do something, especially a feeling that is difficult to control
urge to do sth *I felt a sudden urge to tell him all my problems.*
resist an urge (=not do something, even though you want to) *Sheena resisted the urge to get in her car and go home.*

wish /wɪʃ/ [n C] FORMAL something that you want to happen, especially when this is very important to you: *His last wish was that his body should be buried in his home town.*
sb's dearest/greatest wish (=the thing they want most of all) *She always wanted to see her grandchildren again – it was her dearest wish.*
respect sb's wishes (=do what someone wants you to do because it is important to them) *The doctor has to respect the wishes of the patient.*

7 something that you want to achieve

ambition /æm'bɪʃən/ [n C] something which you want to achieve in the future, especially in your work, and which you will try hard to achieve
sb's ambition is to do sth *Her ambition was to go to law school and become an attorney.*
achieve/fulfil your ambition (=finally do what you wanted to do) *Earlier this year, he achieved his ambition of competing in the Olympic games.*

dream /driːm/ [n C] something very special that you want to do and that you think about a lot, especially something that is not very likely to happen

sb's dream is to do sth *Her dream was to go to Hollywood and become a movie star.*

dream of doing sth *After the accident, Clarke had to give up his dream of becoming a racing driver.*

sb's dream comes true (=they finally do what they want) *Last year her dream came true and she was offered a chance to study in America.*

goal /gəʊl/ [n C] something important that a person, company, or government hopes to achieve in the future, even though it may take a long time

achieve/reach a goal *By 1975, they had achieved their goal of providing free education for every child.*

sb's goal is to do sth *Our goal is to become the biggest-selling brand of coffee in the country.*

short-term goal / long-term goal (=one that you hope to achieve soon/a long time in the future) *I took a job as a teacher with the long-term goal of becoming a principal of a school.*

target /ˈtɑːʳgɪt/ [n C] a particular amount or total that you want to achieve, for example an amount of products you must sell or produce: *We produced 16,000 cars this year, but our target was 17,500.*

achieve/reach/meet a target *The Government is struggling to reach its target of $23 billion in spending cuts.*

set (sb) a target (=say what the target is) *I set myself a target of learning 20 new words each week.*

8 an offer, opportunity etc that makes you want to do something

attractive /əˈtræktɪv/ [adj] an **attractive** offer, idea, opportunity etc makes you want to do something because you think that you would enjoy it or get advantages from it: *It was an attractive offer, and I accepted the job.* | *Cycling would be an attractive alternative to driving if there were better cycle paths.*

+to *Low business taxes make the area attractive to foreign investors.*

> **Formal or informal?**
> **Attractive** is not usually used in informal conversation.

tempting /ˈtemptɪŋ/ [adj] a **tempting** offer or suggestion makes you want to do something, but you have doubts about doing it: *"Why don't you come out with Phil and me tonight?" "It's a very tempting idea, but I have an essay to finish."* | *They made me a tempting offer, but it wasn't quite enough to make me take the job.*

incentive /ɪnˈsentɪv/ [n C/U] something good that makes you want to work harder or do what someone else wants you to do

incentive to do sth *We need to give young people an incentive to stay at school for longer.*

incentive for sb to do sth *When prices are so low, farmers have little incentive to grow more food.*

WAR

➡ opposite **PEACE**

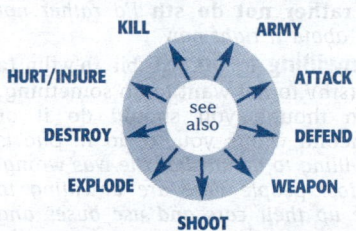

1 fighting between countries or armies

war /wɔːʳ/ [n C/U] a long period of fighting, when the armies, ships, and planes of two or more countries fight against each other in many different places: *the Vietnam War* | *When the war ended in 1945, Europe was in chaos.*

win/lose a war *Who won the Franco-Prussian War?*

civil war (=war between groups of people from the same country) *More*

Americans died in the Civil War than in World War II.

declare war (on) (=make an official statement that you are going to fight another country) *In October 1853, Turkey declared war on Russia.*
+against/with *Iran's seven-year war with Iraq*
+between *the wars between England and Scotland*
war breaks out (=war begins) *In 1874, war broke out in Europe again.*

> ⚠ You can also use **war** before a noun, like an adjective: *a war hero* | *war movies*

battle /'bætl/ [n C] a fight in one area between two armies, or two groups of ships or planes: *a naval battle in the North Sea*
+of *the Battle of the Somme*
win/lose a battle *The French lost the Battle of Agincourt in 1415.*
die/be wounded/be killed in battle *King Olaf died in battle, in 1030.*

conflict /'kɒnflɪkt‖'kɑːn-/ [n C/U] a situation in which two countries or groups are fighting against each other – used especially in newspapers and news reports: *the conflict in the Middle East* | *Can this peace settlement bring an end to years of conflict?*

rebellion /rɪ'beljən/ [n C] an organized attempt to change or destroy the government by fighting against it: *The rebellion spread quickly through the Western Provinces.*
+against *an armed rebellion against the government*
crush/put down a rebellion (=use force to stop it) *The army was brought in to crush the rebellion.*

fighting /'faɪtɪŋ/ [n U] when soldiers fight against each other during a war or battle: *The UN had failed to stop the fighting in Rwanda.*
heavy/fierce fighting (=a lot of fighting when many people are hurt) *The streets of the capital are now quiet again, after three weeks of heavy fighting.*

warfare /'wɔːrfeər/ [n U] the activity of fighting in a war – use this especially to talk about the methods of fighting that are used in war: *the history of modern warfare*
nuclear/chemical warfare (=fighting with nuclear bombs or poison gas) *a*

secret underground chemical warfare plant
guerrilla warfare (=when small unofficial military groups fight against the government) *The rebels aimed to overthrow the government through guerrilla warfare.*

2 to fight a war or be in a war

fight /faɪt/ [v I/T] to take part in a war or battle: *His grandfather fought on the Republican side in the Spanish Civil War.* | *The Boers were fighting the British at this time.*
+for *Most of these young soldiers don't even know what they're fighting for.*
+in *My grandfather fought in World War II.*
fight a war/battle *They were fighting a war of independence against a powerful enemy.*
fighting – fought – have fought

be at war /biː ət 'wɔːr/ if two countries **are at war** with each other, they are fighting a war against each other: *Europe had been at war for nearly two years.*
+with *In 1792, England was at war with America.*

3 during a war

wartime /'wɔːrtaɪm/ [adj only before noun] during or relating to the time when there is a war: *He died on a wartime bombing mission.* | *My grandmother's wartime experiences were still fresh in her memory.*
wartime /'wɔːrtaɪm/ [n U] the time when there is a war
in wartime *the importance of secrecy in wartime*

in the war /ɪn ðə 'wɔːr/ during the particular war that you are talking about: *What did your father do in the war?*

4 the place where a war is fought

battlefield /'bætlfiːld/ [n C] a place where two armies fight a battle: *Thousands died on the battlefields of northern France.*

the front line/the front /ðə ˌfrʌnt 'laɪn, ðə 'frʌnt/ [n singular] the place where

W

an army is closest to the enemy and where the fighting takes place: *We were now just a few kilometres behind the front line.*

the Western/Eastern/Russian etc front *Her grandfather had spent four years on the Western Front.*

war zone /ˈwɔːʳ zəʊn/ [n C] an area which is very dangerous because a war is being fought there: *the latest news from the war zone*

---

5   the people you are fighting against in a war

enemy /ˈenəmi/ [n C] someone that you are fighting against in a war: *Even though these soldiers were our enemies, I still felt sorry for them.*

the enemy (=the army or country that your army or country is fighting against in a war) *They accused him of giving secret information to the enemy.* plural **enemies**

> ⚠ You can also use **enemy** before a noun, like an adjective: *an enemy plane | enemy territory*

WARN

➡ see also **TELL, ADVISE**

warn /wɔːʳn/ [v T] to tell someone about something bad or dangerous that might happen, so that they can avoid it or prevent it: *We tried to warn her, but she refused to listen.*

warn sb (that) *The local people were warned that the volcano might erupt at any time. | We were warned there were going to be delays on the motorway, so we came back by a different route.*

warn sb about sth *Parents should warn their children about the dangers of smoking.*

warn (sb) of sth *Weather forecasters warned of possible flooding in coastal regions.*

warn sb not to do sth/warn sb against doing sth (=tell someone they should not do something because it is dangerous or risky) *Police are warning drivers not to go*

out on the roads unless their journey is really necessary. | I tried to warn him against sending Phil any money.*

warning /ˈwɔːʳnɪŋ/ [n C/U] something that you say or do to warn people about danger or to warn them not to do something: *All cigarette packets carry a government health warning.*

give a warning *The weather report gave a warning of more snow and icy roads.*

+to *Two of the prisoners were publicly beaten, as a warning to the others.*

without (any) warning (=without giving a warning) *Soldiers began firing into the crowd without any warning.*

> ⚠ You can also use **warning** before a noun, like an adjective: *Headaches may be warning signs of a more serious illness.*

beware /bɪˈweəʳ/ [v I only in imperative] WRITTEN used on signs to warn people about something dangerous

+of *Beware of the dog. | Beware of falling rocks.*

WASH

➡ if you mean 'to make something clean', go to **CLEAN 2**
➡ see also **DIRTY, MARK, SHINE**

---

1   to wash your hands/face/body etc

wash /wɒʃ‖wɑːʃ, wɔːʃ/ [v I/T] to clean yourself with soap and water: *Harry went upstairs to wash.*

wash your hands/face/hair etc *She was washing her hair when the phone rang. | Have you boys washed your hands yet?*

> ⚠ Don't say 'I washed myself', 'she washed herself' etc. Say **I washed my hands**, **she had a wash** etc.

have a wash BRITISH **wash up** AMERICAN /hæv ə ˈwɒʃ, ˌwɒʃ ˈʌp‖-ˈwɑːʃ/ to wash your hands and face: *You'll feel better once you've had a wash and something to eat. | You kids go wash up now – dinner's nearly ready.*

have a bath BRITISH **take a bath**
AMERICAN /ˌhæv ə 'bɑːθ, ˌteɪk ə 'bɑːθǁ
-'bæθ/ to wash your whole body while
sitting in a bath full of water: *Is there
enough hot water for me to have a
bath?* | *I just had time to take a bath
and change before we had to go out
again.*

have a shower BRITISH **take a shower**
AMERICAN /ˌhæv ə 'ʃaʊəʳ, ˌteɪk ə 'ʃaʊəʳ/ to
wash your whole body while standing
under a shower: *I'll just have a quick
shower and get changed.* | *She decided
to take a shower before dinner.*

brush your teeth (also **clean your
teeth** BRITISH) /ˌbrʌʃ jɔːʳ 'tiːθ, ˌkliːn jɔːʳ
'tiːθ/ to clean your teeth with a small
brush: *Have you brushed your teeth
this morning?*

○ **freshen up** /ˌfreʃən 'ʌp/ [phrasal verb
I] ESPECIALLY SPOKEN to wash your face
and hands so that you feel more
comfortable, for example when you
have been working hard or travelling:
*The bathroom's on the right if you'd
like to freshen up.* | *She hoped there
would be time to freshen up before the
interview.*

2 to wash a car/floor/wall/object etc

wash /wɒʃǁwɑːʃ, wɔːʃ/ [v T] to clean
something using a lot of water, and
usually soap: *I really must wash the
car this weekend.*
+in *The spinach leaves should be
washed in cold water.*

clean /kliːn/ [v T] to clean something
using soap and water, and usually by
rubbing with a cloth or brush:
*Where's that stuff you use for cleaning
the bathtub?* | *I usually clean the
windows about once a month.*

mop /mɒpǁmɑːp/ [v T] to wash a floor
using a special tool with a long
handle that is dipped in a bucket of
water: *Dan has to mop the floor of the
café every night.*
mopping – mopped – have mopped

scrub /skrʌb/ [v T] to make something
very clean, using a stiff brush and
water, or soap and water: *Lou was on

her knees, scrubbing the kitchen floor.*
| *Scrub the potatoes, then put them in
a pan of boiling water.*
**scrubbing – scrubbed – have
scrubbed**

> ⚠ You can also say **give something a
> wash/a clean/a scrub** (especially in
> British English), and it means the same: *I gave
> the floor a scrub.* Instead of saying that
> something needs to be washed, you can say
> that it **needs a wash/clean/scrub**: *The oven
> needs a good clean* (=needs to be cleaned
> thoroughly).

3 to wash clothes

wash /wɒʃǁwɑːʃ, wɔːʃ/ [v I/T] to wash
clothes, especially in a washing
machine: *Could you wash this shirt for
me?* | *I seem to spend all my time
washing and ironing these days.* | *You
ought to wash that sweater by hand.*

dry-clean /ˌdraɪ 'kliːn/ [v T] to clean
clothes by using special chemicals
instead of soap and water: *Don't put
that dress in the washing machine – the
label says it should be dry-cleaned.*

dry-cleaner's [n C] a shop where you
can get your clothes dry-cleaned:
*Could you collect my suit from the
dry-cleaner's?*

do the washing BRITISH **do the
laundry** AMERICAN /ˌduː ðə 'wɒʃɪŋ, ˌduː
ðə 'lɔːndrilǁ-'wɑːʃ-/ to wash clothes that
need to be washed: *Did you do the
laundry this morning?*

get sth out /ˌget (sth) 'aʊt/ [phrasal verb
T] to remove a mark from clothes or
material: *How can I get this coffee
stain out?*

launderette BRITISH **laundromat**
AMERICAN /lɔːn'dret, 'lɔːndrəmæt/ [n C] a
place where you can pay to wash
your clothes in a washing machine

4 to wash cups/plates/knives/pans etc

wash the dishes/do the dishes /ˌwɒʃ
ðə 'dɪʃɪz, ˌduː ðə 'dɪʃɪzǁ-wɑːʃ-/ to wash
all the cups, plates, knives etc that
you have used during a meal: *My

mom always makes me wash the dishes. | Can I help you do the dishes?

do the washing up/wash up /ˌduː ðə ˈwɒʃɪŋ ˈʌp, ˌwɒʃ ˈʌpǁ-ˌwɑːʃ-/ BRITISH to wash all the cups, plates, knives etc that you have used during a meal: If you'll do the cooking tonight, I'll do the washing up. | Who's going to wash up?

> ⚠ **Wash up** has different meanings in American and British English. In American English it means to wash your hands and face.

5 to wash with water but without soap

rinse /rɪns/ [v T] to wash something with water in order to remove soap or dirt: I'll just rinse the lettuce under the tap. | Rosie rinsed her mouth to get rid of the taste.
rinse out a cup/pan/glass etc (=quickly clean a container, just using water) He rinsed out a glass and poured himself a whiskey.

soak/leave sth to soak /səʊk, ˌliːv (sth) tə ˈsəʊk/ [v T] to leave something in water for a long time in order to clean it or make it easier to wash later: You'll have to soak that shirt to get the blood off it.
leave sth to soak Just leave that pan to soak overnight.

WASTE

to use more than you need, or use something in a way that is not useful

➡ see also **RUBBISH, GET RID OF**

1 to waste something

waste /weɪst/ [v T] to use time, money, food etc in a way that is not useful or sensible: I wasted 40 minutes waiting for a bus this morning. | Don't leave the light on – you're wasting electricity.
waste money/time on sth Bill wastes all his money on beer and cigarettes. | Let's not waste any more time on this.

wasted /ˈweɪstᵻd/ [adj] something that is **wasted** is not used in a sensible

way, or does not produce a useful result: I felt as if my education had been wasted when I couldn't get a job.
a wasted trip/journey I'm sorry you've had a wasted trip. Mr Newton isn't here at the moment.

2 something that wastes time, money etc

be a waste of sth /biː ə ˈweɪst ɒv (sth)/ if something **is a waste of** time, money, energy etc, it annoys you because it uses time, money etc in a way that has no useful results: a pointless war that was a terrible waste of human life | That class was a complete waste of time – I didn't learn anything. | My parents think going to football games is a waste of money.

wasteful /ˈweɪstfəl/ [adj] an activity or method that is **wasteful** uses too much money, food, energy etc, without any useful results: Many people see the new £60 million building as wasteful and extravagant. | wasteful packaging

inefficient /ˌɪnᵻˈfɪʃəntᐸ/ [adj] an organization or system that is **inefficient** does not work well, so it uses more time, money, or energy than it needs to: an inefficient heating system | Local government in the area is seen as corrupt and inefficient.

WATCH

to look at and pay attention to something that is happening

➡ see also **SEE, LOOK AT**

> ⚠ Don't confuse **see, watch,** and **look at.** When you **see** something, you notice it with your eyes, either deliberately or accidentally: I saw an accident on my way to school today. You **watch** films, sports games, or other situations where there is action and movement: Dad was watching a basketball game on TV. When you **look at** people, scenery, pictures, and other things that are not moving, you deliberately pay attention to them: Look at this old picture of Sally!

1 to watch someone or something

watch /wɒtʃ‖wɑːtʃ, wɔːtʃ/ [v I/T] to look for some time at something that is happening or moving, or at a place where something may happen, paying attention to what you see: *A large crowd was watching the football game.* | *Do you want to play with us or just sit and watch?* | *The police were watching the house, but Morgan still managed to escape.*
+as *I watched as the small boat disappeared over the horizon.*
watch sb do sth/watch sb doing sth *He watched them slowly climb the hill.* | *We watched the children playing on the beach.*
watch television/a video/a programme etc *Did you watch that programme about real life murders last night?* | *He's in the living room, watching television.*

see /siː/ [v T] to watch a particular television programme, film, play etc – use this to say whether you watched something or when you watched it or will watch it: *Did you see the news last night?* | *We went to see the new James Bond film last weekend.*
seeing – saw – have seen

 Don't say 'see television'. Say **watch television**: *I enjoy watching television.*

keep an eye on sb/sth /ˌkiːp ən ˈaɪ ɒn (sb/sth)/ ESPECIALLY SPOKEN to make sure someone or something is safe by regularly looking at them over a particular period of time: *Keep an eye on the baby, in case she gets too near the fire.*
+for *Ask a neighbour to keep an eye on the house for you while you're away.*

spy on sb /ˈspaɪ ɒn (sb)/ [phrasal verb T] to watch someone secretly, in order to find out information about them: *Mathers admitted he had followed Ms Evans and spied on her.*

2 always watching to see what happens

alert /əˈlɜːᵗt/ [adj] someone who is **alert** is always watching, and notices if anything strange or unusual happens: *Passengers should try to stay alert at all times, and report any suspicious packages to the police immediately.* | *She owes her life to an alert farmer who spotted her car in a ditch and called the emergency services.*

keep your eyes open /ˌkiːp jɔːr ˈaɪz ˌəʊpən/ ESPECIALLY SPOKEN to keep watching carefully so that you will see something that you are hoping or expecting to see: *We might see a dolphin if we're lucky, so keep your eyes open.*
+for *I always keep my eyes open for discounts and special offers.*

3 someone who is watching something

spectators

spectator /spekˈteɪtəᵗ‖ˈspekteɪtər/ [n C] someone who is watching an event or game: *The game was watched by over 50,000 spectators.* | *Some of the spectators began throwing cans and beer bottles.*

W

When you see **EC**, go to the **ESSENTIAL COMMUNICATION** section.

audience

audience /'ɔːdiəns‖'ɔː-, 'ɑː-/ [n C] all the people who are watching a play, concert, film etc: *The audience clapped and cheered.*
in the audience *There seemed to be quite a lot of young people in the audience.*

⚠ In British English, you can use **audi-ence** with a singular or plural verb: *The audience was/were cheering loudly.* In American English, always use a singular verb.

viewer /'vjuːəʳ/ [n C] someone who watches a television programme – used especially in newspapers and news reports: *The concert was seen by 500 million viewers around the world. | Many television viewers were upset by the violence in last night's movie.*

WAY

➡ look here for ...
• a way or method of doing something
• the way someone behaves
• the way you go from one place to another

1 a way or method of doing something

➡ see also **SYSTEM, ORDER**

way /weɪ/ [n C] *Potatoes can be cooked in many different ways.*
way to do sth *Visiting a country is a great way to learn its language.*
way of doing sth *Is there any way of controlling the heating in here?*
way (that) sb does sth *I'll show you the way we calculate the cost.*

the best/only way *The only way to lose weight is to eat less.*
the right/wrong way *The government does not believe that this approach is the right way to deal with the problem.*

○ **like this** /laɪk 'ðɪs/ SPOKEN in this way – say this when you are showing someone the way to do something: *You have to fold the corners back, like this.*

how /haʊ/ [adv] use this to talk or ask about the way that someone does something: *How do you get your CD player to work? | We don't know how she managed to escape.*
how to do sth *My dad's teaching me how to play chess. | Could you show me how to work the photocopier?*

method /'meθəd/ [n C] a way of doing something, especially one that is well known and often used: *Printing methods have changed completely in the last twenty years. | traditional teaching methods*
+of *You can choose whichever method of payment you prefer.*
method of doing sth *The clinic provides information about various methods of preventing pregnancy.*

means /miːnz/ [n C] a method, system, machine etc that you use to do something or achieve something
means of doing sth *Education and training are the most effective means of improving the nation's economy.*
by means of sth (=using a particular method or system) *Sykes had obtained the money by means of a trick.*
by peaceful/political/unlawful etc means *The enormous political changes in South Africa were achieved by peaceful means.*
means of communication/ transport/transportation *E-mail has become an increasingly important means of business communication.*
plural **means**

technique /tek'niːk/ [n C] a particular way of doing something, for which you need a skill that has to be learned and practised: *More and more heart patients are surviving thanks to improved surgical techniques. | helpful tips on how to improve your exam technique*
technique for doing sth *Chapter 6 describes useful techniques for moving documents about on screen.*

strategy /ˈstrætɪdʒi/ [n C] a set of carefully planned methods for achieving something that is difficult and may take a long time: *the company's new marketing strategy*
strategy for (doing) sth *the government's long-term strategy for reducing crime*
plural **strategies**

tactics /ˈtæktɪks/ [n plural] methods you use in order to achieve what you want, especially in a game or competition: *The team was busy discussing tactics for the game.*

2 the way that someone behaves or talks

way /weɪ/ [n C] *Losing a job affects different people in different ways.*
the way (that) sb does sth *I just love the way she laughs.* | *I could tell by the way he looked at me that he was annoyed.*
sb's way of doing sth *The younger girls admired Louise, and tried to copy her way of dressing and talking.*
in the same/a different way *We try to treat all the children in the same way.*

how /haʊ/ [adv] use this to talk or ask about the way someone behaves or moves: *Watch how Thierry Henry controls the ball.* | *I'll ask her, but I'm not sure how she'll react.*

manner /ˈmænəʳ/ [n singular] ESPECIALLY WRITTEN the way that someone behaves towards someone else and talks to them: *The doctor had a relaxed and friendly manner.*
not like sb's manner *I didn't like her manner – she seemed very impatient.*

3 the way you go from one place to another

➡ see also **DIRECTION**

way /weɪ/ [n singular] the road, path etc that you must follow in order to get to a place: *The road was blocked, so we came back a different way.*
be the way *Are you sure this is the way?*
+to/into/home etc *Is this the way to Grand Central Station?* | *I think this is the quickest way into town.*

the right/wrong way *I don't recognize this part of town – I think we've come the wrong way.*
know the way (=know how to get to a place) *Will you come with me? I don't know the way.*
ask/tell sb the way (=ask or tell someone how to get to a place) *He went into a shop and asked the way to the hospital.*

how to get /ˌhaʊ tə ˈget/ if you ask or tell someone **how to get** to a place, you ask or tell them the way to it
how to get to sth *Can you tell me how to get to the Piazza Venezia?*
how to get there/back/home *Come with me. I know how to get there.*

route /ruːt‖ruːt, raʊt/ [n C] the way from one place to another, especially a way that is used regularly and can be shown on a map: *If you don't enjoy driving on the main highways, try to find another route.*
take a route (=follow a route) *There are two routes we can take – this one along the coast or this one through the mountains.*
+from/to *This is the most direct route from Baghdad to Damascus.*

short cut /ˌʃɔːʳt ˈkʌt/ [n C] a way of getting somewhere that is shorter than the usual way: *Taxi-drivers know all the short cuts.*
take a short cut (=use a short cut) *Let's take a short cut across the field.*

WEAK

➡ if you mean 'not brave', go to **BRAVE/NOT BRAVE 5**
➡ opposite **STRONG**
➡ see also **BREAK**

1 physically weak

weak /wiːk/ [adj] someone who is **weak** is not strong enough to lift heavy things or do a lot of physical work, especially because they are ill: *When you have flu, you feel tired and weak for a long time.* | *I can't go running – I've got a weak heart.*
+from/with *The soldiers were weak from hunger and exhaustion.* | *She felt weak with emotion at the sight of him.*
weakness [n U] *The symptoms of the*

illness are a sore throat, weakness, and dizziness.

frail /freɪl/ [adj] someone who is **frail** is thin and weak, especially because they are old: *a frail 85-year-old lady | He lay in bed, looking very frail.*

puny /ˈpjuːni/ [adj] a man or boy who is **puny** is small and thin, and looks very weak: *Pete was a puny little boy with short hair and glasses. | She was such a big strong woman that she made her husband look puny.*

weedy /ˈwiːdi/ [adj] BRITISH INFORMAL a man or boy who is **weedy** is thin and looks weak: *a weedy young man with glasses*

> It is rude to describe someone as **weedy**.

2 not powerful

weak /wiːk/ [adj] a **weak** leader, manager, or government does not have clear ideas about what should be done, and is too easily influenced by other people: *Weak management led to the failure of the business.*
weakness [n U] *The President has often been accused of weakness.*

3 easy to attack or harm

vulnerable /ˈvʌlnərəbəl/ [adj] someone who is **vulnerable** can easily be harmed or attacked: *a small vulnerable child in need of protection | Wild animals are most vulnerable when they are asleep.*

defenceless BRITISH **defenseless** AMERICAN /dɪˈfensləs/ [adj] not strong enough to protect yourself against an attack: *This was a horrible crime against a defenceless old man. | The UN has condemned the latest bombing of defenseless civilians.*

4 to make someone or something weak

weaken /ˈwiːkən/ [v T] to make someone or something weak: *Her long illness had weakened her. | The city's defences had been weakened by enemy shelling.*

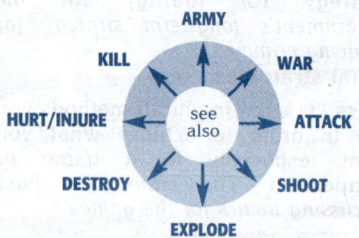

WEAPON

something that you use to fight with

ARMY
KILL
WAR
HURT/INJURE
see also
ATTACK
DESTROY
SHOOT
EXPLODE

1 a weapon

weapon /ˈwepən/ [n C] something that you use to fight with, such as a gun, bomb, or knife: *Drop your weapons and come out with your hands up!*
carry a weapon *The three men were carrying weapons.*
murder weapon *Police have not yet found the murder weapon.*
nuclear / chemical / conventional weapons (=atom bombs, poisonous gases, or ordinary weapons) *a treaty to reduce the number of nuclear weapons*

arms /ɑːʳmz/ [n plural] weapons used for fighting wars: *Foreign governments had been supplying arms to the rebels.*

> You can also use **arms** before a noun, like an adjective: *a major US arms manufacturer | discussions about arms control*

ammunition /ˌæmjʊ̩ˈnɪʃən/ [n U] bullets and other things that are fired from large or small guns: *The soldiers kept on firing until they had no more ammunition. | The terrorist group is believed to have significant quantities of guns, ammunition, and explosives.*
round of ammunition (=a single bullet) *Sixteen pistols and 150 rounds of ammunition were stolen.*

2 having weapons

armed /ɑːʳmd/ [adj] someone who is **armed** is carrying a gun or other weapon: *An armed gang stole jewellery worth £40,000. | The two men may be*

armed, and should not be approached by members of the public. | armed guards
heavily armed (=with lots of weapons) a group of heavily armed soldiers

3 having no weapons

unarmed /ˌʌn'ɑːᵣmd◄/ [adj] someone who is **unarmed** is not carrying a gun or other weapon: It was later discovered that the hijacker was unarmed.
unarmed civilians Police fired shots over the heads of unarmed civilians.

4 to get or provide weapons

arm /ɑːᵣm/ [v T] ESPECIALLY WRITTEN to provide someone with weapons: The rebels were trained, armed, and financed by foreign governments. | The country does not have sufficient funds to arm its troops.
arm yourself with sth We armed ourselves with whatever we could find – sticks, knives, and bricks.

arms race /'ɑːᵣmz reɪs/ [n singular] the competition between different countries to have a larger number of powerful weapons: The situation is dangerous and could start another arms race. | We have to halt the nuclear arms race.

WEATHER

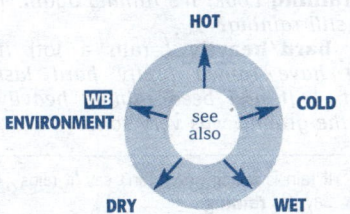

HOT

WB **ENVIRONMENT**   see also   **COLD**

DRY   WET

1 weather

weather /'weðəᵣ/ [n U] use this to talk about whether it is hot or cold outside or whether it is raining, snowing, windy etc

the weather What was the weather like on your holiday? | We're thinking about having a picnic on Saturday, but it depends on the weather.
hot/warm/wet etc weather a period of warm sunny weather | I don't like going to work on my bike in wet weather.
weather forecast (=a report on television or radio, saying what the weather will be like) Here is the weather forecast for central Europe.

it /ɪt/ [pronoun] use this to talk about what the weather is like: What's it like in Spain at this time of year? Is it really hot?
it's lovely/nice/awful etc Isn't it nice today?
it's cold/sunny/cloudy etc The weather forecast says it's going to be cloudy tomorrow.

climate /'klaɪmɪt/ [n C] the usual weather conditions in a particular country or area: Queensland has a warm tropical climate. | These flowers will not grow in a cold climate.
+of The climate of southern Florida attracts thousands of tourists each year.

2 good weather

good weather /gʊd 'weðəᵣ/ [n U] weather that is sunny and warm
get/have good weather We go to Greece every Easter, and we usually get good weather.

glorious/beautiful/gorgeous /'glɔːriəs, 'bjuːtɪfəl, 'gɔːᵣdʒəs/ [adj] very sunny and warm: a beautiful sunny morning | a glorious summer | We had three weeks of absolutely gorgeous weather.

> Don't say 'very glorious', 'very beautiful' etc. Just say **glorious**, **beautiful** etc.

Formal or informal?
Gorgeous is used especially in informal spoken English.

nice (also **lovely** ESPECIALLY BRITISH) /naɪs, 'lʌvli/ [adj] ESPECIALLY SPOKEN pleasantly warm and sunny: Morning, Bill. Nice weather, isn't it?

it's a nice day/it's a lovely morning etc *It's a lovely day – why don't we go for a walk?*

fine /faɪn/ [adj] ESPECIALLY BRITISH if the weather is **fine**, it is not raining and the sky is clear: *Next week will be fine but a little cooler.* | *a fine spring evening*

 Don't say 'very fine'. Just say **fine**.

dry /draɪ/ [adj] if the weather is **dry**, it does not rain: *If it stays dry, I'll hang out the washing.* | *The dry weather will continue for several days.*

the dry season (=the time of year when there is little or no rain) *During the dry season, there are lots of bushfires.*

dry – drier – driest

sunny /'sʌni/ [adj] if the weather is **sunny**, the sun is shining: *a lovely sunny afternoon* | *It's going to be sunny all day.*

sunny spells/intervals ESPECIALLY BRITISH (=short periods of sunny weather – used in weather forecasts) *The weather will remain dry with sunny spells.*

sunny – sunnier – sunniest

sunshine /'sʌnʃaɪn/ [n U] warm bright light from the sun: *We sat in the garden enjoying the autumn sunshine.* | *Northern regions will start dry with some sunshine.*

in the sunshine *The children ran out to play in the sunshine.*

in the sun /ɪn ðə 'sʌn/ where the sun is shining down: *I'm just going to lie here in the sun and get a nice tan.*

3 bad weather

bad weather /bæd 'weðəʳ/ [n U] when it is raining, snowing, or very cold: *The game was cancelled because of bad weather.*

◯ awful/terrible/horrible /'ɔːfəl, 'terɪbəl, 'hɒrɪbəl‖'hɔː-, 'hɑː-/ [adj] ESPECIALLY SPOKEN very unpleasant, cold, wet etc: *Awful weather, isn't it?* | *The weather's been terrible all year.*

 Don't say 'very awful', 'very terrible' etc. Just say **awful**, **terrible** etc.

4 weather that changes a lot

unsettled /ˌʌn'setld/ [adj] if the weather is **unsettled**, it keeps changing and it often rains: *More unsettled weather is forecast for the weekend.*

continue unsettled BRITISH (=used in weather forecasts) *Tomorrow will continue unsettled, with showers in most areas.*

changeable /'tʃeɪndʒəbəl/ [adj] ESPECIALLY BRITISH likely to change suddenly: *The British weather is very changeable.*

5 rain

rain /reɪn/ [n U] water that falls from the sky in small drops

the rain *The rain was beating against the window.*

in the rain *I like walking in the rain.*

heavy/torrential rain (=a lot of rain) *The roads are flooded after a period of exceptionally heavy rain.*

light rain (=a little rain) *Some light rain is likely in the Boston area.*

rain falls (=comes down from the sky) *Four inches of rain have fallen in four days.*

 Don't say 'under the rain'. Say **in the rain**: *I've been standing in the rain for an hour.*

it rains /ɪt 'reɪnz/ if **it rains**, drops of water fall from clouds in the sky: *It's starting to rain.* | *It rained for four days straight.*

it's raining *Look! It's raining again.* | *Is it still raining?*

rain hard/heavily (=rain a lot) *It must have rained pretty hard last night.* | *It had been raining heavily and the ground was very soft.*

 If rain is falling now, don't say 'it rains'. Say **it's raining**.

◯ it's pouring /ɪts 'pɔːrɪŋ/ ESPECIALLY SPOKEN use this to say that it is raining very hard: *As soon as I got outside, it started pouring.*

it's pouring with rain BRITISH *It was pouring with rain, and she had forgotten her umbrella.*

it's drizzling /ɪts ˈdrɪzəlɪŋ/ ESPECIALLY SPOKEN use this to say that it is raining a little, with very small drops of rain: *I think I'll walk to work – it's only drizzling.*

wet/rainy /wet, ˈreɪni/ [adj] if the weather is **wet** or **rainy**, it rains a lot: *It's been wet all week.* | *wet weather* | *a rainy weekend in November*
wet – wetter – wettest

shower /ˈʃaʊəʳ/ [n C] a short period of rain, especially light rain: *It was just a shower, so we didn't get too wet.*
heavy showers (=when a lot of rain falls during short periods) *Heavy showers are forecast for the weekend.*
light showers (=when a small amount of rain falls during short periods) *The weather will be cloudy with light showers in places.*

the rainy season/the Monsoon /ðə ˈreɪni ˌsiːzən, ðə mɒnˈsuːn‖-mɑːn-/ [n singular] a time of the year when it rains a lot in hot countries: *The seeds must be planted in time for the rainy season.*

6 snow and ice

snow /snəʊ/ [n U] soft white pieces of frozen water that fall from the sky in cold weather: *The tops of the mountains were still covered in snow.*
snow falls *Some snow is expected to fall in the Rockies tonight.*
deep snow (=a lot of snow that has fallen on the ground) *Tony and I trudged home through the deep snow.*

it snows /ɪt ˈsnəʊz/ if **it snows**, snow falls from the sky: *It snowed six inches last night.*
it's snowing *Look! It's snowing!* | *It was snowing when he left the house.*
snow hard/heavily (=snow a lot) *It's been snowing heavily all day long.*

> ⚠ If snow is falling now, don't say 'it snows'. Say **it's snowing**.

hail /heɪl/ [n U] frozen raindrops that fall as small balls of ice: *There were frequent showers of rain and hail.*

sleet /sliːt/ [n U] a mixture of snow and rain: *We couldn't see anything because of the sleet and snow.*

frost /frɒst‖frɔːst/ [n U] ice that looks white and powdery and covers things when the temperature is very cold: *The grass was covered with frost.*
frosty [adj] *frosty winter mornings*

icy /ˈaɪsi/ [adj] covered in ice and very slippery: *Be careful – the roads are icy this morning.*
icy – icier – iciest

7 cloudy

cloudy /ˈklaʊdi/ [adj] if the weather is **cloudy**, there are a lot of clouds in the sky: *a cloudy day*
cloudy – cloudier – cloudiest

dull /dʌl/ [adj] if the weather is **dull**, it is cloudy and there is no sunshine: *It will be dry but dull this morning, with the possibility of showers later in the day.*

grey (also **gray** AMERICAN) /greɪ/ [adj] ESPECIALLY WRITTEN cloudy and not at all bright: *It was a grey winter morning.*

overcast /ˌəʊvəʳˈkɑːst◂‖-ˈkæst◂/ [adj] if the sky is **overcast**, it is very cloudy and dark, and there will probably be rain: *The sky was overcast, and a light rain began to fall.*

cloud /klaʊd/ [n C/U] a white or grey mass in the sky that rain falls from: *There wasn't a single cloud in the sky.*
thick/dense cloud (=a lot of cloud) *Dense cloud prevented the rescue helicopter from taking off.*

fog /fɒg‖fɑːg, fɔːg/ [n U] thick cloudy air near the ground, which is very difficult to see through clearly
the fog *I could just make out a dim figure coming towards me in the fog.*
patch of fog *Watch out for patches of fog in low-lying areas.*
thick/dense fog (=a lot of fog) *Dense fog is making driving conditions difficult on many roads.*
the fog lifts/clears (=it goes away) *The fog has almost cleared – our plane will be able to take off soon.*
foggy [adj] *a foggy November evening*

mist /mɪst/ [n singular/U] wet light cloud near the ground, which is difficult to see through clearly: *A light mist lay in the valley.* | *The mist along the river banks had gone by 10 o'clock.*
misty [adj] *It may be misty in the east in the morning.*

8 windy

windy /'wɪndi/ [adj] if the weather is **windy**, there is a lot of wind: *It was a bright windy day in October.* | *The windy conditions made it difficult to put the tent up.*

wind /wɪnd/ [n C/U] a moving current of air near the ground: *We walked home through the wind and the rain.*
the wind blows *A strong wind was blowing from the east.*
in the wind *The flags fluttered gently in the wind.*
strong/high wind *Strong winds caused damage to many buildings.*
gust of wind (=when the wind suddenly blows strongly) *A sudden gust of wind blew the paper out of his hand.*

breeze /briːz/ [n C] a gentle pleasant wind: *A cool breeze blew in off the sea.*
slight/gentle breeze *A gentle breeze ruffled her hair.*

gale /geɪl/ [n C] a very strong wind: *The fence was blown down in the gale last night.*

9 hot weather

➡ see also **HOT**

hot /hɒt‖hɑːt/ [adj] *Isn't it hot today?* | *We had three weeks of very hot weather.* | *It was the hottest summer this century.*
hot – hotter – hottest

boiling/scorching /'bɔɪlɪŋ, 'skɔːʳtʃɪŋ/ [adj] ESPECIALLY SPOKEN extremely hot: *It's boiling out here! Let's go inside and get a cool drink.*
boiling hot/scorching hot *It was a boiling hot day in August and the kids were out playing in the pool.*

warm /wɔːʳm/ [adj] pleasantly hot, but not too hot: *I'm looking forward to some warmer weather.*
nice and warm *It was nice and warm in the sunshine.*

mild /maɪld/ [adj] **mild** weather is pleasant because it is not as cold as it usually is: *It seems quite mild for February.* | *a mild winter*

humid /'hjuːmɪd/ [adj] if the weather is **humid**, the air is hot and wet in a way that makes you feel uncomfortable: *Tokyo is very humid in summer.*

10 cold weather

➡ see also **COLD**

cold /kəʊld/ [adj] *I'd hate to live somewhere where it's always cold.* | *The car is difficult to start, especially on cold winter mornings.* | *There was a very cold winter that year.* | *It's so cold. I wish I was back home in Greece.*
the cold [n singular] cold weather outside: *Come in out of the cold.*

cool /kuːl/ [adj] pleasantly cold, especially compared to the heat of the sun: *It gets much cooler in the evenings.* | *a cool breeze*

chilly /'tʃɪli/ [adj] a little cold, in a way that makes you feel uncomfortable: *It was getting chilly outside, so we went back into the house.*
chilly – chillier – chilliest

freezing /'friːzɪŋ/ [adj] ESPECIALLY SPOKEN extremely cold
it's freezing *Can't we go inside? It's freezing out here.*
freezing cold *a freezing cold day in January*

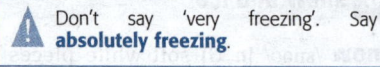
Don't say 'very freezing'. Say **absolutely freezing**.

11 storm

storm /stɔːʳm/ [n C] a period of very bad weather, when there is a lot of rain, wind, and sometimes thunder and lightning: *The Spanish ships were wrecked in the storm.*
severe storm *There had not been such severe storms in southern England for hundreds of years.*
stormy [adj] stormy weather | *The sky was starting to look stormy.*

thunderstorm /'θʌndəʳstɔːʳm/ [n C] a storm when there is a lot of thunder and lightning: *There was a spectacular thunderstorm that night.*

thunder /'θʌndəʳ/ [n U] the loud crashing noise that you hear in a storm
thunder rumbles/crashes *They could hear thunder rumbling in the distance.*
clap of thunder/thunder clap (=one sudden noise of thunder) *There was a thunder clap followed instantly by lightning.*

lightning /ˈlaɪtnɪŋ/ [n U] a bright flash of light in the sky during a storm
flash of lightning *A flash of lightning lit up the whole sky.*

blizzard /ˈblɪzəʳd/ [n C] a storm with a lot of snow and strong winds: *He had to 'drive home through the blizzard.*

hurricane/typhoon /ˈhʌrɪ̩kən, taɪˈfuːn‖ˈhɜːrɪ̩keɪn/ [n C] a severe storm with very strong winds that causes a lot of damage: *The hurricane devastated Florida and killed at least 40 people.*

> ⚠ **Hurricanes** happen in the Western Atlantic Ocean. **Typhoons** happen in the Western Pacific Ocean.

tornado

tornado /tɔːˈneɪdəʊ/ [n C] a small but very powerful twisting mass of air that causes a lot of damage: *A tornado destroyed twelve homes in Ashport, Tennessee yesterday.*

> ⚠ **Tornadoes** usually happen in the southern USA.

WET

➡ opposite **DRY**
➡ see also **WEATHER**

1 wet

wet /wet/ [adj] if something is **wet**, it has a lot of liquid on it or in it; if someone is **wet**, their clothes and hair are wet: *I can't come out yet – my hair's still wet.* | *You'd better change out of those wet clothes.* | *Let's not sit here – the grass is wet.*
get wet *Hurry up with the umbrella – I'm getting wet!*

🔍 **soaking wet/wet through** (=very wet) ESPECIALLY SPOKEN *A pipe had burst and the carpet was soaking wet.* | *By the time the bus arrived, we were wet through.*

🔍 **all wet** SPOKEN (=very wet) *Oh no! My socks are all wet now!*

wet – wetter – wettest

drenched/soaked /drentʃt, səʊkt/ [adj] if you are **drenched** or **soaked**, you are extremely wet, so that drops of water are falling from your clothes: *Everyone got completely drenched when a huge wave hit the boat.* | *Your clothes are soaked. Leave them in front of the fire to dry.*
soaked to the skin (=completely soaked) *When the men came in from the storm, they were soaked to the skin.*

damp /dæmp/ [adj] slightly wet, especially in an unpleasant way: *Don't put that shirt on. It's still damp.* | *Clean the counter with a damp cloth.* | *My hair is still damp.* | *There was a damp spot on the ceiling.*

moist /mɔɪst/ [adj] ESPECIALLY WRITTEN something that is **moist** is slightly wet, and this is the way it should be: *The mixture should be slightly moist, but not sticky.* | *Water the plants regularly to keep the soil moist.*

soggy /ˈsɒgi‖ˈsɑːgi/ [adj] something that is **soggy** is softer than usual and looks or feels unpleasant, because it has become wet: *Breakfast was terrible – the eggs were burnt and the toast was soggy.* | *He always leaves the towels in a soggy heap on the bathroom floor.*

2 when the air feels wet

humid /ˈhjuːmɪ̩d/ [adj] **humid** air or weather is hot and wet in a way that makes you feel uncomfortable: *Summers in Tokyo are hot and humid.* | *the humid heat of a tropical rainforest*

damp /dæmp/ [adj] **damp** air or weather is slightly wet in an unpleasant way, and makes you feel cold: *It's cold and damp outside – make sure you wear a warm coat.* | *At first I hated the damp weather in Britain.*

3 to make something or someone wet

⟨ **get sth wet** /ˌget (sth) 'wet/ ESPECIALLY SPOKEN to make something wet, especially by not being careful enough to keep it dry: *Don't splash me – I don't want to get my hair wet.* | *How did you manage to get the bathroom floor so wet?*

wet /wet/ [v T] to deliberately put water or other liquid onto something: *The hairdresser usually wets my hair before she cuts it.*

wetting – wet (also **wetted** BRITISH) – **have wet** (also **have wetted** BRITISH)

soak /səʊk/ [v T] to leave something in water for a long time in order to make it clean, soft etc: *Soak the beans overnight before cooking them.*

soak sth in sth *Soak a piece of cotton in water and use it to clean the wound.*

WIDE/NARROW

➡ see also **FAT, THIN, THICK**

1 a long distance from one side to the other

wide /waɪd/ [adj] if a road, river, space, object etc is **wide**, there is a large distance between one side of it and the other: *The girl led me down a wide corridor into a large office.* | *a wide leather belt* | *The doorway isn't wide enough to get the piano through.*

wide – wider – widest

broad /brɔːd/ [adj] ESPECIALLY WRITTEN wide – use this especially to describe roads, paths, or parts of someone's body: *a broad, tree-lined avenue* | *He was six feet tall with broad shoulders and strong arms.*

2 how wide something is

how wide /haʊ 'waɪd/ use this to ask or talk about how wide something is: *How wide is the driveway?* | *I'm not sure how wide the window is.*

2 miles wide/1 metre wide etc /(2 miles, etc) 'waɪd/ use this to say exactly how wide something is: *At this point the river is over a mile wide.* | *Cut a piece of paper 3 cm wide.*

width /wɪdθ/ [n C/U] the distance from one side of something to the other: *Carpets are available in several different widths.*

+of *Can you just measure the width of the door?*

3 not wide

➡ see also **THIN**

narrow /'nærəʊ/ [adj] a **narrow** road, river, bed, space etc is not wide: *He led me through the narrow streets of the old city.* | *She climbed through a narrow gap in the fence.* | *The road was too narrow for me to overtake the car in front.*

WIN

➡ opposite **LOSE**

1 to win a race/game/competition/election

win /wɪn/ [v I/T] to win a race, competition, election etc, for example by getting more points, votes etc than everyone else or by being the first to finish: *No-one really expected the Socialist Party to win.*

win a race/game/election etc *Moya won the first set but lost the next two.* | *The competition was won by a Nigerian student.*

win a prize/medal/cup etc *His book won the Pulitzer Prize for literature.* | *She won almost $1 million in the lottery.*

win by 6 votes/2 goals etc (=win by getting 6 votes etc more than the other person or team) *He went ahead of Nolan, winning by 15 seconds.*

win 4–2/20–12 etc (=use this to show the final result of a game) *Do you remember our first game of the season? We won 3–1.*

win at cards/chess/tennis etc *She always wins at table tennis.*

winning – won – have won

be first (also **come first** BRITISH) /biː ˈfɜːʳst, ˌkʌm ˈfɜːʳst/ to win a race or competition in which more than two people or teams are competing: *Who do you think will be first?*

+in *An Australian runner came first in the marathon.*

> ⚠ Use **be/come second**, **be/come third** etc about the teams or players that are the next best, after the winner.

beat/defeat /biːt, dɪˈfiːt/ [v T] if you **beat** or **defeat** another team or player, you win a game, race etc against them: *Brazil beat Italy in the final.* | *Since he was defeated by Jackson, Marquez has announced his retirement.*

beat sb 3–1/by 50 points etc *Short beat Redgrave by nearly 200 votes.* | *The Red Sox defeated the Yankees 6–3.*

beating – beat – have beaten

> **Formal or informal?**
> **Defeat** is more formal than **beat**, and is used especially in written English.

first place /ˌfɜːʳst ˈpleɪs/ [n U] the position of the person or team that wins a race or competition

in first place *Johnson finished in first place, narrowly ahead of Green.*

win first place *Our team won first place.*

> ⚠ Use **second place**, **third place** etc about the teams or players that are the next best, after the winner: *Powell was disappointed to finish in third place.*

2 to win a war/fight/argument

win /wɪn/ [v I/T] to argue, fight etc more successfully than someone else: *I could never win an argument with my father.* | *Who won the first Civil War?*

win a victory *This was the first of many victories won by women's rights campaigners.*

winning – won – have won

defeat /dɪˈfiːt/ [v T] ESPECIALLY WRITTEN if a leader, army, or country **defeats** another leader, army, or country, they win a war or battle against them: *Wellington's army finally defeated Napoleon.*

defeat [n C] *the defeat of the Republican army in Spain*

3 to be winning a game, race etc that has not yet finished

be winning /biː ˈwɪnɪŋ/ to have more points or votes than your opponents in a game or election, or to be at the front in a race when the game, race etc has not yet finished: *I think Myskina is winning at the moment.*

be in the lead /biː ɪn ðə ˈliːd/ to be winning a game, race, election etc: *The Dolphins are still in the lead with only two minutes left to play.*

lead /liːd/ [v I/T] to be winning a game, race, election etc: *At half time, Brazil led 1–0.* | *Polls showed Boxer leading her opponent, 55 percent to 34 percent.*

be ahead /biː əˈhed/ to be doing better than someone else in a game, competition, race, or election: *For the first half of the game, the Dodgers were ahead.*

+of *With over half the votes counted, the Socialists were ahead of all the other parties.*

be 12 points/5 games etc ahead *Schumacher is now 14 points ahead of his nearest rival.*

4 the person or team that wins

winner /ˈwɪnəʳ/ [n C] someone who has won a game, race, competition, or election: *The winner will receive a prize of $500.* | *Tottenham were the winners with a late goal from Defoe.*

+of *On Thursday the judges will be announcing the winner of this year's Booker Prize.*

champion /ˈtʃæmpiən/ [n C] someone who has won a competition, especially in sport: *Roger Federer, the 2004 Wimbledon men's champion*

W

world champion (=the winner of the most important competition in a particular sport) *He finally achieved his dream of becoming Formula 1 World Champion.*

defending champion (=the person who won last time and is trying to win again) *As defending champion, he is expected to reach the final.*

winning /'wɪnɪŋ/ [adj only before noun] **winning team/player/horse etc** the team, player etc that wins: *The winning team will go through to the grand final in London.*

5 an occasion when someone wins

victory /'vɪktəri/ [n C/U] when a country, player, team etc wins a battle, game, race etc: *The crowds were celebrating Italy's victory.* | *Napoleon's victory at Austerlitz* | *We're confident of victory.* | *victory celebrations*
+over/against *Their 24–3 victory over the Australians was completely unexpected.*
win a victory *He had won a comfortable victory in the general election.*
plural **victories**

win /wɪn/ [n C] when a team or player wins in a sport or competition – used especially in news reports: *It was an important win for Manchester United.* | *A couple from London are celebrating a big lottery win.*
+over/against *a 2–0 win over their oldest rivals*

6 something that you get when you win

prize /praɪz/ [n C] something that is given to the person who wins a competition, game, or race: *The prize is a 3-week holiday in the Bahamas.*
first/second/third prize *Second prize is a book token.*
win/get a prize *She won the Booker Prize for her novel 'The Ghost Road'.*

cup /kʌp/ [n C] a special silver or gold container, shaped like a large cup with two handles, that is given to the winner of a sports competition: *The Queen presented the cup to the captain of the winning team.*

medal /'medl/ [n C] a round flat piece of metal that is given to someone who has won a race, game, or competition: *The winning team went up to collect their medals.*
gold/silver/bronze medal (=a medal for coming first/second/third) *The gold medal was won by Kelly Holmes.*

award /ə'wɔːʳd/ [n C] a prize that someone wins for achieving something important or doing something very well
+for *One of the firefighters was given an award for bravery.*
win an award *Charlize Theron won the best actress award.*

> ⚠ Don't use **award** when talking about sports.

WOMAN

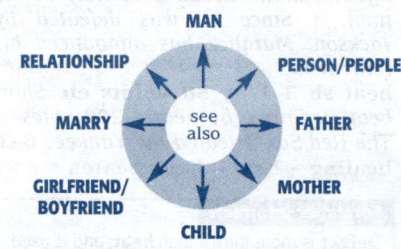

1 a woman

woman /'wʊmən/ [n C] a female adult: *Rebecca Stephens was the first British woman to climb Mount Everest.* | *Who's that woman you were talking to just now?* | *In some African countries, the women do most of the agricultural work.*
plural **women**

> ⚠ **Woman** can also be used before a noun, like an adjective: *Britain's first woman Prime Minister.* Use **women** before a plural noun: *Some companies offer low-cost insurance to women drivers.*

lady /'leɪdi/ [n C] a polite word for a woman, especially a woman who is there when you are speaking about her: *There's a lady here who wants to speak to you about her account.*

○ **ladies and gentlemen** SPOKEN (=use this when you are talking to an audience, making a speech etc) *Ladies and gentlemen, I am delighted to welcome you here tonight.*
old lady *Ella is a lovely old lady.*
plural **ladies**

> ⚠ Some women do not like being called 'ladies' and prefer to be called **women**.

female /'fiːmeɪl/ [adj usually before noun] FORMAL a **female** worker, teacher, singer etc is a woman or girl – use this especially to emphasize that the person you are referring to is a woman or girl and not a man or boy: *Emma is the only female lawyer that the firm has ever employed.* | *Female students tend to get better grades than male students.* | *a company with a mainly female workforce*

girl /gɜːʳl/ [n C] a young woman: *He's going out with that girl who works in the library.*

> ⚠ Many young women do not like being called 'girls' and prefer to be called **women**.

2 what you call a woman when you speak to her or write to her

Mrs BRITISH **Mrs.** AMERICAN /'mɪsɪz/ use this before the family name of a woman who is married: *Mrs Thomas, the doctor is ready to see you now.* | *It's Mrs Hawksworth's 70th birthday this weekend.*

Miss /mɪs/ use this before the family name of a woman who has never been married: *My secretary, Miss Evans, will meet you in reception.*

Ms BRITISH **Ms.** AMERICAN /mɪz, məz/ use this before a woman's family name if you do not know whether she is married, or if it is not important to know whether she is married: *Would you prefer to be called Mrs or Ms Cawley?*

> ⚠ Many women prefer to be called **Ms**, instead of **Mrs** or **Miss**, because they do not think it is necessary for people to know whether they are married or not.

madam /'mædəm/ FORMAL use this when writing a formal letter to a woman. In British English this is also used when talking to a customer in a shop, hotel, restaurant etc: *Can I help you, madam?* | *Dear Madam, I am writing in response to your advertisement.*

○ **ma'am** /mæm, mɑːm, məm‖mæm/ AMERICAN SPOKEN a polite word used when talking to a woman who you do not know: *Would you like some help, ma'am?*

3 for women or like women

women's /'wɪmɪnz/ [adj only before noun] use this about things that are designed for women or done by women, and not designed for or done by men: *She's the fashion editor for a women's magazine.* | *Why don't they ever show women's football on TV?*

female /'fiːmeɪl/ [adj only before noun] use this about behaviour or personal qualities that are traditionally thought to be typical of women, or about physical characteristics that belong to women: *Many women reject the traditional female roles of wife and mother.* | *Patience and kindness are often seen as female qualities.*

feminine /'femɪnɪn/ [adj] looking attractive in a way that is traditionally thought to be typical of a woman: *Hairstyles this autumn are long, soft, and very feminine.* | *Lindsay wears very feminine clothes – pretty dresses with flowers on and things like that.*

effeminate /ɪ'femɪnɪt/ [adj] use this about a man who behaves like a woman or looks like a woman: *He was very young and handsome in a slightly effeminate way.*

WORD/PHRASE/ SENTENCE

➡ see also **LANGUAGE, ANSWER 1, ASK 5**

1 a word or group of words

word /wɜːʳd/ [n C] *Look up any words you don't know in a dictionary.* | *Is 'lunchtime' one word or two?* | *The word 'origami' comes from Japanese.*

word for sth (=word that means something) *'Casa' is the Italian word for 'house'.* | *What's another word for 'way out'?*

phrase/expression /freɪz, ɪkˈspreʃən/ [n C] a combination of two or more words that has a particular meaning: *There are some useful words and phrases at the end of each chapter in the Student's Book.* | *"It'll be alright in the end" – that was my mother's favourite expression.*

term /tɜːʳm/ [n C] a word or group of words that are used in a technical or scientific subject and have an exact meaning in that subject

technical / medical / legal / scientific etc term (for sth) *The medical term for losing your hair is 'alopecia'.*

idiom /ˈɪdiəm/ [n C] a group of words that are used together and have a special meaning that you cannot guess from the meanings of each separate word: *'Full of beans' is an idiom which means lively and energetic.*

cliché /ˈkliːʃeɪ‖kliːˈʃeɪ/ [n C] a phrase that is used so often that it seems boring, annoying, or silly: *It's a cliché I know, but the game isn't over until the final whistle blows.*

W

---

2 **a sentence or part of a sentence**

sentence /ˈsentəns/ [n C] a group of words that begins with a capital letter, ends with a full stop, and includes a verb: *Write a complete sentence for each answer.*

clause /klɔːz/ [n C] a group of words that has a subject and a verb and that is part of a sentence

main clause (=the clause that describes the main action) *We're going to the theatre tonight [main clause] if we can get tickets [subordinate clause].*

subordinate clause/dependent clause (=a clause that is not the main clause)

---

3 **all the words someone knows or uses**

vocabulary /vəˈkæbjŭləri, vəʊ-ll-leri/ [n C usually singular] someone's **vocabulary** is all the words that they know or use: *These stories are written for students with a vocabulary of about 2000 words.* | *Reading is a good way to increase your vocabulary.*

plural **vocabularies**

---

4 **words that someone has written**

writing /ˈraɪtɪŋ/ [n U] words that someone has written or printed: *There's some writing on the back of the photo, but I can't read what it says.*

text /tekst/ [n U] the written part of a book, newspaper etc, not including notes, pictures etc: *The book consisted mainly of colour photographs and not much text.*

> **Formal or informal?**
> **Text** is a fairly formal word.

WORK

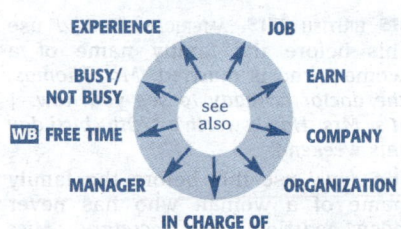

EXPERIENCE   JOB

BUSY/NOT BUSY   EARN

WB FREE TIME   *see also*   COMPANY

MANAGER   ORGANIZATION

IN CHARGE OF

---

1 **to do a job**

work /wɜːʳk/ [v I] to do a job that you get paid for: *I haven't worked since I had my first child seven years ago.*

+for (=for a company or organization) *She used to work for the BBC.*

+in/on/at *Susie works in a supermarket on Saturdays.*

work as a secretary / builder / gardener etc *Russell is now working as a software developer for Microsoft.*

work somewhere *Where do you work?*

work long hours/Sundays/nights/full-time etc *He only works three days a week now.*

> ⚠ Use **work for** to talk about the company or organization that someone is employed by: *I work for Eriksson International.* | *Pam works for a biotechnology company.* Use **work in** with words like 'school', 'bank', 'hospital', 'factory', 'hotel' etc to talk about the kind of place where someone works: *He used to work in a Chinese restaurant.* | *I've worked in a factory all my life.* Don't use **work in** with the name of a company or organization. You can use **work at** to mention a specific shop, hospital, university etc where someone works: *Bill works at McDonald's.* | *During the school vacation, she's working at that bookstore on Ramsey Street.*

be /biː/ [v] if someone **is** a teacher, a doctor etc, that is their job: *She was a journalist for 20 years before she wrote her first novel.* | *"What does your father do?" "He's a dentist."* | *Jill wants to be a professional musician.*

> ⚠ Don't say 'she is nurse/teacher etc'. Say **she is a nurse, she is a teacher** etc.

⌕ **do** /duː/ [v T] ESPECIALLY SPOKEN use this to ask or talk about the type of job that someone does: *What does her father do?* | *Jess isn't sure yet what she wants to do when she finishes school.*

be employed /biː ɪmˈplɔɪd/ FORMAL to work for a company or organization, especially when you have an official contract and a permanent job
+by *She was the first woman pilot to be employed by a commercial airline.*
+in *The number of people employed in the construction industry has been falling for many years.*

2 to be at the place where you usually work

be at work /biː ət ˈwɜːʳk/ to be doing your job at the place where you work, especially at a factory, office etc owned by your employer: *I'm afraid Fran's not here at the moment – he's at work.*

be on duty /biː ɒn ˈdjuːti‖-ˈduːti/ to be at work in a job where there must always be someone working, for example if you are a nurse or a police officer: *You can't drink while you're on duty.*

be on duty from 6.00 p.m./on Mondays etc *I'm on duty from 8 a.m. on Monday until 12 midday on Thursday.*

on business /ɒn ˈbɪznɪs/ if you go somewhere **on business**, you go there as part of your job, especially to another city or country: *I had to fly to Tokyo on business.*

3 to do work that is not part of a job

work /wɜːʳk/ [v I] to do an activity that needs effort and takes time: *I've been working all day in the garden.*
work on sth *I have to work on the car over the weekend.*

do /duː/ [v T]
do the housework / gardening / cleaning/cooking etc to do work that must be done regularly in your home: *Whose turn is it to do the washing-up?*

4 to work independently and not for someone else

self-employed /ˌself ɪmˈplɔɪd◂/ [adj] someone who is **self-employed** does not have a job with one particular employer, but instead works independently and does work for many different people: *Martin is a self-employed builder.* | *How long have you been self-employed?*
the self-employed (=people who are self-employed) *The government gives generous tax allowances to the self-employed.*

freelance /ˈfriːlɑːns‖-læns/ [adj] working for several different organizations instead of being employed by only one – use this especially about people such as writers, designers, and photographers
freelance designer/journalist/photographer etc *Jamie's trying to earn a living as a freelance photographer.*
freelance work/writing/photography etc *Karen stayed at home while the children were small, and made a little money from freelance writing.*

freelance [adv] If you work freelance from home, your hours are completely flexible.

5 to work hard

work hard /ˌwɜːʳk ˈhɑːʳd/ to work hard when you are doing your job, your schoolwork, or anything that takes time and effort: Bruno had been working hard in the kitchen all morning. | I wouldn't mind working so hard if they paid us more.

put a lot of effort into sth /ˌpʊt ə lɒt əv ˈefəʳt ɪntu: (sth)‖-lɑːt-/ to work hard because you think something is important and you want to do it well: She had obviously put a lot of effort into her assignment, and got a good grade. | The company puts a great deal of effort into training its staff.

hardworking /ˌhɑːʳdˈwɜːʳkɪŋ◂/ [adj] always working hard in your job or on your schoolwork: Colleagues described him as a quiet, hardworking young man.

dedicated /ˈdedɪkeɪtɪd/ [adj] someone who is **dedicated** works very hard at something because they care about it a lot, even though the job is difficult or does not earn them much money: Jane's a wonderful nurse – completely dedicated. | The lifeboat service is run by a team of dedicated volunteers.

overworked /ˌəʊvəʳˈwɜːʳkt◂/ [adj] someone who is **overworked** has too much work to do: Teachers often complain that they are overworked and underpaid. | I'd been six months without any holiday, and I was tired and overworked.

6 work that you do at home, in your job etc

work /wɜːʳk/ [n U] the things that you have to do at home or at school or in your job, which need time and effort: She has a busy job, and she often takes work home with her. | I agreed to organize the party, but I didn't realize there would be so much work involved. **do work** I can't go out tonight, I have a lot of work to do for my biology test tomorrow.

secretarial/teaching/bar work etc Have you ever done any secretarial work before?

effort /ˈefəʳt/ [n U] the physical or mental energy that is needed to do something: It seemed like a lot of effort for a very small gain. **take/require effort** (=need a lot of work) This exercise isn't difficult – it shouldn't require much effort.

job /dʒɒb‖dʒɑːb/ [n C] a specific piece of work that you have to do, especially one that you do not get paid for: Repairing the roof – that's going to be the biggest job. | Cleaning the car's one of my least favourite jobs. **do a job** I spent the weekend doing various jobs around the house.

task /tɑːsk‖tæsk/ [n C] a piece of work that you have to do – use this especially about a difficult or unpleasant job, or about a specific part of your work: One of the first tasks Eva set herself was learning the local language. **impossible/difficult/arduous etc task** The UN Peacekeeping Force faces an almost impossible task. **+of** Recovery crews continued the grim task of retrieving bodies from the wreckage.

> **Formal or informal?**
> **Task** is used in writing and in formal spoken English.

duties /ˈdjuːtɪz‖ˈduː-/ [n plural] FORMAL the various things that you have to do as part of your job – used especially in contracts or other official documents **sb's duties** Your duties will include organizing a monthly departmental meeting. | As soon as she returned home from her honeymoon, she resumed her medical duties at the clinic.

housework /ˈhaʊswɜːʳk/ [n U] work that needs to be done in your home, for example, cleaning, washing clothes, or keeping rooms tidy: None of her kids ever help with the housework. **do (the) housework** Saturday is the only day I have enough time to do the housework.

homework /ˈhəʊmwɜːˌʳk/ [n U] the work that a student has to do at home as part of their studies
do your homework *Have you done all your homework?*
for homework *For homework, I'd like you to finish Exercise 3.*
have homework *I don't have any homework tonight.*

schoolwork /ˈskuːlwɜːˌʳk/ [n U] all the work that a student has to do, both at home and in class: *Problems at home have affected Laurie's schoolwork.*

7 someone who works for an organization or company

worker /ˈwɜːˌʳkəʳ/ [n C] someone who works for an organization but is not a manager: *We need better communication between the management and the workers.*
manual worker (=who does physical work, for example in a factory, rather than working in an office) *The report shows that male manual workers earn twice as much as female workers.*
post office / factory / office etc worker *Tony was a retired post office worker.*
skilled/unskilled worker (=someone who has or does not have special skills) *There is a shortage of skilled workers in some industries.*

employee /ɪmˈplɔɪ-iː/ [n C] someone who has a job, especially a permanent job, with a particular company or organization: *We're a multinational corporation with 140,000 employees worldwide.* | *a bank employee*
+of *Employees of American Airlines get generous reductions on the cost of flights.*

staff /stɑːf‖stæf/ [n C/plural] all the people who work for a company, organization, school etc: *The staff were clearly worried about rumours of job losses.* | *The hospital has a staff of around 500 people.*
library/office/hospital/security etc staff *Our library staff will be happy to help if you are unable to find the book you want.* | *The company is looking for part-time sales staff.*
member of staff *Training is provided for all members of staff.*
join the staff *In 2003, she joined the President's personal staff in the White House.*

workforce /ˈwɜːˌʳkfɔːˌʳs/ [n C usually singular] all the people who work in a country, industry, or large organization: *Women make up 40% of the workforce.* | *The company has had to get rid of a third of its workforce in order to save costs.*

8 someone you work with

colleague /ˈkɒliːg‖ˈkɑː-/ [n C] someone you work with – use this especially about people who do professional jobs in offices, schools, government etc: *I'd like you to meet a colleague of mine, Jean-Michel Blanc from our Paris office.* | *Jenny is a hardworking manager, very popular with her colleagues.*

workmate /ˈwɜːˌʳkmeɪt/ [n C] someone that you work with, especially someone who works closely with you and who you are friendly with: *Police are questioning neighbours and workmates of the missing woman.*

W

9 the person or company you work for

→ see also **MANAGER**

employer /ɪmˈplɔɪəʳ/ [n C] someone's **employer** is the person, company, or organization that they work for: *We will need a reference from your last employer.*

> **Formal or informal?**
>
> **Employer** is a rather formal word. In ordinary conversation, it is more usual to say something like 'the company I work for', instead of 'my employer'.

10 to stop working in order to get more money

strike /straɪk/ [n C] when people deliberately stop working in order to get more money, better working conditions etc: *The strike lasted about two months.*
miners'/teachers'/railworkers' etc strike *The railworkers' strike caused chaos in the city.*
coal/rail/dock etc strike *The roads were a nightmare as commuters were hit by a rail strike.*
call a strike (=ask workers to join a strike) *Union bosses have called a strike in protest over low pay.*
call off a strike (=agree to end a strike or not start a strike) *Teachers have called off the strike that was planned for Tuesday.*

on strike /ɒn ˈstraɪk/ if workers go **on strike**, they stop working in order to demand better pay or working conditions, or to protest about something
go on strike *Ford workers threatened to go on strike unless the company improved its pay offer.*
be (out) on strike (=not working) *There were frequent power cuts when the electricity workers were out on strike.*

WORKING

when a machine, car etc is working as it should, and is not broken

→ opposite **BROKEN**
→ see also **REPAIR**

work /wɜːʳk/ [v I] if a machine or piece of equipment **works** or **is working**, it can be used without any problems because there is nothing wrong with it: *We had to go to the laundromat because the washing-machine wasn't working.*
🔍 **work fine/be working fine** ESPECIALLY SPOKEN *I've fixed your heater – it's working fine now.*

be in working order /biː ɪn ˌwɜːʳkɪŋ ˈɔːʳdəʳ/ if something **is in working order**, it is working well and safely, especially because it has been well cared for: *The mill was built in the 16th century and is still in working order.*
be in good/perfect working order *As far as he could tell, the engine was in perfect working order.*

> **Formal or informal?**
>
> **Be in working order** is more formal than **work**, and is not usually used in ordinary conversation.

🔍 **go** BRITISH SPOKEN **run** AMERICAN SPOKEN /gəʊ, rʌn/ [v I] to be working properly – use this especially about a car, clock, or watch: *I dropped my watch, but it's still going.* | *I don't mind what kind of car we rent as long as it runs.*
going – went – have gone

be up and running /biː ˌʌp ənd ˈrʌnɪŋ/ to be working well and without any problems – use this about computers or systems, especially new ones: *As soon as the new computer system is up and running, we can transfer our records onto it.*

WORLD

the planet we live on

➡ see also **COUNTRY, LAND AND SEA**, **WB ENVIRONMENT**

1 the world

the world /ðə ˈwɜːʳld/ [n singular] the planet we live on, and all the people and places on it: *In some parts of the world, clean drinking water is very scarce.*
all over the world *You can buy Coca-Cola all over the world.*
around the world (=in every part of the world) *Scientists around the world have been doing similar experiments.*
the whole world (=everyone and everything in the world) *The two countries are trying to work out a peace deal with the whole world watching.*
the best, fastest etc in the world/ the world's best, fastest etc *It's the world's tallest building.* | *At age 116, she was believed to be one of the oldest people in the world.*
earth/Earth /ɜːʳθ/ [n singular/U] use this especially when you are comparing our world with the moon, stars, and other places in space: *Light from the stars can take millions of years to reach Earth.*
the earth/the Earth *The earth revolves around the sun.* | *Water is one of the Earth's most important resources.*
the largest/oldest/poorest sth on Earth *The Blue Whale is the largest animal on Earth.*
to earth *The space shuttle returned safely to earth on December 9th.*
the planet /ðə ˈplænɪt/ [n singular] use this especially when you are talking about problems that affect the environment: *The massive volcanic eruption could affect the climate of the whole planet.* | *Energy conservation is vital for the future of the planet.*

2 things that affect the whole world or happen everywhere in the world

world /wɜːʳld/ [adj only before noun] use this to talk about something that exists everywhere in the world, or affects the whole world, or is the best or most important in the world: *The top 50 multinational companies control about 80% of world trade.* | *At that time Britain was a major world power.* | *Islam is one of the great world religions.*
world champion/record/expert (=the best in the world) *The world champion, Michael Schumacher, is still in the lead.* | *Jones is a world expert in genetics.*
global /ˈɡləʊbəl/ [adj only before noun] use this especially to talk about political or economic situations: *The fight against AIDS requires a global strategy.* | *Campaigners have called for a global ban on whale hunting.* | *Nuclear war could lead to global catastrophe.*
worldwide /ˌwɜːʳldˈwaɪd◂/ [adj] existing or happening in every country of the world: *There is a worldwide shortage of oil.* | *The concert attracted a worldwide television audience of over a billion people.*

W

WORRYING/ WORRIED

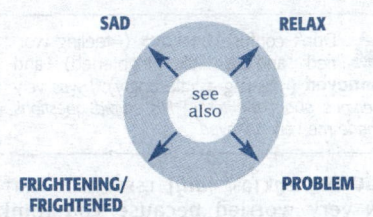

1 feeling worried

worried /ˈwʌrɪd‖ˈwɜːrɪd/ [adj] not feeling happy or relaxed, because you keep thinking about a problem or about something bad that might happen: *Dave could see how worried she was, and tried to reassure her.*

look worried *You look worried – what's the matter?*

+about *Marion was worried about losing her job.*

+(that) *She rushed to the station, worried that she might miss her train.*

get worried *We began to get worried when she didn't come home on Thursday night.*

a worried look/frown/glance *She had a worried look on her face.*

worry /ˈwʌri‖ˈwɜːri/ [v I] to keep thinking about a problem or about something bad that might happen, so that you cannot relax or feel happy: *My parents worry when I'm late home from school.* | *You worry too much.*

+(that) *He began to worry he might lose his job.*

+about *I worry about my kids' future.*

🔾 **don't worry** SPOKEN (say this to tell someone not to worry) *Don't worry, I can pay for both of us.*

worrying – worried – have worried

nervous /ˈnɜːrvəs/ [adj] worried and slightly frightened about something that is going to happen or something new or difficult that you have to do: *I'm always nervous before exams.*

get nervous *Mum gets nervous if we don't call to say we're late.*

look/feel/sound nervous *Bill looked nervous, and I could see that his hands were shaking.*

+about *Kelly was so nervous about her interview that she couldn't sleep.*

nervously [adv] *She waited nervously for him to return.*

> ⚠ Don't confuse **nervous** (=feeling worried and a little frightened) and **annoyed** (=feeling a little angry): *I was very nervous about the test.* | *His stupid questions made me very annoyed.*

anxious /ˈæŋkʃəs/ [adj] ESPECIALLY WRITTEN very worried because you think that something bad has happened or may happen, and you feel that you have no control over the situation: *Anxious relatives waited at the airport for news of the plane crash.*

feel/sound anxious *She knew it was a simple operation, but she still felt anxious.*

+about *Helen is always anxious about travelling alone.*

an anxious face/voice/expression etc *"Please come with me," she said in an anxious voice.*

anxiously [adv] *"Is he going to be all right?" she asked anxiously.*

frightened/scared/afraid /ˈfraɪtnd, skeəʳd, əˈfreɪd/ [adj] worried and frightened because of something bad that might happen

+(that) *She was frightened that the dog might bite her.* | *I was scared she might never come back.*

+of *Many people are frightened of losing their jobs.* | *I was afraid of offending her.*

> **Formal or informal?**
> **Scared** is more informal than **frightened** and **afraid**.

tense /tens/ [adj] so worried about something that you cannot relax, and you easily get angry or upset: *Lesley's problems at work made her tense and irritable.*

tense silence/moment/situation etc *There was a tense silence, then everyone began to laugh.*

stressed out /ˌstrest ˈaʊt◂/ [adj] INFORMAL worried and tired all the time, because you have a lot of problems to deal with and too much work to do: *Rob's been really stressed out since he started his new job.*

+about *She's pretty stressed out about the court case.*

2 to make someone feel worried

worry /ˈwʌri‖ˈwɜːri/ [v T] to make someone feel worried: *Recent changes in the climate are beginning to worry environmental scientists.* | *I could tell that something was worrying her.*

it worries sb that *Doesn't it worry you that Stephen spends so much time away from home?*

🔾 **what worries sb is** ESPECIALLY SPOKEN *What worries me is the difference in age between Rosie and her boyfriend.*

worrying – worried – have worried

worrying /ˈwʌri-ɪŋ‖ˈwɜːri-/ [adj] **worrying** events, changes etc make you feel worried: *The possibility that I might lose my job is very worrying.*

it's worrying that/when *It's worrying that violent crime seems to be on the increase.*

stressful /'stresfəl/ [*adj*] a **stressful** job or situation makes you feel worried and tired all the time, for example because you have too many problems or too much work to do: *Looking after small children can be very stressful.*

make sb nervous /ˌmeɪk (sb) 'nɜːʳvəs/ to make someone feel nervous and unable to relax: *Stop watching me when I'm trying to work – you're making me nervous.*

3 a feeling of being worried

worry /'wʌri‖'wɜːri/ [*n* C/U] the feeling you have when you are worried that something bad has happened or is going to happen: *When he didn't come home that night, we were sick with worry.*
+about/over *worries about the company's poor sales figures*

anxiety /æŋ'zaɪəti/ [*n* U] ESPECIALLY WRITTEN the feeling you have when you are very worried: *After weeks of anxiety, I finally heard that I would not need an operation after all.*
+about *Her anxiety about the pain of childbirth is understandable.*

stress /stres/ [*n* U] the feeling of being worried all the time, for example about work or personal problems, which can make you ill or very tired: *Her financial problems were causing her a lot of stress.*
mental / emotional / psychological stress *Geoff is having trouble dealing with the emotional stress of his recent divorce.*
stress-related illnesses/disorders/ conditions etc (=illnesses, conditions etc caused by stress) *His wife has also suffered stress-related health problems.*
be under stress (=be feeling stress) *He's been under a lot of stress at work lately.*

concern /kən'sɜːʳn/ [*n* U] a worried feeling – use this especially when many people are worried about a problem that affects everyone: *The shortage of water is beginning to cause widespread concern.*
+about/over *Concern over the President's health is increasing.*

hang-up /'hæŋ ʌp/ [*n* C] INFORMAL if you have a **hang-up** about something, for example about your appearance or your relationships with other people, you feel worried and embarrassed about it, and this makes you feel less confident: *They wanted their children to grow up without any hang-ups.*
+about *I don't know why she has such a hang-up about her nose – it looks OK to me.*

4 something that makes you feel worried

worry /'wʌri‖'wɜːri/ [*n* C] something that makes you feel worried: *It is important that children can discuss their worries with their parents.*
sb's main/biggest worry (=the thing someone worries about most) *Her main worry was how the divorce would affect the children.*
plural **worries**

concern /kən'sɜːʳn/ [*n* C] something important or serious that makes you or many people feel worried: *One of the concerns that people have is the possible side effects of the treatment.*

5 not worried any more

relieved /rɪ'liːvd/ [*adj*] feeling relaxed again because you do not need to worry about something that you worried about before: *"Oh," she said, relieved. "I'm so glad you're back."*
seem/feel/look relieved *He seemed relieved to be back home.*
+that *Tim was relieved that the teacher didn't ask him to read out his answer.*
relieved to hear/learn/find/see *Sue was relieved to hear that her mother's illness was not a serious one.*

relief /rɪ'liːf/ [*n* singular/U] the pleasant feeling you have when you no longer have to worry about something
a feeling/sense of relief *He felt a sense of great relief when he finally managed to find a job.*
with relief *Everyone smiled with relief as the plane landed safely.*
to sb's relief (=making them feel relieved) *To Sam's relief, nobody asked to check his ticket.*

W

it is a relief to know/hear/see/find etc *It was such a relief to know that the children were OK.*

WORSE

➡ opposite **BETTER**
➡ see also **BAD, IMPROVE**

1 worse

worse /wɜːʰs/ [*adj*] more unpleasant, annoying, bad etc, or of a lower standard or quality than someone or something else that is also bad: *I really don't think the situation could be any worse.*
+than *Conditions in the prison were worse than anything I had seen before.*
even/far worse (=worse than something that is very bad) *a terrible script and even worse acting | Duncan's handwriting is far worse than his sister's.*
a lot worse/much worse *The traffic is a lot worse after five o'clock.*
make sth worse *I tried to fix the computer myself, but that just made it worse.*

not as good /ˌnɒt əz ˈɡʊd/ of a lower standard, quality, or level than something else: *I like this town better than Harrisburg, but the schools aren't as good.*
+as *This book is not as good as her last one.*
not nearly as good/nowhere near as good as (=of a much lower quality) *Their latest album isn't nearly as good as their last one.*

> ⚠ **Worse** means 'more bad than something that is bad'. **Not as good** means 'less good than something that is good'. Compare these sentences: *The food was awful, and the service was even worse. | It's an enjoyable book, but it's not as good as her last one.*

inferior /ɪnˈfɪəriəʰ/ [*adj*] FORMAL of a lower quality than something else, or less good at doing something than someone else: *Consumers are tired of paying a high price for what is an increasingly inferior service.*
+to *Old Mr Carter was convinced that women doctors were inferior to men.*

of inferior quality/materials/status etc *Their furniture is certainly cheaper, but it's of inferior quality.*

worst /wɜːʰst/ [*adj* only before noun] worse than anything else or worse than at any time before: *I think he's the worst teacher in the school. | In my opinion, that's the worst movie of all time. | The doctor said it was one of the worst cases of food poisoning he'd ever seen.*
by far the worst (=much worse than any other) *It's by far the worst neighborhood in the whole city.*

2 to become worse

get worse /ˌɡet ˈwɜːʰs/ if a situation **gets worse**, it becomes more difficult or more unpleasant: *The weather here appears to be getting worse every day. | The pain continued to get worse so I called a doctor.*
get worse and worse *Paul's behaviour seems to get worse and worse.*

deteriorate /dɪˈtɪəriəreɪt/ [*v* I] FORMAL to gradually become worse: *His health has deteriorated significantly since I last saw him. | If the dispute continues for much longer, conditions in the city could deteriorate.*
deteriorate rapidly *Air quality is rapidly deteriorating in our cities.*
deterioration /dɪˌtɪəriəˈreɪʃən/ [*n* U] when something gradually becomes worse: *the further deterioration of relations between the two countries*

go from bad to worse /ˌɡəʊ frəm ˌbæd tə ˈwɜːʰs/ if a situation **goes from bad to worse**, it is already bad and then becomes even worse: *Things then went from bad to worse, and soon the couple were barely talking to each other.*

decline /dɪˈklaɪn/ [*v* I] FORMAL to become gradually worse – use this especially about the quality or standard of something: *Do you think standards of education are declining? | Britain's economic performance declined noticeably during the 1970s.*
decline [*n* singular] *a steady decline in the standard of healthcare provided in our hospitals*

WRITE

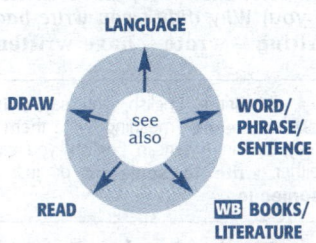

LANGUAGE

DRAW   WORD/
                       PHRASE/
     see   SENTENCE
     also

READ   **WB** BOOKS/
              LITERATURE

1 to write with a pen or pencil

write /raɪt/ [v I/T] to write words or numbers using a pen or pencil: *Over 15 percent of adults have never learned to write.* | *At the bottom he wrote: "with sincere love from your oldest friend".*
write sth on/in/at etc *Write your name at the top of the page.*
write down sth/write sth down (=write information so that you can use it later) *We wrote down everything he told us.* | *I've written the address down for you.*
writing – wrote – have written

◯ **put** /pʊt/ [v T] ESPECIALLY SPOKEN to write something: *I wrote to Marian, but I didn't put anything about Bill being arrested.*
put sth in/on/at sth *Put your name at the top of each answer sheet.*
putting – put – have put

make a note of sth /ˌmeɪk ə ˈnəʊt ɒv (sth)/ to write down information so that you can use it later: *OK, let me make a note of that before I forget it.* | *Did you make a note of the train times?*

take down/get down /ˌteɪk ˈdaʊn, ˌget ˈdaʊn/ [phrasal verb T] to write down what someone says, at the same time as they are saying it
take down sth/get down sth *A group of reporters was following the Senator, trying to get down every word he said.*
take sth down/get sth down *Do you want me to take all this down?*

note down sth /ˌnəʊt (sth) ˈdaʊn/ [phrasal verb T] ESPECIALLY WRITTEN to write down information so that you can use it later: *She noted down the train times.*

fill in/fill out /ˌfɪl ˈɪn, ˌfɪl ˈaʊt/ [phrasal verb T] to write information or answer questions on an official document, for example giving your name, address, and age
fill in sth ESPECIALLY BRITISH **fill out sth** ESPECIALLY AMERICAN *Passengers must fill in a short form before boarding the plane.*
fill sth in/fill sth out *You just fill it out, then send it in to the passport office.*

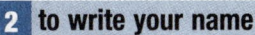
fill in

2 to write your name

sign /saɪn/ [v I/T] to write your name at the end of a letter, document etc, in order to prove who you are or show that you wrote it: *Sign here, please.* | *You forgot to sign the cheque.*
sign your name *The artist had signed his name in the corner of the painting.*
sign for sth (=to show that you have received it) *Could you sign for this package, please?*

signature /ˈsɪgnətʃəʳ/ [n C] your name written by you, for example on a document or at the end of a letter, in order to prove who you are or show that you wrote it: *Who's it from? I can't read the signature.*

autograph /ˈɔːtəgrɑːfǁ-græf/ [n C] the name of a famous person, written by them on a photograph, in a book etc for someone to keep: *She has the autograph of every player in the team.*
sign autographs (=to sign your name for people when they ask) *He refused to sign autographs at a charity event last year.*

3 to write something quickly or carelessly

jot down /ˌdʒɒt ˈdaʊnǁdʒɑːt-/ [phrasal verb T] to quickly write down ideas, notes, or facts
jot down sth *Let me jot down the name of that restaurant.*
jot sth down *If anyone has any suggestions, jot them down on a piece of paper and give them to me.*

W

scribble /'skrɪbəl/ [v T] to write something quickly and untidily: *Andrew scribbled a note and handed it to the chairman.*
scribble down sth/scribble sth down *We'll all scribble down some suggestions, and then compare them.*

4 to write with a computer or typewriter

key in /ˌkiː 'ɪn/ [phrasal verb T] to write something on a computer, especially something that you are copying from somewhere else
key in sth *I spent all morning keying in the latest sales data.*
key sth in *Find out the name of the file, key it in, and it will appear on the screen.*

type /taɪp/ [v I/T] to write with a computer or typewriter: *I'm afraid I don't type very fast.* | *Could you type those letters for me?*
typing [n U] writing with a typewriter or computer: *We need a secretary with good typing speeds.* (=who can type fast)

enter /'entəʳ/ [v T] to make words or numbers appear on a computer screen by pressing the keys: *Enter the filename and click 'OK'.*
enter sth in/into sth *The patients' medical records are entered into a database.*

Formal or informal?
Enter is a more technical word than **key in**.

5 to write a letter

write /raɪt/ [v I/T] to write someone a letter: *Sorry, I haven't had time to write.*
write a letter/postcard/note etc (to sb) *We wrote about 20 postcards while we were in Greece.* | *I try to write a cheerful letter to her at least once a week.*
write sb a letter/postcard/note *Kathleen wrote him dozens of letters, but he never replied.*
+to *He wrote to his father, asking for more money.*
write sb AMERICAN (=write a letter to someone) *Steve wrote me about the wedding.*
write back (=write a letter to someone after they have written one to you) *Why didn't you write back?*
writing – wrote – have written

In British English, you say **write to someone** (meaning 'write them a letter'), but in American English, you can say either **write to someone** or just **write someone**.

get in touch with sb /ˌget ɪn 'tʌtʃ wɪð (sb)/ to write to someone, or phone them, especially someone you have not seen or written to for a long time: *I'd love to get in touch with Monique again. Do you have her new address?*

contact /'kɒntækt‖'kɑːn-/ [v T] to write to someone that you do not know, or phone them, especially in order to ask for help or information: *Elsa contacted several companies to ask if they could offer her part-time work.* | *If the problem continues, try contacting a software expert.*

Formal or informal?
Contact is a fairly formal word.

keep in touch/stay in touch /ˌkiːp ɪn 'tʌtʃ, ˌsteɪ ɪn 'tʌtʃ/ to continue to write to someone or phone them, when you no longer work with them or live near them: *I met Pia in Sweden and we've stayed in touch ever since.*
+with *Do you keep in touch with any of your friends from school?*

6 to write a story, book etc

write /raɪt/ [v I/T] to write a book, story, newspaper article etc: *I can't come out tonight. I have an essay to write.* | *Who wrote 'Madame Bovary'? | When did he write his first novel?*
+about/on *She writes very amusingly about her childhood in Moscow.*
well/badly written *It's a fascinating article, and very well written.*
writing – wrote – have written

writer /'raɪtəʳ/ [n C] someone whose job is to write books, stories: *Terry Pratchett, the science-fiction writer*
+of *a writer of romantic novels*

author /ˈɔːθəʳ/ [n C] someone who writes books, or who wrote a particular book: *Jane Austen is one of my favourite authors.*
+of *Hawking is best known as the author of 'A Brief History of Time'.*

7 to write a song/music

write /raɪt/ [v T] to write music or songs: *Lennon and McCartney wrote over 100 songs.* | *Who wrote the soundtrack for 'The Bodyguard'?*
writing – wrote – have written

compose /kəmˈpəʊz/ [v T] to write a piece of music, especially serious music: *Mozart composed his first symphony when he was still a child.*

composer /kəmˈpəʊzəʳ/ [n C] someone who writes music, especially serious music: *My favourite composer is Beethoven.*

songwriter /ˈsɒŋˌraɪtəʳ‖ˈsɔːŋ-/ [n C] someone who writes songs, especially modern, popular songs: *songwriter Bernie Taupin*

8 to write the letters of a word

spell /spel/ [v I/T] to write a word using the correct letters in the correct order: *In American English, 'organize' is always spelled with a 'z'.* | *I've never been able to spell very well in English.*
spell sth out (=say each letter of a word in the right order) *And your last name is Aitchison? Could you spell that out for me please?*
spelling – spelled (also **spelt** BRITISH) – have spelled (also **have spelt** BRITISH)

spelling /ˈspelɪŋ/ [n C/U] the way in which a word is spelled, or someone's ability to spell words correctly: *The dictionary gives both British and American spellings.* | *This essay is full of spelling mistakes.* | *My spelling isn't very good.*

9 the way someone writes with a pen or pencil etc

writing/handwriting /ˈraɪtɪŋ, ˈhænd,raɪtɪŋ/ [n U] *I can barely read your writing.* | *The children spent hours practising their handwriting.*

10 written, not spoken

written /ˈrɪtn/ [adj] *Some expressions are much more common in spoken English than in written English.*
written statement/agreement/reply/ instructions etc *Don't sign any written agreement until you have read every word of the contract.*

in writing /ɪn ˈraɪtɪŋ/ if you get or give information **in writing**, it is written down, not spoken, so you can prove later what was actually said: *Please confirm in writing the date you intend to leave.* | *I don't have anything in writing, but said they expected me to start work on Monday.*
put sth in writing *You should have asked them to put what they agreed in writing.*
get it in writing ESPECIALLY SPOKEN (=ask someone to write something down) *"They promised to replace the computer if there are any problems." "Make sure you get it in writing."*

on paper /ɒn ˈpeɪpəʳ/ if you put ideas or suggestions **on paper**, you write them down so that you can remember them or organize them more clearly: *If you have any suggestions for improving the course, put them on paper and we'll discuss them.*

handwritten /ˈhænd,rɪtn/ [adj] written by hand, not using a typewriter or computer: *There was a handwritten note on the desk addressed to Paul.*

WRONG

➡ opposite **RIGHT**

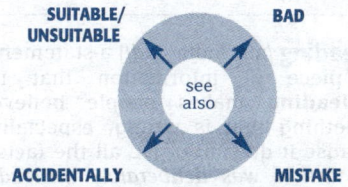

SUITABLE/
UNSUITABLE　　　　　　BAD

see also

ACCIDENTALLY　　　　　　MISTAKE

1 wrong

wrong /rɒŋ‖rɔːŋ/ [adj] not right or not correct: *For every answer that is wrong, you lose five points.* | *I think that clock must be wrong.* (=be showing the wrong time) get sth wrong *You must have got my email address wrong.*

wrong number/address/name etc *I tried to phone her, but it was the wrong number.*

wrong/wrongly [adv] *You've spelled my name wrong – there should be an 'e' at the end. | I think you've added it up wrongly.*

Formal or informal?
Wrong (adverb) is more informal than **wrongly**. Only use it in spoken English.

incorrect /ˌɪnkə'rekt◂/ [adj] facts, figures, answers etc that are **incorrect** are wrong because they are not the same as the correct ones: *The information about current prices was incorrect. | incorrect spelling*
it is incorrect to say/do sth *It's simply incorrect to say that tobacco advertising does not influence young people.*

incorrectly [adv] *If a player answers incorrectly, the question is given to the other team.*

Formal or informal?
Incorrect is more formal than **wrong**.

inaccurate /ɪn'ækjᵿrᵻt/ [adj] information, numbers etc that are **inaccurate** are not exactly right or contain some mistakes: *The old maps were usually inaccurate or incomplete. | inaccurate measurements*
totally/wildly inaccurate (=very inaccurate) *Figures quoted in the article are wildly inaccurate.*

Formal or informal?
Inaccurate is used in writing and in formal spoken English.

misleading /mɪs'liːdɪŋ/ [adj] a statement or piece of information that is **misleading** makes people believe something that is wrong, especially because it does not give all the facts: *The article was deliberately misleading, and the newspaper has apologized.*
give a misleading impression/ statement etc *Agents often gave a false or misleading description of the properties they were selling.*

2 to believe something that is wrong

➡ see also **MISTAKE**

be wrong /biː 'rɒŋ‖-'rɔːŋ/ if you **are wrong**, you think or say something that is not correct: *I thought a holiday in Greece would be cheap, but I was wrong. | Why won't he admit he was wrong?*
+about *You were wrong about that train – it left at 10.30.*

be mistaken /biː mᵻ'steɪkən/ FORMAL to have an incorrect opinion or belief about something: *I thought it was an accident, but I was mistaken.*
+about *Anna realised she had been mistaken about Dennis.*
Ｏ **you must be mistaken** SPOKEN (use this to say politely that someone is wrong) *I think you must be mistaken. He could not have obtained a key to your room.*

3 in the wrong position

wrong /rɒŋ‖rɔːŋ/ [adj only before noun]
the wrong direction/way/place/ order etc *Someone had moved the road sign so that it was pointing in the wrong direction. | The TV antenna is facing the wrong way. | The files had been put back in the wrong order.*

the wrong way around (also **the wrong way round** BRITISH) /ðə ˌrɒŋ weɪ (ə)'raʊnd‖-ˌrɔːn-/ if something is **the wrong way around**, it is pointing in the opposite direction to the correct one: *You've got your T-shirt on the wrong way around! | Someone's put the battery in the wrong way round.*

inside out /ˌɪnsaɪd 'aʊt/ if something, especially a piece of clothing, is **inside out**, the inside of it is on the outside and the outside of it is on the inside: *I put my socks on inside out by mistake. | The wind was so strong that it blew her umbrella inside out.*
turn sth inside out *Before washing your sweater, turn it inside out.*

upside down /ˌʌpsaɪd 'daʊn/ if something is **upside down**, the top of it is at the bottom and the bottom of it is at the top: *You're holding the picture upside down. | The monkey was hanging upside down from a tree.*
turn sth upside down *Turn the cups upside down and leave them to dry.*

Y, y

YOUNG

➡ opposite **OLD**

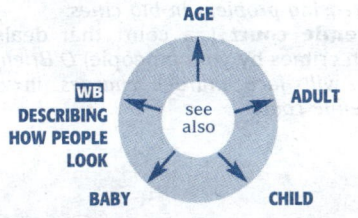

1 young

young /jʌŋ/ [adj] *You're too young to smoke.* | *a single mother with two young children* | *When I was younger, I used to play a lot of baseball.* | *Her youngest son works for a television company.*
younger brother/sister *Hannah has two younger brothers.*
little /'lɪtl/ [adj] ESPECIALLY SPOKEN very young – use this to talk about a young child: *When I was little we used to go camping a lot.*
little brother / sister (=younger brother or sister, who is still a child) *Mike's little brother is doing much better at school than he is.*
little boy/girl (=a young child, or a young son or daughter) *They've been married for ten years and have two little girls.* | *Who's that little boy in the blue sweater?*

2 a young person

teenager /'tiːneɪdʒəʳ/ [n C] someone who is between 13 and 19 years old: *He became a famous actor while still a teenager.* | *The survey showed that three out of five teenagers have experimented with illegal drugs.*
teenage [adj only before noun] *Jenny has three teenage children.*
youth /juːθ/ [n C usually plural] a young man between about 15 and 25 years old – use this especially about groups of young men who behave

badly or do something illegal: *One of the youths pushed her against the wall and took her bag.* | *a gang of youths on motorbikes*
in your teens /ɪn jɔːʳ 'tiːnz/ someone who is **in their teens** is between 13 and 19 years old: *She had run away from home several times in her teens.*
in your early/mid/late teens *Most of the girls at the concert were in their early teens.*
adolescent /ˌædə'lesənt◂/ [n C] someone who is at the age when they change from being a child into a young adult – use this especially when talking about problems that young people have at this age: *John changed from a friendly and cheerful young boy into a confused adolescent.*

> ⚠ You can also use **adolescent** before a noun, like an adjective: *a crowd of screaming adolescent girls*

3 the time when you are young

childhood /'tʃaɪldhʊd/ [n C/U] the time when you are a child: *Nina had happy memories of her childhood on the farm.*
early childhood (=when you are a young child) *His early childhood was spent with his father in Chicago.*

> ⚠ You can also use **childhood** before a noun, like an adjective: *a book about his childhood memories* | *childhood illnesses like measles*

youth /juːθ/ [n U] ESPECIALLY WRITTEN the time when you are young, especially the time between 15 and 25 when you are no longer a child: *She revisited all the places where she had spent her youth.*
in sb's youth (=when they were young) *Caroline had been a ballet dancer in her youth.*
adolescence /ˌædə'lesəns/ [n U] the time when a young person is changing from being a child into a young adult – use this especially when talking about the problems that young people have at this age: *During adolescence, boys are sometimes very shy and lacking in self-confidence.*

4 connected with things that young people do

youth /juːθ/ [adj only before noun]
youth club/group/organization etc
a club, group etc for young people: I met her at the local youth club. | a concert by the National Youth Orchestra

teenage /'tiːneɪdʒ/ [adj only before noun] use this about things produced for teenagers, or things that teenagers do

teenage pregnancy/drug-taking etc
There has been a significant increase in teenage pregnancies recently.
teenage fashions/magazines etc

juvenile /'dʒuːvənaɪlǁ-nəl, -naɪl/ [adj only before noun] FORMAL use this about crimes by young people
juvenile crime/offender (=crime by young people/a young person who is a criminal) *Juvenile crime is an increasing problem in big cities.*
juvenile court (=a court that deals with crimes by young people) *O'Brien, 15, will face murder charges in a juvenile court.*

ESSENTIAL COMMUNICATION

The ESSENTIAL COMMUNICATION section will help you communicate in English. To use it, look up the situation you need to deal with (for example AGREEING or COMPLAINING), and choose the box which best fits what you need to say. The ESSENTIAL COMMUNICATION section has been based on the spoken component of the British National Corpus.

ADVICE

asking for advice

What do you think I should do?

I don't know whether speak to Bob or not. What do you think I should do?

Can I ask your advice/opinion about something?

Can I ask your advice about something? I am really worried about my brother.

Do you think I should ...?

It is only $10 a month. Do you think I should join?

I'm thinking of .... What do you think?

I'm thinking of dyeing my hair. What do you think?

> Don't say, "Can you give me an advice?" Use one of the phrases above.

giving advice

You should ... / You ought ...

You should phone the police if you're really worried about it.
You shouldn't drink so much.

If I were you, ...

If I were you, I'd wait till tomorrow.
If I were you, I wouldn't tell anyone about it.

What you ought to do is ...

What you ought to do is write a letter and explain the situation.

What you need is ...

What you need is a nice long holiday.

You'd better ...

You'd better hide that before Andy gets home.

Make sure (that) you ...

use this to give someone advice that will help them not to make a mistake
Make sure you take enough money for the taxi.

The best thing is to ...

The best thing is to drink lots of water.

> In a conversation, don't say 'I advise you to do this' or 'I recommend that you do this'. These are very formal and are mostly used in writing.

SUGGESTIONS

making a suggestion | replying to a suggestion

making a suggestion

Let's …
Let's have a picnic.

We could … / You could …
We could go for a drink before the concert.
You could ask Simon if he wants to come.

Why don't we/you …?
Why don't we go to Spain this summer?
Why don't you paint it white?

What about …? / How about …?
What about going out one night next week?

Do you want to …?
ESPECIALLY AMERICAN
Do you want to see if we can get a room for the night?

Shall I/we …?
ESPECIALLY BRITISH
Should I/we …? AMERICAN
Shall I organize the drinks for the party?
Should we go to Becky's then?

YES

Yes. / Yeah.

How about finding somewhere to eat?
Yes, I'm starving.

OK. / Right. / All right.

Let's go and visit your brother.
OK.

Good idea!

What about a trip to the beach?
Good idea!

That sounds good/great.

Shall I organise a barbecue on Saturday?
That sounds good.

Sure! ESPECIALLY AMERICAN

Do you want to try some sushi?
Sure!

NO

⚠ When you say no to a suggestion, it is polite to give a reason, or suggest something else instead.

Sorry, I can't.

Let's go out for pizza on Saturday.
Sorry, I can't. I'm going away for the weekend.

How about … instead?

Shall I say that we'll come?
How about staying home instead?

I'd rather (do sth). / I'd prefer to (do sth).

Let's stay over till Saturday.
I'd rather come back straight after the party.

Conversation

Kate: Let's go and see a movie on Saturday.
Richard: Sorry, I can't. I'm going to visit my cousins. Why don't we go next week instead?
Kate: OK. What about Wedneday?
Richard: That's sounds good. Shall I meet you at your house?
Kate: I have a better idea. How about getting something to eat before the movie?
Richard: Good idea! What time? About 7 o'clock?
Kate: Right, see you then.

OFFERS

offering to do something for someone

Would you like me to ...?

use this when you want to be polite

Would you like me to help you with your homework?

Do you want me to ...?

use this with friends and people you know well

Do you want me to get some tickets for the concert?

Shall I ...? BRITISH
Should I ...? AMERICAN

Shall I buy the stuff for the picnic?
Should I make the salad?

offering someone a drink, something to eat etc

Would you like ...?

use this when you want to be polite

Would you like a drink?

Do you want ...?

use this with friends and people you know well

Do you want a cup of coffee?

Can I get you ...?

Can I get you a beer or something?

How about ...? INFORMAL

How about a quick snack before we leave?

Fancy ...? / Do you fancy ...?
BRITISH INFORMAL

Fancy a drink after work, Annie?

saying yes or no to an offer

YES	NO

Yes, please.

> *Do you want a piece of cake?*

> *Yes, please.*

Thanks.

> *Would you like a drink?*

> *Thanks. A glass of white wine, please.*

That's very kind of you. FORMAL

> *Would you like a drink?*

> *That's very kind of you. A glass of white wine, please.*

No, thanks.

> *Would you like a drink?*

> *No, thanks. I have to leave soon.*

No, I'm fine, thanks.

use this to say no when someone offers you more food or drink

> *Do you want another beer?*

> *No, I'm fine, thanks.*

That's very kind of you, but ... FORMAL

> *Would you like a drink?*

> *That's very kind of you, but I'm afraid I can't stay very long.*

INVITATIONS

asking friends

Do you want to ...?
Do you want to go to the movies on Saturday?

asking anyone

Would you like to ...?
Would you like to go out for dinner sometime?

asking someone you do not know very well

I was wondering if you'd like to ...
I was wondering if you'd like to join us for a drink?

> ⚠ Don't say 'I invite you ...' or 'I'd like to invite you ...' Use one of the phrases above.

saying yes or no to an invitation

YES

Yes, I'd like that.

> *Would you like to play tennis one night next week?*
>
> *Yes, I'd like that.*

That sounds great! INFORMAL

> *We're going skating. Do you want to come?*
>
> *That sounds great! Thanks.*

Yes, OK.

> *Do you want to join us for a game of basketball?*
>
> *Yes, OK. What time?*

NO

Sorry, (I'm afraid) I can't.

> *Do you want to come swimming on Thursday?*
>
> *Sorry, I can't. It's my dad's birthday.*

Sorry, but I'm going to ... on Wednesday/Friday etc.

> *Would you like to come for dinner on Tuesday?*
>
> *Sorry, but I'm going to aerobics on Tuesday.*

Thanks for asking me, but ...

> *Do you want to come to a party on Friday night?*
>
> *Thanks for asking me, but I'm going away for the weekend.*

REQUESTS
asking someone to do something for you

> ⚠ Use the polite phrases when you are talking to someone you do not know well, or when you are asking a friend to do something difficult or important.

asking friends

Can you …?
Can you lend me $10 till Saturday?

Will you …?
Will you buy me a newspaper while you're out?

asking anyone

Could you …?
Could you give me a ride to work on Monday?

Would you mind … (doing sth)?
Would you mind feeding the cat while I'm away?

when you want to be polite

Do you think you could …?
Do you think you could check your records again, please?

I wonder if you'd mind … (doing sth)?
FORMAL
I wonder if you'd mind giving this letter to Mr Roberts?

saying yes or no to a request

YES

OK. / All right.

> Can you lend me $10 till Saturday?

> OK. Here you are.

Yes, sure.

> Will you buy me a newspaper while you're out?

> Yes, sure. Which one?

Certainly. FORMAL

> Do you think you could check your records again, please?

> Certainly. Just one moment.

NO

> ⚠ It is polite to give a reason if you say no.

Sorry, but …

> Can you lend me $10 till Saturday?

> Sorry, but I don't really have enough.

I can't really.

> Could you give me a lift into town?

> I can't really. I'm waiting for a phone call.

I'm afraid …

> Can you come to my office tomorrow at 10 o'clock?

> I'm afraid I'm busy tomorrow morning.

ASKING FOR PERMISSION
asking someone to let you do something

 Use the polite phrases when you are talking to someone you do not know well, or when you are asking a friend if you can do something important, such as borrow their car.

asking anyone

Can I ...?
Can I borrow your pen?

Is it OK/all right if I ...?
Is it OK if I bring a friend to your party?

Do you mind if I ...?
Do you mind if I open the window?

when you want to be polite

Would you mind if I ...?
Would you mind if I came with you to the concert?

Would it be OK/all right if I ...?
Would it be all right if I left early today?

saying yes or no to a request

YES	NO

YES

Yes, of course.

Is it OK if I bring a friend to your party?

Yes, of course. Bring anyone you like.

Yes, sure.

Can I borrow your pen?

Yes, sure.

Yes, that's fine.

Is it all right if I keep this photo?

Yes, that's fine.

No, that's fine.
use this to reply to questions that start with Do/Would you mind if ...?

Do you mind if I open the window?

No, that's fine.

NO

 It is polite to give a reason if you say no.

Sorry, but ...

Is it all right if I keep this photo?

Sorry, but I only have one copy.

No, sorry.

Can I borrow your pen?

No, sorry. I need it.

I'm afraid ...

Can I have a look at the files myself?

I'm afraid that's not possible.

I'd rather you didn't.

Do you mind if I open the window?

I'd rather you didn't. It gets really noisy with the window open.

COMPLAINING

writing a letter to complain about something

I am writing to complain about …

I am writing to complain about the service I received in your restaurant.

complaining to someone you know well

I'm sick/tired of you (doing sth)/ I've had enough of you (doing sth)

use this when you are annoyed at someone's behaviour

I've had enough of you two arguing. Stop right now!

You're always (doing sth)

use this when someone keeps doing something that annoys you

You're always flirting with other women.

You never …

use this when someone keeps forgetting to do something or is unwilling to do something

You never listen, do you?

complaining in a shop, restaurant, etc

The usual way to complain is just to explain what is wrong. For example, *The shower in my room isn't working.* You then expect that the person you are talking to will do something to put it right. Only use the following phrases when you have already done this and are complaining because you are still not satisfied.

I'm not satisfied with …

I'm not satisfied with the repairs that you carried out.

I'd like to make a complaint about …

I'd like to make a complaint about the extra charges on my bill.

APOLOGIZING

if you want to say you are sorry when something bad has happened to someone, go to SORRY

when you have made a small mistake, for example if you accidentally stand on someone's foot

Sorry.
Sorry. I didn't mean to kick you.

Excuse me. AMERICAN
Oh, excuse me. That was my fault.

when you have done something wrong or upset someone

Sorry.
Sorry I'm late – the traffic was terrible!
I have forgotten your book. Sorry!
+ about *Sorry about all the mess.*

I'm sorry.
+ that *I'm sorry that you weren't told about the meeting.*
I'm sorry I shouted at you.
+ about *I'm sorry about the mix-up. It was my fault.*

I'm really sorry. (=very sorry)
I'm really sorry, but I've broken one of your CDs.

I apologize FORMAL
use this in formal spoken situations such as meetings
I apologize for mentioning this again, but we still haven't made a decision.

Apologies for ... WRITTEN
Apologies for not replying to your letter sooner.

SAYING THANK YOU

when someone gives you something or when someone says your work is good or that you look good

Thank you. / Thanks.

Here, have some gums.

Thanks.

Your report was really good.

Thank you. It took me ages to do.

Thank you very much. / Thanks very much.

That dress really suits you.

Thanks very much. I got it last year.

⚠ **Thanks** is more informal than **thank you**. Don't say 'very thanks' or 'much thanks'.

when someone has done something for you or has offered to do something

Thank you. / Thanks.

Can I help you with those bags?

Oh, thank you.

+for doing sth *Thanks for getting the tickets.*

Thank you very much. / Thanks very much.

Thanks very much for all your help.

⚠ **Thanks** is more informal than **thank you**.

It's/That's very kind of you. FORMAL

If the meeting finishes late, I'll drive you back to town.

Thank you. That's very kind of you.

I really appreciate it.

say this when someone has done a lot for you

Thanks for helping out on Sunday. I really appreciated it.

when you are writing a letter to thank someone

Thank you for …

Thank you for the book you sent me on my birthday.

+doing sth *Thank you for feeding the cat while I was away.*

Thank you very much for …

Thank you very much for the information about the art course.

Many thanks for … FORMAL

Many thanks for the card and flowers.

what to say when someone thanks you for doing something or for giving them something

In American English you usually reply when someone thanks you for doing something of for giving them something. In British English people often do not reply, but this is not rude.

That's OK.

Thanks for looking after the kids.

That's OK. I enjoyed having them.

You're welcome. ESPECIALLY AMERICAN

Thanks for letting me stay, Mrs Parker.

Oh, you're welcome.

No problem. INFORMAL

Thanks for coming with me.

No problem.

Don't mention it.

Thank you for all your help.

Don't mention it.

Sure. AMERICAN

Thanks for the ride.

Sure.

DIRECTIONS

asking for directions   **giving directions**

⚠️ It is polite to say **excuse me** at the beginning of your question, or **please** at the end. If you use both, you will sound quite formal.

How do I get to ...?
Excuse me, how do I get to the post office?

Is there a ... near here?
Excuse me, is there a bank near here, please?

Could/Can you tell me the way to ...?
Could you tell me the way to the bus station, please?

Could/Can you tell me where the ... is?
Excuse me, could you tell me where the National Gallery is?

⚠️ **Could** is more polite than **can**.

Go straight ahead
(also **Go straight on** BRITISH
Go straight AMERICAN)

Turn left
(also **Take a left** AMERICAN)
Turn left at the crossroads.

Turn right
(also **Take a right** AMERICAN)
Take a right at the bank.

Go past the ...
Go past the lake.

Keep going until you get to ...
Keep on going until you get to the park.   **PARK**

Take the first/second turn on your left/right.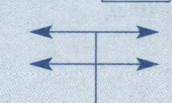

Conversation 1

A: Excuse me. How do I get to the station?
B: I'm sorry. I don't know.

Conversation 2

A: Excuse me. Could you tell me the way to the library, please?
B: Yes, sure. Go straight on and keep going until you get to the post office. Then turn left and keep going until you get to the crossroads. Turn right at the crossroads and the library's on your left.
A: Thanks very much.

OPINIONS

1. **giving your opinion**
2. **saying what other people think**
3. **asking someone for their opinion**

1. giving your opinion

I think (that) …	this is the most common way of giving your opinion	*I think that we should spend more on education.*
		I think it's a waste of time.
I believe (that) …	use this in formal speech or in writing when you have strong opinions about something	*I believe that abortion is wrong.*
		I believe we have made a major financial error.
In my opinion …	use this in writing	*In my opinion, less money should be spend on weapons.*
It seems to me (that) …	use this when you are giving your opinion based on things that have happened or on things that you have noticed	*It seems to me that children have too much freedom these days.*
		It seems to me that you don't have much choice.
As far as I'm concerned …	use this to emphasize that you do not care whether people agree with you or not	*As far as I'm concerned, everything's fine the way it is.*
If you ask me … INFORMAL	use this to say what you think about a particular problem or situation	*If you ask me, they ought to just fire him.*

 Don't say 'according to me' when giving your opinion. Use one of the phrases in the box above.

 Don't talk about 'saying your opinion'. Use **giving your opinion** or **saying what you think**. *We never get a chance to say what we think.*

2. saying what other people think

think (that) …	this is the most common way of saying what other people think	*Most students think that getting a job is the most important thing.* *Some people think the laws on drinking are too strict.*
be in favour of BRITISH **be in favor of** AMERICAN	use this before saying what people think is right or good	*Most people are in favour of greater political freedom.* *Only the liberals are in favor of tax reform.*
be against	use this in writing before saying what people think is wrong or bad	*Over 80% of those surveyed are against the use of animals in experiments.*

3. asking someone for their opinion

To ask for someone's opinion you usually ask a direct question. For example: *Do you think the President should resign?* *Do you think that Sarah will get the job?* You can also use the following ways of asking:		
What do you think of …?	use this to ask whether they like someone or something	*What do you think of Sheila's new boyfriend?* *What do you think of their new CD?*
What do you think about …?	use this to ask for someone's general opinion about something	*What do you think about going to Australia this winter?* *What do you think about the plans to build a new freeway?*

AGREEING

when you agree strongly

Absolutely!

> Men and women should have equal rights.

> Absolutely!

Exactly!

> She shouldn't have come if she didn't want to.

> Exactly!

I couldn't agree more.

> Parents are responsible for making sure their children behave well.

> I couldn't agree more.

You're telling me! INFORMAL
use this to agree with something when you know about it or have personal experience of it

> The buses are always late, aren't they.

> You're telling me! I've been standing here for half an hour.

when you agree

Yes. also **Yeah.** INFORMAL

> I think we should get Ann a birthday present.

> Yes. That's a really good idea.

I know.

> That meeting was really boring.

> I know. I thought it would never end.

I agree.

> It would really help if the bank stayed open longer.

> I agree. If the shops can do it, why can't the banks?

⚠️ **I agree** is more formal than **yes**.

Right. / That's right. / You're right.

> I think we're wasting our time here.

> You're right. Let's go home.

when you agree, but not strongly

I suppose so.

> You should tell Jenny how you feel.

> I suppose so, but it's not easy.

I guess so. AMERICAN

> It's your first date. Chris will be nervous too.

> I guess so.

DISAGREEING

when you disagree, but you want to be polite

when you disagree strongly

Yes, but …

> We should buy computers for every class in the school.

> Yes, but we don't have enough money.

I know, but …

> It would be much simpler to meet at the restaurant.

> I know, but I might get lost. Let's go there together.

I take/see your point, but … INFORMAL

> Famous people can't really expect to keep their private lives secret.

> I take your point, but don't you think everyone have a right to privacy?

But don't you think …?

> We should have the party at a restaurant.

> But don't you think it might be too expensive?

I'm not so sure …

> Well, it looks as if Greece would be the best choice.

> I'm not so sure, Larry. It's a long way to go.

⚠️ Only use these phrases only with people you know well. You will sound rude if you say them to a stranger.

I don't think so.

> The flowers would look really nice over by the window.

> I don't think so. I think they look better here.

No, it isn't./No, she isn't. etc

> The quickest way is to take the train.

> No, it isn't. It's much faster by car.

That's not true.

> Eating meat is bad for you.

> That's not true. It's a really good source of iron.

You must be joking!/No way! INFORMAL

> It'll only take 30 minutes to get there.

> You must be joking! The traffic's really bad at this time of the day.

I can't accept that … FORMAL

> I believe we should close the department until next year.

> I'm sorry. I can't accept that this is the best solution.

Rubbish! INFORMAL

> I'm too tired to do the washing up.

> Rubbish! You haven't done anything all day.

SAYING YES

saying yes to a question

when you want to emphasize that the answer is definitely yes	when the answer is yes	when you think that the answer is yes, but you are not sure

when you want to emphasize that the answer is definitely yes

Definitely!

> Are you going to Sonia's party?

> Definitely!

Of course!

use this when you are surprised or annoyed that someone has asked you something, or to emphasize your answer

> Is it OK if Sara stays with us for a few days?

> Of course! She's welcome to.

Of course I did/ she did etc

> Did you lock the door?

> Yes, of course I did!

when the answer is yes

Yes.

> Is that ring real gold?

> Yes, it is.

That's right.

use this especially when someone is checking facts

> You are Ben's sister aren't you?

> That's right.

Yeah. INFORMAL

> Are you going to the club tonight?

> Yeah. Are you?

I'm afraid so.

use this when you think the person asking the question is hoping for a different answer

> Was she angry?

> I'm afraid so.

when you think that the answer is yes, but you are not sure

I think so.

> Are you coming to the movies with us?

> I think so. It depends what time I finish work.

Probably.

> Will you be home by six o'clock?

> Probably. The class is usually over by five.

I guess so. AMERICAN

> Are you going to take that apartment?

> I guess so. It's a little expensive though.

> Have they already gone home?

> Yes, I guess so.

➡ for saying yes to an invitation, go to **EC** INVITATIONS

➡ for saying yes when someone offers you something, go to **EC** OFFERS

➡ for saying yes when someone suggests something, go to **EC** SUGGESTIONS

➡ for saying yes when someone asks you to do something, go to **EC** REQUESTS

➡ for saying yes when someone asks if they can do something, go to **EC** PERMISSION

➡ for saying that you agree with someone's opinion, go to **EC** AGREEING

SAYING NO
saying no to a question

when you want to emphasize that the answer is no

Definitely not!

So, would you go camping again?

Definitely not! It rained all week.

Of course not!

use this when you are surprised or annoyed that someone has asked you something, or to emphasize your answer

Did he pass any of his exams in the end?

Of course not! he didn't do any work!

Of course I won't/ she didn't. etc

You won't tell Mike about this, will you? It's supposed to be a secret.

No, of course I won't.

No way! INFORMAL

Are you going to go out with Ron?

No way! He's horrible.

when the answer is no

No.

Are you Italian?

No, I'm Spanish.

> ⚠ It often sounds rude or angry if you use **no** on its own. People usually say something else after the word **no**.

Not really.

Did you have a good day?

Not really. The car broke down.

I'm afraid not.

use this when you think that the person asking the question is hoping for a different answer

Did you find the book I wanted?

I'm afraid not. I looked everywhere.

when you think that the answer is no, but you are not sure

I don't think so.

Will it be ready by tomorrow?

I don't think so. There's a lot to do.

Probably not.

Is that enough pasta for four of us?

Probably not. I'd better get some more.

I doubt it.

Do you think Sophie will come?

I doubt it. She's very busy at the moment.

➡ for saying no to an invitation, go to **EC** INVITATIONS

➡ for saying no when someone offers you something, go to **EC** OFFERS

➡ for saying no when someone suggests something, go to **EC** SUGGESTIONS

➡ for saying no when someone asks you to do something, go to **EC** REQUESTS

➡ for saying no when someone asks if they can do something, go to **EC** PERMISSION

➡ for saying that do not you agree with someone's opinion, go to **EC** DISAGREEING

SAYING HELLO

saying hello to friends or someone you already know

Hello.

Hi.

Morning.

use this when you see someone at the start of the day, for example when you arrive at work

saying hello when you are being polite because you are in a formal or business situation

Hello.

Good morning.
(= before 12 noon)

Good afternoon.
(= 12 noon until about 6 p.m.)

Good evening.
(= after about 6 p.m.)

> ⚠ Only use **Goodnight** when you are saying goodbye in the evening, not when you are saying hello.

when you are introducing yourself

Hello, I'm …
Hello, I'm Greg. I'm a friend of Rachel's.

Hello, my name's …
Hello, my name's Lynn. I'll be in the same class as you this year.

saying hello when you have been introduced to someone for the first time

Nice to meet you./ Pleased to meet you.

Mark: *Hello, Colin.*
Colin: *Hello, Mark.*
Mark: *Have you met my cousin Freddie from Canada?*
Colin: *No, I haven't.* (they shake hands)
Freddie: *Hello, Colin.*
Colin: *Hello. Pleased to meet you.*

> ⚠ **How do you do** is very formal, and is not often used.

when you are introducing someone else

This is …
This is my boyfriend, Andy.

Have you met … ?
Have you met my brother, Richard?

Do you know …?
Do you know our Sales Manager, Patsy Morris?

I'd like you to meet …

use this in formal situations, for example at work, or when you are talking to a much older person

I'd like you to meet Linda Davis, the new science teacher.

SAYING GOODBYE

when saying goodbye, you usually say Bye,
but you can say these other things

saying goodbye to a friend you will see again soon

See you.

See you later. /
See you soon.

See you tomorrow/
next week. etc

saying goodbye when it's the end of an evening or you are going to bed

Goodnight.

Night.

> ⚠ **Night** is more
> informal than
> **Goodnight**.

saying goodbye when you want to be formal or very polite

Goodbye.

It was nice
meeting you/talking
to you.

saying goodbye to a friend you may not see very soon

See you sometime.

See you around.

Take care.

saying goodbye when you think it's time to leave – you can use these phrases before you say goodbye

> ⚠ You usually you give a reason when you tell someone that
> you have to leave.

I'd better be going. INFORMAL
I'd better be going. Jack will wonder where I am.

I must go. BRITISH
I must go, or I'll be late for my aerobics class.

I'd better be off. BRITISH INFORMAL
Well, we'd better be off. I've got work in the morning.

I've got to go. ESPECIALLY BRITISH
I have to go. AMERICAN
I have to go or I'll be late.

I'm afraid I have to leave now. FORMAL
I'm afraid I have to leave now. My train leaves at nine.

TALKING ON THE PHONE

when you are making the call

asking for the person you want to speak to

Is ... there please?

Hello, is Monica there, please?

 Don't say "Is there Monica, please?"

Can I speak to ..., please?
May I speak to ..., please?

Can I speak to Dr. Chang, please?

 These are more formal than **is ... there**, please?

Is that ...?

use this when you think you are speaking to the right person, but you are not sure

Hello. Is that Guy?

saying who you are

It's ...

Hello, is Steve there? It's his sister.

This is ...

Can I speak to Catherine Hart, please? This is Grant Davies.

 This is ... is more formal than **It's** ...

when you are answering the call

Hello

In formal or business situations, you usually give your name, or the name of your company. At home, you usually say "hello."

Hello, Gail Block speaking.
Hello, R. W. Motors.

when the right person is there

One moment, please   FORMAL

> Hello. Can I speak to David Schmidt, please?

> One moment please.

Hold on. / Hang on.   INFORMAL

> Hello. Is Liz there?

> Hold on. I'll see if she's in.

I'll (just) get him/her.   INFORMAL

> Is Vanessa there, please?

> Yes, I'll just get her.

Speaking

> Can I speak to Tom, please?

> Speaking.   (=I am Tom)

when the right person is not there

Sorry, he's/she's …

Sorry, he's out.
Sorry, she's away for the weekend.

Can I take a message? / Would you like to leave a message?

Simon's out at the moment. Can I take a message?

Do you want to hold?

(=when the person is already on the phone in an office but the caller could wait for them to finish the conversation)

I'm sorry, her line's busy at the moment. Do you want to hold?

saying goodbye

At the end of the conversation, it sounds rude if you suddenly say Bye or Goodbye, and put the phone down. People usually say something else first.

A: *Well, I'd better go. I have to pick up the kids.*
B: *OK, see you soon, then.*
A: *Yes, see you on Tuesday.*
B: *Goodbye.*

HAVING A CONVERSATION

asking someone to repeat what they said

Sorry? / Pardon?
Sorry? Did you say Tuesday?

Could you repeat …
Could you repeat the address, please?

I didn't quite catch …
I didn't quite catch the number. Could you say it again, please?

when you want to start a new subject or go back to the main subject

So …
use this to continue what you were saying before, or to introduce a new subject, especially a question
So, have you decided where you're going to live yet?

Anyway …
use this to go back to the main point of what you were saying, especially after talking about other things
Anyway, in the end, I decided to buy the black one.

when you want to give yourself more time to think

Um … / Er … / Uh … / Well …
Er … I don't really know.

I mean …
It's so far away. And, I mean, if we have to be there by two o'clock …

checking that someone understands or agrees with you

Do you know what I mean?
I just don't think it's right to treat people like that. Do you know what I mean?

…, you know?
I want to get one of those big leather bags, you know? One with a shoulder strap.

showing that you are listening to what someone is saying

While someone else is talking, you normally show that you are listening by looking at them, nodding your head, and using these words

Yes. / Yeah. / Right. /Mm./ Uh-huh
A: *You know my friend Sam was going to buy a motorcycle …*
B: *Yeah …*
A: *Well, she went to this place where you get them cheap …*
B: *Mm.*
A: *… and got a really good one, which she's going to let me borrow.*
B: *Oh, right.*
A: *So, d'you want to come for a ride sometime?*

when someone is talking and you want to say something

When you want to interrupt someone, you usually show this by leaning forward, making a movement, or taking a breath. You can also use these words and phrases.

Um … / Well …
use these to show that you want to interrupt and then leave a pause to see whether the other person is going to stop or not
A: *So if you come over to my place, then we can all travel there together in my car, and …*
B: *Um …*
A: *What?*
B: *Well, I'm not sure if I can come after all.*

Yes, but … / I know, but …
use these when you want to interrupt in order to disagree
A: *It would be great to travel around while we're there, and maybe visit …*
B: *Yes, but what if we run out of money?*

Sorry to interrupt, but …
use this when you are interrupting a conversation, which you were not involved in before
Sorry to interrupt, but I have an urgent message for you.

LINKING WORDS

use these words and phrases to link your ideas together

1. **AND words**
2. **BUT words**
3. **BECAUSE words**
4. **IF words**
5. **THEREFORE words**
6. **IN ORDER TO words**

1. AND words

and

Use this to join two things, actions, ideas etc in one sentence or in one part of a sentence.

All we had for three days was bread ***and*** water .

Suddenly, she stood up ***and*** started shouting .

Tall ***and*** handsome , *Lionel was very attractive to women.*

I don't know why you think this ***and****, to be honest,* I really don't care .

> Don't start a sentence with the word **and**.

also

Use this when you are linking one idea, thing, action etc to another one in the previous sentence. Put the word **also** directly before the verb or after the first auxiliary or modal.

*François speaks English. He **also** speaks German.*

*A dog provides friendship and exercise. It can **also** be useful for protecting your house.*

> Don't say 'I also can play the piano.'
> Say **I can also play the piano.**

> Don't say 'We also have decided to get a new car.'
> Say **We have also decided to get a new car.**

> Don't use **also** with two negative statements. Use **either**.
> Don't say 'She doesn't smoke. She also doesn't drink.'
> Say **She doesn't smoke. She doesn't drink either.**

too

Use this at the end of a sentence when you are adding something to a list of things that you gave in the previous sentence.

*Gary and Sheila and the kids are coming to visit. They're bringing Sheila's mother, **too**.*

*It's fast and comfortable. It's economical, **too**.*

> Don't use **too** with negative statements. Use **either**.
> Don't say 'He didn't smoke or drink. He didn't gamble, too.'
> Say **He didn't smoke or drink. He didn't gamble either.**

as well

Use this at the end of a sentence when you are adding something to a list of things that you gave in the previous sentence.

Most of them have a cassette and a radio built in. This one's got a CD player ***as well****.*

"I'm going to get bread, cheese, tea, and sugar." "Can you get some milk ***as well****?"*

> Don't use **as well** with two negative statements. Use **either**.
> Don't say 'Carlo's not coming to the party. Maria can't come as well.'
> Say **Carlo's not coming to the party. Maria can't come either.**

anyway/besides INFORMAL

Use this at the beginning of a sentence when you have given one reason for doing something and you want to add another.

I hate asking for a pay rise. ***Anyway****, there's no point.*

I don't really need a new car. ***Besides****, I can't afford one.*

furthermore FORMAL, ESPECIALLY WRITTEN

Use this at the beginning of a sentence to add another important fact that is related to the subject mentioned in the previous sentence.

The drug has powerful side effects. ***Furthermore****, it may be addictive.*

2. BUT words

but

Use this to join two words or phrases when the second one has the opposite meaning to the first one, OR when the second one is surprising after the first one, OR when one is negative and one is positive.

The new Skoda is fast ***but*** *quite cheap to run.*

I called ***but*** *there was no one there.*

He's short and not really handsome, ***but*** *women still find him attractive.*

although/even though

Use this before a statement that makes the main statement seem surprising or unlikely.

Although *we are a small company, we still produce over 10,000 cars a year.*

I enjoyed German, ***even though*** *I wasn't very good at it.*

> **Although** is used especially in writing.

on the other hand

Use this at the beginning of a sentence when you have just mentioned one side of an argument and you are going to mention the opposite side.

Nuclear power is relatively cheap. ***On the other hand****, you could argue that it's not safe.*

still/then again/mind you

Use this when you have just given one opinion about something and you now want to say something which suggests the opposite, for example when you give an advantage and then a disadvantage.

Teaching must be an interesting job. **Then again**, *it must be stressful too.*

This trip is going to be very expensive. **Still**, *we don't go away very often.*

I'd love to travel around the world. **Mind you**, *I wouldn't want to go on my own.*

however/nevertheless

Use **however** and **nevertheless** in fairly formal writing when giving facts the make your previous sentence seem less true or when giving facts that balance what you said in your previous sentence. Use **nevertheless** at the beginning of a sentence. Use **however** at the beginning of a sentence, or in the middle of a sentence, separated from the rest of the sentence by two commas.

Young people can be rude and badly-behaved. That is no reason, **however***, for treating them like criminals.*

The drug is certainly effective. **However***, it is fairly expensive.*

It was a terrible accident. **Nevertheless***, air travel is still the safest form of transport.*

in spite of/despite

Use this to introduce a fact in one half of a sentence when this fact makes the rest of the sentence seem surprising.

In spite of *having lots of money, he was an unhappy man.*

Despite *his lack of education, Jake became a successful businessman.*

In spite of *her injuries, Sandra was able to crawl to safety.*

> ⚠ Don't say 'In spite of he had lots of money ...' Say **In spite of having lots of money** ... If you put a verb phrase after **in spite of** or after **despite**, it must be in the '-ing' form.

3. BECAUSE words

because

Use this to give the reason for something.

I can't come **because** *my car's broken down.*

Bring a coat **because** *it's very cold outside.*

Because *you've been so helpful, I'd like to get you all a drink.*

as

Use this mainly when writing stories or descriptions of events.

As *he wasn't well, I offered to do the shopping.*

We left the party early **as** *we had school in the morning.*

due to/owing to

Use this in written English or formal spoken English, especially when you are saying what has caused a particular problem.

*The dinner was cancelled, **owing** to the President's ill health.*

 Owing to cannot be used after the verb 'to be'.
Don't say 'The delay was owing to engine failure.'
Say **The delay was due to engine failure.**

thanks to

Use this when something has been possible because of someone's actions or because something is very good, very effective etc.

***Thanks to** everyone's hard work, the play was a great success.*

***Thanks to** its excellent suspension, the Mercedes feels very comfortable at high speeds.*

because of/as a result of

Use this when saying what made something happen.

*Hundreds of people lost their homes **as a result of** the war.*

***Because of** an increase in street crime, many old people are afraid to go out.*

 As a result of is more formal than **because of**.

4. IF words

if

***If** I have the time, I'll come with you.*

***If** the snow doesn't stop, I won't be able to get to work.*

***If** I'd known you were there, I would have phoned.*

even if

Use this when something will still happen if a situation changes or if there is a problem.

*I've got to get a job, **even if** it's not well paid.*

***Even if** we leave now, we'll still be late.*

unless

Use this to say that something will happen if something else does not stop it from happening.

*Let's go now, **unless** you're too tired.*
(=if you're not too tired, let's go)

***Unless** you work harder, you'll fail the test.*
(=if you don't work harder, you'll fail the test)

in case

Use this to mention something that might happen, which someone wants to be prepared for.

*Take an umbrella **in case** it rains.*
(=if it rains you'll be able to use it)

***In case** I'm late, here's the key to the apartment.*
(=if I'm late, you'll be able to get inside)

suppose ...? / supposing...?

Use this to mention something that might happen or be true, when you want to consider what the result would be.

***Suppose** you lose your job? What will we do then?*

***Supposing** my Mum finds out we were at the party? She'll kill me.*

or/otherwise

Use this to say there will be a bad result if someone does not do something or if something does not happen.

*Don't eat so much chocolate **or** you'll be sick.*
(=if you eat so much chocolate you'll be sick)

*I'd better go now, **otherwise** Ann will wonder where I am.*
(=if I don't go now, Ann will wonder where I am)

5. THEREFORE words
use these words to say what the result of something is

so

Use this to link two ideas in one sentence.

*John's sick, **so** he won't be able to come tonight.*

*My Dad's in a bad mood, **so** there's no point in asking him if I can borrow the car.*

therefore

Use this in formal written or spoken English to link a result in one sentence with a cause in the previous sentence.

*I would like to spend more time with my family. I have **therefore** decided to resign as chairman.*

*The dollar has gone down against the yen, and **therefore** Japanese goods seem more expensive.*

6. IN ORDER TO words
use these words to say what the purpose of an action is

to
Use this in spoken or written English.
*I went to the bank **to** get some money.*
***To** lose weight, you should exercise more.*

in order to
Use this in more formal written or spoken English.
*Some drug users steal **in order to** buy drugs.*
***In order to** be a doctor, you have to study for six years.*

so (that)
Use this in spoken English or informal written English.
*I'm studying English **so that** I can go to college.*
*I'm saving up **so** I can go to the concert.*

POSITION & DIRECTION

**use these words and phrases to say where someone or something is,
or to talk about the direction they are moving in**

1	in a place	**15**	across/through
2	in a room/box etc	**16**	along
3	into	**17**	above
4	out of	**18**	under/below
5	outside	**19**	up
6	to/towards	**20**	down
7	(away) from	**21**	forward
8	on	**22**	backwards
9	next to	**23**	top
10	opposite	**24**	bottom
11	in front of	**25**	front
12	behind	**26**	back
13	between/among	**27**	side
14	around	**28**	corner

1 in a place

in [preposition]
- use this when you are not saying exactly where someone or something is within a particular area: *in the garden* | *in the sky* | *in the city* | *swimming in the lake*
- use this with names of countries and towns: *My uncle lives in Canada.* | *I work in Birmingham.*

at [preposition]
- use this when you are saying exactly where someone or something is: *I was waiting at the bus stop.* | *Let's meet at Bill's house.* | *Turn left at the church.* | *He was sitting at his desk.* | *They're at the airport.*
- use this with names of buildings, shops, hotels, theatres, schools etc: *We're staying at the Holiday Inn.* | *He studied economics at Harvard Business School.*
- use this with addresses: *The Prime Minister lives at 10 Downing Street.*

on [preposition]
on the beach/coast/shore/island *a city on the west coast of Australia* | *He spent the rest of his life on the island of St Helena.*
on the first/second etc floor *The manager's office is on the third floor.*
on a farm/ranch *She lived with her parents on the farm.*

 Don't say 'in our home'. Say **at home**: We decided to spend a quiet weekend at home.

 Don't say 'I stayed in my bed.' Say **I stayed in bed.**

2 in a box, room etc

in [*preposition/adv*]
in a container, room, building, or vehicle: *There were some pink flowers in the vase.* | *He's in the office.* | *There were four people in the car.*
be in/stay in to be in the building where you live or work: *She's never in when I call.* | *We're staying in this evening.*

inside [*preposition/adv*]
● use this when you are talking about something completely enclosed in a container: *There's a key inside the envelope.*
● use this when you are outside and thinking about what is happening in a room or building: *The lights were on inside the house.* | *It was snowing outside, but inside it was nice and warm.*

indoors [*adv*]
inside a building, especially someone's home: *I hope you're not going to stay indoors on a sunny day like this.*

indoor [*adj* only before noun]
used or happening indoors: *indoor tennis* | *an indoor swimming pool*

the inside [*n* singular]
the part of something that is inside
+of *The inside of the cupboard had not been painted.*

interior [*n* singular]
the inside of a building or car: *The all-leather interior and CD player make this new model a truly luxurious car.*
+of *My eyes gradually became accustomed to the dark interior of the store.*

3 into

into [*preposition*]
I saw him going into a bar. | *She got back into bed.* | *Pour the milk into a pan.*

> ⚠ Don't spell this as 'in to'. The correct spelling is **into**.

> ⚠ After **put**, **throw**, **drop**, and **look** it is more natural to use in as a preposition: *Put it in the drawer* (not 'into the drawer'). | *My gloves are dirty – I dropped them in the mud.* | *Look in the cupboard and see if it's there.*

in [*adv*]
into the place where you are or the place you have just mentioned: *Come in and sit down.* | *Look who's just walked in.* | *All the gates were locked. How did they get in?*

inside [*adv/preposition*]
into an enclosed space such as a cupboard, or into a building from the outside: *Come inside out of the rain.* | *Jane opened the cupboard and looked inside.* | *Go inside the cave and look around you.*

indoors [*adv*]
into a building, especially someone's home: *When it got colder, we went back indoors.*

4 out of

out [*adv*]
moving or looking away from the inside of a building, room, or container: *I sent her out to buy a newspaper.* | *She opened her bag and took out her passport.*
+of *Sharon sat there, staring out of the window.* | *People came rushing out of the office to see what had happened.*

outside [*adv/preposition*]
out of a building or room: *Look outside – it's snowing.* | *Why don't we go outside and sit on the patio?* | *As soon as I got outside the room, I wanted to cry.*

5 outside

outside [*adv/preposition*]
not inside a building, room, or area: *I'm going to sit outside in the sun.* |
Would you wait outside, please | *When I woke up, it was still dark
outside.* | *There's someone outside the door.* | *You do not need to go
outside the building.*
outside Boston/the US/Europe (=not inside a city/country etc):
Clark Air Base is the largest American military base outside the US. |
We live just outside the town.

> ⚠ American English you can also use **outside of** instead of the preposition **outside**.

outdoors/out of doors [*adv*]
not inside any buildings – use this especially to talk about pleasant or healthy things that you
do outside: *We often eat outdoors on summer evenings.* | *I spend my weekends out of doors,
playing golf or working in the garden.*
outdoor [*adj* only before noun] used or happening outdoors: *an outdoor swimming pool* |
outdoor activities such as skiing and climbing

out [*adv*]
out in/out on/out there etc somewhere outside a room or building: *We had to stand out in
the rain.* | *"Where's Martin?" "He's out in the corridor."* | *It's cold out there.*

the outside [*n* singular]
the part of something that you see from outside
+of *We must paint the outside of the house.*
from the outside *From the outside, it looks like an ordinary townhouse.*
on the outside *I can't eat these hamburgers – they're burnt on the outside and raw in
the middle.*
outside [*adj* only before noun] on the outside of a building: *The outside walls of the school
were covered with graffiti.* | *an outside toilet*

6 to/towards

to [*preposition*]
He's gone to Australia. | *She stood up and walked to the door.* | *the road to the airport* | *a trip to
Palm Springs*
on your way to (=while going to a place) *We stopped for a drink on our way to the theatre.*

> ⚠ Don't say 'I came in England.' Say **I came to England.**

> ⚠ Don't say 'We're going to home.' Say **We're going home.**

> ⚠ Don't say 'come to here' or 'go to there'. Say **come here** and **go there**.

towards [*preposition*]
moving, facing, or pointing in a particular direction: *Wright
noticed two policemen walking towards him.* | *All the windows face
towards the sea.*
in the direction of
going towards a place that you know about but cannot see:
Bramwell rode off in the direction of Foxwood. | *Guests were
starting to move in the direction of the dining room.*

up [*adv*]
go/come/walk/drive up to go towards someone or something and stop near them: *He drove up in a red Mercedes and parked it in front of the house.*
+to *An old man came up to me in the street and asked for money.*

7 (away) from

from [*preposition*]
You can fly from St Louis to San Francisco. | He broke his leg when he jumped from an upstairs window.

away [*adv*]
if you walk away, move away, run away etc you move in a direction that takes you further from someone or something: *He turned his back on me and walked away.*
+from *Why did you run away from me?*

off [*adv/preposition*]
away from a place
go/walk/drive/ride etc off (=leave a place) *Travis got into his car and drove off.*
off the field/stage/platform etc *The referee sent him off the field. | She bowed to the audience and walked off the stage.*

8 on

on [*preposition*]
on the surface of something: *There was a glass and an empty bottle on the table. | You'll have to sleep on the floor. | Neil Armstrong was the first man to walk on the moon.*
on the wall/ceiling/door the pictures on the wall | a fly on the ceiling | *You'll see his name on the door.*
on sb's body/finger/dress etc the diamond ring on her finger | *torture that left no mark on his body | There's lipstick on your collar.*

on top of
on the highest part of something: *I found this card on top of the cupboard. | the silver star on top of the Christmas tree*
one on top of the other (=in a pile) *You'll have to stack the boxes one on top of the other.*

onto [*preposition*]
moving to a position on the surface of something: *Nancy walked onto the stage and took the microphone in her hand.*

> ⚠ After **put, throw, drop, land,** and **fall** it is more natural to use **on**: Put the books back on the shelf (not 'onto the shelf').

over [*preposition*]
on something and covering it: *There was a white sheet over the victim's body. | She wore a coat over her sweater.*
put/lay/throw sth over sth *She put a blanket over the child's legs to keep him warm.*
all over (=on all parts of something) *Look, there are pieces of paper all over the floor.*

9   next to

next to

closest to the side of another person room or building – use this especially when there are several people, rooms, buildings etc in a line: *I was sitting next to Mr Gregory.* | *Next to the church was a park.*

right next to (=next to and very close) *I was standing right next to him, but I still couldn't hear what he was saying.*

beside [*preposition*]

close to the side of something or someone: *Leave the medicine on the table beside her bed.* | *She came and sat down beside me.* | *Harriet was walking beside the river with her dog.*

by [*preposition*]

beside something: *I'll meet you by the entrance.* | *Relatives are waiting by the phone for more news of the crash.* | *a hotel by the sea*

along [*preposition*]

continuing or moving close to the side of a river, coast, border etc: *the path along the shore* | *Walk along the canal as far as the bridge.*

all along (=from one end to the other) *There were thousands of tanks and guns all along the border.*

at the side of

next to a road or path: *Richard left his motorcycle at the side of the road and started to walk.*

side by side

if two people are walking, sitting or lying side by side they are next to each other: *We walked along slowly side by side.*

next door

next to another building, house, office etc or living in the house next to someone: *The hotel's very noisy at night – there's a night club right next door.*

the house/office/shop etc next door (=next to the place you are in or the place you have mentioned) *The house next door has been sold.*

+to *There's a bookstore next door to the bank.* | *Mrs Cottrell lived next door to my parents.*

next door neighbour BRITISH *next door neighbor* AMERICAN (=the person who lives next door)

10   opposite

opposite [*preposition/adv*]

in front of a building, thing or person, and on the other side of a street or table from them: *His wife was sitting opposite me at dinner last night.*

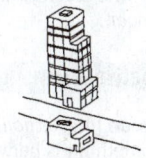

just/right/immediately opposite (=exactly opposite) *There's a bus stop right opposite my house.* | *The Harrisons live just opposite.*

> Don't confuse **opposite** and **in front of**. If there is a bus stop in front of your house, it is on the same side of the street. If there is a bus stop **opposite** your house, it is on the other side of the street.

opposite [*adj only before noun*]

opposite side/end/corner (=the side etc facing you across an area) *I saw him walk past on the opposite side of the street.*

facing sth/sb

a person, seat, or building that is **facing** something or someone is opposite them and has their or its front towards them: *an apartment facing the harbour* | *They sat facing each other across the table.*

across [*preposition*]

on the opposite side of a road, river, border etc from where you are: *My friend lives across the road.*

just across (=on the opposite side and close to where you are) *Tijuana is just across the border in Mexico.*

11 in front of

in front
further forward than someone or something else: *The car in front started to slow down.* | *She walked in front carrying the baby.*

in front of sb/sth
if something is **in front of** you, you are facing it; if something is in front of a building, object etc, the front of the building or object is facing it: *There was a tall man standing in front of me, so I couldn't see what was happening.* | *She parked her car right in front of the main entrance.*

> ⚠ Don't confuse **in front of** (=directly next to the front of a building) and opposite (=on the other side of the street).

ahead [*adv*]
if something or someone is ahead of you, they are in front of you, and are moving in the same direction or towards them: *He knows the way, so let him go on ahead and we'll follow.*
far ahead *I shouted at him to stop, but he was too far ahead and didn't hear me.*
+of *We could still see their car ahead of us.*
the road/way/path ahead (=the road etc in front of you that you are travelling along) *The road ahead was closed because of an accident.*

12 behind

behind [*preposition/adv*]
Put your hands behind your back. | *The sun disappeared behind a cloud.* | *I got here first – the others are following on behind.*

at the back ESPECIALLY BRITISH
behind a building: *There's a small garden at the back.*
+of *The tennis courts were at the back of the main school building.*

in back AMERICAN
behind something, especially a building: *You can park your car in back.*
+of *The garbage cans are in back of the house.*

round the back BRITISH INFORMAL
to or in a place behind a building: *If you go round the back, you can leave your boots next to the door.*

13 between/among

between [*preposition/adv*]
if something is between two or more things, they are on either side of it: *The ball rolled between the goalkeeper's legs.* | *I was standing between my mother and father.*
halfway between *Nagoya is situated roughly halfway between Tokyo and Kyoto.*

in the middle
if someone or something is in the middle, they are in the middle of a group or row, with one or more people or things on either side of them: *Here's a photo of all the family – that's Mario in the middle.* | *My parents sat at either end of the sofa with me in the middle.*
+of *a seat in the middle of the front row*

among [*preposition*]
in a group of people or things so that they are all around you: *I saw him standing among a group of students.* | *The house was hidden among the trees.*

surrounded by sth
if you are **surrounded by** people or things, they are all around you on every side: *Jill was sitting on the floor surrounded by boxes.*

14 around

around (also **round** BRITISH) [preposition]
in a circle or moving in a circle, with something or someone in the middle: *The whole family was sitting around the dinner table talking.* | *A small crowd had gathered round us.* | *He had a bandage round his wrist.* | *People used to believe that the sun went around the earth.*

15 across/through

across [preposition/adv]
from one side of something to the other: *The children ran across the road.* | *sailing across the Atlantic* | *We gazed across the valley.* | *The traffic was heavy so it took a long time to get across.*
+to *He walked across to the window.*

over [preposition]
going from one side of something to the other, especially by flying, jumping, climbing, or using a bridge: *A cat jumped over the fence.* | *the road over the mountains* | *one of the bridges over the Rhine*

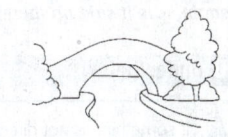

through [preposition/adv]
from one side or end of something to the other – use this about going through a town, a forest, or a crowd, or looking through a hole, window etc: *I pushed my way through the crowd.* | *walking through the forest* | *We drove through Baltimore on our way to Washington.* | *I could see her through the window.* | *The trip through the tunnel takes about 40 minutes.* | *We found a gap in the fence and climbed through.*

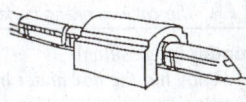

16 along

along/down/up [preposition]
moving or looking from a place on a road, passage, line etc towards the end of it: *walking along the road* | *I could hear him coming along the corridor.* | *I looked down the line of prisoners, but I didn't recognize any of them.* | *Go up Main Street and turn right.*

17 above

above [*preposition/adv*]
in a higher position than something: *There was a light directly above the table.* | *Mexico City is 2400 metres above sea level.*
the floor/room/apartment above (=above where you are) *We could hear noises in the room above.*
from above *Looking down from above, we could see the whole island spread out like a map.*

over [*preposition/adv*]
directly above something or moving across in the air above it: *Black clouds hung over the valley.* | *As the planes flew over, Selim could see the Russian markings on their wings.* | *Riot police fired over the heads of the demonstrators.*

overhead [*adv*]
in the sky directly above your head: *Suddenly, they heard the rumble of thunder overhead.* | *The ship moved away slowly with seagulls circling overhead.*

upstairs [*adv*]
on a higher floor of a building, above where you are: *The bathroom is upstairs.* | *We got a note from the woman who lives upstairs.*
upstairs [*adj* only before noun] *The burglars got in through an upstairs window.*

up [*adv*]
up in/up on/up there etc in a higher position than where you are: *The cat's up on the roof again.* | *Is it safe up there?*

18 under/below

> ⚠ If something is not directly under something else, use **below**: *the path below my bedroom window*

> ⚠ If something is hidden or covered by something else, or is moving directly under it, use **under**: *The cat was hiding under the table.*

under [*preposition*]
Wendy hid the box under her bed. | *The first of the boats was already passing under the Golden Gate Bridge.* | *The ruins of the ancient city now lie under the sea.*

- you can also use this to say that something is covered by clothes, skin, paint etc: *I'm wearing a sweater under my coat.*

below [*adv/preposition*]
in a lower position than something: *We were standing on top of the mountain, looking down into the valley below.* | *He has a nasty scar just below the left eye.*
the floor/room/apartment below (=below where you are) *I work on the fourth floor and Gerry's office is on the floor below.*

underneath [*preposition/adv*]
- directly under an object: *I found your keys on the sofa, underneath a cushion.* | *He got out of the car and looked underneath.*
- you can also use this to say that something is covered by clothes, skin, paint etc: *a disease caused by a tiny insect that lays its eggs just underneath the skin*

underground [*adv*]
under the ground: *The explosives are stored underground in concrete bunkers.*
underground [*adj* only before noun] *An underground passage leads from the castle to a secret cave.*

downstairs [*adv*]
on a lower floor of a building, below where you are: *I can hear someone moving around downstairs.* | *the people who live downstairs*
downstairs [*adj* only before noun] *I think it's in the downstairs cupboard.*

19 up

up [*adv/preposition*]
moving, pointing, or looking up: *Caroline looked up and laughed.*
up a hill/ladder/tree/wall etc *He had climbed up a tree to get a better view.*
+onto/into/at etc *Don't let the cat jump up onto the table.*
straight up (=directly towards the sky)

upwards (also **upward** AMERICAN) [*adv*]
towards a higher position, especially towards the sky: *Most plants grow upwards, towards the light.* | *With a loud bang, the rocket shot upward into the night sky.*
upward [*adj* only before noun] *He signalled with an upward movement of his arm.*

uphill [*adv*]
going up a slope or hill: *It's hard work biking uphill.* | *The path continues uphill for another mile.*

upstairs [*adv*]
going up the stairs to a higher level of a building: *They carried her upstairs to the bedroom.*

20 down

 If you want to say that something comes onto the ground, floor etc from a higher position, use **down**, not downwards: *Come down from that tree!*

down [*adv/preposition*]
moving, pointing, or looking down: *I told you not to climb on the table. Get down!* | *Tears ran down his face.*
+into/at/off/from etc *Dr Morel glanced down at the notepad on his desk.* | *The accident happened as we were coming down off the mountain.*
down a hill/hole/slope etc *We went down some steps into a cellar.*

downwards (also **downward** AMERICAN) [*adv*]
towards a lower position or place: *a path winding downwards through the woods to the valley below* | *He was gazing downward into the pit.*
downward [*adj* only before noun] *the downward pull of gravity*

downhill [*adv*]
going down a slope or hill: *We set off downhill, towards the lake.* | *From here it's downhill all the way to the beach.*

downstairs [*adv*]
going down the stairs to a lower floor of a building: *She said goodnight to the children and went downstairs.* | *After drinking half a bottle of whisky, he had fallen downstairs.*

21 forward

forward (also **forwards**) [*adv*]
moving or looking towards a point in front of you: *She leaned forward to speak to the driver.* | *One of the guards stepped forward and raised his rifle.* | *Sit facing forwards with your legs stretched out.*

ahead [*adv*]
in front of you: *It was impossible to see ahead through the fog.*
straight ahead (=directly ahead) *He was staring straight ahead toward the gates at the end of the road.*

straight on ESPECIALLY BRITISH
if you go **straight on**, you go directly forward, not to the left or right: *When you come to the crossroads, drive straight on.*

22 backwards

back [*adv*]
moving or looking towards a point behind you: *He looked back over his shoulder.* | *I stepped back to let them pass.* | *Police pushed the crowd back, away from the palace gates.*

backwards (also **backward** AMERICAN) [*adv*]
moving back: *She fell backwards onto the bed.* | *Harry took a step backwards and stood on someone's toe.*

23 top

the top [*n* singular]
the top part or surface of something: *When you get to the top, wait for me.*
+of *There is a wonderful view from the top of the tower.*
at the top (=on or near the top) *When I'm painting a wall, I always start at the top.* | *He was waiting for me at the top of the stairs.* | *Write your name at the top of the page.*

top [*adj* only before noun]
top shelf/drawer/floor/layer etc *The books are on the top shelf.* | *Our apartment is on the top floor.*

upper [*adj* only before noun]
upper part/teeth/lip/deck etc the part, teeth etc at the top – use this when there is one part or set at the top and one at the bottom: *Several of his upper teeth are missing.* | *As the ship came in, she could see Henry waving from the upper deck.*

24 bottom

the bottom [*n* singular]
the lowest part of something
+of *There's a crack along the bottom of the wall.* | *The ship sank to the bottom of the ocean.*
at the bottom *Paul was waiting for her at the bottom of the stairs.* | *The answers are at the bottom of Page 51.*
in the bottom (=in the bottom of a container, hole etc) *There's a little paint left in the bottom of the can.*

at the foot of sth
close to the bottom of a mountain, a ladder, a tree, or some stairs: *a hotel situated at the foot of the Lamvern Hills* | *Jean stopped at the foot of the stairs and looked back at him.*

> ⚠ Use **at the foot of** in written descriptions.

bottom [*adj* only before noun]
bottom shelf/drawer/layer etc the shelf, drawer etc at the bottom: *She searched through the bottom drawer of her desk.*

lower [*adj* only before noun]
lower part/lip/deck etc the part, lip etc at the bottom – use this when there is one at the top and one at the bottom: *We drove onto the lower deck of the ferry.*

25 front

the front [n singular]
the part of something that is furthest forward, or the part of a moving object that is facing in the direction that it is moving
+of *The front of the house was painted yellow.* | *You've spilt soup all down the front of your dress.* | *The hijacker walked down to the front of the plane.*
at the front (=at the front of a room, area, or space) *Come and sit at the front – you'll be able to see.*
on the front (=on the front surface or cover of something) *Her picture was on the front of 'Time' magazine.*

front [adj only before noun]
use this about something that is at the front when there are other things of the same kind behind it
front row/seats/page/teeth/legs etc *I don't want to sit in the front row.* | *a story that was on the front page of every newspaper*
front door/garden/room/entrance (=not the one at the back, but the one facing the street) *I walked up to the front door and rang the bell.*

26 back

the back [n singular]
the back part or surface of an object, building, car etc
+of *I wrote a message on the back of an envelope.* | *We walked past the back of the college.*
at the back (=in the back part of the inside of a room, cupboard, drawer etc) *The students who were sitting at the back could not hear what the teacher was saying.* | *I found your passport. It was right at the back of the drawer.*
in the back (=in the back part of the inside of a car) *Just throw all your bags in the back of the car.*
on the back (=on the back of a piece of paper, clothing etc) *If you turn it over, you'll see the artist's signature on the back.*

back [adj only before noun]
use this about something that is at the back when there are other things of the same kind in front of it
back seat/row/page/teeth/legs etc *the back page of 'The New York Times'* | *There were two children and a large dog on the back seat.*
back door/garden/room (=at the back of the house) *You forgot to lock the back door.*

rear [adj only before noun]
in or on the back part of a building, car, train, or plane – used in official or technical information
rear window/exit/carriage etc *The two rear carriages of the train are reserved for non-smokers.*

27 side

side [n C]
the part of an object, building, car etc that faces left or right, not front
or back

+of *A motorcycle crashed into the side of the car, damaging the door on
the driver's side.* | *There's a path along the side of the house.*
side [adj only before noun] at the side: *the side entrance*

sideways [adv]
towards your left or right side, not forward or backwards: *She glanced
sideways out of the corner of her eye.* | *Lift your arm sideways and
hold that position.*

from side to side
towards the left and then the right, and then towards the left again etc:
The ship swayed from side to side.

28 corner

in the corner
at the place in a room where two walls meet, or at the place
where two sides of an area meet: *The phone's over there, in
the corner.*
+of *He had pitched his tent in the corner of the field.*

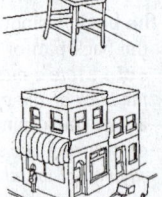

on the corner
where two roads meet: *the shop on the corner*
+of *Ross was standing on the corner of the street, waiting for her.*

around the corner (also **round the corner** BRITISH)
at or to the other side of a corner, either the outside corner of a
building or a corner where two roads meet: *If you go round the
corner, you'll see the side entrance.* | *I think the gas station is just
around the next corner.*

Essential Grammar
by David Crystal

The Essential Grammar covers the areas of English Grammar which most often cause problems for intermediate learners. It has been based on students' needs and analysis of the Longman Learners' Corpus, with natural real-life example sentences taken from the British National Corpus. It provides practical help for students who want to put their grammar to active use when writing or speaking English.

Contents

1 Statements and questions

STATEMENTS

A 'statement' is a sentence which gives information. If you make a statement, you usually give the sentence a subject, and this must go in front of the verb.

> *The children are playing in the garden.*

NEGATIVE STATEMENTS

Negative statements are made in two main ways:

1 If the statement contains an auxiliary verb, such as **is** or **have**, or the main verb is **be**, you usually add **not** or its contracted form **n't**.

> *She is not leaving.* **OR** *She isn't leaving.*

Am and **may** do not allow **n't**. **Will**, **shall**, and **can** have special contracted forms: **won't**, **shan't**, **can't**.

The same rules apply when you make a question negative.

> *Are they in the garden? Aren't they in the garden?*
> *Will he get the job? Won't he get the job?*

2 If the statement has no auxiliary verb, you need to make the negative using a form of **do + not/n't**. Make sure that the main verb is in its basic form.

> *She likes swimming. She doesn't like swimming.* **NOT** *She doesn't likes swimming.*
> *I saw a ship. I didn't see a ship.* **NOT** *I didn't saw a ship.*

QUESTIONS

Questions are sentences which ask for information. They fall into three main types, depending on the kind of reply they expect.

'Yes–no questions' expect a simple **yes** or **no** reply (or a word or phrase which can be used instead of **yes** or **no**). In these cases, you put the subject after an auxiliary or after the main verb **be**.

> *Will Jane resign?* (Possible answers: *yes, no, I don't know, probably, maybe* etc)
> *Are they ready?*
> *Does Dave know about this?*

'**Wh– questions**' begin with a question word, such as **what**, **why**, **where**, or **how**. This kind of question can have a wide range of different replies. The answer may be a full sentence, or one which leaves out the words that you can guess from knowing the question. Here too, you need to put the subject after an auxiliary or **be**, unless the question word is the subject.

> *Where are you going?* (Possible answers: *I'm going to work, downstairs, to the library* etc)
> *What did she say?*
> *Who found the money?*

'**Alternative questions**' give the listener a choice of two possible replies, both of which are mentioned in the question. The two possibilities are connected by the word **or**. Once again, you must change the order of subject and verb.

> *Will you travel by train or by boat?* (Possible answers: *by train, by boat, I don't know* etc)

Tag questions

You can change a statement into a question by adding a 'tag question' at the end of it. When you use a tag question, you are asking the listener to agree with the statement you have just made. If the statement is positive, you expect the answer **yes**. If it is negative, you expect the answer **no**.

A tag question is a type of 'yes–no question', and consists of a personal pronoun after an auxiliary or the main verb **be**. You use the same personal pronoun (**she**, **they** etc) and tense of the verb as in the statement to which the tag question is joined. In the most common kind of tag question, you change from positive to negative, or from negative to positive.

> *She's outside, isn't she?* (Expected answer: *yes*)
> *They were ready, weren't they?* (Expected answer: *yes*)
> *You aren't going, are you?* (Expected answer: *no*)
> *It isn't difficult, is it?* (Expected answer: *no*)

Questions which are not questions

You can also use a sentence which looks like a question, but it is one where you are not actually expecting any reply. Because these sentences are halfway between a question and an exclamation, you will find them sometimes written with a question–mark and sometimes with an exclamation–mark.

In some cases, you already know the answer or you are asking your listener to agree with you. These sentences are called 'exclamatory questions'.

> *Hasn't she grown!*
> *Wasn't the book marvellous?*

In other cases, no answer is possible. (Of course your listener may still give you an answer, whether you like it or not!) These sentences are used when you want to express a strong feeling about something. They are called 'rhetorical questions'.

> *Doesn't everyone know that the whole thing is impossible?*

Polite questions

When using a question to make a request, you can make it sound more polite by using **please** and by using phrases such as **could I ...?** or **may I ...?** For more information about this kind of question, go to **REQUESTS** in the **ESSENTIAL COMMUNICATION** section.

2 Verbs: intransitive and transitive

Most verbs in English belong to either of two types: intransitive verbs or transitive verbs.

INTRANSITIVE VERBS

An intransitive verb does not have an object. You can use it without having to add any more words to the sentence. Here are some examples of intransitive verbs:

> *Something's happening.* | *I'll wait.* | *It doesn't matter.*

You can add other words to these sentences in order to show meanings such as time, place, or manner, but these words do not have to be there for the sentence to make sense.

> *Something's happening in the street.* | *I'll wait for a few minutes.* | *It doesn't matter at all.*

Other intransitive verbs include **appear**, **come**, **go**, **smile**, **lie**, and **rise**.

Intransitive verbs cannot be used in the passive.

> Don't say 'it was happened' or 'they were died'. Say **it happened** or **they died**.

In this dictionary, intransitive verbs are shown like this: [v I].

TRANSITIVE VERBS

A transitive verb must have an object. Without the object, the sentence does not make sense. The object of the verb is usually a noun, a noun phrase, or a pronoun. Here are some examples of transitive verbs:

She bought that dress in Tokyo. **NOT** *She bought in Tokyo.*
Did you find the key? **NOT** *Did you find?*
I really like him. **NOT** *I really like.*

Sometimes the object is a clause which begins + (**that**). For example:

I wish she would stop smoking. **OR** *I wish that she would stop smoking.*

Sometimes the object is a whole sentence. For example:

"It's time to go home," he said.

Other transitive verbs include **make, use, need, thank, enjoy, keep**, and **carry**.

In this dictionary, transitive verbs are shown like this: [*v* T].

VERBS THAT CAN BE TRANSITIVE OR INTRANSITIVE

Several verbs can be used in a transitive or intransitive way. Here are some examples of verbs that can be transitive or intransitive:

There's no need to shout. [*v* I]
Someone shouted my name. [*v* T]
Where do you want to meet? [*v* I]
I'll meet you outside the school. [*v* T]
I'm sorry. I don't understand. [*v* I]
She didn't understand his explanation. [*v* T]

The intransitive uses are very similar to the transitive ones, except that the object been left out.

In this dictionary, these verbs are shown like this: [*v* I/T].

OTHER VERBS

Some verbs can be followed by an adjective or adjective phrase. Here are some examples of these verbs:

You seem tired. | *It all sounds very interesting.* | *Was he angry?*

In this dictionary, these verbs are shown like this: [*v*].

3 Talking about the present

English has two main ways of talking about present time: the simple present and the present progressive.

THE SIMPLE PRESENT

You make the simple present by using the verb in its basic form. You add –s or –es to the verb in the third person singular.

The simple present is used in the following ways:

1 You use the simple present to talk about something which is happening now, and which will continue to happen in the future. You often use the simple present in this meaning to talk about things that are true about your life, for example where you live, your job, or the kinds of things you like.

Martin lives in Canada. | *I work in a hospital.* | *"What kind of music do you like?"*
"I like all kinds of pop music."

2 You use the simple present when you talk about something which happens again and again, or when you say that something happens regularly at a particular time. Use words such as **always**, **often**, **sometimes**, **occasionally**, and **never**, or phrases such as **on Tuesdays** or **every day** with the simple present in this meaning.

They often go out to restaurants. | *I travel to London twice a month.* | *He gets up at 6 o'clock.* | *She goes to church every Sunday.*

3 You use the simple present to talk about something which stays the same for ever – such as a scientific fact.

Oil floats on water. | *Two and two make four.*

4 You can use the simple present when you are describing what is happening at the exact moment when you are speaking. The simple present is used like this, for example, in sports commentaries.

Shearer gets the ball from Gascoigne. He shoots – and scores!

> For descriptions of actions that are happening now, you usually use the present progressive (see below) rather than the simple present. For example:
>
> *"What are you doing?" "I'm making a poster."*   **NOT**   *"What do you do?" "I make a poster."*

THE PRESENT PROGRESSIVE

You make the present progressive by using a form of the verb **be** in the present tense, followed by the main verb with an **–ing** ending, for example **I am waiting**, **she is coming**.

The present progressive is used in the following ways:

1 You use the present progressive to talk about something which is happening now at the time you are speaking or writing. You often use this meaning with words and phrases that express present time, such as **now**, **at the moment**, and **currently**.

"What's Bob doing?" "He's watching television." | *It's raining again.* | *I'm looking for my glasses.*

2 You use the present progressive to say that something is happening now, but will only continue for a limited period of time. Compare these pairs of sentences:

We live in France. (=France is our permanent home)
We're living in France. (=we are living there for a limited period of time)
He cooks his own meals. (=he always does it)
He's cooking his own meals. (=he does not usually do it)

If you want to talk about the subjects you are studying at school or university, you usually use the present progressive.

She's studying law at Harvard.   **NOT**   *She studies law at Harvard.*
I'm studying English.   **NOT**   *I study English.*

Verbs that cannot be used in the progressive
Verbs which express a situation or state, rather than describing a definite action, are not usually used in the progressive. Do not use the progressive with the following verbs:

be	understand	hate	agree
believe	wish	prefer	disagree
know	have	want	mean
recognize	like	belong	need
remember	love	see	deserve

I know the answer. **NOT** *I am knowing the answer.*
She understands me. **NOT** *She is understanding me.*

---

 4 **Talking about the past**

There are several ways of talking about actions that happened in the past. These include the simple past, the past progressive, the present perfect, the past perfect, and the phrase **used to**.

THE SIMPLE PAST

You usually make the simple past by adding **-ed** to the end of the verb. For example:

> I walk   → I walked
> we wait   → we waited
> they jump   → they jumped

Many common verbs have irregular simple past forms, and so you have to use a special ending, or change the verb in some other way. For example:

> I go   → I went
> we buy   → we bought
> they see   → they saw

You use the simple past to talk about an action which happened and finished in the past. There is a space between the time when the action happened, and the time when you are speaking or writing about it.

> He kicked the ball into the net. | I went home early because I had a headache. | The police found a dead body in the river.

You often use words or phrases such as **at midnight**, **on Tuesday**, **in 1992**, **yesterday**, and **last year** with the simple past, to draw attention to the time when something happened. For example:

> Our visitors arrived yesterday. | Where did you go last week? | The war ended in 1945.

THE PAST PROGRESSIVE

You make the past progressive by using **was** or **were**, followed by the main verb with an **–ing** ending, for example **I was looking**, **they were laughing**.

The past progressive is used in the following ways:

1   You use the past progressive when you want to talk about something that happened in the past, and continued to happen for only a limited period of time.

> We were living in France at that time. | I was trying to get the waiter's attention. | The man was looking at me in a very strange way.

2   You use the past progressive to talk about something which continued to happen for a period of time, during which another thing happened.

> I was watching TV when the phone rang. | They met each other while they were staying in London.

 Some verbs are not usually used in the progressive. Don't say, 'I was not believing him'. Say **I did not believe him**. See section **3** for a list of these verbs.

THE PRESENT PERFECT

You make the present perfect by using **has** or **have**, followed by the past participle form of the main verb, for example **I have walked**, **she has gone**, **they have seen**.

The present perfect is used in the following ways:

1   You use the present perfect to talk about something that happened in the past and is finished, but which still affects the situation now.

> Someone has broken the window. (RESULT NOW: it is still broken, and needs to be mended)
> The taxi has arrived. (RESULT NOW: someone needs to go and get into the taxi)
> Jane's hurt her hand, so she can't write. (RESULT NOW: Jane can't write)

You often use **just** and **recently** with the present perfect in this meaning.

> Jane's just left, but you might catch her in the car park.

In American English, people often use the simple past instead of the present perfect in this sense.

British English	American English
I've just seen Carol.	*I just saw Carol.*
You've already told me that.	*You already told me that.*
Have they come home yet?	*Did they come home yet?*

2 You use the present perfect to say that something started to happen in the past, and has continued to happen up to now. There is a clear difference with the past tense, which you use when the action is finished. Compare these sentences:

present perfect: *I have lived in Chicago for many years.* (=I still live there now)
simple past: *I lived in Chicago for many years.* (=now I live somewhere else)
present perfect: *Jim has worked for us since 1992.* (=he still works for us now)
simple past: *Jim worked for us from 1992 to 1996.* (=he does not work for us any more)

 Don't say 'I am living here for 10 years', or 'I live here for 10 years'. Say **I have lived here for 10 years**.

3 You use the present perfect to talk about something that happened at some time in the past before now, when it is not important to say when it happened.

She has had several jobs abroad.
There have been problems with this system in the past.

The present perfect is often used in this way in news reports.

There has been a big earthquake in Japan, and hundreds of people have been killed.

You can emphasize this meaning by using **ever** in questions, or **never** in negative sentences. For example:

Have you ever visited Scotland? | *I've never been in a plane before.*

If you give the date, year, or time when something happened, you must use the simple past, not the present perfect. For example:

I spoke to him yesterday. **NOT** *I have spoken to him yesterday.*
They arrived in the US last week. **NOT** *They have arrived in the US last week.*

THE PRESENT PERFECT PROGRESSIVE

You make the present perfect progressive by using **have been/has been**, followed by the main verb with an **–ing** ending, for example **I have been living**, **she has been studying**. The present perfect progressive has very similar meanings to the present perfect, but draws attention to the period of time during which the action has taken place.

The present perfect progressive is used in the following ways:

1 You use the present perfect progressive to talk about something which has continued to happen for a period of time in the past, and which may still be happening now.

How long have you been learning English? | *We've been expecting them to arrive since last Thursday.*

2 You use the present progressive to talk about something which has been taking place recently and which affects the situation now.

"You look tired." "I've been working really hard."
It's been raining all week, so the ground's very wet.

 Don't say 'I've been knowing John for a long time'. Say **I have known John for a long time**. See section **3** for a list of these verbs.

THE PAST PERFECT

If you want to talk about a past action which took place before another past action, you can use **had**, followed by the past participle of the main verb.

> *After the visitors had left, we watched TV.* | *They told me that the taxi had already arrived*

You can also use the past perfect in a 'progressive' form by using **had been**, and putting it in front of a main verb with an **–ing** ending.

> *We had only been driving for an hour when the car ran out of petrol.*

Using the right time phrases with the past tense

If you use words or phrases about time with the simple past, they must have a meaning which shows there has been a space between the time when the action or event happened and the time when you are talking or writing about it. For example: *I saw John yesterday/a week ago/last Tuesday.*

If you use words or phrases about time with the present perfect, they must have a meaning which shows that the action has continued up to the present, and may still going on. For example: *I haven't seen John since Monday/so far/yet.*

 Don't say 'I've seen him a week ago' or 'I didn't see John since Monday'.

USED TO

You use **used to** when you want to say that something happened in the past over a period of time, but it no longer happens now. It is found only in the past tense. You use **used to** with the basic form of the main verb, for example **used to smoke**, **used to live**, **used to be**.

> *I used to play football a lot when I was at school.* | *She used to smoke 40 cigarettes a day.* | *The club used to be very fashionable.* | *They used to live in Los Angeles.*

In negatives, you say **didn't use to**, or **used not to**.

> *I didn't use to like spicy food.*   **OR**   *I used not to like spicy food.*

In questions, you say **did (you/she/John *etc*) use to ... ?**

> *Did you use to smoke?* | *What did she use to call him?*

5 | Talking about the future

There are several ways of talking about the future in English.

THE FUTURE WITH 'WILL'

You put the verb **will** in front of the main verb. This is the most common way of expressing future time. The short form of **will** is **'ll** and the short form of **will not** is **won't**. You usually use these in spoken English instead of **will** or **will not**. The main verb can be either in its 'simple' form or in its 'progressive' form. For example:

> *I will talk to them.* | *We'll have a break at six o'clock.* | *I'll talk to them.* | *He'll be arriving later.* | *Don't worry – I won't break it.*

You use **will** in this meaning in sentences that begin **I'm sure, I think, I expect, I suppose, I doubt** etc, or with words such as **probably, perhaps, certainly** etc.

> *"Do you think Carla will pass her test?" "Yes, I'm sure she will."* | *I'll see him again soon.* | *They say it'll probably snow tomorrow.* | *Perhaps things will be better next week.*

THE FUTURE WITH 'SHALL'

In British English, you often use **shall** in questions when making suggestions about what to do, or when discussing what to do. This use is rare in American English.

Shall we go now? | *What shall I tell Mike?*

In formal British English, you can sometimes hear **I shall** used to express future time.

I shall try to persuade them.

This is very rare in American English.

THE FUTURE WITH 'BE GOING TO'

You use a form of **be going to** to say that something will happen soon.

It's going to rain. | *Watch out – you're going to hit that tree!* | *I think I'm going to be sick.*

You also use a form of **be going to** to talk about someone's intentions, or what they have decided to do.

I'm going to ask for my money back.
Lucy is going to travel round the world when she leaves school.

THE FUTURE WITH 'BE ABOUT TO'

You use **be about to** to say that something will happen almost immediately.

Take your seats, please. The show is about to begin. | *The situation is about to change.*

THE FUTURE WITH THE PRESENT PROGRESSIVE

You use the present progressive (**he's leaving, they're starting** etc) with a word or phrase expressing future time to talk about something that will happen because you have planned or arranged it.

We're leaving on Saturday morning. | *I'm having a party next week – do you want to come?*

THE FUTURE WITH THE SIMPLE PRESENT

You use the simple present (it starts, we arrive etc) with a word or phrase expressing future time, to say that something will definitely happen at a particular time, especially because it has been officially arranged.

The next plane to Los Angeles leaves at 6:25. | *The meeting is on Thursday.* | *What time does the show start?*

You use the simple present in subordinate clauses to talk about the future, for example in clauses that begin with **when, if, unless, before, after**, and **as soon as**. Don't use **will** in this kind of clause.

I'll call you when I get back. **NOT** *I'll call you when I will get back.*
If the bus leaves on time, it will get there by 6. **NOT** *If the bus will leave on time, it will get there by 6.*

6 Phrasal verbs

WHAT IS A PHRASAL VERB?

A phrasal verb is a verb which consists of more than one word. Most phrasal verbs consist of two words: the first word is a verb, the second word is a preposition or an adverb.

Examples of common phrasal verbs are **get up**, **put off**, **turn on**, **look after**, and **add to**. There are also some three–word phrasal verbs, such as **look forward to** and **get away with**.

You can sometimes guess the meaning of a phrasal verb from the meaning of the words it contains, for example **come in** = come + in. More often, the meaning *of* the phrasal verb is different – often very different – from the meaning of the verb which forms its first part.

For example **put off** (=arrange to do something at a later time) has a very different meaning from **put** (=put something somewhere), and **look forward to** (=when you feel happy because something is going to happen soon) has a very different meaning from **look** (=look at something).

Like single–word verbs, some phrasal verbs are 'transitive' (they must have an object), and some phrasal verbs are 'intransitive' (they do not have an object). For example:

take off [phrasal verb T] (=remove your shirt, coat etc)
She took off her coat and sat down.

get up [phrasal verb I] (=leave your bed in the morning)
I usually get up very early.

Some phrasal verbs can be transitive or intransitive. For example:

join in [phrasal verb I/T] (=start taking part in something that other people are already doing, for example a game or song)
We all joined in the game.
I want you all to join in.

WHERE DO YOU PUT THE OBJECT?

With transitive phrasal verbs, you have to decide where to put the object.

● If the phrasal verb ends with a preposition, the preposition must come after the verb, and you cannot split up the phrasal verb. For example:

look after sb (=make sure someone is safe and has the things they need)
Will you look after the children for me?.

add to sth (=increase an amount that is already large)
This will just add to the confusion.

● If the phrasal verb ends with an adverb, there are three possibilities.

1 If you choose a noun phrase as the object, you can put it either before or after the adverb. For example:

call off (=decide that a meeting, party, strike etc should not happen)
They've called off the strike. **OR** *They've called the strike off.*

turn on (=make a light, television, radio etc start working)
Will you turn on the light? **OR** *Will you turn the light on?*

2 If you choose a pronoun (**him**, **her**, **it**, **them** etc) as the object, you have to put it before the adverb. For example:

turn down (=make a television, radio etc less loud)
Can you turn it down? **NOT** *Can you turn down it?*

3 If the object is a long phrase, you usually put it at the end after the phrasal verb. For example:

They've called off the strike that was planned for next week.
Can you turn down the television in the front room?

7 Modal verbs

The main 'modal verbs' (or 'modals') are:

can	may	will	shall	must
could	might	would	should	

Ought to, **used to**, **dare** and **need** are also used as modal verbs, but they have other uses as well.

WHEN TO USE MODAL VERBS

Modals have several meanings, so you need to think about the meaning of the sentence as a whole to be sure that your choice of modal expresses exactly what you want to say. The main ideas that modals are used to express are shown in the following sections.

Permission (=allowing someone to do something)

If you want to give or ask for permission, use **can** or **may**. **May** is more polite or formal than **can**.

> *You can leave when the bell rings.* | *Customers may purchase extra copies at half price.*

Could is a polite way of asking for permission.

> *Could I leave early today?*

Might is a very formal and old-fashioned way of asking for permission.

> *Might I borrow your umbrella?*

→   see also LET and **EG** PERMISSION

Obligation (=saying what someone must do)

If you want to demand that something happens, or that someone does something (=to express obligation), use **must**. You can also use this idea about yourself, in order to express a sense of duty.

> *The builders must finish the job today.* | *We mustn't leave the house before 6 o'clock.* | *I must remember to bring my notebook.*

→   see also MUST

Intention (=saying what you are going to do)

If you want to say that you intend to do something, use **will** or **shall**. You can emphasize the meaning of intention if you say the modal louder than the surrounding words.

Shall is only used with the first person (**I** or **we**), and is much less common than **will**. It is hardly ever used in American English.

> *This letter says they will definitely give us our money back.* | *I shan't stay long.*

To express an intention at a time in the past, use **would**.

> *I tried to explain, but nobody would listen.*

Use **would** if there are conditions controlling whether something will take place.

> *I would leave tomorrow, if I had the money.*

→   see also INTEND

Ability (=saying whether you are able to do something)

If you want to say whether someone is able to carry out an action, use **can**.

> *Guy can speak Russian.* | *Can you remember her name?* | *I can't find my shoes!*

When you talk about the past, use **could**.

> *He was late for school because he couldn't find his bag.*

Use **could** if there are conditions controlling whether the event will take place.

I could leave tomorrow, if I had the money.

→ see also CAN

Possibility (=saying whether something is possible)

If you want to say that something is possible, use **can** or **may**. May is more polite or formal than **can**.

These chairs can be stored flat. | You may find the manager is still there, if you go to the office now.

If you want to suggest that the event is less likely to happen, use **could** or **might**. If you use **might**, you mean that the event is especially unlikely.

It could be interesting. | It might be interesting. (=it is possible, but unlikely)

→ see also POSSIBLE

Probability (=saying whether something is likely)

If you want to suggest that an event is likely to happen, use **should** or **ought to**. It will probably take place, but you are not completely sure.

If you take these tablets, you should be all right. | They should have had our reply by now. | We ought to be there by 6 o'clock.

→ see also PROBABLY, SURE/NOT SURE

Desirability (=saying that something is the right thing to do)

If you want to say that you think it is a good thing for something to happen, use **should** or **ought to**. If you think that it is a bad thing for something to happen, put these verbs into the negative.

You should get the early flight, if you want to be in good time. | You ought to see the doctor as soon as possible. | You shouldn't say things like that. | You oughtn't to have left the engine running.

→ see also SHOULD

Necessity (=saying that something is necessary)

If you want to say that it is necessary for something to happen, use **must**.

We really must go now. | I must get my hair cut this weekend.

If you want to express the opposite meaning (=it is unnecessary for something to happen) use **needn't/need not** or **not need to**.

There's plenty of time, so you needn't worry.

 Don't use **mustn't** because this gives the meaning of obligation.

→ see also NEED

Certainty (=saying that you are sure about something)

If you want to say that you are sure something is true, use **must**.

You must be tired, after all your hard work. | They must have left by now.

To express the opposite meaning (=you are sure something is not true) use **can't**.

You can't be that tired – you've only been working for an hour! | They can't have left yet.

→ see also SURE/NOT SURE

Prediction

(=saying what you think is going to happen)

If you want to say that something is certain to happen, use either **will** or **shall**. As with the other uses of these words, **shall** tends to be found only with the first person (**I** or **we**), and is much less common than **will**. **Shall** is very rare in American English.

The cars will be there on time, I promise. | *There is no doubt that we shall win.*

→   see also SURE/NOT SURE

HOW TO USE MODAL VERBS

● Modal verbs are used with the basic form of the verb (=the infinitive form, without 'to').

You must pay now. **NOT** *You must to pay now*
They can go home if they want. **NOT** *They can to go home if they want.*

● Modal verbs do not have an **–s** ending in the present tense of the third person singular.

He can speak French. **NOT** *He cans speak French.*

● Modal verbs are not used with **do** in questions or negatives.

Can you remember her name? **NOT** *Do you can remember her name?*
We must not be late. **NOT** *We don't must be late.*
Should we lock the door? **NOT** *Do we should lock the door?*

● Modal verbs do not have an infinitive, a past participle, or a present participle.

● In spoken English, you often use short forms when you use the modal verb in the negative.

cannot	→ can't
could not	→ couldn't
will not	→ won't
must not	→ mustn't
shall not	→ shan't
might not	→ mightn't
would not	→ wouldn't
should not	→ shouldn't
ought not	→ oughtn't

 Mustn't, shan't, mightn't, and **oughtn't** are normal in British English, but American speakers usually say **must not, shall not, might not**, and **ought not**.

8 Conditionals

When you want to say that one situation (described in the main clause) depends on another situation, you use a conditional clause. Conditional clauses usually begin with **if** or (for negative clauses) **unless**.

Jane will pass the exam if she works hard.
Jane will not pass the exam unless she works hard.

They may follow or go in front of the main clause.

If Jane works hard, she will pass her exam.

Conditional clauses are used in two main ways:

● If you see the situation as a real one, and likely to happen, you use the simple present tense in the conditional clause and **will** (**'ll**) or **won't** in the main clause. Don't use **will** in the conditional clause.

If you take a taxi, you will be there in good time. **NOT** *If you will take a taxi ...*
If you wear a coat, you won't get cold. **NOT** *If you will wear a coat ...*

- If you see the situation as unreal, imaginary, or less likely to happen, you use the simple past tense in the conditional clause and **would ('d)**, **might**, or **could** in the main clause. Don't use **would** in the conditional clause.

    If you saw a ghost, what would you do? **NOT** *If you would see a ghost ...*
    If I bought a new coat, I might not feel so cold. (=I would possibly not feel so cold)
    If I found their address, I could write to them. (=I would be able to write to them)

In sentences of this kind, the past tense of the verb **be** appears as **were** after the first and third persons, in formal speech and writing. Only use **was** in informal speech.

    If I were at home, I would be watching television. (informal: *If I was at home ...*)
    If John were playing today, we'd have a chance of winning. (informal: *If John was playing ...*)

- If you want to talk about conditional situations in the past, use **had ('d)** in the conditional clause, and **would have** in the main clause.

    If I'd seen her, I would have asked her to call. (=I did not see her)
    The books wouldn't have been damaged if Mary had moved them. (=Mary didn't move them)

- You can use **when** instead of **if** in sentences of the first type (simple present + **will** etc), but not with those of the second (simple past + **would** etc). **When** is not used for situations that are unlikely or impossible.

    What will John do if he goes home? (=John is probably going home)
    OR *What will John do when he goes home?* (=John is definitely going home)

    What would John do if he went home? (=John is probably not going home)
    NOT *What would John do when he went home?*

    I would shout if I saw a ghost. **NOT** *I would shout when I saw a ghost.*

I wish

If you want to talk about a situation in the present which you are not happy about, and would like to change, use the simple past tense in a clause after **I wish**.

    I wish I had a new bike. (=unfortunately, I don't have a new bike)

If you want to talk about a situation in the past which you are not happy about, and would like to change, use **had**.

    I wish I'd gone by train. (=unfortunately, I didn't go by train)
    I wish I hadn't gone by train. (=unfortunately, I did go by train)

9 Active and passive

In the sentence *The dog chased the cat*, the verb (*chased*) is active. If you turn it around, and say *The cat was chased by the dog*, the verb (*was chased*) is passive. You form the passive by using the verb **be** and the past participle of the main verb. For example, the passive of **attack** is **be attacked**, the passive of **pay** is **be paid**, and the passive of **see** is **be seen**. You can only use the passive with transitive verbs (see section **2**).

WHEN TO USE AN ACTIVE VERB

You use an active verb when you want to say that the subject of a sentence does something. For example:

    She opened the window.

WHEN TO USE A PASSIVE VERB

You use a passive verb when you want to say that something happens to the subject of the sentence. For example:

    President Kennedy was killed in 1963.

You often use a passive verb when talking about the history of something. For example:

The bridge was built in the 19th century. | *The company was established in 1826.*

In these cases, it is much more natural to use the passive than to find a vague, active way of expressing the sentence (such as *Someone built this bridge in the 19th century.*)

You often use a passive verb when you are writing about science, or when you are saying how things are made. For example:

Hydrogen and oxygen can be easily mixed in this way.
Paper is made from wood.

If you used an active verb here, you would have to say who does the action – information which is not known or not important.

If you want to say who does the action of the verb in a passive sentence, use **by** and then say who does it.

President Kennedy was killed by Lee Harvey Oswald in 1963.
The bridge was designed by Brunel.

HOW TO CHANGE AN ACTIVE SENTENCE INTO A PASSIVE ONE

There are three things you need to do in order to change an active sentence into a passive one.

1   Move the subject of the active verb to the end of the sentence, and put **by** in front of it.

2   Move the object of the active verb to the front of the sentence, so that it becomes the passive subject.

3   Change the verb from active to passive. You do this by adding a form of the auxiliary verb **be** and changing the main verb to the past participle form (see section **4**).

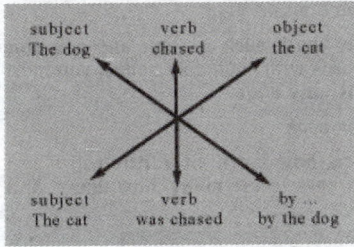

THE PASSIVE WITH 'GET'

You can also make a passive using **get** instead of **be**. This kind of passive is very common in conversation. Do not use it in formal writing. You often use this kind of passive to say that something happened suddenly to someone.

I got sacked by my firm.   **OR**   *I was sacked by my firm.*
He got hit by a car.   **OR**   *He was hit by a car.*

You can also use the passive with **get** when you want to suggest that an action is more forceful or more important to you.

I get paid on Thursday.   **OR**   *I am paid on Thursday.*
We often get asked this question.   **OR**   *We are often asked this question.*

10 Nouns: countable and uncountable

COUNTABLE NOUNS

A noun is 'countable' if you can think of it as one of several separate units, for example **book**, **egg**, or **horse**. As the name suggests, countable nouns can actually be counted.

UNCOUNTABLE NOUNS

A noun is 'uncountable' if you cannot think of it as one of several separate units, but only as a single idea or substance, for example **butter**, **music**, or **advice**. These nouns are sometimes called 'mass' nouns. They cannot be counted.

GRAMMATICAL DIFFERENCES

There are some important grammatical differences in the way you use countable and uncountable nouns.

1 You can use a countable noun in the singular or in the plural, for example **book/books**, **egg/eggs**, **horse/horses**, **ticket/tickets**, **university/universities**. Don't try to use uncountable nouns in the plural. Don't say **butters**, **musics**, **advices**, **informations**, **furnitures**. It is a common mistake to use an uncountable noun in the plural.

You should listen to his advice.   **NOT**   *You should listen to his advices.*

2 You can use a countable noun with **a** or **an**: for example **a book**, **an egg**, **a horse**, **a ticket**, **a university**. Don't use **a** or **an** with uncountable nouns. Don't say **a butter**, **a music**, **an advice**, **an information**, **a furniture**. It is a common mistake to use **a** or **an** with an uncountable noun.

I like listening to music.   **NOT**   *I like listening to a music.*

3 You can use an uncountable noun with quantity words such as **some** and **any**: **some butter**, **any music**. If you want to use these words with countable nouns, you must put the nouns into the plural, and say **some tickets**, **any eggs**.

She bought some books.   **NOT**   *She bought some book.*

4 You can only use the quantity expressions **much**, **how much**, or **a little** with uncountable nouns. With countable nouns, you have to use **many**, **how many**, or **a few**.

uncountable	countable
I don't have much money.	He doesn't have many friends.
How much time do you have?	How many records do you have?
There is a little butter in the fridge.	There are a few rooms still available.

5 You can use an uncountable noun on its own without such words as **the**, **some**, or **any**.

She doesn't eat meat. | *If you need advice, don't be afraid to ask.*

You cannot use a countable noun in the singular in this way – only in the plural.

I like reading books.   **NOT**   *I like reading book.*
Computers are always causing problems.   **NOT**   *Computers are always causing problem.*

NOUNS WHICH CAN BE COUNTABLE OR UNCOUNTABLE

You can use some nouns in either a countable or an uncountable way, depending on their meaning. The following pairs of sentences show how the meaning can change: in each case there is a countable noun in the first sentence, and an uncountable noun in the second.

Would you like a cake? (=one of several cakes which someone can take to eat)
Do you like chocolate cake? (=a type of food)
The lambs were born early this year. (=the animals)
There are several ways of cooking lamb. (=a type of meat)

Most abstract nouns, such as **love**, **anger**, **knowledge**, **intelligence**, or **freedom**, are always uncountable. But some abstract nouns can also be used in a countable way.

uncountable	countable
They did it with difficulty.	*They've had a lot of difficulties.*
Her voice sounded full of doubt.	*I have my doubts about whether he's the right person for the job.*

11 Nouns: singular and plural

Most countable nouns (see section **10**) have both a singular and a plural form, showing the difference between 'one' and 'more than one'.

REGULAR PLURALS

The regular way of changing a noun from singular to plural is to add **–s** or **–es** at the end.

dog – dogs, chair – chairs, difference – differences, dress – dresses, watch – watches

For nouns ending in **–y**, you drop the **–y** and add **–ies** to form the plural, if the **–y** follows a consonant.

dictionary – dictionaries, opportunity – opportunities

For some nouns ending in **–o**, you add **–es** to form the plural, for others you add **-s**.

tomato – tomatoes, potato – potatoes, radio – radios, cello – cellos

IRREGULAR PLURALS

There are also several irregular ways of forming a plural.

1 With seven nouns you change the vowel. They are:

man – men, woman – women, foot – feet, goose – geese, mouse – mice, tooth – teeth, louse – lice

2 With a few nouns you change the final **–f** to **–v** before adding the **–s** ending. They include:

knife – knives, leaf – leaves, wife – wives, half – halves

Some nouns in this group have a regular plural as well: **scarfs** and **scarves**, **hoofs** and **hooves**. Both possibilities are correct.

3 With three nouns you add **–en**. They are:

ox – oxen, child – children, brother – brethren (only in the religious sense)

4 A few nouns which have been borrowed from foreign languages have an irregular plural. They include:

stimulus – stimuli, crisis – crises, criterion – criteria, phenomenon – phenomena

Often these nouns have two plurals: they have developed a regular plural but have also kept their original irregular one. In these cases, the regular form is more informal and popular; the irregular form tends to be used by specialists.

There are no certain formulas for success. (informal)
We have to learn all the relevant chemical formulae. (specialist)

5 A few nouns have no plural ending, but you can still use them in a singular or plural way: they include the names of some animals (such as **sheep**, **deer**, **cod**), some nouns expressing quantity (such as **ton**, **p** (=pence)), and a few others (such as **aircraft**, **crossroads**, **kennels**, **offspring**).

The sheep was making a noise.   *The sheep were making a noise.*

PLURALS FOR COMPOUND NOUNS

Compound nouns combine two or more words into a single unit. You usually make them plural by adding **–s** at the end of the word: **can–openers**, **grown–ups**. But in a few cases, the first part of the compound takes the **–s** ending, especially when the compound contains an adverb or preposition.

runner–up – runners–up, passer–by – passers–by, man–of–war – men–of–war

Sometimes, a regular plural form has developed, which is slowly replacing the irregular one.

spoonfuls (also *spoonsful*)
mother–in–laws (also *mothers–in–law*)

NOUNS WHICH ARE ONLY SINGULAR

Several nouns are used only in the singular. There are three main types:

1 Proper names – names of particular people, places, times, occasions, events, and so on.

John, Robinson, Christmas, Tuesday

You can use these in the plural only if you think of them in a 'countable' way. This is especially common with proper nouns expressing time.

On Tuesdays I go swimming. | *Are the Robinsons coming to the party?* | *We stayed with Mary three Christmases ago.*

2 Most uncountable nouns, such as **music** and **advice**, are only singular (see section **10**).

3 A group of nouns which you use in the singular, even though they end in **–s**. These include the names of certain subjects, diseases, and games.

physics, linguistics, mumps, measles, billiards

A common mistake is to think of these as plural, and use them with a plural verb or form a singular noun from them.

Linguistics is fascinating.   **NOT**   *Linguistics are fascinating.*
Billiards is a game.   **NOT**   *Billiards are a game.*
Poor Mike's got measles.   **NOT**   *Poor Mike's got a measle.*

NOUNS WHICH ARE ONLY PLURAL

Several nouns are used only in the plural. There are three main types:

1 A few nouns are related to things consisting of two joined parts. They include **jeans**, **binoculars**, **trousers**, **pliers**, **scissors**. To talk about these in the singular, you use **a pair of**.

Your jeans are in the wash.   **NOT**   *Your jeans is in the wash.*
I need to buy another pair of jeans.   **NOT**   *I need to buy another jeans.*
                                          NOT   *I need to buy another jean.*

2 A few nouns ending in **–s** are used only in the plural. They include **congratulations**, **outskirts**, **remains**, **clothes**, **thanks**.

His clothes were dirty.   **NOT**   *His clothes was dirty.*
                            NOT   *His clothe was dirty.*

These are not uncountable nouns, because they are used with a plural verb, not a singular verb.

3 A few nouns express the idea of groups of people or animals. They include **people**, **folk**, **police**, **cattle**, **poultry**, **livestock**.

The police are outside. **NOT** *The police is outside.*
NOT *The polices are outside.*

12 Determiners and articles

'Determiners' are used before a noun to 'determine' the character of the noun – in particular, how 'definite' or 'general' a noun it is, and whether it is 'one' or 'more than one'. When you use a noun, you have the choice of using it in one of three possible states.

1 You can use the noun without any determiner at all.

- in the singular, if it is a proper noun   *Boston is on the east coast.*
- in the singular, if it is an uncountable noun   *I can hear music.*
- in the plural, if it is a countable noun   *Tigers have black stripes.*

When you use a plural countable noun without a determiner, you are seeing the noun in a general way – 'tigers in general'.

2 You can use the noun with either of the 'articles', **a** or **the**:

- use **a** with singular countable nouns   *I can see a car.*
- use **the** with singular countable nouns   *I can see the car.*
- use **the** with plural countable nouns   *I can see the cars.*
- use **the** with uncountable nouns   *I can see the water.*

The articles are the most common determiners in English. Their main job is to say whether the noun is 'definite' or 'indefinite'.

3 You can use the noun with one of the other determiners. This adds a further meaning to the noun. For example:

determiner	adds the meaning of
my book	'possession' (also **our**, **his**, **her** etc)
this book	'nearness to the speaker' (also plural **these**)
that book	'distance from the speaker' (also plural **those**)
some books	'quantity' (also **any**)
enough books	'sufficiency'
each book	'item by item' (also **every**)
either book	'one of two' (also **neither**)
no book	'absence'
what book	'unknown item' (also **which**, **whose** etc)

 You cannot use two determiners at the same time. Don't say things like 'the this car', 'my an apple', or 'some the cups'.

You can use other words or phrases expressing quantity in front of a determiner to make the meaning of the noun phrase more exact.

NOTE: *(of)* shows that you can leave out the word **of**.

all (of) the people	*both (of) the cats*	*half (of) the gold*
double the amount	*twice the cost*	*a third of the people*
a few of the cars	*half (of) that cake*	*some of those cakes*

You can also add certain quantity words after the determiner. They include the numerals, as well as a few general expressions of quantity.

*The **three** kittens were playing on the floor.* | *I've just taken my **fourth** examination.* | *He bought it on one of his **many** trips abroad.*

If you want to add adjectives to the noun phrase (see section **13**), they always follow any determiners or other quantity expressions.

> the three little kittens
> my fourth difficult examination
> his many interesting trips

WHEN TO USE 'A' AND 'THE'

A and **the** are called 'the articles'. **A** is called 'the indefinite article', and **the** is called 'the definite article'. They are used in the following ways:

1   The main use of **a** and **the** is to say whether you are talking about a noun for the first time, or whether you have mentioned it before. For a first–time mention, use **a**; for later mentions, use **the**.

> Mary bought a car and **a bike**, but she used **the bike** more often.

2   If you use **the** with a noun that you have not mentioned before, you are actually saying to your listener 'you know which one I mean'. This is usually because there is only one example of the noun in the situation, or you have only one such example in your mind. That is why it is 'definite'.

> Have you fed the cat? (=you have only one cat)
> There's the hotel. (=that is the hotel we have been looking for)
> I met him during the war. (=both you and your listener know which war you mean)
> Pass the salt, please.

3   If you want to talk about something of a particular type in an indefinite way, use **a**.

> I'm training to be an engineer.   **NOT**   I'm training to be engineer.
> I went out to buy a newspaper.   **NOT**   I went out to buy newspaper.

4   Use **a** when you are talking about one of several things or people and it is not important to say which one. Use **the** when it is clear that you are talking about one particular thing or person and there is only one.

> A man I work with told me about it. (=you work with several men)
> The man I work with told me about it. (=you work with only one man)

5   You must use **the** with singular nouns such as **world**, **sky**, or **sun**, because there is only one of these things in the situation that you are talking about.

> We're going to travel round the world.
> Don't look directly at the sun.

6   If you are talking about buildings, places, and organizations as things which you often see or visit, use **the**. For example **the bank**, **the theatre**, **the cinema** etc.

> I went to the theatre last week.
> She's at the gym.

 When **a** is used before a word that begins with a vowel, it changes to **an**.

WHEN NOT TO USE 'A' OR 'THE'

1   If you want to use a countable noun in the plural to talk in general about something, don't use **the**.

> Tigers are very fierce animals. | Prices keep going up.

2   If you want to use an uncountable noun to talk in general about something, don't use **the**.

> There has been a big increase in crime.   **NOT**   There has been a big increase in the crime.

It takes patience and skill to be a teacher. **NOT** *It takes the patience and the skill to be a teacher.*

3 Most names of places or people that begin with a capital letter do not have **the** before them. Don't use **the** with these names.

They're visiting Belgium and Holland **NOT** *They're visiting the Belgium and the Holland.*

However, there are some names that always have **the** in them, for example **the United States**, **the Nile** (=the big river in Egypt) etc. Don't forget to put **the** in these names.

He's from the United States. **NOT** *He's from United States.*

There are also many common nouns and phrases which are not used with **a** or **the**. This is especially true when talking about meals, illnesses, ways of travelling, times, and periods of time.

Will you have lunch with me? **NOT** *Will you have the lunch with me?*
Her mother has cancer. **NOT** *Her mother has the cancer.*
I travel to work by bus. **NOT** *I travel to work by the bus.*
In winter we get a lot of snow. **NOT** *In winter we get a lot of the snow.*
It's time to go to bed. **NOT** *It's time to go to the bed.*
We got up at dawn. **NOT** *We got up at the dawn.*

13 Word order

This section deals with two areas which can cause problems for students: word order with adjectives before a noun, and word order with adverbs.

WORD ORDER WITH ADJECTIVES BEFORE A NOUN

The main way of describing a noun is to use adjectives or words that are like adjectives. You add these words after **a**, **the**, **my**, **her** etc, before the noun. You can add as many as you want, but you sometimes need to be careful about the order in which you use them.

You have a choice of three kinds of word. The largest group consists of adjectives.

*a **lovely** day*   *a **small round** table*   *the **best** students*

You may also use a 'participle' before the noun – the **–ing** or **–ed** form of a verb, but here used to describe the noun.

*a **crumbling** wall*   *her **smiling** face*   *a **cracked** window*   *the **stolen** car*

You may also add one noun before another – the first noun is used to describe the second noun, which is the main noun in the phrase.

*the **school** buildings*   *a **tourist** paradise*   *a **London** bus*

WHICH ORDER?

As soon as you use two or more describing words, you have to decide which order to put them in.

In many cases, there is no rule: you simply say first what comes into your mind first. But many adjectives, and the other kinds of describing word, are typically used in a particular place before the noun. You should think of these patterns only as a guide to help you, because there are a number of cases which do not follow the rule. But the following patterns are common:

1 Nouns go next to the main noun in the phrase, after any other adjectives.

a big London bus **NOT** *a London big bus*
the long country road **NOT** *the country long road*

2 Words which are closely related to nouns, such as the material something is made of or where something is from, also go next to the main noun.

big leather boots **NOT** *leather big boots*

a serious social problem **NOT** *a social serious problem*

3 Participles usually go in front of groups (1) and (2), but after any adjectives.

a broken garden chair **NOT** *a garden broken chair*
a smiling American tourist **NOT** *an American smiling tourist*
a happy smiling American tourist **NOT** *a smiling happy American tourist*

4 Adjectives with an 'intensifying' meaning, for example **entire**, **whole**, **same** go near the beginning, close to **a**, **the**, **my**, **her** etc.

the entire local committee **NOT** *the local entire committee*
the same old battered car **NOT** *the old battered same car*

5 Other adjectives follow (4) and go before (3). Those with a more general meaning usually come first, and those which describe properties of the noun which can be clearly seen, such as size and shape, usually come last. There are typical patterns here, too, as the table shows.

those lovely red curtains **NOT** *those red lovely curtains*
a strange triangular table **NOT** *a triangular strange table*

your opinion about sth	size	age	shape	colour	where sth is from	material
lovely	big	old	round	black	American	wool
beautiful	little	young	square	red	French	plastic
horrible	small	new	L-shaped	brown	Japanese	leather
etc	etc	etc	etc	etc	etc	etc

WORD ORDER WITH ADVERBS

Some adverbs of time and frequency usually come immediately after the subject, an auxiliary or modal verb, or the main verb **be**. These include:

always	**almost**	**just**
rarely	**nearly**	**already**
ever	**never**	**still**

She always looks nice. **NOT** *Always she looks nice.*
They are still working. **NOT** *Still they are working.*
Dinner is almost ready. **NOT** *Almost dinner is ready.*

Always and **never** are sometimes used at the beginning of a sentence in instructions and warnings, when the verb does not have a subject.

Always keep medicines away from children. | *Never look directly at the sun through a telescope.*

Adverbs and adverb phrases should not come between the verb and the object.

I like Japanese food very much. **NOT** *I like very much Japanese food.*

Adverbs and adverb phrases should not come between a main verb and an **–ing** participle, or between a main verb and an infinitive.

Tomorrow we'll go sightseeing. **NOT** *We'll go tomorrow sightseeing.*
In the evenings she likes to watch television. **NOT** *She likes in the evenings to watch television.*

Adverbs and adverb phrases (apart from the ones like **always** mentioned above) should not come between a modal verb (for example **can**, **must**, **could**) and a main verb.

I can speak Spanish quite well. **NOT** *I can quite well speak Spanish.*

OTHER WORD ORDER PROBLEMS

The Essential Activator also has information about word order with the following words:

all ➔ see **ALL** | **both** ➔ see **TWO** | **each** ➔ see **ALL**

14 Comparison

COMPARATIVE AND SUPERLATIVE ADJECTIVES

If you want to compare two things, you use the comparative form of an adjective. For example the comparative form of **big** is **bigger**, and the comparative form of **interesting** is **more interesting**.

Your car is bigger than mine.
His new book is more interesting than his last one.

If you want to say that one thing is bigger, faster, more interesting etc than all the others of a group of things, you use the superlative form of an adjective. For example, the superlative form of **big** is **biggest**, and the superlative form of **interesting** is **the most interesting**.

It's the fastest motorcycle in the world.
What's the most delicious food you've ever eaten?

CHOOSING THE RIGHT FORM OF THE ADJECTIVE

If the adjective is one syllable long, you add **–er** or **–est** to it, sometimes making a change in the spelling.

adjective	comparative	superlative
tall	taller	tallest
big	bigger	biggest
nice	nicer	nicest

If the adjective is three or more syllables long, you add the words **more** or **most** before it.

That's a more interesting question. | *Kim's question was the most interesting one.* | *The new trains are more comfortable than the old ones.* | *That's the most comfortable bed I've ever slept in.*

Most adjectives with two syllables are used with **more** and **most** to form the comparative and superlative, but some two–syllable adjectives have **–er/–est** endings, and some two–syllable adjectives can have either kind of comparative and superlative.

The **–er/–est** endings are possible with adjectives ending in **–y**, **–ow**, **–le**, **–er**, **–ure**. Don't forget that with adjectives that end in **–y**, the **–y** changes to **–i**.

adjective	comparative	superlative
happy	happier	happiest
gentle	gentler	gentlest
narrow	narrower	narrowest
clever	cleverer	cleverest

You keep this pattern when **un–** is added to a two–syllable adjective.

unhappier/unhappiest

Proper and **eager** do not follow this rule: you can use only **more/most** with them.

You use **more/most** with all other two–syllable adjectives.

more/most active   more/most useful   more/most recent

In this dictionary, comparatives and superlatives are shown at the end of the entry if there is anything irregular or unpredictable about them.

ADJECTIVES THAT DO NOT FOLLOW THE NORMAL RULES

Not all adjectives follow the normal rules. Some adjectives have completely irregular forms. The most common ones are:

adjective	comparative	superlative
good	better	best
bad	worse	worst

In this dictionary, we show these irregular forms at the end of the entry.

Words which are formed from a verb, and which end in **–ing**, **–ed**, or other past forms, are always used with **more/most**, no matter how many syllables they have.

His latest film is even more boring than his previous ones.
She was more shocked than I was.

COMPARING TWO THINGS WHICH ARE THE SAME

If you want to say that two things are the same size, the same height etc, you can say that one thing is as big as the other, as tall as the other etc.

She's as tall as her sister.
Do you think this summer will be as hot as last summer?

COMPARING TWO THINGS WHICH ARE NOT THE SAME

If you want to say that two things are not the same size, the same height etc, you can say that one thing is **not as big as** the other, **not as tall as** the other etc.

The meal wasn't as good as the last meal I had there.
I'm not as fat as him.   **OR**   *I'm not as fat as he is.*
London is not as expensive as some other European cities.

You can use **less ... than** to mean the same thing as **not as ... as**, but you usually use it with adjectives that have two or more syllables, for example **less expensive**, **less important**.

Value for money is less important than quality and reliability.

 Don't use **less** with short adjectives such as **good**, **old** etc.

You can leave out the second **as** and the noun after it, if you have already mentioned or suggested the second thing that you are comparing.

The material looks like silk, but it's not as expensive. (=not as expensive as silk)

Similarly, you can also leave out the **than** part of the comparison when you are using **less**, if you have already mentioned or suggested the second thing that you are comparing.

I prefer the old Hollywood movies. They're much less violent. (=than modern films)
The buses are less crowded after 10 o'clock. (=than they are before 10 o'clock)

If you want to say that one type of thing is less expensive, less important etc than all other things of the same type, you can say that it **is the least expensive**, **the least important** etc.

People usually choose the least expensive brand.

 Don't use **least** with short adjectives such as **good**, **old** etc.

15 Reported speech

REPORTING STATEMENTS

Direct speech

If you want to write what someone has said, the simplest way is to repeat the exact words that they used inside quotation marks ("..."). This is called 'direct speech'.

"I really enjoyed the meal," he said. | *She went upstairs and shouted, "Time to get up!"*

If you mention the speaker at the end of the sentence, and do not say **he**, **she**, **I** etc, you usually reverse the order of the subject and the verb. For example:

"It's much too cold to swim," said Frank. | *"Go back to your room," said her mother.*

Indirect speech

You can also report what someone has said without using quotation marks. This is called 'indirect speech'. The usual way of doing this is to use a clause which begins with + **(that)**. For example:

"I'm tired!" (direct speech)
He said he was tired. **OR** *He said that he was tired.* (indirect speech)

That is more common in written English and in formal spoken English.

Changing from direct to indirect speech

When changing from direct to indirect speech, you need to change the grammar in certain ways.

Verb tense forms usually need to change. In most cases, you change the present tense into the past tense.

She said, "I am staying at the Chelsea Hotel."
She said that she was staying at the Chelsea Hotel.

If the direct speech is already in the past tense, you need to put the verb even further back in time, using **had**. This applies to both past tense and present perfect forms of the verb (see section **4**).

He said, "I came by bus." | *He said that he had come by bus.* | *She said, "I've definitely seen John recently."* | *She said that she had definitely seen John recently.*

However, you do not use this rule if the verb in the direct speech already uses **had**.

She said, "I had given up hope of seeing him again." | *She said that she had given up hope of seeing him again.*

The correct relationship between the verbs in the reporting clause and the verb in the reported clause is called the 'sequence of tenses'.

If you report something that someone said which is still true now, you do not need to change the tense of the verb.

"I want to get married."
She said she wants to get married.
"Blue's my favourite colour."
She said that blue's her favourite colour.

If the direct speech contains **will**, **shall**, or **may** (see section **7**), these also need to change.

will → **would**   **shall** → **should**   **may** → **might**
She said, "I will see you soon."
She said that she would see us soon.

Would, **should**, **could**, **might**, and **must** do not change.
She said, "I could visit him on Thursday."
She said she could visit him on Thursday.

You also need to change certain personal pronouns. **I** and **you** have to be changed to **he** and **she**, unless the original people are still taking part in the conversation. Similarly, **my** and **your** need to be changed to **his** and **her**.

> *Mary said to John, "I saw your cat."*
> *Mary said that she had seen your cat.* (if the person who says this is talking to John)
> *Mary said that she had seen his/John's cat.* (if the person who says this is not talking to John)

You also need to change times and places which depend on the speaker's point of view.

> *He said, "I saw the car here yesterday."* | *He said that he'd seen the car there the day before.*

In this case **here** becomes **there** because you are in a different place, and **yesterday** becomes **the day before** because you are now speaking at a later time.

Similarly, **now** becomes **then**, **last week** becomes **the week before**, **two months ago** becomes **two months before**, **tomorrow** becomes **the next day**, and so on. Of course, if the time phrase does not depend on the speaker's point of view, it can be used without change.

> *He said, "I bought the car in November 1996."* | *He said he had bought the car in November 1996.*

REPORTING QUESTIONS

When you are changing a question from direct speech into indirect speech, you follow the same kinds of rules as for statements. The only differences are that you need to use a different word to introduce the reported speech, and the word order of the question becomes like that of a statement. You end the sentence with a full stop, not a question mark.

You use **if** or **whether** to introduce a 'yes–no question'.

> *I asked, "Does he eat meat?"*
> *I asked whether he ate meat.*   **OR**   *I asked if he ate meat.*

You introduce questions where there is a choice in the same way – more usually by using **whether** than by using **if**.

> *I asked, "Is it Karen's book or Michael's?"* | *I asked whether it was Karen's book or Michael's.*

You introduce questions that begin with **who**, **why**, **what**, **how** etc by using the word which begins the question in direct speech.

> *Someone asked, "Why doesn't she resign?"* | *Someone asked why she didn't resign.* | *She asked, "When will you go back to Japan?"* | *She asked when he would go back to Japan.*

You often mention the person who is being asked the question, by using a pronoun (**him**, **her**, **them** etc) or by mentioning their name.

> *I asked him if he ate meat.*
> *She asked Michael when he would go back to Japan.*

REPORTING WHAT SOMEONE HAS TOLD OR ASKED ANOTHER PERSON TO DO

When saying what someone has told or asked another person to do, you usually use an infinitive.

> *"Go home!"* | *She told him to go home.* | *"Can you shut the window?"* | *She asked him to shut the window.*

 Don't confuse **say** and **tell**. Don't say 'He said me to go home.' or 'He told, Go home!' Say **He told me to go home**. or **He said, "Go home!"**

INDEX

INDEX

INDEX

When you see **WB**, go to the **WORD BANKS** section

INDEX

B

INDEX

INDEX

INDEX

When you see **EC**, go to the **ESSENTIAL COMMUNICATION** section

INDEX

INDEX

INDEX

INDEX

When you see **EC**, go to the **ESSENTIAL COMMUNICATION** section

INDEX

When you see **WB**, go to the **WORD BANKS** section

INDEX

E

INDEX

INDEX

F

INDEX

INDEX

When you see **EC**, go to the **ESSENTIAL COMMUNICATION** section

When you see **WB**, go to the **WORD BANKS** section

INDEX

INDEX

H

When you see **EC**, go to the **ESSENTIAL COMMUNICATION** section

INDEX

INDEX

INDEX

INDEX

INDEX

When you see **EC**, go to the **ESSENTIAL COMMUNICATION** section

INDEX

L

INDEX

INDEX

When you see **EC**, go to the **ESSENTIAL COMMUNICATION** section

INDEX

INDEX

When you see **EC**, go to the **ESSENTIAL COMMUNICATION** section

INDEX

INDEX

INDEX

INDEX

pass the time ....SPEND 6
passenger .... **WB** TRAVEL 5
passion ....LOVE 3
passionate ... **WB** DESCRIBING PEOPLE'S CHARACTER 1;
FEEL 7; LOVE 4
passport control.......................... **WB** TRAVEL 9
past .... AFTER 2; LAST 3; PASS 2; PAST 1
past: in the past...PAST 2
past: it's ten past five ....TIME 5
past: sb's past ....PAST 1
past: the past ....PAST 1
paste: cut and paste .... **WB** COMPUTERS/INTERNET 3
pastel ....COLOUR/COLOR 4
pat...TOUCH 2
patch ....AREA 3; MARK 1
paternal ....FATHER 2
path ....ROAD/PATH 4
patient .... **WB** DESCRIBING PEOPLE'S CHARACTER 1;
ILL/SICK 3; WAIT 4
patriotic..COUNTRY 7
pattern ....ORDER 1; PATTERN 1
patterned ....PATTERN 1
pause ....STOP 2, 3
pavement ....ROAD/PATH 4
pay ....EARN 4; PAY 1, 2, 4
pay: not pay any attention ....OBEY/DISOBEY 2
pay attention.................................LISTEN 1; THINK 2
pay attention to sth ....CAREFUL 2
pay back ....PAY 6
pay in/into ....BANKS 2
pay off ....PAY 6
pay rise ....INCREASE 5
pay £5/$10 etc for sth ....SPEND 1
payment ....PAY 1
PC.............................. **WB** COMPUTERS/INTERNET 1
peace ....PEACE 1; QUIET 1
peace: make peace ....PEACE 2
peace treaty ....PEACE 2
peaceful.................................PEACE 1; QUIET 1
peacetime..PEACE 1
peak: be at your peak................................BEST 2
peak: the peak season .... **WB** TRAVEL 3
peck ....BITE 1
peckish ....HUNGRY 1
peculiar ....STRANGE 1
pedestrian ....WALK 7
peek/take a peek.................................LOOK AT 3
peep ....LOOK AT 3
penalty ....PUNISH 2
penalty: the death penalty ....KILL 4
peninsula...LAND AND SEA 11
pension...MONEY 3
pensioner/old age pensioner ....OLD 2
people ....PERSON/PEOPLE 1
people: the people ....PERSON/PEOPLE 3
people: they say/people say........................SAY 12
per person ....PERSON/PEOPLE 5
perceive..NOTICE 1
percentage ....AMOUNT/NUMBER 3; PART 6
perceptive ....NOTICE 3
perfect ....PERFECT 1, 2
perform ....ACTOR/ACTRESS 2; DO 1; **WB** MUSIC 1
perform: be in sth/appear in sth/perform in
sth .... **WB** THEATRE/PLAYS 5
performance ...ACTOR/ACTRESS 2; **WB** FILMS/MOVIES 5;
WB MUSIC 4; **WB** THEATRE/PLAYS 2, 5
perfume ....SMELL 5
perhaps: maybe/perhaps ....MAYBE 1
period ....TIME 13
perm ....HAIR 5
permanent ....ALWAYS 2, 4; CHANGE 9
permission ....LET 3
permission: give permission ....LET 1
permit ....LET 3
permitted: be permitted ....LET 2
persecute ....CRUEL 3
perseverance ....DETERMINED 6
person...PERSON/PEOPLE 1

person: businessman/businesswoman/business
person ....BUSINESS 4
person: in person ....MYSELF/YOURSELF 1
person: per person ....PERSON/PEOPLE 5
personal..PRIVATE 1
personally...............................MYSELF/YOURSELF 1
persuade ....PERSUADE 1, 3
persuade sb not to do sth ....PERSUADE 4
persuasion ....PERSUADE 4
persuasive..PERSUADE 4
pessimist ....EXPECT 4
pessimistic ... **WB** DESCRIBING PEOPLE'S CHARACTER 1;
EXPECT 4
pesticides .... **WB** ENVIRONMENT 3
pet...TOUCH 2
pet: teacher's pet .....FAVOURITE/FAVORITE 1; LIKE/NOT
LIKE 4
petty ....IMPORTANT/NOT IMPORTANT 6
pharmacy ....SHOP 2
phase ....PART 4
PhD: doctorate/PhD .... **WB** EDUCATION 11
phone .... MAIL, PHONE, AND FAX 2, 3
phone: answer the phone/telephone ....MAIL, PHONE,
AND FAX 3
phone: call back/phone back ... MAIL, PHONE, AND FAX 3
phone: call/phone call .... MAIL, PHONE, AND FAX 3
phone: cellular phone ....MAIL, PHONE, AND FAX 2
phone: mobile phone .....MAIL, PHONE, AND FAX 2
phone: pick up the phone .....MAIL, PHONE, AND FAX 3
phone: put the phone down ...MAIL, PHONE, AND FAX 3
phone number/telephone number ....MAIL, PHONE, AND
FAX 2
phone-in .... **WB** TELEVISION AND RADIO 4
photo/picture...PICTURE 2
photocopy ....COPY 1, 2
photograph ....ART 2, 6; PICTURE 2
photographer ....ART 5
photography ....PICTURE 2
phrase/expression ....WORD/PHRASE/SENTENCE 1
physical ....BODY 3
physician ....DOCTOR 1
physiotherapy .... **WB** MEDICAL TREATMENT 3
physique ....BODY 3
pick ....CHOOSE 1, 2
pick at sth ....EAT 4
pick holes in sth ....CRITICIZE 2
pick up ... IMPROVE 1; LEARN 1; LIFT 1; TAKE/BRING 2;
TIDY 2
pick up the phone ....MAIL, PHONE, AND FAX 3
pickpocket...STEAL 4
picky: fussy/picky ....CHOOSE 6
picnic ....MEAL 5
picnic: have a picnic .... **WB** FREE TIME 3
picture ....ART 2; IMAGINE 1; PICTURE 1
picture: photo/picture ....PICTURE 2
picturesque ....BEAUTIFUL 6
piece ....PART 1; PIECE 1
piece: be a piece of cake ....EASY 2
piercing ....HIGH 4
pig ....EAT 6
pig-headed ....DETERMINED 4
piglet...BABY 6
Pilates.. **WB** EXERCISE 1
pile ....GROUP 6; PUT 2
pile-up ....ACCIDENT 2
pinch ....PRESS 1
pinch: nick/pinch...STEAL 4
pirate ....COPY 4
pitch .... **WB** SPORT 6; THROW 2
pity ....SORRY 4
pity: it's a pity/it's a shame ...............UNFORTUNATELY 1
place ....HOME 1; PLACE 1; SIT 3
place: a place to stay/somewhere to stay ....STAY 4
place: every place ....EVERYWHERE 1
place: first place ....WIN 1
place: in place of sth ....INSTEAD 1
place: in sb's place...INSTEAD 2
place: out of place ....SUITABLE/UNSUITABLE 2
place: somewhere to live/a place to live ....HOME 2

INDEX

INDEX

INDEX

INDEX

INDEX

INDEX

INDEX

INDEX

INDEX

When you see **EC**, go to the **ESSENTIAL COMMUNICATION** section

INDEX

INDEX

T

INDEX

INDEX

INDEX

INDEX

INDEX

INDEX

INDEX

World Wide Web/WWW/the Web ...... **WB COMPUTERS/ INTERNET 6**
worldwide .... **EVERYWHERE 1; WORLD 2**
worn out .... **TIRED 1**
worried .... **WORRYING/WORRIED 1**
worry .... **WORRYING/WORRIED 1, 2, 3, 4**
worrying .... **WORRYING/WORRIED 2**
worse .... **WORSE 1**
worse: get worse .... **WORSE 2**
worse: go from bad to worse .... **WORSE 2**
worship .... **RELIGION 6**
worst .... **WORSE 1**
worth: 100 pounds' worth/ten dollars' worth
     etc .... **AMOUNT/NUMBER 1, 2**
worth: be worth .... **COST 3**
worth: be worth a fortune .... **EXPENSIVE 4**
worth: be worth a lot (of money) .... **EXPENSIVE 4**
would: can I/would you like me to .... **OFFER 2**
would like .... **WANT 1**
would love .... **WANT 2**
would prefer .... **WANT 3**
would rather .... **WANT 3**
would you like ...? .... **OFFER 1**
wouldn't: I wouldn't be surprised .... **EXPECT 2**
wouldn't: I wouldn't be surprised if .... **PROBABLY 1**
wouldn't: I wouldn't mind .... **WANT 1**
wound .... **HURT/INJURE 3, 4**
wounded .... **HURT/INJURE 5**
wounded: be wounded .... **HURT/INJURE 1**
wrap up/wrap .... **COVER 1**
wrapper .... **COVER 2**
wreck .... **ACCIDENT 2; DESTROY 1, 2, 4; SPOIL 1**
wreckage .... **DESTROY 4**
wrecked .... **DRUNK 1**
wrestling .... **FIGHT 2**
wrinkles .... **WB DESCRIBING HOW PEOPLE LOOK 7; LINE 2**
write .... **MAIL, PHONE, AND FAX 5; WB MUSIC 6; WB NEWSPAPERS 5; WRITE 1, 5, 6, 7**
write about sb/sth .... **DESCRIBE 1**
write back .... **ANSWER 2**
write off .... **DESTROY 2**
write-off .... **DESTROY 3**
writer .... **WB BOOKS/LITERATURE 6; WRITE 6**
writing .... **WORD/PHRASE/SENTENCE 2**
writing: in writing .... **WRITE 10**
writing/handwriting .... **WRITE 9**
written .... **WRITE 10**
wrong ...... **BAD 8; SUITABLE/UNSUITABLE 2; WRONG 1, 3**
wrong: be wrong .... **WRONG 2**
wrong: get sth wrong .... **MISTAKE 3**
wrong: go wrong .... **BROKEN 5; FAIL 2**
wrong: guess wrong .... **GUESS 3**
wrong: in the wrong order .... **ORDER 3**
wrong: the wrong time .... **TIME 19**
wrong: the wrong way around .... **WRONG 3**
wrong: there's something wrong with sth ...... **BROKEN 4; ILLNESS/DISEASE 4**
wrong: think sth is wrong .... **BAD 12**
wrong: what's wrong?/what's the matter? ..... **PROBLEM 6**
wrong number .... **MAIL, PHONE, AND FAX 3**
WWW: World Wide Web/WWW/the
     Web .... **WB COMPUTERS/INTERNET 6**

X

X-ray .... **WB MEDICAL TREATMENT 3**

Y

yank .... **PULL 1**
yawn .... **TIRED 2**
year: every day/every week/every year etc ..... **REGULAR 1**
year: first year/second year etc .... **WB EDUCATION 6**
year: first/second etc year .... **WB EDUCATION 7**
year: gap year .... **WB HOLIDAY/VACATION 3**
year: the day/week/year before .... **LAST 3**
year: the school year/the academic year ....
     WB EDUCATION 8
year one/two etc .... **WB EDUCATION 7**
years: be 10/15 etc (years old) ... **WB DESCRIBING HOW PEOPLE LOOK 3**
years: hours/months/years .... **LONG 4**
years: hours/weeks/years .... **TIME 14**
years: in the last few
     days/weeks/months/years .... **RECENTLY 2**
years: not in a million years .... **NEVER 1**
yell .... **SHOUT 1**
yell at sb .... **ANGRY 7**
yes: say yes .... **ACCEPT 1**
Yes./Yeah. .... **EC AGREEING**
yet .... **NOW 3**
yet again .... **AGAIN 1**
yoga .... **WB EXERCISE 2**
you can't miss it .... **NOTICE 4**
you can't trust sb .... **DISHONEST 1**
you never know .... **MAYBE 1**
you see .... **EXPLAIN 2**
You should .../You ought .... **EC ADVICE**
you're kidding/you're joking ...... **BELIEVE/NOT BELIEVE 5**
You're telling me! .... **EC AGREEING**
You're welcome. .... **EC SAYING THANK YOU**
young .... **BABY 6; WB DESCRIBING HOW PEOPLE LOOK 3; YOUNG 1**
your honour .... **WB COURT/TRIAL 3**
your mind goes blank .... **FORGET 1**
yourself: alone/on your own/by yourself .... **ALONE 1**
yourself: be pleased with yourself .... **PROUD 2**
yourself: be resigned to sth/resign yourself to
     sth .... **ACCEPT 4**
yourself: be unsure of yourself .... **CONFIDENT/NOT CONFIDENT 3**
yourself: can take care of yourself .... **INDEPENDENT 2**
yourself: dry yourself off .... **DRY 4**
yourself: feeling sorry for yourself .... **SAD 1**
yourself: help yourself .... **OFFER 1**
yourself: kill yourself .... **KILL 2**
yourself: on your own/by yourself .... **ALONE 2**
yourself: sure of yourself ... **CONFIDENT/NOT CONFIDENT 1**
yourself/myself etc .... **MYSELF/YOURSELF 1**
youth .... **YOUNG 2, 3, 4**

Z

zany .... **CRAZY 1**
zero .... **NONE/NOTHING 2**
zigzag .... **BEND 7**
zip up .... **FASTEN/UNFASTEN 1**
zone .... **AREA 1**
zone: war zone .... **WAR 4**

INDEX

Single User Licence Agreement: Longman Writing Coach

IMPORTANT: READ CAREFULLY

This is a legally binding agreement between You (the user or purchaser) and Pearson Education Limited. By retaining this licence, any software media or accompanying written materials or carrying out any of the permitted activities You agree to be bound by the terms of the licence agreement below.

If You do not agree to these terms then promptly return the entire publication (this licence and all software, written materials, packaging and any other components received with it) with Your sales receipt to Your supplier for a full refund.

SINGLE USER LICENCE AGREEMENT

YOU ARE PERMITTED TO:

- ✔ Use (load into temporary memory or permanent storage) a single copy of the software on only one computer at a time. If this computer is linked to a network then the software may only be installed in a manner such that it is not accessible to other machines on the network. If You want to use the software on a network or across a whole site, You need to read the Network version of the User Licence or the Site Licence. You can get these from the email address at the end of this licence
- ✔ Use the software with a class provided it is only installed on one computer
- ✔ Transfer the software from one computer to another provided that you only use it on one computer at a time
- ✔ Print out individual screen extracts from the disk for (a) private study or (b) to include in Your essays or classwork with students
- ✔ Photocopy individual screen extracts for Your schoolwork or classwork with students

YOU MAY NOT:

- ✘ Rent, lease or sell the software or any part of the publication
- ✘ Copy any part of the documentation, except where specifically indicated otherwise
- ✘ Make copies of the software, even for backup purposes
- ✘ Reverse engineer, decompile or disassemble the software or create a derivative product from the contents of the databases or any software included in them
- ✘ Use the software on more than one computer at a time
- ✘ Install the software on any networked computer or server in a way that could allow access to it from more than one machine on the network
- ✘ Include any material or software from the disk in any other product or software materials, except as allowed under "You are permitted to"
- ✘ Use the software in any way not specified above without the prior written consent of Pearson Education Limited
- ✘ Print out more than one page at a time
- ✘ Print, download or save any pictures

ONE COPY ONLY

This license is for a single user copy of the software

PEARSON EDUCATION LIMITED RESERVES THE RIGHT TO TERMINATE THIS LICENCE BY WRITTEN NOTICE AND TO TAKE ACTION TO RECOVER ANY DAMAGES SUFFERED BY PEARSON EDUCATION LIMITED IF YOU BREACH ANY PROVISION OF THIS AGREEMENT.

Pearson Education Limited owns the software. You only own the disk on which the software is supplied.

LIMITED WARRANTY

Pearson Education Limited warrants that the disk or CD ROM on which the software is supplied is free from defects in materials and workmanship under normal use for ninety (90) days from the date You receive it. This warranty is limited to You and is not transferable. Pearson Education Limited does not warrant that the functions of the software meet Your requirements or that the media is compatible with any computer system on which it is used or that the operation of the software will be unlimited or error-free.

You assume responsibility for selecting the software to achieve Your intended results and for the installation of, the use of and the results obtained from the software. The entire liability of Pearson Education Limited and your only remedy shall be replacement free of charge of the components that do not meet this warranty.

This limited warranty is void if any damage has resulted from accident, abuse, misapplication, service or modification by someone other than Pearson Education Limited. In no event shall Pearson Education Limited be liable for any damages whatsoever arising out of installation of the software, even if advised of the possibility of such damages. Pearson Education Limited will not be liable for any loss or damage of any nature suffered by any party as a result of reliance upon or reproduction of or any errors in the content of the publication.

Pearson Education Limited does not limit its liability for death or personal injury caused by its negligence.

This licence agreement shall be governed by and interpreted and construed in accordance with English law.

Technical support: only registered users are entitled to free technical help and advice. As a registered user, You may receive technical help by writing to elt-support@pearson.com or your local agent.